Architecture | **Theory** | since 1968

Columbia University Graduate
School of Architecture,
Planning and Preservation
New York, New York

Architecture | **Theory** | since 1968 | edited by K. Michael Hays

The MIT Press | Cambridge, Massachusetts | London, England

A Columbia Book of Architecture

First MIT Press paperback edition, 2000

This book was set in Meta and Joanna by Graphic Composition, Inc. and was
printed and bound in Canada.

Library of Congress Cataloging-in-Publication Data

Architecture theory since 1968 / edited by K. Michael Hays.
        p.   cm.
     "A Columbia book of architecture"—T.p. verso.
     Includes bibliographical references and index.
     ISBN 978-0-262-08261-7 (hardcover: alk. paper), 978-0-262-58188-2 (paperback)
     1. Architecture, Modern—20th century—Philosophy.   I. Hays, K. Michael.
NA680.A728   1998
724'.6—dc21
                                                            98-13415
                                                              CIP

10

Contents

Introduction

It does not seem particularly controversial to mark the beginning of contemporary architecture theory in "the sixties" (with all the changes in political theory and practice, the history of philosophy, the world economy, and general cultural production that the date connotes), for since then architecture, both built and projected, has notoriously been discussed and debated according to theoretical categories, from such blunt oppositions as "white" versus "gray" or "rationalist" versus "historicist" to more sophisticated and articulate -isms. And, since 1968, "architecture *theory*" has all but subsumed "architecture *culture*," for the prevailing sentiment in these years has been that cultural production in its traditional sense—especially the sense of culture as something that one both belongs to *and* possesses, culture as some precipitate that saturates from top down everything in its domain, culture as a boundary between legitimacy and disestablishment—can no longer be expected to arise spontaneously, as a matter of social course, but must now be constantly constructed, deconstructed, and reconstructed through more self-conscious theoretical procedures.[1]

This collection confirms the unprecedented transformation of architectural discourse in which theory displaced architectural criticism and rivaled the methodological importance of traditional architectural historiography (though it has in no way diminished considerations of history as a determinate factor of architectural production; as Marx taught us, the affirmation of the primacy of theory *just is* the affirmation of history). It also seeks to show the prevailing contours and not a few conceptual details of what many readers still take to be a dim and shapeless mass of texts, for even if the importance of theory can hardly be denied, its historical configuration has not been charted. The chronological rather than thematic ordering of texts here allows the attentive reader to see the weaving of themes, overlaps, starts, and stops that are inevitably reduced by imposed rubrics. My introductions to the texts, which may often be better read as afterwords, attempt to draw out some of their prevalent concepts. And the marginal references point to crossings of ideas.

Certain criteria guided the choice of material in this anthology and, equally, characterize what I take to be the distinguishing features of architecture theory since 1968. First and foremost, architecture theory is a practice of mediation. In its strongest form mediation is the production of relationships between formal analyses of a work of architecture and its social ground or context (however nonsynchronous these sometimes may be), but in such a way as to show the work of architecture as having some autonomous force with which it could also be seen as negating, distorting, repressing, compensating for, and even producing, as well as reproducing, that context. Fredric Jameson, speaking of the production of theory generally, has given a slightly modulated version of this: *transcoding*, "the invention of a set of terms, the strategic choice of a particular code or language, such that the same terminology can be used to analyze and articulate two quite distinct types of objects or 'texts,' or two very different levels of structural reality."[2] Or again: "New theoretical discourse is produced by the setting into active equivalence of two preexisting codes, which thereby, in a kind of molecular ion exchange, become a new one. What must be understood is that the new code (or metacode) can in no way be considered a synthesis between the previous pair. . . . It is rather a question of linking two sets of terms in such a way that each can express and indeed *interpret* the other."[3]

From Marxism and semiotics to psychoanalysis and rhizomatics, architecture theory has freely and contentiously set about opening up architecture to what is thinkable and sayable in other codes, and, in turn, rewriting systems of thought assumed to be properly extrinsic or irrelevant into architecture's own idiolect. And while it is correct to point out that today there still remain vestiges of older, "philosophical" criticisms that simply apply various philosophical systems to architecture in occasional and opportunistic ways, architecture theory has been, in part, a displacement of traditional problems of philosophy ("truth," "quality," and the like) in favor of attention to distinctly and irreducibly *architectural* ideas, and an attempt to dismantle the whole machinery of master texts, methods, and applications, putting in its place concepts and codes that interpret, disrupt, and transform one another.

Thus, for example, Manfredo Tafuri's work on modernism and contemporary architectural production, which I take as initiating one important trajectory of architecture theory, enfolds the old Marxian terms of base and superstructure and makes architecture *when it is most itself*—most pure, most rational, most attendent to its own techniques—the most efficient ideological agent of capitalist planification and unwitting victim of capitalism's historical closure. In a certain sense, this is just the maximization of the classical mediating term of critical theory, *reification* (or *Verdinglichung*, as used from Georg Luckács to Theodor Adorno to Fredric Jameson), but now with the twist that architecture's utopian work ends up laying the tracks for a general movement to a totally administered world.[4]

Or semiology, another dominant paradigm of architecture theory, links architecture and the social city (often including popular culture and consumerism) through the fraction of the sign (signifier/signified), setting off a fission that leads to the theorization of postmodernism itself, whose dust lingers on almost all subsequent discourse. But it should be clear that, while architecture theory preserves the fundamental structuralist apparatus of the sign, and language as the predominant model of that apparatus, it also, early on, mobilized its mediatory techniques in order to query of semiological systems how, by what agents and institutions, and to what ends they have been produced. Theory's situating of architecture in history and production—or, to use different terminology, its interrogation of the structurality of semiological structures[5]—ensures that any simple distinction between structuralism and poststructuralism in architecture theory cannot easily be maintained. One should note, too, that, while the logics of communication and type were the first products of theorizing the architectural sign, the concept of media— understood as including specific technologies and institutions as well as forms— would by the 1980s become the logical elaboration of that of the sign.[6]

Architecture theory's mediatory function releases unnoticed complicities and commonalities between different realities that were thought to remain singular, divergent, and differently constituted. Mediating among different discourses has sponsored a rich literature that addresses itself to a whole range of practical issues—the role of the unconscious, the socially constructed body, ecology, the politics of spatial relations—which connoisseurs of unmediated form nevertheless regard as an occultation of architecture's original object and seekers of certainty find maddeningly frustrating. But a primary lesson of architecture theory is that what used to be called the sociohistorical contexts of architectural production, as well as the object produced, are both themselves *texts* in the sense that we cannot approach them separately and directly, as distinct, unrelated things-in-themselves, but only through their prior differentiation and transmutation, which is shot through with ideological motivation. The world is a totality; it is an essential and essentially *practical* problem of theory to rearticulate that totality, to produce the concepts that relate the architectural fact with the social, historical, and ideological subtexts from which it was never really separate to begin with.

There are other criteria, mentioned in no particular order, that guided the selections for this anthology. Though I believe that the most important texts of architecture theory are included here, I have not tried to reproduce the most used texts, or anthologize history "as it really happened." Rather I have rationally reconstructed the history of architecture theory in an attempt to produce (as Louis Althusser recommended) the *concept* of that history—which is a quite different matter. I have chosen what I regard as the most robust texts of the authors represented, the ones with the most explanatory power and richness of implication, rather than the best known. Moreover, however influential they may have been on architecture theory, I have not included texts that have as their primary object of study other aesthetic modes (Rosalind Krauss's "Grids" and "Sculpture in the Expanded Field" are widely read examples, as are Hal Foster's and Andreas Huyssen's different works on postmodernism); on the other hand, essays do appear here by many authors who are not exclusively or even primarily architecture theorists, but all of whom have had a specific and sustained engagement with architectural material. As a corollary to this, I have tried to find entries that treat specific architectural objects, texts, and design practices even while producing generalizable concepts. One of my aims is to show how architecture enables certain ways of thinking that are irreducible to other modes of thought. While any theory that talks about architecture only—that does not relate architecture to the larger social, material field—is practically useless, at the same time any theory that does not articulate the concrete specificity and semi-autonomy of architecture's codes and operations misses a major medium of social practice.

But if theory's vocation is to produce the concepts by which architecture is related to other spheres of social practice, architecture, too, can be understood as the construction of new concepts of space and its inhabitation; which is to say that buildings and drawings can be theoretical, seeking a congruence between object and analysis, producing concepts as fully objective and material as built form itself. It is one of the characteristics of architecture since 1968 that a few key projects and exhibitions have explicitly sought to do just that. I have entered what I take to be the most important ones.

This anthology is not an introduction to architecture theory (which, if you've gotten this far, you must already know). At least some general background knowledge of the intellectual history of the twentieth century is assumed. Moreover, it is necessary to accompany this volume with some knowledge of the built and projected architecture of the same period, for that is the object on which these texts beat their heads and gnash their teeth. With that knowledge, not only does this anthology become a reconstruction of the history of architectural discourse, but further, the contradictions and aporias, intellectual failures as well as successes of the now highly specialized discipline of architecture theory become also rather precise calibrations of the history of architecture itself. The much decried split between theory and practice, and the tedious laments about theory's relevance, then lose much of their threat.

For the work in architecture theory written before 1977, it is especially helpful to understand the importation and deployment of both structuralist and phenomenological thought as militating against the received models of modernist functionalism and the positivist analyses that had reemerged in the guises of behaviorism, sociology, and operations research in the 1960s. Against these, structuralism and phenomenology each projected questions of "meaning" (it is a prevalent word in the essays presented here) into a structure of sheer relations among architectural elements within a field of signification. Ferdinand de Saussure's disconnection of the sign from the referent may be said to be analogous, in its architecture theoretical versions, to Edmund Husserl's phenomenological bracketing. Both operations suspend the commonsense perception of architecture as a vessel of meaning filled from the outside, or as a collection of behaviors and uses considered as its content. They both install a code of intrinsically and irreducibly architectural elements or phenomena that are related within a generalized system and that individual buildings or projects partially instantiate. In both structuralist and phenomenological thought, architectural signification is autonomous, at a distance from reality, but an architectural concept is still a concept of *something*; an idealized or total system of architecture is still a kind of map of reality, even if the particular coordinates of that map lack a one-to-one correspondence with the everyday world. At the same time, structuralism and phenomenology come down differently on the status of the subject. Structuralism characteristically liquidates the subject, construing it as no more than an effect of the signifying system, while phenomenology relies on concepts like consciousness and presence and tends to privilege the signified over the signifier, interiority over exteriority, subject over system. In the texts presented here, structuralism and phenomenology weave a difficult pas de deux that finishes around 1983 with the emergence of interpretive techniques that cut across such oppositions and open to a more radical heterogeneity.

To those who take the ambition of this anthology to be to render victorious one discourse over all others (that is, the discourse of those included here over those not), it must quickly be replied that the importance of the period in question, from 1968 to 1993, is not one of competing styles or group allegiances (Marxism versus formalism, structuralism versus phenomenology, or the like) but rather of the collective experience of an objective situation to which diverse responses emerged, all attempting to provide maps of the possibilities for architectural intervention, to articulate the specific limiting conditions of architectural practice. I have suggested elsewhere that that historical experience sponsored, among other things, a very particular attitude toward commodification and consumption. For architecture theory during the past quarter of a century seems to have been produced and read mostly by individuals nurtured on popular culture, schooled on contradiction and paradox, and instilled with the belief that things can be changed, that theory can and must make a difference. Highly competent cultural consumers all, these are individuals with some remaining faith in an engaged resistance to "the system" yet still able to be titillated by the ecstatic surrender of the architectural subject to the very forces that threaten its demise.[7] But the almost manic mood swings of those of us who do theory, between exhilaration and contempt for the absolute ease with which signs can be redistributed, the blending of euphoria and bleakness with regard to commercial culture, and the desires and pleasures of things, images, and events, which we ingest, it sometimes seems, through almost mindless consumption—all these cannot, I suggest, be dismissed offhand. They are but a reaction formation against what history has dealt us—a totally reified life—and they are but one side of a demand for something different, *the other side of which is theory itself.*

It may well turn out that a different, younger audience, whose relation to consumption is altogether altered, whose memories may not include any notions of resistance or negation, may have to produce another kind of theory premised on neither the concept of reification nor the apparatus of the sign, both of which have their ultimate referent in the vexatious territory of reproducibility and commodity consumption. Indeed, since 1993, there have been important developments in architecture theory not covered by this anthology.[8] I still believe, however, that the texts included here will then constitute the necessary history on which those new theories will be built. Theory is a practice explicitly ready to undertake its self-critique and effect its own transformation. And, like architecture itself, theory is an appetite for modifying and expanding reality, a desire to organize a new vision of a world perceived as unsatisfactory or incomplete—such will always be architecture theory's proper utopia.

During the course of this book's preparation, I have probably mentioned it to every colleague and student I have passed, many of whom have made helpful comments. I regret that I can formally thank only those who have contributed substantially to the book's formation. Bernard Tschumi has enthusiastically supported the project from the start, made valuble suggestions regarding its contents, and facilitated its development in every way. Special thanks to Renata Hejduk, who helped with the research and coordination of the entire project. Michael Speaks steadied my hand through numerous theory shakes. Luis Carranza, Mary Lou Lobsinger, and Felicity Scott helped research specific areas. Helpful suggestions and information about the general field and particular subjects came from Diana Agrest, George Baird, Micha Bandini, Jean-Louis Cohen, Beatriz Colomina, Peter Eisenman, Rodolphe el-Khoury, Kenneth Frampton, Catherine Ingraham, Jeffrey Kipnis, Sandro Marpillero, Robert McAnulty, Rafael Moneo, Joan Ockman, Colin Rowe, Robert Somol, and Mark Wigley. Marshall Brown and Michael Gamble researched the illustrations and prepared them for publication. Marshall Brown and Leah Ray scanned the texts. Special thanks to Peter Rowe, who has helped create a structure and an atmosphere at Harvard's Graduate School of Design supportive of theoretical work in every way. I am grateful to students who have participated in my courses at the GSD for their insights and provocations. The MIT Press has been particularly supportive of this project and tolerant of its size. I would particularly like to thank Roger Conover for his editorial acumen, advice, and thoughtfulness about the topic, Matthew Abbate for his tireless attention to every detail, Jean Wilcox for the deployment of her extraordinary design talent, and Julie Grimaldi for facilitating this publication.

Notes

1. It is not uninteresting but also not that useful to debate the exact year in which contemporary architecture theory's predominance began. Robert Venturi's *Complexity and Contradiction in Architecture* and Aldo Rossi's *L'architettura della città* both appeared in 1966; one could rightly start there, even though neither of these texts looks much like what goes by the name of theory now. A different trajectory might begin with Christian Norberg-Schulz's *Intentions in Architecture* of 1963. Colin Rowe's "Mathematics of the Ideal Villa" of 1947 already enunciated issues of Gestalt formalism, typology, and the proliferation of formal effects, and even anticipated two camps of postmodern formalism, the "white" rigorists and the "gray" inclusivists. But in the long run, the coupling of Marxian critical theory and post-structuralism with readings of architectural modernism has been what has dominated theory in the main, subsuming and rewriting earlier texts; and "since 1968" covers that formation.

    It should be apparent that *Architecture Theory since 1968* also claims to be both a continuation and a modulation of Joan Ockman's *Architecture Culture 1943–1968* (New York: Columbia University and Rizzoli, 1993); in a certain sense, this is a companion volume.

And yet, however much I may have tried to emulate Joan's effort, I have not made a sequel, for this is a very different time and this had to be a very different kind of book.

2. Fredric Jameson, *The Political Unconscious* (Ithaca: Cornell University Press, 1981), 40.

3. Fredric Jameson, *Postmodernism, or, The Cultural Logic of Late Capitalism* (Durham: Duke University Press, 1991), 394–395.

4. The concept of reification, in convergence with the enormous importance of the work of Aldo Rossi, also spurred a rehabilitation of a realist paradigm that played out in the texts of Bernard Huet, Martin Steinmann, and Jorge Silvetti.

5. I am, of course, referring to the classic essay of Jacques Derrida, "Structure, Sign, and Play in the Discourse of the Human Sciences," in *The Structuralist Controversy*, ed. Richard Macksey and Eugenio Donato (Baltimore: Johns Hopkins University Press, 1972).

6. The mention of the legacies of Marxian critical theory and structuralism immediately brings to mind the most influential conjunction of these in the work of Louis Althusser. And, indeed, a loose kind of "Althusserianism" can be found in much of architecture theory, as my introductions to the essays by Mario Gandelsonas, Diana Agrest, Bernard Tschumi, Jorge Silvetti, and later Fredric Jameson show.

7. K. Michael Hays, "Architecture Theory, Media, and the Question of Audience," *Assemblage* 27 (August 1995).

8. Feminism and identity politics are only the most obvious of themes that have produced massive numbers of studies since 1993 not primarily concerned with reification.

This was the moment when language invaded the universal problematic, the moment when, in the absence of a center or origin, everything became discourse.

JACQUES DERRIDA, *Writing and Difference*

The critical act will consist of a recomposition of the fragments once they are historicized: in their "remontage."

MANFREDO TAFURI, *The Sphere and the Labyrinth*

Architecture | **Theory** | since 1968

Manfredo Tafuri   **"Toward a Critique of Architectural Ideology"** "Per una critica dell'ideologia

architettonica," *Contropiano* 1 (January-April 1969); translated for this anthology

by Stephen Sartarelli

Contemporary architecture's situation was never more radically theorized than by Manfredo Tafuri. Locating architecture's intellectual project in the historical matrix of the bourgeois metropolis, Tafuri formulates the entire cycle of modernism (he refuses any periodization of a *post*modernism) as a unitary development in which the avant-gardes' visions of utopia come to be recognized as an idealization of capitalism, a transfiguration of the latter's rationality into the rationality of autonomous form — architecture's "plan," its ideology. Gathering up the threads that link the sociology of Georg Simmel and Max Weber, the critical theory of Georg Lukács, Walter Benjamin, and Theodor Adorno, the structuralism of Louis Althusser and Roland Barthes, and the negative thought of Massimo Cacciari, Tafuri identifies what for him is contemporary architecture's only condition of possibility: to collapse into the very system that assures its demise or retreat into hypnotic solitude.

see Jameson (**442 ff**) and Cohen (**508 ff**)

Substitute "bourgeois art" for "the individual," and the first lines of Simmel's "The Metropolis and Mental Life" disclose the same problematic as those of Tafuri's essay reprinted here: how the subject — the individual or art — seeks to protect its internal integrity and, at the same time, accommodate itself to the shock of metropolitan experience. Simmel: "The deepest problems of modern life derive from the claim of the individual to preserve the autonomy and individuality of his existence in the face of overwhelming social forces, of historical heritage, of external culture, and of the technique of life."[1] Tafuri: "To dispel anxiety by understanding and internalizing its causes: this would seem to be one of the principal ethical imperatives of bourgeois art. It matters little whether the conflicts, contradictions, and torments that create anxiety are absorbed into a comprehensive mechanism capable of reconciling those differences, or whether catharsis is achieved through contemplative sublimation."

compare 392–393 and Cacciari (**397 ff**)

Following Simmel, Tafuri understands the metropolis as the general form assumed by the process of technical rationalization and objectification of social relations brought about by the monetary economy. This process dissolves individuality into a flow of weightless impressions, abstracts and levels down all particularity and quality, and restructures subjectivity as reason and calculation.[2] The result, at the level of the individual, is the metropolitan subject, what Simmel called the blasé type: the neurasthenic who survives the increase in nervous life by becoming totally intellectualized and indifferent. ("There is perhaps no psychic phenomenon which has been so unconditionally reserved to the metropolis as has the blasé attitude," wrote Simmel.)[3] The conflicted nature of the blasé type fully reflects the metropolis's structure of functional contradictions — contradictions that include a close confrontation with objects and people (shock) *and* an excessive distance from them (agoraphobia), stimulation as the cure for overstimulation, the ascendancy of the life of the intellect (*Verstand* or *Vergeistigung*) only through the life of the nerves (*Nervenleben*), the emergence of extreme individuality in the social totality and the simultaneous internalization of the social totality in the individual. All of which is to say that the blasé type reflects the metropolis from the perspective of the subject's negated autonomy.[4] As Tafuri puts it, "The problem now became that of teaching not how one should 'suffer' that shock, but how one should absorb it and internalize it as an inevitable condition of existence."

Like the blasé personality, bourgeois art and architecture essentially and contradictorily register the very forces that assure their ineffectuality. Having first been exploded by the shock and distress of the metropolis (expressionism), and then, with a sardonic detachment, taken an inventory of its surrounding remains (dadaism), bourgeois architectural thought must conclude that the subject itself is the only impediment to the smooth development of the fully rationalized technocratic plan that was to become the total system of capital. One had to pass from Edvard Munch's cathartic *Scream* to Ludwig Hilberseimer's metropolitan machine—the ultimate architectural sign of self-liquidation through the autonomy of formal construction, its homeostatic regulation of urban form understood as the ideological training ground for life in the desacralized, distracted, posthumanist world. Tafuri again:

To remove the experience of shock from all automatism, to use that experience as the foundation for visual codes and codes of action borrowed from already established characteristics of the capitalist metropolis—rapidity of change and organization, simultaneity of communications, accelerated rhythms of use, eclecticism—to reduce the structure of artistic experience to the status of pure object (an obvious metaphor for the object-commodity), to involve the public, as a unified whole, in a declaredly interclass and therefore antibourgeois ideology: such are the tasks taken on, as a whole, by the avant-gardes of the twentieth century.

The problem, then, was to *plan* the disappearance of the subject, to dissolve architecture into the structure of the metropolis, wherein it turns into pure object. Thus does architectural ideology resolve the contradiction between the internal, subjective resistance to metropolitan shock and the external, structural totality of the production system: *this is its utopia.* For Tafuri, that utopianism—whatever other aims and local concrete effects it may have—ends up ushering into being the universal, systematic planification of capitalism, all the while concealing this fundamental function behind the rhetoric of its manifestos and within the purity of its forms. The struggle of architecture to rationalize itself through autonomous formal operations alerts us not to architecture's success, but to the historical moment of modernity as a limiting condition, one that shuts down certain social functions that architecture had previously performed.

Tafuri's theory takes ideology as its object (it is an ideology of ideologies), and, from his point of view, in modernity all aesthetic ideologies are equivalent if not interchangeable. As such they are equally useless for social production: *this is architecture's destiny.* Such a thesis was received at the time of its first publication as the pronouncement of the death of architecture, to which Tafuri responded:

What is of interest here is the precise identification of those tasks which capitalist development has taken away from architecture. That is to say, what it has taken away in general from ideological prefiguration. With this, one is led almost automatically to the discovery of what may well be the "drama" of architecture today: that is, to see architecture obliged to return to *pure architecture*, to form without utopia; in the best cases, to sublime uselessness. To the deceptive attempts to give architecture an ideological dress, I shall always prefer the sincerity of those who have the courage to speak of that silent and outdated "purity"; even if this, too, still harbors an ideological inspiration, pathetic in its anachronism.[5]

Notes

In its original form this essay had no section headings; as an aid to the reader, they have been added here following the Spanish version of the essay in *De la vanguardia a la metropoli: Critica radical a la arquitectura* (Barcelona: Gustavo Gili, 1972).

Tafuri expanded the essay as *Progetto e Utopia* (Bari: Laterza & Figli, 1973), which appeared in English as *Architecture and Utopia: Design and Capitalist Development*, trans. Barbara Luiga La Penta (Cambridge: MIT Press, 1976).

1. Georg Simmel, "Die Grosstädte und das Geistesleben" (1903); translated as "The Metropolis and Mental Life," in *The Sociology of Georg Simmel*, ed. Kurt H. Wolff (New York: Free Press, 1950), p. 409.
2. "The essence of modernity as such is psychologism, the experiencing and interpretation of the world in terms of the reactions of our inner life and indeed as an inner world, the dissolution of fixed contents in the fluid element of the soul, from which all that is substantive is

Aldo Rossi,
*L' architecture
assassinée*, 1975

filtered and whose forms are merely forms of motion." Georg Simmel, "Rodin," in *Philoso-phische Kultur: Gesammelte Essais* (Leipzig: W. Klinkhardt, 1911), p. 196.

3.   Simmel, "The Metropolis and Mental Life," p. 413.

4.   "In the blasé attitude the concentration of men and things stimulates the nervous system of the individual to its highest achievement so that it attains its peak. Through the mere quanti-tative intensification of the same conditioning factors this achievement is transformed into its opposite and appears in the peculiar adjustment of the blasé attitude. In this phenome-non the nerves find in the refusal to react to their stimulation the last possibility of accommo-dating to the contents and forms of metropolitan life. The self-preservation of certain personalities is bought at the price of devaluing the whole objective world, a devaluation which in the end unavoidably drags one's own personality down into a feeling of the same worthlessness." Simmel, "The Metropolis and Mental Life," p. 415.

Simmel's truth, for Tafuri and Massimo Cacciari, is the recognition of metropoli-tan experience as a form of negative thought. His mistake (the same as Lukács's) was his anachronistic humanism—*"man's 'diabolical' insistence on remaining man*, on taking his place as an 'imperfect machine' in a social universe in which the only consistent behavior is that of pure silence." Tafuri, *Architecture and Utopia*, p. 74. Also see Cacciari, *Architecture and Nihilism: On the Philosophy of Modern Architecture,* trans. Stephen Sartarelli (New Haven: Yale University Press, 1993).

5.   Tafuri, *Architecture and Utopia*, p. ix.

To dispel anxiety by understanding and internalizing its causes: this would seem to be one of the principal ethical imperatives of bourgeois art. It matters little whether the conflicts, contradictions and torments that create anxiety are absorbed into a comprehensive mechanism capable of reconciling those differences, or whether catharsis is achieved through contemplative sublimation. We recognize, in any case, the "necessity" of the bourgeois intellectual in the imperative significance his "social" mission assumes: in other words, there exists, between the avant-gardes of capital and the intellectual avant-gardes, a kind of tacit understanding, so tacit indeed that any attempt to bring it into the light elicits a chorus of indignant protest. Culture, in its intermediary role, has so defined its distinguishing features in ideological terms that in its shrewdness it has reached the point—beyond all intellectual good faith—of imposing forms of contestation and protest upon its own products. And the higher the formal level of the sublimation of conflicts, the more the structures confirming and validating that sublimation remain hidden.

If we are to confront the subject of the ideology of architecture from this perspective, we must attempt to shed light on how one of the most functional proposals for the reorganization of capital has come to suffer the most humiliating frustrations, to the point where it can be presented today as objective and transcending all connotations of class, or even as a question of alternatives, a terrain of direct confrontation between intellectuals and capital.

I must say straightaway that I do not believe it an accident that so many of the recent cultural theories in the architectural debate are devoted to a somber reexamination of the very origins of modern art. Assumed as an indication of a thorough, self-regarding uneasiness, architectural culture's increasingly generalized interest in the Enlightenment has, for us, a precise significance, beyond the mystified manner in which it is explained. By returning to its origins—correctly identified in the period of strict correspondence between bourgeois ideologies and intellectual advances—one begins to see the whole course of modern architecture as a unitary development.

Accepting this approach, we can consider the formation of architectural ideologies comprehensively, particularly as regards their implications for the city.

Moreover, a systematic exploration of the Enlightenment debate will also enable us to grasp, on a purely ideological level, a great many of the contradictions that accompany the development of modern art.

Reason's Adventures: Naturalism and the City in the Century of the Enlightenment

The formation of the architect as ideologue of the "social"; the individuation of the proper area of intervention in the phenomenology of the city; the role of form as persuasion in regard to the public, and as self-criticism in regard to its own concerns; the dialectic—on the level of formal investigation—between the role of the architectonic "object" and that of urban organization: On what level, and with what sort of awareness, do these abstract constants of the modern means of visual communication become concretized in the currents of Enlightenment thought?

When Laugier, in 1765, formulated his theories on the design of the city, officially inaugurating Enlightenment architectural theory, his words betrayed a twofold influence: on the one hand, the desire to reduce the city itself to a natural phenomenon, on the other, the wish to go beyond all *a priori* ideas of urban organization by extending, to the urban fabric, the formal dimensions associated with the aesthetics of the Picturesque.

"Anyone who knows how to design a park well," writes Laugier in his *Observations*, "will draw up a plan according to which a City must be built in relation to its area and situation. There must be squares, intersections, streets. There must be regularity and whimsy, relationships and oppositions, chance elements that lend variety to the tableau, precise order in the details and confusion, chaos, and tumult in the whole."[1]

Laugier's words perceptively capture the formal reality of the eighteenth-century city. It is no longer a question of archetypal schemas of order, but of accepting the anti-perspective character of the urban space. Even the park, as reference point, has a new meaning: in its variety, the nature called upon to form part of the urban structure supplants the comforting rhetorical and didactic naturalism that had dominated the episodic narrativity of Baroque arrangements through the seventeenth century and for the first half of the eighteenth.

Thus Laugier's appeal to naturalism implies, at once, an appeal to the original purity of the act of ordering the environment, and an understanding of the eminently *anti-organic* character typical of the city. But that is not all. The reduction of the city to a natural phenomenon clearly corresponds to the aesthetics of the Picturesque that English Empiricism had introduced in the first decades of the eighteenth century, for which Alexander Cozens, in 1759, had provided a very rich and important theoretical foundation.

We do not know to what degree Cozens's theory of "blots" may have influenced Laugier's notion of the city. What is certain is that the French abbot's urban invention and the English painter's landscape theory share a method based on selection as a tool for critical intervention in a "natural" reality.[2]

Now, taking for granted that for the theorists of the eighteenth century, the city fell within the same formal domain as painting, selectivity and criticism implied the introduction, into urban planning, of a fragmentary approach that places not only Nature and Reason, but the natural fragment and the urban fragment, on the same level.

As a human creation, the city *tends* toward a natural condition, in the same way that the landscape, through the critical selection made by the painter, must necessarily bear the stamp of a social morality.

It is significant that while Laugier, like the English Enlightenment theorists, pointedly grasps the artificial character of the urban language, neither Ledoux nor Boullée, who were far more innovative in their works, are willing to relinquish a mythical, abstract view of Nature and its organic quality. Boullée's polemic against Perrault's perceptive insights into the artificial nature of the language of architecture is very revealing in this respect.

It may be that Laugier's *city as forest* was modeled on nothing more than the varied sequences of spaces that appear in Patte's plan of Paris, which brought together, in a single, comprehensive framework, the projects for the new royal squares. We shall therefore limit ourselves to noting Laugier's theoretical perceptions, which become all the more significant when we recall that Le Corbusier leaned on them in delineating the theoretical principles of his Ville Radieuse.[3]

What does it mean, on the ideological level, to liken the city to a *natural* object? On the one hand we find, in such an assumption, a sublimation of physiocratic theories: the city is not interpreted as a structure that, with its mechanisms of accumulation, transforms the processes of land exploitation and agricultural and property revenues. As a phenomenon likened to a "natural" process, ahistorical because it is universal, the city is freed from any structural considerations whatsoever. At first, formal "naturalism" served to advocate the *objective* necessity of the processes set in motion by the pre-Revolutionary bourgeoisie; later it was used to consolidate and protect these achievements from any further transformation.

On the other hand, this naturalism fulfills its function by ensuring artistic activity an ideological role in the strict sense. It is no accident that at the very moment in which the bourgeois economy began to discover and establish its own categories of action and judgment, assigning "values" contents directly measurable with the gauges dictated by the new methods of production and exchange, the crisis of the former systems of "values" was immediately covered up by new sublimations made artificially objective through an appeal to the universality of Nature.

This was why Reason and Nature now had to be unified. Enlightenment rationalism was unable to take upon itself full responsibility for the operations it was carrying out, and believed it necessary to avoid a direct confrontation with its own premises.

It is clear that, throughout the eighteenth and early nineteenth centuries, this ideological smokescreen played on the contradictions of the *ancien régime*. Nascent urban capitalism and the economic structures based on precapitalist exploitation of the land butted up against one another. It is significant that the theorists of the city, rather than emphasize this contradiction, attempt to hide it, or rather to resolve it by dissolving the city in the great sea of Nature and focusing their attentions entirely on the city's superstructural aspects.

Urban naturalism, the imposition of the *Picturesque* on the city and its architecture, and the emphasis on landscape in artistic ideology, all served to negate the now manifest dichotomy between urban and rural reality, to pretend that there was no gap between the valorization of nature and the valorization of the city as a machine for producing new forms of economic accumulation.

The rhetorical, Arcadian naturalism of seventeenth-century culture was now replaced by a different, but equally persuasive naturalism.

It is important, however, to point out that at first, the deliberate abstraction of Enlightenment theories of the city served to destroy the planning and development schemas of the Baroque city; it later became a way of avoiding, rather than conditioning, the formulation of new, consistent models of development.

Thus, in a manner entirely anomalous with the general trends in Enlightenment criticism, architectural culture played a predominantly destructive role in the eighteenth and nineteenth centuries. Not having at its disposal a mature substratum of production techniques corresponding to the new conditions of bourgeois ideology and laissez-faire economics, architecture was forced to channel its self-critical efforts in two directions:

First of all, for polemical reasons, it tended to glorify everything that might assume an anti-European significance. Piranesi's fragmentationism is a product of the new bourgeois science of historical criticism, which is also, paradoxically, criticism of criticism. The whole fashion of invoking Gothic, Chinese, and Hindu architecture, and the Romantic naturalism of landscape gardens in which fantasies of exotic pavilions and false ruins are inserted without irony, is theoretically connected to the atmosphere of Montesquieu's *Lettres persanes*, Voltaire's *Ingénu*, and Leibniz's caustic anti-Western positions. To integrate rationalism and critical philosophy, one confronted the European myths with anything that might, by contradicting them, reconfirm their validity. In the English landscape garden, the annulment of historical perspective is consummated. But in that accumulation of little temples, pavilions and grottoes, which seem to summon together the most disparate testimonies of human history, it was not really an escape into a fairy-tale world that was sought. Rather, the "picturesque" of Brown, Kent, and Wood, and the "horrid" of Lequeu, pose a question: with the tools of an architecture that has already given up the making of "objects" in becoming a technique of organizing premade materials, they demand a verification extraneous to architecture.

With the utter detachment typical of the great Enlightenment critics, these architects began a systematic and fateful autopsy of architecture and all its conventions.

Secondly, even while bracketing its own formative role in regard to the city, architecture presented an alternative to the nihilistic prospect clearly discernible behind the hallucinatory fantasies of a Lequeu, a Bélanger, or a Piranesi.

Renouncing a symbolic role, at least in the traditional sense, architecture—in order to avoid destroying itself—discovered its scientific vocation. On the one hand it could become an instrument of social equilibrium; in which case it would have to confront the question of types head-on—which Durand and Dubut in fact did. On the other hand it could become a science of sensations; and this is the direction in which Ledoux and, more systematically, Le Camus de Mézières, would steer it. Typology, then, and *architecture parlante*: the same themes that Piranesi brought into conflict with each other, and which, instead of leading to solutions, would accentuate, throughout the nineteenth century, the internal crisis of architectural culture.

Architecture now accepted the task of "politicizing" its own handiwork. As agents of politics, architects had to take up the challenge of continuously inventing advanced solutions at the most generally applicable levels. Toward this end, ideology played a determinant part.

The utopianism that modern historiography has chosen to see in the works of Enlightenment architecture should therefore be precisely defined according to its authentic meanings. In fact, the architectural propositions of eighteenth-century Europe contain nothing that cannot be realized, and it is no accident that among all the theorizing of the *philosophes* of architecture one can find no social utopia in support of the urban reformism advocated at the purely formal level.

The very introduction to the entry under *Architecture*, written by Quatremère de Quincy for the second edition of the great *Encyclopédie*, is a masterpiece of realism, even in the abstract terms in which it is expressed.

"Among all the arts," writes Quatremère, "those children of pleasure and necessity in which man has participated to help him bear the trials of life and pass on his memory to future generations, one cannot deny that *architecture* must hold a most eminent place. Even considered only from the point of usefulness, it surpasses all the other arts. It sees to the salubrity of cities, guards the health of men, protects their properties, and works only for the safety, repose and orderliness of civic life."[4]

Nor is Enlightenment realism belied by the gigantic-scale architectural dreams of a Boullée or the pensioners of the Académie. The glorification of size, geometric distillation, and ostentatious primitivism that are the constants of those projects assume concrete meaning when read in the light of what they want to be: not so much dreams that can never be realized, but experimental models of a new method of design.

From the unbridled symbolism of Ledoux or Lequeu to the geometrical silence of Durand's typology, the process followed by the architecture of the Enlightenment remains consistent with the new ideological role it has assumed. Architecture must redefine itself as it starts to become part of the structures of the bourgeois city, dissolving into the uniformity ensured by preconstituted typologies.

But this dissolution was not without its consequences. The one who took Laugier's theoretical insights to their extreme limit was Piranesi: his ambiguous evocation of the *Iconographia Campi Martii* is a graphic monument to late Baroque culture's openness to the late revolutionary ideologies, just as his *Parere sull'architettura* is its most pointed literary testimony.[5]

In Piranesi's Campo Marzio there is no longer any loyalty to the late Baroque principle of *variety*. Since Roman antiquity is not only a reference charged with ideological nostalgia and revolutionary expectation, but a myth to be contested, every form of classicist derivation is treated as mere fragment, deformed symbol, broken hallucination of an "order" wasting away.

The order in the details does not, therefore, lead simply to *tumulte dans l'ensemble*, but indeed to a monstrous pullulation of symbols bereft of meaning. The Piranesian *forest*, like the sadistic atmospheres of his *Prisons*, shows that it is not only the "sleep of reason" that produces monsters; "reason awake" can also create deformity, even when the goal at which it aims is the Sublime.

There is a prophetic quality to the criticism implicit in Piranesi's Campo Marzio. In it, the most advanced point of the Enlightenment imagination seems to warn, with sorrowful emphasis, of the danger lurking in the definitive loss of organic form: it is now the ideal of the Whole and the universal that has come into crisis.

Architecture, however, could also strive to preserve a fullness that would save it from total dissolution. Yet such an effort was undermined by all the *pieces* of architecture assembled in the city. These fragments, in the city, were pitilessly absorbed and deprived of all autonomy, despite their obstinate wish to assume articulated, composite configurations. In the *Iconographia Campi Martii* we witness an epic representation of the battle waged by architecture against itself. Typology is asserted as an instance of superior organization, yet the configuration of the individual types tends to destroy the very concept of typology; history is invoked as an inherent "value," yet the paradoxical rejection of the archaeological reality casts its civilizing potential into doubt; formal invention seems to proclaim its own primacy, yet the obsessive repetition of the inventions seems to reduce the whole urban organism to a sort of gigantic "useless machine."

Rationalism would seem thus to reveal its own irrationality. In attempting to absorb all of its own contradictions, architectural "reasoning" uses the technique of *shock* as its own foundation. The individual architectural fragments collide with one another, indifferent even to the clash, while their accumulation attests to the uselessness of the inventive effort made to define their form.

The city, here, remains an unknown quantity. Piranesi's Campo Marzio fools nobody as to its reality as an experimental design hidden behind an archaeological mask. Nor is it possible to define new constants of order through the act of designing. This colossal *bricolage* reveals only a single truth: that the rational and the irrational must cease to be mutually exclusive. Piranesi does not have the tools to translate the dialectics of contradiction into form; he must therefore limit himself to proclaiming, emphatically, that the great, new problem is that of balancing opposites, the appointed place for which must be the city, lest the very notion of architecture itself be destroyed.

Essentially, it is the struggle between architecture and the city that assumes an epic tone in Piranesi's *Campo Marzio*. Here the "dialectics of the Enlightenment" attains an unsurpassed potential, as well as an ideal tension so violent that contemporaries could not grasp it as such. Piranesian *excess*—like the excesses of libertine Enlightenment literature in other respects—became, as such, the revelation of a truth: a truth that the architectural culture and urban planning of the Enlightenment would hasten, as they developed, to cover up.

Nevertheless, the urban fragmentationism introduced on the ideological level by Laugier would make itself felt once again in the eclectic theorizations of Milizia, in his *Principi di architettura civile*. Milizia writes:

A city is like a forest, whence it follows that the organization of a city is like that of a park. One must have squares, intersections and broad, straight streets in great numbers. Yet this is not enough; the plan must be designed with taste and verve, so that order, whimsy, eurythmy and variety may coexist in equal measure: here the streets must radiate starlike, there like a goose-foot, on one side in herringbone pattern, on the other like a fan; farther on they should be parallel, with three-street and four-street crossroads everywhere and in different positions, and a multitude of squares of entirely different shape, size and decoration.[6]

It is impossible not to see the influence of a refined sensism in what Milizia says next:

He who knows not how to vary our pleasures, will never give us pleasure. [The city,] in short, should be a varied picture of an infinity of chance occurrences; with great order in the details, and confusion, chaos and tumult in the whole.[7]

He continues:

The city's plan must be so arranged that the magnificence of the whole will be subdivided into an infinity of beautiful details, each so different from the other that one never encounters the same objects, and that, covering it from one end to the other, one always finds something new, something singular and surprising, in each quarter. Order must reign, but amidst a kind of confusion . . . and this multitude of regular parts must create, in the whole, a certain sense of irregularity and chaos, of the sort that so befits great Cities.[8]

Order and chaos, regularity and irregularity, organic unity and inorganic disunity. This is a far cry from the late Baroque precept of *unity in variety*, which had taken on mystical resonances in Shaftesbury.

What the writings of Laugier, Piranesi, Milizia, and—somewhat later, in a more moderate tone—Quatremère de Quincy contributed to the architectural debate was precisely this notion of control over a reality lacking organic structure. Such control was to be achieved by acting upon that very lack, not in order to change its structure, but to elicit from it a complex array of simultaneously present meanings.

Yet immediately the pressures of a rigorous traditionalism rose up against these hypotheses. Giovanni Antolini, in his commentary on Milizia's *Principi*, did not fail to launch a few salvoes against the latter's theories, defending the authority of Vitruvius and the ideal example set by Galiani. And to counter the glorification of empiricism and the picturesque implicit in the Woods, in Palmer's Bath, in the Edinburgh crescents and in the 1803 plan for Milan, there was the strict rationalism of Muratti's Bari and the new plans for St. Petersburg, Helsinki, and Turku.

Of particular interest to our analysis is the intellectual opposition that occurred between Antolini and the members of the commission for the Napoleonic plan for Milan.

The commission had agreed to work dialectically with the city's structure, as it had evolved over the course of history. The problem was that in so doing, they implicitly cast judgment on it. As a product of forces and events determined by prejudice, myth, and the structures of feudalism and the Counter-Reformation, the complex historical fabric of the Lombard capital was, for them, something to be rationalized and clarified in terms of its functions and its form. It was also something to be appraised in such a way that from the clash between the ancient, preexisting parts—centers of obscurantism—and the new demolitions and interventions—centers of *clarté* and *lumières*—there would emerge an obvious and valid choice corresponding to a clear and unequivocal hypothesis of the city's destiny and physical structure.

It is no accident that Antolini was among those opposed to the Napoleonic plan. While the Napoleonic commission in some fashion was open to a dialogue with the historical city and managed to dilute, in the city's fabric, the ideology informing their interventions, Antolini was against such a dialogue. His project for the Foro Bonaparte is, at once, a radical alternative to the history of the city, a symbol loaded with absolute ideological values, and an urban *locus* which, as a totalizing presence, sets itself the goal of transforming the entire urban structure while giving back to architecture a communicative role of a peremptory nature.[9]

The antithesis is not incidental: indeed, it involves every aspect of the city's communicative role. For the 1803 commission, the protagonist of the new intellectual and functional message was the urban structure in and of itself.

For Antolini, on the other hand, the restructuring of the city must be achieved by introducing a disruptive urban locus, capable of radiating induced effects that resist all contamination, into the network of its contradictory values. The city as a universe of discourse or system of communications can be summed up, for Antolini, in an absolute, peremptory "message."

Thus we see the *two paths* of modern art and architecture already delineated. The dialectic is the same as that inherent in all of modern art over the course of its history, which pits those attempting to dig down into the very bowels of reality in order to know and assimilate its values and shortcomings, against those who want to push beyond reality, to construct, *ex novo*, new realities, new values, new public symbols.

The difference between the Napoleonic commission and Antolini is the same as that which will later distinguish Monet from Cézanne, Munch from Braque, Schwitters from Mondrian, Häring from Gropius, Rauschenberg from Vasarely.

Between Laugier's "forest" and Antolini's aristocratic reserve, however, there was a third way, and it was destined to become the main force behind a new way of intervening in and controlling urban morphology. L'Enfant's plan for Washington and William Penn's for Philadelphia, for example, use new tools compared to European models.

The relationship between these pragmatic schemas of development and the value structure typical of American society from its very beginnings has already been analyzed on several different occasions, and this is clearly not the place to reexamine this subject.[10]

The great historical merit of the urban planning adopted by American cities since the mid-1700s is to have explicitly sided with the forces that spurred the morphological transformation of the cities, controlling these forces with a pragmatic approach entirely foreign to European culture.

Using a regular grid of arteries as the simple, flexible support for an urban structure whose perpetual changeability is to be safeguarded, allowed the Americans to achieve a goal that the Europeans had been unable to realize. In the United States, absolute freedom is granted to the single architectural fragment, which is situated in a context that is not formally conditioned by it. The American city gives maximum articulation to the secondary elements that shape it, while the laws governing the whole are strictly upheld.

Here urban planning and architecture are finally separated from each other. The geometric design of the plan does not seek—in Washington, Philadelphia, and later, New York—an architectural counterpart in the forms of the individual buildings. Unlike what happened in St. Petersburg or Berlin, here the architecture was free to explore the most diverse and remote areas of communication. The urban system was given only the task of asserting to what degree this freedom of figuration could be exploited, or rather, of ensuring, through its formal rigidity, a stable frame of reference. In this way the urban structure spurred the incredible wealth of expression that, especially in the second half of the nineteenth century and thereafter, found its way into the open grids of US cities. Free-trade ethics thus met up with the pioneer myth.

Form as Regressive Utopia

Thus far, what emerges most clearly from our summary analysis of the experiences and expectations of eighteenth-century architectural culture is the crisis of the traditional concept of form. This arises from an awareness of the problem of the city as an autonomous field of communicative experiences.

From the very beginnings, the architecture of the Enlightenment had already managed to formulate one of the principles that the path of contemporary art would follow: the disarticulation of form and the inorganic nature of structure. And it is not insignificant that the perception of these new formal values was linked from the start to the problem of the new city that was soon to become the institutional site of modern bourgeois society.

Yet the theorists' calls for a revision of formal principles led not so much to a true revolution of meaning, as to an acute crisis of values. The new dimensions presented by the problems of the industrial city over the course of the nineteenth century would only aggravate the crisis, in the face of which art struggled to find the proper paths by which it might follow the developments of urban reality.

On the other hand, the fragmentation of organic form occurred predominantly in architectural activity, without managing to find an outlet in the urban dimension. When, looking at a "piece" of Victorian architecture, we are struck by the exasperation of the "object" there before us, we rarely take into consideration that eclecticism and linguistic pluralism, for nineteenth-century architects, represented the proper response to the multiple disruptive stimuli produced by the new environment that technology's "universe of precision" had created.

The fact that architects were unable to respond to that "universe of precision" with anything more than a confused "more or less" should not come as a surprise. In actuality it was the urban structure—precisely insofar as it registered the conflicts that witnessed the victory of technological progress—that violently changed dimension, becoming an open structure in which any search for a point of equilibrium became a utopian proposition.

Architecture, however, at least according to the traditional notion, is a stable structure, which gives form to permanent values and consolidates an urban morphology.

Those who may wish to shatter this traditional notion and link architecture with the destiny of the city, can only conceive of the city itself as the specific site of technological production and as a technological product in itself, thereby reducing architecture to a mere moment in the chain of production. And yet in some way, Piranesi's prophecy of the bourgeois city as an "absurd machine" comes true in the nineteenth-century metropolises, which were organized as primary structures of capitalist economy.

The "zoning" that presided over the growth of those metropolises did not trouble, at first, to mask its own class character. Ideologies of radical or humanitarian derivation might well shed light on the irrationality of the industrial city, but they forgot (not coincidentally) that such a world appeared irrational only to the observer who entertained the illusion of being *au dessus de la réalité*. Humanitarian utopianism and radical critiques had one unexpected result: they convinced the progressive elements of the bourgeoisie themselves to pose the question of reconciling rationality and irrationality.

For all of the reasons elaborated thus far, this question would appear to be intrinsic to the formation of urban ideology. Taken in the abstract, it is also familiar to the figurative arts of the nineteenth century in general, since the very origin of Romantic eclecticism was a reassertion of ambiguity as a critical value in and of itself—the very same ambiguity that Piranesi had taken to its highest level.

What had allowed Piranesi to give voice, through primitivistic nostalgias and flights into the Sublime, to the terrifying prophecy of the eclipse of the sacred, is the same thing that allowed Romantic eclecticism to become the mouthpiece of the merciless concreteness of the commodified human environment, filling it with particles of already entirely worn-out values presented as such: as voiceless, false, bent in two, as if to show that no subjective force would ever again succeed in recovering an authenticity forever lost.

Nineteenth-century ambiguity lies entirely in the unrestrained exhibition of a false conscience that strives for final ethical redemption by displaying its own inauthenticity. If the mania for collection is the sign and tool of this ambiguity, then the city is its specific field of application: Impressionist painting, in attempting to redeem this ambiguity, will have to place itself at an observation point immersed in the urban structure but far removed from its meanings by the subtle distortions of lenses imitating an objective, scientific detachment.

While the first political responses to this situation had their roots in a recovery of the traditional utopianism that the Enlightenment seemed to have eclipsed, the specific responses of visual communication methods introduced a new type of utopia: that implicit in realized events, in the concreteness of constructed, verifiable "things." For this reason, the relationships between the whole current of nineteenth-century political utopianism and the ideas of the "modern movement," though plentiful, would remain very indirect. Indeed, we must consider the links normally established by modern historians between the utopias of Fourier, Owen, and Cabet, and the theoretical models of Unwin, Geddes, Howard, and Stein, on the one hand, and those of the Garnier–Le Corbusier current on the other, as hypotheses in need of careful verification. In all likelihood, they will eventually be recognized as dependent upon and integral to the very phenomena they are supposed to explain.[11]

It is clear, in any case, that the specific responses given by Marxist scholarship to the problem around which utopian thought is forever condemned to revolve, had two immediate effects on the formation of the new urban ideologies:

(1) By bringing the general questions back into a strictly structural framework, it made evident the concrete failure to which utopias condemn themselves, revealing as well the secret desire for ruin implicit in the very birth of the utopian notion;

(2) by annulling the Romantic dream of subjective action's having any direct effect on social destiny, it made it clear to bourgeois thinkers that the very concept of *destiny* was a creation linked to the new relations of production; as a sublimation of real phenomena, the virile acceptance of destiny—a cornerstone of bourgeois ethics—could redeem the misery and impoverishment that this same "destiny" had produced at all levels of social life and above all in its quintessential form: the city.

The end of utopianism and the birth of realism are not automatic moments in the formative development of the ideology of the "modern movement." On the contrary, around the 1830s, realist utopianism and utopian realism begin to overlap and complement each other. The decline of social utopianism confirmed ideology's surrender to the *politics of things* created by the laws of profit. Architectural ideology, in both its artistic and urban forms, was left with the utopia of form as a project for recuperating the human Totality in the ideal Synthesis, as a way of mastering Disorder through Order.

Architecture, therefore, insofar as it was directly linked to the reality of production, was not only the first discipline to accept, with rigorous lucidity, the consequences of its already realized commodification. Starting from problems specific to itself, modern architecture, as a whole, was able to create, even before the mechanisms and theories of Political Economy had created the instruments for it, an ideological climate for fully integrating design, at all levels, into a comprehensive Project aimed at the reorganization of production, distribution and consumption within the capitalist city.

Analyzing the course of the modern movement as an ideological instrument of capital (from around 1901, the year of Tony Garnier's "industrial city" project, to around 1939, the year in which its crisis became palpable at all levels and in all sectors), thus implies tracing a history that can be broken down into three successive phases:

(1) the first, which witnesses the formation of an urban ideology as a way of overcoming architectural Romanticism;

(2) the second, which witnesses the rise of the artistic avant-gardes as ideological projects and foregroundings of "unsatisfied needs" that are then handed over in that form—that is, as advanced goals that painting, poetry, music and sculpture can realize only on an ideal level—to architecture and urban planning, the only disciplines capable of realizing them in concrete form;

(3) the third, in which architectural ideology becomes the *ideology of the Plan*. This phase was, in turn, put into crisis and surpassed when, after the crash of 1929, with the formulation of anticyclical theories and the international reorganization of capital, the ideological function of architecture began to appear superfluous, or at least limited to fulfilling rearguard tasks of marginal importance.

The observations that follow do not pretend to any exhaustive treatment of this process; my intention was only to highlight a few of its salient points, in the hope of providing a methodological framework for future investigations and more detailed analyses.

The Dialectic of the Avant-Garde

It is very important to underscore that in criticizing Engels's "moral reaction" to the urban crowd, Benjamin used the latter's observations as a way of introducing the subject of the spread of working-class conditions into the general urban structure.[12]

One may disagree with the partiality with which Benjamin reads *The Situation of the Working Class in England*. What interests us is the way in which he moves from Engels's description of the masses to his thoughts on Baudelaire's relationship with the masses themselves. In judging Engels's and Hegel's reactions to be vestiges of a detachment from the new qualitative and quantitative aspects of urban reality, Benjamin notes that the ease and nonchalance with which the Parisian *flâneur* moves through the crowd have become natural modes of conduct for the modern user of the metropolis.

No matter how great the distance which [Baudelaire] cared to keep from it, he still was colored by it and, unlike Engels, was not able to view it from without. . . . The masses had become so much a part of Baudelaire that it is rare to find a description of them in his works. . . . Baudelaire describes neither the Parisians nor their city. Forgoing such descriptions enables him to invoke the ones in the form of the other. His crowd is always the crowd of a big city, his Paris is invariably overpopulated. It is this that makes him so superior to Barbier, whose descriptive method caused a rift between the masses and the city. In [Baudelaire's] *Tableaux parisiens* the secret presence of a crowd is demonstrable almost everywhere.[13]

This presence—or rather, this immanence—of the real relations of production in the conduct of the "public," who use the city while being unknowingly used by it, can be identified in the very presence of an observer, like Baudelaire, who is forced to recognize his own untenable position as participant in an ever more generalized commodification at the very moment in which he discovers, through his own production, that the only unavoidable necessity for the poet henceforth is prostitution.[14]

The poetry of Baudelaire, like the products exhibited at the universal expositions or the transformation of the urban morphology set in motion by Haussmann, marks a newly discovered awareness of the indissoluble dialectic existing between uniformity and diversity. It is still too early yet to speak of a tension between the exception and the rule, especially as regards the structure of the new bourgeois city. But one may speak of the tension between the forced commodification of the object and the subjective attempts to recuperate—falsely—its authenticity.

The problem is that now the only way left in the search for the authentic is the search for the eccentric. It is not only the poet who must accept his lot as mime—and this, incidentally, may explain why all the art of the time presents itself simultaneously as a deliberately "heroic" act and as a bluff, conscious of its own self-mystification—but the city itself, objectively structured as a machine for extracting social surplus value, reproduces, in its own conditioning mechanisms, the reality of the industrial modes of production.

Benjamin closely links the decline, in industrial labor, of *skill* and *experience*—still operative in handicrafts—to the experience of *shock* typical of the urban condition. He writes:

The unskilled worker is the one most deeply degraded by the drill of the machines. His work has been sealed off from experience; practice counts for nothing there. What the Fun Fair achieves with its Dodgem cars and other similar amusements is nothing but a taste of the drill to which the unskilled laborer is subjected in the factory—a sample which at times was for him the entire menu; for the art of being off center, in which the little man could acquire training in places like the Fun Fair, flourished concomitantly with unemployment. Poe's text [Benjamin here is referring to *The Man of the Crowd*, translated by Baudelaire] makes us understand the true connection between wildness and discipline. His pedestrians act as if they had adapted themselves to the machines and could express themselves only automatically. Their behavior is a reaction to shocks. "If jostled, they bowed profusely to the jostlers."[15]

There is, therefore, a profound affinity between the code of conduct connected to the experience of shock and the technique of the game of chance. "Since each operation at the machine is just as screened off from the preceding operation as a *coup* in a game of chance is from the one that preceded it, the drudgery of the laborer is, in its own way, a counterpart to the drudgery of the gambler. The work of both is equally devoid of substance."[16]
Despite the pointedness of his observations, Benjamin does not link—either in his essays on Baudelaire or in "The Work of Art in the Age of Mechanical Reproduction"—this invasion of the urban morphological structure by the modes of production with the response of the avant-garde movements to the question of the city.
The arcades and large department stores of Paris, like the universal expositions, were clearly places in which the crowd, in becoming its own spectacle, found a spatial and visual instrument for self-education from the point of view of capital. But throughout the nineteenth century, such recreational-pedagogical experiences, being centered around exceptional architectural typologies, continued to reveal the partiality of their propositions. The ideology of the public is not, in fact, an end in itself. It is but one aspect of the ideology of the city as a productive unit in the proper sense of the term, and as an instrument for coordinating the cycle of production-distribution-consumption.
This is why the ideology of consumption, far from constituting an isolated or subsequent moment of the organization of production, must offer itself to the public as an ideology of the *correct use* of the city. (It might be pertinent to recall here how important the question of conduct was to the European avant-gardes, and to the symptomatic example of Loos, who in 1903, upon his return from the United States, published two issues of the review *Das Andere* devoted to introducing, in an ironic, polemical tone, new, "modern" modes of urban conduct into the Viennese bourgeoisie.)
Until the moment the experience of the crowd was translated— as in Baudelaire—into a painful awareness of participation, it served to generalize an operative reality, but did not contribute to its advancement. It was at this moment, and only at this moment, that the linguistic revolution of modern art was summoned to make its own contribution.

To remove the experience of shock from all automatism, to use that experience as the foundation for visual codes and codes of action borrowed from already established characteristics of the capitalist metropolis—rapidity of change and organization, simultaneity of communications, accelerated rhythms of use, eclecticism—to reduce the structure of artistic experience to the status of pure object (an obvious metaphor for the object-commodity), to involve the public, as a unified whole, in a declaredly interclass and therefore antibourgeois ideology: such are the tasks taken on, as a whole, by the avant-gardes of the twentieth century.
To repeat: as a whole—that is, beyond any distinction between constructivism and protest art. Cubism, Futurism, Dada, De Stijl, all the historic avant-gardes arose and followed one another according to the laws typical of industrial production: continuous technical revolution is their very essence. For all the

avant-gardes—and not just in painting—the law of assemblage was fundamental. And since assembled objects belong to the real world, the painting became the neutral field into which the *experience of shock*, suffered in the city, was projected. Indeed, the problem now became that of teaching not how one should "suffer" that shock, but how one should absorb it and internalize it as an inevitable condition of existence.

The laws of production thus came to form part of a new universe of conventions explicitly posited as "natural." Herein lies the reason why the avant-gardes did not raise the question of appealing to the public. Indeed, the question could not even be raised: since they were interpreting something necessary and universal, the avant-gardes could easily accept being temporarily unpopular, knowing full well that their break with the past was the fundamental condition for their worth as models for action.

Art as model for action: this was the great guiding principle of the artistic uprising of the modern bourgeoisie, but at the same time it was the absolute that gave rise to new, irrepressible contradictions. Life and art having proved antithetical, one had to seek either instruments of mediation—and thus all artistic production had to accept problematics as the new ethical horizon—or ways by which art might pass into life, even at the cost of realizing Hegel's prophecy of the death of art.

It is here that the links holding the great tradition of bourgeois art together in a single whole become more concretely manifest. We can now see how our initial consideration of Piranesi as both theorist and critic of the conditions of an art *no longer universalizing and not yet bourgeois* serves to shed light on the problem. Criticism, problematics, programmatics: such are the pillars on which was founded the "modern movement," which as a program for modeling the "bourgeois man" as an absolute "type" undoubtedly had its own internal consistency (even if this is not the same consistency recognized by current historians).

Both Piranesi's *Campo Marzio* and Picasso's *Dame au violon* are "programs," even though the first organizes an architectural dimension and the second a mode of human behavior. Both use the technique of shock, even though Piranesi's etching uses preformed historical materials and Picasso's painting, artificial materials (as later Duchamp, with greater rigor, would also do). Both discover the reality of a machine-universe, even though the eighteenth-century urban project makes that universe abstract and recoils in horror from its discovery, while Picasso's canvas works entirely within it.

More importantly, however, both Piranesi and Picasso "universalize," through an excess of truth attained with the tools of a profoundly critical elaboration of form, a reality that could still have been considered wholly particular. But the "program" inherent in the Cubist painting goes well beyond the canvas itself. The "ready-made" objects introduced in 1912 by Braque and Picasso, and codified as new means of communication by Duchamp, ratify the self-sufficiency of reality and the definitive repudiation, by reality itself, of all representation. The painter can only analyze this reality. His supposed dominion over form merely covers up something that he does not want to accept: that henceforth it is form that dominates the painter.

Except that now "form" has to be understood as the logic of subjective reactions within the objective universe of production. Cubism, as a whole, tends to define the laws of these reactions: it is symptomatic that Cubism began with the subjective and led to an absolute rejection of it (as Apollinaire would realize, with apprehension). As a "program," what Cubism wanted to create was a mode of behavior. Its antinaturalism, however, contained nothing that might persuade the public; we persuade someone only when we maintain that the object of persuasion is outside of and superimposed upon the one to whom we are addressing ourselves. Cubism's intention was instead to demonstrate the reality of the "new nature" created by capital, and its necessary, universal character, in which necessity and freedom coincide.

This is why the canvases of Braque, Picasso, and to an even greater extent Juan Gris adopt the technique of assemblage: to give absolute form to the linguistic universe of the *civilisation machiniste*. Primitivism and antihistoricism are consequences, not causes, of their fundamental choices.

As techniques for analyzing a totalizing universe, both Cubism and De Stijl are explicit invitations to action. In writing about their artistic products, one could easily speak of the *fetishization of the art object and its mystery*.

The public had to be provoked. That was the only way people could be inserted actively into the *universe of precision* dominated by the laws of production. The passivity of Baudelaire's *flâneur* must be overcome and translated into active participation in the urban scene. The city itself is the object to which neither the Cubist paintings, nor the Futurist "slaps," nor the nihilism of Dada referred specifically, but which remained—precisely because it was continually presupposed—the reference value to which the avant-gardes tried to measure up. Mondrian would later have the courage to "name" the city as the final object at which Neoplasticist composition aimed; yet he would be forced to acknowledge that once it was translated into the urban structure, painting—now reduced to a mere model of behavior—would have to die.

Baudelaire discovered that the commodification of the poetic product could be accentuated by the poet's very attempt to free himself from his objective conditions: the prostitution of the artist follows the moment of his greatest human sincerity. De Stijl and, to an even greater extent, Dada, discovered that there were two paths for the suicide of art: silent immersion in the structures of the city through the idealizing of its contradictions, or the violent insertion of the irrational—it, too, idealized, and drawn from the city—into the structures of artistic communication.

De Stijl became a mode of formal control of production, while Dada wanted to give apocalyptic expression to its inherent absurdity. The nihilist critique formulated by Dada, however, ended up becoming a tool for controlling design. It should come as no surprise when one encounters, even in a philological context, the many points of tangency between this most destructive of twentieth-century movements and the more "constructive" ones.

Indeed what are Dada's ferocious dismantling of linguistic materials and its anti-programmatic position, if not sublimations, in spite of everything, of the automatism and commodification of "values" now spread to all levels of existence by capitalist advancements? De Stijl and Bauhaus—the former in a sectarian manner, the latter in eclectic fashion—introduced the *ideology of the plan* into a *design* method that was ever more deeply linked to the city as a productive structure. Dada, through absurdity, demonstrated the necessity of the plan without ever naming it.

All the historic avant-gardes, moreover, adopted the political parties' model of action as their own. While Dada and Surrealism can be seen as particular expressions of the anarchic spirit, De Stijl and Bauhaus did not hesitate to present themselves as global alternatives to political praxis. Alternatives that, it should be noted, assumed all the characteristics of an ethical choice.

De Stijl opposed Chaos, the empirical, and the everyday with the principle of Form. Theirs was a Form that takes into account the thing that concretely renders reality formless, chaotic and impoverished. The horizon of industrial production, which spiritually impoverishes the world, was dismissed as a value in itself, but subsequently transformed into a new value through its sublimation. The Neoplasticist dismantling of elementary forms corresponded to the discovery that the "new wealth" of the Spirit could no longer be sought outside of the "new poverty" subsumed by the civilization of the machine; the disjointed recomposition of those elementary forms then sublimated the mechanical universe, demonstrating that there can no longer be any form of recovery of the whole (of being as of art) that does not derive from the problematics of form itself.

Dada, on the other hand, plunged into Chaos. Representing chaos confirmed its reality; by mocking it, they posited a need and decried the fact that it was unfulfilled. This need was the very same control of the Formless that De Stijl, all the various European constructivist currents, and even nineteenth-century formalist aesthetics—from *Sichtarbeit* on—had embraced as the new frontier of visual communications. It is hardly surprising, therefore, that Dada's Anarchy and De Stijl's Order should have met and converged, in a theoretical context, in the review *Mécano*, and in an operative context, in the formulation of the instruments of a new syntax.

Chaos and Order were thus sanctioned by the historic avant-gardes as the "values," in the proper sense of the term, of the new city of capital.

Chaos, of course, is a given, while Order is a goal. Yet Form henceforth should not be sought beyond Chaos, but within it: it is Order that confers meaning on Chaos and translates it into value, into "freedom." To redeem the formlessness of the city of profit-ruled consumption, one must draw upon all its progressive valences. And it is the Plan that the avant-gardes called upon to carry out this maieutic task, before discovering at once that they were incapable of giving it any concrete form.

It was at this point that architecture was able to enter the scene, by absorbing and overcoming all the demands of the historic avant-gardes—and indeed by throwing them into crisis, since architecture alone was in a position to provide real answers to the demands made by Cubism, Futurism, Dada, De Stijl, and all the various Constructivisms and Productivisms.

The Bauhaus, as the decantation chamber of the avant-gardes, fulfilled this historic task: it selected from among all the contributions of the avant-gardes, testing them against the demands of the reality of industrial production. Design, as a method of organizing production more than of configuring objects, did away with the utopian vestiges inherent in the poetics of the avant-gardes. Ideology was no longer superimposed on activity—which was now concrete because it was connected to real cycles of production—but was inherent in the activity itself.

But design too, despite its realism, presented unsatisfied demands; and in the impetus it gave to the organization of enterprises and production, it too contained a hint of utopianism. (This utopia, however, served the goal of reorganizing production, a goal its promoters fully intended to achieve.) The Plan embraced by the leading architectural movements (the term "avant-garde" is no longer applicable), starting with Le Corbusier's *Plan Voisin* (1925) and the stabilization of the Bauhaus (around 1921), contained the following contradiction: starting from the building sector, architectural culture discovered that only by linking that sector to the reorganization of the city could preestablished goals be satisfactorily met. But this was equivalent to saying that, just as the demands presented by the avant-gardes had pointed to the visual communications sector most directly entrenched in the economic process (i.e., architecture and industrial design), so the planning formulated by architectural and urban theorists likewise pointed toward something other than itself: to wit, toward a restructuring of production and consumption in general—toward a *plan for capital*, in other words. In this sense, architecture—starting with itself—mediated between realism and utopia. The utopia lay in stubbornly continuing to hide the fact that the ideology of planning could be realized in building production only by making clear that the true Plan could only take shape beyond this sector; and that, indeed, once the Plan came within the scope of the general reorganization of production, architecture and urban planning would become its objects, not its subjects.

Architectural culture, in the 1920s, was not ready to accept such consequences. What it understood most clearly was its own "political" task. It was a question of architecture (read: the planned reorganization of building production and the city as a productive organism) over Revolution. Le Corbusier articulated this choice very clearly, and it is also implicit in the writings of others such as Mondrian and Gropius.

In the meanwhile, starting with the most politically engaged circles—from the Novembergruppe, to the review G, to the Berlin Ring—architectural culture defined itself technically. Accepting with lucid objectivity all the avant-garde's apocalyptic conclusions as to the "death of art" and the purely "technical" role of the intellectual, the Central European Neue Sachlichkeit adapted the very method of design to the idealized structure of the assembly line. The forms and methods of industrial labor became part of the organization of design and were reflected in the proposed use of the object.

From the standardized part and the cell to the single block, the Siedlung, and finally to the city: such is the assembly line that architectural culture devised between the wars with exceptional clarity and consistency. Each "piece" in the line is fully resolved and tends to disappear or, better yet, to dissolve formally in the assembly.

The result of all this was the revolutionization of the aesthetic experience itself. No longer is it *objects* that presented themselves for appraisal, but an entire *process*, to be experienced and used as such. The user, called upon to fill the "open" spaces of Mies van der Rohe or Gropius, is the central element in this process. Architecture, in calling upon the public to participate in the design—since the new forms were no longer individualistic absolutes but proposals for organizing community life, as in Gropius's *integrated architecture*—forced the ideology of the public to make a leap forward. The dream of Morris's romantic socialism—an art made by all for all—here takes ideological form within the ironclad laws of profit. In this respect, too, the ultimate test for the theoretical hypothesis would be the city.

"Radical" Architecture and the City

In his fundamental work *Grossstadtarchitektur*, Ludwig Hilberseimer writes:

The architecture of the large city depends essentially on the solution given to two factors: the elementary cell and the urban organism as a whole. The single room, as the constitutive element of the dwelling, will determine its appearance, and since the dwellings in turn form blocks, the room will become a factor in the urban configuration, representing architecture's true goal. Likewise the planimetric structure of the city will have a substantial influence on the design of the dwelling and the room.[17]

The large city is, therefore, a true unity. Reading beyond the author's actual intentions, we may translate his assertions as follows: It is the whole modern city itself which has structurally become an enormous "social machine." This is the aspect of urban economics that Hilberseimer, like almost all the German theorists of the twenties and thirties, chose to isolate in order to analyze and resolve its component parts separately. What he writes on the relationship between the cell and the urban organism is exemplary for its lucidity of exposition and for its skillful reduction of problems to their essential aspects. The cell is not only the first element in the continuous production line whose ultimate product is the city; it is also the element that determines the dynamics of building aggregations. Its value as *type* allows it to be analyzed and resolved in the abstract: the building unit, in this sense, represents the foundational structure of a production program from which all further typological components have been excluded. The single building [*unità edilizia*] is no longer an "object" now. It is only the place in which the individual cells, through elementary assembly, assume physical form. As infinitely reproducible elements, these units conceptually embody the primary structures of a production line that dispenses with the ancient concepts of "place" and "space." In keeping with his own assumptions, Hilberseimer posits the entire city organism as the second term of his theorem. The shape of the cell predetermines the planning coordinates of the urban whole; the city's structure may then alter, by dictating the rules of its assemblage, the typology of the cell.[18]

In the rigid articulation of the production plan, the specific dimension of architecture, in the traditional sense of the term, disappears. As an "exception" to the homogeneity of the city, the architectural object has been completely dissolved. Hilberseimer writes:

As great masses have to be shaped according to a general law, dominated by multiplicity, . . . the general case, the rule, is emphasized while the exception is set aside, the nuance obliterated. Measure reigns, forcing chaos to become form, logical, univocal, mathematical form.[19]

And again:

The need to shape a heterogeneous and often gigantic mass of materials in accordance with a formal law equally valid for each element implies a reduction of architectural form to its most formal, necessary, general need: a reduction, that is, to cubic, geometrical forms, which represent the basic elements of all architecture.[20]

This is not a "purist" manifesto, but a logical conclusion drawn from hypotheses that hew stubbornly to the scientific method in their conceptual elaboration. By not offering "models" for design, but rather presenting the coordinates and dimensions of the design at the most abstract (because the most general) level possible, Hilberseimer reveals—more than do Gropius, Mies, or Bruno Taut around the same time—to what new tasks the capitalistic reorganization of Europe was summoning its architects.

In the face of modernized production techniques and the expansion and rationalization of the market, the architect, as producer of "objects," became an incongruous figure. It was no longer a question of giving form to single elements of the urban fabric, nor even to simple prototypes. Once the true unity of the production cycle has been identified in the city, the only task the architect can have is to *organize* that cycle. Taking the proposition to its extreme conclusion, Hilberseimer insists on the role of elaborating "organizational models" as the only one that fully reflects the need for Taylorizing building production and the new task of the technician, who is now completely integrated into this process.

On the basis of this position, Hilberseimer was able to avoid involvement in the "crisis of the object" so anxiously articulated by such architects as Loos or Taut. For Hilberseimer, the "object" was not in crisis because it had already disappeared from his spectrum of considerations. The only emerging imperative was that dictated by the laws of organization, and therein lies what has been correctly seen as Hilberseimer's greatest contribution.

What, on the other hand, has not been appreciated is Hilberseimer's utter refusal to consider architecture as an instrument of knowledge. Even Mies van der Rohe was divided on this issue. In the houses on the Afrikanische Strasse in Berlin, he is rather close to Hilberseimer's positions, while in the *Weissenhofsiedlung* of Stuttgart, he wavers in his approach. In the project for the curvilinear, glass and steel skyscraper, however, and in the monument to Karl Liebknecht and Rosa Luxemburg, the 1935 housing project, and finally even in the Tugendhat house, he explores what margins of the reflective approach still remained to the architect.

It is of little interest to us, here, to follow the inner workings of this dialectic, which was rife throughout the modern movement. We should, however, note that a good number of the contradictions and obstacles that the movement found in its path arose from the attempt to separate technical propositions and cognitive aims.

Ernst May's plan for Frankfurt, Martin Wagner's Berlin, Fritz Schumacher's Hamburg, and Cornelis van Eesteren's Amsterdam are the most important chapters in the history of modern urban planning. Yet beside the oases of order that were the *Siedlungen*—true *constructed utopias*, on the margins of an urban reality little affected by them—the old cities continued to accumulate and multiply their contradictions. And for the most part, these contradictions would soon appear more vital than the tools established by the architectural milieu to control them.

The architecture of Expressionism succeeded in absorbing the ambiguous vitality of these contradictions. The Viennese *Höfe* and the public buildings of Poelzig or Mendelsohn were clearly foreign to the new methodologies of urban intervention of the avant-garde movements. These experiences refused in numerous ways to be situated within the new horizons discovered by an art that accepted its own "mechanical reproduction" as a means toward bearing upon human behavior. Still, like such art, they seemed to assume a critical value, specifically in regard to the growth of the modern industrial cities.

Works such as Poelzig's Schauspieltheater in Berlin, Fritz Höger's Chilehaus and other Hamburg buildings, and the Berlin buildings of Hans Hertlein and Ernst and Günther Paulus, certainly did not constitute a new urban reality. But by exasperating already existing forms through an excess of pathos, they commented on the contradictions of the operative reality.

The two poles of Expressionism and the Neue Sachlichkeit once again symbolized the inherent rift in European culture.

Between the destruction of the *object*, its replacement by a *process* intended to be experienced as such (a transformation effected by the artistic revolution brought about by the Bauhaus and the Constructivist currents) and the exasperation of the object (typical of the lacerating but ambiguous eclecticism of the Expressionists), there could be no real dialogue.

Yet let us not be deceived by appearances. This was a clash between intellectuals who reduced their own ideological potential to the orchestration of up-to-date programs for a production system in the process of reorganization, and intellectuals whose work involved exploiting the backwardness of European capitalism. The subjectivism of Häring or Mendelsohn, in this sense, assumes a critical import in regard to the Taylorism of Hilberseimer or Gropius; but objectively speaking, it is a critique made from a rearguard position that is therefore incapable, by its very nature, of proposing universal alternatives.

Mendelsohn's self-publicizing architecture involved the creation of persuasive "monuments" in the service of commercial capital, while Häring's intimism played on the late Romantic tendencies of the German bourgeoisie. Still, to present the dialectic of twentieth-century architecture as a unitary cycle is not entirely off the mark, even if such a point of view is tenable only from within this cycle.

The rejection of contradiction as a premise for objectivity and the rationalization of planning revealed its own partiality at the very moment when architecture came closest to the political power structures. The very goal of the social democratic architects of central Europe was the unification of administrative power and the intellectual project. In this sense, it is no accident that May, Wagner, and Taut should have assumed political offices in the administrations of social democratic cities. If the entire city was now to assume the structure of an industrial machine, different categories of problems should find their solutions in it: first and foremost the conflict between parasitic mechanisms of ground rent, which impeded the expansion and technological revolutionization of the building market, and the need to organize, comprehensively, the machine-city by giving it a role in stimulating its own functions.

The architectural project, the urban model it spawned, and the economic and technological premises on which it was based—public ownership of the land and systems of industrialized construction modeled on production cycles programmed within the urban sphere—were indissolubly interconnected. Architectural science became fully integrated into the ideology of the plan, while formal choices themselves were only variables dependent on it. All of May's work in Frankfurt can be read as the highest expression of this concrete "politicization" of architecture. The industrialization of the construction site conformed to the minimum unit of production identified in the *Siedlung*. The primary element of the industrial cycle within this system was centered around the service nucleus (the *Frankfurter Küche*). The modeling of the *Siedlungen* and their displacement within the city to lands directly administered by the city government were made possible by city policies. It was at this point that the formal model of the *Siedlung*, because of its flexibility, granted cultural approval to, and made "real," the political objectives wholly embraced by architects.

Nazi propaganda would later speak of the Frankfurt quarters as *constructed socialism*. We, instead, should read them as realized social democracy. It must be noted, however, that the task befalling this concurrence of political and intellectual authority was merely that of mediating between structures and superstructures. This was clearly reflected in the structure of the city itself: the closed economy of the *Siedlung* was mirrored in the fragmented nature of the intervention, which left intact the contradictions of a city that had not been regulated or restructured as an organic system.

The utopianism of the Central European architectural culture of the 1920s lay precisely in the fiduciary relationship established between leftist intellectuals, advanced sectors of capital, and political administrations. While solutions restricted to specific areas tended, in this relationship, to present themselves as highly generalized models—policies of eminent domain and expropriation, technological experiments, formal elaborations of the *Siedlung* typology—they revealed their limited efficacy when put to the test.

May's Frankfurt, like Mächler's and Wagner's Berlin, certainly tended to reproduce the factory model at the social level, to give the city the "shape" of a production machine, and to produce the appearance of universal proletarianization within the urban structure and the mechanisms of distribution and consumption. (The interclassism of central European urban planning projects was a goal continually proposed by theorists.)

But the unity of the urban image, a formal metaphor of the proposed "new synthesis" and an obvious sign of the thrilling collective dominion over nature and those means of production confined within the sphere of a new "human" utopia, was never realized by the German and Dutch intellectuals. Strictly integrated into specific urban and regional planning policies, they fashioned models of intervention to be applied universally. The model of the *Siedlung* is one such example. Yet a theoretical constant of this sort reproduced in the city the disaggregate form of the early technological production line: the city remained an aggregate of parts functionally unified at the lowest level, and even within each single "piece"—the working-class quarter—the unification of methods soon proved to be a rather uncertain tool.

The crisis, in the specific area of architecture, came to a head in 1930, in Berlin's Siemensstadt. It is quite incredible that modern historians have not yet acknowledged the famous Berlin *Siedlung*, planned by Scharoun, as a crucial historical moment in which one of the most serious ruptures within the "modern movement" occurred.

Siemensstadt revealed the utopian character of the premise that design, in its different dimensional scales, could possess methodological unity. On the basis of an urban design that some, perhaps correctly, have ascribed to the ironic deformations of Klee, such architects as Bartning, Gropius, Scharoun, Häring, and Forbat showed that the dissolution of the architectural object within the formative process of the whole reflects the contradictions of the modern movement itself. In contrast to Gropius and Bartning, who remained loyal to the conception of the *Siedlung* as an *assembly line*, there are the allusive ironies of Scharoun and the ostentatious organicism of Häring. If, to use Benjamin's terminology, "the destruction of the aura" traditionally associated with the "piece" of architecture was consummated in the ideology of the *Siedlung*, Scharoun's and Häring's "objects" aimed instead at recuperating an "aura," however much this aura might be conditioned by the new modes of production and formal structures.

The Siemensstadt episode, moreover, was merely the most clamorous of its kind. In fact, with the exception of Cornelis van Eesteren's plan for Amsterdam, between 1930 and 1940 the ideal of the European constructivist movements—that of founding a *city of a single tendency*—decidedly entered a state of crisis.

All the contradictory aspects assumed by the modern capitalist city—improbability, polyfunctionality, multiplicity and lack of organic structure—remained outside the analytical rationalization pursued by central European architecture.

The Crisis of Utopia: Le Corbusier at Algiers

To absorb that multiplicity, to temper the improbable with the certainty of the plan, to reconcile organic structure and disorganization by exacerbating the dialectical relationship between them, to demonstrate that the highest level of productive planning coincides with the maximum "productivity of the spirit": such were the objectives that Le Corbusier delineated, with a lucidity unparalleled within *progressive* European architectural culture at the time, ever aware of the triple front on which modern architecture had to fight. If architecture was now synonymous with organization of production, it was also true that distribution and use were also determinant factors of the cycle, in addition to production itself. *The architect is an organizer*, not a designer of objects. This statement of Le Corbusier's was not a slogan, but an imperative linking intellectual initiative and *la civilisation machiniste*. As the advance guard of this *civilisation*, architects, in anticipating and determining its plans (however limited to specific sectors), must articulate their activity in three different directions: (1) by addressing an *appel aux industriels*, and a choice of building typologies, to business and industry; (2) by pursuing the search for an *authority* capable of reconciling construction and urban planning with civil reorganization programs through the institution of the CIAM; (3) by exploiting the articulation of form at its highest level in order to make the public an active and conscious user of the architectural product.

To be more precise: form assumed the task of making the unnatural world of technological precision *authentic and natural*. And since this world tended to subjugate nature as a whole in an ongoing process of transformation, the entire anthropogeographic landscape became, for Le Corbusier, the living subject on which the reorganized cycle of building production must lay its emphasis.

But Le Corbusier also discovered that financial prudence, individualism in enterprise, and the persistence of archaic income mechanisms such as ground rent, perilously obstructed the development of civilization, the expression and appraisal of production, and the "human" yield of this expansion.

With the typological formulation of the Dom-ino unit, the *Immeuble-villa*, the City for Three Million Inhabitants, and the *Plan Voisin* for Paris, Le Corbusier, in a "patient search" conducted between 1919 and 1929, arrived at precise scales and tools of intervention, tested general hypotheses in partial realizations—seen as laboratory experiments—and went beyond the models of German "rationalism," intuiting the correct dimension in which the urban question must be considered.

Between 1929 and 1931, with the plans for Montevideo, Buenos Aires, São Paulo, and Rio, and finally with the Obus plan for Algiers, Le Corbusier formulated the most advanced theoretical hypothesis of modern urbanism, which to this day remains unsurpassed on both the ideological and formal levels.

In contrast to Taut, May, and Gropius, Le Corbusier broke the unbroken associative chain of architecture-neighborhood-city. The urban structure in itself, as a physical and functional unity, became the repository of a new scale of values; it was to the dimension of the landscape itself that one should look for the meaning of its communications.

At Algiers, Corbusier took the old Casbah, the hills of Fort-l'Empéreur, and the coastal inlets as raw materials to be reused, veritable, gigantic ready-made objects to which the new structure redefining them would offer a previously nonexistent unity, overturning their original significations. Yet this maximum conditioning must be accompanied by a maximum of freedom and flexibility. The economic premise of the entire operation was clear: the Obus plan would not limit itself to demanding a new "territorial statute" that, by overcoming the early capitalist anarchy of land accumulation, would make the whole area available for the unitary, organic reorganization of what would thereby become an urban system in the proper sense of the term.

The industrial object does not presuppose any univocal situation in space. Underlying the concept of mass production is the radical notion of overcoming all spatial hierarchy. The technological universe does not distinguish between the *here* and the *there*; its natural sphere of operations is the whole human environment—a purely topological field (as the Cubists, Futurists, and Elementarists well understood). In the reorganization of the city, the full availability of the terrain is no longer enough: it is now the whole three-dimensional space that must become available to be shaped by a planned technologization. Thus two levels of intervention within the unified city must be distinguished: the cycles of production and consumption.

The restructuring of the entire urban space and surrounding landscape thus corresponds to the need to rationalize the total organization of the urban *machine*: on this scale, technological structures and transportation systems must constitute a unitary "image" in which the antinaturalism of the *terrains artificiels* laid out at various levels, and the exceptional nature of the road network—the superhighway running at the highest level of the serpentine block designed for the workers' residences—take on a symbolic meaning. The housing blocks of Fort-l'Empéreur, in their formal freedom, assume the values emblematic of the Surrealist avant-garde;

the rounded buildings—like the free forms inside the Villa Savoye or the ironic *assemblages* of the Beistegui attic on the Champs-Elysées—are enormous objects that enact an abstract, sublimated "dance of contradictions."[21]

Even at the level of the urban structure—here finally resolved into an organic unity—what emerges is the positive nature of the contradictions, the reconciliation of the problematic with the rational, and the "heroic" resolution of violent tensions. Only through the structure of the image, *and in no other way*, can the reign of necessity merge with the reign of freedom—even though the former is identified with the rigor of the plan and latter with the recuperation, within the plan, of a higher human consciousness.

Le Corbusier, too, uses the technique of shock: the *objets à réaction poétique*, however, are now connected with one another within a dialectical, organic whole. The formal and functional dynamic is inescapable: at every level of use and interpretation, Le Corbusier's Algiers entails the total involvement of the public. It is worth noting, however, that here this involvement is predicated on a critical, reflective, intellectual participation. An "inattentive reading" of the urban images would in fact produce an obscure result—although there is certainly no saying that Le Corbusier did not perhaps intend this secondary effect as well, as a necessary moment of indirect stimulus.[22]

Le Corbusier's point, however, cannot be reduced to "dispelling anxiety by internalizing its causes." At the lowest level of production—that of the single residential cell—the goal is to gain a maximum flexibility, interchangeability, and possibility of rapid use. The broadest freedom of insertion of preformed residential elements is made possible within the meshes of the larger structures, which are made up of superimposed *terrains artificiels*. To the public, this is an invitation to become active planners of the city: in one illustrative sketch, Le Corbusier actually goes so far as to imagine the insertion of eccentric, eclectic elements within the meshes of fixed structures. The "freedom" granted to the public must be pushed so far that it will allow this same public—the proletariat, in the case of the serpentine edifice uncoiling itself along the sea, and the bourgeoisie, up on the hills of Fort-l'Empéreur—to express its own "bad taste." Architecture thus becomes both a pedagogical act and a tool of collective integration.

For industry, on the other hand, this freedom assumes even greater significance. Unlike May in his *Frankfurter Küche*, Le Corbusier does not crystallize the minimum production unit in standard functional elements. On the level of the individual object, one must consider the need for continuous technological revolution, styling, and rapid use—needs dictated by an active capitalism in the process of expansion. The residential cell, theoretically usable in a very short time, can be replaced with every change that occurs in individual needs—the needs, that is, created by the renovation of the residential models and standards dictated by production.[23]

In this light, the significance of the project becomes quite clear. The subject of the urban reorganization is a public that is called upon and made a critical participant in its own creative role. Through theoretically homogeneous functions, the vanguard of industry, the "authorities," and the users of the city become involved in the impetuous, "exalting" process of continuous development and transformation. From the reality of production to the image and the use of the image, the whole urban machine pushes the "social" potential of the *civilisation machiniste* to the most extreme of its implicit possibilities.

An obvious question now arises: Why is it that the Algiers project, the subsequent plans for European and African cities, and even the smaller projects advanced by Le Corbusier, remain a dead letter? Is there not perhaps a contradiction between what we have said—that is, that these projects should be seen as the most advanced and formally elevated hypothesis of bourgeois culture in the field of design and urban planning to this day—and the failures experienced firsthand by Le Corbusier?

Many answers may be given to this question, all of them valid and complementary. Above all, however, we should remember that Le Corbusier worked as an "intellectual" in the strict sense. He did not become associated—like Taut, May, or Wagner—with local government powers. His hypotheses start from specific realities (the physical geography and historical stratification of Algiers are, of course, exceptions, and the form of the plan taking these into account is unique to those circumstances); but the method guiding them is broadly applicable on a general scale. From the particular to the universal: the exact opposite of the method followed by the intellectuals of the Weimar social democracy. Nor is it coincidental that in Algiers, Le Corbusier worked without a commission and without pay for more than four years. He "invented" his commission and made it universal, ever willing to finance his own active and creative role.

As a result, his models have all the characteristics of laboratory experiments: and in no case can a laboratory model be translated *tout court* into reality. But that is not all. In this case, the universal applicability of the hypothesis clashed with the backward structures that it was supposed to stimulate. When what is needed is a revolutionization of architecture in keeping with the most advanced functions of an economic and technological reality still incapable of giving it coherent, organic form, it should hardly come as a surprise if realistic hypotheses are seen as utopian.

But the failure of Algiers, and Le Corbusier's "failure" in general, cannot only be correctly understood when seen in the context of the international crisis of modern architecture.

Capitalist Development Confronts Ideology

It is interesting to look at how modern historians have attempted to explain the crisis of modern architecture. They place the beginnings of the crisis in the years around 1930, and generally consider its exacerbation to continue to this day. Nearly all the initial "blame" for the crisis they lay at the feet of the Fascisms of Europe on the one hand, and Stalinism on the other. In so doing, they systematically ignore the introduction, throughout the world, immediately after the economic crisis of 1929, of a new and decisive factor: the international reorganization of capital and the establishment of anti-cyclical planning systems.

It is significant that almost all the economic objectives formulated by Keynes in his *General Theory* can be found, in purely ideological form, at the basis of the poetics of modern architecture. The foundation of Keynesian interventionism is the same as that of the poetics of all modern art: "To free oneself from the fear of the future by eyeing that future as present" (Negri). And in a strictly political sense, this also underlies the urban planning theories of Le Corbusier. Keynes comes to terms with the "party of catastrophe," and aims at coopting its threat by absorbing it at ever new levels;[24] Le Corbusier notes the reality of class in the modern city and takes its conflicts to a higher level, giving shape to the most advanced plan for integrating the public, whom he involves as operator and active user of the urban mechanism of development, now rendered organically "human."

Thus is our initial hypothesis confirmed. Architecture as the *ideology of the Plan* is swept away by the *reality of the Plan* the moment the plan came down from the utopian level and became an operant mechanism.

The crisis of modern architecture begins at the precise moment when its natural target—large industrial capital—makes architecture's underlying ideology its own, setting aside the superstructures. As of that moment, architectural ideology has exhausted its own functions: its obstinate insistence on seeing its hypotheses realized will become either a springboard for going beyond backward conditions, or a troublesome disturbance.

The regression and anxious struggles of the modern movement from 1935 to the present day can be read in this light. The most general demands for the rationalization of cities and outlying areas remain unmet, continuing to act as indirect stimuli for realizations compatible with the partial goals established along the way by the system.

At this point something inexplicable, at least at first glance, occurs. The ideology of form seems to abandon its own vocation to realism, turning to the second pole inherent in the dialectic of bourgeois culture. Although the "utopia of the project" is not abandoned, an attempt is made to counteract the processes that have concretely risen above the ideological level by recuperating Chaos, by contemplating the very same anxiety that Constructivism seemed to have forever overcome, and by sublimating Disorder.

Having arrived at an undeniable impasse due to the inherent contradictions of capitalist development, architectural ideology gives up its role as stimulus to the structures of production and hides behind ambiguous slogans contesting the "technological civilization."

Incapable of analyzing the real causes of the crisis of design, and concentrating all its attention on the internal problems of design itself, contemporary criticism has been accumulating symptomatic ideological inventions in an attempt to give new substance to the alliance between techniques of visual communication and industrial production. It is no accident that the area singled out for the redemption of this alliance—now postulated in terms of an ambiguous "neo-humanism" which, compared to the Neue Sachlichkeit of the 1920s, has the serious drawback of mystifying its own role as mediator between Utopia and Production—is the image of the city itself.

City as superstructure, then. Actually, art is now called upon to give the city a superstructural face. Pop Art, Op Art, analyses of the city's *imageability*, and *esthétique prospective*, all these things converge toward a single objective: that of dissimulating the contradictions of the contemporary city, resolving them in polyvalent *images*, figuratively glorifying that formal complexity which, when read with the proper parameters, proves to be nothing more than the explosion of the incurable conflicts that elude the plans of advanced capitalism. The recuperation of the concept of *art* is thus useful to this new task of covering up. Just when industrial design assumes the lead in technological production, influencing its quality for the purpose of increasing consumption, Pop Art, by recycling its residues, places itself at its rear guard. This, however, corresponds precisely to the twofold demand now made of the technologies of visual communication. An art that refuses to place itself in the vanguard of the cycles of production, demonstrates, well beyond all verbal challenges, that the consumption process extends to infinity, and that even *rubbish*, when sublimated into useless or nihilistic objects, can assume a new *use value*, thus reentering, if only by the back door, the cycle of production and consumption.

Yet this rear guard is also an indication of the capitalist plan's refusal—perhaps only temporary—to fully resolve the contradictions of the city and transform the city into a totally organized machine without archaic forms of waste or generalized dysfunctions.

In such a phase as this, one must act to convince the public that the contradictions, imbalances, and chaos typical of the contemporary city are inevitable—that such chaos in itself, in fact, contains unexplored riches, unlimited possibilities to be turned to account, bright and shining values to be presented as new social fetishes.

Carnaby Street and the new utopianism are thus different aspects of one phenomenon. Architectural and supertechnological utopianism; the rediscovery of the *game* as a condition for the public's involvement; the prophecies of "aesthetic societies"; invitations to establish the *primacy of the imagination*: such are the proposals of the new urban ideologies.[25]

There is one text in particular that manages to synthesize and balance all the different exhortations for art to assume a new, persuasive rather than operative role. And it is significant that this book, the *Livre blanc de l'art total*, by Pierre Restany, explicitly brings up all the same themes that arise from a concerned awareness that the objectives pursued until now have been eroding. The result of such erosion is that the "new" proposals for rescuing art have taken on the very same connotations, in different words, as those of the early-century avant-gardes, without possessing any of the clarity or self-confidence that the latter could quite justifiably flaunt. Restany writes:

The metamorphosis of languages is but the reflection of the structural changes of society. Technology, by increasingly reducing the gap between art (the synthesis of new languages) and nature (modern, technical, urban reality), plays a determinant role as catalyst of a sufficient, necessary process.

Beyond its vast potential and the limitless worlds it opens up, technology also displays a flexibility indispensable in a period of transition: it allows the conscious artist to act not upon the formal effects of communication, as before, but upon its very terms: the human imagination. *Contemporary technology, in short, allows the imagination to take power.* Freed of all normative impediments, of all questions of realization or production, the creative imagination can identify itself with global consciousness. *Prospective aesthetics is the vehicle of man's greatest hope: the collective liberation of humanity.* The socialization of art represents the convergence of the forces of creation and production toward a goal of dynamic synthesis and technical metamorphosis: it is through such restructuring that man and reality find their true, modern face, that they become *natural* again, having overcome all alienation.[26]

Thus the circle closes. Marcusian mythology is used to demonstrate that it is possible to achieve a vaguely defined "collective freedom" within the current relations of production, and not through their subversion. One need only "socialize art" and put it at the head of technological "progress": never mind that the entire course of modern art demonstrates the utopianism—perhaps understandable yesterday, merely backward today—of such a proposition. Thus it actually becomes legitimate to assimilate even the most ambiguous slogans of May 1968. *L'imagination au pouvoir* sanctions the reconciliation between revolt and conservation, between symbolic metaphor and productive process, between diversion and *Realpolitik*.

And that is not all. With the reassertion of art's role as mediator one may again assign it the *naturalistic* attributes that Enlightenment culture had given it. The avant-garde critique thus reveals its role as ideological tool of the current critical phase of the capitalist world. Indeed, it is even imprecise to call it a "critique" any longer, since its function, in this sense, is entirely obvious: the confusion and ambiguity that it advocates for art—using all the conclusions of semantic analysis to this end—are only sublimated metaphors for the crisis and ambiguity informing the structures of the present-day city. The critique's refusal to stand outside the circle of planning-production-consumption is therefore symptomatic. Restany goes on:

The critical method must contribute to a generalization of aesthetics: superseding the work and multiple production; making a fundamental distinction between the two complementary orders of creation and production; systematizing operational research and technical cooperation in every domain experimenting with synthesis; structuring the notion of game and spectacle in psycho-sensorial fashion; organizing ambient space with a view to mass communications; inserting the individual environment into the collective space of urban well-being.[27]

Criticism must therefore function within the cycles of production; it must, by becoming *operative*, serve as stimulus in order to shift the Plan to increasingly advanced levels.

But what real novelty is there in all this with respect to the historic avant-gardes? It would not be difficult to demonstrate, through technical analysis, that aside from a relaunching of ideology, the novel elements are extremely limited. Indeed, in propositions of this sort—once we have set aside the Marcusian utopia of redeeming the future dimension through the Great Refusal enacted by the imagination—there is clearly something less with respect to the coherence of the historic avant-gardes.

So how does one explain all this insistence on the waste of form and the recovery of a specific dimension of artistic themes, in the light of the need for increasing integration of formal elaboration into the cycle of production?

There is no denying that we are faced with two concurrent phenomena. On the one hand, the fact that building production remains confined to broad, comprehensive plans continues to reduce the functionality of architecture's ideological role. On the other, the economic and social conflicts exploding with ever greater frequency within urban and outlying areas seem to be imposing a pause on capitalism's Plan. Faced with the notion of the rationalization of the urban milieu—a central, determinant theme—capital seems, for the moment, unable to find within itself the strength and means necessary to fulfill the tasks rightly pointed out by the ideologies of the modern movement.

This has forced a return to activism—to strategies of stimulus, critique, and struggle—on the part of the intellectual opposition, and even of class organizations, which to this day have assumed the task of fighting to resolve such problems and conflicts. The harshness of the struggle over urban-planning laws (in Italy as well as the US), over the reorganization of the building industry, over urban renewal, may have given many the illusion that the fight for planning could actually constitute a moment in the class struggle.

Architects now work in a climate of anxiety, owing to the discovery of their decline as active ideologues, the realization of the vast potential of technology in the rationalization of the city and outlying areas together with the daily awareness of its waste, and the obsolescence of specific planning methods even before they have had a chance to be tested. All this points to a concrete development on the horizon, feared as the worst of all evils: the proletarianization of the architect, and his insertion—with no more neo-humanistic delays—within the planning programs of production.

When this new professional situation—already realized in advanced capitalist countries like the US or in countries of socialized capital such as the USSR—is feared by architects and avoided with the most neurotic sorts of formal and ideological contortions, it shows only the political backwardness of that particular intellectual group.

Having ideologically anticipated the iron law of the Plan, architects, unable to interpret historically the distance traveled, are now rebelling against the extreme consequences of processes that they themselves helped to set in motion. What's worse, they are attempting pathetically to relaunch modern architecture "ethically," assigning it political tasks suitable only for temporarily calming abstract, unjustified frenzies.

We must realize one thing: that the entire course of modern architecture and the new systems of visual communication was born, developed and brought into crisis in a grandiose attempt—the last of bourgeois culture—to resolve, on the level of an ideology all the more insidious because it lies entirely within concrete activities and real production cycles, the imbalances, contradictions and delays typical of the capitalistic reorganization of the world market.

Order and disorder, in this light, cease to be in opposition to each other. If we interpret them according to their true historical significance, it becomes clear that there is no contradiction between constructivism and "protest art," between the rationalism of building production and informal subjectivism or Pop irony, between the capitalist plan and the urban chaos, between the ideology of planning and the poetics of the object.

The *destiny* of capitalist society, in this interpretation, is not at all extraneous to the *project*. The ideology of the project is as essential to the integration of modern capitalism, with all its structures and superstructures, into human existence, as is the illusion of being able to oppose that *project* with the tools of a *different* project or with those of a radical "anti-project."

It may even be that many marginal and rearguard roles exist for architecture and planning. Of primary interest to us, however, is the question of why, until now, Marxist-oriented culture has very carefully, and with an obstinacy worthy of better causes, denied or concealed the simple truth that, just as there can be no such thing as a political economics of class, but only a class critique of political economics, likewise there can never be an aesthetics, art or architecture of class, but only a class critique of aesthetics, art, architecture and the city.

A coherent Marxist critique of architectural and urbanistic ideology can only demystify the contingent, historical—and in no way objective or universal—realities that lie hidden behind the unifying categories of the terms "art," "architecture," and "city."

In assuming its historic, objective role as class critique, architectural criticism must become a critique of urban ideology, and avoid in every way the danger of entering into "progressive" dialogue with the techniques for rationalizing the contradictions of capital.

And first among the intellectual illusions to be dispelled is that which strives to anticipate, through mere imagery, the conditions of an architecture "for a liberated society." Anyone who proffers such a slogan avoids the question of whether, even leaving aside its manifest utopianism, such an objective could ever be sought without a linguistic, methodological and structural revolution reaching well beyond the simple subjective will or the simple updating of a syntax.

Modern architecture has marked the paths of its own destiny by becoming the bearer of ideals of progress and rationalization to which the working class is extraneous, or in which it is included only in a social democratic perspective. One might well recognize the historical inevitability of this phenomenon; yet having done so, one may no longer hide the ultimate reality that makes the choices of "leftist" architects so uselessly anguished.

Uselessly anguished because it is useless to struggle when one is trapped inside a capsule with no exit. The crisis of modern architecture does not issue from "weariness" or "dissipation." Rather, it is a crisis of the ideological function of architecture. The "fall" of modern art is the ultimate testimony of bourgeois ambiguity, poised as it is between "positive" goals—the reconciliation of contradictions—and the merciless exploration of its own objective commodification. There is no more "salvation" to be found within it: neither by wandering restlessly through "labyrinths" of images so polyvalent that they remain mute, nor by shutting oneself up in the sullen silence of geometries content with their own perfection.

This is why there can be no proposals of architectural "anti-spaces":[28] any search for an alternative within the structures determining the mysti-fication of planning is an obvious contradiction in terms.

Reflection on architecture, as a critique of the concrete ideology "realized" by architecture itself, can only push further, and strive for a specifically concrete dimension in which the systematic destruction of the mythologies sus-taining its development is only one of the objectives. But only the future conditions of the class struggle will tell us whether the task we are setting ourselves is that of an avant-garde or a rearguard.

Notes

1. M. A. Laugier, *Observations sur l'architecture* (The Hague, 1765), pp. 312–313.

2. Alexander Cozens, *A New Method of Assisting the Invention Drawing Original Compositions of Landscape* (London, 1786). The words of Alexander Pope, cited by Cozens at the start of his treatise, assume particular importance in this context: "Those rules which are discovered, not devised / are Nature still, but Nature methodized: / Nature, like Monarchy, is but re-strained / by the same Laws which first herself ordained." Cf. G. C. Argan, *La pittura dell'Illuminismo in Inghilterra da Reynolds a Constable* (Rome: Bulzoni, 1965), pp. 153 ff. The civic significance attributed to Nature—the subject and object of ethical and pedagogical ac-tion—comes to replace the traditional principles of authority which rationalism and sensism were in the process of destroying.

3. Cf. Le Corbusier, *Urbanisme* (Paris: Crès, 1925).

4. M. Quatremère de Quincy, "Architecture" entry in the *Encyclopédie méthodique*, vol. I, p. 109.

5. Cf. G. B. Piranesi, *Iconographia Campi Martii* (1761–1762); idem, *Parere su l'architettura*, included in the *Osservazioni* (Rome, 1765); Werner Körte, "G. B. Piranesi als praktischer Architekt," *Zeitschrift für Kunstgeschichte* 2 (1933); R. Wittkower, "Piranesi's *Parere su l'architettura*," *Journal of the Warburg Institute* 3 (1938), p. 2.

6. Francesco Milizia, *Principj di architettura civile* (Bassano, 1813), vol. II, pp. 26–27.

7. Ibid., p. 28.

8. Ibid., p. 29.

9. Cf. G. Antolini, *Descrizione del Foro Bonaparte, presentato coi disegni al comitato di governo della Repubblica Cisalpina . . .* (Milan, 1802); A. Rossi, "Il concetto di tradizione nell'architettura neoclas-sica milanese," *Società* 12, no. 2 (1956), pp. 474–493; G. Mezzanotte, *L'architettura neoclassica in Lombardia* (Naples: Esi, 1966).

10. Cf. L. Benevolo, *Storia dell'architettura moderna* (Bari: Laterza, 1960); M. Manieri-Elia, *L'architet-tura del dopoguerra in U.S.A.* (Bologna: Cappelli, 1966). "On the urbanistic level," writes Ma-nieri about the 1807 plan for the city of New York, "it seems clear that the Puritan, 'antiarchitectural' attitude well coincides with the sense of Jeffersonian libertarian indi-vidualism, according to which the system, as is quite evident in the Declaration of Inde-pendence . . . , consists of the least cumbersome sort of functional support possible: if the government should only be a flexible and alterable instrument at all times in the service of inalienable human rights, then that is all the more reason why an urban plan should provide a maximum guarantee of flexibility and present a minimum of resistance to productive initiative" (pp. 64–65). Cf. also the exceptional documentation of the for-mation of American cities in J. W. Reps, *The Making of Urban America* (Princeton: Princeton University Press, 1965).

11. The historical period of utopian socialism and its proposals for urban reorganization can-not be regarded with the same criteria as the formation of the ideologies of the modern movement. One can only hint at the alternative role utopian Romanticism played as com-pared to those ideologies. Its development, however, particularly in Anglo-Saxon plan-ning practices, should be compared with the models formulated by the New Deal. But such an analysis would well surpass the limits of the present essay.

12. Walter Benjamin, "On Some Motifs in Baudelaire," in *Illuminations*, ed. Hannah Arendt, trans. Harry Zohn (New York: Harcourt, Brace and World, 1968). "Engels is dismayed

by the crowd," writes Benjamin; "he responds with a moral reaction, and an aesthetic one as well; the speed with which people rush past one another unsettles him. The charm of his description lies in the intersecting of unshakable critical integrity with an old-fashioned attitude. The writer came from a Germany that was still provincial; he may never have faced the temptation to lose himself in a stream of people" (p. 169).

13. Ibid., pp. 169–170.

14. "With the rise of the great cities prostitution came into possession of new secrets. One of these is the labyrinthine character of the city itself. The labyrinth, whose image had passed into flesh and blood in the *flâneur*, is at the same time colorfully framed by prostitution." Walter Benjamin, "Central Park," *New German Critique* 34 (Winter 1985), p. 53.

15. Benjamin, "On Some Motifs in Baudelaire," p. 178.

16. Ibid., p. 179.

17. Ludwig Hilberseimer, *Grossstadtarchitektur* (Stuttgart: Julius Hoffmann Verlag, 1927), p. 100.

18. From this derived the model of the "vertical city" which, according to Grassi (introduction to *Un'idea di piano*, a translation of Hilberseimer's *Entfaltung einer Planungsidee* [Padua: Marsilio, 1967], p. 10), was presented as a theoretical alternative to the "city for three million inhabitants" presented by Le Corbusier at the 1922 Salon d'Automne. It should also be noted that despite his detached rigor, Hilbersheimer—who, not coincidentally, was a member of the 1919 Novembergruppe and of all the "radical" intellectual groups thereafter—would come close, after the self-critique he carried out after his transfer to the U.S., to the communitarian and naturalistic myths that were to figure among the ideological ingredients of the New Deal.

19. Hilbersheimer, *Grossstadtarchitektur*, p. 103.

20. Ibid.

21. The drawings in the *Poème de l'angle droit* (Paris: Verve Editions, 1955) clarify the significance Le Corbusier gave to the journey of the intellect through the labyrinth. As for Klee—to whose graphic style these drawings are very close—Order is not a totality external to the human activity that creates it. As much as the search for synthesis is enriched by the uncertainties of memory, by the tension of doubt, even by paths leading elsewhere than to the final destination, such a destination is actually reached in the fullness of an authentic *experience*. For Le Corbusier, too, the absolute of form lies in the full realization of a constant victory over the uncertainty of the future, achieved through the assumption of the problematic position as the only guarantee of collective salvation.

22. Among Le Corbusier's many written testimonies in which architectural intervention is explicitly foregrounded as an instrument of class integration, his passage on the Van Nelle factory in Holland is particularly revealing: "The Van Nelle tobacco factory in Rotterdam," writes Le Corbusier, "a creation of the modern age, redeems the word *proletarian* of its desperate signification. This diversion of the sentiment of egotistical property toward a sentiment of collective action leads us to the felicitous phenomenon of *personal intervention* at every stage of human endeavor. The work remains such as it is in its material state, but the spirit illuminates it. I repeat: everything lies in the words: *proof of love.*

"It is to this point that, through a new form of administration, one should lead, purify and amplify the contemporary event. Tell us what we are, in what way we may be of use, why we work. Give us plans, show us the plans, explain your plans. *Make us united. . . .* If you show us the plans and explain them to us, the propertied classes and the hopeless proletariat will cease to exist. In their place will be a society of belief and action. At this present moment of strict rationalism, the question is one of consciousness." Le Corbusier, *Spectacle de la vie moderne*, in *La ville radieuse* (Paris: Vincent Fréal, 1933), p. 177.

23. On the basis of these considerations, one could rebut Banham's thesis, which criticizes, from a point of view based within technological development, the typological stasis of the "modern movement's" masters. "In opting for stabilised types or norms," he writes, "architects opted for the pauses when the normal processes of technology were interrupted, those processes of change and renovation that, as far as we can see, can only be halted by abandoning technology as we know it today, and bringing both research and mass-production to a stop." Reyner Banham, *Theory and Design in the First Machine Age* (London:

The Architectural Press, 1962), p. 325. It is perhaps unnecessary to point out that all the architectural science fiction that has proliferated from 1960 to this day by redeeming the "image" dimension of the processes of technology, is, compared to Le Corbusier's Obus plan, quite disturbingly backward.

24. Cf. A. Negri, "La teoria capitalista dello stato nel '29: John M. Keynes," *Contropiano*, no. 1 (1968), pp. 3 ff.

25. Cf., as texts symptomatic of the phenomenon: G. C. Argan, *Relazione introduttiva al convegno sulle "strutture ambientali"* (Rimini, September 1968); L. Quaroni, *La Torre di Babele* (Padua: Marsilio, 1967); M. Ragon, *Les visionnaires de l'architecture* (Paris, 1965); A. Boatto, *Pop Art in U.S.A.* (Milan: Lerici, 1967); F. Menna, *Profezia di una società estetica* (Milan: Lerici, 1968). It should not be necessary to point out that this grouping of these texts has nothing to do with their inherent rigor or the quality of their individual contributions.

26. Pierre Restany, "Le livre blanc de l'art total; pour une esthétique prospective," *Domus*, no. 269 (1968), p. 50. Italics mine.

27. Ibid. Obviously I am using Restany's text merely to exemplify a very widespread mythology among the protagonists of the new avant-garde. Moreover, many of my assertions may also hold true for far more serious "disciplinary" attempts at redemption through utopia.

28. The Italian word here is *controspazi*—in the original, an obvious polemical reference to the polemical contemporary architectural journal, *Controspazio*. [Translator's note.]

George Baird   **"'La Dimension Amoureuse' in Architecture"** From Charles Jencks and George

Baird, *Meaning in Architecture* (New York: George Braziller, 1969)

Modern architecture's envy of the theories and methods of the "exact sciences" lasted well into the 1960s, in the form of operational research and design methodologies that held that a careful description of any building's program—the physical conditions required for the performance of specific functions—and a systematic adherence to that description in the process of design should result in a direct transposition of functional demands into built form.[1] A sufficiently minute description of the requisite functions would allow a design solution of singular correctness, free from mediating conventions and the arbitrary choice from among alternative formal organizations— a one-to-one matching of function and form in which the problem of representation or translation seems to disappear. Against the vestiges of this scientism, George Baird's preliminary semiotics of architecture elaborates the basic structuralist insight that buildings are not simply physical supports but artifacts and events with meaning, and hence *signs* dispersed across some larger social text. That insight is then trained on two of the most enduring of modernist myths, the building as a totally designed environment (exemplified by Eero Saarinen's CBS Building, New York) and the building as a value-free servo-mechanism (exemplified by Cedric Price's Potteries Thinkbelt project).

Price diverts architecture to purely utilitarian ends, toward the regenerative potential of accessible education in the economically depressed English Midlands. His commitment is not to architecture but to some value or effect outside architecture, which architecture is to serve. Saarinen's object is "architecture itself," capital A, but likewise distanced from any common sense of the legible physical environment. As total designer, Saarinen claims to purvey no particular local message. Yet, as Baird shows in a dialectical reversal, Saarinen communicates just by the force of his refusal to do so, for the paternalistic totality of his authorship becomes its own message. And Price, society's would-be servant, similarly fails if he succeeds, for if his architecture says nothing, then it has no audience to serve.

The repercussions of the textualization of architecture as a critique of modernist dogma would prove enormous, of course, extending over the next decade of architecture theory. But if the linguistic analogy was perhaps inevitable (semiotics is designed to manage all cultural phenomena, including architecture) and in certain ways already latent in earlier models of architectural interpretation (those of Emile Kaufmann, John Summerson, or Rudolf Wittkower, for example), one must still decide on the most pertinent and fruitful level of homology between architecture and language. Is the individual work or group of works like a language, or is architecture as a whole like a language? The first view has affinities with traditional treatments of buildings as organic units whose origins and intentions of formation must be elucidated, whereas the second view, which Baird adopts, shifts the interpretive vocation considerably. No longer is the interpreter's task to say *what* the individual work means (any more than it is the linguist's task to render the meanings of individual sentences) but rather to show *how* the conventions of architecture enable works to produce meaning. Questions are raised about users' and readers' expectations, about how a structure of expectation enters into and directs the design of a work, about how any architectural "utterance" is a shared one, shot through with qualities and values, open to dispute, already uttered — questions, in short, about architecture's public life.

In semiotic terms, if architecture as a whole is like a language (*langue*) then the individual work is like a speech act (*parole*), which entails that the architect cannot simply assign or take away meaning and meaning cannot be axiomatic.[2] Rather architecture becomes a readable text, and the parameters of its legibility are what we mean by rhetoric. Rhetoric operates within the structure of shared expectations and demands an ethical, even erotic relationship with the reader, an "amorous dimension." But rhetoric is not subjective expression. Its procedures are inseparable from processes of argument and justification with respect to the social function of making architectural sense.

compare Silvetti (**266 ff**)

But the most fruitful dimension of Baird's essay is his setting of Claude Perrault's concepts of positive and arbitrary beauty into active equivalence with the *langue/parole* system — a strong example of the vocation of transcoding that is fundamental to architecture theory after 1968. For what is achieved should not be understood as a simple simile of architecture as a language but rather as the creation out of two previous codes of an entirely new one, capable of recoding vast quantities of discourse, from eighteenth-century French theory's concern with the natural basis of architecture, to modernism's mimetic relationship with industry, to postmodernism's loosening of the components of the classical order.

see x–xii

Within the relatively closed circles of traditional architectural discourse, the perennial dilemmas of taste and style, of eclecticism and the "morality" of materials, of technological determinism, and the like, have been worked through most often without much interference from the discordant claims of other disciplines, even if architecture has its own versions of the philosophical questions of "nature," "beauty," and "truth." Rewriting such dilemmas as components in a complex fraction — positive beauty/arbitrary beauty : *langue/parole* — enables the enlargement of architectural interpretation to include the social communicative function of architecture's handling of style, materials, and technology and to measure the social unconscious of different, competing architectural representations in their specific contexts.[3] Further, it enables the classification of architecture into the different operations based either on the selection-substitution of elements (what in semiotics is called the paradigmatic axis of a language, associated with the *langue* and with metaphor) or on the combination-correlation of elements (the syntagmatic axis, associated with *parole* and metonymy).[4] Indeed, as Baird uses it, this feature seems to anticipate postmodernism's classification as a kind of revenge of the *parole* — of the specific utterance, of dialectics, and idiolects, of the shimmering metonymic surface — against general autotelic and self-reflexive techniques. Finally, though Baird does not mention it, his semiotic fraction is capable of generating a third term out of its binaries that might articulate the reciprocal exchanges between the limiting system of archi-

| *see* 284–286, 332 |

tectural conventions and the individual instances of that system. The reemergent notion of architectural typology, as represented by Alan Colquhoun's essay in the same volume as Baird's, attempted to do just that.[5] Henceforth, worry about empirical method and total design would be completely eclipsed by concerns with the contexts and processes of meaning.

Notes

This is an extensively revised version of a paper that originally appeared in *Arena* 33 (June 1967), the journal of the Architectural Association in London.

1. Christopher Alexander, *Notes on the Synthesis of Form* (Cambridge: MIT Press, 1964), was the paragon of this renewed positivism, but versions flourished in many schools of architecture.

2. As defined by Ferdinand de Saussure, *langue* (connoting "language" but also a particular "tongue") is the specific but abstract linguistic system that preexists any individual use of it and exists perfectly only within a collectivity; *parole*, the individual speech act, is the manipulation of that system to produce concrete utterances and includes localized contingencies and "accidents" like accent or personal style. See Ferdinand de Saussure, *Course in General Linguistics* (1916), ed. Charles Bally and Albert Sechehaye in collaboration with Albert Reidlinger, trans. Wade Baskin (New York: McGraw-Hill, 1959).

3. It should be remembered that this homology is as susceptible as any to vulgar reduction and can be used to generate and identify numerous facile "meanings" in architecture, wherein architecture becomes a mere illustration of concepts in other fields.

4. The classic text that treats these associations is Roman Jakobson, "Two Aspects of Language and Two Types of Aphasic Disturbances," in *On Language*, ed. Linda R. Waugh and Monique Monville-Burston (Cambridge: Harvard University Press, 1990).

5. Alan Colquhoun, "Typology and Design Method," first published in *Arena* 33 (June 1967).

La rhétorique, qui n'est rien d'autre que la technique de l'information exacte, est liée non seulement à toute littérature, mais encore à toute communication, dès lors qu'elle veut faire entendre à l'autre que nous le reconnaissons; la rhétorique est la dimension amoureuse de l'écriture.

ROLAND BARTHES, Essais critiques

It is not unprecedented to suggest that architecture occupies its place in human experience through some kind of communication. By the mid-eighteenth century, Germain Boffrand had already speculated that "the profiles of mouldings and the other parts which compose a building are to architecture what words are to speech."[1]

Nowadays we know all too well that Eero Saarinen's TWA terminal at Kennedy Airport symbolizes "flight"; we have heard him say that the "beauty" of his CBS building "will be, I believe, that it will be the simplest skyscraper statement in New York."[2] In fact, even discussions of "symbolism" and "statement" provoke vigorous protest today. The young English architect, Cedric Price, for instance, recently criticized architects' preoccupation with "the role of architecture as a provider of visually recognizable symbols of identity, place and activity." Call it a fix or the "image of a city," said Price, "such overt self-consciousness is embarrassing only to a few—in general, it is both incomprehensible and irrelevant."[3] Familiar as it may be, then, the issue is a contentious one.

Now Saarinen's and Price's importance for this paper does not only lie in their having made their positions as clear as that. As Saarinen was, so Price is a designer of facility and sophistication. As one might expect, then, both of them have produced designs which aptly reflect their respective views. This means that it is possible to see even more clearly in their work than in their remarks, just how fundamentally they have both misconceived the question which presently concerns me; the question of just how it is that architecture occupies its place in human experience. The designs I mean to discuss are Saarinen's CBS building,[4] and Price's "Potteries Thinkbelt" project for a technical university in the English Midlands.[5] There is no doubt that CBS, the prominent seat of a prestigious American corporation, is a definitive example of what Robert Venturi calls "establishment Modern architecture";[6] it is well-known that the Thinkbelt, conceived in terms of minimum cost and maximum efficiency, has been proposed as the antithesis of a building like CBS. Yet the designs' similarities are really more extensive and more important than their differences. That CBS and the Thinkbelt are thought of as antithetical seems to me only to show the shallowness of the controversy they represent; the depth of their designers' misconception of architecture's place in human experience.

This misconception is neatly summed up in the respective approaches of the two designs to the detailed organization of human occupation of space. In the Thinkbelt project, the designer stops well short of offering the occupant, say, an ash-tray (on the grounds that there is no guarantee that the designer and the occupant have the same cultural values), while at CBS, the designers only *allow* him one approved by Florence Knoll (since there is no guarantee that the designers and the occupant have the same cultural values). But this is just an ironic illustration of my point. To grasp the full scale of the misconception involved requires examination of these designs' historical context. After all, the concept of "total design"[7] underlying CBS, following Gropius's "total theatre" and "total architecture," is nothing more nor less than a Wagnerian *Gesamtkunstwerk*. And Price's idea of architecture as "life-conditioning"[8] rests on essentially the same view of human experience as Jeremy Bentham's *Panopticon*. Both designs' conceptual premises then, lie deep in the intellectual history of the nineteenth century. What we ought eventually to understand, is how CBS and the Thinkbelt, as manifestations of *Gesamtkunstwerk* and "life-conditioning," show the bizarre consequences which even today follow from that century's loss of faith in rhetoric.

The first of those consequences is that modern designers, especially those like Saarinen and Price, become caught up in partly conscious, partly unconscious attempts to assume privileged positions with respect to the groups of people who will occupy the environments they design. The architectural *Gesamtkünstler* assumes a stance towards those groups analogous to that of Wagner *vis-à-vis* his audiences. He takes quite for granted his capacity to enhance the lives of the occupants of his buildings; he believes that enhancement ultimately depends upon the occupants' conscious experience of their environment being dramatically heightened; he is thus committed to a "total" predetermination of their experience of the environment, from every conceivable point of view. In short, were he successful, he would occupy a privileged position in the sense that he would stand utterly *over and above* his fellows' experience of the environment he had designed.

The "life-conditioner," on the other hand, is not paternalistic, but scientistic. He assumes a stance towards his fellows analogous to that of a nineteenth century natural scientist towards an experiment he is conducting. He is anxious to take nothing for granted, to sustain an absolute neutrality with respect to the experience the occupants have of the environment he has designed. He believes his neutrality precludes his taking any account of their experience of it and he thus resorts to a designed anonymity, the purpose of which is a "total" non-determination of the occupants' experience of that environment. Were the life-conditioner successful, he would occupy a privileged position in the sense that he would stand utterly outside his fellows' experience of the environment he had designed. To sum up, the *Gesamtkünstler* treats his fellows as children; the life-conditioner treats them as objects.

Now I introduced this matter of the attempt to assume a privileged position, as one of the bizarre consequences of the nineteenth century's loss of faith in rhetoric. What I should really in the first instance say is that the *Gesamtkünstler* and the life-conditioner forget—or else take completely for granted—just how inescapably the design act is always a gesture in a social context. Their oversight can be seen to have been part of a loss of faith in rhetoric only in the light of the current revival of interest in the ancient subject, which surrounds the work of men such as Roland Barthes, Ernst Gombrich, Claude Lévi-Strauss, and Marshall McLuhan.[9] This revival is due, of course, to the fact that all of these men have attempted to analyze and understand various kinds of gesture-in-a-social-context, by means of either the traditional categories of rhetoric, or the concepts of modern communication theory.

In criticizing Saarinen's and Price's misconceptions, in discussing how it is that architecture occupies its place in human experience, I shall rely most heavily upon the ideas of Lévi-Strauss. The reason is that he has staked the most audacious, yet most intellectually tenable claim of the four, proposing anthropology as the intellectual discipline of most comprehensive human relevance, and doing so in an expansive fashion which appears to accommodate many of the others' most impressive ideas. Lévi-Strauss has explained his claim for anthropology, by calling it the "bona-fide" occupant of the domain of *semiology*. This, the comprehensive theory of communications, the linguist Ferdinand de Saussure introduced half a century ago as the study of the life of signs at the heart of social life.[10] Taking its cue from Lévi-Strauss's "structural" anthropology, modern semiology looks on *all* social phenomena as communication systems; not just the obvious ones such as literature and

Cedric Price,
Potteries Thinkbelt,
Staffordshire, 1964

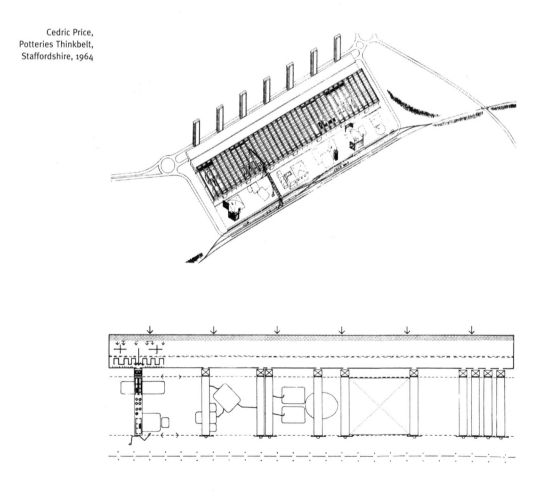

films, but also kinship systems, culinary customs, clothing habits, and, of course, architecture.

The part of semiological theory which bears most directly on the problem of modern designers' attempts to assume privileged positions, is the part Saussure described by means of the *langue/parole* distinction. For semiology, any social phenomenon is made up of both a *langue* and a *parole*. In the first of three senses, the *langue* is the collective aspect of the phenomenon, and the *parole* the individual aspect. Thus, semiology incorporates the fundamental sociological insight that human experience, in so far as it is social, is simultaneously collective and individual.

In the second of the three senses, semiology sees the *langue* as the unconscious aspect of a social phenomenon, and the *parole* as the conscious aspect. In this way, it incorporates one of the most obvious insights of post-nineteenth century psychology, and posits that any conscious gesture in a social context always involves an unconscious component. With respect to these two senses of the *langue/parole* distinction in language, Barthes has said: "The *langue* is both a social institution and a system of values. As a social institution, it is never an act; it utterly eludes premeditation; it is the social part of language; the individual can, by himself, neither create it, nor modify it; it is essentially a collective contract, which, if one wishes to communicate, one must accept in its entirety. What is more, this social product is autonomous, like a game which has rules one must know before one can play it. . . . As opposed to the *langue*, institution and system, the *parole* is essentially an individual act of selection and actualization."[11]

In the most modern sense of the distinction, the *langue* of a social phenomenon is considered to be its "code," and the *parole* its "message." In some respects, this new sense of the distinction is the most interesting, because it introduces into semiology a number of precise mathematical techniques of analysis, commonly grouped under the name "information theory." In terms parallel to the collective/individual and unconscious/conscious senses of the distinction, we may say that the particular "message" which any gesture in a social context constitutes, necessarily involves the use of the "code" which that context entails.

Of course, information theory goes even further than that nowadays, viewing communication systems as dynamic. While the *relation holding between* the *langue* and the *parole* is necessarily constant, the system as a whole is in a continuous process of development. More specifically, "information" occurs as a function of "surprise" within a matrix of "expectancy." In order to register, a message must be somewhat surprising, yet not utterly unexpected. If it is too predictable, the message won't register at all. It is in this sense that "background noise" tends to slip below the threshold of awareness, and that we speak of clichés as not having enough "information value." Conversely, if the message is too unpredictable, the result is the same. As Paul McCartney has said, "if music . . . is just going to jump about five miles ahead, then everyone's going to be left standing with this gap of five miles that they've got to all cross before they can even see what scene these people are on."[12, 13]

We can now, I think, begin to see how the *Gesamtkünstler* and the life-conditioner become involved in their attempts to assume privileged positions. If, for example, we examine their stances in the light of the collective/individual sense of the *langue/parole* distinction, the following becomes apparent. In undertaking "total design," the *Gesamtkünstler* presumes *ipso facto*, either individually, or as part of a small elite, to take over comprehensive responsibility for the *langue* of architecture, and to do so, moreover, in a fashion which leaves the *langue*'s collective validity unimpaired. In other words, "total design" amounts to an attempt to shift the impact of the individual design act from the level of *parole* to that of *langue*. On the other hand, in making his individual design gesture, the life-conditioner pretends to act altogether independently of the *langue* of architecture. But of course, since he, like the *Gesamtkünstler*, is only an individual acting in a social context, his pretense really amounts to a single-handed attempt at a radical modification of the *langue*. And that is just another way of saying that he too attempts to shift the impact of the individual design act from the level of *parole* to that of *langue*.

Then, too, the unconscious/conscious sense of the *langue/parole* distinction throws further light on their attempts at privileged positions. As I have said above, the *Gesamtkünstler* makes his attempt for the purpose of dramatically heightening the occupants' conscious experience of the environment he has designed. The life-conditioner, on the other hand, makes his for exactly the opposite purpose. But what they both do, in this respect, is to take for granted their own capacity for consciously manipulating their fellows' *threshold of awareness* of the environment in question.

An examination of such designers' attitudes in terms of code and message only confirms the picture now emerging. Neither sees fit to modulate his design gesture in terms of either its "surprise" or its "expectancy." Indeed, were it not the case of architecture under consideration, I would say that the emphatic manner in which the CBS environment has been imposed upon its occupants would no doubt result in its being sensed only as "background noise," while Price's look-no-hands gesture would leave the Thinkbelt's occupants with their own gap of five miles to cross before they could make any sense of the environment in which they found themselves. But alas, it is the case of architecture under consideration, and analogies from music don't apply perfectly straightforwardly. Unlike music, architecture is inescapably operative in human experience. When music becomes "background noise," its unconscious impact is incidental; when architecture becomes "background noise," its unconscious impact is still far from incidental.

The illumination provided by the *langue/parole* distinction is also capable of graphic representation. Extracting from it two of its particular senses, unconscious/conscious, and code/message, one can portray the *field of meaning* of any social phenomenon, as shown in the following diagram.

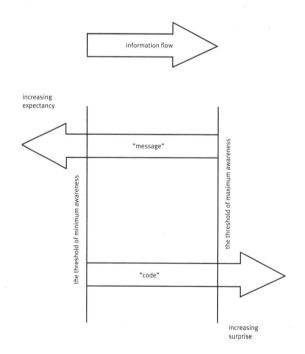

The line across the top of the diagram represents increasing expectancy, and that across the bottom, increasing surprise. In terms of the capacity for registering messages which I described above, the extent of the overlap between the line indicating the threshold of minimum awareness, and that indicating maximum awareness, defines the field of meaning. The length of the bottom line then, from the one threshold to the other, represents the scope of articulation of the social phenomenon in question.

In the language of information theory, the *langue* of architecture is the gamut of conceivable perceptible articulations, while the *parole* comprises the possibility of selective combination across that gamut. But that is only the abstract formulation of the relation. Since, as Barthes says, the *langue* is a "social institution and a system of values," one can say much more. Take as examples those very concepts "house," "overcoat," "commuter service," and "shop," whose "existing definitions" Price deprecated in his introduction to the Thinkbelt.[14] We can consider the *langue* as the gamut of articulation defined in such complex environmental concepts as those. The parole, then, comprises the selective possibility of variation implicit in that gamut. To suggest that the *langue* comprises such a gamut is not to imply that there is anything inherently significant or stable about those particular, or any particular concepts. For the *langue* lies in the gamut of articulation, and not in any primary functional category those concepts might be thought to represent. To suggest that there were such categories would be to fall into the historicism and/or the functional Platonism which, one presumes, have provoked Price's objections.

On the other hand, to suggest that the *langue* comprises such a gamut is very much to claim that the place as "social institution," which such albeit nonprimary concepts hold, can be ignored only at the risk of diminishing the scope of articulation of the whole of the environment. In short, as *langue*, such concepts establish the fixes which allow the corresponding variability of *parole*. The greater the scope of the *langue*, the greater the possible variation of *parole*.

In fact, Price's attack on the "ephemerality" of those definitions is most noteworthy in the way it recalls the linguistic crusade which was launched in immediately postrevolutionary Russia, and which has been described by Roman Jakobson.[15] In that case, a number of theorists argued that phrases such as "the sun is setting" ought to be expunged from Communist speech, on the grounds that they were obsolete remnants of a non-scientific mentality. Obviously, a success in either of these cases would have as its chief result simply an impoverishment of the existing cultural situation.

Up to this point, I have concerned myself with modern designers' attempts to assume privileged positions. But that is only the first of the consequences of the nineteenth century's loss of faith in rhetoric. For the premises underlying the *Gesamtkunstwerk* and life-conditioning also involve such designers in a belief that their designs embody what we might call an *absolute perceptual transparency*; a belief that they can take for granted their fellows' capacity to see each design "as it in itself really is."[16] And, of course, the corollaries of that belief, typical of both the *Gesamtkunstwerk* and life-conditioning, are an aversion to ambiguity, and an incapacity for ever sustaining irony.

Consider again Saarinen's conviction concerning the CBS building. "Its beauty will be," he said, "that it will be the simplest skyscraper statement in New York." Later on, he continued, "when you look at this building, you will know exactly what is going on. It is a very direct and simple structure."[17] What Saarinen has done, it seems to me, is to take the "objectivist" aesthetic of orthodox modernism in its most literally expressionist sense, and then to assume that his design was capable, through its transparent "simplicity," of rendering directly accessible to his fellows an ultimate, universal, even metaphysical reality.

Price, for his part, looks on all such concerns with considerable contempt. He prefers, like his Utilitarian predecessors, to affect a matter-of-fact pragmatism with respect to all aspects of human experience. Nevertheless, his pragmatism rests on an assumption of architecture's perceptual transparency which is just as absolute as Saarinen's. For he takes for granted the capacity of a configuration of built form as elaborate as the Thinkbelt, to unfold *itself* in his fellows' experience as nothing more nor less than a "servicing mechanism," that is to say, as unambiguously and unobtrusively as, say, a coffee-vending machine.

If, however, we take seriously the proposition put above, that there is nothing *inherently* significant, or stable, about any particular environmental condition then we must at the same time recognize the impossibility of taking it for granted that architecture can be perceptually transparent, or that people can *a priori* perceive any environment "as it in itself really is." Indeed, it has been one of the preoccupations of modern philosophers to indicate that we do not even possess any criteria for deciding *in advance* how to measure our fellows' estimates of reality "as it in itself really is." To use Merleau-Ponty's words, "the phenomenological world is not pure being [as Saarinen and Price assume], but rather the sense which is revealed where the paths of my various experiences intersect, and also where my own and other people's intersect and engage each other like gears."[18]

Semiology takes account of these matters in defining the *langue* of a social phenomenon as a set of signs, each of which comprises a *signifier* and a *signified*. That is to say, each signifier is something, which *stands* for something else. It is because social phenomena are coded as such sets of signs, that the reality of human experience is socially representable. In the most general perspective, one can say that the ultimate *signifier* is the social phenomenon's set of signs *itself*, and the ultimate *signified* is the "reality" which that set of signs discloses, and which is accessible to us only through those signs. In other words, for semiology, there is no "getting to the bottom of" any social phenomenon.

Furthermore, semiology looks on the relations holding between *signifiers* and *signifieds* as having been established arbitrarily, or non-isomorphically. For instance, it is not necessary for the purposes of communication, that the signifier "tree" be the most "tree-like" signifier to describe the phenomenon "tree." So long as once a tree is called a "tree," everyone involved agrees to call it that (or at least to call it that sufficiently frequently that occasional ironic, or humorous exceptions will still make sense). Alternatively, it is this same non-isomorphism that accounts for the simultaneous precision and flexibility of a signifier such as "spring," which can, depending on its context, have as its signified either "the season of the year following winter," "a natural source of fresh water," or "a mechanical device for providing flexible support for weight." In short, semiological theory holds that the relations of signifiers and signifieds depend on both a conceptual arbitrariness and an operative nonarbitrariness. And that means, of course, that it is exactly the extent to which signs are capable of misinterpretation, that they are also capable of re-interpretation. To return to the case of architecture, it is just this fact that enables Aldo van Eyck to say that "it is not merely what a space sets out to define in human terms that gives it place-value, but what it is able to gather and transmit."[19]

We can now see why the beliefs underlying the *Gesamtkunstwerk* and life-conditioning both entail such an aversion to ambiguity, such an incapacity for ever sustaining irony. In so far as either conception still allows any appreciation of the fact that the environment consists of a set of signs, it involves designers in an attempt to cut through all that, to "get to the bottom of the situation" in exactly the fashion I have just described as impossible.

Take the case of Saarinen. In assuming that the "ultimate reality" which he intended his design to reveal depended so completely upon its "directness" and "simplicity," he would obviously feel that he could not afford to leave any part of the detail of that design "unsimplified," that is to say unclear or less than utterly straightforward. On the other hand, in taking for granted the capacity of the Thinkbelt to unfold *itself* in human experience "as it in itself really is," Price would obviously see no reason to concern himself with such "ephemeral" matters. The life-conditioner, like the *Gesamtkünstler*, always sees ambiguity as compromise, and irony as hypocrisy.

The irony of ironies is that there is no ambiguity less controlled, no irony less sustained, than that which follows from these naivetés. But to show that requires two further tenets of semiological theory. I have already quoted Merleau-Ponty to the effect that *what we perceive* is "the sense which is revealed where the paths of my various experiences intersect, and also where my own and other people's intersect and engage each other like gears." In other words, not only are we able to perceive only in terms of a past and present context, we inevitably do perceive in such a context, if we perceive at all. Semiology takes account of this by positing that the signs which make up the *langue* of a social phenomenon carry meaning through the fact of their *total mutual interrelatedness*. It is in this sense that Colin Cherry said: "signals do not convey information as railway trucks carry coal."[29] That is, any individual sign in a code has a particular meaning by virtue of its distinctiveness from every other sign in that code. To understand a sign means in this sense to be aware of the set of alternative possible signs from the code that could conceivably take that sign's place. This dimension of meaning Saussure characterized as "the relationship of substitution" between the signs in the code.

However, the distinctiveness of all the signs in the code—one from another—needn't be absolute. For a sign, or to be more precise, a signifier, can stand for, or substitute for, a range of signifieds, the precise reference to be established through the actual context of the sign in question. (Recall again the example "spring" discussed above.) To understand a sign in this sense means to be aware of the extent to which the signs surrounding a particular sign qualify its particular significance. This dimension of meaning Saussure characterized as "the relationship of contiguity" between the signs assembled in any particular message.

Saussure illustrated this distinction by an actual architectural analogy himself, saying: "Each linguistic unit is like a column of an antique temple: this column is in a real relation of contiguity with other parts of the building, the architrave for example; but if this column is Doric, it reminds us of the other architectural orders, Ionic or Corinthian; and this is a relation of substitution."[21]

Jakobson has subsequently argued that Saussure's distinction between contiguity and substitution is capable of further elucidation.[22] While, in Saussure's sense of the distinction, any message would necessarily be defined in terms of both contiguity and substitution, Jakobson thought that at the level of "style," one could point to a possibility of emphasis on one or other of the two poles. He claimed that certain works of art were characterized primarily through relations of substitution (metaphor, in his terminology) while others are characterized more through relations of contiguity (metonymy, in that terminology). Thus, he saw romanticist and symbolist poetry, and Chaplin's films, as emphasizing the pole of metaphor, and realist literature and Griffith's films as emphasizing metonymy. In architecture, one can point to a work like Mies's Farnsworth house as emphasizing the pole of metaphor, not only because of the reductive substitution from the norm "house" which that design involves, but also because each element which remains is thereby supercharged with metaphorical significance. On the other hand, works like Carlo Scarpa's renovation of the mediaeval palace of Verona, or an interior by Alexander Girard, emphasize the role of metonymy, since they do not substitute reductively from their norms, nor powerfully metaphorize their individual elements, but rather build up their significance out of the assembly of relatively diverse parts.

When, however, in this perspective, we get to designs like CBS and the Thinkbelt, we encounter what can only be described as a radical polarization between metaphor and metonymy. The Thinkbelt makes a radical substitution, both reductive (through the complete elimination of anticipated academic elements), and non-reductive (through a major shift from academic to industrial iconography), from the norm "university." CBS on the other hand, undertakes a radical intensification of the assembly of all its diverse elements (from the details of the window wall right down to the relations of the already-mentioned ash trays and potted plants).

It is this radical polarization which results first in the uncontrolled ambiguity and unsustained irony and eventually in the impoverishment of the existing cultural situation, which I referred to above. The first result occurs because polarization has the effect of eroding the occupants' capacity for detecting *in the particular design itself* any very helpful evidence of its relation to the historic and present context in which it has taken its place. Thus, the occupants are obliged all by themselves to bring to their experience of the environment an awareness of alternative possible environments on which that particular environment's whole distinctiveness rests. Far from being perceptually transparent then, CBS and the Thinkbelt are in fact highly opaque; they tend to confront occupants in the first instance as uncontrollably ambiguous, except in so far as those occupants' previous experience lends any stability to the situation. Subsequently, of course, when that previous experience is no longer so effectively operative, the second result of polarization occurs. The precarious ambiguity and irony of the first stage collapse altogether, and the occupants are no longer even able to *conceive of* those alternative possible environments. And that, effectively, amounts to an impoverishment of the existing cultural situation.

Of course, in discussing the results of this polarization, I have moved on a stage in my general argument, from a consideration of the consequences of the nineteenth century's loss of faith in rhetoric, to a consideration in turn, of those consequences' own effects. Let me briefly go back over my argument so far, so that I may try to indicate, in the light of semiological theory, just what *those* effects might be.

My first conclusion in these terms was that both the *Gesamtkünstler* and the life-conditioner attempt to shift the impact of the individual design gesture from the level of *parole* to that of *langue*. Just what that involves is neatly illustrated in the now-so-fashionable quotations from *Through the Looking-Glass*.

"When I use a word," Humpty Dumpty said in a rather scornful tone, "I mean just what I choose it to mean, neither more nor less." "The question is," said Alice, "whether you can make words mean so many different things." "The question is," said Humpty Dumpty, "who is to be master."[23]

Now, short of establishing a dictatorship which is either ruled or managed by designers, neither the *Gesamtkünstler* nor the life-conditioner is likely to have much success on this front. Nor would it seem that their failure in this respect would have any serious consequences. But there is the assumption that they are in a position to consciously manipulate their fellows' threshold of conscious awareness. In this case, it seems to me, the situation is more complicated. After all, it is possible to manipulate others' thresholds of awareness, at least to some extent. And not only that. An attempt at such manipulation which fails has consequences almost as serious as one which succeeds.

Take the case of CBS. To the extent that its designers fail to heighten the occupants' conscious awareness of their environment, the occupants will end up in the position described above, their capacity to conceive of, let alone to respond to alternative possible environments having been correspondingly reduced. On the other hand, to the extent that the designers succeed, they beg the question as to what those occupants will be so dramatically conscious of. After all, the chief part of their extraordinary effort at intensification has been devoted to making the building a ruthlessly simplified symbolic "object" as a whole, and a highly formalized continuum in its minutest details. No effort of equivalent power has been devoted to a reconsideration of peoples' experience of the environment at the crucially important level intermediate between those extremes, the level of workaday experience of an "office-building" in central Manhattan. At the same time, as I indicated above, the designers' extraordinary effort (at the levels where it has been made) erodes the occupants' capacity for detecting in the building itself any evidence of its relation to its context. In other words, it erodes that evidence at every level but the workaday one. This combination of circumstances will guarantee that any heightened awareness of the environment of CBS will reveal not an "ultimate reality" at all, but rather just a monumentalization of the already familiar phenomenon of mass bureaucracy.

In the case of the Thinkbelt, the situation is slightly different. If Price were to fail to leave the Thinkbelt's occupants unconscious of their environment, those occupants would become consciously aware of their environment. The question then arises, what would they perceive? Well, they would perceive a configuration of built form which, in the terms of both the historic and the present kinds of context we have discussed, would demonstrate a quite particular and identifiable set of characteristics. Among those characteristics, as I see it, would be the following: first, a fundamental organizational scheme in terms of a mechanical flow pattern; second, a pattern of human occupation of built form, which is itself articulated mechanistically; third, the restriction upon the potential psychological intensity of any particular space to a maximum level of a "zone"; fourth, a construction technique which formalizes the actual temporariness of the built form involved. In short, although Price claims to have succeeded in devising an environment which stands for no particular "values" at all, what he has in fact done is simply to exchange one set of values for another. What the occupants of the Thinkbelt would consciously perceive would, in my view, be the most concrete symbolization there has yet been of bureaucracy's academic equivalent, the "education-factory."

On the other hand, what of the consequences if Price were to succeed, to some extent, in leaving those occupants unconscious of their environment? The environment would correspond to "background noise," in the sense I discussed above. But of course, as I said at that point, when architecture becomes "background noise," its unconscious impact is still far from incidental. To cite one of the most apt recent McLuhanisms, "the most successful television commercial is the one you are least aware of." So if Price were successful the Thinkbelt's occupants would be *processed* without realizing that was what was happening to them. Faced with an "educational service" which made no claims on their values, the students would be unable to make any claim on that education's values. They would, in short, have become part of the "servicing mechanism."

It seems unnecessary, in conclusion, to do more than repeat: the *Gesamtkünstler* treats his fellows as children; the life-conditioner (and we can see now with what unwitting aptness Price chose that term) treats them as objects.

Part Two

The question that now arises is why, in the mid-twentieth century, there should arise two such strikingly distinctive architectural schemes, which both betray a conception of architecture's place in human experience, and which do so in terms I have described as the bizarre consequences of the nineteenth century's loss of faith in rhetoric. To answer that question, or at least to try to answer a part of it, will require an even larger historical context than that I have used so far. But here as before, the precepts of semiological theory offer illumination.

The issues at stake really began to be unmanageable two centuries before the concepts of *Gesamtkunstwerk* and life-conditioning gained their definitive, nineteenth century formulations. It was at that particular time in European history when, to use Pascal's terms, the relation of "nature" and "custom" in human experience was first seen as such an urgent philosophical question. In 1683 Claude Perrault's *Treatise on the Five Orders* was published, a work which outlined the particularly architectural implications of that question, with astonishing clarity and foresight.

Perrault was convinced that the twin tenets of traditional architectural theory, the authority of classical precedent, and the assumption that "beauty" was a kind of Platonic absolute, were too seriously discredited to guide contemporary practice any longer. Regarding the traditionally acknowledged authority of ancient precedent, he said: "we cannot find, either in the remains of the Buildings of the Ancients, or among the great Number of Architects that have treated of the Proportions of the Orders, that any two Buildings, or any two Authors, agree, and have followed the same rules."[24]

So much then, for classical precedent. As for the assumption of "beauty" as a Platonic absolute, Perrault was so unconvinced of that as to speculate "whether that which renders the proportions of a building agreeable be not the same thing as that which makes a modish Habit please on account of its Proportions, which nevertheless have nothing positively beautiful, and that ought to be loved for itself; since when Custom, and other reasons not positive, which induc'd this Love, come to change, we affect them no longer, tho' they remain the same."[25]

Perrault's controversial suggestion, based on that argument, was: To judge rightly in this case suppose two sorts of Beauties in Architecture, namely those which are founded on solid convincing Reasons (positive beauties, in that terminology, corresponding to nature in Pascal) "and those that depend only on Prepossession and Prejudice (arbitrary beauties for Perrault, corresponding to custom in Pascal)."[26]

It is this argument in terms of a relationship between "positive" and "arbitrary" beauty, which can instructively be set alongside Saussure's distinction of *langue* and *parole*, where the *langue* is the "invariant" and the *parole* the "variant" aspect of a communication system. I have said that in information theory, "information" is a function of "surprise" within a matrix of "expectancy." Or, to return to Perrault's terminology, "architecture has no Proportions true in themselves; it remains to be seen whether we can establish those that are probable and likely ['vraysemblable', in the original French text], founded upon convincing Reason, without departing too far from the Proportions usually received."[27]

As well-known as Perrault's argument is the extraordinary theoretical dispute that followed it. For over a century after its publication, Perrault's treatise dominated French architectural writing. Each successive writer from Blondel to Boullée established his own position primarily with respect to the concepts of "positive" and "arbitrary" beauty as originally discussed by Perrault. However, no influential contributor to that dispute attempted to sustain his concern for "those [proportions] that are probable and likely." Rather, each laid a particular emphasis on either "positive" or "arbitrary" beauty.

Although, as I have said, Perrault's argument and the ensuing dispute are well-known, the consequences of the split emphasis laid by his important successors are not, as far as I can see, well-known at all. If they were, I do not think we should be faced with such designs as CBS and the Thinkbelt. Generally speaking, we seem to be as yet too much a product of that split to recognize the extent of its influence upon our thinking. All the same, I would suggest that all subsequent architectural theory lies in the shadow of this distinction.

Consider the school of thought which, upon following Perrault, chose to assert the primacy of "positive" beauty.[28] Their commitment involved them in a moral obligation to "get to the bottom of" architecture, an effort whose modern guises I have already discussed in Part One. In the three centuries since Perrault, there have of course been numerous proposals put forward, purporting to reveal what that solid "bottom" was, among them Laugier's ethnological primitivism, Choisy's technological determinism, Guadet's elemental geometry, and Hannes Meyer's dialectical materialism. However, as Perrault knew quite well, it is not possible to lay such an exclusive emphasis upon the "positive" aspects of architecture, to the exclusion of the "arbitrary." Indeed, for those who wished to see, the persistent quest for a solid bottom for architecture was shown to be pointless before the eighteenth century was half over. The philosophical experience of David Hume demonstrated that such skeptical rationalism as the advocates of a solid bottom to reality were required to exercise towards the whole of *apparent* reality would end up leaving indubitable virtually no aspect of human experience whatsoever.[29]

Alternatively, consider the school of thought which chose to assert the primacy of "arbitrary" beauty. Their commitment involved them in resolutely sticking close to the diverse surface of architecture as they saw it in all its forms. Once again, three centuries have produced various approaches to the "arbitrary," ranging through early versions of cultural relativism, such as Fischer von Erlach's, Louden's and Schinkel's calculated eclecticism, Gilbert Scott's uncalculated eclecticism, and Philip Johnson's "Camp." But of course, here again, by the mid-eighteenth century, the theoretical premises of the position were already (albeit inadvertently) demolished in Hume's claim that "beauty is no quality in things themselves: it exists merely in the mind which contemplates them, and each mind sees a different beauty."[30]

With that celebrated remark, Hume both out-flanked and superseded the advocates of arbitrary beauty. For were he correct—and all he did was to take the argument for "arbitrary" beauty to its radically subjective conclusion—then the result was not just that there was no such thing as "positive" beauty, but that there was no such thing about which one could generalize at all. From the time of Hume, until that of Marcel Duchamp and John Cage, the unqualified commitment to the "arbitrary" has always ended in utter silence.

Now semiology does not only offer us a simulacrum of the relation of "positive" and "arbitrary" beauty, in terms of *langue* and *parole*. It also suggests a means of correlating the approaches of the various theorists that succeeded Perrault. I have discussed the semiological poles of metaphor (the relationship of substitution) and metonymy (the relationship of contiguity). In the light of those concepts, I think we can see that the three-centuries-old drive to "get to the bottom of" architecture, has been characterized by a continual, radically reductive pattern of substitution for the given architecture at any particular time; while the corresponding effort to stick close to the given architecture's diverse surface has been equally characterized by a pattern of radically inclusive correlation of the forms of that given architecture.

Consider again the first tradition. As each successive proposal of a truly solid "bottom" for architecture was made, the very force of exclusion of some factor previously taken for granted was what imbued the new proposal with a certain plausibility, not to say moral authority. Thus, Laugier proposed to substitute for the accepted architecture of his day a new one which excluded arches, niches, and applied pilasters. And the force of that exclusion lent his argument sufficient plausibility to dominate the development of architecture (especially in France) for several years. In his turn, Choisy proposed to substitute for the history of architecture which was accepted in his day a new one which excluded legitimate formal intention, and that exclusion lent his argument its conviction. And, of course, Hannes Meyer proposed to substitute for architecture in his day simply "building," deriving his moral authority from the exclusion of "architecture" altogether. Thus, the quest for the solid "bottom" has proceeded. In every case, only the passage of time revealed that the particular reductive substitution involved was insufficient to guarantee the indubitability of the new proposal.

As for the second tradition, the defenders of "arbitrary" beauty have taken the opposite tack. Instead of effecting reductive substitutions for the given architecture at a particular time, they have always attempted to correlate all that architecture's forms to the greatest extent possible. Both Louden and Schinkel, for example, devised theoretical systems in which the various stylistic motifs used in their period were carefully correlated, so that each would have a particular program significance (Gothic style for churches, Greek style for public buildings, etc.).[31] For that matter, Saarinen's well-known effort to find the "style for the job" is only another version of the Louden-Schinkel approach. But this school of thought has never established any real authority, since, in the face of its adversaries' reductive skepticism, it has continually failed to demonstrate any conclusive "authenticity" for its elaborate sets of stylistic distinctions.

Now, what I suggest, in the face of designs such as the CBS building and the Thinkbelt, is that we regard both of those traditions as bankrupt. The attempt to "get to the bottom" of architecture has now clearly shown that there is no such "bottom." In this respect, it is only appropriate that Price, who has in the Thinkbelt taken radical reduction to one of its extremes, should himself have been publicly chastised by Reyner Banham, for his unwarranted presumption in taking it for granted that he could even describe *himself* as "in the enclosure business."[32] In its latest stages, "getting to the bottom of" architecture has turned into a game of nihilist oneupmanship. At the same time, the parallel struggle to stick close to architecture's diverse surface would seem to have shown itself as finally self-defeating. When the commitment to the "arbitrary" has been serious, it has always fallen into the trap of making "comprehensibility" an end in itself. In seeking "the style for the job," and in undertaking a *Gesamtkunstwerk* such as CBS, Saarinen has in just this way promoted a kind of petrification of architecture's communicativeness. On the other hand, frivolous commitment to the "arbitrary" has always tended to dissolve that communicativeness. To see this, one has only to think of any modern hotel interior, with its Bali Hai Room, its Charles Dickens Pub, its Old West Saloon, etc., etc. As William Burroughs puts it: "Nothing is true; everything is permitted."[33]

The bankruptcy of both those traditions, and the illumination cast upon them by semiological theory, suggest to me that there would be good reason to look again at Perrault's long-forgotten query as to "whether we can establish those [proportions in architecture] that are probable and likely, without departing too far from the proportions usually received." If Perrault's tone seems cautious, it is no more so than Paul McCartney's. The point is simply the abstract one made by Norbert Wiener: "The essence of an effective rule for a game . . . is that it be statable in advance, and that it apply to more than one case. . . . In the simplest case, it is a property which is invariant to a set of transformations to which the system is subject."[34]

The possibilities for architecture which open up in the perspective of semiological theory are numerous and even exhilarating. Consider again the diagram which I used above to illustrate the "field of meaning" of a social phenomenon. As I said at that point, one dimension of that field can be considered to represent the "scope of articulation" of architecture. Then too, in terms of the overall "social context" of which I spoke, that "scope of articulation" is co-extensive with our society's total social awareness of architecture, both historically and geographically.

Take the case of our relation to architecture which is distant in time, yet nearly within our own cultural tradition. A semiological perspective reveals how it is that so long as we take the trouble to observe the buildings of the past, they will assume a greater and greater distinctiveness, simply by virtue of the "perceptual distance" as it were, which separates us from, yet connects us to them. In other words, semiology provides a kind of theoretical apparatus to back up T. S. Eliot's famous remark: "what happens when a new work of art is created is something that happens simultaneously to all the works that preceded it."[35] We may even conclude that there is a sense in which Wiener's "effective rule" applies to history. Like the human unconscious, it is inexhaustible, since present action perpetually transforms it. At the same time, an acknowledgment that the distinctiveness of our architectural heritage is so largely a function of "perceptual distance," has an important reverse implication. For example, once we recognize that the "visual coherence" which we admire in mediaeval towns is so much due to our own historical perceptual position, then we can see that attempts to reproduce that coherence are really attempts to seize hold of our own shadows.

On the other hand, if we take the case of our relation to an exotic architecture which is remote geographically, and therefore completely incommensurable with our own historically, such as that of a "primitive" society, then the implications are even more interesting. As Lévi-Strauss has said; "the paradox is irresolvable; the less one culture communicates with another, the less likely they are to be corrupted one by the other; but, on the other hand, the less likely it is, in such conditions, that the respective emissaries of these cultures will be able to seize the richness and significance of their diversity."[36] In other words, if it is the case that there exists no overlap at all between the architectural "fields of meaning" of our own society, and those of the "primitive" society in question, then what we can say that we perceive in their architecture will be nothing but a shallow (if diverting) reflection of our own. If, on the other hand (the more likely possibility nowadays), there is a partial overlay between the two "fields of meaning," then what we perceive of their architecture may indeed bear some relation to that society's own perception of it. However, in such circumstances, our threshold of conscious awareness of that architecture still does not coincide with that society's threshold. There will be a large area of meaning of which the society is conscious, but which we can only take for granted; there will be another area, which we will consciously perceive, but which they will take for granted. It is exactly this discrepancy which, in my view, prompts certain observers, such as Bernard Rudofsky, to extol the formal precocity of primitive architecture,[37] and others, such as Christopher Alexander, to savor its "well-adaptedness" and "unself-consciousness."[38] One hopes the realization that both of these characteristics are so largely a function of our own position as observers, that it will indicate how condescending it is of Alexander to attribute such "well-adaptedness" to an "unself-conscious design process."[39]

For that matter, while it is not possible here to examine Alexander's views in a general way, it is, I think, important to point out that semiological theory sees virtually all current versions of functionalism, whether "organicist" like Alexander's, or not, as inadequate to explain or generate *any* social phenomenon. Since those social phenomena are socially representable structures of reality, they obviously "go far beyond any possible considerations of utility."[40] Indeed, although semiology nowhere yet includes a full-scale refutation of functionalism, it does very strongly imply the kind of critique which Hannah Arendt has formulated. "The perplexity of utilitarianism," according to Arendt, "is that it gets caught in the unending chain of means and ends without ever arriving at some principle which could justify the category of means and ends, that is, of utility itself. The "in order to" has become the content of the "for the sake of"; in other words, "utility established as meaning generates meaninglessness."[41]

Arendt's point is particularly important in my present context, for in continuing her argument, she then charged that utilitarian ideas had become so pervasive in the late eighteenth century as to affect even the thinking of Kant. His characterization of the only objects that are not "for use," namely works of art, cannot, in her view, deny its origins in utilitarian thinking, since he describes them as objects in which we take "pleasure without any interest." That charm has the most remarkable implications for architecture, for in the perspective of the subsequent century, it shows that the attitudes of "arts for art's sake," and "utilitarianism" are really two sides of the same coin. In the light of that revelation, we could conclude that the *Gesamtkünstler* and the life-conditioner do not only follow parallel paths, but in fact derive their design attitudes from the same philosophical premises.

But we must not be *too* surprised at this revelation. After all, to have understood that, we need not have turned to anthropology, communication theory and social philosophy. All we need to have done is to remember the eloquent statement (well within the normal scope of our discipline) by this century's greatest interpreter of "meaning in architecture," in defense of the ideas of Marsilio Ficino and Pico della Mirandola. What concerned Erwin Panofsky was their "conviction of the dignity of man, based on both the insistence on human values (rationality and freedom) and the acceptance of human limitations (fallibility and frailty); from this," argued Panofsky, "two postulates result—responsibility and tolerance. Small wonder," he continued, "that this attitude has been attacked from two opposite camps whose common aversion to the ideas of responsibility and tolerance has recently aligned them in a common front. Entrenched in one of these camps are those who deny human values: the determinists . . . the authoritarians. . . . In the other camp are those who deny human limitations in favor of some sort of intellectual or political libertinism."[42]

Responsibility and tolerance. At the intersection of those two postulates lies the role of the architect who attempts to take the measure of "la dimension amoureuse." In assuming that role, in designing in his fellows' experience, rather than above it, or outside it, such an architect will devise forms analogous to those of Lévi-Strauss's projected anthropology; forms, that is, which "correspond to a permanent possibility of man."[43] In short, that architect will *offer*, with neither the arrogance of the *Gesamtkünstler*, nor the indifference of the life-conditioner, "ideal" images of human existence, "ideal" frames for human action.

Notes

1. Germain Boffrand, quoted in Peter Collins, *Changing Ideals in Modern Architecture* (London: Faber & Faber, 1965), p. 174.
2. *Eero Saarinen on His Work* (New Haven: Yale University Press, 1962), p. 16.
3. Cedric Price, "Life-Conditioning," *Architectural Design*, October 1966, p. 483.
4. *Eero Saarinen on His Work.* See also *Progressive Architecture*, July 1965, pp. 187–192.
5. Cedric Price, "Potteries Thinkbelt," *Architectural Design*, October 1966, pp. 484–497.
6. Robert Venturi, *Complexity and Contradiction in Architecture* (New York: Museum of Modern Art, 1966), p. 103.
7. *Life*, April 29, 1966, pp. 50–58, and Chris Welles, "How Does It Feel to Live in Total Design?," ibid., pp. 59–60a.
8. Price, "Life-Conditioning."
9. Roland Barthes, *Essais critiques* (Paris: Editions du Seuil, 1964). See also his *Elements of Semiology* (London: Jonathan Cape, 1967); Ernst Gombrich, *Art and Illusion* (London: Phaidon Press, 1962), and *Meditations on a Hobby Horse* (London: Phaidon Press, 1963); Claude Lévi-Strauss, *A World on the Wane* (London: Hutchinson, 1961), *La pensée sauvage* (Paris: Plon, 1962), and *Structural Anthropology* (New York: Basic Books, 1963); Marshall McLuhan, *Understanding Media* (New York: McGraw-Hill, 1966). Barthes's is the best short introduction

to the thought of Lévi-Strauss, and that of Peter Caws: "Structuralism," *Partisan Review*, Winter 1968, pp. 75–91.

10. Claude Lévi-Strauss, *The Scope of Anthropology* (London: Jonathan Cape, 1967), p. 16.

11. Barthes, *Elements of Semiology*, p. 93.

12. Paul McCartney, quoted in *International Times*, London, January 29, 1967.

13. Readers of Gombrich's *Art and Illusion* and *Meditations on a Hobby Horse* may have noticed the striking conceptual similarity between semiology's use of *langue* and *parole*, and Gombrich's use of schema and correction, which he has derived from perception psychology. Then too, of course, Professor Gombrich has been influenced as much as the semiologists by the precepts of information theory.
    Readers of Christian Norberg-Schulz's *Intentions in Architecture* (London: Allen & Unwin, 1963) will also recognize how the semiologists' use of information theory is similar to his own use of it, as well as of perception psychology.

14. Price, "Life-Conditioning."

15. Roman Jakobson, "Aspects linguistiques de la traduction," in *Essais de linguistique générale* (Paris: Editions de Minuit, 1963), p. 81.

16. The phrase comes, of course, from Matthew Arnold's "The Function of Criticism at the Present Time," of 1864, but it is characteristic of a whole nineteenth century tradition. Compare, for example, Ranke's description of the proper scope of historical studies, "to know only what really happened."

17. *Eero Saarinen on His Work*, p. 16.

18. Maurice Merleau-Ponty, *The Phenomenology of Perception* (London: Routledge and Kegan Paul, 1962), p. xx.

19. Aldo van Eyck, quoted in *Team 10 Primer*, ed. Alison Smithson (London: Stoddard Catalogue Co.), p. 40.

20. Colin Cherry, quoted by Gombrich in *Meditations on a Hobby Horse*, p. 61.

21. Saussure, quoted by Barthes in "Eléments de sémiologie," *Communications* no. 4, p. 115.

22. Jakobson, "Deux aspects du langage et deux types d'aphasie," in *Essais de linguistique générale*, pp. 43–67.

23. Lewis Carroll, *Alice in Wonderland, and Through the Looking-Glass* (New York: New American Library, 1960), p. 186.

24. Claude Perrault, *A Treatise on the Five Orders*, translated by John James (London, 1722), p. ii.

25. Ibid., p. v.

26. Ibid., p. vi.

27. Ibid., p. xi.

28. Admittedly, not all members of this school have talked in terms of "beauty." But they have all taken a consistent attitude to what architecture "ought" to be, as opposed to what it "is," at any particular point in time (using "is" as "ought" in the manner of modern sociology).

29. Colin Cherry, *Enlightenment* (Boston: Beacon Press, 1960), p. 307.

30. David Hume, *A Treatise of Human Nature*.

31. My information regarding Louden's efforts I owe to George L. Hersey, of the Department of Art at Yale University, that regarding Schinkel's, to Professor Christian Norberg-Schulz, of the State School of Architecture, Oslo, Norway.

32. The incident is described by Robin Middleton in *Architectural Design*, July 1966.

33. William Burroughs, *Dead Fingers Talk* (London: Tandem Books, 1966), p. 197.

34. Norbert Wiener, *Cybernetics* (Cambridge: MIT Press, 1965), p. 50.

35. T. S. Eliot, *The Sacred Wood* (London: Methuen, 1964), p. 49.

36. Lévi-Strauss, *A World on the Wane*, p. 45.

37. Bernard Rudofsky, *Architecture without Architects* (New York: Museum of Modern Art, 1965).

38. Christopher Alexander, *Notes on the Synthesis of Form* (Cambridge: Harvard University Press, 1964). See especially chapter 3.

39. Ibid., pp. 32 ff.

40. Caws, "Structuralism," p. 80.

41. Hannah Arendt, *The Human Condition* (Garden City, N.Y.: Doubleday Anchor Books, 1959), p. 135.

42. Erwin Panofsky, "The History of Art as a Humanistic Discipline," in *Meaning in Visual Arts* (Garden City, N.Y.: Doubleday Anchor Books, 1955), p. 2.

43. Lévi-Strauss, *The Scope of Anthropology*, p. 49.

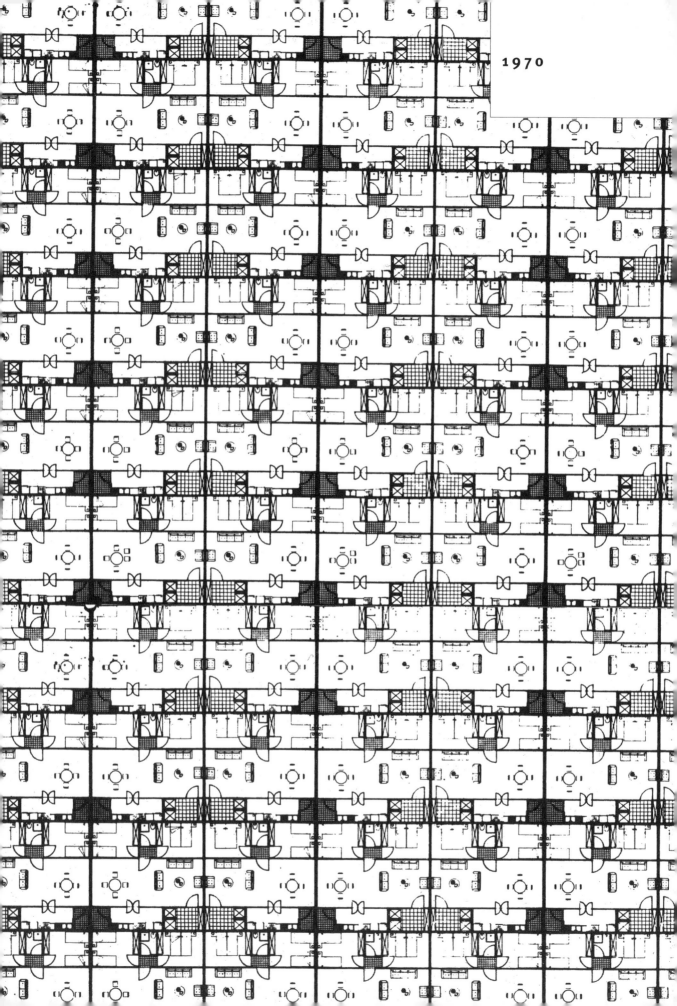

1970

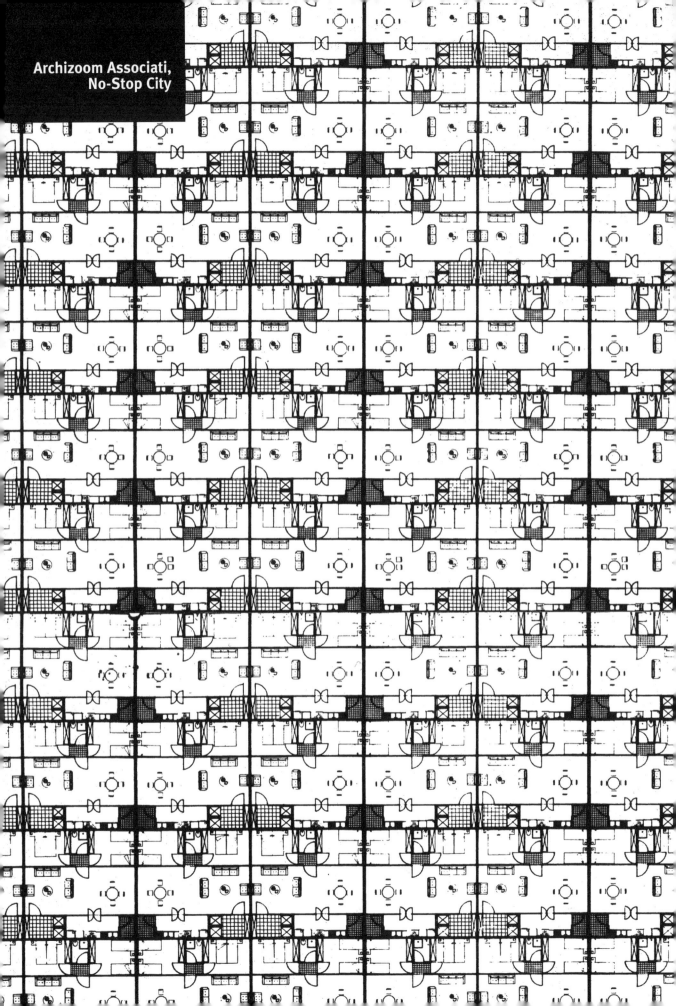

Archizoom Associati,
No-Stop City

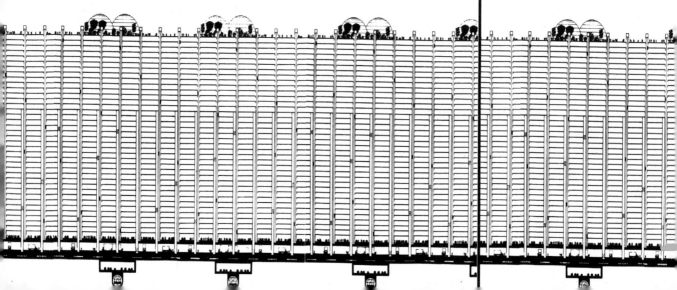

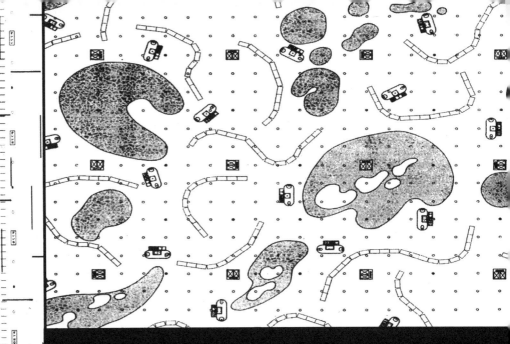

The carrying out of a social organization of labor by means of Planning eliminates the empty space in which Capital expanded during its growth period. In fact, no reality exists any longer outside the system itself: the whole visual relationship with reality loses importance as there ceases to be any distance between the subject and the phenomenon. The city no longer "represents" the system, but becomes the system itself, programmed and isotropic, and within it the various functions are contained homogeneously, without contradictions. Production and Consumption possess one and the same ideology, which is that of Programming. Both hypothesize a social and physical reality completely continuous and undifferentiated. No other realities exist. The factory and the supermarket become the specimen models of the future city: optimal urban structures, potentially limitless, where human functions are arranged spontaneously in a free field, made uniform by a system of micro-acclimatization and optimal circulation of information. The "natural and spontaneous" balance of light and air is superseded: the house becomes a well-equipped parking lot. Inside it there exist no hierarchies nor spatial figurations of a conditioning nature.

Andrea Branzi, "No-Stop City, Residential Parking, Climatic Universal System," *Domus* 496 (March 1971)

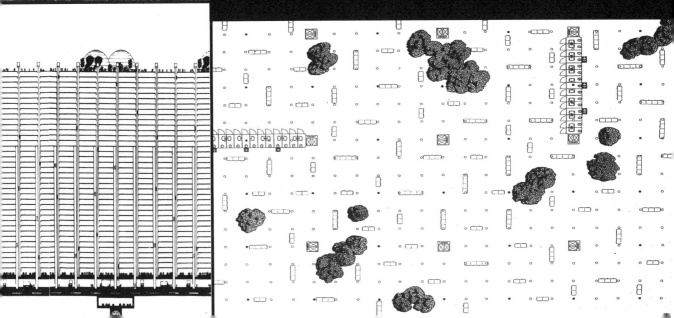

Denise Scott Brown   **"Learning from Pop"** *Casabella* 359–360 (December 1971)

"But Today We Collect Ads," an essay by Alison and Peter Smithson published in *Ark* 18, November 1956, together with the exhibition "This Is Tomorrow," mounted by the Independent Group at the Whitechapel Art Gallery in London in August of the same year, marked architecture's entry into an overt relationship with pop culture. Emphasizing the technology of reproduction, the transparency of information, and the sheer abundance and vividness of images as manifest in 1950s advertising, the Smithsons sought to displace the monofunctional grain silo–steamship–design object paradigm of Gropius, Le Corbusier, and Perriand with the mass consumerist ideals of diversified fabrication, interchangeability, novelty, and disposability: "For us it would be the objects on the beaches, the piece of paper blowing about the street, the throw-away object and the pop-package. For today we collect ads."

Such interests characterized the London milieu of Denise Scott Brown's intellectual formation. After 1958 and her move to the University of Pennsylvania, they converged with another important current (which was part of the distinction between her and Archigram, for example) comprising the populism of Herbert Gans, the "advocacy planning" of Paul Davidoff, and the "probabilistic planning" of Melvin Webber, which, together with the first current, found their ultimate topos in Las Vegas, Levittown, and the architecture of the Venturi–Scott Brown office.

"Learning from Pop" — commissioned by the Institute for Architecture and Urban Studies for publication in a special issue of *Casabella*[1] — synthesizes these two currents, pop culture and populist planning, develops the theses of "A Significance for A&P Parking Lots, or Learning from Las Vegas" (with Venturi, *Architectural Forum*, March 1968) and "On Pop Art, Permissiveness and Planning" (*Journal of the American Institute of Planners*, May 1969), and anticipates the publication of *Learning from Las Vegas* (1972). The essay states two fundamental propositions: first, that the communication of social values across space has superseded mere function and even space itself as the primary substance of architecture; second, that permissiveness, deferred judgment, and the separation of variables for independent study (such as affective properties of artifacts separated from functional and economic criteria) are part of a necessary transitional moment away from the unreflective acceptance of received forms, and in particular of those forms presumed to arise from functional criteria alone.

compare Lefebvre (181–186)

Behind both propositions lies a powerful conceptual reversal of modern architecture's emphasis on the production of objects, via a diagnosis of modernity through its ephemeral, surface-born appearances and modes of reception. *Learning from Las Vegas* developed that reversal into a full-blown analysis, complete with a Smithson-like matrix of desiderata for the new architecture. But "Learning from Pop" is an early signal of a shift that would become fundamental to much of architecture theory after 1968: the motivation for new interventions would no longer be the clearing of space for some bright, new, functionally efficient utopia that architecture might help install, but rather the affirmation of the preexisting context in all its messy heterogeneity and informational flux.[2]

Notes

"Learning from Pop" was reprinted in Robert Venturi and Denise Scott Brown, *A View from the Campidoglio: Selected Essays, 1953–1984,* ed. Peter Arnell, Ted Bickford, and Catherine Bergart (New York: Harper & Row, 1984).

1. Among other articles in the same issue, these are noteworthy: Peter Eisenman, "Notes on Conceptual Architecture: Towards a Definition"; Joseph Rykwert, "The Necessity of Artifice"; Stanford Anderson, "Environment as Artifact: Methodological Implications"; Thomas Schumacher, "Contextualism: Urban Ideals + Deformations"; and Emilio Ambasz, "Institutions and Artifacts for a Post-technological Society."

2. In the same issue of *Casabella*, Kenneth Frampton made the point that the absolute effacement of the distinction between architecture and the popular culture would be a far from untroubling development, harboring the prospect of an architecture cynically fused with the degradation of daily life. "Is it that the inevitability of kitsch is only to be transcended through such a perverse exultation of our industrial capacity to induce and satisfy mass taste in the endless promotion and repetition of kitsch? Or is it that the present triumph of kitsch is testament in itself, without the illuminations of Pop Art, that our urban society is organized towards self defeating ends, on a sociopolitical basis that is totally invalid?" Frampton, "America 1960–1970: Notes on Urban Images and Theory," *Casabella* 359–360 (1971), p. 36.

Las Vegas, Los Angeles, Levittown, the swinging singles on the Westheimer Strip, golf resorts, boating communities, Co-op City, the residential backgrounds to soap operas, TV commercials and mass mag ads, billboards, and Route 66 are sources for a changing architectural sensibility. New sources are sought when the old forms go stale and the way out is not clear; then a Classical heritage, an art movement, or industrial engineers' and primitives' "architecture without architects" may help to sweep out the flowery remains of the old revolution as practiced by its originators' conservative descendants. In America in the sixties an extra ingredient was added to this recipe for artistic change: social revolution. Urban renewal, supplier of work for architects for two decades and a major locus of the soft remains of the Modern movement, was not merely artistically stale, it was socially harmful. The urgency of the social situation, the social critique of urban renewal and of the architect as server of a rich narrow spectrum of the population—in particular the criticism of Herbert Gans—have been as important as the Pop artists in steering us toward the existing American city and its builders. If high-style architects are not producing what people want or need, who is, and what can we learn from them?

Needs, Plural
Sensitivity to needs is a first reason for going to the existing city. Once there, the first lesson for architects is the pluralism of need. No builder-developer in his right mind would announce: I am building for Man. He is building for a market, for a group of people defined by income range, age, family composition and life style. Levittowns, Leisureworlds, Georgian-styled town houses grow from someone's estimation of the needs of the groups who will be their markets. The city can be seen as the built artifacts of a set of subcultures. At the moment, those subcultures which willingly resort to architects are few.

Of course learning from what's there is subject to the caveats and limitations of all behavioristic analysis—one is surveying behavior which is constrained, it is not what people might do in other conditions. The poor do not willingly live in tenements and maybe the middle classes don't willingly live in Levittowns; perhaps the Georgian-styling is less pertinent to the townhouse resident than is the rent. In times of housing shortage this is a particularly forceful argument against architectural behaviorism since people can't vote against a particular offering by staying away if there is no alternative. To counteract this danger one must search for comparison environments where for some reason the constraints do not hold. There are environments which suggest what economically constrained groups' tastes might be if they were less constrained. They are the nouveau riche environments; Hollywood for a former era, Las Vegas for today, and the homes of film stars, sportsmen, and other groups where upward mobility may resemble vertical takeoff, yet where maintenance of previous value systems is encouraged.

Another source is physical backgrounds in the mass media, movies, soap operas, pickle and furniture polish ads. Here the aim is not to sell houses but something else, and the background represents someone's (Madison Avenue's?) idea of what pickle buyers or soap opera watchers want in a house. Now the Madison Avenue observer's view may be as biased as the architect's, and it should be studied in the light of what it is trying to sell—must pickle architecture look homey like my house or elegant like yours if it is to sell me pickles? But at least it's another bias, an alternative to the architectural navel contemplation we so often do for research; i.e., ask: What did Le Corbusier do? Both Madison Avenue and the builder, although they can tell us little of the needs of the very poor, cover a broader range of the population and pass a stiffer market test than does the architect in urban renewal or public housing, and if we learn no more from these sources than that architecture must differ for different groups, that is a great deal. But an alternative to both is to examine what people do to buildings—in Levittowns, Society Hills, gray areas and slums—once they are in them. Here, costs and availability are less constraining forces since the enterprise is smaller. Also, changes tend often to be symbolic rather than structural, and aspirations can perhaps be more easily inferred from symbols than from structures.

Attention to built sources for information on need does not imply that asking people what they want is not extremely necessary as well. This is an important topic, as is the relation between the two types of survey, asking and looking; but it is not the subject of this enquiry, which is on what can be learned from the artifacts of pop culture.

Formal Analysis as Design Research

A second reason for looking to pop culture is to find formal vocabularies for today which are more relevant to people's diverse needs and more tolerant of the untidinesses of urban life than the "rationalist," Cartesian formal orders of latter-day Modern architecture. How much low-income housing and nineteenth-century architecture has been cleared so some tidy purist architect or planner could start with a clean slate?

Modern architects can now admit that whatever forces, processes, and technologies determine architectural form, ideas about form determine it as well; that a formal vocabulary is as much a part of architecture as are bricks and mortar (plastics and systems, for futurists); that form does not, cannot, arise from function alone, newborn and innocent as Venus from her shell, but rather that form follows, *inter alia*, function, forces, and form. Formal biases, if they are consciously recognized, need not tyrannize as they have done in urban renewal; and formal vocabularies, given their place in architecture, can be studied and improved to suit functional requirements, rather than accepted unconsciously and unsuitably—some old hand-me-down from some irrelevant master. The forms of the pop landscape are as relevant to us now as were the forms of antique Rome to the Beaux Arts, Cubism and Machine Architecture to the early Moderns, and the industrial Midlands and the Dogon to Team 10, which is to say extremely relevant, and more so than the latest bathysphere, launch pad, or systems hospital (or even, *pace* Banham, the Santa Monica pier). Unlike these, they speak to our condition not only aesthetically, but on many levels of necessity, from the social necessity to rehouse the poor without destroying them to the architectural necessity to produce buildings and environments that others will need and like. The pop landscape differs from the earlier models in that it is also the place where we build; it is our context. And it is one of the few contemporary sources of data on the symbolic and communicative aspects of architecture, since it was untouched by the Modern movement's purist reduction of architecture to space and structure only. But formal analysis presents a problem. First, since form has for so long been an illegitimate topic, we have lost the tradition of analyzing it, and second, the forms we are dealing with are new and don't relate easily to traditional architectural or planning techniques of analysis and communication. Orthographic projection hardly covers the essence of the Stardust sign, and, although this sign is a block long and has an overpowering visual impact *in situ*, it doesn't show well on a land use map. Suburban space, being automobile space, is not defined by enclosing walls and floors and is therefore difficult to portray graphically using systems devised for the description of buildings. In fact, space is not the most important constituent of suburban form. Communication across space is more important, and it requires a symbolic and a time element in its descriptive systems which are only slowly being devised.

New analytic techniques must use film and videotape to convey the dynamism of sign architecture and the sequential experience of vast landscapes; and computers are needed to aggregate mass repeated data into comprehensible patterns. Valuable traditional techniques should also be resuscitated by their application to new phenomena; for example, when Nolli's mid-eighteenth-century technique for mapping Rome is adapted to include parking lots, it throws considerable light on Las Vegas. It could also lend itself fairly easily to computer techniques.

Formal analysis should be comparative, linking the new forms, by comparison, to the rest of the formal tradition of architecture thereby incorporating them into the architectural discipline and helping us to understand our new experience in the light of our formal training. By suggesting that form should be analyzed, I do not imply that function (the program), technologies, or forces (urban social processes or land economics) are not vital to architecture, nor indeed, that they too can't serve as sources of artistic inspiration to the architect. All are necessary and they work in combination. The others are merely not the subject of this particular enquiry.

Tanya billboard, from *Learning from Las Vegas*, 1972

The Soup Can and the Establishment

There is an irony in the fact that the "popular" culture and the "popular" landscape are not popular with those who make the decisions to renew the city and rehouse the poor. Here is John Kenneth Galbraith, an important and influential liberal, quoted in *Life* magazine:

For the average citizen there are some simple tests which will tell him when we have passed from incantation to practical action on the environment. Restriction of auto use in the large cities will be one. Another will be when the billboards, the worst and most nearly useless excrescence of industrial civilization, are removed from the highways. Yet another will be when telephone and electric wires everywhere in the cities go underground and we accept the added charge on our bills.

My own personal test, for what it may be worth, concerns the gasoline service station. This is the most repellent piece of architecture of the past two thousand years. There are far more of them than are needed. Usually they are filthy. Their merchandise is hideously packaged and garishly displayed. They are uncontrollably addicted to great strings of ragged little flags. Protecting them is an ominous coalition of small businessmen and large. The stations should be excluded entirely from most streets and highways. Where allowed, they should be franchised to limit the number, and there should be stern requirements as to architecture, appearance and general reticence. When we begin on this (and similar roadside commerce), I will think that we are serious.[1]

He does not even mention the need for low-income housing as an urgent environmental problem, and in my opinion he should stick to economics. But the conventional wisdom which Galbraith expounds is shared by his colleagues, the elderly architectural radicals who man America's fine arts commissions, the "design" departments of HUD and the planning and redevelopment agencies, who plan and build for the larger public and private corporations and have the ear of the city makers. If the public is to be well served by their decisions, these members of the architectural establishment must learn to separate out for a different type of scrutiny their aesthetic from other preoccupations with "environmental pollution." Fouled water and billboards are not of the same magnitude or order of problem. The first cannot be done well, but the second can; particularly if we are given the opportunity to study them for awhile, nonjudgmentally.

When "blighted" neighborhoods are swept away together with billboards and gasoline stations in the name of the avoidance of "visual pollution," the social harm can be irreparable. However, an old aesthetic formula, even though it is shown to be obstructive, will not be relinquished until it is replaced by a new one, since, as we have seen, form depends on form for its making. And, for the architectural establishment, the new vocabulary must have a respectable lineage. Hence, if the popular environment is to provide that vocabulary, it must be filtered through the proper processes for its acceptance. It must become a part of the high-art tradition; it must be last year's avant garde. This is another reason to submit the new landscape to traditional architectural analysis: for the sake of its acceptance by the establishment. They can't learn from pop until Pop hangs in the academy.

Hop on Pop

I have recommended an investigation of the forms of the new, existing city on both social and aesthetic grounds for architects who hope to hone their skills to a sharp new edge. High art has followed low art before and vice versa; in fact, where did the McDonald's parabola and the split-level ranch come from in the first place?

In the movement from low art to high art lies an element of the deferral of judgment. Judgment is withheld in the interest of understanding and receptivity. This is an exciting heuristic technique but also a dangerous one since liking the whole of pop culture is as irrational as hating the whole of it, and it calls forth the vision of a general and indiscriminate hopping on the pop bandwagon, where everything is good and judgment is abandoned rather than deferred. Yet artists, architects, actors, must judge, albeit, one hopes, with a sigh. After a decent interval, suitable criteria must grow out of the new source. Judgment is merely deferred to make subsequent judgments more sensitive.

Note

1. John Kenneth Galbraith: "To My New Friends in the Affluent Society—Greetings," *Life*, March 27, 1970.

Together, all of the buildings read as a city in which the private relationship with death happens to be the civil relationship with the institution. Thus the cemetery is also a public building with an inherent clarity in its circulation and its land use. Externally, it is closed by a fenestrated wall. The elegiac theme does not separate it much from other public buildings. Its order and its location also contain the bureaucratic aspect of death. The project attempts to solve the most important technical issues in the same manner as they are solved when designing a house, a school, or a hotel. As opposed to a house, a school, or a hotel, where life itself modifies the work and its growth in time, the cemetery foresees all modifications; in the cemetery, time possesses a different dimension. Faced with this relationship, architecture can only use its given elements, refusing any suggestion not born out of its own making; there-

**Aldo Rossi,
Cemetery of San Cataldo,
Modena**

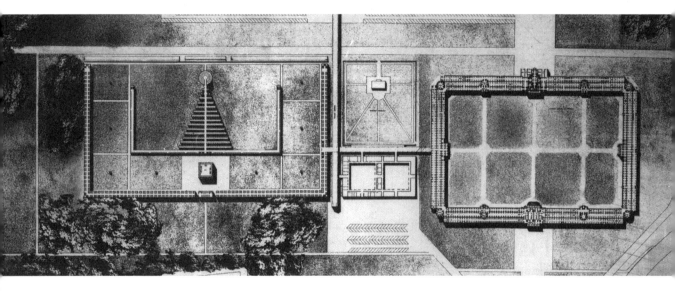

fore, the references to the cemetery are also found in the architecture of the cemetery, the house, and the city. Here, the monument is analogous to the relationship between life and buildings in the modern city. The cube is an abandoned or unfinished house; the cone is the chimney of a deserted factory. The analogy with death is possible only when dealing with the finished object, with the end of all things: any relationship, other than that of the de-   serted house and the abandoned work, is consequently untransmittable. Besides the municipal exigencies, bureaucratic practices, the face of the orphan, the remorse of the private relationship, tenderness and indifference, this project for a cemetery complies with the image of cemetery that each one of us possesses.

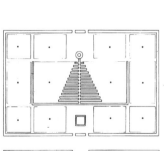

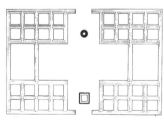

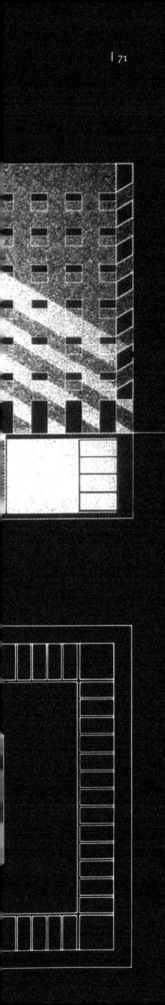

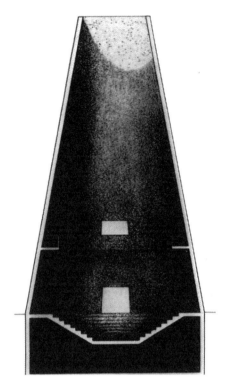

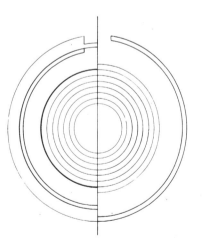

Colin Rowe   Introduction to *Five Architects* (New York: Wittenborn, 1972)

If the historical architectural avant-garde shared common ideological roots with Marxism, it also shared a Marxian philosophical ambition to interfuse form and word — variously articulated as expression and content, system and concept, practice and theory, building and politics. That the fusion process ultimately failed entailed a shift in the terms in which the experience of modernity itself was thought, a shift from modernity, fully developed, as the essential desired achievement of architecture to modernity as architecture's limiting condition.

| *compare 146–147* ▌

Feeling the force of this shift, Colin Rowe, in his introduction to the work of five of the American neo-avant-garde, forthrightly exposes what seems to be the only possible choice: adhere to the forms, the *physique*-flesh of the avant-garde and relegate the *morale*-word to incantation. For if the latter has been reduced to "a constellation of escapist myths," the former "possess an eloquence and a flexibility which continues now to be as overwhelming as it was then." The measure of architecture no longer lies in the efficacy with which it prefigures a new and better world, but rather in its achievement, within the contingent conditions of the modern, of meeting the demands of the flesh, as it were, of elevating form as its own language without reference to external sentiments, rationales, or indeed social visions: "the great merit of what follows lies in the fact that its authors are not enormously self-deluded as to the immediate possibility of any violent or sudden architectural or social mutation." The plastic and spatial inventions of cubism and constructivism, Terragni and Le Corbusier, remain the standard specific to the ideologically indifferent medium of architecture itself. The neo-avant-garde are "belligerently second hand," Scamozzis to modernism's Palladio, a series of simulacra. But it is through acceptance of that standard and the repetition of just those simulacra that the architect aspires to be intelligible. From this position, the true potential of architecture lies not in the prospect of its popular or technological relevance, but in the possibility of its autonomy.

While Rowe's later project, *Collage City,* has received more critical attention, this short introduction has proved more theoretically powerful. For his argument entails his final question: "Can an architecture which professes an objective of continuous experiment ever become congruous with the ideal of an architecture which is to be popular, intelligible, and profound?" And that question fixes the opposition that has haunted most of subsequent architectural practice.

> What you should try to accomplish is built meaning. So get
> close to the meaning and build.
>
> **ALDO VAN EYCK,** *Team 10 Primer,* p. 7

When, in the late 1940s, modern architecture became established and institutionalized, necessarily, it lost something of its original meaning. Meaning, of course, it
had never been supposed to possess. Theory and official exegesis had insisted that
the modern building was absolutely without iconographic content, that it was no
more than the illustration of a program, a direct expression of social purpose. Modern architecture, it was pronounced, was simply a rational approach to building; it
was a logical derivative from functional and technological facts; and—at the last
analysis—it should be regarded in these terms, as no more than the inevitable result
of twentieth century circumstances.

There was very little recognition of meaning in all this. Indeed
the need for symbolic content seemed finally to have been superseded; and it was
thus that there emerged the spectacle of an architecture which claimed to be scientific but which—as we all know—was in reality profoundly sentimental. For very
far from being as deeply involved as he supposed with the precise resolution of
exacting facts, the architect was (as he always is) far more intimately concerned
with the physical embodiment of even more exacting fantasies.

Fantasies about ineluctable change were combined in his mind
with further fantasies about imminent and apocalyptic catastrophe and with still
others about instant millennium. Crisis threatened; but hope abounded. A change
of heart was therefore required—for, if a new world might still rise, like a phoenix,
from out of the ashes of the old, it was up to all men of good will to help bring
this about; and thus while a holocaust of conventional vanities now ensued, the
architect called upon himself simultaneously to assume the virtues of the scientist,
the peasant and the child. The objectivity of the first, the naturalness of the second
and the naivete of the third indicated the values which the situation required; and
the architect, transformed in terms of this image, could now assume his proper
role—part Moses, part St. George—as the leader and the liberator of mankind.

The idea was grand and, for a time, the messianic program
was productive. The architect found himself to be an enthusiast for speed and for
sport; for youth, sunbathing, simple life, sociology, Canadian grain elevators, Atlantic liners, Vuitton trunks, filing cabinets and factories. And his buildings became
the illustrations of these enthusiasms. But they became also the outward and visible
signs of a better world, a testament in the present as to what the future would
disclose; and there was always the proviso that his buildings were the agents of this
future, that the more modern buildings were erected the more the hoped for condition would ensue.

The hoped for condition did not ensue. For, when modern architecture became proliferated throughout the world, when it became cheaply available, standardized and basic, as the architect had always wished it to be, necessarily there resulted a rapid devaluation of its ideal content. The intensity of its social vision became distanced. The building became no longer a subversive proposition about a possible Utopian future. It became instead the acceptable decoration of a certainly non-Utopian present. The *ville radieuse*—that city where life would become intelligent, educated and clean, in which social justice would be established and political issues resolved—this city was not to be built. Compromise and accommodation were therefore in order; and hence, with deflation of conviction, there followed divergence of interest.

The scene was now ripe for the cheap politician and the commercial operator. The revolution had both succeeded and failed. The cautious and the careful could, therefore, now emerge; but, while they could acclaim revolutionary success and repudiate suggestion of failure, there still remained the predicament of "the true believer" who, above all else, was obliged to detach himself from success.

The camp of success—always eclectic, facile and agreeable—proceeded to modify and to use the revolution. The camp of "the true believer"—always anxious for authenticity—attempted to work over the results of the revolution so as to make them strange, arcane, difficult; interesting to the few and inaccessible to the many. And both parties were prone, as advantage seemed to dictate, to employ sometimes the polemics of revolution and sometimes its forms.

Thus there ensued that succession of fractional style phases: the cult of townscape and the new empiricism, Miesian neo-classicism, neo-Liberty, the New Brutalism, Team X, the Futurist Revival, Archigram, in terms of which involutions any consideration of architecture in the 1970s must be based, and, indeed, the two camps—of success and "the true believer"—have, by now, so much interpenetrated, so infected one another, so much exchanged arguments and apologetic, appearances and motifs, that to discriminate either is becoming a major operation.

So much is largely true today of modern architecture in general; but it should go without saying that these remarks do not wholly describe its *modus vivendi*—either past or present—within the United States. Thus, while with regard to Europe, it is possible to argue that modern architecture was conceived as an adjunct of socialism and probably sprang from approximately the same ideological roots as Marxism, in America an indigenous modern architecture was very conspicuously unequipped with any such implicit social program or politically critical pedigree. That is: an indigenous modern architecture was the result of no largely obtrusive collective social concern and its exponents seem scarcely to have been obsessed by any overwhelming vision of either impending cataclysm or of unitary future world. These visions were distinctively European and, in extreme form, perhaps more specifically Germanic; but, whatever their place of origin and concentration, rooted as they were in the circumstances of World War I and the Russian Revolution, they qualified European production as they never could American. In post–World War I Europe, the combined promise and threat of *Architecture or Revolution* could seem to many important innovators to be a very real one; but, in the United States, the presumption that only architecture could turn a "bad" revolution into a "good" one, that only a Wagnerian recourse to "total" design could avert social catastrophe, this could never seem to be very highly plausible. For in the United States the revolution was assumed to have already occurred—in 1776, and it was further assumed to have initiated a social order which was not to be superseded by subsequent developments. In other words, with the revolutionary theme divested by circumstances of both its catastrophic and futurist implications, with this theme rendered retrospective, legalistic and even nationalist, an indigenous modern architecture in America deployed connotations quite distinct from its European counterparts. Its tacit assumptions were infinitely less grand. It was clean, efficient, empirically reasonable, simple, evidently to be related to the time-honored Yankee virtues; and while a Frank Lloyd Wright could—and did—claim revolutionary antecedents, could represent his buildings as the natural sequel to something latent and libertarian in American air, as the *Usonian* efflorescence of a politically democratic society; still, in doing so, he proposed no intrinsic challenge to the social order and inferred no scheme of radical social reconstruction. Instead, such an architecture as his was essentially a call for a particular political society to become more completely itself.

But, if the Architecture-Revolution confrontation (whatever value is attached to either of its components) is one of the more obviously unexplored ingredients of modern architecture's folklore, and if any attempt to explore it would, almost certainly, meet with the most strenuous disavowal of its significance, and if it might be possible to demonstrate the action or the inaction of this fantasy, for present purposes it should be enough simply to reiterate that the revolutionary theme was never a very prominent component of American speculation about building. European modern architecture, even when it operated within the cracks and crannies of the capitalist system, existed within an ultimately socialist ambiance: American modern architecture did not. And it was thus, and either by inadvertence or design, that when in the 1930s, European modern architecture came to infiltrate the United States, it was introduced as simply a new approach to building—and not much more. That is: it was introduced, largely purged of its ideological or societal content, and it became available, not as an evident manifestation (or cause) of socialism in some form or other, but rather as a *décor de la vie* for Greenwich, Connecticut or as a suitable veneer for the corporate activities of "enlightened" capitalism.

Depending on our values, this was either triumph or tragedy; but the presentation of modern architecture primarily in terms of formal or technological construct, its disinfection from political inference, its divorce from possibly doubtful ideas, in other words, its ultimate American qualification, should be recognized as being important—both inside and outside the United States—and as having direct bearing upon developments at the present day. For, by these means, and for better or worse, the message of modern architecture was transformed. It was made safe for capitalism and, with its dissemination thereby assisted, the products of a movement which became crystallized in the stress and the trauma of the central European 1920s became agreeably available to be catalogued—on either side of the Atlantic—among the cultural trophies of the affluent society.

The ironies of a European revolution which, perhaps, tragically failed to make it, do not comprise the most gratifying of spectacles. When these are compounded with the further ironies of trans-Atlantic architectural interchange and their physical results, in America, Europe and elsewhere, we find ourselves confronted with an evidence—an adulteration of meaning, principle and form—which is far from easy to neglect. The impeccably good intentions of modern architecture, its genuine ideals of social service, above all the poetry with which, so often, it has invested random twentieth century happening may all conspire to inhibit doubts as to its present condition, to encourage a suppression of the obvious; but, conspire as they may, and however reluctantly we recognize it, the product of modern architecture compared with its performance, the gap between what was anticipated and what has been delivered, still establishes the base line for any responsible contemporary production and, in doing so, introduces the context for consideration of such buildings and projects as are here published.

These, had they been conceived c. 1930 and built in France, Germany, Switzerland or Italy, had then they been illustrated by Alberto Sartoris or even F. R. S. Yorke, would today very likely be approached as ancient monuments; and as exemplary of the heroic periods of modern architecture, they would be visited and recorded. Indeed one can imagine the tourists and almost concoct the historical evaluations. But these buildings were not conceived c. 1930. They are of comparatively recent origin; they are built in, or proposed for, the vicinity of New York City; and therefore, whatever their merits and demerits, such is the present constellation of critical ideas, they can only be regarded as constituting a problem.

For we are here in the presence of what, in terms of the orthodox theory of modern architecture, is heresy. We are in the presence of anachronism, nostalgia, and, probably, frivolity. If modern architecture looked like this c. 1930 then it should not look like this today; and, if the real political issue of the present is not the provision of the rich with cake but of the starving with bread, then not only formally but also programmatically these buildings are irrelevant. Evidently they propound no obvious revolution; and, just as they may be envisaged as dubiously European to some American tastes, so they will seem the painful evidence of American retardation to certain European and, particularly, English judgments.

Now these evaluations will not be made to go away. A grass roots Neo-Populist Americanism will approve of these buildings no more than a Pop-inspired and supercilious European, or English, neo-Marxism; and, given the situation in which opposite but sympathetic extremes will, alike, both smell abomination, it might be best to address arguments to neither of these two states of mind but, instead, to withdraw attention to that body of theory, alleged or otherwise, of which these buildings, like so many of their predecessors of the twenties and thirties, may be construed as violation.

With the establishment and institutionalization of modern architecture, not only was much of its original meaning lost; but it also became apparent that it was scarcely that synthesis it had so widely been proclaimed to be. It became apparent that never had it been so much the limpid fusion of content and form, that famous integration of feeling and thinking, which Sigfried Giedion had supposed—a symbiosis of highly discrete and ultimately incompatible procedures; and, if the incompatibility between the form of modern architecture and its professed theoretical program, however apparently happy was their brief co-existence some thirty to forty years ago, has now long been evident, it has also been the subject of, in general, sardonic comment. The configuration of the modern building was alleged to derive from a scrupulous attention to particular and concrete problems, it was supposed to be induced from the empirical facts of its specific case; and yet modern buildings looked alike whether their specific case was that of a factory or an art museum. Therefore there was no one to one correspondence between practice and theory. Thus it could come to be argued that, from almost the beginning, the buildings erected in the name of modern architecture had comprised an enormous series of misunderstandings; that they had represented no intrinsic renewal; that, ultimately, they had constituted no more than a simultaneously sophisticated and naive rearrangement of surfaces. Reyner Banham's *Theory and Design in the First Machine Age* celebrated just this problem and it concluded with what amounted to a repudiation of modern architecture's forms and an endorsement of what the modern movement, theoretically, was supposed to be. And this is a style of critique which, for obvious reasons, has now become very well known. For, at one and the same time, it allows its exponents the pleasures of condemning, or of patronizing, most of modern archi-

Peter Eisenman,
House II, 1969

tecture's classic achievements and, also, of annexing that revolutionary tone which, though it may be ancient, can still posture as new.

But, if it is possible to speak of the theoretical program of modern architecture and to observe how, almost invariably, it was largely honored in the breach, then, by now, the logical contradictions within this alleged theory itself should, equally, be glaring—though, perhaps, it would be more correct to speak of this theory not in terms of its logical contradictions. For in the light of any critical perspective, what we have here is very little more than an incoherent bundle of highly volatile sentiments, not so much the stipulation of a consistent dogma as the registration of a general tendency of thought and the evidence of a highly pronounced climate of feeling.

As already suggested, in its theory, modern architecture was conceived to be no more than a rational and unprejudiced response to twentieth century enlightenment and its products; and, if we subject this theoretical conception to a slight caricature, we might distinguish what is still a prevalent and orthodox position. It may be outlined as follows:

Modern architecture is no more than the result of the age; the age is creating a style which is not a style because this style is being created by the accumulation of objective reactions to external events; and hence, this style is authentic, valid, pure and clean, self-renewing and self-perpetuating.

Thus compressed and rendered absurd, it becomes, of course, difficult to understand how passion could, and can still, revolve around such a statement as this one; that is until we recognize that what we have here is the conflation of two powerful nineteenth century tendencies of thought. For here, in varying degrees of disguise, we are presented with both "science" and "history." We are provided with the Positivist conception of fact (without any great epistemological reservations as to what does constitute a fact) and we are provided with the Hegelian conception of manifest destiny (without any doubts as to the substantial reality of the inexorable *zeitgeist*) and then, as a corollary, we have the implicit assertion that when these two conceptions are allied, when the architect recognizes only "facts" and thus, by endorsing "science," becomes the instrument of "history," then a situation will infallibly ensue in which all problems will vanish away.

But again, although in these notices we may touch upon one of the central motivations of twentieth century architecture, it is only when we introduce subsidiary arguments into this scene that it fully begins to acquire color and momentum. And thus, the idea of relying upon the "facts," however ill determined these may be, the idea that when once the relevant data are collected then the controlling hypothesis will automatically divulge itself, becomes very easily allied with the so many attacks upon "art" (the gratuitous transformation of private concern into public pre-occupation) which, even though "art" is bought and consumed to its destruction, is typically conceived to be a reprehensible activity. And, correspondingly, attacks upon "architecture" conducted by the architect have always expressed irritation at the continued existence of the institution and dismay that the item is still to be found available. For architecture, so it is consistently inferred, is only morally acceptable so long as the architect suppresses his individuality, his temperament, his taste and his cultural traditions; and unless, in this way, he is willing to win through to "objectivity" and to a scientific state of mind, then all his work can do is to obstruct the inexorable unrolling of change and thereby, presumably, retard the progress of humanity.

However, if we are here presented with what might seem to be an argument for pure passivity, with an argument that the architect should act simply as the midwife of history, then we might also recognize an entirely contrary strand of thought which no less urgently clamors for attention. The idea that any repetition, any copying, any employment of a precedent or a physical model is a failure of creative acuity is one of the central intuitions of the modern movement. This is the deep seated idea that repetition establishes convention and that convention leads to callousness; and thus, almost constitutionally, modern architecture has been opposed to the dictatorship of the merely received. Opposed to the imposition of *a priori* pattern upon the multifariousness of events, instead it has set pre-eminent value upon "discovery"—which, characteristically, it has been unwilling to recognize as "invention." Without an unflagging consciousness of flux and of the human efforts which this implies, without a continuous ability to erect and to dismantle scaffolds of reference, then—so proceeds an argument—it is entirely impossible to enter and to occupy those territories of the mind where, alone, significant creation moves and flourishes.

The idea can only deserve respect; but, if it is pressed, then like so many ideas which also deserve respect, it can only become something doctrinaire and destructive of its own virtues; and, with its heroic emphasis upon the architect as activist, the notion of architecture as ceaseless moral experiment must now be subjected to the presence of yet another equally coercive but contrary proposition. This, quite simply, is the idea that modern architecture was to instigate order, that it was to establish the predominance of the normative, the typical and the abstract.

However we may estimate the record of nineteenth century building, it is not hard to see how ideas of order and type should have recommended themselves to the modern movement. For, in contrast to the products of Romantic individualism and political *laissez faire*, there was always the evidence of previous centuries, of Bath or Potsdam, Amsterdam or Nancy; and, if there was always involved some sort of fantasy concerned with a contemporary simulacrum of just such cities as these, then, in the *Siedlungen* of Frankfurt or at Siemenstadt, among the early triumphs of modern architecture, one may presumably discern the influence of this intention.

But such developments belonged to the age of innocence; and while in them the reasonable demands of the particular versus the abstract, of specific function versus general type might seem to have been approximately met, there still remained to prevent the multiplication of such achievements the overriding inhibition as to repetition, the conviction that to reproduce something, to allow precedent to enforce itself, was to betray the forces of change and to deny the drive of history.

Now whether it was thus that the demand for order became vitiated by the competing necessity to illustrate the action of experiment or the behavior of first principles, it should be enough to state that it seems likely—whatever value we may wish to attribute to change and order—that a high valuation of change must, in the end, cancel out a high valuation of order, that, given the perpetual redefinition of a situation, no theory of types can survive, that, if the terms of a problem are constantly altered before approaching solution, then that problem never can be solved. But if, with this statement, though it is rarely made, there is nothing remarkable announced, then attention might usefully be directed towards another of those paradoxes which sprout so irresistibly the more the theory of modern architecture is, even casually, scrutinized.

Modern architecture professed to address itself to the great public. What was believed to be its intrinsic rationality was never overtly intended for the delectation of minor professional interest groups; but rather the architect was to address himself to *the natural man*. Enlightenment won by bitter struggle was to speak to enlightenment which was innate. As simply a scientific determination of empirical data modern architecture was to be understood by *the natural man*; and hence the modern building, believed to be purged of mythical content, became conceivable as the inevitable shelter for a mythical being in whose aboriginal psychology myth could occupy no place.

The notion, of course, continues to possess a certain eighteenth century decency. Without rhetoric the truth will be accepted as the truth. But, in practice, it has always allied with an alternate ambition. The modern building should—and can—act as a prophetic statement. Retrospection is to be tabooed; the memory is to be exercised no more; nostalgia can only corrupt; and it is with reference to this ambition, perhaps never explicitly uttered, that we revert again to the thesis of an architecture which does not involve itself with minor sophistications, which is no way concerned with local ambiguities, ironical references and witty asides, which is absolutely not at all addressed to the few, but which, of its nature, is absolutely available and intelligible to the uninstructed (or to the however instructed) many. For there should be no doubt whatsoever that this was the objective, and it is here, when the ideal of public intelligibility makes its extreme claim, that it might be proper to obtrude the issue of prophecy versus memory.

The concept of the modern building as a compilation of recognizable empirical facts is, evidently, immediately compromised by the more suppressed concept of the building as a prophetic statement (for are prophetic speculations empirical facts?); but the simultaneous orientation towards both the prophetic and the intelligible should now be related to modern architecture's emphatic anathema of retrospection and its products. And it should not be necessary to itemize the details of this anathema. Simply it should be enough to ask the question: *How to be intelligible without involving retrospection?*; and, without being unduly sententious, it should be enough to observe that except in terms of retrospection, in terms of memory upon which prophecy itself is based, upon recollection of words with meaning, mathematical symbols with values and physical forms with attendant overtones, it is difficult to see how any ideal of communication can flourish. In a better world, no doubt, the problem would not exist; but if, in conceiving a better world, modern architecture here conceived no problem, then we might abruptly conclude this issue by suggesting that, unless a building in some way or other evokes something remembered, it is not easy to see how it can enlist even a shred of popular interest. The ideal of order based upon public understanding, if it is to be insisted upon, requires some suppression of both experimentalist and futurist enthusiasm.

The foregoing remarks have been an attempt, admittedly overcompressed and far too generalized, to identify—not without critical asides—the complex of sentiments about architecture in terms of which the buildings here published are likely to be condemned—for formalism, bourgeois lack of conscience, esoteric privacy and failure to keep pace with the social and technological movement of the age. But the moment that this body of ideas is subjected to even the most casual skeptical analysis, the moment that it ceases to be unexamined gospel, then it also becomes evident that, while it may serve to illustrate what was once a creative state of mind, it can no longer very seriously serve the purposes of useful criticism. The theoretical presumptions of modern architecture, located as they once were in a matrix of eschatological and utopian fantasy, began to mean very little when the technological *and* social revolution whose imminence the modern movement had assumed failed to take place. For with this failure, if it became obvious that theory and practice were disrelated, it could also become apparent that theory itself was never so much a literal directive for the making of buildings as it was an elaborately indirect mechanism for the suppression of feelings of guilt: guilt about the products of the mind—felt to be comparatively insignificant, guilt about high culture—felt to be unreal, guilt about art—the most extreme anxiety to disavow the role of private judgment in any analytical or synthetic enterprise. In the end what is understood as the theory of modern architecture reduces itself to little more than a constellation of escapist myths which are all active in endeavoring to relieve the architect of responsibility for his choices and which all alike combine to persuade him that his decisions are not so much his own as they are, somehow, immanent in scientific, or historical, or social process.

And this realization breeds another. For if these once convincing and still seductive doctrines—with their strong determinist and historicist bias—are very readily susceptible to demolition, and if that they are not yet demolished is surely a tribute to modern architecture's public virtues, then one might still ask why it is that an attitude of mind which places so much emphasis upon change, which sets such a high value upon exploration and discovery, itself continues not to change. The *sense* of what was said some fifty years ago prohibits repetition; but then the repetition of what was said persists. . . .

Now, either statements made about architecture in the 1920s comprise an immutable revelation valid for all time (which is contrary to the meaning of these statements), or they do not. But if, logically—in terms of the principle which it tends to stipulate—the use and re-use of a verbal or polemical model deriving from the 1920s should be conceived as subject to the same reservations as the use of a physical model belonging to the same years, then that such logic does not widely apply is easy to explain. For, while the forms of words can still seem to provide an heroic litany of revolution, the form of buildings does not so readily offer itself as any religious intoxicant; and, if the steady incantation of, now, very old revolutionary themes will encourage the further joys of rhetorical excursion into areas of assumed social and technological relevance, the recapitulation of the themes of building offers no present career so blissful and free from trouble: and thus, while the derivative argument continues to thrive, its exponents, conceiving themselves to be the legitimate and sole heirs of the modern movement, display very little tolerance for what ought to be recognized as the absolutely parallel phenomenon of the derivative building.

Which is again to establish that the *physique* and the *morale* of modern architecture, its flesh and its word, were (and could) never be coincident; and it is when we recognize that neither word nor flesh was ever coincident with itself let alone with each other, that, without undue partiality, we can approach the present day. For under the circumstances what to do? If we believe that modern architecture did establish one of the great hopes of the world—always, in detail, ridiculous, but never, *in toto*, to be rejected—then do we adhere to *physique*-flesh or to *morale*-word?

To repeat: this choice became visible once it became almost too evident to bear that the central and socialist mission of modern architecture had failed—or alternatively that this mission had become dissolved in the sentimentalities and bureaucracies of the welfare state. The simple fusion of art and technology, of symbolical gesture and functional requirement was now not to be made: and in default of this fusion, a variety of alternatives have offered themselves.

These have included what has already been listed: Miesian neo-classicism (with some kind of dependent theory of Platonic form); the New Brutalism (with the inference that self-flagellation may elicit the better world); the Futurist Revival (with the very popular supposition that science fiction might provide the ultimate hope), and the neo-art nouveau (which, both in its Shingle Style and Italian ramifications, insists that if we only retreat to the 1890s—and also simulate a naivete—then health will inevitably ensue.

And, to this catalogue, there must also be added the notion that we ignore the situation altogether: that, in default of that convenient anti-"art" entity

of the twenties called the "machine," we substitute the equally useful entities designated "the computer" and "the people" and that, if these two abstractions are absolutely at variance with each other, we will not indulge ourselves in too many scruples
about this problem. It is a problem which exists only in the minds of the far too
sensitive; and if research and data-collection are the wave of the future—if the public
wisdom so indicates—then it is certainly to the future we belong.

It is in this context of choices (none of them very agreeable)
that we should place what is here published; and, having recognized this context, we
should not then be too ready to impute charges of irresponsibility. It is difficult to
generalize the work of these five architects. Eisenman seems to have received a revelation in Como; Hejduk seems to wish affiliation both to Synthetic Cubist Paris and
Constructivist Moscow. Nor will the more obviously Corbusian orientation of Graves,
Gwathmey and Meier so readily succumb to all encompassing observations. But, for
all this, there is a point of view shared which is quite simply this: that, rather than
constantly to endorse the revolutionary myth, it might be more reasonable and more
modest to recognize that in the opening years of this century, great revolutions in
thought occurred and that then profound visual discoveries resulted, that these are
still unexplained, and that rather than assume intrinsic change to be the prerogative
of every generation, it might be more useful to recognize that certain changes are
so enormous as to impose a directive which cannot be resolved in any individual
life span.

Or, at least, such would seem to be the argument. It concerns
the plastic and spatial inventions of Cubism and the proposition that, whatever may
be said about these, they possess an eloquence and a flexibility which continues now
to be as overwhelming as it was then. It is an argument largely about the physique
of building and only indirectly about its morale: but, since it should also be envisaged
as some sort of interrogation of the mid-twentieth century architect's capacity to
indulge his mostly trivial moral enthusiasm at the expense of any physical product,
it might also be appropriate to conclude what has been a largely negative introduction—an attack upon a potential attack—with a series of related questions which
might, ambiguously, help to establish the meaning—if any—in Aldo van Eyck's terms,
of what is here presented.

- Is it necessary that architecture should be simply a logical derivative from functional and technological facts; and, indeed, can it ever be this?
- Is it necessary that a series of buildings should imply a vision of a new and better
world; and, if this is so (or even if it is not) then how frequently can a significant
vision of a new and better world be propounded?
- Is the architect simply a victim of circumstances? And should he be? Or may he
be allowed to cultivate his own free will? And are not culture and civilization the
products of the imposition of will?
- What is the zeitgeist; and, if this is a critical fiction, may the architect act contrari-
wise to its alleged dictates?
- How permissible is it to make use of precedent; and therefore, how legitimate
is the argument that the repetition of a form is a destruction of authenticity?
- Can an architecture which professes an objective of continuous experiment ever
become congruous with the ideal of an architecture which is to be popular,
intelligible, and profound?

Erratum
Submitted to the Second Edition
These are reasonably important questions which it is ostrich-like not to consider. They propound problems which are not any less real because the "theory" of modern architecture failed to give them attention; and, by the introduction of such problems, there is immediately implied a concept of society very radically different from that which modern architecture presumed. This is the concept of society and building implied by our five architects. It is all indisputably bourgeois (but what, in the United States, is not?); most of it makes a parade of cosmopolitan erudition (but, given the information explosion, how to avoid?); and it is all of it belligerently second hand, what Whitehead called "novelty in the use of assigned pattern" (but, assuming a present hiatus so far as creative breakthrough is concerned, how do otherwise?). However, perhaps the great merit of what follows lies in the fact that its authors are not enormously self-deluded as to the immediate possibility of any violent or sudden architectural or social mutation. They place themselves in the role, the secondary role, of Scamozzi to Palladio. Their posture may be polemical but it is not heroic. Apparently they are neither Marcusian nor Maoist; and, lacking any transcendental sociological or political faith, their objective—at bottom—is to alleviate the present by the interjection of a quasi-Utopian vein of poetry. There could be less worthy objectives, less tolerable options; and, in a truly pluralist society (supposing such a society could ever exist) what is here published would no doubt receive acknowledgment—as one possibility among many. It is what *some* people and *some* architects want; and therefore, in terms of a general theory of pluralism, one must wonder how, in principle, it can be faulted. Faults in detail may perhaps be recognized; but faults in principle? For, in terms of a general theory of pluralism, how can any faults in principle be imputed?

Which is to suggest that these five architects (who sometimes seem to regard buildings as an excuse for drawing rather than drawings as an excuse for building) are highly likely to be crudely manhandled by an allegedly pluralist, but, intrinsically, a determinist, technocratic and historicist establishment; and which is further to suggest that the apologetic which has here been made is by way of being a critical umbrella almost too catholic in its functions—an umbrella which is not only intended to protect the graphic contents of this book but which is also to be understood as outspread to protect a good deal else which is by no means necessarily comparable in *maniera*.

This project is the result of a twenty-year effort and search into generating principles of form and space. There is an attempt to understand certain essences in regard to an architectural commitment with the hope of expanding a vocabulary. The discovery of the workings and dictates of an organic development of specific ideas becomes a necessary function of the search. It was from the understanding of these projects that I hoped to establish a point of view, a belief; the belief that through self-imposed discipline, through intense contained study, through an aesthetic, a liberation of the mind and hand would be possible leading to certain visions and transformations of form regarding space.

The realization that profound works in the arts are the embodiment of specific plastic points of view, that the hand and mind are one, working on first principles, and on filling these principles with meaning through juxtaposition of basic relationships such as point, line, plane, volume opened up the possibility of argumentation. The mind played a most significant part in the support of the creative act. The first gropings were arbitrary; but once the arbitrary beginning was committed, once the initial intuitions were experienced, it was necessary that the organism go through its normal evolution—and whether the evolution of form continued or stopped depended on the use of the intellect not as an academic tool, but as a

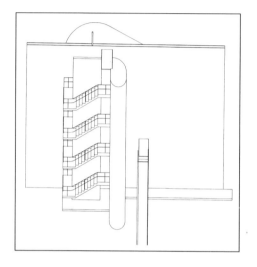

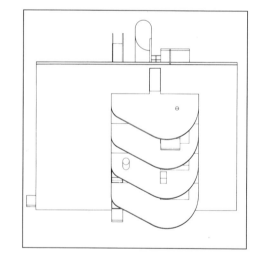

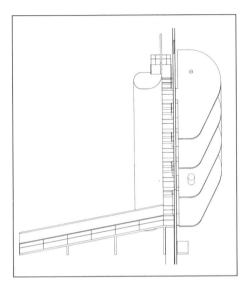

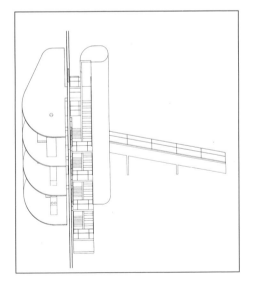

passionate living element. The problems of point-line-plane-volume, the facts of square-circle-triangle, the mysteries of central-peripheral-frontal-oblique-concavity-convexity, of right angle, perpendicular, perspective, the comprehension of sphere-cylinder-pyramid, the questions of slab, vertical-horizontal, the arguments of two dimensional–three dimensional space, the extent of a limited field, of an unlimited field, the meaning of plan, of section, of spatial expansion–spatial contraction–spatial compression–spatial tension, the direction of regulating lines, of grids, the meaning of implied symmetry to asymmetry, of diamond to diagonal, the hidden forces, the ideas of configuration, the static with the dynamic, all these begin to take on the form of a vocabulary.

The project started not knowing the above, but knowing that basic orders needed to be searched for, becoming known as the work progressed, as the work was analyzed, as the work was criticized, as the work was formed. In order to have a-priori principles meaningful, and to give up and put forth organic revelations, there had to be a given form. The arguments and points of view are within the work, within the drawings; it is hoped that the conflicts of form will lead to clarity which can be useful and perhaps transferable.

1972

Colin Rowe and   From *Collage City* Manuscript in circulation from 1973; published later

Fred Koetter   (Cambridge: MIT Press, 1978)

On the occasion of the publication of *Collage City*, Colin Rowe delivered the 1979 Cubitt Lecture in London. The lecture began with an obituary for modern architecture, whose characteristic use of conceit (here unabashedly gendered) as much as its concise autopsy merits reporting in full:

We may ascribe her death (Modern architecture is surely a she) to the ingenuousness of her temperament. Displaying an extraordinary addiction to towers and completely unconstructed spaces, when young she possessed a high and romantically honorable idea of life and her excess of sensibility could only lead to later chagrin. Like one of Jane Austen's more extreme heroines — though she was simultaneously morally reserved, passionate, and artless — it was her juvenile notion that, once she was perfectly wedded to society, this so much desired husband would, by the influence of her example, become redeemed of errors, tractable, pliant, and ready to act with her in any philanthropy which she might have in mind. But the marriage did not prove to be a success. Modern architecture was admired by society but not for what she conceived to be her inherent virtues. Her spouse was attracted by her many external charms but was utterly unwilling to award recognition of what she conceived to be the ethical principle of her being. And, in spite of the elevated model which she offered, he remained stubbornly confirmed in his old ways. Moral regeneration he did not seek. For him the ethical posture of modern architecture was too much like that of a Victorian heroine and, correspondingly, he looked for his delinquent pleasures elsewhere. He, society, was in no way ready to envisage those limpid possibilities of the New Jerusalem which she so enthusiastically advertised and, as she continued, he increasingly became fatigued. Indeed, he (society) came to discover that, though admired, he too was not accepted; and, gradually, the rift became irretrievable. Not surprising, therefore, should be modern architecture's agitated and long decline; but, though this death was to be expected, it is greatly to be regretted and the extinction of this once pristine creature (with her elaborately Victorian standards) has been desperately sad to witness. But, a late nineteenth-century character and never fully knowing it, she addressed herself to a moral condition of permanent rapture, to an ecstatic condition which could only endanger her frail physique; and, to repeat, excessive sensibility abused by inadequate experience, motivated by a quasi-religious sentiment not well understood and complicated by the presence of physics envy, *Zeitgeist* worship, object fixation, and stradaphobia must be considered the greatest factors contributing to the demise.[1]

Rowe's critique of modern architecture, far more accessible than Tafuri's and exactly counter to Tafuri's politics, could easily claim to be the most influential of the period here documented. What is more, the "therapies" that emerged out of his etiology of modernism were developed by generations of architects and students, well before and after the publication of *Collage City*.[2] Among his prescriptions ("stimulants" they are called) are (1) reconsider the dense texture of traditional cities such as Rome "in order to reduce the mental inflammation which has always demonstrated itself as moral excess and undue preoccupation with over-articulated solids"; (2) invert objects to obtain figurative voids, as Vasari's Uffizi palace is the inversion of Le Corbusier's Marseilles Unité; (3) play "the long skinny building game," using continuous thin set pieces either as "filters" or facades in order to discriminate certain conditions of building texture or landscape; (4) look to the French *hôtel* for "habitable *poché*" and Soane's Bank of England for a collision of set pieces; (5) use "magically useless stabilizers" and "nostaglia-producing instruments"; and (6) reconstitute the urban garden.

Rowe's concept of collage — conjoining as it does a critique of modern utopianism (as in his obituary) and a proposal for a radical heterogeneity of appropriated form (as in his prescriptions) — would seem to summarize much of architectural postmodernism, which, indeed, may partly account for the concept's influence. Yet Rowe's theory of collage city is specified by its incorporation of Claude Lévi-Strauss's distinction between the bricoleur and the scientist, Karl Popper's anti-utopianism and fallibilism, and the law as a model for architecture, even if that literature was in circulation well before Rowe and Koetter's early published condensation of their 1973 text, "Collage City," *Architecture Review* 158 (August 1975).[3]

compare 240–241, 306–307

Rowe construes each of these references as components in an ostensibly ideologically neutralized technique of composition that might balance scaffold and exhibit, structure and event, the ideal and the empirical, to achieve, in short, both the autonomy and the heterogeneity of architectural form — form understood as the foremost sign and support of culture itself. The city as museum, along with Mondrian's *Victory Boogie-Woogie,* stand as adequate tropes for Rowe's political liberalism and cultural relativism as well as his collage aesthetic. In his own words, "it is because, to my mind, the relationship of figure to matrix in *Victory-Boogie Woogie* is the relationship of object to texture, solid to void, randomness to order, incident to norm, even individual to state — because *Boogie-Woogie* allows figures to augment and to contract, to congeal and to dissolve, to erupt from matrix and to return to it again — that, in terms of the imaginary city which I have been examining, I feel compelled to cite this Mondrian performance as what I believe to be the instigation of anything useful which might have been said here."[4]

see Somol (789–791)

To establish his system of autonomous grid and heterogeneous fragments, Rowe must expel any history other than architectural history from his account, must eschew any material external to the architectural language itself. In an effort to avoid any sort of historical determinism, the architecture of collage becomes transhistorical even if historically motivated, collapsing its categories into a set of repetitive variations on the themes of scaffold and exhibit. Rowe's earlier separation of the *physique*-flesh from the *morale*-word of architecture here reaches its fullest development even as the ideology of his nonideological liberal-legal humanism is revealed.

see Rowe (82)

Which is not to deny to subtle power of Rowe's liberal formalism, but only to mark it as such. For it is a formalism born of a certain architecture coming to grief against a desire for social relevance. In the same year as his Cubitt Lecture, criticizing the city proposed by *architettura razionale*, Rowe allows as much:

see 124–125

With the nitty-gritty of the Welfare State and the appalling bureaucratic details of pseudo-Capitalist administration we will have nothing to do; instead we will simplify, abstract, and project to the degree of extravagance a highly restricted, private, and not very hospitable version of what the good society might be assumed to be.[5]

Collage City is presumably Rowe's attempt at a more consensual and hospitable version of the same.

Notes

1. Colin Rowe, "The Present Urban Predicament: Some Observations," The Second Thomas Cubitt Lecture at the Royal Institution, London (London: Thomas Cubitt Trust, 1979); reprinted in *As I Was Saying: Recollections and Miscellaneous Essays* (Cambridge: MIT Press, 1996), vol. 3, pp. 167–168.
2. Thomas Schumacher, "Contextualism: Urban Ideals + Deformations," *Casabella* 359–360 (1971), and Stuart Cohen, "Physical Context/Cultural Context: Including It All," *Oppositions* 2 (January 1974), are two of the early theorizations of Rowe's urban design teaching at Cornell University after 1963, whose tenets were grouped under the construct of "contextualism."
3. See for example Charles Jencks and Nathan Silver, *Adhocism* (New York: Doubleday, 1973), for a mention of Lévi-Strauss and bricolage; see Stanford Anderson, "Architecture and Tradition That Isn't 'Trad, Dad,'" in *The History, Theory, and Criticism of Architecture*, ed. Marcus Whiffen, papers from the 1964 AIA-ACSA Teacher Seminar, Cranbrook (Cambridge: MIT Press, 1965), for a use of Popper in an attempt to resolve the apparently conflicting claims of science and tradition; and see Peter Collins, *Architectural Judgement* (London: Faber, 1971), for the use of law as a model for architecture.

    Rowe knew Popper (through Ernst Gombrich) while in Cambridge, England, in 1958–1962. In a letter to this editor in May 1996, Rowe indicated that, along with Popper's work, crucial to the formation of the ideas that would be developed in *Collage City* were Michael Polanyi, *Beyond Nihilism* (1960); Norman Cohn, *The Pursuit of the Millennium* (1957); Judith N. Shklar, *After Utopia: The Decline of Political Faith* (1957); and P. B. Medawar, *The Art of the Soluble* (1967).
4. Rowe, "The Present Urban Predicament," p. 216.

Peter Carl, Judith DiMaio, Steven Peterson, and Colin Rowe, Nolli: Sector Eight, from *Roma Interrotta*, 1978

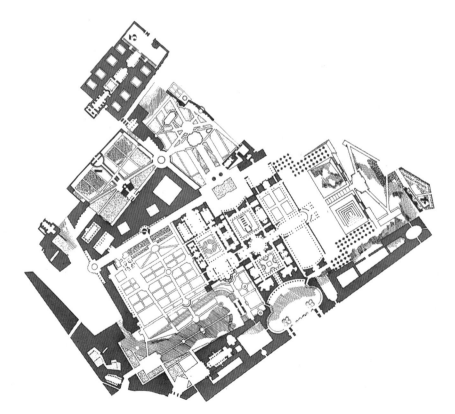

5. Colin Rowe, foreword to Rob Krier, *Urban Space* (London: Academy Editions, 1979); reprinted in *As I Was Saying*, vol. 3, p. 262. Rowe continues: "We will give a nod to Kaufmann; we will give three muted cheers for the Stalinallee; we will adore the manifesto pieces of Boullée; we will (mostly) refuse to observe the built work of Soane; instead we will unroll a few hundred yards of neutral Adolf Loos facade, build a lot of little towers and stand around on top of them a quantity of Ledoux villas, wave quietly but not too exuberantly to Louis Kahn . . . , insinuate a reference to the metaphysic of Giorgio de Chirico, display a conversance with Leonidov, become highly enthusiastic about the more evocative aspects of Art Deco, exhibit the intimidation of curtains waving in the wind, and, then, gently warm up the ensuing goulash in the *pastoso* of Morandi."

from "Crisis of the Object: Predicament of Texture"

To summarize: it is here proposed that, rather than hoping and waiting for the withering away of the object (while, simultaneously manufacturing versions of it in profusion unparalleled), it might be judicious, in most cases, to allow and encourage the object to become digested in a prevalent texture or matrix. It is further suggested that neither object nor space fixation are, in themselves, any longer representative of valuable attitudes. The one may, indeed, characterize the "new" city and the other the old; but, if these are situations which must be transcended rather than emulated, the situation to be hoped for should be recognized as one in which both buildings *and* spaces exist in an equality of sustained debate. A debate in which victory consists in each component emerging undefeated, the imagined condition is a type of solid-void dialectic which might allow for the joint existence of the overtly planned and the genuinely unplanned, of the set-piece and the accident, of the public and the private, of the state and the individual. It is a condition of alerted equilibrium which is envisaged; and it is in order to illuminate the potential of such a contest that we have introduced a rudimentary variety of possible strategies. Cross-breeding, assimilation, distortion, challenge, response, imposition, superimposition, conciliation: these might be given any number of names and, surely, neither can nor should be too closely specified; but if the burden of the present discussion has rested upon the city's morphology, upon the physical and inanimate, neither "people" nor "politics" are assumed to have been excluded. Indeed, both "politics" and "people" are, by now, clamoring for attention; but, if their scrutiny can barely be deferred, yet one more morphological stipulation may still be in order.

Ultimately, and in terms of figure-ground, the debate which is here postulated between solid and void is a debate between two models and, succinctly, these may be typified as acropolis and forum.

from "Collision City and the Politics of 'Bricolage'"

"There still exists among ourselves," says Claude Lévi-Strauss, "an activity which on the technical plane gives us quite a good understanding of what a science we prefer to call 'prior' rather than 'primitive' could have been on the plane of speculation. This is what is commonly called 'bricolage' in French";[1] and he then proceeds to an extended analysis of the objectives of "bricolage" and of science, of the respective roles of the "bricoleur" and the engineer.

In its old sense the verb "bricoler" applied to ball games and billiards, to hunting, shooting and riding. It was however always used with reference to some extraneous movement: a ball rebounding, a dog straying or a horse swerving from its direct course to avoid an obstacle. And in our time the "bricoleur" is still someone who works with his hands and uses devious means compared to those of the craftsman.[2]

Now there is no intention to place the weight of the argument which follows upon Lévi-Strauss's observations. Rather the intention is to promote an identification which may, up to a point, prove useful and, so much so, that if one may be inclined to recognize Le Corbusier as a fox in hedgehog disguise, one may also be willing to envisage a parallel attempt at camouflage: the "bricoleur" disguised as engineer. "Engineers fabricate the tools of their time. . . . Our engineers are healthy and virile, active and useful, balanced and happy in their work. . . . Our engineers produce architecture for they employ a mathematical calculation which derives from natural law."[3]

Such is an almost entirely representative statement of early modern architecture's most conspicuous prejudice. But then compare Lévi-Strauss:

The "bricoleur" is adept at performing a large number of diverse tasks; but, unlike the engineer, he does not subordinate each of them to the availability of raw materials and tools conceived and procured for the purpose of the project. His universe of instruments is closed and the rules of his game are always to make do with "whatever is at hand," that is to say with a set of tools and materials which is always finite and is also heterogeneous because what it contains bears no relation to the current project, or indeed to any particular project, but is the contingent result of all the occasions there have been to renew or enrich the stock or to maintain it with the remains of previous constructions or destructions. The set of the "bricoleur's" means cannot therefore be defined in terms of a project (which would presuppose besides, that, as in the case of the engineer, there were, at least in theory, as many sets of tools and materials, or "instrumental sets," as there are different kinds of projects. It is to be defined only by its potential use . . . because the elements are collected or retained on the principle that "they may always come in handy." Such elements are specialized up to a point, sufficiently for the "bricoleur" not to need the equipment and knowledge of all trades and professions, but not enough for each of them to have only one definite and determinate use. They represent a set of actual and possible relations; they are "operators," but they can be used for any operations of the same type.[4]

For our purposes it is unfortunate that Lévi-Strauss does not lend himself to reasonably laconic quotation. For the "bricoleur," who certainly finds a representative in "the odd job man," is also very much more than this. "It is common knowledge that the artist is both something of a scientist and of a 'bricoleur'";[5] but, if artistic creation lies mid-way between science and "bricolage," this is not to imply that the "bricoleur" is "backward." "It might be said that the engineer questions the universe while the 'bricoleur' addresses himself to a collection of oddments left over from human endeavors";[6] but it must also be insisted that there is no question of primacy here. Simply, the scientist and the "bricoleur" are to be distinguished "by the inverse functions which they assign to event and structures as means and ends, the scientist creating events . . . by means of structures and the 'bricoleur' creating structures by means of events."[7]

But we are here, now, very far from the singular notion of an exponential increasingly precise "science" (a speedboat which architecture and urbanism are to follow like highly inexpert water-skiers); and, instead, we have not only a confrontation of the "bricoleur's" "savage mind" with the "domesticated" mind of the engineer, but also a useful indication that these two modes of thought are not representatives of a progressive serial (the engineer illustrating a perfection of the "bricoleur," etc.) but that, in fact, they are necessarily coexistent and complementary conditions of the mind. In other words, we might be about to arrive at some approximation of Lévi-Strauss's "pensée logique au niveau du sensible."

There could, of course, have been other routes followed. Karl Popper might have put us down in, very approximately, the same place; Jürgen Habermas might have helped to somewhat equivalent conclusions; but we have preferred Lévi-Strauss because, in his discussion, with its emphasis upon making, it is far more possible for the architect to recognize something of himself. For, if we can divest ourselves of the deceptions of professional *amour propre* and accepted academic theory, the description of the "bricoleur" is far more of a "real-life" specification of what the architect-urbanist is and does than any fantasy deriving from "methodology" and "systemics."

Indeed, one could fear that the architect as "bricoleur" is, today, almost too enticing a program—a program which might guarantee formalism, ad hocery, townscape pastiche, populism and almost whatever else one chooses to name. But . . . The savage mind of the bricoleur! The domesticated mind of the engineer/scientist! The interaction of these two conditions! The artist (architect) as both something of a bricoleur and something of a scientist! These evident corollaries should alleviate such fears. However, if the mind of the bricoleur should not be expected to sponsor universal ad hocery, it must still be insisted that the mind of the engineer need not be imagined as supporting the idea of architecture as part of a unified comprehensive science (ideally like physics). And, if Lévi-Strauss's conception of "bricolage," which patently includes science, may now be placed in some relationship with Popper's conception of science, which evidently excludes "methodology," there is here the illustration of some more restrictive intention in the present argument. For the predicament of architecture—which, because it is always, in some way or other, concerned with amelioration, by some standard, however dimly perceived, of making things better, with how things ought to be, is always hopelessly involved with value judgments—can never be scientifically resolved, least of all in terms of any simple empirical theory of "facts." And, if this is the case with reference to architecture, then, in relation to urbanism (which is not even concerned in making things stand up) the question of any scientific resolution of its problems can only become more acute. For, if the notion of a "final" solution through a definitive accumulation of all data is, evidently, an epistemological chimera, if certain aspects of information will invariably remain undiscriminated or undisclosed, and if the inventory of "facts" can never be complete simply because of the rates of change and obsolescence, then, here and now, it surely might be possible to assert that *the prospects of scientific city planning should, in reality, be regarded as equivalent to the prospects of scientific politics.*

For, if planning can barely be more scientific than the political society of which it forms an agency, in the case of neither politics nor planning can there be sufficient information acquired before action becomes necessary. In neither case can performance await an ideal future formulation of the problem as it may, at last, be resolved; and, if this is because the very possibility of that future where such formulation might be made depends upon imperfect action now, *then this is only once more to intimate the role of "bricolage" which politics so much resembles and city planning surely should.*

Indeed, if we are willing to recognize the methods of science and "bricolage" as concomitant propensities, if we are willing to recognize that they are—both of them—modes of address to problems, if we are willing (and it may be hard) to concede equality between the "civilized" mind (with its presumptions of logical seriality) and the "savage" mind (with its analogical leaps), then, in reestablishing "bricolage" alongside science, it might even be possible to suppose that the way for a truly useful future dialectic could be prepared.

A truly useful dialectic?[8] The idea is simply the conflict of contending powers, the almost fundamental conflict of interest sharply stipulated, the legitimate suspicion about others' interests, from which the democratic process—such as it is—proceeds; and then the corollary to this idea is no more than banal: if such is the case, if democracy is compounded of libertarian enthusiasm and legalistic doubt, and if it is, inherently, a collision of points of view and acceptable as such, then why not allow a theory of contending powers (all of them visible) as likely to establish a more ideally comprehensive city of the mind than any which has, *as yet*, been invented.

And there is no more to it than this. In place of an ideal of universal management based upon what are presented as scientific certainties there is also a private, and a public, emancipatory interest (which, incidentally, includes emancipation from management); and, if this is the situation and, if the only outcome is to be sought in collision of interest, in a permanently maintained debate of opposites, then why should this dialectical predicament be not just as much accepted in theory as it is in practice? The reference is again to Popper and to the ideal of keeping the game straight; and it is because, from such a criticist point of view, collision of interest is to be welcomed, not in terms of cheap ecumenicism which is only too abundantly available, but in terms of clarification (because, in the battlefield engendered by mutual suspicion, it is just possible that—as has been usual—the flowers of freedom may be forced from the blood of conflict) that, if such a condition of collisive motives is recognizable and should be endorsable, we are disposed to say: why not try?

The proposition leads us (like Pavlov's dogs) automatically to the condition of seventeenth century Rome, to that collision of palaces, *piazze* and villas, to that inextricable fusion of imposition and accommodation, that highly successful and resilient traffic jam of intentions, an anthology of closed compositions and *ad hoc* stuff in between, which is simultaneously a dialectic of ideal types plus a dialectic of ideal types with empirical context; and the consideration of seventeenth century Rome (the complete city with the assertive identity of its subdivisions: Trastevere, Sant'Eustachio, Borgo, Campo Marzio, Campitelli . . .) leads to the equivalent interpretation of its predecessor where forum and thermae pieces lie around in a condition of inter-dependence, independence and multiple interpretability. And imperial Rome is, of course, far the more dramatic statement. For, certainly with its more abrupt collisions, more acute disjunctions, its more expansive set pieces, its more radically discriminated matrix and general lack of "sensitive" inhibition, imperial Rome, far more than the city of the High Baroque, illustrates something of the "bricolage" mentality at its most lavish—an obelisk from here, a column from there, a range of statues from somewhere else, even at the level of detail the mentality is fully exposed; and, in this context, it is amusing to recollect how the influence of a whole school of historians (Positivists, no doubt!) was, at one time, strenuously dedicated to presenting the ancient Romans as inherently nineteenth century engineers, precursors of Gustave Eiffel, who had somehow, and unfortunately, lost their way.

So Rome, whether imperial or papal, hard or soft, is here offered as some sort of model which might be envisaged as alternative to the disastrous urbanism of social engineering and total design. For, while it is recognized that what we have here are the products of a specific topography and two particular, though not wholly separable, cultures, it is also supposed that we are in the presence of a style of argument which is not lacking in universality. That is: while the physique and the politics of Rome provide perhaps the most graphic example of collisive fields and *interstitial debris*, there are calmer versions of equivalent interests which are not hard to find.

. . .

However this is to introduce conjecture; and, rather than dwell upon Rome, London, Houston and Los Angeles as differing versions of the same paradigm, it might, once more, be useful to return to the Cartesian co-ordinates of happiness, to the neutral grid of equality and freedom—and the reference must be to Manhattan.

Some two thousand blocks were provided, each theoretically two hundred feet wide, no more, no less; and ever since, if a building site was wanted, whether with a view to a church or a blast furnace, an opera house or a toy shop, there is, of intention, no better place in one of these blocks than in another.[9]

But, like all despairing observations, Frederick Law Olmsted's was never completely true. For if, in Manhattan, the unrolling of the blanket grid simultaneously extinguished local detail and illustrated the expertise of the land marketeer in action, it was impossible that the operation could ever be complete. For, while the grid remains belligerently "neutral" and while its major qualifiers are only to be found on the most general and crude levels (continuous waterfront, Central Park, lower Manhattan, the West Village, Broadway . . .), in spite of circumstance, the evidences of idiosyncratic coagulation present themselves and demand to be exploited; nor is the situation—which was clearly visible to Mondrian—one of total defeat. But if, in offering a highly energetic scaffold for fluctuating and casual event, New York City might constitute the best of apologias for the all-prevailing grid, the satisfactions which its grid provides are, perhaps, principally of a conceptual and intellectual order. The, apparently, infinitely extended field, just as it tends to defeat politics, tends to defeat perception; and it is presumably in an effort to institutionalize what can only be a felt and a necessary presence that there have emerged such propositions as "what a democratic New York would look like"[10]—demands for the political cantonization of unrealistically centralized government, demands which, interestingly, tend to align themselves with what might be the results of more purely morphological analysis.

Somewhat irrationally the ongoing tradition of modern architecture would now tend to look with favor upon such proposals as these. Somewhat irrationally because, however democratic such cantonization can only appear, the bias which the architect has inherited from long indulgence of total design fantasies tends to make him incapable of following through to where such alternative propositions might lead. For, while there has emerged an awareness of the untenable prospects of total politics, there remains, or so it would seem, a large lack of interest or belief in the analogous prospects of any physical counterpart to such a conclusion. In other words, while in politics the existence of finite fields (interacting with each other but all protected from ultimate infringement) is once more to be considered profitable and desirable, this message seems not, as yet, to have been fully translated into the language of perception; and thus the production of any spatial or temporal equivalent of the finite field is, characteristically, liable to be received with mistrust—again as a blockage of the future and as a dangerous impediment to the freedoms of open-endedness.

Whatever survives of the present argument is now inconsiderable and will carry no conviction whatever for those who, as a basis of operation, are still obliged to conceive of a totally integrated world society, a combination of innate goodness and scientific *savoir faire*, in which all political structures, major or minor, will have become dissolved. We concede the values of this persuasion; but we are also obliged to suggest that the ideally open and emancipated society is not likely to be made this way, that the open society depends upon the complexity of its parts, upon competing group-centered interests which need not be logical but which, collectively, may not only check each other but may, sometimes, also serve as a protective membrane between the individual and the form of collective authority. For the problem should remain that of a tension between quasi-integrated whole and quasi-segregated parts; and, lacking the segregated parts, one can only imagine that "open society" where, in despite of the theorems of liberty and equality, all the compulsions of fraternity—elective affinities, team sweatshirts, group dynamics, revolutionary communes providing the joys of pleasurable alienation, the Society of Jesus, Lambda Chi, annual conventions, regimental dinners—would break out yet again.

But the issue may, and without extravagance, be equipped with a far more literal illustration; and such words as integration and segregation (related to both politics and perception) can scarcely lead us elsewhere than to the predicament of the American black community. There was, and is, the ideal of integration and there was, and is, the ideal of segregation; but, if both ideals may be supported by a variety of arguments, proper and improper, there remains the evidence that, when gross injustice begins to be removed, the barriers which were formerly maintainable from the outside are just as reconstructable from within. For, whatever fantasies of the ideally open society are maintainable (and Popper's "open society" may be just as much a fiction as the ideally "closed society" which he condemns), in spite of the abstract universal goals demanded by theoretical liberalism, there still remains the problem of identity, with its related problems of absorption and extinction of specific type; and it is yet to be proved that such problems should be considered temporary. For the truly empirical order was never liberty, equality, fraternity; but it was rather the reverse: a question of the fraternal order, a grouping of the equal and like-minded, which, collectively, assumes the power to negotiate its freedoms. Such is the history of Christianity, continental freemasonry, the academic institution, trades' unionism, women's suffrage, bourgeois privilege and all the rest. It is a history of the open field as an idea, the closed field as a fact; and it is because, in this continuous eruption of closed fields which has contributed so much to genuine emancipation, the recent history of black liberties in the United States is so illuminating (and surely so "correct" in both its aggressive *and* protective attitudes) that we have felt compelled to cite it as a classical—perhaps *the* classical—illustration of a general predicament.

The argument, such as it is, may now be condensed. It certainly concerns the theological extremes of predestination versus free will; and, just as certainly, it is both conservative and anarchistic in its drive. It supposes that, beyond a point, protracted political continuities should neither be postulated nor hoped for and that, correspondingly, the continuities of hyper-extended "design" should also be viewed with doubt. But it does not suppose that, in the absence of total design merely random procedures can be expected to flourish. Instead, whatever may be the empirical and whatever may be the ideal (and both positions can be distorted by intellectual passion or self-interest to appear their opposites), the ongoing thesis presumes the possibility and the need for a two-way argument between these polar extremes. To a point it is a formalist argument; but, then, to the degree that it contains formalist characteristics, this is not without intention.

"Men living in democratic ages do not readily comprehend the utility of forms." The date is the early 1830s and the author of the statement is Alexis de Tocqueville who continues:

Yet this objection which the men of democracies make to forms is the very thing which renders forms so useful to freedom; for their chief merit is to serve as a barrier between the strong and the weak, the ruler and the people, to retard the one and to give the other time to look about him. Forms become more necessary in proportion as the government becomes more active and powerful, while private persons are becoming more indolent and feeble. . . . This deserves most serious attention.[11]

And, if it still may deserve at least some attention, it is with such a statement as this, a curiously pragmatic base for a theory of forms, that we again propose the analogue of politics and perception.

To terminate: rather than Hegel's "indestructible bond of the beautiful and the true," rather than ideas of a permanent and future unity, we prefer to consider the complementary possibilities of consciousness and sublimated conflict; and, if there is here urgent need for both the fox and the "bricoleur," perhaps it can only be added that the job ahead should be envisaged as no matter of making the world safe for democracy. It is not totally different; but, certainly, it is not this. For, surely, the job is that of making safe the city (and hence democracy) by large infusions of metaphor, analogical thinking, ambiguity; and, in the face of a prevailing scientism and conspicuous *laissez-aller*, it is just possible that these activities could provide the true *Survival Through Design*.

from "Collage City and the Reconquest of Time"

To move now from the consideration of a collision of physical constructs to the further consideration of collision, this time on a psychological and, to some degree, a temporal plane. The city of collisive intentions, however much it may be presentable in terms of pragmatics, is evidently also an icon, and a political icon signifying a range of attitudes relating to historical process and social change. So much should be obvious. But, if Collision City, as so far discussed, has only incidentally betrayed an iconic intention, questions of symbolic purpose or function begin now increasingly to rise to the surface.

For one mode of thought it is a psychological necessity that things are what they are; for another something like the reverse is true: things are never what they seem to be and the phenomenon always disguises its own essence. For the one state of mind facts are readily ascertainable, concrete and always susceptible to laconic description. For the other facts are essentially fugitive and will never yield themselves to specification. The one intellectual party requires the supports of definition, the other the illuminations of interpretation; but, if neither attitude enjoys a monopoly of empirical understanding or idealist fantasy, their characterization need not be unduly prolonged. Both mental conditions are only too familiar; and, if it is all too simple (and not completely accurate) to speak of the one attitude as iconoclast and the other as iconophile, it is just such an elementary distinction that is here proposed.

Iconoclasm is and should be an obligation. It is the obligation to expurgate myth and to break down intolerable conglomerates of meaning; but, if one may perfectly well sympathize with the type of the Goth and the Vandal in his efforts to free the world from a stifling excess of reference, one is also obliged to recognize the ultimate uselessness—in terms of original intentions—of any such endeavors. Temporarily they may induce elation, self-gratification and a whole release of hyper-thyroid excitements; but permanently—and as one knows—such efforts can only contribute to yet another iconography. For, if one can agree with Ernst Cassirer and the many of his following[12] that no human gesture can be wholly free from symbolic content, this is only to acknowledge that, while we go through all the public motions of expelling myth through the front door, then, even while (and because) we are doing so, myth is still effecting an insidious re-entry via the kitchen. We may claim rationality. We may insist that reason is always simply reasonable—no more and no less; but a certain stubborn totemic *matériel* will still refuse to go away. For, to iterate Cassirer's primary intuition, however much we may aspire to logic, we are still confronted with the circumstance that language, the prime instrument of thought, inevitably antedates and casts a cloud over all elementary programs of simple logical procedure.

It has been the splendor and the tragic limitation of the revolutionary tradition to have disregarded (or to have affected to disregard) this predicament. Revolutionary light will banish obscurity. With the revolution achieved human affairs will become located in the full radiance of enlightenment. Such, again and again, has been the revolutionary presumption; and, deriving from it, again and again there has ensued an almost predictable disillusion. For, whatever the abstract height of the rational project, the totemic stuff has simply refused to be expunged. Merely it has discovered for itself a new disguise; and in this way, concealing itself in the sophistications of freshly invented camouflage, it has invariably been enabled to operate quite as effectively as ever.

Such has been the history of twentieth century architecture and urbanism: the overt expulsion of all deleterious cultural fantasy and the simultaneous proliferation of fantasy not conceived to be such. On the one hand, the building and the city were to advertise no more than a scientifically determined pattern of performance and efficiency: but, on the other, as the evidence of a complete integration of subject and content, either imminent or already achieved, they could only be charged with an emblematic role. Their covert purpose was sententious; they preached; and indeed so much so that, if one must think of the city as inherently a didactic instrument, then the city of modern architecture will surely long survive in the critical literature of urbanism as a prime illustration of an irrepressible tendency to edify.

The city as didactic instrument. It is not then a question as to whether it should be so. It is rather a matter that it cannot be otherwise. And, this being so, it is therefore a question of the nature of the instructive information which is deliverable, of approximately how a desirable discourse is to be formulated, of what criteria are to determine the city's preferred ethical content.

Now this is an issue involving the highly uncertain roles of custom and innovation, of stability and dynamism, of—in the end—coercion and emancipation which it would be happiness to evade; but the lines of the much travelled escape routes—"Let science build the town," "Let people build the town"—have already been delineated and dismissed. For, if an allegedly cool rationale of "facts" and numbers may disclose an ethical tissue full of dubieties, may justify not only the city of deliverance but also the moral catastrophes of an Auschwitz or a Vietnam, and if the lately resurrected "power to the people" can only be preferred to this, this too cannot be without massive qualification. Nor, in the context of a model city, a city of the mind, can simply functional or simply formal preoccupations be allowed to suppress questions relating to the style and substance of discourse.

Which is to notice that in the arguments which follow it is supposed that, in a final analysis, there are only two reservoirs of ethical content available for our use. *These are: tradition and utopia, or whatever intimations of significance our notions of tradition and utopia may still provide.* These, whether separately or together, positive or negative, have been the ultimate servicing agents of all the various cities of "science" and "people," of "nature" and "history" already noticed; and, since there is no doubt that, practically, they have acted as a very coherent litmus of action and reaction (perhaps the most coherent of any) they are here cited as final, though far from absolute, references.

This is not entirely to proclaim paradox. We have already stated reservations about utopia. We shall go on to stipulate reservations about tradition;

but it would be facetious further to indulge speculation in this area without first directing some attention to the still insufficiently regarded evaluations of Karl Popper.[13] Popper, the theorist of scientific method who believes that objective discernible truth is not available, who proposes the necessity of conjecture and the subsequent obligation towards every degree of refutation, is also the Viennese liberal long domiciled in England and using what appears to be a Whiggish theory of the state as criticism of Plato, Hegel and, not so incidentally, of the Third Reich. The *philosophe engagé*, dedicated via experience to attack upon all doctrines of historical determinism and all assumptions of the closed society: it is in terms of this background that Popper, the apostle of scientific rigor, further presents himself as the critic of utopia and the exponent of tradition's usefulness; and it is in these identical terms that he may also be seen to emerge as, by implication, the greatest of critics of modern architecture and urbanism (though in practice it might be doubted whether he possesses the technical capacity, or the interest, to criticize either).

So Popper's theory of traditional value may seem, logically, to be unfaultable; and it may also seem, emotionally, to be unpalatable. Tradition is indispensable—communication rests upon tradition; tradition is related to a felt need for a structured social environment; tradition is the critical vehicle for the betterment of society; the "atmosphere" of any given society is connected with tradition: and tradition is somewhat akin to myth, or—to say it in other words—specific traditions are somehow incipient theories which have the value, however imperfectly, of helping to explain society.

But such statements also require to be placed alongside the conception of science from which they derive: the largely anti-empirical conception of science not so much as the accumulation of facts but as the criticism, in terms of their non-performance, of hypotheses. It is hypotheses which discover facts and not vice versa; and, seen in this way—so the argument runs—the role of traditions in society is roughly equivalent to that of hypotheses in science. That is: just as the formulation of hypotheses or theories results from the criticism of myth,

Similarly traditions have the important double function of not only creating a certain order or something like a social structure, but also of giving us something on which we can operate; something that we can criticise and change. [And] . . . just as the invention of myth or theories in the field of natural science has a function—that of helping us to bring order into the events of nature—so has the creation of traditions in the field of society.[14]

And it is, presumably, for such reasons that a rational approach to tradition becomes contrasted by Popper with the rationalist attempt to transform society by the agency of abstract and utopian formulations. Such attempts are "dangerous and pernicious"; and, if utopia is "an attractive . . . an all too attractive idea," for Popper it is also "self-defeating and it leads to violence." But again to condense the argument:

1. It is impossible to determine ends scientifically. There is no scientific way of choosing between two ends. . . .
2. The problem of constructing a utopian blueprint [therefore] cannot possibly be solved by science alone. . . .
3. Since we cannot determine the ultimate ends of political actions scientifically . . . they will at least partly have the character of religious differences. And there can be no tolerance between these different utopian religions . . . the utopianist must win over or else crush his competitors. . . . But he has to do more . . . [for] the rationality of his political action demands constancy of aim for a long time ahead. . . .

4. The suppression of competing aims becomes even more urgent if we consider that the period of utopian construction is liable to be one of social change. [For] in such a time ideas are liable to change also. [And] thus what may have appeared to many as desirable when the utopian blueprint was decided upon may appear less desirable at a later date. . . .

5. If this is so, the whole approach is in danger of breaking down. For if we change our ultimate political aims while attempting to move towards them we may soon discover that we are moving in circles . . . [and] it may easily turn out that the steps so far taken lead in fact away from the new aim. . . .

6. The only way to avoid such changes of our aims seems to be to use violence, which includes propaganda, the suppression of criticism, and the annihilation of all opposition. . . . The utopian engineers must in this way become omniscient as well as omnipotent.[15]

. . .

Such is the real burden of Popper's position. Simply that, in so far as the form of the future depends upon future ideas this form is not to be anticipated; and that, therefore, the many future-oriented fusions of utopianism and historicism (the ongoing course of history to be subject to rational management) can only operate to restrain any progressive evolution, any genuine emancipation.

And perhaps it may be at this point that one does distinguish the quintessential Popper, the libertarian critic of historical determinism and strictly inductivist views of scientific method who surely more than anyone else has probed and discriminated that crucial complex of historico-scientific fantasies which, for better or worse, has been so active a component of twentieth century motivation.

But we here approach Popper, who it has already been suggested is—inferentially—the most completely devastating critic of almost everything which the overtly twentieth century city has represented, with the anxiety to salvage at least *something* from the results of his analysis. We approach him, that is, with some of the surviving prejudices (or from the traditional point of view) of what used to be called the modern movement; and our own disagreements with his position are comparatively easy to state. Briefly: his evaluations of utopia and tradition seem to present irreconcilable styles of critical involvement; the one is heated, the other cool, and his distinctly abrupt denunciations of utopia are slightly less than pleasing when they are brought into conjunction with the sophistications of his endorsement of tradition. Apparently much can be forgiven tradition; but, if nothing can be forgiven utopia, one may still feel disturbed by this evidence of special pleading. For the abuses of tradition are surely not any less great than the abuses of utopia; and, if one may feel obliged to concede the accuracy of Popper's condemnation of a prescriptive utopia, one may also ask: *How is it that, if enlightened traditionalism may be distinguished from blind traditionalist faith, the concept of utopia cannot be comparably articulated?*

For, if Popper is able to attribute a sort of proto-theoretical status to tradition and if he is able to envisage social progress as ensuing from a continuous criticism of tradition, that he cannot make these accommodations with reference to utopia can only be considered unhappy.

Utopia has achieved great universality by evincing great understanding and sympathy with all men. Like tragedy it deals with the ultimates of good and evil, virtue and vice, justice and continence and the judgment that is to come. The whole is suffused with two of the tenderest of all human feelings: pity and hope.[16]

But Popper, with his admirable condemnation of political excess, finding literal utopia to promise nothing more than sociological nightmare, seems deliberately to render himself obtuse to the promptings of that great body of manifestations which, particularly in the arts, the myth of the absolutely good society has engendered. He condemns utopian politics and seems unprepared to make any accommodation of utopian poetics. The open society is good, the closed society is bad; therefore utopia is bad and let us have no thought for its by-products. Such would seem to be a very crude digest of his position which we would wish to qualify in the following terms: utopia is embedded in a mesh of ambiguous political connotations and this is to be expected; but, since utopia is something perhaps by now ingrained (and certainly ingrained in the Hebreo-Christian tradition), it cannot, and should not, be something wholly made to go away. A political absurdity, it might remain a psychological necessity. Which, translated into architectural terms, could be a statement concerning the ideal city—for the most part physically insufferable, but often valuable to the degree that it may involve some kind of dimly perceived conceptual necessity.

But, if Popper's rejection of utopia (while he seems surreptitiously to posit a tacit utopian condition in which all citizens are involved in rational dialogue, in which the accepted social ideal is that of a Kantian self-liberation through knowledge) might seem strange, the twentieth century architect's comparable rejection of tradition (while, not so surreptitiously, he maintains a tacit affiliation to what is by now a distinctly traditional body of attitudes and procedures) is surely more explicable. For if, as Popper has surely demonstrated, tradition is unavoidable, then, among the definitions of the word, there is one to which traditionalists do not often refer. A tradition is "a giving up, surrender, betrayal." More particularly it is "a surrender of sacred books in times of persecution"; and this involvement of tradition with treachery is quite possibly some deeply rooted thing which is given in the origins of language. *Traduttore-traditore*, translator-traitor, *traiteur-traité*, traitor-treaty: in these senses the traditionalist traitor is always that person who has abandoned a purity of intention in order to negotiate meanings and principles, perhaps ultimately to treat or to trade with hostile circumstances. An etymology which is eloquently indicative of social prejudice. By the standards of aristocratic, military, or merely intellectual rationalism the traditionalist, in these terms, ranks very low. He corrupts and he accommodates; he prefers survival to the intransigence of ideas, the oases of the flesh to the deserts of the spirit; and, if not criminally feeble, his capacities for the most part are at the level of the mercantile and the diplomatic.

These are among the aspects of tradition which explain the twentieth century architect's loudly paraded distaste for it; but, if much the same distaste may also be felt for utopia (though it has rarely been felt by the architect), these largely uncritical or all-encompassing reactions have, in some way, to be overcome. For, in the end (or so it is here assumed), one is still obliged to struggle with the manifold emanations, legitimate and illegitimate, positive and negative, of both tradition *and* utopia.

But to introduce a concrete illustration of the problem (not wholly unlike the problem of today) which is presented by a utopia in which one has ceased completely to believe and a tradition from which one is critically detached. Napoleon I entertained the project of turning Paris into a species of museum. The city was, to some degree, to become a sort of habitable exhibition, a collection of permanent reminders which were to edify both the resident and the visitor; and the substance of the instruction, one guesses right away, was to be some kind of historical panorama not only of the greatness and continuity of the French nation but, also, of the comparable (though surely slightly less) contributions of a mostly subservient Europe.[17]

So, instinctively one recoils from the idea; but, if it must for the present day command something less than enthusiasm (one is apt to think of Albert

Speer and his unfortunate sponsor), one is still, with Napoleon's idea, presented with the fantasy of a great emancipator, still provided with the embryonic program for what, in its day, could be regarded as a genuinely radical gesture. For this is perhaps one of the first appearances of what was to be a recurrent, and maybe not a repressive, nineteenth century theme: the city as museum.

The city as museum, the city as a positive concert of culture and educational purpose, the city as a benevolent source of random but carefully selected information, was perhaps to be most abundantly realized in the Munich of Ludwig I and Leo von Klenze, in that Biedermeier Munich with its supremely conscientious profusion of references—Florentine, medieval, Byzantine, Roman, Greek—all of them looking like so many plates from Durand's *Précis des Leçons*. But, if the idea of this city, which seems to have found its time in the decade of the 1830s, is surely implicit in the cultural politics of the early nineteenth century, its significance has remained unassessed.

. . .

But, if this is some attempt to identify the city as museum, the city of precisely presented discrete objects/episodes, then what to say about it? That, in mediating the residue of classical decorum and the incipient optimism of the liberal impulse, it operates as interim strategy? That, though its instructive mission is paramount, it addresses itself to "culture" rather than technology? That it still incorporates both Brunelleschi *and* the Crystal Palace? That neither Hegel, Prince Albert nor Auguste Comte were strangers to this city?

These are all questions which the equivocal and eclectic conception of city as museum (the first sketch for the city of a ruling bourgeoisie?) may elicit; and they are probably all to be answered in the affirmative. For whatever our reservations (this city is a rattling of dead bones, a mere anthology of historical and picturesque high spots), it is difficult not to concede its amiability and its hospitality. An open city and, to a degree, a critical one, receptive—in theory at least—to the most disparate stimuli, hostile to neither utopia nor tradition, while by no means value free the city as museum discloses no intimations of urgent belief in the value of any all-validating principle. The reverse of restrictive, implying the entertainment rather than the exclusion of the manifold, by the standards of its day it surrounds itself with the minimum of customs barriers, of embargoes, of restraints upon trade; and, accordingly, the *idea* of the city as museum, felicitous in spite of many valid objections, may, today, be not so readily dismissible as one at first imagines. For, if the city of modern architecture, open though it has always professed to be, has displayed a lamentable lack of tolerance for any import foreign to itself (open field and closed mind), if its basic posture has been protectionist and restrictive (tight controls to stimulate more of the same), and if this has resulted in a crisis of internal economy (increasing poverty of meaning and decline of invention), then the presumptions of formerly unquestionable policy can no longer provide any plausible framework for exclusion.

. . .

As a public institution the museum emerged consequent to the collapse of classical visions of totality and in relation to the great cultural revolution which is most dramatically signified by the political events of 1789. It came into existence in order to protect and display a plurality of physical manifestations representing a plurality of states of mind—all assumed to be in some degree valuable; and, if its evident functions and pretensions were liberal, if the concept of museum therefore implied some kind of ethical ballast, hard to specify but inherent in the institution itself (again the emancipation of society through self-knowledge?), if, to repeat, it was a mediating concept, then it is in terms analogous to the museum that one might postulate a possible solution for the more eminent problems of the contemporary city.

It is suggested that the museum predicament, a predicament of culture, is not readily to be overcome; it is further suggested that its overt presence is more readily to be tolerated than its surreptitious influence; and it is obviously recognized that the designation "city as museum" can only be repulsive to contemporary sensibility. The designation *city as scaffold for exhibition demonstration* almost certainly introduces a more palatable terminology; but, whichever designation is the more useful, both of them in the end are faced with the issue of museum-scaffold versus exhibits-demonstrations; and, depending upon the working up of the show, this can first lead to two major questions. Does the scaffold dominate the exhibits? Or do the exhibits overwhelm the scaffold?

This is a matter of Lévi-Strauss's precarious balance: "between structure and event, necessity and contingency, the internal and the external—constantly threatened by forces which act in one direction or the other according to fluctuation in fashion, style and general social conditions";[18] and, in general, modern architecture resolved its understanding of these questions in favor of an all-pervasive scaffold which largely exhibited itself, a scaffold which pre-empted and controlled any incidentals. This being the case, one also knows, or can imagine, the opposite condition in which the exhibits take over, even to the degree of the scaffold being driven underground or wished away (Disney World, the American romantic suburb, etc.). But, apart from these alternatives which both exclude the possibilities of competition, if the scaffold tends to simulate necessity and the exhibited object freedom, if one of them might simulate utopia and the other tradition, there remains the obligation—for those who are predisposed to envisage architecture as dialectic—further to conceive of a two-way commerce between scaffold and object, "structure" and "event," between the fabric of the museum and its contents, a commerce in which both components retain an identity enriched by intercourse, in which their respective roles are continuously transposed, in which the focus of illusion is in constant fluctuation with the axis of reality.

. . .

The tradition of modern architecture, always professing a distaste for art, has characteristically conceived of society and the city in highly conventional artistic terms—unity, continuity, system; but the alternative and apparently far more "art"-prone method of procedure has, so far as one can see, never felt any need for such literal alignment with "basic" principles. The alternative and predominant tradition of modernity has always made a virtue of irony, obliquity and multiple reference. We think of Picasso's bicycle seat (Bull's Head) of 1944:

You remember that bull's head I exhibited recently? Out of the handlebars and the bicycle seat I made a bull's head which everybody recognized as a bull's head. Thus a metamorphosis was completed; and now I would like to see another metamorphosis take place in the opposite direction. Suppose my bull's head is thrown on the scrap heap. Perhaps some day a fellow will come along and say: "Why there's something that would come in very handy for the handlebars of my bicycle. . ." and so a double metamorphosis would have been achieved.[19]

Remembrance of former function and value (bicycles and minotaurs); shifting context; an attitude which encourages the composite; an exploitation and re-cycling of meaning (has there ever been enough to go around?); desuetude of function with corresponding agglomeration of reference; memory; anticipation; the connectedness of memory and wit; the integrity of wit: this is a laundry list of reactions to Picasso's proposition; and, since it is a proposition evidently addressed to people, it is in terms such as these, in terms of pleasures remembered and desired, of a dialectic between past and future, of an impacting of iconographic content, of a temporal as well as a spatial collision, that resuming an earlier argument, one might proceed to specify an ideal city of the mind.

With Picasso's image one asks: what is false and what is true, what is antique and what is "of today"; and it is because of an inability to make half way adequate reply to this pleasing difficulty that one, finally, is obliged to identify the problem of composite presence in terms of *collage*.

Collage and the architect's conscience, collage as technique and collage as state of mind: Lévi-Strauss tells us that "the intermittent fashion for 'collages', originating when craftsmanship was dying, could not . . . be anything but the transposition of 'bricolage' into the realms of contemplations"[20] and, if the twentieth century architect has been the reverse of willing to think of himself as a "bricoleur" it is in this context that one must also place his frigidity in relation to major twentieth century discovery. Collage has seemed to be lacking in sincerity, to represent a corruption of moral principles, an adulteration. One thinks of Picasso's *Still Life with Chair Caning* of 1911–12, his first collage, and begins to understand why.

In analyzing this, Alfred Barr speaks of:

the section of chair caning which is neither real nor painted but is actually a piece of oilcloth facsimile pasted on the canvas and then partly painted over. Here in one picture Picasso juggles reality and abstraction in two media and at four different levels or ratios . . . [and] if we stop to think which is the most "real" we find ourselves moving from aesthetic to metaphysical contemplation. For what seems most real is most false and what seems most remote from everyday reality is perhaps the most real since it is *least an imitation*.[21]

And the oilcloth facsimile of chair caning, an *objet trouvé* snatched from the underworld of "low" culture and catapulted into the superworld of "high" art, might illustrate the architect's dilemma. Collage is simultaneously innocent and devious.

Indeed among architects only that great straddler Le Corbusier, sometimes hedgehog, sometimes fox, has displayed any sympathy towards this kind of thing. His buildings, though not his city plans, are loaded with the results of a process which might be considered more or less equivalent to that of collage. Objects and episodes are obtrusively imported and, while they retain the overtones of their source and origin, they gain also a wholly new impact from their changed context. In, for instance, the Ozenfant studio one is confronted with a mass of allusions and references which it would seem are all basically brought together by collage means.

Disparate objects held together by various means, "physical, optical, psychological," "the oilcloth with its sharp focussed facsimile detail and its surface apparently so rough yet actually so smooth . . . partly absorbed into both the painted surface and the painted forms by letting both overlap it."[22] With very slight modifications (for oilcloth caning substitute fake industrial glazing, for painted surface substitute wall, etc.) Alfred Barr's observations could be directly carried over into interpretation of the Ozenfant studio. And further illustrations of Le Corbusier as collagiste cannot be hard to find: the too obvious De Beistegui penthouse, the roofscapes—ships and mountains—of Poissy and Marseilles, random rubble at the Porte Molitor and the Pavillon Suisse, an interior from Bordeaux-Pessac and, particularly, the Nestle exhibition pavilion of 1928.

But, of course, beyond Le Corbusier the evidences of this state of mind are sparse and have been scarcely well received. One thinks of Lubetkin at Highpoint II with his Erectheion caryatids and pretended imitations of the house painter imitating wood; one thinks of Moretti at the Casa del Girasole—simulated antique fragments in the *piano rustico*; and one thinks of Albini at the Palazzo Rosso, also one may think of Charles Moore. The list is not extensive but its briefness makes admirable testimony. It is a commentary upon exclusiveness. For collage, often a method of paying attention to the left-overs of the world, of preserving their integrity and equipping them with dignity, of compounding matter of fastness and cerebrality, as a convention and a breach of convention, necessarily operates unexpectedly. A rough method, "a kind of *discordia concors*; a combination of dissimilar images, or discovery of occult resemblances in things apparently unlike," Samuel Johnson's remarks upon the poetry of John Donne,[23] which could also be remarks upon Stravinsky, Eliot, Joyce, upon much of the program of Synthetic Cubism, are indicative of the absolute reliance of collage upon a juggling of norms and recollections, upon a backward look which, for those who think of history and the future as exponential progression towards ever more perfect simplicity, can only prompt the judgment that collage, for all its psychological virtuosity (Anna Livia, all alluvial), is a willfully interjected impediment to the strict route of evolution.

. . .

      It is suggested that a collage approach, an approach in which objects are conscripted or seduced from out of their context, is—at the present day—the only way of dealing with the ultimate problems of, either or both, utopia and tradition; and the provenance of the architectural objects introduced into the social collage need not be of great consequence. It relates to taste and conviction. The objects can be aristocratic or they can be "folkish," academic or popular. Whether they originate in Pergamum or Dahomey, in Detroit or Dubrovnik, whether their implications are of the twentieth or the fifteenth century, is no great matter. Societies and persons assemble themselves according to their own interpretations of absolute reference and traditional value; and, up to a point, collage accommodates both hybrid display and the requirements of self-determination.

      But up to a point: for if the city of collage may be more hospitable than the city of modern architecture, it cannot more than any human institution pretend to be *completely* hospitable. The ideally open city, like the ideally open society, is just as much a figment of the imagination as its opposite. The open and the closed society, either envisaged as practical possibilities, are both of them the caricatures of contrary ideals; and it is to the realms of caricature that one should choose to relegate all extreme fantasies of both emancipation and control. The arguments of Popper and Habermas may be conceded; the desideratum of the open society and the emancipatory interest is evident; the need for the reconstruction of an operative critical theory after its long negation by scientism, historicism, psychologism should be equally so; but one may still be concerned, in this Popperian area, with an imbalance comparable to that in his critiques of tradition and utopia. This can seem to be a too exclusive focus upon concrete evils and a corresponding reluctance to attempt any construction of abstract goods. Concrete evils are identifiable—there can be consensus about them, but abstract goods (apart from the highly abstract emancipatory interest) remain a difficult commodity—they evade agreement; and therefore, while the criticist pursuit and eradication of concrete evil becomes libertarian, all attempts to stipulate abstract good—because of their inevitable foundation in dogma—begin to be envisaged as coercive.

      So it is with the problems of dogma (hot dogma, cool dogma, mere dogma), all abundantly segregated by Popper, that the issue of ideal type again emerges. The Popperian social philosophy is an affair of attack and détente—of attack upon conditions and ideas not making for détente; and it is, up to a point, sympathetic. But this intellectual position which simultaneously envisages the existence of heavy industry and Wall Street (as traditions to be criticized) and then also postulates the existence of an ideal theatre of argument (a Rousseau version of the Swiss canton with its organic *Tagesatzung*?) may also inspire skepticism.

The Rousseau version of the Swiss canton (which had very little use for Rousseau), the comparable New England town meeting (white; paint and witch hunt?), the eighteenth century House of Commons, the ideal academic faculty meeting (and what to say about that?): undoubtedly these—along with miscellaneous soviets, kibbutzim and other references to tribal society—belong to the few theatres of logical and equal discourse so far projected or erected. But, if there should obviously be more of them, then, while one speculates about their architecture, one is also compelled to ask whether these are simply traditional constructs. Which is first to intrude the ideal dimension of these various theatres; and which is then to ask whether specific traditions (awaiting criticism) are in any way conceivable without that great body of anthropological tradition involving magic, ritual and the centrality of ideal type, and presuming utopia as an incipient presence.

In other words, conceding the criticist argument and conceding the categorical imperative of emancipation, we return to the problems of scaffold and exhibit, the problems of the exhibit/demonstration/critical act which will remain invisible (and unprovoked) so long as not supported by a far from auxiliary apparatus of isolation, framing and light. For, just as utopia has traditionally been a mandala, a device for concentrating and protecting ideas, so—and equally—tradition has never been without its utopian component. "This is a government of laws not men," an important, a dogmatic and a highly American statement which is both absurd and eminently comprehensible—absurd in its utopian and classical protestation, comprehensible (in despite of "people") in its appeal to a magical efficacy which, occasionally, may even serve pragmatic purpose.

And it is the notion of the law, the neutral background which illustrates and stimulates the particular ("the law entered that the offense might abound"),[24] the notion of the law, inherently a matter of precedent but also conceiving itself to be an ideal formulation, either given in nature or imposed upon it by divine will—in any case magically sanctioned and not man made, it is the constitution of this sometimes incredible but always necessary fiction, which equips itself with both empirical and ideal, traditional and utopian overtones, which operates with a double ethic, which evolves in history but which insists on platonic reference, it is this very public institution which must now be gainfully employed in commentary upon the scaffold-exhibit relationship.

Renato Poggioli speaks of "the failure of the attempt to realize a modern marvelous (almost always scientific in content, almost exclusively urban in ambiance)";[25] and, in the concept of "modern marvelous," we can easily recognize the presence of those visions of a permanently limpid social order by which the modern city was to be animated and sustained, visions of a social order that was to derive and maintain its value by means of a wholly accurate and automatically self-renewing perception of fact, a perception at once scientific and poetic, which could only assign to fact the role of miracle. This is the type of *miracle scaffold of the measurable* which presents itself as benign (a government of neither laws *nor* men), as a cathedral of popular faith in the scientific imagination (excluding the need for both imagination and faith), as an edifice where all contingencies have been taken care of (where questions no more remain). But it is also the type of miracle-marvel, the icon whose presence speaks for itself, which, presuming its legality, eradicates the requirements of both judgment and debate, which can neither accept nor be accepted by any degree of reasonable scepticism, and which is infinitely more dreadful than any legal construct. Certainly the government of neither laws nor men: at this stage Hannah Arendt's "most tyrannical government of all . . . the government of nobody, the totalitarianism of technique"[26] can only enter the picture.

The overt proclamation of liberty and the surreptitious insistence that liberty (founded in fact) must exist apart from human volition, the determination to leave unconsidered such structures of mediation as are obviously man made ("I do not like the police"),[27] the nihilistic gesture which is rooted in misunderstood, and misinterpreted, abundance: it is in connection with all this that we have proposed a contemplation of the elementary and enlivening duplicities of law, "natural" and traditional, of that conflict between an ethical and a "scientific" ideal which, so long as maintained, at least facilitates interpretation.

But all of this, proposing an order of release through the media of both utopia and tradition, through the city as museum, through collage as both exhibit and scaffold, through the dubieties and duplicities of law, through the precariousness of fact and the eel-like slipperiness of meaning, through the complete absence of simple certainty, is also to propose a situation (which may seem utopian) in which the demands of activist utopia have receded, in which the time bomb of historical determinism is at last defused, in which the requirements of composite time have become finally established, and in which that strange idea, the eternal present, becomes effectively reinstated alongside its equally strange competitors.

The open field and the closed field: we have already suggested the value of the one as a political necessity, of the other as an instrument of negotiation, identity, perception: but, if the conceptual functions of both of them should not require to be emphasized, it might still be noticed that the predicament of the open spatial field and the closed temporal field must, of necessity, be as absurd as that of its opposite. It was the lavish perspectives of cultural time, the historical depths and profundities of Europe (or wherever else culture was presumed to be located) as against the exotic insignificance of "the rest," which most furnished the architecture of previous ages; and it has been the opposite condition which has distinguished that of our own day—a willingness to abolish almost all the taboos of physical distance, the barriers of space, and then, alongside this, a corresponding determination to erect the most relentless of temporal frontiers. One thinks of that chronological iron curtain which, in the minds of the devout, quarantines modern architecture from all the infections of free-wheeling temporal association; but, while we recognize its former justification (identity, incubation, the hot house), the reasons for artificially maintaining such a temperature of enthusiasm can now only begin to seem very remote.

For when one recognizes that restriction of free trade, whether in space or time, cannot, forever, be profitably sustained, that without free trade the diet becomes restricted and provincialized, the survival of the imagination endangered, and that, ultimately, there must ensue some kind of insurrection of the senses, this is only to identify one aspect of the situation which may be conceived. Like the open society as a fact, the ideal of unrestricted free trade must be a chimera. We are apt to believe that the global village will only breed global village idiots; and it is in the light of this supposition that the ideal Swiss canton of the mind, trafficked but isolated, and the New England village of the picture postcard, closed but open to all the imports of mercantile venture, begin again to clamor for attention. For an acceptance of free trade need not require complete dependence upon it and the benefits of free trade are not entirely obliged to lead to a rampage of the libido.

In issues such as these the ideal Swiss canton of the mind and the New England community of the picture postcard are reputed to have always maintained a stubborn and calculated balance of identity and advantage. That is: to survive they could only present two faces; and, if to the world they became exhibit, for themselves they could only remain scaffold. Which, because it is a qualification that must be laid upon the idea of free trade, could, before conclusion, allow occasion to recall Lévi-Strauss's precarious "balance between structure and event, necessity and contingency, the internal and the external . . ."

Now a collage technique, by intention if not by definition, insists upon the centrality of just such a balancing act. A balancing act? But:

Wit, you know, is the unexpected copulation of ideas, the discovery of some occult relation between images in appearance remote from each other; and an effusion of wit, therefore, presupposes an accumulation of knowledge; a memory stored with notions, which the imagination may cull out to compose new assemblages. Whatever may be the native vigor of the mind, she can never form many combinations from few ideas, as many changes can never be rung upon a few bells. Accident may indeed sometimes produce a lucky parallel or a striking contrast; but these gifts of chance are not frequent, and he that has nothing of his own, and yet condemns himself to needless expenses must live upon loans or theft.[28]

Samuel Johnson, again, provides a far better definition of something very like collage than any we are capable of producing; and surely some such state of mind should inform all approaches to both utopia and tradition.

We think of Hadrian. We think of the "private" and diverse scene at Tivoli. At the same time we think of the Mausoleum (Castel Sant'Angelo) and the Pantheon in their metropolitan locations. And particularly we think of the Pantheon, of its oculus. Which may lead one to contemplate the publicity of necessarily singular intention (keeper of Empire) and the privacy of elaborate personal interests—a situation which is not at all like that of *ville radieuse* versus the Villa Stein at Garches.

Habitually utopia, whether platonic or Marxian, has been conceived of as *axis mundi* or as *axis istoriae*; but, if in this way it has operated like all totemic, traditionalist and uncriticized aggregations of ideas, if its existence has been poetically necessary and politically deplorable, then this is only to assert the idea that a collage technique, by accommodating a whole range of *axes mundi* (all of them vest pocket utopias—Swiss canton, New England village, Dome of the Rock, Place Vendôme, Campidoglio, etc.) might be a means of permitting us the enjoyment of utopian poetics without our being obliged to suffer the embarrassment of utopian politics. Which is to say that, because collage is a method deriving its virtue from its irony, because it seems to be a technique for using things and simultaneously disbelieving in them, it is also a strategy which can allow utopia to be dealt with as image, to be dealt with in *fragments* without our having to accept it *in toto*, which is further to suggest that collage could even be a strategy which, by supporting the utopian illusion of changelessness and finality, might even fuel a reality of change, motion, action and history.

Notes
1. Claude Lévi-Strauss, *The Savage Mind* (London, 1966; New York, 1969), p. 16.
2. Ibid., p. 16.
3. Le Corbusier, *Towards a New Architecture* (London, 1927), pp. 18–19.
4. Lévi-Strauss, *The Savage Mind*, p. 17.
5. Ibid., p. 22.
6. Ibid., p. 19.
7. Ibid., p. 22.
8. The possibilities of an exponential, progressive dialectic—whether Marxian or Hegelian—are not here assumed to be "useful."
9. Frederick Law Olmsted and James R. Croes, *Preliminary Report of the Landscape Architect and the Civil and Topographical Engineer, upon Laying Out of the Twenty-third and Twenty-fourth Wards*, City of New York, Doc. No. 72, Board of Public Parks, 1877. Extracted from S. B. Sutton, ed., *Civilizing American Cities* (Cambridge, Mass., 1971).
10. We are indebted for this image to Charles Jencks, *Modern Movements in Architecture* (New York and London, 1973).

11. Alexis de Tocqueville, *Democracy in America*, trans. Henry Reeve (London, 1835–40; New York, 1848), part 2, p. 347.

12. Ernst Cassirer, *Philosophy of Symbolic Forms*, trans. Ralph Manheim (New Haven and London, 1953), and, for instance, Suzanne Langer, *Philosophy in a New Key* (Cambridge, Mass., 1942). But also—and not so incidentally—the whole Warburgian tradition should surely be here cited.

13. Particularly, Karl Popper, "Utopia and Violence," 1947; and "Towards a Rational Theory of Tradition," 1948. Published in *Conjectures and Refutations* (London and New York, 1962).

14. Popper, *Conjectures and Refutations*, pp. 120–135.

15. Ibid., pp. 355–363.

16. Edward Surtz, S.J., *St. Thomas More: Utopia* (New Haven and London, 1964), pp. vii–viii.

17. At least such an idea, or so we believe, is reported in one of the earlier volumes of *La Revue Générale de l'Architecture*—though at the time of writing this note, the exact location of the source seems to evade our retrieval. In any case, a reading of such a document as Emmanuel de Las Cases, *Mémorial de Sainte Hélène* will provide at least some intimations of such a meditated policy. Napoleon's conversations at Longwood were mostly of a military or political concern; but, from time to time, matters of architecture and urbanism did arise and, then, the drift of thought is characteristic. Napoleon is concerned with "practical" performance (harbors, canals, water supply); but he is concerned, quite as much, with "representational" gesture. And thus from Las Cases (ed. Paris, 1956), the following quotations may be suggestive:
On Paris, vol. 1, p. 403,

> Si le ciel, alors, continuait-il, m'eut accordé quelques années, assurément j'aurais fait de Paris la capitale de l'univers et de toute la France un véritable roman.

On Rome, vol. 1, p. 431,

> L'Empereur disait que si Rome fût restée sous sa domination elle fût sortie de ses ruines; il se proposait de la nettoyer de tous ses décombres, de restaurer tout ce qui eût été possible, etc. Il ne doutait pas que le même esprit s'étendant dans le voisinage, il eût pu en être en quelque sorte de même d'Herculaneum et de Pompeia.

On Versailles, vol. 1, p. 970,

> De ces beaux bosquets, je chassais toutes ces nymphes de mauvais goût . . . et je les remplaçais par des panoramas, en maçonnerie, de toutes les capitales où nous étions entrés victorieux, de toutes les célèbres batailles qui avaient illustré nos armes. C'eût été autant de monuments éternels de nos triomphes et de notre gloire nationale, posés à la porte de la capitale de l'Europe, laquelle ne pouvait manquer d'être visitée par force du reste de l'univers.

And, finally, vol. 2, p. 154,

> Il regrettait fort, du reste, de n'avoir pas fait construire un temple égyptien à Paris: c'était un monument, disait-il, dont il voudrait avoir enrichi la capital, etc.

But the notion of the city as museum, as a monument to the state and a representative of its culture, is an index and an instrument of education, which might seem to be implicit in Neo-Classical idealism also receives a microcosmic reflection in the notion of the house as museum: and we think here of Thomas Hope, Sir John Soane, Karl Friedrich Schinkel and, possibly, John Nash. For the Egyptian temple which Napoleon wished to have built in Paris, and which would have "enriched" the capital, substitute the sarcophagus of Seti I with which Soane succeeded in "enriching" his own domestic basement and the analogy begins to take shape. Add Soane's Parlour of Padre Giovanni and his Shakespeare Recess to Hope's Indian Room and Flaxman Cabinet (see David Watkin, *Thomas Hope and the Neo-Classical Ideal* [London, 1968]) and the traces of what Schinkel was to attempt in Berlin and Potsdam are abundantly present. Indeed we are surprised that the category: city as museum, with its sub-category the "museum street" (visible in places so far apart as Athens and Washington) has, so far, remained unidentified.

18. Lévi-Strauss, *The Savage Mind*, p. 30. Also refer to Claude Lévi-Strauss, *The Raw and the Cooked* (New York, 1969; London, 1970).

19. Alfred Barr, *Picasso: Fifty Years of His Art* (New York, 1946), p. 241.

20. Lévi-Strauss, *The Savage Mind*, p. 11.

21. Barr, *Picasso*, p. 79.

22. Ibid.

23. "Abraham Cowley," in *Lives of English Poets, Works of Samuel Johnson Ll.D.* (London, 1823), vol. 9, p. 20.

24. St. Paul, Epistle to the Romans, 5:20.

25. Renato Poggioli, *The Theory of the Avant-Garde* (Cambridge, Mass., and London, 1968), p. 219.

26. We are indebted to Kenneth Frampton for this quotation from Hannah Arendt. He is unable to specify its source.

27. O. M. Ungers, a much repeated remark addressed to students at Cornell University, c. 1969–70.

28. Samuel Johnson, *The Rambler*, no. 194 (Saturday, 25 January 1752).

Mario Gandelsonas   **"Linguistics in Architecture"** *Casabella* 374 (February 1973)

see 199 n.1

Strongly marked by their experience of the Parisian intellectual scene around 1968, Mario Gandelsonas and Diana Agrest were the first architecture theorists to admix the French model of the intellectual *engagé* with Italian semiotics and the American neo-avant-garde. In its post-Sartrean version, the radical intellectual can appreciate the art of the avant-garde (think of Julia Kristeva's work, much admired by Gandelsonas), is anti-humanist and anti-empiricist (concerned to avoid any naïveté about representations of an unconstructed "reality"), and often tries to effect a triple alliance with Marxism, psychoanalysis, and structuralist linguistics. The provenance of one such alliance is the work of Louis Althusser, to which Agrest and Gandelsonas explicitly turn in "Semiotics and Architecture," their critique of Charles Jencks and George Baird. The clearer exposition of Gandelsonas's position, however, is the present essay of the same year, which uses what Gandelsonas had already termed Peter Eisenman's experiments in "syntactic structures" to make its general points.[1] And it is Gaston Bachelard as read by Althusser that guides the argument.

According to Althusser, Marxist philosphy is a "theory of the production of knowledges" and knowledge is an intratheoretical affair. Some theoretical practices are scientific, producing scientific knowledge, while others are ideological, producing ideological "knowledge." To theorize this distinction, Althusser adopted Bachelard's concept of epistemological break, which maintained that there was a complete disjunction, *une rupture épistémologique*, between scientific knowledge and *connaissance commune*, the aconceptual, unconscious common sense that is scattered with "epistemological obstacles." Althusser conceived ideology as a *kind* of knowledge, but an inferior one. As a representation of an "imaginary" relation to reality, ideological theory is not mere false consciousness or error but an objective reality, a material practice. Yet ideological theory is governed by adventitious factors, a "practico-social function" that is external to science; it designates existences but does not give the concepts by which they can be understood; and it is therefore a repetition of its own ideological closure rather than a transformation or development. Scientific knowledge can be obtained only by first breaking with the immediate existences in order to produce the knowledge of real objects by first producing adequate concepts of the objects. Thereafter, the scientific theoretical practice achieves a radical inwardness, a cognitive autonomy, its verifiability being internal to the theory, requiring no external confirmation. "For theoretical practice is indeed its own criterion. . . . [Scientific practices] have no need for verification from *external* practices to declare the knowledges they produce to be 'true,' i.e. to be *knowledges*."[2]

Gandelsonas links the prescientific or ideological theoretical practice to the vestigial "semantic" dimension of Eisenman's work, which aids in the reproduction of Western social formations even as it works as an obstacle to real knowledge. A theory of the production of knowledge in architecture can proceed only "through methodically erasing the boundaries separating different practices within a culture and through looking towards other cultures and situated *at other points in time*"[3] — which is to say, given that even highly autonomized architectural practices

compare Agrest (200–202, 206–208)

like Eisenman's still exhibit an *internal* discontinuity between *episteme* and *doxa*, that a fully adequate account of the transformation of concepts must be a historical one.

compare Jameson (**445 ff**)

Notes

1. See Diana Agrest and Mario Gandelsonas, "Semiotics and Architecture: Ideological Consumption or Theoretical Work," *Oppositions* 1 (September 1973); Mario Gandelsonas and David Morton, "On Reading Architecture," *Progressive Architecture* 53 (March 1972), reprinted in *Signs, Symbols, and Architecture,* ed. Geoffrey Broadbent (New York: Wiley, 1980). Gandelsonas returned to Eisenman's work in "From Structure to Subject: The Formation of an Architectural Language," *Oppositions* 17 (Summer 1979).
2. Louis Althusser and Etienne Balibar, *Reading Capital*, trans. Ben Brewster (New York: Pantheon, 1971), pp. 59–60.
3. Agrest and Gandelsonas, "Semiotics and Architecture," p. 99, emphasis added. Agrest would elaborate the possibility of traveling across boundaries of practices in her essay "Design and Non-Design," *Oppositions* 6 (Fall 1976), reprinted in this volume. The historical imperative entailed in their proposal was never fully developed.

Linguistics, Social Sciences, Architecture

In the last ten years linguistics has played a fundamental role in the field of the so-called social sciences: anthropology, psychoanalysis, aesthetics and philosophy have been, among others, the disciplines most profoundly influenced by linguistics, adopting it as a model and therefore accepting its role as a "pilot science." From this position linguistics has provoked theoretical production in these disciplines of which both its positive aspects and its limitations have been widely discussed.[1] Architecture has also been affected by linguistics. But in comparison to these other fields, with the exception of very limited attempts, this effect cannot be referred to in positive terms.[2] First, because there is the problem of the limited knowledge in architecture about linguistics and semiotic concepts derived from linguistics, and consequently about their transference to architecture. Second, there is in architecture itself a confusion between what is technical practice and what is theoretical practice; that is, between the introduction of theoretical models either to solve technical problems, or to produce descriptive or explicative theories as an activity in itself.[3] Finally, and the most important for articulating our position on current architectural theory, is the necessity to distinguish between what we shall call ideological functioning and theoretical functioning in these theories, which can be seen specifically in the transference of theoretical models from one field to another. From the analysis of this transference a new fact comes to light: one must choose between building ideology or producing theory. It is on the basis of both this particular choice and also the more general problem of transference that we will base our critique of Peter Eisenman's approach to what he terms syntactic structures, or more generally, Conceptual Architecture.[4]

Proposition

This problem of ideology and theory is in reality nothing but the general problem of the relationship of science to ideology. It will be my position that the clarification of this point must precede any work of theoretical development.

     The dialectical relationship between theory and ideology is a problem common to any science and for that reason should be redefined in the specific case of architecture before any theoretical work may begin. As a first step in the redefinition, recall Gaston Bachelard's proposition about the nature of the relationship between theory and ideology.[5] In analyzing this relationship in Bachelard's terms, it is possible to say first that any scientific theory seen as the production of knowledge is built on the basis of a dialectical relationship with an ideology—that is, on the basis of an ideology and at the same time radically opposing it. It is this dialectical relationship which separates scientific theory from ideology. Second, that ideology functions as an obstacle in the production of knowledge.[6]

     We will call architectural ideology the summation of Western architectural "knowledge" considered as a whole, from commonplace intuition to sophisticated theories and histories of architecture. What has been called up to now theory in architecture has presented itself as having a practical purpose, such as the ordering and amelioration of the environment or the development of aesthetic codes. Explicitly or not, these theories aim to renovate and revitalize architecture. In our terms, theories have an ideological function inasmuch as they contribute to the survival and continuity of architecture.

To these essentially ideological theories we will oppose a theory of architecture which must be placed outside ideology. This second type of theory must expose, describe and explain architectural ideologies as they exist as part of a bourgeois society and culture.[7] This type of theory defines an Architecture with a capital A as the theory of many different architectural ideologies or architectures with a small a, e.g., the history of Chinese architecture between 1500 and 1600. Ideology provides a type of knowledge whose major effect is the preservation of existing social systems and their institutions rather than the explanation of that reality. For example, the Church supported for centuries Ptolemy's theory of the universe which corroborated biblical texts against any other models which could explain more accurately the same reality, i.e., Galileo's theory, as opposed to Ptolemy's ideology. We will say that any analysis of architecture which shows its function as a mechanism which distorts and hides knowledge about reality—the world out there—should also be considered as part of this second type of theory. Thus, in order to make the separation or distinction between an architectural ideology and Architecture (theory), one needs to define the former as the object of study of the latter. It must be accepted that no theory of architecture exists. Therefore, if one wants to analyze Peter Eisenman's work it must be seen in such an ideological context. First because there is no dialectical relationship between his theory and the ideological context, and second because the definition of the theoretical object is lacking. In other words, his work is neither opposed to nor outside of the existing architecture, and therefore it is linked to its continuation.[8] Nevertheless, his work must be considered as a particular approach within Western architectural ideology, and as such is a useful model for our critique. But more importantly, and quite by accident, since he is not aware of it, some of his propositions could be used to formulate a more purely theoretical context. For us it will be important to attempt to show the conditions which would be necessary in order to do this. We will start by isolating the aspects of his approach which are particular within Western architecture. We will see that some of these aspects could be related under certain conditions to what we have called a theory of architecture.

To this end we will point out one of the characteristics of architecture that is the semantic dimension which is implied by his approach. From this we will be able (1) to locate his work within Western architecture; (2) to determine what existent "materials" in terms of "ideas" and "forms" he uses;[9] and (3) to isolate the particular characteristics of his approach such as the definition of a deep structure which may be reformulated to lead us to this more theoretical context.

Critique

Architecture as a technical practice was instituted in the Renaissance. It is mainly articulated in what we will call the "semantic dimension."[10] We mean by this that any description or interpretation of either a whole building or parts of a building is made by linking physical "indicators" to functional or expressive meanings. For example, a column is a physical indicator which, while it has the structural meaning of support, may have at the same time the expressive meaning of, for example, "Ionic." While the functioning of the semantic dimension is not as simple as this example of the column would at first suggest, it indicates the fundamental role of the relationship between a building (either in terms of its elements or as a whole) and an "external" meaning "residing" in that object whether it is an aesthetic, a functional, or a structural meaning.[11]

The production of this external meaning has always been considered as the first step in any building—that is its program. But as we have seen, it is also its final objective. It becomes then both the determining and resulting aspect of the building itself,[12] and perhaps for this reason it has been predominant over other aspects of building such as syntactics. It would also be possible to define the syntactic dimension in architecture from the Renaissance onwards in a way in which certain procedures such as the alignment of windows and columns, considerations of symmetry and proportions would probably be included.[13] But these considerations have always been thought of, with a few, rare exceptions, as secondary to the semantic dimension, in that they are not done as ends in themselves but to convey meaning.[14]

The relationships in the semantic dimension between a physical indicator such as a building and meaning are not fixed. There are many possible types of modifications of meanings or functions attributed to buildings which themselves are unchanged through time. The superficial modifications of the semantic dimension could be understood by analyzing Robert Venturi's work. For example, he introduces into architecture some elements such as new shapes and meanings belonging to a mass culture which are implicitly considered by him as outside of high culture and thus, in his terms, outside of architecture. However, by this gesture Venturi only changes certain elements which are integrated within the traditionally dominant semantic dimension, but this does not affect the structure of the semantic dimension itself. This process of modification, or more appropriately of assimilation of new ideas without changing the whole is characteristic of an architectural ideology. By means of this kind of modification, architecture has survived for five hundred years, "adapting" to the changes which have occurred in Western society.

In the case of Peter Eisenman's work, this traditional play of modifications within a semantic dimension has been abandoned. In our judgment, one of the most interesting and original aspects in the work of Eisenman is the discovery of the possibility of modifications within architecture which are the result of a shift in the dominant characteristic of architecture from the semantic to the syntactic. By "paralyzing" the semantic dimension, the syntactic dimension is seen in a new light. In this way both the syntactic and the semantic dimensions of architecture stand uncovered, thus permitting not only new access to their makeup but also a potential point of departure for the development of a nonideological theory. The fact that this type of approach appears now seems not to be by chance. It is instead the result of an historical process—a situation which can be seen as the apparent exhaustion of the possibilities for semantic variation and modification which have served to characterize and vitalize architectural production throughout the 1960s. In exploring the mechanisms and the limits of Western architectural ideology, Eisenman's work is interesting to us mainly because of its capacity to serve both as a mark and a touchstone.

Eisenman's work has been in development since the mid-1960s. His first works, however, were not published until the 1970s, during the decline of avant-garde attitudes—attitudes which themselves had resulted from the perpetuation, in the semantic dimension of architecture, of the classic vicious circle of intuition versus reason or art versus technique. Art and intuition are represented by the utopian formalism of Archigram or the "reformist" formalism of Venturi's attempt to incorporate and absorb the mass culture into architecture. Technique and reason are represented in the direct rejection of forms per se expressed by the adoption of computer methods and the primacy of the "design process."

Eisenman's work stands in opposition to the impasse described above and within a line of thinking first proposed by Colin Rowe, which considers the Modern Movement and the Renaissance for the analysis of some essential characteristics of architecture which are no longer seen in terms of two poles of comparison. Further, he has also taken from Reyner Banham the hypothesis of rereading the Modern Movement in terms of separating what is really new from what is only a continuation of classical themes. These two propositions allow Eisenman to regard the Modern Movement as a process which has been "stopped" or sidetracked and which must be restarted, became this process is thought by both Rowe and Banham to have been invested with something which can be best called the "classical" nature of architecture. As we will see below, Eisenman interprets this "classical" nature as something which is archetypal or universal. From Rowe's and Banham's hypotheses, Eisenman draws a rationale for his own approach to architecture. The works of Scamozzi and Palladio contrasted with those of Le Corbusier and Terragni as models: in his article "Notes on Conceptual Architecture" he separates his own work from the mainstream of the Modern Movement. In a sense Terragni has been "reinvented" by Eisenman to represent a model of the syntactic aspect of architecture. This is then contrasted with Le Corbusier who is taken to represent the semantic aspect. Such a formulation, while deforming the actual record, allows Eisenman to see their work in a new way, and in turn to use this way as a basis for his own theoretical construct. In a sense both Le Corbusier and Terragni are made to stand for a "monolithic" or traditional conception of architecture, which Peter Eisenman then breaks down. The first move in this break is when he defines two aspects of form. In "Notes" he puts forward the term semantic to indicate those aspects of building which can be explained in cultural terms, and the term syntactic to indicate those aspects which exclude the notion of culture—aspects which, therefore, can be seen as universal. The exclusion of the notion of culture or of the cultural aspects is the basis for a model which considers the perceived phenomena as only the manifestation of a system which defines two structures called "deep" structure and "surface" structure.[15]

The deep structure in Eisenman's terms is similar to the linguistic concept of deep structure as defined by Noam Chomsky, who says that deep structure is partly defined by "universal rules . . . which specify an abstract underlying order of elements that makes possible the functioning of transformational rules . . . that map deep structures into surface structures."[16] Eisenman postulates a syntactic component in architecture which, as in linguistics, would be capable of generating deep and surface structures. "The deep structure is made up of syntactic integers which are a set of irreducible formal oppositions which become manifest in an actual environment (surface structure) via a set of transformational rules and operations."[17]

From a more detailed analysis of Eisenman's model in relation to Chomsky we can see two things happening: first, what in Chomsky's model is changed after it is transposed into an architectural context; second, some of the elements of Peter Eisenman's notion of deep structure upon which our critique will be focused.

Deep structure as defined by Eisenman is a duality, a "dialectic" of two categories which he calls conditions and qualities. "Conditions are concerned with the relationships in architectural space which are abstract and thus with syntactic information which is notational. Within the conditions of deep structures it is possible to identify from the above two irreducible sets of formal integers. The first is solid and void; the second, centroidal and linear. These conditions do not exist without each other; they are interdependent."[18] "Qualities are concerned with the relationships in architectural space which are three-dimensional, physical, and thus with syntactical meaning which is spatial. The qualities of an architectural deep structure are linear, planar and volumetric (and not line, plane and volume which are the actual forms in a specific physical environment). Linear, planar and volumetric in the sense in which they are being used here are not objects or elements, but again relationships between elements."[19]

From the above, one could conclude that Noam Chomsky's model—specifically the linguistic rewriting rules and the lexicon—have been explicitly transformed by Peter Eisenman in their transposition to architecture. Chomsky's concepts are substituted by a new set of categories and notions, which, according to Eisenman, could serve to describe some aspects of the specific nature of architecture. However, the categories of notational and spatial would represent a structural characteristic of architecture which could not be perceived in a direct way, by simply looking at existing buildings, and which have no particular corollary in Chomsky's model, or in linguistics. It is this distortion of deep structure from Chomsky to Eisenman which we feel might be used as a beginning point in the generation of theoretical concepts. If such a model is to work theoretically, the use of a concept such as deep structure must be distinguished from a mechanical importation of such a concept. This distinction has not been made by Eisenman. But equally it has not been made by anyone else. The theoretical development of a concept implies among other things the act of transferring it from its original context. This process also presupposes its modification in its comprehension and extension and its generalization by the incorporation of external features which originally were not part of the concept.[20] Furthermore, in transposing a concept such as deep structure from one field to another, the relation between it and other concepts in the original context also has to be modified. If this distinction is not made, one implicitly carries over other concepts from the original context.

It is this implicit transposition of linguistic notions into architecture which is one of the limitations of Eisenman's work. Three concepts which are implicitly imported by him have to be analyzed: creativity, intuition, and the universal. The distinction between the idea of creativity from intuition and the universal is important because there are some aspects of the notion of creativity which could be used in order to produce a non-ideological theory of architecture. But there are aspects of the terms intuition and the universal which function as ideological obstacles.

The most important characteristic of Chomsky's model which Eisenman preserves, in an implicit way, is the concept of a system which permits creative action. This concept describes in language the capability of the speaking subject to generate an unlimited number of utterances, making infinite use of finite means. In our opinion there is a particular type of creativity in architecture which is different from language. This difference should be considered in terms of the differences between the nature of language and the nature of architecture. Language contains a supra-institutional level, explained in Chomsky's model as the syntactic component, which is probably linked to the biological characteristics of man. This allows each child to incorporate at a similar age and in a short period of time a grammatical mechanism which he or she retains forever. This does not, obviously, happen in architecture. Only a few persons learn the architectural mechanisms in a process which, as opposed to the acquisition of grammar in childhood, starts in their adolescence and may continue throughout their whole lives. This process might be seen as a sociological process rather than as coming from a biological characteristic of man.

We think that it is therefore of major importance to distinguish between a linguistic syntactic component which explains creativity in language and an architectural syntactic dimension which accounts for creativity in architecture. This syntactic dimension of architecture is comparable to the rhetorical mechanism of the literary discourse more than to the syntactic component of language. For literature, like architecture, is performed by a few in a community of users of language.

Rhetoric must be understood here without any of the pejorative connotations with which "modernity" has loaded this term during this century. This term is more appropriately used in the sense in which it is used in semiotics;[21] as an analytic concept to designate a certain practice in language in the Western world from the fifth century to the nineteenth, and that has been reintroduced recently in the study of literature as well as in the study of other fields removed from language, such as advertising,[22] cinema,[23] etc. Rhetoric indicates a discourse built upon another discourse. For example, in the novel in Western culture it is possible to distinguish two superimposed "discourses": (a) a narration which can be abstracted in a few pages (e.g., the classic love triangle) but which is stretched and sustained by (b) a rhetorical discourse. The rhetorical discourse allows the rewriting of the same narration in various ways.[24]

Architectural ideological theories never thought of architecture as rhetoric but in terms of creation or invention. However, it is possible to recognize in architecture a similar rhetorical mechanism not in the sense in which Alison and Peter Smithson define rhetoric, but as a discourse built on a discourse. The term "house," for instance, has a constant meaning, while houses may be given different forms. That the meaning "house" is present in the beginning and the end of the design process is one discourse. The form of the house meanwhile is transformed, distributed, combined, done and undone. This process, which is typical of architecture, is a second discourse. The functioning of the two discourses in architecture can be considered similar to their functioning in literature. They are a product of complementary but contradictory discourses. The first one, the functional meaning, which is not changed during the process—the house is always a house—insures a first and more obvious level of communication. Meanwhile, the second meaning, the rhetorical, which is totally outside of the first and in a sense autonomous to it, coexists with the first without destroying its original meaning. This second meaning represents an aspect of what we call the syntactic dimension of architecture. This rhetorical meaning defines a certain type of creativity in architecture; a creativity in terms of an integral system which is purely syntactic, which has been recognized by Peter Eisenman and which is a first step in defining a rhetorical mechanism. For example, his use of a numeric game, or the movements of displacement and rotation, or the transformations which allow one to pass from column to wall and from wall to volume, respond to a system that has nothing to do with a use, structure, or aesthetic. By doing this, Eisenman is stretching to its limit the existing rhetorical mechanisms of Western architecture developed since the Renaissance. Inasmuch as his work consistently exposes the limitations of these existing mechanisms, it furnishes a point of departure to develop a theoretical model. However, there are problems which derive from the simultaneous importation of other notions, specifically intuition and the universal. These notions are linked with concepts of syntax and deep structure in language, but must be carefully distinguished and separated from them when transferred to architecture. The function of these notions in architecture is ideological and they can only play the role of epistemological obstacles inasmuch as they imply two other ideological notions that characterize Western architecture: the theological notion of creation in classical aesthetics and the "ethnocentrist" notion of history of architecture. This latter is a retrospective projection in a linear time of a particular "architecture," namely Western architecture, which is seen as having precedence over all other architectures.

Concerning the problem of intuition, we find first that the intuition of the speaking subject who develops an "objective creativity" by means of an unmodifiable mechanism, such as the Chomskyan syntactic component, should be distinguished from the subject of design in architecture whose intuition can be "worked." The implications of the lack of such a distinction between intuition in language and intuition in architecture can be seen in Peter Eisenman's work. This is reflected by his assumption that the term linear is an intuition inherently possessed by any subject of architecture. How would we characterize the term linear, which appears both as condition and as quality in his deep structure, and which also structures the movements according to an ordered series which link the planes in layers or the transitions between qualities (linear/planar/volumetric)? We have seen that linear is not a line but a type of relationship. This relationship produces a virtual state only when "conceived" by a subject starting from notions such as shear, compression or tension. We deny, from our materialistic standpoint, any autonomous concept. Therefore, the term linear cannot be autonomous as an intuition or imaginary formation. We will propose that line is linked to philosophic categories, ideological notions or scientific concepts. And as each of those three classes has a history, it is possible to indicate that the conception of "linearity" in the work of Eisenman has more to do with Euclidean geometry and mechanical physics than with topology, microphysics or nuclear physics.[25] When Eisenman speaks about linear, he presupposes that the architect has an inbuilt conception of linearity. But this conception is nothing but an intuition linked to the particular concept. As Gaston Bachelard demonstrates in the "elementary spatial connections,"[26] a scientific activity upon a common intuition can produce a worked intuition loosening the hierarchies imposed by common intuition, thus allowing the construction of finer structures in an unlimited process. "The common intuition of the line is a 'totalitary' intuition which has wrongly accumulated an excess of teleology on the trace of the line: the line is thus determined not only step by step as it should be but from its origin to its end."[27] A primary task in the work of the constitution of a theory of architecture would be to transform the Euclidean or, at most, a Cartesian conception of geometry into a worked intuition.

We think, however, that besides the introduction of the notion of worked intuition to define more precisely the subject of design, it would be necessary to introduce also the notion of various deep structures, even "deeper" than the one defined by Eisenman in his work. Such deep structures would be defined by mechanisms such as those which are linked to the unconscious, and whose role is impossible to ignore in the production of the architectonic object. This deep structure (with a capital D), which functions by means of displacements and condensations, is analogous to the work of the dream as explained by Freud.[28] These are operations of another productive mechanism directly linked to the "matter" they work with—phonic, graphic, and "material."[29] This concept of materiality is excluded in Eisenman's approach. The ideological bonds that link his conceptual system to the traditional notion of creation will begin to dissolve by mutating the notion of intuition into the notion of worked intuition, and by considering Eisenman's deep structure as only one within a series of mechanisms.

The notion of universality—the classical nature of architecture—which is linked with the other notions in the syntactic structures of Eisenman, is one of the key constructions in bourgeois ideology. Any notion which is linked to the idea of "man" as an ecological or communicative animal which hides, among other things, the concept of social class and the particularity and limits of Western culture to which this notion is related must be considered ideological. Furthermore, the transposition of the notion of man's innate capacity to master languages from linguistics to architecture carries with it the notion of a universal inbuilt ability for man to master architecture. This notion of universal intuition has the complementary function of erasing the fact that architectural knowledge is owned and produced by a limited sect for the service of a certain social class. It is the notion of culture as private which functions in a way to "exclude" other cultures. For example, in the West "primitive" cultures named savage and/or barbarian are excluded from the notion of culture, as are cultures from the Orient, named "chinoiserie." This exclusion is a double one: of culture and of "other" cultures.[30] The exclusion of culture implied by the notion of the universal can only reinforce the ideological machinery built over centuries by the histories of art and architecture. These histories have always been an indispensable support of architectural ideology, inasmuch as they permit the imposition of the values of a given culture upon other cultures through the notion of an ever-present "human artistic activity" of a supracultural nature. History orders buildings and objects in a hierarchical way through its uses of the implied opposition between Western culture and the rest of the world. The latter is always thought of as the inferior replica of the former, without even the slightest suspicion that the inferiority might only reflect the inadequacy of a conceptual apparatus.[31] The options seem to be quite clear: to collaborate in the maintenance of architecture or to work outside of architecture not only by refusing to serve, to adorn, to justify but also by pointing out constantly the nature of these functions. Hence, the role of theoretical productions is a primary one in this task.

The work of Peter Eisenman is situated in terms of this option within an architectural ideology, but with the potential of being displaced towards the outside. The "form" of Peter Eisenman is still related to function and to the notions which are tied together with it in architecture. Eisenman's form is a "deep" form of an architectural surface form—form which is what remains of function. The work of Peter Eisenman has for us the virtue of accentuating even to a level of antagonism the internal contradictions of the existing architectural ideology. We believe that this antagonism is a potential, which despite its ideological character, can serve as a basis for a theoretical work of articulation with historic and dialectical materialism.

Notes

1. Concerning the positive aspects see Claude Lévi-Strauss, "Langage et parenté," in *Anthropologie structurale* (Paris: Plon, 1958). In reference to the limitations see Julia Kristeva, "L'expansion de la sémiotique," in Julia Kristeva, Josette Rey-Debove, and Donna Jean Umiker, eds., *Essays in Semiotics* (The Hague: Mouton, 1971); and Eliseo Veron, "Pour une sémiologie des opérations translinguistiques," to be published in *Versus* (Milan: Achille Mauri Editore).

2. Diana Agrest and Mario Gandelsonas, "Critical Remarks in Semiotics and Architecture," *Semiotica* 9, no. 3 (1973).

3. Theories of Architecture per se should be distinguished from any theory (or analysis) which is determined by a project, or from any theory which is used for a specific purpose. Overlooking such a distinction can only lead, as has so often happened, to misunderstandings. A theory of architecture may be used in designing, in teaching, in establishing norms, etc.; only by accident will it become a tool. (A theory may become a tool once applied to a specific task.)

4. Peter Eisenman, "Notes on Conceptual Architecture," *Casabella* 359–360 (1971), pp. 49–56.

5. Gaston Bachelard, *La formation de l'esprit scientifique* (Paris: Librairie Philosophique J. Vrin, 1972).

6. On the analysis of the relationship between theories in electricity and magnetism (in physics), and prescientific or ideological theories on the same subject, see Michel Pecheux, *Sur l'histoire des sciences* (Paris: Maspéro, 1969).

7. Diana Agrest and Mario Gandelsonas, "arquitectura Arquitectura," *Materia, Cuadernos de Trabajo* (Buenos Aires, 1972).

8. Although we are far from a theory of Architecture, we can state, a priori, that such theory cannot be built by rewriting architectural ideology.

9. Peter Eisenman, "From Golden Lane to Robin Hood Gardens, or If You Follow the Yellow Brick Road, It May Not Lead to Golders Green," *Architectural Design* 9 (1972). This title as well as the name of the author "disappeared mysteriously" in the process of publication.

10. The term "semantic dimension" refers to a specific mechanism of architecture and includes notions such as function or expression.

11. Structure, here, is meant in the sense of structure of the building.

12. Mario Gandelsonas, "On Reading Architecture," *Progressive Architecture*, March 1972.

13. Emilio Garroni, "Semiotica e architettura," *Op. Cit.* (Naples, 1970).

14. J. N. L. Durand's (1760–1834) work might be one of the few which represents a syntactical trend within classic architecture.

15. Eisenman, "Notes on Conceptual Architecture," p. 51.

16. Noam Chomsky, *Aspects of the Theory of Syntax* (Cambridge: MIT Press, 1965), p. 141.

17. Eisenman, "Notes on Conceptual Architecture." [Editorial note: Though the ideas Gandelsonas refers to are present in Eisenman's essay, this and the following quotations do not correspond exactly to the version published in *Casabella*. Perhaps Gandelsonas is working from a different, unpublished version. See also Peter Eisenman, "Notes on Conceptual Architecture (II): Double Deep Structure," *A + U* 3 (March 1974; Japanese version only), and "Notes on Conceptual Architecture II A," in *Environmental Design Research*, proceedings of the fourth international Environmental Design Research Association conference, ed. Wolfgang F. E. Preiser (Stroudsburg, Pa.: Dowden, Hutchinson & Ross, 1973–1974), vol. 2.]

18. Ibid.

19. Ibid.

20. Georges Canguilhem, quoted in *Cahiers pour l'analyse 1/10* (Paris: Editions du Seuil, 1966–69).

21. Roland Barthes, "L'ancienne réthorique," *Communications* 16 (1970).

22. Jacques Durand, "Rhétorique et image publicitaire," *Communications* 15 (1970).

23. Christian Metz, *Langage et cinéma* (Paris: Larousse, 1979).

24. We are paraphrasing Julia Kristeva, *Le texte du roman* (The Hague: Mouton, 1970).

25. The possibility of thinking of the plane by taking the line as a point of departure, or the movements as compressions, indicates the specific type of line which Eisenman considers as a formal category.

26. Gaston Bachelard, *La philosophie du non* (Paris: Presse Universitaire de France, 1940).

27. The beam (of light) and the mechanic trajectory have been considered as the true symbols of this determination. But yet, microphysics has developed the notion of a circumstantiated trajectory, which sets aside the postulated continuity of the whole. Bachelard shows how the intuition worked by microphysics, incorporating Heisenberg's principle of uncertainty, allows us to abandon the "ballistic intuition" of the line. See Bachelard, *La philosophie du non*, p. 95.

28. Sigmund Freud, *The Interpretation of Dreams* (London: Allen & Unwin, 1961).

29. Agrest and Gandelsonas, "Critical Remarks in Semiology and Architecture."

30. Diana Agrest, "Materia y lugar," unpublished manuscript.

31. Chang Tung Sun, "La logique chinoise," *Tel Quel* 38 (1969).

Massimo Scolari   **"The New Architecture and the Avant-Garde"** "Avanguardia e nuova architettura,"

from Massimo Scolari et al., *Architettura razionale*, XV Triennale, international

session of architecture (Milan: Franco Angeli, 1973); translated for this anthology

by Stephen Sartarelli

Surely the architects assembled in the fifteenth Triennale of Milan, 1973, under the
formula "Rational Architecture," were not the only ones pursuing an autonomous architecture made out of architecture's own purified elements and its elements only.[1]
But to construct out of that gathering a new international program of architectural
research — the "Tendenza," in Massimo Scolari's resonant appellation — put the theoretical fine point on a contradiction that was paramount in the architecture theory
of the 1970s: the contradiction between the universality of architecture's historical
contingency and the universality of its autonomy. For by 1973, against historical constructions like Manfredo Tafuri's — which understood formal autonomy as a sublimation of architecture's guilty relation to capitalist rationality, a reaction formation that
removes architecture from its functional and economic contexts — practicing architects were experimenting with disciplinary autonomy as a form of counterideological
resistance to, or liberation from, the very rationalized, consumption-driven society
that Tafuri saw as autonomy's sponsor.

see Tafuri (28–33)

    While semiotics and structuralist linguistics had already been
enlisted as models for a nonhistoricist, epistemic analysis of architecture, Scolari
finds in the new experiments "principles [that] guide the formal choices through a
genealogy of reference spanning the typologies of history and materials projected,
written, and thought." These typological principles (the revived interest in which was
due in large part to Aldo Rossi's *L'architettura della città* of 1966) enable architecture
to reflect on its own self-generated, internally coherent laws or norms, and to display
these, or at least their visible traces, as constitutive elements of a building or architectural drawing. The logic of types is a classificatory operation that produces objects
specific to the discipline of architecture, logically distinct from everything that is not
architecture. The object must be understood, then, not as determined by some historical imperative but rather as a cognitive object, one that, through the nuances of its
very form, gives epistemic access to the defining conventions or limiting conditions
of architecture. Scolari:

compare Vidler (291–294)

For the Tendenza, architecture is a cognitive process that in and of itself, in the acknowledgment
of its own autonomy, is today necessitating a refounding of the discipline; that refuses interdisciplinary solutions to its own crisis; that does not pursue and immerse itself in political, economic,
social, and technological events only to mask its own creative and formal sterility, but rather
desires to understand them so as to be able to intervene in them with lucidity — not to determine
them, but not to be subordinate to them either.

The cognitive object is not a representation of some sociohistorical condition that
precedes and determines it and can be interrogated in other than purely architectural
terms, but an image of the interrogative process itself. Architectural design becomes
a mode of research in its own right.

    Pitting the new architecture against both the anti-avant-gardist
dogma of continuity and the *architettura radicale* of groups like Archizoom, Superstudio, and 9999 — who alternatively appealed to the historical avant-garde for its

culturally destructive strategies or twisted the procedures of pop art into ironically ❚ *compare* 56–59 ❚ liberating therapies — Scolari offers a rational reconstruction of a contemporary architecture's relation to the history of modernism. Whether or not Scolari was himself "making an ironic Dadaist 'gesture'" in his construction of the Tendenza,[2] both his notions of the fading of the avant-garde and of a disciplinary refunctioning through autonomous research reverberated through architecture theory for nearly a decade.

Notes

1. These were Aldo Rossi, Leon Krier, Nino Dardi, Adolfo Natalini, Carlo Aymonino, and Ludwig Leo, together with the New York Five — Peter Eisenman, John Hejduk, Michael Graves, Richard Meier, and Charles Gwathmey. The exhibition generated a number of critiques and countercritiques, including accusations of a return to a rhetoric dangerously reminiscent of totalitarianism. See especially the special issues of *Parametro* 21–22 (1973) and *Controspazio* 6 (1973); and Joseph Rykwert, "XV Triennale," *Domus* 530 (1974).
2. As reported by Manfredo Tafuri, *History of Italian Architecture, 1944–1985*, trans. Jessica Levine (Cambridge: MIT Press, 1989), p. 236 n. 3.

To define contemporary Italian architecture, there is probably no more accurate description than the one Camillo Boito gave in response to the whimsy and confusion of late nineteenth-century architecture: "Nowadays," said Boito, "there is no architecture, only buildings and architects. Architecture, except in rare cases, is a plaything of the imagination, a clever combination of forms, a game of pencils, compasses, lines and squares."[1]

In 1973, almost a century later, the observations one may make concerning the "misery of recent architecture," as it is designed and realized, are the same, *except in rare cases.*

Current Italian architectural history is entirely incapable of explaining this misery or of suggesting a way to overcome it. Bruno Zevi and Leonardo Benevolo, in their histories of architecture (1952 and 1960, respectively), do not manage to shed any light on the present; and if they do manage in their occasional "updatings" of the topic, it is only in a *defensive capacity.*

In rebutting the pluralistic theses of Christian Norberg-Schulz, Zevi provides us with the paradigm of this defensive support: "The alternative to the harsh responsibility of remaining faithful to the modern tradition lies not in pluralism, but in the open, courageous suicide proposed by Pop architecture. Rejecting all cultural models, all open or closed order, and returning to the primordial chaos, to triviality and artifice. Whoever decides to abandon the modern movement can choose between Versailles and Las Vegas, between sclerosis and drugs."[2]

While recognizing the consistency and seriousness of Zevi's ongoing cultural commitments, we cannot accept these "operative instructions" as the only alternatives to the dogma of the modern movement. The modern movement's legacy is still rife with unexplored possibilities, deep strata to be investigated, and the potential heresies that may arise from it will have to be grounded in the recognition of that doctrinaire legacy, or at least in its utilization.

Zevi is right when he asserts (in 1965) that no new architectural avant-garde has emerged,[3] and that the anti-avant-garde (neoliberty, neorealism, environmental perceptionism, historicism, mannerism) had produced no substantial shifts, but only works of regressive retreat.

It must be said, however, that it is incorrect to preclude any sort of critical advance along the modern movement's track, with the only alternative being derailment. The interesting debate, in the review *Controspazio*, that pitted the dogma of the modern movement against "pure architecture" demonstrated how arid the defensive strategy is, and pointed out just how many and what sort of real alternatives exist to chaos and "pop suicide."[4]

Zevi's conclusion constitutes a dangerous, and useless, encouragement of "triviality" in architecture: of that picturesque disorder which in the name of the imagination chooses, in planning, only chaos, "as a redemption from the methodological discipline of rationalism and as an alibi for the sociopolitical goals of urbanism"[5]—or which, for dubious demands of objectivity, opts for the placeless, cultureless formalism of geometrical exercises.

Opposed to this rigid "conservative" front, which bands together the "secular arm of functionalism" and the "organicism" now overflowing with the uncontrolled imagination, are the few but clear voices of heresy.

The present essay seeks to clarify the meaning of this heresy, which informs the most vital works of the new Italian architecture. It aims to establish, that is, a sense of avant-garde, progress and architecture within the opacity in which we are immersed, in an attempt to grasp those few centimeters of difference that, as Le Corbusier used to say, separated a good architect from a bad one.

We shall therefore have to give up the idea of tracing a precise, distinctive movement, not because this would be too arduous or simplistic, but because it would prove too inadequate to describe the *Alexandrian situation of contemporary Italian architecture.*

The wide range of historicistic recuperations and the breadth of figurative interest would render pointless any attempt at systematization using the normal tools of architectural criticism. Moreover, even the recent theoretical contributions of Manfredo Tafuri, Vittorio Gregotti, and Nino Dardi fail to reassure us about the death of architecture as much as they convince us of its programmatic ambiguity and complexity and encourage us about the assumptions of a relaunching inferred from penetrating readings of international architecture.

We shall therefore proceed according to differences, negatively, seeking to remain as farsighted as possible, without the comfort of European, American, or Japanese examples.

We shall begin by saying that there is no avant-garde in Italy, or that if there is, and such is what we wish to call it, it has nothing to do with architecture.

It is rather in the field of design and its most recent extensions into the utopias of the city and its outlying areas that such a term, with all its cultural ambiguities, may be applied. The recent promotion of Italian design at the clamorous fair of the Museum of Modern Art in New York (1972) certainly provided positive and useful publicity to Italian industrial crafts; it did not, however, produce clarity.

The "killing fields" of the most politically ruthless designers (the Strum group), Rosselli's accordions, or Zanuso's caravans have been associated, with typical commercial cynicism, with the offerings of the Florentine groups (9999, Archizoom, Superstudio), which some time ago, with their Anglo-Saxon companions, had won their place in the confused organs of the avant-garde, such as *AD* and *Casabella*.

It is therefore necessary to state precisely the terms of this avant-garde and the reasons for its absence in the world of architecture.

Usually anything that regresses, in this case Italian architecture, implies the logic of progress in a state of pause, the formulation, sometimes purely negative, of a new order of theoretical values and principles. This pause or change of mind, which is often and improperly singled out as the locus of the avant-garde, may present two different and contrasting paths of development: the utopia of the avant-garde, and the refounding of the discipline.

The first takes shape with the formulation of a negative thought that projects into the future all the figurative potential triggered by the rejection of the past. In its will to start over again from nothing, it denies history in order to find another point of departure, however illusory; and in so doing it easily achieves utopia and its isolation from reality. In short, it plays an essentially reactionary role since, with its self-exclusion, it helps to reinforce the situation it wanted to destroy.

Thus the groups of the Florentine avant-garde are of assistance to us the way dreams, not science, may be of assistance to us: they constitute a stimulus, a judgment, an apprehension, but they are unable, in fact, "to link together, as required, analysis and rapture." Pursuing a critique of social practice with essentially romantic slogans and attitudes, they arrive at an analysis that in its depth grasps the most corrosive sort of darkness but shrinks from the most evident necessities.

A typical example is provided by the "academics" of the Archigram group, who have a large following in Florence: the Plug-In City, which piles together traditional typologies, in disorderly fashion and with a bent for "disruption," in open organizational systems, producing nothing more than a rather unfortunate metaphor for the traditional figurations already in crisis.

In fact, in seeking new truths, these figurational experiences disperse, in the immediate, didactic image—which is not, at times, without a certain artistic appeal—the real raison d'être of scientific research: that is, the *refutation of mistakes*, which requires a vastly greater amount of time than that needed to know new realities.

Even if the pronouncement of new truths involves an area typical of the discipline, in asking itself the question of what the new city will be like and how it should be inhabited—and thus in advancing hypotheses of formal or purely cultural prefiguration—this avant-garde aspires to architecture without managing to be structured by it. Thus the urbanistic propositions of Archizoom converge, even while coming from the opposite side, with the abstractions of the most far-flung, second-rate prefigurations, such as those exhibited in the architecture section of the recent Kassel show ("Dokumenta 5," 1972).

Louis Kahn, with whom one might well not share certain formalistic "contaminations," has expressed an opinion, with considerable irony, concerning these positions. In a conversation with the students of Rice University, he emphasized how certain utopian propositions are nothing more than transpositions of language from other more scientifically advanced disciplines already capable of technically resolving the projected image. "When we set about planning the future," Kahn said, "something rather ridiculous might come out, because it is all that can be done at the present time. Some are able to concretize an image. But it is what is possible today, not a foreshadowing of how things will be tomorrow." And Paolo Soleri's termitariums in the Arizona desert are obvious proof of this.

The world of advanced technologies becomes the reference point, even if it is only romantically felt, for getting smoothly beyond utopianism. It is therefore natural that the most technologically advanced countries serve as the continuous reference point for this avant-garde, which in Italy is particularly well entrenched in Florence.

Although it would be simpler to single out the reasons for these sympathies in the provincialism of Italian culture, and of Florentine culture in particular, it is perhaps more useful to attempt briefly to discuss the historical assumptions of this attitude, which one also encounters, with more disconcerting results, in the professional activity of certain Tuscan architects.

To Michelucci we owe the revival, in 1925, of the *need for the fantastic* in Florentine architectural culture, which was launched in a magazine bearing the significant name of *Fantastica*. At a time when rationalism had not yet consolidated itself in Italy, Michelucci wrote: "For reasons of environment and tradition we feel the need for melodious, musical movements. . . . Modern constructions should conquer a few illogical, unexpected elements. . . . Movement is an indication of inner life and of lasting conquest." Later, after rationalism had acquired an indisputable authority and diffusion, "rationalist Florence" managed to absorb and neutralize the very same open rejection of historicism and naturalism that rationalism championed. Thus Pagano, in 1931, speaking of the exhibition of drawings at the School of Architecture at the University of Florence, could say: "In modern architectural history Florence has slept in the shadow of the eternal construction of the Biblioteca Nazionale, or has racked her brains in the disciplines of restoration, or has resigned herself to the nonchalant stylism of Piazza Vittorio Emanuele; San Miniato was left to the observations of Berenson, and the arcade of the Badia of Fiesole was downright lacking in 'details' for having taken a lesson in parsimony from the former church."

The experiences of Ricci, and those of Savioli and his picturesque school, are the autobiographical episodes of a culture that through history, local traditions, and the overcoming of rationalism by the fantastic and by informalism, would culminate in the later Michelucci's "fables" in his church along the Autostrada del Sole.[6] ("If under the guise of fables—*si sub velamento fabuloso*—there lies a meaning, it is not useless to compose fables.")

In this cultural hinterland, the Florentine avant-gardes develop in accordance with the typical Italian model, which, in Edoardo Persico's words, "is shaped in imitation of the foreign and resorts to every trick in the book to hide the fact that it has no doctrine."[7]

These Florentine groups (with the exception of Superstudio, given their special attention to disciplinary debates), after a quick pass through those sciences that are supposed to verify them, fall apart when the technological cloud dissolves in the "final unmasking": the production of graceful, disruptive objects. Technology, apparently exorcised in comic-book shrieks, thus reveals itself to be the crude ideological expression of the very same system one had wanted to negate. The stylistic seal, as presupposition of commodification, reduces these formal prefigurations to the world of objects, consumption, and obsolescence.

The definition of style and its "variations" resolves the utopian tension simply in a kind of design that is different from the rest, perhaps more costly, but equally petulant and banal.

The clarity and simplicity of the mechanism linking the arrow with its target run undramatically through the "histories" of Archizoom, Superstudio, and 9999. Their stage lies above reality, even if a few of its most disturbing fragments appear in reality. But nothing is dramatic: everything is capable of slipping into the everydayness of a Superstudio checked table, or refreshing itself with the vegetables of 9999, or arousing our curiosity with the candidness of Archizoom's No-Stop City.

But it is actually not the images that disturb, but their motivations; the images remain silent before the progress of the discipline, since they understand progress simply as change, mutation, *diversity*, and not as active, operative *clarification*. If in some way they happen to be stimulating or thought-provoking, this occurs, in the best of cases, as if by way of a Sironian suburb or a De Chirican Piazza d'Italia.

These positions are of interest not so much for their contents, then, as for their raisons d'être, for the conditions that they implicitly denounce.

Their cultured infantilism provides us with useful information toward an understanding of the *difficulty of architecture* and, on a more culturally problematic level, of its impossibility, in certain respects. Toward an understanding, that is, of how, nowadays, the figure of the architect sees the possibility of *collective salvation*, especially in the professional sphere, as forever receding; and of how the strategy of confusion, which mixes commodity and culture, works continually and daily on the scale of values with the imitative mobility typical of talent that always accompanies any attempt to surpass this scale, thus leading one to identify, as the target disappears, that which one wishes to combat as the combat itself.

In this colossal intellectual waste the avant-garde manages not even to be harmful, but simply to be useless. It is, however, a uselessness that is not a subtraction, but an ideological begging of the question, which finds the quality of art to be the most stimulating autobiographical goal.

This "artistic" uselessness, which one can also trace in the new architecture, is subtended, in the avant-garde, by a refusal; architecture, on the other hand, attains it through the necessity that binds the image to reality. And it is precisely on the basis of a common *feeling of the times*, of the futility sensed in the face of cultural and political irrationalism, that the two positions each choose a different road.

Valéry's *Eupalinos* evokes, in exemplary fashion, what the avant-garde alternative is for us: the constructive will-to-form that logically orders life's spontaneity. "I am niggardly of musings," says Eupalinos, "I conceive as though I were executing. No more now, in the shapeless void of my soul, do I contemplate those imaginary edifices, which are to real edifices what chimaeras and gorgons are to true animals. But what I think, is feasible, and what I do, is related to the intelligible."[8]

What Eupalinos is describing is the tautology of architecture, the necessity of its logical clarity, its simplicity and its operative rationality: the image that describes itself. Naturally, however, it is a real image, built from real materials, for a real world: the place of the possible, today.

But if on the one hand we deny the evasiveness of art, the sterile abstractness of geometrical exercises, or the planning of the metropolis "in a single stroke," then what sort of operative field do we have? And in what way can we realistically set in motion impulses of renewal of the discipline?

It must be said at once that there is no precise answer, since solutions are not the exclusive domain of our will. They depend fundamentally on the fate of the democracy and civic progress of a country: they are collective, not individual choices.

The "will-to-form" is, in architecture, a necessary and autonomous condition, but it does not in itself constitute a need for more effective political action; and even if it did, one would have to show in what way a certain type of architecture projects onto a given society and vice versa.

Thus it is not a question of "recognizing an autonomy alongside the social function of architecture, but an autonomy as a corollary to the social function of architecture."[9]

Thus once we have dismissed the possibility of prefiguring a new reality only through the power of ideas or images, all that is left is to refuse compromise, take cognizance of the social reality in which we are immersed, and prepare ourselves technically with properly "honed" tools and forms.

Italian architecture, which is sullying our suburbs and ruining our historic city centers, is "tired"; it is unable to answer our questions because political and interdisciplinary compromise have used up whatever stimulus to renewal it might have had.

The new architecture's "renunciation" is actually a full historical awareness. The many projects designed in the universities or for the sham of competitions clearly exhibit instances of disciplinary renewal in those alternative settings that are the *universities* and the *competitions*. The new architecture's will to progress, though it has little chance of being realized in construction, gives rise to patient, precise research, without compromises but also without dreams.

The wait for better times and better tools, which in the 1950s saw Italian progressivist architectural culture delegate its own activity to professionalism, and which today is proposing that one abandon the discipline for political involvement or avant-garde escapism, is the most present of historical traps today. And if much of the new architecture is still only designed or written, the reason should be sought in that operative trap which since the days of Fascist dictatorship has created a deep split between intellectuals and politicians. This is why the so-called reconstruction of the postwar period "had no experience in willing, projecting or even constructing the physical city, because there no longer existed that idea of the city—the moral city, the political city, the economic, social, human city—by means of which alone, and by measure of which alone, it is possible to build the city of architects, made up of houses, streets, ports, factories, and other such things."[10]

This situation of profound mistrust and inherent cultural crisis, which separates, as we have said, the destinies of the avant-garde from those of the new architecture, still has an area of light: those *rare cases* mentioned at the start of this essay. Today the healthiest architectural culture, the one that concretely defends architecture as an autonomous fact, as a discipline, works both individually in its search for congenial themes and techniques, and collectively in those free zones that certain university architecture departments (as in Venice) manage to maintain for the hope of many and the benefit of few.

Architecture thus quietly carries on, even though, despite all the drama of its insolvency, it is becoming only a will-to-planning and a "memory" of architecture, and the architect's situation has been reduced to that of a man at a drafting table.

With the *geometric locus* where it was formed and developed (the university) having been destroyed, progressivist architectural culture continues to consolidate its own *logical locus* through writings, competitions, conferences and the creative imagination as free human experience.

Even though government repression after 1968 led to the forced diaspora of the best professors, their intentions, programs, ideas and images have remained, even in the minds of individuals, and they have constituted the most dependable reference-point for the sort of pause and change of mind that, at the start of this essay, I juxtaposed with the bombast of the avant-garde.

This second sort of critical attitude, which in its analysis is creating the new architecture, opts not for invention or the great idea, but rather moves patiently and perhaps more surely through a process of *clarification*. Like every truly scientific attitude, this position, which for the sake of brevity we shall call the "Tendenza," does not discover new truths, but aims at the elimination of errors in a process of knowledge centered on historical and formal analysis, on the study of the city as a product, and on the characteristics that lead a certain kind of architecture to be projected onto a certain part of society.

For the Tendenza, architecture is a cognitive process that in and of itself, in the acknowledgment of its own autonomy, is today necessitating a refounding of the discipline; that refuses interdisciplinary solutions to its own crisis; that does not pursue and immerse itself in political, economic, social, and technological events only to mask its own creative and formal sterility, but rather desires to understand them so as to be able to intervene in them with lucidity—not to determine them, but not to be subordinate to them either.

This cultural position, which has its roots in the legacy of the modern movement as handed down by such masters as Giuseppe Samonà and Ludovico Quaroni, defines itself negatively, opposing what Nino Dardi calls the "*Picturesque International*," which, in accordance with optico-perceptual evaluations, "brings together the secondary derivatives of expressionism and constructivism—Sacripanti's proposals and Moshe Safdie's associations, Michelucci's plasticisms and Scharoun's huts, Archigram's pop architecture, Candilis's inlaid plates, Venturi's geometrisms, Frei Otto's structures, Paolo Soleri's anamorphisms, Gunnar Bikerts's constructions, St. Florian's space capsules—and inevitably reduces the experience of architecture to a series of formal preconceptions in which the apparent freedom of the gesture is actually a limitation to unmotivated choices."[11]

Yet the Tendenza's recognition of a heritage in the modern movement does not mean mechanically absorbing it: the Tendenza accepts all history as *event*, as a "pile of simulacra," and perceives "our architectural culture as a static twilight bathing all forms, all styles, in an equal light."[12]

In this sense, one cannot recognize the Tendenza in the general principles "around which modern architecture has come to be developed, according to the content-oriented and ethical interpretation of it provided by Giulio Carlo Argan: (1) the priority of urban planning over architectural planning; (2) a maximum of economy in the use of the terrain and construction, for the purpose of resolving, if only at the level of a *minimum of existence*, the problem of housing; (3) the rigorous rationality of the architectural forms, which are seen as logical deductions (effects) from objective needs (causes); (4) the systematic use of industrial technology, standardization, mass prefabrication—that is, the progressive industrialization of the production of things having to do with everyday life (industrial design); (5) the conception of architecture and industrial production as factors conditioning the progress and the democratic education of the community."[13] The gap between, as Montale puts it, "the roaring thirties and the rattling fifties," prompts the new generations to look critically on the legacy of the modern movement, particularly on its choice of antihistoricism.

In this way, the book of architectural history, next to the universal drafting device, can become a real image for representing a new critical attitude and a new relationship with history, which for some has actually become the painful stuff of planning, if not the project itself.

The discussion of history thus assumes, for some of the most representative architects, a veritable unit of measure, not only for evaluating mutual differences, but also for calculating the individual *heretical distances* separating contemporaries from the modern movement.

Sigfried Giedion, recapitulating the architectural development of the 1920s in eight points, foregrounded, in the architects of the "third generation," a very strong relationship with the past. It might therefore be interesting to gauge the extent of this relationship in the work of Italian architects. But given the occasion for this essay, we would do well to limit ourselves to certain significant positions as examined by the Tendenza.

Manfredo Tafuri, one of the liveliest architectural historians in Italy, is, on this subject, at least as categorically defensive in his position as Bruno Zevi. Tafuri unequivocally asserts that "even today, we are obliged to recognize history not as a great reservoir of codified values, but as a vast collection of utopias, failures and betrayals." On the subject of its new instrumentalization, Tafuri's judgment leaves no way out: "As a tool of planning, history is sterile; all it can offer are solutions already taken for granted."

Tafuri, though an architect, is an excellent historian—that is, an architect who has chosen history as his field of autobiographical research. And he has done so with such dramatic, trenchant emphasis that in him, the historian's mask has taken on the dignity of the face. In a certain sense Tafuri can be considered one of the most passionate "planners" of the Tendenza, since the relationship to history, though "forbidden" in the designed architecture that he personally does not practice, contains a well-defined project, entirely thought out but no less important or suggestive than those that are "only" designed: a kind of meta-project that extends to all the architecture that is thought, designed and written.

One could say paradoxically that Tafuri is the Italian architect most "dripping with history." In fact Tafuri, who in Venice has succeeded in creating an important, aristocratic school of historians, does not claim *tout court* the death of architecture, as is commonly believed.

In a recent updating of an essay of his,[14] he partially withdrew the apocalyptic prophecy born of the complex cauldron of 1968. The drama of architecture today, for Tafuri, is that of "seeing ourselves forced to turn back to 'pure architecture,' an instance of form devoid of utopia, a sublime uselessness in the best of cases. Yet to the mystified attempts to dress architecture in ideological clothing, we shall always prefer," says Tafuri, "the sincerity of those who have the courage to speak of that silent, unrealizable purity." The reference to the planned and written work of Aldo Rossi is quite explicit here.

Aldo Rossi has the merit of having succeeded in lucidly formulating a Tendenza position which, in the Italian debate, constitutes, if not the only one, at least the most precise, and the one most pregnant with possible developments.

In defining the architecture of Aldo Rossi, the relationship to history is quite useful: "Roman monuments," says Rossi, "Renaissance palaces, castles, Gothic cathedrals, constitute architecture. They are part of its construction. As such they shall always return, not only and not so much as history and memory, but as elements of planning."[15] With a new kind of "operative critique," which Tafuri defines as "typological critique," Rossi assumes history as an uninterrupted event to be studied and explored, to be drawn and written; a world pregnant with magical evocations and inscrutable correspondences.

In planning, Rossi looks to history with an attitude that we shall define as *laconic*. As Ezio Bonfanti acutely noted in his fine essay on Rossi, we find ourselves "before an architecture that underscores its own sectionality and the existence of a limited number of elements"; and "the fact of using finished parts, veritable architectures, as elements, is the very precise choice of an architecture."[16]

By other routes, somewhat more tortuous and twisting, we find the relationship to history in the architectures of an "enlightened" professional such as Vittorio Gregotti.

His very situation as a mannerist compels him to look at history but not to touch it; the anxiety of contemporaneity, consumed in the lacerating convulsions of professional compromise, requires novelty, mutation; every imitation is closely watched. "History," says Gregotti, "presents itself . . . as a curious tool, the knowledge of which is indispensable; but once this is attained, it is not directly usable. It is a kind of corridor through which one must pass in order to gain access, but which teaches us nothing about the art of walking."[17]

Unlike Rossi, who composes *parts* and *pieces* of history without preclusions of time, Gregotti seems more ready to assume history by grasping its possible *variations*, digging out and eroding its most recent and sedimented layers, as in a refined *collage* using fragments with which we are already familiar.

History, for Gregotti, is above all the history of the modern movement, analyzed with the impatience of the gaze more than with the calm of the collector. Gregotti constructs contemporary ambiguity and complexity through complex erosions of form. He starts with the tautological and crystalline, at the very point, that is, where Rossi's project ends.

The true essence of comparison, most useful in tracing the paths of the new architecture, is thus to be found between simplicity and complication, between evocation and description, between the possibilities of the *type* and the repeatability of the *model*.

Complexity and *ambiguity* are qualities that Gregotti describes and Rossi evokes. With the historians lies the task of evaluating which road will have proved more fertile.

In the architectures of Gregotti and Rossi, beyond all autobiographical differences, we find echoed and measured all the observations that Manfredo Tafuri had made about the competition for the new offices of the Chamber of Deputies (1968).

"One thing," said Tafuri, "is certain: between experimentalism, whether positive or negative, and professionalism, no mediations are any longer possible." The *order* and *disorder* that characterized the projects presented [in the competition] were unable, in the dialectics between rationality and irrationality, to create a new order: "Wrapping oneself in silence and diving into the amusement park now confront each other, hermetic, disillusioned, abstracted. . . . Chaos and geometry: the two paths of modern art once again present themselves severed from each other, in a state of tension, searching for complementarity. In Berlin they confront one another symbolically: Scharoun's Philharmonie and Mies van der Rohe's pure prism seem, in their contrary absoluteness, to close the dialectic first opened by the German avant-gardes in the early decades of this century."[18]

For Italian architectural culture, the 1970s began with the gradual extinction of the debate and the pronounced decline of collective commitment. After the shameful government repression of 1970, 1971, and 1972, and the paralysis of the architectural departments hardest hit (Milan, Pescara, Rome, Florence, etc.), the cultural debate that had been most tenaciously rooted in such faculties is also now undergoing a long and dangerous apnea. And the outpatient coalition of rare and exhausted architectures is not enough to keep it alive. The rare projects given form or designed by the new generation of architects are not enough to constitute a new logic or to produce a sufficiently compact and substantial front to create a clash. Yet even if such were possible, one might ask: a clash with whom? The old guard formed by the likes of Albini, BPR [Belgiojoso-Peressuti-Rogers], Gardella, Ridolfi, Quaroni, and Samonà has not, in recent years, produced any works likely to spur the discipline, and the respect that the new generations do not hesitate to show them once again demonstrates how they have gradually "lost the center."

It is therefore no accident that the clearest voices are to be heard today in the avant-garde, despite all the mistakes we have seen, or else they are coming from the surviving bastions that progressive architectural culture is still able to maintain in the architecture faculties at Venice (Aymonino, Tafuri) and Palermo (Gregotti, Benevolo, Alberto Samonà) and around certain individual personalities barred from the universities after the repression (such as Aldo Rossi in Milan).

Quite rightly Vittorio Gregotti devoted the last paragraph of his pamphlet on Italian architecture to the "revolt of the architecture faculties": in 1969, Gregotti could still say that "it is no longer in the magazines, the factional groups, or professional production, but in the faculties that the discussion and even the planning of *Italian architecture* is carried forward, however laboriously, the little that it is carried forward today."[19]

And in the geography of university architecture departments, it is Milan that in the late 1960s made the most fundamental contribution to carrying forward the debate and realization of a school of thought bearing the characteristics of disciplinary autonomy.

It will therefore be useful to dwell a moment on the experience of the Milanese Sperimentazione (experimentation), since it was there, more than in other venues, that democratic instruction and student engagement were best able to create, if only for a few short years, a singular and perhaps unique meeting-point.

By 1967–68, at Milan, a number of well-defined politico-cultural positions emerged and faced off against each other, positions which for their exemplary nature managed to echo within the school of architecture the most conspicuous elements of the ongoing national debate.

Ernesto N. Rogers, Guido Canella, Aldo Rossi, Vittorio Gregotti, Franco Albini, Lodovico Belgiojoso, and Piero Bottoni are the cultural spearheads around which the most vital forces of the student movement took up positions.

In particular, the multi-chair course given by Rogers, Rossi, and Canella, centered around the planning-related subject of the "Theater in the City," gave rise to a clash of ideas that managed for the first time to involve architectural discourse in political engagement, and the analysis of the system of production in a profound critique of the university institutions themselves. And it succeeded in clarifying individual positions in the *facts of planning*, overcoming programmatic ambiguities and laying down the foundations for the institution of a Tendenza faculty.

What clearly emerges from this is first of all an overall critical vision. One realizes that in the university architecture departments—because of, on the one hand, the objective marginality of their institutional and economic role and the subsequent lack of development of an explicit demand for research aimed in this direction, and on the other, the cultural backwardness of professional arrangements within the discipline—no comprehensively organized and systematic work of research has ever been developed that might fit into the whole as a way of advancing the dispositions of the discipline.

Thus in 1967–68 the architecture faculty of Milan was the first to individuate, in dismantling the program of studies, the tool most essential for overturning the institutional relationships of power and thereby opening up a political space for establishing a new work of cultural and scholarly production.

The dialectical confrontation of forces, following diversified roles, brought out a series of politico-cultural positions, a development that outlined the direction of research in which to articulate the new organization of university labor.

This new articulation gave rise to three general, highly differentiated orientations that one still encounters today in the architectural debate.

The first denies disciplinary discourse in the specific sense in order to address itself to more general political problematics. The second is the one that may be defined as professionalism. The third attempts to posit the establishment of a school of architecture by restoring dignity and specificity to the disciplinary problem of architecture.

Of the first orientation, we may say that it is positive in those instances where it denounces the academic character of the disciplines and brings the themes of our society as a whole back into the university. Fatefully, however, it presumes a generality of intents, since it must make a choice even as it is spelling itself out.

Thus, beyond a series of motifs based on the "feelings of the times," this current ends up lacking in substance.

Professionalism, instead, represents the commodification of culture and establishes its objectives in the area of personal profit within a traditional bourgeois society, considered the model in which one should acritically insert oneself. From this derive, on the one hand, the processes of rationalization of the system (planning, industrialization, etc., considered in themselves to be absolute resolutions of architecture), and on the other, the didactic codification of the professional routine.

Lastly, the third orientation, the one informing the actions of the group directed by Aldo Rossi, proposes a *global refounding of architecture* in the terms set forth by the Tendenza; they want to give free rein to architecture without political, sociological or technological subordination or tutelage.

Within the Sperimentazione, the Tendenza broke down according to positions echoed in the nationwide architectural debate.

The position of those who had brought the need for a refounding of the architectural discipline into the schools, as its proper venue, clashed in programmatic fashion with the other two positions present in the Sperimentazione.

It is on the basis of these positions, which I have described, that the most substantial line of research was developed within the university in the late 1960s and early 1970s. In other faculties as well, the argument for the refounding of the discipline assumes ever greater import, though sometimes with a more "urbanistic" slant or with more attention being paid to the planning of the urban territory. In a special issue of the review *Controspazio* (nos. 5–6, 1972), an attempt was made for the first time to provide a framework for these researches, which could, with due caution, be considered the main vehicle of a renewal of the discipline.

I have, thus far, attempted to present a series of arguments that might shed light on what I consider to be the red thread of contemporary architecture in Italy: the Tendenza.

We have discussed the reactionary character of both the avantgarde and the dogmatism of the modern movement. And these critiques, in their mutual difference, have informed the discourse of the concept of architecture as discipline and of progress as a will to *clarification* and not simply change.

The discourse of history has been positively introduced not only to characterize the need for a foundational rethinking of the new progressivist forces, but also as the measure of an autobiographical relationship with architecture. Thus we have come to speak of that geometrical locus that played such a large, important part in the debates of the late 1960s: the architecture departments in the universities.

It might, at this point, seem logical to attempt to complete the picture and present the situation of contemporary Italian architecture with a vast panorama of works and ideas.

But this will not happen, for two reasons. First of all because the need for clarity cannot really be satisfied with descriptive digression; and one would run the risk of seeing the few theories in the process of formation debased by so many ridiculous attempts at application.

And secondly because, to use the words of Francesco Milizia, in every art reason dictates few rules, while pedantry multiplies them. Rules and models must therefore possess a maximum *typicality* in order to be comprehensible, to be able to acquire that didactic, transmissible value that becomes a necessity in scientific progress.

This conclusion will therefore be extremely partial and "tendentious" in the sense referred to by Baudelaire: in other words, "partial, passionate, political; that is, a point of view that opens the most horizons."[20]

We shall first discuss just what the Tendenza is in the new architecture. In confronting this difficult task I shall use few examples and a number of *historical references*. I shall also attempt to point out in what way the Tendenza situates itself on the progressivist front of the *New Architecture* that Nino Dardi has recently brought together and defined in his interesting book.[21]

Dardi, however, dwells predominantly on the international panorama, thus losing an opportunity to concretize a number of Italian resonances that deserved perhaps to be treated more centrally.

It would therefore be useful to outline briefly, with all the injustices that brevity implies, the configuration of the progressivist front, which can, in a certain sense, bear directly on the New Architecture.

In 1963 Francesco Tentori (editor-in-chief of *Casabella-Continuità*, under the direction of E. N. Rogers) presented a group of architects from Milan, Udine, and Trieste, who had joined together in an association under the name of "Incontri del Biliardo" (The Billiard Encounters).[22]

The group—which was actually very heterogeneous (A. Rossi, N. Dardi, V. Gregotti, C. Pellegrini, P. L. Crosta, G. U. Polesello, F. Tentori, G. Canella, E. Mattoni, etc.)—revolved around Rogers's *Casabella* and presented itself in the Italian debate with a profoundly critical attitude toward the 1950s, which had been "a distressing example, for architects, of the Italian path to *arrivisme*."

In subsequent years, many of them made significant contributions as professors (in Milan and Venice) and as the central figures of the most important architectural competitions (the Administrative Center of Turin, the Reconstruction of the Teatro Paganini at Parma, etc.). What they had in common was a militant critical engagement, aimed at calling into question, in the praxis of planning as in university teaching, the entire "doctrine" of the modern movement. This engagement succeeded in bringing the discipline, through the measure of politics, into a broader confrontation with the realities of the whole country, using "the written page not as occasional, detached activity, but as an expression fully consistent and commensurable with the planned work, almost the extension of a single cognitive process."[23]

On the occasion of his survey, Nino Dardi underscored, in the prospects for renewal, the need for a "reinvention of the architectural organisms," proposing the recuperation of certain fundamental moments in modern architecture. Guido Canella, like Vittorio Gregotti already active professionally, posited the need for "overturning the conventional relationship between abstraction and reality, where in the name of reality we are accustomed to accepting the brutal conditioning of an improvident, rapacious society, labeling all radical alternatives as abstract, and where what prove to be abstract are those propositions . . . in which one achieves an effective view of the essential politico-cultural themes of our age that await decisive revolutions."[24]

In more or less explicit ways, the common perspective was that of *architecture as a cognitive problem*, whether specifically as the "conscious call to the city on the part of the most recent modern architecture" (Canella) or as an autobiographical or personal matter (Rossi).

Already at that time, the work of Aldo Rossi (based on studies in Lombard neoclassicism, in Antonelli, Ledoux, Loos, and Le Corbusier, and in the urban morphology and building typologies of Milan) appeared to be the leanest, the most linear, unbendingly aiming at a process of essentialization. "In my projects," said Rossi, "or in what I write, I seek to focus on a rigid world, with few objects, a world already established in its givens. . . . A position of this sort denies, and is unaware of, the whole process of *redemptive* attribution that the modern movement wanted to impute, as both attitude and formal result, to architecture and art. For this reason I personally—not polemically, but because the problem has a different dimension for me—have never distinguished between modern and non-modern architecture, with the understanding that it is simply a question of making a choice between certain types of models."

And on the subject of urbanism and the city, Rossi continued: "I wonder, and have wondered from the start, what urbanism really is. For now I am unable to see it as anything other than a morphological problem whose field of study is the cities and, in part, other territories. The description of the city's forms, and thus the invention—that is, the new formulation—of these forms, can help us to know and understand something extremely useful."[25]

Yet beyond the individual declarations that we have presented here, what "markings," what "pedigree" precedes the majority of these architects?

For many, Ernesto N. Rogers was an invaluable reference point. Director of one of the most prestigious international architectural reviews (*Casabella-Continuità* from 1953 to 1963), Rogers at the time was the only Italian architect with any international stature.

A friend of Gropius, Wright, and Le Corbusier and an active member of the CIAM, he brought the method and maieutic system of Gropius to his magazine and later to the architecture faculty of Milan (1953). His profound commitment to civil society and democracy, together with his acute syncretic intelligence, found in teaching a particularly congenial field of action. His editorials and lectures serve as the central argument for the most advanced sector of Italian architectural culture.

In the classroom, in particular, Rogers shaped the best of the latest generation. His lectures on the problems of the modern movement, on Wright, Behrens, van de Velde, Pagano, and Terragni, on democratic commitment in the university, remain exemplary; as does his slogan—*the utopia of reality*—utopia as "the teleological charge that projects the present into the possible future," and reality as the reasonable surpassing of contingent boundaries.[26]

Equally important is the second reference point, represented by the "culture" and irrepressible action of Giuseppe Samonà. Author of a book of fundamental importance to Italian architectural culture,[27] he was the outstanding dean, professor, and teacher of that miraculous creation that since 1945 has been the Istituto Universitario di Architettura di Venezia.

Alongside these two masters, an unusual and in some ways unique role was played by the "urbanist" Ludovico Quaroni, who, together with the typological studies of Saverio Muratori,[28] the formal rigor of Luigi Moretti and the solitary civic engagement of Mario Ridolfi, constitutes the most incisive point of reference that the Roman school has to offer to the "Incontri del Biliardo."

Here one could extend the "genealogical" picture of this group by discussing the refinement of Ignazio Gardella and the subtle poetics of Franco Albini rather than the rationalism of Piero Bottoni, but I shall resist this nevertheless tempting prospect in order to limit this brief portrait to the essential.

It should suffice to add that the "Incontri del Biliardo" have had increasing difficulty taking place, and that personal affairs and the passage of time have gradually led some away, pushed others to the background, and brought still others to the foreground.

The internal struggles at *Casabella*, followed by the liquidation of the "Rogers staff," eventually shattered that syncretism that had already begun to crack with the polemics over neoliberty and the departure of Vittorio Gregotti in 1961.

This is a good point at which to make an observation. The scattering of the group into various university sites (Rossi, first to Venice and then Milan, Canella to Milan, Aymonino to Venice, Gregotti to Palermo) slowly led to the eclipse of their genealogical references, due to the emphasis of the different directions of their research. Thus when speaking today of the Tendenza, we can no longer include Gregotti's research on the *environment* or Canella's studies of the "consolidation and integration of several functions," and scarcely, and only because of the common theoretical foundations, can we liken the researches of Carlo Aymonino and Aldo Rossi, though they are now clearly differentiated from each other on the planning level.

The "scuola di Rossi" in Milan, for example, became wide-spread. One could say that the numerous thesis projects appearing in architectural reviews[29] and exhibition catalogues starting in 1967 bear witness to an unusual consistency and homogeneity that acquires the dignity of "contribution," freeing itself from the formal mimesis of the epigone. Moreover, from his array of assistants have come some theoretical and planning contributions of great value: one need only mention Giorgio Grassi's book[30] and his didactic role first as Rossi's assistant in Milan and later as professor in the department of architecture at the University of Pescara.

It is therefore necessary to realize that the Tendenza has by now achieved an unquestionable presence and authority thanks to the precision of its *forms* and to the clarity of its *principles*. From Aldo Rossi's book[31] to the contributions of Giorgio Grassi and Carlo Aymonino,[32] to the work of *diffusion* conducted after 1969 by a few editors of *Controspazio* (up to the dissolution of the Milanese editorial staff in 1973), the Tendenza succeeded in providing a real alternative to the facile utopias, to the abstraction of "revolutionary" discourse, and to geometrical research as an end in itself, and in finally confronting the sovereignty of the most accredited Italian professionalism in the field (Gio Ponti, P. L. Nervi).

An early attempt to historicize the Tendenza was made in Vittorio Gregotti's book.[33] In defining the three new orientations of Italian architecture, Gregotti individuated the Tendenza in the orientations present in Milan and Venice. Its "center of attention [lies] in the relationship between urban typology and morphology and especially in that aspect which defines the idea of architecture" as testimony and persistence. This follows a line of reasoning that through the notion of monument tends to link the neoclassical architects of the French Revolution with the example of Loos and one side of Le Corbusier, and manages (via the most rigorously objective German rationalists such as Hannes Mayer and Klein) to include as well one aspect of Kahn."

This attitude, which Tafuri defined more precisely as one of "typological critique," contrasts with the other two singled out by Gregotti (the "environmentally" oriented one, and that concerning "methods" of planning).

From Gregotti's description emerge a number of elements that constitute some, if not all, of the principles to which one may legitimately link the concept of Tendenza: the strict relationship to history, the predominance of urban studies, the relation between building typology and urban morphology, monumentality, and the importance of form.

Actually, certain particularly important concepts are left out of this classification, and even those listed might seem insufficient if we did not explain them in greater depth.

The concept of monument, which Italian critics have savagely and naively attacked, has a specific tradition within the progressive ranks of the modern movement.

Giedion himself, who can rightly be considered the "founder" of the modern movement, had already found a "new monumentality" to be the requirement and most advanced element of certain kinds of progressivist architecture. And one could go back to the criticism and projects of Edoardo Persico (at the Salone d'Onore of the 6th Triennial) to better understand how the "question of monumentality" presented itself to Italian rationalist architecture in the 1930s.

Persico himself, in a 1934 article, warned against the dilettantism of *content-oriented critics* who, faced with the monumental style of the Palace of the Soviets and the similar Palazzo del Governo in Taranto, found themselves forced to express a paradox: "Does a Fascist house have the same 'content' as a house for the Soviets?"[34] This paradox still has its latter-day supporters today, who counter the "reactionary content" of the "monument" with the democracy of formal emptiness, and in simplistic, banal fashion distinguish between the "free" plan and the "closed" (central) plan, between *monolithism* and formal mushiness, placing each on opposite ideological sides in almost Manichean fashion.

We shall not pause to refute these paradoxical positions, since good sense prevents us from doing so. A few clarifications might, however, be in order.

Monumentality is based above all on a need that emerges from a more than superficial examination of the *urban phenomenon*. Indeed, the destiny of the community seems to express itself "with characteristics of permanence" at those physically and psychologically pivotal points that are urban monuments. One of the most important contributions of the "scuola di Rossi" to the foundation of an urban science is having individuated within the *city as product* the dialectic between primary elements (monuments) and residential areas. In particular, says Rossi, "monuments, signs of the collective will expressed through the principles of architecture, seem to present themselves as primary elements, fixed points of the urban dynamic."[35]

This conception of the *city as work of art* has specific reference points in the work of Lévi-Strauss and even more in the thought of Maurice Halbwachs, who finds the typical nature of urban reality to lie in the characteristics of imagination and *collective memory*.[36]

In this conception of the city, the monumental highlights above all the outgrowths (dimensional and qualitative) around which the urban topography revolves. For the Tendenza, however, its role, which might be seen only to concern the results of historical and formal analysis, lies also and above all in planning as an *indication of simplicity and formal rarefaction*.

The choice of monumentalism thus comes to convey a new vision of the city. It critiques the undifferentiated expansion and misery of quantity deceptively guided by the tools of *zoning*, in a city in which one might instead recognize and design the *parts* organically related to its structure: *city parts* within which the *relationship between urban morphology and building typology* would isolate and foreground those collective fixed points around which the private city builds and transforms itself.

What the city today is in danger of losing forever is its own consciousness, its individuality, its character of civilization. It is on the verge of losing (like Milan) its historic center, devastated by the service-industry invasion, which has destroyed those precious signs that once culturally anchored the city's transformations and development to an awareness of its own history.

The *new monumentality* thus implies a demand for *unity* and *simplicity*. It is a response that is supposed to counter the disorder of the modern city with the clarity of *few but decisive rules*. It expresses a wish to recuperate definitively a *character* of the city, by starting with *simplicity* of the needs of the collective spirit and with the feeling of *unity* in the means used to satisfy them.

The concept of monumentality also aims to recuperate a new dignity for art, whether it is the art identifiable in the city plan, in the city's texture as product [*manufatto*], or in the single building. Moreover, "the monument" foregrounds the collectivity dominant in the very structure of the city and controls it, so to speak, "democratically." On a more broadly social level, the choice of monumentalism opposes the consumerism of the private city, the artificial demand for the new—since, with the growth of the needs of capitalist society, private interests tend to search for *minute combinations* unable to satisfy real needs but efficient in continually creating new ones, both on the physical and psychological levels. And satisfying the *desire for novelty* seems in the end to be one of those circumstances shaped by the few to the detriment of the many.

But as we said at the start, progress is not novelty and change, or at least it does not necessarily presuppose them. If anything, progress is clarification, a passage from the complicated to the simple. In architecture it implies simplicity, unity, symmetry and correct proportions, typological clarity, homogeneity between plan and elevation, and negation of disorder, however justified it may be to represent symbolically the crisis of a culture.

Here we have attempted to present a new meaning of "monument" (*mnema*): that concept which in architecture has always expressed, in the solidity and size of the edifice, the collective *character* as a *demonstrative property* of the common goal by means of formal expression.

A particularly convincing definition of monumentality as compositional and theoretical system is presented in Dardi's book: "The systematic use of geometry, the frequent manipulation of scale and distortion of dimension, and the renewed attention paid to orchestrating the different materials within the disciplinary sphere of composition, constitute the distinctive features of the monumentalist tendency; but they are also, at the same time, the elements that make up the research of the most interesting currents in the architectural production of recent years. This is why the only way to spur the monumentalist revival, if we wish to avoid the shoals of an aberrant idealism . . . must be based on the conviction, to quote Aldo Rossi once again, that architecture is a permanent, universal, and necessary fact."[37]

It must be pointed out, however, that Dardi offers a definition deduced from *readings* of architectural objects, objects not his own: the "distinctive features" he singles out are eminently formal and scarcely theoretical at all.

I instead would like to foreground the fact that the Tendenza, despite its "distinctive features," cannot make up its mind, and wears itself out in the search for a *style*, methodologically sought. The Tendenza, in its methods, denies the determinism between form and function, which is based on a faith in the "positive" objectivity of the givens. It sets itself up as a *system*, with its own geography of choices and theoretical principles that style measures and brings into form.

It is therefore useful to proceed with an analysis of the principles we singled out above.

We have seen that the city as product, and the relationship between residential areas and monuments, define the main field of interest of the Tendenza. We have attempted to explore the concept of monument. Now we shall discuss a second aspect of this conception of the city: the foregrounding of *typological questions*.

In this second perspective, typology is singled out as the foundation of architecture. And *type* is defined as "something permanent and complex, a logical proposition that is prior to form and comes to constitute it."[38]

The notion of type, for the Tendenza, represents one of the principles of architecture, a rule that is far more important in ordering images than in creating them, and which in any case helps to keep "violations" within the path of the discipline.

Quatremère de Quincy has given an exemplary definition of type, one worth quoting here to shed light on our discussion:

The word "type" presents less the image of a thing to copy or imitate completely than the idea of an element which ought itself to serve as a rule for the model. . . . The model, as understood in the practical execution of the art, is an object that should be repeated as it is; the type, on the contrary, is an object after which each [artist] can conceive works of art that may have no resemblance. All is precise and given in the model; all is more or less vague in the *type*. At the same time, we see that the imitation of types is nothing that feeling and intellect cannot recognize, and nothing that cannot be opposed by prejudice and ignorance. . . . In every country, the art of regular building is born of a preexisting source. Everything must have an antecedent. Nothing, in any genre, comes from nothing, and this must apply to all of the inventions of man. Also we see that all things, in spite of subsequent changes, have conserved, always visibly, always in a way that is evident to feeling and reason, this elementary principle, which is like a sort of nucleus about which are collected, and to which are coordinated in time, the developments and variations of forms to which the object is susceptible. Thus we have achieved a thousand things in each genre, and one of the principal occupations of science and philosophy, in order to understand the reasons for them, is to discover their origin and primitive cause. This is what must be called "type" in architecture, as in every other field of inventions and human institutions.[39]

The idea of architecture that arises from this definition is an unequivocal one, and its clarity may be of great help to us in developing, on the one hand, an historico-analytical discourse, and on the other, the discourse of greatest interest to us at the moment, that is, that of planning.

In confronting the problem of planning we must thus give up the idea of treating the problems of *history, type,* and *monument* with the methods of historical and formal analysis—those, that is, that rely on scientific knowledge and experimentation (observation, classification, and comparison).

The persistence of the central plan or the elongated lot (as in Gothic mercantile building) over the different urban forms (radiocentricity, linearity) constitute, in the project, not objects for classification, comparison and observation, but possibilities on the basis of which one may make real choices.

Of essential concern to planning, therefore, is a *theory of architecture* in which the theoretical principles guide the formal choices through a *genealogy of reference* spanning the typologies of history and materials projected, written, and thought. This genealogy reaches the project through the *techniques* that extend beyond the autobiographical moment without excluding it.

In this complex gamut of elaboration lies a dialectic between the generality that practical thought tends to maintain and the breakdown of principles that art stimulates as it approaches the object.

The *relationship to history* is resolved as a scenario in which the object is perceived against a background of other objects, and in relation to them. The range of techniques is expressed in the *variations* with respect to the type, just as the techniques distort the formal vocations of the model.

The type, on the other hand, can be rationalized and defined according to its rules; the more it evokes form, the more it tends to elude the crystallization of the model, enriching itself with unforeseen experiences and attributions. And if it is true that the fundamental content of form is formal, and that beauty is what best adapts to the useful, it can also be asserted that the formal content of a beautiful form is, so to speak, functional. Reversing the terms of a noted axiom, the New Architecture may show that function follows form. Indeed, form as tangible manifestation of type, of norm, is either itself functional (in all its variations) to the norm, finding its usefulness in the beautiful, or else typological form embraces the utilitarian dimension through its openness to the transformations of use—i.e., to function.

By way of concluding this essay, I shall attempt to explore a number of "established" compositional rules on the basis of which further research may be pursued. In short, the goal of these final considerations should be to outline a *treatise of composition,* but given the limitations of space, I shall only set forward a number of assertions.

We have seen how history can be viewed from different angles (Tafuri, Gregotti, Rossi) and how, in particular, having established its necessity, the Tendenza opted for a relationship with a history understood as the *history of types* and of constitutive elements, and not as a training ground for stylistic and formal imitation (*contaminatio*) or as a demonstration of its uselessness. From this angle one may note a characteristic intrinsic to the concept of type: I am referring to its *migratory* possibilities in time and space, and thus to its openness to *transformations of use*. We are well aware, in fact, of how, in leaping over certain sacred, privileged areas (like the modern movement), history may tend to reassert types whose use derived from remote social conditions and different or no longer current functions. One need only think of how, in the New Architecture, the classical has recovered, with varying degrees of success, a centrality that would have been unthinkable to the dogma of the modern movement; or of those compositional procedures aimed at inserting elements and entire individuated architectures into new logical and functional contexts.

In many of his projects, Aldo Rossi has demonstrated the *correctness* of this procedure, which he calls *distributive indifference* and juxtaposes with *typological indifference*, i.e., disorder.

"Distributive indifference," explains Rossi, "is proper to architecture; the transformation of ancient buildings . . . is factual proof of this. It has the power of law; such examples as the transformations of the amphitheaters (Arles, the Coliseum, Lucca, etc.), even more than urban transformations, show that maximum architectonic specification—in this case the monument—potentially offers maximum distributive freedom, and in a more general sense, maximum functional freedom. Architecture's independence of function is demonstrated by many different paths."[40]

It seems clear that the point of transfer between history and planning can be summarized in the conception of type as architectural principle, and that invention in design can be practiced from a perspective indifferent to functions and references of time and place—that is, through *analogies*.

A further observation can be made concerning the migratory nature of the type through history. In the gamut of projects the type, as a rule, is carried to the point where, once a formal choice has to be made, it precipitates of necessity into a model. It is at this point that a process of rarefaction occurs, similar to that which presided over the formation of a logical universe of principles (theory of architecture).

The project thus acts upon the hypothetical model by attempting to bring it back as closely as possible to the type. With a procedure typical of art, it attempts—to use Paul Klee's words—to liberate the crystalline from the murkiness of the real.

In the best of cases what the project gives back is a new *description* of the type; but it is in this very description that we realize the analogical role played by creative individuality.

Without entering too deeply into the difficult terrain of creativity, we can observe, by looking once again at the architecture of Aldo Rossi, that distributive indifference is not only a different way of using the type, but also involves a graduated selection from among the constituent elements of architecture. What happens, in other words, is that in Rossi's architecture the additive approach, proceeding by pieces and parts, exhibits techniques that are differentiated in the description of like or contiguous elements.

The *off-scale*, the *repetition* of like elements, the juxtaposition of a gigantic order with a dwarf order, the use of like objects in *different logical contexts*, all this acts upon the objects of history with a laconic astonishment, as though they were being encountered for the first time.

We shall call this method *estrangement*—with reference to the literary procedure, proper to the Russian formalist school (Shklovsky), that consisted of describing a familiar object or situation as though it were being seen for the very first time, without acknowledging or naming it.

By way of summary, we may thus suggest some elements to serve as guides for planning.

Once a *theory of architecture*, based on logically interconnected principles (monument, type, city as product, and their interrelationships, etc.), has been formulated, we may move on to the definition of a *treatise of composition* for which we have, for now, isolated several rules: *distributive indifference* as to the *type as principle of architecture*; the *migratory characteristics* of types, with "types" intended as recurrent themes; and the *estrangement* of models or their parts.

One final consideration is in order here. I would like to underscore the importance ascribed to architecture as *form* and to recapitulate, from a compositional point of view, the implications underlying the concept of monument. The concept of monument of interest here is not that which one might encounter in the range of the plan, the elevation of masses, the solidity of the construction, the symmetry and beauty of the proportions; or at least it is not only and exclusively this.

I have already pointed out its implications on an urban level (monument as opposed to residential area); now I would like to define it in terms of the programmatic character that naturally underlies the monument.

The image of the monument is the one perhaps most easily grasped by everyone, and for this very reason we shall use its *realism* as an *indication of simplicity*.

From the compositional point of view, the monument immediately hearkens to a demand for *simplicity and compactness* of form: what we might call the *conciseness* of beauty.

Leonidov, who will one day take his rightful place alongside Le Corbusier and Mies van der Rohe, has said: "If, in spite of everything, form is necessary (content must have a form), then form too must be perfect."[41]

The monumentalist choice lies in this search for the perfection that is classicism in architecture. It would be too easy to renounce these affirmations for fear of being accused of neoclassicism and neo-Enlightenmentism. I shall say only that what classicism the monumental expresses lies in the simplicity and dignity of the volumes, or better yet, in "the assumption of a given logical structure, the *rational consideration of the fundamental rules of architecture*."[42]

The architectural works of Oud, Behrens, or Tessenow would thus be attributable to "a monumental simplification . . . that draws them from its essentiality, that is, from its absolute focus on expressing itself as intelligible and rational . . . as the stimulus of a fundamental idea."[43]

Notes

1. Camillo Boito, "Sullo stile futuro dell'architettura italiana," introduction to *Architettura del Medioevo in Itaia* (Milan, 1880).
2. Bruno Zevi, "Pluralismo e pop-architettura," in *L'Architettura* 143 (September 1967).
3. Bruno Zevi, "Architettura," in *L'Espresso*, special issue, December 1965.
4. Polemic between Aldo Rossi, Carlo Melograni, Paolo Portoghesi, et al., presented in *Controspazio* 10–11 (1971), and 5–6 (1972).
5. G. C. Argan, *Arte moderna 1770–1970* (Rome: Sanson, 1970), p. 612.
6. The "Sun Highway," which runs from Florence to the Tyrrhenian Sea. [Translator's note.]
7. Edoardo Persico in *Il Rosai*, November 1930.
8. Paul Valéry, *Eupalinos, or, The Architect*, trans. William McCausland Stewart (London: Oxford University Press, 1932), p. 21.
9. E. Bonfanti, "Autonomia dell'architettura," *Controspazio* 1 (1969), pp. 24–29.
10. Ludovico Quaroni, "L'architettura, crisi e speranza," in *Architettura italiana anni sessanta* (Rome: Stefano De Luca, 1972).
11. N. Dardi, *Il gioco sapiente, tendenze della nuova architettura* (Padua: Marsilio, 1971), p. 21.
12. F. Tentori, "D'où venons-nous? Qui sommes-nous? Où allons-nous?" in *Aspetti dell'arte contemporanea*, catalogue of the exhibition at L'Aquila, July 28–October 6, 1963 (Rome: Edizioni dell'Ateneo, 1963), pp. 264–265.

13. Argan, *Arte moderna*, pp. 324–325.

14. Manfredo Tafuri, "Per una critica dell'ideologia architettonica," *Contropiano* 1 (1969) [translated in this volume]; now updated in *Progetto e utopia* (Bari: Laterza, 1973).

15. A. Rossi, letter to F. Tentori in Tentori, "D'où venons-nous?"

16. E. Bonfanti, "Elementi e costruzione—note sull'architettura di Aldo Rossi," *Controspazio* 8–9 (1970).

17. V. Gregotti, *Il territorio dell'architettura* (Milan: Feltrinelli, 1966), p. 133.

18. M. Tafuri, *Il concorso per i nuovi uffici della camera dei deputati* (Rome: Edizioni Universitarie Italiane, 1968), p. 85.

19. V. Gregotti, *Orientamenti nuovi nell'architettura italiana* (Milan: Electa, 1969).

20. C. Baudelaire, "Salon de 1846," in *Oeuvres complètes* (Paris: Gallimard, 1961).

21. Dardi, *Il gioco sapiente*.

22. Tentori, "D'où venons-nous?"

23. Ibid.

24. Ibid.

25. Ibid.

26. E. N. Rogers, "Utopia della realtà," *Casabella* 259 (1962).

27. G. Samonà, *L'urbanistica e l'avvenire della città negli stati europei* (Bari: Laterza, 1959).

28. On the role played by S. Muratori in the founding of urban science, see M. Scolari, "Un contributo per la fondazione di una scienza urbana," *Controspazio* 7–8 (1971).

29. See the special issue of *Controspazio*, no. 5–6 (1972), devoted to planning research in university architecture departments in Italy.

30. G. Grassi, *La costruzione logica dell'architettura* (Padua: Marsilio, 1967).

31. A. Rossi, *L'architettura della città* (Padua: Marsilio, 1966).

32. C. Aymonino, *Origini e sviluppo della città moderna* (Padua: Marsilio, 1971); see also C. Aymonino, A. Rossi, et al., *La città di Padova* (Rome: Officina, 1970).

33. Gregotti, *Orientamenti nuovi*.

34. E. Persico, "Due palazzi: a Ginevra e a Mosca," *Casabella*, October 1934.

35. Rossi, *L'architettura della città*, p. 13.

36. M. Halbwachs, *La mémoire collective* (Paris, 1950).

37. Dardi, *Il gioco sapiente*.

38. Rossi, *L'architettura della città*, p. 31.

39. Antoine Chrysostome Quatremère de Quincy, "Type," in *Encyclopédie Méthodique, Architecture*, vol. 3, pt. II (Paris, 1825), trans. Anthony Vidler, *Oppositions* 8 (Spring 1977), pp. 148–149.

40. A. Rossi, "Due progetti," *Lotus* 7 (1970).

41. P. A. Aleksandrov, *Ivan Leonidov* (Moscow, 1971).

42. Grassi, *La costruzione logica dell'architettura*.

43. Ibid.

Manfredo Tafuri   **"L'Architecture dans le Boudoir: The Language of Criticism and the Criticism of**

Language" *Oppositions* 3 (1974); expanded in Manfredo Tafuri, *The Sphere and*

the Labyrinth: Avant-Gardes and Architecture from Piranesi to the 1970s, trans.

Pellegrino d'Acierno and Robert Connolly (Cambridge: MIT Press, 1987); slightly

modified here

see Tafuri (31–33)   Though Tafuri's position on contemporary architecture had already been enunciated in his 1969 *Contropiano* essay, it was necessary that he elaborate his thesis in an explicit engagement with the most advanced architecture of the American neo-avant-garde and of the Italian experiments of Rossi and others—necessary because the formation of his own theoretical and historiographic position owed a great deal to a confrontation with those contemporaneous architectural practices. First presented as a lecture, "A Theory of Criticism," in April 1974 at the conference "Practice, Theory and Politics in Architecture," organized by Diana Agrest at Princeton University,[1] "L'Architecture dans le Boudoir" was first published the same year in *Oppositions* as the introduction of Tafuri's work to an American audience.

see Scolari (133–134)

For Tafuri, the historical avant-garde was a premonitory aestheticization of precisely the subjective alienation and dispersion that would arrive fully geared up (or wound down to nothing) in the postwar consumer culture of America; and the advanced architecture of the present is little but a bathetic replay of the avant-garde's self-destructive project, now relegated to the boudoir. Though his title is taken from the Marquis de Sade's *Philosophie dans le boudoir*, and the theme of the return of language from Michel Foucault's readings of Sade, Tafuri's conceptualization of the estranged, eroticized space of a self-isolated language could equally have come from Roland Barthes. Throughout the first paragraphs of his essay reverberates the painful discovery in Barthes's "Myth Today" of counterideologies' utter uselessness against the hegemony of bourgeois culture and of critical language's impossible alternation between the destruction and the mystification of its object.[2]

"The return to language is a proof of failure," asserts Tafuri; but that return is not so much chosen by the architect as it is imposed by the regressive conditions of present consumer society, "bored and in need of sedatives."[3] The "removal of form from the sphere of the quotidian" is not "because of any incapacity on the part of the architect, but rather because this 'center' [of discourse, of order] has been historically destroyed." *Erlebnis*, the space of life as actually experienced, now excludes the space of form; architecture's position in the relations of production is limited, if, indeed, it has any influence at all. And thus architecture faces the aporia of the desire to communicate and the awareness that communication is no longer possible. An architectural language that takes itself as its object is the experience of this historical limiting condition.

compare 72

The result is an architecture of excess and emptiness; criticism must violate and pass through the object of such an architecture to the system that gives the object's meaning. A passage from Foucault aptly summarizes Tafuri's problematic:

Words are like so many objects formed and deposited by history; for those who wish to achieve a formalization, language must strip itself of its concrete content and leave nothing visible but those forms of discourse that are universally valid; if one's intent is to interpret, then words become a text to be broken down so as to allow that other meaning hidden in them to emerge and become clearly visible; lastly, language may sometimes arise for its own sake in an act of writing that designates nothing other than itself.[4]

And yet, the lesson of Barthes is that there is a certain legitimate pleasure to be taken in the neo-avant-garde's architecture of the boudoir. Tafuri, citing Barthes's *The Pleasure of the Text*, allows as much in the final passages of "The Ashes of Jefferson," his last statement on the neo-avant-garde.

The pleasure of the subtle mental games that subjugate the absoluteness of forms . . . : there is clearly no "social" value in this. And, in fact, is not pleasure perhaps on the whole egoistic and private? It is too easy to conclude that these architectures perpetrate a "betrayal" vis-à-vis the ethical ideals of the modern movement. They register, rather, the state of mind *of someone who feels himself betrayed*; they reveal to the very depths the condition in which he who still wants to make "Architecture" is confined.[5]

Notes

1. The other speakers at the conference were: "on practice," Rem Koolhaas, Jorge Silvetti, Mario Gandelsonas, and Adolfo Natalini; "on theory," Peter Eisenman and Lionel March; "on politics," Kenneth Frampton, Melvin Charney, and Franco Raggi.
2. "In a bourgeois culture, there is neither proletarian culture nor proletarian morality, there is no proletarian art; ideologically all that is not bourgeois is obliged to *borrow* from the bourgeoisie. Bourgeois ideology can therefore spread over everything and in so doing lose its name without risk: no one here will throw this name of bourgeois back at it. . . . It can exnominate itself without restraint when there is only one single human nature left. The fact that we cannot manage to achieve more than an unstable grasp of reality doubtless gives the measure of our present alienation: we constantly drift between the object and its demystification, powerless to render its wholeness. For if we penetrate the object, we liberate it but we destroy it; and if we acknowledge its full weight, we respect it, but we restore it to a state which is still mystified. It would seem that we are condemned for some time yet always to speak *excessively* about reality." Roland Barthes, "Myth Today," in *Mythologies,* trans. Annette Lavers (New York: Hill and Wang, 1972), pp. 139, 159.
3. Manfredo Tafuri, "The Ashes of Jefferson," in *The Sphere and the Labyrinth: Avant-Gardes and Architecture from Piranesi to the 1970s*, trans. Pellegrino d'Acierno and Robert Connolly (Cambridge: MIT Press, 1987), p. 301.
4. Michel Foucault, *The Order of Things: An Archaeology of the Human Sciences* (New York: Random House, 1970), p. 304.
5. Manfredo Tafuri, "The Ashes of Jefferson," p. 302.

To work with degraded materials, with refuse and fragments extracted from the banality of everyday life, is an integral part of the tradition of modern art: a magical act of transforming the formless into aesthetic objects through which the artist realizes the longed-for repatriation in the world of things. It is no wonder, then, that the most strongly felt condition, today, belongs to those who realize that, in order to salvage specific values for architecture, the only course is to make use of "battle remnants," that is, to redeploy what has been discarded on the battlefield that has witnessed the defeat of the avant-garde. Thus the new "knights of purity" advance onto the scene of the present debate brandishing as banners the fragments of a utopia that they themselves cannot confront head-on.

Today, he who wishes to make architecture speak is thus forced to resort to materials devoid of all meaning; he is forced to reduce to degree zero every ideology, every dream of social function, every utopian residue. In his hands, the elements of the modern architectural tradition are all at once reduced to enigmatic fragments—to mute signals of a language whose code has been lost—shoved away haphazardly in the desert of history. In their own way, the architects who from the late fifties until today have tried to reconstruct a universe discourse for their discipline have felt obliged to resort to a new "morality of restraint." But their purism and their rigorism are those of someone who is aware that he is committing a desperate action whose only justification lies in itself. The words of their vocabulary, gathered from the lunar wasteland remaining after the sudden conflagration of their grand illusions, lie precariously on that slanting surface that separates the world of reality from the solipsism that completely encloses the domain of language.

It is precisely several of these salvage operations that we wish the language of criticism to confront: after all, to historicize such deliberately antihistorical projects means nothing more than to reconstruct, as rigorously as possible, the system of ambiguity of metaphors that are too clearly problematic to be left isolated as disquieting monads.

We must immediately point out that we have no intention of reviewing recent architectural trends. We shall, instead, focus attention on a few particularly significant attitudes, questioning ourselves about the specific tasks that criticism must assume in confronting each case. It is necessary, however, to bear in mind that every analysis that seeks to grasp the structural relations between the specific forms of recent architectural writing and the universe of production of which they are functions requires doing violence to the object of analysis itself. Criticism, in other words, finds itself forced to assume a "repressive" character, if it wishes to liberate all that which is beyond language; if it wishes to bear the brunt of the cruel autonomy of architectural writing; if it wishes, ultimately, to make the "mortal silence of the sign" speak.

As has been perceptively pointed out, to Nietzsche's question "Who speaks?" Mallarmé answered "the Word itself."[1] This would seem to preclude any attempt to question language as a system of meanings whose underlying discourse it is necessary to "reveal." Therefore, wherever contemporary architecture ostensibly poses the problem of its own meaning, we can discern the glimmering of a regressive utopia, even if it simulates a struggle against the institutional functions of language. This struggle becomes evident when we consider how, in the most recent works, the compositional rigorism hovers precariously between the forms of "commentary" and those of "criticism."

The most striking example of this is the work of the British architect James Stirling. Kenneth Frampton, Reyner Banham, Mark Girouard, Alvin Boyarsky, Joseph Rykwert, and Charles Jencks have all contributed to the difficult task of determining the meaning of Stirling's enigmatic and ironic use of the "quotation."[2] But in some of his more recent works such as the headquarters of the Siemens A.G. near Munich, the Olivetti Training Centre in Haslemere, and the housing development for Runcorn New Town, one has wanted to detect a change of direction, a breaking away from the disturbing composition of constructivist, futurist, Paxtonian, and Victorian memories of his university buildings at Leicester, Cambridge, and Oxford and of the Civic Centre designed with Leon Krier for Derby.[3] And yet, the parabola covered by Stirling does possess a high degree of internal coherence. It clearly demonstrates the consequences of reducing the architectural object to a syntax in transformation, to a linguistic process that wishes, nevertheless, to challenge the tradition of the Modern Movement, that is, to be measured against a body of work strongly compromised in an "antilinguistic" sense. Stirling has rewritten the "words" of modern architecture, constructing an authentic "archaeology of the present."

Let us examine the design of the Civic Centre in Derby. An ambiguous and wry dialogue with history is established by the old Assembly Hall facade, tilted at a forty-five-degree angle and serving as the proscenium for the theatrelike space created by the U-shaped gallery. In fact, the entire architecture of Stirling has this "oblique" character. The shopping arcade at derby echoes the Burlington Arcade in London. But it also recalls the bridge of Pyrex glass tubing in the Johnson Wax Building by Frank Lloyd Wright and, even more strongly, an architectural scheme that was never built nor even designed: the shopping arcade in the form of a circular Crystal Palace, which, according to the description of Ebenezer Howard, was to have surrounded the central space of the ideal Garden City. In fact, the Civic Centre in Derby is also an urban "heart." Except that it is part of a real city, not a utopian model, and, consequently, the allusion to Paxton takes on the flavor of a disenchanted but timely *repêchage*.

Unlike Kevin Roche and I. M. Pei, for whom every formal gesture is a hedonistic wink addressed to the spectator, Stirling has revealed the possibility of an endless manipulation of the grammar and the syntax of architectural signs, exercising with extreme coherence the formalist procedures of contrast and opposition: the rotation of axes, the montage of antithetical materials, and the use of technological distortions.[4] With Stirling's work a new *ars rhetorica* is installed at the heart of an investigation that has very little to do with those of Denis Lasdun or Leslie Martin, both of whom are also committed to employing hermetic metaphors under the sign of a self-satisfied "Englishness." Stirling's "symbolism," in fact, is based upon the extenuation of form, an extenuation that, as in his most recent works, can very well reach the point of deforming language, of exhausting it. But it always remains an exhaustion that stops short of a complete shattering of language. The works of Stirling are "texts," not explosions of an imaginary utopia. The results of such an operation of controlled *bricolage* can be seen in a metaphoric reference to one of the subjects most dear to the English architect: the architecture of ships.

James Stirling and
Leon Krier, Derby Town
Centre, 1970

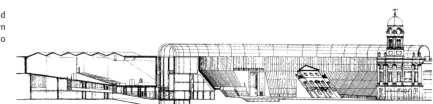

"A dream with marine associations" is how Kenneth Frampton has accurately described the Leicester University Engineering Laboratory, a virtual iceberg that navigates in the sea of the park in which it is casually placed, according to a mysterious course.[5] And even though Stirling does not seem to enjoy the "fishing for references" on the part of the critic, the porthole that emerges ironically from the podium of the laboratories at Leicester, alongside the jutting Melnikovian halls, would seem to confirm that constructivist poetics are one of his occasional sources—an all-too-obvious reference to the design for the Palace of Labor (1923) by the Vesnin brothers. But the theme of the ship returns, this time freighted with literary allusions, in the terracing, in the overall organization, and in the planning of the common passageways of the Andrew Melville Hall of St. Andrews University. It is again Frampton who observes that here the naval metaphor has a deeper meaning:[6] the ship, like the phalanstery, is the symbol of a community will that proves unattainable. (Is it mere coincidence that the fourth meeting of CIAM was held aboard a ship?) The ship, the monastery, and the phalanstery are thus equivalent; in striving to reach a perfectly integrated community, they isolate themselves from the world. Le Corbusier and Stirling seem—at La Tourette and St. Andrews respectively—to set forth a painful discovery: social utopia is only worthwhile as a literary document and can enter into architecture only as an element, or better, as a pretext. The dynamic atmosphere of the English "angry young men" of the fifties and of the Independent Group, of which Stirling was a member from 1952 to 1956, thus has a coherent result. Stirling's articulation of language, based on the interweaving of complex syntactic valences and ambiguous semantic references, also includes the "function," the existential dimension of the work. The problem is that it deals only with a "virtual function" and not an effective function. Andrew Melville Hall "represents" in theatrical form the space of community integration that—from the Spangen superblock (1912–21) of Michael Brinckman to the Narkomfin housing project (1927) of Moisei Ginzburg, to the postwar plans of Le Corbusier and of Alison and Peter Smithson, to the construction of the Park Hill residential complex (1957–65) in Sheffield and the Robin Hood Gardens complex (1960–64) in London[7]—the orthodoxy of the Modern Movement had hoped to make act as a nucleus of social precipitation.

Suspending the public destined to use his buildings in the limbo of a space that oscillates between the emptiness of form and a "discourse on function"—that is, architecture as an autonomous machine, as is announced in the library of the history faculty building at Cambridge and made explicit in the project for the Siemens A.G.—Stirling executes the cruelest operation possible by violating the sacred canons of the semantic universe of the modern tradition. Neither attracted nor repelled by the autonomous articulation of Stirling's formal machines, the spectator is compelled, in spite of himself, to recognize that this architecture does indeed speak a language of its own, one that is, however, perversely closed within itself. It is impossible to participate in this language "by living it"; instead, one can only tread water or swim in it, forced into a vacillating course, itself just as vacillating as the sadomasochistic game the architect plays with his linguistic materials. Stirling, usually so reluctant to "explain" his own architecture, confirms these last observations in some notes written in 1974 as an outline for a lecture delivered at Carnegie Mellon University in Pittsburgh:

The combination of neutral forms and significant forms, sometimes focusing on a central significant point with neutral extensions (Olivetti Training Centre), or vice versa (Andrew Melville Hall, St. Andrews), sometimes placing a projection that "acts as a facade" against a neutral background, even when an urban context is involved (Civic Centre, Derby; the Arts

Centre, St. Andrews). The "causal" exhibition of maintenance tools, such as ladders, tracks, cranes, etc.[8]

Neutral forms juxtaposed against evocative images, then, and attributions of semantic depth—the "casual exhibition"—to accessories elevated to the rank of protagonists: a full-fledged poetics of the *objet trouvé* is contained in the words of Stirling, who confirms his intention to "clear away" the traditional logic of structures in order to allow them to fluctuate in a metaphysical play.[9] This claim is borne out by the close reading, deliberately confined to the syntactic level, that Peter Eisenman has performed on the Leicester Engineering Building.[10] According to Eisenman, Stirling carries out at Leicester a systematic "conceptual destruction": where the nature of the materials seems to call for a "full" iconic figure—the laboratory tower, composed of brick cut into by bands of raked glass windows—Stirling reduces the solid volume to a paper-thin surface; where the glass would seem to suggest a dematerialization—the block of sheds or the office tower—he treats the glass as a prism, thereby making it contradict its "natural" evanescence. Thus a process of erosion appears to pervade the "strong" forms—typical is the handling of the cement columns of the office tower, emphasized just at the point at which they are about to be absorbed by the glass prism—whereas the "weak" forms undergo an inversion of their function. But in the cantilevered struts that support the body of the sheds, this play of programmatic inversions reveals itself in all its ironic force: their "literal void," as Eisenman points out,[11] is, at the same time, a conceptual solid."

Eisenman contends that the writing of the building for Leicester University represents a unicum in the work of Stirling and cannot be placed in a unhistorical continuum with the writings employed by him at Cambridge or Oxford.[12] And yet, all of Stirling's work takes place under the sign of *distortion*. That which at Leicester appears the product of conceptual inversion takes form elsewhere as the opposition between linguistic elements and the context, an opposition no less polemical than those inversions. The problem is always how to mediate the hermetic metaphors, intrinsic to the finds uncovered by his archaeological excavations of the tradition, and their assemblage. Not only in the Florey Building at Oxford, but also in the projects for the Olivetti headquarters in Milton Keynes, the Wallraf-Richartz Museum in Cologne, and the Landesgalerie Nordrhein-Westfalen in Düsseldorf,[13] the reassemblage follows two seemingly divergent laws: on the one hand, it imitates the mechanical world; on the other, it reduces the formal assemblages, obtained by the accumulation of forms, to a succession of "events." The "casual exhibition" is not limited to secondary elements, but applies as well to principal structures. The *objets trouvés* are set into astonishing juxtapositions, either through their surreal encounter with the landscape—the Olivetti headquarters in Milton Keynes—or their no less surreal encounter with preexisting seventeenth-century and Victorian structures—the Arts Centre of St. Andrews University or the Olivetti Training Centre in Haslemere. Here irony turns into self-irony, as if to demonstrate that a rewriting based on fragments of other texts requires the use of a hieroglypics whose code can be cracked only by a chain of subjective associations.

This explains in large part why many of Stirling's formal machines appear to be crystallized in the moment of their collapse. The projects for Selwyn College, for the Florey Building, for the Olivetti headquarters at Haslemere assume the aspect of structures violated and fixed by a photographic lens an instant before their explosion. The aggregation follows, then, the path of uncertainty and alliteration. Like Raymond Roussel, Stirling is imprisoned within the chains of associations evoked by the "available words" selected by him: in this light, the frequent references to the architecture of Hawksmoor take on a new significance.[14]

Commentary and criticism, as we have previously mentioned, prove to be superimposed in such an operation. Commentary takes the form of a repetition desperately in search of the origins of signs; criticism takes the form of an analysis of the functions of the signs themselves, once that search for the pristine meaning of signs has been abandoned. The operation carried out by Stirling is exemplary: it condemns the utopia inherent to the attempt to salvage an architecture as "discourse." In this light, the criticisms that are constantly leveled at Stirling in the name of functionalism are at the same time correct and unwarranted.[15] Once having artificially reconstructed the autonomous system of linguistic structures, these criticisms can only play themselves out in an interplay of tensions between the world of signs and the real world.

All of this leads us back to our initial problem: in what manner does criticism become compromised in such a "perverse play," under whose ambiguous sign the entire course of modern architecture wavers? At the origins of the critical act, there always lies a process of destroying, of dissolving, of disintegrating a given structure. Without such a disintegration of the object under analysis—as we have already made clear in the introduction to this book—no further rewriting of the object is possible. And it is self-evident that no criticism exists that does not retrace the process that has given birth to the work and that does not redistribute the elements of the work into a different order, if for no other purpose than to construct typological models. But here criticism begins what might be called its "doubling" of the object under analysis. The simple linguistic analysis of architecture that confines itself to speaking only of the work's status as language laid bare would result in mere description. Such an analysis would be unable to break the magic circle that the work has drawn around itself, and, consequently, it would only be able to manipulate the very process by which the text produces itself, thereby repeating the laws of this productivity. The sole external referent of such a completely "intrinsic" reading of the object under analysis would have to be found in the gaps, in the interstices of the linguistic object. Thus, this "doubling" engendered by criticism must go beyond the mere construction of a "second language" to be kept floating above the original text, as theorized by Barthes and realized by Stirling.[16]

The discourse on language requires still further elaboration. Criticism must determine with precision its tasks with regard to architectural proposals that fold in upon themselves, that refer to and reflect themselves, if only because today they are the most apparent. We arrive at the limit-case: wherein the nonlinguistic residues in the architecture of Stirling and Louis Kahn—those aspects of the real world that have not been converted into form—are suddenly eliminated; wherein the absolute presence of form renders "scandalous" the presence of chance—and even that expression *par excellence* of chance, human behavior. The work of Rossi is an excellent litmus paper for checking the effects of a problematic that inexorably divides the entire course of contemporary art.[17] Rossi answers the poetics of ambiguity of a John Johansen, of a Charles Moore, or of a Robert Venturi with the freeing of architectural discourse from all contact with the real, from all incursions by chance or by the empirical into its totally structured system of signs.

The "scandal" of Stirling's architecture is constituted by man, as he is forced to ricochet between architecture as pure object and the redundancy of hermetic messages, deranged by a "rhetoric of interruption." The architecture of Aldo Rossi eliminates such a scandal. Its reliance upon form excludes all justifications from outside. The distinctive features of architecture are inserted into a world of rigorously selected signs, within which the law of exclusion dominates. From the monument of Segrate (1965) to the projects for the cemetery in Modena (1971) and for student housing in Chieti (1976), Rossi elaborates an alphabet of forms that rejects all facile articulation. As the abstract representation of the inflexibility of its own arbitrary law, it makes artifice into its own domain. By such means, this architecture reverts to the structural nature of language itself. By deploying a syntax of emptied signs, of programmed exclusions, of rigorous limitations, it reveals the inflexibility of the arbitrary—the false dialectic between freedom and norm inherent to the linguistic order.

The emptied sign is also the instrument of the metaphysics of De Chirico, of the oneiric realism of the *neue Sachlichkeit*, and of the mute enigma projected onto the object by the Ecole du Regard.[18] "The world is neither significant nor absurd"—writes Robbe-Grillet, placing himself anachronistically *before* Weber, Wittgenstein, and Mies—"It is, quite simply. . . . And suddenly the obviousness of this strikes us with irresistible force." This gives rise to the poetics of the inhuman declaimed with a contradictory anguish, barely disguised: "to construct from nothing a world that stands on its own feet without having to lean on anything external to the work." With these three attempts, Rossi has in common only a sort of frustrated nostalgia for the structures of communication. But for him it is a communication that has nothing to speak about except the finite character of language as a closed system.[19] Mies van der Rohe had already experimented with the language of emptiness and silence—the *unio mystica* of solipsism. But for Mies, the reification of the sign still occurred in the presence of the real, that is, in direct confrontation with the "swamp of the cities." In Rossi's work, however, the categorical imperative of the absolute estrangement of form is in effect, to the point of creating an emptied sacrality: an experience of fundamental immobility and of the eternal recurrence of geometrical emblems reduced to ghosts.[20] There is a specific reason for this phenomenon. The result at which Rossi arrives is that of demonstrating, conclusively, that his removal of form from the sphere of the quotidian is forced continually to circumnav-

Aldo Rossi, *The Analogous City*, 1976

igate the central point from which communication springs forth, without being able to draw from that primary source. This is not so because of any incapacity on the part of the architect, but rather because that "center" has been historically destroyed, because that "source" has been dispersed into multiple streams, each without beginning or end. It is precisely this "revelation" that Rossi's architecture seems to offer; the superimposition of the triangular hollow on the emptied cube, in the courtyard of the De Amicis School (1971) in Broni, is clearly emblematic of this. Around those "cuttlefish bones" circles the question that they disdainfully drive away from themselves.

If a neo-Enlightenment attitude is discernible in Rossi, it can be understood as a mode of compensating for the irreparable act perpetrated in the eighteenth century: the fragmentation of the "order of discourse." Only the ghost of that lost order can be held up today. And the accusations of "fascism" hurled at Rossi mean nothing, given that his attempts to recover an aristocratic ahistorical status for forms preclude naive verbalizations of content and all compromise with the real.[21] Through such attempts, this research loses itself in one last endeavor to save a humanistic ordinance for architecture. The thread of Ariadne with which Rossi weaves his typological research does not lead to the "reestablishment of the discipline," but rather to its dissolution, thereby confirming in extremis the tragic recognition of Georg Simmel and György Lukács: "a form that preserves and is open to life, does not occur."[22] In his search for the Being of architecture, Rossi discovers that only the "limit" of Being there is expressible.

This gives rise to a theoretical result of fundamental importance, one that has, in fact, been taken for granted by contemporary culture, but that is continually laid aside. The rejection of the naive manipulation of forms, maintained by Rossi, concludes a debate that was fought personally by Loos in his early years and that in Karl Kraus has its strongest spokesman. Kraus writes in 1914:

In these great times, which I knew when they were small, which will become small again, provided they have time left for it . . . in these loud times, which boom with the horrible symphony of deeds that produce reports, and of reports that cause deeds; in these unspeakable times, you should not expect any word of my own from me—none but these words which barely manage to prevent silence from being misinterpreted. Respect for the immutability, the subordination of language before this misfortune is too deeply rooted in me. In the empires bereft of imagination, where man is dying of spiritual starvation while not feeling spiritual hunger, where pens are dipped in blood and swords in ink, that which is not thought must be done, but that which is only thought is inexpressible. Expect from me no word of my own. Nor should I be capable of saying anything new; for in the room where someone writes the noise is so great, and whether it comes from animals, from children, or merely from mortals shall not be decided now. He who addresses deeds violates both word and deed, and is twice despicable. This profession is not extinct. *Those who now having nothing to say because it is the turn of deeds to speak, talk on. Let him who has something to say step forward and be silent!*[23]

If it is the turn of deeds to speak, then nothing else remains except to let deeds speak and to preserve in silence the holy ark of great values: of these—Kraus, Loos, and Tessenow all agree on this—"one cannot speak," at least not without contaminating them. Loos expresses it clearly. Only that which evades life can elude the refusal to speak through architecture: the monument (the artificial creation of a collective memory, the true "parallel action" of men "without qualities") and the tomb (the illusion of a universe beyond death).[24] One can construct such virtual spaces, only in the service of virtual, that is, illusory functions.

It is useless to dismiss Kraus and Loos from such considerations with too much haste, while it is even more harmful to make Kraus and Loos serve as the introit to the thought of Wittgenstein.[25] He who must "step forward" to "be silent" certainly has nothing in common with the lapidary proposition seven of the *Tractatus logico-philosophicus*: "What we cannot speak about we must pass over in silence." If the Krausian critique of language is only a *beginning*, if it is still part of the *ethical* sphere, it is also true that its lucidity—"I am only one of the late followers, who inhabits the old house of Language"—makes Kraus "our contemporary" by virtue of its excessiveness. Much more Krausian than one thinks is the caustic irony of the "architects without architecture," or the silent manipulators of their own modesty. Contemporary architecture, in fact, is far too fascinated with not wanting or not knowing how to decide whether the noise that enters the room "comes from animals, from children, or merely from mortals" not to follow Kraus's ineluctable command to make out of keeping silent the new, last word. It is certainly true, as Brecht cruelly remarked in *On the Rapid Fall of an Ignoramus*, that Kraus always "spoke about the ice at the North Pole to those who already were cold" or showed "how useless is the desire to proclaim the truth when one does not know what is true." And yet, our neo-avant-gardes, more or less knowingly, operate today *under the sign of Kraus*. This obliges us to come to terms with their "indecent" fascination.

"The word is indecent": Hugo von Hofmannsthal had come to this conclusion already in his youth, only to repeat it later in *The Difficult Man* (1918). In the *Letter to Lord Chandos* (1902), he declared: "In truth, the language in which I would have wished not only to write but also to think is not Latin, nor English, Italian, or Spanish, but the *language in which mute things speak to me* and in which perhaps one day from the tomb I will be able to exculpate myself in front of an unknown judge." The language in which "mute things" speak is the one spoken by the "islands of the air" that Hofmannsthal writes about in *Andreas*: it is the language that Rossi would like to hear and *to make heard*.

The ineffable attracts all the more strongly the less we are conscious that words which are unpronounceable and yet utterable "do not produce," precisely because they cancel—by wishing to make it manifest—the *mystical* of Wittgenstein. For this reason, the late followers who delude themselves into thinking themselves able to inhabit "the old house of Language" believe that the "return to nature"—the *tristes tropiques* of Aldo van Eyck or the landscapes inhabited by the *silent witnesses* of Hejduk—involves, as an inevitable consequence, biting into the apple of knowledge offered by an Eve eager to accept the serpent's invitation. They find themselves "beyond good and evil," and for their mute writing, the "beyond" is proposition seven. The wearing out of material suffered by Klimt, by Mahler, by Mies has apparently taught them nothing. Or better, they think they can remain in that state of suspended animation which accompanies that wearing out. But if the long voyages of no return that, from Piranesi to Mahler's *Lied von der Erde*, mark the stages of the long goodbye to the ancient homeland of certitudes have enabled us to recognize the *necessity of the lie*, it would be a grave error to mistake for one's new "duty" the standing at the edge of the dock to wave goodbye perpetually to the "friend" who is leaving. To split oneself in two, to make oneself at the same time the friend who departs and the friend who remains behind: and yet, this is certainly not the plurality to accept or, at any rate, not the one to celebrate. However, it is also useless to hand lighted matches to a man who is freezing. The instancy of form is nothing but such a "match": time consumes it rapidly, without offering an *Erlebnis* to redeem the suffering.

The aforementioned statement by Lukács, at this point, could very well be inverted: the space of life, of time as it is actually experienced, excludes the space of form or, at least, holds it constantly in check. In the Gallaratese Quarter in Milan, in opposition to the moderated expressionism of Carlo Aymonino, who articulates his residential blocks as they converge upon the hub of the open-air theatre in a complex play of artificial streets and tangles, Rossi sets the hieratic purism of his geometric block, which is kept aloof from every ideology, from every utopian proposal for a "new lifestyle."

The complex designed by Aymonino wishes to underscore each solution, each joint, each formal artifice. Aymonino declaims the language of superimposition and of complexity, in which single objects, violently yoked together, insist upon flaunting their individual role within the entire "machine." These objects of Aymonino's are full of "memories." And yet, quite significantly, Aymonino, by entrusting to Rossi the design for one of the blocks in this quarter, seems to have felt the need to stage a confrontation with an approach utterly opposed to his own, that is, with a writing in which memory is contracted into hieratic segments. It is here that we find, facing the proliferation of Aymonino's signs, the *absolute sign* of Rossi, involuntarily and cunningly captured by the play of that proliferation.

The position taken by Kraus and Loos is not negated; it is only rendered more ambiguous. Since it is the turn of deeds to speak, form may keep silent: the new word, the "eternal lament," is condensed into allusive symbols. The coexistence of objects, heaped together in constructivist fashion and obstinately forced to communicate impossible meanings, and a mute object, closed within its equally obstinate timidity, recapitulates in an exemplary fashion the entire "drama" of modern architecture. Architecture, once again, has fashioned a discourse on itself. But, this time, in an unusual way: as a dialogue, that is, between two different modes of architectural writing that arrive at the same result. Not by chance, in the *liceo* in Pesaro, Aymonino pays homage to his silent friend. The noise of Aymonino and the silence of Rossi: two ways of declaiming the guttural sounds of the yellow giants in which, as we have already noted, Kandinsky had personified the "new angels" of mass society.

These observations are validated by a significant document: the illustration presented by Aldo Rossi at the Biennial of Venice in 1976, a graphic metaphor of his theory of the "analogous city." For that matter, Rossi had already accustomed us to evaluate as formal machines designs based on the combinatory manipulation of real and ideal places.[26] Analogical thought as an archaic symbolism only expressible through dehistoricized images? And why, now, such a belated proposal for an itinerary in the labyrinth of an urban dream, within which the fragment of a Renaissance treatise is equivalent to an eighteenth-century design or to one of Rossi's?

Even for Rossi's "analogous city," there is no real "site." Beneath the composition, there could very well appear the inscription, scrawled in childish handwriting, *ceci n'est pas une ville*, which would produce the same discursive slippage that occurs in Magritte's *Pipe*.[27] Nothing else remains except to play out the game proposed by the architect, throwing oneself into the deciphering and the recognition of the elements of his puzzle. As logbooks of elliptical voyages into *temps passé*, the montages of Aldo Rossi renew the desire for an ecumenical embrace with the dreamt-of reality. Yet such a wish to take in the whole of reality—object and subject, history and memory, the city as structure and the city as myth—expresses a state of mind that Michelstaedter has defined as "the anxiety of the persecuted beast." The "colossal humming" coming from the social machine (is it not the same noise heard by Kraus?), "which creaks in all its joints . . . but does not breakdown [because] this is its way of being, and there is no change in this smog,"[28] provokes, in the interlocutor of the *Dialogue on Health*, written by Michelstaedter in 1910, the anguishing question: "How can this cursed smog be broken through?" The answer offered by the Triestine writer is concise and concedes no alternatives either to the aloof *flâneur*, deluded into thinking he can pose as a "new Baudelaire," or to the man who would "save himself" by making his own stream of consciousness into the object of his own voyeurism:

Do you understand? The path is no longer a path, because paths and ways are the eternal flowing and colliding together of things that are and things that are not. But health belongs to the man who "subsists" in the midst of all this; who lets his own need, his own desire flow through himself and still "subsists"; who even if a thousand arms seize him and try to drag him along with them still "subsists," and through his own stability imparts stability to others. He has nothing to keep from others and nothing to ask from them, since for him there is no future, because nothing "awaits."[29]

"Subsisting" is thus elevated into a symbol for the contemplation of pain: the course of the real is immutable, but in such an acceptance of suffering, in such a negation of utopian alternatives, there lives the *duty of being aware*. Of this "duty"—the highest expression of upper-middle-class introspection—perhaps only Mies, in the architecture of our century, speaks by making of silence a mirror. Such a road excludes every further "voyage." Why take a "path that is no longer a path," especially if it only leads to self-description?[30] If, as Rossi has written,[31] "the lucidity of the design is always and only the lucidity of thought," there is no longer any room for those disturbing heterotopias that "shatter and entangle common names." Rossi, in his allegory of the "analogous city," attempts a magical operation: to unite the declaration of his own "subsisting" to a dried-up nostalgia. *Trieste and a Woman* is how he titles in 1974 his own project for the regional building in Trieste, explicitly alluding to those aspects of the city immortalized by Umberto Saba. But the Trieste of Saba had already been set into crisis by Svevo. The "woman" of Rossi is the Angiolina that Emilio creates for himself as a lie in *Senilità* (As a Man Grows Older). In this sense, the "subsisting" of Aldo Rossi is, contradictorily, in desperate search of a place in which to deposit its own "stability."

That such a place should be the labyrinth of "many beauties" gathered together in an ideal montage has an equally contradictory meaning. It indicates the need of a public to which to "ask something" and from which to expect responses. It is necessary to restore these reciprocal roles to their rightful places. It behooves one not to respond to those who seek a conscious "stability," yet actually wish at all costs to solicit assent. The keeping silent of criticism means, in such a case, rejecting the fragility of the poet, who expresses, *coram populo*, his own desire to stretch himself out, in front of his public, on a comforting Freudian couch.

To expose oneself even more than Rossi has done means to transfer architecture into a realm dominated by the "Icarus complex"; it means renewing Breton's dream of a purity entrusted to a waiting without hope. But then architecture would have to levitate, to take off and fly, like the *Sanity* of Malevich, like the *Letatlin*, like the utopian projects of Krutikov, or like, with greater coherence, the oneiric landscapes of Massimo Scolari.

Having lost its roots, the *contaminatio* between architectural graphics and dream deposited on paper indicates, in Scolari's work, that the "dwelling" place no longer is the city. The detailed watercolors of Scolari reveal neither the cynical play of Koolhaas nor the utopian tensions of the Krier brothers. Writing is everything in them; therefore, they speak of nothingness. The architectural landscape lives on as a private memory within which forms regain, without the use of subterfuges, a Kantian "beauty without purpose." Such coherence has an unquestionable critical value, even if it does not coincide with the one spelled out by the author:[32] it demonstrates that the incessant transformation of language, in the absence of matter—once the "spirit of the old mole" has been accepted[33]—is presented solely as an evocation of *autres* labyrinths. One can exit from these labyrinths only by agreeing to "sullying oneself" without restraint; the anxiety of purity is completely dissipated in them. Even the *boudoir* of Scolari is crowded with portraits of De Sade, but there is no place in it for the De Sade of Bataille.

Throughout this discussion, we have deliberately intertwined the analysis of specific phenomena with the search for a correct use of the instruments of critical inquiry. The examples chosen have proven useful precisely because in confronting them the very function of criticism becomes problematic and because, as limit-cases, they encompass a great part of the current debate on architectural language, as it extends from the work of Louis Kahn to that of the American neo-avant-gardes and of the Italian experimentalists such as Vittorio De Feo, Franco Purini, and Vittorio Gregotti.[34]

In writing about De Feo, Dal Co has spoken of "architecture as a suspended form."[35] And, in fact, the works of De Feo oscillate between the creation of virtual spaces and mannered typological exercises. The experimentation with the deformation of geometric elements is his dominant concern. From the project for the new House of Representatives in Rome, devised with the Stass Group (1967), to the Technical School at Terni (1968–74), the competition for an Esso service station (1971), and the project for the new communal theatre in Forlì (1976), De Feo treats geometry as a primary element to be made to clash with the chosen functional order. Compared with the purism of Rossi, the architecture of De Feo certainly appears more empirical and more open to chance. However, in its attempt to lay bare the intrinsic qualities of form, his architecture possesses a self-critical and self-ironic force that manifests itself most clearly in the exorbitant Pop image, in which the exasperated geometric play of the project for the Esso station is resolved. One can detect a warning here: once form has been "liberated," the geometric universe becomes the site of the most uncontrollable "adventure."

Certainly, similar works come about historically from reflections upon the new thematics introduced by Louis Kahn; but, in the particular case of the Italians, the exploration of linguistic instruments is conducted without any mystic aura and without any misplaced faith in the charismatic power of institutions. We find ourselves, therefore, faced with an apparent paradox. Those who concentrate on linguistic experimentation have lost the old illusions about the innovative powers of communication. Yet by accepting the relative autonomy of syntactic research, they must then own up to the arbitrary nature of the original choice of a reference code. Neither De Feo nor Purini are willing, however, to link that choice of reference code to an act of *engagement*, when such a social commitment can be more fully expressed through other means. It is perhaps not by chance that Gregotti and Purini have "met" on several schemes for large-scale projects; even though for Gregotti the "dimension," the inscription of a sign-structure onto a regional geography appears to be the primary objective, while for Purini the question of dimension is unimportant. But it is no accident that in 1968 Purini undertook a "classification by sections of architectural systems." Was not the abstract typology of Durand in effect a reductive instrument capable of placing architecture "on hold," with respect to the new *programmatics*, stemming from "other technologies"? Furthermore, the studies on the relationship of the *Dasein* of the sign, which Purini continues to elaborate, express a similar "placing on hold." Without doubt, his signs are in search of articulation; their purism is always dangling between eloquence—the desire for metaphoric "transparencies"—and the retreat into self-contemplation. In a project from 1976, a pavilion in cement and glass, Purini alludes to the Farnsworth house by Mies, the pavilion as a forest of columns in a garden by Tessenow, the glass house by Figini, and the *Victory Room* by Persico; but no direct "quotation" is present in the project, which seems to call for a comparison between history and a form impervious to all external forces.

For Gregotti, form is not absolute. And yet his projects on a regional scale adopt a poetics of rigorous structural definition as a "defense" against that which they intend to assault. To show and then to withdraw, to create new thresholds and then to load them with "incidents," to wall up "places" and then to make them visible tombs: Purini and Gregotti have also met on this. Nor is it insignificant that Gregotti has arrived at such a position only after feverish *recherches* for subjective and collective memories. But today there is no Académie des Sciences to intervene by offering to the typological openness of current architectural writing, contracted as it is into essential alphabets, the kind of overall program that is translatable into typologies. That architecture which is made only of "relations" continues "on hold": its experimentalism produces "models" unwittingly.

And yet neither Gregotti's project for the Zen Quarter in Palermo nor those for the University of Calabria and the University of Florence cast a glance toward heavenly expanses. Instead, this architecture that seeks to saturate the landscape with techniques contracts into atonal narrations: it recites its own "contraction." But even this architecture is "on hold." It waits, first of all, to make itself into matter—but perhaps this is not its primary concern—and, ultimately, to force its "suspended tonality" into a resolution. But this is impossible. The formal play that wishes to present itself as thoroughly "calculable" and verifiable, that wishes to impose its own *ratio* upon the infinity of nature, condemns itself once again to heterotopia, and this time in a deceitful way. The calculability of Gregotti's architecture is still an evasion. Certainly, it attempts to play/transform the "great city" or the "great land." In this lies the merit of its having made architecture into a managerial product. But too great a desire for synthesis is contained in those "bridges" and in those excessively transparent grids: their serenity, their desire to go beyond the "tragic vision" of the "disquieting Muses"—the Italian masters of the fifties and sixties[36]—is imbued with hidden nostalgia. Distortions are still present in the project for the Rinascente Department Store in Turin; the utopias of "radical" architecture clearly flourish in the Zen Quarter, closed into itself like a "new Jerusalem" (in fact, the biblical theme is even mentioned in a report by Gregotti);[37] and the axis of multiple expansions in the project for the University of Calabria alludes to possible adventures of forms, beginning with the inflexible sign that restrains them. On the same open page, but on the two facing leaves, Euclid and Breton try to shatter the *difference* that the page imposes on their messages.

To what degree are these attitudes comparable to those of such architects as Peter Eisenman, Michael Graves, and John Hejduk, who, in the panorama of international architecture, appear to be closest to a conception of architecture as a means of reflecting upon itself and upon its internal articulations? Is it really possible to speak of their work as a "mannerism amongst the ruins"? Mario Gandelsonas has correctly singled out the specific areas of concern in the work of Michael Graves: the classicist code, cubist painting, the traditions of the Modern Movement, and nature.[38] However, it should be remarked that we are again dealing with closed systems, within which the themes of polysemy and pluralism are already "orchestrated" and controlled, and within which the *possession of the aleatory* is made to take on a form that, to say the least, is "monumental." The only source that seems to defy such an interpretation is the one that refers to the Modern Movement; nevertheless, it is read nonproblematically by Graves as meaning "metaphysical" and "twentieth-century," thus permitting the previous schema to stand intact. Having established a system of limitations and of exclusions, Graves can manipulate his materials in a limited series of operations; but at the same time, this system permits him to demonstrate how a clarification or explication of his own linguistic procedures exerts an indirect control of the plan, always *from within the system of predetermined exclusions.*

In other words, both Graves and Hejduk renew a method based on the "laying bare" of syntactic procedures. The essence of formalism— "formalism" understood in its original sense—is perpetuated in their work. "Semantic distortion," the *priëm* (device) of the Russian formalists, is thus taken up again in a most obvious way in works like Graves's Benacerraf and Snyderman houses. And these works as well as the more hieratic and atemporal syntactic decompositions of Eisenman should be regarded as a sort of analytic laboratory dedicated to experimentation on select stylemes, rather than merely as reworkings of Terragni's rationalism or as expressions of a taste for the abstract.

We cannot try to analyze here the meaning of such research within the context of American culture. Their objective function, however, is without doubt to provide a well-tested catalogue of design approaches, applicable to predetermined situations. It is useless then to ask if their "neopurist" tendencies are actual or not.[39] As instances of the baring of linguistic structures, they are asked simply to be rigorous in their absolute ahistoricity. Only in this way can their nostalgic isolation be neutralized, thereby permitting the recognition of the necessity of their estrangement to emerge from those meticulous exercises. (A recognition, by the way, that would never spring from the self-satisfied stylistic gestures of Philip Johnson or from the equally self-satisfied fragmentism of Paul Rudolph.)

But what is the meaning of this isolation of pure *design*, not only, or not so much, for the latest work of Stirling and Gregotti—which is "obligated" to it—but rather for the work of Rossi, Scolari, the Kriers, Pichler, Purini, Hejduk, and Eisenman? Leo Castelli, in New York, immediately seized the opportunity to merchandise the images consigned to the sheets on which our "untimely ones" deposited "images as deeds." Those *designs* wish to resist the attack of time; they demonstrate in their absoluteness the sole possibility of "narrating clearly." In this sense, they are *texts in which form lies inert*; it "reposes"; it narrates its own fractures attempting to possess them totally. They do not represent "interrupted architectures," but rather universes that attempt to heal the radical rift that Le Corbusier had originally established between painting and constructing. Now, the "clear narration"—which Graves and Stirling renounce voluntarily—is there to declare that real differences are expressible only at the price of an absolute reification. The path taken by Lissitzky with the *Proun* is thus followed in reverse.

Let us try to synthesize the argument made so far. It requires a specific reading of the languages under examination as well as a use of diverse critical approaches. For example, in treating the work of Stirling and Gregotti, it is necessary to refer to technological aesthetics and to information theory, for they prove to be instruments essential to a full understanding of the rationale behind the semantic distortions employed by both architects. But information theory sheds very little light on Rossi's study of typological invariants, especially since Rossi's formalism seems to want to contest the original formulation of linguistic formalism by Shklovsky and Eichenbaum.

To dismantle and reassemble the geometric metaphors of "the compositional rigorists" may prove an endless game, which may even become useless when, as in the case of Peter Eisenman, the process of assemblage is all to explicit and presented in a highly didactic form. In the face of such products, the task of criticism is to begin from within the work only to break out of it as quickly as possible in order not to remain caught in the vicious circle of a language that speaks only of itself, in order not to participate guiltily in the "infinite entertainment" that it promises.

Clearly, the problem of criticism is of another order. We do not give credence to the artificial "New Trends" attributed to contemporary architecture.[40] But there is little doubt that a widespread attitude does exist that is intent upon reclaiming the dimension of the object and its character as unicum by removing it from its economic and functional contexts; by marking it as an exceptional—and thus surreal—event by placing it between parentheses within the flux of "things" generated by the system of production. One could describe such acts as an *architecture dans le boudoir*. And not simply because, as we have already emphasized in treating the opposed but complementary examples represented by the work of Stirling and Rossi, we find ourselves facing an "architecture of cruelty"—the cruelty of language as a system of exclusions—but further because the magic circle drawn around linguistic experimentation reveals a significant affinity with the structural rigor of the texts of the Marquis De Sade. "Where sex is involved, everything must speak of sex": that is, the utopia of eros in Sade culminates in the discovery that the maximum liberty leads to the maximum terror and indifference, while that utopia itself remains completely inscribed within the supreme constriction of the inflexible geometric structures of narrativity. But as we have already pointed out with respect to Piranesi, this means making nonlinguistic forces break into the domain of language. And yet the *boudoir* of the great new writers of architecture, however well furnished with mirrors and instruments of pleasure it may be, is no longer the place where the maximum degree of "virtuous wickedness" is consummated. The modern libertines become horrified when faced with the theme of the inflexibility of the limit. Their vivisections are performed after they have skillfully anesthetized the patients. The torturer now works in padded operating rooms; the *boudoir* is aseptic and has too many safety exits. The recovery of the border of discourse," after its destruction by the historical avant-gardes in their struggle against the techniques of mass communication and the dissolution of the work of art into the assembly line, serves today to safeguard the possibility of salvation for the "nouvelles Justines" attracted by the recesses in which "gentle tortures" are consummated.

There are two contradictions, however. On the one hand, as with the Enlightenment utopia, such attempts to recover a discursive order are forced to discover that those exits from the castle serve only to make silence speak. On the other hand, they try to go beyond this aporia by offering themselves as the foundation for a new institutional format for architecture. These contradictions are actually given theoretical form in Louis Kahn's work from the mid-fifties on. But, with his work, we have already exited from the hermetic game of language that collapses upon itself.

The questions that criticism ought to ask at this point are: what makes these "gentle tortures" possible? In what contexts and in what structural conditions are they rooted? What is their role within the present-day system of production? We have responded in part to these questions in the course of our discussion. But we can add, however, that these works are the by-products of a system of production that must, simultaneously: (a) renew itself on a formal level, by delegating to marginal sectors of its professional organizations the task of experimenting with and developing new models (in fact, it would prove useful to analyze the way in which the models devised by the isolated form makers come to be introduced within the process of mass production); and (b) consolidate a highly diversified public, by assigning the role of "vestals of the discipline" to figures bent on preserving the concept and the role of architecture, in its accepted meaning as a traditional object endowed with certain permanent and inalienable powers of communication.

As you see, we pass from the object itself to the system that gives meaning to it. What we meant in affirming that the task of criticism is to do violence to the object under analysis now becomes clear. From the examination of the most contrary attempts to bring architecture back into the realm of "discourse," we have passed to pinpointing the role of architectural discourse itself, thereby casting serious doubt on the overall function of those attempts. Now, we must even go further.

On several occasions we have tried to demonstrate that throughout the adventures of the historical avant-gardes the alternatives that appear as opposites—order and disorder, law and chance, structure and formlessness—are in reality completely complementary. We have seen this exemplified in the Gallaratese Quarter, within which the dialectic between purism and constructivism is fully manifest. But the historical significance of such complementarity extends well beyond this specific example. To degrade the materials of communication by compromising them with the commonplace, by forcing them to be reflected in the agonizing swamp of the world of merchandise, by reducing them to emptied and mute signs: this is the process that leads from the tragic buffoonery of the Cabaret Voltaire to the *Merzbau* of Kurt Schwitters, to the constructivist pictures of László Moholy-Nagy, and to the false constructions of Sol LeWitt. Yet the result is surprising. The desecrating immersion into chaos permits these artists to reemerge with instruments that, by having absorbed the logic of that chaos, are prepared to dominate it from within.

Thus we have the *form of formlessness* as both conquest and project. On the one side, the manipulation of pure signs as the foundations of an architectural constructivism; on the other, the acceptance of the indefinite, of dissolution. The control of chaos and of chance requires this twofold attitude. As Rudolf Arnheim has keenly observed, "the earlier insistence on minimal shapes of the utmost precision (in the work of Jean Arp, which is illustrative of our argument) and the subsequent display of corrosion, seemingly at extreme opposites, were in fact symptoms of the same abandonment."[41] But it is the testimony of Arp himself that makes clear the process binding the affirmation of form to the "death wish" of form itself:

About 1930 the pictures torn by hand from paper came into being. . . . Why struggle for precision, purity, when they can never be attained. The decay that begins immediately on completion of the work was now welcome to me. Dirty man with his dirty fingers points and daubs at a nuance in the picture. . . . He breaks into wild enthusiasm and sprays the picture with spittle. A delicate paper collage of watercolor is lost. Dust and insects are also efficient in destruction. The light fades the colors. Sun and heat make blisters, disintegrate the paper, crack the paint, disintegrate the paint. The dampness creates mould. The work falls apart, dies. The dying of a picture no longer brought me to despair. I had made my pact with its passing, with its death, and now it was part of the picture for me. But death grew and ate up the picture and life. . . . Form had become Unform, the Finite the Infinite, the Individual the Whole.[42]

The formlessness, the risk of existence, no longer generates anxiety once it is accepted as linguistic material, as in the "combine-paintings" of Rauschenberg, as in *Homage to New York* by Jean Tinguely (1960), as in the corrosive manipulations of sound by John Cage. And vice versa: language can speak of the indeterminate, the casual, the transient, since in them it greets the advent of the Whole. Yet this is but an endeavor to give a form of expression to the phenomenon of *mass consumption*. It is not by chance that a great many of such celebrations of formlessness take place under the banner of a technological utopia. The ironic and irritating metaphors of the Archigram and Archizoom groups, or Johansen's and Gehry's notion of architecture as an explosion of fragments (not to mention the cynicism of the Site group) have their roots in the technological myth. Technology can thus be read mystically, as a "second nature," the object of mimesis; indeed, it may even become the object of formalist small talk, as in some of the work of Russian Constructivism in which the form self-destructs in order to emit messages stemming from the same process of self-contestation. There are even those who, like Bruno Zevi, try to construct a code for such programmed self-destruction.[43] What remains hidden in all of these "abstract furors" is the general sense of their agreeable masochism. And it is precisely to such experiences that a critical approach inspired by the technological aesthetics of Max Bense or by the information theory of Abraham Moles may be fruitfully applied. But this is only possible because, much more than Stirling, these architects attempt to convert into discourse the indeterminacy of the technological world: they attempt to saturate the entire physical environment with excessive amounts of revved-up information in an effort to reunite "words and things" and impart to commonplace existence an autonomous structure of communication. It is no accident, then, that the already outmoded images of Archigram and the artificial and deliberate ironies of Robert Venturi and Denise Scott Brown or of Hans Hollein simultaneously expand and restrict the sphere of architectural intervention. They expand it insofar as they introduce the theme of dominating visible space in its entirety; they restrict it insofar as they interpret that space solely as a network of superstructures.

A definite result, however, emerges from projects like the one designed by Venturi and Rauch for Benjamin Franklin Avenue in Philadelphia.[44] Here, the desire to communicate no longer exists; architecture is dissolved into a deconstructed system of ephemeral signals. In place of *communication*, there is a flux of *information*; in place of architecture as language, there is an attempt to reduce it to a mass medium, without any ideological residues; in place of an anxious effort to restructure the urban system, there is a disenchanted acceptance of reality, bordering on extreme cynicism.

In this manner, Venturi, placing himself within an exclusively linguistic framework, has arrived at a radical devaluation of language itself: the meaning of the *Plakatwelt*, of the world of publicity, cannot be sought in referents external to it. Venturi thus obtains a result that is the exact opposite of that reached by the compositional rigorists. For the latter, it is the metaphysical recovery of the "being" of architecture extracted from the flux of existence; for Venturi, it is the process of rendering language useless, having discovered that its intrinsic ambiguity, upon contact with reality, makes any pretext of autonomy purely illusory.

Note well: in both cases, language undeceives itself. We shall return to this problem in the next chapter. It should now be observed that if the protagonists of contemporary architecture often take on the role of Don Quixote, such a posture has a less superficial meaning than is readily apparent.

Language has thus reached the point of speaking about its own isolation, regardless of whether it chooses to retraverse the path of rigorism by focusing on the mechanisms of its own writing, or to explode outward toward the Other, that is, toward the problematic space of existence. But does not such a journey, which was originally undertaken in the period that extends from the early fifties to the present, simply repeat an adventure already lived out? Is not Mallarmé's reply to the question regarding the subject of discourse, "It is the Word itself that speaks," complementary to that at once tragic and comforting recognition of Kraus and Loos, "it is the turn of deeds to speak, and that which is only thought is inexpressible?" And furthermore, has not the destiny of the historical avant-gardes been to dissolve into a project—a historically frustrated one at that—for the intellectual management of the Whole? The homecoming to language constitutes a roof of failure. But it remains necessary to determine the extent to which such a failure is due to the intrinsic character of the discipline of architecture and the extent to which it is due to uncertain causes not yet fully understood.

Michel Foucault has pointed out the existence of a kind of gradation between different types of discourses:

Discourse "uttered" in the course of the day and in casual meetings, and which disappears with the very act which gave rise to it; and those forms of discourse that lie at the origins of a certain number of new verbal acts, which are reiterated, transformed or discussed; in short, discourse which is *spoken* and remains spoken, indefinitely, beyond its formulation, and which remains to be spoken.[45]

It is a question of a gap clearly not absolute, but sufficiently defined to permit a distinction between levels of linguistic organization to be made. The Modern Movement, overall, had tried to eliminate that gap: here we are thinking specifically of the polemical position of Hannes Meyer, the radicalism of Hans Schmidt, the stances of magazines like *ABC* and *G*, and the aesthetic theories of Karel Teige, Walter Benjamin, and Hans Mukarhovsky.[46] But it is Foucault himself who recognizes the final results of such an attempt:

The radical denial of this gradation can never be anything but play, utopia or anguish. Play, as Borges uses the term, in the form of commentary that is nothing more than the reappearance, word for word (though this time it is solemn and anticipated) of the text commented on; or again, the play of a work of criticism talking endlessly about a work that does not exist.[47]

Is this not, in fact, the position upon which not only Stirling and Kahn converge, but also those whom Jencks has called the "Supersensualists"[48]—namely Hans Hollein, Walter Pichler, and Ricardo Bofill—who were preceded, however (and Jencks makes no note of this), by much of the late work of Frank Lloyd Wright and the imposing prefigurations of the technological avant-gardists (Leo Ludwig and Piano & Rogers)? The elimination of the gap between the discourses "which are uttered" and those "which are spoken" cannot be realized at the level of language. The tight-lipped humor that emanates from the architecture of Hollein or from the formal paradoxes of Arata Isozaki—the Fujimi Country Clubhouse (1972–74), the Kitakyushu Central Library (1973–75), and even the chair *Marilyn on the Line* (1972)[49]—may contrast with the equally sophisticated but more genuine humor of Carlo Scarpa; but for all of them, it is a question of the "comical that does not make anyone laugh," of "play as utopia and anguish."

On the other hand, the explosion of architecture outward toward the real contains within it a comprehensive project that becomes evident once we take into consideration that the tradition of this sector of research is based on the activity of such figures as Raymond Unwin, Barry Parker, Clarence Stein, Henry Wright, and Martin Wagner. There is, nevertheless, a certain undercurrent in such a shifting of the discipline of architecture from form to *reform* that might lead to a possible overcoming of its own equivocations. In fact, at least the start of a trend is discernible in this body of attempts: the premise for a "new technique," submerged within the organizations that determine the capitalistic management of building and regional planning.

But this forces us to abandon almost entirely the paraphernalia of the traditional categories of judgment. Since an individual work is no longer at stake, but rather an entire cycle of production, critical analysis has to operate on the material plane that determines that cycle of production. In other words, to shift the focus from what architecture wishes to be, or wishes *to say*, toward what building production represents in the economic game means that we must establish parameters of reading capable of penetrating to the heart of the role played by architecture within the capitalist system. One could object that such an economic reading of building production is *other* than the reading of architecture as a system of communication. But we can only reply that it will never be repeated too often that, when wishing to discover the secret of a magician's tricks, it is far better to observe him from backstage than to continue to stare at him from a seat in the orchestra.

Clearly, however, to interpret architectural ideology as an element—secondary perhaps, but an element nonetheless—of the cycle of production results in the overturning of the pyramid of values that are commonly accepted in the treatment of architecture. Indeed, once such a criterion of judgment is adopted, it becomes absolutely ridiculous to ask to what extent a linguistic choice or a structural organization expresses or tries to anticipate "freer" modes of existence. What criticism ought to ask about architecture is, instead, in what way does it, as an organized institution, succeed or not in influencing the relations of production.

We regard it, then, as absolutely crucial to take up the questions that Walter Benjamin posed in one of his most important essays, "The Author as Producer":

Instead of asking, "What is the attitude of a work to the relations of production of its time? Does it accept them, is it reactionary—or does it aim at overthrowing them, is it revolutionary?"—instead of this question, or at any rate before it, I should like to propose another. Rather than ask, "What is the *attitude* of a work to the relations of production of its time" I should like to ask, "What is its *position* in them?" This question directly concerns the function the work has within the literary relations of production of its time. It is concerned, in other words, directly with the literary *technique* of works.[50]

This viewpoint, by the way, represents for Benjamin a radical surpassing of the more ideological positions he had expressed in the conclusion to "The Work of Art in the Age of Mechanical Reproduction." In the questions posed in "The Author as Producer," there are no concessions made to proposals for salvation by means of an "alternative" use of linguistic techniques; there is no longer any ideological distinction between a "communist art" as opposed to a "fascist art." There is only a genuinely structural consideration of the productive role of intellectual activities and, consequently, a series of questions regarding their possible contribution to the development of the relations of production. Certainly, Benjamin's text still contains many dubious points concerning the political value of certain technological innovations—here we are thinking of the connections drawn between dada-

Massimo Scolari,
*La macchina
dell' oblio*, 1978

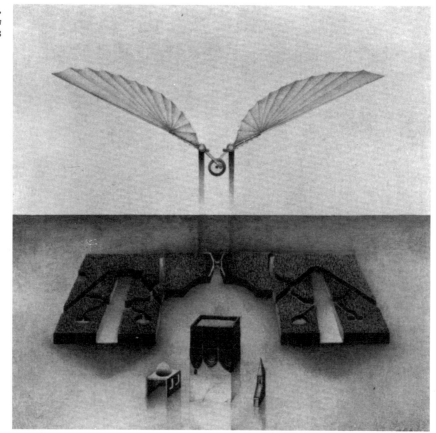

ism and the content of a political photomontage by Heartfield, considered by Benjamin to be "revolutionary." But the substance of his argument remains profoundly valid today, so much so as to point the way to a radical revision of the criteria for determining the fundamental problems of the history of contemporary art and architecture. By keeping in mind the central question—what is the position of a work of art in the relations of production—many of the so-called masterpieces of modern architecture come to take on a secondary or even marginal importance, while a great many of the current debates are relegated to the status of peripheral considerations.

The judgment we have advanced regarding the present research aimed at restoring to architecture its original "purity" therefore proves to be valid. These attempts are confirmed as "parallel actions," bent on building an uncontaminated limbo that floats above (or below) the real conflicts in the social formation of which it only picks up a distant echo.

L'art pour l'art has been, in its own way, a form of blasé upper-class protest against the universe of *Zivilisation*. In defending *Kultur* against "civilization and its discontents," Thomas Mann found it necessary to formulate "the reflections of a nonpolitical man," which, if carried to their extreme, reassert the kinship between art and play posited by Schiller. After all, "the courage to speak of roses" can always be appreciated, provided that the courage is true enough to confess and to bear witness to a deeply felt inadequacy.

We do not, however, wish to be misunderstood: the critic is also an "angel with dirty hands." The very same questions that criticism puts to architecture it must also put to itself: that is, in what way does *criticism* enter *into* the process of production? How does it conceive its own role within that process? As is evident, the knotty problems set out in the introduction to this book return intact and with full force. Only with great difficulty can such questions be answered *theoretically*. They are beyond any "general theory." The "project" that they designate places the present-day formation of intellectual work on trial, even if, for the time being, only a line of march can be pointed out, one that lacks a fully formed and expressible *telos*.

The conclusion of our discourse can only be problematic. Once again, it is the questions posed by Benjamin—by the same Benjamin, mind you, who wrote about his experiences with hashish—that present themselves to us as an obstacle to be confronted. And to the architect (or to the critic) who accepts the new roles that today's difficult reality proposes, we shall never desist from asking:

Does he succeed in promoting the socialization of the intellectual means of production? Does he see how he himself can organize the intellectual workers in the production process? Does he have proposals for the *Umfunktionierung* [transformations] of the novel, the drama, the poem? The more completely he can orient his activity toward this task, the more correct will the political tendency, and necessarily also the higher technical quality, of his work.[51]

"The disenchanted avant-garde," completely absorbed in exploring from the comfort of its charming *boudoirs* the profundities of the philosophy of the unexpected writes down, over and over again, its own reactions under the influence of drugs prudently administered. Its use of hashish is certainly a conscious one: but it makes of this "consciousness" a barrier, a defense. Of the "perfidious enchantment" of the products that come out of the new laboratories of the imaginary it is good to be distrustful. With a smile, we have to catalogue them in the imaginary museum of the bad conscience of our "small age," to be used as rearview mirrors by whoever recognizes himself to be caught in the midst of a crisis that obliges him to remain stuck in the minefield of the "evil present."

Notes

1. See Michel Foucault, *The Order of Things* (New York: Pantheon Books, 1970), p. 382; original ed., *Les mots et les choses* (Paris: Gallimard, 1966). Note, in any case, that the expression "mortal silence of the sign" is Nietzsche's.

2. See principally Kenneth Frampton, "Leicester University Engineering Laboratory," *Architectural Design* 34, no. 2 (1964), p. 61, and idem, "Information Bank," *Architectural Forum* 139, no. 4 (1968), pp. 37–47; "Andrew Melville Hall, St. Andrews University, Scotland," *Architectural Design* 40, no. 9 (1970), pp. 460–462, and "Transformations in Style: The Work of James Stirling," *A + U* 50 (1975), pp. 135–138; Mark Girouard, "Florey Building, Oxford," *Architectural Review* 152, no. 909 (1972), pp. 260–277, in which, in addition to the references that Frampton makes to the images of Sant'Elia, constructivism, Wright, Chareau, Brinckman, and van der Vlugt, a relationship is established between the contrived geometricism of Stirling and the Victorian unreality of Butterfield. See also Joseph Rykwert, "Un episodio inglese," *Domus* 415 (1964), pp. 3 ff; idem, "Stirling a Cambridge," *Domus* 491 (1969), pp. 8–15; "Stirling in Scozia," *Domus* 491 (1970), pp. 5–15; Charles Jencks, the chapter "James Stirling or Function Made Manifest," in *Modern Movements in Architecture* (Garden City, N.Y.: Anchor Press, 1973), pp. 260–270; Reyner Banham, "History Faculty, Cambridge," *Architectural Review* 146, no. 861 (1968), pp. 329 ff., which lists the poetics of Scheerbart among Stirling's sources; and idem, "Problem x 3 = Olivetti," *Architectural Review* 155, no. 926 (1974), pp. 197–200; John Jacobus, introduction to *James Stirling, Buildings and Projects 1950–1974* (New York: Oxford University Press, 1975). In his article, "Stirling 'Dimostrazioni,'" *Architectural Design* 38, no. 10 (1968), pp. 454 ff., Alvin Boyarsky presents Stirling as a typical member of an "angry generation" that was quickly disillusioned, thus explaining his "apocalyptic" architectural structures, mixtures of "succulent memories." In his personal statements, Stirling avoids dealing with the question of his sources, constantly bringing the discussion back to the invention of the organism as a unitary structure; see Stirling, "An Architect's Approach to Architecture," *RIBA Journal* 72, no. 5 (May 1965), pp. 231–240; also in *Zodiac* 16 (1967), pp. 160–169; and idem, "Anti-Structure," *Zodiac* 18 (1968), pp. 51–60. See also nn. 8 and 9 below.

3. This opinion is expressed, for example, by Frampton in "Andrew Melville Hall," pp. 460–462, and by Rykwert in "James Stirling, 4 progetti," *Domus* 516 (1972), pp. 1–20. On the residential complex built by Stirling in Runcorn, see Werner Seligmann's article, "Runcorn: Historical Precedents and the Rational Design Process," *Oppositions* 7 (1976), pp. 5–22, with a postscript by Anthony Vidler, p. 23.

4. Think, for example, of the Melnikov-like hall, fastened sideways to the pillars, and of the beams supported by the weight of the tower above, both in the Engineering Laboratory at the University of Leicester. But Rykwert has rightly observed that there is a structural dissonance in the Olivetti building in Surrey caused by the truncated metal trusses on brackets in the wedge-shaped foyer (see J. Rykwert, "Lo spazio policromo: Olivetti Training Centre, Haslemere, Surrey, 1968–1972," *Domus* 530 [1974], pp. 37–44). On the Olivetti building at Haslemere, see also Charles Jencks, "Stirling's Olivetti Training Centre," *Archithese* 10 (1974), pp. 41–46. Regarding the opening out of the wings of Stirling's building, Jencks writes: "A comparable feeling in music would be the suspensions and tensions of Stravinsky, in art the distortions of Francis Bacon."

5. Frampton, "Leicester University," p. 61. But see also William Curtis, "L'université, la ville et l'habitat collectif," *Archithese* 14 (1975), pp. 32–34.

6. Frampton, "Andrew Melville Hall."

7. See Peter Eisenman, "From Golden Lane to Robin Hood Gardens: Or If You Follow the Yellow Brick Road, It May Not Lead to Golders Green," *Oppositions* 1 (1973), pp. 28–56.

8. James Stirling, "Appunto per la Hornbostel Lecture alla Carnegie Mellon University, Pittsburgh, aprile 1974," in the catalogue *James Stirling*, exhibition at the Castel Nuovo, Naples, 18 April–4 May 1975 (Rome: Officina, 1976).

9. Stirling, however, contradicted himself when he stated at the Second International Iranian Architectural Congress (Persepoli-Shiraz, September 1974): "It seems essential to me that a building contain a whole series of forms, which the general public can relate to, be familiar with, and identify with. These forms will stem from staircases, windows, corridors, statues, entranceways, etc., and the entire building will be thought of as a composi-

tion of everyday elements which can be recognized by the average man and not only an architect" (see the catalogue *James Stirling*, pp. 28–29). This contradiction is not in itself significant, but rather shows how, for architects like Stirling, formal writing follows laws that cannot be verbalized or translated into other writings.

10. Peter Eisenman, "Real and English: The Destruction of the Box. I," *Oppositions* 4 (1974), pp. 6–34.

11. Ibid., p. 20.

12. Ibid., pp. 27–31.

13. On these projects, see *Lotus International* 15 (1977), pp. 58 ff. See also David Stewart, "Three Projects by James Stirling," *A + U* 67 (1976), pp. 55–56, with graphic and photographic documentation on pp. 22 ff. Stewart examines the Town Centre Housing of Runcorn New Town, as well as the projects for the new Gallery on Grabbeplatz in Düsseldorf, and for the Wallraf-Richartz Museum, finding in them echoes of Schinkel and of Hadrian's Villa at Tivoli.

14. See Cesare De Seta, "La storicità dialettica di Stirling," in *James Stirling*, pp. 22–24.

15. See, for example, Alan Johnson and Stephen N. Games, "Florey Building, Oxford" (Letters to the Editors), *Architectural Review* 152, no. 910 (1972), pp. 384–385.

16. Roland Barthes, *Critique et verité*.

17. We shall consider Aldo Rossi here only as an architect, pointing out that his theoretical works are but "poetics" in the strictest sense. It is useless to contest a literary work of his: it has but one use, that of helping to understand the spiritual autobiography that the author inscribes within his formal compositions. The bibliography on Rossi suffers in general from partiality; we will thus cite only these texts: Ezio Bonfanti, "Elementi e costruzione: Note sull'architettura di Aldo Rossi," *Controspazio* 2, no. 10 (1970), pp. 19 ff.; Massimo Scolari, "Avanguardia e nuova architettura," in (various authors) *Architettura razionale: XV Triennale di Milano, Sezione internazionale di architettura* (Milan: Franco Angeli, 1973), pp. 153–187; the catalogue *Aldo Rossi, Bauten Projekte* (with Martin Steinmann's introduction "Architektur") of the exhibition held in Zurich in November-December 1973; Renato Nicolini, "Note su Aldo Rossi," *Controspazio* 4 (1974), pp. 48–49; Vittorio Savi, *L'architettura di Aldo Rossi* (Milan: Franco Angeli, 1976), with an ample bibliography; the special issue dedicated to Rossi by the Japanese magazine *A + U* 65 (1976), pp. 55 ff.; and the catalogue *Aldo Rossi* (Florence: Centro Di, 1979).

18. Fossati writes of the "metaphysical" De Chirico using words that could also be applied to the architecture of Rossi: "The play of contradictions and suspensions of meaning from the network of common relationships by and of objects is not just an ordinary technical expedient: it is the expedient par excellence, the ritual, with its preparatory and evocative minute details, the epiphany as sublimation, its healing and miraculous effects. Sublimation, *par excellence*, the play hides the game, and each slowly and deliberately reveals the other, with painting as a thing in itself, as a counterpoint to the crisis between appearance and substance, and as an alternative as well. . . . The line having been severed between reality and its objects, the game is completed; faith in making, in knowing, in concealing, becomes an object more objective than the real objects at stake with which it should concern itself, a truth truer than actual exigencies and relationships, a thing in itself" (Paolo Fossati, *La pittura a programma: De Chirico metafisico* [Venice: Marsilio, 1973], pp. 24–25).

19. We are obviously referring to the noted passage by Walter Benjamin in "Theses on the Philosophy of History," which Frampton places at the beginning of his essay in *Oppositions* 1 (1973). And yet the theme of Klee's *Angelus Novus* is found throughout Benjamin's mature works: "The average European has not succeeded in uniting his life with technology, because he has clung to the fetish of creative existence. One must have followed Loos in his struggle with the dragon 'ornament,' heard the stellar Esperanto of Scheerbart's creations or have escorted Klee's New Angel, who preferred to free men by taking from them, rather than make them happy by giving to them, to understand a humanity that proves itself by destruction. . . . Like a creature sprung from the child and the cannibal his conqueror stands before him: not a new man; a monster, a new angel." Walter Benjamin, "Karl Kraus," in *Reflections*, ed. Peter Demetz, trans. Edmund Jephcott (New York: Schocken, 1986), pp. 272–273; originally in *Frankfurter Zeitung* (10, 14, 17, and 18 March 1931), reprinted in *Schriften*, vol. 2 (Frankfurt: Suhrkamp Verlag, 1955), pp. 159–195.

20. This can achieve notable poetic effects, as in the "magical" bursting through of a truncated cone into the grid, forcing it apart, at the City Hall in Muggiò in 1972. This project perhaps explains what Aldo Rossi means when he speaks of an "analogous city"—a kind of "magical realism," related to a conceptual experience, resonant with memories: "We can utilize the reference points of the existing city, placing them on a vast, illuminated surface: and thereby let architecture participate, little by little, in the creation of new events."

21. Numbers 21–22 (1973) of the magazine *Parametro*, dedicated to the XV Triennale of Milan, and edited by Rossi, Franco Raggi, Massimo Scolari, Rosaldo Bonicalzi, Gianni Braghieri, and Daniele Vitale, bear the title *La Triennale modello Starace* (Starace was a leading Fascist party official); harsh criticism in the same vein appears in Glauco Greslieri's article, "Alla XV Triennale di Milano," on p. 6 of the same issue; in the letter sent by Giovanni Klaus König to the magazine *Architettura: cronache e storia* 19, no. 8 (1973), pp. 456–467; and in Joseph Rykwert's article, "XV Triennale," *Domus* 530 (1974), pp. 1–15. We cannot agree with these criticisms. There are far stronger reasons for criticism than those found in the above-mentioned articles: evidently no one has observed how objectively "reactionary" were the city-scale projects drawn up by obviously "nonacademic" architects for Rome and Venice. But to attack the Triennale to strike at Rossi—his "school" is something else again—is simply inadmissible. The enthusiasm of the historian has nothing to do with that of the sports fan. We have long ceased to wonder about whose body is buried in the cellar, or to hurl curses at a too-partial referee even if our friend Rykwert, with a superficiality that oddly enough we do not find in his studies on nudist paradises, attributes to us ideas and preferences that we have never expressed. The point is another. If "fascism" is thought to mean dedicating oneself to the "scandalous" autonomy of art, then one should have the courage to break with sclerotic and ambiguous criteria of judgment, which directly influence the destiny of the Modern Movement. But once having agreed to descend to infantile criteria of judgment, is it really necessary to recall that it was Gropius who explained to Goebbels that modern architecture was the only kind capable of expressing the supremacy of the Germanic race? And why has it not occurred to anyone that if the mute symmetries of Rossi can be labeled "à la Starace," then the constructivist products of the Kennedy era—of Kallmann and Kevin Roche, for example—should be thought of as symbols of American democracy and of its "civil" colonization of Vietnam? Only by avoiding the use of such puerile parallels is it possible to make history. Personally, we feel obliged to advise Rossi not to teach architecture: not out of a hysterical and conformist desire to ostracize him, but rather to help him to be more consistent in his fascinating, albeit superfluous, silence. On the XV Triennale, see also the issue of *Controspazio* dedicated to it (no. 6, 1973), especially the estimable article in defense of the basic choices of the exhibit, by Renato Nicolini, "Per un nuovo realismo in architettura," pp. 12–15. From today's vantage point, however, we may thank the XV Triennale for having instigated the debate, and affording the occasion for international criticism to reveal its inhibitions and its naïveté. A prime example of this is Charles Jencks's article, "Irrational Rationalists: The Rats since 1960. Part 1," *A+U* 76 (1977), pp. 110–113, with its simplistic concept of "rationality" and of the epistemological debate on the crisis of dialectic thought.

22. See György Lukács, "Georg Simmel," 1918, reprinted in *Buch des Dankes an Georg Simmel*, ed. Kurt Gassen (Berlin: Duncker & Humbolt, 1958), p. 173.

23. Karl Kraus, *In These Great Times* (Montreal: Engendra Press, 1976); "In Dieser grossen Zeit . . ." was originally given as a speech on 19 November 1914. See Benjamin, "Karl Kraus," pp. 242–243.

24. See Adolf Loos, *Spoken into the Void* (Cambridge: MIT Press, 1982); original ed., *Architektur*, 1910 (conference), reprinted in *Sämtliche Schriften, Adolf Loos*, vol. 1 (Vienna and Munich: Herold Verlag, 1962), pp. 302 ff. But Loos's position is anything but an isolated one; in a certain way it is linked to the teachings of Theodor Fischer and to the elementarism of his pupils, and even more so to the deeply felt purism of Heinrich Tessenow (see Heinrich Tessenow, *Hausbau und dergleichen* [Berlin: B. Cassirer, 1920]; Italian trans., introduction by Giorgio Grassi [Milan: Franco Angeli, 1974]). On the other hand, the position of an artist like Georg Muche, in the midst of the Weimar Bauhaus, proves to be very close to that of Loos: see Georg Muche, Memorandum of 18 February 1922 to the college of

professors of the Bauhaus, and "Bildende Kunst und Industrieform," *Bauhaus* 1, no. 1 (1926), pp. 5–6; English trans. in Hans M. Wingler, *The Bauhaus: Weimar, Dessau, Berlin, Chicago* (Cambridge: MIT Press, 1969), pp. 113–114. See also Marcel Franciscono, *Walter Gropius and the Creation of the Bauhaus in Weimar* (Urbana: University of Illinois Press, 1971); and, on the relationship among Loos, Kraus, and Wittgenstein, the volume *Letters from Ludwig Wittgenstein: With a Memory by Paul Engelmann* (Oxford: Blackwell, 1967), as well as Francesco Amendolagine and Massimo Cacciari, *Oikos: Da Loos a Wittgenstein* (Rome: Officina, 1975). Useful only as a documentary source is Bernhard Leitner, *The Architecture of Ludwig Wittgenstein* (New York: New York University Press, 1976).

25. We refer to Albert Janik and Stephen Toulmin, *Wittgenstein's Vienna* (New York: Simon & Schuster, 1973), which, with disconcerting naïveté, connects Kraus's preservation of "values," once they are separated from the "facts," to the solipsism of the early Wittgenstein; and, conversely, to the too-hasty dismissal of Kraus on the part of Cacciari, in *Krisis* and in the article "La Vienna di Wittgenstein," *Nuova corrente* 72–73 (1977), pp. 59 ff., but particularly in the passage "American Kraus," pp. 101–106. Benjamin's essay "Karl Kraus," on the other hand, seems to be a highly reflective text, in which the new "messengers of the old engravings" can find infinite material upon which to meditate.

26. The ultimate referent of this coexistence of real and imaginary spaces, which Rossi symbolizes by invoking a "world rigid and with few objects," is the museum. In *L'architettura di Aldo Rossi*, pp. 126–127, Savi writes: "For Rossi, the word museum conveys a carefully ordered arrangement, in which all the elements converge in a single direction. Rossi has not designed a project for a museum. . . . He has made numerous sketches on the subject and its installations for the XV Triennale. The basic scheme in the design is the skeleton. A cutout dividing wall—already seen along the one side of the piazza of Segrate used as a quint, and in the axonometric drawing of the project, similar to a stele—is repeated along the entire wing of the palazzo of the Triennale. Even Zevi in *L'Espresso* noted that the cells divided by the walls were reminiscent of the cells of a convent. In fact, typologically, there is little difference between a convent and a museum. The only difference: Rossi places an opening in the center of the single wall, obtaining, by repetition, an effect of central perspective, Weinbrunner-like. The cross axis that intersects the partitions is analogous to the spinal cord. From one partition to the next, the exposition space is eaten up. The exhibitors cannot fill the exhibition structure. The result is disconcerting for everyone when it is realized that the iconographic model of the skeleton dominates the installations. Thus, if in the House of the Dead Rossi portrays architecture abandoned by life, here he shows architecture abandoned by things. Only the row of rooms of a deserted house gives the same sensation. Rossi feels that a true museum is a void and that therefore a museum symbolizes isolation, and that every time we think of a museum, in reality we are thinking of museification, that is, of a void, of squalor." Savi's observations can be compared with the two essays by Aldo Rossi, "Adolf Loos, 1870–1933," *Casabella continuità* 233 (1959), pp. 5–12, and "Architettura per i musei," in (various authors) *Teoria della progettazione architettonica* (Bari: Dedalo, 1974), pp. 122–137. This comparison confirms how "Krausian" is the musing upon the void that Rossi proposes, and how far it is, by contrast, from Mies's "theater of absence," as we described it in chapter three of the present volume.

27. See Michel Foucault, *This Is Not a Pipe* (Berkeley: University of California Press, 1983); original ed., *Ceci n'est pas une pipe* (Montpellier: Fata Morgana, 1973).

28. Carlo Michelstaedter, "Dialogo sulla salute," (1910) in *Opere* (Florence: Sansoni, 1958), p. 356.

29. Ibid., p. 366. See Alberto Abruzzese, "Da Trieste a Firenze: Lavoro e tradizione letteraria," in (various authors) *La classe dei colti* (Bari: Laterza, 1970), pp. 236 ff.

30. See Savi, *L'architettura di Aldo Rossi*, pp. 150–152.

31. Aldo Rossi, introduction to Hans Schmidt, *Contributi all'architettura: 1924–1964* (Milan: Franco Angeli, 1974), p. 17; original ed., *Beiträge zur Architektur* (Berlin: Verlag für Bauwesen, 1965).

32. See Massimo Scolari, "Les apories de l'architecture," *Architecture d'Aujourd'hui* 190 (1977), pp. 82–93. Extremely unconvincing is the interpretation of Scolari's watercolors found in M. Gandelsonas, "Massimo Scolari: Paesaggi teorici" *Lotus International* 11 (1976), pp. 57–63.

33. We are obviously referring here to the dispute between Breton and Bataille, the latter accusing Breton, in the name of the "spirit of the old mole" of "baseness"and "dirtiness," of gross and physical corporeity, of having an "Icarus complex," of wanting to fly to a lofty spot where the "full word," unsullied and pristine, flies toward a happy but nonexistent land, where "the words make love" in ecstatic moments far from the physicality of the real.

34. It is obvious that we mention these widely dissimilar experiments in the same breath merely for convenience's sake. More than a mere trend, today they are part of a vaguely defined "climate," examined in Francesco Dal Co and Mario Manieri-Elia, "La génération de l'incertitude," *Architecture d'Aujourd'hui* 181 (1975), pp. 948 ff.

35. Francesco Dal Co, "Architettura come forma sospesa," in Vittorio De Feo, *Il piacere dell'architettura* (Rome: Magma, 1976), pp. 13–17. A useful, if somewhat schematic, summing-up of the most recent tendencies in Italian architecture, can be found in the volume by Cina Conforto, Gabriele De Giorgi, Alessandra Muntoni, and Marcello Pazzaglini, *Il dibattito architettonico in Italia 1943–1973* (Rome: Bulzoni, 1977), particularly pp. 177 ff. On Purini's projects, see Franco Purini, *Luogo e progetto* (Rome: Kappa, 1976); the catalogue of the exhibition of his engravings published by the Centro Di (Florence, 1977); the article "Doppio tempo," *Controspazio* 9, nos. 4–5 (1977), pp. 54–55; and the article by Paolo Melis, "Il 'timore' e il 'bisogno' dell'architettura," ibid., pp. 61–63.

36. See M. Tafuri, "Les 'muses inquiétantes,' ou le destin d'une génération de 'Maîtres,'" *Architecture d'Aujourd'hui* 181 (1975), pp. 14–33.

37. See the report concerning the project for the Zen Quarter in Palermo in *Controspazio* 3 (1971), pp. 12–17: "This reduction to elementary clarity of the general structure of the design of the district is in marked contrast to the attempt . . . to complicate, stratify, and differentiate the image of the district itself, *to actually create a historical depth, a Biblical story, an interior monologue* . . . established by means of a critical reflection on its own condition of social utilization, of *its distance from and immersion in* the present model of culture and its contradictions" (ibid., p. 12; the italics are mine). See also the article by Massimo Scolari, "Tre progetti di Vittorio Gregotti," *Controspazio* 3, no. 3 (1971), pp. 2–6, in which he offers an early interpretation of Gregotti's "turnabout in his projects." The Zen Quarter is illustrated extensively in *Lotus International* 9 (1975), pp. 6–27, and the designs for the University of Calabria appear in the same magazine in issue 11 (1976), pp. 146–153, with a note by Pierluigi Cerri. There is a vast documentary bibliography on the works of Gregotti, but we know of no critical study on them worth mentioning. Observations of a general nature can be found in Oriol Bohigas, "Vittorio Gregotti," in *Once arquitectos* (Barcelona: La Gaya Ciencia, 1976), pp. 67–82. See also M. Tafuri, "Le avventure dell'oggetto: Architetture e progetti di Vittorio Gregotti," in the catalogue of the traveling exhibition dedicated to the artist (Milan: Electa, 1982).

38. M. Gandelsonas, "On Reading Architecture," *Progressive Architecture*, no. 3 (1972), pp. 68–87. On Graves's architecture, and particularly on the Gunwyn Office in Princeton (1971–72), see also Peter Carl's article, "Towards a Pluralist Architecture,"' *Progressive Architecture*, no. 2 (1973), pp. 82–89; on one of his most notable works, the Medical Office of Ear, Nose, and Throat Associates, in Fort Wayne, Indiana (1971), see C. Ray Smith, "Painterly Illusion and Architectural Reality," *Interiors* (September 1974). Finally, see the chapter "Michael Graves: l'immagine e il suo doppio," on pp. 20–22 of the essay by M. Tafuri, "Les bijoux indiscrets," in the catalogue *Five Architects, New York* (Rome: Officina, 1976). We might point out, incidentally, that what Argan has sought to identify in the architecture of Louis Kahn is perhaps more applicable to this type of research: "Today, the currents that are most strongly committed, most aware of the crisis, adopt a methodical, almost scientific, and in any event, critical, analysis of the structural components of the artistic 'phenomenon': in order to establish whether art can still 'phenomenize' itself, they try to discover why a surface is a surface, a volume a volume, a building a building, a painting a painting. Recognizing that art cannot be defined by its position and its function within the system, they ask whether it can be defined as a system unto itself, an autonomous structure" (Giulio Carlo Argan, "I due stadi della critica," in "Dove va l'arte," the special issue of *Ulisse* 13, no. 76 [1973], pp. 14–26; citation on p. 25). On these topics, see also Filiberto Menna, *La linea analitica dell'arte moderna: Le figure e le icone* (Turin: Einaudi, 1975).

39. See Walter Segal, "The Neo-Purist School of Architecture," *Architectural Design* 42, no. 6 (1972), pp. 34–45.

40. We refer here both to "Nuova Architettura," defined with a capital N and A, if not with valid arguments, in Nino Dardi's *Il gioco sapiente* (Padua: Marsilio, 1971), and to the "Nuova Tendenza" (note the persistence of the capitals), discussed by Scolari in "Avanguardia e nuova architettura." If the problem is to establish a continuity with the abstract tendencies of the period from 1920 to 1930, one ought to have the courage to speak not of something new, but rather of revival or survival; if the intent is to emphasize the importance given to linguistic considerations, greater care should be taken in indicating what is included and what excluded.

41. Rudolf Arnheim, *Entropy and Art: An Essay on Disorder and Order* (Berkeley: University of California Press, 1971), pp. 53–54.

42. Jean Arp, *On My Way: Poetry and Essays 1912–1947* (New York: Wittenborn, 1948), p. 77. A perceptive analysis of Arp's poetics is found in Laura Mancinelli, *Il messaggio razionale dell'avanguardia* (Turin: Einaudi, 1978), pp. 50–73.

43. See Bruno Zevi, *Il linguaggio moderno dell'architettura: Guida al codice anticlassico* (Turin: Einaudi, 1974).

44. See *Architecture d'Aujourd'hui* 169 (1973), pp. 63–69.

45. Michel Foucault, "The Discourse on Language," inaugural lecture at the Collège de France, 2 December 1970, in *The Archaeology of Knowledge and The Discourse on Language*, trans. A. M. Sheridan Smith (New York: Pantheon, 1972), p. 220.

46. On the views of the Swiss architect Hannes Meyer, see the fundamental preface by Francesco Dal Co to the Italian edition of his writings, *Architettura e rivoluzione*, 2d ed. (Padua: Marsilio, 1973); for a contrasting opinion, however, see Massimo Scolari's "Hannes Meyer e la pretesa negazione dell'arte," *Controspazio* 1, no. 7 (1969), pp. 58–59, in addition to the noted work by Claude Schnaidt. See also Hans Schmidt, *Beiträge zur Architektur*, and *Werk* 10 (1972), an issue devoted in part to the work of Schmidt.

47. Foucault, "The Discourse on Language," p. 220.

48. Jencks, *Modern Movements in Architecture*, pp. 51–59 (the chapter "Dolce Vita or the Supersensualists").

49. Among the many publications concerning the work of Arata Isozaki, perhaps the most complete and anthologylike is the issue dedicated to him of the Japanese magazine *SD* (*Space and Design*) 140 (1976), which contains articles by Hans Hollein, "Position and Move: The Architect as a Work of Art, or Mr. Isozaki Marries the Fresh Window," pp. 4–9; Kazuhiro Ishii, "A Guide to the World of Arata Isozaki," pp. 11–23; "28 of Isozaki's Works with Notes by the Architect Himself," pp. 24 ff; and a "Chronological Review," pp. 179–188. See also the article by Kenneth Frampton, "The Japanese New Wave," in the catalogue *A New Wave of Japanese Architecture* (New York: Institute for Architecture and Urban Studies, 1978), pp. 2–13.

50. Walter Benjamin, "The Author as Producer," in *Reflections*, p. 222. This essay of Benjamin's was cited by Paolo Portoghesi to refute our thesis concerning the loss of function of architectural ideologies (see Paolo Portoghesi, "Autopsia o vivisezione dell'architettura," *Controspazio* 1 [November 1969], pp. 5–7). Actually, here, too, Benjamin is ambiguous and open to diverse interpretations. But it would be misleading to consider, as Portoghesi does, only the more traditional aspects of the essay. On the subject of the *neue Sachlichkeit*, Benjamin writes: "This school made a great display of its poverty. It thereby shirked the most urgent task of the present-day writer: to recognize how poor he is and how poor he has to be in order to begin again from the beginning. . . . Nothing will be further from the author who has reflected deeply on the conditions of present-day production than to expect, or desire [new masterpieces in which to display the long-since-counterfeit wealth of creative personality]. His work will never be merely work on products but always, at the same time, on the means of production. In other words, *his products must have, over and above their character as works, an organizing function*" (p. 233; the italics are mine). Benjamin himself points out that this organizational function goes beyond any propagandistic intention.

51. See Benjamin, "The Author as Producer," p. 238.

Henri Lefebvre   **From *The Production of Space*** From *La production de l'espace* (Paris: Editions

Anthropos, 1974); trans. Donald Nicholson-Smith (Cambridge: Blackwell, 1991)

Henri Lefebvre launched his search for a unitary theory of physical, mental, and social space with this declaration: "The fact is that around 1910 a certain space was shattered. It was the space of common sense, of knowledge (*savoir*), of social practice, of political power, a space thitherto enshrined in everyday discourse, just as in abstract thought, as the environment of and channel for communications. . . . Euclidean and perspectivist space have disappeared as systems of reference, along with other former 'commonplaces' such as the town, history, paternity, the tonal system in music, traditional morality, and so forth. This was truly a crucial moment."[1]

The very concept of *moment* is crucial for Lefebvre. Moments are points of rupture—ephemeral, euphoric, revelatory of the total, radical, sometimes revolutionary possibilities latent in everyday life (or the *quotidien* as he called it, a condition that emerged with the competitive capitalism of the nineteenth century, where new types of alienation were most blatant and oppressive, but which alone could measure the dialectical progress of alienation and becoming). Around 1910 Picasso, Frank Lloyd Wright, and the artists and architects later associated with the Bauhaus all heralded the new space of modernity that was entangled with imperialism, social revolution, a world market, and the explosion of the historical city—heralded, in Lefebvre's phrase, "abstract space," with all its attendant limitations as well as contradictions and possible openings. By around 1950 the process of global urbanization of society completely absorbed and superseded the aspects of social life formerly marked by distinctions between city and country, center and periphery, industry and agriculture, commodity and art, and precipitated the passage from the production of things *in* space to the production of space itself. Around 1968, the moment of a "new praxis" of urbanism emerged within abstract space, in which "the term 'political' is restored to its oldest meaning—the theoretical and practical knowledge of the social life in the community."[2]

Lefebvre's conception of the historical specificity and originality of the production of space, which is lived distinctively and differently from other modes of production, counters the Kantian treatment of space and time as universal, empty containers whose forms stand as frameworks that structure experience but are not themselves part of that experience. The production of space is the way in which the capitalist mode of production maintains itself, creates more space for itself; and urbanization is capitalism's primary extension. The abstract space of capitalism depends on global networks of banks and businesses, on highways and airports, on flows of energy, raw materials, and information. "Natural space" and its particularities like climates and topographies are irrevocably reduced to materials on which society's productive forces operate: ground, underground, air, even light become products that can be manipulated, exchanged, and controlled; space is utilized to produce surplus value; space is consumed in tourism and leisure. Like equipment in factories, the spatial arrangements of cities, regions, nations, and continents increase production and reproduce the relations of production. Even time is spatialized in capitalism's repetition, circularity, and immobility; distances between things (in the sense of

compare Virilio (542 ff)

Benjamin's "aura") are collapsed and our felt perception of our own place in history is distorted.

Abstract space is at once fragmented and homogeneous; capitalism compartmentalizes and routinizes all activity, yet relentlessly saturates any remaining voids with its wavelike flows. Abstract space is pulverized by private property relations, but as a productive force it is global. Such contradictions cause differences to assert themselves even as abstract space tends to dissolve all difference. And it is precisely the instability of abstract space that produces the potential to resist its domination, to produce an "other" space, by what Lefebvre calls the "appropriation" of space from its alienation in capitalism — "the 'real' appropriation of space, which is incompatible with abstract *signs* of appropriation serving merely to mask domination."[3]

The Production of Space is a philosophy of history, not an architecture theory. Yet contained within it is an architecture theory properly understood as a mediation between architecture, broadly conceived, and social practice; indeed, this mediation is primary to Lefebvre's thesis that space is a social product whose particularity is revealed only to the extent that it is distinguished from epistemological space (the "absolute" space of philosophy and mathematics) and physical space (as defined by purely practical activities or the perception of "nature"). What is more, architecture theory is credited with an adumbration of a history of space (Giedion), a notion of the body as a totality with spatial qualities and energetic properties (Zevi), and a perception of the ascendancy of the logic of visualization (Panofsky). What architecture theory has not grasped, however, is the ideology of such a logic based only on speech and writing or vision. For when communication and the spectacle (Debord) displace social practice, the twin illusions of innocent transparency and substantiality of meaning rush in to fill the void. Lefebvre here speaks directly to the semiotic theories of architecture prevalent in the early 1970s when he insists that spatial practice is, precisely, *acted* and not read.

❚ *see* x–xii ❚

Despite his acute criticism of abstract space, Lefebvre remained optimistic (if vague) that the very contradictions of abstract space could be deployed against it to produce a differential space in the future. "Insofar as we can conceive it, given certain current tendencies, socialist space will be a *space of differences*."[4] In his existentialist, utopian version of the role of Marxism, according to which ideology might project some future, he directly counters the bleak prognosis of Tafuri. Yet his program has not been fully developed in architecture theory.

❚ *compare* 146–147 ❚

Notes

1. Henri Lefebvre, *The Production of Space*, trans. Donald Nicholson-Smith (Cambridge: Blackwell, 1991), p. 25.

2. Henri Lefebvre, *The Explosion: Marxism and the French Revolution*, trans. Alfred Ehrenfeld (New York: Monthly Review Press, 1969), p. 155.

3. Lefebvre, *The Production of Space*, p. 393.

4. Henri Lefebvre, "Space: Social Product and Use Value," in *Critical Sociology: European Perspectives*, ed. J. W. Freiberg (New York: Irvington, 1979), p. 293. It should not be supposed, however, that this space of differences will be brought into being by architects. "Turning the world 'back on its feet,' according to Marx, implies overturning dominant spaces, placing appropriation over domination, demand over command and use over exchange. . . . It is space as a whole that would be redefined, that would bring about a conversion and subversion." (Ibid., p. 294.)

It might be asked if there is any way of dating what might be called the moment of emergence of an awareness of space and its production: when and where, why and how, did a neglected knowledge and a misconstrued reality begin to be recognized? It so happens that this emergence can indeed be fixed: it is to be found in the "historic" role of the Bauhaus. For the Bauhaus did more than locate space in its real context or supply a new perspective on it: it developed a new conception, a global concept, of space. At that time, around 1920, just after the First World War, a link was discovered in the advanced countries (France, Germany, Russia, the United States), a link which had already been dealt with on the practical plane but which had not yet been rationally articulated: that between industrialization and urbanization, between workplaces and dwelling places. No sooner had this link been incorporated into theoretical thought than it turned into a project, even into a program. The curious thing is that this "programmatic" stance was looked upon at the time as both rational and revolutionary, although in reality it was tailor-made for the state—whether of the state-capitalist or the state-socialist variety. Later, of course, this would become obvious—a truism. For Gropius or for Le Corbusier, the program boiled down to the production of space. As Paul Klee put it, artists—painters, sculptors or architects—do not show space, they create it. The Bauhaus people understood that things could not be created independently of each other in space, whether movable (furniture) or fixed (buildings), without taking into account their interrelationships and their relationship to the whole. It was impossible simply to accumulate them as a mass, aggregate or collection of items. In the context of the productive forces, the technological means and the specific problems of the modern world, things and objects could now be produced in their relationships, along with their relationships. Formerly, artistic ensembles—monuments, towns, furnishings—had been created by a variety of artists according to subjective criteria: the taste of princes, the intelligence of rich patrons or the genius of the artists themselves. Architects had thus built palaces designed to house specific objects ("furniture") associated with an aristocratic mode of life, and, alongside them, squares for the people and monuments for social institutions. The resulting whole might constitute a space with a particular style, often even a dazzling style but it was still a space never rationally defined which came into being and disappeared for no clear reason. As he considered the past and viewed it in the light of the present, Gropius sensed that henceforward social practice was destined to change. The production of spatial ensembles as such corresponded to the capacity of the productive forces, and hence to a specific rationality. It was thus no longer a question of introducing forms, functions or structures in isolation, but rather one of mastering global space by bringing forms, functions and structures together in accordance with a unitary conception. This insight confirmed after its fashion an idea of Marx's, the idea that industry has the power to open before our eyes the book of the creative capacities of "man" (i.e. of social being).

The Bauhaus group, as artists associated in order to advance the total project of a total art, discovered, along with Klee,[1] that an observer could move around any object in social space—including such objects as houses, public buildings and palaces—and in so doing go beyond scrutinizing or studying it under a single or special aspect. Space opened up to perception, to conceptualization, just as it did to practical action. And the artist passed from objects in space to the concept of space itself. Avant-garde painters of the same period reached very similar conclusions: all aspects of an object could be considered simultaneously, and this simultaneity preserved and summarized a temporal sequence. This had several consequences.

1. A *new consciousness of space* emerged whereby space (an object in its surroundings) was explored, sometimes by deliberately reducing it to its outline or plan and to the flat surface of the canvas, and sometimes, by contrast, by breaking up and rotating planes, so as to reconstitute depth of space in the picture plane. This gave rise to a very specific dialectic.

2. *The facade*—as face directed towards the observer and as a privileged side or aspect of a work of art or a monument—*disappeared*. (Fascism, however, placed an increased emphasis on facades, thus opting for total "spectacularization" as early as the 1920s.)

3. *Global space* established itself in the abstract as a void waiting to be filled, as a medium waiting to be colonized. How this could be done was a problem solved only later by the social practice of capitalism: eventually, however, this space would come to be filled by commercial images, signs and objects. This development would in turn result in the advent of the pseudoconcept of the environment (which begs the question: the environment of whom or of what?).

The historian of space who is concerned with modernity may quite confidently affirm the historic role of the Bauhaus. By the 1920s the great philosophical systems had been left behind, and, aside from the investigations of mathematics and physics, all thinking about space and time was bound up with social practice—more precisely, with industrial practice, and with architectural and urbanistic research. This transition from philosophical abstraction to the analysis of social practice is worth stressing. While it was going on, those responsible for it, the Bauhaus group and others, believed that they were more than innovators, that they were in fact revolutionaries. With the benefit of fifty years of hindsight, it is clear that such a claim cannot legitimately be made for anyone in that period except for the Dadaists (and, with a number of reservations, a few surrealists).

It is easy enough to establish the historic role of the Bauhaus, but not so easy to assess the breadth and limits of this role. Did it cause or justify a change of aesthetic perspective, or was it merely a symptom of a change in social practice? More likely the latter, *pace* most historians of art and architecture. When it comes to the question of what the Bauhaus's audacity produced in the long run, one is obliged to answer: the worldwide, homogeneous and monotonous architecture of the state, whether capitalist or socialist.

How and why did this happen? If there is such a thing as the history of space, if space may indeed be said to be specified on the basis of historical periods, societies, modes of production and relations of production, then there is such a thing as a space characteristic of capitalism—that is, characteristic of that society which is run and dominated by the bourgeoisie. It is certainly arguable that the writings and works of the Bauhaus, of Mies van der Rohe among others, outlined, formulated and helped realize that particular space—the fact that the Bauhaus sought to be and proclaimed itself to be revolutionary notwithstanding.[2]

The first initiative taken towards the development of a history of space was Sigfried Giedion's.[3] Giedion kept his distance from practice but worked out the theoretical object of any such history in some detail; he put space, and not some creative genius, not the "spirit of the times," and not even technological progress, at the center of history as he conceived it. According to Giedion there have been three successive periods. During the first of these (ancient Egypt and Greece), architectural volumes were conceived and realized in the context of their social relationships—and hence from *without*. The Roman Pantheon illustrates a second conception, under which the *interior* space of the monument became paramount. Our own period, by contrast, supposedly seeks to surmount the exterior-interior dichotomy by grasping an interaction or unity between these two spatial aspects. Actually, Giedion succeeds here only in *inverting* the reality of social space. The fact is that the Pantheon, as an image of the world or *mundus*, is an opening to the light; the *imago mundi*, the interior hemisphere or dome, symbolizes this exterior. As for the Greek temple, it encloses a sacred and consecrated space, the space of a localized divinity and of a divine locality, and the political center of the city.[4] The source of such confusion is to be found in an initial error of Giedion's, echoes of which occur throughout his work: he posits a pre-existing space—Euclidean space—in which all human emotions and expectations proceed to invest themselves and make themselves tangible. The spiritualism latent in this philosophy of space emerges clearly in Giedion's later work *The Eternal Present*.[5] Giedion was indeed never able to free himself from a naive oscillation between the geometrical and the spiritualistic. A further problem was that he failed to separate the history he was developing from the history of art and architecture, although the two are certainly quite different.

The idea that space is essentially empty but comes to be occupied by visual messages also limits the thinking of Bruno Zevi.[6] Zevi holds that a geometrical space is animated by the gestures and actions of those who inhabit it. He reminds us, in a most timely manner, of the basic fact that every building has an interior as well as an exterior. This means that there is an architectural space defined by the inside-outside relationship, a space which is a tool for the architect in his social action. The remarkable thing here, surely, is that it should be necessary to recall this duality several decades after the Bauhaus, and in Italy to boot, supposedly the "birthplace" of architecture. We are obliged to conclude that the critical analysis of the facade mentioned above has simply never taken hold, and that space has remained *strictly visual*, entirely subordinate to a "logic of visualization." Zevi considers that the visual conception of space rests upon a bodily (gestural) component which the trained eye of the expert observer must take into account. Zevi's book brings this "lived" aspect of spatial experience, which thanks to its corporal nature has the capacity to "incarnate," into the realm of knowledge, and hence of "consciousness," without ever entertaining the idea that such a bodily component of optical (geometrico-visual) space might put the priority of consciousness itself into question. He does not appear to understand the implications of his findings beyond the pedagogical sphere, beyond the training of architects and the education of connoisseurs, and he certainly does not pursue the matter on a theoretical level. In the absence of a viewer with an acquired mastery of space, how could any space be adjudged "beautiful" or "ugly," asks Zevi, and how could this aesthetic yardstick attain its primordial value? To answer one question with another, how could a constructed space subjugate or repel otherwise than through *use*?[7]

Contributions such as those of Giedion and Zevi undoubtedly have a place in the development of a history of space, but they herald that history without helping to institute it. They serve to point up its problems, and they blaze the trail. They do not tackle the tasks that still await the history of space proper: to show up the growing ascendancy of the abstract and the visual, as well as the internal connection between them; and to expose the genesis and meaning of the "logic of the visual"—that is, to expose the *strategy* implied in such a "logic" in light of the fact that any particular "logic" of this kind is always merely a deceptive name for a strategy.

Historical materialism will be so far extended and borne out by a history so conceived that it will undergo a serious transformation. Its objectivity will be deepened inasmuch as it will come to bear no longer solely upon the production of things and works, and upon the (dual) history of that production, but will reach out to take in space and time and, using nature as its "raw material," broaden the concept of production so as to include the production of space as a process whose product—space—itself embraces both things (goods, objects) and works.

· · ·

As for dialectical materialism, it also is amplified, verified—and transformed. New dialectics make their appearance: work *versus* product, repetition *versus* difference, and so on. The dialectical movement immanent to the division of labor becomes more complex when viewed in the light of an exposition of the relationship between productive activity (both global labor—i.e. social labor—and divided or parceled-out labor) and a specific product, unique in that it is also itself a tool—namely, space. The alleged "reality" of space as natural substance and its alleged "unreality" as transparency are simultaneously exploded by this advance in our thinking. Space still appears as "reality" inasmuch as it is the milieu of accumulation, of growth, of commodities, of money, of capital; but this "reality" loses its substantial and autonomous aspect once its development—i.e. its production—is traced.

There is one question which has remained open in the past because it has never been asked: what exactly is the mode of existence of social relationships? Are they substantial? natural? or formally abstract? The study of space offers an answer according to which the social relations of production have a social existence to the extent that they have a spatial existence; they project themselves into a space, becoming inscribed there, and in the process producing that space itself. Failing this, these relations would remain in the realm of "pure" abstraction—that is to say, in the realm of representations and hence of ideology: the realm of verbalism, verbiage and empty words.

Space itself, at once a product of the capitalist mode of production and an economico-political instrument of the bourgeoisie, will now be seen to embody its own contradictions. The dialectic thus emerges from time and actualizes itself, operating now, in an unforeseen manner, in space. The contradictions of space, without abolishing the contradictions which arise from historical time, leave history behind and transport those old contradictions, in a worldwide simultaneity, onto a higher level; there some of them are blunted, others exacerbated, as this contradictory whole takes on a new meaning and comes to designate "something else"— another mode of production.

· · ·

It is not certain that systems of non-verbal signs answer to the same concepts and categories as verbal systems, or even that they are properly systems at all, since their elements and moments are related more by contiguity and similarity than by any coherent systematization. The question, however, is still an open one. It is true that parts of space, like parts of discourse, are articulated in terms of reciprocal inclusions and exclusions. In language as in space, there is a before and an after, while the present dominates both past and future.

The following, therefore, are perfectly legitimate questions.

1. Do the spaces formed by practico-social activity, whether landscapes, monuments or buildings, have meaning?

2. Can the space occupied by a social group or several such groups be treated as a message?

3. Ought we to look upon architectural or urbanistic works as a type of mass medium, albeit an unusual one?

4. May a social space viably be conceived of as a language or discourse, dependent upon a determinate practice (reading/writing)?

The answer to the first question must, obviously, be yes. The second calls for a more ambiguous "yes and no": spaces contain messages—but can they be reduced to messages? It is tempting to reply that they imply more than that, that they embody functions, forms and structures quite unconnected with discourse. This is an issue that calls for careful scrutiny. As for the third and fourth questions, our replies will have to include the most serious reservations, and we shall be returning to them later.

We can be sure, at any rate, that an understanding of language and of verbal and non-verbal systems of signs will be of great utility in any attempt to understand space. There was once a tendency to study each fragment or element of space separately, seeking to relate it to its own particular past—a tendency to proceed, as it were, etymologically. Today, on the other hand, the preferred objects of study are ensembles, configurations or textures. The result is an extreme formalism, a fetishization of consistency in knowledge and of coherence in practice: a cult, in short, of *words*.

This trend has even generated the claim that discourse and thought have nothing to express but themselves, a position which leaves us with no truth, but merely with "meaning"; with room for "textual" work, and such work only. Here, however, the theory of space has something to contribute. Every language is located in a space. Every discourse says something about a space (places or sets of places); and every discourse is emitted from a space. Distinctions must be drawn between discourse *in* space, discourse *about* space and the discourse *of* space. There are thus relationships between language and space which are to a greater or lesser extent misconstrued or disregarded. There is doubtless no such thing as a "true space," as once postulated by classical philosophy and indeed still postulated by that philosophy's continuation, namely epistemology and the "scientific criteria" it promotes. But there is certainly such a thing as a "truth of space" which embodies the movement of critical theory without being reducible to it. Human beings—why do we persist in saying "man"?—are in space; they cannot absent themselves from it, nor do they allow themselves to be excluded from it.

Apart from what it "remarks" in relation to space, discourse is nothing more than a lethal void—mere verbiage. The analogy between the theory of space (and of its production) and the theory of language (and of its production) can only be carried so far. The theory of space describes and analyses textures. As we shall see, the straight line, the curve (or curved line), the check or draftboard pattern and the radial-concentric (center *versus* periphery) are forms and structures rather than textures. The production of space lays hold of such structures and integrates them into a great variety of wholes (textures). A texture implies a meaning—but a meaning for whom? For some "reader"? No: rather, for someone who lives and acts in the space under consideration, a "subject" with a body—or, sometimes, a "collective subject." From the point of view of such a "subject" the deployment of forms and structures corresponds to functions of the whole. Blanks (i.e. the contrast between absence and presence) and margins, hence networks and webs, have a *lived* sense which has to be raised intact to the *conceptual* level.

. . .

Semiology is the source of the claim that space is susceptible of a "reading," and hence the legitimate object of a practice (reading/writing). The space of the city is said to embody a discourse, a language.[8]

Does it make sense to speak of a "reading" of space? Yes and no. Yes, inasmuch as it is possible to envisage a "reader" who deciphers or decodes and a "speaker" who expresses himself by translating his progression into a discourse. But no, in that social space can in no way be compared to a blank page upon which a specific message has been inscribed (by whom?). Both natural and urban spaces are, if anything, "over-inscribed": everything therein resembles a rough draft, jumbled and self-contradictory. Rather than signs, what one encounters here are directions—multifarious and overlapping instructions. If there is indeed text, inscription or writing to be found here, it is in a context of conventions, intentions and order (in the sense of social order *versus* social disorder). That space signifies is incontestable. But what it signifies is dos and don'ts—and this brings us back to power. Power's message is invariably confused—deliberately so; dissimulation is necessarily part of any message from power. Thus space indeed "speaks"—but it does not tell all. Above all, it prohibits. Its mode of existence, its practical "reality" (including its form) differs radically from the reality (or being-there) of something written, such as a book. Space is at once result and cause, product and producer; it is also a *stake*, the locus of projects and actions deployed as part of specific strategies, and hence also the object of *wagers* on the future—wagers which are articulated, if never completely.

As to whether there is a spatial code, there are actually several. This has not daunted the semiologists, who blithely propose to determine the hierarchy of levels of interpretation and then find a residue of elements capable of getting the decoding process going once more. Fair enough, but this is to mistake restrictions for signs in general. Activity in space is restricted by that space; space "decides" what activity may occur, but even this "decision" has limits placed upon it. Space lays down the law because it implies a certain order—and hence also a certain disorder (just as what may be seen defines what is obscene). Interpretation comes later, almost as an afterthought. Space commands bodies, prescribing or proscribing gestures, routes and distances to be covered. It is produced with this purpose in mind; this is its *raison d'être*. The "reading" of space is thus merely a secondary and practically irrelevant upshot, a rather superfluous reward to the individual for blind, spontaneous and *lived* obedience.

So, even if the reading of space (always assuming there is such a thing) comes first from the standpoint of knowledge, it certainly comes last in the genesis of space itself. No "reading of the space" of Romanesque churches and their surroundings (towns or monasteries), for example, can in any way help us predict the space of so-called Gothic churches or understand their preconditions and prerequisites: the growth of the towns, the revolution of the communes, the activity of the guilds, and so on. This space was *produced* before being *read*; nor was it produced in order to be read and grasped, but rather in order to be *lived* by people with bodies and lives in their own particular urban context. In short, "reading" follows production in all cases except those in which space is produced especially in order to be read. This raises the question of what the virtue of readability actually is. It turns out on close examination that spaces made (produced) to be read are the most deceptive and tricked-up imaginable. The graphic impression of readability is a sort of *trompe-l'oeil* concealing strategic intentions and actions. Monumentality, for instance, always embodies and imposes a clearly intelligible message. It says what it wishes to say—yet it hides a good deal more: being political, military, and ultimately fascist in character, monumental buildings mask the will to power and the arbitrariness of power beneath signs and surfaces which claim to express collective will and collective thought. In the process, such signs and surfaces also manage to conjure away both possibility and time.

We have known since Vitruvius—and in modern times since Labrouste, who was forever harping on it—that in architecture form must express function. Over the centuries the idea contained in the term "express" here has grown narrower and more precise. Most recently, "expressive" has come to mean merely "readable."[9] The architect is supposed to construct a signifying space wherein form is to function as signifier is to signified; the form, in other words, is supposed to enunciate or proclaim the function. According to this principle, which is espoused by most "designers," the environment can be furnished with or animated by signs in such a way as to appropriate space, in such a way that space becomes readable (i.e. "plausibly" linked) to society as a whole. The inherence of function to form, or in other words the application of the criterion of readability, makes for an instantaneousness of reading, act and gesture—hence the tedium which accompanies this quest for a formal-functional transparency. We are deprived of both internal and external distance: there is nothing to code and decode in an "environment without environs." What is more, the significant contrasts in a code of space designed specifically to signify and to "be" readable are extremely commonplace and simple. They boil down to the contrast between horizontal and vertical lines—a contrast which among other things masks the vertical's implication of hauteur. Versions of this contrast are offered in visual terms which are supposed to express it with great intensity but which, to any detached observer, any ideal "walker in the city," have no more than the appearance of intensity. Once again, the impression of intelligibility conceals far more than it reveals. It conceals, precisely, what the visible/readable "is," and what traps it holds; it conceals what the vertical "is"—namely, arrogance, the will to power, a display of military and police-like machismo, a reference to the phallus and a spatial analogue of masculine brutality. Nothing can be taken for granted in space, because what are involved are real or possible acts, and not mental states or more or less well-told stories. In produced space, acts reproduce "meanings" even if no "one" gives an account of them. Repressive space wreaks repression and terror even though it may be strewn with ostensible signs of the contrary (of contentment, amusement or delight).

This tendency has gone so far that some architects have even begun to call either for a return to ambiguity, in the sense of a confused and not immediately interpretable message, or else for a diversification of space which would be consistent with a liberal and pluralistic society.[10] Robert Venturi, as an architect and a theorist of architecture, wants to make space dialectical. He sees space not as an empty and neutral milieu occupied by dead objects but rather as a field of force full of tensions and distortions. Whether this approach can find a way out of functionalism and formalism that goes beyond merely formal adjustments remains (in 1972) to be seen. Painting on buildings certainly seems like a rather feeble way of retrieving the richness of "classical" architecture. Is it really possible to use mural surfaces to depict social contradictions while producing something more than graffiti? That would indeed be somewhat paradoxical if, as I have been suggesting, the notions of "design," of reading/writing as practice, and of the "signifier-signified" relationship projected onto things in the shape of the "form-function" one are all directed, whether consciously or no, towards the dissolving of conflicts into a general transparency, into a one-dimensional present—and onto an as it were "pure" *surface*.

I daresay many people will respond to such thinking somewhat as follows.

Your arguments are tendentious. You want to re-emphasize the signified as opposed to the signifier, the content as opposed to the form. But true innovators operate on forms; they invent new forms by working in the realm of signifiers. If they are writers, this is how they produce a discourse. The same goes for other types of creation. But as for architects who concern themselves primarily with content, as for "users," as for the activity of dwelling itself—all these merely reproduce outdated forms. They are in no sense innovative forces.

To which my reply might be something like this:

I have no quarrel with the proposition that work on signifiers and the production of a language are creative activities; that is an incontestable fact. But I question whether this is the whole story—whether this proposition covers all circumstances and all fields. Surely there comes a moment when formalism is exhausted, when only a new injection of content into form can destroy it and so open up the way to innovation. The harmonists invented a great musical form, for instance, yet the formal discoveries about harmony made by the natural philosophers and by theorists of music such as Rameau did not take the exploration and exploitation of the possibilities that far. Such progress occurred only with the advent of a Mozart or a Beethoven. As for architecture, the builders of palaces worked with and on signifiers (those of power). They kept within the boundaries of a certain monumentality and made no attempt to cross them. They worked, moreover, not upon texts but upon (spatial) textures. Invention of a formal kind could not occur without a change in practice, without, in other words, a dialectical interaction between signifying and signified elements, as some signifiers reached the exhaustion point of their formalism, and some signified elements, with their own peculiar violence, infiltrated the realm of signifiers. The combinatorial system of the elements of a set—for our purposes a set of signs, and hence of signifiers—has a shorter life than the individual combinations that it embraces. For one thing, any such combinatorial system of signs loses its interest and emotional force as soon as it is known and recognized for what it is; a kind of saturation sets in, and even changing the combinations that are included or excluded from the system cannot remedy matters. Secondly, work on signifiers and the production of a discourse facilitate the transmission of messages only if the labor involved is not patent. If the "object" bears traces of that labor, the reader's attention will be diverted to the writing itself and to the one who does the writing. The reader thus comes to share in the fatigue of the producer, and is soon put off.

It is very important from the outset to stress the destructive (because reductive) effects of the predominance of the readable and visible, of the absolute priority accorded to the visual realm, which in turn implies the priority of reading and writing. An emphasis on visual space has accompanied the search for an impression of weightlessness in architecture. Some theorists of a supposed architectural revolution claim Le Corbusier as a pioneer in this connection, but in fact it was Brunelleschi, and more recently Baltard and then Eiffel, who blazed the trail. Once the effect of weightiness or massiveness upon which architects once depended has been abandoned, it becomes possible to break up and reassemble volumes arbitrarily according to the dictates of an architectural neoplasticism. Modernity expressly reduces so-called "iconological" forms of expression (signs and symbols) to surface effects. Volumes or masses are deprived of any physical consistency. The architect considers himself responsible for laying down the social function (or use) of buildings, offices, or dwellings, yet interior walls which no longer have any spatial or bearing role, and interiors in general, are simultaneously losing all character or content. Even exterior walls no longer have any material substance: they have become mere membranes barely managing to concretize the division between inside and out-side. This does not prevent "users" from projecting the relationship between the internal or private and a threatening outside world into an invented absolute realm; when there is no alternative, they use the signs of this antagonism, relying especially on those which indicate property. For an architectural thought in thrall to the model of transparency, however, all partitions between inside and outside have collapsed. Space has been comminuted into "iconological" figures and values, each such fragment being invested with individuality or worth simply by means of a particular color or a particular material (brick, marble, etc.). Thus the sense of circumscribed spaces has gone the same way as the impression of mass. Within and without have melted into transparency, becoming indistinguishable or interchangeable. What makes this tendency even more paradoxical is the fact that it proceeds under the banner of structures, of significant distinctions, and of the inside-outside and signifier-signified relationships themselves.

> . . .

We already know several things about abstract space. As a product of violence and war, it is political; instituted by a state, it is institutional. On first inspection it appears homogeneous; and indeed it serves those forces which make a *tabula rasa* of whatever stands in their way, of whatever threatens them—in short, of differences. These forces seem to grind down and crush everything before them, with space performing the function of a plane, a bulldozer or a tank. The notion of the instrumental homogeneity of space, however, is illusory—though empirical descriptions of space reinforce the illusion—because it uncritically takes the instrumental as a given.

Critical analysis, by contrast, is immediately able to distinguish three aspects or elements here, aspects which might better be described—to borrow a term from the study of musical sounds—as "formants." These formants are unusual (though not unique) in the following respect: they imply one another and conceal one another. (This is not true of bipartite contrasts, the opposing terms of which, by reflecting each other in a simple mirror effect, illuminate each other, so to speak, so that each becomes a signifier instead of remaining obscure or hidden.) What, then, are these three elements?

1. *The geometric formant.* This is that Euclidean space which philosophical thought has treated as "absolute," and hence a space (or representation of space) long used as a space of *reference.* Euclidean space is defined by its "isotopy" (or homogeneity), a property which guarantees its social and political utility. The reduction to this homogeneous Euclidean space, first of nature's space, then of all social space, has conferred a redoubtable power upon it. All the more so since that initial reduction leads easily to another—namely, the reduction of three-dimensional realities to two dimensions (for example, a "plan," a blank sheet of paper, something drawn on that paper, a map, or any kind of graphic representation or projection).

2. *The optical (or visual) formant.* The "logic of visualization" identified by Erwin Panofsky as a strategy embodied in the great Gothic cathedrals now informs the entirety of social practice. Dependence on the written word (Marshall McLuhan) and the process of spectacularization (Guy Debord) are both functions of this logic, corresponding respectively to each of its two moments or aspects: the first is metaphoric (the act of writing and what is written, hitherto subsidiary, become essential—models and focal points of practice), and the second is metonymic (the eye, the gaze, the thing seen, no longer mere details or parts, are now transformed into the totality). In the course of the process whereby the visual gains the upper hand over the other senses, all impressions derived from taste, smell, touch and even hearing first lose clarity, then fade away altogether, leaving the field to line, color and light. In this way a part of the object and what it offers comes to be taken for the

whole. This aberration, which is normal—or at least normalized—finds its justification in the social importance of the written word. Finally, by assimilation, or perhaps by simulation, all of social life becomes the mere decipherment of messages by the eyes, the mere reading of texts. Any non-optical impression—a tactile one, for example, or a muscular (rhythmic) one—is no longer anything more than a symbolic form of, or a transitional step towards, the visual. An object felt, tested by the hands, serves merely as an "analogon" for the object perceived by sight. And Harmony, born through and for listening, is transposed into the visual realm; witness the almost total priority accorded the arts of the image (cinema, painting).

The eye, however, tends to relegate objects to the distance, to render them passive. That which is merely *seen* is reduced to an image—and to an icy coldness. The mirror effect thus tends to become general. Inasmuch as the act of seeing and what is seen are confused, both become impotent. By the time this process is complete, space has no social existence independently of an intense, aggressive and repressive visualization. It is thus—not symbolically but in fact—a purely visual space. The rise of the visual realm entails a series of substitutions and displacements by means of which it overwhelms the whole body and usurps its role. That which is merely seen (and merely visible) is hard to see—but it is spoken of more and more eloquently and written of more and more copiously.

3. *The phallic formant.* This space cannot be completely evacuated, nor entirely filled with mere images or transitional objects. It demands a truly full object—an objectal "absolute." So much, at least, it contributes. Metaphorically, it symbolizes force, male fertility, masculine violence. Here again the part is taken for the whole; phallic brutality does not remain abstract, for it is the brutality of political power, of the means of constraint: police, army, bureaucracy. Phallic erectility bestows a special status on the perpendicular, proclaiming phallocracy as the orientation of space, as the goal of the process—at once metaphoric and metonymic—which instigates this facet of spatial practice.

Abstract space is *not* homogeneous; it simply *has* homogeneity as its goal, its orientation, its "lens." And, indeed, it renders homogeneous. But in itself it is multiform. Its geometric and visual formants are complementary in their antithesis. They are different ways of achieving the same outcome: the reduction of the "real," on the one hand, to a "plan" existing in a void and endowed with no other qualities, and, on the other hand, to the flatness of a mirror, of an image, of pure spectacle under an absolutely cold gaze. As for the phallic, it fulfills the extra function of ensuring that "something" occupies this space, namely, a signifier which, rather than signifying a void, signifies a plenitude of destructive force—an illusion, therefore, of plenitude, and a space taken up by an "object" bearing a heavy cargo of myth. The use value of a space of this kind is political—exclusively so. If we speak of it as a "subject" with such and such an aim and with such and such means of action, this is because there really is a subject here, a political subject—power as such, and the state as such.

Thus to look upon abstract space as homogeneous is to embrace a representation that takes the effect for the cause, and the goal for the reason why that goal is pursued. A representation which passes itself off as a *concept*, when it is merely an image, a mirror, and a mirage; and which, instead of challenging, instead of refusing, merely *reflects*. And what does such a specular representation reflect? It reflects the result sought. "Behind the curtain there is nothing to see," says Hegel ironically somewhere. Unless, of course, "we" go behind the curtain ourselves, because someone has to be there to see, and for there to be something to see. In space, or behind it, there is no unknown substance, no mystery. And yet this transparency is deceptive, and everything is concealed: space is illusory and the secret of the illusion lies in the transparency itself. The apparatus of power and knowledge that is revealed once we have "drawn the curtain" has therefore nothing of smoke and mirrors about it.

Notes

1. In 1920 Klee had this to say: "Art does not reflect the visible; it renders visible."
2. See Michel Ragon, *Histoire mondiale de l'architecture et de l'urbanisme modernes*, 3 vols. (Tournai: Casterman, 1971–1978), esp. vol. 2, pp. 147ff.
3. Sigfried Giedion, *Space, Time and Architecture* (Cambridge, Mass.: Harvard University Press, 1941).
4. Cf. Heidegger's discussion of the Greek temple in *Holzwege*.
5. Sigfried Giedion, *The Eternal Present*, 2 vols. (New York: Bollingen Foundation/Pantheon, 1962–1964).
6. See Bruno Zevi, *Architecture as Space: How to Look at Architecture*, tr. Milton Gendel, rev. ed. (New York: Horizon Press, 1974).
7. Ibid., pp. 23ff. See also Philippe Boudon's comments in his *L'espace architectural* (Paris: Dunod, 1971), pp. 27ff.
8. See Roland Barthes in *Architecture d'Aujourd'hui*, nos. 132 and 153.
9. See Charles Jencks, *Architecture 2000: Predictions and Methods* (New York: Praeger, 1971), pp. 114–116.
10. See Robert Venturi, *Complexity and Contradiction in Architecture* (New York: Museum of Modern Art/Doubleday, 1966).

Denis Hollier   **"Architectural Metaphors"** From *La prise de la Concorde* (Paris: Editions Gallimard, 1974), translated as *Against Architecture*, trans. Betsy Wing (Cambridge: MIT Press, 1989)

compare Wigley
(**660 ff**)

"We shall begin with architecture," Denis Hollier tells us in the first line of *Against Architecture*, his study of the writings of Georges Bataille. It is one of two beginnings, an exegesis of Hegel's aesthetics and its privileging of architecture as a model for an entire philosophical system. The second beginning is an analysis of Bataille's earliest text — *Notre-Dame de Rheims*, a religious meditation on that cathedral and a plea for its restoration after its bombing in World War I — a text that reproduces unawares Hegel's initial architecture metaphor and a Hegelian three-part progression. The cathedral is the symbol of continuity, goodness, whiteness and youth, safety and faith. The war, destroyer of the cathedral, is connected to contemporary materialism, to the negation of the cathedral. The exhortation to restore the cathedral is the negation of the negation, Hegel's *Aufhebung*.

Bataille did not write again for ten years after this first published text, at which point he began his "labyrinthian," surrealist work that aimed at the undoing of structures both linguistic and architectural — erotic, excessive, radically incomplete and formless. Hollier sees this hiatus as a slow burial in which the early text on architecture is covered over with layers of silence. The task of the subsequent work is against the first, against the self-constituting and repressive hierarchies of systems building, against the architectural metaphor of the cathedral — writing against architecture.

In some ways all of Bataille's work will be a rewriting of this initial text, a reworking intended to dismantle such a beginning and draw out its silences . . . not because of a paralyzed guilt; rather because this text itself is the almost anonymous (and for this reason negligible) result of the vast ideological system symbolized and maintained by architecture. In order to loosen the structure that is hierarchical and at the same time creates hierarchy, Bataille will introduce the play of writing. Writing in this sense would be a profoundly antiarchitectural gesture, a nonconstructive gesture, one that, on the contrary, undermines and destroys everything whose existence depends on edifying pretensions.[1]

In his article "Architecture," published in *Documents* in 1929, Bataille began his denunciation of architecture's complicity with authoritarian hierarchies. As Hollier puts it, "Architecture is society's authorized superego; there is no architecture that is not the Commendatore's."[2] In his article "Informe," Bataille used the term *besogne* — job, with connotations of drudgery — to designate the work of a word in terms not of its meaning but of the effects it induces. In "Architectural Metaphors," Hollier considers the work of the word *architecture* and its constitutive-constraining functions, the critique of which might then be accomplished through the polyphonic, intertextual play of writing.

Hollier's essay represents an indictment of architecture's fundamental and unavoidable confinement and violence that would later, with the writings and projects of Bernard Tschumi, Rem Koolhaas, Mark Wigley, and others, be seen as a potential for new areas of investigation, for an architecture that undoes *itself*.

Notes

1. Denis Hollier, *Against Architecture*, trans. Betsy Wing (Cambridge: MIT Press, 1989), pp. 22–23.
2. Ibid., p. ix.

Books are not made like children but like pyramids.

FLAUBERT TO FEYDEAU, 1858

The "jobs" taken on by the word "architecture" certainly have more import than its meaning. When architecture is discussed it is never simply a question of architecture; the metaphors cropping up as a result of these jobs are almost inseparable from the proper meaning of the term. The proper meaning itself remains somehow indeterminate, which is all the more surprising since it is associated with jobs that are strikingly clear and urgent. Architecture refers to whatever there is in an edifice that cannot be reduced to building, whatever allows a construction to escape from purely utilitarian concerns, whatever is aesthetic about it. Now this sort of artistic supplement that, by its addition to a simple building, constitutes architecture, finds itself caught from the beginning in a process of semantic expansion that forces what is called architecture to be only the general locus or framework of representation, its ground. Architecture represents a religion that it brings alive, a political power that it manifests, an event that it commemorates, etc. Architecture, before any other qualifications, is identical to the space of representation; it always represents something other than itself from the moment that it becomes distinguished from mere building. This encroachment by an irreducibly metaphorical situation, with architecture defined as the representation of something else, extends to language, where architectural metaphors are very common. There is the facade, generally concealing some sordid reality; there is the secret, hidden architecture itself that one discovers in seemingly the freest works of art, in living beings, indeed in the universe itself where one acknowledges the creator's unified plan; pillars are not all literally pillars of the church; keystones prevent systems (whether political, philosophical, or scientific) from collapsing; to say nothing of foundations, etc., etc. These metaphors seem too inevitable for us to see them as sought-after literary effects. Their cliche nature and their anonymity are, however, an indication that they are not innocent, but rather surreptitiously accomplishing some ideological task for which they are the instruments. Never mind if the proper meaning of architecture remains subject to discussion. What is essential is that it always do its job. No metaphor is innocent; and the less it is contrived the less it is innocent. Its self-evidence is the ground floor where thought can safely walk in its sleep.

Hubert Damisch has shown that Viollet-le-Duc's *Dictionnaire de l'architecture française* followed a structuralist analytical method (one since developed by Saussure and the linguists) before the term was invented.[1] This homology is not purely coincidental. Instead of seeing the architect's discourse as a preformation of the linguist's, the homology requires in fact that linguistic analysis be thought of as dominated by the importation of an architectural vocabulary. The term "structure" itself is not the least of the evidence. That it is used today to describe practically all organizations and all systems shows just how far the domination extends.

(In memoriam. The metaphor here will be borrowed from Jacques Lacan in his praise for an "edifice": the theoretical work of Ernest Jones, to contrast it with the pragmatism reigning in what he calls the professional psychoanalytic "building." "This edifice is appealing to us. For, metaphoric though this may be, it is perfectly constructed to remind us of what distinguished architecture from building: that is a logical power organizing architecture beyond anything the building supports in terms of possible use. Moreover no building, unless reduced to a shack, can do without this order allying it with discourse. This logic coexists harmoniously with efficacy only when dominating it, and in the art of construction their discord is not just a possibility.")[2]

There is consequently no way to describe a system without resorting to the vocabulary of architecture. When structure defines the general form of legibility, nothing becomes legible unless it is submitted to the architectural grid. Architecture under these conditions is the architstructure, the system of systems. The keystone of systematicity in general, it organizes the concord of languages and guarantees universal legibility. The temple of meaning, it dominates and totalizes signifying productions, forcing them all to come down to the same thing, to confirm its noologic system. Architecture is a compulsory loan burdening all of ideology, mortgaging all its differences from the outset.

It is as if, by allowing themselves to be named metaphorically by a vocabulary borrowed from architecture, the various fields of ideological production uncovered a unitary vocation. This metaphor provides the system's form in every area where it appears. Which results in the repression of anything resembling play, exteriority, or alterity. The system tends to be monodic: it has only one voice, the other voice is not heard there. There is a sort of gigantic internal monologue that it organizes. Otherness is excluded; it has no other place than outside. In an exterior which, reduced to silence, has no voice in the matter.

(Félibien counts Noah's ark as a work of architecture and suggests the tight connection between this art and religion. "This people," he writes, speaking of the Jewish people, "held architecture in special esteem, no doubt because this art has some divine element, and because God not only is called in the Scripture the sovereign architect of the Universe, but because he was willing himself to teach Noah how the Ark should be built.")[3]

The great architect is, by metaphor, God, or to use the rationalist litotes, the Supreme Being. Starting with the activity of the architect conceiving his work as its analogon, ideology gives hints of what the final word will be, the word on which its entire meaning hangs. But the impact of the analogy is not limited to cause, it is equally valid for effect. The image of the world itself is caught in the architectural analogy. But this analogy programs architecture in advance in a religious and theological perspective, imposing a cosmic function on it. The world is legible only if one starts with the temple's dome, and God is the great architect only because the temple the architect has constructed celebrates the divine work. Such a metaphor only functions on the basis of the architect's commitment to the economy of faith. In other words, it is faith that makes the architect. Cosmic symbolism is not self-evident and the homology between temple and cosmos is not a given but a requirement, a must with which the architect must comply. But faith is what upholds the resemblance.

Let's not forget this shattering of the economy of mimesis that defines the ideology function of architecture: it does not produce copies, but models. It produces itself as model. It does not imitate an order but constitutes it: whether the order of the world or of society.

In Quatremère de Quincy's *Dictionnaire d'architecture* the autoproduction of architecture produces a similar breakaway beyond mimesis. The structure of mimesis is called into question there by "accomplished" architecture, which has no existing model anywhere for itself and which thus must itself produce what it is to imitate. In fact Quatremère says: If architecture begins by imitating itself, by mechanically reproducing its own origins (as it still does for mere buildings—sheds, houses, etc.); and if then it imitates the human body, doubtless not as sculpture (which only deals with external forms) does, but by studying and drawing on its knowledge of the proportions and the organization that make up its beauty, whose relationships it will reproduce in its edifices; in its most accomplished stage architecture "imitates" nature itself, it "reproduces" the harmonious system of cosmic laws:

It is no longer from wooden frames or huts that it will obtain its origins, nor from the human body whose proportions it will use to regulate its relationships; it is nature itself, in its abstract essence, that it takes for its model. It is nature's order par excellence that becomes its archetype and its genius. . . . It is thus that this art, seemingly more materially dependent than others, in this last respect was able to become more ideal than they, that is, more fitted to exercise the intelligent side of our soul. Nature, in fact, beneath its material exterior, provides only intellectual analogies and relationships for it to reproduce. This art imitates its model less in material than in abstract qualities. It does not follow it but goes alongside. It does not make things it sees, but watches how they are made. It is not interested in the results but in the cause producing them.

As nature's emulator, its efforts are bent to the study of nature's means and to reproducing its results on a smaller scale. Thus, whereas other arts of delineation have created models that they imitate, architecture must create its own, without being able to seize upon it anywhere in reality.[4]

Architecture, consequently, has no "created" model; it must create this. It follows an archetype, but one that does not exist independent of itself. Far more importantly, it must itself produce this archetype. Which is how the unity of plan between architecture and nature is guaranteed. By constituting itself as a microcosm, architecture delineates the world and projects the shadow of the great architect behind it. Without architecture the world would remain illegible. Nature is the archetype of architecture only insofar as architecture is the archetype of nature. It is less that architecture is cosmic than that the cosmos itself is architectured.

Taine in *Philosophie de l'art* defines architecture as the production of a harmonious whole whose example is not found in nature: "In every art there must be a whole made up of connected parts modified by the artist so as to manifest some character; but it is not necessary in every art that this whole correspond to real objects; it is enough for it to exist. Hence, if it is possible to encounter wholes made of connected parts that are not imitative of real objects, there will be arts that do not have imitation as their point of departure. This does happen, and thus architecture and music are born. In fact, apart from the connections, proportions, organic and moral dependencies copied by the three imitative arts, there are mathematical relationships worked out by the other two that imitate nothing.")[5]

Vitruvius begins his book (in some ways the bible of architecture) with this definition: "Architecture is a science that must be accompanied by a great diversity of studies and knowledge, by means of which it judges all the works of the other arts." Omniscience is the architect's greatest virtue. It is the quality permitting him, whether he is "great" or of lesser stature, according to Boullée, to "make himself the one who implements nature,"[6] which is what distinguishes his art from the simple art of building, which concerns merely the execution of a plan: first it must be conceived. Conception as a precondition implies recourse to all branches of knowledge, so as to judge, for example, the appropriateness of the mathematical proportions of the edifice to its purpose, as well as its geographical surroundings or its insertion into communal life, etc. All branches of knowledge converge thus in architecture, which for this reason occupies a position that can be very exactly defined as *encyclopedic*. And, if we are to believe Perrault, in his edition of Vitruvius, this would even be the word's etymological sense: "Architecture is of all the sciences the one to which the Greeks gave a name signifying superiority and stewardship over the others."

The primacy of architecture is assured by its unifying function. It constitutes the unity of the sciences, no matter if following a theological or mathematical inspiration: it sets unity as the required vocation. Locus of peace, *Place de la Concorde*.

(Alberti, in *Della tranquillità dell'animo* [1442], recommends that, to flee anxiety and pain, one devote oneself to mathematics or to architectural reverie: "Sometimes I have designed and built finely proportioned buildings in my mind, arranging their orders and numerous columns with cornices and panels. And I have occupied myself with constructions of this kind until overcome by sleep."[7] Architecture restores peace to the soul.)

Architecture represents this silent, homologous, gravitational mass that absorbs every meaningful production. The monument and the pyramid are where they are to cover up a place, to fill in a void: the one left by death. Death must not appear, it must not take place: let tombs cover it up and take its place. Death comes with time as the unknown borne by the future. It is the other of everything known; it threatens the meaning of discourses. Death is hence irreducibly heterogeneous to homologies; it is not assimilable. The death wish, whose action Freud recognized whenever a return to the inanimate could be noted, whenever difference was denied, wears the elusive face of this expanding homology that causes the place of the Other to be imported into the Same. One plays dead so that death will not come. So nothing will happen and time will not take place.

Notes

1. Hubert Damisch spoke of "the specifically structural—one would say today, structuralist—notion formed by Viollet-le-Duc concerning the relationship between the architectural whole and its constituent elements." If only the *Dictionnaire de l'architecture française* were read, he continues, "with attention to the dialectic of the whole to its parts and the parts to the whole which is the avowed motivation for this 'descriptive' dictionary it will inevitably seem to be the manifesto, or at least the oddly precocious, definite outline of the method and ideology of the sort of structural thought that is famous today in linguistics and anthropology." Introduction to *L'architecture raisonnée*, extracts from the *Dictionnaire de l'architecture française* of Viollet-le-Duc (Paris: Hermann, 1964), p. 14.

2. Jacques Lacan, "A la mémoire d'Ernest Jones: Sur sa théorie du symbolisme," *Ecrits* (Paris: Seuil, 1966), p. 698.

3. André Félibien, *La vie des architectes*, book 1.

4. M. Quatremère de Quincy, *Encyclopédie méthodique: Architecture*, vol. 1 (Paris, 1788), p. 120 (from the article "Architecture").

5. Hippolyte Taine, *Philosophie de l'art*, I, I, VI.

6. Etienne Louis Boullée, *Architecture, essai sur l'art*, ed. Jean-Marie Pérouse de Montclos (Paris: Hermann, 1968).

7. Leon Battista Alberti, *Della tranquillità dell'animo*, quoted in Franco Borsi, *Leon Battista Alberti*, trans. Rudolf C. Carpanini (New York: Harper & Row, 1977).

1974

Diana Agrest   **"Design versus Non-Design"** Paper presented at the First International Congress of
Semiotic Studies, Milan, July 1974; published in *Oppositions* 6 (Fall 1976)

| *see* 112–113 |

| *compare* Gandelsonas (114–115) |

Among the five essays in the inaugural issue of *Oppositions*, the last, Diana Agrest
and Mario Gandelsonas's "Semiotics and Architecture: Ideological Consumption or
Theoretical Work," stood out for its intense theoretical language adopted from the
Parisian *Tel Quel* group, its thoroughgoing European approach based on structuralist
Marxist principles, and its searing criticism of the Anglo-American absorption of semiotics into architectural theory.[1] The essay advanced what would become a primary theme
for Diana Agrest: the structure of the exchange between architecture and ideology, of
architecture *as* ideology, which was based on the pivotal work of Louis Althusser.

"Design versus Non-Design," the centerpiece of her theoretical
oeuvre, continues the elaboration of this theme within an Althusserian paradigm, but
now avoids the problematic distinction of the earlier essay between ideology and
theory or "science," concentrating instead on the discursive specificity of architectural
codes which are nevertheless permeable to other cultural codes — what Althusser
called the relative autonomy of levels in a social formation organized in a structured
but decentered totality. Borrowing the Freudian concept of overdetermination, Althusser insisted that no instance or practice (architecture, say) was ever determined by
one or even a set of other instances or practices (economy and politics, say); neither
was any instance ever fully autonomous. Rather, each was determined by the effects
and interactions of *all* the other instances at once — a set of insides and outsides
enfolded in the structural totality.[2] Agrest sees the interaction of these zones as an
exchange of ideological codes, each of which has its own designations of relevance,
propriety, regularity, and so forth, but which can *transcode*, that is, act as a kind of
commutation device, moving and sorting among other discourses and levels in the
cultural field. A code is like an ideological prospect, constantly shifting its point of
view, constantly being produced, constantly seeking to compare itself to the conceptual possibilities of other codes. And architecture is therefore not confined to its own
narrow idiolect of design, but rather transcodes between design and non-design,
throwing discursive forces into multiple play.

Design can achieve a certain plurality. Within its necessary enclosure of specificity — its cultivation of its own autonomous techniques and occlusion
of other cultural codes — it is unconstrained by an imperative of representation; it can
combine multiple networks of self-reflexive meaning and provide various points of
access for filtering material from outside, as Agrest's examples of metaphor attest.
Nevertheless, design classically conceived produces what Roland Barthes called a
lisible text (classical and *lisible* are synonyms for Barthes), in which the whole range
of institutionalized techniques and habits necessary for its legibility — and that make
it an integral whole, a traditionally "good" design — limit the plurality of the text.[3]
Non-design, in contrast, produces a *scriptible* text, permeable, fluctuating, giving no
indications as to how it is to be read, demanding that its reading be in effect its
rewriting. To maintain the architectural text's plurality, a reading is called for that
refuses to make hierarchies, integrations, or syntheses of the heterogeneous constituent codes, that instead simply juxtaposes fragment by fragment — a productive reading, Agrest's *mise-en-séquence*.

New theoretical discourse is produced in this active exchange between design and non-design. The rewriting of the Althusserian structure in terms of codes allows Agrest to construct a powerful if still skeletal model of the line of impingement between the autonomy of architectural discourse as it was understood in the mid-1970s and the larger sociocultural field from which it was emergent and whose structures were immanent in its forms. Both the causal model of an economic-technological base determining an architectural superstructure and the formalist model of a unified, freestanding architectural object can be rejected when it becomes "possible to discern the mode of articulation between the various systems and, in this way, to define the cultural and ideological overdetermination of the built environment, or rather the process by which culture is woven into it."

Notes

"Design versus Non-Design" was reprinted in Agrest, *Architecture from Without: Theoretical Framings for a Critical Practice* (Cambridge: MIT Press, 1991).

1. Diana Agrest and Mario Gandelsonas, "Semiotics and Architecture: Ideological Consumption or Theoretical Work," *Oppositions* 1 (September 1973). "In opposition to ideology, we propose a *theory* of architecture, which is necessarily placed outside ideology. This theory describes and explains the relationships between society and the built environments of different cultures and modes of production. . . . The *relationships* between theory and ideology might be viewed as a continuous struggle where ideology defends a type of knowledge whose major effect is the preservation of existing social systems and their institutions, rather than the explanation of reality." This is a concise summation of the distinction made by Althusser between ideology and knowledge or "science"—what Agrest and Gandelsonas call theory—differentiating the *imaginary* political function of ideologies, whose purpose is to secure the conditions for reproducing the forms of social domination, from the *epistemological* function of science, which is to produce descriptions of the real nature of objects. This means neither that we can do without ideology nor that science is more valuable than ideology. Rather the two are different registers of social being, with different vocations and different material conditions of existence. See Louis Althusser, "Ideology and Ideological State Apparatuses," in *Lenin and Philosophy and Other Essays*, trans. Ben Brewster (New York: Verso, 1971); and *For Marx*, trans. Ben Brewster (New York: Pantheon, 1969).

2. The conception implies, of course, that each instance is not simply determined by the economic level, as in reductionist Marxism. Althusser does not allow this conception of the social formation to mean an equality of interaction between all instances, however; rather he affirms that in each social formation there is one instance that is dominant, thus securing a certain kind of unity.

     Note, too, that the shift in Agrest's language from "instance" to "discourse" is not inconsistent. Althusser regarded the work on medical and psychiatric discourses produced by his student, Michel Foucault, as exemplary investigations of the conditions of the production of knowledge.

3. Roland Barthes, *S/Z*, trans. Richard Miller (New York: Hill and Wang, 1974). Agrest attended Barthes's lectures on Honoré de Balzac's *Sarrasine* at the Ecole Pratique des Hautes Etudes in Paris, 1968, lectures that became *S/Z*.

The specific relationship of architecture to ideology has been generally excluded from consideration in traditional architectural criticism. Concerned only to relate architecture formally, or internally, to itself, or at best to relate architecture externally to society in general, criticism has failed to truly incorporate the *cultural* problematic of architecture into its domain of concern. When the cultural dimension has been introduced, it has more often been as a simple explanation of architecture as "reflecting" a particular culture—the notion of style as the expression of the spirit of the age—than as a problem to be confronted independently from a consistent theoretical standpoint.

Practicing architects and critics of architecture have repeatedly emphasized the need to relate architecture to its social or cultural context. Positions have been developed around such concepts as "contextualism" and "ugly and ordinary" by writers like Colin Rowe and Denise Scott Brown and Robert Venturi. Rowe, for example, speaks of an architectural contextualism that situates the object of design or analysis in its physical-historical surroundings in terms of formal elements and relations; Venturi and Scott Brown speak of the need to recognize mass culture as *the* necessary cultural product of our time and as a new source of inspiration for designers. However, rather than attempting to appeal to the notion of collage—a familiar architectural strategy in periods of transition—or to the simulation of the objects of mass culture, this analysis will attempt to investigate the mechanisms of the built environment at this specific historical moment.

I wish to explore here the *external* or cultural relations of architecture—that is, between architecture and its social context—by means of a theoretical model that posits two distinct forms of cultural, or symbolic, production. The first, which I shall call *design*, is that mode by which architecture relates to cultural systems outside itself; it is a normative process and embraces not only architecture but also urban design. The second, which is more properly called *non-design*, describes the way in which different cultural systems interrelate and give form to the built world; it is not a direct product of any institutionalized design practice but rather the result of a general process of culture.

In thus examining the mechanisms which relate architecture to culture—the processes by which meaning is produced, not only within architecture or design, but also in the domain of non-design—we are, of course, analyzing ideology itself. For ideology is no more than the social production of meaning. Thus, all cultural production, such as architecture, when articulated at the economic and political levels, manifests the ways in which ideology is produced as part of a given social structure.[1]

In this sense, it is unnecessary to compare one type of architecture to any other type of architecture—as in the accepted mode of "formal," internal criticism—or to compare it to society in general. Rather, one must oppose the notion of architecture as *design* to the notion of a radically different kind of symbolic configuration—*non-design*. This opposition allows a reading of the built environment in terms of the relationship between different cultural systems. Design and non-design, in fact, can be seen as two modes of social discourse; and to consider them in this way opens up the question of what might be called the "active relationship" between design, as one cultural system, and other cultural systems.

Design and Culture

Design, considered as both a practice and a product, is in effect a closed system—not only in relation to culture as a whole, but also in relation to other cultural systems such as literature, film, painting, philosophy, physics, geometry, etc. Properly defined, it is reductive, condensing and crystallizing general cultural notions within its own distinct parameters. Within the limits of this system, however, design constitutes a set of practices—architecture, urban design, and industrial design—unified with respect to certain normative theories. That is, it possesses specific characteristics that distinguish it from all other cultural practices and that establish a boundary between what is design and what is not. This boundary produces a kind of *closure* that acts to preserve and separate the ideological identity of design. This closure, however, does not preclude a certain level of permeability toward other cultural systems—a permeability which nevertheless is controlled and regulated in a precise way.

Culture, on the other hand, is understood to be a system of *social codes* that permit information to enter the public domain by means of appropriate signs. As a whole, culture can be seen as a hierarchy of these codes, manifested through various texts.[2]

The relationship between design and culture may, then, be stated as the mode by which design is articulated as one cultural system in relation to other cultural systems at the level of codes. The transformations in these articulations are historically determined, and they display themselves as changes in the structures of meaning. Thus, the development of specific forms of articulation between design and other cultural systems can be seen as a dynamic process, the study of which opens up the problem of the production of meaning.

The relationship between design and other cultural systems is heightened and intensified at certain moments in this process, and its precise articulations become clearer. In architecture, this occurs when new economic, technical, functional, or symbolic problems force the production of new formal repertories, or the expansion and transformation of existing vocabularies.

Thus, during the French Enlightenment, elementary geometrical figures (the sphere, the pyramid, the cube, etc.) were introduced as the primary constituents of a new formal vocabulary by the "revolutionary" architects Boullée and Ledoux. For Ledoux these forms expressed the new notions of the *sublime*, while for Boullée they represented the universe and its scientific explanation developed in the context of profound social and political change.[3]

Specificity

This recognition of articulations between design and other cultural systems also implies the recognition of differences between them—differences which may be understood through the notion of *specificity*.[4] This is a notion which permits the clarification of codes according to their relation to design or to other cultural systems.

Three types of codes regulate the interpretation and production of texts in design. First, there are those codes which may be seen as exclusive to design, such as codes establishing relationships between plans and elevations or plans and cross-sections. Second, there are those codes which are shared by various cultural systems, among which design is included (i.e., spatial, iconic). Third, there are those which, while they are crucial to one cultural system (such as rhythm to music), participate—albeit transformed—in another (such as architecture) by virtue of a shared characteristic, i.e., in the case of rhythm, the temporality of the sequence, auditory in one case and visual in the other.[5] In a decreasing order of specificity, the first type of codes are specific to design, the second have a multiple specificity, and the third are non-specific.

The specificity of a signifying system is not, however, defined solely by the specificity of its codes, but also by the form in which those codes are articulated; that is to say, the combination of codes may be specific, although the codes themselves may or may not be specific to the system in question.[6] Examples of specific code articulation in architecture are found in classical theories of harmony that utilize the articulation of musical codes and arithmetical proportional series for the invention of specific *architectural* codes, which are then used to determine the proportions of and relationships among the different elements of a building.

Specificity manages to maintain the limits of architecture despite the apparent changes that occur under the pressures of history, technology, social action, or symbolic change. On the one hand, the most specific codes remain within the system of architecture; on the other hand, the less specific codes link design with other systems through the opening and closing of its limits. This mechanism allows for the articulation of design with some systems and not with others, a process which operates according to the "internal" determinations of design—that is, according to the rules of architectural language, to the logic of the configuration, and to the meaning proper of the "text" of design.[7]

The Mannerist inversion of the established architectural rules—by which each element is used in contradiction to what should be its prevailing ideological function—is an excellent example of such internal determination, in which the inversions so weaken the limits of architecture as to allow an opening to codes external to it; thus the "painterly" architecture of the sixteenth century in Italy.[8]

This process of articulation might, however, take place according to "external" determinations   to the forces of economics, politics, or other ideologies foreign to design. The influence of hermetic thought on the design of the Escorial Palace, for example, demonstrates the role of such external factors in architecture. Both the plan and the general configuration seem to have been derived from mystical or hermetic geometric regulating lines, based partly on parallel developments in quantitative mathematics, and partly on chapters eliminated from Renaissance editions of Vitruvius,[9] but not, as might be assumed, directly from classical architectural theory. Magic codes were thus substitutes for the Albertian geometric codes. Geometry, while represented by similar figures, was imbued with an entirely different meaning. At the same time, these geometric magic codes remained distinctly separate from other magic codes, such as those based on verbal or gestural practices which never entered in their physical-spatial implications into architecture.

Metaphoric Operations in Design

The concept of the closing and opening of limits introduces the notion of an ideological *filtering* in the production of design, which takes place by means of certain processes of symbolization. In this case an equivalence, or exchange, of sense is produced by restricting the access of certain codes and figures from other systems into architecture.

The notions of *metaphor* and *metonymy* allow for a more systematic analysis of this symbolic functioning. These should be considered as the mechanisms of opening and closure, ultimately revealing the way in which design maintains its limits in relation to culture and acts as a filter in relation to meaning.[10]

Metaphor and metonymy are, of course, notions that have been used principally in the analysis of discourse and text. Since in this context we are analyzing the *production* of meaning and not its structure, the reference in general will be to metaphoric or metonymic *operations* rather than to these figures as they are applied to classical rhetoric.[11]

These tropes or rhetorical figures represent the most condensed expression of two basic kinds of relationship in discourse: the relation of similarity, which underlies the metaphor, and the relation of contiguity, which determines the metonymy. Each may exist in the relationship between the figure and the content or in the relation between figure and figure.

The development of any discourse (not necessarily a spoken one, and in this case the architectural discourse) may develop along two semantic-syntactic lines; one theme in the expression or content may lead to another either by means of similarity or by means of contiguity.[12] The most appropriate term for the former relation is "metaphoric" while the latter might be termed "metonymic."[13]

In its relationship to other cultural systems, a necessary condition for the regeneration of sense, architecture takes part in a game of substitutions which, thought of in terms of metaphoric or metonymic operations, explains at the most specific level of form the translation from extra-architectural to intra-architectural systems in a recoding which, by means of reducing meanings, maintains the limits of architecture.

The well-known nautical metaphor in Le Corbusier's Villa Savoye exemplifies this functioning. Here, two different signifying systems are related: dwelling and ocean liner. The necessary condition for this relationship is provided by the existence of an element common to both, in this case the window. Through a metaphoric operation, a figurative substitution of the signifying element common to both systems is produced (dwelling/window—liner/window), carrying and transferring codes from one system (liner) to the other (house). The new form is thus loaded with the new meanings required to translate into figures the proposed new architectural ideology.

The operation involved may be explained by the following propositions:

$$\text{Housing Code:}\quad \frac{\text{House}}{\text{Inhabit}} \;:\; \frac{\text{Window}}{\text{Passage of Light}} \;:\; \frac{\text{Wall}}{\text{Boundary, Protection}} \;:\; \text{etc.}$$

$$\text{Liner Code:}\quad \frac{\text{Boat}}{\text{Sail + Inhabit + Movement + Technology}} \;:\; \frac{\text{Window}}{\text{Passage of Light + View + Seat + Sun}} \;:\; \frac{\text{Decks}}{\text{Promenade}} \;:\; \text{etc.}$$

$$\text{Metaphor:}\quad \frac{\text{House Window}}{\textit{Liner Window}} \times \frac{\textit{Liner Window}}{\text{Light + View + Movement + Technology} + \ldots} = \frac{\text{House Window}}{\text{Light + View + Movement + Technology} + \ldots}$$

The similarity of functions—in this case, both liner and house are forms of habitation—makes the metaphor possible.

To these metaphoric transpositions other metonymic operations are added—for example, the *promenade architecturale*—which also carry further meanings related to the liner.

Functionalist Metaphors

At an urban scale, where the system of architectural design co-exists with many others almost by definition, the role of the metaphor as a filtering device becomes particularly evident, especially in the functional approach to urban design.

At the moment when urbanism was constituted as an institutionalized practice in the first decade of this century, urban formal codes were developed on the basis of the prevailing architectural codification. From the set of possible systems that give meaning to form, the functional approach was emphasized almost exclusively. Le Corbusier may serve once more to exemplify the type of functionalism that is at work in a filtering operation in the substitutive relation between architecture and other systems.

In Le Corbusier's texts *Vers une architecture* (1923) and *Urbanisme* (1925), these metaphoric operations function clearly as a mechanism for contact between different cultural systems and, on other levels, as a means to architectural recodification.[14]

At the building scale, Le Corbusier establishes a connection between architectural systems and other systems, such as technology, tourism, sports, and geometry. This connection is established through a metaphor based on similarity of function.[15]

Geometry, for example, had acted as an internal code for formal control from the classical period of Greek architecture. It had not, however, functioned as the provider of the formal vocabulary itself, geometric regulating lines being the "invisible" elements in the construction. For Le Corbusier, however, geometry became not only an instrument of formal control, but also the provider of the formal vocabulary itself in two and three dimensions. The instrument (tool) for representation, that is, drawing, became first the project itself, and then the construction, without alteration.

At the urban scale, Le Corbusier's metaphoric operation establishes a relation between geometry as a signifying system and the city by means of the common element of "order," which is manifested as a "grid"; a system of equivalences is established between the geometric grid with its connoted codes and the city grid with the set of values ascribed to it by Le Corbusier.

Thus, in *Urbanisme*, the existing city is seen as equivalent to disorder, chaos, illness, and irrationality. On the other hand, the grid, the geometric order, is seen as equivalent to order, health, beauty, reason, modernity, and progress. "Geometry is the foundation. . . . It is also the material basis on which we build those symbols which represent to us perfection and the divine."[16]

In the plans for the Ville Contemporaine, and later for the Ville Radieuse, Le Corbusier establishes the equivalence between those two systems by means of the common element of grid-order. The appropriate connoted codes of the geometric grid are transferred through a figurative substitution to the city plan and become the codes of the city itself.

It can be seen, in this case, that while there is an initial opening of the system, its closure is produced by means of a metaphorical equivalence by which the means of representation are imposed as ideological filters in order to develop an architectural recodification. In this substitution, meanings are limited and filtered by a system (geometry) which, while it may not be specific to architecture, will, in its recoding, become specific to urban design. This is made possible by the fact that a system such as geometry may participate in a double "game": symbolic at a formal-cultural level, and instrumental, or representative, at the level of the specific practice where physical configuration becomes the device that allows for translation and recoding.

The relationship between geometry as a symbolic system on the one hand, and as a basic organizational system on the other, is not, of course, a new problem and may be found at other points in the history of architecture. In the work of Piranesi, for example, the figurative and the geometric coexist, juxtaposed in a clear dialectical relationship. The rear of the altar of S. Maria del Priorato, for example, crudely displays the set of geometric volumes which serve as its support, while the face presents itself as almost pure allegory. The architectural contradiction between geometry and symbolism is here critically posed.[17]

When Boullée and Ledoux adopted geometry in itself as a formal system, the sacred symbology was substituted for a more secular symbology—that of man. In Le Corbusier, however, there is no longer a separation between the geometric and the symbolic; rather geometry itself represents the symbolic aspect of form, and carries with it an entire set of implicit values.

The Critique of Functionalism

With the waning of the enthusiasm for functionalism in the late 1940s, a series of works appeared which, conscious of the cultural reductivism of the heroic period, were explicitly concerned with the cultural rather than the functional aspects of design. This cultural concern was demonstrated by an intention to make explicit the articulation between architecture and other cultural systems.[18] The work of the active members of Team 10 (Alison and Peter Smithson) reintroduces culture in this sense, and again new openings and closures are produced by means of metaphoric operations: openings to incorporate "the culture"; closures to preserve the specificity of the system.

However, while in Le Corbusier the metaphor was reductive in terms of the possible inclusion of other cultural systems—a product of the exclusive nature of geometry and its concomitant modernism—the intention of Team 10 was to establish relations between architecture and other systems. "Our hierarchy of associations," they stated, "is woven into a modulated continuum representing the true complexity of human associations. . . . *We must evolve an architecture from the fabric of life itself,* an equivalent of the complexity of our way of thought, of our passion for the natural world and our belief in the ability of man."[19]

This criticism addresses itself precisely to the functionalist reductivism of the 1920s and to its elimination of cultural aspects, here described as "human associations" and "the fabric of life itself." These aspects were considered as an intrinsic aspect of architecture by Team 10.

Once more, metaphor is being used as the substitutive operation to incorporate "vital" aspects into design. Two types of metaphor are used. The one, which accounts for urban form in general, resembles Le Corbusier's use of geometry at an urban scale. The other, which accounts for the realization of ideas at a building scale, is itself conceived as a fundamental element of urban design.

The first metaphoric operation links two systems through the common element "life," and thus relates the city to nature (a tree). Hence the plans for Golden Lane. The city is overlaid with the attributes of a tree and given qualities of growth, organicity, movement; at the level of form, the city is understood as a tree possessing a stem, branches, and leaves.

$$\frac{\text{city/life}}{\text{tree/life}} = \frac{\text{tree/life}}{\text{branches, leaves, etc.}}$$

The second type of metaphoric operation articulates the relationship between design and life at the scale of the building and operates on the basis of a common function: circulation of people (street). In the proposal for Sheffield, the corridor is transformed through substitution into a street, carrying with it the urban codes which, when transferred to the building, give it "life."

Despite the explicit intent of Team 10 to open the system of architecture to culture, however, the result does not, in the end, differ much from the reductive system they criticize. The type of substitution utilized—the recodification of architecture by means of yet another formal analogy—is fundamentally similar to that effected by Le Corbusier. The process by which the Smithsons assimilate "life" to design is described exclusively in socio-cultural terms, even though "nature" is invoked, while the form adopted is taken directly from nature, that is, from organic, physical life. The other systems to which architecture is supposed to be actively linked (in this case, life or nature) are, in this way, filtered and reduced through the metaphor of one system, that of architectural forms. Thus, there is little real difference between the street in the air and the open corridor; the symbolic functioning which would make an architecture "out of life itself" is in fact absent. We may now see that metaphoric operations, rather than functioning to open the design system beyond its limits, in fact operate as filtering mechanisms which precisely define those limits.

It is paradoxical that the metaphor which allows for the interrelation of different codes is here used as a closing mechanism. Design is once again a sieve which allows the passage of certain meanings and not others, while the metaphor, which is used as a translating device from other codes to architecture, provides a mechanism by which ideology operates through design. In the infinite field of signifying possibilities, the metaphor defines, by a complex process of selection, the field of "the possible," thus consolidating itself in different regions by means of a language or languages.

Design/Non-Design

There is, however, another possible way of stating the relationship between design and culture. Rather than seeing systems of culture from a point of view that imposes a hierarchical relationship in which architecture or design is dominant, we may posit a notion of the "non-designed" built environment—"social texts," as it were, produced by a given culture.

The act of placing design (that is, both architecture and urban design) in relation to the rest of the built environment—the non-designed environment—immediately changes the level at which the problem is formulated. While in the work of Team 10 the problem is stated as internal to a single cultural system (architecture or urban design)—the relating of architecture to the city in such a way that the former acquires the "life" of the latter, here the signifying function of design is considered to relate to and, in relating, to oppose the rest of the built environment. It is regarded as a problem *internal to culture*, and thus to an entire set of cultural systems.

In these terms, architecture is no longer either implicitly or explicitly seen as the dominant system, but simply *one* of many cultural systems, each of which, including architecture, may be closed or "designed." But it is the entire set of different cultural systems configuring the built environment which we call non-design.

In the world of non-design, that no-man's-land of the symbolic, the scene of social struggle, an internal analysis of single systems is revealed as inadequate and impossible to apply. Here there is no unique producer, no subject, nor is there an established rhetorical system within a defined institutional framework. Instead there is a complex system of intertextual relationships.

The opposition between design and non-design is fundamentally defined by three questions: first, the problem of *institutionality*; second, the problem of *limits and specificity*; and third, the problem of the *subject*. While the first establishes the relationship between design and non-design, the second establishes their respective types of articulation within culture (ideology), and the third establishes the processes of symbolization.

Design may be defined as a social practice that functions by a set of socially sanctioned rules and norms—whether implicit or explicit—and therefore is constituted as an institution. Its institutional character is manifested in the normative writings and written texts of architecture, which fix its meaning and, therefore, its reading. These texts insure the recording of the codes of design and guarantee their performance as filters and preservers of unity. They assure the homogeneity and closure of the system and of the ideological role it plays. The absence of a normative written discourse in non-design, on the other hand, precludes defining it as an institution and makes possible the inscription of sense in a free and highly undetermined way; we are here presented with an aleatory play of meaning. Thus, while design maintains its limits and its specificity, these defining aspects are lost in the semiotically heterogeneous text of non-design.[20]

Non-design is the articulation—as an explicit form—between different cultural systems. This phenomenon may be approached in two ways: as empirical fact—the actual existence of such systems found, for example, in the street, where architecture, painting, music, gestures, advertising, etc. coexist—and as a set of related codes. In the first instance, at the level of "texts," each system remains closed in itself, presenting juxtaposed manifestations rather than their relationships. At the level of codes, on the other hand, it is possible to discern the mode of articulation between the various systems and, in this way, to define the cultural and ideological overdetermination of the built environment, or rather the process by which culture is woven into it.[21] The predisposition of non-design to openness implies permeable limits and an always fluctuating or changing specificity.

Finally, if design is the production of an historically determined individual subject which marks the work, non-design is the product of a social subject, the same subject which produces ideology. It manifests itself in the delirious, the carnivalesque, the oneiric, which are by and large excluded or repressed in design.

To study the reality of non-design and its symbolic production in relation to culture, it is necessary to perform an operation of "cutting"—"cutting" and not "deciphering," for while deciphering operates on "secret" marks and the possibility for discovering their full depth of meaning, cutting operates on a space of interrelations,[22] *empty* of meaning, in which codes substitute, exchange, replace, and represent each other, and in which history is seen as the form of a particular mode of symbolizing, determined by the double value of use and exchange of objects, and as a symbolic *modus operandi* which may be understood within that same logic of symbolic production and which is performed by the same social subject of ideology and the unconscious.[23]

The moment one object may be substituted for another beyond its "functional" use-value, it has a value added to it which is the value of exchange, and this value is nothing but symbolic. Our world of symbolic performances is comprised of a chain of such exchanges in meaning; that is how we operate within the realm of ideology. Non-design leaves this ideology in a "free state," while design hides it.

The mode of analysis for these two phenomena of design and non-design (at least from the first moment that the difference between them is recognized) must therefore vary.

Reading. Mise-en-Séquence

As a complex social text, a semiotically heterogeneous object in which many different signifying matters and codes intervene, non-design has a disposition to be open to a situation which we will call here a *mise-en-séquence*.

We propose here for non-design a productive reading, not as the re-production of a unique or final sense, but as a way of retracing the mechanisms by which that sense was produced.[24] Productive reading corresponds to the expansive potential of non-design and permits access to the functioning of meaning as an intersection of codes. The object of analysis is not the "content," but the conditions of a content, not the "full" sense of design but, on the contrary, the "empty" sense which informs all works.[25] Instead of reading by following a previously written text, the reading starts from a "signifier of departure," not only toward an architectural text but toward other texts in culture, putting into play a force analogous to that of the unconscious, which also has the capacity to traverse and articulate different codes.

The metaphoric operation participates asymmetrically in both readings, design and non-design. While in design the metaphor is not only the point of departure but also the final point of the reading, in non-design the metaphoric and metonymic operations function similarly to dreams, as chains which permit access to meanings that have been repressed, thus acting as expansive forces. This expansive mechanism may be seen to be a device used for the purpose of criticism in the work of Piranesi. His opposition to the typological obsession of his time is an indication of his perception of the crisis of architecture and the consequent need for change and transformation. His *Campo Marzio* is a true architectural "explosion" that anticipates the destiny of our Western cities.[26] Piranesi's "explosive" vision comprises not just the architectural system per se but rather a system of relationships, of contiguity and substitution.

Non-design may also be seen as an explosive transformation of design. This kind of explosion implies in some way the dissolution of the limits of architecture, of the ideological limits which enclose different architectural practices.

In front of two drawings of Piranesi's *Carceri*, one of the Carcere Oscura of 1743 from the series of the *Opere varie* and the other of the Carceri Oscure from the *Invenzioni*, the Russian filmmaker Eisenstein makes a reading which may be considered as an example of this type of analysis. Eisenstein applies a cinematographic reading to the first prison, his reading producing displacements with respect to the limits imposed by pictorial and architectural codes, thereby making it "explode" in a kind of cinematographic sequence.[27] This is the starting point of a reading that travels across literary, political, musical, and historical codes, multiplying in this way perceptions which are potential in the Piranesian work. A proof of this potential lies in Eisenstein's reading of Piranesi's second engraving, done eighteen years later, in which Eisenstein finds that the second is actually an explosion of the first prison, done by Piranesi himself.[28] It should be noted that Eisenstein is here dealing with a closed cultural system, such as architecture or painting. What Eisenstein takes, however, is not just *any* closed work from these fields but rather the work of someone like Piranesi, who poses the problem of the explosion in form (or form as explosion) in his *Carceri*, or in his *Campo Marzio*, which is a delirium of typological chaining. Although this Piranesian strategy touches problems specific to architecture, it also comes very close to the problem of the explosion of sense in architecture, to the problem of meaning as signifying chaining. In creating this extreme situation, Piranesi is implicitly assessing the problem of the limits of architecture as a "language," that is, as a closed system.

Fragments of Reading

One evening, half asleep on a banquette in a bar, just for fun I tried to enumerate all the languages within earshot: music, conversations, the sounds of chairs, glasses, a whole stereophony of which a square in Tangiers (as described by Severo Sarduy) is the exemplary site. That too spoke within me, and this so-called "interior" speech was very like the noise of the square, like that amassing of minor voices coming to me from the outside: I myself was a public square, a sook; through me passed words, tiny syntagms, bits of formulae, and no sentence formed, as though that were the law of such a language. This speech, at once very cultural and very savage, was above all lexical, sporadic; it set up in me, through its apparent flow, a definitive discontinuity: this non-sentence was in no way something that could not have acceded to the sentence, that might have been before the sentence; it was: what is eternally, splendidly, outside the sentence.[29]

The urban environment as the object of reading is not "seen" as a closed, simple unity but as a set of *fragments*, or "units of readings." Each of these units may be replaced by others; each part may be taken for the whole. The dimension of the built environment, empirically determined, depends upon the density of meanings, the "semantic volume."

Since these fragments appear as an articulation of different texts belonging to various cultural systems—e.g., film, art, literature—it is possible to read them by starting from any of these systems, and not necessarily from design.

Certain types of configurations, like public places (streets, plazas, cafes, airports), are ideal "fragments of readings," not only for their "semantic volume," but also for the complexity they reveal as to the signifying mechanisms in non-design. They may be characterized as signifying "nodes," where multiple codes and physical matter are articulated, where design and non-design overlap, and where history and the present are juxtaposed.[30]

The reading that can be produced by these places is not a linear discourse but an infinite and spatialized text in which those levels of reading, organized along various codes, such as theater, film, fashion, politics, gesture, are combined and articulated. The reading example we choose to present below is in itself metaphorical. It is the metaphor of architecture as theater. It is not a specific detailed analysis, but rather it exemplifies the mechanisms of chains and shifters.

Chains:

A metaphor begins to function by articulating the referential codes in relation to other codes by means of replacing the referential codes in the signifier of departure with another code. In this way, a chain linking the codes is developed. Once the intersemiotic metaphor, such as that between architecture and theater, is produced and a possible level of reading is established, the chain of signifiers along the codes and subcodes of that cultural system is organized by "natural association"—that is metonymically.

Signifiers appear and disappear, sliding through other texts in a play that moves along the codes of, for instance, the theater (i.e., scenic, gestural, decorative, acting, textual, verbal, etc.) in an intertextual network. This play continues until some signifier becomes another departure signifier, opening the network toward new chains through what we have called the *mise-en-séquence*, thus starting other readings from other cultural systems like film, fashion, etc. These signifiers which open to other systems may be called *shifters*.[31]

Shifters:

Such a reading presents a symbolic structure of a "decondensed" kind. By decondensation we refer to an operation which is the reverse of that in the elaboration of dreams. Condensation and displacement are the two basic operations in the work of elaboration of dreams. By them, the passage is produced from the latent level to the manifest level of the dream. These two operations of condensation and displacement are two ways of displacing meanings, or of overdetermining, or giving more than one meaning to, some elements; they are produced precisely by means of the two operations already discussed, namely metaphor and metonymy. The metaphor corresponds to condensation, and metonymy to displacement.[32] In this way, it is possible to see the relationship between ideology (cultural codes) and subject (of ideology and of the unconscious) in the logic of symbolic production in the environment as determined by a particular mode of production.

Some signifier fragments function as "condensers" from which decondensation is possible through a network of meanings. These will be called "shifters." A set of readings could be regarded as a musical staff in which various signifiers are situated in a polyphonic organization with each voice at a different level of reading. Certain of these signifiers organize several different readings and allow for the intercrossing of codes and for the shifting from one to the next. These are the shifters; they are part of a process of exchange of codes. They are the conditions of the probability of producing different readings; they are structures of transition, the organizers of symbolic space. These connective, condensing structures are the key to the understanding of the complexity of the built environment as an infinite text. They are not concerned with signification but with the linking of signifiers. They are the key to an intertext where meanings are displaced, thereby forming a network in which the subject of the reading, the laws of the unconscious, and the historico-cultural determinants are articulated. The importance of this notion of shifter is that it accounts for the process of configuration and for the dynamic aspect of a configuration, rather than for objects and functions. It accounts for the symbolic aspect of exchange. It provides an insight into the problem of the mode of operation of ideology within the built world. It allows us to enter into a mechanism of production of sense that corresponds to an ideology of exchange.

If the system of architecture and of design, even when we play with it, is always closed within a game of commentaries of language—a metalingual game—it is interesting to speculate on the outcome of a similar "game" of *non-design*, a game of the built world. For non-design is a non-language, and by comparison with a language, it is madness since it is outside language, and thus outside society. This non-language, this non-sense constitutes an explosion of the established language in relation to a sense already established (by conventions and repressive rules). It is symbolic of the built world outside the rules of design and their internal "linguistic" games. It permits us finally to understand another logic which informs the significance of building.

The Productive Reading

The outdoor part of the "cafe-terrace" establishes the relationship cafe/street and is organized in terms of the opposition sidewalk as passage or circulation/sidewalk as cafe; another element in the sidewalk-circulation is introduced; people link the first opposition with the second one. Some people walk in the sidewalk/street; some people sit in the sidewalk/cafe. People are distributed in a field of objects that may be distinguished as objects for use and objects for background. Buildings are objects and façades; the background is a continuous façade; the façade of the cafe stands out as a mediating element which because of its transparency creates a relationship between the exterior cafe or cafe/street and the interior cafe. The interior cafe repeats the same oppositions between people/objects and background/mirrors, which themselves now become mediators between exterior and interior in a reflection in which objects, sidewalk, people, street, and interior space are superimposed. . . .

The seats, which are distributed in rows and in which people are clustered, resembles a pit. This substitution produces a point of departure, from cafe/street to cafe/pit.

$$\frac{Cafe\ seats}{Pit\ seats} \times \frac{Pit\ seats}{Theater}$$

$$\frac{Background\ plane\ cafe}{Background\ plane\ scene} \times \frac{Background\ plane\ scene}{Theater}$$

New readings may be produced:

The Gaze:
The gaze from the cafe as pit transforms the street into a scene and sweeps through the codes both of the cafe and the theater. Codes organize the gaze: the people from whom and to whom they are directed—Observer/Observed; the places from where and to where they are directed—Public/Private; the desire which generates them—Voyeurism/Exhibitionism. In their interrelation, places configure the gaze: frontal—oblique—side view. Scene and pit are confused in a general scene where gaze and desire are structured and articulated together. The pleasure in the realization of desire is generated not only at the visual level but also at the level of language in action: that is, discourse.

Discourse within the "theater" is fragmented, dispersed among various actors and spectators, articulating itself without either dominating or subordinating, with the body in action, with the gesture.

Gesture:

Gesticulating bodies form a chain with clothes as a second skin, regulated by the gestures of fashion which play a role in the marking and disguising of sex differences. Cafe, the domain of men, is incorporated in the city as theater, articulated with fashion, the domain of women, as costume. The two together transform the visual codes, which link cafe/masculinity and fashion/femininity, thereby confounding them.

The gesture is not only that of a static pose, but the multiplied gesture of the body in movement, engaged in entries and exits from the scene.

Discourse and gesture configure the scene; meanwhile, time and volume perforate the plane of decoration and configure the space.

The scene in the streets:
The scene in the streets is in turn the explosion of the cafe/theater.

The street as a scene of scenes:
The street as a scene of scenes in turn projects into the cafe, opening it up to new paradigms and their codes.

The system of cafes:

Each cafe is not a cafe in itself but is part of a system of cafes, which speaks of its history, of its origins, of its transformations, thus establishing the paradigm of the cafe.

The system of the fragments of public places:

The cafe belongs to the paradigm of streets, plazas, monuments. In turn, each of these is not only physically juxtaposed but also textually juxtaposed. This transforms these places into complex entities: cafe-square, cafe-market, cafe-street. The street is transformed into a new point of departure. We are again in the street, but now the street is a scene.

Street:

A scene in movement. The street is the scene of struggle, of consumption, the scene of scenes; it is infinitely continuous, unlimited in the motion of objects, of gazes, of gestures.

It is the scene of history.

It is a scene, but it is also what is behind the scene, what is not seen, or not allowed to be seen. When what is behind the scene is shown, it produces a demystifying effect, like that of exposing the reasons for the split between individual and social, between private and public.

The façades frame the street. They function as scenery or decoration and control the demystifying effect. The decoration may or may not correspond to the content of representation. This accentuates its mask-like character.

People as decoration:

Fashion transforms people into objects, linking street and theater through one aspect of their common ritual nature.

Rituals:

People meet at corners, people promenade, defining a ritual space, participating in ceremonies, and. . . .

Notes

1. Accordingly, architecture itself must be approached as a particular form of cultural production—as a specific kind of overdetermined practice.
2. Jury Lotman, "Problèmes de la typologie des cultures," in *Essays in Semiotics*, ed. Julia Kristeva, Josette Rey-Debove, and Donna Jean Umiker (The Hague: Mouton, 1971).
3. See Jean-Marie Pérouse de Montclos, *Etienne-Louis Boullée* (New York: George Braziller, 1974); Emil Kaufmann, *Architecture in the Age of Reason* (Cambridge, Mass.: Harvard University Press, 1955).
4. See Christian Metz, *Langage et cinéma* (Paris: Klincksiek, 1971); Emilio Garroni, *Progetto di semiotica* (Bari: Laterza, 1973).
5. Ibid.
6. Christian Metz, "Spécificité des codes et/ou spécificité des langages," *Semiotica* 1, no. 4 (1969).
7. The role of specificity in maintaining the limits of architecture becomes evident, for example, in the development of the steel industry in the nineteenth century, which determined the development of its own independent techniques according to a reason and coherence of its own (exemplified in works of such architects as Eiffel and Paxton), while the world of architectural forces developed according to a logic neatly dissociated from technology. Such technical-formal developments are absorbed through symbolic mechanisms that incorporate the structural system as one of the expressive elements of the architectonic vocabulary. This prevents the fusion of architecture with engineering and its disappearance as an autonomous practice.
8. Heinrich Wölfflin, *Renaissance and Baroque* (Ithaca: Cornell University Press, 1966).

9. René Taylor, "Architecture and Magic: Considerations on the Idea of the Escorial," in *Essays in the History of Architecture Presented to Rudolf Wittkower*, ed. Douglas Fraser, Howard Hibbard, and Milton J. Lewine (New York: Phaidon, 1967).

10. The notions of closing and opening would allow rethinking of certain aspects of design at the level of meaning in a manner more systematic and specific than the traditional historical analysis that looks for the explanation of the meaning of formal architectural structures in the sociocultural context in general and considers it as a problem of content.

11. Pierre Fontanier, *Les figures du discours* (1821; Paris: Flammarion, 1968).

12. Roman Jakobson, *Studies on Child Language and Aphasia* (The Hague: Mouton, 1971).

13. This is developed by Mario Gandelsonas, "On Reading Architecture," *Progressive Architecture*, May 1972; idem, "Linguistics and Architecture," *Casabella 373* (February 1973).

14. I refer in this article to the Le Corbusier of *Towards a New Architecture* and *The City of Tomorrow*, although it is possible to say that there are several Le Corbusiers.

15. Le Corbusier, *The City of Tomorrow* (London: John Rodker, 1929).

16. Ibid.

17. Manfredo Tafuri, *Giovanni Battista Piranesi: L'architettura come "Utopia negativa"* (Turin: Accademia delle Scienze, 1972).

18. This articulation has, of course, always been present in architectural treatises from the Renaissance to Le Corbusier. But it is important here, however, to posit it in this functionalist context where the conception of culture is universalist, reductivist, and imperialistic.

19. Alison Smithson, ed., *Team 10 Primer* (Cambridge, Mass.: MIT Press, 1968).

20. See Diana Agrest and Mario Gandelsonas, "Critical Remarks in Semiotics and Architecture," *Semiotica* 9, no. 3 (1973).

21. Diana Agrest, "Towards a Theory of Production of Sense in the Built Environment" (1968–1973), in *On Streets*, ed. Stanford Anderson (Cambridge, Mass.: MIT Press, 1972). Here I proposed considering the street as a signifying system.

22. Roland Barthes, *Sade/Fourier/Loyola* (Paris: Editions du Seuil, 1972). See the following works on architectural typology: Garroni, *Progetto di semiotica*; Giulio Argan, "Sul concetto della tipologia architettonica," in *Progetto e destino* (Milan: Alberto Mondadori, 1965); Aldo Rossi, *L'architettura della città* (Padua: Marsilio Editori, 1966); Alan Colquhoun, "Typology and Design Method," in *Meaning in Architecture*, ed. Charles Jencks and George Baird (New York: George Braziller, 1970), pp. 267–277.

23. See J. J. Goux, *Economie et symbolique* (Paris: Editions du Seuil, 1973).

24. Roland Barthes, *S/Z* (Paris: Editions du Seuil, 1970).

25. An important difference between the reading of design and non-design is the existence or non-existence of a written text. In the case of design one may reconstruct a discourse in such a way as to illuminate its meaning by a previous reading. When we read Le Corbusier, we reconstruct a reading made by him. In the case of non-design, however, we must put ourselves in the position of direct reading.

26. Tafuri, *Giovanni Battista Piranesi*.

27. S. M. Eisenstein, "Piranesi e la fluidità delle forme," *Rassegna Sovietica* 1–2 (1972).

28. Manfredo Tafuri, "Piranesi, Eisenstein e la dialettica," *Rassegna Sovietica* 1–2 (1972).

29. Roland Barthes, *The Pleasure of the Text* (New York: Hill and Wang, 1975), p. 49.

30. These nodes, thought of as referents to non-design, permit a more precise formulation of its meaning and distinguish it from the term "place" with which we designate the signifying structure.

31. Roman Jakobson, "Les catégories verbales et le verbe Russe," in *Essais de linguistique générale* (Paris: Editions de Minuit, 1963); Roland Barthes, *Système de la mode* (Paris: Editions du Seuil, 1967). The shifter should not be mistaken as being in itself possessed of "double meaning," a notion which has become almost classical in architecture. It does not refer to language. Double meaning on the contrary, refers to the issue of content, to the problem of ambiguity in relation to language and to metaphor. While the shifter accounts for the chaining of fragments, double meaning refers to a totality with different meanings. There is no chaining and no process involved in this notion.

32. Sigmund Freud, *Interpretation of Dreams* (London: G. Allen & Unwin, 1961); idem, *Psychopathology of Everyday Life* (New York: Norton, 1966).

Bernard Tschumi   **"The Architectural Paradox"** *Studio International*, September-October 1975; revised

in Bernard Tschumi, *Architecture and Disjunction* (Cambridge: MIT Press, 1994)

"The concept of space is not a space": Bernard Tschumi begins with an Althusserian distinction between space as the object of knowledge and actually existing spaces in order then to superimpose several other distinctions on this first one, all mobilized toward a theory of "the pleasure of architecture." Tschumi textualizes architecture by obliquely registering the post-'68 languages of Henri Lefebvre and situationism, Philippe Sollers and the *Tel Quel* group, Roland Barthes and Jacques Derrida, as well as the earlier critical theory of the Frankfurt School, and dragging these, in turn, across a firsthand knowledge of Italian *architettura radicale*, conceptual art, and performance art, all of which creates one of the more startlingly expansive intertexts of architecture theory.[1]

The Althusserian formula is, of course, based on the older Marxian distinction of science and ideology and reaffirms that, while we can conceptualize the world and its totality in an abstract way, there is a rift between that knowledge and the here and now of immediate perception and practice. But Tschumi further associates this distinction with Georges Bataille's economy of the pyramid and the labyrinth, which does not oppose the two spaces of conception and perception so

much as infold them. The pyramid is a substantive; it is proof of architecture's power and its limitations. It names the entire tradition of architecture, all the recognizable categories and entities and their "proper" concepts, but in a void—the conceptual knowledge of the pyramid can never be positioned or actualized in any concrete way. The labyrinth, on the other hand, is a copula. It has no substantive meaning but only a function of circulating signs in an erotic interplay—copulation—which serves to undermine the "proper" identities of conceptual entities in order to break through to everything that that sameness excludes. And yet the labyrinth produces the pyramid; we can reach the experience of the new and of the other only through conceptuality: "This flight toward the summit (which, even dominating empires, is the composition of knowledge) is but one of the routes of the 'labyrinth.' Yet this route, which we must follow, false lead after false lead, in search of 'being,' cannot be avoided by us, no matter how we try."[2] Architecture, being both conceptual and perceptual, in its very nature is both pyramid and labyrinth. That is its paradox.

The only "solution" to the paradox produced in architecture theory thus far, Tschumi reminds us, is "silence, a final nihilistic statement that might provide modern architectural history with its ultimate punchline, its self-annihilation." But Tschumi suggests a possible alternative to silence, one that might accelerate and instensify the architectural paradox rather than negate it: "experienced space," which, more than a concept or a perception, is a *process*, a way of *practicing space*, an *event* related to both Bataille's *expérience intérieure* and the situationists' *événements*, but now rewritten in terms of Roland Barthes's textual pleasure. For Barthes's *plaisir/ jouissance* formulation, which first opposes and then joins the two types of pleasure, not only provides a way of thinking this fundamental paradox but also coordinates other binaries like architecture's "selective historicism" as against its avant-garde ambitions, its conformist disciplinary constraints as against its revolutionary political

compare Hollier (192 ff)

compare 146–147

compare Lefebvre (182–183)

potentials, its rigor as against its sensuality, its closed and open processes of signification. Barthes:

Text of pleasure [*texte de plaisir*]: the text that contents, fills, grants euphoria; the text that comes from culture and does not break with it, is linked to a *comfortable* practice of reading. Text of bliss [*texte de jouissance*]: the text that imposes a state of loss, the text that discomforts (perhaps to the point of a certain boredom), unsettles the reader's historical, cultural, psychological assumptions, the consistency of his tastes, values, memories, brings to a crisis his relation with language.

But Barthes's point, and Tschumi's, is not merely to invade the proper with the improper but to recognize the "anachronic" process *before* their separation.

Now the subject who keeps the two texts in his field and in his hands the reins of pleasure and bliss is an anachronic subject, for he simultaneously and contradictorily participates in the profound hedonism of all culture . . . and in the destruction of that culture: he enjoys the consistency of his selfhood (that is his pleasure) and seeks its loss (that is his bliss). He is a subject split twice over, doubly perverse.[3]

The *texte de plaisir* promotes a self-conscious, reflected appreciation within a bounded inventory of entities, techniques, and evaluative categories of the discipline; the *texte de jouissance* cuts the reader adrift from the standard topoi of culture. *Plaisir* pertains to the propriety, the comfort, and the security of pyramidal knowledge, the realm of a unified but dematerialized conceptuality. *Jouissance* is the orgasmic breaking up of that unity through the constant labyrinthine detours of Text, the fragmentation of experience. (Tschumi: "You don't really see the cube. You may see a corner, or a side, or the ceiling, but never all defining surfaces at the same time. You touch a wall, you hear an echo. But how do you relate all these perceptions to one single object?") The *texte de jouissance* liquidates its own discursive categories for the sheer thrill of transgression. In his 1977 "The Pleasure of Architecture," Tschumi wrote,

The architecture of pleasure lies where conceptual and spatial paradoxes merge in the middle of delight, where architectural language breaks into a thousand pieces, where the elements of architecture are dismantled and its rules transgressed. No metaphorical paradise here, but discomfort and unbalanced expectations. Such architecture questions academic (and popular) assumptions, disturbs acquired tastes and fond architectural memories. Typologies, morphologies, spatial compressions, logical constructions, all dissolve. Inarticulated forms collide in a staged and necessary conflict: repetition, discontinuity, quotes, clichés and neologism. Such architecture is perverse because its real significance lies outside any utility or purpose and ultimately is not even necessarily aimed at giving pleasure.[4]

But *jouissance* cannot be absolute, for if a text is to be read, if a space is to be experienced, it will be so according to or against cultural codes. And if culture, then *plaisir*, too. The experience of architecture is wedged in a gap between two architectural surfaces, two edges of the pyramid and the labyrinth, two types of pleasure, one conceptual, culturally conservative, and rule-bound, the other sensual, transgressive, even violent.[5] It is the gap that is erotic.

Furthermore, it is the erotic that reorders the relationship between architecture and politics. Before, we were to wait for the realization of a new mode of production that would necessitate a new architecture — a utopia that would never come. Now architecture's social power is its very uselessness to society, and only the paradox of transgression rubbing against rule can figure utopia.

Since the 1970s, following his own analysis of the architectural paradox through his architectural projects, Tschumi has used a series of techniques that he calls crossprogramming, transprogramming, and disprogramming, each of which associates a given spatial type with alien and unintended activities ("pole vaulting in the cathedral"), seeking different modes of experiencing space, training architecture's inhabitants in new ways of practicing space. These techniques refuse the distinctions between concept and percept, container and action, and install the new processes of event-space. "I would like to propose," Tschumi is fond of saying, "that the future of architecture lies in the construction of events."[6]

| compare **408–411** |

Notes

1. It is perhaps worth reminding the reader that "Text" is not an exclusively literary or even essentially linguistic phenomenon. Indeed, Roland Barthes encountered the idea of Text in a North African landscape (see Roland Barthes, *The Rustle of Language*, trans. Richard Howard [New York: Hill and Wang, 1986], p. 60) and went on to produce Text out of the space of a bar (see Roland Barthes, *The Pleasure of the Text*, trans. Richard Miller [New York: Hill and Wang, 1975], pp. 49–50).

2. Georges Bataille, "L'expérience intérieure," in *Oeuvres complètes* (Paris: Gallimard, 1971–1988), vol. 5, p. 102; cited in Denis Hollier, *Against Architecture: The Writings of Georges Bataille,* trans. Betsy Wing (Cambridge: MIT Press, 1989), p. 73.

3. Barthes, *The Pleasure of the Text*, p. 14.

4. Bernard Tschumi, "The Pleasure of Architecture," *Architectural Design* 3 (March 1977), p. 218.

5. "1. There is no architecture without action, no architecture without events, no architecture without program. 2. By extension, there is no architecture without violence." Bernard Tschumi, "Violence of Architecture," *Artforum,* September 1981, p. 44.

6. Such statements can be found throughout Tschumi's writings and lectures, but this one comes from "Six Concepts," *Columbia Documents of Architecture and Theory (D)* 2 (1993), p. 93.

1. Most people concerned with architecture feel some sort of disillusion and dismay. None of the early utopian ideals of the twentieth century has materialized, none of its social aims has succeeded. Blurred by reality, the ideals have turned into redevelopment nightmares and the aims into bureaucratic policies. The split between social reality and utopian dream has been total, the gap between economic constraints and the illusion of all-solving technique absolute. Pointed out by critics who knew the limits of architectural remedies, this historical split has now been bypassed by attempts to reformulate the concepts of architecture. In the process, a new split appears. More complex, it is not the symptom of professional naivete or economic ignorance but the sign of a fundamental question that lies in the very nature of architecture and of its essential element: space. By focusing on itself, architecture has entered an unavoidable paradox that is more present in space than anywhere else: the impossibility of questioning the nature of space and at the same time experiencing a spatial praxis.

2. I have no intention of reviewing architectural trends and their connection to the arts. My general emphasis on space rather than on disciplines (art, architecture, semiology, etc.) is not aimed at negating academic categorization. The merging of disciplines is too worn a path to provide a stimulating itinerary. Instead, I would like to focus attention on the present paradox of space and on the nature of its terms, trying to indicate how one might go beyond this self-contradiction, even if the answer should prove intolerable. I begin by recalling the historical context of this paradox. I will examine first those trends that consider architecture as a thing of the mind, as a dematerialized or conceptual discipline, with its linguistic or morphological variations (the Pyramid); second, empirical research that concentrates on the senses, on the experience of space as well as on the relationship between space and praxis (the Labyrinth); and third, the contradictory nature of these two terms and the difference between the means of escaping the paradox by shifting the actual nature of the debate, as, for example, through politics, and the means that alter the paradox altogether (the Pyramid and the Labyrinth).

3. Linguistically, to define space means both "to make space distinct" and "to state the precise nature of space." Much of the current confusion about space can be illustrated by this ambiguity. While art and architecture have been concerned essentially with the first sense, philosophy, mathematics, and physics have tried throughout history to give interpretations to something variously described as a "material thing in which all material things are located" or as "something subjective with which the mind categorizes things." Remember: with Descartes ended the Aristotelian tradition according to which space and time were "categories" that enabled the classification of "sensory knowledge." Space became absolute. Object before the subject, it dominated senses and bodies by containing them. Was space inherent to the totality of what exists? This was the question of space for Spinoza and Leibniz. Returning to the old notion of category, Kant de-

scribed space as neither matter nor the set of objective relations between things but as an ideal internal structure, an a priori consciousness, an instrument of knowledge. Subsequent mathematical developments on non-Euclidean spaces and their topologies did not eliminate the philosophical discussions. These reappeared with the widening gap between abstract spaces and society. But space was generally accepted as a *cosa mentale*, a sort of all-embracing set with subsets such as literary space, ideological space, and psychoanalytical space.

4. Architecturally, to define space (to make space distinct) literally meant "to determine boundaries." Space had rarely been discussed by architects before the beginning of the twentieth century. But by 1915 it meant *Raum* with all its overtones of German esthetics, with the notion of *Raumempfindung* or "felt volume." By 1923 the idea of felt space had merged with the idea of composition to become a three-dimensional continuum, capable of metrical subdivision that could be related to academic rules. From then on, architectural space was consistently seen as a uniformly extended material to be modeled in various ways, and the history of architecture as the history of spatial concepts. From the Greek "power of interacting volumes" to the Roman "hollowed-out interior space," from the modern "interaction between inner and outer space" to the concept of "transparency," historians and theorists referred to space as a three-dimensional lump of matter.

To draw a parallel between the philosophies of a period and the spatial concepts of architecture is always tempting, but never was it done as obsessively as during the 1930s. Giedion related Einstein's theory of relativity to cubist painting, and cubist planes were translated into architecture in Le Corbusier's Villa Stein at Garches. Despite these space-time concepts, the notion of space remained that of a simplistic and amorphous matter to be defined by its physical boundaries. By the late 1960s, freed from the technological determinants of the postwar period and aware of recent linguistic studies, architects talked about the square, the street, and the arcade, wondering if these did not constitute a little-known code of space with its own syntax and meaning. Did language precede these socioeconomic urban spaces, did it accompany them, or did it follow them? Was space a condition or a formulation? To say that language preceded these spaces was certainly not obvious: human activities leave traces that may precede language. So was there a relationship between space and language, could one "read" a space? Was there a dialectic between social praxis and spatial forms?

5. Yet the gap remained between ideal space (the product of mental processes) and real space (the product of social praxis). Although such a distinction is certainly not ideologically neutral, we shall see that it is in the nature of architecture. As a result, the only successful attempts to bridge this philosophical gap were those that introduced historical or political concepts such as "production," in the wide sense it had in Marx's early texts. Much research in France and in Italy opposed space "as a pure form" to space "as a social product," space "as an intermediary" to space "as a means of reproduction of the mode of production."

This politico-philosophical critique had the advantage of giving an all-embracing approach to space, avoiding the previous dissociation between the "particular" (fragmented social space), the "general" (logico-mathematical or mental spaces), and the "singular" (physical and delineated spaces). But by giving an overall priority to historical processes, it often reduced space to one of the numerous socioeconomic products that were perpetuating a political status quo.[1]

6. Before proceeding to a detailed examination of the ambivalence of the definition of space, it is perhaps useful to consider briefly this particular expression of space in architecture. Its territory extends from an all-embracing "everything is architecture" to Hegel's minimal definition. This latter interpretation must be pointed out, for it describes a difficulty that is constitutive to architecture. When Hegel elaborated his aesthetic theory,[2] he conventionally distinguished five arts and gave them an order: architecture, sculpture, painting, music, and poetry. He started with architecture because he thought it preceded the others in both conceptual and historical terms. Hegel's uneasiness in these first pages is striking. His embarrassment did not really proceed from his conservative classification but was caused by a question that had haunted architects for centuries: were the functional and technical characteristics of a house or a temple the means to an end that excluded those very characteristics? Where did the shed end and architecture begin? Was architectural discourse a discourse about whatever did not relate to the "building" itself? Hegel concluded in the affirmative: architecture was whatever in a building did not point to utility. Architecture was a sort of "artistic supplement" added to the simple building. But the difficulty of such an argument appears when one tries to conceive of a building that escapes the utility of space, a building that would have no other purpose than "architecture."

Although such a question may be irrelevant, it finds a surprising echo in the present search for architectural autonomy. After more than half a century of scientific pretense, of system theories that defined it as the intersection of industrialization, sociology, politics, and ecology, architecture wonders if it can exist without having to find its meaning or its justification in some purposeful exterior need.

The Pyramid: Stating the Nature of Space (or The Dematerialization of Architecture)

7. Little concerned with Hegel's "artistic supplement," architects have nevertheless not regarded the constructed building as the sole and inevitable aim of their activity. They have shown a renewed interest in the idea of playing an active role in fulfilling ideological and philosophical functions with respect to architecture. Just as El Lissitzky and the Vesnin brothers sought to deny the importance of realizing a work and stressed an architectural attitude, so the avant-garde feels reasonably free to act within the realm of concepts. Comparable to the early conceptual artists' rejection of the art commodity market and its alienating effects, the architects' position seems justified by the very remote possibility they had of building anything other than a "mere reflection of the prevalent mode of production."

Moreover, historical precedents exist to give enough credibility to what could paradoxically be described either as a withdrawal from reality or as a takeover of new and unknown territories. "What is architecture?" asked Boullée. "Will I define it with Vitruvius as the art of building? No. This definition contains a crass error. Vitruvius takes the effect for the cause. One must conceive in order to make. Our forefathers only built their hut after they had conceived its image. This production of the mind, this creation is what constitutes architecture, that which we now can define as the art to produce any building and bring it to perfection. The art of building is thus only a secondary art that it seems appropriate to call the scientific part of architecture."[3] At a time when architectural memory rediscovers its role, architectural history, with its treatises and manifestos, has been conveniently confirming to architects that spatial concepts were made by the writings and drawings of space as much as by their built translations.

The questions, "is there any reason why one cannot proceed from design that can be constructed to design that concerns itself only with the ideology and concept of architecture?" and "if architectural work consists of questioning the nature of architecture, what prevents us from making this questioning a work of architecture in itself?"[4] were already rhetorical questions in 1972. The renewed importance given to conceptual aims in architecture quickly became established. The medium used for the communication of concepts became architecture; information was architecture; the attitude was architecture; the written program or brief was architecture; gossip was architecture; production was architecture; and inevitably, the architect was architecture. Escaping the predictable ideological compromises of building, the architect could finally achieve the sensual satisfaction that the making of material objects no longer provided.

8. The dematerialization of architecture into the realm of concepts was more the characteristic of a period than of any particular avant-garde group. Thus it developed in various directions and struck movements as ideologically opposed as, for example, "radical architecture"[5] and "rational architecture."[6] But the question it asked was fundamental: if everything was architecture, by virtue of the architect's decision, what distinguished architecture from any other human activity? This quest for identity revealed that the architect's freedom did not necessarily coincide with the freedom of architecture.

If architecture seemed to have gained freedom from the socio-economic constraints of building processes, any radical counter-designs and manifestos were inevitably reinstated in the commercial circuits of galleries or magazines. Like conceptual art in the mid-1960s, architecture seemed to have gained autonomy by opposing the institutional framework. But in the process it had become the institutional opposition, thus growing into the very thing it tried to oppose.

Although some architects, following a political analysis that we shall soon describe, were in favor of doing away with architecture altogether, the search for autonomy inevitably turned back toward architecture itself, as no other context would readily provide for it. The question became: is there an architectural essence, a being that transcends all social, political, and economic systems?" This ontological bias injected new blood into a concept that already had been well aired by art theorists. Investigations into Hegel's "supplement" received the support of structural linguistic studies in France and Italy. Analogies with language appeared en masse, some useful, some particularly naive and misleading. Among these linguistic analogies, two figure prominently.

9. The first theory claims that the Hegelian "supplement," added to the simple building and constitutive of architecture, is immediately struck by some semantic expansion that would force this architectural supplement to be less a piece of architecture than the representation of something else. Architecture is then nothing but the space of representation. As soon as it is distinguished from the simple building, it represents something other than itself: the social structure, the power of the King, the idea of God, and so on.

The second theory questions an understanding of architecture as a language that refers to meanings outside itself. It refuses the interpretation of a three-dimensional translation of social values, for architecture would then be nothing but the linguistic product of social determinants. It thus claims that the architectural object is pure language and that architecture is an endless manipulation of the grammar and syntax of the architectural sign. Rational architecture, for example, becomes a selected vocabulary of architectural elements of the past, with their oppositions, contrasts, and redistributions. Not only does it refer to itself and to its own history, but function—the existential justification of the work—becomes virtual rather than real. So the language is closed in on itself, and architecture becomes a truly autonomous organism. Forms do not follow functions but refer to other forms, and functions relate to symbols. Ultimately architecture frees itself from reality altogether. Form does not need to call for external justifications. In a critical article in *Oppositions*, Manfredo Tafuri can thus describe Aldo Rossi's architecture as "a universe of carefully selected signs, within which the law of exclusion dominates, and in fact is the controlling expression," and the trend it represents as "l'architecture dans le boudoir" because the circle drawn around linguistic experimentation reveals a pregnant affinity with the obsessively rigorous writings of the Marquis de Sade.[7]

Freed from reality, independent of ideology, architectural values are striving toward a purity unattained since the Russian formalist criticism of the 1920s, when it was argued that the only valid object of literary criticism was the literary text. Here, the tautology of architecture—that is, an architecture that describes itself—becomes a syntax of empty signs, often derived from a selective historicism that concentrates on moments of history: the early modern movement, the Roman monument, the Renaissance palace, the castle. Transmitted through history, and removed from the constraints of their time, can these signs, these diagrams of spaces, become the generative matrices of today's work?

10. They might. Architectural theory shares with art theory a peculiar characteristic: it is prescriptive. So the series of signs and articulations that has just been described may undoubtedly prove a useful model for architects engaged in a perpetual search for new support disciplines, even if it is not clear whether systems of nonverbal signs, such as space, proceed from concepts similar to verbal systems. However, the real importance of this research lies in the question it asks about the nature of architecture rather than in the making of architecture. This is not without recalling the perverse and hypothetical search for the very origins of architecture. Remember: at the outset, does architecture produce copies or models? If it cannot imitate an order, can it constitute one, whether it be the world or society? Must architecture create its own model, if it has no created model? Positive answers inevit-

ably imply some archetype. But as this archetype cannot exist outside architecture, architecture must produce one itself. It thus becomes some sort of an essence that precedes existence. So the architect is once again "the person who conceives the form of the building without manipulating materials himself." He conceives the *pyramid*, this ultimate model of reason. Architecture becomes a *cosa mentale* and the forms conceived by the architect ensure the domination of the idea over matter.

The Labyrinth: Making Space Distinct (or The Experience of Space)

11. *Should I intensify the quarantine in the chambers of the Pyramid of reason? Shall I sink to depths where no one will be able to reach me and understand me, living among abstract connections more frequently expressed by inner monologues than by direct realities? Shall architecture, which started with the building of tombs, return to the Tomb, to the eternal silence of finally transcended history? Shall architecture perform at the service of illusory functions and build virtual spaces? My voyage into the abstract realm of language, into the dematerialized world of concepts, meant the removal of architecture from its intricate and convoluted element: space. Removal from the exhilarating differences between the apse and the nave of Ely Cathedral, between Salisbury Plain and Stonehenge, between the Street and my Living Room. Space is real, for it seems to affect my senses long before my reason. The materiality of my body both coincides with and struggles with the materiality of space. My body carries in itself spatial properties and spatial determination: up, down, right, left, symmetry, dissymmetry. It hears as much as it sees. Unfolding against the projections of reason, against the Absolute Truth, against the Pyramid, here is the Sensory Space, the Labyrinth, the Hole. Dislocated and dissociated by language or culture or economy into the specialized ghettos of sex and mind, Soho and Bloomsbury, 42nd Street and West 40th Street, here is where my body tries to rediscover its lost unity, its energies and impulses, its rhythms and its flux . . .*

12. This purely sensory approach has been a recurrent theme in this century's understanding and appreciation of space. It is not necessary to expand at length on the precedents witnessed by twentieth-century architecture. Suffice it to say that current conversation seems to fluctuate between (a) the German esthetic overtones of the *Raumempfindung* theory, whereby space is to be "felt" as something affecting the inner nature of man by a symbolic *Einfühlung*, and (b) an idea that echoes Schlemmer's work at the Bauhaus, whereby space was not only the medium of experience but also the materialization of theory. For example, the emphasis given to movement found in dance the "elemental means for the realization of space-creative impulses," for dance could articulate and order space. The parallel made between the dancer's movements and the more traditional means of defining and articulating space, such as walls or columns, is important. When the dancers Trisha Brown and Simone Forti reintroduced this spatial discussion in the mid-1960s, the relationship between theory and practice, reason and perception, had to take another turn, and the concept of theoretical praxis could not be simply indicative. There was no way in space to follow the art-language practice. If it could be argued that the discourse about art was art and thus could be exhibited as such, the theoretical discourse about space certainly was not space.

The attempt to trigger a new perception of space reopened a basic philosophical question. Remember: you are inside an enclosed space with equal height and width. Do your eyes instruct you about the cube merely by noticing it, without giving any additional interpretation? No. You don't really see the cube. You may see a corner, or a side, or the ceiling, but never all defining surfaces at the same time. You touch a wall, you hear an echo. But how do you relate all these perceptions to one single object? Is it through an operation of reason?

13. This operation of reason, which precedes the perception of the cube as a cube, was mirrored by the approach of concept-performance artists. While your eyes were giving instructions about successive parts of the cube, allowing you to form the concept of cube, the artist was giving instructions about the concept

of cube, stimulating your senses through the intermediary of reason. This reversal, this mirror image, was important, for the interplay between the new perception of "performance" space and the rational means at the origin of the piece was typically one aspect of the architectural process: the mechanics of perception of a distinct space, that is the complete space of the performance, with the movements, the thoughts, the received instructions of the actors, as well as the social and physical context in which they performed. But the most interesting part of such performance was the underlying discussion on the "nature of space" in general, as opposed to the shaping and perception of distinct spaces in particular.

It is in recent works that the recurring etymological distinction appears at its strongest. Reduced to the cold simplicity of six planes that define the boundaries of a more or less regular cube, the series of spaces designed by Bruce Nauman, Doug Wheeler, Robert Irwin, or Michael Asher do not play with elaborate spatial articulations. Their emphasis is elsewhere. By restricting visual and physical perception to the faintest of all stimulations, they turn the expected experience of the space into something altogether different. The almost totally removed sensory definition inevitably throws the viewers back on themselves. In "deprived space," to borrow the terminology of Germano Celant, the "participants" can only find them-selves as the subject, aware only of their own fantasies and pulsations, able only to react to the low-density signals of their own bodies. The materiality of the body coincides with the materiality of the space. By a series of exclusions that become significant only in opposition to the remote exterior space and social context, the subjects only "experience their own experience."

14. Whether such spaces might be seen as reminiscent of the behaviorist spaces of the beginning of the century, where reactions were hopefully triggered, or as the new echo of the *Raumempfindung* theory, now cleaned-up of its moral and esthetic overtones, is of little theoretical importance. What matters is their double content: for their way to "make space distinct" (to define space in particular) is only there to throw one back on the interpretation of the "nature of space" itself. As opposed to the previously described pyramid of reason, the dark corners of expe-rience are not unlike a *labyrinth* where all sensations, all feelings are enhanced, but where no overview is present to provide a clue about how to get out. Occasional consciousness is of little help, for perception in the Labyrinth presupposes immedi-acy. Unlike Hegel's classical distinction between the moment of perception and the moment of experience (when one's consciousness makes a new object out of a per-ceived one), the metaphorical Labyrinth implies that the first moment of perception carries the experience itself.

It is hardly surprising, therefore, that there may be no way out of the Labyrinth. Denis Hollier, in his book on Georges Bataille,[8] points out that from Bacon to Leibniz the Labyrinth was linked with the desire to get out, and science was seen as the means to find an exit. Rejecting such an interpretation, Bataille suggested that its only effect was to transform the Labyrinth into a banal prison. The traditional meaning of the metaphor was reversed: one never knows whether one is inside or not, since one cannot grasp it in one look. Just as language gives us words that en-circle us but that we use in order to break their surround, the Labyrinth of experience was full of openings that did not tell whether they opened toward its outside or its inside.

The Pyramid and the Labyrinth: The Paradox of Architecture

15. To single out particular areas of concern, such as the rational play of language as opposed to the experience of the senses, would be a tedious game if it were to lead to a naive confrontation between the mind and the body. The architectural avant-garde has fought often enough over alternatives that appeared as opposites—struc-

ture and chaos, ornament and purity, permanence and change, reason and intuition. And often enough it has been shown that such alternatives were in fact complementary: our analysis of a dematerialization of architecture in its ontological form (the Pyramid) and of a sensual experience (the Labyrinth) is no different. But if the existence of such an equation does not raise doubts over its complementarity, it certainly raises questions about how such equations can go beyond the vicious circle of terms that speak only of themselves.

The answer may lie in the context in which such an equation takes place. A common accusation of analyses or even of works that concentrate on the specific nature of architecture is that they are "parallel," that is, they fold and unfold in some Panglossian world where social and economic forces are conveniently absent. Not affecting the determining forces of production, they constitute harmless forms of private expression. We shall therefore briefly consider the ambiguous particularities of the relationships between architecture and politics.

16. These have been well researched in the past few years. The role of architecture and planning has been analyzed in terms of a projection on the ground of the images of social institutions, as a faithful translation of the structures of society into buildings or cities. Such studies underline the difficulty architecture has in acting as a political instrument. Recalling the nostalgic and attenuated cry of the Russian revolutionary "social condensers" of the 1920s, some advocated the use of space as a peaceful tool of social transformation, as a means of changing the relation between the individual and society by generating new lifestyles. But the "clubs" and community buildings proposed not only required an existing revolutionary society but also a blind belief in an interpretation of behaviorism according to which individual behavior could be influenced by the organization of space. Aware that spatial organization may temporarily modify individual or group behavior but may not change the socioeconomic structure of a reactionary society, architectural revolutionaries looked for better grounds. Their attempts to find a socially relevant, if not revolutionary, role for architecture culminated in the years following the May 1968 events with "guerrilla" buildings, whose symbolic and exemplary value lay in their seizure of urban space and not in the design of what was built. On the cultural front, plans for a surrealistic destruction of established value systems were devised by Italian "radical" designers. This nihilistic prerequisite for social and economic change was a desperate attempt to use the architect's mode of expression to denounce institutional trends by translating them into architectural terms, ironically "verifying where the system was going" by designing the cities of a desperate future.

Not surprisingly, it was the question of the production system that finally led to more realistic proposals. Aimed at redistributing the capitalistic division of labor, these proposals sought a new understanding of the technicians' role in building, in terms of a responsible partnership directly involved in the production cycle, thus shifting the concept of architecture toward the general organization of building processes.

17. Yet it is the unreal (or unrealistic) position of the artist or architect that may be its very reality. Except for the last attitude, most political approaches suffered from the predictable isolation of schools of architecture that tried to offer their environmental knowledge to the revolution. Hegel's architecture, the "supplement," did not seem to have the right revolutionary edge. Or did it? Does architecture, in its long-established isolation, contain more revolutionary power than its numerous transfers into the objective realities of the building industry and social housing? Does the social function of architecture lie in its very lack of function? In fact, architecture may have little other ground.

Just as the surrealists could not find the right compromise between scandal and social acceptance, architecture seems to have little choice between autonomy and commitment, between the radical anachronism of Schiller's "courage to talk of roses" and society. If the architectural piece renounces its autonomy by recognizing its latent ideological and financial dependency, it accepts the mechanisms of society. If it sanctuarizes itself in an art-for-art's-sake position, it does not escape classification among existing ideological compartments.

So architecture seems to survive only when it saves its nature by negating the form that society expects of it. *I would therefore suggest that there has never been any reason to doubt the necessity of architecture, for the necessity of architecture is its non-necessity. It is useless, but radically so.* Its radicalism constitutes its very strength in a society where profit is prevalent. Rather than an obscure artistic supplement or a cultural justification for financial manipulations, architecture is not unlike fireworks, for these "empirical apparitions," as Adorno puts it, "produce a delight that cannot be sold or bought, that has no exchange value and cannot be integrated in the production cycle."[9]

18. It is hardly surprising, therefore, that the non-necessity of architecture, its necessary loneliness, throws it back on itself. If its role is not defined by society, architecture will have to define it alone. Until 1750, architectural space could rely on the paradigm of the ancient precedent. After that time, until well into the twentieth century, this classical source of unity progressively became the socially determined program. In view of the present-day polarization of ontological discourse and sensual experience, I am well aware that any suggestion that they now form the inseparable but mutually exclusive terms of architecture requires some elucidation. This must begin with a description of the apparent impossibility of escaping from the paradox of the Pyramid of concepts and the Labyrinth of experience, of immaterial architecture as a concept and of material architecture as a presence.

To restate my point, the paradox is not about the impossibility of perceiving both architectural concept (the six faces of the cube) and real space at the same time but about the impossibility of questioning the nature of space and at the same time making or experiencing a real space. Unless we search for an escape from architecture into the general organization of building processes, the paradox persists: architecture is made of two terms that are interdependent but mutually exclusive. Indeed, *architecture constitutes the reality of experience while this reality gets in the way of the overall vision. Architecture constitutes the abstraction of absolute truth, while this very truth gets in the way of feeling.* We cannot both experience and think that we experience. "The concept of dog does not bark"; the concept of space is not in space.

In the same way, the achievement of architectural reality (building) defeats architectural theory while at the same time being a product of it. So theory and praxis may be dialectic to one another, but in space, the translation of the concept, the overcoming of the abstraction in reality, involves the dissolution of the dialectic and an incomplete statement. This means, in effect, that, perhaps for the first time in history, architecture can never be. The effect of the great battles of social progress is obliterated, and so is the security of archetypes. Defined by its questioning, architecture is always the expression of a lack, a shortcoming, a noncompletion. It always misses something, either reality or concept. Architecture is both being and nonbeing. The only alternative to the paradox is silence, a final nihilistic statement that might provide modern architectural history with its ultimate punchline, its self-annihilation.

19. Before leaving this brief exploration of architecture as paradox, it is tempting to suggest a way of accepting the paradox while refuting the silence it seems to imply. This conclusion may be intolerable to philosophers, in that it alters the subject of architecture, you and I (and one knows logicians are never drunk). It may be intolerable to scientists who want to master the subject of science. It may be intolerable to artists who want to objectify the subject.

Let us first examine the Labyrinth. In the course of this argument, it has been implied that the Labyrinth shows itself as a slow history of space, but that a total revelation of the Labyrinth is historically impossible because no point of transcendence in time is available. One can participate in and share the fundamentals of the Labyrinth, but one's perception is only part of the Labyrinth as it manifests itself. One can never see it in totality, nor can one express it. One is condemned to it and cannot go outside and see the whole. But remember: Icarus flew away, toward the sun. So after all, does the way out of the Labyrinth lie in the making of the Pyramid, through a projection of the subject toward some transcendental objectivity? Unfortunately not. The Labyrinth cannot be dominated. The top of the Pyramid is an imaginary place, and Icarus fell down: the nature of the Labyrinth is such that it entertains dreams that include the dream of the Pyramid.

20. But the real importance of the Labyrinth and of its spatial experience lies elsewhere. The Pyramid, the analysis of the architectural object, the breaking down of its forms and elements, all cut away from the question of the subject. Along with the spatial praxis mentioned earlier, the sensual architectural reality is not experienced as an abstract object already transformed by consciousness but as an immediate and concrete human activity—as a praxis, with all its subjectivity. This importance of the subject is in clear opposition to all philosophical and historical attempts to objectify the immediate perception of reality, for example, in the relations of production. To talk about the Labyrinth and its praxis means to insist here on its subjective aspects: it is personal and requires an immediate experience. Opposed to Hegel's *Erfahrung* and close to Bataille's "interior experience," this immediacy bridges sensory pleasure and reason. It introduces new articulations between the inside and the outside, between private and public spaces. It suggests new oppositions between dissociated terms and new relations between homogeneous spaces. This immediacy does not give precedence to the experiential term, however. *For it is only by recognizing the architectural rule that the subject of space will reach the depth of experience and its sensuality. Like eroticism, architecture needs both system and excess.*

21. This "experience" may have repercussions that go far beyond man as its "subject." Torn between rationality and the demand for irrationality, our present society moves toward other attitudes. If system plus excess is one of its symptoms, we may soon have to consider architecture as the indispensable complement to this changing praxis. In the past, architecture gave linguistic metaphors (the Castle, the Structure, the Labyrinth) to society. It may now provide the cultural model.

As long as social practice rejects the paradox of ideal and real space, imagination—interior experience—may be the only means to transcend it. By changing the prevalent attitudes toward space and its subject, the dream of the step beyond the paradox can even provide the conditions for renewed social attitudes. Just as eroticism is the pleasure of excess rather than the excess of pleasure, so the solution of the paradox is the imaginary blending of the architecture rule and the experience of pleasure.

Notes

1. For these issues, see the interpretation offered by Henri Lefebvre in *La production de l'espace* (Paris: Editions Anthropos, 1973), and the texts of Castells and Utopie. See also Bernard Tschumi, "Flashback," on the politics of space, in *Architectural Design*, October-November 1975.

2. Friedrich Hegel, *The Philosophy of Fine Art*, vol. 1 (London: G. Bell and Sons, 1920).

3. Etienne-Louis Boullée, *Essai sur l'art*, ed. Jean-Marie Pérouse de Montclos (Paris: Hermann, 1968).

4. On the ideological crisis of architecture and the emergence of radical architecture, see Germano Celant (quoted here) in *The New Italian Landscape* (New York: Museum of Modern Art, 1972), p. 320.

5. Originated in Florence from 1963 to 1971 by groups such as Superstudio, Archizoom, UFO, and so forth, radical architecture explored the destruction of culture and its artifacts. "The ultimate end of modern architecture is the elimination of architecture altogether" (Archizoom Associates).

6. One of the first and most significant events of rational architecture was the XV Milan Triennale, organized by Aldo Rossi, whose catalogue bore the title of *Architettura razionale* (Milan: F. Angeli, 1973).

7. "The return to language is a proof of failure. It is necessary to examine to what degree such a failure is due to the intrinsic character of the architectural discipline and to what degree it is due to a still unresolved ambiguity." Manfredo Tafuri, *Oppositions* 3 (May 1974), where the author develops a historical critique of traditional approaches to theory and shifts from a central focus on the criticism of architecture to the criticism of ideology.

8. Denis Hollier, *La prise de la Concorde* (Paris: Gallimard, 1974), the reading of which suggested the opposition between the labyrinth and the pyramid. See also Georges Bataille, *Eroticism* (London: Calder, 1962) and "L'expérience intérieure," in *Oeuvres complètes* (Paris: Gallimard, 1971).

9. Bernard Tschumi, "Fireworks," 1974, extract from *A Space: A Thousand Words* (London: Royal College of Art Gallery, 1975): "Yes, just as all the erotic forces contained in your movement have been consumed for nothing, architecture must be conceived, erected and burned in vain. The greatest architecture of all is the fireworker's: it perfectly shows the gratuitous consumption of pleasure."

Accepted for years as a worthy successor to Philip Johnson, American mandarin of the modern movement, Drexler has finally flipped. He now loathes the architecture that the modern movement has spawned and is intent to make known his disillusion. Eighteen months ago he organized a superlative exhibition at the Museum of Modern Art, of about 200 drawings, dating largely from the mid-nineteenth century, done in the main by students and architects from the Ecole des Beaux-Arts in Paris. The historicist revival that he thus propounded was made the more telling in that the architectural section of the historic institution was dissolved finally in 1968—by rioting students. The Ecole des Beaux-Arts is dead; long live the Ecole des Beaux-Arts!

Robin Middleton, "Vive l'Ecole," in *Architectural Design 48/11–12: The Beaux-Arts,* ed. Robin Middleton (1978)

In the establishment of the modern state during the nineteenth century the role of the Beaux-Arts must be viewed not so much as a cultural phenomenon but as a political operation, where culture becomes both a trade and an instrument of domination in the hands of the bourgeoisie.

The Beaux-Arts was, therefore, concerned with large-scale composition, with the act of ordering rather than the search for order. Science also is concerned with ordering rather than with order.

And politics, above all, is concerned with ordering rather than with order.

While the Beaux-Arts had little to do with architecture (the art of building), it had everything to do with that gloriously emphatic (and finally pathetic) victory of necessity over pleasure, of ordering over order, of propaganda over communication, of the state over the community, of law over order, of the future over the present. . . .

Architecture after all is concerned with meaning and beauty, and to my mind the Beaux-Arts was concerned with neither. And to understand our own problems we have to look back—much further back than the Beaux-Arts.

Leon Krier, "Law and Disorder," in *Architectural Design 48/11–12: The Beaux-Arts,* ed. Robin Middleton (1978)

The Beaux-Arts exhibition was mounted with the intent to shock, and it has succeeded. Arthur Drexler sees it as a frontal challenge to the current practice of mainstream modern architecture. And Ada Louise Huxtable thinks the exhibition focuses a "crisis" of modern architecture.

I don't think the exhibition *itself* offers any very explicit new lessons for a redirected approach to architecture.

On the one hand, the impact of the show may be beneficial. It may contribute to the growing movement toward the new and more sensitive relationship of building typologies and urban morphologies. (This despite the fact that the exhibition does not illustrate this particular aspect of Beaux-Arts practice.) It may strengthen various tendencies which take a more supple stance vis-à-vis architectural history and the historical artifacts amongst which almost all our new buildings are erected. It may contribute to a greater formal facility amongst designers, as compared with the club-footed moral earnestness which has too often passed for facility during the past decade.

Yet, given its lack of explicit directives, I don't think we have much *assurance* that these beneficial outcomes will follow. I have fears of possible—and perhaps equally likely—*unfortunate* impacts of the exhibition. I fear that we may well hear a Yamasaki of the 1980s speak of a new "architecture of delight"; I fear the architects of major public buildings will find in the Beaux-Arts a new justification for designing buildings like Edward Stone's Embassy in India, or Kennedy Center. Then, too, we may face a resurgent vulgar historicism.
George Baird, in "Forum: The Beaux-Arts Exhibition," ed. William Ellis, *Oppositions* 8 (Spring 1977)

The bizarre union of MOMA and the Beaux-Arts is spawning misinterpretations of architectural history as individual protagonists realign themselves to meet the new alliance. In the reshuffle, the Beaux-Arts itself is being reinterpreted to teach, I fear, the wrong lessons.

The Modern architectural establishment is picking up the Beaux-Arts for several wrong reasons: for its elitist programs ("history," "urbanism," and "*pro bono publico*" in the catalogue preface sound like code words for upper class architecture), for its good drawings, and to find some way of accepting, at last, the fifteen-year-old critique of the Modern movement, without appearing to cave in; particularly without having to accept the call of Modern architecture's critics for social relevance, openness to the pluralist aesthetic and understanding of the everyday environment. Beaux-Arts will enable Arthur Drexler, for instance, to "reexamine our architectural pieties," as he puts it, without having to heed Herbert Gans or learn from Las Vegas.
Denise Scott-Brown, in "Forum: The Beaux-Arts Exhibition," ed. William Ellis, *Oppositions* 8 (Spring 1977)

The nineteenth century believed in an architecture which did not concern itself merely with a functional, constructional, spatial fit. It struggled toward semantic articulateness. To the Vitruvian triad it added a fourth goal—appropriateness—and it is in the continuous struggle to make forms which are meaningful in a broad cultural context that the architecture of the nineteenth century offers great lessons for today. Venturi and Moore began to redefine for us a modern position in architecture that draws on historic issues—modernism and nineteenth century eclecticism—to establish a new working strategy which I will call post-modernism for want of a better term. I believe that to succeed, the post-modernist attitude must be re-established or reaffirmed in word and deed, and the beliefs which were implicit in the vast amount of architecture of the nineteenth century, especially the belief in the power of architecture to achieve symbolic meaning through allusion not only to other moments in architectural history but to historical and contemporary events of a social, political, and cultural nature, are central to the emerging post-modern position. And a post-modernist attitude must also carry with it an affirmation of belief that architecture is for the eye as well as the mind. Such seems to be our best hope for capturing the affection of our very disaffected constituency: the public.
Robert Stern, in "Forum: The Beaux-Arts Exhibition," ed. William Ellis, *Oppositions* 8 (Spring 1977)

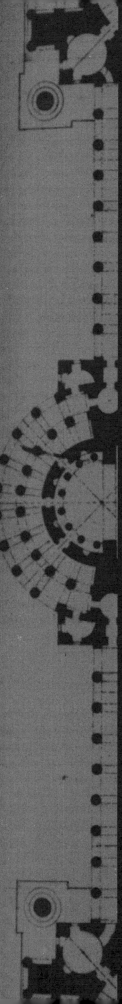

In assessing the present exhibition, we are not fighting the same battles as the Europeans—our defenses, in America, are not aroused for the new spirit, nor for the carefully worked aesthetics of neo-plasticism or purism; nor, and this is more significant, are we fighting any form of rearguard action for a lost social ethic. In the U.S. modern architecture was, and is, not the same as in Europe; its ends, its aspirations, its forms, and its roles have not been the same from the very beginning. In Europe modern architecture forged itself not only as an aesthetic but as a social movement; its was the expression (however misplaced in retrospect) of social democracy, sometimes even socialism in action—it was avant-garde, and progressive, when the idea of progress was not a cheap dream of cars and suburbs; it was the restoration of conditions of life, on the premises of a new technology, a new equality, a new vision of world order. The merging of Saint-Simon the technocrat, and Fourier the social harmonist, was premised by the Radiant City.

But, in America this was never the case. As with the first adoption of the Beaux-Arts in the nineteenth century, the only recognizable export from Europe was the style; its forms may have been meticulously correct—even as Le Corbusier now shelters the beach house elite of Long Island—but its ends were different. The Beaux-Arts monument in the U.S. was the elegant shelter of a society in full development—the confirmation of the expanding world of industry and capital.

Similarly, when finally the Modern Movement was imported into the U.S. (by the mechanism, it is interesting to note, of an exhibition at the Museum of Modern Art), it was as International Style, not movement. . . . Americans, always uncomfortable with the brief, and temporary, identification of modern style with the social premises of the new deal, were now relieved to see the divorce between art and society ratified by the art exhibition.

So now, when the Beaux-Arts is again imported, a great deal of talk is heard about the end of social engagement—as if there ever had been any; the death of modern architecture—as if it had ever been more than an imported style, readily discarded when the packaging of space demanded a different economy, a different image. . . .

Thus the event is not an event; merely a confirmation of a situation, a symptom of a mode of conceiving architecture that was always academic in essence, and perhaps, until some critique or progress finally takes hold in the U.S. to allow movements to emerge as fully fledged criticisms of the existing order, it always will be.

Anthony Vidler, in "Forum: The Beaux-Arts Exhibition," ed. William Ellis, *Oppositions* 8 (Spring 1977)

Some architects and journalists have assumed that there were ulterior motives attached to the exhibition, especially because it was presented by the Museum of Modern Art. Some observers thought the show was meant to bring on a Beaux-Arts revival. That was not the case. But insofar as such fears are prompted by the show being an implied criticism of the Modern Movement, the fears are understandable.

Arthur Drexler, in "Forum: The Beaux-Arts Exhibition," ed. William Ellis, *Oppositions* 8 (Spring 1977)

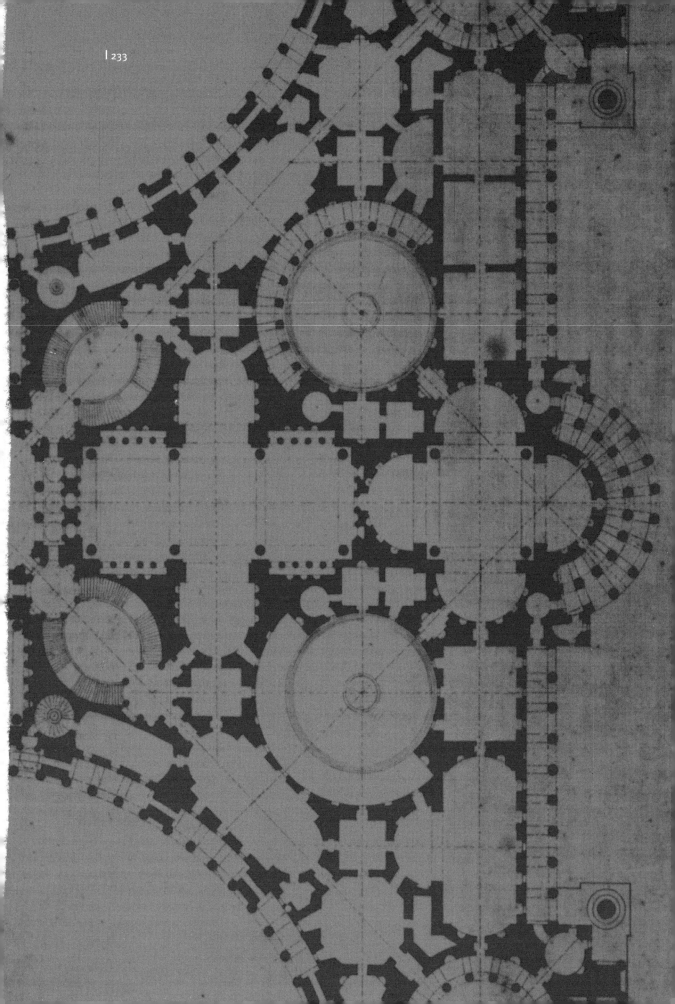

233

Peter Eisenman   **"Post-Functionalism"** *Oppositions* 6 (Fall 1976)

The Institute for Architecture and Urban Studies, an independent research, design, and educational corporation directed by Peter Eisenman, was founded in New York in 1967. *Oppositions*, the Institute's primary organ, first appeared in September 1973 and remained the single most important journal of architecture theory until 1982. In issues 4, 5, 6, and 7 of the journal, each of its editors, Kenneth Frampton, Mario Gandelsonas, Peter Eisenman, and Anthony Vidler, published an independent editorial that together marked out many of the major categories of architecture theory in the 1970s and 1980s.

Frampton's reading of the Heideggerian *Raum* as a place of possible resistance to the techno-scientific and mass-cultural attacks on the fundamentally phenomenological aspect of architectural experience prompted his proposal for a dialectic of ends and means, of "place" and "production," that already anticipated his later work.[1] Gandelsonas's "Neo-Functionalism" categorized dialectically, for the first time, the position epitomized by the work of Robert Venturi — "neorealism" — and that represented by Aldo Rossi, Peter Eisenman, and John Hejduk — "neorationalism" — and identified modernist functionalism's underdeveloped concern with the problem of meaning ("since function is itself one of the meanings that could be articulated by form") as a possible third term.[2] Vidler's apologia for Rossi and the Tendenza, the "third typology," identified its "ontology of the city" as a possible base for the restoration of a critical role to architecture.[3] Eisenman, in his editorial reprinted here, gathered up his preoccupations with structural linguistics, conceptual art, and avant-garde autotelic procedures, and characterized a "post-functionalist" position that would recognize architecture's epistemological status.

As its title suggests, Eisenman's essay enters into a mode of thinking that Gregory Ulmer has called "post-criticism," which is constituted primarily by the application of certain devices of modernism (such as the direct incorporation of a formal fragment into a collage, or the aleatory process of montage) to critical *representations*.[4] Rather than simply deriving its forms from functional needs, Eisenman sees modernism as "work on the language itself. . . . It fundamentally changed the relationship between man and object away from an object whose primary purpose was to speak *about* man to one which was concerned with its own objecthood."[5] A properly modernist architecture should be not so much a subjective innovation (on the model of the artist-as-genius) as a search for objective knowledge that lies outside the artist, within the very materials and formal operations of architecture. Such a research discovers the new in the given "language," immanently, through an articulation and redistribution of its elements. Hence the importance of representation: the architectural object, on this view, is just a representation of architectural logic itself.

Eisenman earlier called such a formal object-become-simulacrum-of-process "cardboard architecture": "Cardboard is used to shift the focus from our existing conception of form in an aesthetic and fuctional context to a consideration of form as a marking or notational system. The use of cardboard attempts to distinguish an aspect of these forms which are designed to act as a signal or a message and at the same time the representation of them as a message."[6] Further, he

| *see* 358–360 ▌

| *see* 284–286 ▌

associated cardboard architecture's effects with the defamiliarization and alienation effects of a Brechtian modernism.[7] In the present essay, he historicizes such concerns as part of a new episteme, a posthumanist paradigm heralded by James Joyce, Arnold Schönberg, Hans Richter, and others, and theorized in the antihumanism of Michel Foucault and Claude Lévi-Strauss.

But as important as its effort to push architecture into this new paradigm is what is entailed when architecture represents the very process of "architecting": that the effort to represent the inner logic of the object *in the object itself* is made not because of some preordained decision to exclude other considerations but because of the felt consequence of a historical evolution crucial, if not unique, to the discipline of architecture itself. This evolution, which began with modernism, fuses the practice of architecture with the *critique* of architecture and replaces the functional object with a theoretical one.

Notes

1. Kenneth Frampton, "On Reading Heidegger," *Oppositions* 4 (October 1974).
2. Mario Gandelsonas, "Neo-Functionalism," *Oppositions* 5 (Summer 1976).
3. Anthony Vidler, "The Third Typology," *Oppositions* 7 (Winter 1977).
4. Gregory L. Ulmer, "The Object of Post-Criticism," in *The Anti-Aesthetic: Essays on Postmodern Culture*, ed. Hal Foster (Port Townsend, Wash.: Bay Press, 1983).
5. See Peter Eisenman, "Postscript [to Alan Colquhoun's]: The Graves of Modernism," *Oppositions* 12 (Spring 1978).
6. Peter Eisenman, "Cardboard Architecture: House I," in *Five Architects* (New York: Wittenborn, 1972), p. 16. See also Peter Eisenman, "Notes on Conceptual Architecture: Towards a Definition," *Casabella* 359–360 (1971).
7. "While the architectural system may be complete, the environment 'house' is almost a void. And quite unintentionally — like the audience of the film — the owner has been alienated from his environment. In this sense, when the owner first enters 'his house' he is an intruder; he must begin to regain possession — to occupy a foreign container. In the process of taking possession the owner begins to destroy, albeit in a positive sense, the initial unity and completeness of the architectural structure." Peter Eisenman, "To Adolf Loos & Bertold Brecht," *Progressive Architecture* 55 (May 1974), p. 92.

The critical establishment within architecture has told us that we have entered the era of "post-modernism." The tone with which this news is delivered is invariably one of relief, similar to that which accompanies the advice that one is no longer an adolescent. Two indices of this supposed change are the quite different manifestations of the "Architettura Razionale" exhibition at the Milan Triennale of 1973, and the "Ecole des Beaux Arts" exhibition at The Museum of Modern Art in 1975. The former, going on the assumption that modern architecture was an outmoded functionalism, declared that architecture can be generated only through a return to itself as an autonomous or pure discipline. The latter, seeing modern architecture as an obsessional formalism, made itself into an implicit statement that the future lies paradoxically in the past, within the peculiar response to function that characterized the nineteenth century's eclectic command of historical styles.

What is interesting is not the mutually exclusive character of these two diagnoses and hence of their solutions, but rather the fact that both of these views enclose the very project of architecture within the same definition: one by which the terms continue to be function (or program) and form (or type). In so doing, an attitude toward architecture is maintained that differs in no significant way from the 500-year-old tradition of humanism.

The various theories of architecture which properly can be called "humanist" are characterized by a dialectical opposition: an oscillation between a concern for internal accommodation—the program and the way it is materialized—and a concern for articulation of ideal themes in form—for example, as manifested in the configurational significance of the plan. These concerns were understood as two poles of a single, continuous experience. Within pre-industrial, humanist practice, a balance between them could be maintained because both type and function were invested with idealist views of man's relationship to his object world. In a comparison first suggested by Colin Rowe, of a French Parisian hôtel and an English country house, both buildings from the early nineteenth century, one sees this opposition manifested in the interplay between a concern for expression of an ideal type and a concern for programmatic statement, although the concerns in each case are differently weighted. The French hôtel displays rooms of an elaborate sequence and a spatial variety born of internal necessity, masked by a rigorous, well-proportioned external façade. The English country house has a formal internal arrangement of rooms which gives way to a picturesque external massing of elements. The former bows to program on the interior and type on the façade; the latter reverses these considerations.

With the rise of industrialization, this balance seems to have been fundamentally disrupted. In that it had of necessity to come to terms with problems of a more complex functional nature, particularly with respect to the accommodation of a mass client, architecture became increasingly a social or programmatic art. And as the functions became more complex, the ability to manifest the pure type-form eroded. One has only to compare William Kent's competition entry for the Houses of Parliament, where the form of a Palladian Villa does not sustain the intricate program, with Charles Barry's solution where the type-form defers to program and where one sees an early example of what was to become known as the *promenade architecturale*. Thus, in the nineteenth century, and continuing on into the twentieth, as the program grew in complexity, the type-form became diminished as a realizable concern, and the balance thought to be fundamental to all theory was weakened. (Perhaps only Le Corbusier in recent history has successfully combined an ideal grid with the architectural promenade as an embodiment of the original interaction.)

This shift in balance has produced a situation whereby, for the past fifty years, architects have understood design as the product of some oversimplified form-follows-function formula. This situation even persisted during the years immediately following World War II, when one might have expected it would be radically altered. And as late as the end of the 1960s, it was still thought that the polemics and theories of the early Modern Movement could sustain architecture. The major thesis of this attitude was articulated in what could be called the English Revisionist Functionalism of Reyner Banham, Cedric Price, and Archigram. This neo-functionalist attitude, with its idealization of technology, was invested with the same ethical positivism and aesthetic neutrality of the prewar polemic. However, the continued substitution of moral criteria for those of a more formal nature produced a situation which now can be seen to have created a functionalist predicament, precisely because the primary theoretical justification given to formal arrangements was a *moral* imperative that is no longer operative within contemporary experience. This sense of displaced positivism characterizes certain current perceptions of the failure of humanism within a broader cultural context.

There is also another, more complex, aspect to this predicament. Not only can functionalism indeed be recognized as a species of positivism, but like positivism, it now can be seen to issue from within the terms of an idealist view of reality. For functionalism, no matter what its pretense, continued the idealist ambition of creating architecture as a kind of ethically constituted form-giving. But because it clothed this idealist ambition in the radically stripped forms of technological production, it has seemed to represent a break with the pre-industrial past. But, in fact, functionalism is really no more than a late phase of humanism, rather than an alternative to it. And in this sense, it cannot continue to be taken as a direct manifestation of that which has been called "the modernist sensibility."

Both the Triennale and the "Beaux Arts" exhibitions suggest, however, that the problem is thought to be somewhere else—not so much with functionalism *per se*, as with the nature of this so-called modernist sensibility. Hence, the implied revival of neo-classicism and Beaux Arts academicism as replacements for a continuing, if poorly understood, modernism. It is true that sometime in the nineteenth century there was indeed a crucial shift within Western consciousness: one which can be characterized as a shift from humanism to modernism. But, for the most part, architecture, in its dogged adherence to the principles of function, did not participate in or understand the fundamental aspects of that change. It is the potential difference in the nature of modernist and humanist theory that seems to have gone unnoticed by those people who today speak of eclecticism, post-modernism, or neo-functionalism. And they have failed to notice it precisely because they conceive of modernism as merely a stylistic manifestation of functionalism, and functionalism itself as a basic theoretical proposition in architecture. In fact, the idea of modernism has driven a wedge into these attitudes. It has revealed that the dialectic form and function is culturally based.

In brief, the modernist sensibility has to do with a changed mental attitude toward the artifacts of the physical world. This change has not only been manifested aesthetically, but also socially, philosophically, and technologically—in sum, it has been manifested in a new cultural attitude. This shift away from the dominant attitudes of humanism, that were pervasive in Western societies for some four hundred years, took place at various times in the nineteenth century in such disparate disciplines as mathematics, music, painting, literature, film, and photography. It is displayed in the non-objective abstract painting of Malevich and Mondrian; in the non-narrative, atemporal writing of Joyce and Apollinaire; the atonal and polytonal compositions of Schönberg and Webern; in the non-narrative films of Richter and Eggeling.

Abstraction, atonality, and atemporality, however, are merely stylistic manifestations of modernism, not its essential nature. Although this is not the place to elaborate a theory of modernism, or indeed to represent those aspects of such a theory which have already found their way into the literature of the other humanist disciplines, it can simply be said that the symptoms to which one has just pointed suggest a displacement of man away from the center of his world. He is no longer viewed as an *originating agent*. Objects are seen as ideas independent of man. In this context, man is a discursive function among complex and already-formed systems of language, which he witnesses but does not constitute. As Lévi-Strauss has said, "Language, an unreflecting totalization, is human reason which has its reason and of which man knows nothing." It is this condition of displacement which gives rise to design in which authorship can no longer either account for a linear development which has a "beginning" and an "end"—hence the rise of the atemporal—or account for the invention of form—hence the abstract as a mediation between pre-existent sign systems.

Modernism, as a sensibility based on the fundamental displacement of man, represents what Michel Foucault would specify as a new *épistème*. Deriving from a non-humanistic attitude toward the relationship of an individual to his physical environment, it breaks with the historical past, both with the ways of viewing man as subject and, as we have said, with the ethical positivism of form and function. Thus, it cannot be related to functionalism. It is probably for this reason that modernism has not up to now been elaborated in architecture.

But there is clearly a present need for a theoretical investigation of the basic implications of modernism (as opposed to modern style) in architecture. In his editorial "Neo-Functionalism," in *Oppositions* 5, Mario Gandelsonas acknowledges such a need. However, he says merely that the "complex contradictions" inherent in functionalism—such as neo-realism and neo-rationalism—make a form of neo-functionalism necessary to any new theoretical dialectic. This proposition continues to refuse to recognize that the form/function opposition is not necessarily inherent to any architectural theory and so fails to recognize the crucial difference between modernism and humanism. In contrast, what is being called post-functionalism begins as an attitude which recognizes modernism as a new and distinct sensibility. It can best be understood in architecture in terms of a theoretical base that is concerned with what might be called a modernist *dialectic*, as opposed to the old humanist (i.e., functionalist) opposition of form and function.

       This new theoretical base changes the humanist balance of form/function to a dialectical relationship within the evolution of form itself. The dialectic can best be described as the potential co-existence within any form of two non-corroborating and non-sequential tendencies. One tendency is to presume architectural form to be a recognizable transformation from some pre-existent geometric or platonic solid. In this case, form is usually understood through a series of registrations designed to recall a more simple geometric condition. This tendency is certainly a relic of humanist theory. However, to this is added a second tendency that sees architectural form in an atemporal, decompositional mode, as something simplified from some pre-existent set of non-specific spatial entities. Here, form is understood as a series of fragments—signs without meaning dependent upon, and without reference to, a more basic condition. The former tendency, when taken by itself, is a reductivist attitude and assumes some primary unity as both an ethical and an aesthetic basis for all creation. The latter, by itself, assumes a basic condition of fragmentation and multiplicity from which the resultant form is a state of simplification. Both tendencies, however, when taken together, constitute the essence of this new, modern dialectic. They begin to define the inherent nature of the object in and of itself and its capacity to be represented. They begin to suggest that the theoretical assumptions of functionalism are in fact cultural rather than universal.

       Post-functionalism, thus, is a term of absence. In its negation of functionalism it suggests certain positive theoretical alternatives—existing fragments of thought which, when examined, might serve as a framework for the development of a larger theoretical structure—but it does not, in and of itself, propose to supply a label for such a new consciousness in architecture which I believe is potentially upon us.

Robert A. M. Stern   **"Gray Architecture as Post-Modernism, or, Up and Down from Orthodoxy"**

L'Architecture d'Aujourd'hui 186 (August-September 1976); reconstructed for

this anthology

The richness of architectural practice in the late 1970s, particularly in the United States, demanded an articulation of the postmodern. Yet, at this relatively early stage of theorizing — eight years before the debates on postmodernism were played out in journals like *New Left Review*, *New German Critique*, and *October* — architecture seemed ineluctably partitioned into binary oppositions variously labeled modern/ postmodern, rationalist/realist, exclusivist/inclusivist, New York/Yale-Penn, white/ gray, and the like. Robert Stern's "Gray Architecture," part of a special issue of *L'Architecture d'Aujourd'hui* titled "New York in White and Gray," and his "At the Edge of Modernism," the postscript to the second edition of his *New Directions in American Architecture* (1977), summarized what at the time were generally understood to be the attributes of these dichotomies.

For the May 1973 issue of *Architectural Forum*, Stern had organized "Five on Five," a polemical response to the publication of *Five Architects* by five other architects loosely associated with Yale or the University of Pennsylvania (alternatively, with Robert Venturi and Louis Kahn).[1] For the April 1975 issue of *A + U*, Stern and Peter Eisenman coedited the special feature "White and Gray: Eleven Modern American Architects," with Colin Rowe and Vincent Scully as the respective intellectual sponsors.[2] In 1976, in a forum held at the Institute for Architecture and Urban Studies in New York, and again in the present essay, Stern hooked the various characteristics of "grayness" to a now certain and general shift in mood represented by Arthur Drexler's "The Architecture of the Beaux-Arts" exhibition at the Museum of Modern Art.[3] By 1980, the signs of the complete institutionalization of such characteristics included the inaugural issue of the student-edited *Harvard Architecture Review*, entitled "Beyond the Modern Movement," the editorial of which itemized desiderata of postmodernism that seem to be direct elaborations of Stern's principles of contextualism, allusionism, and ornamentalism: (1) history (as the repository of past forms), (2) cultural allusionism (or pluralism and populism), (3) anti-utopianism ("working with what 'is' rather than what 'should be'"), (4) urban design and contextualism (*à la* collage city), and (5) formal concerns (by which is meant symmetry, closed and static spaces, landscape as form, and the diminution of programmatic concerns) — all of which is presumed to lead to (6) referential form ("that is, the search for meaning").[4]

| *see* 232 |

| *see* Rowe and Koetter (**104 ff**) |

Postmodernism's much-touted search for meaning oscillates between a renunciation of the modernist claim to radical difference through formal innovation (and the resultant identification of postmodern architecture with the commercial spaces of advertisement and product packaging) and a claim for postmodernism's pluralism and populism, or, in Stern's words "a new way of gathering up the diverse threads of the architecture and the culture or our polyglot nation."[5] The most interesting theoretical issue, however, one that attends both these declarations, is the effacement of the distinction between so-called high and mass culture. For it is a distinction on which modernism depended for its utopian vocation (the radical disjunction of the new from the status quo in order to invent new forms adequate for a new society) and its search for authentic experiences over and against the degraded

| *see* Scott Brown (**62 ff**) and Jencks (**308 ff**) |

culture of commerce. The collapse of the difference between high and low is in some sense a collapse of *difference*, and as such must still be regarded as ambiguous, hovering between an enlargement of the cultural realm and a mere symptom of further degradation.

Notes

Because *L'Architecture d'Aujourd'hui* published a full-length French version and only an abstract in English, and the original English text has been lost, the present version of this essay incorporates some translations of the French text back into English as well as minor revisions made by Stern.

1. *Architectural Forum* 138, no. 4 (May 1973). The respondents were Robert Stern, Jacquelin Robertson, Charles Moore, Alan Greenberg, and Romaldo Giurgola.

2. *A + U* 52 (April 1975). The "whites" were Peter Eisenman, Michael Graves, John Hejduk, Richard Meier, and Werner Seligmann. The "grays" were Robert Stern, Charles Moore, Giovanni Pasanella, Jaquelin Robertson, Richard Weinstein, and T. Merrill Prentice. The issue included Japanese translations of parts of Colin Rowe's *Collage City* and Vincent Scully's *The Shingle Style Today, or, The Historian's Revenge*.

3. See Stern's intervention in "Forum: The Beaux-Arts Exhibition," held at the Institute for Architecture and Urban Studies in January 1976, published in *Oppositions* 8 (Spring 1977), pp. 169–171, and excerpted in this volume as part of the document on the Beaux-Arts exhibition.

4. *Harvard Architecture Review* 1 (Spring 1980), pp. 4–9. Stern's own contribution to the *Harvard Architecture Review*, "The Doubles of Post-Modern," which aspired to give the new architecture a pedigree within the "ongoing culture which we call the Western Humanist tradition," in fact adds little more than decorative obfuscation to the blunt symmetry of "white" and "gray." Stern's "doubled" categories are traditional modernism/schismatic modernism, and traditional postmodernism/schismatic postmodernism. The latter double is doubled again: traditional postmodernism that breaks with modernism in order to reintegrate with humanism/traditional postmodernism that is a continuation of modernism's effort to break with humanism; and schismatic postmodernism that is a continuation of modernism (the realization of modernism's desired break with humanism)/schismatic postmodernism as a continuing tradition (the postmodern breakthrough to postmodernity, "a totally new state of consciousness").

5. Robert Stern, "Postscript: At the Edge of Modernism," in his *New Directions in American Architecture*, 2d ed. (New York: Braziller, 1977), p. 136.

At the outset of this brief essay, I would like to suggest that the "White and Gray" debate is not (as has been suggested in the press) an encounter between polarities such as might have occurred in 1927 between advocates of the Beaux-Arts and apostles of International Style modernism. Rather, this debate, beginning at the University of California at Los Angeles in May 1974, has grown into an ongoing dialogue between two groups of architects who, in their built work and theoretical investigations, share our active to chart out and clarify a direction which architecture can take now that the orthodox Modernist Movement has drawn to a close.

Peter Eisenman, to my mind the principal theorist among the "White" architects, sees this new direction in a particular way, which he labels "Post-Functionalism." Eisenman seeks to free architecture from explicit cultural associations of any kind. My view of this new direction differs from Eisenman's: I call it "Post-Modernism" and see it as a kind of philosophical pragmatism or pluralism which builds upon messages from "orthodox Modernism" as well as from other defined historical trends.

For "Post-Modernism," and probably for "Post-Functionalism" as well, it is safe to say that the orthodox Modernist Movement is a closed issue, an historical fact of no greater contemporaneity than that of nineteenth-century academicism; and though messages can be received from both these historical periods, as from the past in general, nostalgia for either cannot be substituted for a fresh, realistic assessment of the issues as they are now. The struggle for both groups, then, is to return to our architecture that vitality of intention and form which seems so absent from the work of the late Modernists.

"Post-Modernism" and "Post-Functionalism" can both be seen as attempts to get out of the trap of orthodox Modernism now devoid of philosophic meaning and formal energy, and both are similar in their emphasis on the development of a strong formal basis for design. Beyond this, however, they are widely divergent, in that "Post-Functionalism" seeks to develop formal compositional themes as independent entities freed from cultural connotations, whereas "Post-Modernism" embodies a search for strategies that will make architecture more responsive to and visually cognizant of its own history, the physical context in which a given work of architecture is set, and the social, cultural, and political milieu which calls it into being. Contrary to what was said at the end of the 1960s, "Post-Modernism" is neither a sociology of the constructed nor the technico-socio-professional determinism of the orthodox Modern Movement; it affirms that architecture is made for the eye as well as for the mind, and that it includes both a conceptualized formation of space and the circumstantial modifications that a program can make this space undergo.

Implicit in this emergent Post-Modernist position is a recognition that the more than fifty-year history of the Modernist movement has been accompanied by no notable increase in affection on the part of the public for the design vocabulary that has been evolved. This is partially so because that movement has been obsessively concerned with abstraction and has eschewed explicit connections with familiar ideas and things. (Even the pipe railings of the 1920s are by now, for most of us, cut off from everyday reference; who among us has been on an ocean liner in the last twenty-five years?) For a Post Modernist attitude to take root in a meaningful way, an effort must be made toward recapturing the affection of architecture's very disaffected constituency, the public.

The exhibition of drawings of the Ecole des Beaux Arts which was presented in 1975 at the Museum of Modern Art in New York, and the discussion of the significance of that exhibition in the press, at the Institute for Architecture and Urban Studies, at the Architectural League of New York, and within the frame of seminars at the School of Architecture at Columbia University, made it possible for architects of New York—many of the "Whites" and "Grays," in particular—to begin to reweave the fabric of the Modern period, which was so badly rent by the puritan revolution of the Modern Movement. It is not surprising that the tradition represented by the Ecole des Beaux Arts—the poetic tradition of design—should be examined with renewed sympathy, and that one of the hallmarks of the Ecole's design methodology, the beautiful drawing, should be restored to a position of influence. A large part of the work of the "Grays" tends to establish connections with the formal, spatial, and decorative invention of the nineteenth century.

For the "Grays," at least, Venturi and Moore have laid the foundation for the philosophical structure of Post-Modernism. In the search for an architectural position able to draw on historic issues, including both Modernism and nineteenth-century eclecticism, they have reminded us of the power to achieve symbolic meaning through allusion—not only allusion to other movements in architectural history, but to historical and contemporary events of a social, political, and cultural nature as well. In organizing the Beaux Arts exhibit, Arthur Drexler, long associated with the position of orthodox Modernism, has also made a contribution to the philosophical structure of Post-Modernism. The Beaux Arts exhibit suggests that Modern architecture might find a way out of the dilemma of the late Modern Movement by entering a period where symbolism and allusion would take their place alongside issues of formal composition, functional fit, and constructional logic. In his introduction to the Beaux Arts show's catalogue, Drexler admonished that "we would be well advised to examine our architectural pieties 'in the light of an increased awareness and appreciation of the nature of architecture' as it was understood in the nineteenth century."

The Beaux Arts exhibition reminded us of the poverty of orthodox Modern architecture: trapped in the narcissism of its obsession with the process of its own making, sealed off from everyday experience and from high culture alike by its abstraction and the narrowing of its frame of reference within the Modern period to the canonical succession of events and images and personalities delimited by Giedion and Pevsner, and drained of energy as a result of a confusion between the values assigned to minimalism by a Mies van der Rohe with those assigned by an Emery Roth.

The work of the "Grays" presents certain strategies and attitudes that distinguish it from that of the "Whites." These strategies include (in no particular order):

- *The use of ornament.* Though ornament is often the handmaiden of historical allusion, the decoration of the vertical plane need not be justified in historical or cultural terms; the decorated wall responds to an innate human need for elaboration and for the articulation of the building's elements in relation to human scale.

- *The manipulation of forms to introduce an explicit historical reference.* This is not to be confused with the simplistic eclecticism that has too often in the past substituted pat, pre-digested typological imagery for more incisive analysis. The principle is rather that there are lessons to be learned from history as well as from technological innovation and behavioral science, that the history of buildings is the history of meaning in architecture. Moreover, for the Post-Modernist these lessons from history go beyond modes of spatial organization or structural expression to the heart of architecture itself: the relationship between form and shape and the meanings that particular shapes have assumed over the course of time. This Post-Modernist examination of historical precedent grows out of the conviction that appropriate references to historical architecture can enrich new work and thereby make it more familiar, accessible, and possibly even meaningful for the people who use buildings. It is, in short, a cue system that helps architects and users communicate better about their intentions.

- *The conscious and eclectic utilization of the formal strategies of orthodox Modernism, together with the strategies of the pre-Modern period.* Borrowing from forms and strategies of both orthodox Modernism and the architecture that preceded it, Post-Modernism declares the past-ness of both; as such it makes a clear distinction between the architecture of the Modern period, which emerged in the middle of the eighteenth century in western Europe, and that puritanical phase of the Modern period which we call the Modern Movement.

- *The preference for incomplete or compromised geometries, voluntary distortion, and the recognition of growth of buildings over time.* This is manifest in a marked preference for the Aalto of the fifties over the Corbusier of the twenties, for the plans of Lutyens over those of Voysey, and for the long love affair with the American Shingle Style of the nineteenth century. These preferences are paired with an architecture that appeals to Platonic geometry, particularly in its general composition. Thus, geometrically pure rooms are linked together in an unaccustomed manner and create larger and frankly hybrid forms, tied together visually by the envelope of the exterior walls. These hybrid forms are rarely perceptible at first glance. For lack of a more appropriate term, I would call this an "episodic composition," which must be distinguished from the determinist composition of Modernist orthodoxy.

- *The use of rich colors and various materials that effect a materialization of architecture's imagery and perceptible qualities,* as opposed to the materialization of technology and constructional systems that remain so overtly significant in brutalist architecture.

- *The emphasis on intermediate spaces, that is, the "pochés" of circulation, and on the borders, that is, on the thickness of the wall.* From this comes an architecture made of spaces whose configuration is much more neutral and supple, from a functional point of view, than the so-called continuous spaces of the orthodox Modern Movement.

- *The configuration of spaces in terms of light and view as well as of use.*

- *The adjustment of specific images charged with carrying the ideas of the building.* It is thus possible for the architect to create simultaneously two premises or spatial units within one building or two buildings in a complex that do not resemble each other even if their compositional elements are the same. An attitude of this sort permits us to see the work of Eero Saarinen in a new light.

To return to the philosophical intentions of "Gray" architecture, the importance of the writings of Vincent Scully is evident: his vision of architecture as part of a larger whole, which is at the heart of the cultural formation of the "Grays" (many of whom were his students at Yale), often runs counter to arbitrary stylistic and cultural categories and puts a particular emphasis on the interrelationship of the building, the landscape, and culture. Scully has begun to influence not only architects but also historians like Neil Levine who, in his account of the Beaux Arts, assigns great importance to questions of communication and in particular to that of an *architecture parlante*. He has equally influenced George Hersey, whose studies on the associationism of mid-nineteenth-century English architecture make an important contribution to the philosophical foundation of the eclecticism emerging in the "Grays."

Not surprising, then, that Hersey should have been a client for whom Venturi achieved one of his most stunning houses. One finds at the root of the "gray" position a rejection of the anti-symbolic, anti-historical, hermetic and highly abstract architecture of orthodox Modernism. Grayness seeks to move toward an acceptance of diversity; it prefers hybrids to pure forms; it encourages multiple and simultaneous readings in its effort to heighten expressive content. The layering of space characteristic of much "gray" architecture finds its complement in the overlay of cultural and art-historical references in the elevations. For "gray" architecture, "more is more."

"Gray" buildings have facades which tell stories. These facades are not the diaphanous veil of orthodox Modern architecture, nor are they the affirmation of deep structural secrets. They are mediators between the building as a "real" construct and those allusions and perceptions necessary to put the building in closer touch with the place in which it is made and beliefs and dreams of the architects who designed it, the clients who paid for it, and the civilization which permitted it to be built; to make buildings, in short, landmarks of a culture capable of transcending transitory usefulness as functional accommodation. "Gray" buildings are very much of a time and place: they are not intended as ideal constructs of perfected order; they select from the past in order to comment on the present.

Martin Steinmann   **"Reality as History: Notes for a Discussion of Realism in Architecture"** *A + U* 69

(September 1976)

see Scolari
(126 ff)

The most complete realization of the so-called Tendenza outside of Italy was in the Swiss region of Ticino.[1] While the deeper roots of the Ticinese architecture go to prewar Italian rationalism (primarily Alberto Sartoris) and Switzerland's own *Neues Bauen* (Hans Schmidt et al.), the Tendenza's theorization of architecture's autonomy gave the means to conceptualize the specific design techniques of the new architecture in reciprocal relation to both its modern predecessors and the precisely planned and detailed "vernacular" buildings of the region, without abdicating a thoroughly progressive, critical, and international position.

see Huet (256 ff)
and Cohen
(512–513)

Martin Steinmann, together with Thomas Boga, organized an exhibition of the work of twenty young Ticinese architects at the Eidgenössische Technische Hochschule, Zurich, in November and December of 1975, and turned what might have been an approbation of a particular regionalism into an important contribution to the discourse on realism that was intensely played out in 1976–1977. The present essay, an expansion of Steinmann's introduction to the exhibition catalogue, *Tendenzen. Neuere Architektur im Tessin*, was written for *A + U*'s special issue on Ticino. A related essay, coauthored with Bruno Reichlin, was the lead article in *Archithese*'s special issue on realism, guest-edited by the two and extracted in *L'Architecture d'Aujourd'hui*.[2] Steinmann continued to develop his characterization of realism through his editorship of *Archithese* from 1980 to 1986 and in essays that linked the sober rationalism of Aldo Rossi, the populism of Robert Venturi, and the new architecture of Switzerland.[3]

compare Silvetti
(270–274)

"Reality as history" diverges from a vulgarly theorized autonomy that understands architecture undialectically as a purely negative withdrawal — a position that always runs the risk of separating and trivializing architecture in advance, so that demonstrations of its "distance from degraded life" become redundant — as well as from a realism that construes architecture as a "natural" and direct reflection of its socioeconomic base — a position out of which develops a *ressentiment* for the aesthetic supplement in all its forms. Steinmann attempts to articulate an immanent reality of architecture that is both positive and as profoundly historical and social as history and society themselves. For Steinmann, such an architecture's vocation is primarily epistemological: architecture, with practical techniques of design that relate it to specific social uses of buildings of the past, produces a concept of its history even as it verifies its own place in that history. "An architecture referring to itself — reflecting its own nature — is able to discover more and more meaning in its own structures, in the literal sense of the word 'discover': it is as if veils that covered these structures were drawn away. Architecture that is autoreflexive in this way communicates its historicity." The originality of his concept of realism lies largely in this epistemological status.

But it should be noted that Steinmann's sense of architecture's epistemological endeavor is modulated by a well-nigh manual, Brechtian practicality (witness the ironic epigraph to the essay) — architecture understood as an experimental, transformative activity that ties an ideal of practice to concrete production and "le droit au plaisir."[4] This ensures a principle of play and populism in architecture's

"reality" and a theoretical way of appreciating the density of genuine aesthetic gratification, an appreciation that would generally characterize architectural theories of
realism.

Notes

1. For the origin of the term Tendenza, see the essay by Massimo Scolari in this anthology.
    Ticino's connections to the Italian Tendenza are primarily through Aldo Rossi, who taught
    at the Eidgenössische Technische Hochschule in Zurich from 1972 to 1974.

2. Bruno Reichlin and Martin Steinmann, "Zum Problem der innerarchitektonischen Wirklich-
    keit," *Archithese* 19 (1976); extracted as "A propos de la réalité immanente," *L'Architecture
    d'Aujourd'hui* 190 (April 1977). The other authors of the *Archithese* special issue were Alan
    Colquhoun, Giorgio Grassi, Aldo Rossi, Denise Scott Brown, Hans Heinz Holz, Otakar Mácel,
    and Karel Teige (an excerpt from an essay of 1950–1951).

3. See, for example, Martin Steinmann, "Von 'einfacher' und von 'gewönlicher' Architektur,"
    Archithese, new series 1 (January-February 1980), reprinted as "On Simple and Ordinary
    Architecture," *Parametro* 141 (November 1985).

4. Reichlin and Steinmann, "A propos de la réalité immanente," p. 73.

> Nowadays, complained Mr. K., countless people pride them-
> selves on being able to write thick books all alone, and this
> meets with general approval. . . . There is no thought then
> which could be adopted and no formulation of a thought
> which could be quoted. How little they need to do so! A pen
> and a bit of paper is all they can present! And without help,
> only with the pitiful material that a single man can carry in
> his arms, they erect their huts! The largest buildings they
> know are the ones that can be built by a single man!
>
> **BERTOLT BRECHT,** *Tales of Mr. Keuner*

The following statements, made on the occasion of an exhibition on "Recent Architecture in Ticino" last November in Zurich, do not claim to attribute the works
represented there to a well-defined theory of architecture. Such an attempt would
not succeed except with the help of tools like the ones Procrustes used—at the
expense of the works. The statements therefore serve to indicate some of the
common traits that united these works in an exhibition, despite the differences
which persist among them. These common traits rest in the "manière de penser
l'architecture."

Architecture is an important part of material production.
Therefore it is particularly responsive to the ruling powers, which were once called
the mirrors of a kaleidoscope, thanks to which an image of order can always be
brought into being. Under these conditions, to what extent can architecture be an
element of the general social progress?

Architecture is subject to the realization of capital, to be sure;
but its social function may not be restricted to the economic dimension. The social
and cultural dimension are not determined solely by the economic dimension. Architecture is conditioned and is conditioning: architecture as a collective fact is
inseparable from society, but "its principles are of a specific nature; they are derived
from architecture itself," as Aldo Rossi writes (*Zürcher Vorlesungen*, 1974). In other
words, architecture is a discipline possessing its own principles and maintaining
them under the conditions just mentioned. I think that the recognition of such an
autonomy of architecture is one of the common traits of the architects represented
in the exhibition.

Approaches scorning these principles (supposedly more ratio-
nal because more calculable) are condemned to fail. In this sense, Luigi Snozzi
writes (in his contribution to the catalogue) that the approach to the problems
of architecture has to start from form and that other approaches (from sociology,
economy, etc.) only represent an evasion by architects of their true responsibilities.

The approach from form is not opposed to acknowledging the indispensable support of these sciences, but all the more to the "laboratory coat" of scientism, with which the lack of architectural principles is so often covered. I think that it is the disguise of an ideology attempting to attribute a false naturalness to forms, thus creating things without explication except the immediate one of first function. It is such false naturalness that Roland Barthes identified as an element of bourgeois ideology (*Mythologies*, 1957). The recognition of an autonomy of architecture means compromising this system of myths that passes itself off as a system of facts.

To the extent that architecture develops according to its own principles, courageously accepting the contradictions that ensue, it is rational (being an element of progress by what Hegel calls "the ruse of reason"). These principles are contained in the works themselves, as Rossi states: "L'architettura sono le architetture." This leads to the conclusion (which Bruno Reichlin and Fabio Reinhart drew in an article on history as part of architectural theory, in *Archithese*) that the meaning of architecture defines itself in relation to its own tradition, where by tradition we understand the works as well as our comprehension of them.

If I refer to Reichlin and Reinhart repeatedly, this is not in order to explain with their conceptions the architectures that are the subject of the exhibition. Rather, it is because in their writings they suggest a way of speaking about architecture which to me seems promising. It is based on "the relationship—and the nature of this relationship—which connects the empirical object, architecture, to the cognitive experience belonging to it and developing from it." In other words: architecture is understood to be the signifier of a sign having its signified in socio-cultural usage but also creating its signified itself, insofar as each work essentially reflects its own "nature." If architecture makes reference to itself in this way, then history (to continue the thoughts of Reichlin and Reinhart) is not merely a vast depository of experiences already made, but is rather the place where the meaning of architecture defines itself. "Understanding the meaning of a work of architecture implies situating it in a dense network of relationships."

History is then no place for those who, as Nietzsche put it, wish to stroll in the "Garden of Knowledge" on mild evenings: history is the place where one's own age forms a constellation together with a definite earlier one, in a manner defined by tradition. Thus Trotsky could say that it was not an altogether new world which was entered with the October Revolution, but rather "a world that we had already made our own as tradition" (*Futurism*, 1922). In this manner, tradition is more than a relationship which we may or may not have to history. It is an epistemological category; it dictates that a new meaning can only be derived from a familiar one, a new norm only from the old one that it replaces—a nice example of the ambiguity of the word "replace."

No society, determined to develop its culture in a rational manner, can therefore renounce the decision for a definite tradition, designating the conscious relationship in which a society makes its aims understood to itself. Of the works that become points of reference for a rational architecture, those belonging to the *Neues Bauen* of the period between the wars occupy a preferential place, if only because the problems the *Neues Bauen* stated have lost nothing of their significance, and the solutions have kept their value. I am thinking in the first place of the *Siedlungen*, which are called, with good reason, the true monuments of the twentieth century. Thus the row of houses erected by the Collettivo-2 (Tita Carloni, Lorenzo Denti, and Fosco Moretti) in Balerna refers, in a fragment, to some *Siedlung* in Frankfurt, not only in its manner of stating the problem of the minimal dwelling, but also in its clear forms.

I have to admit that a certain tradition of the *Neues Bauen* seems to be a general one of building after the Second World War, namely the professionalism of building. It is not the widespread vulgarization of rationalism of which I speak (a tradition which, for its part, reveals the general aims of society). In fact, the notion of tradition as a progressive category in the sense of Trotsky, which has to be saved each moment anew from becoming a tool of the ruling powers, is another common trait of these architects.

A work of art is perceived by association and dissociation with other works of art. "Its form is defined in relation to other, already existing forms," as the Russian formalist Viktor Shklovsky formulated his "general rule," where the term "form" must be understood in its broadest sense. No one was more aware of this than Le Corbusier when he summarized his norms in the "Five Points for a New Architecture." When in his illustrations he continually opposed the "maison sur pilotis" to the conventional house, this was precisely because the latter represented the inventory of existing norms which the former was to overthrow, one by one, until the breaking point of this relationship: the "maison sur pilotis" acquired its meaning (modernity, etc.) from its antithetical relationship to the conventional house.

The architect then does not invent his language from nothing: he makes use of the language of his predecessors for his own intentions, changing it little by little, enriching it with new meanings, but meanings deduced from the old ones, as I indicated before. In this sense, Arnold Hauser, the great sociologist of art, remarked that a work owes more to works that preceded it than to the "invention" of the artist who created it.

This is, in part, a question of intelligibility. It is not hard to explain that man makes use of conventional forms to make his ideas understood, even

Bruno Reichlin and Fabio Reinhart, Tonini House, Torricella, 1972–1974

if these ideas lose some of their meaning in the process of conventionalization. But there is another explanation as well: Hauser went on to remark that art uses conventional forms not only for their intelligibility, but also because these forms themselves partly create the content to be expressed. "It belongs to the dialectic nature of the events of consciousness that forms not only serve to express ideas but also become their starting point" (*Kunst und Gesellschaft*, 1972).

Applied to the tradition of rationalism of which I spoke, this observation may say: the forms of the *Siedlungen* themselves contain a certain way of stating the problem of housing. I understand the words of Roberto Bianconi in this sense, who writes about his apartment buildings in Bellinzona: "The reference to the languages of architecture of the twenties and thirties allowed me to state the problem in a clear, precise manner" (catalogue).

In the face of architecture after the Second World War, which hastened from one architectural "invention" to the other, Ernesto Rogers, in *Casabella*, stressed the importance of making use of conventional forms. He did so under the term "mannerism": "Mannerism is necessary to concretize the architecture of a period in its generality: our time cannot evade this necessity."

At the occasion of my introduction to the exhibition in Zurich, the term gave rise to some criticism. In the positive sense that Rogers gave it (or rather gave it back), it means, as I think: to establish a defined relationship between a work and its tradition, so that the work as the actualization of a code measures itself intelligibly with the code it actualizes. The term means moreover that architecture is understood as something that can be traced back to determinable and describable elements, i.e., as something of a technical nature. The programmatic Rotalinti House, built by Aurelio Galfetti after travels in France dedicated to studying the works of Le Corbusier, the house in Morbio Inferiore by Flora, Ruchat House, and other works, all give evidence of the cognitive value of such mannerism or *maniera*.

In one of his novels, Peter Handke gives an impressive description of his method of work which bears on my remarks about the relation between form and content: "In the beginning, I started from facts and looked for ways of formulating them. Then I noticed that my very search for formulations removed me from the facts. So instead, I now started from existing formulations and sorted out the occurrences . . . already foreseen by these formulations. . . . From the convergences and contradictions my actual writing then developed" (*Wunschloses Unglück*, 1972). Applied to architecture, this suggests the repeated use of forms from the past in which the relation between form and meaning is established, so that a design, sustained by experience, cannot but be tautological: tautological in the positive sense of a deeper penetration into the aforementioned relationship, for signs are ambiguous (and their interpretation implies a choice that has to be probable, but cannot be true). Repetition constantly transforms the signified into the signifier of a new signified: it can therefore be considered an instrument of recognition.

A sign *means* something that lies outside of the sign itself and is defined by its use: it means the use that a certain society makes of it. (From this follows the importance of history for architectural design as the place where the meaning of architecture defines itself.) The meaning of a sign is not founded in its formal properties; therefore it is not stable, it changes continually. In his book, Hauser stressed this point: "The history of art shows the image of a dialectic movement: the new results from the old, but at the same time the old changes in light of the new." This indicates that the idea of an architecture referring to itself—reflecting its own nature—is able to discover more and more meaning in its own structures, in the literal sense of the word "discover": it is as if veils that covered these structures were drawn away. Architecture that is autoreflexive in this way communicates its historicity.

At this point it can do no harm to give an example. It comes from Pop Art, which uses familiar forms as its material in an obvious manner, the ideological-critical statements remaining secondary to the statements about the nature of painting. Pop Art represents a breaking with the conventions of tachism. Thus, in his "brushstroke" pictures, Roy Lichtenstein uses color application as his material, repeating a brushstroke, but with his own tools: spray gun and stencil. The result is "the same and not the same": it is the goal of the "répétition différente" (to use the term proposed for this operation) to create this tension.

The example is particularly suitable, since the place where this "répétition différente" achieves its objective is the museum, the place in which a work is measured by the works that surround it. (That is the meaning of Cézanne's statement that he painted only for the museum—used by Rossi as the title of his important text "Architettura per i musei.") The museum is our architectural knowledge. Insofar as there exists a rational cognition in architecture, this museum is the institution that represents it. In this museum, a work explains itself from the other works, including the newer ones, thanks to analogy, which is, in Rossi's definition, "a way to understand the world of forms and of things so directly . . . that they can hardly be expressed otherwise than by other things" (L'architettura analoga, 1975).

Lichtenstein's painting shows the double nature that, according to Barthes, begins in literature with "the first tremors of the bourgeois conscience in the nineteenth century": it is "parler et se parler" (Littérature et méta-langage, 1959). Saying that architecture reflects its own nature means just that: "se parler."

In "répétition différente," whose critical character is evident, can be found the basis for the intervention that Reichlin and Reinhart suggested for the restoration of the Castello Grande in Bellinzona. It runs along the wall, partially through eighteenth-century houses that last served as arsenals, at the level of the former parapet walk, from which it differs technologically and morphologically but to which it is related by a parallelism on the typological level: both are walks. The intervention is a "répétition différente" of the parapet walk, and the differentiation implementing it lies primarily in the area of sociocultural usage. The parapet walk, used to overlook the surrounding terrain, now becomes itself an object to be looked at. Nothing could better illustrate its historicity!

The basis for repetition is the recognition of the technical "nature" of architecture, which may always be traced back to describable elements and procedures. It is therefore meaningful to think of criticism and design as activities that are structurally related. The expression "architectural research," used in Italian discussions of architecture, means precisely this convergence of two activities in one: criticism in the form of design. (Baudelaire says that the best criticism of a work of art is another work of art.) In the nineteenth century, Poe was the first to call attention to this technical "nature" of literature. "The wires," Poe writes, "are not only not concealed, but displayed as things to be admired, equally with the puppets they set in motion. The result is" (and here follows one of the most concise descriptions of the alienation-effect I have ever heard) "that . . . we say to ourselves, without shedding a tear: Now, there is something which will be sure to move every reader to tears" (Marginalia).

Poe continues, "The poetic effect of a work comes about when the procedures which accomplish it, do not only serve the content of the work but constitute it, being displayed as things to be admired." Its meaning for architecture can be illustrated by the restoration of the Castello Montebello in Bellinzona by Mario Campi, Franco Pessina, and Niki Piazzoli. In a study of the project that may reveal primarily their own intentions, Reichlin and Reinhart discuss the project's use of antithesis at different levels as its poetic procedure. "The first antithesis concerns two different static principles: a metal structure is suspended from the thick walls of the tower. The second concerns different technological conceptions: a minimum of differentiation in the coarse stone construction of the castle, a maximum degree of differentiation in the new metal and wood construction. . . . The third antithesis regards the different morphologies: geometric indifference in the irregular old building, perfect geometry with the square as the basic form of the new construction." In addition, this restoration shows clearly how these antitheses define themselves in the autoreflexivity of the language of architecture. Studies attempting to take an inventory of typological, morphological, technological, and other norms that were developed from a definite socio-cultural usage permit a rational discussion of architecture, in the form of a design. Or, as the English Rococo painter Reynolds said to his students: "The more comprehensive your knowledge of distinguished works is, the greater will be your inventiveness" (quoted by Hans Heinz Holz in *Tradition und Traditionsbruch*, 1972).

These recent restoration designs (for the Castello Montebello and the Castello Grande, both in Bellinzona) show with particular clarity how architecture creates its meaning insofar as it refers to itself. Restoration becomes in this manner a measure for the cognitive value of architecture. But these designs represent only the most evident case of a general problem, i.e., the problem that all construction is construction in a defined social and cultural context, even if it takes place in a natural landscape. (Landscape is also permeated with meaning, insofar as we perceive it in coded form: recall the influence of the paintings of Caspar David Friedrich on the perception of nature in the nineteenth century.)

As the historian Carlo Cattaneo noted, landscape is an immense deposition of labor: "Landscape is not at all a work of nature, it is a work of man" (*Notiziario su la Lombardia*, c. 1860).

A comprehension of landscape that finds its definition in the term "territory" is another common trait of these architectures. As Mario Botta writes (in the catalogue), it is not so much the question of a building's site as of building the site itself, so that the work, making the general properties of the site its motives, in a sense, serves to better define it. "In this view of things, architecture becomes a critical instrument of our awareness."

This is true, for example, of the house designed by Botta in Riva San Vitale, or more precisely, somewhat outside this village. The site led Botta to a building type that in previous times was often encountered in similar locations, the *roccolo*. This was a part of the country estates of the wealthier families, "which spent the summer months there, enjoying country life and passing their time catching birds" (*La casa borghese*, vol. 26). This was precisely the purpose served by the *roccoli*, which were erected like small towers in somewhat secluded areas. Through its relationship to these historic buildings, it appears to me that Botta's project succeeds in characterizing the particularities of its site with great accuracy. (I recall a *roccolo* in Carona which, when I was a child, greatly intrigued me precisely because it was located "outside" the village.)

Architecture is not able to designate the real—of which this one characteristic of this site is a part—directly, but only indirectly, by repeating forms which draw their meaning from appropriate socialized experiences—connotations. Architecture is able to connote the real, but not denote it (except at the level of the immediate "first function"). Having established this, if we now propose the question of realism in architecture, we notice that we must return to architecture for the answer: there we find the confirmation that the meaning of architecture derives from its relationship to itself, from its autoreflexivity.

I think that this indicates a path on which the discourse on realism in architecture can advance, a discourse that cannot ignore history as the place where the meaning of architecture defines itself: reality as history.

Bernard Huet   **"Formalism — Realism"** "Formalisme — réalisme," *L'Architecture d'Aujourd'hui* 190

(April 1977); translated for this anthology by Brian Holmes

Aside, even, from the contingencies of its historical variations, the concept of realism in architecture is peculiar in principle. Realism imbricates two contradictory claims, one aesthetic and one epistemological. The aesthetic claim tends to mark off the work from everyday life, isolating it in a realm of heightened aesthetic intensity where concepts such as style, typology, and technique are understood self-consciously, synchronically, and reflexively — a realm almost unmediated by circumstance. The epistemological claim, on the other hand, operates to bind the work to the real itself, to situate it in a historically specific context and value the work for the knowledge it affords of a particular reality rather than for its autonomy and mobility.

Pushed to their respective extremes, the aesthetic claim recognizes the architectural sign in all its materiality and opacity but splits the sign off from its referent (as Bernard Huet asserts, for example, "If we admire again the architecture of Terragni, it is in spite of his active allegiance to Fascism, right up to the time of his death"),[1] while the epistemological claim depends on a certain transparency of the sign to its referent, to some preexisting image, function, process, technology, or context — a denotational system (like documentary writing or film) from which all aesthetic manipulations and distortions, if not entirely erased, simply "share the virtues and the vices of the regime that produces them." Pushed to their extremes, the two claims would evacuate the category of realism altogether, collapsing it into sheer free play of aesthetic signs on one side and a reflection or copy theory of "truth" on the other. Yet no conception of realism seems possible without maintaining both claims together.[2]

compare Steinmann (**248 ff**) and Silvetti (**268 ff**)

A theory of a realist architecture retains this fundamental contradiction between an autonomous aesthetic production and a representation of reality and adds further complications. While the forms of realism in painting, literature, or film share the very appearance of what they represent (a "common sense" about how things look or how we speak and act), the forms of architecture represent visibly, most fundamentally, architecture itself. The "real" represented by architectural realism is a real that architecture itself has produced, so its "verification" becomes even more complex.

see **246** and Cohen (**512–513**)

In a special issue of *L'Architecture d'Aujourd'hui*, "Formalisme — réalisme," and the debate that it sponsored, the antinomies of realism (already under the surface in the earlier discussions in the "realism" issue of *Archithese*) make cracks that are fully apparent.[3] In his own plea for an appreciation of the qualities of socialist realism, Bernard Huet, who edited the issue, draws a less than satisfactory conclusion: "Architecture is not fascist or Stalinist in its 'form.' There is only architecture of the fascist or Stalinist periods," to which Anatole Kopp and Claude Schnaidt retorted, "Can one seriously study the architectural qualities of false villages set up along the same routes traveled by the Empress Catherine II or Field Marshal Potemkin? The Stalinist 'socialist realist' architecture's essential function was not to express reality but, on the contrary, to conceal behind decorations and false appearance a reality which we know and of which we understand the costs. The difference with Marshal Stalin is that Marshal Potemkin hadn't discovered 'theoreticians.'"[4] Insofar as Huet wants to avoid the pure formalist pole of realism, how can he also completely avoid the realm in which architecture acquires its worldly baggage?

Surely Huet is right to warn against the unwarranted confidence in deducing political and ideological positions from a protocol of merely formal architectural properties. But that does not provide escape from the question of the possible uses anticipated and controlled by architectural forms — not only of how spaces were meant to be inhabited, but of how they *might* be inhabited. As T. J. Clark once queried, "What are we supposed to say, for example, about a photo of Mussolini's shock troops marching through the Arch of Constantine? Put the blame on the Arch somehow? Pretend that Mussolini got Roman architecture right? (To which the reply might reasonably be, in fact: Are you saying he got it wrong? What else, after all, was the Arch of Constantine for?)"[5]

Notes

1. Bernard Huet, "Le temps des malentendus . . . ," *L'Architecture d'Aujourd'hui* 192 (September 1977), p. x.
2. This general formulation of realism is at least tacitly adopted by theorists of realism from Georg Lukács and Bertolt Brecht to Fredric Jameson and Naomi Schor. I have drawn the notion of a double claim of realism from Fredric Jameson, "The Existence of Italy," in *Signatures of the Visible* (New York: Routledge, 1990).
3. See, for example, Francesco Dal Co's critique of Martin Steinmann's *Tendenzen. Neuere Architektur im Tessin* (the revised version of the latter is published in this volume) and the response by Steinmann and Bruno Reichlin in *Archithese* 19 (1976).
4. Anatole Kopp and Claude Schnaidt, "Bernard Huet entre le rationalisme et le kitsch stalinien," *L'Architecture d'Aujourd'hui* 192 (September 1977), p. viii.
5. Timothy J. Clark, "Jackson Pollock's Abstraction," in *Reconstructing Modernism*, ed. Serge Guilbaut (Cambridge: MIT Press, 1990), p. 176.

Every realist in art is also a realist outside art.

BERTOLT BRECHT

Neither figurative nor "articulate," architecture shared little in the nineteenth-century literary and artistic debates over the question of "realism." Only with the German avant-garde did the idea of realism emerge, in the form of the Neue Sach-lichkeit. But this had few relations to "realism." As early as 1935, Ernst Bloch showed that its apparent functionalist radicalism agreed perfectly with the reformist policy of the German and Austrian Social Democrats, and that it satisfied the middle classes above all, to the extent that it proposed to overcome class differences.[1]

In addition, the political consciousness of the architects in the modern movement was vague enough to allow a clever mix of opportunism and moralism.[2]

In Praise of Socialist Realism
The question of "realism" did not become historically important for architecture until the Russian revolution and the great debate over the new revolutionary art, which began to galvanize intellectuals in 1917.[3] The complexity of the Soviet cultural context in the twenties and thirties, the absence of any serious historical analysis of the phenomenon of socialist realism, the disarray of Marxist historians where the Stalinist period is concerned, all invite prudence and dissuade from adherence to hasty or simplistic hypotheses. For example, the 1934 "turnabout" is a simple reaction of good sense in the face of "the constructivists' incapacity and utopianism"; or again, socialist realism is an epiphenomenon of the "personality cult"; or finally, it is the revenge of the "die-hard classicists" and academics of the régime, temporarily squeezed out of public commissions. These interpretations have their share of truth, but none account for the historical context and the real power relationships (at a time when Stalin had not yet consolidated his control), nor above all for the original work that brought socialist realism into being.

Socialist realism arose from the efforts of writers and theorists; it was not artificially imposed by "cultural bureaucrats."

This debate, whose influence on the field of architecture came very late, was dominated by the personality of Gorky and by Lenin's inclination toward "realist" writers; but fifteen years of quarreling and the liquidation of the Proletkult were necessary before the notion of socialist realism would be proclaimed at the First Congress of Soviet Writers in 1934.[4]

Socialist realism proposed, for the first time, an integral response to the question of culture in the framework of the construction of socialism and not in that of the revolution: it dealt with the relations and function of art in the new society, and the status and role of the "intellectual worker" faced with the duties imposed by a precise social commission.

The definition offered by the *Short Dictionary of Aesthetics* (Moscow, 1965) perfectly illuminates the aim: to create a new humanism.

Socialist realism is an artistic procedure whose essence consists in reflecting reality captured in its revolutionary development, in a truthful and historically concrete way. It demands that the artist realize a definite aim . . . the formation of the new man in whom ideological wealth, spiritual beauty, and physical perfection coexist harmoniously.

Standing against "the death of art," which it sees as a consequence of art's commercialization by capitalist society, socialist realism reaffirms the importance of aesthetic values as a vital need of man, on a par with other material needs. Artists must clearly and effectively express these needs and "reflect"—according to Lenin's theory—socialist reality, including the description of the most complex social relations (the class struggle) and the affirmation of the values of the collective consciousness (the positive hero and the monument). It is less a question of forming a hypothetical "proletarian" culture than of restoring to the people the "heritage" (another Leninist idea) of erudite, national, and popular cultures.

The theory of socialist realism implies dialectical relations between form and content. Any conception which privileges content to the detriment of aesthetics (contentism, sociologism, functionalism), or which lingers over a purely formal play with language or figurative abstraction, will therefore be called "formalist."[5]

The Avatars of Realism

The application of socialist realism to architecture was slow and problematic. From 1934 onward, increasingly threatening accusations of "formalism" were brought to bear against the constructivists and their "progressive" allies: André Lurçat, Mart Stam, Hannes Meyer, Ernst May, and Hans Schmidt.[6] They were reproached for a vulgar functionalism that failed to integrate aesthetic and monumental values, an internationalism cut off from historical-cultural and national realities, and a utopian individualism imposing a way of life detached from collective aspirations.

In Stalin's words, as restated by Otakar Mácel: "socialist architecture is socialist for the content, nationalist for the form. Its national form rests on the development of national traditions and not on a mechanistic or intuitive explanation."[7] The exemplarity of the creations of socialist realism from 1945 to 1955—the Moscow metro and university, the Karl-Marx-Allee in East Berlin, the reconstruction of Warsaw—springs from the popular, collective, rational, and national character of this architecture.

Socialist realism is not only a glorious episode in the history of contemporary architecture, but also the sole alternative proposed to the "formalisms" born of the failure of the avant-garde in the West: the International Style, "international picturesque," "kitsch," professional commercialism.[8] The scornful laughter, incomprehension, and stupor which greeted the architectural creations of socialist realism testifies to the blindness of critics, historians, and other zealots of progress and modernity. This blindness finds a convenient and oversimplified justification in the "excesses" of the Zhdanovian phase of socialist realism, and in the caricature that sometimes resulted from bureaucratic codification and the "personality cult." Monuments can share the vices and virtues of the régimes that produced them. As Brecht has noted, socialist realism then becomes its own content, and sows the seeds of a new "formalism": a "style" for the régime, condemned to Stalinist hagiography and an absurd and ridiculous evaluation of the history of architecture. Mechanically applied, the Leninist theory of "reflection" reduces that history to alternating periods of progress and decline, and tends to demonstrate the absolute superiority of the neoclassical style. As to nationalism, it is transformed into an incredible display of pan-Russian chauvinism.

The choice of a codified language comprehensible by everyone certainly facilitated the expression of collective contents, offering architects an operative system that could guarantee the coherency of the collective work. But these explanations cannot justify such a conception of style. Rather, it was a means to overcome the subjectivity of discourse and to attain what Engels had called a "typical character in typical situations."

From Neo-Realism to the Tendenza

In 1945, the intellectuals who had engaged in the resistance felt the imperious desire to carry out an exacting and exalting inventory of the humblest details of Italian reality, to conjure away twenty years of fascist lies and mythology. Twenty years of political "formalism."

Filmmakers (Rossini, Visconti) and writers (Pasolini) invented neo-realism, while at the same time discovering Soviet cinema, the writings of Georg Lukács, and the posthumous work of Antonio Gramsci. The latter's imprisoned thinking, cut off from the world and reduced to inactivity, would now lend its original, non-conformist imprint to the Italian progressive movement, permitting an escape from Stalinist dogmatism. For once, the architects followed. Having learned a lesson from the Mussolini regime, which fascinated them and then repressed them, they had lost all illusions about the progressive, redemptive virtues of modern architecture. They were the first in Europe to recognize the ambiguity of International Style "formalism," to doubt the usefulness of the "avant-garde," and to distrust the reduction of reality to "utopias." Their neo-realist quest (Ludovico Quaroni, Mario Ridolfi) led them to explore history and look to a national and popular tradition for a mode of expression that could match the collective and democratic aspirations of the Italian people.

This debate over "realism" ran parallel to, but did not merge with, certain principles of socialist realism. It was expressed in the journal *Casabella*, where a generation of young architects gathered around Ernesto Rogers. Among these, figures such as Vittorio Gregotti, Aldo Rossi, and Tullio Tentori would play a key role in the 1960s when neo-realism, secreting its own "formalism," strayed into the aristocratic refinements of the eclectic and historicist anti-avant-garde.

This crisis of "language" is inscribed in the generalized crisis that struck European architecture in its professional structures and teaching systems. It attained its apogee in 1968. Two irreducible positions then came into confrontation: one was "contentist," predicting the death of Architecture with a capital *A* and denying it any disciplinary specificity; the other was "formalist" and called for a cynical and opportunistic professionalism exploiting the confusion "of styles" (kitsch) for commercial ends.

In the face of these positions, a certain number of architects formed the Tendenza, which presented itself as a critical and operational alternative.[9]

Its first objective was a double critical clarification. The historical criticism developed by Manfredo Tafuri and the Istituto Universitario di Architettura di Venezia proposed an ideological deconstruction and reevaluation of the history of architecture as an integral part of the history of labor. The "typological" criticism developed by Carlo Aymonino and Aldo Rossi attempted to situate architecture as a typical production in the historical process of the formation of cities.

Second, the Tendenza sought to reconstruct the architectural "discipline." It opposed the functionalism of modern architecture with an "enlightened" rationalism in which form implies architecture as an instrument of knowledge. The irreducible specificity of architecture and its disciplinary autonomy reside in its capacity to produce "typical" forms of general and popular import, requiring precise knowledge: a "trade" or *métier*. For the Tendenza, architecture's only justification lies in its very "being"; it is not infused with any content, it has no redemptive value, it can express nothing by itself. And if it refers to a monumentality, it is the monumentality designated by collective memory, through the history of types. In a word, it is "realist." It is easy to establish a kind of affiliation (admitted by Rossi) between the Tendenza and socialist realism. Those who are scandalized thereby, and who identify the Tendenza with formalism, fascism, or a return to academism, do no more than nourish the confusion and perpetuate the "formalist critique" denounced by Brecht as early as 1938.

Broadened Notions of Realism and Formalism

It is once again necessary to clarify the terms of the formalist/realist debate, and to broaden its meaning. As Brecht said, "realism is not a matter of form." One is tempted to paraphrase him by saying that formalism, too, is not a matter of form. It is time to finish off the gross simplifications of a certain kind of "formalist" criticism. Architecture is not fascist or Stalinist in its "form." There is only architecture of the fascist or Stalinist periods.

It is now clear and well established that the *métier* of the architect is to produce the most perfectly usable form; there can be no "formalism" on that level.

Formalism is above all political: Walter Benjamin remarked that fascism is the worst formalism, because it effects an aestheticization of social relations in order to mask conflicts. To the extent that such an attempt is visible in the work of certain architects, whose projects lend figure to the utopia of a social "order" without conflict, one can speak of "formalism." Formalism is bureaucratic. Any system that tends to reduce reality to a certain number of norms, standards, and styles leads to formalism. By extension, it can be said that architects who conceive architecture in simple adequacy to functional norms, without any concern for social relations or for the monumental values that are implicit in social demands, are liable to the accusation of "formalism."

Formalism is technocratic. The mechanical application of technology to reality masks the latter and transforms it into abstraction. Any architecture which is reduced to a series of financial, distributive, or constructive techniques is "formalist." Finally, formalism is irrational. The architects who seek architecture's own rationality outside architecture (in sociology, contentism, etc.) run the serious risk of formalism.

To be "realist" is not to accept reality, but to take hold of it in order to transform it "politically." It is not to impose a new style of life upon the inhabitants, but to offer them the typologies they expect. It is not to make a myth of technology, but to use it effectively. It is not to create "meaning" that is incomprehensible to the greater population, but to call upon common sense. It is not to create a proletarian culture, but to make a heritage available for use.

"Realism is not only a literary matter, it is an important political, philosophical, and practical matter, and must be proclaimed and treated as such: as a matter that affects all human life."[10]

Thus there is no single form of realism. Realism is multiple like the reality it reflects: Maurice Culot's action in Brussels and the city management of Bologna are just as "realist" as the Tendenza or the paper architects.

Notes

1. Ernst Bloch, *Erbschaft dieser Zeit* (Zurich: Oprecht & Helbling, 1935), p. 127.
2. See the correspondence between Karel Teige and Le Corbusier, in 1929, published in *L'Architecture d'Aujourd'hui* (special issue), 1933, and reprinted in *Oppositions* 4 (1975).
3. It must also be recalled that the Soviet avant-garde (Mayakovsky) was linked to the group of "formalist" linguists (Eichenbaum, Shklovsky, etc.), of which Roman Jakobson was a protagonist.
4. In 1921, Voronsky judged that the new style—"neo-realism"—would be a combination of romanticism, symbolism, and realism. In 1927, Lunacharsky spoke of a "definitive turn toward social realism"; then in 1924 Zonin published a book entitled *For a Proletarian Realism*; finally, between 1932 and 1934, Marx and Engels's writings on art were published, with a commentary by Georg Lukács, who would remain the theorist of socialist realism par excellence until 1956.
5. This is how Teige, in his critique of socialist realism (1951), defines realism in architecture: as a simple functional and technical adequacy to the natural and spiritual needs of mankind.
6. When Herman Muthesius visited Siedlung Weissenhof in 1927 he declared, "Form is the major recognizable demand of the buildings in the exhibition and of the so-called new architecture. This should come as no surprise, since artistic currents are always of a formal nature."
7. Otakar Mácel, "Le réalisme socialiste en architecture," in *Archithese*, 1975.
8. In 1938 Hannes Meyer said: "The call for an international architecture at a time of national autarchy and of progress for colonial peoples . . . is a fantasy of architectural aesthetes cut off from social reality, who dream of a compact architectural world of glass and steel (for the greater profit of the glass, cement, and steel monopolies)."
9. The name Tendenza originated in an article by Aldo Rossi written in 1966, "L'architettura della ragione come architettura di tendenza" (the architecture of reason as architecture of tendency).
10. Bertolt Brecht, *Über Realismus* (Frankfurt: Suhrkamp, 1971).

Jorge Silvetti   **"The Beauty of Shadows"** *Oppositions* 9 (Summer 1977)

"The Beauty of Shadows" is most explicitly a mobilization of Roland Barthes's concept of critical play to construct a response to Manfredo Tafuri's "L'Architecture dans
le Boudoir." It is also, though less overtly, a mobilization of Louis Althusser's concept
of ideology as a countercritique of Diana Agrest and Mario Gandelsonas's Althusserian "Semiotics and Architecture: Ideological Consumption or Theoretical Work."[1]
Outstretching its rather localized and focused origins, however, the essay conjoins
the discourse of realism with the general tendency of architectural theory in the 1970s
to look to (post)structuralist studies of language as a possible paradigm for architectural thought, and develops a theory of architectural production, which Silvetti calls
"criticism from within," that is a concise description of what many felt to be the predominant working conditions and operations of contemporary architectural practice.[2]
      Of relevance here is the Foucauldian distinction between com-
mentary and criticism—the first of which essentially reproduces and legitimizes the
work or language under analysis, the latter of which "judges" the language itself and
"profanes it." Criticism from within is both a *re*presentation of architectural language
and a subversion of architecture's conventional "linguistic" material or design procedures—what Barthes calls "a mask which points to itself."[3] This type of criticism is
consonant with the difficult complicity of Barthes's mythologist (the critic, not the
creator of myth). Like myth, the architecture Silvetti discusses "is made of material
which has *already* been worked on so as to make it suitable for communication"; it
appears as a "second-order semiological system," but one whose signified is itself a
signifying system—an architectural language.[4] It is this formal aspect, not its content,
that characterizes myth. But whereas myth surreptitiously naturalizes and essential-
izes structures that are in fact arbitrary, the mythologist, still working from within
language, deploys myth's own form against it, transposes it to another level of signification, and then suspends its artifice in a play of connotations and demystifications.
"Truth to tell," writes Barthes, "the best weapon against myth is perhaps to mythify
it in its turn, and to produce an *artificial myth*: and this reconstituted myth will in fact
be a mythology. Since myth robs language of something, why not rob myth? All that
is needed is to use it as the departure point for a third semiological chain, to take its
signification as the first term of a second myth."[5]
      Silvetti aims to expose not so much any particular instance of
architecture as the fundamental mechanisms by which elements of the architectural
language are lifted out of their historical sediment and recombined, transformed, or
distorted into the language's various instances, forming constellations of related
structures and strategies, each producing different effects already latent in the language but heretofore unrealized. He uses the categories of rhetoric to label the sets of
rules that govern the production of these effects. "The goal of all structuralist activity,
whether reflexive or poetic," Barthes writes, "is to reconstruct an 'object' in such a
way as to manifest the rules [that structure] this object. Structure is in fact a *simulacrum* of the object, but a controlled and interested *simulacrum*, since the copy of the
object brings out something previously invisible, or . . . unintelligible in the natural
object."[6] In the sense that the practice of criticism from within dissolves the individual

unit of signification back into the generalized structure that it partially instantiates —
in the sense, that is, that it operates as a "third semiological chain" — Silvetti
broaches the issue of ideology, understood as that which manages the structures that
structuralist operations reveal.

By placing itself within the act of making and by not using the instruments of language but those
of architecture itself, [criticism from within] becomes compromised by the ideological nature of
all objects produced by culture; but, at the same time, paradoxically, the very identification of
this type of criticism depends on the fact that these same objects possess the capacity to expose
certain meanings of the work that are otherwise obscured by ideological veils.

In "Semiotics and Architecture," Agrest and Gandelsonas distin-
guish between architectural ideology and architectural theory on the model of Althusser's distinction of ideology and science. They maintain that "theoretical work cannot
be realized from inside architectural ideology, but from a theoretical 'outside' separated from and against that ideology."[7] It is at this crucial moment — the moment of
insisting on theory as *outside* ideology — that Silvetti swerves from the otherwise
foundational arguments of Agrest and Gandelsonas and attempts to project criticism
from within as a provisional practice in between the hegemonic force field of cultural
and disciplinary ideologies as analyzed by Agrest and Gandelsonas and the implacable silence of Tafuri's historical closure.

see 112–113,
199 n.1

Perhaps what is most promising about [criticism from within] is precisely the awareness that we
will not gain from it access to objective, scientific knowledge . . . , but rather that through it we
may aim at unfolding the imaginary-symbolic universe that architecture simultaneously proposes and represses. The clear objective of such criticism should be the production of a kind
of "qualified" knowledge, even if short-lived, which will emerge as an "apparition" against a
background of transparent myths. It should not be expected that the effects of a theory [in the
sense of Althusserian science] will be achieved. . . . [But] perhaps through the exercise of this
criticism it will be possible to produce the "subtle subversion" that Barthes suggests . . . , the
subversion that does not accept the play with opposites that are merely accomplices within the
same structure . . . , but one that seeks another term beyond the game of oppositions, a term
not of synthesis but of an eccentricty that frustrates false oppositions.

Criticism from within is launched from the recognition that the
production of architectural meaning is a notion understandable only as the transformation of a meaning already emergent, Althusser's *toujours-déjà-donné*, the always-
already-given. Meaning is never just *there*; rather meaning is always already given in
the process of its transformation into another meaning. As important, the domain of
architectural meaning is not a theoretical outside but rather the Althusserian "imaginary," which is to say the domain of ideology itself.[8] Architecture needs some ideology; it requires some *chiaroscuro*. Silvetti's is a conception of architecture that
accepts and acts within ideological limits, but exposes and subverts them through

formal operations: "the beauty of shadows," of anamorphosis, of obliqueness, of fictions that make manifest the fact that they are fictions.

Notes

1. Manfredo Tafuri, "L'Architecture dans le Boudoir: The Language of Criticism and the Criticism of Language," *Oppositions* 3 (May 1974), reprinted in this volume; Diana Agrest and Mario Gandelsonas, "Semiotics and Architecture: Ideological Consumption or Theoretical Work," *Oppositions* 1 (September 1973).

2. For a more explicit discussion of realism, see Jorge Silvetti, "On Realism in Architecture," *Harvard Architecture Review* 1 (Spring 1980).

3. Roland Barthes, "Literature and Metalanguage," in *Critical Essays*, trans. Richard Howard (Evanston: Northwestern University Press, 1972), p. 98.

4. Barthes expands Louis Hjelmslev's model of semiotics to construct a tripartite scheme, within which the *sign* of the first-order, denotative language produces a *meaning* that in turn becomes a signifer, or *form*, of the second-level, connotative, mythical *concept*; together the form and the concept produce the mythical *signification*. Barthes identifies the connotative level with ideology; myth deploys the signs at this level to naturalize the dominant values of a given historical period. See Roland Barthes, "Myth Today," in *Mythologies*, trans. Annette Lavers (New York: Hill and Wang, 1972).

5. Barthes, "Myth Today," p. 135.

6. Roland Barthes, "The Structuralist Activity," in *Critical Essays*, pp. 214–215.

7. Agrest and Gandelsonas, "Semiotics and Architecture," p. 99.

8. See Louis Althusser, "Ideology and Ideological State Apparatuses," in *Lenin and Philosophy and Other Essays*, trans. Ben Brewster (New York: Verso, 1971). Althusser considered art to be a special case on the continuum from ideology to science or knowledge, inhabiting a space "midway" between the two. The presentation of ideology in art places the reader or spectator — for the moment and within the context of the work's ideological materials — outside the particular ideology being presented. The work of art thus allows for the distantiation of ideology and sets the spectator on the track toward understanding its workings. This culminates in theoretical knowledge, the epistemological explanation of the lived experience of ideology by descriptive concepts, which is the realm of Althusserian science.

"There is nothing more essential for a society than to classify its own languages," wrote Roland Barthes in 1966.[1] This imperative seems to underlie much theoretical work of the present decade in the fields of literature, music, and particularly in architecture. What follows is an attempt to discuss and reaffirm the validity of contemporary inquiries that focus their attention on architecture as language: that is, architecture as a specific ideological practice concerned with the production of cultural symbols; architecture understood or "read" as a "text," as material that supports a signification which includes but goes beyond the functions it involves. Specifically, this essay seeks to contribute to such classificatory tasks by concentrating on one mode of architectural discourse of which we have become recently aware: architecture as a discourse critical of itself. Such a discourse does not itself make use of language, but instead places itself at the very moment of producing an architectural object, aiming through this at a critical reading of the system of architecture. The idea of "criticism from within" is not a new notion, and indeed it has been equated at times with the very notion of art. What is new, however, is the possibility of defining it more clearly by using new conceptual tools.

As defined, this type of criticism seems to differ from other more conventional and well established types of criticism by virtue of the instruments it uses. We shall see later that its identity depends on many other characteristics that include the type of "effects" it produces as well as its relationship with theory. For the moment, we need only make clear that the "realm" of criticism has traditionally been divided between two opposing modes: one that tries to evaluate the degree of "fitness" or "non-fitness" of a solution to a particular architectural question and another that attempts to see both the question and that solution as parts of a larger historical, cultural, or ideological process. The former, typical of architectural journals and chronicles, is mainly concerned to "evaluate facts"; it is in the end trapped within its own ideological perspective. This kind of critical discourse constitutes in most cases an obstacle for theory, and should perhaps be better termed "technical" or "evaluative" criticism. The latter is related more to historical and scholarly endeavors and has theory, to which it is a prolegomena and constant check, as its final aim. This is indeed the only discourse that can safely claim the name of criticism in that it enjoys the more "comfortable" situation of being distanced from the act of making.[2]

Undoubtedly, the third type of critical discourse which I am introducing here, and which I shall call "criticism from within," does not appear to have the same conceptual clarity as these two traditional forms, particularly in its relation to theory and ideology. By placing itself within the act of making and by not using the instruments of language but those of architecture itself, it becomes compromised by the ideological nature of all objects produced by culture; but, at the same time, paradoxically, the very identification of this type of criticism depends on the fact that these same objects possess the capacity to expose certain meanings of the work that are otherwise obscured by ideological veils.

One might expect that among the copious writings that have appeared in the last decade which have attempted a description and explanation of architecture as language, attention would have been given to this third type of criticism if only because it is itself, as a criticism of architecture, one of the many discourses of language itself. Following the logic of the analogy between architecture and language (and noting that important contributions on this area of theory have concentrated heavily on the problems of theory versus ideology), the parallel contains the possibility of making, or at least proposing, the existence of such a criticism in architecture. But few have analyzed this notion of criticism, while many have abused the usage of the term.

Manfredo Tafuri has recently attempted to evaluate the historical significance of internal criticism, particularly for the present time.[3] In his writings, Tafuri takes a rather pessimistic view both of the historical and the cultural value of an attitude that concerns itself with the problem of language—"the return to language," he writes, "is a proof of failure"[4]—an attitude to which "criticism from within" belongs, and especially of the critical intentions that he sees as pervading the objects of present production. And yet, one of the central conclusions that emerge from his argument is that there are no fundamental differences between such architects as Aldo Rossi, James Stirling, Peter Eisenman, Robert Venturi, since they "all return to language." One may suspect that such frustration might well be a typical initial reaction to a work of criticism of such stature and originality that it shatters hitherto unchallenged systems of ordering and classifying and subverts our previously held values, rearranging what is known according to a more enlightened conceptual framework and thus transforming the object of analysis into a new, unexpected reality.

Nonetheless, such classifications as Tafuri's, which polarize the objects of analysis into categories that are too broad, thus erasing significant differences, or into trivial labeling systems as in the case of the originally amusing but by now boring chromatic grouping into "the whites," "the grays," and "the silvers" (a taxonomy which has retarded any serious understanding of the problem of architecture as language), are in the end still frustrating in themselves. Further treatment of the subject seems warranted, if for no other reason than because there has been no systematic discussion of the nature of "criticism from within" and its relation to a more general "return to language." As yet I do not know what mechanisms and operations it uses or how it differs from other types of work on language. Indeed, to test and evaluate Tafuri's macroscopic, global view it is indispensable to shift attention to the internal workings of language and to possess a clear model of its structure. I will begin my discussion at a microscopic, yet generalizable level, describing certain mechanisms and operations, which I hope will later enable me to establish the role that such "criticism from within" might play today in the development of architecture in its relation to theory, criticism, and ideology.

I would like for the purpose of my analysis to follow an opposite path to Tafuri and start with a general characterization of the common traits shared by most contemporary production concerned with architecture as language, ending with a more particularized analysis that is intended to help differentiate what is "criticism from within" from what is not.

Let us begin by assuming that the "return to language" has indeed occurred (a trend that seems to characterize the seventies, as has been said, but which also can be traced back to Kahn and even to the early Johnson). That is, this "return to language" is marked by an unusual degree of self-consciousness in architecture, which starts with the recognition that architecture, like any other cultural product, can be studied as a system of signification, establishing different levels, accumulating layers of meaning and sense, and constituting one of the many symbolic spheres instituted by society. As a consciousness of itself, architecture can only, and only willingly, operate with the known: its past, immediate or distant, and the existent world. It is, then, a work of reflection, essentially anti-utopian, one which automatically establishes a basis for criticism since criticism is a speculative reflection on the known.

It is undoubtedly for this reason that on so many occasions we hear the analogy drawn between the present moment and that of Mannerism, that "universal malaise" as Colin Rowe called it, that appeared in Italy during the Cinquecento.[5] This is probably because, for the first time since the twenties, we find ourselves looking back on the Modern Movement itself from a real historical perspective. Its "classicism" has by now been experienced, its effects sensed, and its postulates questioned; yet with all this nothing seems to have appeared to replace it. Like the Mannerist architect we can only manipulate the known. Such is, in my view, all that can be said in general terms about the state of architecture today.

But as soon as we begin to scrutinize these modern "manners" and their mechanisms for the production of meaning, we realize that the conscious reference either to past architectures or to contemporary realities can be established and expounded in many forms (some of them of antagonistic character), so that self-consciousness and the "return to language" are not sufficient categorizations upon which to reject or accept them; that there might be specific differentiations, much more useful than Tafuri's universalist label, to be made between Charles Moore's "wit" and Aldo Rossi's "silence"; that, in short, as a parallel to the general treatment we need to establish with clarity: (1) how operations on language work; (2) what their relations to theory and ideology are; (3) what their historic-cultural status is.

What then is it possible to do with an established code, or how can we operate on it? Without risking much, we could say that it is only possible either to transform it or to reproduce it. By transformation we mean those operations performed on the elements of a given existent code which depart from the original, normative, or canonical usage of the code by distorting, regrouping, reassembling, or in general altering it in such a way that it *maintains its reference to the original, while tending to produce a new meaning.* (For the purposes of our discussion, we need not enter into the problem of reproduction.)[6] From this very general point of view, the Renaissance becomes a transformation of Antiquity, Mannerism of Quattrocento architecture, Neo-Classicism of Classicism, eclecticism of the past as a whole, etc. We might usefully illustrate these transformational operations by means of an analogy with the classical figures of rhetoric. We can see, for example, the "hyperboles" to which the architect-monk submitted the classical code in the Cartuja de Granada, the "paradox" which Bernardo Buontalenti presents to us in the stair of the choir of Santo Stefano in Florence, the "ironies" in Giulio Romano's Palazzo del Te, the "metaphors" of most of the work of Charles Moore, the "ellipses" of Fascist architecture, of Robert Venturi, and of Aldo Rossi.[7] All these examples exhibit the same general characteristics: they all operate with known architectural codes, and they all re-deploy these codes by effecting some easily perceivable changes. Yet all the resulting effects are different; for while in one case we might be induced to smile with a certain conde- scension, in another we are puzzled by what seems an impossible mistake, and in another we might even need to close our eyes to imagine what is not there. An almost endless list could be compiled for the purpose of showing how powerful rhetoric can be in assisting a theoretical and hence systematic classification of these architectural operations, and for demonstrating the similar structure of production of meaning of most of man's products. My interest here is to concentrate on specific effects pro- duced by some of these transformations. For this, it is enough to say that rhetoric is a *metalanguage*, a discourse built on another discourse. As we will see later, this concept that comes out of logic and semiotics provides us with a tool that will help us under- stand and delimit the problems posed at the beginning of this paper in relation to "criticism from within."

To begin with, it is clear that much of what is produced today in architecture consists of a discourse that comments on other already constituted architectural discourses: that is, the very special case of metalanguage in which both discourses belong to the same practice; architecture commenting on architecture, architecture "speaking" of itself. One way to clarify the concept of metalanguage in relation to our subject is to classify the range of possible object-languages; that is to say, the codes or elements that can be referred to or commented on by the meta- language. For example, the metalanguage may refer to or comment on *the formal codes*; it may also refer to the functional codes, that is, the set of systematized, normalized functions (the program) and the uses they promote. Because they are the most con- scious codes of modern architecture, both of these seem to have been rather thor- oughly explored. But it is also possible to conceive of a commentary on the rhetorical codes themselves, and on the moral codes. In reality, these commentaries seem to concentrate on *elements of the codes*. This can be illustrated by the example of the column. The column has undoubtedly been one of the most significant elements of architec- ture, and as such it has become one of the favorite elements of architectural language, attracting commentaries of metalinguistic nature, as illustrated by the Désert de Retz by François Barbier of 1771, the inverted half-shaft column of the William Henry Seward Memorial by Hornbostel & Wood of 1929, and by Adolf Loos's Chicago Trib- une competition entry of 1923. These examples all refer, on the first reading, not to the body of referents peculiar to the classical code, but to the element itself or to the code itself (in this case the column, in its denotative state). Thus, these examples refer not to the supposed contents of classical architecture (beauty, the human body, proportions, etc.) but to the classical element, column; that is to say, all these ex- amples (each of them a fully constituted significant system of signified/signifier) contain in themselves another significant system previously constituted (i.e., the clas- sical column). In most of these cases the metalinguistic operation is constituted by a simple change of scale or the substitution of a different function for the original one. Again, it is interesting to note that all of these displacements do not produce the same effect. In some cases, a certain surplus of meaning appears beyond the simple commentary, and in some cases this "beyond" approaches a dimension of *criticism*. The famous triglyphs of Giulio Romano might serve to further the analysis. The her- esy perpetrated by Giulio Romano against the classical language seems to be more than a heresy, more than a trivial game: in it we find it extremely difficult to experi- ence the principles of humanism. We are forced to refer back to architecture itself, since the disordered order within the order disturbs us. There is no change of scale, no inversion, no second stage; we are confronted with a wall conceived *within* a canon. However, if only one triglyph were loose, we would not see it; it would be an accident. It is precisely the insistent and systematic disorder within the order which disorders the old one, and which forbids us to experience the transparent effect of what it should have been—something classic. Giulio Romano thus invents, in a single heretical gesture, a new meaning—perhaps proving that the impossible is possible—by showing up the conventionality of the classical code. The operation is one of altering syntactic relationships. The rhetorical figure is irony, and its effect can be interpreted as critical. It is only at the end of this process of deciphering that we turn back to the original referent (beauty, the human body, proportions, etc.) in order to sense the strength of the new effect; but now we accept the reference only after de-mythifying it. This results in a de-naturalization of the code that has been interrogated. The object-language is thus questioned *in its own terms*. Indeed, this is an apparently trivial detail if considered by itself. It is only as part of the spirit that pervades the entire work that we can establish its place in a more complex system of critical meanings. Giulio Romano's building acquires a startling power when we discover that a similar attack has been carried at all levels, intentionally profaning the integrity of all the iconographic, compositional, structural codes of the classical language.

Shocking at first, the object impatiently unfolds before us a universe of meanings hitherto hidden from us; and our initial feeling of disturbance gives way to a pleasurable sensation of intellectual complicity between the architect and ourselves after we have, not without effort, succeeded in disclosing the building's arcane messages. The object appears as a revelation, not of sacred but of heretical nature because it confronts us with a subversive meaning whose opaque effect proposes and obliges us to perform a certain intellectual task of deciphering. The object cannot be consumed, but must be interpreted; indeed, we must wander along the same path that the architect followed; we must work with it.

Although we cannot place ourselves at the same comfortable distance with the present that we are able to do with the Italian Cinquecento, perhaps it is possible, tentatively, to propose a similar reading of some recent architecture. We can recognize in some works of Charles Moore, for example, the same type of transformations to which we have alluded. Kresge College *re-presents* the known and all too familiar in a disjointed, unexpected, disturbing manner, and we can apply our previous remarks in relation to the effects of the "criticism from within" to describe what we are told through these buildings.

The effectiveness of such "criticism from within," however, does not necessarily depend on such ironic manipulations of architectural codes. Rather, the critical effect depends on a subversion of known meanings and on the production of knowledge itself;[8] and to that end no rhetorical operation, per se, can offer guarantees. Lévi-Strauss, commenting on Duchamp's "ready mades," expresses eloquently the complex mixture of operations and effects in these types of works: "You then accomplish a new distribution between the signifier and the signified, a distribution that was in the realm of the possible but was not openly effected [in the primitive condition of the object]. You make then, in one sense, a work of learning, discovering in that object latent properties that were not perceived in the initial context; a poet does this each time he uses a word or turns a phrase in an unusual manner."[9] It is this test, and not the simple manipulation of known codes, which the work of "criticism from within" must pass. Thus, works like those of Rossi and Graves that are neither ironic nor paradoxical nonetheless impose on us an *oeuvre de connaissance*, make us discover latent properties, and open to us a poetic dimension. And, recalling Barthes, we may use and interpret the notion of "anamorphism" as a metaphor that can help us to circumscribe even more precisely this still evasive notion of "criticism from within."[10] In fact, anamorphism expresses almost literally the mechanism, effects, and dilemmas of this type of criticism. For example, the techniques used widely in painting during the sixteenth century and illustrated here by the "skull" depicted at the bottom of Holbein the Younger's *The Ambassadors* can be read in two different ways. We can see them as tricks, games, diversions; but it is also possible to read in them a much more subversive content than can be apprehended if we concentrate only on the technique of distortion employed. In this case, it is necessary to understand the implications of perspective as "symbolic form" (in Panofsky's sense) to see that the technique of anamorphism effects also a criticism of a mode of representation, making explicit the illusion of perspective and producing, if only for a moment, a condensed knowledge that must be unraveled by the beholder.

We can, then, base our understanding of the nature of "criticism from within" on this constellation of attributes, and this, in turn, helps us to differentiate it from other types of transformation. This distinction is important because there exists another possibility of transformation, which is opposed to criticism, an understanding of which should help us in the task of clarifying contemporary productions. If we analyze, for instance, some current architectures that abound in historical allusions and quotations, we find that neither the operations nor the effects produced belong to the category of criticism described, in spite of sharing with it a certain self-consciousness and transformational character. In these cases the material that supports meaning is not substantially altered in order to bring out any latent properties; rather, it is strategically marked—simply "quoted"—with the resulting effect of veiling, covering, wrapping as it were, the original sign in a new meaning. It tends to emphasize features of the already known, seeking an external, larger association. It seeks a connotation. And paradoxically, in the cases of historical quotation, it denies the history contained in it by erasing the contingencies by which it is or was determined; by denying history it naturalizes the object. It is a process of mythification of the known.[11] As such, this type of transformation is often found in the architecture of mass consumption, where nothing could be more alien to its aim than the deciphering activity which characterizes "criticism from within." But it is also, and at a more profound level, at the root of many of the present attempts to consciously work with architecture as language. Examples could be listed endlessly, but suffice it to say that it is probably the effect sought after by most of the iconographers of the present, so-called "populist" tendencies. For it is not history in its most profound sense that is the desired object of exploration, exposition, and unraveling, but rather the immediate, uncritical, almost urgent rapport between the architecture and the beholder.

Thus, in terms of mechanisms of transformation, we can differentiate clearly between "criticism from within" and mythification. "Criticism from within" is a signifying system in which the content is in itself a signifying system; that is to say, the form and the content of the original object are both, in turn, the content of another form (the transformed object). Mythification, conversely, institutes a new signifying system in which its form remains almost untransformed, but by subtle accents, a new content covers the object. The respective effects can also be seen as dichotomous: criticism generates opaqueness, intrigue, questioning, subversion; mythification generates transparency, complacency, naturalization, and conformism.

Using this reading, one cannot any longer group the members of the New York "Five" together simply on the basis of their use of similar superficial elements. Of all of them, only John Hejduk and Michael Graves seem to achieve the effects produced by critical operations. Hejduk does so by elevating certain architectural components to the category of signs of themselves, and by virtue of this, he achieves an architecture almost devoid of any metaphorical or representative value except that of itself; plans and facades become the vehicles for unprecedented discoveries, while the myths of function and structure are dissipated by poetry. Graves, on the other hand, concentrates insistently on the metaphorical dimensions of architecture and thereby brings about a completely new reading of all the elements implicated (columns, walls, ceilings, colors, etc.), and as a result his architecture yields as surplus an enrichment of a vocabulary and mechanisms that were deemed exhausted. In both cases, our reading of the early work of Le Corbusier and of general architectural notions is both demythified and enriched.

We see then that the "return to language" deserves more than the merely perfunctory treatment which discards it altogether as senseless. In rather schematic fashion, we have been able to establish the existence of at least two opposite effects resulting from different ways of constructing the architectural discourse that reflects upon itself: the possibility of criticism and that of mythification. This analysis suggests other levels of investigation. As both criticism and myth produce a certain type of knowledge—criticism by digging into the object itself in a relentless search for fundamental meaning, mythification by re-presenting the object as a confirmation of our previous knowledge and then by naturalizing it—we must ask what kind of relations this very special type of criticism "from within" establishes with theory and ideology, what its locations are in regard to these two realms of human knowledge. We might even ask whether, indeed, this type of "production of knowledge" deserves the label of criticism. The consideration of this question seems imper-

Rodolfo Machado,
Fachada Mascara,
Cuernavaca, 1972

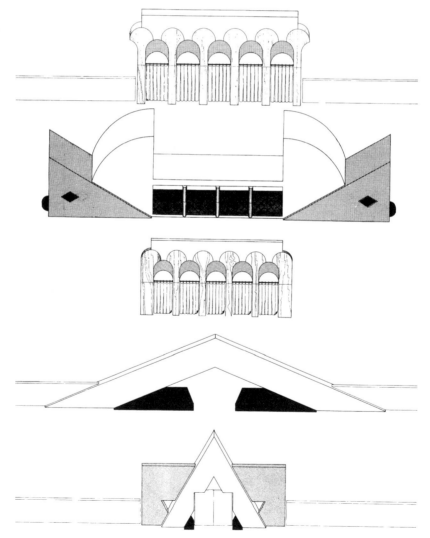

ative, since, as we said at the beginning, we are confronted with an apparently blatant contradiction: we assume that an object produced by culture (and as such marked by ideology) also has the capacity to present a critique of itself (and as such to contribute to theoretical knowledge). But, at the risk of constructing a tautology, it is this paradox itself that constitutes its own explanation and is the foundation of its own richness and uniqueness. For it is senseless to ask of this "criticism from within" a guarantee that it will discover some "truth" of scientific nature. As a discourse it can only be read through the object in which it is rooted and not through language, which manipulates concepts that are organized logically and provides the "matter" that science and theory transform. As criticism contained in an object (whether a painting, a sculpture, a work of architecture), it proposes itself to us as a totality, which cannot be reproduced or tested as a scientific or theoretical proposition. Once it has appeared, its own critical nature is compromised by its very object-nature, and it cannot escape the destiny that our culture reserves for its objects: its critical meaning becomes consumable after its operations are discovered. It is possible to transform these operations into techniques, or into normative principles (as, for example, in the efforts of Venturi to institutionalize irony), and l'enfant terrible becomes a desired connotation with time. This condition thus defines the difference between this type of criticism and the criticism involved in the production of scientific or theoretical knowledge: while both are subversive at the beginning, one becomes the object of consumption, the other, of systematic knowledge. "Criticism from within" is, then, a short-lived phenomenon in the continuum of knowledge, its initial power being recoverable only through exegesis and archaeology, although never to be experienced again with its own original vigor and authority. But this limitation only serves to clarify its role, not to suggest that it should be dismissed. Because of this specific and unique condition, there is a liberating effect: not being able to exercise the power of "truth," criticism from within institutes in its place the domain of art as poetry. The consequences of acknowledging its dependence on and its contradictory, ambiguous relationship with ideology becomes its force.

It is especially at such a time of questioning as the present that the mass of ideological formations cracks, that "criticism from within" penetrates the solidity of mythical constructions with the aim of exposing the multiplicity of meanings that lie hidden in it. Perhaps what is most promising about this type of criticism is precisely the awareness that we will not gain from it access to objective, scientific knowledge (a task that returns to the discipline where it belongs: history), but rather that through it we may aim at unfolding the imaginary-symbolic universe that architecture simultaneously proposes and represses. The clear objective of such criticism should be the production of a kind of "qualified" knowledge, even if short-lived, which will emerge as an "apparition" against a background of transparent myths. It should not be expected that the effects of a theory will be achieved. However, the poetical dimension which finds in this criticism its natural realm in the present moment may be rediscovered. And perhaps through the exercise of this criticism it will be possible to produce the "subtle subversion" that Barthes suggests as a possible solution to the contradictions of art;[12] that is to say, the subversion that does not accept the play with opposites that are merely accomplices within the same structure (i.e., the endless oscillation between formalism and functionalism), but one that seeks another term beyond the game of oppositions, a term not of synthesis but of an eccentricity that frustrates false oppositions. Therefore, one cannot conclude with Tafuri that "behind this laborious digging into architecture's own existence, there is a constant fear of an authentic critical process."[13] Both "criticism from within" as well as the criticism of theory and history have, de facto, a precisely delimited field of action, so that it is not necessary to engage in a discussion as to which criticism is "authentic." "Authentic" is too loaded a term to be useful in defining the boundaries of different practices. But if the possibilities of inquiry offered by historical criticism are not the same as those offered by the work of art, the distinction between them does not preclude their dialectical relationship. History aims at scientific explanation, and it has, consequently, an undeniable lead in the field of knowledge. It helps the artist to establish and become conscious of his own location. This consciousness has consequences for the artist's work, although these consequences are not automatic. But conversely, the artist's products provide the material for theory, and theory must wait for their appearance; for no matter how advanced a structural model of society theory might possess, it cannot forecast and depict the artistic products that that structure will produce.

Our inquiry into the nature of "criticism from within" cannot, however, be concluded here. In addressing the questions of its place in the sphere of knowledge, we found that some aspects of it are neither explained by a description of its internal mechanisms nor by its relationships with theory and ideology; more specifically, we implied that there is some temporal aspect to "criticism from within." It seems, then, that in order to understand the paradoxical nature of this criticism, we need to consider its relation with both of its coordinates: not only the structural, which we have just touched upon, but also the historical-cultural, which we will consider next.

As the concept of "criticism from within," or even the general notion of transformation implies, its operation requires the existence of well established codes on which to work. It is not, then, surprising that throughout history its appearance has been rather discreet and sporadic. In this context we might re-invoke the analogy of contemporary architecture to that of Mannerism, an architecture that responded to the "very human desire to impair perfection when once it has been

Rodolfo Machado
and Jorge Silvetti,
Fountain House,
Los Angeles, 1975

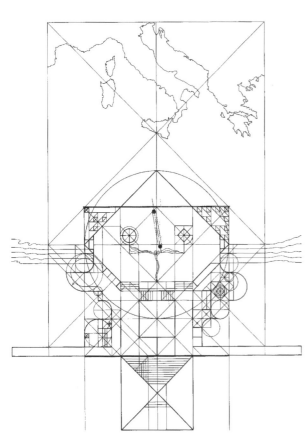

achieved."[14] Mannerist architecture was, like the works of today, essentially a reflective task, a critical experimentation with Classicism, which effected the subversive dismembering of the classical language through the heretical and revealing work of Giulio Romano, Michelangelo, Serlio, and the like, at the same time as it unfolded an unexpected treasure from which the classical language could re-emerge renovated and ready for its most fulfilling moment, pregnant with a seemingly inexhaustible richness.

This sporadic nature of "criticism from within," which appears as it were as an irregular necessity of history, forms its principal historical differentiation from other types of transformational work, and specifically from that type we have defined as its opposite: mythification. Mythification appears as a continuum in history; it is the most basic, rudimentary, and unavoidable manner of signifying of any object of the material culture. The prevailing forces in architectural ideologies, throughout history, are those that try to "naturalize" the cultural constructs of architecture, to justify and rationalize it through mythification. The forms of objects are thus constantly wrapped and veiled with secondary meanings, establishing chains which can only be interrupted momentarily by the reversing act of criticism. But it is important, since we are testing these arguments against the historical coordinate, to differentiate within mythification the existence of two different and opposed modes of effecting the naturalization of historical contingencies, two clear and typical forms that correspond to two very well differentiated historical moments: one (and this applies specifically to recent history) is the avant-garde moment, and the other, the moments that correspond to crisis or disbelief. Firstly, mythification (which attempts to achieve a particular transformation in men's consciousness—that of transforming the contingencies of the cultural and the historical into the natural) acquires in the avant-garde a positive value insofar as it is a genuine act of creation and insofar as it represents an intentional break with the past, placing the language in question within new terms and establishing its own parameters of production and criticism. Since no artistic movement can precede a general change in the historical determinants, the ideological work of the avant-garde—its mythification—consists precisely in making intelligible these determinants within a new ideological discourse; thus, for example, the aesthetics of the machine is a mythification, a naturalization of the historical *contingencies* of the machine itself, which does not explain it but rather borrows it uncritically, yet which, however, performs the role of establishing an iconography that symbolizes a positive utopia that is historically correct and forward looking. Now, this discourse that tells us about a new reality, that makes that reality legible and intelligible, is, because of its ideological nature, a distortion of those historical determinants. But although this fact is proven by time, it does not provide an automatic knowledge of what has been falsified; this is the work of criticism.

Secondly, in periods of disbelief, such as that which began in the late fifties and culminated during the sixties, mythification acquires the role of a cynical accomplice because it has nothing to propose and yet it continues to mimic the gestures of creation. At this point, there is only one positive option as to what to do with the "classic" language, and that is to demythify it. This act, together with theoretical work, can close a historical period. The counterpart of this proposition is—if I may be permitted the term—the mythification of myth, and as such it represents a reactionary force. It invariably implies a degradation of what is being transformed.

The type of mythification that is of interest for an analysis of the present moment then, is that which converts an already established architectural language into the material support of a sign which connotes what has already been sanctioned, approved, and digested by the system of architecture; that is to say, not into a language that connotes itself, but into one that seeks as a unique objective to signify the value that the system has acquired already in history. Hence, in many cases, the uses of the International Style, rationalism, "Corbusianism," etc. do not necessarily imply an intent to continue the tasks set forth in the heroic period of modern architecture or an attempt to realize the program of the avant-garde; rather, the style is often selected because of the connotations of "art" and "modernity" that it carries, and finally because it permits the architect to play safely within architecture.[15]

At this point it might be of help to introduce a more specific nomenclature, one that might serve to differentiate even further and with more precision the possibilities of work with language. These are the notions of "criticism" and "commentary" as elaborated by Michel Foucault in *The Order of Things*: "Since the classical age, commentary and criticism have been in profound opposition. By speaking of language in terms of representation and truth, criticism judges it and profanes it. Now as language in the irruption of its being, and questioning it as to its secret, commentary halts before the precipice of the original text, and assumes the impossible and endless task of repeating its own birth within itself: it sacralizes language. These two ways by which language establishes a relation with itself were now to enter into a rivalry from which we have not yet emerged—and which may even be sharpening as time passes."[16] For, to interrogate a language as to what, how, and why it represents, as criticism does, is to begin to disturb it at the very point where the ideological operation takes place; it is indeed to attempt to "profane" its inner sanctum and to judge its truth. Commentary, on the other hand, reproduces language, represents it with no other intention than to sanction its truth. And without attempting to generalize these two notions for the history of architecture, Foucault's categories are useful in separating present productions precisely and in regulating the use of the two terms which are loosely used in architecture today.

It is possible now to respond with more clarity to some of the questions that were posed at the beginning. We know it is possible to discern two types of discourse that are based on transformations of existing architectural codes, and that they are opposed in their mechanisms and in their effects. While one— criticism—attempts a reading of architecture in depth, unfolding the latent layers of meaning, the other—mythification—slides on the surface of the veils with which it has covered architecture. We have found that, historically, this seemingly simple duality is in fact a more complex, asymmetrical cultural phenomenon, since it is possible to sketch for the latter two opposing pictures, corresponding to two different historical moments, and for the former a sporadic appearance.[17] What our analysis has also yielded is the conviction that the critical reflection of language upon itself, "criticism from within," although sporadic, appears as an inevitable part of the architect's endeavor, in turn part of a more general phenomenon of a "return to language." Hence, as such, the phenomenon implies neither advancement nor regression. It is a historical reality, a common background against which we find ourselves working today. Within it, the searches, means, and objectives, which are marked by the subject and its contingencies, can be as varied as in any historical moment. Of course, it is not only possible, but necessary that the theoretical/historical criticism that analyzes these phenomena be carried out with different focuses and at different scales. Thus the general view that Tafuri offers is more than necessary: it is indispensable to talk about the "return to language" and to try to disentangle the historical meaning that such an attitude, as a whole, might have as opposed to other historical possibilities, contemporary, past, or hypothetical. But such a view, when expounded in disregard of the meaning of the nuances and eccentricities that the historical material offers, might become unconstructive if not informed dialectically by an internal analysis of such an attitude toward architecture. Tafuri's principal theoretical objective justifies his level of generalization because in his analysis he seeks to oppose the architect as a "producer" to the architect as an "expert in language";[18] however, his analysis of these two categories, which might have important theoretical consequences, is not altogether convincing because of his ambiguous use of the concept of "production." It is confusing because both types of work imply the "production" of something and as such both are historically and theoretically relevant; both operate upon and transform a given material by using and manipulating determinate means of production; both are related to ideology as well as to technique. Therefore, if it is true that a critic may find that some of the products of some of the "experts in language" have no cultural or historical relevance, obviously the same may be found for some of the producer's products, so that it is simply incorrect to try to establish the supremacy or importance of one over the other. Tafuri may consider that the work of certain contemporary architects is, in the end, irrelevant, but to generalize in such a way as to say that "the return to language [in this moment] is a proof of failure" obscures this fundamental principle: the production of "building" and the production of "meaning" are both parts of the production of architecture. Of course Tafuri would agree with this, but he seems to imply that the problem of the language of architecture ("as a system of communication . . .") should be left aside, to "happen" as it were, and that it is more important to concentrate on the nature of "building construction in reality."[19]

But what is building construction in reality? It does not stop at the moment when all economic, managerial, and political problems have been taken into account. The building still has to be created, and at that moment, whether the agent involved is an architect, a planner, a politician, a builder, or a layman does not matter: the whole problem of architecture as language, architecture as symbol, architecture as material culture, starts all over again; the dialectical process between creativity and history is again put into motion; and however uncultivated or underdeveloped the agent is, the problem of the transformation of a language is posed.

It therefore seems that this consciousness about "language" which characterizes the present moment, these attempts at a real criticism "from within," are a positive step. To extend Tafuri's own parable of the magician,[20] an understanding of the position where the architect-critic places himself might help us to understand more fully "the tricks of the magician" since these tricks can only be explained from both vantage points; from "behind the scene" (as Tafuri would want it) one sees the *techniques* of the tricks, and from the "seat in the audience" one sees the way in which the trick is delivered and the effects it produces. Both positions are needed to explain the magician and his tricks. If this is true, then there is no way by which we can escape our involvement with language. And regardless of whether or not one agrees with the view that the architect may be a "producer," such a view is not an "either/or" option when considered in relation to architecture as language.

It is important now to move a step forward, to change the level of discourse and enlarge the focus as it were, in order to establish the place of the "concern for language" and specifically of "criticism from within" within the system of production. We should recall that we started our work by assuming that what characterizes architecture today is its capacity to be studied as a system of significations that establishes different levels and layers of meanings and sense and constitutes one of the symbolic spheres instituted by society. If our assumption was correct, we can further conclude that architecture defines its place and role in the spheres of the production of knowledge and the production of meaning, as well as in the technical production of artifacts, as being within the social practices, and that as such it can be regarded mainly as a technical-ideological practice insofar as it transforms both matter and man's consciousness and utilizes both techniques and human relations. But within the realm of the production of meaning and knowledge—that with which we have been specifically concerned in our analysis of "criticism from within"—it is necessary to establish with certainty what role and place this criticism occupies, its extensions and limits.

For it is clear, as has already been implied in our discussion of the multi-layered nature of the phenomena of meaning in architecture, that this aspect of "criticism from within" cannot be the only discourse proposed by architecture. This peculiar discourse, as is obvious to many and disturbing to most, concerns mainly the most hermetic level of meaning that architecture can articulate. What may be read in this architecture of "criticism from within" pertains only to the closed domain of architecture itself as a discipline, and requires a trained reader, one who knows the symbolic universe proposed and instituted by it, and one whose intimate knowledge of the universe of, for instance, classical and modern architecture enables him to decipher the depth of the critical messages of Giulio Romano and John Hejduk respectively. Thus, this "hermetic" language of "criticism from within" must be understood and used as an internal disciplinary mechanism, whose social value is delimited by the boundaries that any specialized language establishes in society. It is pointless, then, to argue about "elitism" or "hermeticism" as the socially and politically undesirable results of these internal elaborations, since they are by their very nature "hermetic" and "elitist" in their relations with the collective realm. However, that they are only as hermetic as any internal criticism of any contemporary discipline is a fact that we can easily test, for example, by attempting to decipher the communications among physicists. But if we can refrain from discarding physics for its seemingly "hermetic" quality, we should at the same time demand that its products have a more positive collective value. This also goes for architecture where the issue seems even more pressing because of the unavoidable impingement of its products upon the public realm. So there should be no controversy over whether architecture language should deal with one or the other. The two discourses, the hermetic and the collective, seem to define the two poles of the scale of possible discourses that architecture is capable of handling. Considering these terms as dichotomic and exclusive is an error that seems to explain much of the confusion and poverty pervading architectural discussion today—confusion insofar as there is no awareness that architecture operates, communicates, and speaks at many levels as a polyphonic composition, and poverty, as a consequence, because most seem to want to suppress this potential richness in favor of a monochord discourse which "speaks" solely the language of "the people" or of "the elite," as if such a thing were possible. It is only after establishing with clarity the place and limits of "criticism from within" in the system of production as an inescapable, indispensable, "elitist" language that we can assess more thoroughly and correctly some of the architecture produced today. If there is something to be questioned in architecture, it is not its preoccupation with language, which is a concern that it can rightfully display and dutifully respond to; rather, it should be questioned on its lack of articulation between the internal, speculative discourse implied by the return to language and the domain of architecture as a collective discourse.

At this point we return to the problem of Mannerism. It was precisely a moment of profound moral and intellectual crisis that produced the reflective attitude, the "signifying consciousness" and critical mind of the Mannerist artist of the sixteenth century. This chapter of history has been thoroughly explained, but what is important to note is that the magnificent Baroque explosion that followed it could only have happened after Mannerism demonstrated to what limits the classical language of architecture could be extended. The excesses and heresies of Mannerism cleared the way for the majestic and sure moves of the Baroque architect, opening the path to one of the most successful chapters in the history of architecture, when the bonds between a political and social program (the Counter Reformation) and an artistic program (based on the rhetoric of persuasion) seem to have been stronger than they are today. The optimistic conclusion that might be drawn from this analogy as far as our own future is concerned is not necessarily convincing, and one can only wish it were true. But we believe that one must, at the least, accept the necessity of this reflective moment, when architecture turns into itself to recognize its signifying nature and to search for its limits, as indispensable for any future. The period that followed the heroic years of the Modern Movement did not produce much knowledge about its own nature, but rather a pragmatic, over-optimistic and simplified application of its universalist principles. Slowly it withdrew into the most banal forms of consumerism, undoubtedly as a result of this uncritical application of its principles. Whereas some serious theoretical and historical criticism was produced, the practice of architecture proceeded with blind confidence in its language and its ethical codes, and culminated in stagnation and in premature failure.

As often with historical parallels, their value lies not so much in the points where coincidence occurs, but rather where the analogy no longer holds; indeed, it is at the moment when a difference appears that we can begin to gain knowledge. For this reason, the analogy between Mannerism and the present can only be stretched so far. The two moments in fact derived from two very different methodological commitments, each consciously established: the classical view was *typological*, the modern view was *programmatic*. The former furnished a symbol to be operated upon, the latter supposedly furnished a set of social demands from which a form could be derived if reason and the spirit of the age were invoked. It is beyond the scope of this paper to analyze further the contradictions inherent in this last distinction, but some observations are possible. The tenets of modern architecture, simplified to pure formulae, continued to champion the programmatic approach at the same time that they generated architectural typologies, rooted in culture in the deepest sense, and instituted in practice but unacknowledged as such. This fact prevented and even forbade any conscious attempt to investigate the language of architecture "from within." The trap of the "form/function" ideology which reappeared, renovated and transformed into all the variants that characterized the dispersion of architecture during the sixties—"systems analysis," behaviorism, planning, "problem solving techniques," etc.—prevented any consideration of architecture as a fact of culture. (In this country, the work of Kahn stands out as a powerful reaction to it, although his work had to be wrapped in obscure and metaphysical rationalization.)

It is tempting to think, then, that a reconsideration of the implications of a typological approach in architecture today might suggest a possible articulation between those two unavoidable discourses that architecture must institute. For if we look at the problem of a typology of architecture as not just functional recipes or formal dictionaries, but rather as an ever changing, symbolic discourse articulated by culture as a whole and from which we can nurture our search, it becomes clear that it is *only* with a *conscious* "return to language" that we can successfully operate upon transform, and invent *from architecture*. For this reason this approach, and the consciousness that arises from it, can establish the basis for a new type of creativity, one that allows us to depart from a collective intelligibility and to accept consciously the notion of transformation as a means of operation, thus dissipating the anguish that results from either "scientific" demands or from the myth of the genius. It seems possible, then, to find place for both internal speculation and social responsibility, "criticism from within" and "collective myths," the two inescapable voices that are uttered through architecture. This new consciousness does not stop with the memory of the type, but begins with it only to forget it at the moment of poetic transformation. It furnishes us with the conceptual foundations upon which it is possible to reestablish an intelligent discussion about representation and iconography in architecture, two subjects that have been denied or treated obliquely by modern architecture. Finally, such a typological approach to architecture, which recognizes the multiplicity of meanings of the built world, also affords the possibility of accepting and incorporating the ever present and unresolvable contradictions between myth and critique, the two substances that inform the space in which we inescapably act.

If these very tentative conclusions seem to pose more questions than answers, and to cast some doubt upon the exactitude of some of the previous speculations, at least this last fact of the double, paradoxical nature of architecture together with all its implications, seems to be undisputable. Through asserting this fact, we have attempted to erase the remaining traces of the false dilemma of "scientific versus intuitive" that still haunts us. Neither pure fact nor pure myth, architecture must unashamedly depict its ambiguous nature. It seems appropriate to recall Barthes in closing: "There are those who want a text (an art, a painting) without a shadow, without the 'dominant ideology'; but this is to want a text without fecundity, without productivity, a sterile text. . . . The text needs its shadows; this shadow is *a bit* of ideology, *a bit* of representation, *a bit* of subject: ghosts, pockets, traces, necessary clouds: subversion must produce its own chiaroscuro."[21]

Notes

1. Roland Barthes, *Critique et vérité* (Paris: Editions du Seuil, 1966), p. 45. Translation by the author.

2. For a substantive discussion on the concept of ideology and its implications for architecture see Diana Agrest and Mario Gandelsonas, "Semiotics and Architecture: Ideological Consumption or Theoretical Work," *Oppositions* 1 (September 1973); see also Mario Gandelsonas, "Linguistica nell'architettura," *Casabella* 374 (February 1973).

3. Manfredo Tafuri, "L'Architecture dans le Boudoir," *Oppositions* 3 (May 1974); Manfredo Tafuri, *Teoria e storia dell'architettura* (Bari: Laterza, 1971), ch. 3.

4. Tafuri, "L'Architecture dans le Boudoir," p. 55.

5. Colin Rowe, "Mannerism and Modern Architecture," *Architectural Review*, May 1950, p. 292: "that universal 'malaise' which in the arts, while retaining the externals of classical correctness, was obliged at the same time to disrupt the inner core of classical coherence."

6. I leave aside the general problem of which reproduction and transformation are part: a larger system that includes the invention of a code. In the context of this article I will avoid a discussion of invention as well as reproduction and the problems they pose for theory.

7. Hyperbole: rhetorical figure that consists of an exaggeration of the terms.

Anacoluthon: rupture in the syntactic structure.

Ellipsis: grammatical figure which consists of suppressing unnecessary elements as far as intelligibility can be maintained.

Irony or antiphrasis: rhetorical figure that consists of expressing the contrary of the meaning intended (it is a connotation): "irony goes together with a sentiment of superiority."

Metaphor: rhetorical figure of substitution of one term for another both of different classes. The term present in the sentence stands for the one that is meant but is absent. Based on association.

Paradox: rhetorical operation that consists of presenting a meaning contrary to common sense. Absurd and shocking affirmation at first, it should conform to reality after analysis.

These definitions, which are a sample of rhetorical figures and operations, have been taken from Henri Morier, *Dictionnaire de poétique et de rhétorique*, and Roland Barthes, "L'ancienne réthorique," *Communications* 16 (Paris: Editions du Seuil, 1970). It is interesting to note that at different times in history, architects and artists were well versed in the arts of rhetoric, which they tried consciously to apply to their work. See, for instance, Giulio Carlo Argan, "La retorica e l'arte barocca" and "Retorica e architettura," in *Studi e note. Dal Bramante al Canova* (Rome: Mario Bulzoni Editore).

8. We talk about subversion in very precise terms, as the discourse whose purpose or effect is to unveil the fallacies of another well established ideological discourse. In that sense, Galileo's theories were as subversive in their moment as Marcel Duchamp's work on its own. The efficiency of subversion is diverse, and we will see later the differences of effects between the type of Galilean subversion (science) and that of art.

9. Georges Charbonnier, *Entretiens avec Claude Lévi-Strauss* (Paris: René Julliard et Librairie Plon, 1961). Translation by the author.

10. Barthes, *Critique et vérité*, p. 64.

11. For a suggestive treatment of the idea of myth and mythification in present western society, see Roland Barthes, *Mythologies* (Paris: Editions du Seuil, 1957).

12. Roland Barthes, *Le plaisir du texte* (Paris: Editions du Seuil, 1973).

13. Manfredo Tafuri, *Teorie e storia dell'architettura* (Bari: Laterza, 1970), p. 161.

14. Rowe, "Mannerism and Modern Architecture," p. 292.

15. Although it would be possible to trace this process of degradation back into history, probably to the moment in which the notions of progress and change became active in history, it seems peculiar and characteristic of our present times, a result of the structural changes in society that have occurred in this century, which shifted the emphasis from us to consumption, from aesthetic contemplation to stylistic degradation. Degradation and consumption: these two words in this context recall the modern notion of kitsch—the operation which entails an uncritical debasement of the work of art, oriented toward an easy consumption. It takes very little effort to discover that the definition of kitsch applies to what we have been discussing in terms of mythification in architecture, and only the classic content that the artistic elite has attached to the notion of kitsch to defend its own lesser works has so far prevented us from seeing the parallel. It is only a matter of how inclusive one wants this notion to be. And, if we only take into account the type of operations involved in it, we might surprisingly find that kitsch is not only a reproduction of Mona Lisa on a towel, but also much of the present exquisite architecture.

16. Michel Foucault, *The Order of Things* (New York: Vintage Books, 1973), p. 81.

17. And while this theoretical model seems to account for both Mannerism and the present, we need at this point further discussion and clarification because of the immediately apparent contradictions that a comparison with other views of the same problem produces. Particularly for its historical importance and the brilliance of its arguments, Colin Rowe's "Mannerism and Modern Architecture" needs to be discussed in this light. Rowe's contention that it is possible to understand not only some of the products of the early Modern Movement, but also the "mental climate" that produced them by drawing a parallel between this time and that of Mannerism, is at least in opposition to what has been said here about the avant-garde, insofar as it is a period of positive ideological impetus, while Mannerism is one of critical reflection. I believe it is not a case of two opposing tenets, but rather one of different focus: in my view what characterizes a "Mannerist" period is the absence of any attempt to produce new codes and rather to operate with them (as in Rowe's words: "it demands an orthodoxy within whose framework it might be heretical") in a critical fashion, which in turn eliminates the heroic period of the Modern Movement as the candidate for the Mannerist label (it was mainly concerned with a new codification). It is also true that some of Rowe's arguments and parallels help us to understand unequivocally at what levels modern architecture was still dependent on a pre-existing order, and that modern architecture does not represent a total break with its past. The divergence in interpretation seems to arise from the fact that Rowe's impeccable characterization of Mannerism seems not to include the notion of criticism that is central in the present argument. While my present use of the term "criticism" seems to imply a degree of consciousness and intention on the part of the artist that might indeed be consciously manifest neither in the late Cinquecento architect nor in the present one, the actual effect produced by these operations on the codes of architecture in both cases belongs unquestionably, in my view, to the category of "criticism from within" as characterized so far. And this differs widely from the effect produced by early modern architecture. It seems that the work of deciphering proposed by these works of the heroic period had to do with discovering the new relationships between form and content, trying to match the symbols with their intended meanings, whereas today this interpretative task concentrates on the questioning of the nature of those bonds. In the end, as we will see

later, what is important is not how far the analogy can be carried between two historical periods, but rather what type of knowledge its use might produce, and in this respect, Rowe's discussion of modern architecture continues to be a model of anti-empirical criticism, that type of criticism that relentlessly unfolds the object of analysis, uncovering its hidden meanings, and which, by its implacable scholarly precision, transforms that object into a treasure of knowledge.

18. Tafuri, "L'Architecture dans le Boudoir," p. 57.
19. Ibid.
20. Ibid. "We can only answer that, wishing to discover the tricks of a magician, it is often better to observe him from behind the scenes rather than to continue to stare at him from a seat in the audience."
21. Barthes, *Le plaisir du texte*, p. 53.

Anthony Vidler   **"The Third Typology"** *Oppositions* 7 (Winter 1977); expanded in *Rational*

Architecture: The Reconstruction of the European City (Brussels: Editions des

Archives d'architecture moderne, 1978)

The work of Anthony Vidler frequently spans between the modes of architectural history, critical commentary, and theory. His historical analyses of Claude-Nicolas Ledoux, Etienne-Louis Boullée, Antoine-Chrysostome Quatremère de Quincy, and others found a receptive audience among architects interested in issues of character and type, even as contemporaneous architectural production influenced Vidler's own research trajectory. The present essay first appeared in a shorter version as an editorial

| *see 234* |

in *Oppositions* 7, as part of that journal's introduction of Italian "neorationalist" architecture to an English-speaking audience. In 1977, the essay was solicited by Maurice Culot and Leon Krier for republication in expanded form in *Rational Architecture* and

■ *compare 124–125* |

soon became something of an anthem for that loosely banded movement. Its importance here lies in its distinction between different theories of type according to different epistemes and its concise formulation of typology as an agent of regeneration in an era of dispirited functionalism.

Giulio Carlo Argan's 1962 essay "On the Typology of Architecture" revived interest in Quatremère de Quincy's idea of type, and Aldo Rossi's 1966 *L'architettura della città* strengthened its importance. But there was a need for a distinction between the modern use of types and the "first typology" of Quatremère and the Abbé Laugier whom he followed.[1] In 1967 Alan Colquhoun formulated the first theory of types to appear in English, in an epistemological argument that recognized the discursive categories of architecture and reintroduced the ideological dimension

| *see 332* ■

of design operations. Colquhoun's is fundamentally a critique of the pseudoscientific claims of architectural empiricists to arrive at a nonarbitrary form from purely functional determinants (which is related to what Vidler terms the second typology). During the design process, Colquhoun reminds us, in the inevitable absence of enough determinate information, certain formal choices must intervene, and in selecting and arranging certain conventionally constituted organizations of a building "the architect thus makes his voluntary decisions in the world of types, and these voluntary decisions explain his ideological position in architecture."[2] In a properly structuralist way, Colquhoun foregrounds the arbitrary, conventional, cultural nature of architectural codes, and the use of types in the design process comes to be seen as a kind of *catachresis*: not so much a misapprehension of an architectural organism's origins as the necessary and inevitable substitution and distortion of already known configurations to fill the gaps in an architectural "vocabulary" that can never be completely, and certainly not functionally, determined.

Vidler builds on Aldo Rossi's discussions of "autonomous" architecture, "analogous" architecture, and the city, as well as the emergent neorationalist design projects of the 1970s, and goes beyond Colquhoun's catachretic model to construct what might be called an interactive model of types. He seizes, first, on the conceptual open-endedness of types. By inviting the "reader" of a building to consider the primary subject (say, Rossi's Trieste City Hall project) in the light of associated implications characteristic of the commonplace conception of a secondary subject (say, a late-eighteenth-century prison), a type operates something like a literary metaphor. "The dialectic is clear as a fable: the society that understands the reference to prison will still have need of the reminder, while at the very point the image finally loses all meaning, the society will either have become entirely prison, or, perhaps, its opposite."

Vidler seizes, second, on the inductive open-endedness of types, revealed in the fact that, at its ultimate level, the interactive subject of a type is the city itself, considered as a whole, whose nature is induced from its architectural elements. What is most distinctive about the inductive open-endedness of types is that, from this "ontology of the city," an architecture may be constructed that *creates* the very typological analogies on which it depends, rather than merely picking out metaphorical similarities that existed antecedently. Rossi's Modena cemetery, for example, derives its poignancy from the constructed interaction of tomb, house, city, ❚ *see* 68–71 ❚ and cemetery. Within each of these primary subjects are insinuated—obliquely, ana-morphically—all the others, producing a kind of overprinting of types and a concep-tual pass through registers whose analogous moments did not exist before the architecture that conflated them.

Architecture in its very autonomy thereby enables the concep-tion of a world that may not yet have actually existed, but is nevertheless verifiable. Rossi's meditation on Canaletto's painting of Venice captures this paradoxical possi-bility of an analogous architecture:

In this view, the Palladian project for the Rialto bridge, the Basilica Palladiana, and the Palazzo Chiericati are brought together and described as if the painter rendered an urban context in perspective from his own observation. The three Palladian monuments, one of which is a project, are constructed as an analogous architecture, as well as the city. The geographic transposition of the monuments to the site of the Rialto project constitutes a city that we know which conforms to a place of purely architectural values.

The analogous Venice that was born there is real and necessary; we assist at a logical-formal operation, at a speculation on the monuments and on the disconcerting urban character in the history of art and in thought. A "collage" of Palladian architecture that conforms to a new city, and in the reunion, reconfirm themselves.[3]

In the paradoxical ability of architecture to produce an entire image and structure of subject-object relations in the city—to propose an under-standing and experience of an actual, concrete, historical life—within what is never-theless an irreducibly architectural modality, Vidler finds the critical role of the third typology.

Writing around the same time as Vidler, and similarly historiciz-ing contemporaneous events, Rafael Moneo generalized the importance of typology and its mediatory potential:

To understand the question of type is to understand the nature of the architectural object today. It is a question that cannot be avoided. The architectural object can no longer be considered as a single, isolated event because it is bounded by the world that surrounds it as well as by its history. It extends life to other objects by virtue of its specific architectural condition, thereby establishing a chain of related events in which it is possible to find common formal structures.[4]

Notes

1. For a history of eighteenth- and nineteenth-century typologies, see Anthony Vidler, "The Idea of Type: The Transformation of the Academic Ideal, 1750–1830," *Oppositions* 8 (Spring 1977).
2. Alan Colquhoun, "Typology and Design Method," *Arena* 83 (June 1967), p. 18. In this publication Colquhoun's formulation is pitted against Tomás Maldonado's design methodology.
3. Aldo Rossi, "L'arquitectura analoga," *2c. Construcción de la Ciudad* 2 (1975), p. 8.
4. Rafael Moneo, "On Typology," *Oppositions* 13 (Summer 1978), p. 44.

From the middle of the eighteenth century two dominant typologies have served to legitimize the production of architecture: The first returned architecture to its natural origins—a model of primitive shelter—seen not simply as historical explanation of the derivation of the orders but as a guiding principle, equivalent to that proposed by Newton for the physical universe. The second, emerging as a result of the Industrial Revolution, assimilated architecture to the world of machine production, finding the essential nature of a building to reside in the artificial world of engines. Laugier's primitive hut and Bentham's Panopticon stand at the beginning of the modern era as the paradigms of these two typologies.

Both these typologies were firm in their belief that rational science, and later technological production, embodied the most progressive forms of the age, and that the mission of architecture was to conform to and perhaps even master these forms as the agent of material progress.

With the current re-appraisal of the idea of progress, and with this the critique of the Modern Movement ideology of productivism, architects have turned to a vision of the primal past of architecture—its constructive and formal bases as evinced in the pre-industrial city. Once again the issue of typology is raised in architecture, not this time with a need to search outside the practice for legitimation in science or technology, but with a sense that within architecture itself resides a unique and particular mode of production and explanation. From Aldo Rossi's transformations of the formal structure and institutional types of eighteenth century urbanism, to the sketches of Leon Krier that recall the "primitive" types of shelter imagined by the eighteenth century philosophes, rapidly multiplying examples suggest the emergence of a new, third typology.

We might characterize the fundamental attribute of this third typology as an espousal, not of an abstract nature, not of a technological utopia, but rather of the traditional city as the locus of its concern. The city, that is, provides the material for classification, and the forms of its artifacts over time provide the basis for recomposition. This third typology, like the first two, is clearly based on reason, classification, and a sense of the public in architecture; unlike the first two, however, it proposes no panacea, no ultimate apotheosis of man in architecture, no positivistic eschatology.

I

The small rustic hut is the model upon which all the wonders of architecture have been conceived; in drawing nearer in practice to the simplicities of this first model essential faults are avoided and true perfection is attained. The pieces of wood raised vertically give us the idea of columns. The horizontal pieces that surmount them give us the idea of entablatures. Finally, the inclined pieces that form the roof give us the idea of pediments. This all the masters of the art have recognized.

M. A. LAUGIER, 1755

The first typology, which ultimately saw architecture as imitative of the fundamental order of Nature itself, allied the primitive rusticity of the hut to an ideal of perfect geometry, revealed by Newton as the guiding principle of physics. Thus, Laugier depicted the four trees, types of the first columns, standing in a perfect square: the branches laid across in the form of beams, perfectly horizontal, and the boughs bent over to form the roof as a triangle, the type of pediment. These elements of architecture, derived from the elements of nature, formed an unbreakable chain and were interrelated according to fixed principles: if the tree/column was joined in this way to the bower/hut, then the city itself, agglomeration of huts, was likewise susceptible to the principle of natural origin. Laugier spoke of the city—or rather the existing, unplanned and chaotic reality of Paris—as a forest. The forest/city was to be tamed, brought into rational order by means of the gardener's art; the ideal city of the late eighteenth century was thereby imaged on the garden; the type of the urbanist was Le Nôtre, who would cut and prune an unruly nature according to the geometrical line of its true underlying order.

The idea of the elements of architecture referring in some way to their natural origin was, of course, immediately extensible in the idea of each specific kind of building representing its "species" so to speak, in the same way as each member of the animal kingdom. At first the criteria applied to differentiate building types were bound up with recognition, with individual physiognomy, as in the classification systems of Buffon and Linnaeus. Thus, the external affect of the building was to announce clearly its general species, and its specific subspecies. Later this analogy was transformed by the functional and constitutional classification of the early nineteenth century (Cuvier), whereby the inner structure of beings, their constitutional form, was seen as the criterion for grouping them in types.

Following this analogy, those whose task it was to design the new types of public and private buildings emerging as needs in the early nineteenth century began to talk of the plan and sectional distribution in the same terms as the constitutional organization of species; axes and vertebrae became virtually synonymous. This reflected a basic shift in the metaphor of natural architecture, from a vegetal (tree/hut) to an animal analogy. This shift paralleled the rise of the new schools of medicine and the birth of clinical surgery.

Despite the overt disgust that Durand showed toward Laugier—laughing at the idea of doing without walls—it was Durand, professor at the Polytechnique, who brought together these twin streams of organic typology into a lexicon of architectural practice that enabled the architect, at least, to dispense with analogy altogether and concentrate on the business of construction. The medium of this fusion was the graph paper grid which assembled on the same level the basic elements of construction, according to the inductively derived rules of composition for the taxonomy of different building types, resulting in the endless combinations and permutations, monumental and utilitarian. In his *Recueil* he established that the natural history of architecture resides so to speak in its own history, a parallel development to real nature. In his *Lessons* he described how new types might be constructed on the same principles. When this awareness was applied in the next decades to the structural rationalism inherited from Laugier, the result was the organic theory of Gothic "skeletal" structure developed by Viollet-le-Duc. The operation of the romantics on classic theory was simply at one level to substitute the Cathedral for the Temple as the formal and later the social type of all architecture.

II

The French language has provided the useful definition, thanks to the double sense of the word type. A deformation of meaning has led to the equivalence in popular language: a man = a type; and from the point that the type becomes a man, we grasp the possibility of a considerable extension of the type. Because the man-type is a complex form of a unique physical type, to which can be applied a sufficient standardization. According to the same rules one will establish for this physical type an equipment of standard habitation: doors, windows, stairs, the heights of rooms, etc.

LE CORBUSIER, 1927

The second typology, which substituted for the classical trinity of commodity, firmness and delight a dialectic of means and ends joined by the criteria of economy, looked upon architecture as simply a matter of technique. The remarkable new machines subject to the laws of functional precision were thus paradigms of efficiency as they worked in the raw materials of production; architecture, once subjected to similar laws, might well work with similar effectiveness on its unruly contents—the users. The efficient machines of architecture might be sited in the countryside, very much like the early steam engines of Newcomen and Watt, or inserted in the fabric of the city, like the water pumps and later the factory furnaces. Centralized within their own operative realm, hermetically sealed by virtue of their autonomy as complete processes, these engines—the prisons, hospitals, poor houses—needed little in the way of accommodation save a clear space and a high wall. Their impact on the form of the city as a whole was at first minimal.

The second typology of modern architecture emerged toward the end of the nineteenth century, after the takeoff of the Second Industrial Revolution; it grew out of the need to confront the question of mass-production, and more particularly the mass-production of machines by machines. The effect of this transformation in production was to give the illusion of another nature, the nature of the machine and its artificially reproduced world.

In this second typology, architecture was now equivalent to the range of mass-production objects, subject themselves to a quasi-Darwinian law of the selection of the fittest. The pyramid of production from the smallest tool to the most complex machine was now seen as analogous to the link between the column, the house and the city. Various attempts were made to blend the old typology with the new in order to provide a more satisfactory answer to the question of specifically architectonic form: the primary geometries of the Newtonian generation were now adduced for their evident qualities of economy, modernity and purity. They were, it was thought, appropriate for machine tooling.

Equally, theoreticians with a classical bias, like Hermann Muthesius, stressed the equivalence of ancient types—the temple—and the new ones—the object of manufacture—in order to stabilize, or "culturalize," the new machine world. A latent neoclassicism suffused the theories of typology at the beginning of the contemporary epoch, born of the need to justify the new in the face of the old. The classical world once again acted as a "primal past" wherein the utopia of the present might find its nostalgic roots.

Not until the aftermath of the First World War was this thrown off, at least in the most advanced theories—articulated with more and more directness by Le Corbusier and Walter Gropius. A vision of Taylorized production, of a world ruled by the iron law of Ford supplanted the spuriously golden dream of neoclassicism. Buildings were to be no more and no less than machines themselves, serving and molding the needs of man according to economic criteria. The image of the city at this point changed radically: the forest/park of Laugier was made triumphant in the hygienist utopia of a city completely absorbed by its greenery. The natural analogy of the Enlightenment, originally brought forward to control the messy reality of the city, was now extended to refer to the control of entire nature. In the redeeming park, the silent building-machines of the new garden of production virtually disappeared behind a sea of verdure. Architecture, in this final apotheosis of mechanical progress, was consumed by the very process it sought to control for its own ends. With it, the city, as artifact and polis, disappeared as well.

In the first two typologies of modern architecture we can identify a common base, resting on the need to legitimize architecture as a "natural" phenomenon and a development of the natural analogy that corresponded very directly to the development of production itself. Both typologies were in some way bound up with the attempts of architecture to endow itself with value by means of an appeal to natural science or production, and instrumental power by means of an assimilation of the forms of these two complementary domains to itself. The "utopia" of architecture as "project" might be progressive in its ends, or nostalgic in its dreams, but at heart it was founded on this premise: that the shape of environment might, like nature herself, affect and hereby control the individual and collective relations of men.

III

In the first two typologies, architecture, made by man, was being compared and legitimized by another "nature" outside itself. In the third typology, as exemplified in the work of the new Rationalists, however, there is no such attempt at validation. Columns, houses, and urban spaces, while linked in an unbreakable chain of continuity, refer only to their own nature as architectural elements, and their geometries are neither naturalistic nor technical but essentially architectural. It is clear that the nature referred to in these recent designs is no more nor less than the nature of the city itself, emptied of specific social content from any particular time and allowed to speak simply of its own formal condition.

This concept of the city as the site of a new typology is evidently born of a desire to stress the continuity of form and history against the fragmentation produced by the elemental, institutional, and mechanistic typologies of the recent past. The city is considered as a whole, its past and present revealed in its physical structure. It is in itself and of itself a new typology. This typology is not built up out of separate elements, nor assembled out of objects classified according to use, social ideology, or technical characteristics: it stands complete and ready to be decomposed into fragments. These fragments do not reinvent institutional type-forms nor repeat past typological forms: they are selected and reassembled according to criteria derived from three levels of meaning—the first, inherited from the ascribed means of the past existence of the forms; the second, derived from the specific fragment and its boundaries, and often crossing between previous types; the third, proposed by a recomposition of these fragments in a new context.

Such an "ontology of the city" is, in the face of the modernist utopia, indeed radical. It denies all the social utopian and progressively positivist definitions of architecture for the last two hundred years. No longer is architecture a realm that has to relate to a hypothesized "society" in order to be conceived and understood; no longer does "architecture write history" in the sense of particularizing a specific social condition in a specific time or place. The need to speak of nature of function, of social mores—of anything, that is, beyond the nature of architectural form itself—is removed. At this point, as Victor Hugo realized so presciently in the 1830s, communication through the printed work, and lately through the mass media, has apparently released architecture from the role of "social book" into its own autonomous and specialized domain.

This does not, of course, necessarily mean that architecture in this sense no longer performs any function, no longer satisfies any need beyond the whim of an "art for art's sake" designer, but simply that the principal conditions for the invention of objects and environments do not necessarily have to include a unitary statement of fit between form and use. Here it is that the adoption of the city as the site for the identification of the architectural typology has been seen as crucial. In the accumulated experience of the city, its public spaces and institutional forms, a typology can be understood that defies a one-to-one reading of function, but which at the same time ensures a relation at another level to a continuing tradition of city life. The distinguishing characteristic of the new ontology beyond its specifically formal aspect is that the city polis, as opposed to the single column, the hut-house, or

Aldo Rossi, Regional Administration Building, Trieste, 1974

the useful machine, is and always has been political in its essence. The fragmentation and recomposition of its spatial and institutional forms thereby can never be separated from their received and newly constituted political implications.

When typical forms are selected from the past of a city, they do not come, however dismembered, deprived of their original political and social meaning. The original sense of the form, the layers of accrued implication deposited by time and human experience cannot be lightly brushed away, and certainly it is not the intention of the new Rationalists to disinfect their types in this way. Rather, the carried meanings of these types may be used to provide a key to their newly invested meanings. The technique or rather the fundamental compositional method suggested by the Rationalists is the transformation of selected types—partial or whole—into entirely new entities that draw their communicative power and potential criteria from the understanding of this transformation. The City Hall project for Trieste by Aldo Rossi, for example, has been rightly understood to refer, among other evocations in its complex form, to the image of a late eighteenth century prison. In the period of the first formalization of this type, as Piranesi demonstrated, it was possible to see in prison a powerfully comprehensive image of the dilemma of society itself, poised between a disintegrating religious faith and a materialist reason. Now, Rossi, in ascribing to the city hall (itself a recognizable type in the nineteenth century) the affect of prison, attains a new level of signification, which evidently is a reference to the ambiguous condition of civic government. In the formulation, the two types are not merged: indeed, city hall has been replaced by open arcade standing in contradiction on prison. The dialectic is clear as a fable: the society that understands the reference to prison will still have need of the reminder, while at the very point that the image finally loses all meaning, the society will either have become entirely prison, or, perhaps, its opposite. The metaphoric opposition deployed in this example can be traced in many of Rossi's schemes and in the work of the Rationalists as a whole, not only in institutional form but also in the spaces of the city.

This new typology is explicitly critical of the Modern Movement; it utilizes the clarity of the eighteenth century city to rebuke the fragmentation, decentralization, and formal disintegration introduced into contemporary urban life by the zoning techniques and technological advances of the twenties. While the Modern Movement found its Hell in the closed, cramped, and insalubrious quarters of the old industrial cities, and its Eden in the uninterrupted sea of sunlit space filled with greenery—a city became a garden—the new typology as a critique of modern urbanism raises the continuous fabric, the clear distinction between public and private marked by the walls of street and square, to the level of principle. Its nightmare is the isolated building set in an undifferentiated park. The heroes of this new typology are therefore not among the nostalgic, anti-city utopians of the nineteenth century nor even among the critics of industrial and technical progress of the twentieth, but rather among those who, as the professional servants of urban life, have directed their design skills to solving the questions of avenue, arcade, street and square, park and house, institution and equipment in a continuous typology of elements that together coheres with past fabric and present intervention to make one comprehensible experience of the city. For this typology, there is no clear set of rules for the transformations and their objects, nor any polemically defined set of historical precedents. Nor, perhaps, should there be; the continued vitality of this architectural practice rests in its essential engagement with the precise demands of the present and not in any holistic mythicization of the past. It refuses any "nostalgia" in its evocations of history, except to give its restorations sharper focus; it refuses all unitary descriptions of the social meaning of form, recognizing the specious quality of any single ascription of social order to an architectural order; it finally refuses all eclecticism, resolutely filtering its "quotations" through the lens of a modernist aesthetic. In this sense, it is an entirely modern movement, and one that places its faith in the essentially public nature of all architecture, as against the increasingly private and narcissistic visions of the last decade. In this it is distinguished from those latter-day romanticisms that have also pretended to the throne of post-modernism—"town-scape," "strip-city" and "collage-city"—that in reality proposed no more than the endless reduplication of the flowers of bourgeois high culture under the guise of the painterly or the populist. In the work of the new Rationalists, the city and its typology are reasserted as the only possible bases for the restoration of a critical role to public architecture otherwise assassinated by the apparently endless cycle of production and consumption.

Georges Teyssot   **"Heterotopias and the History of Spaces"** From Georges Teyssot et al., *Il*

dispositivo Foucault (Venice: Libreria Editrice, 1977); revised in *A + U* 121

(October 1980), trans. David Stewart

"Think of the ship," Michel Foucault asks of us. "It is a floating part of space, a place-less place, that lives by itself, closed in on itself and at the same time poised in the infinite ocean, and yet, from port to port, tack by tack, from brothel to brothel, it goes as far as the colonies, looking for the most precious things hidden in their gardens. Then you will understand why it has been . . . the greatest reserve of imagination for our civilization from the sixteenth century down to the present day. The ship is the heterotopia *par excellence*. In civilizations where it is lacking, dreams dry up, adventure is replaced by espionage, and privateers by the police."[1]

In "Of Other Spaces: Utopias and Heterotopias," Foucault lists six characteristics of heterotopias. (1) Though they assume a wide variety of forms, heterotopias are a constant feature of all cultures. (2) Over the course of its history, a society may take an existing heterotopia and make it function in a different way. (3) The heterotopia has the power of juxtaposing in a single real place different spaces and locations that are incompatible with each other. (4) Heterotopias are linked to time, entering fully into function when traditional time is breached (as in, for example, the cemetery, where the loss of life and the perception of eternity coincide). (5) One does not usually enter a heterotopia by one's own will (think of the prison), and, as a visitor by force or permission, one must perform certain gestures only to be still excluded from its true heart. (6) Heterotopias perform the contradictory functions of revealing the illusory quality of all space and compensating for that illusion with a perfect, meticulous, and well-arranged real space.

A seminar at the Istituto Universitario di Architettura di Venezia was the occasion for architecture theory to criticize Foucault's fundamental concept of heterotopia along with that of panopticism, Jeremy Bentham's architectural device and, for Foucault, the principle of a system of spatial control.[2] In the present paper, his contribution to that seminar, Georges Teyssot elaborates Foucault's theory of heterotopia, providing examples of its occurrence in the history of architecture. Further, he reiterates the important Foucauldian point that architectural "discourse" — discourse understood as the organization and manipulation of knowledge — must be

compare Agrest
200–202,
206–208

studied in its own irreducible terms *and* in its relation to other discourses; or, in other words, that architecture has an autonomy, an "epistemic" status of its own — its own canons of truth, its own designations of relevance, propriety, normalcy, and so forth — but must nevertheless be mediated by other discursive formations of its context. "Architectural discourse is not enough in itself to explain the appearance of specific forms, the derivation of typologies and the whole concatenation of a spatial genealogy. And the reason for this is that the discourse only makes itself felt within a *context* that is provided by a network of interactions combining various levels of action and transformation."

The filled, activated structure or contextual field of a given epoch is an episteme; the filling is discourse. In order to think discursive events in all their immediacy, different events must be correlated; hence Teyssot's point that discursivity emerges as an intertextual relationship. But according to Foucault, discourse tends to gradually efface itself, to dissemble and appear merely as writing — or as

Teyssot would say, as discourse *about* architecture—thus masking the systematic rules of its formation and its concrete affiliations with knowledge-as-power. It is important to remember that Foucault's archaeological analyses of discursive systems are premised on the Marxian thesis that every society develops elaborate procedures to select, organize, and control the production of discourse in such a way as to avert its powerful materiality.

Teyssot links the historical formation of heterotopias in architecture to the irruption of the particular discourse of environment (understood as a *milieu*)—a habitat that impinges on its inhabitants. Habitat, and its correlated concerns of hygiene, behavioral patterns, and functional distributions, are themselves part of an episteme whose "beginning" has, as its minimum preconditions, first, that spatial relations are perceived in topological and experiential terms rather than in terms of formal resemblance or homologies of order and proportion, and second, that interactions between habitat and inhabitant are defined in mechanical terms. It was in his meditations on this episteme, and the ways in which one discourse repeats another in a different mode, that Foucault made his descriptions of institutions and power in terms of architecture, revealing the administrative, psychological, and moral economy of architecture's panoptic places.[3]

compare Foucault (430 ff)

Notes

1. Michel Foucault, "Des espaces autres," in *Architecture Mouvement Continuité* 5 (October 1984); English version in *Lotus International* 48/49 (1985/86), trans. Jay Miskowiec; reprinted in Joan Ockman, *Architecture Culture 1943–1968* (New York: Columbia Books of Architecture and Rizzoli, 1992).
2. The main participants were Teyssot, Massimo Cacciari, Franco Rella, and Manfredo Tafuri.
3. See Michel Foucault, *Discipline and Punish: Birth of the Prison*, trans. Alan Sheridan (New York: Pantheon, 1977); *Power/Knowledge: Selected Interviews and Other Writings 1972–1977*, ed. Colin Gordon (New York: Pantheon, 1980), especially "The Eye of Power" and "Questions on Geography"; and "Space, Knowledge, and Power," interview with Paul Rabinow, trans. Christian Hubert, *Skyline,* March 1982, reprinted in this anthology.

> The architecture that intervenes between us and the exercise of power is our real adversary. . . .
>
> But who erects this obstacle, who creates this distance? No one does. . . .
>
> The obstacle is an ambiguous one, for it is a matter of fashioning a world we cannot escape from as much as one we may not enter.
>
> These two self-opposing impossibilities are identical in fact. . . .
>
> What matters is the separation. . . .
>
> This space will, therefore, always remain sealed off yet at the same time perilously exposed. . . .
>
> Its edifices, like strange organisms, are threateningly proliferous.
>
> **Jean Starobinski**, "The Illusion of Architecture"

At the beginning of *The Order of Things*[1] Michel Foucault refers to a "certain Chinese encyclopedia" quoted by J. L. Borges, in which the animals of the world are catalogued. "Animals," he says, "are divided into: (a) belonging to the Emperor, (b) embalmed, (c) tame, (d) suckling pigs, (e) sirens, (f) fabulous, (g) stray dogs, (h) included in the present classification, (i) frenzied, (j) innumerable, (k) drawn with a very fine camelhair brush, (l) *et cetera*, (m) having just broken the water pitcher, (n) that from a long way off look like flies."[2]

This list, which is bound to elicit a smile at its incongruity and heteroclite composition, gives Foucault the chance to enter into a discussion of the ways of organizing "things" within a given historical period; even the incongruity of an alphabetical series, as revealed when a dictionary or an encyclopedia is read as if it were a novel, is more logical than the disjointedness to be found here, where the structure no longer defines a common locus of classification. After all, an encyclopedia is heterogeneous while the example from Borges may be said to be *heterotopic*.

Here, we find ourselves face to face with a true and proper "heterotopia." Thus, one of the first definitions assigned to this word—as a "literary" term—is given by Foucault as follows:

Utopias afford consolation: although they have no real locality there is nevertheless a fantastic, untroubled region in which they are able to unfold; they open up cities with vast avenues, superbly planted gardens, countries where life is easy, even though the road to them is chimerical. *Heterotopias* are disturbing, probably because they secretly undermine language, because they make it impossible to name this *and* that, because they shatter or tangle common names, because they destroy "syntax" in advance, and not only the syntax with which we construct sentences but also that less apparent syntax which causes words and things (next to and also opposite one another) to "hold together." This is why utopias permit fables and discourse: they run with the very grain of language and are part of the fundamental dimension of the *fabula*; heterotopias (such as those to be found so often in Borges) desiccate speech, stop words in their tracks, contest the very possibility or grammar at its source; they dissolve our myths and sterilize the lyricism of our sentences.[3]

In addition to this definition of heterotopia in the epistemological domain that consists of those systems or taxonomies that structure thought at a given moment in history, Foucault has also formulated a spatial notion of heterotopia applicable to the classification of real *places*. In order to illustrate the meaning that heterotopia, in this second sense, might assume within a city we shall take an example. Let us try to explain the matrix of institutions established with respect to health measures prior to the Revolution and still existing in the period 1740–1750 in the Norman city of Caen in France, as studied by J.-C. Perrot. The pattern of hospitals and related facilities in that city may be represented as a "grid" of eight spaces, each of which corresponds to a separate institution, as summarized in the following diagram:

1	2	3	4
5	6	7	8

The first box corresponds to an institution known as *Bon Sauveur* where prisoners of the nobility or the king were detained. Box 2 is the Châtimoine Tower, for madmen, prisoners and detainees confined by royal warrant. Box 3 contains the important *Hôpital Général*,[4] whose inmates included indigent children of legitimate family between the ages of two and nine, invalids, old people, beggars, prostitutes, syphilitics, those afflicted with mental diseases, the feeble, imbeciles, delirious persons, epileptics, and others. (These "taxonomies" of confinement—or exclusion—are for us today as absurd as those heterotopias invented by Borges.)

To continue, in Box 4 we find the *petits renfermés*, namely foundlings above the age of nine, the indigent, bastards, and so forth; in Box 5 the so-called *Baillage* or city gaol, which held the condemned and accused in general. Box 6 is the *Charité*, a convent to which persons might be committed for prostitution and other crimes by their own families. In 7, a venerable and ancient institution, the *Hôtel-Dieu*, that admitted the ill, whether residing in the town or elsewhere, as well as soldiers, foundlings, and so on. Finally, the eighth space represents an institution that was an extension of Box 4 and thus accommodated the *petits renfermés*. In short, the "grid" allows for transition from a structure of total confinement to one of semi-internment but clearly does not correspond to either the modern hospital or prison systems. It is evident, therefore, that between the combined Poor Law Administration and Security measures of the eighteenth century and the modern welfare state there exists a hiatus. Such discontinuities within the general "order of things" have always received special emphasis in the work of Foucault.

Discontinuity, it has been said, for this is the apposite term: a smooth evolutionary history of hospitals, from a mythical inception, proceeding by way of examples confirming a progressive linear development, to the modern hospital in its definitive state—even if it be admitted that certain improvements were yet to be made—could scarcely be written. The above examples of the organization of welfare and public assistance at Caen in the eighteenth century will serve to illustrate the meaning assumed by the word *heterotopia* when applied to a real historical situation at a given time and place. It is in this way that Foucault has been able to speak of "heterotopia" in a topological rather than a literary sense. There exist, he tells us, "real and effective spaces which are outlined in the very institution of society, but which constitute a sort of counterarrangement, of effectively realized utopia, in which all the real arrangements, all the other real arrangements that can be found within society, are at one and the same time represented, challenged, and overturned: a sort of place that lies outside all places and yet is actually localizable. In contrast to the utopias, these places which are absolutely *other* with respect to all the arrangements that they reflect and of which they speak might be described as heterotopias."[5] In this manner the term acquires a dual significance—spatial as well as temporal. It signifies a "discontinuity" in time, an interruption of sorts, a sudden rupture within the order of "knowing" and—at the same time—a detached heterogeneous place disposed against the background of the spatial continuum.

A clear idea of this phenomenon of a "spatially discontinuous ground" is essential for an understanding of the structure of spaces fixed by modern society; but before proceeding with our analysis, let us provide a summary indication of the notion of "historical discontinuity," as it appears at the center of Foucault's argument.

It is evident from his book *The Order of Things: An Archaeology of the Human Sciences* that its implicit and explicit method of historical enquiry, Foucault's *archaeology*, defines history as a manifestation of various systems of discontinuity. He introduces the concept of *episteme*, or epistemological field within the "space" of knowledge, as a totality endowing thought with a particular Order during a given historical period. The *episteme* is, then, a conceptual structure or distributional concept that does not contain the Order itself, as such: Within a specified culture and at a given historical period, there is only one *episteme* capable of defining the conditions of possibility of any knowledge, whether manifest as theory or latent as practice. The term episteme is above all connected with what Foucault calls the Classical Age[6] (the middle of the seventeenth century through the end of the eighteenth) by opposition to the Renaissance, which preceded it, and the modern age from which we are about to "emerge." In attempting to reconstruct the classical episteme, Foucault's analysis turns on three cognitive axes: namely "speaking (Language)," "classifying (Life)," and "exchanging (Labor)," which in the modern age comprises philology or linguistics, biology, and economics but in the Classical Age were known respectively as "general grammar," "natural history," and "analysis of wealth."

The 400 pages of *The Order of Things* sets forth the problem of the discontinuity, or disjunctions, between one particular system of ordering and the next. Foucault demonstrates that there can be no transition (in the sense of "evolution" or "progress") between, for example, the natural history of Buffon or Linnaeus—still related, as it was, to the task of a *mathesis universalis*, as a science of universal order—and modern biology (from Cuvier onward) where the concepts "history," classification, structure, and "table" are replaced by anatomy, organism, and series. Science, as a cognitive practice, encounters epistemological "obstacles" at certain moments, the resolution of which is achieved through "ruptures" that constitute *events*. It was the anti-evolutionary and anti-positivist thinking of Gaston Bachelard which introduced these notions of discontinuity to the history of science in France. For Bachelard and for his successor Georges Canguilhem, every science generates, at each moment of its history, its own truth criteria. While Bachelard's epistemology is historical, Canguilhem's history of science is epistemological: to set an analysis of the object and the "ruptures" in cognitive organization against the subject and its *continuity* is—for Foucault—"to achieve a form of historical analysis able to take into account the subject's position in the network of history." The "truth" of a science occasions an "irruption," and it is the discovery of a number of such occurrences in simultaneous fashion that allows Foucault to define the episteme. Nevertheless, the fact, as Canguilhem notes, that not *all* the sciences are taken into account by Foucault poses, paradoxically, a doubt with respect to the epistemological existence of the "Classical episteme": the Foucauldian edifice gives no place to the relative *continuity* of physics from, for example, Newton to Maxwell. It is perhaps for this very reason that the term episteme is relatively little used in his subsequent writings. However, the aim and scope of Foucault's work is not so much to construct a universal system of knowledge as to write an archaeology of the science of Man, thereby forestalling any attempt to discover in the age of the late Renaissance or the Enlightenment the origins of contemporary social science.

In the foregoing sense, Foucault may be viewed as situating his endeavors within the radical criticism of the notion of *origins*, accomplished by Nietzsche in his introduction to the *Genealogy of Morals* (1887), or *The Wanderer and His Shadow* (1880).[7] Genealogy, or the genealogical approach, is—for Foucault—"a form of history that takes into account various areas of knowledge, fields of discourse, categories of objects, and so forth, without requiring reference to any subject whatsoever transcending the field of actual occurrences concealing the emptiness of his identity throughout the course of history." He ignores, therefore, the problem of *origins* in order to concentrate upon the beginnings of a particular science or field of knowledge—a given concept.[8] In the same sense, but more concretely, the "beginnings of technology" or the "beginnings" of mathematics as applied to social and political questions have been analyzed. In such "histories" it becomes a question of the modes of appearance of particular "concepts." Being able to formulate a "concept" (within a given science) means—for Canguilhem—being able to define a *problem*: the problem must be capable of being formulated, its very appearance heralded by the possibility of its formulation.

"Concepts" are not words. A concept may be stated in different ways by using different words. The opposition of two concepts frequently embodies the configuration of knowledge at a given moment: as in the case of concepts related to the organism and the machine. In the biological domain, at the beginning of the nineteenth century, the supporters of the first fought in favor of the (organic) *cell* theory against apologists of the (mechanical) *tissue* theory supported, for example, by Bichat. Thus arose the opposition between *normal* and *pathological* which was to institute a new notion of *normalcy* with respect to vital processes.

Another pair of terms of great significance is given in the binomial contrast between Life and Medium. From where does the concept of medium (*milieu* in French) "appear"? Out of the mechanically conceived notion of space. Newton required the notion of an *ether* in answer to the problem posed by the definition of a given space in which forces acted upon one another (Descartes, by way of parenthesis, was unable to conceive of the action of force without contact between two bodies). The *Encyclopedia* affirms, in a still purely mechanical sense, that water is a medium for the fish who move about in it. According to the numerous translations of the Hippocratic treatise *Airs, Waters, and Places*, all known fluids (air, water, light) assume this characteristic of substances through which effects may be transmitted.

Auguste Comte, the founder of positivism, placed himself within this mechanistic tradition when he established the dialectic between *life* and *medium*, which he conceived in the form of a mathematical problem. "In a particular medium given an organ, find its function and vice versa," thereby, and at the same time, formulating the biological relationship of an organism with its surroundings.

The formative value of these "concepts" lies not only within a given science; the concept of medium once arrived at, the modern notion of *habitat* (in the biological, geographical and ecological senses) was able to develop: thus was born the modern concern for habitat as part of the human environment. A "discourse" comprehending the dwelling, housing in general, health measures and density. Moreover, none of these was a perennial concern within the space of knowledge, rather all are instruments of cognition that have their "beginnings" around 1830. And that is the very moment at which "population" and its "growth" in cities (potential storehouses of manpower) became privileged fields of investigation.

These instruments may assume an analogical value (in historical terms) from the moment they enter into circulation as concepts. Often enough it is this metaphorical transformation that reveals the effective strength of a particular "discursive practice." Let us recall the importance of "concepts," such as that of "function," which acquires a new meaning about 1750, as used by Physiocrats, such as Quesnay or Baudeau; or by Turgot, the French minister who, for the first time (about 1770), used the word "functionary" in its present sense of "civil servant." Later on, Bichat anchored this concept within biology when he pronounced in 1800: "Life is the ensemble of functions that resist death." The moment would not be long in coming when the "function" of the city and, later, the "urban nucleus," urban "tissue" and the "evolutions" and "organic growth" of cities were to be spoken of, all precisely in their capacity to evoke analogy.

It is now time to ask ourselves whether there is any sense in "applying" this method of enquiry to architecture. In what way can architecture be said to depend upon the episteme that characterizes a particular period? What are the "discursive practices" of architecture? Is the architectural "discourse" to be understood as *about* architecture in general or as an "architectural discourse" *proper*, that is to say the *logos* constituted by the architectural space as disposed and constructed.

Three distinct approaches can be differentiated:

First. Architecture constitutes a practice ("discursive" as well as social, "technical" and so on). This aspect is revealed at the "compositional" level (that is, design) which consists in: the manipulation of behavioral patterns (*habitus*) or the organization of a locus of productive facilities (program, the spatial transcription of an organigram . . .) or the distribution of activities (flow and so on . . .) or the designation of forms (either as concerns a single building or architectural complex, or more generally in terms of a typology . . .).

Second. Architecture is, in itself, a form of material production that includes drawing plans and making models: it is here in the process of representation that an epistemological analysis might be based.

Third. Lest it be forgotten, architecture belongs to a sector of economic activity (the construction industry in combination with the field of speculation) that merits study for its own sake.

A further difficulty of a methodological sort is that the content to be analyzed is twofold: as raw material, there is on the one hand a written discourse (treatises and briefs) about architecture in general, some particular building or a certain program. On the other, we are first confronted by the design in the form of a representational apparatus and, after that, by the work itself in all the opacity of its forms, in short its material reality.

If desired, architecture may be considered as a "text," but (owing to the multiple nature of the practices with which it is connected) the knowledge it comprises is not reducible to a *general* epistemology of the field. Still—having made clear the limits of such an enquiry—it is possible to individuate certain instruments (the "concepts"), certain "discursive practices" having figured at a given moment in the architectural discourse proper, or, more aptly, in the discourse about architecture (an example of this second type of discursive practice would be the opposition between "*regular*" and "*irregular*" so important for the entire eighteenth century).

The discourse *about* architecture, therefore, provides material for a so-called "reading." The analysis of discourse, of the logic peculiar to it, should allow us to individuate conceptual instruments and "discursive practices" having served to structure the design process at a certain moment. But the *text* must not be regarded merely as a collection of statements to be analyzed in terms of grammar or syntax. On the contrary, its fundamental aspect as "discourse" is logical and semantic. The purpose of the analysis is to reveal the universe to which the discourse refers. In this sense, the text has been defined as a "translinguistic" apparatus; it is related to other texts, both anterior to and synchronic with itself. The text "produces" and embodies this productivity as a form of production and a technique. It functions within a given historical space that is itself a space of texts (discursive practices, hence signifying, hence semiotic). The productivity of the text consists in its "intertextuality," offering "a point of intersection for what has been said in other texts."[9]

In a history of "discursive practices" in architecture, there can be no theories to confute: truth and falsity have equal worth as indicators within discourse. "Within its own limits, every discipline recognizes true and false propositions," says Foucault in the "Discourse on Language," "but it repulses a whole teratology of learning. The exterior of a science is both more, and less, populated than one might think. . . . Perhaps there are no errors in the strict sense of the term, for error can only emerge and be identified within a well-defined process."[10]

However, our particular concern is that the analysis of this architectural discourse is not enough in itself to explain the appearance of specific forms, the derivation of typologies and the whole concatenation of a spatial genealogy. And the reason for this is that the discourse only makes itself felt within a *context* that is provided by a network of interactions combining various levels of action and transformation.

Other difficulties arise, therefore, when this *context*, which is that of the space of the city and the countryside, is itself subjected to analysis. The discontinuity between city and country (including both historical and geographical aspects) has been dealt with—following the extremely clear notes on the subject compiled by Karl Marx (*Grundrisse* II, 181)[11]—by Max Weber, for example, in *The City*.[12] There, it is shown how the city grew out of the confines of feudal jurisdiction, where property could only be transmitted by inheritance; how it later became the object of special statutes (take the case of borough franchises) under which the notion of economic regions developed, the same notion that was to result in the phenomenon of the conurbation; and so forth. But "discontinuity" is to be found equally within the city: and here we are not speaking *only* of the fragmentation resulting from speculation; in fact, we know relatively little about the urban dwelling in the seventeenth and eighteenth centuries, at the moment when neighborhoods, tenements, and individual families first became the object of improvement programs concerning health measures.

The work of demographers and historians—such as Philippe Ariès[13] and Louis Chevaliers[14]—and of Foucault himself, demonstrate that there is no linearity as concerns the history of *habitat*. When it became a question of piecing together a historical morphology of the city by devising an "evolution" of residential "typologies," deductions had to be made *a posteriori*, based on nineteenth-century reconstructional diagrams as well as civil archives, including tax and assessment records, that at best provided an account of housing development based on a study of the subdivision of building plots and the functions of rooms. (However, Ariès, Perrot, et al. qualify such functional distinctions as problematic before about 1820.) Moreover, Boudon reminds us that until the end of the seventeenth century "documents concerning residential buildings in the district of Les Halles are almost exclusively *hand-written*."[15] While this is scarcely astonishing, it does suggest the extent to which copying out, or redrawing and interpreting such materials is the practical equivalent of a rewriting of history.

While such a procedure is fully justified in the field of historical conservation studies, it can scarcely be approved of as a legitimate method of historical enquiry. Thus, discontinuity in the history of housing, echoing discontinuity in the city "appeared with respect to its main spatial variables as (yet another) object of the introduction of health measures." One such variable was *habitat* (dangerously promiscuous, thoroughly undifferentiated); another was the street ("where the most disreputable professions are exercised" in indecent confusion between public and private spaces); others included certain so-called "designated areas" within the city (think of those treatises, scientific or otherwise, concerning hospitals, abattoirs, cemeteries, sewers, and public water facilities . . .). In accepting the axis of investigation opened up by Foucault, the problem is not to fall prey to a mythical notion of *habitat*—primitive or "natural" as the case may be (even though one is well aware of the small degree to which the classical encoding of architecture should be regarded as "natural" in contrast to being merely "undifferentiated")—as opposed to a somehow definitively modern conception of *habitat* as "objective" or "functional."

Yet, there is a more substantial criticism to be leveled against the "archaeology" of the vast movement to contain the pathogenesis of the city, as sketched by Foucault. He delineates a sort of biopolitics, or "nosopolitics," we might say, which "would isolate within the urban configuration areas to 'sanitize' urgently," to be "insularized" from the continuum of the urban "tissue." Having accompanied Foucault thus far, a number of unsolved issues await resolution. It remains for us to reconstruct the ways in which this supposed "insularization" was actually carried out at the level of existing social relationships. Briefly and in the most schematic fashion: the replanning of the city and the development of urban services in the nineteenth century followed a course that can scarcely be taken for granted by present-day research. Foucault has outlined the general "strategy" of this movement, but often—especially in his most recent works—he fails to individuate the actual techniques of *realization*. In the particular case under review, that of the "insularization" of the city, it needs to be stressed that policy was implemented according to historically defined procedures: a *program* was set forth (with its "*laws*" and "*statutes*"); a project was drawn up based on a preestablished architectural *type* for the required institution; finally, the project had to pass institutional and administrative scrutiny (in the form of a commission or assembly) where it was modified in actual confrontation with the body politic. Each program was "confronted" by varied and opposed vested interests with their diverse *modes* of expression (an elected council, a petition circulated by a pressure group, and so on; in brief, all the modes of political utterance and conflict). Each program, therefore, took shape (*architecturally* speaking, as well) and had to conform in accordance with a complex relationship of political and professional interventions that made possible its effective realization. This field of intervention (both theoretical and actual) embodies all the political and professional "practices," as well as the institutional processes, codified to a greater or lesser extent, that every design had to submit to before it could be realized. These "practices" went to make up a "democratic" strategy, laid down the technique of realization and established the "rules of the game" by which modern spaces have been structured.

This is a history that remains largely to be written, the importance of which is suggested in an observation made by Foucault himself: "history as it is practiced today does not withdraw from events; on the contrary, it seeks only to broaden their scope. . . . The significant aspect of this is that there can be no taking account of events without a definition of the set to which each belongs." Foucault's writings can, at the very least, serve to inspire fellow historians with a "general fear of anachronism" (Canguilhem). Moreover, the intensification of rigor which should result would not be in vain.

Notes

1. English title of *Les mots et les choses* as suggested by Foucault. This work was translated from the French by Alan Sheridan, who is the English translator of most of Foucault's works.
2. Michel Foucault, *The Order of Things: An Archaeology of the Human Sciences*, trans. Alan Sheridan (New York: Pantheon, 1971), preface, p. xv.
3. Ibid., p. xviii.
4. 1656 was the date of the royal decree that founded the Hôpital Général in Paris, 1676 for the rest of France. "From the very start," writes Foucault, "one thing is clear: the Hôpital Général is not a medical establishment. It is rather a sort of semijudicial structure, an administrative entity. . . . The Hôpital Général is a strange power that the King establishes between the police and the courts, at the limits of the law: a third order of repression." *Histoire de la folie* (Paris: Librairie Plon, 1961), from the translation of the abridged edition by Richard Howard: *Madness and Civilization: A History of Insanity in the Age of Reason* (New York: Pantheon, 1965), p. 40.
5. Michel Foucault, "Des espaces autres," *Architecture Mouvement Continuité* 5 (October 1984); English version in *Lotus International* 48/49 (1985/86), p. 3.
6. This term follows a more or less established usage in French. In addition to the literal translation here, "Age of Reason" and "Age of Humanism" are also found in translations and commentary.
7. In the original, reference is made to paragraph 3 of this work.
8. In short, the relatively recent concept of man himself articulated upon the "already begun of labor, life and language."
9. For the ideas in this paragraph, the reader is referred to Julia Kristeva, *Semeiotiké* (Paris: Seuil, 1969).
10. English translation by Rupert Swyer from "L'ordre du discours," in Michel Foucault, *The Archaeology of Knowledge* (New York: Harper and Row, 1976), appendix, p. 223.
11. Karl Marx, *Grundrisse: Foundations of the Critique of Political Economy*, trans. Martin Nicolaus (New York: Vintage, 1973).
12. Max Weber, *The City*, trans. and ed. Don Martindale and Gertrud Neuwirth (New York: Free Press, 1966).
13. For example Philippe Ariès, *Centuries of Childhood: A Social History of Family Life*, trans. Robert Baldick (New York: Vintage, 1962).
14. Chevalier is considered by T. H. Hollingsworth to be the "true father . . . of parish register studies" in English; see also Peter Laslett, *The World We Have Lost* (London: Methuen, 1965).
15. *Annals Economies-Sociétés-Civilisations*, no. 4 (1975), p. 816.

Charles A. Jencks   **"Post-Modern Architecture"** From *The Language of Post-Modern Architecture*

(London: Academy Editions, 1977; New York: Rizzoli, 1977)

Architecture theory owes the concept and category of postmodern to Charles Jencks. Though the theoretical "inhibitions" of modern architecture against past forms and the actual plurality of its modes had already been developed by Paolo Portoghesi, Jencks, and others,[1] it was the convergence of Jencks's search for a multivalent or multicoded architecture with certain design practices of the 1970s that enabled the theorization of postmodern architecture as a distinct, articulate, and affirmative position rather than as merely a reaction formation against modernism or a synonym for the contemporary.

In his *Modern Movements in Architecture* (1973) Jencks had already formulated what would become the foundational condition of postmodern architecture—an antideterministic, self-sustaining "multivalence"; Le Corbusier's Unité d'Habitation was his primary example. Following the precepts of the New Criticism (particularly the new critical readings of I. A. Richards), Jencks finds architecture to be fundamentally about human experience and the *organization* of such experience obtained through perception and reflection. The use and configuration of a self-conscious architectural "language"—an analog of the New Critics' poetic language—involve structure and pattern together with rhetorical devices such as metaphor, paradox, and irony, all of which serve to organize the complexity of human experience. A multivalent architecture is thus emotive *and* cognitive. Jencks:

The more one analyses [Le Corbusier's Unité d'Habitation], the more one finds link after link between the different levels of experience and the more experience becomes self-validating as one discovers not only Le Corbusier's intentions, but more possible meanings which are latent within the architecture. It is this power of the multivalent work to engage the perceiver's powers of creation which is significant here. Not only does this allow the architecture to become alive in different ways to each generation and thus result in a lasting architecture, but it also stimulates each generation to reach beyond its familiar abstractions. Multivalent architecture acts as a catalyst on the mind, provoking wholly new interpretations which, in however small a way, affect the individual. The range, delicacy and complexity of meanings which exist in a multivalent work have an analogous effect on the mind that interacts with them. Ultimately, we are transformed by what we experience, and the quality of a work is transferred, even if indirectly, into organizational states of the mind.[2]

It is one of the paradoxes of the modern/postmodern relation that the concept of multivalence can then be transferred to the proposed postmodern architectural language, where it is modulated by a notion of double-coding: "A Post-Modern building is . . . one which speaks on at least two levels at once: to other architects and a concerned minority who care about specifically architectural meaning, and to the public at large, or the local inhabitants, who care about other issues concerned with comfort, traditional building and a way of life."[3] Such "schizophrenia" was surely part of modernism's historical condition as well, but it must be self-consciously and ironically exacerbated in order for Jencks to arrive at his semiotics of the nonsynchronous.

Postmodern architecture is concerned with the complex texture of reality ("It can include ugliness, decay, banality, austerity, without becoming depressing"), yet it avoids all stance-taking ("The particular motivation or 'interests' of men are momentarily dropped") in order to reach its "disinterested fulfilment." Its function is to create meaning in a balance of irresolvables through related structured levels and a density of connotativeness rather than the random heterogeneity or neat arrangement of individual elements. Meaning must be forged always in tension with other potential meanings, employing explicit denotations, everyday associations, reference to other buildings, and inherent or contrived simile or "seeing-as," all of which aids communication.

compare Scott Brown (**62 ff**)

While Jencks's manner of reading buildings as similes and metaphors sometimes results in a kind of architectural Rorschach text ("Now tell me what this reminds you of"), his work also initiated a powerful new mode of perception that Fredric Jameson later summarized as "difference relates."[4] Together with other efforts like Portoghesi's 1980 exhibition "The Presence of the Past" and Heinrich Klotz's *The History of Postmodern Architecture*,[5] Jencks helped popularize and institutionalize a label that would dominate architecture journals and the academy for a decade.

Notes

1. Paolo Portoghesi, *Le inibizioni dell' architettura moderna* (Bari: Laterza, 1974); Charles Jencks, *Modern Movements in Architecture* (New York: Anchor, 1973). See also Robert Venturi, *Complexity and Contradiction in Architecture* (New York: Museum of Modern Art, 1966).

2. Jencks, *Modern Movements*, p. 26. Charles Jencks, "The Rise of Post-Modern Architecture," *Architectural Association Quarterly* 7, no. 4 (October–December 1975), also contains many of the constitutive characteristics found in the 1977 book.

3. Charles Jencks, introduction to the third edition of *The Language of Post-Modern Architecture* (New York: Rizzoli, 1981), p. 6.

4. Fredric Jameson, "Architecture and the Critique of Ideology," in *Architecture, Criticism, Ideology* (Princeton: Princeton Architectural Press, 1985), p. 86; reprinted in this anthology.

5. Heinrich Klotz, *Moderne und postmoderne: Architektur der Gegenwart 1960–1980* (Braunschweig: F. Vieweg, 1984), published in English as *The History of Postmodern Architecture* (Cambridge: MIT Press, 1988); *The Presence of the Past: First International Exhibition of Architecture*, ed. Gabriella Borsano (Venice: Edizioni La Biennale di Venezia, 1980).

Recent Departures

Several architects are moving beyond modern architecture in a tentative way, either adapting a mixture of modernist styles, or mixing these with previous modes. The results as yet are not convincing enough to speak of a totally new approach and style; they are evolutionary, not a radical departure. And it is in the nature of the case that practicing architects now in their forties and trained in modernism can only make hesitant, evolutionary changes. When the present students of architecture start practicing, we should begin to see much more convincing examples of radical eclecticism, because it is only this group which is really free enough to try their hand at any possible style—ancient, modern, or hybrid.

A few Japanese architects, Kurokawa, Kikutake and Isozaki among them, have on occasion produced work in several different styles, and single buildings which use various aesthetic systems in a semantic way. Also they have been able to incorporate a traditional language without necessarily being coy or ironic. Why they, unlike Westerners, have been able to be modern *and* traditional without compromising either language remains something of a mystery. Partly it is explained by the persistence of traditional Japanese culture in all areas, and the absence of a revolutionary avant-garde which establishes its credentials by inverting those of the previous generation. But also it is due to the Japanese sophistication towards signs: they have traditionally absorbed alien cultures, or modified the Chinese to their own purposes. Whatever the explanation, the results are there as a lesson to pluralist societies. The architect can design tea-ceremony rooms in a straightforward, sensitive way, or push the latest technology to its expressive limits.

Kikutake, in his Tokoen Hotel, has used a version of the Torii gate to acknowledge the entrance, and has employed traditional bracket construction—but in concrete not wood—to articulate the main public areas. The hotel rooms near the top mix tatami proportions and modern architecture; while the restaurant on the roof is under a gentle curve, in blue tile, that manages to recall traditional roof forms and modern hyperbolic parabolas (which in fact it is). Two different structural systems and two aesthetics thus give a legibility and dynamism missing in Western modern architecture.

Kurokawa's Odakyu Drive-In Restaurant is similar in its use of mixed systems. Again the traditional bracket construction is a departure point for the joint, but here the joint has exploded to such prominence that it has swallowed the building and, conversely, the building has swallowed the joint. This witty piece of advertising architecture is in the best roadside tradition—a gigantic metaphor proclaiming its function. The red tent, slung under the top joints, signifies outdoor activities, in this case a beer garden, while the plug-in capsule of brown steel signifies the main dining room.

Minoru Takeyama, another young Japanese architect, has pushed the use of popular, commercial codes even further in what is perhaps the most convincing Pop building yet designed from within the architectural tradition.

His Ni-ban-Kahn makes use of gigantic supergraphics, optical patterns, written signs, and combines these commercial codes with a geometric discipline and volumetric expression more common in the high game of serious architecture. Architect's architecture and commercial motifs can be combined without compromising either code: in fact their mutual confrontation is a positive gain for both sides. The resultant hybrid, like all inclusive architecture, is not easily subverted by an ironic attack, an unsympathetic viewpoint, because it balances and reconciles opposed meanings. Instead of gaining a tenuous integration by denial, by excluding inharmonious meanings in a search for consistency, this inclusive architecture absorbs conflicting codes in an attempt to create "the difficult whole."

      This phrase, borrowed from Robert Venturi, should not be regarded as a facile panacea, as his own work shows. It is considerably more difficult to design works which unify disparate material than to unify already homogeneous meanings and styles; just as it is more difficult to write a tragedy than a farce. By the same token, an inclusive architecture brings much more of our personality and behavior into focus; just as tragedy articulates a greater wealth of experience than any other genre.[1] The rare, inclusive building—as rare as the true tragedy (most are melodramas)—does not sublimate unattractive aspects of the world. It can include ugliness, decay, banality, austerity, without becoming depressing. It can confront harsh realities of climate, or politics without suppression. It can articulate a bleak metaphysical view of man—Greek architecture and that of Le Corbusier—without either evasion or bleakness.[2] The extraordinary power of tragedy when it is really tragic, or inclusive architecture when it really unifies disparate material, is its disinterested fulfillment. The particular motivation or "interests" of men are momentarily dropped as they watch a configuration of particularly disturbing events unfold—murders, betrayals slow disintegration—they watch these monstrosities with detached pleasure, as long as they are balanced or reconciled within an overall tragic pattern. The catharsis this can produce, irrespective of whether it is looked at psychologically (I. A. Richards), or metaphysically (Nietzsche), is of a higher order than the reactions produced by other genres. Inclusive architecture and tragedy, simply, are the pinnacles of expressive modes: there is nothing else as rich, mature and honest towards the complexities of life.

      Having staked out grandiose claims for such work, it is unfortunate not to be able to illustrate it with convincing modern examples. But, again, only the first steps have been taken in this direction, and one doesn't expect them to be accomplished or perfect. Certain buildings of Le Corbusier definitely articulate this kind of experience, but they do so with a Purist language purged of symbolic signs, writing and vulgarity. By contrast, the buildings of Venturi and his team use an inclusive language without attempting much of a reconciliation between opposed meanings. Only one architect manages to be convincingly profound with a hybrid language, Gaudí; but before discussing him, I'd like to instance several examples of this language itself since it is the precondition for an inclusive architecture.

In general terms it can be described as radical eclecticism, or adhocism.[3] Various parts, styles or sub-systems (existing in a previous context) are used in a new, creative synthesis. Radical eclecticism stresses the aspect that these parts must find a semantic justification; eclecticism in itself is a senseless shuffling of styles, as incoherent as Purism, its opposite. Adhocism stresses the aspect that these parts must be unified creatively for a specific purpose (the definition of *ad hoc*). Several recent architectural examples make it clear what this language looks like. It is variegated rather than homogeneous, witty rather than somber, messy rather than clean,

Charles Moore (with Perez Associates, Inc., U.I.G., and Ron Filson), Piazza d'Italia, New Orleans, 1976–1979

picturesque but not necessarily without a classical, geometric order (usually it is made from several orders in contrast).

A key *ad hoc* building group, perhaps the largest built to date, is the students' residence and social zone at Louvain University, just outside Brussels. Designed with the aid of Lucien Kroll (who acted as orchestra leader for the various design groups), this set of structures resembles a child's building-block hill town more than a traditional group of university buildings. The reason is simply that many students participated in its design, and they used small bits of plastic foam in working out a model. They shuffled these bits around, combining various functions, such as individual rooms with restaurant. But disputes arose and the inevitable specialization of teams led to an impossible fragmentation. Kroll reorganized these teams several times, letting them become more familiar with each other's problems, until a possible solution was in sight. Not until then did he draw up the plans and sections which made it workable.

The resultant buildings show a complexity and richness of meaning that usually takes years to achieve and is the result of many inhabitants making small adjustments over time. The fact that a simulation of such piecemeal tinkering and pluralism can be built in from the beginning through such a process, should not be underrated. It takes, of course, the commitment and understanding that Kroll and his group had from the start; but the process is definitely generalizable, and similar results have been achieved elsewhere with similar processes of consultation, if not participation—Ralph Erskine and his team at Byker, for instance.

Kroll's orchestration even went so far as allowing the builders a certain improvisation while constructing. They changed the siding of one building from rough rubble stonework to brick and tile as the work progressed, so this building seems to grow up from the ground like a variegated tree. The students wished to combine functions while distinguishing them visually, so five different building systems were used—tile, plastic, aluminum and glass, wood, and concrete—in a finely-grained patchwork. No explicit semantic modeling was used, as far as I know, but the parts bespeak their use with a certain eloquence and mutual toleration. Perhaps this was due to Kroll himself, as participation won't automatically produce such sensitivity. There was clearly an aesthetic intention consciously brought to bear on the scheme at some point; and it is this skill, which has been delicately keyed into the process without dominating it, that distinguishes this result of participation from others, and from the very large self-build movement.

Perhaps participation has been oversymbolized. Kroll boasts that no two bedroom windows next to each other are the same; and when I was there in 1976 I found parts of the building had graffiti and political slogans written on them before they were being used. It was as if the street art of May '68 was being preapplied down at the factory. Perhaps the scheme may be overarticulated and somewhat too fussy in its insistent attempt to humanize and individualize.

Nonetheless, the spirit of the place really captures the feeling of what *ad hoc* design can be—a continually renewed improvisation on themes coming from every possible source. There are pitched roofs here which tumble about the roof-scape of an amoeboid community building; other popular signs, such as trellis-work, greenhouse sheds, and primitive figurative sculpture, punctuate the main blob of the scheme (one has to apply new architectural terms to these units—perhaps "hills" is a better word). The syncopation of various materials over the surface of these blob-hills can only be described as rich and riotous; tumultuous in the detail and violent in the whole—and yet still very personal and small-scaled. It is a kind of language very appropriate to student life and desires (at least *some* desires). I'm sure certain critics are going to condemn this as the totalitarianism of enforced participation, where there is no normalized architectures for the student who just wants to be his ordinary, privatized self. Indeed, perhaps improvisation has gone too far spread all over the site in every detail. But this excess is the price often paid for innovating a new process of design, and there is nothing inherent in the process which precludes ordinary building for those who really want it. They will just have to make their voices heard in the future as the university continues to expand.

Multivalent Architecture

The direction that Kroll and these other architects are moving towards is a pluralistic language which incorporates traditional and modern elements, vernacular and high art meanings. The Japanese designers, Charles Moore, the Venturi team, Bruce Goff, and countless individuals building their own handmade houses, do not yet constitute a single coherent tradition; but they have enough in common to make a very loosely defined group departing from the orthodoxies of the modern movement They find support, if not identity of approach, in the emergent philosophies of the ecological movement "small is beautiful," intermediate technology, and the general trend towards decentralization which is being called for around the world. These last movements are neutral concerning a new language of architecture, they aren't concerned with the way buildings communicate one way or another, but their underlying pluralism is to be welcomed.

If this pluralism is going to amount to anything it will really have to become more tough-minded. The architect will have be trained in four or five different styles and trained as an anthropologist, or at least a good journalist, to learn and be able to use the particular architectural codes that prevail among the subcultures that persist in any large city. He will have to learn the particular metaphors and symbolic signs which have a short-lived potency, and the slow-changing traditional signs, and use all these with wit and precision. This is not going to be an easy thing to do because the other part of his training, in the new technologies and abstract methodologies of planning, will inevitably remove him, as they have done in the past, from the users of his buildings. He will continue to have a professional ideology induced by the modern movement on a world-wide scale; he will respond to formal inventions coming from Italy and Japan, theory that emanates from London and New York, and individual practice coming from everywhere. He will build for multinational and large corporations and indefinable clients; he will still love the manipulation of pure form and the high game of Architects' Architecture. All these

Michael Graves, The Portland Building, 1980

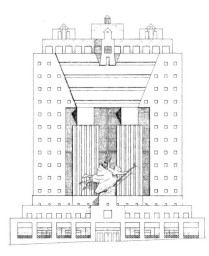

forces will alienate him from the people who ultimately use his buildings and there is little hope of changing these forces (barring the collapse of international communications and all economies, not a very happy solution).

A realistic assessment of the situation suggests that schizophrenia is the only intelligent approach. The architect should be trained as a radical schizophrenic (everything must be radical today), always looking two ways with equal clarity: towards the traditional slow-changing codes and particular ethnic meanings of a neighborhood, and towards the fast-changing codes of architectural fashion and professionalism. If he doesn't make this schizophrenia quite explicit and incorporate it as part of his basic training, then he will be an inadvertent victim of one pressure or the other.

On the other hand, if he does adopt this dual approach, his enjoyment of architecture might actually increase, as he becomes more responsible for its various meanings. The more he can know about how people will react to the forms he uses, the more he can confidently use and decode them. The pleasure of manipulating various languages will easily repay the effort at learning them.

Ultimately however, it is the way a language is used that matters, the actual messages sent as much as the particular language used. Obviously if an architect has nothing important to say, his facility with communication is just going to advertise this fact clearly; so ideology, and ideas, are also preconditions for effective discourse. A multivalent architecture, opposed to a univalent building, combines meanings imaginatively so that they fuse and modify each other. A multivalent architecture, like the inclusive building, makes use of the *full arsenal of communicational means*, leaving out no area of experience, and suppressing no particular code (although of course any building is inevitably limited in range).

The only architect I could say really uses a pluralist language to produce multivalent works, Antonio Gaudí, has sometimes been classified as an Art Nouveau designer. The problem with this classification is that it obscures Gaudí's universality, not to say peculiarity. He was a man deeply committed to Barcelona's separatist movement, and to "modernismo," its artistic expression, as well as more general social issues, such as workers' control and Christian humanism.

Gaudí's version of Art Nouveau was highly inclusive, even cannibalistic: it swallowed Moorish elements, tiles and domical vaults; it absorbed Gothic motifs, buttresses, pinnacles, and stained glass; it borrowed nature's plants and animals, metaphors of any living creature; and incorporated emergent forms of engineering (the parabola and hyperbolic parabola were practically invented by Gaudí). Spatially it flowed and curved around solid elements, while structurally it not only articulated the lines for force, but dramatized them as twisting muscles and tendons. Symbolically, his work followed the local Christian and social meanings existing in Barcelona at the time. And Gaudí was not even intimidated by vulgarity— he'd write various slogans across the tops of his building, early Cubist advertisements. There wasn't a communicational mode Gaudí didn't use at least once.

His Casa Battló, finished in 1907, is a particularly multivalent work, where meanings modify one another. You come upon it near the corner of a main boulevard in Barcelona, past a phalanx of plane trees on the Paseo de Gracia. On one side is a typical nineteenth-century apartment block in the classical style; on the other, the stepped shops and polychromy of another Art Nouveau building. Gaudí has filled this hole with a building that respects the street facade and unites the two adjoining structures (or at least did until one of them was added to). He also adopts a variation of the window treatments on either side.

On inspecting the entrance facade, you can discover a series of metaphors and symbolic signs. The balconies stare back like so many death masks or skulls. The middle part of the architecture also recalls vegetable and marine meta-phors, with some people seeing it as a violent blue sea breaking over rocks, which then turn into kelp (the codes of Barcelona are, after all, sensitive to the sea).

The lower two floors adopt a related organic metaphor of skele-tons and bones (the architecture was known as "the house of bones"), and you can see this exoskeleton go internal on two sides of the third floor. A recent designer has incorporated a wandering, blue neon sign suggesting, if we continue the metaphor, that the "legs have varicose veins"—a rather ludicrous example of the way multiva-lent architecture forces meanings to modify each other.

It is quite possible to see these "bones" as tendons, or a ductile metaphor of wax or lava. If a mixed metaphor is more dramatic than a single, obvious one, then it is Gaudí's particular strength to find a multiplicity of meanings for these mixtures.

For instance, they divide the architecture into three main func-tional parts (following the classical convention): a base of two floors with the bone/wax metaphor which can denote "shops," "entrance" and "main apartment"; a shaft of four floors in the marine/mask metaphor which can denote "similar apartments of a lesser nature"; finally a capital, a roof in the dragon metaphor which can denote "roof garden, water tanks, skylight, mechanical equipment." Thus strange, regional codes are used to signify different functions and break up a large apartment block into identifiable and personal areas. How far this is from the recent practice of anony-mous slab blocks it is not necessary to emphasize.

The pre-eminent role of the architect is to articulate our envi-ronment, not only so we can comprehend it literally, but also so we can find it psy-chologically nourishing, create meanings we hadn't even imagined were possible.

In this sense the overall message, or symbol, of the Casa Battló is truly extraordinary: it articulates meanings which are much more profound than the surface metaphors of which it is composed. For a long time I puzzled over the meaning of the roof dragon—that sleeping monster sprawled out at the top who looks down on the passerby with one eye lazily half open. The ceramic tile of what appears at first its tail (the three-dimensional cross) shades slowly from golden or-ange on the left to blue green on the right. Gaudí was a very devout Christian and he announced the fact with the cross and initials of the Holy Family encrusted on the cylinder. But what sort of Christianity is this? I had assumed the dragon was a typical Art Nouveau conceit, taken perhaps from Chinese garden walls which undulate this way, but I couldn't see its relation to a religious message. Was it a kind of Tao-Christianity, a form of nature-worship akin to pantheism? I assumed this until I was told the conventional reference to these signs. The missing clue was supplied by the architect David Mackay, and the correct interpretation came into focus with all the vividness of a suddenly solved crime.

St. George, it turns out, is the patron saint of this city, and Barce-lona has always been the center of a separatist, Catalonian movement. It has its special Catalan dialect and has always sparked off regional groups and extreme individualists. Anarchism has had a foothold there: Picasso, Sert, Salvador Dalí, Miró, are some of the more pronounced individualists. When you walk along the back streets and main commercial avenues and eat the highly sophisticated seafood, you realize that this city is European, not just Spanish; it has had Mediterranean roots (and routes) for several thousand years. The nationalist movement to which Gaudí belonged was try-ing to assert independence from Spanish domination. The Casa Battló then apparently represents this struggle in its metaphors: the dragon—Spain—is being slain by that three-dimensional cross wielded by Barcelona's patron saint. The bones and skulls refer to the dead martyrs who have been victimized in the struggle.[4] All this in an apartment building! But coded with enough subtlety to be apparent only to those who care to read it in depth. The deeper symbol, the knowledge of which transforms your whole view of the building, is not absolutely necessary in order to grasp its more obvious meanings. But like multivalent works in other fields it speaks to many different people on different levels.

These kinds of work, the six major tragedies of Shakespeare for instance, have the power to engage the mind and open our imaginations to new meaning. They are catalytic, provocative and creative, stimulating each generation to reach beyond its familiar abstractions and discover new interpretations; whereas the univalent work is reductive, dull, and ultimately repressive. A multivalent architecture remains alive because its meanings are so related as to allow new paths to be discovered between them. Finally, then, it is because of its effect on us that such architecture is mandatory—because it will shape us in multiple ways and speak to various groups, to the whole spectrum of society rather than just one of its elites. In the long run we are transformed by what we experience and inhabit; and the quality of architecture affects the quality of our minds at least as much as any other artifact we make.

No doubt many architects are now as disenchanted with modernism as the public, and a new paradigm, or theory, is beginning to form. This paradigm is still loosely defined and it doesn't yet enjoy a large consensus, but the outlines of what it is becoming are clear, particularly to the generation of architects now in their thirties. The next five years promise to be extremely interesting for architects, as the paradigm takes shape—but also probably confused and uncertain. The adage "may you be cursed to live in interesting times" is good warning for the architect now about to practice, because he will invariably spend a large part of his time fighting battles of taste, with differing publics. But this is not necessarily a bad thing. After all, the modern movement itself came into existence through struggle, and it won't exit without a fight. Every change in paradigm entails struggle, and the paradox facing our generation of architects is that it has to go backwards to previous theories, and reweave several strands which have been cut away, in order to go forward.

We must go back to a point where architects took responsibility for rhetoric, for how their buildings communicated intentionally, how "decorum" and *bien-séance* were consciously achieved, and then combine insights from such a study with a relevant theory of semiotics, so that an updated rhetoric can be consciously taught along with other specialties—no, as the unifying agent of these other disciplines. For an architect's primary and final role is to express the meanings a culture finds significant, as well as elucidate certain ideas and feelings that haven't previously reached expression. The jobs that too often take up his energy might be better done by engineers and sociologists, but no other profession is specifically responsible for articulating meaning and seeing that the environment is sensual, humorous, surprising and coded as a readable text. This is the architect's job and pleasure, not, let us hope, ever again his "problem."

Notes

1. The organizing powers of tragedy and its pre-eminence is discussed by I. A. Richards in his *Principles of Literary Criticism* (1925; New York: Harcourt Brace, 1961), pp. 245–250.
2. I have partly explored this notion in *Le Corbusier and the Tragic View of Architecture* (Cambridge: Harvard University Press, 1973), but my discussion of tragedy there was severely curtailed.
3. In *Adhocism* (New York: Doubleday, 1972), Nathan Silver and I showed many examples of various styles and building systems being lifted from their former contexts and being put together *ad hoc* in a new synthesis. Arthur Koestler has illuminated the general principle involved in his *Act of Creation* (London: Hutchinson, 1964).

4. This is third-hand information, and a guess on my part. Gaudí told the architect Martorell that the roof represented a dragon being slain; Martorell told his son, Josep Maria, who told his partner, David Mackay, who told me. Given the separatist ideals of *Modernismo* it then seems logical to me that the dragon would represent Spain, the bones and skulls becoming veiled symbols of the Catalan martyrs. Surely many Catalans must have seen it this way, since St. George and the dragon appear on other separatist buildings, and Catalan Nationalism was very closely associated with *Modernismo* (for a while its style).

    Some critics might say that Gaudí's work is too highly wrought to act as a model for the present city—a veritable zoo of animalistic and other meanings—but the basic lessons are there to follow: a full use of the expressive means, all the modes of communication. In one sense, Gaudí had it easy. He was in a rich traditional society, immersed in everyday Catholic faith, and working at a time (during the *Renaixenca* and *Modernismo*) when architects could use metaphors and symbols as a matter of course, without reflection. Animal and vegetable metaphors cover many *Modernismo* buildings—not just mythic beasts such as the dragon, but domestic ones such as cats and dogs. Thus this culture did a lot of work for Gaudí, something which we can't expect today. And yet in the mass culture of the West, there are many of the same values and forces at work, even if they are finely spread out across society, and operative in a commercial and debased form. They are there, and it is theoretically possible that some individual and group can reweave these disparate aspects together and achieve something as deep and intense as *Modernismo.*

I hope this building will evoke an association of Museum and I'd like the visitor to feel it "looks like a museum." In its built details it may combine traditional and new elements though old elements are used in a modern way; for instance, the histrionic coving is not a cornice used throughout, but only defining the sculpture terraces. Similarly, there are assemblages of constructivist canopies which define a hierarchy of entrances. . . . The axiality of the plan is frequently compromised, set piece rooms conjoin with the free plan and the public footpath meanders either side of a central axis — thus the casually monumental is diminished by the deliberately informal. . . . In addition to Representational and Abstract, this large complex I hope supports the Monumental *and* Informal, also the Traditional *and* High Tech.

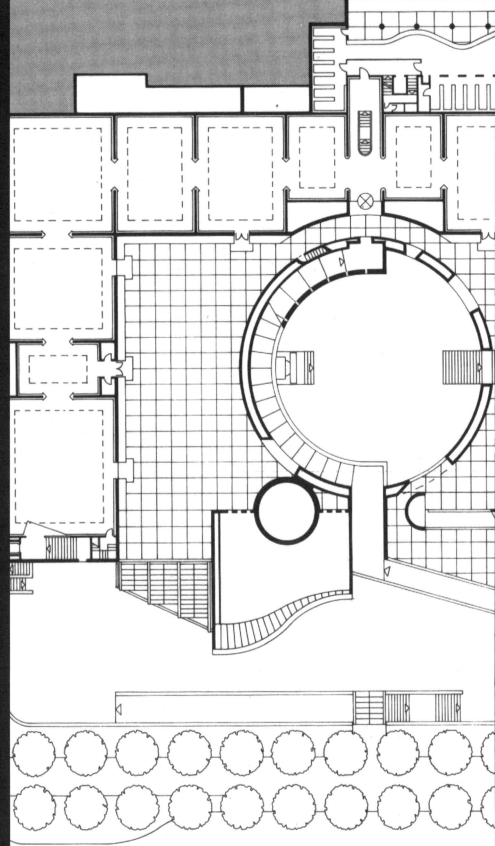

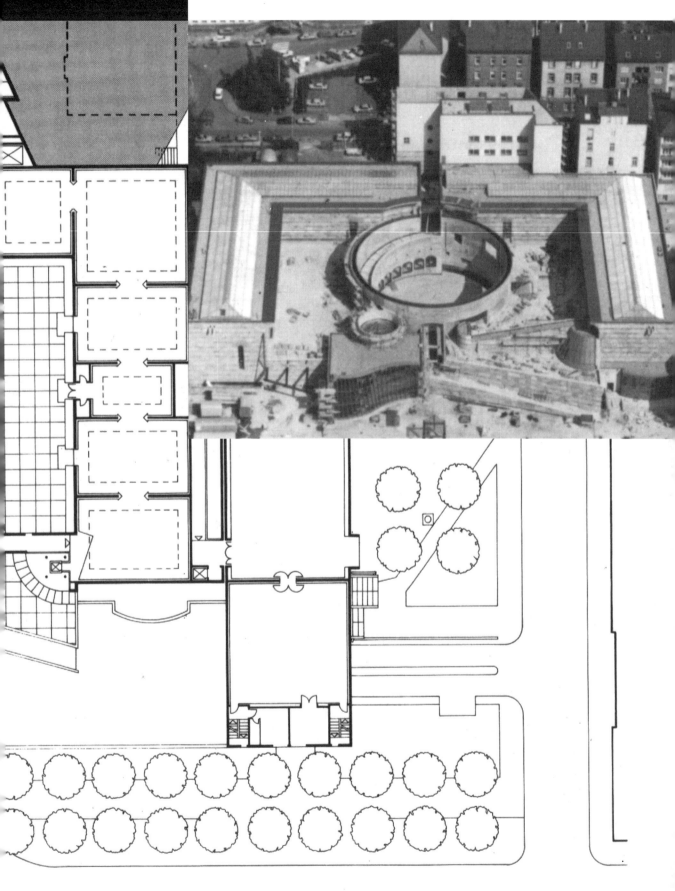

James Stirling, Neue
Staatsgalerie,
Stuttgart

Rem Koolhaas   **"'Life in the Metropolis' or 'The Culture of Congestion'"** *Architectural Design* 47,

no. 5 (August 1977)

In the very midst of an antimodernism that vilified the utopian aspirations of architecture between the wars as a manifest will to power whose desire for a collective freedom had been converted into the totalizing formula of a steel and glass cage, there arose a sensibility altogether different, characterized by its ironic, parodic take on the psycho-aerobic exercises of modernism and its maintenance of what should still be seen as functionalist and programmatic concerns, but now directed toward almost surreal scenarios. Between 1975 and 1977, in projects like the Welfare Palace Hotel, The Hotel Sphinx, and the Floating Pool, Rem Koolhaas and his associates in the Office for Metropolitan Architecture (an international firm founded in London in 1975) produced what could easily be mistaken for the paranoid hallucinations of a Georg Simmel, Charles Fourier, or Ludwig Hilberseimer — the sociological-elementarist apprehensions of capitalism's madness. In their research and design projects, Koolhaas and OMA looked to Manhattan's "culture of congestion" for a demonstration of a link between commercial architecture and an avant-garde program of accelerated technological effects. The new "ecstasy about architecture" — comprising almost equal parts

OMA and Rem
Koolhaas, Parc de La
Villette, Paris,
1982–1983

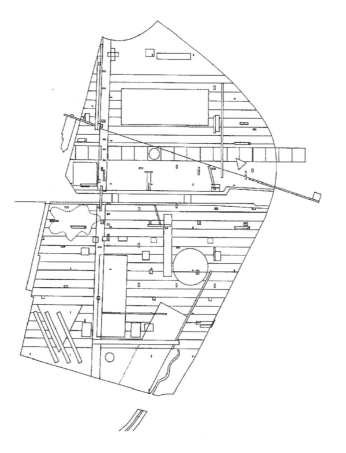

of constraint and elation, resignation and intoxication — is the essence of the ambivalent life in the metropolis, where the antinomies of modern utopianism are played out. It finds its most perfect object in Manhattan, the principal site of laissez-faire development, congestion, consumption, and all manner of worldliness.[1]

| see 706 |

One of the primary examples of Manhattan's "techno-psychic" machines discovered by Koolhaas is the Downtown Athletic Club, in which the vast urban grid and the elevator couple horizontally and vertically to produce previously unimaginable experiential effects out of an economically engineered servomechanism. "Eating oysters with boxing gloves, naked, on the 9th floor" is but one of the surrealist programmatic promises of what is, in itself, an almost unrepresentable infrastructure, but one whose liberative potentials can be thwarted only by a failure of nerve. What is more, this machine (the grid-elevator-skyscraper combination) came into being without a single architect's intention. It is the almost automatic by-product of a collective metropolitan subject that refused to adopt a discourse at odds with the realities of actual practice — an avant-garde without a manifesto, which must then be written retroactively.

In 1978, *Delirious New York: A Retroactive Manifesto for Manhattan*, the full study of Manhattan metropolitanism, was published. In 1982 the Downtown Athletic Club was rotated ninety degrees, from section into plan, to form the diagram of OMA's entry to the competition for the Parc de La Villette, which further explored the relationship between a rigid, nonarchitectural device and the contingent programmatic effects it can generate.

Note

"If Manhattan is still in search of a theory, then this theory, once identified, should yield a formula for an architecture that is at once ambitious *and* popular. Manhattan has generated a shameless architecture that has been loved in direct proportion to its defiant lack of self-hatred, respected exactly to the degree that it went too far. Manhattan has consistently inspired in its beholders *ecstasy about architecture*." Rem Koolhaas, *Delirious New York: A Retroactive Manifesto for Manhattan* (New York: Oxford University Press, 1978), p. 10.

Why do we have a mind, if not to get our own way?

DOSTOEVSKY

Somewhere in the 19th century certain parts of the globe—negligible in terms of surface—developed an unprecedented condition: through the simultaneous explosion of modern technologies and human population on their limited territories, they found themselves supporting the mutant form of human coexistence that is known as Metropolis.

The Metropolis invalidates all the previous systems of articulation and differentiation that have traditionally guided the design of cities. The Metropolis annuls the previous history of architecture.

But if the Metropolis is a true mutation, it can be assumed that it has also generated its own Urbanism: an architecture that is exclusively concerned with the "splendeurs et misères" of the Metropolitan Condition; an architecture with its own theorems, laws, methods, breakthroughs and achievements that has remained largely outside the field of vision of official architecture and criticism, both unable to admit a fundamental rupture that would make their own existence precarious.

Manhattan

By an unspoken consensus, Manhattan is considered the archetype of the Metropolitan Condition, to the point where the two are often interchangeable. Manhattan's spectacular growth coincided exactly with the definition of the concept of Metropolis itself. Manhattan represents the apotheosis of the ideal of density per se, both of population and of infrastructures; its architecture promotes a state of congestion on all possible levels, and exploits this congestion to inspire and support particular forms of social intercourse that together form a unique *culture of congestion*.

The following episodes of Manhattan's history circumscribe such an Urbanism that is specifically Metropolitan.

Coney Island

Coney Island is a clitoral appendage at the mouth of New York harbor, discovered one day before Manhattan itself.

From 1600 to 1800 the shape of the peninsula changed under the combined impact of natural forces—(shifting sands)—and human intervention—(the cutting of a canal that turned Coney actually into an island). These modifications together followed a "design" that turned the Island more and more into a miniature of Manhattan.

From the mid-19th century, the obstacles of geography that had so far ensured relative inaccessibility to the island were one by one transcended by new transportation technologies.

In 1883 the Brooklyn Bridge removed the last obstruction that had kept Manhattan's inhabitants in place. From then on they escaped to the Atlantic beach in a weekly Exodus that concentrated more than 1 million people on the minuscule island on a good day.

The virgin nature that is the destination of this frantic migration disappeared under the onslaught of the unprecedented hyper-density. As compensation for this loss of nature, a battery of new technologies was developed to provide equivalent conditions on a scale that was commensurate with the new Metropolitan numbers.

Coney Island became a laboratory of the collective unconscious: the themes and tactics of its experimentation were later to reappear in Manhattan.

Cow

The first natural element to be converted was the cow. Since no amount of real cows could deal with the insatiable thirst of the million, a machine was designed and built: the Inexhaustible Cow. Its milk is superior to the natural product in terms of quantity, regularity of flow, hygiene, and controllable temperature.

Bathing

Similar conversions follow in rapid succession. Since the total surface of the beaches and the total length of the surfline were finite and given, it followed with mathematical certainty that not each of the hundreds of thousands of visitors could find a place to spread out in the sand, let alone succeed in reaching the water within the limit of a single day.

Toward 1890, the introduction of electricity in this impasse made it possible to create a second daytime—intense electric lights were placed at regular intervals along the surfline, so that the sea could be enjoyed in a truly Metropolitan shift system. Those unable to reach the water in the day were given a 12-hour extension. What is unique in Coney Island—and this syndrome of the Irresistible Synthetic sets the tone for later events in Manhattan—is that this illumination was not seen as a second-rate experience, but that its very artificiality was advertised as an attraction in itself: Electric Bathing.

Horses

The preferred activity of the happy few who had enjoyed the island in its virgin state had been horseback riding. Of course, that experience was unthinkable on the scale of the new masses. Real horses in adequate numbers would require a separate infrastructure as big as the island itself.

Also, the ability to ride a horse was a form of "knowledge" not available to the proletariat that had made the island its playground.

In the mid-1890s George Tilyou laid out a mechanical track that leads through Coney's natural landscapes, along the oceanfront and across a number of man-made obstacles. He named it "Steeplechase" . . . "an automatic racetrack with gravitation as its motive power. . . . Its horses resemble in size and model the trackracer. Staunchly built, they are to a certain extent under the control of the rider, who can accelerate the speed by the manner in which he utilizes his weight and his position on the ascending and descending grades."

Steeplechase combined in a single attraction the provision of entertainment with a form of emancipation through machinery—the elite experience of horseback riding democratized through technology.

Love
Two years later, even the most intimate processes of human nature were converted.

It is often alleged that the Metropolis creates loneliness and alienation. Coney Island responded to this problem with the "Barrels of Love."

Two horizontal cylinders—mounted in line—revolve in opposite directions. At either end a narrow staircase leads up to the entrance; one feeds men into the apparatus, the other women. It is impossible to remain standing in the machine; men and women are thrown on top of each other. The unrelenting rotation then creates synthetic intimacy between couples who would never have met without its assistance.

If necessary, this intimacy could be further processed in the "Tunnels of Love," an artificial mountain next to the couple-forming machine. The freshly formed pairs would board a small boat that disappears inside a system of dark tunnels where complete obscurity ensues—or at least—visual privacy.

The rocking movement of the boats on the shallow water was supposed to increase sensuality.

Conclusion: 1
With the sequence of: Cow, Electric Bathing, Steeplechase and Barrels of Love, all the natural elements that had once defined the attraction of the Island, were systematically replaced by a new kind of machinery that converted the original nature into an intricate simulacrum of nature, a compensatory technical service.

This technology is not the agent of objective and quantifiable improvements—such as raising the levels of illumination, controlling temperature, etc.—it is a superior substitute for the "natural" reality that is being depleted by the sheer density of human consumers.

Together, this apparatus constitutes an alternative reality that is invented and designed, instead of accidental and arbitrary.

Since this "instrumentarium" of true modernity creates states and situations that have never existed before, it can never escape its aspect of fabrication—of being the result of human fantasy.

The Metropolis is irrevocably the resultant of such identifiable mental constructions, and that is the source of its fundamental "otherness" from all previous Urbanisms.

Elevator
In 1853, at Manhattan's first World's Fair, the invention that would, more than any other, become the "sign" of the Metropolitan Condition, was introduced to the public in a singularly theatrical format.

Elisha Otis, the inventor of the elevator, mounts a platform. The platform ascends. When it has reached its highest level, an assistant presents Otis with a dagger on a velvet cushion. The inventor takes the knife and attacks what appears the crucial component of his invention: the cable that has hoisted the platform upward and that now prevents its fall. Otis cuts the cable; nothing happens to platform or inventor.

Invisible safety-catches prevent the platform from rejoining the surface of the earth. They represent the essence of Otis's invention: the ability to prevent the elevator from crashing.

Like the elevator, each technical invention is pregnant with a double image: the spectre of its possible failure. The way to avert that phantom disaster is as important as the original invention itself.

Otis introduced a theme which would become a *leitmotiv* in the performance of the Metropolis: a spectacle that features a neck and neck race between an astronomical increase in the potential for disaster that is only just exceeded by a still more astronomical increase in the potential to avert disaster.

Elevator 2

From the 1870s, the elevator became the great emancipator of all the floors above the ground floor. Otis's apparatus recovered the innumerable planes that had so far been purely speculative, and revealed their superiority in the first Metropolitan paradox: the greater the distance from the earth—the more unnatural the location—the closer the communication with what remains of nature (i.e., light, air, views, etc.).

The elevator is the ultimate self-fulfilling prophesy: the further it travels upward, the more undesirable the circumstances it leaves behind.

Through the mutual reinforcement of the elevator and the steelframe (the latter with its uncanny ability to support the newly identified territories without itself taking any space), any given site in the Metropolis could now be multiplied ad infinitum, a proliferation of floorspace that was called Skyscraper, prime instrument of the architecture of density.

Theorem

In 1909 the "layering" of the world's surface through the action of the elevator was posited in the form of a visual theorem that appeared in the popular press.

A slender steel structure supports 84 horizontal planes, all the size of the original plot. Each of these artificial levels is treated as a *virgin site* to establish a private domain around a single countryhouse and its attendant facilities such as stables, servants' cottages, gazebos, etc., all implanted in an airborne meadow.

Emphatic permutations of the styles of the villas suggested that each of the elevator stops corresponded to a different lifestyle—an implied ideological variation—all of them supported with complete neutrality by the steelframe rack.

Life inside this building is fractured to the extent that it could not conceivably be part of a single scenario: on the 82nd floor a donkey shrinks back from the void, on the 81st a cosmopolitan couple hail a plane.

The privacy and isolation of each of the aerial plots seemingly conflicts with the fact that, together, they form a single building. In fact, the diagram implies that the structure is successful exactly to the extent that the individuality of each plot is respected. The structure "frames" their coexistence without interfering with their contents.

The Building is an accumulation of privacies.

Only 5 of the 84 floors are visible on the drawing. Hidden in the clouds other activities occupy other plots; the use of each platform can never be known in advance of its construction. Villas go up and collapse, other facilities replace them, but that does not affect the framework.

100-Story Building

In 1911 a project for a "100-Story Building" was unveiled that incorporated many of the breakthroughs which, only two years earlier, seemed entirely theoretical. The Building was a straightforward extrusion of the block it occupies multiplied by 100.

The lower third of the Building is devoted to industry, the middle part to business, the upper part to living. On every 20th story is a public plaza that occupies a whole floor and articulates the demarcation between the different functional sectors: a "general market" on the 20th, a cluster of theatres on the 40th, a "shopping district" on the 60th, a hotel on the 80th, and an "amusement park, roof garden and swimming pool" on the roof.

At first sight, the rooms inside this structure are conventional, equipped with fireplaces and wood panelling. But they are also equipped with 7 outlets for "temperature and atmosphere regulating tubes" which demonstrate once more the antipragmatic, in fact, poetic usage of the Metropolitan infrastructure: "A = salt air, B = fresh air, C = dry salt air, D = dry fresh air, E = medicated air (to suit disease), F = temperature switch, GHI = perfumes."

The outlets of this techno-psychic battery are the keys to a scale of synthetic experiences that ranges from the hedonistic to the hyper-medical. Some rooms can be "set" on Florida, others on the Canadian Rocky Mountains The perfumes and the medicinal air suggest even more abstract destinations. In the 100-story Building each cubicle is equipped to pursue its private existential journey.

The building has become a laboratory for emotional and intellectual adventure; the fact that it is implanted in Manhattan has become—almost—immaterial.

Downtown Athletic Club

Within 20 years, the promise of the 100-story Building—that of a skyscraper fully conquered by higher forms of social intercourse than mere business—was realized in 1931 with the Downtown Athletic Club.

Rem Koolhaas, *A Machine for Metropolitan Bachelors . . .*, painting by Madelon Vriesendorp, from *Delirious New York*, 1978.

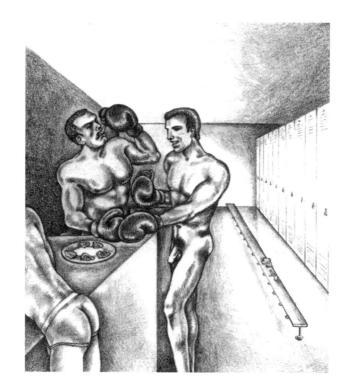

All the latent potential of the skyscraper as a type is exploited in a masterpiece of the Culture of Congestion, a Constructivist Social Condenser materialized in Manhattan.

It is one of the rare 20th century buildings that is truly revolutionary: it offers a full inventory of the fundamental modifications—technical and psychological—that are caused by life in the Metropolis, and that separate this century from all previous ones. Its existence allows a spectrum of experiences on a single place that was previously unthinkable.

The Club—externally indistinguishable from the other skyscrapers in the Wall Street area—is located on the Hudson near Battery Park on a lot 23 meters wide and 54 meters deep.

The Club is the 1909 theorem made concrete: a sequence of superimposed platforms that each repeat the original rectangle of the site, connected by a battery of 13 elevators concentrated along the north wall of the structure.

"The plan is of primary importance, because on the floor are performed all the activities of the human occupants"; that is how Raymond Hood (the most theoretical of Manhattan's architects) defined Manhattan's interpretation of functionalism: each plan as a collage of functions that describes on the synthetic platforms an episode of Metropolitan ritual. Each of the rectangles of the Downtown Athletic Club is such a scenario with a highly suggestive—if abstract—plot.

Each floor is a separate installment of a complex intrigue—their sequence as random as only the elevator man can make them—this form of architecture is a form of Modernistic writing: the planning of choreography of mankind through experimental techno-psychic apparatus designed by themselves to celebrate their own redesign.

The lower 15 floors of the building are accessible only to men. Their sequence from the ground to the top corresponds to an increasing refinement and artifice. From the 17th to the 18–1/2th floor, the men, perfected in the lower floors, are allowed to communicate with the opposite sex in the dining room, the roof terrace and the dance floor. The final 20 floors are devoted to Hotel accommodation.

Floors 7, 9, 11 and 12 deserve special analysis for their extreme daring: Emerging from the elevator on the 9th floor, the visitor—probably a Wall Street stockbroker—finds himself in a vestibule that leads directly to a locker-room at the center of the floor (where there is no daylight). There he undresses, puts on gloves and enters an adjoining space that is equipped for boxing and wrestling. But on the southern side, the locker-room is also served by a small oyster bar.

Eating oysters with boxing gloves, naked, on the 9th floor—such is the plot of this floor—the 20th century in action.

The 10th floor is devoted to preventive medicine. On one side of a large dressing room and lounge an array of body manipulations—sections for massage and rubbing, an 8-bed station for artificial sunbathing (open to the river), a 10-bed rest area—is arranged around a Turkish bath. The south-east corner of the floor is a medical facility capable of treating five patients at once. A doctor is charged with the process of "colonic irrigation," the literal invasion of the human body with cultivated bacteria that modify and accelerate the natural metabolism of the human body.

This final step completes the sequence of radical intervention and voluntary self-experimentation initiated by such apparently innocent attractions as Coney Island's "Barrels of Love."

On the 12th floor, a swimming pool occupies almost the full rectangle. At night, it is illuminated by an underwater lighting system, so that the entire slab of water with its frenetic swimmers appears to float in space, between the electric scintillation of the Wall Street skyline.

Of all the floors, the Interior Golfcourse is perhaps the most significant enterprise: an interior English garden landscape of small hills and valleys, a little river that curls across the rectangle, green grass (real), a bridge. . . . A mural extends the landscape toward a nebulous horizon, but the regular punctuation of the lighting fixtures on the ceiling reminds, irrevocably, of fabrication.

The presence of the Golfcourse argues that nature, obliterated by all the Metropolitan structures, will now be resurrected as merely one of the layers of the Metropolis. After its total eclipse, nature returns as one of the services of the Culture of Congestion.

Conclusion: 2

Through the medium of the Skyscraper, each site in the Metropolis accommodates— in theory at least—an unstable and unforeseeable combination of superimposed and simultaneous activities whose configuration is fundamentally beyond the control of architect or planner.

As a vehicle of Urbanism, the indeterminacy of the Skyscraper suggests that—in the Metropolis—no single specific *function* can be matched with a single *place*.

Through this destabilization it is possible to absorb the "change that is life" by continuously rearranging functions on the individual platforms in an incessant process of adaptation that does not affect the framework of the building itself.

Exteriors and interiors of such structures belong to two different kinds of architectures. The first—external—is only concerned with the appearance of the building as a more or less serene sculptural object, while the interior is in a constant state of flux—of themes, programs, iconographies—in which the volatile metropolitan citizens, with their overstimulated nervous systems, combat the perpetual threat of ennui.

Radio City Music Hall

The application of technology at the service of metaphor occurs at a still more explicit level and on a larger scale than the Athletic Club in Radio City Music Hall, a theater for 6200.

Rem Koolhaas with Zoe Zenghelis, *The City of the Captive Globe*, painting by Madelon Vriesendorp, from *Delirious New York*, 1978

It is a prototype of a strictly interior architecture inserted in the neutral envelope of Rockefeller Center. Its cosmogony was not invented by its official architects, but by their client, the impresario Samuel Rothafel, known as Roxy.

In the early 1930s a group of architects—among them Wallace Harrison—took Roxy on a European tour—all the way to Moscow—in an attempt to convert him to Modern Architecture.

But Roxy remained indifferent to the antiseptic accommodations which modern architects had designed for the fundamentally irrational culture of the theater. On his return to New York, he had a revelation when he watched a mid-Atlantic sunset. "I didn't conceive of the idea. I dreamed it. I believe in creative dreams. The picture of Radio City Music Hall was complete and practically perfect in my mind before architects and artists put pen on drawing paper." His theater is to be a simulation of the spectacle he beheld from the railing of the ship: a sunset.

Roxy's architect dutifully executed the metaphorical theme. A vast ovoid space is covered with plaster "rays" that extend across the ceiling of the entire theatre, embracing the audience like a firmament. The curtain is made of an especially developed synthetic fiber—so glittering that it outshines the real sun. When the lights are slowly dimmed, the impression of a sunset is inescapable.

But the lights have to go on again. And off again. There are three or four such cycles for each complete performance. If the metaphor is taken seriously, the audience lives through three or four accelerated days.

Then Roxy discovered that the air-conditioning system could be used for more creative purposes than simple cooling and heating—i.e., to increase the density of metaphor in the auditorium. First he considered adding laughing gas to its atmosphere, so that his 6200 clients would be transported to "another world" where they would be more receptive to the impact of the movies. However, he desisted after urgent pleading by his lawyers, but only after substituting health-giving Ozone for the N2O. Now his theater combines "Supertime" with "Superhealth," a union that is caught perfectly in his advertisement: "A visit to Radio City Music Hall is as good as a month in the country."

Conclusion: 3

As in the example of Radio City Music Hall, planning in Manhattan consists of the imposition on the explosive substance of the Metropolis of metaphoric models—at once primitive and efficient—that replace literal organization—impossible in any case—with a form of conceptual control.

Such hermetic, self-contained enclaves offer emotional shelter to the disinherited Metropolitan masses, ideal worlds removed in time and space, protected against the corrosion of everyday reality in their interior locations. These sub-Utopian fragments are all the more convincing for having no territorial ambitions beyond occupying their interior allotments through a private hyperdensity of symbolism and localized paroxysms of the particular. Together, such moments form a matrix of frivolity, a system of poetic formulas that replaces traditional quantifiable planning in favor of metaphoric planning.

Movement in the Metropolis becomes ideological navigation between the conflicting claims and promises of "islands" of a metaphoric archipelago.

Postscript

The three episodes above present a provisional triangulation of a truly Metropolitan architecture. If they appear extravagant, or even unreal, that is only a sign of the narrowness of our architectural focus and of our refusal to admit that a fundamental break has occurred between traditional and modern Urbanisms.

These "stories" describe a tradition of modernity that insists on systematically exploiting all available apparatus and all the fresh infrastructures of the age to establish fantasies as realities in the world. The cumulative effect of such scattered episodes—and no doubt the cause of the anxieties they inspire—is that they discredit the idea of Reality as an immutable and indestructible presence—of reality as an ultimate safety net under our flawed acrobatic performances.

Instead, the "hysterical" structures of the Metropolis represent a free fall in the space of human imagination, a fall with unpredictable outcome, not even the certainty that it will end on the ground.

The true ambition of the Metropolis is to create a world totally fabricated by man, i.e., to live *inside* fantasy. The responsibilities of a specifically Metropolitan architecture have increased correspondingly: to design those hermetic enclaves—bloated private realms—that comprise the Metropolis. Such an architecture not only creates the "sets" of everyday life, but it also defines its contents with all possible means and disciplines such as literature, psychology, etc. Through the magical arrangement of human activities on all possible levels, it writes a scenario for the scriptless Metropolitan extras.

If that appears a form of megalomania, such a megalomania is tempered by the fact that its expressions are always localized, since they address, by definition, only a part of the total audience, never the whole. Metropolitan architecture is megalomaniac on a modest scale.

Metropolitan architecture thus defined implies a 2-fold polemic: against those who believe that they can undo the damage of the Modern Age—i.e., the Metropolis itself—through the artificial respiration and resuscitation of "traditional" architecture of streets, plazas, boulevards, etc.; empty spaces for dignified and decent forms of social intercourse, to be enforced in the name of a stoic good taste . . . and against that Modern architecture which—with its implacable aversion to metaphor—has tried to exorcise its fear of chaos through a fetish for the objective and to regain control over the volatility of the Metropolis by dispersing its bulk, isolating its components, and quantifying its functions, and render it predictable once more. . . . Both squander the potential of the Culture of Congestion.

The Urbanism of the 3 episodes was subconscious and spontaneous, not the result of an explicit doctrine. It was followed by an interval in which the architecture of the Metropolis has regressed, or at least fallen under the domination of official architecture.

Alan Colquhoun **"From Bricolage to Myth, or How to Put Humpty-Dumpty Together Again"**

Oppositions 12 (Spring 1978)

see **284–286**;
compare
262–264

In his early essay "Typology and Design Method," written in 1966 and published in the 1967 *Arena* edited by George Baird, Alan Colquhoun had already taken up a position akin to Roland Barthes's "mythologist": he set about dissolving purportedly "objective" design decisions into their historical and ideological concepts with the seemingly simple and implicitly semiotic recognition that "a plastic system of representation such as architecture has to presuppose the existence of a given system of representation."[1] In 1972, Colquhoun published the first of his many explicit meditations on semiology, structuralism, and architecture, "Historicism and the Limits of Semiology," where he again insisted on the fundamental and inescapable dilemma of architectural practice: to be meaningful, architecture must recombine elements already invested with conventional meanings, yet that same recombinatory act can itself be neither normative nor neutral; it is a value judgment of the individual designer with tractable ideological effects.[2]

Several other threads of architectural discourse converge in Colquhoun's essay on the work of Michael Graves, reprinted here. In 1972 Mario Gandelsonas had theorized, for the first time, the work of Graves as a semiotic system, opposing Graves's concern with the "semantic dimension" of architecture to Peter Eisenman's exclusively "syntactic" operations.[3] By 1978, Colin Rowe's undermining of any critical claims of American post-Corbusianism and Manfredo Tafuri's relegation of the same to the confines of the boudoir had further polemicized the terrain on which Graves's work was to be interpreted. And the widely accepted partitioning of critical categories like neorationalism and neorealism forced most commentators on contemporaneous design production to steer through that terrain accordingly. Finally, 1978 marked an internal turning point for Graves's work, from a post-Corbusian experimentation to an overtly anthropomorphic and classicizing collage of forms.

Colquhoun's essay on Graves should further be seen in relation to his "Form and Figure," written at the same time and published together with the former in *Oppositions* 12. In "Form and Figure," Colquhoun makes his uneasiness felt about the neorealists' cynical technical and economic exploitation of graphic fragments from the mass-media sign system (Charles Moore and Robert Venturi are examples), and the neorationalists' abnegation of certain technological imperatives in order to achieve their archetypal figures (Aldo Rossi et al.).

When he turns to the work of Graves, Colquhoun throws these two positions into dialectical relationship, situating Graves's work not exactly as the resolution of the conflict between the architectural sign and technical structure but as the mythification of the terms of conflict. Graves exploits the technical openness of the American balloon frame and strives to achieve an ahistorical, archetypal representation, but by reducing all functional, constructional, and representational elements to the condition of tautology: architecture represents architecture. It is no longer possible to distinguish between elements that derive from functional or structural considerations—walls, windows, columns, frames—and those more purely compositional elements lifted from cubist and purist painting. Images from the landscape—clouds, trees, hedges—exist on the same level as images from building—

soffits, stairs, door frames, handrails. Spatial typologies from academic Beaux-Arts plan systems are combined with figural fragments from the Corbusian repertoire, all bleached of their original historical reference and reconfigured in new constellations.

Then, Colquhoun observes, Graves seeks to coordinate the resulting series of isolated, fragmented elements in a narrative or ritual of controlled "anecdotal and episodic" encounters. Clusters of contiguous elements are sorted into thematic oppositions—zones of interstitial passage and transition versus zones of arrival and stasis; perspectival "real" space versus "virtual" spaces layered or flattened into murals; metaphorical realms counterposing a "sacred" interior to a "profane" exterior. Sequences of architectural frames momentarily fix certain locations as thresholds distinguishing and conjoining the different themes. Thus do architectural elements, organizational *partis*, and ritualized exchanges between the body and architectural form all move from a "*bricolage* made from figural fragments which are still recognizable"[4] to become prime examples of what Barthes called "the privation of history": "In [myth], history evaporates. It is a kind of ideal servant: it prepares all things, brings them, lays them out, the master arrives, it silently disappears: all that is left for one to do is to enjoy this beautiful object without wondering where it comes from."[5]

In a postscript to Colquhoun's essay, Peter Eisenman accuses him of uncritically following Rowe's split between form and content, too easily accepting a nonideological method of analysis, and overlooking Graves's shift away from a modernist "work on the language." But, though characteristically uncensorious, Colquhoun's structuralist use of the title "from bricolage to myth" already pins Graves's work to, precisely, ideology. For what constitutes myth is not its content but its form; and myth is not just a message, but a message that is political by virtue of its own depoliticizing. Myth turns culture into nature, history into essence, and obscures just those socioeconomic forces that legitimate its being.

Notes

"From Bricolage to Myth" was reprinted in Alan Colquhoun, *Essays in Architectural Criticism: Modern Architecture and Historical Change* (Cambridge: MIT Press, 1981).

1. Alan Colquhoun, "Typology and Design Method," *Arena* 33 (June 1967), reprinted in Colquhoun, *Essays in Architectural Criticism*, p. 49.

As part of his mythological analyses, Barthes formulated a multitiered semiotics that seizes on the inherent reiterability of the signifier/signified unit. In myth, the first-order sign, operating at what Barthes calls the level of denotation, becomes, in turn, the form or signifier of the second-level, connotative sign, which produces a new and more insidious message. He identifies the level of connotation with the operation of ideology or myth, which consists of the deployment of preformed signs from the level of denotation for the purpose of expressing and surreptitiously legitimating the dominant values of a given period. The denotative message belongs to a self-sufficient but contingent, historical order, which myth abstracts, naturalizes, and uses as an alibi. Through this "theft of language," the mythical message comes to impose itself with the straightforwardness of an empirical fact, making the historical seem natural and the contingent eternal and inevitable, and reducing the complexity of culture's artifacts to a circumscribed set of privileged signifieds. See Roland Barthes, "Myth Today," in *Mythologies,* trans. Annette Lavers (New York: Hill and Wang, 1972).

2.   Alan Colquhoun, "Historicism and the Limits of Semiology," *Op. Cit.* 25 (September 1972), reprinted in Colquhoun, *Essays in Architectural Criticism.* In 1988 Colquhoun returned to his meditations on structuralism, now historicizing the emergence of the theoretical method itself and linking it to postmodernism's critique of modernist functional and historical determinism. See Alan Colquhoun, "Structuralism and Postmodernism: A Retrospective Glance," *Assemblage* 5 (February 1988).

3.   Mario Gandelsonas and David Morton, "On Reading Architecture," *Progressive Architecture* 53 (March 1972), pp. 68–88; reprinted in *Signs, Symbols, and Architecture,* ed. Geoffrey Broadbent (New York: Wiley, 1980).

4.   Alan Colquhoun, "Form and Figure," *Oppositions* 12 (Spring 1978), p. 31. It is important to note that this definition of bricolage was made with reference to Ledoux, Boullée, and Lequeu, architects closely studied by the neorationalists but also strongly present at Princeton (where Colquhoun has taught since 1978) in the historiography of Anthony Vidler. Leon Krier's visit to Princeton around 1978 also contributed to Graves's assimilation of this neoclassicism and, no doubt, to Colquhoun's interpretation of the same.

5.   Roland Barthes, "Myth Today," p. 151.

Criticism occupies the no-man's-land between enthusiasm and doubt, between poetic sympathy and analysis. Its purpose is not, except in rare cases, either to eulogize
or condemn, and it can never grasp the essence of the work it discusses. It must try
to get behind the work's apparent originality and expose its ideological framework
without turning it into a mere tautology.

  This applies particularly to the work of Michael Graves, with
its appearance of being *sui generis* and its sensitivity to outside influences which it
immediately absorbs into its own system. This essay, therefore, will attempt to discuss his work in terms of these broad contexts: the American tradition, the tradition
of modern architecture, and the classical tradition. It is not suggested that a discussion of his work in these terms exhausts its meaning. It merely provides a rough
and ready scaffold—a way of approaching the work obliquely.

  Graves's work is so clearly related to the international Modern
Movement that it is at first sight difficult to see in it any reference to purely American traditions. But some of the ways in which it differs (and differs profoundly)
from European interpretations of the Modern Movement seem to be traceable to
specifically American sources. Graves's apparent rejection of modern architecture as
a social instrument—and his insistence that architecture communicates with individuals and not classes—does not operate in a social void. His work is made possible by social conditions which are probably unique to the United States at the
present moment (though they existed in Europe between 1890 and 1930). The
chief of these is the existence of a type of client (whether institutional or private)
which regards the architect not only as a technician who can solve functional problems, or satisfy a more or less pre-formulated and predictable set of desires, but
also as an arbiter of taste. In this role he is called upon not only to decide matters
of decorum; like the modern painter, he is expected to say something "new," to
propound a philosophy. No doubt this only applies to a minority of clients (and
even these are probably often puzzled at the results), but their very existence explains how an architect as intensely "private" as Michael Graves can insert himself
within the institutionalized framework of society despite the absence of a clearly
defined "market." If his work reflects a nostalgia for "culture" which is characteristically American, and which, as Manfredo Tafuri has pointed out,[1] can be traced
back at least to the City Beautiful movement, it depends on the existence of a type
of client who has similar—though less well defined—aspirations. In Europe the
critique of a materialistic modern architecture has usually taken place under the
banner of a betrayed populism. It is perhaps only in America that it could be
launched in the name of intellectual culture. Certainly the importance in Graves's
work of the French tradition—its assimilation, initially through the example of Le
Corbusier, of the Beaux Arts discipline of the plan—has its origins in a purely
American tradition going back to Richardson and McKim.

  But there also exists a technological condition peculiar to the
United States which seems especially favorable to Graves's architecture and which

is related to the social, insofar as it depends on the fact that most of his commissions are for private houses or additions. This is the balloon frame—a system of construction whose lightness and adaptability gives the designer great freedom and allows him to treat structural matters in an ad hoc way. Without this form of construction an architectural language like that of Graves, which depends on a blurring of the distinction between what is real and what is virtual, and between structure and ornament, would hardly be conceivable. By using a system of construction which provides so few constraints, Graves is able to treat structure as a pure "idea." The regular grid, for example, which is such an important ingredient of his work, is relieved of those positivistic and utilitarian qualities which it had for Le Corbusier (e.g. in the Maison Domino). For Graves structure has become a pure metaphor, and he thus reverses the postulates of the Modern Movement, in which the split between perception and calculation resulted in an emphasis on instrumentality.

The openness and transparency of Graves's houses are made possible by the use of the frame, while their complexity and ambiguity are made possible by the fact that the frame can be manipulated at will. These are qualities which his work shares with the Shingle Style, even more than with its Shavian counterpart, and seem characteristic of later nineteenth century American domestic architecture. In Europe the houses of the Modern Movement were relatively box-like. The Neo-Plasticist projects of Van Doesburg and Mies van der Rohe were the exception, and it is these projects, as Vincent Scully has pointed out, which have such a striking resemblance to the houses of Frank Lloyd Wright, with their hovering planes and strong vertical accents. If the houses of Graves also have closer ties with Neo-Plasticism than with the more typical houses of the European movement, it may be that, as in the case of Wright, there is a coincidence between Cubist spatial principles and an American tradition which, in its response to climate, in its attitude toward nature, and in a certain kind of sociability, creates an intermediate zone between the private realm of the house and the public realm of its environment. Not only the openness of the nineteenth century American house, but also the proliferation of verandas, porches, and bay windows, and the frequent placing of these on the diagonal suggest a parallel with the way Graves weaves secondary spaces in and out of the periphery of the cage, or superimposes a diagonal fragment on an otherwise orthogonal parti.

All this is perhaps to say no more than that the picturesque nineteenth century house is a precursor of a modern architecture which combines Cubist devices with an anecdotal and episodic elaboration of the program. This should surprise us no more than similar connections in the other arts, for instance the fact that modern music took over from romantic music its rejection of classical symmetry and classical cadence.

In the context of contemporary American architecture, there are two figures with whom one is tempted to compare Graves.

Among the architects of the New York Five, with whom Graves has become associated, it is Peter Eisenman with whom he seems to have the greatest affinity. In the mid-sixties, when they worked together on a competition for a site located on the upper west side of Manhattan, they both shared the same influences—notably that of the Como School—and attempted to construct a new architectural language out of the basic vocabulary of the Modern Movement. But from the start they diverged—Eisenman toward a syntactic language of exclusion, Graves toward a language of allusion and metaphor. This semantic inclusiveness has led Graves to direct historical quotation, which now puts his work at the opposite pole from that of Eisenman. But in the work of both one finds an architecture in which the ideal completely dominates the pragmatic. It is true that Graves—in contrast to Eisenman—starts from the practical program, the distribution of living spaces. But these quotidian considerations are merely a point of departure; they are immediately ritualized and turned into symbols—for example, the ritual of entry. With Eisenman the semantic dimension is conceptual and mathematical; with Graves it is sensuous and metaphysical.

Graves's later work might seem to bear some resemblance to (and even the imprint of) the work of Robert Venturi, with his parodistic use of traditional motifs. But this similarity is superficial. Graves shows no interest in what seems to be Venturi's chief concern: the problem of communication in modern democratic societies, and of "architecture as mass medium." If Venturi wants to bridge the gap between "pop music and Vivaldi," Graves remains exclusively a "serious" composer, for whom the possibility of communication is predicated on the existence even in a fragmentary form of a tradition of high architecture. This no doubt explains Venturi's preference for the romantic and populist overtones of vernacular architecture, as against that of Graves for the architecture of the classical and academic traditions.

Though the degree of dependence of Graves's work on American traditions is perhaps arguable, its affiliations with the Modern Movement are beyond dispute. The nostalgic quality of these affiliations has been stressed by other critics, but it should not be forgotten that Graves belongs to a generation for whom the Modern Movement still represented all that was vital and creative in architecture. To return to the 1920s and Le Corbusier was not an eclectic choice but a return to sources. What was new about this return was its rejection of functionalism and its claim that architecture had never exploited the formal and semantic possibilities of modernism as the other arts had. There was also the conviction that the "new tradition" of avant-garde art constituted a historical development from which it was impossible to turn back.

It is certainly true that the development of the avant-garde marks a radical break with the form of artistic language which existed until the latter part of the nineteenth century. Traditionally, language was always thought of as describing something outside itself, in the "real" world. The difference between natural language (considered as an instrument rather than a poetics) and artistic languages was merely that in the latter the form was an integral part of the message—the "how" was as important as the "what." At whatever date we put the moment when the epistemological foundations of this "rhetorical" world began to disintegrate, it was not until the end of the nineteenth century, and in the context of avant-garde art, that the content of a work began to become indistinguishable from its form. External reality was no longer seen as a donnée with its own preordained meanings, but a series of fragments, essentially enigmatic, whose meanings depended on how they were formally related or juxtaposed by the artist.

In modern architecture this process took the form of demolishing the traditional meanings associated with function. But these were replaced by another set of functional meanings, and architecture was still seen in terms of a functional program which was translated, as directly as possible, into forms. In the work of both Graves and Eisenman, this linear relation between content and form has been rejected. Function has been absorbed into form. "Functional" meanings still exist, but they no longer constitute a prior condition to derive their nourishment from a pragmatic level of operation. They are reconstructed on the basis of the building as a pure work of art, with its own internally consistent laws.

By returning to the sources of modern architecture Graves attempted to open up a seam which had never been fully exploited, as it had been in Cubist painting. In his work, the elements of *techné* and those of architecture (windows, walls, columns) are isolated and recombined in a way which allows new metonymic and metaphoric interpretations to be made. At the same time rhythms, symmetries, perspectives, and diminutions are exploited in a way which suggests the need, in discussing his work, for a descriptive vocabulary such as existed in the Beaux Arts tradition, and still exists in musical criticism, but which is generally lacking in modern architectural discourse.

Within this process no semantic distinction exists between functions and forms. They reinforce each other to produce meanings which extend in an unbroken chain from the most habitual and redundant to the most complex and information-laden. To respond to Michael Graves's architecture it is essential to understand the "reduction" which is involved in such a process, for it is this which makes his work specifically "modern." It involves the dismantling of the preconceptions which would allow one to have a ready-made idea of what a "house" is, and insists that the observer or user carry out a reconstruction of the object. Graves's elementarism is related both to the architecture of the Modern Movement and to modern art in general. It is tied to an elementarization resulting from industrialization and the disappearance of craft, and it strives for the condition of the *tabula rasa*, the primal statement.

The reconstruction of the object, made necessary by this process of analysis and reduction, involves the use of codes which are themselves meaningful and internally coherent. But what interests Graves is not the way in which these syntactically organized and semantically loaded elements already form a system whose meaning has been ideologically internalized. For him all the elements must be reduced to the same condition of "raw material." They have become de-historicized and "potential," and must be reconstructed consciously as a "structure." He is interested in how such a structure works perceptually as the product of conflicts and tensions in the psyche of the individual. He demonstrates the *process* by which meanings are generated, and this leads him to a language whose articulation depends on oppositions, fragmentation, and the visual pun.

In this process of reduction Graves does not attempt (as Peter Eisenman does) to strip the elements of their connotations. Columns, openings, spaces all retain their qualities of body image and the meanings which have accumulated around them. Not only do the basic architectonic elements have meanings which relate to their functions, but their very isolation allows them to become metaphors. There is, indeed, a danger that these metaphors may remain private and incommunicable, and in his earlier work this danger is increased because of the reliance on relatively abstract forms. Where meanings are clear in his earlier work, they tend to be those which have already become established in modern architecture.

The most fundamental source of Graves's work (and it is this which links him with the other members of the so-called New York Five) is Le Corbusier. In Le Corbusier's work there is always a tension between the figurations and symmetries of the French classical tradition and the infinite improvisations which are demanded by modern life and which are made possible by the neutral grid. It is this tension which Graves exploits. But he superimposes on this Corbusian system—whose chief vehicle is the "free plan"—an open three-dimensional cage which was seldom used by Le Corbusier. The vertical planes of Graves's work are closely related to the work of Giuseppe Terragni—to such buildings as the Casa del Fascio and the Asile Infantile at Como, with their open structural cage, their delicate layering of structural planes, and their frequent absorption of the frame within the wall surface. The transparency of the cage enables Graves to provide an adumbration of the building's limits without destroying the flow of space between inside and outside. The dialectic between solid and planar elements and the structural grid becomes a basic architectural theme, not only in plan but as perceived in three dimensions, and dominates the whole plastic organization in a way which it seldom does in the work of Le Corbusier.

Apart from these purely architectural sources, Graves's work is directly related to Cubist and Purist painting. His work as a painter is closer to his architecture than Le Corbusier's was to his. For Le Corbusier painting provided a lyrical outlet to some extent constrained by the logical and systematic researches of the architect, but Graves develops parallel themes in both painting and architecture,

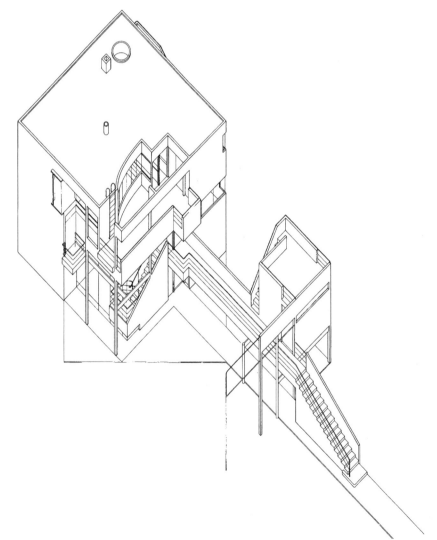

Michael Graves,
Hanselmann
House, 1967

among which one finds the typically Cubist notion of a world built out of fragments, related to each other not according to the logic of the perceived world, but according to the laws of pictorial construction. His buildings are, as it were, projections into real three-dimensional space of a shallow pictorial space, and his spaces are frequently made up of planes which create an impression of Renaissance perspective or of successive planes of the Baroque theater.

Although the dominance of the three-dimensional frame suggests, as in Neo-Plasticism, the parity between all three dimensions, in Graves's work the plan is still thought of as possessing figural qualities which actually generate the vertical and spatial configurations, in the manner of Le Corbusier and the Beaux Arts. It is in the development of the plan that the influence of his painting can be felt most strongly. The paintings suggest collages built up out of fragments which create diagonal fault lines or, as if with torn paper, trembling profiles suggestive of the edges of bodies. These elements reappear on his plans and create a nervous interplay of fragmentary planes, a web of countervailing spatial pressures inflected with slow curves or overlaid with diagonal figures.

Unlike the plans of Le Corbusier, with their muscular, vertebral sense of order, Graves's plans tend to be dispersed and episodic, and often resemble, perhaps fortuitously, the plan of Chareau's Maison de Verre, with its multiple centers, complex spatial subdivisions, and gentle inflections. There is, in Graves's plans, a sense of almost endless elaboration and half-statement, every function being a clue for syntactic complexity or metaphorical qualification.

This elaboration is not arbitrary; it comes from an extreme sensitivity to context, and this is perhaps its chief difference from the tradition of the Modern Movement, with its attempt to create architectural types of a new order in polemical contrast to the existing built environment. I have said that many of Graves's projects are additions. These additions draw attention to their difference from the existing buildings, but they do not ignore them. The old house is considered as a fragment which it is possible to extend and qualify in a way unforeseen in the original. In the Benacerraf House, for example, the wall separating the original house and the extension is removed, and the cage of the addition penetrates into the living spaces of the existing house to form a transparent veil which transforms the original space and overlays it with a new spatial meaning.

But sensitivity to context is equally apparent in completely new structures. The houses respond to the natural environment, which itself is modified by the building. The more typical houses of the Modern Movement tended to respond to the gross features of the environment (particularly orientation) by setting up elementary oppositions, for example that between an open side which was fully glazed and a closed side which was solid. Graves uses this basic opposition as a compositional point of departure, as can be seen in the Hanselmann House of 1965, where the theme open/closed is almost obsessively stated, and is reinforced by a ritualistic frontalization and a displacement of the front facade to form an additional plane of entry. But in other works, for instance the Snyderman House of 1969, the opposition closed/open is used with greater subtlety, and is qualified by a number of conflicting contextual demands. The "closed" surface is punctured by a variety of openings, and its function as a limiting plane is actually enhanced by its greater transparency. The way in which this and other diagrammatic expressions of opposition are modified in the design process is illustrated by comparing the sketches for the Snyderman House with the final design. In the early sketches the plan consists of two equal axes at right angles, the east-west axis being bounded on the west by a solid wall punctured by only one opening and on the east by an open surface with fragmentary obstructions. As the design progresses these ideas are retained but are overlaid with counterstatements. The west wall becomes a perforated screen. At the same time the east-west axis is strengthened by a caesura in the structural grid, while the north-south axis is suppressed. A diagonal is introduced by the erosion of the south-east corner and the skewing of the second floor accommodation—a diagonal which is reinforced by raising the south and east facades to three stories. These moves suggest entry from the south-east corner and act in contrapuntal opposition to the plan's biaxial symmetry. The house is no longer a statement of simple oppositions, but an overlay of several *different* oppositions, each element separately inviting contradictory interpretations.

Other ways in which Graves's buildings differ from more orthodox modern buildings can be seen by analyzing the Gunwyn office conversion at Princeton of 1972. The elements used in this design are those which one might expect to find in a typical "systems approach" building of the West Coast—tubular steel columns, exposed I-beams, standard lighting tracks, and office furniture. The basic imagery is industrial, efficient, smooth.

But there is another language superimposed on this. Whereas, according to functionalist practice, the systems should be logically independent, Graves (starting, as always, from Le Corbusier's poetic use of mechanical forms but going further into a world of free fantasy) deliberately overlaps them to produce ambiguities which gently subvert their primary and unequivocal meanings, and give rise to less obvious correspondences.

The space of the office is complex, with various penetrations through three stories. A hatch to the second floor office projects over one of these voids. Its waferthin work-top is carried on a bracket attached to the column on the *opposite* side of the void, which thus reaches out to receive an unexpected but hardly onerous burden and at the same time provides the hatch with a frame which it has borrowed from the nearby tubular balustrade at floor level. Similar ambiguities are created when the glass-brick wall to the office is prized open and an I-beam inserted to support its upper half. This I-beam, seen from alongside the office, appears as a jagged fragment mysteriously projecting from a column. Most of the columns are circular, but when they occur in a wall they turn into pilasters and merge with the wall surface above. All these fragments and transpositions have a local, internal logic of their own. Their shock effect is a result of the way they undermine expected hierarchies. The fragments are differentiated by means of color, for the most part brilliant, but intermixed with grass greens, sky blues and flesh pinks. Just as these colors suggest elements of nature, so does the metaphorical play of functional elements have anthropomorphic, and sometimes surreal, overtones relating mechanical functions to our own bodies, and making us question reality.

Graves's buildings, in the phase of his work most directly influenced by the Modern Movement, consist of a large number of variations on a limited number of themes. The most persistent idea is that of the open frame defining a continuous space partially interrupted by planes and solids. Not only is horizontal space continuous but vertical penetrations occur at crucial points to create three-dimensional continuity. Through this space the frame is threaded, creating a dialectic between a rational *a priori* order and a circumstantial, sensuous, and complex plastic order. This is in essence the "free plan" of Le Corbusier, but developed with greater complexity in a repetition, transformation, and interweaving of formal themes reminiscent of musical structure. Tensions develop around the periphery of the building, and there is a maximum exploitation, by means of layered screenings and shallow recessions, of the plane of the facade—an intense moment of transition between the "profane" world outside the house and the "sacred" world inside.

Graves's work cannot be called "classical" in any strict sense. But his thought is permeated with a kind of eighteenth century deism, and a belief that architecture is a perennial symbolic language, whose origins lie in nature and our response to nature. He finds support for these views in such modern writers as Geoffrey Scott and Mircea Eliade. The frequent use in his writings of the words "sacred" and "profane" shows that he regards architecture as a secular religion which is in some sense revelatory.

In his earlier work the symbolic images and metaphors are very generalized and are drawn from a repertoire of abstract forms chiefly derived from Le Corbusier and Terragni. This language is autonomous within an architectural tradition and operates through the use of certain graphic codes, the most important of which is the plan. But during the early 1970s Graves seems to have become dissatisfied with the expressive possibilities of this language and, above all, of the plan as an abstraction, and this dissatisfaction coincides with a radical change of style. The attitude behind it is expressed in the following program notes for a student project: "The design of a guest house addition to an existing villa is given . . . to focus the students' attention on the perceptual elements of a building, the wall surfaces, and the spaces they describe. . . . The plan is seen as a conceptual tool, a two-dimensional diagram or notational device, with limited capacity to express the perceptual elements which exist in three-dimensional space."[2]

Graves's buildings have always laid stress on these "perceptual elements"—especially on the function of the plane as a method of stratifying space, and as symbolic of the spaces which it defines or conceals. But in his earlier projects the solid and planar elements in themselves were reduced to the degree zero of expressiveness, in accordance with the functionalist precept of minimum interference with the industrial product as "ready-made." In his more recent work these elements have begun to be semantically elaborated. They are no longer the minimal ciphers which go to form a rich metonymy; they become overlaid with meanings belonging to the architectural tradition. Columns develop shafts and capitals; openings are qualified with architraves and pediments; wall surfaces become ornamented. A new dimension of purely architectural metaphor is added to the functionalist and natural metaphors of his earlier work.

It is possible that these ideas developed initially less from a process of deduction than from particular design problems. The use of figural elements seems, for example, to be connected with his habit of extracting the maximum of meaning from a given context. In the Claghorn House of 1974—which seems a pivotal work—the humble motif of a chair rail with bolection moldings is used as a way of linking the new to the old. This seems to have been suggested by the fact that the existing house had few spatial qualities, but a strong nineteenth century flavor. This carrying through of motifs is similar to the use of the frame in the Benacerraf House. But here the process is reversed. Instead of the new extending its language back into the old, the thematics of the old are re-used in the new. As if in sympathy with this, the outside of the addition has a heavily figural quality, with a broken pediment and a wall trellis, turning what would have been an inconsequential statement into one which is dense with parabolic meanings. At the same time, somber colors echoing the period taste of the old house replace the clear colors of the earlier work.

At about the same time, architraves and other figural elements appear in Graves's paintings, and these underline the fact that the change to a figurative, ornamental architecture has not altered his method of composition, with its dependence on *collage*. It is like the change from analytical to synthetic Cubism. Traditional figures are introduced as quotations and fragments, as were the functionalist motifs of the earlier work. Because these figures already exist in our memory, and because they are ornamental and not structural, they can be transposed, split up, inverted or distorted without losing their original meanings. The chief sources of this "metalanguage" are Italian Mannerism, eighteenth century "romantic classicism," and the later Beaux Arts. But in developing a language of ornament which is simple and allows for repetition, Graves has recourse to the language of Art Deco—that "debased" style which tried to unite the more decorative aspects of Cubism with a remembered tradition of architectural ornament.

In Graves's earlier buildings the fundamental element is the frame or grid, creating a Cartesian field in which the planes and volumes locate themselves. It is impossible, in such a system, for the wall to develop any density; its function is simply to modulate space. In his more recent work the wall—or the wall fragment—takes the place of the frame as the main organizing element. Two consequences follow from this. First, the space is no longer continuous but is made up of discrete spatial figures bounded by walls or colonnades. The walls develop thickness, and the negative, solid spaces are read as poché. Figural space is seen as carved out of solid mass. During the preliminary stages of the design, the plan is allowed to suggest the spatial composition independently of its three-dimensional consequences; thus, in the Crooks House, the early sketches show no distinction between house walls and garden hedges; according to the code of the plan, they both define space in terms of void and solid, figure and poché. But this results in a metaphorical relationship between house and garden; topiary defines internal spaces, whose "ceiling" is the sky. We see here that ambiguity between fully enclosed space and semi-enclosed space which has always been a feature in Graves's buildings. The second consequence of the new importance given to the wall is that the shallow layering of space in the frontal plane of the building, which was previously created by parallel and separate planes suspended in the cage, is now flattened onto the wall surface itself. The wall becomes a bas-relief with layers of ornament which are built up or peeled away. Fragments of architectural motifs are assembled to create a balanced asymmetrical whole.

The massive architectural elements which occur on the facade are frequently distorted and transposed. Thus, in the studies for the Plocek House, several simultaneous interpretations of the same figures are invited. The main entry is monumentalized by the presence of two giant columns supporting a flat arch. But this monumentality is subverted by contradictions. The traditional flat arch with voussoirs is established, but subjected to a figure-ground reversal by the removal of the keystone. The expected pyramidal composition is reversed; the center is a void between the masses on either side, which become a "split pair." The voussoirs are read both in their normal sense as radiating wedges on a flat plane and as the receding lines of a trompe l'oeil perspective. The columns are structurally redundant in voussoir construction. Their role as pylons constricting and guarding the entrance is reinforced by the absence of capitals and the insertion of an architrave between them and the arch. Such transformations can be seen as an extension of the Mannerist permutation of a repertoire of figures, whereby two systems of meaning are superimposed, and their paradigmatic relations are stated explicitly in the same object, e.g. in the "Gibbs surround."

In Graves's earlier work metonymic and metaphoric meanings had to be created by the relationship between elements which were themselves relatively mute. As soon as established architectural figures become the basic counters, relationships are established, not between irreducible forms, but between the semantic contents existing in the figures. His buildings now become bricolages of recognizable figures complete with their historical connotations. For example, on the bridge of the Fargo-Moorhead project, there is an overt reference to Ledoux's barrel-shaped "House for the Director of the river Loüe" in the Saline de Chaux, and this image is conflated with a frozen waterfall reminiscent of the ornamental urne à congélations on the main gate. But it is the way in which Ledoux has reduced the classical repertoire to pure geometrical figures which enables his forms to release primary and archetypal sensations. The historical reference by itself is not enough. Graves's work there-fore depends on eighteenth century sensationalist theory, and not on pure historical associations.

Perhaps the most important single aspect of Graves's work lies in the attitude toward nature which it reflects. There is, in his work, a continual dialectic between architecture as the product of reason, setting itself against nature, and architecture as a metaphor for nature. The drama of this dialectic is played out in the architecture itself. The open structure characteristic of his earlier work allows the virtual space of the building to be penetrated by outside space, and itself frames the natural landscape. Thus defined by its structural elements, the building remains incomplete, as if arrested in the process of marking out a habitable space. References to the primitive act of building are filtered through the language of Cubism and advanced technology (itself a metaphor since the actual technology is mostly pre-industrial). The round column, isolated against the sky, suggests the tree as primor-dial building material; free-form profiles either in plan or (as in the Benacerraf House) in elevation, suggest the presence of nature within the man-made world of the building. There are references to a domesticated nature, as in the perforated steel beams with their suggestion of pergolas. An all-pervading nature is also evoked by the association of colors with the primary aspects of nature—sky, earth, water, and vegetation. The earlier buildings recall both conservatories and bowers or arbors, which protect man from nature by means of nature's own materials.

In the later work, Graves's classicist preferences are for garden structures (topiary, trellises) or for those architectural motifs which are associated with a mythologized nature—rustication, grottos, cascades, ruins. The fragmenta-tion of the buildings suggests the presence of natural obstacles to conceptual com-pleteness, and the inability of man to establish order in the face of Time and Chance. One has the impression of an arcadia which is not only irretrievable, but also some-how flawed.

These are the qualities which unite the two phases of Michael Graves's work, and which allow him to use the language of Cubism or of the classical tradition to recreate an architecture out of its primordial elements; to offer a new and intense interpretation of architecture itself and of man's cultural predicament in relation to nature.

Graves's work is a meditation on architecture. This is to say much more than it is concerned exclusively with the aesthetic. Such a concern is perfectly compatible with the problem of construction, which, in the case of a Le Corbusier or a Mies, is the *sine qua non* of aesthetic choice and is based on the (aes-thetic) principle of economy of means. With Graves this problem is excluded; archi-tectural meaning withdraws into the realm of "pure visibility"; the substance of the building does not form a part of the ideal world imagined by the architect. Structure becomes a pure representation. The objective conditions of building and its subjec-tive effect are now finally separated. Architecture is created and sustained in the psy-che, and its legitimate boundaries are established by voluntary judgment acting on an imagination nourished by history.

The difference between these two systems of representation, and the different status which they attribute to the "real," can be seen if we compare two works by an engineer—Gustave Eiffel. The Tower and the Statue of Liberty repre-sent the two poles toward which structure gravitates at the end of the nineteenth century. In the first case structure is the sufficient and necessary condition of mean-ing; in the second, the structure is purely "enabling" and plays no part in the object as a sign. So long as one accepts the traditional distinction between sculpture and architecture the paradoxical relation between these two attitudes remains obscured. But it becomes apparent the moment one sees sculpture and architecture as two modes of representation, where meanings are derived either from the traditional subject of sculpture—the human form—or from architecture. Both the human form and its "house" are perceived as cultural "traces," not as natural and objective "referents." If architecture becomes the subject of representation, this representation necessarily includes the memory of the "problem" of structure.

This system of representation is the exact opposite of the "classical" process by which the ephemeral was translated into the durable, according to which durability as such was a value and materiality a symbol of the transcendental. With the instrumentalization of structure, the mythic is rechanneled, and, in the Modern Movement, takes up its abode in instrumentality itself. In the architecture of Michael Graves, the alternative route is taken. The myth becomes pure myth, recognized as such, and the architectural sign floats in the dematerialized world of *Gestalt*, and the de-historicized world of memory and association.

Notes

1. Manfredo Tafuri, "'European Graffiti.' Five $\times$ Five = Twenty-five," *Oppositions* 5 (Summer 1976).
2. "The Swedish Connection," *Journal of Architectural Education*, September 1975.

Maurice Culot and   **"The Only Path for Architecture"** "L'unique chemin de l'architecture," *Archives*

Leon Krier   *d' Architecture Moderne* (Brussels) 14 (2d trimester 1978); translated in *Oppositions* 14

(Fall 1978), trans. Christian Hubert

A century ago William Morris declared, "Romance is the capacity for a true conception of history, a power of making the past part of the present."[1] In this sense, it may be correct to understand the position taken in this essay by Maurice Culot and Leon Krier as representative of a left-wing conservative romance paradigm dragged into the twentieth century. For Morris's definition and Culot and Krier's position are both based on a poignantly felt break in cultural continuity and a conviction that the rupture must be sealed by an effort of historical imagination, both in theory and in practice. (As Robert Maxwell, one of the most sympathetic and balanced critics, put it, "Whereas Krier sees architecture as an immediate source of ideological values by means of which the new conditions of life may be envisaged, Culot looks rather to its established ideological values as a source of political clarification and confrontation, and hence as the occasion for political action. One sees architecture as a value to be conserved and recuperated; the other as a resource to be expended in the political struggle.")[2] The cultural rupture is associated by Culot and Krier, as by Morris before them, not only with the architectural stylistic machinations of vulgar appropriationists (for Morris, neoclassicism, for Culot and Krier, Venturi) but also with the continual acceleration of modern industrial capitalism. And its overcoming will be effected in terms of the history of form: in particular, of the survival and readaptation of a form developed within one mode of production—a preindustrial, collective, manual tradition—within the very different environment of a later one—the culture of consumption and individual profit.

"La reconstruction des Marolles," from *La reconstruction de Bruxelles*, 1982

By an act of critical imagination akin to that of the historical novelist, Culot and Krier — in their writings, architectural projects, and pedagogy at the Ecole Nationale Supérieure de La Cambre, Brussels, where Culot has taught since 1968 — convey the experience of another time to be set against our own. And, indeed, their call for anti-industrial resistance and a "savagely European" ethos is something of a return of the Ruskinian repressed — a recurrence of the archaic and the communitarian, which is romance. But their position is not nostalgic. It does not involve the recovery or substitution of some more ideal world for ordinary reality (as in mystical experience or as in other genres such as the idyll or the pastoral). They aim rather at a condition that will have delivered the subject from the offenses and injuries of present reality yet will still contain that reality.

Even if the theory of Culot and Krier should be understood as a general proposition, the particular situation of Brussels is the best context for an understanding of their position. During the 1960s and 1970s the insertion of slab buildings into the urban fabric without regard for the small-scaled local context resulted in a uniformly bureaucratic and scaleless environment that begged for "counterprojects," even if only as critiques or only as a heuristic. However, if such counterprojects are projected onto sites (in Brussels or elsewhere) where an older fabric was never established and where the last vestiges of craft production have long since been displaced, critique and romance are easily converted into ersatz urbanity. It is that dilemma that frames the poignancy of Krier's declaration: "Nowadays I cannot build because I am an architect."[3]

| see 357 |

Notes

1. *William Morris: Artist, Writer, Socialist*, ed. May Morris, 2 vols. (Oxford: Blackwell, 1948), vol. 1, p. 148.
2. Robert Maxwell, "Architecture, Language, and Process," *Architectural Design* 47, no. 3 (1977), p. 190.
3. Leon Krier, *Drawings 1967–1980* (Brussels: Archives d'Architecture Moderne, 1980), p. 82.

You need a good black coffee to find something attractive about these reinforced concrete buildings. I read with horror (in the publicity brochure of an American contractor) that these skyscrapers survived the San Francisco earthquake. Having thought about it a little, however, I think they are more perishable than peasants' huts: these have stood upright for a thousand years, they were interchangeable, quickly wore out and grew up again effortlessly. I'm happy that this idea came to me, because I think with pleasure on these long lasting and glorious houses. I think the surface of the earth is destined for a great future. In civilized countries there are no fashions: it is an honor to resemble the models.

BERTOLT BRECHT, *Things Which Pass,* 1925

Unbridled industrialization with no aim but consumption has led to the destruction of the cities and countryside. The perspectives of "progress" are henceforth clear: everything will be destroyed, everything will be consumed! In the years to come the increasing unemployment engendered by industrialization[1] will widen and accelerate the process of destruction of the cities and, as a corollary, increase the alienation of individuals. Progress has reached a stage scarcely conceivable to the first socialist thinkers, and today it would be pointless to want to base ourselves on this tradition, to magnify the urban struggles, and "to exalt, with the help of the imagination, the work to be done to recapture the spirit of revolution rather than put chimeras back into circulation."[2]

It is too late to evoke the shadows of the past for the sake of putting them to our own use. Borrowings from history can be considered only within the framework of precise strategies for urban struggles, but they cannot in themselves reconstitute a coherent language.

What we wish to say is that a change in style or fashion is not enough this time. After all, we are dealing with a generation who, in the last thirty or forty years of its professional life, has changed styles more often than it has changed neckties. And it would be naive to see the current interest in architecture as an unmistakable sign of its renaissance. The only characteristic that the more recent experiences have in common—from Venturi to Kroll, by way of the stars of Ivry and the typological fever that ravages the architecture schools is their fragmentary nature and provocative formal eclecticism. The barbarous profusion of the "innovations" applauded by the journalists of post-modernism and commercially promoted under the slogan of "complexity and contradiction" culminates in the kitsch which perverts every level of life and culture and constitutes the most important cultural phenomenon of industrial civilization.

Our proposal in terms of the European urban tradition is to take up the discourse of the city where it was brutally interrupted by "industrial civilization"; to continue this discourse in order to elaborate the project of reference in which urban struggles and the aims of democratizing the decision-making process that they imply—will become recognized and find a necessary and fortifying theoretical coherence. The daily struggles which activate the inhabitants of European cities, menaced by the threat of "modern" urbanism, have led them to set up committees of inhabitants that, in the best of cases, have themselves federated to present a united front against the misfortune of capitalism. In Brussels, for instance, the inhabitants themselves are the only ones who have really developed a global alternative to industrial voracity and not the administrations, be they Socialist or otherwise. But we are not dupes. Associations of inhabitants are not necessarily progressive. To locate the urban struggle within the framework of the class struggle requires a considerable internal effort, and encouraging local conditions cannot make us forget that it is necessary to refer them to a social utopia, since it is to this that one must return to precipitate a coherent opposition front to the process of fragmentation resulting from the social division of labor—a process by which the capitalist order successfully opposes change and which it uses as a solvent against the fact of class struggle.

It is important to note here that the city and its neighborhood can no longer be used as a field of experimentation for architects. The problem of the reconstruction of the European city is not posed at the level of individual prowess, but rather at the level of *architecture* and *construction*. The symbolic and iconographic vacuity of "modern" architecture can of course be explained by the fact that it has never been architecture but rather a form of packaging. And in its most ambitious examples, it can sometimes have been an "art" of packaging. Certainly even the most ambitious will never succeed in constructing the city through packaging. Nor does "modern" architecture derive from construction. The latter, with its roots in artisanal disciplines, was transmitted as a culture through history by the collective memory until its final destruction by the industrial division of labor and by an education based both on the alienation of knowing from doing and on the glorification of "creativity." *Architecture* and *construction* have thus disappeared both as intellectual and manual cultures. The city of stone, the European city, has become, in the eyes of the prophets of mobility at any price, a synonym for a dangerous— mortal—inflexibility, even a sign of laziness.

As the European cities are being pitilessly ruined by the brutal construction of the new infrastructures of the advanced industrial state, the architectural profession has entered a state of crisis which no one since 1968 has beenable to escape. Only the most retrograde faction of the profession persists in its self-delusion by brandishing ideals whose necessity and inevitability are convincing only to itself. Today there is no hope for the more conscious architects who desire to unify a professional practice with the practice of a progressive ideology. One can only oppose the process of merciless destruction of the cities through, on the one hand, urban action, which, in the current phase of industrial development of the cities, can only hope to avoid further destruction and gain time,[3] and on the other hand, through theoretical work which strategically reinforces this action.

One cannot be at once in the camp of the architect-constructors, as well intentioned as they might be, and in the camp of the architect-theoreticians, who are the only ones who might be able to learn through a rational mode of thought something other than the more or less servile reproduction of the dominant cultural model. As reproduction, one must include both the actual pastiche indulged in by "modern" architecture as well as the fact of its acceptance of the myth of industrialization with all its negative consequences. The fact that this editorial is appearing with our joint signatures takes on a significance surpassing friendship or the existence of any international coterie. By this act we wish to make clear the existence of a movement of convergent theoretical reflection on the European level. We wish to define a movement in which intellectuals who engage in the struggle for neighborhoods at a daily level and others who develop a project for the city on the basis of a personal reflection on architecture gather together in the midst of pedagogical work and in the context of political and social preoccupations, outside of any spirit of avant-garde aesthetic. This convergence has nothing in common with the publicity campaign for industrialization orchestrated yesterday by the Congrès Internationaux d'Architecture Moderne; instead it reflects a desire to escape the trap of fragmentation and situates itself within the framework of a specific project for social democracy, even if its modalities are not yet precisely defined. But, after all, the essential today is not to weigh the respective merits of popular democracy, the dictatorship of the proletariat, or some system of worker control. What is shared by all is the certainty that the constitutive elements of the pre-industrial European city—the quarter, the street, the square—must form the basis for any reconstruction of cities destroyed by "modern" urbanism. This certainty has been acquired by those engaged in the practice of urban struggle, who have shown that socially, economically, and politically, only the traditional urban fabric can lead to satisfactory counter-measures to the social and physical disintegration of the city. It is now clear that the traditional fabric lends itself to step-by-step operations that are of greater social and economic interest than the poetics of the bulldozer. This fabric ensures the best conditions for mixed use, reduces the costs of maintenance of public space, and permits precisely by virtue of its familiar character the mobilization of the population towards tangible goals, etc. . . . For the others, this certainty derives from an intellectual undertaking that includes, in addition to analyses of the Bologna experience and of the urban struggle, theoretical work on the definitions of architecture and construction or even critical research on the so-called progress of the industrialization of construction, etc. . . . The latter as well as the former reject "modern" architecture and urbanism to the extent that they have been vehicles for the physical and social destruction of the cities (and countryside) and have relied upon the separation of functions, the myth of prefabrication, the useless typological works undertaken for themselves in the name of sacrosanct "creativity," the principle of the mechanical mobility of individuals, the arrogant and obtuse refusal to accept the difference between architecture and construction. . . .

Thus, for the first time in the history of architecture since the Industrial Revolution, there appears a coherent European project capable of opposing the brutal repercussions of profit. A convergence of thought, a convergence of directions. The paths for architecture are not many but singular. The only objective, and several generations will have to harness their energies to achieve it, is the elaboration of a common language. For everything has to be relearned: by means of historiography the capitalist order has even consumed our memory.

We must begin by rediscovering the forgotten language of the city that achieved its formal perfection in the eighteenth century, and at the same time we must work at modernizing it, so that this language can incorporate the contradictions issuing from the European anti-industrial resistance.

It is a matter of specifying the fields of action of architecture and of construction. To be more restricted during the years of re-education, housing must stem only from the urban fabric, that is to say, from construction and not architecture; the typology of dwellings must be completely subject to the constraints of urban morphology, etc. . . . It is only much later, when the language will have become familiar, that one will be able to consider exceptions and divergences. It is through the rational mode of thought that topics of research and the important questions, matters of useful reflection, can be raised at the very interior of the utopian project itself. What are the conditions for an art of building that gives manual (as well as intellectual) workers the dignity that industrialization refuses them? How can the articulation between architectural utopia and social project be organized? Etc. . . .

Against the Moral Resignation of the Architect into a Collective Immorality

Because the cities are threatened with total destruction; because belief in the virtue of the positivist example today reveals an innocence of mind, a humanist dream; because we are witnessing a convergence of efforts both at the level of urban struggles and at the level of theoretical work on the city; because the contradictory, gratuitous, and dangerous architectural experiments against the cities are proliferating with the objective only of game, of fashion, or of scandal.

Because of all of this, we will speak, in the manner of Kraus and of Loos, in order to show that there is a difference between a vase and a chamber pot, between a street and a pseudo-street, between a square and a pseudo-square, between a complex quarter and a factitious one. . . .[4]

An indispensable difference which allows architecture and construction to find their proper fields of application.

It is still important to point this out, not out of any "taste for energetic surgical methods," but because at the moment when the process of regionalization gains hold throughout Europe, the anemic state of urban culture could lead to even more savage acts of vandalism than those perpetuated by centralized authorities who have maintained here and there a sense of decency.

There is thus nothing to be "learned from Las Vegas," except that it constitutes a widespread operation of trivialization, a cynical attempt to recuperate and accommodate the leftovers of the greatest of all cannibalist feasts, a desperate attempt to give the profession of architecture a final justification of its bad conscience: to make believe in its social utility despite its lack of project. The European city is a creation of the intelligence; the very trace of this intelligence embarrasses "the builders of today" who are all too happy to find in Venturi and the other consorts of post-modernism unexpected intellectual allies who do not hesitate to propose the forgetting of any pre-industrial tradition in favor of a mercantile conception of architecture. Opposing any direct communication between individuals and unquestioningly accepting the principle of feverish and obligatory mechanical mobility, they reject the very basis of any urban culture.

A Copernican Revolution

When we allude to the necessity for a global project, we do not intend by any means to say that we wish to cover the territory with plans, but rather that basic models which take man as their measure must be studied as a first priority—man as he is normally constituted, not man stricken with elephantiasis as he wanders through the projects of Speer, or that deaf and dumb man who surveys from his automobile the empty and discontinuous spaces of modern urbanism.

In Bologna, the ancient parishes have finally become an authentic model for democratic administration; in Brussels, the inhabitants of the most popular district have obliged a reactionary municipal administration to reconstruct their quarter in terms of real streets and real squares.

For the concept of streets and squares does not derive from fashion, but rather constitutes a historic concept inscribed within the European tradition, and it is not a matter of imitating them as style but as precise types.

A street is a street, and one lives there in a certain way not because architects have imagined streets in certain ways. As opposed to television and the automobile, which have already succeeded in changing the physical qualities of American man, the terrorism of modern architecture has fortunately not yet succeeded in changing the character of European man. (Scenario for a horror film: crab-man from Barbican meets oblique-man from the city of Claude Parent.)

We must forcefully reject the American city and become savagely European; our objective is not a sort of supernationalism incompatible with the very notion of culture, but aims at the development of an intense social life, at the development of the highest and most differentiated levels of communication, in complete opposition to the industrialized media. *Against the agglomeration of buildings and of individuals we posit the city and its communities.* The inevitable results for a society which refuses the pleasure in work are suicide or collective fascism, toward which the most industrialized countries are inevitably drawn. The only means of avoiding this fate lie in the rejection of the social and industrial division of labor as well as in the espousal and even reinforcement of the professional division of labor, and at the same time the rejection of the social stratification between manual and intellectual work. Our project for architecture works in this direction: it tends to reduce the differentiation of social divisions. This is precisely where the essence of its political nature lies.

To "augment our well-being without reducing our pleasure"[5] or at the limit to insure our survival, we must immediately take part in the recognition and reconstruction of artisanry, of manual work. The latter, which has always been the basis for human creativity and personal realization, has become an exercise in degradation through the division of labor. And it is the schools themselves that have proceeded to destroy the culture and intelligence of the people.

Yesterday this willful destruction was still dictated by a "bourgeois coldness"; today this illegitimate rationality is weighed down further by stupidity and cynicism. More than ever before, the Modern Movement, in all its expressions—written, built, and pedagogical—presents the European city as a natural field for the experiments of the "creators." Those who are experiencing the destruction of the cities directly through the urban struggles know that administrative and artistic neutrality is a delusion and that technicians (engineers and architects) have played a determining role in the contagion and generalization of the destructuring models of the Athens Charter. This is why we insist upon participating in the urban struggles while at the same time developing new architectural models that anticipate a decentralized and self-governed society, as opposed to the Athens Charter, which stands on an argument based on a principle of outrageous levels of industrialization, of unbridled mobility, of zoning, of political and cultural centralization, etc. The freedom sold daily by the media through every possible trick is none other than the slavery of mobility, which has become today the cause and means of social fragmentation—a fragmentation necessary for the destruction of any resistance, of all intelligence awakening against the industrial system, the suicidal alienation of those with no other project but consumption.

Within the framework of an anti-industrial resistance carried out at the European scale, we are engaged in theoretical exercises and their practical applications (to the architectural project), with the reconstruction of the cities in mind. These stimulating exercises have no innocent character; they permit us to verify hypotheses, to stimulate questions, debates, and works that are all situated along the only path of architecture.

Notes

1. Two figures give some indication of the evolution taking place: German industry currently provides the same output as it did in 1974 with one million fewer workers. A French report, which has remained secret for good reason, estimates that within ten years thirty percent of the employees in banks, insurance companies, and administration will be eliminated (according to Michel Bosquet, in *Le Nouvel Observateur*, no. 702, April 1978).
2. Marx quoted in Manfredo Tafuri, *Theories and History of Architecture*, trans. Giorgio Verrecchia (New York: Harper and Row, 1980), apropos of the value of the "heroic resurrection" of antiquity.
3. To gain the necessary time to integrate the urban struggle into the class struggle.
4. Cf. the chapter on Karl Kraus in Allan Janik and Stephen Toulmin's *Wittgenstein's Vienna* (New York: Simon and Schuster, 1973).
5. William Morris in "Useful Work versus Useless Toil."

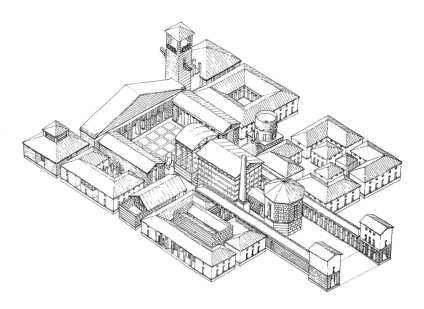

This school conforms strictly to the requirements laid down by the French Ministry of Education and Culture. It is a simple proposition, neither spectacular in its composition nor extraordinary in its construction or use of materials (stone, wood and bricks).

After two and a half years of preparation and discussions, it was concluded that this modest school exceeded its budget by 240%. The use of natural materials would have raised the excess to 500%.

It then became obvious that however unspecific government briefs may be in terms of aesthetics, construction and materials, school classrooms may not be higher than three meters and walls no thicker than twenty centimeters. The use of natural materials would thus be impossible.

"That which is shabby and false must henceforth be the rule." From this state of affairs a thinking architect may draw two conclusions. First: "NOWADAYS I CANNOT BUILD BECAUSE I AM AN ARCHITECT." Second: "NOBODY WHO BUILDS NOWADAYS CAN BE CALLED AN ARCHITECT." If it is true that the phenomena of the ephemeral, of kitsch and of self-destruction are the major products of our industrial civilization, then to be involved in building must be seen as one of the most corrupt forms of collaboration.

Kenneth Frampton   **"The Status of Man and the Status of His Objects: A Reading of _The Human_**

Condition" From _Hannah Arendt: The Recovery of the Public World_, ed. Melvyn A.

Hill (New York: St. Martin's Press, 1979)

Kenneth Frampton's essays on critical regionalism are arguably his most important, if important is understood to mean influential and widely read. The first was first published in Hal Foster's 1983 edition, _The Anti-Aesthetic: Essays on Postmodern Culture_, a collection that promulgated decisive new terms for architecture-theoretical discussions, with Frampton's set of five dialectical pairs foremost among them: space/place, typology/topography, scenographic/architectonic, artificial/natural, and visual/tactile.[1]

The terms of critical regionalism, however, turn out to be but a specific instance of the overarching structure and character of Frampton's thought, which is most fully developed in his meditations on Hannah Arendt's _The Human Condition_. Behind each of his five binaries we are able to detect the presence of what Arendt conceived as the fundamental duality of the human condition, her unusual distinction between labor and work. Labor corresponds to the never-ending "biological" cycles of reproduction and consumption. It is the source of property and wealth; it is private and impermanent; and it is ultimately quantitative and systemic, a "victory of exchange value over use value" and "finally the devaluation of all values." Work corresponds to a dense variety of things that together make up "the human artifice," the "home for mortal men." It yields stability and solidity; it is public and durable; and in modernity, it is ultimately sacrificed to labor's demand for abundance.

Arendt's oppositional framework is thus also the underpinning for Frampton's reading of Jürgen Habermas's "lifeworld" versus "system" and Paul Ricoeur's "universal civilization" versus "national cultures," both of which intend to give dialectical accounts of the globally operational technology that enables the liberative aims of modernization but also drives its rationalizing, optimizing thrust and its tendency to level, if not utterly eradicate, regional and national traditions, including the continuing craft of building.

Within Frampton's own dialectical scheme, the first opposition, space/place, is derived from his gloss on Martin Heidegger's 1954 essay "Building, Dwelling, Thinking,"[2] already presented in his editorial for _Oppositions_ 4 (October 1974). Frampton relates Heidegger's two alternative conceptions of space, the Latin _spatium in extensione_ and the Teutonic _Raum_, to two modes of experiencing built form and the environment: the unobstructed clarity of the measured, rationalized opticality of formal representation versus the phenomenologically thick, bounded, material experiences of touch, hearing, and smell. Second, the socio-spatial, typological conception of building organizations is paired against the concrete, site-specific rootedness of constructions that incorporate factors of topography, ecology, and climate. Third, Frampton's scenographic category is literally "representational in nature," whereas the architectonic is a kind of constructed narrative of the logic of building — a verisimilar "myth of the reality of [a] structural achievement" or of the building's "durability with regard to the erosive agencies of climate and time."[3] The final, more general dyads of artificial/natural and visual/tactile are thus already anticipated in the first three pairs of opposites.

In the building practices of traditional or rooted cultures, Frampton attributes primary significance to Arendt's "work" mode, understood as the normative means of building as against building's instrumental value according to utility-
maximizing criteria. In this mode, the value of a building is immanent in its means, in
building as an activity, and is thus qualitatively distinct from any separate economic
or functional ends to which the building might be put. In the case of such traditional
production, building conventions (like all cultural behavior) have been collectivized
and ritualized — "socially integrated," Jürgen Habermas would say — and, as a result,
any ulterior purpose of the activity seems beyond any single individual's direction and
control. In contrast, in the totally administered, technical-scientific world of universal
civilization and "labor," ends transcend means. Forms of human activity are no longer
seen in terms of their unique differences as distinct types of work but are "systems-
integrated," reorganized under the common denominator of sheer efficiency or instrumentality, which now becomes the sole basis for their value. Building no longer has
any qualitative worth in itself, is no longer intrinsically satisfying; rather value exists
only to the extent that the activity can be directed toward some quantifiable, self-
interested purpose. Technology has become radically autonomous, optimized, and
alienated; the subjective agent has lost its ritualized means and localized equipment
for making and representing shelter and is now left to float without the benefit of
traditional habits.

compare Baird (53–54)

Within this binary work/labor, means/ends organization, Framp-
ton sees architecture as a potentially resistant practice, construed as a proper third
term that mediates between the two primary, impossible or intolerable terms of
opposition.

In my view, the constituent elements of architecture are to be seen as being determined by the
way in which such oppositions are mediated through form. . . . As far as I am concerned, this
recalcitrance of the *métier* vis-à-vis modernization is a blessing in disguise, since it provides the
fundamental basis from which to cultivate a "critical" architecture. It affords, above all, a hybrid
situation in which rationalized production (even partially industrialized production) may be combined with time-honored craft practices, provided that the scale of the investment remains sufficiently modest to permit idiosyncratic forms of disjunction and that the local culture retains a
capacity to evaluate the results in terms which are not exclusively economic.[4]

Frampton summarizes the mediating practice of architecture in the phrase "critical
regionalism."

I wish to employ the term to allude to a hypothetical and real condition in which a local culture
of architecture is consciously evolved in express opposition to the domination of hegemonic
power. In my view, this is a theory of building which, while accepting the potentially liberative
role of modernization, resists being totally absorbed by forms of optimized production and
consumption.[5]

| compare 61 n.2 |

As ends overtake means and labor overtakes work, the lifeworld is reorganized according to the "techno-science" and consumerist logic of the system, which, in turn, produces pathological symptoms in architectural culture. Frampton labels two of these symptoms "neo-Situationist" and "neo-Historicist," corresponding to the escalating modernization of the one position and the reactionary pseudo-traditionalism of the other, but sees them as two sides of the same coin of system integration, two reaction formations equally uncritical of the "master-narrative of techno-science."[6] Frampton's solution, then, is to invert the priorities of system and lifeworld, of means and ends, insisting that an architecture sensitive to the ecological, tectonic, and tactile dimensions of building can push its way into the edges and cracks of rationalized production and abrade the slick surface of consumption, that "a peripheral or *interstitial* architecture may still be capable of generating a more appropriate, sensitive and responsive physical environment than that generally found today in the centers of hegemonic power."[7]

Frampton thus spans theoretical and normative discourses and constructs one of the most specific and concrete of models for practice, deploying architecture's dialectical means/ends structure and building's inherent material characteristics as a kind of impedance to the flow of commodification.

Notes

"The Status of Man and the Status of His Objects: A Reading of *The Human Condition*" was reprinted in Kenneth Frampton, *Modern Architecture and the Critical Present* (New York: St. Martin's Press, 1982).

1. Kenneth Frampton, "Towards a Critical Regionalism: Six Points for an Architecture of Resistance," in *The Anti-Aesthetic: Essays on Postmodern Culture,* ed. Hal Foster (Port Townsend, Wash.: Bay Press, 1983). Frampton elaborated his thesis in "Place-Form and Cultural Identity," in *Design after Modernism,* ed. John Thackara (New York: Thames and Hudson, 1988). The same basic themes appear in his *Studies in Tectonic Culture: The Poetics of Construction in Nineteenth and Twentieth Century Architecture* (Cambridge: MIT Press, 1995).
2. In Martin Heidegger, *Basic Writings*, ed. David Farrell Krell (New York: Harper and Row, 1977).
3. Frampton, "Place-Form and Cultural Identity," p. 59.
4. Ibid., p. 57.
5. Ibid., p. 56.
6. Ibid., p. 63.
7. Ibid., p. 64.

The only philosophy which can be responsibly practiced in
the face of despair is the attempt to contemplate all things as
they would present themselves from the standpoint of redemption; all else is reconstruction, mere technique. Perspectives must be fashioned that displace and estrange the world,
reveal it to be, with its rifts and crevices, as indigent and distorted as it will appear one day in the messianic light.

THEODOR ADORNO, *Minima Moralia,* 1947

The Architectural Corollaries of Labor and Work

In her book *The Human Condition,* significantly subtitled "a study of the central dilemmas facing modern man," Arendt designated three activities—*labor, work,* and *action*—as being fundamental to the *vita activa.* She established at the beginning of her
argument the particular meaning that she would consistently assign to each of these
terms. Of *labor* she wrote: "Labor is the activity which corresponds to the biological
process of the human body, whose spontaneous growth, metabolism, and eventual
decay are bound to the vital necessities produced and fed into the life process by
labor. The human condition of labor is life itself."[1]

Of *work* she wrote: "Work is the activity which corresponds to
the unnaturalness of human existence, which is not imbedded in, and whose mor-
tality is not compensated by, the species' ever-recurring life cycle. Work provides
an 'artificial' world of things, distinctly different from all natural surroundings.
Within its borders each individual life is housed, while this world itself is meant to
outlast and transcend them all. The human condition of work is worldliness."[2]

In her definition of the public and private attributes of the *vita
activa*—the former having a dependency on the latter—Arendt amplified further
her unusual distinction between *work* and *labor.* She argued that labor by being a
constantly transforming but repetitive procedure—akin to the cycle of biological
survival—is inherently *processal, private,* and *impermanent,* whereas work, by virtue of
being the precondition for the reification of the world as the space of human appearance, is by definition *static, public,* and *permanent.*

An architect could hardly fail to remark on the correspondence
between these distinctions and the fundamental ambiguity of the term "architecture"; an ambiguity that finds reflection in the *Oxford English Dictionary* in two significantly different definitions—first, "the art or science of constructing edifices for
human use" and second, "the action and process of building."[3] These definitions
with their potential hierarchy latent even in the etymology of the Greek term *archi-
tektōn*—meaning chief constructor—proffer themselves as paralleling the distinction that Arendt draws between work and labor.[4]

The designation "for human use" imparts a specifically human, if not humanist, connotation to the whole of the first definition, alluding to the creation of a specifically human world, whereas the phrase "the action and process of building" in the second definition clearly implies a continuous act of building forever incomplete, comparable to the unending process of biological labor. The fact that the dictionary asserts that the word "edifice" may be used to refer to "a large and stately building such as a church, a palace, or a fortress" serves to support the work connotation of the first definition, since these building types, as the "representations" of spiritual and temporal power, have always been, at least until recent times, both public and permanent. Furthermore, the word "edifice" relates directly to the verb "to edify," which not only carries within itself the meaning "to build" but also "to educate," "to strengthen," and "to instruct"—connotations that allude directly to the poetical restraint of the public realm. Again the Latin root of this verb—*aedificare*, from *aedes*, a "building," or, even more originally, a "hearth," and *ficare*, "to make," has latent within it the public connotation of the hearth as the aboriginal "public" space of appearance. This aspect persists even today in the domestic realm, where surely no place is more of a forum in the contemporary home than the hearth or its surrogate, the television set, which as an illusory public substitute tends to inhibit or usurp the spontaneous emergence of "public" discourse within the private domain.

Within the corpus of modern architectural theory, no text is more aware of the respective statuses of architecture and building than Adolf Loos's essay "Architecture 1910," wherein he characterizes the eminently biological, innate, and repetitive nature of vernacular construction in the following terms:

The peasant cuts out the spot on the green grass where the house is to be built and digs out the earth for the foundation walls. Then the mason appears. If there is loamy soil in the vicinity, then there will also be a brickworks to provide the bricks. If not, then stone from the riverbanks can be used for the same purpose. And while the mason places brick upon brick and stone upon stone, the carpenter has established himself nearby. The strokes of the axe ring out merrily. He makes the roof. What kind of roof? One that is beautiful or ugly? He does not know. The roof. . . . His aim was to build a house for himself, his family and his livestock and in this he has succeeded. Just as his neighbors and ancestors succeeded. As every animal which allows itself to be led by its instincts, succeeds.[5]

Loos was aware that, like the pure instrumentality of engineering, this rooted vernacular had nothing whatsoever to do with the traditionally representative role of architecture. Later in the same text he wrote:

Only a very small part of architecture belongs to art: the tomb and the monument. Everything else, everything which serves a purpose should be excluded from the realms of art. . . . If we find a mound in the forest, six feet long and three feet wide, formed into a pyramid, shaped by a shovel, we become serious and something within us says, someone lies buried here. This is architecture.

The Public Realm and the Human Artifice

While the representative scope of architecture had already become severely curtailed by the turn of the century, the space of public appearance could still serve not only to house the public realm, but also to represent its reality. Where in the nineteenth century the public institution was exploited as an occasion on which to reify the permanent values of the society, the disintegration of such values in the twentieth century has had the effect of atomizing the public building into a network of abstract institutions. This dissipation of the *agora* reflects that mass society whose alienating force stems not from the number of people but from "the fact that the world between them has lost its power to gather them together, to relate and to separate them."[6]

While the political life of the Greek *polis* did not directly stem from the physical presence and representation of the city-state, Arendt emphasizes, in contrast to our present proliferation of urban sprawl, the spontaneous "cantonal" attributes of concentration:

The only indispensable material factor in the generation of power is the living together of people. Only where men live so close together that the potentialities of action are always present can power remain with them, and the foundation of cities, which as city-states have remained paradigmatic for all Western political organization, is therefore indeed the most important material prerequisite for power.[7]

Nothing could be further from this than our present generation of motopia and our evident incapacity to create new cities that are physically and politically identifiable as such. By the same token, nothing could be more removed from the political essence of the city-state than the exclusively economic categories of rationalistic planning theory; that theory espoused by planners such as Melvin Webber, whose ideological conceptions of *community without propinquity* and the *non-place urban realm* are nothing if not slogans devised to rationalize the absence of any adequate realm of public appearance within modern suburbia.[8] The manipulative and "apolitical" bias of such ideologies has never been more openly expressed than in Robert Venturi's *Complexity and Contradiction in Architecture*, wherein the author asserts that the Americans don't need piazzas, since they should be at home watching television.[9] These and similar reactionary modes of beholding seem to emphasize the impotence of an urbanized populace who have paradoxically lost the object of their urbanization. That their power grew initially out of the city finds corroboration in Arendt's conception of the relations obtaining between politics and built form:

Power preserves the public realm and the space of appearance, and as such it is also the life-blood of the human artifice, which, unless it is the scene of action and speech, of the web of human affairs and relationships and the stories engendered by them, lacks its ultimate *raison d'être*. Without being talked about by men and without housing them, the world would not be a human artifice but a heap of unrelated things to which each isolated individual was at liberty to add one more object; without the human artifice to house them, human affairs would be as floating, as futile and vain, as the wanderings of nomad tribes.[10]

It was a similar realization that the monuments of the Ringstrasse, built around Vienna during the second half of the nineteenth century, were nothing but a sequence of "unrelated things," that caused Camillo Sitte to demonstrate that each of these isolated public structures could be restored to being a *res publica* in itself. In his *City Planning According to Artistic Principles* (1889), he revealed how the fabric of the medieval town had had the capacity of enclosing as a single "political" entity both the monument and its civic piazza.[11]

The Private Realm and the Rise of the Social

While Arendt acknowledges that the rise of modern intimacy and individualism has largely eliminated the aspect of privation from the term "privacy," she nonetheless remains aware that a life excluded from the public realm is still "deprived" by virtue of its being confined to the shadowy domestic interior of the *megaron*—that traditional single cell volume of the Greek peninsular, whose very etymology reveals the household as the domain of darkness.[12] Unlike the Greeks, who despised the individual domain or *idion* as the province of idiocy,[13] but like the Romans, who valued the interdependence of both realms, Arendt conceives of the private as the essential "darker" ground that not only nourishes the public realm but also establishes its experiential depth. At the same time she recognizes that the rise of the social—to which the intimate is of course related—has had the ultimate effect of impoverishing both the public and private spheres and with this the mediatory capacity of built form to articulate one from the other. Arendt argues that the flowering of the social art form, the novel, after 1750 effectively coincided with the progressive decline of all the public arts, especially architecture.[14] The ultimate triumph of the social in collectivized life has, as Arendt puts it, given rise to a "mass society [that] not only destroys the public realm but the private as well, [and] deprives men not only of their place in the world but of their private home, where they once felt sheltered against the world and where, at any rate, even those excluded from the world could find a substitute in the warmth of the hearth and the limited reality of family life."[15]

This thesis, as to the loss of the private realm at the hands of the social, finds some corroboration in the fragmentary writings of the Mexican architect, Luis Barragán, who has criticized the overexposed landscape of the contemporary suburb in the following terms: "Everyday life is becoming much too public. Radio, TV, the telephone all invade privacy. Gardens should therefore be enclosed, not open to public gaze." Elsewhere, Barragán continues: "Architects are forgetting the need of human beings for half-light, the sort of light that imposes a tranquillity, in their living rooms as well as in their bedrooms. About half the glass that is used in so many buildings—homes as well as offices—would have to be removed in order to obtain the quality of light that enables one to live and work in a more concentrated manner."[16]

Arendt's insight that the triumph of laboring society has condemned man to perpetual movement[17] finds a further echo in Barragán texts wherein he asserts:

Before the machine age, even in the middle of cities, Nature was everybody's trusted companion. . . . Nowadays, the situation is reversed. Man does not meet with Nature, even when he leaves the city to commune with her. Enclosed in his shiny automobile, his spirit stamped with the mark of the world whence the automobile emerged, he is, within Nature, a foreign body. A billboard is sufficient to stifle the voice of Nature. Nature becomes a scrap of Nature and man a scrap of man.[18]

This tendency towards global reduction, not to say of a total fusion, between man, machine, and Nature—latent in the processal triumph of industrial production—finds its ideological corollary in the behavioral sciences of which Arendt has written:

To gauge the extent of society's victory in the modern age, its early substitution of behavior for action and its eventual substitution of bureaucracy, the rule of nobody, for personal rulership, it may be well to recall that its initial science of economics, which substitutes patterns of behavior only in this rather limited field of human activity, was finally followed by the all-comprehensive pretension of the social sciences which, as "behavioral sciences," aim to reduce man as a whole, in all his activities, to the level of a conditioned and behaving animal.[19]

The Duality of the *Homo Faber*: Artifice versus Instrumentality

The dependency of the human artifice on the work of *homo faber* stems from the intrinsic durability of objects and their capacity to withstand (*Gegenstand*) both the erosions of nature and the processes of use. As Arendt has written:

The man-made world of things, the human artifice erected by *homo faber*, becomes a home for mortal men, whose stability will endure and outlast the ever-changing movement of their lives and actions, only insomuch as it transcends both the sheer functionalism of things produced for consumption and the sheer utility of objects produced for use. Life in its non-biological sense, the span of time each man has between birth and death, manifests itself in action and speech, both of which share with life its essential futility. . . . If the *animal laborans* needs the help of *homo faber* to ease his labor and remove his pain, and if mortals need his help to erect a home on earth, acting and speaking men need the help of *homo faber* in his highest capacity, that is, the help of the artist, of poets and historiographers, of monument-builders or writers, because without them the only product of their activity, the story they enact and tell, would not survive at all. In order to be what the world is always meant to be, a home for men during their life on earth, the human artifice must be a place fit for action and speech, for activities not entirely useless for the necessities of life but of an entirely different nature from the manifold activities of fabrication by which the world itself and all things in it are produced.[20]

No other passage in *The Human Condition* formulates the essential duality of the *homo faber* so succinctly as this—man as the maker split between the fabrication of useless things, such as works of art, which are ends in themselves, and the invention and production of useful objects, which serve as various predetermined means to a given set of ends. For Arendt, *homo faber* is at once both artificer and tool-maker; the builder of the world and the maker of the instruments with which it is built. Where the one addresses itself to the "what" of representation and reification—that is to say, to that object of commemoration which Loos was to consign to the province of art—the other concerns itself with the "how" of utility and process, in which tools tend, at least in the modern world, to be the sole things to survive the occasion of their use. Nothing reveals this second condition of production more than the machine fabrication of goods for consumption, nor the first than the cyclical history of built monuments which, from inception to demolition, testify to a continual transference of value from the past into the future.

The ambiguity of architecture—its status as "edification" or as "building" and often as different aspects within the same physical entity—reflects the parallel ambiguity of the *homo faber*, who is neither pure artist nor pure technician. In a similar manner, representation and commemoration can never be entirely prized apart and the present embodiment of past value already assures its availability for the future. All signification in built form thus embodies a sense of immortality. This much Arendt attempts to make clear in her discussion of art:

In this permanence, the very stability of the human artifice, which, being inhabited and used by mortals, can never be absolute, achieves a representation of its own. Nowhere else does the sheer durability of the world of things appear in such purity and clarity, nowhere else therefore does this thing-world reveal itself so spectacularly as the non-mortal home for mortal beings. It is as though worldly stability had become transparent in the permanence of art, so that a premonition of immortality, not the immortality of the soul or of life but of something immortal achieved by mortal hands, has become tangibly present, to shine and to be seen, to sound and to be heard, to speak and to be read.[21]

While fabrication invariably terminated in the ancient world in either an instrument of use or an art object, it came with the emergence of empirical science to insinuate its process into the methodology of research and, with this deviation, to remove itself from the traditional teleology of artifice in favor of achieving the abstract instruments of cognition. The Renaissance, split between the liberal and the mechanical arts—already anticipatory of the industrial division of labor—led to the rise of the *homo faber* as a man of invention and speculation; of which the architect and *uomo universale*, Filippo Brunelleschi, was one of the earliest examples. As G. C. Argan has shown, this rise of the *homo faber* as architect resulted in widening the incipient division between invention and fabrication and led to the degradation of the traditional craftsmen into the status of the *animal laborans*.

Brunelleschi thought that a new technique could not be derived from the past, but must come from a different cultural experience, from history. In this way he refuted the old "mechanical" technique and created a new "liberal" technique based on those typically individualistic actions which are historical research and inventiveness. He abolished the traditional hierarchical form of the mason's lodge where the head was the co-ordinator of the specialized work of the various groups of skilled workers who made up the lodge of the masters. Now, there was only one planner or inventor; the others were merely manual laborers. When the master mason rose to the status of sole planner, whose activity was on a par with the other humanistic disciplines, the other members of the team of masons fell from the rank of *maestri* in charge of various aspects of the job to that of simple working men. This explains the impatience of the masons and their rebellion against the master mason who had become "architect" or "engineer."[22]

This willful creation of distance between conceiving and building pervades the entire Renaissance. It was as much present in Brunelleschi's invention of perspective or in his machines for the building of the cupola over Santa Maria del Fiore in Florence in 1420, as it was in Galileo Galilei's invention of the telescope in 1610, with which men first established the proof of the Copernican universe. The effective split of appearance and being that was the consequence of this proof, served to institute Cartesian doubt as the fundamental basis of the new scientific perspective. As Arendt has written:

The Cartesian method of securing certainty against universal doubt corresponded most precisely to the most obvious conclusion to be drawn from the new physical science: though one cannot know truth as something given and disclosed, man can at least know what he makes himself. This, indeed, became the most general and most generally accepted attitude of the modern age, and it is this conviction, rather than the doubt underlying it, that propelled one generation after another for more than three hundred years into an ever-quickening pace of discovery and development.[23]

Just as the shift to a heliocentric model of the universe was developed with the aid of an optical tool—the telescope—so the *homo faber* came to his place in the modern world through a reevaluation of his traditional role. From Galileo on, he was not so much valued for his product as an end result but for his process as a means to an end. As Arendt shows, fabrication, which had hitherto disappeared into the product, now became an end in itself since pure science was not interested in the appearance of objects, but in the capacity of objects to reveal the intrinsic structure lying behind all appearance. It abandoned the passive contemplation of objects *per se* for the instrumental penetration of the laws of nature. This effectively reversed the traditional hierarchy of contemplation and action—a shift which, as Arendt shows, had profound consequences for the object of architecture.

As far as *homo faber* was concerned, the modern shift of emphasis from the "what" to the "how," from the thing itself to its fabrication process, was by no means an unmixed blessing. It deprived man as maker and builder of those fixed and permanent standards and measurements which, prior to the modern age, have always served him as guides for his doing and criteria for his judgment. It is not only and perhaps not even primarily the development of the commercial society that, with the triumphal victory of exchange value over use value, first introduced the principle of interchangeability, then the relativization, and finally the devaluation, of all values. . . . It was at least as decisive that man began to consider himself part and parcel of the two superhuman, all-encompassing processes of nature and history, both of which seemed doomed to an infinite progress without ever reaching any inherent *telos* or approaching any preordained idea.[24]

This shift from the "what" to the "how" found its reflection in the division of engineering from architecture during the Enlightenment; first in Colbert's categorically anti-guild creation of the various royal academies for the arts and sciences including the Académie Royale d'Architecture (1677), whose "architectural" graduates were to dedicate themselves solely to the "what," that is, to the reification of public structures commissioned by the State; and then in 1747, with Perronet's creation of the Ecole des Ponts et Chaussées, whose "engineering" graduates were to concern themselves largely with the "how," namely, with the processal means of gaining permanent access to the realm. That these two aspects of the *homo faber* had already become professionally divided over the defense and siege of the walled city may be gauged from the fact that according to Michel Parent and Jacques Verroust: "In the sixteenth century the defense of towns and castles was the work of *architects*. The word *engineer* remained reserved for those who not only built the siege machines but also handled them."[25] The progressive invasion of the city of artifice by the machine—first the siege engine and later the locomotive, and then of course the electric tram and the automobile—accompanied the ultimate dissolution of the walled city in the middle of the nineteenth century. Aside from its monumental rhetoric and its simultaneous reduction of honorific built-form to the status of being a rentable commodity, the Ringstrasse that came to replace Vienna's fortification in the second half of the century was coincidentally the initial proving ground for the horse-drawn tram.[26]

        Deprived by Cartesian doubt of its faith in the received culture of the Renaissance, architectural theory was compelled to search for its authority in the knowledge of an objective archaeology. At the same time it began to look for its creative principle in the all-encompassing processes of nature. Thus while architects began to record and emulate the surviving models of antiquity, natural law came to be asserted as the prime universal principle. Our modern concepts of archaeology and history were both the outcomes of developments such as these. Stripped by science of its magical coalescence, the modern world began to fragment. Since appearance now belied truth, it became necessary to regard form as being separate from content and to this end the modern science of esthetics came into being with Baumgarten's *Aesthetica* (1750). At the same time architectural theoreticians, such as the Abbé Laugier in his *Essai sur l'architecture* (1753), began to advocate "natural" primitive structures of self-evident lucidity. Pure reduced structure became the paradigm of architecture and light came to be regarded as a metaphor for the illumination of reason itself.

The ascendance of the bourgeoisie, the rise of the social and the intimate, the rediscovery of antiquity, the duality of light and nature as the sublime emanence of the Supreme Being, and above all the influence of Rousseau and Newton combined to distract architecture from the task of realization and to project it into either an archaeologically remote past or an unattainable utopian future. This ideological distraction is prominently displayed in the works of Etienne Boullée, who imagined spectacular masses of masonry, at the scale of natural escarpments—vast megaliths of prohibitive size, penetrated by endless galleries of often inaccessible space. Is it not just such a figure that Arendt had in mind when she wrote of the *homo faber* renouncing his traditional calling in favor of the *vita contemplativa*? "All he had to do was let his arms drop and prolong indefinitely the act of beholding the *eidos*, the eternal shape and model he had formerly wanted to imitate and whose excellence and beauty he now knew he could only spoil through any attempt at reification."[27]

While architectural theory tended toward total dematerialization, as in the writings of Laugier, or toward the sureality of sublime, unrealizable form, as in the images of Boullée, engineering proceeded to work upon nature and to subject its untamed wastes to a measured infrastructure of metalled roads and embanked canals. Its province was now no longer the bastions and counterscarps of the fortified city, but the viaducts, bridges, and dams of a universal system of distribution. Its technique not only outstripped the performance of traditional materials and methods but also afforded a more explicit form of structural expression—one in which structure was transparently penetrated by process. From now on architecture looked to such structure for much of its symbolic substance and we find a late neo-classical architect, such as Karl Friedrich Schinkel, totally ignoring contemporary architecture on his first visit to England in 1826 and recording instead the distributive and productive achievements of the time; the Menai Straits suspension bridge and the "processal" mill buildings of Manchester.

The *Animal Laborans* and the Fungibility of the World

The brute concentration of natural labor-power, as though it were akin to water power, preceded, as Robin Evans has attempted to show, the late-eighteenth-century development of industrial production as it is now generally understood. The workhouse as a place of production, secrecy, and moral improvement (this last being nothing more than forcibly obtaining "desirable" behavior from the human animal) was fully instituted long before the invention of such important productive instruments as Newcomen's engine or Arkwright's spinning jenny. That this workplace was invariably a closed world only served to emphasize the essential *worldlessness* of labor for all that the privacy arose primarily out of a need for industrial secrecy. It was in any event a hermetic domain, where deprivation in the original sense was coupled with the work ethic and placed at the disposal of the machine. In the earliest workhouse the imprisoned vagrants, who had hitherto only been subjected to pillory, were punished for their nomadic idleness, after the mid-sixteenth century, by being forced to engage in both useful and useless production. Useful in the sense that Jeremy Bentham's Panopticon project of 1797—to cite a highly developed workhouse type—was a machine for the extraction of improving labor from those "on whose part neither dexterity nor good will were to be depended."[28] Useless, in the sense that William Cubitt's treadmill installed in the Brixton House of Correction in 1821 powered a rotating windsail on top of the mill house that indicated only too well the inutility of the prisoners' efforts.

The fundamental worldlessness of the *animal laborans* that manifested itself in the eighteenth century with the "blind" mechanical production of the workhouse and the mill was paralleled in the twentieth century by the equally blind processes of mass consumption. As Arendt has written:

In our need for more and more rapid replacement of the worldly things around us, we can no longer afford to use them, to respect and preserve their inherent durability; we must consume, devour, as it were, our houses and furniture and cars as though they were the "good things" of nature which spoil uselessly if they are not drawn swiftly into the never-ending cycle of man's metabolism with nature. It is as though we had forced open the distinguishing boundaries which protected the world, the human artifice, from nature, the biological process which goes on in its very midst as well as the natural cyclical processes which surround it, delivering and abandoning to them the always threatened stability of a human world.[29]

Arendt goes on to argue that the modern age has increasingly sacrificed the ideas of permanence and durability to the abundance ideal of the *animal laborans* and that we live in a society of laborers inasmuch as the labor-power has been divided in order to eliminate from the thrust of its natural metabolism the "unnatural" and conscious obstacle of the human artifice—the original object of the *homo faber*.

That the *animal laborans* cannot construct a human world out of its own values is borne out by the accelerating tendency of mass production and consumption to undermine not only the durability of the world but also the possibility of establishing a permanent place within it. The science fiction forms projected by the utopian urbanists of the twentieth century have arisen out of either elitist or populist attempts to reify industrial process as though it were some "ideal" manifestation of a new nature. From the futurist architect Antonio Sant'Elia's Città Nuova (1914), of which, to quote from the *Manifesto of Futurist Architecture*, he stated that "our houses will last less time than we do and every generation will have to make its own,"[30] to Constant Nieuwenhuys's spontaneously dynamic New Babylon (1960), where urban change would be so accelerated as to render it pointless to return home—in each instance we are presented with equally kinetic images that project through prophetic exaggeration the fundamental placeless tendency of our present urban reality. Nieuwenhuys wrote: "There would be no question of any fixed life pattern since life itself would be as creative material. . . . In New Babylon people would be constantly travelling. There would be no need for them to return to their point of departure as this in any case would be transformed. Therefore each sector would contain private rooms (a hotel) where people would spend the night and rest for a while."[31]

From the point of view of machine or rationalized production, architecture has been as much affected as urbanism by the substitution of productive or processal norms, for the more traditional criteria of worldliness and use. Increasingly buildings come to be designed in response to the mechanics of their erection or, alternatively, processal elements such as tower cranes, elevators, escalators, stairs, refuse chutes, gangways, service cores, and automobiles determine the configuration of built form to a far greater extent than the hierarchic and more public criteria of *place*. And while the space of public appearance comes to be increasingly over-run by circulation or inundated at the urban scale by restricted high-speed access, the free-standing, high-rise megaliths of the modern city maintain their potential status as "consumer goods" by virtue of their isolated form. At the same time the prefabricated elements from which such forms are increasingly assembled guarantee the optimization of their production and consumption within the overall industrial economy. Their potential for rapid amortization, convenient demolition, and replacement begins to invalidate the traditional distinction of *meubles* from *immeubles*, a diffusion of meaning that was first announced in the nineteenth century, with the wholesale "removal" of structures intact.[32] In a related but more immediate way automation imposes equally processal conditions on all industrial design, for it tends towards the servo-mechanization of consumption, wherein machine rhythms amplify the fundamental tendency of life to destroy the durability of the world.[33] In this manner even the worldly category of use is to be absorbed by consumption inasmuch as use objects—in this instance, tools—become transformed by abundance into disposable "throwaway" goods; a subtle shift whose real significance resides in the intrinsic destructiveness of consumption as opposed to use.

The consequence of all this for contemporary architecture is as distressing as it is universal. Elevated on freeways or pedestrian decks or alternatively sequestered behind security fences, we are caused to traverse large areas of abstract, inaccessible urban space that can be neither appropriated nor adequately maintained. In a similar way we are confronted by piazzas whose hypothetical public status is vitiated by the vacuousness of the context or alternatively we are conducted down streets evacuated of all public life by the circulatory demands of traffic. We pass across thresholds whose public-representative nature has been suppressed or we enter foyers which have been arranged or lit in such a manner as to defeat the act of public promenade. Alternatively we are caused to depart from airports whose processal function defies the ritual of leave-taking. In each instance our value-free commodity culture engenders an equivalency wherein museums are rendered as oil refineries and laboratories acquire a monumental form. By a similar token public restaurants come to be rudely incarcerated in basements, while schools find themselves arbitrarily encased within the perimeters of windowless warehouses. In each case a ruthless cultural reduction masks itself by the rhetoric of *kitsch* or by the celebration of technique as an end in itself.[34]

The Identity of Consumption and the Worldlessness of Play

The earliest concentrations of labor-power, beginning first with the workhouse and then with the mill, brought about the uprooting of agrarian populations who then became as alienated from their traditional culture as they were from the objects of industrial production. This loss of "vernacular" was to return to haunt the descendants of these populations as soon as they became the "emancipated" consumers of their own output. While the specific form of "worldlessness" that resulted from this induced consumption varied with successive generations and from class to class, the initial loss of identity enforced by the conditions of industrial production was eventually sublimated, irrespective of class, by an identity to be instantly acquired through consumption. The phenomena of *kitsch*—from *Verkitschen*, "to fake"—appears with the advent of the department store, around the middle of the nineteenth century, when bourgeois civilization achieves for the first time an excessive productive capacity and is brought to create a widespread culture of its own—a culture that was to remain strangely suspended between the useful and the useless, between the sheer utility of its own puritan work ethic and a compulsive desire to mimic the licentiousness of aristocratic taste.[35]

While Marx, writing just before mass consumption began in earnest, projected the eventual liberation of all mankind from the necessity of remorseless labor, he failed to account for the latent potential of machine production to promote a voracious consumer society wherein, to quote Arendt, "nearly all human 'labor power' is spent in consuming, with the concomitant serious social problem of leisure."[36] In such a society the basic problem is no longer production but rather the creation of sufficient daily waste to sustain the inexhaustible capacity for consumption. Arendt's subsequent observation that this supposedly painless consumption only augments the devouring capacity of life, finds its corroboration in a world where shorter working hours, suburbanization, and the mass ownership of the automobile have together secured for the realm of consumption the ever-accelerating rate of daily commutation within the megalopolis, a situation in which the hours saved from production are precisely "compensated" by the hours wasted in the consumptive journey to work.

The victory of the *animal laborans* with which Arendt concludes her study of the dilemmas facing modern man turns not only on the reduction of art to the problematic "worldlessness" of free play, but also on the substitution of social gratification for the fabricating standards of function and use. For, as Arendt has argued:

Nothing perhaps indicates clearer the ultimate failure of *homo faber* to assert himself than the rapidity with which the principle of utility, the very quintessence of his world view, was found wanting and was superseded by the principle of "the greatest happiness of the greatest number."[37]

While utility originally presupposed a world of use objects by which man was significantly surrounded, this world began to disintegrate with the "tool-making" tendency of each object not to be an end in itself but rather a means of other objects and other ends. At this juncture where, as Arendt has put it, "the 'in order to' has become the content of the 'for the sake of,' . . . utility established as meaning generates meaninglessness."[38]

Art, on the other hand, as the essence of inutility—and this of course includes the non-functional aspect of architecture—is rendered worldless in such a society, insofar as it is reduced to introspective abstraction or vulgarized in the idiosyncratic vagaries of *kitsch*. In the first instance it cannot be easily shared and in the second it is reduced to an illusory commodity. If, as Arendt insists, the world must be constructed with thought rather than cognition,[39] then insomuch as it is not essential to the life processes of a laboring society, art loses its original worldliness and comes to be subsumed under play. This, of course, raises the problematic question as to the conditions under which play may be considered to be worldly. Be this as it may, freedom in laboring society is perceived solely as release from labor, namely, as play, and it is Arendt's recognition of this fact that makes her text such a perceptive, if partial, critique of Marx.

Marx predicted correctly, though with an unjustified glee, "the withering away" of the public realm under conditions of unhampered development of the "productive forces of society," and he was equally right, that is, consistent with his conception of man as an *animal laborans*, when he foresaw that "socialized men" would spend their freedom from laboring in those strictly private and essentially worldless activities that we now call "hobbies."[40]

The Human Condition and Critical Theory: A Postscript

Given Hannah Arendt's skepticism as to the redemption promised by the Marxist prognosis it will no doubt appear extraneous to compare her discourse to the critical theory of the Frankfurt School.[41] The reserve which Arendt publicly exercised in respect to this school of Marxist criticism should be sufficient caution against making such a comparison. Yet despite the disdain she seems to have felt for those whom she regarded as renegade Marxists, a common concern and even method may be found to relate the arguments developed in *The Human Condition* to the socio-cultural analyses of the Frankfurt School. It is clear that both Arendt and the Frankfurt School were equally obsessed with the interaction of structure and superstructure in advanced industrial society, even if such terms were entirely foreign to her thought.

These qualifications accepted, one may argue that the succession of the Frankfurt School, specifically the theoretical progression that links the later thought of Herbert Marcuse to the writings of Jürgen Habermas, takes up a number of themes that were either suppressed or suspended at the conclusion of *The Human Condition*. Amongst these issues one may arguably posit two. First, the problematic cultural status of play and pleasure in a future laboring society after its hypothetical liberation from the compulsion of consumption (Marcuse) and, second, the problematic possibility for mediating the autonomous rationality of science and technique through the reconstitution of the space of public appearance as an effective political realm (Habermas).

If one derives from *The Human Condition* the implication that a highly secular, laboring, and industrialized order must inevitably prevail in either state-capitalist, capitalist, or socialist societies, and if one posits some future state in which the "fatality" of an ever-accelerating consumption is, in some measure, redeemed, then the question arises as to what are the minimum environmental priorities that such a transformed state could realistically envisage?

While the *vita activa* in the ancient sense would no doubt initially remain in abeyance, some upgrading of the private habitat, essential to the quality of domestic life, would surely assert itself as a priority once this life was no longer subject to either rapacious consumption or optimized production. For while it is true, as Arendt asserts, that from the point of view of nature, it is *work* rather than *labor* that is destructive, this observation overlooks that qualitative dimension of consumption beyond which "man's metabolism with nature" becomes even more destructive of nature than *work*, beyond that frontier that we have already crossed, where non-renewable resources such as water and oxygen begin to become permanently contaminated or destroyed.[42] At this juncture, labor, as optimized consumption, stands opposed to it own Benthamite cult of life as the highest good, just as privacy *per se*, as the quintessence of labor and life, is underlined by the productive reduction of all built objects to the status of "consumer goods"; a threshold that has again been reached in the mobile-home industry of the United States.

Human adaptability notwithstanding, the basic criterion of privacy asserted by Barragán, posits itself not only as the necessary "figure" to the public ground, but also as the only standard by which a *balanced and rhythmic* life for the species could eventually be maintained. The urban consequences of applying such criteria as economic densities would be to spontaneously create the boundaries of a "negative" urban form—namely, some kind of public realm, even if this would not immediately constitute a "world" in the Arendtian sense. That the public space of the medieval city was the physical counterform of the private fabric Arendt herself has recognized in her assertion that it is the exterior perimeter of the private realm that effectively shapes the space of the city.

As to art, that is to say, as to the symbolization of common values and the manner in which they might be represented, this immediately introduces the cultural dilemma of "play" and the extent to which communal expression may or may not be reified. Permanence is not the absolute precondition for reification, music being an obvious exception, as Arendt herself acknowledges: "In music and poetry, the least 'materialistic' of the arts because their 'material' consists of sounds and words, reification and the workmanship it demands are kept to a minimum."[43]

Twentieth-century avant-garde art has frequently resorted to collective play or at least to aleatory forms of art as the necessary expression of an essentially "social" and dynamic future, although in many instances innate "laboring" values have assured that nothing could be achieved save the tautology of production itself.[44] While this strategy may capitalize on the indisputable authority of instrumentality, the parallel tendency of art to survive through the reductive assertion of its own autonomy is yet a further illustration of the general tendency of a laboring society to move toward privatization. It is hardly an accident that both these avant-garde strategies first emerged in the early years of the Soviet Union; the former, the *productivist sensibility*, being typified at its most extreme in the self-referential films of Dziga Vertov where the production of films about production exemplified production itself;[45] and the latter, the cult of *autonomous structure*, being reflected in the general artistic formalism of the period. The failure of this avant-garde to find its ostensible public led to the familiar withdrawal of the Soviet state into the *kitsch* of social realism. Only the repres ˙d Proletcult with its political theater and its program for the "theatricalization of everyday life" retained some lucid potential for a collective realization of an alternative culture.

Whether architecture, as opposed to building, will ever be able to return to the representation of collective value is a moot point. At all events its representative role would have to be contingent on the establishment of a public realm in the political sense. Otherwise limited by definition to the act of commemoration it would remain exactly where Adolf Loos left it in 1910. That this commemorative impulse would remain alive even in a laboring society became manifest after the First World War in the numerous memorials to the "unknown soldier"; those testaments to an unidentifiable somebody whom four years of mass slaughter should have revealed.[46]

Nothing less is outlined in *The Human Condition* than the teleological abyss that has progressively opened up before the path of industrialized man. That Arendt and the Frankfurt School perceived the same void but drew different conclusions from it, may be sensed in the following passage from Herbert Marcuse's *Eros and Civilization*:

The argument that makes liberation conditional upon an ever higher standard of living all too easily serves to justify the perpetuation of repression. The definition of the standard of living in terms of automobiles, television sets, airplanes, and tractors is that of the performance principle itself. Beyond the rule of this principle, the level of living would be measured by other criteria: the universal gratification of the basic human needs and the freedom from guilt and fear—internalized as well as external, instinctual as well as "rational." . . . Under optimum conditions, the prevalence, in mature civilization, of material and intellectual wealth would be such as to allow the painless gratification of needs, while domination would no longer systematically forestall such gratification. In this case, the quantum of instinctual energy still to be diverted into necessary labor . . . would be so small that a large area of repressive constraints and modifications no longer sustained by external forces would collapse. Consequently the antagonistic relation between pleasure principle and reality principle would be altered in favor of the former. Eros, the life instincts, would be released to an unprecedented degree.[47]

While this utopian projection of a future where "the elimination of surplus repression would *per se* eliminate if not labor, then the organization of human existence into an instrument of labor" does nothing if not stress the life-bound values of the *animal laborans*, Marcuse's recognition that the cult of *productivity* as an end in itself is the primary impasse of industrial society brings him surprisingly close to Arendt.

Efficiency and repression converge: raising the productivity of labor is the sacrosanct ideal of both capitalist and Stalinist Stakhanovism. The notion of productivity has its historical limits: they are those of the performance principle. Beyond its domain, productivity has another content and another relation to the pleasure principle: they are anticipated in the processes of imagination which preserve freedom from the performance principle while maintaining the claim of a *new* reality principle.[48]

That one day such a reality might still be achieved seems to be anticipated to an equal degree by Arendt's appraisal of the earliest Russian soviets and Jürgen Habermas's prognostications for the future of the *vita activa*. The two relevant passages are given below, the former from Arendt's study of revolutionary politics entitled *On Revolution* and the latter from Habermas's essay, dedicated to Marcuse on his seventieth birthday, bearing the title "Technology and Science as Ideology." Of the soviets, Arendt was to write:

The councils, obviously, were spaces of freedom. As such, they invariably refused to regard themselves as temporary organs of revolution and, on the contrary, made all attempts at establishing themselves as permanent organs of government. Far from wishing to make the revolution permanent, their explicitly expressed goal was "to lay the foundations of a republic acclaimed in all its consequences, the only government which will close forever the era of invasions and civil wars"; no paradise on earth, no classless society, no dream of socialist or communist fraternity, but the establishment of "the true Republic" was the "reward" hoped for as the end of the struggle. And what had been true in Paris in 1871 remained true for Russia in 1905, when the "not merely destructive but constructive" intentions of the first *soviets* were so manifest that contemporary witnesses "could sense the emergence and the formation of a force which one day might be able to effect the transformation of the State."[49]

And was it not just such a transformation that Habermas had in mind when he attempted to establish the following necessary limits for the emergence of a truly scientific rationality?

Above all, it becomes clear against this background that two concepts of rationalization must be distinguished. At the level of subsystems of purposive-rational action, scientific-technical progress has already compelled the reorganization of social institutions and sectors, and necessitates it on an even larger scale than heretofore. But this process of the development of the productive forces can be a potential for liberation if and only if it does not replace rationalization on another level.

Rationalization at the level of the institutional framework can only occur in the medium of symbolic interaction itself, that is through removing restrictions on all communication. Public, unrestricted discussion, free from domination, of the suitability and desirability of action-ordering principles and norms in the light of the socio-cultural repercussions of developing subsystems of purposive-rational action—such as communication at all levels of political and repoliticized decision-making processes—is the only medium in which anything like "rationalization" is possible.[50]

We are confronted in this complex passage with an existential political perspective that for Arendt and Habermas alike is the only possible vehicle for the rational determination of human ends. Such a decentralized "cantonal" conception, tends, I would submit, to return us to the dependency of political power on its social and physical constitution, that is to say, on its derivation from the living proximity of men and from the physical manifestation of their public being in built form. For architecture at least, the relevance of *The Human Condition* resides in this—in its formation of that political reciprocity that must of necessity obtain, for good or ill, between the status of men and the status of their objects.

Notes

1. Hannah Arendt, *The Human Condition* (Chicago: University of Chicago Press, 1958), p. 7.
2. Ibid.
3. *The Shorter English Dictionary*, 3d ed. (Oxford: Clarendon Press, 1947).
4. Arendt provides the following etymological footnote on p. 136 of *The Human Condition*: "The Latin word *faber*, probably related to *facere* ('to make something' in the sense of production), originally designated the fabricator and artist who works upon hard material, such as stone or wood; it also was used as translation for the Greek word *tektōn*, which has the same connotation."
5. Adolf Loos, "Architecture 1910," in Tim and Charlotte Benton, eds., *An International Anthology of Original Articles in Architecture and Design, 1890–1939* (New York: Watson Guptill, 1975),

pp. 41–45. In her essay "Thinking and Moral Considerations" Arendt directly relates representation with thought in her footnote on Augustine: "The image, *the representation of something absent* is stored in memory and *becomes* a thought object, a 'vision of thought' as soon as it is wilfully remembered." See *Social Research* 38, no. 3 (Autumn 1971), p. 424.

6. Arendt, *The Human Condition*, p. 53.

7. Ibid, p. 201.

8. See Melvin Webber, *Explorations into Urban Structure* (Philadelphia: University of Pennsylvania, 1964). See also his article in Wingo Lowdon, Jr., ed., *Cities and Space* (Baltimore: Johns Hopkins University Press, 1963).

9. Robert Venturi, *Complexity and Contradiction in Architecture* (New York: Museum of Modern Art, 1966), p. 133.

10. Arendt, *The Human Condition*, p. 204. See also her "Thinking and Moral Considerations," pp. 430, 431. In this text Arendt opposes the house to the nomadic tent. "We can use the word house for a great number of objects—for the mud hut of a tribe, the palace of a king, the country home of a city dweller, the cottage in the village, or the apartment house in town—but we can hardly use it for the tents of some nomads. The house, in and by itself, *auto kath'auto*, that which makes us use the word for all these particular and very different buildings, is never seen, neither by the eyes of the body, nor by the eyes of the mind; . . . the point here is that it implies something considerably less tangible than the structure perceived by our eyes. It implies 'housing somebody' and being 'dwelt in' as no tent could house or serve as a dwelling place which is put up today and taken down tomorrow." This recognition of the house as a *place of dwelling* is fundamentally Heideggerian and as such relates to the "darkness" of the *megaron*. As in Martin Heidegger's "Building, Dwelling, and Thinking," the argument implicitly links "house-building" to agriculture and to rootedness.

11. Camillo Sitte, *City Planning According to Artistic Principles*, trans. George R. Collins and Christiane Craseman Collins (New York: Random House. 1965). As the translators point out, Sitte made pointed use of the term *Platz* ("place") rather than the word "square," which has geometrical connotations antipathetic to Sitte's urban principles. Sitte's work was polemically against the normative gridded city as advocated by Reinhard Baumeister.

12. Arendt provides the following etymological footnote on p. 71 of *The Human Condition*: "The Greek and Latin words for the interior of the house, *megaron* and *atrium*, have a strong connotation of darkness and blackness." She cites Mommsen, *Römische Geschichte*, 5th ed., Book 1, pp. 22, 236.

13. Arendt, *The Human Condition*, p. 38.

14. Ibid., p. 39.

15. Ibid., p. 59.

16. Clive Bamford-Smith, *Builders in the Sun: Five Mexican Architects* (New York: Architectural Book Publishing Co., 1967), p. 74.

17. Arendt, *The Human Condition*, p. 122.

18. Bamford-Smith, *Builders in the Sun*, p. 77.

19. Arendt, *The Human Condition*, p. 45.

20. Ibid., pp. 173–174.

21. Ibid., pp. 167–168.

22. G. C. Argan, *The Renaissance City* (New York: Braziller, 1969), pp. 25–26.

23. Arendt, *The Human Condition*, pp. 282–283.

24. Ibid., p. 307.

25. Michel Parent and Jacques Verroust, *Vauban* (Paris: Editions Jacques Fréal, 1971), p. 60.

26. The horse-drawn tram of the Ringstrasse gave way to the electric tram in the early 1890s. In his *Teoría general de urbanización* (1867), Ildefonso Cerda, the planner of modern Barcelona and inventor of the term *urbanization*, argues that "the form of the city is, or must be, derived from the necessities of locomotion." From this date onwards the city becomes inundated by mechanized movement.

27. Arendt, *The Human Condition*, p. 304.

28. See Robin Evans, "Regulation and Production," *Lotus* 12 (September 1976).

29. Arendt, *The Human Condition*, pp. 125–126.

30. See Reyner Banham, *Theory and Design in the First Machine Age* (New York: Praeger, 1960), p. 135.

31. For the complete text see Constant Nieuwenhuys, "New Babylon," *Architectural Design*, June 1964, pp. 304, 305.

32. See Stanley Buder, *Pullman: An Experiment in Industrial Order and Community Planning, 1880–1930* (London: Oxford University Press, 1967). George Pullman, founder of the Pullman Palace Car Company, had, in fact, made his start in Chicago in 1855 raising buildings above the then-existing ground level.

33. Arendt, *The Human Condition*, p. 132.

34. Innumerable examples exist of the specific displacement of the public realm in contemporary building. Among the more recent instances, one might cite the following: The Ford Foundation Building, New York, for its provision of a false "public" foyer which is programmed in such a way as to assure that no public realm may be allowed to come into existence. The Centre Pompidou, Paris, for its reduction of its "users" to the same status as the "services"—the users being piped-in, so to speak, on one side, and the services fed into the structure on the other. In short, the reduction of a museum to the status and the model expressiveness of an oil refinery! The Richards Laboratories at the University of Pennsylvania where service towers are rendered as monumental elements and where the whole structure is pervaded by a sense of "religiosity" inappropriate to the processal nature of a laboratory building. In this last example a misplaced monumentality fails to transcend the manifest absence of an appropriately "representative" or "commemorative" program, whereas in the first case the presence of a "representative" program is rendered null and void by the rhetoric of the machine. Consciously designed as a cultural supermarket, art in the name of populism is reduced to a commodity.

35. See Herman Broch, "Notes on the Problem of Kitsch," in Gillo Dorfles, ed., *Kitsch: The World of Bad Taste* (New York: Universe Books, 1969), p. 54.

36. Arendt, *The Human Condition*, p. 131.

37. Ibid., pp. 307–308.

38. Ibid., p. 154.

39. Ibid., p. 171. Arendt's distinction between "thought" and "cognition" is worth repeating here: "Thought and cognition are not the same. Thought, the source of art works, is manifest without transformation or transfiguration in all great philosophy, whereas the chief manifestation of the cognitive processes, by which we acquire and store up knowledge, is the sciences." Ibid., p. 170.

40. Ibid., pp. 117–118.

41. For a historical account of the Frankfurt School and Institute of Social Research see Martin Jay, *The Dialectical Imagination* (Boston: Little, Brown, 1973).

42. Earl F. Murphy, *Governing Nature* (Chicago: Quadrangle Books, 1967), p. 31. See also p. 118 for an interesting comment on the nature of industrial consumption: "Men have assumed that there was a direct line from production to consumption to disappearance. Now it is evident that man, whether as producer or consumer, is part of a cycle. The residue streaming from his production and consumption do *not* disappear."

43. Arendt, *The Human Condition*, p. 169. See also p. 127 and Johan Huizinga, *Homo Ludens: A Study of the Play Element in Culture* (Boston: Beacon Press, 1950). As to the limits of play in respect of art we find Huizinga writing: "The 'music' arts live and thrive in an atmosphere of common rejoicing; the plastic arts do not" (p. 167).

44. The history of the Proletcult movement in the Soviet Union and its cult of production has yet to be written. For an introduction to the founding principles of the movement and work of Alexander Malinowsky, otherwise known as Bogdanov, see J. B. Billington, *The Icon and the Axe* (New York: Knopf, 1968), p. 489.

45. See Annette Michelson, "The Man with the Movie-Camera: From Magician to Epistemologist," *Art Forum*, March 1972.

46. Arendt, *The Human Condition*, p. 181.

47. Herbert Marcuse, *Eros and Civilization* (New York: Vintage Books, 1962), p. 139.

48. Ibid., p. 141.

49. Hannah Arendt, *On Revolution* (New York: Viking Press, 1965), p. 268.

50. Jürgen Habermas, *Towards a Rational Society*, trans. Jeremy Shapiro (Boston: Beacon Press, 1970), pp. 118–119.

1979

Frank Gehry, Gehry House, Santa Monica, California

The only important thing about my house is the neighborhood it's in. The house isn't a significant example of period architecture. It' was just a dumb little house with charm and I became interested in trying to make it more important. I became fascinated with creating a shell around it, one that allowed the old house to exist as an object, and, in a sense, defined the house by only showing parts. When you look through the new house you see featured parts of the old house in an edited fashion. It's very surreal, and I'm interested in surrealism. . . .

Working in this fashion is a way of learning. I wasn't trying to make a big or precious statement about architecture, or trying to do an important work. I was trying to build a lot of ideas, and when I got caught in the game of the old house, it became serious. I began to engage the house in a dialogue by cutting away from it, exposing some parts and covering up others. I found myself trying to create conflict and collision between the new and the old.

In using the rough carpentry and materials, I wanted to prove you could make an art-object out of anything. This is being done, of course, in sculpture, and I find myself influenced by artists such as Rauschenberg, Serra, Carl André, Donald Judd, Heizer. . . .

I was concerned with maintaining a "freshness" in the house. Often this freshness is lost—in our over-working details, in over-finishing them, their vitality is lost. I wanted to avoid this by emphasizing the feeling that the details are still in the process: that the "building" hasn't stopped. The very finished building has security and it's predictable. I wanted to try something different. I like playing at the edge of disaster.

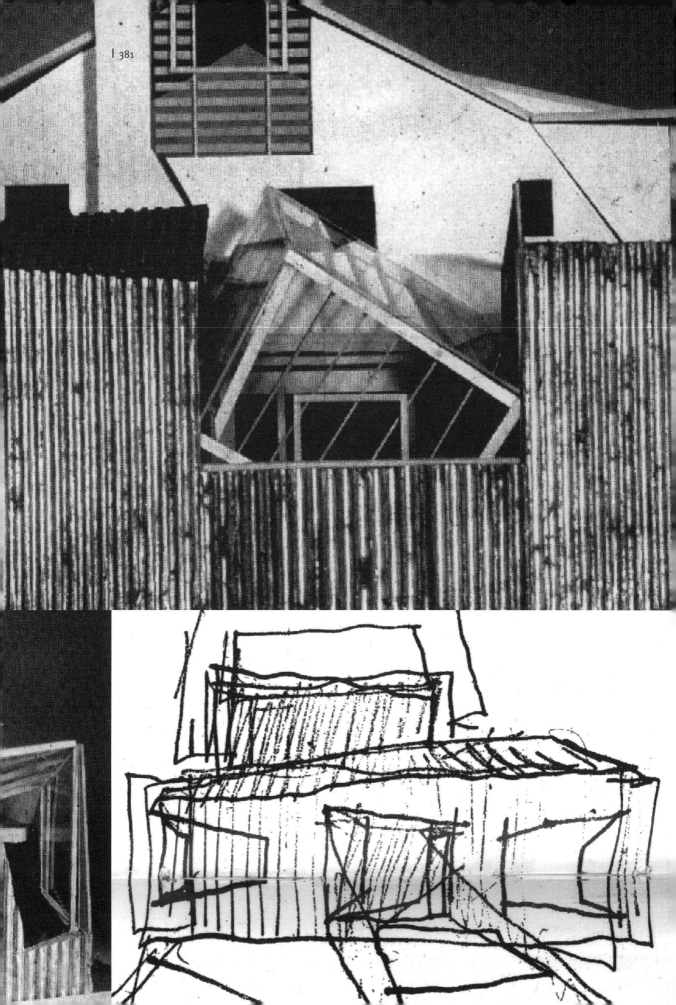

José Quetglas | **"Loss of Synthesis: Mies's Pavilion"** "Pérdida de la síntesis: el Pabellón de Mies,"

Carrer de la Ciutat 11 (April 1980); translated for this anthology by Luis E. Carranza

A 1938 photograph of Walter Benjamin in the garden of Bertolt Brecht's house, along with a translation of the "Angelus Novus" passage from "Theses on the Philosophy of History,"[1] appeared in the inaugural, "o," issue of *Carrer de la Ciutat* as what the editors called a "fetish." Benjamin—the aura of Benjamin—must have been a poignant specter for a group of young intellectuals in Barcelona in 1977, two years after Franco's death, the same year as the first democratic general elections. In this and twelve subsequent issues, the editors—including Beatriz Colomina, Juan José Lahuerta, Helio Piñón, Josep Maria Rovira, and others—foregrounded the work of Aldo Rossi, focused the "otherness" of Adolf Loos, constructed Filippo Brunelleschi as a kind of Benjaminian "destructive character," and in general elaborated urban, theatrical, literary strategies for the interpretation of architecture (many of which were influenced by Manfredo Tafuri), all in an attempt to shatter what they saw as the small-minded barriers of the academic and professional bureaucracies. *Carrer de la Ciutat* was launched also as an alternative to the more established Barcelona journal *Arquitecturas bis*, whose editors included Oriol Bohigas, Federico Correa, Rafael Moneo, Helio Piñón, and Manuel de Solà-Morales.

So, too, Benjamin's comments on the functionality of the bourgeois fear of glass—its essential poverty, its *Ungemütlichkeit*—must have resonated with José Quetglas, the journal's primary director. "It is not for nothing that glass is such a hard and smooth material upon which nothing attaches itself," Benjamin wrote. "Also a cold and concise material. Things made of glass have no aura. In general, glass is the enemy of secrecy. It is also the enemy of possession."[2] In a lyrical but corrosive writing style Quetglas recodes and crosses the local reception of Mies's German Pavilion in Barcelona, the canonic photographs, and a theatrical reconstruction of its context. Moreover, in the background of his meditations is the fact of the recent reconstruction of the pavilion in Barcelona, which occasioned the essay. As Beatriz Colomina would later point out, "not only is the pavilion known to us through its 'reproduction,' but, as Quetglas shows, it in itself comprises a set of reproductions of preceding works and projects by Mies himself, by Bruno Taut, and by Peter Behrens. It also operates in much the same way as a theatrical re-presentation"—all of which situates the theoretical problematic in the relation of architect, audience, the

compare 624–625 building, and its reproducibility.[3]

Notes

1. For its influence on this group and an entire generation of architecture theorists, it is worth reproducing the passage in full: "A Klee painting named 'Angelus Novus' shows an angel looking as though he is about to move away from something he is fixedly contemplating. His eyes are staring, his mouth is open, his wings are spread. This is how one pictures the angel of history. His face is turned toward the past. Where we perceive a chain of events, he sees one single catastrophe which keeps piling wreckage upon wreckage and hurls it in front of his feet. The angel would like to stay, awaken the dead, and make whole what has been smashed. But a storm is blowing from Paradise; it has got caught in his wings with such violence that the angel can no longer close them. This storm irresistibly propels

him into the future to which his back is turned, while the pile of debris before him grows skyward. This storm is what we call progress." Walter Benjamin, "Theses on the Philosophy of History," in *Illuminations*, ed. Hannah Arendt (New York: Harcourt, Brace & World, 1968), pp. 257–258.

2. Walter Benjamin, "Erfahrung und Armut," in *Illuminationen. Ausgewählte Schriften* (Frankfurt: Suhrkamp, 1969), p. 314.

3. Beatriz Colomina, "Architecture, Production and Reproduction," introduction to *Architectureproduction,* ed. Beatriz Colomina (New York: Princeton Architectural Press, 1988). For this edition, Colomina commissioned "Fear of Glass: The Barcelona Pavilion," an expanded version of Quetglas's original essay. Yet another version was published as *Der gläserne Schrecken: Imágenes del Pabellón de Alemania* (Montreal: Section b, 1991).

The architect van der Rohe has created something very modern with only straight horizontal and vertical lines, with very rich materials such as local and Italian marble blocks and double walls of mysterious glass.

His complex appears distinguished: strange because of its structure, with two pools, official room, and wide corridors. It was said that the glass was mysterious because a person standing in front of one of these walls can see himself reflected as in a mirror and if the person moves behind the glass he can see the outside perfectly. Not all visitors notice this odd peculiarity whose cause is unknown.

ELISEO SANZ BALZA, *Notas de un visitante,* Barcelona, 1930

For an explorer, it is important to pay close attention to what is said by the natives, because it is there that he will noticeably find—without translation or any restriction—the true emotions that each received impression awakens in the immaculate savage. Retracing, then, the route toward the sources—starting from the spoken word, moving through the expressed emotion, leaving behind the received impression—the explorer, in this way, can arrive at the object that has produced it all: in our case, the German Pavilion, but in a way unknown to any modern investigator.

But, in order to obtain this reencounter with the primitive object, not any native will do: only the ingenious ones. Never the pedantic ones, who add surprises on their own, who create false tracks that lead nowhere, who describe emotions produced only with the desire to interest the foreigner.

An example of inadequate natives: Hawaiians, who always wear their undergarments beneath their flower necklaces and their grass skirts.

Another example: those that Nicolás Rubió cites in his moving article on the Pavilion published in 1929: "Des touristes et des indigènes d'extrême avant-garde, ont pu lui reprocher: 'Ce pavillon n'est pas tout à fait dernier cri.' Ils en ont voulu à l'architecte, ils ont dit qu'il ne faut pas apporter des *sous-nouveautés* aux Expositions Internationales." One does not know, or does not dare to imagine, who these uncompromising natives could have been that, in the Barcelona of 1929, found Mies's Pavilion barely "modern": Rubió, discreetly, forgets to mention their names.

More examples, because those perverse natives form part of a tough and prolific race: the person who writes, in no. 57 of the *CAU* magazine, that perhaps it is time to oppose "new interpretations" to the "old interpretations" that have always granted the monopoly of quality and interest to the German Pavilion. It is very possible that there is more than one person who would be interested in the pavilions of Yugoslavia, of the Casa Jorba Warehouses, of the Ebro Hydrographic Confederation, or in any other of the rancid exercises that vulgarly combine futurist jokes, poorly evoked expressionist effects, and quickly suspended neoplastic decompositions. And perhaps someone will enjoy this. Far from these nuances, I have only been taught that Mies's Pavilion in and of itself can be used to explain the passage of modern architecture from the trusted heroic years of the avant-garde to the languid and more resigned contemplation of the International Style, and that the Pavilion is also, or perhaps above all, a beautiful and emotive object, indifferent to competitions of more or less modernity that pass by its side.

Because of the pleasure that it always gives me to look at its photographs or to follow the drawings that represent it, I find it gratifying, as a recollection of this pleasure and as an acknowledgment to its author—who also looks so much like Gregorio López Raimundo—to write about the Pavilion.

It is a house without doors. Open or closed?

The question is not irrelevant. For many years, architectural critics have agreed, nobody really knows why, that an open space, fluid in its interior development and spilling toward its exterior, must be judged superior to a compartmentalized, boxed space.

Perhaps it was because of the excitement of the discovery of late Roman space that, from the hand of Wickhoff and Riegl, naturally reached architects a few decades later than the cultured public, or perhaps it was because of the memory, even more distant, of that mythic birth of an autochthonous architecture on the North American prairies: in the house of the pioneer that identified himself with the Nature that he competed against, building his home as an extension of it, as the expression and result of the pact between both, and not as a defensive opposition. The truth is that the myth of "open spaces" encouraged all sorts of valorizations, more than descriptions, of the architecture of our century.

Mies's Pavilion had the obligation, in that it was a work of quality, to explain space as open and fluid, especially when the absence of closure between the interior and exterior was so obvious. A caricatural example: in only sixteen lines of narrow printed columns in the amusing article already mentioned in *CAU* magazine, one can read in reference to the Pavilion: "The themes of spatial fluidity and continuity . . . , the spatial fluidity and transparency . . . , a space in which the fluidity, the continuity. . . ."

Mies's Pavilion is a closed space.

How can this be, in a house without doors, without roofs, almost without walls and with glass walls? Nicolás Rubió, in the same 1929 article, has been the first to point it out and explain it: "Certaines de ces salles manquent de plafond: ce sont des vrais *demi-patios*, où l'espace n'est limité que par trois murs et par la surface horizontale de l'eau d'un bassin, mais où il est 'retenu' par la géométrie."

The space of the Pavilion remains "retenu par la géométrie," according to the constant method in all of Mies's architecture. It deals with the arrangement of one or various horizontal planes, detached from the ground, where the lower plane always designates a strict surface. Think of the coffee tray of a waiter or the surface of a table: there are no "limits" to the virtual space that they construct, but that space becomes perfectly contained, cylindrical in one case and prismatic in the other, despite the absence of material closures that oppose its expansion. To be in that space means being on a cut plane; whereas in North American architecture, for example—to cite a case of true spatial continuity—*to be in* a space never means *to be on* the ground, but rather *to be toward* one or many, precise or ambiguous, directions.

In the Pavilion, the plane that separates the ground and contains the space is formed by the rectangular travertine platform, more than a meter in height. It is a base that hides, to whomever approaches the Pavilion from the front, the way to climb up to it: the eight stairs have been hidden behind the piece that serves as a baseboard, at the same level as the platform.

This segregation of the platform still remains reinforced by the very placement of the Pavilion in the space of the Exposition: opposite the gigantic colonnade at the end of the transversal avenue. The first image of the Pavilion was always one of a solitary object placed behind this fragment of a virtual peristyle, of a cage formed by columns and the unending blind wall of the Victoria Eugenia Palace. The visitor had to leave behind the site of the Exposition and cross the threshold in order to reach the Pavilion.

If the platform is enough to define the space of the Pavilion as different, to segregate it as a stage separated from the ground that the public of the Exposition walks on, the plane defined by the two covers, reduced to a sheet, will serve to transform this space, not only into something different but into something enclosed, into an interior.

It is a theme present in all of Mies's architecture, from his first projects until his death. In an article written some years ago, "Architettura per i musei," Aldo Rossi declared: "I believe that the first principle of every theory consists in the obstinacy of some issues, and that it is proper of artists, of architects in particular, to focus on an issue to develop, to carry out an option in the interior of architecture and to desire to always solve the same problem." This is true for the masters of our century: for Wright, Le Corbusier, Gropius, and for Mies. In Mies, we would find always repeated that obsessive volition to build a segregated and enclosed space where every inhabitant will be excluded.

In his projects of the 1910s—in the Kröller House or in the Bismarck Monument, for example—architecture was not defined as placed on the ground, but rather as elevated, distanced through a previously constructed platform, clearly foreign to the natural terrain. That same elevation (but repeated indefinitely) in the twenties will give rise to his glass skyscraper projects, which are not a vertical sketch but a difficult floor-by-floor ascension of an unlimited series of horizontal platforms, all of which originate on a ground different from that of the city, more profound, and grow in between neighboring buildings without accepting any dialogue with them.

It will no longer be indifference but rather obstinate closure that appears in the courtyard houses of his last years in Germany: hermetically enclosing the interior space with an impassable enclosure as if art or a friendly scenario—the home—could emerge only where all dependence on life has been severed. His North American houses—Resor, Farnsworth, Fifty-by-Fifty—present a more bitter and radical exaggeration of this caesura. The lack of communication between interior and exterior, between art and life, is so assured, even before architecture, that the enclosures don't seem necessary. In fact, to show the lack of necessity of the barriers will show the impassability of the differences. In these projects, space remains definitely retained as a fissure between two platforms, extended by capillary action and levitating at the edge of the natural ground.

In all of Mies's architecture, the first line on the paper is horizontal. The formal definition of space is always and only produced by horizontal planes. Vertical planes will appear later, once the stage has been arranged. That is why they exhibit their mobility, their capacity to slide or stop arbitrarily on any point of the foundational plane which they cannot alter. Then, the screens appear, the partitions of ebony, onyx, or silks, the marble sheets or the cutouts of a landscape through the glass. Or, the objects oversaturated with form appear, regressive, anxious only of themselves: the armchairs, the sculptures, all of the complaining subjects that inhabit the solitary Miesian stage. Can one call them furniture? One could answer: What is not "furniture" on the platform of Mies's architecture? The very representational technique of the project—the collage: on an already drawn sheet on which the horizontal planes appear and therefore the stage, pasting cutouts that represent virtual objects, wandering, hopelessly foreign to the space, delicately deposited on it—indicates clearly the different instant of creation of the one and the other, sentenced to be heterogeneous, to be built of different materials and in different times.

The objects will never form part of the stage. The stage is prepared to remain empty. "Il ne referme que l'espace," Rubió would write about the Pavilion. One could exaggerate his comment, increasing its exactitude even more: *il ne referme que de l'espace refermé.*

We should also note the coincidence, not only functional but also visual, produced in the interior photographs of Mies's houses—especially in the Tugendhat House where all of the photographs seem to be old—between the veining of the blurred exterior landscaping and the veining of the interior marble sheets. The exterior has been negated as a more or less distant landscape and has been converted into a sheet adhered to the window, into a representation of itself: to the point that a project like the Resor House can be simply explained by the intersections of the visual cone of the person looking out with the plane of glass. The exterior will never be able to make itself present, to become noticeable as a material reality, not even when it is more imposing, such as in the mountains of Wyoming: only their representation will be accepted.

The reference to the visual cone—to Alberti, therefore, and, correlatively, to some conceptual Thomist or Platonic matrixes—is not arbitrary. Mies's is an antisensorial architecture formed more by representations than by plastic values. Similar to the facade of Alberti's Sant'Andrea in Mantua, which, in a plane, represents the three-dimensional structure of the naves of Brunelleschi's San Lorenzo in Florence, what makes the *interior elevations* of the Resor House is a conceptualized landscape: represented two-dimensionally, reduced to an image of itself.

It is possible that more than one reader has already been thinking, for some time, of a project by Mies that would prove to be an exception or even a denial of the interpretation explored up to now. I am referring to the project for a brick country house of 1922: an obvious Wrightian exercise, placed at the beginnings of Mies's mature work, finalizing his years of experimentation. From there, the rest of his work could be interpreted in a different way. But let us try, before anything, to understand this project; the most predisposed, apparently, to be explained in terms of a spatial interpretation.

The influence of Wright reaches Mies in two waves. The first, in his years of work with Peter Behrens, would proceed without any doubt from the Wasmuth portfolio, directly known by him or perhaps pointed out by Gropius, who also worked in Behrens's office during this time and who, in his 1914 model factory for the Deutscher Werkbund exposition, would show only all too well his interest in the North American architect, including the literal citation of some fragments. The second wave, more related to the brick country house project, would come from the Low Countries, with Van't Hoff, Oud, and the group gravitating around the magazine *Wendingen*.

The conscious influence of Wright, therefore, cannot be denied. But also it cannot be denied that there is little relation between the role of space in Mies and in Wright. What is it that grows, develops, flows and spills over toward the exterior in Mies's project? Space? No. What grows are the walls: exactly the opposite of space. In Mies's project, spaces remain perfectly defined, static once they have reached their form, in contact with each other but not in contagion. Only that which is not space, or the space where we will never be able to penetrate, space that we are denied—that is to say, the solidness of the wall—shows its capacity to unfold, to organically meld itself with the forceful lines of the exterior world.

It is an inverse situation to Wright's, for whom, beginning with a period that would end with the Husser House, space possesses its own entity, developing toward the walls like wind over reeds: leaning, they point and appear to channel the gusts of wind. In the Husser House, space, although already continuous, is still defined from its perimeter, from the different values that the wall adopts, as a result of the wall, like what had already taken place in Richardson's libraries, primitive precedent to the Wrightian sense of space.

The apparently Wrightian project of Mies is the exact photographic negative of any prairie house. We could interpret it by assuming that the Monument to Karl Liebknecht and Rosa Luxemburg was a magnified detail of the brick country house, an enlarged fragment of any of its walls, which exhibits, provocatively, our exclusion, similar to what the mirrors of the Pavilion do, by reflecting our gaze without permitting it to penetrate, returning back to us our image always placed outside of the Pavilion.

To look into the Pavilion is to find oneself excluded.

The "theme" of Mies is not the same as Wright's, not even in this 1922 project, although he might be experimenting with the materials that Wright uses. It is worth noting that similar relations are also established between Mies and the neoplasticists. Mies is not van Doesburg, even though he is trying out the very tools of neoplastic composition. Zevi has estimated, correctly, that "perhaps there is not one cultured architect . . . that did not pick up, in any phase of his professional development, the decompositional investigations derived from the Dutch group"; but we also must measure just how much neoplasticism there is in the 1929 Pavilion.

Let us recall an important corner, the one where the Kolbe sculpture is situated. What is a dihedral there? There is no doubt: it is the intersection of two planes. Look, at the back, at the dark wall: it comes from some place on the left, through that corridor where the opening is exposed, and it grows toward the right, until it meets another wall made of the same material and dimensions that has been growing constantly in the opposite direction, from some place to our right, until it reaches the back. Where both meet, a straight line is produced, the final result of both, the conclusion of their movement. What is a dihedral in a project by Rietveld, van Eesteren, or van Doesburg? The opposite to that in Mies's Pavilion: it is the *beginning* axis of the composition or analysis, not its final result; it is the support and impulse of the movement in three directions to which all of the planes of space will be referring. Also because of this, in neoplasticist drawings, the straight line that a dihedral would point to occupies an empty or central place: the planes either have already escaped, having slid beyond their guide, or they are spread out, extending beyond their straight intersection, forming, therefore, four dihedrals. This never happens in Mies's Pavilion, where one never finds rough edges, overlaps, or extensions in the intersections of two planes. Returning to the corner of the small pool: notice the exact equivalence between the two light-colored horizontal planes that stop exactly over the same straight line, or the repetition between the two planes, of inverse visual value and, thus, symmetrical and equal, of the deep and clear canopy of the sky and the deep and dark layer of the water, or the screen of dark glass to the left and the virtual, transparent screen that joins, in the center, the end of the cover with the edge of the pool. These multiple pairs of parallel planes define and surround a series of perfectly cut prismatic spaces, of inverse plastic and conceptual values. The whole of the Pavilion could be broken down this way into different prisms united only by tangency, without offering any doubt at the moment of attributing, to one or another box, any of the places of the Pavilion.

A house without doors, closed, where every visitor is excluded; a house formed by spaces that are impermeable to one another: these are the materials of the Pavilion. For what reason could Mies have gathered them here?

"A glass house does not catch fire, there is no need for a fire brigade"; "Parasites are not nice, they will never get into the glass house": these are two of the fourteen verses that Paul Scheerbart writes to be incorporated into the Glass House that Bruno Taut built in Cologne, in 1914, as a pavilion for the glass industries in the Deutscher Werkbund exposition. Fifteen years later, in Barcelona, Mies would want to build this pavilion.

A few photographs and only a few general drawings remain of Taut's pavilion; even the model, as Scheerbart recalls in his correspondence, was lost at the same time that the pavilion was lost, and nothing can restore now the effect that it had on those who penetrated into its interior. In the exterior, the form can be interpreted, simultaneously, as that of a natural bud and that of a polished crystal. Image of synthesis, then: representation of the reconquered harmony between Nature and Thought, between the organic impulse of growth and the conceptual structure of the Universe. The pavilion arose, precisely, above this very exposed and unsolved contradiction: the base was an unconscious bulb, soft and malleable concrete, on which there had been placed, miraculously without rolling down, fourteen very hard, shiny, crystal spheres. To step into the pavilion meant, for the visitor, an unequivocal ceremony of initiation. First, purification of the conditions of the exterior world was guaranteed by surpassing the non-pacified platform: the neophyte ascends up a curved stairway, with glass surfaces to his left, to his right, under his feet, and above his head. He advances without direction between translucent impressions, illuminated and immaterial. Any reference to a stabilized sense of direction has been eliminated. "We are suspended in space yet we still do not know the new order": when Gropius responds in 1919 to the survey of the Arbeitsrat für Kunst, he is exactly describing that instant of purification that comes upon entering the Glass House. The purified neophyte penetrates into an unknown space. When he is under the glass cupola and moves around, he will understand that it is not the environment that is unknown but rather himself, his own body, that becomes the point of interest of the pavilion: the double cupola of white rhomboidal glass on the outside, and of hundreds of polished and colored crystals on the inside, that tinges with dozens of colors and marks of light any object—and person—that is within its interior.

To move under that cupola means to notice how one changes color at each step. The force of the glass has revealed the enormous energy present in the interior of the visitor: dormant, unbeknownst to him. The *Glasarchitektur*, Adolf Behne pointed out, does not *announce* new worlds, it does not imagine them: it *constructs* them. The visitor has approached the Glass House much as a spectator approaches a stage, but once there notices that it is he who is representing the scene. As a total theater, the Glass House will cover any distance between seeing and making, between spectator and actor, between Art and Life.

Explaining this reconquered resonance between the revealing universe and the Subject, to notice in the Subject the restless unfolding of the energy of glass: that is the exulting message of Taut's pavilion. In the grotto of the pavilion—really the ground level, reached only by descending from the interior of the cupola—the new man recognizes in the other objects of the glass world identical qualities to those recently discovered in himself: the waterfall over a glass staircase where the water leaps tinged by the changing colored light, the projections of abstract photographic slides and of kaleidoscopic figures, the cladding of all surfaces with glass mosaics, the very presence of the cupola seen through the central opening of the upper floor, the rhythmic sound of the water: an unequivocal *Gesamtkunstwerk* in harmony—and this is what is important—with the qualities that the visitor has recognized in himself.

In the Barcelona Pavilion, what vanished would be precisely this revealed harmony. The visitor will notice himself differently in this space which he will never be able to cross, a space built precisely to appear empty, a space which the presence of masses will not be able to fill.

"A home is intended for nothing but to be beautiful. It is there for no other purpose; it must stand empty in accordance with the saying of Meister Eckhart: 'I never want to ask God to give himself to me. I want to ask him to make me empty and pure; for if I were empty and pure, God by his very nature would give himself to me and be enclosed within me.'" This is how Bruno Taut begins his *Haus des Himmels*, presenting the project of the same name.

Mies's Pavilion is, again, the Glass House, but this time the light will no longer tinge us and give us its confidence; rather we will never be able to touch it. The only source of light in the interior of the Pavilion is enclosed between four screens of translucent, pink onyx in the interior of a space that we will never enter. We know of its presence at the other side of the wall: prohibited. There still remains one more light that can only be seen by he who is in the corridor at the back of the Pavilion. From there, the sculpture by Kolbe can be seen flooded by an avalanche of terrible light, brighter and clearer because of its contrast with the semi-darkness of the corridor where the spectator stands. But the dancer does not irradiate it, but rather, crushed by its weight, tries to reject it with its arms. At its feet grows the dark pool where the inert, melted glass is gathered, without being able to summon God any more in the empty and pure house.

If a *Gesamtkunstwerk* can still be proposed, Mies's Pavilion constructs it either as an empty stage or as a theater where the Subject must be absent, looking from the other side of the wall. Manfredo Tafuri, in "Il teatro come 'città virtuale.' Dal Cabaret Voltaire al Totaltheater," has explained the Pavilion precisely as a scenic presence:

In 1929 Mies van der Rohe, in the Barcelona Pavilion, constructed a stagelike space whose neutrality had profound affinities with that of the rhythmic geometries of Appia's or Graig's stage designs. In that space, an empty place of *absence*, man, aware of the impossibility of restoring "syntheses," and having once understood the "negativeness" of the metropolis, as the spectator of an entertainment which is truly "total" because it does not exist, is forced into a pantomime. This reproduces the wandering of sign-beings through the urban labyrinth among signs devoid of sense, experienced daily by man. In the absolute silence, the audience at the Barcelona Pavilion can thus "be reintegrated" with that *absence*.

There are no more attempts to synthesize "the trick and the soul." In a place that refuses to be a space and is destined to vanish like a circus tent, Mies injects life into a language of empty spaces and significations, in which all "familiarity" is shown up as a lie. The lottery of the avant-garde theater dies out as the spectator wanders about, with no way out of Mies's pavilion, in the "forest" of pure "data." The liberatory laugh freezes in the perception of a new "duty." Utopia no longer inhabits the city nor its spectacular metaphor, except as a game of productive structure dressed up as imaginary.

The question can reappear constantly: why that bitter distance between Taut's pavilion and Mies's? It is not only the distance separating the two persons—although Mies's concept of space can be easily explained based on the characteristics of his Catholic thinking, so distant from the cosmic communism of Taut. Between 1914 and 1929, in just one generation, Taut's "Magdeburg-in-Color," the Arbeitsrat für Kunst, the participation in the social democratic municipal governments would have taken place, but also the Great War, the crushing of the revolution, the body of Rosa Luxemburg floating in a canal, with her skull crushed by blows also from the butt of a social democratic gun, the crisis of 1924 . . .

1929. it is not worth stressing this emblematic year. Not by chance, two years later the proposal of the avant-garde would be already, only, International Style.

That passage is what the mysterious glass wishes to explain when it returns the visitor's gaze, without allowing him to enter it, without encouraging him to fantasize, waiting in vain for the arrival of God to this empty and pure stage.

"It was only made to be beautiful" is what is usually said about the Pavilion that Mies van der Rohe built in Barcelona. And this is very true if, as the angels told Rilke, that which is beautiful is nothing more than that degree of the terrible that we are still able to tolerate.

Massimo Cacciari   **"Eupalinos or Architecture"** *Oppositions* 21 (Summer 1980), trans. Stephen
Sartarelli

The farmhouse in the Black Forest is not really visible from the glass skyscrapers of
the metropolis; the poetic dwelling of Heidegger's stout, speechless peasants is but
the absent form of life that makes the chattering inauthenticity of *das Man*, the metropolitan Anyone, perceivable as such. If the building-dwelling-building cycle is shattered, if modern man dwells unpoetically, then the architectural *Fragwürdiges*, the
question worth asking, is, What is the authentic form to house this inauthenticity?
Loos gives a partial answer in his Café Nihilismus, in its effort to *become* the city itself
in all its technical and social contradictions. Or Mies, whose "language of absence,"
Massimo Cacciari concludes, "here testifies to the absence of dwelling. . . . The 'great
glass windows' are the nullity, the silence of dwelling. They negate dwelling as they
reflect the metropolis."

   "Eupalinos or Architecture," in the guise of a review of Manfredo
Tafuri and Franceso Dal Co's *Modern Architecture*, is a concise meditation on the problem that has preoccupied Cacciari in all of his architecture-theoretical writings: the
relation of architecture, the metropolis, and nihilism.[1] From the profanation of concrete experience described by Georg Simmel and his ascription of the *legitimacy* of
the nervous logic of the blasé personality, to the functionality of poverty, shock, and
the destructive character perceived by Walter Benjamin, the basic principles for thinking the project nihilism are sketched out. The metropolis is the extreme utopia of
rationalization *and* the site of that rationalization's failure; the metropolis generates
highly differentiated elements only to level all difference in a numbing oneness. Such
aporias produce an architecture at once of the city, made in its own image, and at the
same time striving to overcome that city's limits.

see 2–4

The drama is the emergence, over the course of the past century, of an architecture of *nihilism
fulfilled* as this architecture comes to pervade the image of the Metropolis: it is the very figure
of pro-ducing, of leading-beyond, of continuous and undefinable *overcoming*. The obsession
with overcoming is embodied in the work of "radical uprooting" carried out by this architecture:
an uprooting from the limits of *urbs*, from the social circles dominant in it, from its *form*—an
uprooting from the place (as a place of dwelling) connected to dwelling. The city "departs" along
the streets and axes that intersect with its structure. The exact opposite of Heidegger's *Holzwege*, they lead to no place. . . . The architecture "without qualities" of the Metropolis—a conscious image of fulfilled nihilism—excludes the characteristic of the place.[2]

The architecture of fulfilled nihilism presents its own order as if it were but the direct
transcription of the logic of the metropolis, and, at the same time, it appears uprooted
from its place, from any place, for to be uprooted is just the nature of metropolitan
life.

   Nevertheless, "the uprooted spirit of the metropolis is not 'ster-
ile,' but *productive* par excellence"; its passionate refusal of the illusions of dwelling
is an active self-affirmation in the sense of will-to-power. Cacciari follows Nietzsche,
for whom the most extreme nihilism "places the value of things precisely in the lack
of any reality corresponding to these values and in their being merely a symptom

of strength on the part of the value-positers." "Radical nihilism," Nietzsche further instructed, "is the conviction of the absolute untenability of existence [*Dasein*] when it comes to the highest values one recognizes."[3]

One should not, however, associate Cacciari with the irrationality of some post-Nietzschean positions; for him, the failure of reason is integral to the total rationalization of the metropolis. There can be no radical overcoming of this rationalization—neither solution nor the end of all solutions; that would be utopia. According to Cacciari, we must, rather, "listen" to the differences between no-place and our place, between dwelling and non-dwelling.

| compare 413–414 |

| compare 615 |

Notes

1. Massimo Cacciari, *Architecture and Nihilism: On the Philosophy of Modern Architecture*, trans. Stephen Sartarelli (New Haven: Yale University Press, 1993), is the English-language collection of Cacciari's writings on architecture. Cacciari participated in the seminars of the Istituto Universitario di Architettura di Venezia, Dipartimento di Storia dell'Architettura, directed by Manfredo Tafuri from 1968 to 1996. The writings of Tafuri and Cacciari are closely related.
2. Cacciari, *Architecture and Nihilism*, pp. 199–200.
3. Friedrich Nietzsche, *The Will to Power*, ed. Walter Kaufmann, trans. Walter Kaufmann and R. J. Hollingdale (New York: Random House, 1967), §13, 3.

Manfredo Tafuri and Francesco Dal Co's book *Architettura contemporanea (Modern Architecture)* ends with the name of Heidegger. "Difference" and "renunciation" constitute the *tragic* point of view from which the developments of this architecture are described.[1] The book therefore has nothing to do with "history"—but rather with the problem of modern architecture, with its *Fragwürdiges*: its fundamental relation to the world and to things, its language as the existence of such a relation. To invoke Heidegger thus is *necessary*, since he had long since given thought to precisely that which seems "worthy of question" in architecture's present situation. But that is not all; he formulated it in such a way as to render impossible or inconceivable the Values and Purposes on which this architecture nourishes itself. The "desperate" analysis of this inconceivability constitutes the fulcrum of Tafuri and Dal Co's work. But its relations to Heideggerian criticism are complex, numerous, and themselves irreducible to reconcilable unities. By deconstructing these relations, subjecting them to analysis, we shall perhaps enable ourselves to see the fundamental aspects of this development that we call "contemporary architecture" in a disciplinarily less tenuous light. At stake are not the old criteria—the political, the sociological, the aesthetic, which from time to time are used in order to seize upon this "name"— but this "name" itself. Why "architecture" today? *Wofür Dichter?*

It *is the tectonic* aspect of architecture that interests Heidegger. Architecture produces—in the Greek sense of "technique" (*tekne*), which signifies "neither art nor handicraft, but rather: to make something appear, within what is present."[2] Architecture builds in so far as it produces, in so far as it conducts something to presence. This something is dwelling. Dwelling is not the result of building, but is that which building produces into presence. It becomes produced, made to appear, not determined by building. "Only if we are capable of dwelling, only then can we build."[3]

Lodging (*l'allogiare*), not dwelling, may be conceived as the result of building. Building as the pro-duction of dwelling, however, posits an original identification between the two terms "building" and "dwelling." By means of a typical etymological-allegorical chain Heidegger explains: to build (*bauen*) originally also meant to reside, to remain in a place—but remaining is the form in which "I am" (*bin*). The mode in which "I am" is the "cycle": dwelling-building-dwelling. Not to dwell in a lodging, nor to build a lodging; but to remain, as *colere* or to cultivate, as *cultura* or cultivation: to be in the *Geviert*, in the fourfold—on the *earth* and beneath the *heavens*, before the *gods* and in the community of *men*. To build is to produce dwelling, but dwelling is being in the *Geviert*: architecture is tectonic activity in so far as it makes the *Geviert* happen, makes it appear, and *preserves* it.[4]

We might also ask: what is a built thing? A *bridge*. The bridge makes the banks appear, reunites the earth around itself, "gathers" its elements; it reconciles "in its own way, earth and sky, divinities and mortals."[5] The bridge is a location: "building puts up locations that make space and a site for the fourfold,"[6] that guard it, that take care of it. Before the bridge only spaces exist—*a* space, by virtue of the bridge, becomes a site. To build means to make place, to give rise to. To build is to make a place for the *Geviert* and to stay there.

But what is problematic in all of this? Why should this dis- course call building-dwelling into question? There is a vulgar, idiotically rationalis- tic way of reading this part of Heidegger, reducing him to a "philosophy of architecture" à la Spengler. Spengler spoke of the absence of "house" in the world- city, the absence of houses where "Vesta and Janus, Penates and Lares" might be able to reside. The house appears uprooted and man lives there only as tenant or guest. The spirit is a stranger in this space, whose landscape is systematically de- stroyed by mere *aedificare*, by mere *ars aedificandi*. This spirit, no longer a "plant," no longer organically connected to "heaven and earth," becomes sterile and leads an errant existence amid the "artificial natures" of the metropolis.[7] All of this is at the origin of "radical" architecture and the billions of pseudo-sociological pages on "alienation." But it is the exact opposite of the intention implicit in Heidegger's argument. The uprooted spirit of the metropolis is not "sterile," but *productive* par excellence. It is the definitive rupture of the Subject's natural being that permits it the will-to-power over nature. Heidegger knows this. And Simmel had already said this. But there is an even more substantial difference. The problem is not with the form of building in itself. What is absent is not the "fitness" of building to spirit, in which case spirit would be foreign to its home. The problem lies in the fact that spirit may no longer dwell—it has become estranged from dwelling. And this is why building cannot "make" the Home (*Dimora*) "appear."

How does Heidegger proceed? Simply by radically assuming *the claims and the intentions* of architecture, carrying them to their logically extreme con- sequences: "You say build. But perhaps building is simply a means to dwelling? You build lodgings—and yet you assert that man 'resides' in these lodgings. Your end is to make man 'reside'. But how can you claim this end if you are unaware of the fact that to pro-duce dwelling is conceivable only if dwelling is first connected to building? You must then demonstrate to me the *existence* of this connection. And does 'to reside' only mean 'to shelter oneself' or not also 'to cultivate' and to 'build bridges' between the elements of the *Geviert*?" Such indeed is architecture's response: it preaches the relation between lodging and labor, between shelter and nature. It appears to tend toward this end. And yet this end is never called into question; it is assumed to be "natural" when instead it is part and parcel of the *Fragwürdiges* of architecture's present situation—not as a means with which to resolve the *Fragwür- diges*, but as an end in itself and for itself. No nostalgia, then, in Heidegger—but rather the contrary. He *radicalizes* the discourse supporting any possible "nostalgic" attitude, lays bare its logic, pitilessly emphasizes its insurmountable distance from the actual condition.

It is not a matter of changing the forms by means of which architecture thinks of building homes. One must ask oneself what kind of thing the Home (*Dimora*) is. The Home *is* only if residing (*dimorare*) exists as a precondition for building, only if residing is connected at its origins to building. The Home *is*, only if building pro-duces the place of the *Geviert*. "Aesthetic" or "economic" accommodations to this exigency are not possible. But this does not mean that such accommodations do not exist; what is illusory and mystifying is the belief that interior design or the construction of housing resolves the problem of dwelling. To avert the housing crisis is necessary and fundamental. But this program should be kept *radically distinct* from any other claim, especially that of the problem of the home. The problem of dwelling lies not in the quality of the edifice, of services, or of design. We should either speak of it in its own language or not speak of it at all: dwelling is being in the *Geviert*, experiencing dwelling as a fundamental condition of one's own being, feeling oneself to be a "dweller." But is it possible to build for "dwellers"? Only "dwellers" can do so. And it is precisely the "dweller" that is absent today.

Heidegger limits himself to reconfirming man's uprootedness in the face of false and useless attempts to recompose him organically, to make him again organism, plant, root. That architecture which pretends to this "recompositioning" should be asked, "You want to produce homes [*dimore*]? Then do you know how to dwell?" Heidegger says that it is necessary to "learn to dwell." He keeps listening for the call to dwell. But no god calls. It is rather the present crisis itself that calls. But how can the crisis call to dwell? Heidegger cannot say. In fact, his essay confirms the *non-existent logic* of the dwelling-building-dwelling cycle—and thereby dismantles *a priori* any claim that assumes such logic to be purposeful or denotative. This logic, in a Wittgensteinian way, says nothing—it only forms premises.

Heidegger so detaches from us the idea of building-dwelling that he renders absolutely problematic not only its effectuality, but even the nostalgia for it. There is no doubt that Heidegger keeps listening for the call to dwell. But this listening is just silence. What speaks is not dwelling but the *crisis* of dwelling. And its language is *critical*: to be exact, division, detachment, difference. In illustrating the conditions of dwelling, Heidegger describes the difference that divides us from dwelling—in demonstrating the built thing in terms of a bridge, he shows us the actual inconceivability of a bridge. Indeed, he shows us the actual wretchedness of accommodations that would call themselves bridges. He tells us of the total impotence of shelters disguised as homes, of cities disguised as places.

In Heidegger, this critique appears in the form of listening, of waiting. But this wait is recognized to be *a priori* indefinable. The reasons for our separation from dwelling-building are contained in the overall history of Western thought—in the very translation of Greek *tekne* into European technique. The representation, the presentation of the present, has been up to this day the fundamental characteristic of thought. Western thought treats being as presence.

But *where* does our thought relegate that which we call presence?[8] Being-present presupposes an "unconcealedness." In Being conceived as presence a fundamental unconcealedness is in force which, however, Western thought is unable to grasp. Western thought assumes the equivalence of being and presence to be natural, and its efforts are concentrated on the technical analysis of this presence, on its understanding, and on its use. On this note ends Heidegger's essay "What Is Thinking?" But what is building if not the bringing to presence of the fundamental unconcealedness of dwelling? Dwelling and the thinking about the essential origins of being are connected: thinking for dwelling. But this essential origin remains hidden and mysterious for Heidegger—his thought does not reach that far. In addition, history and the destiny of Western thought are moving in the direction of technique—not in that of pro-duction, but in that of scientific productivity. Can a sense of dwelling reemerge in this destiny, a sense of building as the pro-duction of the unconcealedness of dwelling? In his waiting, Heidegger unmasks all false appeals—

but he remains waiting, listening. Nor could the implications of his inquiry be con-
ducive to anything else. The irreversible "translations" that have marked the history
of thought have left their mark on the history of dwelling as well.

To repeat: the form and quality of the edifice are not at all at
issue here. In reality, it is only about them that we are able to speak; but form and
quality have nothing to do with the *Fragwürdiges* of architecture: to build is to dwell,
to dwell is to build. But since today this idea is given neither to be realized nor even
effectively heard, there remains but the continuous wait in the silence of listening,
or the option of building lodgings or constructions. Heidegger does not call for the
construction of homes—he doesn't criticize, like Spengler, the absence of homes.
Instead, he debunks the pretense of calling homes those buildings that are just lodgings or constructions; and debunks the incredible linguistic confusion between lodging and nostalgia for home that constitutes the specific form of architectural
ideology.[9] How could Heidegger call for the construction of homes by those who
are no longer dwellers? For he knows that this is an essential condition, the fate of
contemporary man.

But Heidegger, of course, remains waiting, listening, hoping for
the call. The essence of dwelling lies in "remaining," in "staying on"—not in any
place, but in a place that provides peace. Dwelling is being-in-peace; it is not a passive
protection, but rather a causing of the fourfold to appear where mortals dwell. Here,
not in refuges, not in hidden places, but here, in the unconcealedness itself, lies
being-at-home.

"*Shepherds,*" says Heidegger, "dwell in this unconcealedness out-
side of the desert of the desolated earth."[10] They guard "the hidden law of the earth"
against the violence of the technical will that drags it toward exhaustion by forcing
it beyond its possibilities. But these shepherds are *invisible*, and the law that they guard,
in which the earth stays within the safety of its limits of possibility, is also *invisible*.
Nostalgia vanishes in the very same moment in which it is first glimpsed. No subject
remains in the home, in an essential relation with the earth. The subject is manifest
solely in its relation with the will to power over the earth. In defining dwelling,
Heidegger describes the possible conditions of a mode of living that today is impossible. To be-at-home is to be *invisible* guardians of *invisible* laws.[11]

Nietzsche's thought in the face of the "great city"[12] is of course
harsher, more sobering (*nüchternes*), since he is no longer even listening. His thought
begins where the very silence of the wait breaks off and the analysis of homelessness
(*Heimatlosigkeit*) begins.

What is meant by not-being-at-home, not being a "dweller"?
We Subjects who make nature *mathémata*, who violate the earth beyond its possibility,
we are the non-dwellers. For us Subjects, what counts is the essential uprootedness
of technique, of the will to power. Contrary to what is commonly believed and said,
the Subject does not live in the home, nor does he yearn for it, but can exist only in
the absence of home and in uprootedness: only here is he *able* and potent, is he *productive*. The language—the functions and conventions—through which the subject expresses his will to power is the sole theme of Nietzschean thought. Spengler, not
Heidegger, is Zarathustra's monkey, who would like to drive the sage back to the
mountain in the face of the "great city." And yet, Heidegger remains waiting for the
Event, the *Ereignis*, that will transform man and bring him back to the path of building-dwelling. But that is not all; even though he cannot see any homes being constructed (and he denies himself any illusions of hope on this matter), at times he
indicates traces of them. The home has left traces in the word of poetry. Into poetry,
into the poetry of this epoch of misery, the home has withdrawn. Poetry *is not*,
is invisible—and yet poetry is Word—the word of the retreat of the home, of the

fourfold.[13] Poetry preserves (in the non-being of its word) that tectonic element of architecture to which the edifice, in so far as it participates in the devastation of the earth, can only allude tragicomically.

This characteristic reversal of Heideggerian disenchantment—or better, this oscillating dialectic between *Andenken* as tragic theory and *Andenken* as nostalgic pro-position, which I have analyzed elsewhere[14]—seeks a foundation for the building-dwelling-building cycle in a late poem by Hölderlin, *In leiblicher Bläue*. The essence of the poem consists for Heidegger in the affirmation "dichterisch woh-net der Mensch"—poetically man dwells. Dwelling is thus grounded in poetry. The building that dwelling allows is poetic: to build is to make poetry, its doing is *poiesis*. The essence of writing poetry is a measure-taking, "in the strict sense of the word, by which man first receives the measure for the breadth [*Weite*] of his being."[15]

This measure is God, not as he is known in himself, but as he is manifest in the heavens. The divinity is absent as such, but precisely as *hidden* he is manifest in the heavens. The heavens manifest the divinity as unknown: and this relation *measures* the being of man—it is the measure of *poiesis*. In this measure man dwells—in it, he is a "dweller." "Poetry builds up the very nature of dwelling."[16] Only if man builds, in the sense of the poetic taking of measure, does he dwell. If he dwells, man dwells poetically.

Do we dwell poetically today? Heidegger is quick to point out that Hölderlin does not speak of the real conditions of modern dwelling. He adds that the poetic taking of measure is foreign to us today, and that only our intuition of poetry enables us to experience the fact that today we dwell in a totally unpoetic world: *undichterisch wohnet der Mensch*. But the reversal of this condition is explicitly hoped for. The attention turned upon the poetic permits *hope*. Hölderlin's lines are com-mented upon with this in mind but in my opinion, however, this intention seems to be totally lacking. At the beginning of the poem the unconcealedness of a place is described: the church's tower "blossoms into sweet azure"; "like doors to beauty" are the windows from which the bells ring. So "simple and sacred" (*einfältig und heilig*) are the images (*Bilder*) "that often I truly fear to describe them." This is the place of dwelling—it is the fourfold. But man may measure himself against it only "as long as Kindness, the Pure, still stays with his heart" (*so lange die Freundlichkeit noch am Herzen, die Reine, dauert*). *Freundlichkeit*, as Heidegger makes clear, is the translation of *kàris*, a con-dition of mutual belonging between man and landscape, man and home. But the measure of which Heidegger speaks is only possible here, in the poem. On the earth that has destroyed the bridge along with the other elements of the *Geviert*, on this earth no longer "beneath the heavens," no measure is conceivable. "Is there a measure on earth? There is none." (*Giebt es auf Erden ein Mass? Es giebt keines.*) Man's living-as-dwelling, the *wohnend Leben*, fades into the distance, *in die Ferne geht*. It does not call him back, but detaches him—it is not reclaimable, it is conceivable only as form, form that measures difference.

Undichterisch wohnet der Mensch. . . . The manifold forms of this un-*dichterisch wohnen* comprise the subject of Tafuri and Dal Co's "history." *Dichterisch wohnen* is never directly named, but it is the "absent form" that makes possible the critique of the ideology of the home and the ridiculous claims that architecture puts forth (which *are* architecture itself) regarding the reconciliation of man and landscape, man and city.

It is strange that alongside the name of Heidegger and in this context Tafuri and Dal Co should make no mention of that of Paul Valéry.[17] And yet in his essays on architecture Heidegger takes up again the fundamental themes of Eupalinos, whose motto is, in fact: *pròs kàrin*. Phaedrus tells Socrates the story of Eupa-linos of Megara and his architectural work. By means of nothing other than "orders and numbers," that is, by *measuring*, he built homes. There were no "details" in his execution[18]—all was essential, of equal value. To build, for Eupalinos, was to know oneself—since building is dwelling and dwelling is being, being-in-peace, being-at-home. To build is to know oneself as a dweller. And homes are cherished by the dweller as beloved objects.

Eupalinos expresses the original, tectonic meaning of architecture. Building is *poiesis*. There exist *mute* edifices—constructions and lodgings; and there exist edifices that speak; but there are others still—and they are the most rare—which *sing*. The edifices which speak must limit *themselves* to speaking clearly: "here the judges deliberate. Here captives moan." In the residences of justice, everything must pronounce sentences and speak of penalties. "The stone gravely declares that which it shuts in; the wall is implacable, and this work of stone, conforming so closely to the truth, strongly proclaims its stern purpose."[19] Markets, tribunals, prisons, theaters speak of *stern purposes*—and they are able to speak of nothing else, not without "disguising" themselves.

The architect must control these purposes, but he must recognize at the same time that they do not express the essence of the dwelling, nor do they fulfill by any means the essence of building poetically. A radical distinction intervenes between them and the masterpiece that seems to "sing for itself." The edifices that sing are Homes. Only there is man a dweller. They are the monuments that measure man's being: "being inside the work of man as fishes are in the sea, being entirely immersed in it, living in it, and belonging to it."[20] These monuments must have solidity and lastingness,[21] since they express the mutual, original belonging between building and dwelling. This is the same limit that Loos imposed on the architecture of the edifice, the technique of the lodging—the same Loosian affirmation of the shadowy possibility of consonance between music and monumental architecture; the same Loosian form in the sense of Hölderlin's "void," of architecture as *poiesis*.[22] It is according to these "Loosian dialectics" that Valéry's dialogue also proceeds.

But which are, indeed, the monuments that sing? Where is the city as harmony? In Valéry's dialogue it seems that the tectonic element of architecture is propounded for the sake of its effect, in contrast with the dialectical element: "It served no purpose, I fear, to seek this God, whom I have tried all my life to discover, by pursuing him through the realm of thought alone. . . . The God that one so finds is but a word born of words, and returns to the word."[23] Thought has been severed from building—or has rendered building merely technique. However, it is building—in the strictest Heideggerian sense—that appears to Socrates to be "of all acts the most complete"; by comparison with "this great act of constructing" he considers incomplete the work of the Demiurge who "organized inequality," who "in his rage to disunite everything" formed and separated the elements. "The converse of this must come to pass":[24] namely the fourfold, the home "on the earth and beneath the heavens," the conciliatory Muse.

Is this an appeal to pass beyond the listening wait? Is it a real possibility? Loos believed that only in sepulchral monuments could architecture become *poiesis*. Socrates erects his own architecture in the word after his time is irreversibly spent. He is an architect *in death*. Not only does he conceive the form of building in the word alone—but his is the word of a *dead man*. It is silence. Socrates and Phaedrus come together on the banks of the Ilissus, in the transparent realm of shadows, in a *here* that does not exist—and all that they have said "is as much a natural sport of the silence of these nether regions as the silly fancy of some rhetorician of the other world who has used us as puppets."[25]

Undichterisch wohnet der Mensch. . . . The home is past, it no longer is.[26] The unity of dwelling and building, which forms the home, has become nothing. The nullification of the home is a fundamental aspect of the conviction peculiar to Western metaphysics, that pure Being (*l'ente*) is nothing (*niente*). The separation of lodging from home, in which the lodging *is* only in time, is not a literary allegory for the fundamental separation of being-in-time (*esse*) from pure Being (*ente*)—the separation through which the Subject of metaphysics takes possession of pure Being—but *is* this separation itself. The home is posited as nothing, or is made to remain solely as ruin or memory, for the purpose of demonstrating even more clearly its nullity, its achieved nullification. On this basis, the Subject is "free," it can *move* freely, can carry on its work and its destiny of separating all atemporal Being from being-in-time, of reducing all Being to time—to the time of the Subject's own movement. The Subject lodges in time—it does not dwell in homes. The difference between dwelling, building, and making poetry is not reversible or reconcilable; and the significance of this difference is essential for the understanding of the fundamental nihilism of Western metaphysics-technics. For this reason, architecture takes on great importance in this "history." It represents one of the decisive forces which separates pure Being from its connection to being-in-time and which obscures the vision of Parmenides, for whom all Being is eternal and united, at its origins, with being-in-time. Architecture *may* be valid as one of these forces—as silence may also be valid, the silent custody of the home's empty form. What condemns architecture to the most despicable misery is the adornment of our deserts with traditional forms and archaic ruins, the disguising of artifice with nature and of Being with eternity, the branding of technical functions as "poetic," and the "ennobling" of the harsh conventions of the *diverse politics* that comprise technique.

      Undichterisch wohnet der Mensch. . . . In no way should this be taken in a moral or "literary" sense; what we are concerned with here is the practical result of the analysis of form, or the *a priori* conditions of possibility, of *dichterisch wohnen*. This result should be kept "pure" of any form of nostalgia or utopian transcendence. Of interest here are only the conditions and the phenomenology of *undichterisch wohnen*. Such is the theme—and method of approach—of Tafuri and Dal Co's "history."

      This "history" describes a result: the result is *undichterisch wohnen*. But how does this non-dwelling manifest itself concretely? Non-dwelling is the essential characteristic of life in the metropolis.[27] When speaking of poetic dwelling neither Heidegger nor Valéry mentions the metropolis; and yet it is here that dwelling is really debased. The "history" of contemporary architecture is therefore a phenomenology of metropolitan non-dwelling. Or it should be such, since contemporary architecture aims at restructuring itself as the possibility of dwelling *within* the metropolis.[28] The preaching of such a possibility is at the base of "urban planning" as a discipline within contemporary architecture. And therefore the acknowledgment of this variegated terrain implies the need for a structural analysis of metropolitan functions. Through its very origin and nature, "urban planning" creates a change in perspective: the impotence of "classic" dwelling; but it also addresses the multiple languages of metropolitan functions (and the consequent destruction of the very possibility of dwelling) as languages intrinsically capable of being "sublimated" into a logical system, into the very logic that "urban planning" would represent or incarnate. Although "classic" dwelling is acknowledged to be henceforth impossible, the idea of city as *organism* remains *possible*: a Plant growing from the root of the architectural-urban planning Logos. The idea of such a Plant represents the imperative, the *Sollen*, of metropolitan organization.

      We could say, "'urban planning' originates in the effort to represent contemporary *undichterisch wohnen* as an *organism*." But of what does this "unpoetical dwelling" consist if not of the multiplicity and the "homelessness," the becoming *heimatlos*, of the various disciplines making up the metropolis? Thus, while "urban planning" advances the claim to an "organic organization" of "unpoetical dwelling," it affirms the *possibility* of reducing to a unity the multiplicity of these languages and functions—it claims to be able to represent a sort of logic of them. But "urban planning" can neither provide the foundations for this claim, since it is itself a language among all the others, nor can it show its Logic to be effectual. For this reason it is forced to transform Logic into *Sollen*, into ethical imperative, into paradoxical ethics—or to assert it as *pure form*, within the other-than-form, within a play of reason centered about the com-posing, de-composing, and re-composing of the signs of the metropolis. Logic, ethics, and play thus follow one another in the formulations of contemporary "urban planning" as more or less disenchanted variants of a fundamental "misery": the idea of the "harmonization" of metropolitan functions, of the creation of a "homeland" common to all of them—and of the assessment of their real conflict as a mere appearance that hides and mystifies a "profound," "substantial" *Gemeinschaft*. This "homeland" claims to announce "urban planning"—and it is this "annunciation" which provides the foundation for its diverse "compositional" proposals. But what indeed would this composition "re-compose"?—of what is this composition composed if not of the "substantial" community of dwelling?

This language of "urban planning" is as logically unfounded as it is historically blind. Contemporary "urban planning," on the basis of its "logic," *does not see*—or, better yet, sees the "vampire of speculation" wherever the industrial capitalist metropolis thrives; it sees social and political disintegration wherever the functional multiplicity of metropolitan "disciplines" finally "liberates" all of its conflicting valences: it sees individual solitude and nostalgia for *dichterisch wohnen* wherever the composition of classes is transformed and the *diverse* political organizations of the *Gesellschaft* spring up. Between this "vision" and the metropolis itself is generated an irresolvable tension—an incurable contradiction within the particular historical context. The discourse does not change when "urban planning" "gives in" to the metropolis, since this too is not *seeing*, is not *making-visible*: the metropolis is assumed to be the natural and obvious scene of compositional planning participation; its arbitrary forms are assumed to be laws and its conventions to be immutable rules of the game. And this position ends up by becoming profoundly intertwined in the false disenchantment of the urban planning game.

Of course, "ethical-compositional" *values* are predominant in the origins of contemporary "urban planning." "The depersonalization, alienation, and disintegration in the large metropolis seem to be able to be overcome by the articulated and organized re-emergence of nuclei in which 'quality' and 'community' are once again protagonists"—Parker, Unwin, and Howard work within this perspective.[29] But soon enough the "model" tends to move away from the "ethical-compositional," to use the above terms: "urban planning" tends to assert itself as a possible *logic* of metropolitan organization. This "turning-point" manifests itself in many different forms, without however altering the idea of "urban planning" as a *rebalancing*: there is the rationalization of urban growth, the territorial equilibrating of productive factors, the "harmonization" of city and country—the idea of urban planning as "a process of *apolitical* integration of the historical contradictions, which are redressed by an optimistic technological evolutionism."[30] In this way the work of Olmsted "seriously turns on the problem of political and institutional reforms . . . the control over the exploitation of resources at the territorial level . . . the deterioration of the old methods of urban management, as evidenced in the failure of Pullman Town," and it is *at once* a struggle against the deterioration of the community and a utopian alliance of science, technique, and *nature*—nature, which becomes once again "a formidable source of urban income."[31] In this way the ideology and language of the Beaux-Arts are "harmonized" in "City Beautiful" with the reaffirmation of the "absolute priority of free-market mechanisms."[32]

Even the proclaimed "realism" of German urban planning, which "aims at reconstituting a condition of *naturalness* for the mechanisms of income" through "the elimination of any artificial 'distortion' of the land market brought about by the monopoly over buildable ground," is accompanied by "implicit nostalgia for the pre-metropolitan 'city.'"[33] The pure free-market vision remains an ideology of balancing. Moreover, within the metropolis that has been rendered a "balanced organism," the role of architectural form is justified as an "event and creation," without which the individual can never feel "in his element."

The plays of reason and the poems of forms[34] of the Masters—who remain awaiting the new Colberts ready to realize their utopias, which will be political in the "classic" sense of the term or philanthropic-collectivist, but in any case anti-metropolitan—are thus profoundly rooted in the ideology of contemporary "urban planning."[35] Nor is the "disenchantment" of Hilberseimer's *Grosstadt-architektur* an effective critique of the ethical formalism of the Masters: his image of the city-machine with its integrated function, of the city as "naked structure," is typical of the naive "machinism," the mechanistic obsession pervading all of the criticism within the metropolis of traditional conciliatory "urban planning." Hilberseimer sees no "alternatives" to this *precise image* of the metropolis. The refutation of utopia thus finishes by reconfirming the reasons for the utopian tension. And the idea of the "alternative city," the "communal island," enjoys its most extreme and perhaps highest manifestation in the Viennese *Höfe*—the residence of those individuals proudly opposed to metropolitan reality, Schillerian heroes, as it seems to me still more than, as Tafuri and Dal Co explain it in several very beautiful pages, protagonists of the great bourgeois novel, of "the haut-bourgeois myths [that] shape the most highly achieved 'magic mountain' of Austrian Marxism."[36]

"Urban planning" as logic and play—in an uncritical framework, amid unclarified languages intrinsically equivocal with regard to their own limits—dominates the scene following the decline of the synthesis between form and ethics, the decline of form as an expression of the *ethical* criticism of the capitalistic metropolis. The utopias of post-World War II "urban planning" are logic and play only. But even these occur as intrinsically contradictory terms. Such utopias present themselves, in fact, as *totalistic* conceptions: no longer *Höfe* or *Siedlungen*, no longer specific functions of the metropolis (however much they are emphasized) make up their content, but rather the *totality* of functions. The consciousness of the utopian nature of this "design" does not change its *groundlessness*: play exists only *in the singular*. To attempt to play a totality of games—or to represent all of them in one game—is intrinsically nonsensical. For this reason "the totalistic conception is again reduced to a decorative enrichment of the metropolitan chaos that it intended to dominate."[37]

This totalistic image is in reality the metropolitan "aura." Far from being the ironic play that it often claims to represent, this image, which has overcome the ethical denunciation of the metropolis (or, in so far as it has overcome it), often emphatically "publicizes" the metropolis's functions, transposing them into the dimension of sacred aura. Metropolitan "aura" surrounds the skyscraper-monuments of New York, Chicago, Boston, "confident that the fascination for the exceptional which had dazzled the tycoons of 1890 Chicago still obtains."[38] But in the "aura" of a naively all-inclusive technological utopia—a simplistic apology for a metropolis assumed to be an unstoppable "creative nature"—also sprang up the monuments of the Brutalism and Neo-Expressionism of the fifties and sixties.[39] It is necessary to reflect upon the presence of the monument: whether in the "technological" versions of it just mentioned, or in its forays into "memory" (a constant sign of the nostalgia for dwelling, a constant struggle to exorcise the "loss of center," as in Kahn), its refusal of the "negligible object" of a contemporary architecture "without quality"[40] is a struggle to prevent the already achieved desacralization of time from ultimately extending to a desacralization of space. The significance of this latest vicissitude of "urban planning" can only be explained in the terms of Foucault.[41]

We are in an era, says Foucault, in which the world is perceived as a network that simultaneously joins juxtaposed and distant points. This space alienates the "pious descendants of history," for whom the world was like a large street which developed different "meanings" through the different ages. Neither does this space resemble the hierarchical space of the medieval city, where the juxtaposition of places referred to the "value" of their respective functions. The present-day space of the metropolis is made up of the non-hierarchical flow of information connecting disciplines and functions, of discrete, aleatory currents, whose movements are not teleologically comprehensible but only stochastically analyzable.

But this desacralization of space—which is in the essence of metropolitan life—is far from complete. It is unfinished not because the "singing" edifices of Eupalinos are still flourishing, nor because dwelling might still be possible; but because in this space, whose function is by now perfectly desacralized, real edifices still find place, but as though entirely out of place—they are at once actual and absolute (ab-soluti): they are heterotopias. Foucault speaks of these heterotopias as "constants" of the practical organization of space. But they become important only when they contradict the purely sequential nature of metropolitan organization, when they attempt to stand in opposition to it as new "places of worship," as "symbols resisting history."[42] Wright spoke of his Guggenheim Museum as a new Pantheon.[43] Heterotopias are places where "abnormal" individuals "set themselves apart"— places of "exceptional conduct" against which the metropolitan space breaks like the waves of a rising tide. But the heterotopia also often inserts itself within "normal" functions, within the metropolis's "normal" systems of information: for example, this happens within the "empty and transparent" inside world of the Ford Foundation, which is "treated like a giant hothouse."[44]

The heterotopia becomes interesting when it develops a function of compensation and consolation in the face of the space that surrounds it. It wants to appear as a denunciation of the desacralization of the surrounding space, as the "salvation" of the hierarchical and cultural values of the city's time. The "Good Form" to which the heterotopia tends would decry the disorder, the bad management, the loss of center of the metropolis. The monument, the perfectly organized "colony," the garden, are not utopian designs, but real places, although other with respect to the information of the metropolis. It is not an issue of the logical organization of the metropolis, nor of the play of reason in the combination of its signs, nor of a utopian overcoming of the alienation which prevails there—but rather of space for the construction of monuments, that is, for the defining of places of worship as monuments for nonexistent "peoples," functions and languages of the metropolis itself. The intrinsic falsity of the heterotopia ultimately does not allow it to consider itself a new home—even if certain memories, certain "recaptured pasts" of contemporary architecture touch upon such nostalgia. But the heterotopia is still always Home: not for the individual, not for the dweller, but for the Values of the community of individuals. They themselves remain forever errant, but in this way they regain possession of places to return to, of promised lands, of churches which console one against the Diaspora of languages and disciplines.

But in the "ideological continuity" of contemporary "urban planning"—or in the architecture which attempts to remedy the problem of dwelling in the metropolis—one like Mies van der Rohe finds no space. The final words of Tafuri and Dal Co's book revolve about Mies—and it is with Mies that we "resolve" the problematic initially set forth in terms of Heidegger. Let us begin with the 1923 text *Building*: "We want building to signify truly and only building." Therefore, *not* dwelling. And indeed, in his 1923 project for the brick house, "the fragmentation of the spatial components is total: the continuity of volumes with respect to the plan is only a seeming one, since the arrangement of the parts does not create a path of circulation, does not refer to any order; yes, they are markings, but they suggest that the labyrinth has no exits."[45] And in the German Pavilion in Barcelona of 1929: "the building is an assemblage of parts, each of which speaks a different language, specific to the materials used."[46] Only building: assembling different languages, attending to details without looking for the "great syntheses" of classical Form, without pretending that this trade of building can satisfy the nostalgia for the Home. This nostalgia even has its own language, but it is untranslatable into that of architectural techniques. The sign must remain a sign, must speak only of its renunciation of having value—and only by means of this renunciation will it be able to recognize its true functions and its own destiny: only a language illuminated by its own limits will be able to operate.[47]

Mies's use of glass manifests his anti-dialectic. Glass is the concrete negation of dwelling. Not only because architectural form drowns in it, but because glass, when so used, renders visible those who seek shelter within it. From the 1920–1921 project for a glass skyscraper in Berlin, an extraordinary negation of Expressionist transcendence à la Scheerbart, up to the Seagram Building in New York, one can trace this constant in all of Mies's work: a supreme indifference to dwelling, expressed in neutral signs: "to the maximum formal structuring corresponds a maximum absence of images."[48] The language of absence here testifies to the absence of dwelling—to the consummate separation between building and dwelling which no heterotopia is capable of remedying. The "great glass windows" are the nullity, the silence of dwelling.[49] They negate dwelling as they reflect the metropolis. And reflection only is permitted to these forms.

Notes

1. Manfredo Tafuri and Francesco Dal Co, *Architettura contemporanea* (Milan: Electa Editrice, 1976), p. 379.
2. Martin Heidegger, "Bauen Wohnen Denken," in *Vorträge und Aufsätze* (Pfullingen, 1954). Eng. trans. by Albert Hofstadter, "Building Dwelling Thinking," in *Poetry, Language, Thought* (New York: Harper & Row, 1976), p. 159. Heidegger treats the same problem in *Einführung in die Metaphysik* (1953) and in *Gelassenheit* (1959). The essay "Bauen Wohnen Denken" goes back to 1951.
3. Heidegger, "Building Dwelling Thinking," p. 160.
4. Ibid., p. 161.
5. Ibid., p. 153.
6. Ibid., p. 158.
7. Oswald Spengler, *The Decline of the West*, trans. Charles Atkinson (New York: Knopf, 1957).
8. Martin Heidegger, *What Is Called Thinking?*, trans. J. Glenn Gray (New York: Harper & Row, 1968).
9. Cf. Manfredo Tafuri, "Per una critica dell'ideologia architettonica," *Contropiano*, no. 1 (1969) [translated in this volume].
10. Martin Heidegger, "Overcoming Metaphysics," in *The End of Philosophy*, trans. Joan Stambaugh (New York: Harper & Row, 1973), p. 109.
11. Here the reference to Kierkegaard's "knights of the faith" should be evident.
12. Cf. my own *Metropolis* (Rome, 1972) and G. Pasqualotto, "Considerazioni attuali," *Nuova Corrente*, no. 68–69 (1975–76).
13. Martin Heidegger, "What Are Poets For?," in *Poetry, Language, Thought*; and "Language in the Poem: A Discussion on Georg Trakl's Poetic Work," in *On the Way to Language*, trans. Peter D. Hertz (New York: Harper & Row, 1971).
14. In "La Vienna di Wittgenstein," *Nuova Corrente*, no. 72–73 (1977), and in the introduction to E. Fink, *La filosofia di Nietzsche* (Venice, 1977).
16. Martin Heidegger, ". . . Poetically Man Dwells . . ." (1951), in *Poetry, Language, Thought*, p. 222.
16. Ibid., p. 227.

17. Paul Valéry's "Eupalinos ou l'architect" appeared in 1921, and can now be found in *Oeuvres*, vol. 2 (Bibliothèque de la Pléiade), pp. 79 ff. This essay was broadly directed toward the "poets of architectural form" between the two world wars, but its tragic-disenchanted aspect remained totally misunderstood, and it is this aspect that I should like to emphasize here. It is perhaps for such reasons that this work was not analyzed by Tafuri and Dal Co. Page numbers correspond to vol. 4 of the Bollingen series of *The Collected Works of Paul Valéry*, trans. W. M. Stewart (New York, 1956).

18. Ibid., p. 71.

19. Ibid., pp. 83–84.

20. Ibid., p. 94.

21. Ibid., p. 129.

22. Cf. my essay "Loos-Wien," in M. Cacciari and F. Amendolagine, *Da Loos a Wittgenstein* (Rome, 1975).

23. Valéry, "Eupalinos," p. 145.

24. Ibid., pp. 145–148.

25. Ibid., p. 180.

26. In relation to the following paragraph, cf. the important essay by E. Severino, "Temporalità e alienazione," in *Archivio di Filosofia* (Rome, 1975).

27. One ought therefore to expand in this direction the analyses of Simmel and Benjamin and my own study on this subject in *Metropolis*.

28. The strength of anti-urban ideology is not only owing to architectural ideology. It is a general function of contemporary culture—up to and including the "new philosophers." The "nomadism" which they preach, unable to be remedied by the institution, is defined by D. Grisoni in *Politiques de la philosophie* (Paris, 1976) as a refutation of the codes of techno-urban civilization. Even the Zivilization-Kultur dichotomy is solved by these "new ones"! Not to mention the "reactionaries par excellence," the "Germans" of Nietzsche! And of course the avant-garde! Even the miseries of ideology present themselves again only as farce.

29. Tafuri and Dal Co, *Architettura contemporanea*, p. 39.

30. Ibid., p. 66.

31. Ibid., pp. 24–25.

32. Ibid., p. 48.

33. Ibid., pp. 51–52. A decisive development in this period, however, is the formation of the "discipline" of the technical administration of territory, of "bureaucrats" of territory. It is a "discipline" having Weberian tendencies and its "culture" profoundly influenced the politico-intellectual climate of Wilhelm's Germany. Cf. G. Piccinato, ed., *La costruzione dell'urbanistica. Germania 1871–1914* (Rome: Officina, 1977).

34. This is the title of the chapter on Le Corbusier in Tafuri and Dal Co, *Architettura contemporanea*, p. 133.

35. It is true that in his old French edition of Zarathustra, next to Zarathustra's first words to the dawn, the nascent sun, "I should like to share my gifts, until wise men should come to rejoice at their folly and the poor at their wealth," Le Corbusier noted down, "à la Main Ouverte" (Tafuri and Dal Co, *Architettura contemporanea*, p. 143), but this is evidence not of Nietzsche's proximity to, but rather total absence from, the "architectural ideology" of the "Master." What gift does Zarathustra bring to men? Is it fidelity to the earth? Simply pagan "good form," Celsus versus Origen? He tells of "the hour of great disdain" when the meaning of the earth is not man himself, but the overcoming of man—the sea that can receive the "dirty river" that is man, as final shelter, as the ultimate refuge of the dead God. Certainly Le Corbusier has nothing to do with the Nietzsche transformed by Van de Velde—and Nietzsche's sister—into a Nuremberg "Champ de Mars" (cf. Van de Velde's project for a Nietzsche *Denkmal* at Weimar, a project which shows how one can "stretch" the research of Mosse, which was conducted anyway on too *völkisch* ground). Nor does Le Corbusier give any indication of the subtle understanding of the Nietzschean "sign" that is discernible, as we shall see, in Mies.

36. Tafuri and Dal Co, *Architettura contemporanea*, p. 193.

37. Ibid., p. 396.

38. Ibid., p. 403.

39. Cf. chap. IV, p. 371.
40. Ibid., p. 408.
41. Michel Foucault, "Des espaces autres," in *Cercle d'Etudes Architecturales*, March 14, 1967.
42. Tafuri and Dal Co, *Architettura contemporanea*, p. 408. The reference is to Kahn.
43. Ibid., p. 362.
44. Ibid., p. 403.
45. Ibid., p. 153.
46. Ibid., p. 154.
47. Cf. pp. 342–345.
48. Ibid., p. 346.
49. The dialectics of "glass" is, however, much more complex than appears here. I intend to address myself to it in subsequent works.

The Manhattan Transcripts differ from most architectural drawings insofar as they are neither real projects nor mere fantasies. They propose to transcribe an architectural interpretation of reality. To this aim, they use a particular structure indicated by photographs that either direct or "witness" events (some would say "functions," others would call them "programs"). At the same time, plans, sections, and diagrams outline spaces and indicate the movements of the different protagonists—those people intruding into the architectural "stage set." The effect is not unlike an Eisenstein film script or some Moholy-Nagy stage directions. Even if the *Transcripts* become a self-contained set of drawings, with its own internal coherence, they are first a device. Their explicit purpose is to transcribe things normally removed from conventional architectural representation, namely the complex relationship between spaces and their use; between the set and the script; between "type" and "program"; between objects and events. Their implicit purpose has to do with the twentieth-century city.

Bernard Tschumi, *The Manhattan Transcripts* (New York and London: St. Martin's Press, 1981)

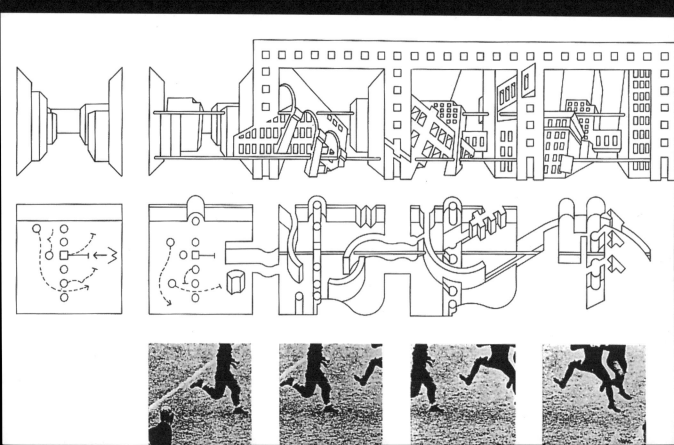

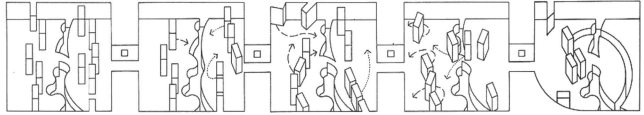

Jürgen Habermas   **"Modern and Postmodern Architecture"** Presented as a lecture at the opening

of the exhibition "The Other Tradition: Architecture in Munich from 1800 up to

Today," November 1981; published in a new translation in Habermas, *The New*

Conservatism: Cultural Criticism and the Historians' Debate, trans. Shierry

Weber Nicholsen (Cambridge: MIT Press, 1989)

In his influential Adorno prize essay of 1980, "Modernity—An Incomplete Project,"
Jürgen Habermas allies himself with Theodor Adorno to rescue what both see as the
critical, utopian force of modernism.[1] But, in a break with Adorno's account of the
bourgeois Enlightenment as but the initial stage in the development of an utterly
instrumentalizing system of thought, Habermas seeks to maintain the Enlightenment's promise of emancipation over and against the actual failure of its ideals within
the trajectory of capitalism. It is this promise, modernity's unfinished project, that
frames Habermas's exploration of the links between the politics of conservatism and
the aesthetic recommendations of postmodernism.

     The 1980 essay begins, significantly enough, with a comment
on recent architecture: "In 1980, architects were admitted to the Biennial in Venice,
following painters and filmmakers. The note sounded at this first Architecture Biennial was one of disappointment. I would describe it by saying that those who exhibited in Venice formed an avant-garde of reversed fronts. I mean that they sacrificed
the tradition of modernity in order to make room for a new historicism. . . . 'Postmodernity definitely presents itself as Antimodernity.' This statement describes an emotional current of our times which has penetrated all spheres of intellectual life."[2]
Habermas then differentiates three types of conservatism: that of the "old conservatives," who long for a return to premodern forms of life; that of the "neoconservatives," who welcome the development of modern science and capitalist growth but
assert the traditional quality of art and its separateness from the lifeworld; and that
of the "young conservatives," who embrace a post-Nietzschean aestheticism and cultural irrationality. The present essay modulates the categories of conservatism to a
specifically architectural field.

     To understand Habemas's pro-modern/anti-postmodern posi-
tion,[3] it is helpful to inflect the term "modern" into three distinct substantives: *modernization*, which involves industrial and scientific progress, the reorganization and
rationalization of production and administration, and the emergence of a mass market; *modernism*, which is the cultural, aesthetic response to such developments; and
modernity, which is the project, since the eighteenth-century Enlightenment, "to develop objective science, universal morality and law, and autonomous art according to
their inner logic."[4] In his definition of modernity, Habermas (building on the analyses
of Max Weber) reviews the story of the developments of the autonomous and nonsynchronous cultural spheres of science, morality, and art—institutionalized, profession-
alized, and separated from the everyday lifeworld—and of the emergence of a
decentered subjectivity that relates to the world through different attitudes—an ob-
jectifying facticity, a norm-conformative intersubjectivity, and the pure subjectivity of
the self's inner experiences. The autonomization and self-legitimation of the cultural
spheres have enabled the unprecedented construction of their own inherent meanings and produced indubitable benefits of technical expertise, political justice, and
aesthetic experience. On the other hand, the instrumental reason of science and technology has attained dominance over the other spheres, allied itself with the economy

and state administration, and colonized the lifeworld, disturbing the communicative, intersubjective domain of everyday life.

Architecture in modernity has its own internal divisions brought on by developments of new industrial and infrastructural supports, new materials and methods of mass production, and the general mobilization of living conditions. Nineteenth-century historicist architecture failed to address (even when it recognized) these new challenges, and completely isolated architecture from everyday life in a self-legitimating aestheticism. Yet that very autonomization and the aesthetic experiments it fostered ultimately enabled modern architecture to reintegrate most, if not all, of everyday life with a new, immanent aesthetic logic.

While the old conservatives reject the modern *tout court*, the neoconservatives focus their critique on the unbridled hedonism, anarchism, and subjectivist culture which they see as irreconcilable with the professional, bureaucratic, rational conduct of life. For them, art's traditional values, stripped of any critical utopian content, must be maintained in a purely private aesthetic experience. But Habermas points out that they have confused the levels of the modern, attributing to cultural modernism what are in fact the very effects of the successful technical, managerial colonization of modernity, which they seek to preserve. "Neoconservative doctrines turn our attention precisely away from such societal process: they project the causes, which they do not bring to light, onto the plane of a subversive culture and its advocates."[5] The young conservatives, meanwhile, indict the instrumentality of modernization yet relish aesthetically the very irrationality and destabilization that it brings. "They claim as their own the revelations of a decentered subjectivity, emancipated from the imperatives of work and usefulness, and with this experience they step outside the modern world. On the basis of modernistic attitudes they justify an irreconcilable antimodernism."[6] Neoconservatism and young conservatism, then, are but two sides of the same coin of the postmodern.

Habermas's discourse on architecture in modernity is an eloquent restatement of architecture's social power as constructed dialectically through its immanent processes, what he calls the "inherent aesthetic logic of functionalism." One is convinced by his argument that the wholesale dumping of modernism constitutes a regression. And surely he is right that an adequate account of the modern or the postmodern must attend to both societal modernization and cultural modernism, not just one or the other. What he fails to account for, however, is not only the antimodernization attendant to certain canonic modernisms (Frank Lloyd Wright's antiurbanism, Alvar Aalto's romanticism, Giuseppe Terragni's classicism, and Louis Kahn's historicism), or the nihilism of Loos or Mies as perceived by Massimo Cacciari, but also the nihilistic, subversive strands of constructivist functionalism itself (Hannes Meyer's productivism, for example). Moreover, though the structure of Habermas's thought may give us a way to think the critical, emancipatory strategies located within postmodernism as well as modernism, he himself seems blind to that possibility. Nevertheless, Habermas's "Modern and Postmodern Architecture" is a crucial reminder

see Cacciari (403–404)

see 358–360

for architecture theory of the 1980s that, though the post-Nietzschean, post-Heideggerian emphasis on the changeable, contingent, and irrational is a necessary response to the traditional preoccupation with the timeless and universal, it can be no less one-sided for that.

Notes

This essay was first published in German in the Süddeutsche Zeitung 5–6 (December 1981), and in an English version in *9H* 4 (1982).

1. "Die Moderne: Ein unvollendetes Projekt" was delivered on the occasion of Habermas's receipt of the Adorno prize awarded by the city of Frankfurt, and was published in Habermas, *Kleine politische Schriften* (Frankfurt: Suhrkamp, 1981). That essay first appeared in English as "Modernity versus Postmodernity," *New German Critique* 22 (Winter 1981); it was reprinted as "Modernity—An Incomplete Project," in *The Anti-Aesthetic*, ed. Hal Foster (Port Townsend, Wash.: Bay Press, 1983).
2. Habermas, "Modernity—An Incomplete Project," p. 3
3. Fredric Jameson categorized Habermas as pro-modern/anti-postmodern in "The Politics of Theory: Ideological Positions in the Debate," *New German Critique* 53 (Fall 1984).
4. Habermas, "Modernity—An Incomplete Project," p. 9
5. Ibid., p. 8.
6. Ibid., p. 14.

The exhibition "The Other Tradition: Architecture in Munich from 1800 to the Present" provides an occasion to reflect on the meaning of a preposition. For the exhibition has unobtrusively taken sides in the debate on *postmodern* architecture. Those who use this "post" want to set themselves apart from a past; they cannot yet give a new name to the present, since we do not yet have answers for the identifiable problems of the future. Terms like "post-Enlightenment" or "post-history" serve the same function. Such gestures of hasty dismissal are suited to periods of transition.

At first the "postmodernists" of today seem to be only reiterating the credo of the "postrationalists" of yesterday. Leonardo Benevolo, an important historian of modern architecture, characterizes this postrationalist tendency, which was widespread precisely among young architects between 1930 and 1933, in this way: "Now that the modern movement had been reduced to a system of formal precepts, it was assumed that the origin of its present uneasiness lay in the narrowness and schematic nature of these rules, and it was believed that the remedy still lay in a change of formal direction, in a lessening of the stress on technical features and regularity, in the return to a more human architecture, warmer, freer, and inevitably more closely attached to traditional values. The economic crisis meant that the debate was compressed into a very short space of time; the Nazi dictatorship that followed saw to it that it was cut short once and for all and at the same time acted as a touchstone, openly revealing what choices had been concealed beneath the stylistic controversy."[1] I do not want to draw false parallels but rather to note that this is not the first time that modern architecture has been dismissed—and it continues to survive.

The prefix that we encounter in such terms for tendencies and points of view does not always have the same meaning. Common to the -isms formed with the prefix "post" is the sense of *standing back* from something. They express an experience of discontinuity but take different attitudes toward the past that is put at a distance. With the word "postindustrial," for instance, sociologists are only trying to say that industrial capitalism has *developed further*, that the new service sectors have expanded at the expense of the domain of immediate production. With the word "postempiricist," philosophers are indicating that certain normative concepts of science and scientific progress have been *rendered obsolete* by recent research. The "poststructuralists" are trying to carry the familiar theoretical approach of structuralism *to its conclusion* rather than to overcome it. We call "postavant-garde," finally, the contemporary painting that makes expert use of the formal language created by the Modern Movement while renouncing its extravagant hopes for a reconciliation of art and life.

At first the expression "postmodern," as it was applied in America during the 1950s and 1960s to literary trends that wanted to set themselves apart from works of the early modern period, was also used merely to designate new variants within the broad spectrum of late modernism.[2] "Postmodernism" became an emotionally loaded outright political battle cry only in the 1970s, when two opposing camps seized the expression: on the one side the *neoconservatives*, who wanted to get rid of the supposedly subversive contents of a "hostile culture" in favor of revived traditions; and on the other side the radical *critics of growth* for whom the *Neues Bauen*, the New Architecture, had become a symbol for the destruction produced by modernization. Only then did postavant-garde movements, which had formerly shared the orientation of modern architecture—and were correctly described by Charles Jencks as representative of "late modernism"³—become caught up in the conservative mood of the 1970s, paving the way for an intellectually playful but provocative repudiation of the moral principles of modern architecture.⁴

These examples of expressions formed with the prefix "post" do not exhaust the spectrum of attitudes one may take toward a past from which one wants to distance oneself. It is only the presupposition that remains constant: the experience of a discontinuity, a detachment from a form of life or consciousness that one had previously trusted "naively" or "unreflectively."

These are the expressions with which Schiller and Schlegel, Schelling and Hegel sought at one time to comprehend the experiences of discontinuity of their time. The period of the Enlightenment had broken irrevocably the continuum joining their present with the world of immediately experienced traditions, both Christian and Greek. The historical Enlightenment did not determine the historicist thought of the late nineteenth century. Still, the classicists and romanticists born in the eighteenth century did not want to simply accommodate to the break in continuity: rather, they wanted to find *their own* way through a *reflective appropriation* of history. This impulse from the German Idealist philosophy of reconciliation also lies behind the quest for a new, synthetic architectural style that dominated the first half of the nineteenth century.⁵ The announcement in which, in 1850, Maximilian II of Bavaria challenged architects to a competition that was to produce the desired new style—and which in fact produced the Maximilianstrasse—reads like an echo of this vividly felt need. It was not until the second half of the nineteenth century that people settled down to living with a pluralism of styles that art history had made contemporary and also objectified.

It was only then that the great accomplishments of historical scholarship, which had distanced the past a second time after the Enlightenment had done so the first time, settled into the form of a Janus-faced *historical consciousness*. On the one hand, historicism signified a continuation and radicalization of the Enlightenment, which, as Nietzsche recognized immediately, defined the conditions for the development of modern identities even more sharply, more mercilessly than before; on the other hand, historicism made historical traditions available in an ideal simultaneity and made it possible for a present that was unstable and trying to escape from itself to dress itself up in borrowed identities. Stylistic pluralism, which had previously been something of an affliction, now became an accomplishment.

First the *Jugendstil* and then classical modernity arrived at a response to this situation that remains relevant today. The designation "classical," to be sure, also indicates the distance we have achieved in the meantime on the Modern Movement of our century. This is why we have to be willing to face the question of our own position vis-à-vis the discontinuity that is now opening up again.

Ten years ago Wend Fischer, director of the Neue Sammlung, put together a highly regarded exhibition. His intention was to counteract a veneration with neohistoricist overtones, a nostalgia that at that time had taken possession of the contrast-filled eclecticism of the nineteenth century, the "masked ball of styles." Fischer wanted to reveal tendencies of a "hidden reason" by presenting the nineteenth century as the *prehistory* of modern architecture and functional design. The city's enormous glass palace and its market hall notwithstanding, one has to conduct an incomparably more demanding search to discover similar traces of reason in Munich, a place that tends to turn away from the modern—and to follow them into the present. But the weakness of the impressions that modernity has left here in Munich cannot fully explain the change in the tenor of the exhibition: in comparison with the exhibition of ten years ago, defensive characteristics are more evident today. The debate over postmodernism, which is no longer confined to architectural journals, has reached the points of reference involved in these two attempts at reconstruction. This battle concerns the standpoint from which one looks back into the prehistory of the Modern Movement.

It is not easy to sort out the fronts in this battle. For all agree in their critique of a soulless container architecture, of the absence of relationship to the environment and the solitary arrogance of blocklike office buildings; of monstrous department stores and monumental university buildings and conference centers; of the lack of urbanity and the misanthropy of commuter towns; of housing developments, the brutal posterity of bunker architecture, the mass production of A-frame doghouses; of the destruction of city centers for the sake of the automobile, and so forth[6]—so many catchwords, and no dissent to be found anywhere. From Sigfried Giedion, a passionate advocate of modern architecture for more than a generation, there are critical statements dating from the year 1964 that could have been written today by Oswald Matthias Ungers or Charles Moore.[7] Of course, what one group presents as immanent critique is *opposition to modernity* in the other group; the same grounds on which the one side is encouraged to continue an irreplaceable tradition from a critical perspective are sufficient for the other side to proclaim the postmodern era. And these opposing groups, furthermore, draw opposite conclusions depending on whether they approach the problem as a cosmetic one or in terms of criticism of the system. The *conservatively minded* are content to cover up stylistically what will go on in any case—whether they do so as traditionalists, like Branca, or, like the contemporary Robert Venturi, as a pop artist who turns the spirit of the Modern Movement into a quotation and mixes it ironically with other quotations to form garish texts that glow like neon lights. The radical antimodernists, in contrast, attack the problem at a more fundamental level, wanting to undermine economic and administrative constraints on industrial construction with the aim of dedifferentiating architecture. What one group sees as problems of style the other understands as problems of the decolonization of devastated lifeworlds. Thus those who want to continue the uncompleted project of a modernity that is on the skids see themselves confronted with a variety of opponents who are in accord only in their determination to bid farewell to modernity.

The modern architecture whose origins in Frank Lloyd Wright and Adolf Loos were both organic and rationalist, and which flowered in the most successful works of a Gropius and a Mies van der Rohe, a Le Corbusier and an Alvar Aalto—this architecture remains the first and only binding style, the first and only style to have shaped even everyday life, since the days of classicism. It is the only architectural movement to have sprung from the spirit of the avant-garde, the only one equal in stature to the avant-garde painting, music, and literature of our century. It continued the line of tradition of Western rationalism and was powerful enough to create models, that is, to become classical itself and to establish a tradition that from the beginning transcended national boundaries. How are we to reconcile these indisputable facts with the fact that those monstrosities we unanimously condemn arose after World War II as the successors to, even in the name of, this International Style? Is the true face of modernity revealed in them—or are they falsifications of its true spirit? I will move toward a provisional answer by listing the problems that faced architecture in the nineteenth century, describing the New Architecture's programmatic responses to them, and showing the kinds of problems that could *not* be solved with this program. These considerations, finally, should permit a judgment on the recommendation that this exhibition, if I understand its intentions correctly, is making. How sound is the advice that we steadfastly appropriate the tradition of modernity and continue it critically, instead of pursuing the escapist movements dominant today—whether the escape be to a tradition-conscious neohistoricism, to the ultramodern "stage-set" architecture presented at the Venice Biennale in 1980, or into the vitalism of the simple life in an anonymous, deprofessionalized vernacular architecture?

1. In the course of the nineteenth century the industrial revolution and the accelerated social modernization that followed it confronted architecture and town planning with a new situation. To note the three best-known challenges: qualitatively new needs for architectural design, new materials and construction techniques, and the subjection of building to new functional, primarily economic imperatives.

With industrial capitalism there arose new *spheres of life* that evaded both the monumental architecture of court and church and the old European architecture of the cities and the country. The diffusion of culture to the middle class and the formation of a broader educated public interested in the arts called for new libraries and schools, opera houses and theaters. But those are conventional tasks. A transport system revolutionized by the railroad presented a different task; not only did it raise the locomotive to a symbol of dynamization and progress, it also gave a new meaning to bridges and tunnels, the familiar structures of transport, and with the construction of railway stations it presented a new task. Railway stations are the characteristic settings for dense and varied but also anonymous and fleeting contacts, the kinds of overstimulating but interpersonally impoverished interactions that were to characterize the sense of life in the big cities. As freeways, airports, and television transmission towers demonstrate, the development of transportation and communication systems has always provided the impetus for innovations.

At that time the same thing was true of commerce, which not only required warehouses and covered markets on a new scale but also brought with it unconventional construction projects: the department store and the exhibition hall. The first large glass palaces, built for industrial exhibitions in London, Munich, and Paris, are fascinating examples. But it was above all industrial production, with its factories, workers' housing developments, and goods produced for mass consumption, that gave rise to areas of life into which principles of form and architectural design did not at first penetrate. The social misery of early industrialism took precedence over its ugliness; its problems called into action the state, bourgeois social reformers, and finally a revolutionary labor movement, not the shaping fantasy of architects—if one disregards utopian designs for the new industrial city (from Robert Owen to Tony Garnier). In the second half of the century, mass-produced articles for daily use that were not subject to the stylistic force of traditional craftsmanship were the first to be perceived as an aesthetic problem. John Ruskin and William Morris tried to bridge the gap between utility and beauty that had arisen in daily life in the industrial world by reforming the applied arts. This reform movement was guided by a broader, forward-looking concept of architecture that was accompanied by the demand that the *whole* physical environment of bourgeois society be given architectural form. Morris in particular recognized the contradiction between democratic demands for what amounted to universal participation in culture and the fact that in industrial capitalism more and more domains of life become alienated from the stamp of cultural forces.

A second challenge for architecture arose from the development of *new materials* (such as glass and iron, steel and cement) and *new methods of production* (especially the use of prefabricated units). In the course of the nineteenth century engineers advanced construction techniques, thereby opening up to architecture construction possibilities that shattered classical limits on the constructive manipulation of surfaces and spaces. Glass palaces made with standardized parts, which had developed out of greenhouse construction, provided fascinated contemporaries with their first impressions of new orders of magnitude and new principles of construction; they revolutionized habits of seeing and altered spectators' spatial sense no less dramatically than the railway altered passengers' experience of time. In the interior of the London Crystal Palace, repetitive and without a center, it must have seemed to contemporaries that the constraints on all the familiar dimensions of formed space had been removed.

The third challenge is the capitalist *mobilization* of labor power, land, and buildings, of urban *living conditions* in general. This led to the concentration of large masses of people and to the incursion of speculation into the domain of private housing. The processes that led to the recent protests in Kreuzberg [a section of Berlin with an active squatters' movement] and elsewhere originated then: to the extent to which housing construction became an amortizable investment, decisions about the buying and selling of real estate, about construction, demolition, and new construction, about renting and vacating became detached from their ties to family and local tradition; they became, in a word, independent of orientation to use-values. Laws governing the market in construction and housing changed attitudes toward construction and housing. Economic imperatives also determined the uncontrolled growth of the cities, resulting in the need for a kind of town planning that had not been involved in the development of the Baroque cities. The way those two kinds of functional imperatives, those of the market and those of communal and state planning, interacted, intersected, and entangled architecture in a new system of dependencies is demonstrated in grand style in the redevelopment of Paris by Haussmann under Napoleon III. Architects played no appreciable role in this planning.

To understand the impulse from which modern architecture arose, one must bear in mind that the architecture of the second half of the nineteenth century was not only overwhelmed by this third challenge of industrial capitalism; in addition, although it had sensed the other two challenges, it had not met them.

Arbitrary disposition of decontextualized, scientifically objectified styles enabled historicism to veer off into an impotent idealism and to *separate* the sphere of architecture from the banalities of everyday bourgeois life. The plight of the new spheres of life that were alienated from architectonic design was turned into the virtue of releasing utilitarian architecture from artistic demands. Opportunities offered by new possibilities for technical design were seized only to divide the world up between architects and engineers, between style and function, between magnificent facades on the exterior and autonomous arrangements of space in the interior. This is why an architecture that has become historicist cannot oppose the internal dynamic of economic growth, the mobilization of urban living conditions, and the social misery of the masses with much more than a flight into the triumph of spirit and culture over the (disguised) material base. The Berlin "rent barracks" becomes an impressive symbol of this: "The front building, whose historicizing facade was designed to ensure the prestige value of the building, was reserved for the middle bourgeoisie, while the poorer people lived in the back buildings."[8]

2. In historicist architecture, Idealism abandoned its original intentions. To be sure, Schelling and Hegel had also placed architecture lowest in the hierarchy of the arts, for "the material for this first art form is the inherently nonspiritual, i.e., heavy matter, shapeable only according to the laws of gravity."[9] For this reason Hegel thinks that "the spiritual meaning does not reside exclusively in the building . . . but in the fact that this meaning has already attained its existence in freedom outside architecture."[10] But he conceives the purpose that architecture is to serve as the totality of the social context of communication and life: "as human individuals assembled as a company or nation."[11] Historicist architecture abandons this idea of reconciliation—the spirit, no longer a force of reconciliation, now feeds the compensatory dynamics of a reality that has been plastered over and hidden behind facades. In the reformist tendencies of the *Jugendstil*, from which modern architecture emerged, protest against this falseness, against an *architecture of repression* and symptom-formation, was already making itself felt. It is no accident that Sigmund Freud developed the bases of his theory of neurosis at the same time.

The Modern Movement took up the challenges to which the architecture of the nineteenth century had not been equal. It overcame stylistic pluralism and the distinctions and divisions to which architecture had accommodated.

To the alienation of the various domains of life from culture in industrial capitalism, the Modern Movement responded with the claim of a style that not only stamped public buildings but also penetrated the practice of everyday life. The spirit of modernity was to spread to the totality of social life-expressions. In this way industrial design could be linked to the reform of the applied arts, the functional design of utilitarian buildings could be linked to the engineering techniques used in buildings for transportation and commerce, and the design of business districts could be linked to the models of the Chicago School. In addition, the new language of form took possession of the exclusive domain of monumental architecture, of churches, theaters, court buildings, ministries, town halls, universities, spas, and so forth; and on the other side it extended into the core domains of industrial production, into housing developments, social housing, and factories.

The new style could not have penetrated all domains of life if modern architecture had not dealt with the second challenge, that of the immensely expanded range of technical design possibilities, with an *inherent aesthetic logic*. The term "functionalism" covers specific key ideas, principles for the construction of spaces and the use of materials, methods of production and organization; functionalism is based on the conviction that forms are supposed to express the use-functions for which a structure is created. But that idea is not so new; even the classicistically inclined Hegel writes, "Need introduces into architecture forms which are wholly and entirely purposeful and belong to the [mathematical] intellect, viz. the straight line, the right angle, level surfaces."[12] Furthermore, the expression "functionalism" suggests false ideas. It disguises the fact that the features of modern buildings associated with it are the result of consistently applied autonomous aesthetic laws. What is falsely attributed to functionalism owes its existence instead to an aesthetically motivated constructivism that emerged from new problems posed within art itself. In this constructivism modern architecture was following the experimental path of avant-garde painting.

Initially, modern architecture found itself in a paradoxical situation. On the one hand, architecture had always been a use-oriented art. In contrast to music, painting, and lyric poetry, it is as difficult for architecture to detach itself from practical contexts as it is for literary prose to detach itself from the practice of everyday language—these arts remain caught in the net of everyday practice and everyday communication: Adolf Loos even saw architecture, along with everything that serves a specific purpose, as excluded from the domain of art. On the other hand, architecture is subject to the laws of cultural modernity—like art in general, it succumbs to the compulsion of radical autonomization, the differentiation of a domain of genuine aesthetic experience, a domain that a subjectivity freed from the imperatives of everyday life, from the routines of action and the conventions of perception, can explore in the company of its own spontaneity. Avant-garde art, which has freed itself from perspectivistic perception of the object and from tonality, from imitation and harmony and turned to its own media of representation, was described by Adorno in terms like construction, experiment, and montage. According to him, exemplary works of avant-garde art devote themselves to an esoteric absolutism "at the expense of the reality-oriented purposefulness in which functional structures like bridges or industrial plants seek their formal laws. . . . The autonomous work of art, in contrast, functional only within itself, hopes to achieve what was once known as beauty through its immanent teleology."[13] Adorno, then, opposes the work of art that is functional "in itself" to the structure that is functional for "external purposes." In its most convincing examples, however, modern architecture does not fit within the dichotomy Adorno outlined.

The functionalism of modern architecture coincides instead with the inner logic of a development in art. There were three main groups that concerned themselves with the problems that emerged from Cubist painting: the Purists around Le Corbusier, the circle of Constructivists around Malevich, and especially the De Stijl movement (with van Doesburg, Mondrian, and Oud). Just as de Saussure analyzed the structures of language during that period, so the Dutch Neoplasticists, as they called themselves, investigated the grammar of expressive and formative means, the most universal techniques of the plastic arts, in order to incorporate the latter into the *Gesamtkunstwerk* of a comprehensive architectonic designing of the environment. "In the future," Mondrian wrote, "the realization of pure figurative expression within the encompassable reality of our environment will replace the work of art."[14] In Malevich's and Oud's very early architectural sketches one can see how structures like those of functionalist Bauhaus architecture came out of this experimental relationship to formative means. In 1922, van Doesburg moved to Weimar and argued for the constructivist bases of functional construction and form in debates with the Bauhaus staff. Despite these controversies, the line of development, which Gropius also followed in his striving for a "new unity of art and technology," is clear; in Bruno Taut's slogan "What functions well, looks good," it is precisely the *inherent aesthetic logic of functionalism*, expressed so clearly in Taut's buildings, that is lost.

While the Modern Movement recognized and, in principle, responded correctly to the challenges presented by qualitatively new needs and new technical design possibilities, it was essentially helpless in the face of systemic dependencies on the imperatives of the market and administrative planning.

3. The expanded concept of architecture that had inspired the Modern Movement from William Morris on and provided the encouragement to overcome a stylistic pluralism detached from everyday reality was a mixed blessing. It directed attention to important connections between industrial design, interior decoration, domestic architecture and town planning, but it was also godfather to the attempt on the part of the theoreticians of the New Architecture to see lifestyles and forms of life as a whole subjected to the dictates of their design tasks. Totalities such as these, however, elude the grasp of planning. When Le Corbusier was finally

able to realize his design for an *"unité d'habitation,"* to give concrete form to his idea of a *"cité jardin verticale,"* it was precisely the communal facilities that remained unused—or were gotten rid of. The utopia of a preconceived form of life, on which in an earlier period the sketches of Owens and Fourier had been based, could not be brought to life. And this was due not only to a hopeless underestimation of the complexity and changeability of modern lifeworlds but also to the fact that modernized societies with their systemic interrelationships extend beyond the dimensions of a lifeworld that could be measured by a planner's imagination. The current manifestations of a crisis in modern architecture derive less from a crisis in architecture than from the fact that architecture voluntarily allowed itself to become overburdened.

In addition, with the ambiguities of functionalist ideology, architecture was ill equipped to confront the dangers that the reconstruction period after World War II—the period in which the International Style finally became widespread—brought with it. Gropius, of course, emphasized time and time again that architecture and town planning were intertwined with industry, the economy, transportation, politics, and administration. He was also aware of the process character of planning. But in the framework of the Bauhaus these problems came up in a format tailored to didactic purposes. And the successes of the Modern Movement misled the pioneer to the unfounded expectation that a "unity of culture and production" could be created in *another* sense as well: in this transfiguring light, the economic and political-administrative constraints to which the designing of the environment was subject seemed to be merely questions of organization. When at their meeting in 1949 the Association of American Architects wanted to adopt a regulation that architects were not to operate as building contractors, Gropius protested not against the inadequacy of this means but against the purpose and rationale of the proposal. He reiterated his credo: "Made into an educational discipline, [participation in the arts] would give our environment the unity that is the very basis of culture, embracing everything from a simple chair to the house of worship."[15] In this grand synthesis the contradictions that characterize capitalist modernization precisely in the area of town planning vanish—contradictions between the needs of a formed lifeworld on the one hand and the imperatives transmitted through the media of money and power on the other.

No doubt this false expectation was abetted by a linguistic misunderstanding or rather a categorial error. The means suited to a certain *purpose* are called "functional." A functionalism that tries to construct buildings in accordance with the purposes of their users should be understood in this sense. But we also call decisions that stabilize an anonymous complex of the results of action "functional," without the contents of this *system* necessarily being desired or even recognized by any of those involved in it. What is "system-functional" for the economy and for administration in this sense, as for example an increase in the density of the inner city with rising real estate prices and increasing tax revenues, will prove to be not "functional" at all within the horizon of the lifeworld of the inhabitants and those living nearby. The problems of town planning are not primarily problems of design but rather problems of steering failures, problems of controlling and managing anonymous system imperatives that invade urban lifeworlds and threaten to consume their urban substance.

Today everyone is thinking and talking about the traditional European city; but in 1889 Camillo Sitte, one of the first to compare the medieval with the modern city, was already issuing warnings against *forced naturalness*: "Can one," he asks, "invent and construct, according to a plan, contingencies that history has produced over the course of centuries? Could one have genuine unfeigned pleasure in such *false naiveté*, in such *artificial naturalness*?"[16] Sitte's starting point was the idea of a restoration of urbanity. But after a century of criticism of the metropolis, after a century of innumerable fruitless attempts to keep the cities in equilibrium, to rescue the city centers, to divide urban space into residential and commercial areas, industrial zones and garden suburbs, private and public areas; after efforts to build livable commuter towns, to clean up slum areas, to regulate traffic rationally and so forth, the question arises whether the very *concept* of the city has not been superseded. The traces of the occidental city that Max Weber described, the city of the European bourgeoisie in the High Middle Ages or the urban nobility in Renaissance Upper Italy, the princely *Residenz* city restored by the Baroque master builders—these historical traces have blended in our minds into a diffuse and many-layered concept of the city. It is the kind of concept that Wittgenstein found in the habits and the self-understanding of everyday activity: our concept of the city is connected to a form of life. But in the meantime that form of life has changed so much that the concept that grew out of it can no longer keep pace. As a lifeworld that could be surveyed and grasped, the city could be given architectural form, sensory representation. The social functions of urban life, political and economic, private and public, the functions of cultural and ecclesiastical representation, of work, habitation, recreation, and celebration could be *translated* into purposes, into functions of the time-regulated use of formed spaces. But in the nineteenth century at the latest the city became the point of intersection of functional relationships of a *different* kind. It came to be embedded in abstract systems that as such could no longer be represented aesthetically in concretely existing form. The fact that from the middle of the century up into the late 1880s the great industrial exhibitions were planned as major architectural events betrays an impulse that now seems touching, an impulse of which the Olympiads of today are reminiscent. In arranging an international comparison of the products of their industrial production in vivid and festive form in magnificent halls, governments were literally trying to put the world marketplace on stage and to bring it back within the bounds of the lifeworld. But even the railway stations could no longer give visual form to the functions of the transportation system to which they linked the passengers in the way the city gates had once given visual form to the city's concrete ties to surrounding villages and neighboring cities.

Today, moreover, airports are located far outside the cities, for good reasons. And in the faceless office buildings that dominate the city centers— the banks and government buildings, court buildings and corporate headquarters, the publishing and printing houses, the private and public bureaucracies—one cannot recognize the functional relationships whose nodal points they form. The graphics of company logos and neon advertisements show that differentiations must be made in a medium *other* than that of the architectural language of forms. Venturi, in fact, drew the conclusions from this—when he compared the shopping center signs along the Autobahn to a duck-house in the shape of a duck, thus ridiculing the unity of exterior and interior, of beauty and utility demanded by modern architecture. Another indication that the urban lifeworld is becoming increasingly mediated by *system relationships that cannot be given form* is the failure of what was probably the most ambitious project of the New Architecture: to this day it has not been possible to integrate social housing projects and factories into the city. The urban agglomerations have outgrown the old concept of the city to which we gave our hearts; that is not the failure of modern architecture, or of any architecture at all.

4. If this diagnosis is not completely wrong, then it merely confirms, first of all, the reigning perplexity and the necessity of seeking new solutions. It also raises doubts about the reactions aroused by the disaster of the simultaneously overburdened and instrumentalized New Architecture. To orient myself at least provisionally in the complex terrain of countermovements, I have made a typology— oversimplified, of course—and distinguished three tendencies that have one thing in common: in contrast to the self-critical continuation of modernity that this ex-

hibition is implicitly advocating, they rupture the modern style by dissolving the conjunction of avant-garde form-language and uncompromising functionalist principles. Form and function once again diverge programmatically. This is true in the trivial sense of a neohistoricism that transforms department stores into a medieval row of houses and subway ventilation shafts into pocketbook-size Palladian villas. This return to the eclecticism of the previous century is due, as it was then, to compensatory needs. This traditionalism conforms to the pattern of political neoconservatism in that it redefines problems that lie at a different level as questions of style and thus removes them from public consciousness. The escapist reaction is linked to a move toward the affirmative: everything *else* is to remain as it is.

The separation of form and function also characterizes a postmodernism that fits the definition given by Charles Jencks and is completely free of nostalgia—whether it be Eisenman and Graves, who give artistic autonomy to the formal repertoire of the 1920s, or Hollein and Venturi, who, like surrealistic stage designers, use modern design techniques to entice painterly effects from an aggressive mixture of styles.[17] The language of this stage-set architecture is pledged to a rhetoric that tries to express in code the systemic relationships that can no longer be given architectonic form.

The unity of form and function is ruptured in another way by the alternative architecture that takes as its point of departure questions of ecology and the preservation of historically developed quarters of the city. These efforts, occasionally called "vitalist,"[18] aim primarily at achieving a close connection between architectural design and spatial, cultural, and historical environmental contexts. Something of the impulse of the Modern Movement survives here—now, however, on the defensive. Especially noteworthy are steps toward a community architecture in which those affected are included in the planning process in a way that goes beyond mere rhetoric and plans city districts in dialogue with clients.[19] When the steering mechanisms of the market and administrative bodies function in town planning in such a way as to have dysfunctional consequences for the lifeworld of those concerned—thus canceling out the "functionalism" that was once intended—then it is only consistent to allow the will-formative communication of participants to enter into competition with the media of money and power.

The longing for dedifferentiated forms of life does, it is true, often give these tendencies a veneer of antimodernism. Then they ally themselves with the cult of the vernacular and the worship of the banal. This ideology of the uncomplicated renounces the rational potential and the inherent aesthetic logic of cultural modernity. Praising anonymous construction and an architecture without architects indicates the price that this vitalism become critical of the system is ready to pay, even if it has in mind another *Volksgeist* than the one whose glorification in its time supplemented the monumentalism of the Führer's architecture most admirably.

There is a good deal of truth in this opposition to modernity; it takes up the unsolved problems that modern architecture pushed into the background—that is, the colonization of the lifeworld through the imperatives of autonomous economic and administrative systems of action. But we can learn something from all these opposition movements only if we keep one thing in mind: At a fortunate moment in modern architecture, the inherent aesthetic logic of constructivism encountered the use-orientation of a strict functionalism and united spontaneously with it. Traditions live only through such moments, even the one that, from the perspective of Munich, represents "the other tradition."

Notes

1. Leonardo Benevolo, *History of Modern Architecture*, vol. 2 (Cambridge, Mass., 1971), p. 552.
2. M. Köhler, "Postmodernismus," *Amerikastudien* 22 (1977), pp. 8 ff.

3. Charles Jencks, *Late Modern Architecture and Other Essays* (New York, 1980).

4. Charles Jencks, *The Language of Postmodern Architecture*, 4th ed. (New York, 1984).

5. M. Brix and M. Steinhauser, "Geschichte im Dienste der Baukunst," in their *Geschichte allein ist zeitgemäss* (Giessen, 1978), p. 255.

6. These descriptions are derived from H. Klotz, "Tendenzen heutiger Architektur in der Bundesrepublik," *Das Kunstwerk* 32 (1979), pp. 6 ff.; and J. Paul, "Kulturgeschichtliche Betrachtungen zur deutschen Nachkriegsarchitecktur," *Das Kunstwerk* 32 (1979), pp. 13 ff.

7. Sigfried Giedion, *Space, Time and Architecture: The Growth of a New Tradition* (Cambridge, Mass., 1965), pp. xxvi ff.; Charles Moore, "Eine persönliche Erklärung," in G. R. Blomeyer and B. Tietze, *In Opposition zur Moderne* (Braunschweig, 1977), pp. 64 ff.

8. M. Brix and M. Steinhauser, *Geschichte allein ist zeitgemäss*, p. 220.

9. G. W. F. Hegel, *Aesthetics*, trans. T. M. Knox (Oxford, 1975), p. 624.

10. Ibid., p. 661.

11. Ibid., p. 655.

12. Ibid.

13. Theodor W. Adorno, *Aesthetic Theory* (London, 1984), p. 89 (translation altered).

14. Quoted in Benevolo, *History of Modern Architecture*, 2:409.

15. Quoted in ibid., 2:786.

16. Camillo Sitte, *Der Städtebau* (Leipzig, 1889).

17. V. M. Lampugnani, "Theorie und Architektur in den USA," *Architekt* 5 (1980), pp. 252 ff.

18. W. Pohl, "Plädoyer für eine unbefriedete Tradition," *Bauwelt* 19/20 (1981), pp. 768 ff.

19. L. Kroll, "Stadtteilplanung mit den Bewohnern," in Blomeyer and Tietze, *In Opposition zur Moderne*, pp. 160 ff.

Michel Foucault   **"Space, Knowledge, and Power"** Interview with Paul Rabinow, *Skyline,* March 1982, trans. Christian Hubert

While Michel Foucault's "archaeologies" of modern reason and institutions had a formative influence on architecture theory after 1968, architecture had received the attention of his very first studies on the institutionalization of the medical and penal gazes.[1] Jeremy Bentham's Panopticon systematized a technology of surveillance that Foucault found crucial for a historical understanding of the spatial inscription of power. "Perrot: So the key was architecture! Indeed, what of architecture as a mode of political organization? For after all, in this eighteenth-century current of thought everything is spatial, on the material as well as the mental level. Foucault: The point, it seems to me, is that architecture begins at the end of the eighteenth century to become involved in problems of population, health and the urban question.... It becomes a question of using the disposition of space for economico-political ends."[2]

Paul Rabinow's interview with Foucault for the architectural tabloid *Skyline* is something of a commemoration as well as a clarification of Foucault's thoughts on the spatialization of knowledge and power. It should be underscored that, for Foucault, it is a misunderstanding to hold that architecture simply represents power, or, even more so, that architecture can have inherent political significance or function. Rather it is the techniques for *practicing* social relations, which are framed and modulated spatially, that allow for the efficient expansion of power, or alternatively, for resistance.

compare 296–297 Nevertheless, Foucault makes a decisive break from the internal, "homogeneous and empty space" of Gaston Bachelard and phenomenology, training his concern, instead, on the exteriority of socially produced and actually lived sites.

The space in which we live, from which we are drawn out of ourselves, just where the erosion of our lives, our time, our history takes place, this space that wears us down and consumes us, is in itself heterogeneous. In other words, we do not live in a sort of vacuum, within which individuals and things can be located, or that may take on so many different fleeting colors, but in a set of relationships that define positions which cannot be equated or in any way superimposed.[3]

Space is the material wherein discourses about knowledge and power are transformed into actual relations of power. In different historical conditions, such techniques may come more or less in architecture's purview.

Furthermore, Foucault's comments here on the "debate" with Jürgen Habermas suggest that our notion of reason may have to be expanded beyond its former boundaries to include certain aspects of what used to be demonized as irrational, since, for example, certain sexual practices, or new technologies of memory and communication, look far more transparent to us than they did to cultures that needed a concept of the irrational to domesticate the offenders of norms of reason. The "irrational," indeed, may amount to an enlargement of the social production of space by means that are not so unreasonable after all.

Notes

"Space, Knowledge, and Power" was reprinted *The Foucault Reader,* ed. Paul Rabinow (New York: Pantheon, 1984).

1. Foucault's "Des espaces autres" was delivered as a lecture in 1967 but remained almost unknown until its publication in *Architecture Mouvement Continuité* 5 (October 1984). In that essay, Foucault identifies many heterotopias: the cemetery and the theater, the museum and the library, the brothel and the colony, Moslem hammams and Scandinavian saunas. The juxtapositions of continuity and discontinuity, power and discourse, are enunciated in his *Madness and Civilization: A History of Insanity in the Age of Reason* (1961; English translation 1965). The most extensive treatment of Bentham's Panopticon is *Discipline and Punish: The Birth of the Prison* (1975; English translation 1977). For an early treatment of the Panopticon in the architectural literature, see Robin Evans, "Panopticon," *Controspazio* 2 (October 1970) and *Architectural Association Quaterly* 3, no. 2 (April–June 1971).

2. Michel Foucault, "The Eye of Power," a conversation with Jean-Pierre Barou and Michelle Perrot published as a preface to Jeremy Bentham, *Le Panoptique* (Paris, 1977), reprinted in *Power/Knowledge: Selected Interviews and Other Writings by Michel Foucault, 1972–1977,* ed. Colin Gordon (New York: Pantheon Books, 1980), p. 148. See also, in the same edition, "Questions on Geography" (1976).

3. Michel Foucault, "Of Other Spaces: Utopias and Heterotopias," in *Architecture Culture 1943–1968,* ed. Joan Ockman (New York: Columbia Books of Architecture and Rizzoli, 1992), p. 421.

P.R.: In your interview with geographers at *Herodote,* you said that architecture becomes political at the end of the eighteenth century. Obviously, it was political in earlier periods, too, such as during the Roman Empire. What is particular about the eighteenth century?

M.F.: My statement was awkward in that form. Of course I did not mean to say that architecture was not political before, becoming so only at that time. I only meant to say that in the eighteenth century one sees the development of reflection upon architecture as a function of the aims and techniques of the government of societies. One begins to see a form of political literature that addresses what the order of a society should be, what a city should be, given the requirements of the maintenance of order; given that one should avoid epidemics, avoid revolts, permit a decent and moral family life, and so on. In terms of these objectives, how is one to conceive of both the organization of a city and the construction of a collective infrastructure? And how should houses be built? I am not saying that this sort of reflection appears only in the eighteenth century, but only that in the eighteenth century a very broad and general reflection on these questions takes place. If one opens a police report of the times—the treatises that are devoted to the techniques of government—one finds that architecture and urbanism occupy a place of considerable importance. That is what I meant to say.

P.R.: Among the Ancients, in Rome or Greece, what was the difference?

M.F.: In discussing Rome one sees that the problem revolves around Vitruvius. Vitruvius was reinterpreted from the sixteenth century on, but one can find in the sixteenth century—and no doubt in the Middle Ages as well—many considerations of the same order as Vitruvius; if you consider them as *reflections upon.* The treatises on politics, on the art of government, on the manner of good government, did not generally include chapters or analyses devoted to the organization of cities or to architecture.

The *Republic* of Jean Bodin (Paris, 1577) does not contain extended discussions of the role of architecture, whereas the police treatises of the eighteenth century are full of them.

P.R.: Do you mean there were techniques and practices, but the discourse did not exist?

M.F.: I did not say that discourses upon architecture did not exist before the eighteenth century. Nor do I mean to say that the discussions of architecture before the eighteenth century lacked any political dimension or significance. What I wish to point out is that from the eighteenth century on, every discussion of politics as the art of the government of men necessarily includes a chapter or a series of chapters on urbanism, on collective facilities, on hygiene, and on private architecture. Such chapters are not found in the discussions of the art of government of the sixteenth century. This change is perhaps not in the reflections of architects upon architecture, but it is quite clearly seen in the reflections of political men.

P.R.: So it was not necessarily a change within the theory of architecture itself?

M.F.: That's right. It was not necessarily a change in the minds of architects, or in their techniques—although that remains to be seen—but in the minds of political men in the choice and the form of attention that they bring to bear upon the objects that are of concern to them. Architecture became one of these during the seventeenth and eighteenth centuries.

P.R.: Could you tell us why?

M.F.: Well, I think that it was linked to a number of phenomena, such as the question of the city and the idea that was clearly formulated at the beginning of the seventeenth century that the government of a large state like France should ultimately think of its territory on the model of the city. The city was no longer perceived as a place of privilege, as an exception in a territory of fields, forests, and roads. The cities were no longer islands beyond the common law. Instead, the cities, with the problems that they raised, and the particular forms that they took, served as the models for the governmental rationality that was to apply to the whole of the territory.

There is an entire series of utopias or projects for governing territory that developed on the premise that a state is like a large city; the capital is like its main square; the roads are like its streets. A state will be well organized when a system of policing as tight and efficient as that of the cities extends over the entire territory. At the outset, the notion of police applied only to the set of regulations that were to assure the tranquillity of a city, but at that moment the police become the very *type* of rationality for the government of the whole territory. The model of the city became the matrix for the regulations that apply to a whole state.

The notion of police, even in France today, is frequently misunderstood. When one speaks to a Frenchman about police, he can only think of people in uniform or in the secret service. In the seventeenth and eighteenth centuries, "police" signified a program of government rationality. This can be characterized as a project to create a system of regulation of the general conduct of individuals whereby everything would be controlled to the point of self-sustenance, without the need for intervention. This is the rather typically French effort of policing. The English, for a number of reasons, did not develop a comparable system, mainly because of the parliamentary tradition on one hand, and the tradition of local, communal autonomy on the other, not to mention the religious system.

One can place Napoleon almost exactly at the break between the old organization of the eighteenth-century police state (understood, of course, in the sense we have been discussing, not in the sense of the "police state" as we have come to know it) and the forms of the modern state, which he invented. At any rate, it seems that, during the eighteenth and nineteenth centuries, there appeared—rather quickly in the case of commerce and more slowly in all the other domains—this idea of a police that would manage to penetrate, to stimulate, to regulate, and to render almost automatic all the mechanisms of society.

This idea has since been abandoned. The question has been turned around. No longer do we ask, What is the form of governmental rationality that will be able to penetrate the body politic to its most fundamental elements? but rather, How is government possible? That is, what is the principle of limitation that applies to governmental actions such that things will occur for the best, in conformity with the rationality of government, and without intervention?

It is here that the question of liberalism comes up. It seems to me that at that very moment it became apparent that if one governed too much, one did not govern at all—that one provoked results contrary to those one desired. What was discovered at that time—and this was one of the great discoveries of political thought at the end of the eighteenth century—was the idea of *society*. That is to say, that government not only has to deal with a territory, with a domain, and with its subjects, but that it also has to deal with a complex and independent reality that has its own laws and mechanisms of reaction; its regulations as well as its possibilities of disturbance. This new reality is society. From the moment that one is to manipulate a society one cannot consider it completely penetrable by police. One must take into account what it is. It becomes necessary to reflect upon it, upon its specific characteristics, its constants and its variables.. . .

P.R.: So there is a change in the importance of space. In the eighteenth century there was a territory and the problem of governing people in this territory: one can choose as an example *La métropolite* (1682) of Alexandre LeMaître—a utopian treatise on how to build a capital city—or one can understand a city as a metaphor or symbol for the territory and how to govern it. All of this is quite spatial, whereas after Napoleon, society is not necessarily so *spatialized*. . . .

M.F.: That's right. On one hand, it is not so spatialized, yet at the same time a certain number of problems that are properly seen as spatial emerged. Urban space has its own dangers: disease, such as the epidemics of cholera in Europe from 1830 to about 1880; and revolution, such as the series of urban revolts that shook all of Europe during the same period. These spatial problems, which were perhaps not new, took on a new importance.

Secondly, a new aspect of the relations of space and power were the railroads. These were to establish a network of communication no longer corresponding necessarily to the traditional network of roads, but they nonetheless had to take into account the nature of society and its history. In addition, there are all the social phenomena that railroads gave rise to, be they the resistances they provoked, the transformations of population, or changes in the behavior of people. Europe was immediately sensitive to the changes in behavior that the railroads entailed. What was going to happen, for example, if it was possible to get married between Bordeaux and Nantes? Something that was not possible before. What was going to happen when people in Germany and France might get to know one another? Would war still be possible once there were railroads? In France a theory developed that the railroads would increase familiarity among people and that the new forms of human universality made possible would render war impossible. But what the people did not foresee—although the German military command was fully aware of it, since they were much cleverer than their French counterpart—was that, on the contrary, the railroads rendered war far easier to wage. The third development, which came later, was electricity.

So, there were problems in the links between the exercise of political power and the space of a territory, or the space of cities—links that were completely new.

P.R.: So it was less a matter of architecture than before. These are sorts of technics of space. . . .

M.F.: The major problems of space, from the nineteenth century on, were indeed of a different type. Which is not to say that problems of an architectural nature were forgotten. In terms of the first ones I referred to—disease and the political problems—architecture has a very important role to play. The reflections on urbanism and on the design of workers' housing—all of these questions—are an area of reflection upon architecture.

P.R.: But architecture itself, the Ecole des Beaux-Arts, belongs to a completely different set of spatial issues.

M.F.: That's right. With the birth of these new technologies and these new economic processes one sees the birth of a sort of thinking about space that is no longer modeled upon the police state of the urbanization of the territory, but that extends far beyond the limits of urbanism and architecture.

P.R.: Consequently, the Ecole des Ponts et Chaussées . . .

M.F.: That's right. The Ecole des Ponts et Chaussées and its capital importance in political rationality in France are part of this. It was not architects, but engineers and builders of bridges, roads, viaducts, railways, as well as the Polytechnicians (who practically controlled the French railroads)—those are the people who thought out space.

P.R.: Has this situation continued up to the present, or are we witnessing a change in relations between the technicians of space?

M.F.: We may well witness some changes, but I think that we have until now remained with the developers of the territory, the people of the Ponts et Chaussées, etc.

P.R.: So architects are not necessarily the masters of space that they once were, or believe themselves to be.

M.F.: That's right. They we not the technicians or engineers of the three great variables—territory, communication, and speed. These escape the domain of architects.

P.R.: Do you see any particular architectural projects, either in the past or the present, as forces of liberation or resistance?

M.F.: I do not think that it is possible to say that one thing is of the order of "liberation" and another is of the order of "oppression." There are a certain number of things that one can say with some certainty about a concentration camp to the effect that it is not an instrument of liberation, but one should still take into account—and this is not generally acknowledged—that, aside from torture and execution, which preclude any resistance, no matter how terrifying a given system may be, there always remain the possibilities of resistance, disobedience, and oppositional groupings.

On the other hand, I do not think that there is anything that is functionally—by its very nature—absolutely liberating. Liberty is a *practice*. So there may, in fact, always be a certain number of projects whose aim is to modify some constraints, to loosen, or even to break them, but none of these projects can, simply by its nature, assure that people will have liberty automatically; that it will be established by the project itself. The liberty of men is never assured by the institutions and laws that we intended to guarantee them. This is why almost all of these laws and institutions are quite capable of being turned around. Not because they are ambiguous, but simply because "liberty" is what must be exercised.

P.R.: Are there urban examples of this? Or examples where architects succeeded?

M.F.: Well, up to a point there is Le Corbusier, who is described today—with a sort of cruelty that I find perfectly useless—as a sort of crypto-Stalinist. He was, I am sure, someone full of good intentions—and what he did was in fact dedicated to liberating effects. Perhaps the means that he proposed were in the end less liberating than he thought, but, once again, I think that it can never be inherent in the structure of things to guarantee the exercise of freedom. The guarantee of freedom is freedom.

P.R.: So you do not think of Le Corbusier as an example of success. You are simply saying that his intention was liberating. Can you give us a successful example?

M.F.: No. It *cannot* succeed. If one were to find a place, and perhaps there are some, where liberty is effectively exercised, one would find that this is not owing to the order of objects, but, once again, owing to the practice of liberty. Which is not to say that, after all, one may as well leave people in slums thinking that they can simply exercise their rights there.

P.R.: Meaning that architecture in itself cannot resolve social problems?

M.F.: I think that it can and does produce positive effects when the liberating intentions of the architect coincide with the real practice of people in the exercise of their freedom.

P.R.: But the same architecture can serve other ends.

M.F.: Absolutely. Let me bring up another example: The *Familistère* of Jean-Baptiste Godin at Guise (1859). The architecture of Godin was clearly intended for the freedom of people. Here was something that manifested the power of ordinary workers to participate in the exercise of their trade. It was a rather important sign and instrument of autonomy for a group of workers. Yet no one could enter or leave the place without being seen by everyone—an aspect of the architecture that could be totally oppressive. But it could only be oppressive if people were prepared to use their own presence in order to watch over others. Let's imagine a community of unlimited sexual practices that might be established there. It would once again become a place of freedom. I think it is somewhat arbitrary to try to dissociate the effective practice of freedom by people, the practice of social relations, and the spatial distributions in which they find themselves. If they are separated, they become impossible to understand. Each can only be understood through the other.

P.R.: Yet people have often attempted to find utopian schemes, to liberate people, or to oppress them.

M.F.: Men have dreamed of liberating machines. But there are no machines of freedom, by definition. This is not to say that the exercise of freedom is completely indifferent to spatial distribution, but it can only function when there is a certain convergence; in the case of divergence or distortion it immediately becomes the opposite of that which had been intended. The panoptic qualities of Guise could perfectly well have allowed it to be used as a prison. Nothing could be simpler. It is clear that, in fact, the *Familistère* may well have served as an instrument for discipline and a rather unbearable group pressure.

P.R.: So once again the intention of the architect is not the fundamental determining factor.

M.F.: Nothing is fundamental. That is what is interesting in the analysis of society. That is why nothing irritates me as much as these inquiries—which are by definition metaphysical—on the foundations of power in a society or the self-institution of a society, etc. These are not fundamental phenomena. There are only reciprocal relations, and the perpetual gaps between intentions in relation to one another.

P.R.: You have singled out doctors, prison wardens, priests, judges, and psychiatrists as key figures in the political configurations that involve domination. Would you put architects on this list?

M.F.: You know, I was not really attempting to describe figures of domination when I referred to doctors and people like that, but rather to describe people through whom power passed or who are important in the fields of power relations. A patient in a mental institution is placed within a field of fairly complicated power relations, which Erving Goffman analyzed very well. The pastor in a Christian or Catholic church (in Protestant churches it is somewhat different) is an important link in a set of power relations. The architect is not an individual of that sort.

After all, the architect has no power over me. If I want to tear down or change a house he built for me, put up new partitions, add a chimney, the architect has no control. So the architect should be placed in another category—which is not to say that he is not totally foreign to the organization, the implementation, and all the techniques of power that are exercised in a society. I would say that one must take him—his mentality, his attitude—into account as well as his projects, in order to understand a certain number of the techniques of power that we invested in architecture, but he is not comparable to a doctor, a priest, a psychiatrist, or a prison warden.

P.R.: "Post-modernism" has received a great deal of attention recently in architectural circles. It is also being talked about in philosophy, notably by Jean-François Lyotard and Jürgen Habermas. Clearly, historical reference and language play an important role in the modern episteme. How do you see post-modernism, both as architecture and in terms of the historical and philosophical questions that are posed by it?

M.F.: I think that there is a widespread and facile tendency, which one should combat, to designate that which has just occurred as the primary enemy as if this were always the principal form of oppression from which one had to liberate oneself. Now, this simple attitude entails a number of dangerous consequences: first, an inclination to seek out some cheap form of archaism or some imaginary past forms of happiness that people did not, in fact, have at all. For instance, in the areas that interest me, it is very amusing to see how contemporary sexuality is described as something absolutely terrible. To think that it is only possible now to make love after turning off the television! and in mass-produced beds! "Not like that wonderful time when . . ." Well, what about those wonderful times when people worked eighteen hours a day and there were six people in a bed, if one was lucky enough to have a bed! There is in this hatred of the present or the immediate past a dangerous tendency to invoke a completely mythical past. Secondly, there is the problem raised by Habermas: if one abandons the work of Kant or Weber, for example, one runs the risk of lapsing into irrationality.

I am completely in agreement with this, but at the same time, our question is quite different: I think that the central issue of philosophy and critical thought since the eighteenth century has always been, still is, and will, I hope, remain the question, *What* is this Reason that we use? What are its historical effects? What are its limits, and what are its dangers? How can we exist as rational beings, fortunately committed to practicing a rationality that is unfortunately crisscrossed by intrinsic dangers? One should remain as close to this question as possible, keeping in mind that it is both central and extremely difficult to resolve. In addition, if it is extremely dangerous to say that Reason is the enemy that should be eliminated, it is just as dangerous to say that any critical questioning of this rationality risks sending us into irrationality. One should not forget—and I'm not saying this in order to criticize rationality, but in order to show how ambiguous things are—it was on the basis of the flamboyant rationality of Social Darwinism that racism was formulated, becoming one of the most enduring and powerful ingredients of Nazism. This was, of course, an irrationality, but an irrationality that was at the same time, after all, a certain form of rationality. . . .

This is the situation that we are in and that we must combat. If intellectuals in general are to have a function, if critical thought itself has a function, and, even more specifically, if philosophy has a function within critical thought, it is precisely to accept this sort of spiral, this sort of revolving door of rationality that refers us to its necessity, to its indispensability, and at the same time, to its intrinsic dangers.

P.R.: All that being said, it would be fair to say that you are much less afraid of historicism and the play of historical references than someone like Habermas is; also that this issue has been posed in architecture as almost a crisis of civilization by the defenders of modernism, who contend that if we abandon modern architecture for a frivolous return to decoration and motifs, we are somehow abandoning civilization. On the other hand, some post-modernists have claimed that historical references per se are somehow meaningful and are going to protect us from the dangers of an overly rationalized world.

M.F.: Although it may not answer your question, I would say this: One should totally and absolutely suspect anything that claims to be a return. One reason is a logical one; there is in fact no such thing as a return. History, and the meticulous interest applied to history, is certainly one of the best defenses against this theme of the return. For me, the history of madness or the studies of the prison . . . were done in that precise manner because I knew full well— this is in fact what aggravated many people—that I was carrying out an historical analysis in such a manner that people *could* criticize the present, but it was impossible for them to say, "Let's go back to the good old days when madmen in the eighteenth century . . ." or, "Let's go back to the days when the prison was not one of the principal instruments. . . ." No; I think that history preserves us from that sort of ideology of the return.

P.R.: Hence, the simple opposition between reason and history is rather silly . . . choosing sides between the two . . .

M.F.: Yes. Well, the problem for Habermas is, after all, to make a transcendental mode of thought spring forth against any historicism. I am, indeed, far more historicist and Nietzschean. I do not think that there is a proper usage of history or a proper usage of intrahistorical analysis—which is fairly lucid, by the way—that works precisely against this ideology of the return. A good study of peasant architecture in Europe, for example, would show the utter vanity of wanting to return to the little individual house with its thatched roof. History protects us from historicism—from a historicism that calls on the past to resolve the questions of the present.

P.R.: It also reminds us that there is always a history; that those modernists who wanted to suppress any reference to the past were making a mistake.

M.F.: Of course.

P.R.: Your next two books deal with sexuality among the Greeks and the Early Christians. Are there any particular architectural dimensions to the issues you discuss?

M.F.: I didn't find any; absolutely none. But what is interesting is that in Imperial Rome there were, in fact, brothels, pleasure quarters, criminal areas, etc., and there was also one sort of quasi-public place of pleasure: the baths, the *thermes*. The baths were a very important place of pleasure and encounter, which slowly disappeared in Europe. In the Middle Ages, the baths were still a place of encounter between men and women as well as of men with men and women with women, although that is rarely talked about. What was referred to and condemned, as well as practiced, were the encounters between men and women, which disappeared over the course of the sixteenth and seventeenth centuries.

P.R.: In the Arab world it continues.

M.F.: Yes; but in France it has largely ceased. It still existed in the nineteenth century. One sees it in *Les enfants du paradis*, and it is historically exact. One of the characters, Lacenaire, was—no one mentions it—a swine and a pimp who used young boys to attract older men and then blackmailed them; there is a scene that refers to this. It required all the naivete and antihomo-sexuality of the Surrealists to overlook that fact. So the baths continued to exist, as a place of sexual encounters. The bath was a sort of cathedral of pleasure at the heart of the city, where people could go as often as they want, where they walked about, picked each other up, met each other, took their pleasure, ate, drank, discussed. . . .

P.R.: So sex was not separated from the other pleasures. It was inscribed in the center of the cities. It was public; it served a purpose. . . .

M.F.: That's right. Sexuality was obviously considered a social pleasure for the Greeks and the Romans. What is interesting about male homosexuality today—this has apparently been the case of female homosexuals for some time—is that their sexual relations are immediately translated into social relations and the social relations are understood as sexual relations. For the Greeks and the Romans, in a different fashion, sexual relations were located within social relations in the widest sense of the term. The baths were a place of sociality that included sexual relations.

One can directly compare the bath and the brothel. The brothel is in fact a place, and an architecture, of pleasure. There is, in fact, a very interesting form of social-ity that was studied by Alain Corbin in *Les filles de noces* (Aubier, 1978). The men of the city met at the brothel; they were tied to one another by the fact that the same women passed through their hands, that the same diseases and infections were communicated to them. There was a sociality of the brothel; but the sociality of the baths as it existed among the ancients—a new version of which could perhaps exist again—was completely different from the sociality of the brothel.

P.R.: We now know a great deal about disciplinary architecture. What about confessional archi-tecture—the kind of architecture that would be associated with a confessional technology?

M.F.: You mean religious architecture? I think that it has been studied. There is the whole problem of a monastery as xenophobic. There one finds precise regulations concerning life in common; affecting sleeping, eating, prayer, the place of each individual in all of that, the cells. All of this was programmed from very early on.

P.R.: In a technology of power, of confession as opposed to discipline, space seems to play a central role as well.

M.F.: Yes. Space is fundamental in any form of communal life; space is fundamental in any exercise of power. To make a parenthetical remark, I recall having been invited, in 1966, by a group of architects to do a study of space, of something that I called at that time "heterotopias," those singular spaces to be found in some given social spaces whose functions are different or even the opposite of others. The architects worked on this, and at the end of the study someone spoke up—a Sartrean psychologist—who firebombed me, saying that *space* is reactionary and capitalist, but *history* and *becoming* are revolutionary. This absurd discourse was not at all unusual at the time. Today everyone would be convulsed with laughter at such a pronouncement, but not then.

P.R.: Architects in particular, if they do choose to analyze an institutional building such as a hospital or a school in terms of its disciplinary function, would tend to focus primarily on the walls. After all, that is what they design. Your approach is perhaps more concerned with space, rather than architecture, in that the physical walls are only one aspect of the institution. How would you characterize the difference between these two approaches, between the building itself and space?

M.F.: I think there is a difference in method and approach. It is true that for me, architecture, in the very vague analyses of it that I have been able to conduct, is only taken as an element of support, to insure a certain adoration of people in space, a *canalization* of their circulation, as well as the coding of their reciprocal relations. So it is not only considered as an element in space, but is especially thought of as a plunge into a field of social relations in which it brings about some specific effects.

For example, I know that there is an historian who is carrying out some interesting studies of the archaeology of the Middle Ages, in which he takes up the problem of architecture, of houses in the Middle Ages, in terms of the problem of the chimney. I think that he is in the process of showing that beginning at a certain moment it was possible to build a chimney inside the house—a chimney with a hearth, not simply an open room or a chimney outside the house; that at that moment all sorts of things changed and relations between individuals became possible. All of this seems very interesting to me, but the conclusion that he presented in an article was that the history of ideas and thoughts is useless.

What is, in fact, interesting is that the two are rigorously indivisible. Why did people struggle to find the way to put a chimney inside a house? Or why did they put their techniques to this use? So often in the history of techniques it takes years or even centuries to implement them. It is certain, and of capital importance, that this technique was a formative influence upon new human relations, but it is impossible to think that it would have been developed and adapted had there not been in the play and strategy of human relations something which tended in that direction. What is interesting is always interconnection, not the primacy of this over that, which never has any meaning.

P.R.: In your book *Les mots et les choses* you constructed certain vivid spatial metaphors to describe structures of thought. Why do you think spatial images are so evocative for these references? What is the relationship between these spatial metaphors describing disciplines and more concrete descriptions of institutional spaces?

M.F.: It is quite possible that since I was interested in the problems of space I used quite a number of spatial metaphors in *Les mots et les choses*, but usually these metaphors were not ones that I advanced, but ones that I was studying as objects. What is striking in the epistemological mutations and transformations of the seventeenth century is to see how the spatialization of knowledge was one of the factors in the constitution of this knowledge as a science. If the natural history and the classifications of Linnaeus were possible, it is for a certain number of reasons: on the one hand, there was literally a spatialization of the very object of their analyses, since they gave themselves the rule of studying and classifying a plant only on the basis of that which was visible. They didn't even want to use a microscope. All the traditional elements of knowledge, such as the medical functions of the plant, fed away. The object was spatialized. Subsequently, it was spatialized insofar as the principles of classification had to be found in the very structure of the plant: The number of elements, how they were arranged, their size, etc., and certain other elements, like the height of the plant. Then there was the spatialization into illustrations within books, which was only possible with certain printing techniques. Then the spatialization of the reproduction of the plants themselves, which was represented in books. All of these are spatial techniques, not metaphors.

P.R.: Is the actual plan for a building—the precise drawing that becomes walls and windows—the same form of discourse as, say, a hierarchical pyramid that describes rather precisely relations between people not only in space but also in social life?

M.F.: Well, I think there are a few simple and exceptional examples in which the architectural means reproduce, with more or less emphasis, the social hierarchies. There is the model of the military camp, where the military hierarchy is to be read in the ground itself, by the place occupied by the tents and the buildings reserved for each rank. It reproduces precisely through architecture a pyramid of power; but this is an exceptional example, as is everything military—privileged in society and of an extreme simplicity.

P.R.: But the plan itself is not always an account of relations or power.

M.F.: No. Fortunately for human imagination, things are a little more complicated than that.

P.R.: Architecture is not, of course, a constant: it has a long tradition of changing preoccupations, changing systems, different rules. The *savoir* of architecture is partly the history of the profession, partly the evolution of a science of construction, and partly a rewriting of aesthetic theories. What do you think is particular about this form of *savoir*? Is it more like a natural science, or what you have called a "dubious science"?

M.F.: I can't exactly say that this distinction between sciences that are certain and those that are uncertain is of no interest—that would be avoiding the question—but I must say that what interests me more is to focus on what the Greeks called the *techne*, that is to say, a practical rationality governed by a conscious goal. I am not even sure if it is worth constantly asking the question of whether government can be the object of an exact science. On the other hand, if architecture, like the practice of government and the practice of other forms of social organization, is considered as a *techne*, possibly using elements of sciences like physics, for example, or statistics, etc., that is what is interesting. But if one wanted to do a history of architecture, I think that it should be much more along the lines of that general history of the *techne*, rather than the histories of either the exact sciences or the inexact ones. The disadvantage of this word *techne*, I realize, is its relation to the word "technology," which has a very specific meaning. A very narrow meaning is given to "technology": one thinks of hard technology, the technology of wood, of fire, of electricity. Whereas government is also a function of technology: the government of individuals, the government of souls, the government of the self by the self, the government of families, the government of children, and so on. I believe that if one placed the history of architecture back in this general history of *techne*, in this wide sense of the word, one would have a more interesting guiding concept than by considering opposition between the exact sciences and the inexact ones.

Fredric Jameson   **"Architecture and the Critique of Ideology"** Paper presented at the Institute for Architecture and Urban Studies, New York, 1982; published in *Architecture, Criticism, Ideology,* ed. Joan Ockman et al. (Princeton: Princeton Architectural Press, 1985)

see 2–5, 146–147

see x–xii

In his matrix of possible ideological positions on modernism and postmodernism, Fredric Jameson places Manfredo Tafuri in the "anti-modernist/anti-postmodernist" square, "perhaps the bleakest of all and the most implacably negative."[1] Tafuri's position is the diagonal inversion of one (which Jameson associates with Jean-François Lyotard) committed to the emergent and the new, to a triumphant world-to-come. Tafuri's "dialectical historiography" allows architecture no purchase in the creases of history's flow but, rather, wraps it so tightly in an ideological veil of intellectual, cultural, and economic forces that it can hardly be extricated. In Tafuri's demonstration of the ways in which architecture's aesthetic formulation comes to entail both cognitive and sociopolitical consequences, Jameson finds reconfirmation of his own conviction that the very concept of space has a mediatory function. And yet, whereas Tafuri narrates the deployment of rationalized planning techniques and multinational capital to create a system so total and all-encompassing that it has no conceivable outside, Jameson is concerned to maintain architecture's utopian vocation in a properly postmodern political aesthetic that, allegorically, turns the geopolitical system inside out so that it can again be seen.

Jameson's now-classical construction of the postmodern as a cultural dominant encompasses practices from literature, film, and video to economics, and contains within it just such allegorical strategies. "It is in the realm of architecture, however," according to him, "that modifications in aesthetic production are most dramatically visible, and that their theoretical problems have been most centrally raised and articulated; it was indeed from architectural debates that my own conception of postmodernism . . . initially began to emerge."[2] If architectural discourse was a spur to his investigations of the new media and aesthetic modes of postmodernism, his confrontation with the resolutely negative thought of Tafuri virtually forced the production of the important, correlated, and positive ideology of cognitive mapping. For the imperative to think totality—and very specifically the complexities of urban and technological totalities—is one on which Tafuri and Jameson agree. Yet for Jameson, architecture still has the important social functions of articulating urban and technological forces that might otherwise remain ungraspable, and linking the most intimate, local experiences of a site to the ongoing development of capitalism itself.

In the present essay (which was presented in 1982 to the reading group that would later constitute *Revisions*), the possibility of an aesthetic practice that would endow the individual subject with some new, intensified sense of its place in the global system is tentatively staged as an "enclave theory"—a counter-hegemonic impulse modeled in some ways on the modern architecture repudiated by Tafuri, which radically separates a new utopian space from the hegemonic and fallen city fabric out of which it first appeared, and construed as a "Gramscian architecture," an alternative to which Tafuri assiduously refused recourse. Jameson would later rewrite Kevin Lynch's notion of mentally mapping one's urban surroundings as a spatial allegory of Louis Althusser's redefinition of ideology as "the representation of the subject's *Imaginary* relationship to his or her *Real* conditions of existence."[3] Within

Tafuri's ideological veil, then, Jameson finds the threads of what used to be called "class consciousness" (itself a mapping of one's social place), except now of a paradoxical kind premised on the representation of the global structure in each of the local, experiential moments that are the effects of that structure.

Notes

1. Fredric Jameson, "The Politics of Theory: Ideological Positions in the Debate," *New German Critique* 53 (Fall 1984); reprinted in Jameson, *Postmodernism, or, The Cultural Logic of Late Capitalism* (Durham: Duke University Press, 1991), p. 60.
2. Jameson, *Postmodernism*, p. 2.
3. Kevin Lynch, *The Image of the City* (Cambridge: MIT Press, 1960); Louis Althusser, "Ideology and Ideological State Apparatuses," in *Lenin and Philosophy and Other Essays*, trans. Ben Brewster (New York: Verso, 1971). For a discussion of cognitive mapping, see Jameson, *Postmodernism*, pp. 50–54 and 406–417; and Jameson, "Cognitive Mapping," in *Marxism and the Interpretation of Culture*, ed. Cary Nelson and Lawrence Grossberg (Houndmills, Basingstoke, Hampshire: Macmillan Education, 1988).

How can space be "ideological"? Only if such a question is possible and meaningful—leaving aside the problem of meaningful *answers* to is—can any conceptions or ideals of nonideological, transfigured, Utopian space be developed. The question has itself tended to be absorbed by naturalistic or anthropological perspectives, predominantly based on conceptions of the human body itself, most notably in phenomenology. The body's limits but also its needs are then appealed to as ultimate standards against which to measure the relative alienation either of older commercial or industrial space of the overweening sculptural monuments of the International Style or of the postmodernist "megastructure." Yet arguments based on the human body are fundamentally ahistorical and involve premises about some eternal "human nature" concealed within the seemingly "verifiable" and scientific data of physiological analysis. If the body is in reality a social body, if therefore there exists no pregiven human body as such, but rather the whole historical range of social experiences of the body, the whole variety of bodily norms projected by a series of distinct historical "modes of production" or social formations, then the "return" to some more "natural" vision of the body in space projected by phenomenology comes to seem ideological, if not nostalgic. But does this mean that there are no limits to what the body, socially and historically, can become, or to the kind of space to which it can be asked to "adapt"?

Yet if the "body" ceases to be the fundamental unit of spatial analysis, the very concept of space itself becomes problematized: What space? The space of rooms or individual buildings, or the space of the very city fabric itself, in which those buildings are inserted, and against whose perceptual background my experience of this or that local segment is organized? Yet the city, however it is construed, is space-in-totalization; it is not given in advance as an object of study or analysis, after the fashion of the constructed building. (Perhaps even the latter is not given in this way either, except to the already abstract sense of sight: individual buildings are then "objects" only in photographs.)

It is important to recognize (or to admit) that this second series of questions or problems *remains* essentially phenomenological in its orientation; indeed, it is possible that the vice of our initial question lies there, that it still insists on posing the problem of the relationship of the individual subject and of the subject's "lived experience" to the architectural or urban, spatial object, however the latter is to be construed. What is loosely called "structuralism" is now generally understood as the repudiation of this phenomenological "problematic," of such presuppositions as "experience"; it has generated a whole new counter-problematic of its own, in which space—the individual building or the city itself—is taken as a text in which a whole range of "signs" and "codes" are combined, whether in the organic unity of a shared code, or in "collage" systems of various kinds, in structures of allusion to the past, or of ironic commentary on the present, or of radical disjunctures, in which some radically new sign (the Seagram Building or the Radiant City) *criticizes* the older sign system into which it dramatically erupts.

Yet in another perspective it is precisely this last possibility that has been called back into question, and which can be seen as a replication, in more modern "structuralist" language, of our initial question. In all the arts, the new "textual" strategies stubbornly smuggled back into their new problematic the coordinates of the older political question, and of the older unexamined opposition between "authentic" and "inauthentic." For a time, the new mediations produced seemingly new versions of the older (false?) problem, in the form of concepts of "subversion," the breaking of codes, their radical interruption or contestation (along with their predictable dialectical opposite, the notion of "cooptation"). It is the viability of these new solutions that is today generally in doubt: they now are taken to be more Utopianism, only of a negative or "critical" variety. They seemed at first to have repudiated the older positive and nostalgic ideals of a new Utopian—authentic, nonalienated—space or art; yet their claim to punctual negativity—far more modest at first glance—now seems equally Utopian in the bad sense. For even the project of criticizing, subverting, delegitimating, strategically interrupting, the established codes of a repressive social and spatial order has ultimately come to be understood as appealing to some conception of critical "self-consciousness," of critical distance, which today seems problematic; whereas on a more empirical level, it has been observed that the most subversive gesture itself hardens into yet another form of being or positivity in its turn (just as the most negative critical stance loses its therapeutic and destructive shock value and slowly turns back into yet another critical ideology in its own right).

Is some third term beyond these two moments—the phenomenological and the structural—conceivable? Pierre Bourdieu, in his *Outline of a Theory of Practice*, explicitly attempts such a dialectical move beyond these two "moments," both of which are for him indispensable, yet insufficient: the concept of "practice"—the social body's programming by its spatial text, not taken to be the "bottom line" both of everyday experience and of the legitimation of the social structure itself—while offered as just such a solution, has only been "tested" on the much simpler materials and problems of precapitalist space in the Kabyl village. Meanwhile, Henri Lefebvre's conception of "space" as the fundamental category of politics and of the dialectic itself—the one great prophetic vision of these last years of discouragement and renunciation—has yet to be grasped in all its pathbreaking implications, let alone to be explored and implemented; while Lefebvre's influential role as an ideologist and a critic of French architecture today must be noted and meditated upon.

It is precisely a role of this kind that yet another logically possible position—faced with the dilemmas we have outlined above—explicitly repudiates: this is the position of Manfredo Tafuri, which in at least some of its more preemptory expressions has the merit of stark and absolute simplicity. The position is stated most baldly in the "Note" to the second Italian edition of *Theories and History of Architecture*: "one cannot 'anticipate' a class architecture (an architecture 'for a liberated society'); what is possible is the introduction of class criticism into architecture."[1] Although Tafuri's working judgments—in texts written over a number of years—are in fact far more nuanced and ambiguous than such a proposition might suggest, certain key elements can at once be isolated: (1) The architectural critic has no business being an "ideologist," that is, a visionary proponent of architectural styles of the future, "revolutionary" architecture, and the like; her role must be resolutely negative, the vigilant denunciation of existent or historical architectural ideologies. This position then tends to slip into a somewhat different one. (2) The practicing architect, in this society and within the closure of capitalism as a system, cannot hope to devise a radically different, a revolutionary, or a "Utopian" architecture or space either. (3) Without any conceivable normative conception of architectural space, of a space of radical difference from this one, the criticism of buildings tends to be conflated with the criticism of the ideologies of such buildings; the history and criticism of architecture thus tends to fold back into the history and criticism of the various ideologies of architecture, the manifestos and the verbal expressions of the great architects themselves. (4) Political action is not renounced in such a position, or not *necessarily* (although more "pessimistic" readings of Tafuri are certainly possible). What is, however, affirmed here is consonant with the Althusserian tradition of the "semi-autonomy" of the levels and practices of social life: politics is radically disjoined from aesthetic (in this case architectural) practice. The former is still possible, but only on *its* level, and architectural or aesthetic production can never be immediately political; it takes place somewhere else. Architects can therefore be political, like other individuals, but their architecture today cannot be political (a restatement of proposition 2, above). It follows, then, that: (5) An architecture of the future will be concretely and practically possible only when the future has arrived, that is to say, after a total social revolution, a systemic transformation of this mode of production into something else.

This position, which inevitably has something of the fascination of uncompromising intransigence and of all absolutes, must be understood, as I will try to show below in more detail, first of all within the history of contemporary Marxism, as a repudiation of what the Althusserians called Marxist "humanism" (including very specifically its "Utopian" component as symbolically represented by Marcuse or by Henri Lefebvre himself). Its refusal to entertain the possibility of some properly Marxian "ideology" (which would seek to project alternate futures), its commitment to a resolutely critical and analytical Marxian "science"—by way of a restriction to the operation of denouncing the ideologies of the past and of a closed present—all these features betray some kinship with T. W. Adorno's late and desperate concept of a purely "negative dialectic." The ambiguity of such a position lies in its very instability, and the way in which it can imperceptibly pass over into a post-Marxism of the type endorsed by the French *nouveaux philosophes* or by Tafuri's collaborator, Massimo Cacciari. This is to suggest that Tafuri's position is *also* an ideology, and that one does not get out of ideology by refusing it or by committing one's self to negative and critical "ideological analysis."

Yet at this stage, such an evaluation remains at the level of mere opinion and in that form has little if any interest. In what follows I will try to give it more content by examining Tafuri's work—and most notably his short, widely read, but dense and provocative *Architecture and Utopia*[2]—in three distinct perspectives. The first must be that of the Marxist context in which it was first produced, a context in which a series of significant but implicit moves may go unrecognized by the non-Marxist or American reader for want of the appropriate background. The second perspective (in no special order) will be that of the discursive form in which Tafuri works, namely historiography itself, and most particularly narrative history, whose formal dilemmas and problems today may be seen as determining (or at least overdetermining) certain of Tafuri's organizing concepts. Finally, it will be appropriate to reconsider this considerable body of work (now largely available in English) in the context of a vaster contemporary event, which has its own specifically American equivalents (and which is by no means limited to the field of architecture, although the battle lines have been drawn more dramatically there than in any other art)— namely the critique of high modernism, the increasingly omnipresent feeling that the modern movement itself is henceforth extinct; this feeling has often been accompanied by the sense that we may therefore now be in something else, sometimes called postmodernism. It is incidentally a matter of no small significance, to which we will return, that this second theme—the dawning of some new postmodernist moment or even "age"—is utterly alien to Tafuri himself and plays no role in his periodizing framework or in his historical narrative.

I want to deal first with the second of my three topics, namely that which has to do with historiography, with the problem of writing history, and in this case of writing the history of a discipline, an art, a medium. That there has been a crisis in narrative or storytelling history since the end of the nineteenth century is well known, as is the relationship between this crisis and that other crisis in the realistic novel itself: narrative history and the realistic novel are indeed closely related and in the greatest nineteenth-century texts virtually interchangeable. In our own time, this ongoing crisis has been rethematized in terms of the critique of representation, one of the fundamental slogans of poststructuralism: briefly, the narrative representation of history necessarily tends to suggest that history is something you can see, be a witness to, be present at—an obviously inadmissible proposition. On the other hand, as the word itself suggests, history is always fundamentally storytelling, must always be narrative in its very structure.

This dilemma will not bother those for whom history-writing is not an essential task; if you are satisfied to do small-scale semiotic analyses of discrete or individual text or buildings, presumably the problem of the writing of history, the telling of a historical story, will not unduly preoccupy you. I say "presumably" because I think that this problem also leaves its traces on such static analyses, and indeed it seems to be an empirical fact that the issues of history are returning everywhere today, not least within semiotics itself (the history of semiotics, the turn of semiotic analysis to the problem of genres, the problem of a semiotic of historical representation).

However, leaving other people to their concerns, it will be clear that no issue is more central or more acute than for those with some commitment to a dialectical tradition, since the dialectic has always for better or for worse been associated with some form or other of historical vision. For myself, I am much attracted by Louis Althusser's solution, which consists in proposing, in the midst of the crisis of historical representation and of narrative history, that the historian should conceive her task not as that of producing a representation of history, but rather as that of producing the *concept* of history, a very different matter indeed.

But how is this to be done? Or rather, to be more modest about it, how has this actually been done in practice? From this perspective, it will be of interest to read *Architecture and Utopia* with a view toward determining the way in which it suggestively "produces the concept" of a dialectical history of architecture. But this is a rare enough achievement for one to want, initially, to juxtapose Tafuri's text with those very rare other realizations of this particular genre or form. I can think of only two contemporary dialectical histories of comparable intensity and intellectual energy: T. W. Adorno's *Philosophy of Modern Music* (a seminal text, on which Thomas Mann drew for his musical materials in *Doktor Faustus*), and in the area of the history of literature, Roland Barthes's early and unequaled *Le degré zéro de l'écriture* (*Writing Degree Zero*). You will understand that this limited choice does not imply a lack of interest in the contributions that a Lukács, a Sartre, an Asor Rosa, a Raymond Williams, among others, have made to the restructuration of traditional paradigms of literary history. What the three books I have mentioned have in common is not merely a new set of dialectical insights into literature, but the practice of a peculiar, condensed, allusive discursive form, a kind of textual *genre*, still exceedingly rare, which I will call dialectical history.

Let me first single out a fundamental organizational feature that these three works share, and which I am tempted to see as the ultimate precondition to which they must painfully submit in order to practice dialectical thinking: this is the sense of Necessity, of necessary failure, of closure, of ultimate unresolvable contradictions and the impossibility of the future, which cannot have failed to oppress any reader of these texts, particularly readers who as practicing artists— whether architects, composers, or writers—come to them for suggestions and encouragement as to the possibility of future cultural production.

Adorno's discussion of musical history culminates, for instance, in Schoenberg's extraordinary "solution"—the twelve-tone system—which solves all the dilemmas outstanding in previous musical history so completely as to make all musical composition after Schoenberg superfluous (or at least regressive) from Adorno's perspective, yet which at the same time ends up as a baleful replication or mirror image of that very totalitarian socioeconomic system from which it sought to escape in the first place. In Barthes's *Writing Degree Zero*, the well-known ideal of "white writing"—far from being what it often looks like today, namely a rather complacent account of postmodernist trends—stood in its initial historical context and situation as an equally impossible solution to a dilemma that rendered all earlier practices of writing or style ideological and intolerable. Tafuri's account, finally, of the increasing closure of late capitalism (beginning in 1931 and intensifying dialectically after the war), systematically shutting off one aesthetic possibility after another, ends up conveying a paralyzing and asphyxiating sense of the futility of any kind of architectural or urbanistic innovation on this side of that equally inconceivable watershed, a total social revolution.

It would be silly, or even worse, frivolous, to discuss these positions in terms of optimism or pessimism. I will later make some remarks about the political presuppositions that account for (or at least overdetermine) some of Tafuri's attitudes here; what I prefer to stress now is the formal origin of these somber visions of the total system, which, far worse than Max Weber's iron cage, here descends upon human life and human creature praxis. The strengths of the readings and insights of Adorno, Barthes, and Tafuri in these works is for one thing inextricably bound up with their vision of history as an increasingly total or closed system: in other words, their ability to interpret a given work of art as a provisional "solution" is absolutely dependent on a perspective that reads the artwork against a context reconstructed or rewritten as a situation and a contraction.

More than this, I find confirmation in these books for an intuition I have expressed elsewhere, namely that the dialectic, or powerful dialectical history, must somehow always involve a vision of Necessity or, if you prefer, must always tell the story of failure. "The owl of Minerva takes its flight at dusk": dialectical interpretation is always retrospective, always tells the necessity of an event, why it *had* to happen the way it did; and to do that, the event must already have happened, the story must already have come to an end. While this may sound like an indictment of the dialectic (or as yet one more post-Marxist "proof" of its irrecuperably Hegelian character), it is important to add that such histories of necessity and of determinate failure are equally inseparable from some ultimate historical perspective of reconciliation, of achieved socialism, of the "end of prehistory" in Marx's sense.

The restructuration of the history of an art in terms of a series of situations, dilemmas, contradictions, in terms of which individual works, styles, and forms can be seen as so many responses or determinate symbolic acts—this is, then, a first key feature of dialectical historiography. But there is another no less essential one that springs to mind, at least when one thinks in terms of historical materialism, and that is the reversal associated with the term "materialism" itself, the anti-idealistic thrust, the rebuke and therapeutic humiliation of consciousness forced to reground itself in a painful awareness of what Marx called its "social determination." This second requirement is of course what sets off the present texts sharply from old-fashioned Hegelian spiritual historiography, but which in turn threatens to undermine the historiographic project altogether, as in Marx's grim reminder in *The German Ideology*:

We do not set out from what people say, imagine or conceive, nor from people as narrated, thought of, imagined, conceived, in order to arrive at people in the flesh. We set out from real, active human beings, and on the basis of their real life-process we demonstrate the development of the ideological reflexes and echoes of this life-process. The phantoms formed in the human brain are also, necessarily, sublimates of their material life-process, which is empirically verifiable and bound to material premises. Morality, religion, metaphysics, all the rest of ideology and their corresponding forms of consciousness, thus no longer retain their semblance of independence. They have no history, no development, in their own right; but it is rather human beings who, developing their material production and relationships, alter, along with this their real existence, their thinking and the products of their thinking. Life is not determined by consciousness, but consciousness by life.[3]

Now the slogan of "materialism" has again become a very popular euphemism for Marxism. I have my own reasons for objecting to this particular ideological fashion on the Left today: facile and dishonest as a kind of popular-front solution to the very real tensions between Marxism and feminism, the slogan also seems to be extraordinarily misleading as a synonym for "historical materialism" itself, since the very concept of "materialism" is a bourgeois Enlightenment (later positivist) one and fatally conveys the impression of a "determinism by the body" rather than, as in genuine dialectical Marxism, a "determination by the mode of production." At any rate, in the context that concerns us here—the description of "dialectical historiography"—the drawback of the word "materialism" is that it tends to suggest that only one form of dialectical reversal—the overthrow of idealism by materialism or a recall to matter—is at work in such books.

Actually, however, the dialectical shock, the reversal of our habits of idealism, can take many forms: and it is evident that in the dialectical history of an art its privileged targets will be the idealistic habits we have inherited in thinking about such matters, and in particular Hegelian notions of the history of forms and styles, but also empiricist or structuralist notions of isolated texts. Still, it is best to see how these reversal-effects have been achieved in practice, rather than deducing them a priori in some dogmatic matter. And since none of these works ever raises one key issue of concern to everyone today, it is appropriate to preface a discussion of them with the indication of a fundamental form of contemporary "reversal" which may not leave them unscathed either: namely the way in which contemporary feminist critiques cut across the whole inherited system of the histories of art and culture by demonstrating the glaring absence from them, not merely of women as such, but, in the architectural area, of any consideration of the relationship between women's work and interior space, and between the domination of women and the city plan itself. For male intellectuals, this is the most stunning materialist reversal of all, since it calls *us* effectively into question at the same time that it disturbingly seems to discredit the very foundations and institutional presuppositions of the disciplines in question.

Indeed, the lesson for us in criticism of this kind may well be, among other things, precisely this: that a materialist or dialectical historiography does its work ultimately by undermining the very foundations, framework, constitutive presuppositions of the specialized disciplines themselves—by unexpectedly demonstrating the existence, not necessarily of "matter" in that limited sense, but rather in general of an *Other* of the discipline, an outside, a limit, the revelation of the *extrinsic*, which it is believed to be scandalous and unscholarly to introduce into a carefully regulated traditional debate.

Adorno's book perhaps goes least far in this direction: the *Philosophy of Modern Music* operates its particular reversal by shifting from the subject (the great composers and their styles and works) to the object, the raw material, the tonal system itself, which as a peculiar "logic of content" has its own dynamics and generates fresh problems with every solution, setting absolute limits to the freedom of the composer at every historical moment, its objective contradictions increasing in intensity and complexity with each of those new moments until Schoenberg's "final solution"—the unification of vertical and horizontal, of harmony and counterpoint—seems to produce an absolute that is a full stop, beyond which composition cannot go: a success which is also, in genuine dialectical fashion, an absolute failure.

Barthes's reversal is useful because his problematic (which is essentially that of the Sartre of *What Is Literature?*) is the most distant from the rhetoric of materialism and materiality and consists rather in a vision of the nightmare of history as blood guilt and as that necessary and inevitable violence of the relationship of any group to the others which we call class struggle. Both writers—Sartre and Barthes himself—reverse our placid conceptions of literary history by demonstrating how every individual text, by its institutionalized signals, necessarily selects a particular readership for itself and thereby symbolically endorses the inevitable blood guilt of that particular group or class. Only, where Sartre proposed the full Utopian solution of a literature of praxis that would address itself to a classless society, Barthes ingeniously imagines a different way of escaping from the "nightmare of history," a kind of neutral or zero term, the projection of a kind of work from which all group or class signals have been eliminated: white or bleached writing, an escape from group blood guilt on the other side of group formation (which in later Barthes will be reoriented around reception rather than production and become the escape from class struggle into an equally nonindividual kind of *jouissance* or punctual schizophrenic or perverse ecstasy, in *The Pleasure of the Text*).

This is the moment to observe the temptation of the "zero degree" solution in Tafuri himself, where it constitutes one, but *only* one, of the provisional working possibilities very sparsely detectable in his pages. A Barthesian reading of Tafuri's account of Mies and the Seagram Building seems more plausible, as well as more historical, than a Heideggerian one, particularly if we attend to the content of Tafuri's pro-Mallarméan celebration of the glacial silence of this building, rather than to its rather Germanic language:

The "almost nothing" has become a "big glass" . . . reflecting images of the urban chaos that surrounds the timeless Miesian purity. . . . It accepts [the shift and flux of phenomena], absorbs them to themselves in a perverse multi-duplication, like a Pop Art sculpture that obliges the American metropolis to look at itself reflected . . . in the neutral mirror that breaks the city web. In this, architecture arrives at the ultimate limits of its own possibilities. Like the last notes sounded by the Doctor Faustus of Thomas Mann, alienation, having become absolute, testifies uniquely to its own presence, separating itself from the world to declare the world's incurable malady.[4]

This is, however, less the endorsement of a Miesian aesthetic than a way of closing the historical narrative, and, as we will see in a moment, of endowing the implacable and contradictory historical *situation* with an absolute power that such desperate non-solutions as Barthesian "bleached writing" or Miesian silence can only enhance.

Returning for the moment to the strategies of the materialist reversal, we see that Tafuri's use of such strategies is original in that it includes an apologia for the primacy of architecture over all the other arts (and thereby of architectural theory and criticism as well); but the apologia is distinctly untraditional and, one would think, not terribly reassuring for people professionally committed to this field of specialization. Architecture is for Tafuri supreme among the arts simply because its Other or exterior is coeval with History and society itself, and it is susceptible therefore to the most fundamental materialist or dialectical reversal of all. To put it most dramatically, if the outer limit of the individual building is the material city itself, with its opacity, complexity, and resistance, then the outer limit of some expanded conception of the architectural vocation as including urbanism and city planning is the economic itself, or capitalism in the most overt and naked expression of its implacable power. So the great Central European urbanistic projects of the 1920s (the *Siedlungen*, or workers' housing in Berlin, Frankfurt, and Vienna) touch their Other in the seemingly "extrinsic" obstacle of financial speculation and the rise in land and property values that causes their absolute failure and spells an end to their Utopian vocation. But whereas for some traditional history of forms this is an extrinsic and somehow accidental, extraneous fact, which essentially has "nothing to do" with the purely formal values of these designs, in Tafuri's practice of the dialectic, this seemingly extrinsic situation is then drawn back into the dialectical spiral itself and passes an absolute judgment of History proper upon such Utopian forms.

These two dialectical reversals—the judgment on the project of an individual building, text, or "work of art" by the preexisting reality of the city itself—the subsequent judgment on aesthetics of urban planning and ensembles by that vaster "totality" which is capitalism itself—these are only two of the modes of reversal among many in Tafuri's little book; and it is this very richness of the forms of an anti-idealist turn, the dialectical suppleness of Tafuri's use of varied thematic oppositions, which makes his text both so fascinating and exemplary, and so bewilderingly dense and difficult to read. Other modes of reversal could be enumerated: most notably the unpleasant reminder of the professional status of intellectuals themselves and the ideological and idealistic distortions that result from such status; as well as the thematics of a Keynesian management of the "future"—a kind of credit and planning system of human life—which is one of the more novel subthemes of this work and of its staging of the critique of modernist Utopianism.

What must be stressed at this point, however, is the way in which the principal "event" of such dialectical histories—the contradiction itself, the fatal reversal of this or that aesthetic solution as it comes to grief against its own material underside—necessarily determines the form of their narrative closure and the kind of "ending" they are led to project. In all three, the present is ultimately projected as the final and most absolute contradiction, the "situation" that has become a blank wall, beyond which History cannot pass. Such an "end of history," or abolition of the future, is most obvious in Adorno, where it is paid for by the tragic "blind spot" of the philosopher-composer, who must on the one hand systematically reject the "other" of his culture (including the movement of popular or mass culture—contemptuously dismissed by Adorno under the all-purpose term "jazz" or "easy music," and that whole movement of Third World history and culture, which is the "repressed" of his Eurocentrism); at the same time he must refuse even the development of advanced music beyond his "final stage," repudiating Stockhausen, electronic music, all the developments of the 1950s and 1960s, with the same stubborn passion that leads him to bracket any conceivable *political* future in *Negative Dialectics.*

We have already examined the more ingenious conception of a "negative way" in Barthes's ideal of a zero degree of writing or in Tafuri's passing homage to Mies. What must now be underscored is the constitutive relationship between Tafuri's possibility of constructing dialectical history and his systemic refusal of what, in *Theories and History of Architecture,* is called operative criticism. This type of criticism, most strikingly employed in classical works like Giedion's *Space, Time and Architecture,* reads the past selectively and places an illusory historical analysis, the *appearance* of some "objective" historical narrative, in the service of what is in reality an architectural *manifesto,* the "normative" projection of some new style, the *project* of future work and future possibilities: "the planning of a precise poetical tendency, anticipated in its structures and derived from historical analyses programmatically distorted and finalized" (T&H, p. 141)—in short, ideological criticism [which] substitutes ready-made judgments of value (prepared for immediate use) for analytical rigor" (p. 153). But this judgment on the spurious appropriation of the past in the service of an endorsement of aesthetic action in the present implies that "rigorous" analytical history must in turn be bought by a stoic renunciation of action and of value, and a well-nigh Hegelian renunciation of all possible futures, so that the owl of Minerva can wing its flight into the past. Tafuri's "pessimism" is thus to be seen as a formal necessity of the generic structure of his text—dialectical historiography—rather than as an "opinion" or a "position" in its own right.

Unfortunately, it must *also* be read as just such an opinion or position; and at this point a purely formal and textual necessity intersects with and is overdetermined by ideology, and becomes the vehicle for a whole set of ideological messages and signals which have real content and which can best be appreciated by way of the Marxian traditions in which they emerge.

It seems to me most convenient to decode these signals in the context of a current and general Left appropriation of the older right-wing "end of ideology" slogans of the late 1950s. In that period, the period of the Eisenhower era and the great American celebration, the "end of ideology" meant not merely the death of Marxism, but also the good news of the end of the classical capitalism anatomized by Marx, and the apparition of some new social order whose dynamics were no longer based on production and associated with social classes and their struggle, but rather on a new principle, which was therefore to be seen in all those senses as "beyond ideology." This new social system will then be named, by the ex-Marxist right-wing theorists of an "end of ideology," most notably Daniel Bell, as "postindustrial society"[5] (others will call it consumer society, media society, consumer capitalism, and so forth); and its dynamic will be characterized by the primacy of knowledge, of scientific and technological know-how, and by the primacy of a new social group (no longer a class in the Marxian sense), namely the technocrats.

For obvious reasons, the Left repudiated this kind of analysis for a number of years, remaining intent on demonstrating that the classical analyses and concepts of Marx's *Capital* were still valid for the period that Bell and others were intent on describing as the dialectical mutation of "postindustrial society." It is clear that something of the force of Bell's theory derived from the optimism of the Eisenhower era, the period of American empire and a global *pax americana*; and that History itself, better than any left countertheories or critiques, undertakes to pronounce judgment on the "end of ideology," "postindustrial society" thesis and to lay it to rest in our own moment of the return of more classical global economic crisis, worldwide depression, unemployment, and the like.

Paradoxically, however, it was precisely in the intervening years that the Left itself caught up with the thesis of a new historical moment, a radical historical break, and produced its own version of the "end of ideology" thesis. This also had something to do with changes in social atmosphere and temperature) and with the alteration of the quality of life in the advanced world, that is to say, with mutations in the appearance or surface of social life. It became clear to everyone, in other words, that with consumerism, with the enormous penetration and colonization of the apparatus of the media, with the release of new nonclass social forces in the 1960s—forces associated with race and gender, with nationalism and religion, with marginality (as with students or the permanently unemployed—something decisive had changed in the very "reality of the appearance" of capitalism. The new Marxian version of the "state" will explain the originality of the features of so-called postindustrial society as a new stage of capitalism proper, in which the old contradictions of capital are still at work, but in unexpectedly new forms. The features enumerated by people like Bell—for example, the primacy of science, the role of bureaucracy—will be retained, but interpreted very differently in the light of a new moment which can be called "late capitalism" or the multinational world system (in the traditional Marxian periodization this would be a third moment of capitalism, after those of classical market capitalism, and the stage of imperialism and monopoly, and could be dated from the immediate postwar period in the United States and the late 1950s in Europe).[6] Although we do not have time for a detailed discussion of this extremely important new Marxian theory of the contemporary world, we must, before returning to Tafuri, underscore two significant features of that theory.

First, it is the theory of something like a total system, marked by a global deployment of capital around the world (even, on many accounts, reaching into the still far from autonomous economic dynamics of the nascent socialist countries), and effectively destroying the older coherence of the various national situations. The total system also is marked by the dynamism with which it now penetrates and colonizes the two last surviving enclaves of Nature within the older capitalism: the Unconscious and the precapitalist agriculture of the Third World— the latter is now systematically undermined and reorganized by the Green Revolution, whereas the former is effectively mastered by what the Frankfurt School used to call the Culture Industry, that is, the media, mass culture, and the various other techniques of the commodification of the mind. I should also add that this enormous new quantum leap of capital now menaces that other precapitalist enclave within older capitalism, namely the nonpaid labor of the older interior or home or family, thereby in contradictory fashion unbinding and liberating that enormous new social force of women, who immediately then pose an uncomfortable new threat to the new social order.

On the other hand, if the new expansion of multinational or late capitalism at once triggers various new forms of struggle and resistance, as in the great revolts of the 1960s, it also tends to be accompanied by a mood of pessimism and hopelessness that must naturally enough accompany the sense of a total system, with nothing outside itself, within which local revolts and resistances come to be seen, not as the emergence of new forces and a new logic of a radically different future, but rather as mere inversions within the system, punctual reversals of this or that systemic feature—no longer dialectical in their force, but merely structural(ist). The Marxist response to this increasing windless closure of the system will be varied: it can take the form of a substitution of the time-scale of the prognosis of the *Grundrisse*, for that, far more imminent, of *Capital* proper. In the *Grundrisse*, indeed, Marx seems to project a far greater resiliency for capitalism than in *Capital* itself, one which better accommodates the unexpected new vitality and dynamism of the system after World War II. The key feature of this position will be the insistence on what is, after all, a classical notion of Marx, namely that a socialist revolution and a socialist society are not possible until capitalism has somehow exhausted all its possibilities, but also not until capitalism has become a worldwide and global fact, in which universal commodification is combined with a global proletarianization of the work force, a transformation of all humanity (including the peasants of the Third World) into wage workers. In that case, the chances for socialism are relegated into some far future, while the ominous nature of the current "total system" becomes rather positive again, since it marks precisely the quantum progression toward that final global state. But this means, in addition, that not only can there not be socialism in one country, there cannot be anything like socialism in one bloc of countries: socialist revolution is here by definition global revolution or it is nothing. And equally obviously, there can be no emergence of a different social system within the interstices of the old, within this or that sector of capitalism proper. Here, I think, you will have already recognized the perspective that is characteristic of Tafuri's work: there can be no qualitative change in any element of the older capitalist system—as, for instance, in architecture or urbanism—without beforehand a total revolutionary and systemic transformation.

(Total-systems theory can of course also be explained in terms of the kind of textual determinism already evoked above: the purpose of the theorist is to build as powerful a model of capital as possible, and as all-embracing, systemic, seamless, and self-perpetuating. Thus, if the theorist succeeds, he fails: since the more powerful the model constructed, the less possibility will be foreseen in it for any form of human resistance, any chance of structural transformation.)

Yet the meaning of this stark and absolute position, this diagnosis of the total system of late or multinational capital, cannot fully be grasped without taking into account the alternative position of which it is the symbolic repudiation; this is what may be called neo-Gramscianism, the more "optimistic" assessment of some possible "long march through the institutions," which counterposes a new conception of some gradualist "war of position" for the classical Leninist model of the "war of maneuver," the all-or-nothing seizure of power. There are, of course, many reasons why radical Italian intellectuals today should have become fatigued with the Gramscian vision, paradoxically at the very moment when it has come to seem reinvigorating for the Left in other national situations in Europe and elsewhere. The most obvious of these reasons is the thirty-year institutionalization of Gramsci's thought within the Italian Communist party (and the assimilation of Gramsci, in the Italian context, to that classical form of dialectical thought which is everywhere systematically repudiated by a Nietzschean post-Marxism). Nor should we forget to underscore the structural ambiguity or polysemousness of the basic Gramscian texts, written in a coded language beneath the eyes of the Fascist censor, these texts either can be "translated back" into classical Leninism or, on the contrary, can be read as a novel inflection of Leninism in a new direction, as post-Leninism or a stimulating new form of neo-Marxism. There are therefore "objectively" many distinct Gramscis, between which it would be frivolous to attempt to decide which is the "true" one. I want, however, to suggest that with some Gramscian alternative, the possibility of a very different perspective on architecture and urbanism today is also given, so that the implications of this further digression are not a matter of Marxist scholastics, nor are they limited to purely political consequences.

At least two plausible yet distinct readings of the Gramscian slogan, the struggle for "hegemony," must be proposed at this point. What is at stake is the meaning of that "counterhegemony" which oppositional forces are called upon to construct within the ongoing dominance of the "hegemony" of capital; and the interpretive dilemma here turns on the (false) problem of a materialist or an idealist reading. If the Gramscian struggle, in other words, aims essentially at the *preparation* of the working class for some eventual seizure of power, "counterhegemony" is to be understood in purely superstructural terms, as the elaboration of a set of ideas, countervalues, cultural styles, which are virtual or *anticipatory*, in the sense that they "correspond" to a material, institutional base that has not yet "in reality" been secured by political revolution itself.

The temptation is therefore to argue for a "materialist" reading of Gramsci on the basis of certain key figures or tropes in the classical Marxian texts. One recalls, for example, the "organic" formulations of the 1859 Preface to the *Critique of Political Economy*: "new, higher relations of production never appear before the material conditions of their existence have matured within the womb of the old society"; "productive forces developing in the womb of bourgeois society create the material conditions for the solution of the antagonism [of all previous history as class conflict]."[7] One must also note the celebrated figure with which, in passing, the Marx of *Capital* characterizes the status of "commerce" within the quite different logic of the "ancient" mode of production: "existing in the interstices of the ancient world, like the gods of Epicurus in the *intermundia* or the Jews in the pores of Polish society."[8]

Such figures suggest something like an *enclave* theory of social transition, according to which the emergent future, the new and still nascent social relations that announce a mode of production that will ultimately displace and subsume the as yet still dominant one, is theorized in terms of small yet strategic pockets or beachheads within the older system. The essentially *spatial* nature of the characterization is no accident and conveys something like a historical tension between two radically different types of space, in which the emergent yet more powerful kind will gradually extend its influence and dynamism over the older form, fanning out from its initial implantations and gradually "colonizing" what persists around it. Nor is this some mere poetic vision. The political realities that have been taken as the "verification" and the concrete embodiment of "enclave theory" in contemporary society are the legendary "red communes" of Italy today, most notably Bologna, whose administration by the Communist party has seemed to demarcate them radically from the corruption and inefficiency of the capitalist nation-state within which, like so many foreign bodies, they are embedded. Tafuri's assessment of such communes is particularly instructive:

The debate over the historical centers and the experience of Bologna have shown that architectural and urbanistic proposals cannot be put to the test outside definite political situations, and then only within improved public structures for control. This has effected a substantial modification in the role of the architectural profession, even further redimensioned and characterized by an increasing change in the traditional forms of patronage and commissioning. . . . Although what [the new left city administrations] have inherited is in a desperate state and the financial difficulties are staggering, one can hope that from this new situation may come the realization of the reforms sought for decades. It is on this terrain that the Italian workers' movements are summoned to a historical test whose repercussions may prove to be enormous, even outside Italy. (*MA*, p. 322)

These lines (written, to be sure, in the more favorable atmosphere of 1976) betray a rather different Tafuri than the somber historiographer of some "end of history" who has predominated in the preceding pages.

What complicates this picture, however, is the discovery that it is precisely some such "enclave theory" which on Tafuri's analysis constitutes the "Utopianism" of the modern movement in architecture; that, in other words, Tafuri's critique of the international style, the informing center of all his works, is first and foremost a critique of the latter's enclave theory itself. Le Corbusier, for example, spoke of avoiding political revolutions, not because he was not committed to "revolution," but rather because he saw the construction and the constitution of new space as the most revolutionary act, one that could "replace" the narrowly political revolution of the mere seizure of power (and if the experience of a new space is associated with a whole transformation of everyday life itself, Le Corbusier's seemingly antipolitical stance can be reread as an *enlargement* of the very conception of the political, and as having an anticipatory kinship with conceptions of "cultural revolution" that are far more congenial to the spirit of the contemporary Left). Still, the demiurgic hubris of high modernism is fatefully dramatized by such visions as the towers of the Plan Voisin, which stride across a fallen landscape like H. G. Wells's triumphant Martians, or the gigantic symbolic structures of the Unités d'Habitation, the Algiers plan, or Chandigarh, which are apocalyptically to sound the knell of the cramped and insalubrious hovels that lie dwarfed beneath their prophetic shadow. We will shortly enter into the terms of Tafuri's critique of modernism itself. Suffice it to say for the moment that its cardinal sin is precisely to identify (or conflate) the political and the aesthetic, and to foresee a political and social transformation that is henceforth at one with the formal processes of architectural production itself. All of this is easier to demonstrate on the level of empirical history, where the new enclaves of the international style manifestly failed to regenerate anything around them; or where, when they did have the dynamic and radiating influence predicted for them by the Masters, the results, if anything, were even more depressing, generating a whole series of dismal glass boxes in their own image, or a multiplication of pseudo-Corbusian towers in the desolation of parks which have become the battleground of an unending daily war of race and class. Even the great emblem of the "red communes" can, from this perspective, be read differently: for it can equally well be argued that they are not enclaves at all—not laboratories in which original social relations of the future are being worked out, but rather simply the administration of inherited capitalistic relations, albeit conducted in a different spirit of social commitment than that of the Christian Democrats.

       This uninspiring balance sheet would settle the fate of the Gramscian alternative if the "enclave theory" were its only plausible interpretation. The latter may, however, be seen as an overly reductive and rather defensively "materialist" conception of the politics of space. But it can equally well be argued that Gramsci's notion of "hegemony" (along with the later and related idea of "cultural revolution") attempts rather to displace the whole distinction of materialism versus idealism (and, along with it, of the traditional concept of base and superstructure). It would therefore no longer be "idealist" in the bad old sense to suggest that "counterhegemony" means producing and keeping alive a certain alternate "idea" of space, the urban, daily life, and the like. It would then no longer be so immediately significant (or so practically and historically crippling) that architects in the West (with the possible exception of France)—owing to the private property system—do not have the opportunity of projecting and constructing collective ensembles that express and articulate original new social relations (and needs and demands) of a collective type. The essential would rather be that they are able to form conceptions and Utopian images of such projects, against which to develop a self-consciousness of their concrete activities in this society (it being understood, in Tafuri's spirit, that such collective projects would only practically and materially be possible after a systemic transformation of society). But such Utopian "ideas" are as "objective" as material buildings: their possibilities—the possibility of conceiving such new space—have conditions of possibility as rigorous as any material artifact. Those conditions of possibility are to be found, first and foremost, in the uneven development of world history and in the existence, elsewhere, in the second and Third Worlds, of projects and constructions that are not possible in the First; this concrete existence of radically different spaces elsewhere (of whatever unequal realization) is what objectively opens the possibility for the coming into being and development of "counterhege-monic values" here. A role is thereby secured for a more "positive" and Gramscian architectural criticism, over against Tafuri's stubbornly (and therapeutically) negative variety, his critical refusal of Utopian speculation on what is not possible within the closure of the multinational system. In reality, both of these critical strategies are productive alternatively according to the situation itself, and the public to which the ideological critic must address herself; and there is no particular reason to lay down either of these useful weapons. It is at any rate worth quoting yet another appreciation of Tafuri—this one, unexpectedly, of the Stalinallee (now the Karl-Marx-Allee) in East Berlin—in order to show that his practical criticism is often a good deal more ambivalent than his theoretical slogans (and also further to dispel the feeling that the celebration of Mies's negative mysticism, quoted above, amounts to anything like a definitive position):

However, in the case [of the Stalinallee, in East Berlin] it would be wrong to regard what resulted as purely ideological or propagandistic; in reality, the Stalinallee is the fulcrum of a project of urban reorganization affecting an entire district, establishing an axis of development toward the Tiergarten different from that developed historically. In addition, this plan inverts the logical manner in which a bourgeois city expands by introducing into the heart of the metropolis the residence as a decisive factor. The monumental bombast of the Stalinallee— now renamed Karl-Marx-Allee—was conceived to put in a heroic light an urbanistic project that set out to be different. In fact, it succeeds perfectly in expressing the presupposition for the construction of the new socialist city, which rejects divisions between architecture and urbanism and aspires to impose itself as a unitary structure. (*MA*, pp. 332, 326)

Such a text can evidently be used to support either position: the negative one—that such a collective project, with its transcendence of the opposition building/city, is only possible *after* a revolutionary transformation of social relations as a whole; or the more Gramscian one outlined above, that the very existence of such an ensemble in some other space of the world creates a new force field which cannot but have its influence even over those architects for whom such a project is scarcely a "realistic" possibility.

Still, until now we have not considered what kind of "total system" sets limits to the practical transformation of space in our time; nor have we drawn the other obvious consequence from the neo-Marxian theorization of "consumer society" or of the new moment of late capitalism, namely that to such a new moment there may very well correspond a new type of culture or cultural dynamic. This is therefore the time to introduce our third theme or problem, namely that of postmodernism and of the critique of classical or high modernism itself. For the economic periodization of capital into three rather than two stages (that of "late" or multinational capitalism being now added to the more traditional moments of "classical" capitalism and of the "monopoly stage" or "stage of imperialism") suggests the possibility of a new periodization on the level of culture as well. From this perspective, the moment of "high" modernism, of the International Style and of the classical modern movement in all the arts—with their great *auteurs* and their "Utopian" monuments, Mallarméan "Books of the World" fully as much as Corbusian Radiant Cities—would "correspond" to that second stage of monopoly and imperialist capitalism which came to an end with the Second World War. Its "critique" therefore coincides with its extinction, its passing into history, as well as with the emergence, in the third stage of "consumer capital," with some properly postmodernist practice of pastiche, of a new free play of styles and historicist allusions now willing to "learn from Las Vegas," a moment of surface rather than of depth, of the "death" of the old individual subject or bourgeois ego, and of the schizophrenic celebration of the commodity fetishism of the image, of a now "delirious New York" and a countercultural California, a moment when the logic of media capitalism penetrates the logic of advanced cultural production itself and transforms the latter to the point where such distinctions as those between high and mass culture lose their significance (and where the older notions of a "critical" or "negative" value of advanced or modernist art may also no longer be appropriate or operative).

As I have observed, Tafuri refuses this periodization and we will observe him positioning his critique of the "postmoderns" beneath the general category of a still high modernist Utopianism, of which they are seen merely as so many epigones. Still, in this country and for this public, the thrust of his critique of Utopian architecture will inevitably be associated with the generalized reaction here against the older hegemonic values and norms of the International Style, about which we must attempt to take an ambivalent and nuanced position. It is certain, for instance—as books like Tom Wolfe's recent *From Bauhaus to Our House* readily testify—that the critique of high modernism can spring from reactionary and "philistine" impulses (in both the aesthetic and the political sense) and can be belatedly nourished by all the old middle-class resistances which the modern movement met and aroused in its first freshness. Nor does it seem implausible that in certain national situations, most notably in those of the former fascist countries, the antimodernist position is still essentially and unambiguously at one with political reaction, as Habermas has suggested.[9] If so, this would explain Tafuri's decision to uncouple a reasoned critique of modernism from the adoption or exposition of any more "positive" aesthetic ideology. In the United States, however, whatever the ultimate wisdom of applying a similar strategy, the cultural pull and attractiveness of the concept of postmodernism clearly complicates the situation in ways that need to be clarified.

It will therefore be useful to retrace our steps for the moment, and however briefly to work through the terms of Tafuri's critique of modernism as he outlines it for us in *Architecture and Utopia*, where we meet a left-wing version of the "end of ideology" roughly consistent with the periodizations of some new stage of capital that have just been evoked. On this view, ideas as such—ideology in the more formal sense of a whole system of legitimizing beliefs—are no longer significant elements in the social reproduction of late capitalism, something that was obviously not the case in its earlier stages. Thus the great bourgeois revolutionary ideology of "freedom, equality, and fraternity" was supremely important in securing the universal consent of a variety of social classes to the new political and economic order; this ideology was thus also, in Tafuri's use of the term, a Utopia, or rather, its ideologizing and legitimizing function was concealed behind a universalizing and Utopian rhetoric. In the late nineteenth century—particularly in the French Third Republic (the "Republic of the Professors")—the rise of positivism, with its militant anticlericalism and its ideal of a lay or secular education, suggests the degree to which official philosophy was still thought to be a crucial terrain of ideological struggle and a supreme weapon for securing the unity of the state; whereas in our own time, until recently, what is generally called New Deal Liberalism (or in Europe, the social democracy of the welfare states) performed an analogous function.

All of this would seem to be in question today. We will want, Adorno says somewhere, to take into account the possibility that in our time the commodity is its own ideology: the practices of consumption and consumerism, on that view, themselves are enough to reproduce and legitimate the system, no matter what "ideology" you happen to be committed to. In that case, not abstract ideas, beliefs, ideologies, or philosophical systems, but rather the immanent practices of daily life now occupy the functional position of "ideology" in its other larger systemic sense. And if so, this development can clearly serve as one explanation for the waning power of the Utopian ideologies of high modernism as well. Indeed, Tafuri explicitly associates the demiurgic value of architectural planning in the modern masters with the Keynesian ideal of the control of the future. In both versions, "Utopia" is the dream of "a 'rational' domination of the future, the elimination of the risk it brings with it" (*A&U*, p. 52): "Even for Le Corbusier the absolute of form is the complete realization of a constant victory over the uncertainty of the future" (p. 129). It is therefore logical enough that both these ultimate middle-class ideologies or Utopias—Keynesianism *and* high modernism—should disappear together, and that their concrete "critique" should be less a matter of intellectual self-consciousness than simply a working out of history itself.

But "ideology" has a somewhat different focus in Tafuri's schematic overview of bourgeois architectural thinking from the dissolution of the Baroque to our own time, where these varied aesthetic Utopias are analyzed in terms of something closer to a Hegelian "ruse of reason" or of History itself. Their Utopian form thus proves to be an instrument in the edification of a business system and the new dynamism of capital; whatever content they claimed in themselves, their concrete effects, their more fundamental function, lay in the systematic destruction of the past. Thus the emergence of secular conceptions of the city in the eighteenth century is primarily to be read as a way of clearing away the older culture: "the deliberate abstraction of Enlightenment theories of the city served . . . to destroy baroque schemes of city planning and development" (p. 8). In much the same way, the dawn of modernism proper—the moment when ideology is overtly transformed into Utopia, when "ideology had to negate itself as such, break its own crystallized forms and throw itself entirely into the 'construction of the future'" (p. 50)—this supreme moment of Freud and Nietzsche, of Weber and Simmel, and of the birth of high modernism in all the arts, was in reality for Tafuri a purely destructive operation in which residual ideologies and archaic social forms were systematically dissolved. The new Utopianism of high modernism thus unwittingly and against the very spirit of its own revolutionary and Utopian affirmations prepared the terrain for the omnipotence of the fully "rationalized" technocratic plan, for the universal planification of what was to become the total system of multinational capital: "the unmasking of the idols that obstructed the way to a global rationalization of the productive universe and its social dominion became the new historical task of the intellectual" (p. 51). It also became the historic mission of the various cultural avant-gardes themselves, for which, in reality although not according to their own manifestos, "the autonomy of formal construction" has as its deepest practical function "to plan the disappearance of the subject, to cancel the anguish caused by the pathetic (or ridiculous) resistance of the individual to the structures of domination that close in upon him or her" (p. 73). Whatever avant-garde or architectural aesthetic Utopias thought they were intent on achieving, therefore, in the real world of capital and in their effective practice, those ends are dialectically reversed and serve essentially to reinforce the technocratic total control of the new system of the bureaucratic society of planned consumption.

We may now return to the beginnings of Tafuri's story in the eighteenth century. The Enlightenment attempt to think urbanism in some new and more fully rational way generates two irreconcilable alternatives: one path is that of architecture as the "instrument of social equilibrium," and "geometric silence of Durand's formally codified building types," "the uniformity ensured by preconstituted formal systems" (p. 13); the other is that of a "science of sensations" (p. 11), a kind of "excessive symbolism" (p. 13) which we may interpret as the conception of a libidinal resistance within the system, the breakthrough of Desire into the grids of power and control. These two great Utopian antitheses—Saint-Simon versus Fourier, if you like, or Lenin versus Marcuse—are, then, for Tafuri the ideological double-bind of a thinking imprisoned in capitalist relations. They are at once unmasked in Piranesi's contemporaneous nightmarish synthesis of the Campo Marzio and are also, unexpectedly, given a longer lease on life in the New World, where, with the open frontier and in the absence of feudalism, the new urban synthesis of Washington, D.C., retains a vitality henceforth forbidden to European efforts.

Interestingly enough, in our present context, these two alternatives also roughly correspond to the analyses of Adorno and Barthes respectively. The first Utopian alternative, that of rationalization, will little by little formulate its program in terms of overcoming the opposition between whole and part, between urban plan and individual architectural monument, between the molar and the molecular, between the "urban organism as a whole" and the "elementary cell" or building blocks of the individual building (Hilberseimer). But it is precisely this "unified field theory" of the macro and the micro, toward which the urbanistic work of a Corbusier strives, which is projected, in Adorno's book, by Schoenberg's twelve-tone system, the ultimate abolition of the gap between counterpoint and harmony, between overall form and the dynamics of the individual musical "parole" or theme. But Schoenberg's extraordinary synthesis is sterile, and in architecture the "unified field theory" destroys the individual work or building as such: "the single building is no longer an 'object'; it is only the place in which the elementary assemblage of single cells assumes physical form; since these cells are elements reproducible ad infinitum, they conceptually embody the prime structure of a production line that excludes the old concepts of 'place' or 'space'" (p. 105). This Utopian impulse has then ended up rationalizing the object world more extensively and ferociously than anything Ford or Taylor might have done on their own momentum.

Yet the second, or libidinal, strategy is no less "ideological" in its ultimate results: Barthes's intellectual trajectory is complicated, and I will not take the time here to insert him neatly back into this scheme (although I think something like this could be done). Suffice it to observe that, following Benjamin, Tafuri sees this second, libidinal strategy in its emergence in Baudelaire as having unexpected subjective consequences which harmonize with the objective external planification achieved above: "Baudelaire had discovered that the commercialization of the poetic product can be accentuated by the poet's very attempt to free himself from his objective conditions" (p. 92). The new vanguard subjectivity, in other words, ends up training the consumer for life in the industrial city, teaching "the ideology of the correct use of the city" (p. 84), freeing the aesthetic consumer from "objects that were offered to judgment" and substituting "a process to be lived and used as such" (p. 101). This particular strategy now prolongs itself into, and revitalizes itself in, the postmodernist ideologies and aesthetics of the present period, denounced by Tafuri in a memorable passage:

Thus the city is considered in terms of a suprastructure. Indeed art is now called upon to give the city a suprastructural guise. Pop art, op art, analysis of the urban "imageability," and the "prospective aesthetic" converge in this objective. The contradictions of the contemporary city are resolved in multivalent images, and by figuratively exalting that formal complexity they are dissimulated. If read with adequate standards of judgment this formal complexity is nothing other than the explosion of the irremediable dissonances that escape the plan of advanced capital. The recovery of the concept of art thus serves this new cover-up role. It is true that whereas industrial design takes a lead position in technological production and conditions its quality in view of an increase in consumption, pop art, reutilizing the residues and castoffs of that production, takes its place in the rear guard. But this is the exact reflection of the twofold request now made to the techniques of visual communication. Art which refuses to take its place in the vanguard of the production cycle actually demonstrates that the process of consumption tends to the infinite. Indeed, even the rejects, sublimated into useless or nihilist objects which bear a new value of use, enter into the production-consumption cycle, if only through the back door.

This art that deliberately places itself in the rear guard is also indicative of the refusal to come to terms with the contradictions of the city and resolve them completely; to transform the city into a totally organized machine without useless squanderings of an archaic character or generalized dysfunction.

In this phase it is necessary to persuade the public that the contradictions, imbalances, and chaos typical of the contemporary city are inevitable. Indeed the public must be convinced that this chaos contains an unexplored richness, unlimited utilizable possibilities, and qualities of the "game" now made into new fetishes for society. (pp. 137, 139)

The power of such negative critiques of ideology (which construe ideology exclusively in terms of "false consciousness") lies in the assumption that everything that does not effectively disrupt the social reproduction of the system may be considered as part and parcel of the reproduction of that system. The anxieties provoked in almost everyone by such an implacable and absolute position are probably healthy and therapeutic in one way or another. As I have begun to suggest before, however, the real problem in such an analysis lies elsewhere, in the assumption that "social reproduction" in late capitalism takes much the same form as in the earlier period of high modernism, and that what some of us call the "postmoderns" simply replicate the old modernist solutions at lower levels of intensity and originality. Thus Philip Johnson's "ambiguous eclecticism ends up as mere jugglery" (MA, p. 397); "the work of Louis Kahn and the British architect James Stirling represent two opposite attempts to breathe life into a seemingly moribund art" (MA, p. 400); Robert Venturi's *Complexity and Contradiction in Architecture* flattens out the new-critical concepts of ambiguity and contradiction, dehistoricizing them and emptying them of all their tragic (and properly high modernist) tension, with a view toward "justifying personal planning choices rather more equivocal than ambiguous" (T&H, p. 213).

Yet there would seem to be a certain inconsistency in the reproach that the newer architects fail to achieve even that tragic tension which was itself considered to be Utopian and ideological in the masters. The other fact of this inconsistency can then be detected in the consonance and profound historical kinship between Tafuri's analysis of modernism and the onslaughts of the postmodernists, most notably Venturi himself, a critique which goes well beyond the usual themes of the hubris of central planning,[10] the single-function conception of space and the puritanism of the streamlining abhorrence of ornament. Venturi's analysis, particularly in *Learning from Las Vegas* (1972), centers specifically on the dialectic (and the contradiction) between the building and the city, between architecture and urbanism, which forms one of the major strands in the historiography of the Italian theorist. The monumental duck of the international style—like Mallarmé's *Livre*, like Bayreuth, like *Finnegans Wake*, or like Kandinsky's mystical painting—proposes itself, as we have already suggested, as a radically different, revolutionary or subversive enclave from which little by little the whole surrounding fabric of fallen social relations is to be regenerated and transformed. Yet in order to stage itself as a *foyer* of this kind, the "duck" must first radically separate itself from that environment in which it stands; it thereby slowly comes to be, by virtue of that very inaugural disjunction, that constitutive self-definition and isolation, not a building but a *sculpture*. After the fashion of Barthes's concept of connotation, the duck ends up—far from emitting a message with a radically new content—simply designating itself and signifying itself, celebrating its own disconnection as a message in its own right.

Whatever else may be said about the architecture of postmodernism—and however it is to be judged politically and historically—it seems important to recognize that it does not seek to do *that* but rather something very different. It may no longer embody the Utopian ideology of high modernism, may indeed in that sense be vacuous of any Utopian or protopolitical impulse, while still, as the suspicious prefix "post" suggests, remaining in some kind of parasitic relationship with the extinct high modernism it repudiates; yet what must be explored is the possibility that with postmodernism a whole new *aesthetic* is in the process of emerging, an aesthetic significantly distinct from that of the previous era.

The latter—high modernism—can perhaps most effectively be characterized (following Althusser's notion of "expressive causality") as an aesthetic of identity or of organic unification. To demarcate the postmodernist aesthetic from this one, two familiar themes may serve as points of reference: the dialectic of inside and outside and the question of ornament or decoration. For Le Corbusier, as is well known, "the plan proceeds from within to without" in such a way that the outside of the building expresses its interior; stylistic homogeneity is thus here achieved by unifying these two opposites, or, better still, by assimilating one of them—the exterior—to the other. As for ornament, its "contradiction" with the reality of the wall itself is overcome by the hygienic *exclusion* of the offending term.[11] What may now briefly be observed is that Robert Venturi's conception of the "decorated shed" seeks, on the contrary, to reinforce these oppositions and thereby to valorize *contradiction* itself (in a stronger way than his earlier terminology of "complexity" or "ambiguity" might suggest). The philosophical formulation of this very different aesthetic move might be found in the (properly poststructural or postmodernist) idea that "difference relates": an aesthetic of homogeneity is here displaced, less in the name of a random heterogeneity, a set of inert differences randomly coexisting, than in the service of a new kind of perception for which tension, contradiction, the registering of the incompatible and the clashing, is in and of itself a strong mode of relating two incommensurable elements, poles, or realities. If, as I believe, something like this characterizes the specific internal logic of postmodernism, it must be seen at the very least as constituting an original aesthetic and one quite distinct from the high modernism from which it seeks to disengage itself.

It will no doubt be observed that the symbolic act of high modernism, which seeks to resolve contradiction by stylistic fiat (even though its resolution may remain merely symbolic), is of a very different order and quality from that of a postmodernism that simply ratifies the contradictions and fragmented chaos all around it by way of an intensified perception of, a mesmerized and well-nigh hallucinogenic fascination with, those very contradictions themselves (contenting itself with eliminating the affective charge of pathos, of the tragic, or of anxiety, which characterized the modern movement). In this sense, no doubt, Marx's early critique of Hegel's theory of religion retains its force for postmodernism: "self-conscious man, insofar as he has recognized and superseded the spiritual world . . . then confirms it again in this alienated form and presented it as his true existence; he reestablishes it and claims to *be at home in his other being.*"[12]

I must add, to this juxtaposition, my feeling that *moralizing* judgments on either of these aesthetics are always the most unsatisfactory way to reach some ultimate evaluation of them; my own perspective here is a historicist one, for which any position on postmodernism must begin by being a self-critique and a judgment on *ourselves*, since this is the moment when we find ourselves and, like it or not, this aesthetic is a part of us.

That is, however, not the most important point to be made in the present context. One of the more annoying and scandalous habits of dialectical thought is indeed its identification of opposites, and its tendency to send off back to back seemingly opposed positions on the grounds that both share and are determined and limited by a common problematic, or, to use a more familiar language, represent the two intolerable options of a single double-bind. One is tempted to see something of the sort at work here, in the opposition between Tafuri's cultural pessimism, with all its rigor and ideological asceticism, and the complacent free play of a postmodernism content to juggle the pregiven tokens of contemporary social reality, from which even the nostalgic memory of earlier commitments to radical change has vanished without a trace.

Is it possible that these two positions are in fact the same, and that as different as they may at first seem, both rest on the conviction that nothing new can be done, no fundamental changes can be made, within the massive being of late capitalism? What is different is that Tafuri's thought lives this situation in a rigorous and self-conscious stoicism, whereas the practitioners and ideologues of postmodernism relax within it, inventing modes of perception in order to "be at home" in the same impossible extremity: changes of valence, the substitution of a plus sign for a minus, on the same equation.

Perhaps, in that case, something is to be said for Lefebvre's call for a politics of space and for the search for a properly Gramscian architecture after all.

Notes

1. Manfredo Tafuri, *Theories and History of Architecture*, trans. Giorgio Verrecchia (New York, 1980), p. iii. Hereafter referred to as *T&H*.
2. Manfredo Tafuri, *Architecture and Utopia*, 2d ed., trans. Barbara Luigia La Penta (Cambridge, Mass., 1980). Hereafter referred to as *A&U*.
3. Karl Marx and Friedrich Engels, *The German Ideology*, ed. R. Pascal (New York, 1947).
4. Manfredo Tafuri and Francesco Dal Co, *Modern Architecture* (New York, 1979), p. 342. Hereafter referred to as *MA*.
5. See Daniel Bell's two books, *Postindustrial Society* (New York, 1973) and *The Cultural Contradictions of Capitalism* (New York, 1976).
6. The most systematic and powerful exposition of this theory is to be found in Ernest Mandel, *Late Capitalism* (London, 1978), on which I draw heavily here.
7. Karl Marx, *Contribution to a Critique of Political Economy* (New York, 1970), p. 21.
8. Karl Marx, *Capital*, vol. 1, trans. Ben Fowkes (London, 1976), p. 172.
9. See Jürgen Habermas, "Modernity versus Postmodernity," *New German Critique* 22 (Winter 1981), pp. 3–18.
10. The critique of central planning, as in Peter Blake, as powerful and persuasive as it is, seems to me extremely ambiguous for the following reason: a perfectly correct and well-documented thesis of this kind can *also* be the occasion for the production of, or investment by, a whole ideology or metaphysics, most notably in the binary opposition between intention or plan and tradition or organic growth. This ideology is already present in Christopher Alexander, "A City Is Not a Tree," but its full-blown transformation into a metaphysic can be observed most dramatically in Deleuze and Guattari's "Rhizome" (in *Mille plateaux*). In this form, of course, it recapitulates the oldest counterrevolutionary position of all, that of Edmund Burke in the *Reflections on the Revolution in France*, where Jacobin hubris is counterposed against the slow and organic growth of social life. On the political level, the Left traditions include a number of counterpositions that work against the emergence of such a stark and ideological opposition, especially in concepts of federation and the "withering away of the state" (the Paris Commune), of *autogestion* or worker's self-management, and of council communism. But in the area of architecture or urbanism it is rather hard to see what form such counterpositions might take. Least persuasive, to my mind, is the idea that people will rebuild their own dwellings as they go along (see, for example, P. Boudon, *Lived-In Architecture* [Cambridge, Mass., 1972], where the idea that Le Corbusier would have approved of all this, let alone intended it to happen that way, seems most disingenuous indeed). I have been attracted by Rem Koolhaas's *Delirious New York* (New York, 1978) for a rather different (and highly idiosyncratic) way of cutting through this ideological double-bind; he *historicizes* the dilemma by transforming "planning" into the unique and historical decision, in 1811, to impose the "grid" on Manhattan. From this single "centralized" decision, then, both the anarchy and the urban classicism (streets and blocks) at once develop.
11. A somewhat different example of such homogenizing repression can be found in Venturi's account of Frank Lloyd Wright's exclusion of the *diagonal*, in *Complexity and Contradiction in Architecture* (New York, 1977), p. 52.
12. Karl Marx, *Early Writings*, ed. T. B. Bottomore (New York, 1964), p. 210.

Alberto Pérez-Gómez   **Introduction to *Architecture and the Crisis of Modern Science*** (Cambridge: MIT

Press, 1983)

As its title indicates, Alberto Pérez-Gómez's 1983 book (which reviews the process by which the mystical, numerological uses of geometry in buildings were transformed into the technical, utilitarian ones Pérez-Gómez sees as dominant since J.-N.-L. Durand instrumentalized theory at the beginning of the nineteenth century) is a juxtaposition of architecture theory and Edmund Husserl's *The Crisis of European Science*.[1] In Husserl's phenomenology, it is modern science itself that is laid open to question, a science that begins with the Greek idea of knowledge and truth and ends with the development of that thought in what Husserl sees as a misguided rationality cut off from its roots in the empirical *Lebenswelt*. While this modern, Western conception of reason presupposes that the world is a rationally structured system and therefore accessible to knowledge on the grounds of our own similarly structured, rational knowledge, Husserl argues that such a conception puts the validity and authority of reason above place and time, in a purely ideational realm, not in being as we actually experience it through our bodily perceptions. The modern conception of reason has proved successful only in the positive sciences and in the technological conquest of nature, where reason becomes utterly instrumental, an unquestioned means to the end of mastering the environment and fellow human beings. Husserl's (and Pérez-Gómez's) science is an opaque and occlusive one wherein knowledge and truth are themselves enfolded with illusion and repression.

see Frampton
(**367–369**)

compare Frampton
(**366 ff**)

Phenomenological criticism in architecture — and in particular what might be called the "Essex school" of Dalibor Vesely, Pérez-Gómez, and others, whose program is put forth under the banner of Husserl's "return to things" and Maurice Merleau-Ponty's notion of the primacy of perception[2] — is an important therapeutic corrective to the often overly bleak, cerebral, and "antihumanist" machinations of architecture theory, an attempt to restore the sensory plenitude of lived experience. Phenomenology has always seen itself as the bearer of humanist values. Vesely (whose influence on architecture theory since 1968 has been mainly through his teaching) has argued again and again that architectural knowledge is grounded not in abstract, mechanistic principles but in representations derived from the experience of things.

But the Essex school seems to stake its hopes on the insertion of individuality as *Dasein* over and against the collective, transindividual phenomena of modern history: "It is the development of modern culture itself which led to the development of phenomenology," Vesely instructs. "The idea that the unfolding of culture engenders phenomenology should not be taken lightly, because phenomenology is a much less calculated response to a recognized condition than one might think. Rather, we are involved in a certain way of living through *a situatedness which we are experiencing as individuals* in culture."[3] Or Pérez-Gómez: "Technology substitutes a 'picture' for the world of our primary experience. However mutable and historically determined this world of primary experience may be, phenomenology discloses it as one where the universal and the specific are given *simultaneously* in the mystery of perception, in the space *between* Being and Becoming."[4]

One cannot but agree that in modernity there is a growing contradiction between a phenomenological description of an individual's lived experience and a structural model of the conditions of existence of that experience. But from Pérez-Gómez's perspective, any interpretive study that analyzes the architectural work for historically specific functions, forms, and structural peculiarities runs directly counter to the effort to simultaneously universalize and repersonalize experience. It comes to seem that if an individual's experience is "authentic" in terms of some phenomenologically disclosed "mystery," then it no longer coincides with the place and time in which it takes place.

For Pérez-Gómez, the errors of architecture are effects of an increasing distance from some original mystery; and technology — which he links with "the prevalent obsession with mathematical certainty in all its various forms: design methodologies, typologies, linguistic rules of formalism, any sort of explicit or disguised functionalism" — plays the lead role in the sapping and distortion of that mystery. But one may suspect that the talismanic use of terms like "mystery," "poetry," and "experience," and their opposition to the monovalent role alloted to technology, are impoverished and unhistorical, recognizing neither the plurality nor the historical variability of technology's actual uses.

If technology is not simply the meaninglessness of being and brute function that Pérez-Gómez makes it out to be, if technology is, rather, counted among those contexts that architecture theory characteristically mediates with considerations of a more obviously aesthetic or bodily kind, then the "proper" use of the technological explanation may well be to further reveal the poverties, outworn idealistic pretenses, and "excessive formalism of systems" that Pérez-Gómez himself combats. One might go so far as to assert that the theorization of the technological fact has as its vocation, or at least its ultimate theoretical service, the demystification of the work of architecture — that is, the opening up of the work to a whole new range of factors and forces that overdetermine the work and whose marks are inscribed in its very forms. But as such the technological explanation tends to recast questions of inspiration, intuition, poetry, creative impulse, and the like in a materialist (anti-idealist but also anti-spiritualist) form, which Pérez-Gómez finds deterministic.

To some extent, the unaccommodating opposition of "science" — rational objectivity, technology, and functionalism — to "experience" — mystery, poetry, and Being — dooms the phenomenologists to just the polarizations they aim to heal. With this, Pérez-Gómez's phenomenology as an interpretive *position* becomes apparent, for within its purview the value of science is decided in advance, and architecture's experiences are as much imposed as historically discovered.

Notes

1.   Edmund Husserl, *The Crisis of European Science and Transcendental Phenomenology* (1936), trans. David Carr (Evanston: Northwestern University Press, 1970).

2.   After his move to England in 1968, Dalibor Vesely's teaching at Essex was influential on an important group of architecture theorists including Peter Carl, Marco Frascari, Daniel

Libeskind, as well as Alberto Pérez-Gómez. *Architecture and the Crisis of Modern Science* was originally presented as a doctoral dissertation under the direction of Vesely and Joseph Rykwert. See Dalibor Vesely, "Architecture and the Conflict of Representation," *AA Files* 8 (January 1985); and "Architecture and the Poetics of Representation," *Daidalos* 25 (September 1987).

3.   Dalibor Vesely, "On the Relevance of Phenomenology," in *Form; Being; Absence. Pratt Journal of Architecture* 2 (Spring 1988), p. 59; emphasis added.

4.   Alberto Pérez-Gómez, introduction to *Architecture, Ethics, and Technology*, ed. Louise Pelletier and Alberto Pérez-Gómez (Montreal: McGill-Queen's University Press, 1994), p. 5. See also Alberto Pérez-Gómez, *Polyphilo, or The Dark Forest Revisited: An Erotic Epiphany of Architecture* (Cambridge: MIT Press, 1992).

The creation of order in a mutable and finite world is the ultimate purpose of man's thought and actions. There was probably never human perception outside a framework of categories; the ideal and the real, the general and the specific, are "given" in perception, constituting the intentional realm that is the realm of existence. Perception is our primary form of knowing and does not exist apart from the a priori of the body's structure and its engagement in the world. This "owned body," as Merleau-Ponty would say, is the locus of all formulations about the world; it not only occupies space and time but consists of spatiality and temporality. The body has a dimension. Through motion it polarizes external reality and becomes our instrument of meaning; its experience is therefore "geo-metrical." The extension of this "geometry of experience," in Husserl's phrase, beyond the body's (and the mind's) spatiality constitutes the thrust of architectural design, the creation of an order resonant with the body's own.

The historical awareness and utilization of geometrical form among architects has by no means resulted in a consistent or universal approach to architecture itself. In fact, the malaise from which architecture suffers today can be traced to the collusion between architecture and its use of geometry and number as it developed in the early modern period. An analysis of the architectural intentions of the seventeenth and eighteenth centuries in relation to the changing world view ushered in by Galilean science and Newton's natural philosophy is necessary before we can understand the dilemmas still confronted by architects. Such an analysis becomes particularly significant in light of the prevalent obsession with mathematical certainty in its various forms: design methodologies, typologies, linguistic rules of formalism, any sort of explicit or disguised functionalism. Contemporary architects, who encounter a proliferation of these forms whenever they make design decisions, find it difficult to reconcile mathematics' demands for invariance (the *mathemata*) with their conception of architecture as an art rather than a science.

The assumption that architecture can derive its meaning from functionalism, formal games of combinations, the coherence or rationality of style understood as ornamental language, or the use of type as a generative structure in design marks the evolution of Western architecture during the past two centuries. This assumption, whose implication is no less than the algebraization or "functionalization" of architectural theory as a whole, the reduction of architecture to a rational theory, began to gain ascendancy toward the middle of the seventeenth century, culminating in the theories of Jacques-Nicolas-Louis Durand and his critics. Durand's functionalized theory is already a theory of architecture in the contemporary sense: replete with the modern architect's obsessions, thoroughly specialized, and composed of laws of an exclusively prescriptive character that purposely avoid all reference to philosophy or cosmology. Theory thus reduced to a self-referential system whose elements must be combined through mathematical logic must pretend that its values, and therefore its meaning, are derived from the system itself. This formulation, however, constitutes its most radical limitation since any reference to the perceived world is considered subjective, lacking in real value.[1]

      This fictionalization of architectural theory implies its transformation into a set of operational rules, into a tool of an exclusively technological character. Its main concern becomes how to build in an efficient and economical manner, while avoiding questions related to why one builds and whether such activity is justified in the existential context.[2] The inception of functionalism coincided, not surprisingly, with the rise of positivism in the physical and human sciences. This set of circumstances, according to Edmund Husserl, marks the beginning of the crisis of European science.[3]

      When a physician talks about a crisis in the condition of a patient, he is describing a moment when it is unclear whether the patient will survive or succumb. In a true sense, this is now the condition of Western culture. In the last century and a half, man has done his utmost to define the human condition and ironically has lost the capacity to come to terms with it; he is unable to reconcile the eternal and immutable dimension of ideas with the finite and mutable dimension of everyday life.[4] Moreover, contemporary man, while recognizing this dilemma, seems incapable of deriving from this tension the ultimate meaning of his existence.[5]

      The elucidation of this crisis marks the writing of the most profound thinkers of our century, but perhaps only Husserl has been able to reveal its unique character.[6] According to Husserl, the beginning of the crisis coincides with the end of classical geometry, still a geometry of the *Lebenswelt*, the world as lived, and the appearance of non-Euclidean geometries, which occurred around 1800. This development in mathematics augured the possibility that the external world of man could be effectively controlled and dominated by a functionalized theory subsumed by technology.[7] One result of the crisis has been an unprecedented inversion of priorities: Truth—demonstrable through the laws of science—constitutes the fundamental basis upon which human decisions are made over and above "reality," which is always ambiguous and accessible only through the realm of "poetics."[8] Today, theory in any discipline is generally identified with methodology; it has become a specialized set of prescriptive rules concerned with technological values, that is, with process rather than ultimate objectives, a process that seeks maximum efficiency with minimum effort. Once life itself began to be regarded as process, whether biological or teleological, theory was able to disregard ethical considerations in favor of applicability. Modern theory, leaning on the early nineteenth-century model of the physico-mathematical sciences with their utopian ideals, has designated the most crucial human problems illegitimate, beyond the transformation and control of the material world.[9]

      According to Husserl, there are two dimensions from which every system derives its meaning: (1) the *formal*, or syntactic, dimension, which corresponds to the structure of the system itself, that is, to the relations among its elements; and (2) the *transcendental*, or semantic, dimension, that is, the reference of each element to the reality of the *Lebenswelt*, including its historic constitution.[10] Although not without difficulty, Western thought managed to reconcile these two dimensions of logic until about 1800. The radical ambiguities of existence were always explained by acknowledging a residual but most important *mythos*.[11] It has only been during the last two centuries that the transcendental dimension of meaning has been questioned. Culminating perhaps in the recent structuralist approach to the human sciences, Western thought seems to be floundering in the excessive formalism of systems, unable to accept the reality of specific phenomena. The already classic failure of C. Norberg-Schulz's *Intentions in Architecture* and other applications of linguistics to architectural theory over the past ten years reveal a passion for structural rules and their limitations. In terms of architecture, structuralism has consciously rejected the importance of the transcendental dimension, thereby denying the importance of the historical horizon of meaning.

The problem that determines most explicitly our crisis, therefore, is that the conceptual framework of the sciences is not compatible with reality.[12] The atomic theory of the universe may be true, but it hardly explains real issues of human behavior. The fundamental axiom of the sciences since 1800, as well as of the humanities, has been "invariance," which rejects, or at least is unable to cope with, the richness and ambiguity of symbolic thought.[13] This attitude is endemic to the modern crisis and is reinforced by those scientists and intellectuals who still believe in a utopian future, who maintain that regardless of present limitations, a time will come when their specific disciplines will arrive at a full understanding of phenomena and thereby become at last truly meaningful for mankind.

The consequences of all this for architectural theory are enormous. The poetical content of reality, the a priori of the world, which is the ultimate frame of reference for any truly meaningful architecture, is hidden beneath a thick layer of formal explanations. Because positivistic thought has made it a point to exclude mystery and poetry, contemporary man lives with the illusion of the infinite power of reason. He has forgotten his fragility and his capacity for wonder, generally assuming that all the phenomena of his world, from water or fire to perception or human behavior, have been "explained." For many architects, myth and poetry are generally considered synonymous with dreams and lunacy, while reality is deemed equivalent to prosaic scientific theories. In other words, mathematical logic has been substituted for metaphor as a model of thought. Art can be beautiful, of course, but only seldom is it understood as a profound form of knowledge, as a genuine, intersubjective interpretation of reality. And architecture, particularly, must never partake of the alleged escapism of the other fine arts; it has to be, before anything else, a paradigm of efficient and economical construction.

This inversion of priorities that originated in the scientific and philosophical speculations of the seventeenth century has never, at a popular level, been corrected. Although Cartesian dualism is no longer a viable philosophical model, faith in mathematics and logic as the only legitimate way of thinking is still commonplace. Decisions concerning planning or the establishment of new towns, for example, continue to be made on the basis of statistics. The immediate perception of the reality of quality of place is disregarded as a subjective interpretation of traditional urbanism. The evident shortcomings of such a view could not be more dramatic; our cities are becoming a vast world village where the external reality of man is at odds with man himself and whose reason for being is to express a mute universal process embodying the values of technology rather than to establish a meaningful framework for man's finite existence. The well-known failures of modern planning continue to be a source of embarrassment. And still the modern professional waits for a set of objective and universal standards, either formal, ideological, or functional, that will determine his design and contribute to truly meaningful buildings.

Many years have passed since architects began their search for a universal theory grounded in absolute rational certainty. Gottfried Semper, for one, drawing on some of the insights first expressed by Durand, postulated functionalism as a fundamental premise of architectural intentionality. In those of his writings that appeared toward the middle of the nineteenth century, Semper clearly attempted to make the process of design analogous to the resolution of an algebraic equation. The "variables" represented the manifold aspects of reality that architecture had to take into account; the solution was simply a "function" of these variables.[14] This reductionist strategy has since become the fundamental framework of architectural theory and practice, whether one examines the forms of structural determinism or the more subtle attempts to utilize psychological, sociological, or even aesthetic variables. More recently, various sophisticated methodologies and even computers have been applied to design, always failing, however, to come to terms with the essential question of meaning in architecture.[15]

The main problem of architectural intentionality is the genesis of form. Prior to the nineteenth century, the architect's concern for *mathemata* was never merely formal. Even the traditional Vitruvian categories: *firmitas*, *commoditas*, and *venustas*, were not perceived as independent entities, as values in their own right. Architectural intentionality was transcendental, necessarily symbolic.[16] Its mode of operation was therefore metaphor, not mathematical equations. Not only did form not follow function, but form could fulfill its role as a primary means of reconciliation, one that referred ultimately to the essential ambiguity of the human condition.

A simplistic view of human experience, derived from the projection of scientific models onto human reality, exemplified by certain aspects of behaviorism and positivistic psychology, has hampered our understanding of the essential continuity between thought and action, between mind and body.[17] Because architectural theory is assumed to imply absolute rationality, it has been considered capable of standing on its own, free of all relations to fundamental philosophical questions.[18] Subject to the values of technology, its interest is not in meaning, but in a conceptual or material efficiency dominating design and construction. This naturally has created a peculiar tension between theory and practice. Theory may work smoothly on a formal level, but it is unable to come to terms with reality. Correlatively, practice has been transformed into a process of production without existential meaning, clearly defined aims, or reference to human values. Or else practice has ignored its connections to theory in order to recover its poetic dimension. This last situation is evident in some of the best examples of contemporary architecture. Obviously, certain buildings by Le Corbusier have very little to do with stated theoretical intentions.

The illusion remains, however, that practice can be reduced to a system of rational prescriptive rules. This is particularly evident in architectural education and obstructs our perception of how the relation between theory and practice operated until the end of the eighteenth century. This uniquely modern relation should not be taken for granted; it epitomizes the crisis of contemporary architecture. Consequently, we must examine its historical origin, studying the process of the transformation of theory into a set of technical rules (*ars fabricandi*) and the implicit intentions in other works related to architecture. An analysis of the changing meaning of geometry and number for architectural intentionality during the seventeenth and eighteenth centuries will illustrate the development of the mathematization of theory.

The Mythical Horizon

Geometry and number, prototypes of the ideal, since time immemorial have been symbols of the highest order, their immutability contrasting with the fluid and changing reality of the sublunar world. The concept of *mathesis* appeared in preclassical Greek culture around the seventh century B.C. It referred to what could be taught and learned: the invariable, the familiar, the accessible; its exemplar was number. *Mathesis* was also the first step toward *theoria*, the apprehension of reality at a distance; as such, it was the first symbol of reality, becoming the basic element in a coherent conceptual system that enabled man to disengage himself from the involvement of his embodied being in ritual, allowing him to come to terms with the external world and his own existence within an independent universe of discourse.

Originally, the knowledge of *mathesis* was confined to the magician. Only he dared to manipulate numerical entities, affecting the world on a level separated from physical reality. Traditional numbers were always material entities, never purely formal. To engage them was equivalent to tampering with the order of the real world, a powerful form of magic.

Positing the invariable in the universe of perception corresponded to ancient astronomical thinking. It was in the supralunar sphere that absolute truths of Euclidean geometry were to be found. Astronomers discerned in the heavens logicomathematical systems, and throughout most of human history such invariable laws were perceived as transcendental symbols. Astronomy was never free of ontological presuppositions; it was traditionally astrobiology, with implications of a magical or religious nature.[19] Reality was perceived as an organic totality directed by the regularity of the heavens, and knowledge was synonymous with the elucidation of the transcendental order of the cosmos.

Before the seventeenth century, the primacy of perception as the ultimate evidence of knowledge was never questioned. *Mathesis* explicitly maintained its symbolic connotations, and the hierarchical structure of the cosmos established by Aristotle remained valid. It was a world of predominantly mythical character, qualitatively different from our present universe of precision.

The discovery of *theoria* in Greece permitted the beginnings of architectural theory, a *logos* of architecture. Such theory, however, always contained the necessary complement of *mythos*, maintaining it explicitly until the end of the Renaissance and implicitly during the seventeenth and eighteenth centuries. Alberti postulated a distance between theory and practice, between design and real building. Vignola and others, during the second half of the sixteenth century, emphasized the prescriptive character of the rules of the classical orders rather than their meaning. Nonetheless, the Renaissance was a profoundly traditional world. Liberated from theological determinism, the architect became conscious of his power to transform the physical world. He was often a *magus*, but his intention was reconciliatory; art was a privileged form of metaphysics—metaphysics made into matter. Architecture was not concerned exclusively with the cathedral or temple, but the physical configuration of the new human world had to conform to the *mathesis* that linked microcosm and macrocosm.

During the Renaissance, theory was not merely a series of technical precepts but was underlined by metaphysical preoccupations often implicit in the mathematical rules themselves. The mythical, ancient world embodied in the writings of Vitruvius and the visible ruins was never lost sight of. In this Aristotelian world, there could be no split between architectural theory and practice. The former maintained its role as the elucidation and justification of the latter, while practice retained its primordial meaning as *poiesis* (not merely *praxis*), as a form of reconciliation between man and the world, which were perceived as the two poles of a sacred, living totality.

Geometry descended from the heavens and lost its sacred character as a result of the epistemological revolution brought about by Galileo's speculations during the first decades of the seventeenth century.[20] The "spatiality" that referred to the immediate network of intentions relating man's embodied being with the *Lebenswelt*, and that allowed for the apprehension of his place in a hierarchical order, could now be replaced by geometrical space.[21] At this historical juncture, geometry and number were able to become instruments for the technical control of practical operations and, eventually, for an effective technological domination of the world. Through the new science of mechanics, man began to subject matter to his will.

The Rational Horizon

The present work argues that modern architecture, and the crisis it faces, has its roots in a historical process touched off by the Galilean revolution, a process whose development is marked by two great transformations, the first of which occurred toward the end of the seventeenth century, and the second, toward the end of the eighteenth.

In the first transformation, the assumption, which had been inherited from medieval and Renaissance cosmology, that number and geometry were a *scientia universalis*, the link between the human and the divine, was finally brought into question by philosophy and science. At the same time, technique and the crafts were freed from their traditional magical associations. In architecture, this laid the basis for a new approach. Architects began to consider their discipline a technical challenge, whose problems could be solved with the aid of two conceptual tools, number and geometry.

But in the eighteenth century, the transcendental dimension of human thought and action was sustained through the myth of Divine Nature. This myth lay at the root of Newtonian natural philosophy. The eighteenth century rejected as fiction the closed geometrical systems of seventeenth-century philosophers, but accepted Newton's empirical methods as universally valid. The influence of Newton paved the way for the systematization and mathematization of knowledge, a knowledge that held that immutable, mathematical laws could be derived from the observation of natural phenomena, and that would eventually take on the form of nineteenth-century positivism. Implicit in eighteenth-century Newtonianism, though to the modern mind it may seem thoroughly empiricist, was a Platonic cosmology, usually complemented by some form of deism, in which geometry and number had transcendental value and power in and of themselves. Architectural theory absorbed the fundamental intentions of Newtonian science, and in doing so, it sidetracked earlier developments.

Around 1800 a second great transformation took place. Faith and reason were truly divorced. Scientific thought came to be seen as the only serious and legitimate interpretation of reality, denying any need for metaphysics. Euclidean geometry was functionalized. Infinitesimal calculus was purged of its residual symbolic content. Geometry and mathematics were now purely formal disciplines, devoid of meaning, value, or power except as instruments, as tools of technological intentionality.[22]

It is around this time that the great obsessions of contemporary architecture were first clearly expressed. Practice was supposed to follow theory since theory now assumed that one day, through the limits of mathematical reason, it would thoroughly control design and building. Eventually, the split between thinking and doing became a critical problem. The belief in the symbolic richness of the external world, in a Divine Nature that ultimately revealed its meaning through observation, was replaced by the notion, by now familiar, of the material world as a mere collection of inanimate objects. In such a framework, architecture could no longer be an art of imitation. Once it adopted the ideals of a positivistic science, architecture was forced to reject its traditional role as one of the fine arts. Deprived of a legitimate poetic content, architecture was reduced to either a prosaic technological process or mere decoration.

It was now that style, that is, the articulation and coherence of architectural "language," became a theoretical problem. The obsession to find immutable laws also invaded the field of aesthetics. But once architecture was reduced to the status of material structure, even the best architects concerned with the problem of meaning could not avoid insurmountable contradictions. History of architecture itself came to be regarded during the nineteenth century as the evolution of rational structure, and style, or *mélange*, was judged on purely rational terms. The problem "In which style should we build?" was not a problem of traditional architecture; an invisible *mathemata* had guaranteed the value of its work, and a symbolic intention had generated both structure and ornament. Only after 1800 do we find a distinction between "necessary" structure, that is, prosaic construction, and "contingent" ornament; the Ecole des Beaux-Arts did not merely continue a traditional "academic" practice in France. The transformation after Durand was profound, and the illusion of stylistic continuity between the eighteenth and nineteenth centuries has created much confusion in our understanding of modern architecture.

Even today, architects who recognize an affinity between their profession and art usually play formal games, but fail to understand the transcendental dimension of meaning in architecture. The lively discussions over the possibility of applying typological or morphological strategies in design also betray the same illusion. Before 1800 the architect was never concerned with type or integrity of a formal language as a source of meaning. Form was the embodiment of a style of life, immediately expressive of culture and perhaps more analogous to a system of gestures than to articulated language. Today architects often work under the absurd assumption that meaning and symbol are merely products of the mind, that they can be manufactured a priori and that they possess somehow the certainty of number.

from "Theoretical Sequel"

Today, practicing architects and their clients are also becoming aware of the limitations of functionalism and formalism, of the impossibility of reducing architecture to decoration, sociology, or psychology. So far, powerful computers, methodologies, and geometrical strategies have failed to provide a mathematical solution to urban and architectural problems. Thus Viel's critique, in spite of transformations in the means of production, should be taken seriously by architects who are concerned with meaning.

The misleading division between rational and intuitive architecture, between scientific and artistic architects, between functionalism, typological methodologies or formalism, and all types of expressionisms, has marked only the least two centuries of architecture. This profound rift was the inevitable outcome of a world view that posited the absolute separation of the objective and subjective realms of human reality. In fact, before the late eighteenth century, architects did not have to choose between two irreconcilable options. It was only with the work of Durand that architects began to perceive the dilemma that still engages them today.

Even the contemporary "schools" of capitalist formalism and Marxist rationalism fall into the same trap, believing that one can separate structure from meaning. Capitalist formalism emphasizes the possibility of architecture as a hermetic, elitist manipulation of forms, with no intended culturally biased meanings. Marxist rationalism pretends that art is not individual expression and that architecture is a craft, a direct result of typological analysis, pure ahistorical content, for which form is irrelevant. Both positions obviously fall short of the truth. There are no structures without meaning; perception is the body's, not merely the mind's. Buildings may be identical typologically (urban and rural "hotels," or Early Christian and Renaissance basilicas), but their meaning is, indeed, very different. Furthermore, art is necessarily personal expression, much more so than science and language (which are, nonetheless, also forms of interpretation). On the other hand, architecture cannot be a private game of combinations, a "formal language" invented a priori (architecture for architects), or a question of merely decorating technological structures with arbitrary historical quotations; the necessarily transcendental (semantic) dimension of meaning cannot be disregarded.

Only contemporary phenomenology, with its rediscovery of the primacy of perception, where structure or mathesis is given and yet embodied in the mutable and specific, has been capable of overcoming the fundamental dilemma that modern philosophy inherited from Descartes. By revealing the limitations of mathematical reason, phenomenology has indicated that technological theory alone cannot come to terms with the fundamental problems of architecture. Contemporary architecture, disillusioned with rational utopias, now strives to go beyond positivistic prejudices to find a new metaphysical justification in the human world; its point of departure is once again the sphere of perception, the ultimate origin of existential meaning.

The reconciliatory mission of the architect is poetic. This is necessarily an individual task, encompassing personal expression and reference to the totality. There is no meaningful logic without acknowledging the intersubjective world, best revealed in dreams and myths. Even in the eighteenth century, poetic wisdom was not without its supporters. Giambattista Vico was perhaps the first to speak up for the primordial knowledge of all people, a knowledge that stemmed not from reason but from imagination. Today Heidegger has given new validity to this idea; we may be condemned to live in the absence of gods, but the void is evident.

The ever present enigma of the human condition is only denied by the foolish. And it is this mystery that architecture must address. Part of our human condition is the inevitable yearning to capture reality through metaphors. Such is true knowledge, ambiguous yet ultimately more relevant than scientific truth. And architecture, no matter how much it resists the idea, cannot renounce its origin in intuition. While construction as a technological process is prosaic—deriving directly from a mathematical equation, a functional diagram, or a rule of formal combinations—architecture is poetic, necessarily an abstract order but in itself a metaphor emerging from vision of the world and Being.

Notes

1. In connection with the primacy of perception and the limitations of intellectual reductionism, see Maurice Merleau-Ponty, *Phenomenology of Perception* (London, 1970) and *The Primacy of Perception* (Evanston, Ill., 1971). See also Mikel Dufrenne, *The Notion of the A Priori* (Evanston, Ill., 1966), and John F. Bannan, *The Philosophy of Merleau-Ponty* (New York, 1967). Reality appears meaningfully in embodied perception. It is in the sense of Merleau-Ponty's phenomenology that I use the notion of perception in this book.

2. The distinction between technology and technique, between how and why, is set forth by Jacques Ellul in *The Technological Society* (New York, 1964). Technology has become a dominating force in the last two centuries, one that has radically determined both thought and action. Its purpose is to subjugate external reality to interests of efficiency, thereby postponing indefinitely the human need for reconciliation. Traditional knowledge and technique, in contrast, have always ultimately been concerned with the most fundamental existential problems. This view is shared in good measure by Martin Heidegger in his late philosophy. See Vincent Vycinas, *Earth and Gods: An Introduction to the Philosophy of Martin Heidegger* (The Hague, 1964), and Jürgen Habermas, *Toward a Rational Society* (London, 1971), chapter 6.

3. Edmund Husserl, *The Crisis of European Sciences and Transcendental Phenomenology* (Evanston, Ill., 1960) and *Phenomenology and the Crisis of Philosophy* (New York, 1965).

4. I use "idea" and "everyday life" also with a horizon of meaning taken from phenomenology. Idea implies figure even in the case of the most abstract notions, while the specific perceptions of everyday life are given a priori in a framework of categories. See Merleau-Ponty, *Phenomenology of Perception*, and Stuart Spicker, *The Philosophy of the Body* (New York, 1970), pp. 334 ff. I use "symbol" as does Alfred Schutz in *Collected Papers I: The Problem of Social Reality* (The Hague, 1973), part III.

5. This notion has been a common point of departure for existential phenomenology. See A. de Waelhens, *La philosophie de Martin Heidegger* (Louvain, 1942), or William Luijpen, *Existential Phenomenology* (Pittsburgh, 1960).

6. See also José Ortega y Gasset, *Man and Crisis* (New York, 1958), and Oswald Spengler, *The Decline of the West* (1918; New York, 1976).

7. Edmund Husserl, *L'origine de la géométrie* (Paris, 1974); Leon Brunschvicg, *Les étapes de la philosophie mathématique* (Paris, 1972); and José Ortega y Gasset, *La idea de principio en Leibniz*, 2 vols. (Madrid, 1967).

8. Mikel Dufrenne, *Le poétique* (Paris, 1973). I use this term in its widest sense as "metaphorical reference," relating it to not only the realm of written poetry but primarily art and myth. See also Paul Ricoeur, *The Rule of Metaphor* (London, 1977).

9. Habermas, *Toward a Rational Society*, and Theodore Roszak, *Where the Wasteland Ends* (London, 1973).

10. Edmund Husserl, *Formale und transzendentale Logik* (Halle, 1929). See Herbert Spiegelberg, *The Phenomenological Movement*, 2 vols. (The Hague, 1971), 1:91 ff. See also Ernest Nagel and James Newman, *Gödel's Proof* (London, 1959).

11. The *logos* has excluded the *mythos* only during the last 180 years of Western history. This is one more symptom of the crisis described by Husserl.

12. I use "reality" also in the phenomenological sense, as the realm of intentionality existing between our embodied selves and the outside world.

13. The precondition of a true symbol is the acceptance of the transcendental dimension of human existence. Thus symbolization becomes a problem, that is, a private language of the genius in art and architecture, only after the crisis has begun.

14. Gottfried Semper's explicit formulation was first brought to my attention by Dalibor Vesely.

15. See, for example, Christopher Alexander, *Notes on the Synthesis of Form* (Cambridge, Mass., 1964), and Nicholas Negroponte, *The Architecture Machine* (Cambridge, Mass., 1970).

16. In his *Collected Papers*, Schutz defines "symbol" as an "appresentational" pair that relates the finite and mutable with the immutable and eternal, lived reality with ideas. Symbolization is human existence, the basis for the perpetuation of culture.

17. See Merleau-Ponty, *Phenomenology of Perception*, pp. 3–63.

18. In the text, I generally use "metaphysics" as does José Ortega y Gasset, *Unas lecciones de metafísica*, translated as *Some Lessons on Metaphysics* (New York, 1974). Ortega defines metaphysics as a radical coming to terms with the fundamental problems of human life (reality as it appears in the field of intentions); it is a basic orientation that allows man's thoughts and actions to be ordered in a meaningful hierarchy. Although it implies the intention to address the question of being, it is not necessarily synonymous with the speculative metaphysics of seventeenth-century philosophy. One of the issues that I shall touch upon in this book is precisely how the metaphysical question was taken up in the natural philosophy of the eighteenth century and the manner in which it was finally excluded from nineteenth-century science, coinciding with Kant's final rejection of legitimate speculative metaphysics. Today it seems that the question of metaphysics cannot be addressed through a still more sophisticated conceptual system. The failure of Husserl's "philosophy as a rigorous science" opened the way for the insights of later philosophers who have placed the question in the realm of mythopoesis, implying an "unthinking" of issues (Ortega), a return to the "Lebenswelt" (Merleau-Ponty). See also Georges Gusdorf, *Mythe et métaphysique* (Paris, 1953). It is Gusdorf who refers to the possible philosophy of today as "mythopoesis," a term that seeks to recover the lost connection between thinking and doing, which the Greek notion of *poiesis* still involved. This "second mythology" is

not "an architecture of concepts, but a justification of real existence in the plenitude of its lived years."

19. See Georges Gusdorf, *Les origines des sciences humaines* (Paris, 1966), and Alexandre Koyré, "Les étapes de la cosmologie scientifique," *Revue de Synthèse* (1951–1952), p. 11. I owe much of my understanding of science and its implications in a wider cultural context to Gusdorf's fascinating (untranslated) history of the human sciences. The work, whose general title is *Les sciences humaines en la pensée occidentale,* is already eight volumes long. It concentrates on the seventeenth and eighteenth centuries.

20. Elsewhere in the text I use the terms "Galilean" and "epistemological revolution" to describe a fundamental transformation that took place during the last decades of the sixteenth century and the beginning of the seventeenth. The terminology and its implications are taken from Georges Gusdorf, *La révolution galiléenne,* 2 vols. (Paris, 1969). Keeping in mind that intentionality, understood phenomenologically, covers the span from thought to action, what is in question is a transformation of the world picture, not only as the articulation of beliefs and ideas (although it certainly started at that level; thus the term "epistemological"), but as the given historical context of human life, art, and architecture. The new relation between man and his external reality was best understood in the seventeenth century by Galileo; it only became accepted at a popular level 200 years later with the "success" of the Industrial Revolution. The Galilean revolution obviously is not the cause of the phenomena that I shall be describing and analyzing. It should be understood as a metaphor for a radical change in the order of the world and the cosmos in which these phenomena originate.

21. For a discussion of "spatiality" and "intellectual space," see Merleau-Ponty, *Phenomenology of Perception,* pp. 98–147.

22. I use "technological intentionality" in the sense of Habermas (see note 2).

Daniel Libeskind, Chamber Works

This work in search of Architecture has discovered no permanent structure, no constant form and no universal type. I have realized that the result of this journey in search of the "essentials" undermines in the end the very premise of their existence. Architecture is neither on the inside nor the outside. It is not a given nor a physical fact. It has no History and it does not follow Fate. What emerges in differentiated experience is Architecture as an index of the relationship between what was and what will be. Architecture as non-existent reality is a symbol which in the process of consciousness leaves a trail of hieroglyphs in space and time that touch equivalent depths of Unoriginality.

Daniel Libeskind, *Chamber Works: Architectural Meditations on Themes from Heraclitus* (London: Architectural Association, 1983)

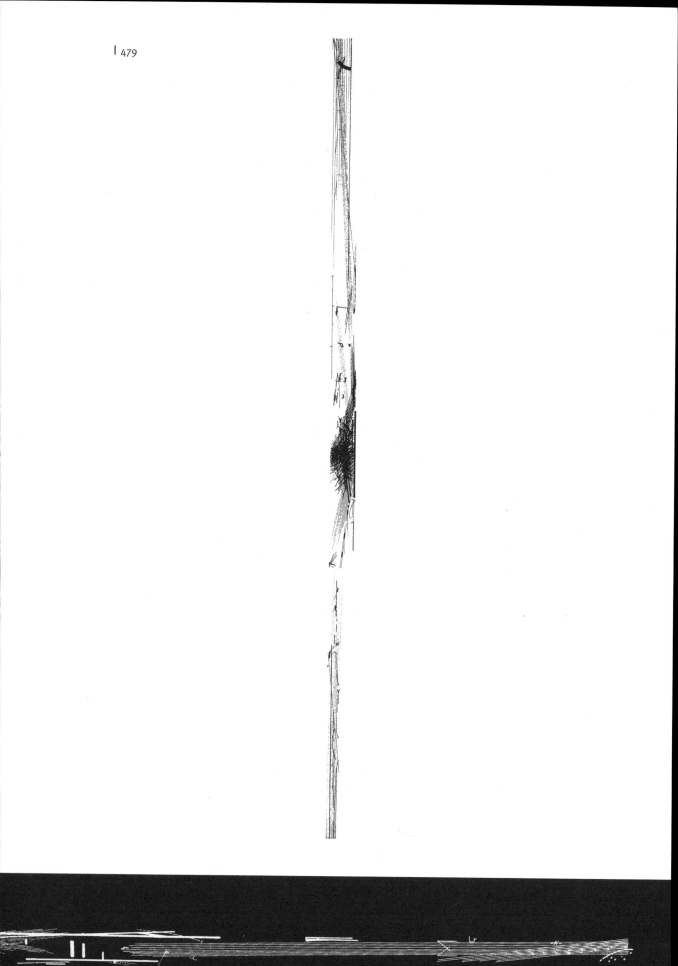

Robin Evans   **"In Front of Lines That Leave Nothing Behind"** *AA Files* 6 (May 1984)

Traditionally, architectural drawings have been seen as means to an end: instruments in a series of steps from idea toward built realization, essential components of a notational system that Nelson Goodman called the "allographic" art of architecture.[1] Historical and theoretical analyses, even when discussing drawings qua drawings, have granted epistemological priority to the referent of the drawings, the imagined, projected building-to-be. In the cases that constitute his major work, *The Projective Cast* (1995), Robin Evans studies the ways in which architecture always exceeds its representations ("Architecture begins and ends in pictures, but I would urge resistance to the idea that pictures give us all we need. . . . The question is, how much more is ever brought within the scope of the architect's vision of a project than what can be drawn?");[2] in his review of the 1983 exhibition of Daniel Libeskind's *Chamber Works*, he queries the attempt to neutralize architecture drawing as an allographic practice and theorizes an architecture of maximal reduction produced *in* the drawings.

What is at stake in the *Chamber Works*, Evans shows, is an interpretive logic and performativity of *reading* that negates visual representation and likeness. This negation must now be understood not as a generic discordance nor as a simple splitting of signifier from signified, but as a telescoping of different registers of the architectural sign onto the same immanent plane — the real system, the notational signs, and the connotative signs (rhetoric and ideology).[3] Bluntly put, the drawing and the reading performance it elicits become architectural significations in their own right, producing a new kind of architectural entity or event, for which theory perhaps does not yet have a concept, but which might have a model in Merleau-Ponty's "significative intention":

The reason why a language finally intends to say and does say something is not that each sign is the vehicle for a signification that allegedly belongs to it, but that all the signs together allude to a signification which is always in abeyance when they are considered singly, and which I go beyond them toward, without their ever containing it. . . . The significative intention . . . is . . . no more than a *determinant gap* . . . the excess of what I intend to say over what is being said or has already been said.[4]

As Libeskind himself has said (in what could almost be a gloss on Merleau-Ponty), we are compelled "to rethink the widely held belief that there is a predestined and correct expression assigned a priori to each form by the 'language of Architecture' itself, as if this 'language' belonged to the ceremonies and rituals themselves."[5] In Libeskind's tumbling of signifiers from one level to another, meaning must be understood as *always yet to come* rather than as residing in some preexisting repository of language.

All of which is beyond the domain of an architecture theory based either on semiotics or on models of aesthetic skill. There is no meaning or experiential realm behind or beneath these drawings waiting to be discovered by the viewer like the "real thing" behind a frottage; and the drawing technique itself disqualifies the architect's traditional skill to enclose an area, to join parts, to mark paths, or to distinguish one territory from another. Evans demonstrates what might be termed the "deskilling" of the architect through, first, the negation of figuration or anthropomorphic attributes: "the lines themselves are expressive of neither velocity, force nor animation"; second, the negation of spatiality; and third, the negation of fragmentation: "Fragmentation assumes the possibility . . . of reconstructing an original that has been broken. . . . The *Chamber Works* do not move towards unity, nor are they subject to fragmentation. . . . Lines that do not make bodies cannot be broken." "Then," he concludes,

whatever is renounced in the drawings . . . would be excluded from architecture's central concerns. Whatever is detached from the drawings will fall away from the word. Building, space, image, program; the essences and crutches of architecture in Portland would be centrifuged to the outer edge of the subject, maybe beyond. At the center, a way of drawing that makes use of architectural instruments — set-square, parallel motion, drafting pens, drawing board — but otherwise requires little external sustenance. Architecture would be moved from building to drawing.

Notes

1.   In fact, Goodman sees architecture as a rather difficult case. "Plainly enough, all houses complying with the plans for Smith-Jones Split-Level #17 are equally instances of that architectural work. But in the case of . . . the Taj Mahal, we may bridle at considering another building from the same plans to be an instance of the same work rather than a copy. We are not as comfortable about identifying an architectural work with a design rather than a building as we are about identifying a musical work with a composition rather than a performance. In that architecture has a reasonably appropriate notational system and that some of its works are unmistakably allographic, the art is allographic. But insofar as its notational language has not yet acquired full authority to divorce identity of work in all cases from particular production, architecture is a mixed and transitional case." Nelson Goodman, *Languages of Art* (Indianapolis: Hackett, 1976), pp. 220–221.
2.   Robin Evans, *The Projective Cast* (Cambridge: MIT Press, 1995), pp. 359–360.
3.   See Roland Barthes, *Elements of Semiology*, trans. Annette Lavers and Colin Smith (New York: Hill and Wang, 1967). Barthes associates second-order connotative signs with mythification and ideology.
4.   Maurice Merleau-Ponty, "On the Phenomenology of Language," in *Signs*, trans. Richard C. McCleary (Evanston: Northwestern University Press, 1964), pp. 88, 89.
5.   Daniel Libeskind, "Symbol and Interpretation," in *Between Zero and Infinity* (New York: Rizzoli, 1981), p. 29.

The Frontal Subject

The trouble with most criticism, and particularly that brand of interpretive criticism associated with iconology, is that meaning is assumed to exist behind, beneath or within the subjects of criticism. The task of the critic is to delve into, uncover, disclose, reveal, divulge, discover, unfold and show to the reader what lies hidden or unseen, to get to the bottom of things, to plumb the depths, to see beneath the surface, behind the curtain. Behind and beneath are metaphors, since there is no real space surrounding events or objects that is made visible by criticism, but if we allow ourselves to be drawn into the trope, then we might well ask what lies beside, above and in front of the subjects of criticism too. What is it that excludes these other positions from notice?

The spatial metaphor places the critic as well as the things he regards. Whatever he talks about, he faces, and by a trick of anthropomorphization the subject faces him. Or at least this is frequently imagined to be the relation. The metaphor of looking would alone be enough to ensure the positioning of the subject in front of the critic (and if we do not look into subjects, we approach them— no less frontal an attitude). Yet it is the face-to-face relationship between the critic and his subject that has the greatest effect because with it comes the idea that the phenomena which are presented to us through our senses are presented as front-ages, facades, things that signify what they stand in front of. So it is that the critic may look at his subject as if it were some kind of projection whose meaning is assured by the fact that it is addressed toward him. All the world can still be a stage, and it is then our business to find out what supports the illusion or what gives rise to the representation. Aspects of reality that cannot be thought of in terms of this privileged orientation become more recalcitrant to interpretation because no clue is given as to where we should stand or what we should look toward. As it is, the spatial metaphor leaves us in no doubt; it leads under the skin, beneath the surface, through the frame, behind the stage, beyond the facade.

Often the spatial metaphor is itself already a metaphor of time, but in this instance space and time are interchangeable. Beneath and behind translate easily into a chronological before. Time passes; we look back. Sediments accumulate; we dig. The face-to-face relationship, no longer possible across time, is replaced by an equivalent arrangement in which the present is construed as a projection of the past, an accessible reality offering evidence of previous events that can only be recovered through it. Extending from the past it eclipses, the present is turned into the facade of history.

The line of sight engendered by the spatial metaphors of hidden meaning, whether single or doubled, whether expressed in space or spatialized time, sets the critic in search of origins, essences, intentions, motives, causes, for these are the things that lie behind appearances. He looks therefore to find some animating or authenticating agency that will account for whatever he confronts. The critic's task is always to confront. The pressure of these harmless metaphors which bear on language at so many points will ease him into position face-to-face with reality, but will also leave him in no doubt that it is his duty not to take things at face value.

Complaint may be made about the covert anthropomorphism imported by metaphors into the critical vocabulary and the frontalizing of the subject as general issues but, in the particular case of architectural criticism or art criticism, there would seem rather less to cavil at, since the face-to-face relationship is given far greater plausibility by the presence of architects and artists who present their work often with considerable care as to how it will be shown and how seen. Would we not be perfectly justified in taking the face-to-face relationship for granted when such is the situation? Can we not, after all, rely on the architect's or artist's intention to orient the work towards us? It would seem so, but Daniel Libeskind's recent drawings may suggest otherwise.

Lines without Bodies

Not that *Chamber Works*, twenty-eight drawings exhibited in October 1983 at the AA, were anything but frontal in their mode of presentation. Nothing oblique or unpremeditated here. A conventionally hung, neatly mounted, uniform series of abstract line compositions in black ink on white paper. At sufficient distance the overall effect is one of staid politeness. It is only when the observer steps within close range of any one of the drawings, close enough for the regulating propriety of the rectangular frame to be diminished, that he becomes aware of the demonic energy of line within. It is energy hard to describe, for the lines themselves are expressive of neither velocity, force nor animation. A drawn line will normally render something visible of the action that gave rise to it, which allows us to attribute human qualities—febrile, agitated, delicate, rapid or hesitant—to mere lines. Because these are architectural drawings, made with architectural instruments, because the lines are constructed, not thrown, it is impossible to do this. An approach that would lead through the drawing back to the event of its being made is denied us. Similar denials occur again and again within the series. Whenever an attempt is made to pass through and beyond the drawings, it proves abortive. They are opaque to this line of critical enquiry.

Tigers, though performing the most elaborate excursions when stalking their quarry in the jungle, will, when presented with a slab of meat in front of their cage, pounce, apparently oblivious to the iron bars that lie between. Theirs is a failure of reflex, not of intelligence; likewise, it seems to me, the commentators who pounce on Libeskind's work in an effort to catch and devour its meaning, the meaning, that is, that might lie hidden within it. Together with the folio reproduction of *Chamber Works* are four short introductory essays by Peter Eisenman, Kurt Forster, John Hejduk and Aldo Rossi. While admitting the barriers to ordinary comprehension, the essayists say that his drawings are hieroglyphics (Rossi) or that they are illustrations of a process of thought (Hejduk) or that they are a kind of writing (Eisenman); that they are spatialized scores, musical translations (Forster), pictures of the soul (Hejduk), anamorphoses (Forster). It is not that they lack circumspection. Eisenman is aware that his recommending that *Chamber Works* be read like writing "insists on their having a significance that as graphics they could not have." Hejduk and Rossi (whose contribution is, incidentally, very good) recognize the inexplicable in them. Yet they cannot help but treat *Chamber Works* as having hidden meaning. The machinations of appreciative language force them to fabricate virtual meanings for the drawings to represent in place of what they know they cannot find—and remarkably inventive about it they are—but can their claims to have discovered the modes of representation (if not the content made apparent by the representation) be sustained?

Take the hieroglyphic. For several centuries the deciphering of Egyptian hieroglyphics posed immense problems in Europe, but at the same time held the promise of revealing the secrets of arcane knowledge direct from the fount of civilization. In the popular imagination, which remembers when men and dinosaurs shared the earth, the hieroglyphics are still undeciphered. We do not so easily allow such exquisite mysteries to be trampled on by the advance of palaeography, the quest for the secret being so much more interesting than its eventual recovery. It is in this state of latent revelation that Rossi employs the word hieroglyphics to describe Libeskind's drawings. Behind the indecipherable marks there lies locked *something* about which we remain ignorant, perhaps a lost empire of meaning which we could disinter if only we had the key. It is an enchanting thought, almost irresistible and nonetheless so for one obvious difference. The men who carved the hieroglyphs knew what they meant. Daniel Libeskind claims no such authority in regard to his own work.

His procedure is therefore more like augury than writing: first form the signs, knowing only how, never what, and then look to see if they signify anything: sometimes they do, sometimes they don't, sometimes good news, sometimes bad, sometimes nothing. Such a procedure shifts the weight of meaning from behind to in front, from before to after, from the verifiable to the unverifiable, and, as we have already noted, twentieth-century interpretation finds these positions difficult to identify—let alone deal with.

There can be little doubt that *Chamber Works* are in some way systematic, but they are certainly not a system of conventionalized notation or representation. Nor are they writing, hieroglyphics, scores, pictures of the soul or of any other part substantial or ineffable. They are more like the tea-leaves in the cup, the spilt entrails of the eviscerated dove, distributions made in such a way that they cannot be fully understood even by their author.

Returning now to the issue of opacity, it may be useful to compare the *Chamber Works* with *Micromegas*, a series exhibited by Libeskind in 1979 and similar to *Chamber Works* in technique and format. Employing the ambiguities of architectural projection as their starting-point, *Micromegas* disrupt the homogeneous, continuous space of axonometry and isometry into a multitude of conflicting spaces. The series is easy to place within the context of modern art, if not modern architecture; it belongs to the class of works that investigate fluctuating representations of space and surface. Synthetic Cubist paintings are of this class, so are some of Lissitzky's Proun compositions, the drawings of Josef Albers and the canvases of Al Held. All are occupants of that fascinating world of visual ambiguity extolled by Ernst Gombrich. The *Micromegas*, however unrelenting their destruction of unified picture space, are masterly compositions; abstract but eminently three-dimensional, belonging to an established convention of pictorial fragmentation.

After *Micromegas*, Libeskind's drawings turned back from abstraction. *The Secret Life of Vegetables* (1981) and *Se guarderai le stelle sanza razzi* (*As Is Done through a Little*

Hole) (1981), for instance, are built up from recognizable fragments of machines, instruments, architecture, furniture, limbs and diagrams. Composed of figurative elements embodied in space, they are relatively transparent to normal interpretation, the iconographer's dream, in fact: piles of recondite images, lashings of derived expression. Let loose on these, our essayists would not need to have racked their own brains so hard and could more easily have ransacked Libeskind's; the door of the safe was wide open.

By complete contrast, figure and space are nearly absent in *Chamber Works*, not quite absent but nearly so. A floating nest of semi-breves here, comical crotchets on ruptured staves there; resolution into cipher-like bits is occasional and partial, no more than enough to suggest a resemblance, never allowing the sign-like element, whether decapitated stick figure, cross, checkerboard or mascot Mondrian, to break free of the lines of which it is made, lines which refuse to synthesize into bodies, but which for courtesy's sake leave clues as to sources of inspiration. Like animal crackers in my soup, these little hints are more diverting than nutritional. The tendency in the work, in any case, is away from recognizability toward what Libeskind himself refers to as "remoteness."[1] What is so remarkable is the near total disengagement from signification of any kind. Such a condition is immensely difficult to achieve; mere abstraction does not begin to approach it.

But are the *Chamber Works* not in some way spatial representations, as suggested by Forster, however far removed from ordinary experience? The answer turns out to be no, not, anyway, the kind of space that has to be thought and constructed into existence by the draftsman. *Micromegas*, which derive ultimately from the Cubist enterprise and look similar to the works of Al Held, were easy to place in the history of modern art; *Chamber Works* are not. Family likenesses are harder to come by. They have something to do with Kandinsky's musical compositions, perhaps also with the architectural sketches by Erich Mendelsohn that were drawn while listening to records on the phonograph and titled according to their inspiration. Perhaps the graphical work of Hans Hartung or Roberto Crippa in the 1950s, of Joel Fisher or Sol LeWitt more recently, all distant relatives at best. Another kind of opacity. No one to talk about. No transactions to record. No past to reconstruct.

Micromegas were eminently spatial; *Chamber Works* allow of only the most detached and uncertain spatial interpretation. The drawings are made of lines that intersect but hardly ever meet. Each of the myriad is a separate construction that begins and ends in its own good time, not joining to another of its kind. The work of a line, its functions, the things it does other than just being a line, are to divide one territory from another, to enclose areas, to join points, to mark paths. This is what they do as edges, traces, contours, trajectories, vectors. The lines of *Chamber Works* do not do any of these things. Though perfectly regular in construction, and looking as if they belonged to geometry, they may well be amongst the least geometrical lines ever drawn.

Since Descartes demonstrated the relationship between geometrical figures and algebraic functions, mathematicians have understood that geometry can do without lines, but here are neat Euclidean lines that do without geometry or, to qualify the absolute proscription, lines which on occasion more or less accidentally deposit geometrical figures in the same way that they occasionally engender signs. Yet despite their lack of employment in normal business, despite their individualization, the lines do interact by drifting in parallel sets, intersecting, pairing up into ribbon forms which sometimes intertwine in complex knots (the only deliberately illusionistic device, since the first strip drawn ends up appearing to be on top, as if it had been the last laid). They float together in loose formation or condense into tight fibrous bunches.

Without *representing* space, any of the *Chamber Works* can be fantasized into three dimensions, given sufficient volition in the observer, for the space is thought into them by him, not projected out of them by the draftsman. The uniform line of the architectural pen helps Libeskind to avoid constructing illusions of space in the drawings, but what is curious, and very impressive, is that even within the narrow confines of his chosen medium a dynamic potency emanates from somewhere. The mechanically regulated line is not an obvious choice for the evocation of movement.

Engraving, which permits far greater expression of line than a Rotring pen, proved incapable of transferring the vital qualities of cartoons or paintings into prints. Marcantonio, excellent in his craft, tried to perform this service for Raphael, and the world he managed to recreate in lines looked as if it had been steeped in toffee in between times. Libeskind has found a way to make the laborious traipse of upright pen into a frigid calligraphy which does not transfer real qualities of movement into lines (making them porters of their own origin) but invokes kinds of motion unconnected to actions previously performed.

Fragmentation has been the leitmotif of Libeskind's work. First impressions of *Chamber Works* might lead one to think that it continues to be so. Even the subtitle, "Architectural Meditations on Themes from Heraclitus," helps by implication to confirm it, since Heraclitus is known to us only through fragments. A collection of odd epigrams and sentences from diverse sources, he, Heraclitus, has to be reconstituted from bits like an amphora stuck together by archaeologists. Fragmentation assumes the possibility, theoretical if not practical, of reconstructing an original that has been broken, of putting together the busted vase. In the past, Libeskind has exploited the psychotic ambivalence of the technique which may either register a delight in smashing things up or sadness in surveying the shattered scene. Yet fragmentation has to be figurative because only things with a constitution can be broken.

Unity and fragmentation are the two major contrasted modes of twentieth-century composition in architecture as well as painting. A classic dialectical pair, married and bickering, they are unable to carry on without each other. The *Chamber Works* do not move towards unity, nor are they subject to fragmentation. It took me a while to realize that there was nothing to be broken, no virtual space, no subject matter, no substructure, no geometry. Lines that do not make bodies cannot be broken. The discovery of this area outside of unity and fragmentation may be the greatest single achievement of the series.

So it looks as if all direct communication from the draftsman through the drawing to the observer has been sabotaged by the former. The remaining signs we may call politenesses; the carry-over of resemblances from earlier works, residua; the words surrounding the project, extraneous. Despite being under the protection of an ancient sage, the past of these drawings is vanishing before our eyes. Yet one transmitted message comes through clearly, and it is propagated not by the individual drawings but by their assembly into a set.

The twenty-eight drawings divide into two groups of fourteen, one group vertical in format, one horizontal. They were, it turns out, exhibited incorrectly. Hung in straightforward sequence, 1 to 14, they should rather have been paired: numbers 1 and 14, 2 and 13, 3 and 12, 4 and 11, 5 and 10, 6 and 9, 7 and 8 in the horizontal series, and likewise with the vertical. Pythagoras, referred to in Libeskind's introduction through a quotation from Heraclitus as "the prince of impostors," makes his presence felt. The number 28 is a summation of integers 1 to 7, a Pythagorean operation. There are 7 pairs in each group of drawings and the sequence numbers of each pair add always to 15.

The drawings decrease in breadth or width from 2:1 (nothing could be more reverent to convention) to 200:1 (nothing could be less like the things we recognize as drawings). The drawings made out of lines end up turning into a line, provoking the thought that every line could be a world to itself composed also of a multitude of lines, and so on.

As exhibited, there was a strong suggestion of a plane rotating on a horizontal, then a vertical axis. The anamorphosis, noted by Forster, is this appearance of rotation into the oblique. Hung as Libeskind would have wished, this effect would be largely obliterated; the proportional contraction in the drawings would then be easier to imagine as a compression than as a three-dimensional rotation.

Which leaves the numbers; they are, I think, hardly more than a framing to the drawings, an external principle of organization. Rossi, though, sees them as a pointer towards integral meaning. If they are, it is a pity because, by pointing straight backwards, they break through the opacity to frontal interpretation constructed with such careful brilliance by Libeskind. Ironic, too. Pythagorean mathematics is not only ancient, it is antiquated. It is the subject of intense mystification arising from the belief that Number is the informing principle behind reality. Now, *Chamber Works*, as we have seen, manage to disengage the drawing from its own history—an awesome accomplishment, as the draftsman, allowing himself no certainty at any point, gives himself nothing to lean on except his elbows. The separation between systems of representation and the aspects of reality they normally stand for (the celebrated uncoupling of signifier and signified in linguistics) has not been applied to architecture in this or any other way before, despite large importations of devalued semiological currency into architectural journalism. Nor is it an idea derived exclusively from linguistics. While Saussure was giving his seminal lectures in Lausanne in 1913, modern painting was well on the way to disengaging itself from illustration. But the most conclusive and spectacular severance between reality and its bonded representation occurred nearly a century before, when the mathematician Carl Friedrich Gauss devised logically rigorous geometries, as internally consistent as the common-sensical Euclidean variety, but which could not apply to real space. From which developed the now common idea that mathematics has absolutely no preordained affinity with nature but is an independently derived system of correlations. Capable, perhaps, of sometimes running in step with nature, it is capable also of traversing vast areas of the possible but unreal: a marvelous new power. So, whether or not Pythagoras was in his own time "prince of impostors," he certainly plays that role in *Chamber Works*, for his magical numbers that make the world—the ultimate hidden meaning—are as alien from Libeskind's project as it is possible to be.

Architecture without Building

So far the drawings have been reviewed without particular reference to architecture in an attempt to find out how they are constituted. In describing how opaque they are to frontal interpretation, how they refuse to make manifest a meaning that lies behind them, they have been characterized in largely negative terms. But then if we cannot look behind them, we must look in front for the things that the drawing might yet suggest, might lead to, might provoke; in short, for what is *potent* in them rather than what is *latent*. Such a posture of observation is maintained by Libeskind himself when he talks of Rossi's Teatro del Mondo, suggesting the question as to "whether the 'no longer' of modern architecture actually *belongs* to its very own 'not yet.'"[2]

If this posture is adopted, then criticism as we know it would have only a marginal function, soon exhausted, that of showing the inexplicability of the work. Interpretation would otherwise have to mutate into another form, with an entirely different orientation, revealing potency not latency. It would become as uncertain an enterprise as any kind of search not assured of at least the possibility of verification. In the meantime my intention is no more than to indicate the empty space outside the interpretive cone of vision, pointing out its qualitative difference from the space within.

The much exercised question "What have they to do with architecture?" may overshadow some qualities of *Chamber Works* not entailed in the answer. Nevertheless, it can hardly be ignored. Nothing, some say. Then there are those who would admit them as a boundary condition, anything further removed from the basic business of making buildings being inadmissible. There are those who might follow Eisenman in describing them as Not-Architecture, a category related by direct opposition. There may be those who would see them the way Werner Oechslin saw *Micromegas*,[3] as a graphic exemplification of qualities that could not so well be achieved in building, an imaginative overspill (he compared Libeskind to Piranesi).

Always metaphors of extremity are employed, and there is good cause for this, but I would like to treat the question differently by altering the position of *Chamber Works* in the metaphor. Suppose the word "architecture," instead of having its center somewhere over a block in Portland, Oregon, had its center close to these drawings. It is not just a center of interest that is being talked about, but a center of activity, an epicenter. Then whatever is renounced in the drawings (and there is a strong renunciation in them) would be excluded from architecture's central concerns. Whatever is detached from the drawings will fall away from the word. Building, space, image, program; the essences and crutches of architecture in Portland would be centrifuged to the outer edge of the subject, maybe beyond. At the center, a way of drawing that makes use of architectural instruments—set-square, parallel motion, drafting pens, drawing board—but otherwise requires little external sustenance. Architecture would be moved from building to drawing, which is more like moving from Chicago to Paris than discovering the Antipodes, in so far as the manner of working is concerned. In one way this is a restoration: drawing once again the fountainhead of architectural creation. In another way it is a truncation. Architecture, which has always involved drawing before building, can be split into prior and subsequent activities: design and construction. The building can be discarded as an unfortunate aftermath, and all the properties, values, and attributes that are worth keeping can be held in the drawing; perhaps a better way of putting it would be to say that they retract back into the drawing.

And it is true that the imaginative work of architecture has for a long time been accomplished almost exclusively through drawing, though manifested almost exclusively in building. The great peculiarity of architecture as a visual art (a peculiarity it nevertheless shares with orchestral, choral, operatic works and, to a lesser extent, film) is the considerable distance between the process of composition and the thing being composed. By truncating architecture and disposing of building, an intimacy between a way of designing and the thing designed is achieved.

The architect can travel light. His work does not now involve him in the tedious entropy of getting something built, nor in the dubious politics of improving social conditions, nor in the appalling sycophancy of client-sucking, nor in reconstructing his personality to fit his job. Libeskind, when asked to explain his work, will talk instead about architecture in general. Sometimes he will say that architecture is no longer possible. Once it was, but not now. Sometimes, when drawn, he will nevertheless claim that his work is architecture. He moves with the tools of his trade, like a refugee. He does the same thing in a different place, starting from scratch, not as a colonist but as an emigrant. The *Chamber Works* are prefaced with a luminous quotation which I repeat in full:

"What do you suppose that white line in the sky that you saw from the crack in the cattle-car on your way to Stutthof really was?" the interviewer asked Elaine some thirty years later in her Brooklyn home.

"You see, in order to survive you must believe in something, you need a source of inspiration, of courage, something bigger than yourself, something to overcome reality. The line was my source of inspiration, my sign from heaven.

"Many years later, after liberation, when my children were growing up, I realized that the white line might have been fumes from a passing airplane's exhaust pipe, but does it really matter?"[4]

In the uncompleted there is always possibility. In an event cut off from its origins there is promise.

There are plenty of people who, either practicing architecture as we know it, or having given it up, regard it, like Libeskind, as fundamentally corrupt, but it is just opinion and it makes no real difference to the way anything happens. Except one. Those who stay console themselves with dreams of a Golden Age. Contemporary architecture, they say, is in a state of degeneracy, has lost its meaning and, although it cannot recover its original significance in full, its lost past becomes, for them, a subject of endless reminiscence, a droning noise of quotations, images, models and derivations. The great mumble.

Libeskind too believes that much has been lost, but because the loss is irretrievable, he realizes there is no point in repetition and only sentiment in reminiscence. Instead, by cutting out the aspects of architecture that are brimful of meaning—its all too vivid meaning as a social, economic and political process of construction—he allows for the construction of lines in the sky. Like Elaine in the cattle-truck, Libeskind invokes a principle of transcendence conditionally, the lost past of architecture, perhaps even now recognized as an enabling fiction.

So, yes, if the center of architecture moved over here it would leave a lot behind. Marvelous. More to be said. Not now. Soon someone might even ask whether it is possible to escape from the truck, and how.

Notes

1. Daniel Libeskind, "Versus the Old Established Language of Architecture," *Daidalos* 1, no. 1 (1981), p. 98.
2. Daniel Libeskind, "Deus ex Machina/Machina ex Deo: Aldo Rossi's Theatre of the World," *Oppositions* 21 (1980), p. 20.
3. Werner Oechslin, "From Piranesi to Libeskind," *Daidalos* 1, no. 1 (1981), pp. 15–19.
4. The source is Yaffa Eliach, *Hasidic Tales of the Holocaust* (New York: Oxford University Press, 1982).

Stanford Anderson   **"Architectural Design as a System of Research Programs"** *Design Studies* 5, no. 3

(July 1984)

compare Pérez-
Gómez
(**466–469**)

While many theoretical positions since 1968 insist on the centrality of a naïve but perniciously instrumental functionalism within modern architecture, Stanford Anderson, in almost all of his writings, has infused his critiques of modernism with an ideologically very different spirit intended to reawaken us to the modernist principles of worldmaking. Le Corbusier's private houses can stand as an example. Commenting on a photograph of the kitchen of the Villa Savoye, Anderson notes,

Le Corbusier offered a vision of certain eternal goods: the loaf of bread, the can of milk, the bottle of wine, light and air, access to the earth and the sky, physical health, all made available more fully and to greater numbers thanks to new potentials that were both spiritual and technical. . . . To the extent that the Villa Savoye permits *that we live according to that vision*, it does something more [than engage the iconographic dimension of architecture]. It "makes a world" that does not determine, but does allow us to live and think differently than if it did not exist. If this fiction can only exist, precariously, in the Villa Savoye, it may indeed be "merely" a fiction, as valuable to us as other great stories. If its vision can be generalized, we may have a literal grasp on a world that could not have been ours without the originating fiction.[1]

Where some would see modern architecture bowing to technical or social imperatives, Anderson sees in modernism (or at least much of it) more of an invitation to dwell differently, to invent new forms of habitation that are the psychological, ethical, and political consequences of changes in architectural form.

compare Rowe and
Koetter
(**100–102**)

Even with his Popperian revulsion against any kind of determinism or any suppression of competing social aims, coupled with his desire to articulate the plurality of modernist stories, Anderson must nevertheless find a theoretical way to grant the architect a nonarbitrary, reasonable conviction about the new life being proposed, about the story being told.[2] It is Imre Lakatos's notion of scientific research programs that provides Anderson with a model of the construction of competing architectural conventions (or what, in the present essay, he calls competing architectural research programs).

Anderson draws two basic premises from Lakatos's model. First, from the field of competing architectural programs (whether this is understood to involve the work of a single architect or many different ones) it is possible to reasonably say that some are more "progressive" or robust than others. Conventions of architectural production are epistemologically compelling only insofar as they involve considerations of relevant alternatives to the beliefs they support and the worlds they construct, and can show themselves capable of being sustained over time. Second, though a convention must have a degree of autonomy and internal coherence, architecture is never fully independent of larger concerns. A convention will be methodologically compelling only to the extent that the domain it organizes can be systematically and rationally related to other features of the cultural world, independent of those of the primary program. It is these two features that can account for architecture's social value. Anderson states:

A triumph in the construction of conventions that is not simultaneously a triumph of discovery is less than the highest triumph of which the construction of conventions is capable. That is to say, a convention is not to be valued primarily for its novelty, beauty, or internal consistency, or for its autonomy, or for the law and order it brings to practice, but rather for its (culturally framed) true or liberating relations to other conventions of practice. This mitigation of the autonomy of the convention, this insistence on the convention's quasi-autonomous address to social practice is what protects the convention from the suspicion of being merely made up. It is only this reciprocity of convention and practice that can sustain the convention. But it is also only such a critically sustained convention that can guide practice without the appeal to arbitrary authority.[3]

While Anderson construes the architectural propositions themselves — their conceptual and artifactual programs — as the proper level of convention construction, it should be observed that the model of competing conventions works at the level of interpretation as well; the same kind of adaptive equilibrium between background theories, interpretive conventions, and social practice can help decide between alternative accounts of architecture.[4] Anderson's effort, in general, is to remind us of the extreme *generosity* of architecture, its working through the immense variety of human cultural production and offering new ways of thinking and inhabiting.

Notes

Anderson's essay was orginally published as two consecutive essays, "Architectural Design as a System of Research Programmes" and "Architectural Research Programmes in the Work of Le Corbusier," in the same volume of *Design Studies*.

1. Stanford Anderson, "The Fiction of Function," *Assemblage* 2 (1987), pp. 24–28.

2. Anderson's early involvement with the thought of Karl Popper is most apparent in Stanford Anderson, "Architecture and Tradition That Isn't 'Trad, Dad,'" in *The History, Theory and Criticism of Architecture*, papers from the 1964 AIA-ACSA Teacher Seminar, Cranbrook, ed. Marcus Whiffen (Cambridge: MIT Press, 1965). The paper is a critique of Reyner Banham and an attempt to resolve what Banham sees as the conflicting claims of science and tradition.

3. Stanford Anderson, "Critical Conventionalism in Architecture," *Assemblage* 1 (1986), pp. 21–22. This paper was originally presented in April 1982 at a conference held at the American Academy of Arts and Sciences, Cambridge, Massachusetts, organized by Anderson and entitled "Conventions, Canons, and Criticism." The conference served to focus Anderson's thinking regarding the construction of conventions and propelled his subsequent research. See also Stanford Anderson, "Types and Conventions in Time: Towards a History for the Duration and Change of Artifacts," *Perspecta* 18 (1982).

4. For a discussion, see K. Michael Hays, "Theory-Constitutive Conventions and Theory Change," *Assemblage* 1 (1986).

"Design" has various meanings ranging from purposive planning to plotting with evil intent. In any case, it invokes notions of rationality and carefully conceived effectiveness. To speak of "design method" only increases the stakes. If we are to conduct "design research," it seems we must seek to reveal the orderliness which can be brought to human action.

Yet we are dismally aware of the numerous failures of design—be it low-income housing or nuclear energy systems. We are also aware of designs that have succeeded in ways unintended. What are we to make of these puzzles and problems of design? Will a more concerted inquiry termed "design research" reveal the ways to avoid failures and anticipate the unintended? I think not.

In every field, our knowledge is imperfect, is not open to ultimate verification, is the product of a particular history. Our knowledge and other cultural forms might have been otherwise, and to that extent we recognize their conventionality—that they are, to a degree, arbitrary. But it is arbitrariness to a degree. Who is to say whether the medicine of the west or the cognate practices of China has set out on a better course? Yet it is clear that both systems, marked by some arbitrariness of beginnings and course, have improved themselves because their respective conventions eventually encounter empirical problems which challenge them and channel further inquiry.

While avoiding notions of total arbitrariness, pure conventionalism and utter relativity, it is necessary to recognize the conventional, partially arbitrary construction of a culture. These conventions encounter testing and limiting empirical conditions which we may hypothesize as the sources of problems and thus as the impetus for change of our conventions.

A decade or more ago, some of the searchers for design method may have thought that a rigorous and infallible design procedure might be revealed. Today, in our own group, I doubt if anyone harbors such hopes. The question now seems to be where will we locate the arbitrariness embedded in our practices, and how will we seek to deal with it rationally?

One way to compare discussions about design method or design research, then, might be to characterize where and how one proposes to deal with arbitrariness. Alternative positions can be suggested without attempting to characterize any specific proposals. One can imagine, for example, the proposition that some level of infrastructure, perhaps even including certain space-defining architectural elements, can and should result from a thoroughly systematic design process, but that the completion and transformation of that environment will be set by the conventionalized, partially arbitrary actions of its inhabitants. Under such a model, design is conceived to be a nonarbitrary process, but its domain is restricted.

One can also imagine a participative design process in which numerous people with differing and not fully-known values, resources and persuasiveness engage in the resolution of design decisions. The most sanguine view of such a process is clearly attractive relative to authoritarian design imposition, though this sanguine view may not be easily sustained either in concept or practice. In any case, under such a model of design process, arbitrariness is not eliminated but rather diffused.

Both hypothetical examples raise difficult questions. If one accepts the first model, is there a fundamental arbitrariness of human thought and action which is not addressed within the realm of design it retains? Does the participatory model, in its pursuit of immediate conflict resolution, obscure the arbitrariness embedded in its own process? In both cases, does the avoidance of direct address of the arbitrariness which must be present in some degree undermine the search for a rational process and a coherent product?

If these two models are "straw men," they may nonetheless sensitize us to alternative positions on design process, including the one explored in what follows.

Hypotheses

In the initiation of any human activity some ultimate arbitrariness will be introduced. Design only begins with that risk. The search for rationality in design is not a matter of eliminating that risk, but rather one of turning that gamble to our advantage. Alternative risks are available, or can be invented by us. Both the design process and its implementation are means to give those risks coherent fulfillment while also testing, revising, learning from, and, if need be, rejecting them.

Design, seen in this way, is not some arcane, special process, but is rather allied to common sense and to the pursuit of rationality. As such, it may be hypothesized that other studies of rational thought and practices may serve as the basis, or as models, for the understanding of design.

In the discussion that follows immediately, and in three studies of architectural production by our group, we seek to investigate whether a qualified version of Imre Lakatos's methodology of scientific research programs may provide an explanatory and normative model of design processes.

Part 1: Lakatos's Methodology of Scientific Research Programs

Only a sketch can be attempted here of the epistemological program which Lakatos advanced.[1]

Lakatos developed his program within the epistemological tradition known as "falsificationism." A naive version of falsificationism might run like this. In science, we seek to put forward internally consistent theories from which we may deduce empirical claims that are subject to experimental test. Now, since true consequences may follow from false premises, a corroborating experimental result is no more than that—a corroboration, not a verification, of the theory under test. However, false consequences cannot follow from true premises, so negative test results assure us that the theory is wrong. By this asymmetry of test results, it is claimed that our only secure knowledge comes in the failure of our theory—thus falsificationism. Since falsification is our only secure ground, it is claimed that the success of science relies on its construction of falsifiable theories, the strenuous pursuit of experimental failure, and thus the establishment of the ground for a new, more advanced cycle of theory building.

Such a naive falsificationism is subject to both logical and historical criticism. Every experiment has among its premises not only the theory under test but also initial conditions stated, for example, as meter readings or other measures. Not only might these initial conditions be stated in error, but they also assume other background knowledge, perhaps theories of optics or heat or whatever that are not considered to be under test. Yet, logically, one can as well direct the negative test results against these initial conditions or against the background knowledge as against the theory under test. Not only can one do this logically, but the history of science is replete with instances of such deflection of falsification away from the theory under test. Furthermore, such deflection need not be, and often is not, an *ad hoc* stratagem wrongfully saving a pet theory. The deflection may reveal weakness in the background theory and provide a step in the corroboration of the theory under test.

Thus we must recognize that we always test large systems of theories rather than isolated ones, and naive falsification cannot account for the locus to which negative test results are directed. A sophisticated version of falsificationism, primarily associated with the work of Karl Popper,[2] recognizes the difficulty just discussed, but would solve the problem through an appeal to the institutional structure of scientific inquiry. Popper recognizes that large systems of theory are under test, but he argues that the scientific community can, and does, guess and agree as to what part of the system has failed. It is then by convention, by agreement among those scientists who succeed in deciding for the whole of the scientific community, that falsification is saved from its logical and historical critique. This is a conventionalism introduced at the level of fact, or at least at the level where fact will be directed against the theoretical system.

The possible arbitrariness of this procedure is highlighted by the further epistemological problem that falsification offers no unique characterization of the background knowledge which is assumed to be necessary for corroboration. It is quite conceivable that a redrafting of the background knowledge would lead to a different agreement within the scientific community.

It is within (or is it from?) this epistemological setting that Lakatos makes his contribution. Lakatos abandons the notion of a strong test even as modified by Popper's conventions of the scientific community. In abandoning strong tests, Lakatos, nonetheless, wishes to maintain an account of the success and rationality of scientific method.

Lakatos's distinctive contribution is the shift of the methodological unit of epistemological analysis from the theory to the "research program." A research program is strongly temporal and historical, though Lakatos is concerned more with the logic of its development than with a historical account. A research program is built around a particular problem situation. Lakatos recognizes that more than one research program may be addressed to any problem situation. Indeed, it is in the competition and comparison of research programs that Lakatos locates much of the success and rationality of science.

Constitution of a Research Program
In the course of a research program there is a series of theoretical states. Each of these theoretical states retains a common element, and it is the constancy of this common element which identifies the series as a single program.

Lakatos refers to this common element as the "hard core," the postulates upon which the program of research is based. According to Lakatos's construction, the hard core is methodologically inviolable. That is, from within its own research program, neither criticism nor test results may be directed against the hard core. Neither the origin, nor the structure, nor the completeness of the hard core are stipulated by Lakatos; these would be historical questions. It may indeed be that the hard core was not articulated by the researchers within a program and that important elements of the hard core were held implicitly. The rationality of assuming the hard core is not known *a priori*; it is a matter of agreement, of convention, to assume the hard core. The fruitfulness of doing so, the efficiency of this particular agreement in the pursuit of knowledge, can only be adduced through the development of the program itself.

With Lakatos, then, the conventional element of science has invaded, to accept his terminology literally, the very core of the scientific enterprise. Convention is an aspect of that which assures the maintenance of the program. It is also this hard core which yields and shapes what Lakatos calls the "negative heuristic" of the program: those possible hypotheses or steps which are not to be entertained because of their inconsistency with the hard core. This conventionalism, this resistance to criticism, this degree of arbitrariness is necessary to the construction and development of the program, but it is tested and controlled in the larger construction of the scientific enterprise.

While coherent development of the program is, on the one hand, facilitated by the maintenance of the hard core, there must also be that which is open to change. So Lakatos's hard core is surrounded by what he sometimes called the "protective belt" of auxiliary hypotheses. It is these hypotheses which must bear the brunt of test. Negative experimental results are directed against the auxiliary hypotheses which are then altered to maintain the coherence of the hard core with the data.

This account of the protective belt explains its logical role, but one can also note a more positive aspect of the auxiliary hypotheses. Additional or improved hypotheses perfect and extend the reach of the hard core.

So then, anything goes? May it not be that the hard core is accepted by convention and protected while auxiliary hypotheses are adapted *ad hoc* to maintain and elaborate an illusionary explanatory power? Such an inadequate state of affairs could indeed arise and be recognized within Lakatos's account, but it would not be justified by his account. Much of Lakatos's text is devoted to the analysis of the development of a research program and the comparison of competing research programs. Lakatos seeks to distinguish progressive and degenerative problem shifts within programs. For his detailed position and some of its difficulties one must consult the literature, but one may say that the inadequate programmatic course mentioned in this paragraph would be recognized as a degenerative program expected to suffer neglect and extinction. But even here, Lakatos expects no death blows. Artificial maintenance of an apparently weak program may yet prove to have been the courageous tenacity of its researchers. Such assessments may change and are unpredictable, but the information on which those assessments are to be made is rationally structured and publicly available.

Finally, a summary and one addition in the explication of Lakatos's methodology of research programs. The research program is characterized and maintained by its conventionally accepted hard core. The hard core is protected by a body of auxiliary hypotheses which can be adjusted to maintain internal agreement among the hard core, the auxiliary hypotheses, and the data. The negative heuristic is closely allied to the hard core, a set of injunctions against possible hypotheses or research strategies inconsistent with the hard core. Finally, Lakatos also posits a positive heuristic, methodological directives or suggestions which help to drive the program. So much for the nature of a research program, but it is the assessment of that program in its empirical, explanatory power and in its strength relative to competing programs that lends us conviction, at least provisionally, about the programs and thus also about the risk that was taken in asserting its hard core.

Lakatos's Methodology and Design Research

If now one proposes to adopt Lakatos's methodology of scientific research programs in the consideration of design—more specifically of architectural design—is one committed to a view of design as science, or to the scientizing of design?

Such a concern is usually advanced by critics who hold that science is positivistic. Whether the inquirer defends or attacks such positivism and whatever may be the implicit valuations of science and design is irrelevant in the face of the critic's conviction that science and design are distinguished by the positivity of science.

But it is just this positivist view of science against which Popper fought as he confronted the Vienna Circle. Lakatos goes further in his increasingly conventional and historical reconstruction of science. He is not just interested in the history of science; the history of science becomes integral to the epistemology itself. From the other side of the divide, the historian, Thomas Kuhn, contemporarily forced reconsiderations in the epistemology of science.[3] Yehuda Elkana presses the issue to the point where the distinction between the history and philosophy of science hardly exists. Science comes to be seen as one more—very important, but one more—cultural system.[4]

Arriving at this point, we are neither forced nor inclined to deny distinctions between such cultural systems as science and art, but neither are we inclined to draw hard and fast boundaries. The acceptance by convention of certain assumptions in order to initiate and drive a body of work; the examination of a body of work for internal structure and for its relation to other systems and to empirical conditions; the embedding of this work in a historical and cultural setting; the necessity of institutional support and constraints—all of these appear as crucial features of human production. Insights into the condition of this production within one subdomain may serve, at least, as a potential model for other domains.

Thus the ambition of the current work is not to make a science of architecture or design. Within the broader claim that such activities as science and architecture share certain features as cultural systems, there is no desire to deny distinctions or to force methodologies from one of these systems upon another. Rather, we propose, Lakatosian style, the agreement that one attempt a research program concerned with architectural design as a rational enterprise subject to an analysis related to Lakatos's methodology of research programs. How our program ends up, how different it may be from that of Lakatos, is best left to the results of the effort itself.

Artifactual Research Program

Whether one thinks of a single work of architecture or certain sustained patterns of work by one or more architects, it is not implausible to think of something like a "hard core" that sets and maintains the direction of the work. Other architectural projections or hypotheses might well be adaptable in the way of Lakatos's auxiliary hypotheses, adaptable in order to maintain a coherence between the hard core and empirical conditions. Lakatos's elimination of the concept of "strong test" and his consequent acceptance of the elusiveness of definitive rejection of a program are more consistent with criticism in architecture than earlier emphases on decisive experimental results.

If, then, one begins with some positive associations between Lakatos's methodology of scientific research programs and programs of architectural design, where does one identify problematic distinctions between these two areas of cultural production?

In Lakatos's case, one has a nonmalleable hard core and an equally obdurate empirical reality mediated by the adaptable auxiliary hypotheses. In architecture, the very nature of the enterprise is to transform the empirical conditions—obviously within physical constraints, but nonetheless significantly for the cultural system under consideration. Thus the artifact that is architecture is malleable; it, along with the auxiliary hypotheses, may be shaped to maintain coherence within the entire program.

To speak a bit poetically, the architect is involved in making his own reality as well as his theory. As just mentioned, this new reality may serve as the fulfillment of the theory rather than as its empirical constraint. Still more important, however, is that every artifact will also be something other or more than the fulfillment of one programmatic theory. The artifact will be open to other interpretations; it has a quasiautonomy relative both to any given theory or interpretation and relative to external factors. This argues that the architect (or any designer and no doubt many other actors in cultural production) is simultaneously involved in two related but not deterministically controlled activities: a conceptual program (similar to that of Lakatos) and what might be called an artifactual program, concerned with the systematic exploration of physical models.

Models (artifacts in the artifactual research program which may include graphic representations of other artifacts) always implicate more than is intended or than can be subsumed under any single conceptual program. Consequently, there is necessarily a quasiautonomy between the two series. While the two series of theories and models may alternate in providing a critique of one another, they do not exhaust one another. Other conceptual research programs may be directed to any given artifact just as other artifacts may stand in a rational relation to a given conceptual program.

In positing these two parallel research programs, no priority is given to either one. The two programs are not deterministically linked; either one may anticipate and influence the other; one may terminate without implying termination of the other. As already stated, each may provide a critique of the other, but no more than in science does one expect a "strong test." Perhaps still more than in science, competing programs can and should proliferate. Yet in practice, such programs do thrive or falter according to their perceived fruitfulness, their success at innovating or in better meeting perceived needs. The attempt to adapt methodology of research programs to architectural production is not seen as a revolution in architectural thought and practice, but rather as a potentially more detailed and rigorous manner of clarifying and judging competing practices.

Internal and External History of Research Programs

For Lakatos, the structure of a research program and its logical development establishes a quite autonomous, what he called "internal," history. Indeed, he sees science, properly conceived, as possessing such autonomy. Lakatos recognizes an "external" history as having its place in accounting for sociological and psychological features that may enhance or impede the achievement of science; but such matters do not, for Lakatos, effect the rational reconstruction offered by the internal history of a research program.

Whether even science possesses this degree of autonomy is widely challenged.[5] In a field such as architecture, I would suggest that this issue—the degree of autonomy of the practice—is usually part of the theoretical program.

That is, explicit or implicit claims are made within the program's hard core or aux-iliary hypotheses as to whether and how social, economic, political, technolog-ical, psychological or other factors are internalized in the theory and practice of architecture.

Thus in proposing a schema of two parallel research programs for the analysis of architectural production we may parallel Lakatos's distinction of an internal history (that history required by the programs themselves) versus an ex-ternal history. But in doing so, one is not prejudging the issue of the degree of auton-omy of a field such as architecture. Rather, one is making two other claims. The first is that the range of factors to be considered and the manner in which they become determinant are formulated in terms of the program's own methodology. Thus, sec-ond, important debate on the degree of autonomy of a discipline such as architecture may be sharpened and advanced by a more rigorous comparison of programs.

The study of Le Corbusier that follows examines the develop-ment and refinement of an architectural program through a series of works.

Part 2: Architectural Research Programs in the Work of Le Corbusier

The present essay does not offer the scope for a detailed analysis of an architectural research program, but will rather illustrate such an approach through selected works of Le Corbusier. Two early projects, the young Jeanneret-Le Corbusier's sketches at the Acropolis and his Maison Dom-ino, will be presented as independent, not fully developed architectural programs. These rudimentary programs are then seen as weakly conflated in the Maison La Roche. With the Five Points of the mid 1920s, the Maison Dom-ino receives an important reinterpretation capable of subsuming the earlier concepts in a new, coherent program which is progressively realized in the major villas of the late 1920s.[6]

Promenade Architecturale

The first fragmentary program turns on the concept which Le Corbusier was later to call the *promenade architecturale*. Perhaps this term could be read as "architecture consid-ered as the orchestration of spatial experience."

Such a concept may not sound so startling today, but one must remember that well into the nineteenth century treatises on architecture relied primarily on an objective view of the autonomous rules of architecture itself, best exemplified in the study of the classical orders. Even movements, such as the "pictur-esque," that put new emphasis on the viewer interpreted the relation between viewer and object as one based more on association than on abstract issues of perception and comprehension.

When Jeanneret-Le Corbusier, on his "voyage d'orient" of 1911, came to the ultimate canonic site of Western architecture, the Acropolis in Athens, he did not repeat or seek to make more precise the earlier researches into the orders, the temple form, or their sophisticated formal nuances. Le Corbusier rather produced a set of sketches which vividly evoke the sequential experience of the ascent of the Acropolis. From outside the Propylaea, we are already embraced by the heights of the Acropolis and the Temple of Athena Nike above. Passing into the Propylaea, the Parthenon appears through a screen of columns. Though these columns are just before the viewer, or precisely because they are so near, one does not see them as wholes. These columns *are* a screen, not sophisticated elements of precise proportions and prescribed relations to the whole of which they are a part.

The Parthenon itself, more distant, suggests an ordered whole, but for now that order is a matter both of prior knowledge and the anticipation of our fuller experience of it. For the moment, the Parthenon appears not only partially obscured but also viewed from angles, from the side and from below. We hold no vantage point from which we may possess the building objectively. And if we did possess such a vantage point, this drawing tells us we would be missing something else—experience itself and the knowledge which comes only through such experience. Architecture is known by the temporal experience of a sentient being, and Le Corbusier's drawing reveals the Acropolis in such a way as to make this proposition plausible.

Though this material offers only the rudiments of a program, I do see here elements which fit the model I am advancing. At a conceptual level, Le Corbusier is concerned with how we correlate experience and knowledge. He proposes an abstract experience of architecture. We need not know anything of Greek architecture or culture; we do not rely on associations. The manner of experience and how we learn through that experience is transferable to other settings. If it is important that this exercise considers the Parthenon, it is precisely because this insistence on experience is more forceful when made in the presence of a work for which we have previously instilled modes of appropriation. Yet the "physical models"—the Acropolis itself as well as Le Corbusier's drawings—are crucial to this fragmentary research program: the Acropolis affording the opportunity to test out the propositions which the drawings advance.

The Maison Dom-ino

For the moment, we turn to another rudimentary and wholly independent research program well known under the name Maison Dom-ino.[7] The devastation of Flanders in the First World War urgently required the rehabilitation of that region at the earliest possible date. Already interested in the relatively new building material, reinforced concrete, Le Corbusier sought a way to provide a rational and economic solution to the emergency housing need.

The drawing which shows the standardized skeleton used in this research project, a drawing summary in nature and rich in suggestive ambiguity, came to stand for the Maison Dom-ino. We too will wish to return to this famous drawing, but if we are to understand the housing research program which generated it, we must also consider other contemporary drawings. The reflected ceiling plan reveals that floor and roof slabs of the construction are not monolithic as they appear in the Maison Dom-ino drawing, but are rather articulated as girders and joists formed by lightweight tiles. Thus the floor construction is directional and has preferred locations for attachments such as non-bearing partitions. Indeed, possible floor plans drawn by Le Corbusier show close adherence not only to the structural lines of the floor construction, but even especially to such dominant structural characteristics as the columns and the edges of the slabs. Nonbearing walls bury the columns at the end walls. Nonbearing partitions uniformly frame into internal columns. These partitions, not as thick as the columns, are normally placed so as to obscure the presence of the columns in the more important rooms; the projecting part of any column remains in closets, vestibules, or service spaces.

These few observations together with the architect's own commentary permit a reconstruction of the main lines of Le Corbusier's Maison Dom-ino research. The reinforced concrete frame provides the entire structure and thus permits a rationalization of the construction process. Government, in support of a modern construction industry (which Le Corbusier sought to form), would effectively provide the standardized structural frame. The infill of that frame could be carried out according to the needs and constraints imposed locally; on whatever schedule local, not necessarily skilled, workmen using local, perhaps rubble, materials would complete the houses to variant plans and elevations.

Conceptually, the Maison Dom-ino, as a housing research project, proposes that new materials and new techniques in the hands of a rationalized industry can efficiently provide a primary structure which will facilitate the solution of a crucial housing problem without inhibiting the efficient and positive employment of local resources.

The Maison Dom-ino, seen in the context of the entire housing research project, does not imply other readings which the skeletal drawing has induced. That famous drawing appears to emphasize primary structure so forcefully that an unintended reading must also have been immediately available: architecture, or this new architecture based on a modern technology, should give direct expression to structural elements. Yet the plastering of the ceiling surfaces in this drawing and the burying of the columns in the typical plans render the structure mute. Neither here nor in any work in his career did Le Corbusier make expression of structure dominant.

Other readings of the Maison Dom-ino, some of them proffered and exploited by Le Corbusier later in his career, were not immediately available if we consider the original housing research as a whole. Some of these readings are: the primary structure as the ordering of space, as an aesthetic order, as the facilitator of the "free plan," as a module of an indefinitely vast system, as a modernist self-referential system. Most of these readings are too commonly diffused to be given specific references. Le Corbusier's "free plan" is discussed below. The Maison Dom-ino as a modernist self-referential system is an anachronistic reading offered by Peter Eisenman.[8] Such readings reveal the fruitfulness of continued inquiry into such a rewardingly ambiguous drawing as that of the Maison Dom-ino. It is a nonconservative model. But the very limits of the complete Maison Dom-ino research project preclude the inclusion of these innovations in the historical moment of the Maison Dom-ino.

Towards an Architecture

The remainder of this paper argues that the two rudimentary research programs already introduced gradually merged in the career of Le Corbusier, yielding a series of brilliant works within a research program (or programs) of increasingly rich implication.

The first work I introduce, the Maison La Roche in Paris, offers a marvelously diverse architectural promenade which can still be enjoyed today in this house, which is now the Fondation Le Corbusier. Indeed, the Maison La Roche is so dominantly "architecture considered as the orchestration of spatial experience" that one wishes only to encourage a visit. If words can have any hold on this house, they must be used almost solely in the service of description.

The Maison La Roche flanks and closes the end of a small private street. The house, or one part of the house, announces itself from afar, a taut convex surface that immediately conveys more of the interior volume than of the entrance, or plan, or larger organization of the house. To the left of the convex surface projects a small balcony, too small but to be a moment for recapitulation in our later itinerary. Coming nearer, the flank of the house at the right side of the street becomes more prominent. The humble openings of the ground floor of this lateral wing, the now obvious open space under the convex volume, and the retreat of that convexity into the juncture of the two wings continue to lead us into the angle of the L. Near enough, the recessed wall in that angle finally reveals a still simple, but larger blank metal door. The conviction of entrance is given less by the door than by the large window above, through which we perceive a small skylight obliquely above the entrance space which rises to the flat roof. Just behind the second floor window is a bridge that assures continuity of movement between the two wings. Admitted to the house, one is under the bridge, initiated to a large space that is compressed in its depth by the proximate, blank party wall, but released in the three-story-high volume of this central, communicating space. The party wall beyond slides continuously out of the entrance hall to the left defining a small, high space for the stair, confirmed by another small balcony at the head of the stair, projecting back into the space in which we now stand, and a perfect pendant to the exterior balcony we still anticipate at the far end of the convex volume. Turning on the half landing of the stair, at the furthest corner of the house and site, we are afforded the best, most distanced view of the entrance hall with its galleries at each floor. At the head of the stair, the balcony suspends us in the entrance hall, a gallery carries us either to the bridge to the lateral wing or directly to the salon in the convex volume: a two-story space lit by high clerestories. To reach the curving ramp that ascends at the interior of the convex, now concave wall one must go to the far corner, to the exterior balcony from which one can recapitulate one's every movement from initial entrance to the street to the interior bridge we have yet to cross. Ascending the ramp (more of a sensory-motor experience than any code would permit) one comes first to a gallery overlooking the salon and then to a gallery room overlooking the entrance hall. The flat roof is now so close over one's head that that plane too plays its distinctive role, as have so many other surfaces, in defining place and movement within this orchestration of spatial experience.

One could, and perhaps should continue this verbal tour, particularly to do justice to the roof garden and its potential link with the other unit of this double house fully known as the Maison La Roche-Jeanneret. Enough has been said to expose one's conviction that Le Corbusier achieved here an exceptional architectural promenade, devoid of easy associations, yet as lyrical and compelling as it is abstract. If at the Acropolis, the concept of architectural promenade afforded another and valuable reading of a canonic site, then at the Maison La Roche Le Corbusier invents an architecture that offers another compelling promenade.

Still, there are reservations. For all the qualities of this house, of this promenade, the experience is very particular, self-indulgent, lacking in convincing relation to other aspects of architecture. The awkward narrow L-shape of the La Roche site is well exploited by Le Corbusier, but the only generalization to be drawn is just that: exploit the site. The Maison La Roche does use some reinforced concrete construction; but this and all other matters of structure, form and function are placed in *ad hoc* service to the promenade which is, finally, too arbitrary. The Maison La Roche offers an artifactual research program that is all enticing auxiliary hypotheses, devoid of hard core principles and played out in a special context that constrained all empirical conditions to ensure realization of the not fully developed program.

If Le Corbusier creatively advanced a new reading of the Acropolis, there his architectural promenade stood alongside, did not displace, earlier formal, systemic and iconographic readings. Architecture, and most notably the Parthenon, remains for Le Corbusier "a pure creation of the mind,"[9] even as it is revealed to us experientially. The architectural promenade of the Maison La Roche received too little support from the other dimensions of architecture.

The Five Points

A few years later, in his well-known "Five Points," Le Corbusier economically integrated many aspects of architecture including a new reading of his Maison Dom-ino and an implicit architectural promenade.

The crucial and first of the Five Points is the point support of the modern concrete or steel frame. The minimal footprint of these columns—pilotis in Le Corbusier's terminology—was an obvious feature of the new structural systems, but Le Corbusier drew some not so obvious, pregnant architectural conclusions.

Contrasting the modern frame system with traditional bearing wall construction, Le Corbusier emphasized that walls as space dividers and enclosure need not coincide with structure, indeed need not be present at all. The building need no longer stand on a basement but could rise free of the ground save for its sparse array of columns. At each floor, and without traditional constraints due to vertical structural continuities, walls and partitions could be located at will, yielding a "free plan." The structurally efficient flat slabs also yielded the flat, and thus usable roof surface. Cantilever construction placed the columns inward from the edge of the building, further enhancing the free plan and fulfilling what was already implicit in the free plan: the free facade. At all points, the wall might be present or not. No vertical structural element existed at the outer limits of the construction; thus the facade might assume any configuration.

It is here that one notes a significant anomaly both in Le Corbusier's diagrams and in his inclusion of a fifth point. The diagram for the free plan suggests a bold exploitation of this freedom except at the edges of the building. The implicit radicalness of the free facade is not diagrammed save in the inclusion of a fifth point: the strip window. Logically, the strip window (though importantly distinctive in that it reveals the absence of vertical structural members) should be only one instance of the general freedom of the facade. Indeed, the strip window is in many ways a rather constraining element; it requires uniformity in the extension of the facade and limits variation of the floor levels or other manipulations in section.

The Five Points reveal a distinctive, positive relation of architecture and new technology as conceived by Le Corbusier. The new architecture Le Corbusier proposes is not possible without the new materials and new structural systems. Yet what Le Corbusier advocates is neither the necessary conclusion (the modern frame had been, and continues to be, used otherwise) nor the ultimate exploitation of the new technology. Le Corbusier is not concerned with the exhibition of structure or of structural principle, but rather with the architectural potential afforded by the new technology. By the time of the Five Points, Le Corbusier seeks an architecture that is consonant with larger forces that he wishes both to identify and advance: an *esprit nouveau*. The free plan and free facade are generated by new conceptions of the environment and the city, of manner of life and thought generated by such matters and only facilitated by the new technologies. By the same token, there is no compulsion to use the technology to its limits; one uses technology to the extent and in the way it serves one's program. And this *esprit nouveau* is not solely about new potentials and freedoms; it is also heir to a Western rationalist tradition that expects these freedoms to exist within a cognitive and moral order. It is for such reasons, I believe, that Le Corbusier restrained himself from the more extravagant readings of free plan or free facade. In the Five Points he sought what was not adequately present in the Maison La Roche, a knowing interrelation of many aspects of architecture, including materials, structure, pragmatic use considerations, systemic relations of elements, iconography, and intellectual order.

The Five Points and the "Satisfaction of the Mind"
The first projects for the villa at Garches reveal a coincidence rather than a coordination of the subsidiary research programs we have been tracing. Early sketches show Le Corbusier considering a systematic use of a reinforced concrete frame: a system of square bays, one of which provides a central enclosed core throughout the height of the building and off which other bays radiate to form a complex of enclosed and open spaces, terraces and covered gardens. The L-plan of the Maison La Roche reappears and a passion for the architectural promenade overwhelms all else including the facilitating frame. After several such early projects, Le Corbusier quickly designed

the villa Stein much as it came to be built: a compact rectangular volume coherent with the implications of the Five Points.

A photograph taken by or for Le Corbusier is a key to the understanding of the Villa Stein. The photographer places us just off the suburban street, under the functionally gratuitous canopy of the porter's lodge. From this position, just as when one viewed the Maison La Roche from afar, one can anticipate much about the eventual experience of the house. However, unlike the Maison La Roche, here the first impression also yields many clues that are simultaneously part of our intellectual framework and characteristic of the house. The ground surface on which we stand not only extends in a continuous plane up to the facade of the house but implicitly extends through the body of the house itself. It is extraordinary for a European house, particularly a house of distinction, to provide such unmediated access to its interior. The Villa Stein, as built, does not stand free on pilotis, but virtually it does.

Reflecting again on the photograph, we are positioned under the too high canopy that stands in the midst of a huge suburban space, distant from the house to which it refers. Such a canopy has little reference to our actual physical needs. It reaches out into a space with stronger reference to the distant villa than to the lodge to which it is attached. It documents the scale of the villa. Between ground and canopy we already know the physical reality of floor planes marked out by the strip windows of the facade of the villa. The orthogonality of the spatial grid of the villa and its site is immediately available to us in the planes of the ground, the canopy and the perspectively recessive plane of the wall of the lodge at our right which contrasts with the frontal plane of the villa. The necessity of our movement and sequential appropriation of this site is obvious, but we also know that this acquisition will be facilitated by correspondences between our preexisting mental structure of a gridded space and the actual deployment of architectural form. There is an assumption that our rationality rests on certain categories and an order which architecture— "pure creation of the mind"—makes manifest.

The present context does not permit a description of the experience of the Villa Stein comparable to that already given for the Maison La Roche. But if this were done it would be clear that the vitality of the architectural promenade has lost nothing for being located within an ordering framework which the architecture makes concrete just as the framework facilitates the appropriation of the architectural order.

The Villa Stein is a successful integration of the architectural promenade and of the Maison Dom-ino programs, but only if we recognize an interpretation of the Maison Dom-ino other than that of its origins. Like the Maison Dom-ino, the Villa Stein distinguishes primary structure and infill. Now, however, this distinction has nothing to do with staging of construction or other pragmatic issues. Nor is the primary structure assertive in the establishment of a spatial or other architectural order. It is well known that the Villa Stein is set out on a plaid grid of 3 x 5 bays or 4 × 6 columns.[10] Here as in the Maison Dom-ino the columns at the end walls are suppressed. At the principal floor of the house, if we consider the 16 internal column locations, two columns are completely eliminated and only five stand free, in positions that yield no easy clues to the larger order. The architectural order of the Villa Stein relies on the structurally secondary planar organization; the concrete frame permits a free plan which secures this desired order.

Space does not here permit discussion of another of the great villas of the late 1920s, the Villa Savoye at Poissy. While the columnar system of the Villa Savoye takes on architectural prominence, a sustained analysis would show, I argue, that the columnar system here too is subservient to the planar organization of the secondary structure. The columnar system becomes apparent; it is not, however, an overall coherent system and, where it is ordered, it reinforces the planar system.

The Four Compositions

After the design of the Villa Savoye, Le Corbusier made a diagram which reflected on the research program presented here. The diagram is called "The Four Compositions," presenting a sketch plan, aerial view and comments on four houses: the Maison La Roche, the villa at Garches, a house identified as that at Stuttgart though it has more affinities with the villa at Carthage, and the Villa Savoye.

Only the aerial view of the Maison La Roche is in perspective, a fact that accords with Le Corbusier's own comments, freighted with implicit criticism. He sees this house as of a "very facile genre, picturesque, eventful; one could, however, discipline it by classification and hierarchy." In contrast, the other three houses are first grouped as "cubic compositions (pure prisms)" and then differentiated. Of the rigorous, prismatic composition of the villa at Garches, Le Corbusier notes "very difficult (satisfaction of the mind)."

The third composition exploits the five points as they seem literally to invite but which, as we have seen, Le Corbusier resisted. The column grid is taken as given and the plan and elevation may be what they will. Le Corbusier again appears to imply a self-criticism of the third composition: "very easy, practical, combinable."

Le Corbusier's comments on the Villa Savoye suggest his sense of a satisfactory conclusion of this search for an architectural order simultaneously practical and satisfying to the mind: "very generous; one recognizes at the exterior an architectural will; at the interior, one satisfies all the functional needs (admission of sunlight, contiguities, circulation)."

Conclusion

In this presentation I did not seek to marshal a detailed analysis of Le Corbusier's work using the full battery of Lakatos's methodological concepts and terminology. I did seek to present a number of works, the earliest of which are too limited to represent architectural research programs but which nonetheless contributed to such a full program as delineated in the period of the Five Points.

What was constant before and after that juncture is a dialectic conducted between sets of conceptual issues and developing physical models which explicate, test, and induce revision of those conceptual issues.

A detailed analysis of these works, making claims as to what constituted the hard core, the auxiliary hypotheses and the heuristics of both the conceptual and artifactual research programs would itself be a historiographic research program. No doubt a first version would fall to criticism, but in that exposition and criticism our understanding would be enlarged and reinforced. Even the present informal presentation correlates certain physical features and programmatic concerns, denying other available readings and thus opening an arena of debate.

An important issue arose with the most famous of the Maison Dom-ino drawings. Its ambiguity as a source for influential alternative readings is readily welcomed. However, these alternatives are not acknowledged until they are identified and employed in larger patterns of discussion, quite possibly new research programs. This is true within the career of Le Corbusier himself. The Maison Domino bore meanings in the mid-1920s which it could not have possessed before. In a full exposition I would like to continue this story down to the Carpenter Center for the Visual Arts at Harvard. By that time Le Corbusier's understanding of architecture and cognition was sufficiently different that a much fuller exploitation of the freedoms of the Five Points was necessary and, with that, the acceptance of another reading of the Maison Dom-ino. On the success or failure of such claims stand not only our understanding of a work such as the Carpenter Center, but also what value and role we accord it in the career of Le Corbusier and in the continuing debates about architecture.

Notes

1. Imre Lakatos, *The Methodology of Scientific Research Programmes* (Cambridge: Cambridge University Press, 1978).
2. Karl Popper, *The Logic of Scientific Discovery* (New York: Basic Books, 1959).
3. Thomas Kuhn, *The Structure of Scientific Revolutions* (Chicago: University of Chicago Press, 1962).
4. Yehuda Elkana, "A Programmatic Attempt at an Anthropology of Knowledge," typescript distributed at the conference "Conventions, Canons and Criticism," Massachusetts Institute of Technology, April 1982.
5. See, for example, Elkana's paper cited in note 4.
6. Le Corbusier and Pierre Jeanneret, *Oeuvre complète 1910–1929* (1929; Zurich: Girsberger, 1964), pp. 23, 128–129, 189, and passim.
7. E. Gregh, "The Dom-ino Idea," *Oppositions* 15/16 (Winter/Spring 1979), pp. 65–87.
8. Peter Eisenman, "Aspects of Modernism: Maison Dom-ino and the Self-Referential Sign," *Oppositions* 15/16 (Winter/Spring 1979), pp. 118–128.
9. Le Corbusier, *Towards a New Architecture* (1923; London: The Architectural Press, 1964), pp. 185 ff.
10. Colin Rowe, "The Mathematics of the Ideal Villa," in Rowe, *The Mathematics of the Ideal Villa and Other Essays* (Cambridge: MIT Press, 1976); Colin Rowe and Robert Slutzky, "Transparency: Literal and Phenomenal," in ibid.

Jean-Louis Cohen   **"The Italophiles at Work"** "Les italophiles au travail," from *La coupure entre*

architectes et intellectuels, ou les enseignements de l'italianophylie (Paris: In

extenso, 1984); translated for this anthology by Brian Holmes

❚ *see* **x–xii** ❚   Theory is ready to travel. While at its best theory will stay close to the historicity of its material, mediating between architectural practice and specific historical and social contexts, theoretical constructions also possess an uncanny capacity to cross over, drift, and expand in culture, however much authors, institutions, and orthodoxies try to confine them. Theory is nourished by circulation — by borrowing and trading, by unconscious influence or wholesale appropriation — but, through the accidents of its own history, a body of theory can also be dislodged and pressed into the service of a quite different one, reinvested with unexpected content, and refunctioned to perform unsuspected functions.

The mid-1980s seemed to be a time when theoretical movements of different sorts became recognizable, not the least of which were the transactions among French poststructuralism, the architecture theory of Italy, and professional architectural practice in both those countries — all of which constitutes Jean-Louis Cohen's problematic of traveling theory — to which one could add the analogous Italophilia of North America and Spain.[1] While Cohen's concise and specific history of these movements is in no way a condemnation of the instrumentalization of theory as an aid in the retooling of design practice, it is a reminder that, if theory's real subject is history, theory must also constantly historicize itself. Theory, as much as architecture, has to be grasped in the place and time out of which it emerges; we must attend to the different reasons theory is begun and the unforeseen uses to which those beginnings can actually be put.

Perhaps we could go so far as to say that part of the job of theory is to partially undo itself by taking as part of its subject the historical reality of its different audiences, its institutionalization, its oppositions. This, lest it assume that what was once responsive and expansive will always be so.

Note

1.   On the American appropriation of Derrida and other traveling theories, see Jean-Louis Cohen, "L'architettura intellettualizzata: 1970–1990," *Casabella* 586–587 (January–February 1992).

In the mid-1970s the French became fascinated with Italian architectural culture. This fascination was to provide a key resource for the reconstruction of architecture as a discipline, as it converged with new state policies and with the specific questions asked by architects in the period after 1968. A radical reform of architectural education giving official sanction to the introduction of the social sciences into the architecture schools was matched, after 1972, by the actions of the Architectural Research group founded in the wake of the Lichnérowicz report in 1970. The report proposed:

The rapid creation of a research community, a milieu bringing together people and teams of all types;

The acquisition and dissemination of methods and knowledge, including the new fundamentals on which architectural creativity must rest, and the processes of programming, design, and realization which are necessary to give shape to this creativity.[1]

Among the themes which emerged from this field of research, those of urban architecture and history rapidly came to be seen as essential, alongside the sociological concerns which had marked the beginnings of the inquiry. These themes not only contributed to the production of research but also spread into the domain of the project, as if to demonstrate the close ties between intellectual culture and architecture which characterize the Italian scene. Thus, even as the idea of urban architecture made headway and the notions of typology and morphology worked their way into the thinking of certain professors, a building by one of the theorists of typo-morphology—the Gallaratese complex by Carlo Aymonino—lent its stimulus to the projects of Paul Chemetov.[2] The identification of such lines of influence enables us to note once again how the Italophile phenomenon acted to reveal the split between architects and intellectuals. What was at stake in Carlo Aymonino's work, as his interest in the *section* demonstrates, is in fact a reference to Le Corbusier's Unité d'Habitation. This is the reference that Chemetov picked up at one remove, allowing him to go beyond the neo-brutalist touches in the details and trim of his buildings—an earlier form of homage to Le Corbusier—and to add a consideration of the large dimension to more linear projects.

The French Sources of Italian Discourses

Such indirect relations to a tradition rooted in French culture would not only show up in architectural references, but above all, and much more importantly for our study, in a series of theoretical themes which are seemingly exterior to the field of architecture. It is striking, for instance, to see the extent to which Aldo Rossi's work, as summarized in *The Architecture of the City*, is inscribed in the French tradition of urban geography, whose influence extended to the Institut d'Urbanisme at the University of Paris in the time of Marcel Poëte, and indeed, to the entire French school of geography. Rossi had actually rediscovered Poëte before the latter's work was reprinted in France (thanks to the clairvoyance of Hubert Tonka)[3] and at a moment when his contribution had been practically forgotten in the very places where his activity had developed, at least to judge from the rather technocratic city planning class taught by Robert Auzelle at the Institut d'Urbanisme.[4] But in his search for historical and theoretical references authorizing his understanding of the city as an architectural ensemble, Rossi took a broader interest in the production of the French social sciences, from *La mémoire collective* by Maurice Halbwachs to *Tristes tropiques* by Lévi-Strauss.[5] In addition to the in-house tradition of the Institut d'Urbanisme, from Poëte to Lavedan, he evoked the work of geographers like Georges Chabot and Jean Tricart, whose respective contributions to the notions of urban function and of morphology he stressed.[6] Rossi also took an interest in Max Sorre's thinking on urban geography and ecology.[7] One may suppose that his familiarity with these undertakings is a result of Pierre Georges's efforts to spread the doctrines of French geography through Italy, from an initial point of contact in Turin.

In the field of philosophy, the ideas of Sartre and Merleau-Ponty remained a dead letter for French architects in the fifties, and were to find no more than a weak echo thirty years later through an often superficial reading of *The Phenomenology of Perception*. In Italy, however, these ideas were taken up and promulgated by Enzo Paci, who communicated them to the Milanese architectural milieu.

As for Roland Barthes, he was mentioned by Manfredo Tafuri as early as *Theories and History of Architecture*,[8] long before French architectural circles paid any real attention to the *nouvelle critique*; Tafuri used Barthes to help unravel the tangle of semiotic theories that had been hastily applied to architectural objects. Only some six years later would the reference to Barthes be made official, in the debates of a conference staged by the Institut de l'Environnement in 1974, "Histoire et théories de l'architecture."[9] This event, whose title paraphrased Tafuri's subtle play of plurals, was practically the birth announcement of Italophilia. It also constituted the first outlines of a reference to Michel Foucault, whose work had already inspired a few undertakings by the CORDA group.[10] But once again, it was in Venice that Foucault's discourse would be most actively sought, though not always well understood. The same would be true of Deleuze, further along in the catalogue of theoretical fashions: it was again Tafuri who drew upon the French philosopher, following the work of Rella.[11]

In a less immediate way, Tafuri's latest attempts to redefine his "historical project" resonate both with Lacan's analytic discourse, through the comparison between historical inquiry and "interminable analysis,"[12] and with a type of historical work which itself has emerged from the *histoire des mentalités*, another product of French culture. Thus while the contact between the social sciences and architectural theory was only being made rather timidly by a few fringe figures in France, it was much more rapid and apparently more fruitful in Italy. No doubt this explains why French readers should have turned to Italian texts to discover themes that were easily accessible to them in terms of language, and yet at the same time very distant, because of the split.

The Breadth of Interest in Italy

What paths would the discovery of Italian architectural culture follow to a wider audience in France? Adopting multiple channels, from teaching to research, from journals to organized tours, from conferences to translations of books and articles, a veritable network of relatively unequal exchanges grew up between the two countries. This import business had its brokers, its insurance men, its creditors and debtors, and it permitted small quantities of symbolic capital to be amassed on either side of the Alps, to borrow Bourdieu's image.

Long-standing personal connections would be complemented by new friendships, allowing the most fertile initiatives to appear: thus behind the special Italy sections of journals like *Architecture Mouvement Continuité* or *L'Architecture d'Aujourd'hui*, it is easy to uncover the special relations between Roman or Venetian groups and particular figures on the Paris scene.

This curiosity toward Italian architectural culture must nonetheless be situated within a far larger current of interest in Italian culture, a current which marked the early 1970s and extended far beyond the spheres of cinema and literature (even if the discovery of figures such as Bertolucci and Sciascia was considerable). The political situation of Italy after *mai rampant*, with the strategy of union unity, and even more importantly, the presence of a communist party whose deep connection to cultural and intellectual life made it very different from its counterpart across the Alps, proved fascinating for many intellectuals on the French left, particularly since it was combined with the discovery of Gramsci's work, which had finally been well translated.[13] Gramsci's importance should not be underestimated; the discovery of the concept of *hegemony*, for example, brought into question an entire dogmatic tradition concerning the relation between politics and culture (a tradition already shaken up by Althusser's work). At the same time, Gramsci's analysis of the question of the state would allow for a less schematic approach to the total set of state functions.[14] This climate of interest in the world of Italian theory and politics is not unrelated to the echoes raised in France by experiments like the renovation of the city center of Bologna, which was precisely at the crossroads between the innovative political strategies of the PCI (Italian Communist Party) and the architectural doctrines derived from the research of the Venice group. A trip to Bologna became a must for architecture and city planning students, architects, and decision makers of every stripe, on a par with an excursion to the new British cities. Publications on the subject piled up,[15] and critiques of the PCI's municipal policy emanating from the left were also admitted to the pages of the journal *Espaces et Sociétés*.[16] In a certain way, the Bologna experiment made it possible for a non-reductive, guilt-free articulation of architecture and politics to be reformulated for French use, as Bernard Huet's remarks indicate:

The problem is no longer to strengthen peripheral "red" positions, but to reconsider the urban strategy in its territorial totality. Bologna must be credited for clearly demonstrating the terms of this reversal, and daring to return decision-making power to neighborhood inhabitants. . . . After Bologna, it can be said that the problem of safeguarding historical centers is no longer an aesthetic problem but a social and political one.[17]

The case of Bologna thus bore witness to a reconciliation of democracy and architecture which no longer involved the sacrifice of professionalism (as it had in the populist endeavors of the period immediately following 1968) and which also escaped from the vision of the architect as the single, willful *creator* of a space stripped of all urbanity:

> In Bologna, the problem of urban growth has been linked to the territorial dimension of the region, just as the preservation of the historical center is no more than a *structural* aspect of the overall city plan. Here, interventions based on centralized, technocratic planning are demystified, and actual results calmly demonstrate how to invent and employ new tools and methods for effective operations benefiting the inhabitants alone. In Bologna, even architects have become modest.[18]

The Quest for Urban Architecture

The rediscovery of the "modesty" so prized by Huet was accompanied by a use of tools which were none other than those of typology and morphology, approached less in their theoretical dimension than in their practical import. Thus the fascination for the Bologna experiment provided the gateway whereby French architectural culture opened up to the theme of urban architecture, both on the level of texts and of projects. The effects of an educational effort like that of Unité Pédagogique no. 8, for example, where a concern for the urban played a federating role during the founding years, could now reveal themselves fully, in combination with a better understanding of Italian authors and architects. A series of articles and fundamental inquiries proposed a vision of typology and morphology somewhat different from that of Carlo Aymonino and Aldo Rossi, though still based on their work. Architectural research allowed for the emergence of such analyses as "De l'îlot à la barre, contribution à une définition de l'architecture urbaine," by Jean Castex, Philippe Panerai, and Jean-Charles Depaule, in 1975,[19] or *Morphologie urbaine et typologie architecturale*, by Ahmet Gülgönen, François Laisney, and their team, in 1977.[20] The role of journals, however, was to prove essential in this debate. "Typologie de l'habitat et morphologie urbaine," an article published in 1974 by Christian Devillers, in the inaugural issue of *L'Architecture d'Aujourd'hui* under the directorship of Bernard Huet, is the first attempt to set these two inseparable notions rigorously into place.[21] Indeed, this text takes on a programmatic value in what can be considered the turning point of French architectural culture. Not only did the idea of urbanity appear in this issue, but also echoes of the analysis of the historical failure of the avant-garde as studied by Tafuri and his Institute, evoked indirectly in the editorial by Bernard Huet:

> For us, in 1974, remaining faithful to the spirit that presided over the creation of this journal means resuming the struggle begun by André Bloc some forty years ago. Of course, our struggle can no longer be stated in the same terms; it is not a question of fighting to defend some other form of modern architecture nostalgically attached to its origins, but rather of drawing the conclusions from the failure of the avant-garde, and discovering whether the preconditions of a contemporary architectural practice can now be stated clearly.[22]

A few years later, Devillers's analysis would be echoed in an article by Henri Raymond, who had been one of the first to familiarize himself with the Italian literature. Published in *Communications*, the article was an attempt to connect typological analysis with the work done by a French branch of urban sociology on the notion of the *cultural model*.[23] Raymond analyzed typology as a "structure of correspondence" between the spatial regularities of the project and the practices that the projected building would enclose. Both Raymond and Devillers shifted the emphasis of the Italian theorists by linking their ideas to the discourse of a certain type of social science which had emerged in the French context. This shift served to clarify aspects of the original analysis: unlike the typological abstraction of the projects in the center of Bologna, where architects sought to reconstruct the types *as they should have been* (an approach which Viollet-le-Duc had long ago suggested for his restorations), Devillers's and Raymond's consideration of the "practical/symbolic" dimension provided a glimpse into a wholly different way to introduce typology into work on projects.

For their part, Ahmet Gülgönen and François Laisney engaged in a much more literal reading of the Italian theories of typology and morphology, in accord with their intention to focus their research on the city and its space. They juxtaposed Italian studies to nineteenth-century French architectural theories from Durand to Guadet, but in the end contributed little more than a jumble of sometimes cloudy reflections on the question of the type. Rather than a fundamental development of operative ideas, their work was above all a preliminary exposé presenting three disparate fields of inquiry from which they drew few comparative conclusions: the recourse to Italian authors served more as a protective shield or screen than a solid frame of reference.[24]

The analyses carried out by Devillers, who drew on the final paper he had written at Unité Pédagogique no. 8, as well as the studies of Raymond, Gülgönen, and Laisney, who taught in the same department, clearly demonstrate that the world of architectural education was the initial echo chamber for the Italian discourse (the work of Castex, Panerai, and Depaule would show the same). Even before the Italian theorists' ideas were relayed by the journals or the studies, they were crystallized in lecture courses and in pedagogical exercises that were unprecedented in the French tradition. This presence of the educational institution is witnessed by the publication of two term papers in the study by Gülgönen and Laisney. It explains the efforts these two authors made to combine the Italian reference with a reference to Louis Kahn, another primary source for the teaching at U.P. no. 8. It also explains Devillers's mix of references, both to the typology of Carlo Aymonino or Giorgio Grassi and to the sociological influences he had received.

Bernard Huet and L'*Architecture d'Aujourd'hui*

The impact of the Italian ideas appeared first in teaching; but the field of the press would prove no less decisive. In his fleeting attempt to give L'*Architecture d'Aujourd'hui* the content of a genuine architectural journal, in contrast to the strategy of the *catalogue* pursued before and after him, Huet was not content simply to propagate a lifeless Italian culture, or merely to attract attention to urban experiments such as that of Bologna. Rather, it was with the direct and ongoing collaboration of Italian authors that L'*Architecture d'Aujourd'hui* became, under his direction, an instrument for a kind of reintellectualization of French architectural culture. Indeed, almost fifteen years after the legendary period of *Casabella Continuità*, it was with the same signatures—Tafuri, or former assistants of Rogers such as Aldo Rossi—that Huet attained his successes. This shift toward the press, after the relationship with Italy had initially prospered in teaching circles, was carried out as a direct exegesis of Italian culture: it was either exalted as a whole, as in the issue "Italie 75," or in one of its particular dimensions (industrial patronage) in the issue on "the Olivetti case."[25]

But there is more: beyond this reference to specific features of the Italian scene, which fascinated the members of the journal's editorial board, a series of phenomena on the world architectural scene would be considered through the eyes of Italian historians and critics. Thus, alongside Oriol Bohigas, Vittorio Gregotti presented his reading of Alvaro Siza.[26] More importantly, Manfredo Tafuri and the Venetian historians trained the spotlights on the problem of the skyscraper, clearing away all technological shortsightedness,[27] and then turned more broadly to the leading figures of the New York architectural scene, from gray to white: it was with the direct concourse of Tafuri that the New York Five appeared on the conceptual map of French architects and students of architecture, like diamonds amid "the ashes of Jefferson."[28]

It was not simply through the mix of historical and critical articles that the influence of Italian culture could be felt in *L'Architecture d'Aujourd'hui*. It was also present in the very problematics of some of Bernard Huet's editorials, especially those that moved away from institutional critique to focus on points of doctrine. In his text "Formalism-Realism," which opens an issue devoted to the exegesis of *La Tendenza*,[29] Huet courageously attempted to articulate a position on Soviet architecture that overturned the common discourse on "formalism." To this end he adopted Aldo Rossi's positive judgment on the Stalinallee in East Berlin, and proclaimed the social import of work on architectural form which refuses the exclusive quest for *originality*. No doubt it is useful to stress why Huet's position—which would soon earn him a chorus of reprimands[30]—was so courageous: it is because he considered, and rightly so, that the urban plans and buildings constructed in the name of socialist realism did not merit repression and exemption from any reflection on architecture and on the city, and that the relation between architecture and politics should be seriously analyzed. Unfortunately Huet's position, sharply attacked by Anatole Kopp and Claude Schnaidt, was built on indirect references to Rossi's ideas, to certain theorists of socialist realism, and to other authors such as the Czech critic Karel Teige, quoted from a very short text published in the journal *Archithese*.[31] It was not the expression of a collective effort, as was the case for the polemics developed on the basis of the Italian *Tendenza*, but rather was a somewhat fragile cultural position: it lacked an anchor in the French architectural debate, where no sustained discussion had ever dealt with the problematic of realism (so crucial in literature, cinema, and theater) and where the question of the relations between the vanguards of modern architecture had never been seriously explored. Huet's dizzying attempt to combine all these dimensions in condensed form could only provoke defensive reactions, which came, what is more, at the very moment when his tenure at *L'Architecture d'Aujourd'hui* was drawing to a close. It remains nonetheless that the editorial invites a double process of "revision," to use one of Rogers's terms, in that it questions both the *political pertinence* of modern architecture and the *formalism* of socialist realism; this process of revision is still an incomplete project.

Paradoxically, it was in this same issue of *L'Architecture d'Aujourd'hui*—marking at once the apogee and the abrupt end of Huet's experiment, whose Italophile dimension has been stressed—that Aldo Rossi chose to express his dismay at not being sufficiently heard, or loved, in France:

Unfortunately, my love for France is unrequited. Unless memory fails me, it was Stendhal who claimed that love has but a single disadvantage: it takes two to make it. In reality, I think that French culture, heir to a great tradition which is inseparable from the greatest cultural imperialism, is still closed in on itself. . . . This will surely be a difficult love.[32]

The Case of *Architecture Mouvement Continuité*

It is true that Rossi's positions would not be known in detail until the French translation of *L'architettura della città* in 1981. But another love story, seemingly more on the order of love at first sight than of Rossi's long seduction, had appeared with the relations that brought together the editorial boards of *Architecture Mouvement Continuité*, in Paris, and of *Controspazio*, which was in the process of moving from Milan to Rome. The idyll was to culminate in the parallel publication of a special issue of *AMC* on Italy and an issue of *Controspazio* on the French scene.[33]

This initiative was already, in a way, an attempt to go beyond the first phase of Italophilia, as Olivier Girard indicates:

The special interest for Italy displayed over the last four or five years by certain fourth-generation circles (the *urban* tendency) has essentially resulted in the appearance of projects more or less directly influenced by Italian publications, and by the emergence of debate and research around the theme of *architectural typologies and urban morphology*, which was paradoxically able to find its own field of enquiry, despite fifteen years of Italian speculations on the same subject, because of the rarity of translated texts until very recently. It now seems indispensable to understand in a more immediate way the Italian attempts to go beyond the modern movement.[34]

With this special issue, the second in a series dubbed *L'autre*, or "The Other"—a no doubt involuntary homage to the journal *Das Andere*, published in Vienna by Adolf Loos—Girard drew on an aspect of Italian architectural culture to support his doctrinal line, in opposition to the ideas for which Huet had also summoned the Italians as character witnesses. Despite the static generated by a clumsy and rather approximate translation, it is possible to grasp the message sent out by Renato Nicolini and Alessandro Anselmi, who indicated the way to read the projects presented: both proposed a critique of the typo-morphological theories, either in the name of a struggle against the "new mannerism" (Nicolini) or the "positivism" of typology (Anselmi). And though the projects themselves included a few proposals issuing from the orbit of the University Institute of Architecture in Venice, they tended to shift the Italian references circulating in the French press toward an understanding of the research undertaken by several Roman teams on geometry and proportion, or on the large territorial scale.

The Translations of Tafuri

The fertile season which saw the flowering of Italophilia in teaching, then a prolongation of these pedagogical positions in the press, would be followed by a season most fruitful in books.

The single work which so far had born witness to Italian debates in France, the translation of *Saper vedere l'architettura*, would gradually be complemented by more recent texts, though these were already dated and contested in Italy itself: for example, Leonardo Benevolo's *Origine e sviluppo della città moderna*, published in 1972, at a date when the same author's *Storia dell'architettura moderna* had already been translated into German and English. But the real indicator marking the appearance of the source texts for the Italian debate was the French publication of Manfredo Tafuri's *Theories and History of Architecture* in 1976. This publication marked the high point of the activities of the SADG (Society of Architects holding Government Diplomas), which published the volume as part of a series of actions contributing to the emergence of a debate on architecture in France. It also marks in the clearest possible way the difficulty of introducing Tafuri's themes into the French context, as attested by the occasional dark spots in the translation, which add to the density of the author's concepts and references. These translation problems—actually very slight compared to those met by Tafuri in the United States, where *Architecture and Utopia* would literally be massacred—are an index of how strange the ideas in *Theories and History* were for the French public; for this was a book which situated the crisis of architecture in a little-known historical and theoretical field. The publication was praised in such distant sites as the pages of *Oppositions*, where Yve-Alain Bois provided a user's guide to the book, indicating its full significance in the overcoming of the semiological discourse on architecture, while at the same time revealing the limits of Tafuri's ideas before certain architects such as Louis Kahn.[35]

It was precisely as an instrument for critical reading of architecture and its doctrines that Yve-Alain Bois analyzed Tafuri's writing, in its rhetorical excesses as well as its theoretical innovations. But it seems that this dimension of

Theories and History was not clearly perceived by its French readers, despite Tafuri's own efforts to indicate how it should be read:

Theories and History—at least in Italian culture—was the first book to draw parallels between the history of the artistic avant-garde and that of contemporary architecture. This is because I was pursuing two distinct aims. The first was to use the discipline as a means of testing its tools; the second followed on from the discovery that the discipline itself was rotten to the core. It wasn't so much that we were in crisis, but that all history had to be reassessed from the bottom up, to discover its theoretical foundations. We found—and personally speaking, I was appalled—that even those foundations were rotten to the core, as Piranesi said. It was no longer possible to move on with such foundations by backtracking. . . . This was true of the language of the avant-garde, the theoretical framework of architectural history and modern art history in general. . . . We were locked in a castle under a spell, the keys were lost, in a linguistic maze—the more we looked for a direction, the more we encountered magic halls full of tortured dreams.[36]

The trip that the French reader would take, from this first text to others such as *Architecture and Utopia*, translated almost five years later,[37] was not only another fantastical episode added to *Sleeping Beauty*: Tafuri led his readers to the discovery of major themes in philosophy and aesthetics. The reference to Barthes, which some French professors had already brought to bear in the field of architecture, was complemented by the more central references to Benjamin and Adorno. The theme of architecture's loss of aura in the era of technical reproducibility thus came before the eyes of architects who, for the most part, had paid no attention to the French publication of Benjamin's texts.[38] Thus it was the detour through the Italian discourse that allowed, by the most twisted of possible paths, the introduction into the French debate of indispensable theoretical references, rendered inaccessible by the split between architectural discourse and the social sciences.

From the consideration of theories of urban architecture and the interest in restoration strategies for city centers to the discovery of entire fields of philosophical thought which could be more or less directly applied to architecture, the Italophile current and its production covered a vast range of territories.

Blind Spots in the Italophile Gaze

The form of the window frame through which the Italian landscape was seen are not insignificant. This frame betrays the very contour of French architectural culture; it reveals the blockages of the French scene by its selection of themes from Italian culture. The relation to history, to theory, and to the urban that could be glimpsed in Italian architecture is exactly what the fashionable sociology and semiology of the early seventies had been unable to provoke in a French context dominated by a vision which reduced architecture to a "combinatory system" of more or less "proliferating" volumes, thought to be "innovative" by the simple force of their proliferation.

But though the Italophile gaze was able to seize a series of cultural movements on the Italian scene, thus uncovering the gaps in French architectural thinking, still the reverberations of this appropriation of Italian discourse were to prove very uneven. The introduction of Tafuri's discourse and the interest in Rossi's architecture, the evocation of typology or of the Bologna experiment would all play an undeniable role in the turn towards the rediscovery of history in architectural discourse, the reinvention of draftsmanship, the new attention to urban space, and the refusal of the mute singularity of the architectural object. More broadly, a certain taste, a certain pleasure of the text would appear. The references to Italy nourished the written production of architects and the production of critical texts on the subject of architecture, which came to know the joys of prose, and even more, of quotation.

But it would be inexact to claim that all the themes raised in the Italian debates crossed the border without difficulty. Take the case of urban architecture. The discourse on the historical centers and the techniques of architectural analysis and intervention were well integrated when it was a matter of considering urban centers and ensembles up to the eighteenth and nineteenth centuries, but this was no longer true when the metropolitan dimension had to be taken into account: in reality, the exponents of urban architecture remained stuck with a rather static vision of the neoclassical city and the city during the early industrial revolution. Cacciari and Tafuri's analyses of the ideologies of the big city and their opposition to the anti-urban discourse of the garden city movement did not come across, and the morphology of the garden cities irresistibly gained ground in the new cities of the Paris region. Thus in the end the new urban culture of French architects fixed upon the somewhat nostalgic vision of a city that had not attained metropolitan scale. The same incomprehension of the specific forms of growth of the twentieth-century city and the same disdain for the doctrines and techniques that can shape it, from its transformed center to its swollen peripheries, crops up again when one measures the echoes of the Venetian research into the question of the avant-garde. While all the Italian analyses pointed to the dead end met by avant-garde approaches and the failure of the attempt to rationalize social contradictions by means of architecture (even when architecture attempts to fit into an all-encompassing plan), the dominant discourse in France remains convinced of the idea of the totally positive nature of avant-garde construction in the interwar years. In particular, the tragic aspect of the experiments in Vienna and Weimar has not been truly grasped, even as their metropolitan dimension has been forgotten: the memory fixes visually on icons representing, at best, the neighborhood scale (the *horseshoe* of Berlin-Britz), and never on an entire urban structure—a trend in no way contradicted by those two great moments of public fanfare, the "Paris-Berlin" and "Paris-Moscow" exhibitions at the Georges Pompidou Center. These events gave a chance to expose two cultural conjunctures in their totality, and yet in both cases, architecture was treated more in counterpoint to the artistic movements than in step with them as it really was, and as had already been proved in the case of Russia by the publication of texts by the Venetians in the journal *VH 101*.[39] Another effect made patent by the two exhibitions is the way the tragic dimension of modern architecture's forced regression in Germany and the USSR becomes the manifestation of blameworthy "forces of evil," but is in no way ascribed to the very nature of the avant-garde, whose both Promethean and suicidal character is clear for anyone who takes the trouble to analyze the theoretical and critical production.

Linguistic Contamination

For everything dealing with the metropolis as well as the temporal unfolding of twentieth-century architectural culture, and even for the very notion of the avant-garde, it seems that a very important part of the themes explored in Italian architectural culture have been and still are misunderstood—even when some of the texts dealing with them have been translated, as is the case for Tafuri. Yet there is another field in which communication was exceptionally successful: that of the fixed formulas and linguistic tics borrowed from Italy, which soon would pepper a great many articles, books, and research reports. What better illustration of the fruitfulness of the Italophile trend than this irruption of terms directly translated—or more precisely, transposed—from Italian? Rather than speaking of work on projects, or coining a prosaic term like *projetage*, French architects began to use the word *projétation*; work on urban form was no longer designated with the American term "urban design" but became a discipline called *urbanistique*; and we'll skip over the erroneous use of the word *illuminisme*, not for the theories of Böhme or Swedenborg, but to describe the

Enlightenment—just as we might bypass the use of strange abbreviations in bibliographies, like *AA.VV.* instead of *Coll.*, to reference multi-author works. No doubt the confusion is at its greatest around the question of typology. Indeed, typology is seen in many French texts from the late seventies not as a classificatory operation allowing for the isolation of distinct types, but instead as a synonym for the notion of type. A given type identified in an urban analysis becomes *une typologie remarquable*: the analytic exercise lends its name to the empirical object.

Let us simply consider this linguistic contamination as the trace of a transferal of knowledge carried out in a discipline rather uncertain of its semantic resources, as French architecture was in its post-1968 mourning for the traditional jargon it had borrowed from the Ecole des Beaux-Arts.

The most recent episodes in the chronicle of Franco-Italian relations have taken on a dimension at once more public and more polemical. The activities of the Institut Italien de Culture had regularly included architectural themes since its exhibition of the architecture of rationalism in 1977[40]—but a great deal more public attention was raised by the presentation in the 1981 Festival d'Automne of an exhibition organized by Paolo Portoghesi for the Venice Biennial in 1980, under the banner of *The Presence of the Past*.

Curiously, it was through a cultural project inspired by an American's reading (Jencks) of a French philosopher's idea (Lyotard) that the vitality of the Italian architectural scene would be perceived far beyond the circle of Parisian architects.

The confusion introduced by the foggy discourse of the exhibition organizers was not dissipated by the belated echoes it found in the press. Thus the idea of post-modernism was definitively linked to the world of architecture, as witnessed by the cluster of texts in the first issue of the journal *Babylone*, published in 1983.[41]

A year after the spotlights had been trained on Portoghesi's machinations, the major voice of the opposition to the 1980 Venice Biennial, Vittorio Gregotti—himself the organizer of the less equivocal but less showy exhibition of architecture at the 1976 Biennial—was presented to the French public in his turn. Gregotti, the author in 1980 of a vehement article against *The Presence of the Past*,[42] was thus thrown into the ring at the very moment when the question of the 1989 Exposition Universelle was being debated in Paris. Among the groups preparing that event, he would associate himself with Renzo Piano, Antoine Grumbach, and other consultants such as Pontus Hulten.

The presence of both Gregotti and Piano in Paris, at the moment when Gae Aulenti had been called to work on the Orsay museum, should be understood in its full significance. No doubt Gregotti was not exempt from a fascination for the supposed capacities of the French technocracy to launch huge, exalting projects. But this presence was also a kind of just deserts for an architectural culture that had been able to assimilate teachings lost for French architecture itself: the lessons of Auguste Perret, for Gregotti, or Jean Prouvé, for Piano. Thus one of the major directions in modern French architecture was reopened through the choice of these men, whose culture helped them craft a highly specific "presence of the past."

It can be useful to linger over the reasons for this strange return of a part of the potential contained in the ideas and forms of twentieth-century French architecture, which has come back via Italy to take on a timeliness that it would not have had without this foreign contribution. Nor is it superfluous to inquire into the reasons that authorized the reexportation to France of theoretical and philosophical discourses which had first come to light here, but which remained outside the field of architecture, because of the split between architects and intellectuals.

Alongside causes external to the field of architecture, such as the solidarity of the generations that had emerged from the struggle against fascism, or the importance of regional poles stimulating the creation of journals and of autonomous, competitive forums of debate, the analysis of trends in the Italian architectural culture of the postwar period has shown the important role played by the educational system, research, and the professional press in the establishment of basic references.

The constitution of meeting places between architects and intellectuals, both real and virtual, is among the phenomena emerging today in France, of which the growing interest for architecture in the press is both an effect and an instrument. The interest that certain intellectuals, philosophers in particular, have shown for architecture—which is quite different from the way that sociologists from the field of housing intervened some twenty years ago—bears witness to these new encounters.

But such meetings may well remain exceedingly fragile, so long as intellectual production in the field of architecture itself is not grounded in an institutional system allowing professors, researchers, and critics to engage in an activity with some stability. In this sense, the institutional dimensions of architectural policy are fundamental, whether it be a matter of doctoral programs allowing for a veritable intellectual investment from young researchers and opening up courses to researchers from other disciplines than architecture, or of recruiting and promoting professors who accord culture and theory their full due. The mix of an obligation to publish and the institution of publishing grants in the framework of a public policy carried out at a national level is therefore indispensable, especially since the historical heritage of centralization does not permit us to imagine the appearance, in the near future, of those regional poles whose importance is so great in Italy.

The resources of living memory lead us inevitably to a reflection on the institutional problems of today's architectural culture. But these problems can only be fully grasped when one keeps in sight the ways in which the activity of the architectural project has reconstituted itself, beneath the impact of the movements analyzed above.

Notes

1. *La fonction architecturale, la recherche architecturale, rapport de la commission formée par André Lichnérowicz* (Paris: Ministère des Affaires Culturelles, 1970), p. 14.

2. To perceive this impact it suffices to analyze certain projects carried out by Paul Chemetov in the early 1970s, such as the housing projects in Romainville, Saint-Ouen, and Vienne.

3. Marcel Poëte, *Introduction à l'urbanisme* (Paris: Anthropos, 1967), preface by Hubert Tonka. Tonka's enterprise is all the more laudable in that his own theoretical positions led him far from Poëte, as he admits in his introduction.

4. Robert Auzelle, ed., *Cours d'urbanisme*, vol. 1, introductory lectures (Paris: Vincent, Fréal et Cie, 1967).

5. Aldo Rossi, *The Architecture of the City*, trans. Diane Ghirardo and Joan Ockman (Cambridge: MIT Press, 1982), pp. 141–144 (Halbwachs), p. 101 (Lévi-Strauss).

6. Georges Chabot, *Les villes: Aperçu de géographie humaine* (Paris: Armand Colin, 1948), pp. 31–34.

7. Max Sorre, "Géographie urbaine et écologie," in *Urbanisme et architecture: Etudes écrites et publiées en l'honneur de Pierre Lavedan* (Paris: Henri Laurens, 1954), pp. 341–346; Max Sorre, *Rencontres de la géographie et de la sociologie* (Paris: Librairie Marcel Rivière et Cie, 1957), p. 140.

8. Manfredo Tafuri, *Theories and History of Architecture*, trans. Giorgio Verrecchia (New York: Harper and Row, 1979); original edition *Teorie e storia dell'architettura* (Bari: Laterza, 1968); French translation *Théories et histoire de l'architecture* (Paris: Editions SADG, 1976).

9. "Histoire et théories de l'architecture," conference on pedagogy, June 17–20, 1974 (Paris: Institut de l'Environnement-Cedra, 1975).

10. Cf. in particular one of the most seminal: Blandine Barret-Kriegel, François Béguin, Bruno Fortier, Daniel Friedmann, and Alain Montchablon, *La politique de l'espace parisien (à la fin de l'Ancien Régime)* (Paris: Corda, 1975).

11. Franco Bella, "Una tomba per Edipo," *Aut Aut* 144 (1974).

12. Manfredo Tafuri, "The Historical 'Project,'" in *The Sphere and the Labyrinth*, trans. Pellegrino D'Acierno and Robert Connolly (Cambridge: MIT Press, 1987).

13. Cf. the parallel undertakings by different publishers: Antonio Gramsci, *Ecrits politiques*, 2 vols., trans. and preface by Robert Paris (Paris: Gallimard, 1974–1975); *Gramsci dans le texte*, anthology edited by François Ricci and Jean Bramant (Paris: Editions Sociales, 1975). Also see the various special issues of journals and books published in the heyday of the PCI: "Révolutions d'Italie," *Esprit*, November 1974; "L'Italie et nous," *Dialectiques* 18–19 (Spring 1977); Dominique Grisoni and Hugues Portelli, *Les luttes ouvrières en Italie (1960–1976)* (Paris: Aubier-Montaigne, 1976); Marcelle Padovani, *La longue marche du P.C. Italien* (Paris: Calmann-Lévy, 1977); Patrick Meney, *L'Italie de Berlinguer* (Jean-Claude Lattès, 1977), etc.

14. Christine Buci-Glücksmann, *Gramsci et l'Etat* (Paris: Fayard, 1975).

15. Cf. the many special sections in journals, the on-site studies, and among the books praising the effort, one authored by its principle protagonist, Pierluigi Cervellati: *La nouvelle culture des villes* (Paris: Seuil, 1980).

16. Marco De Michelis, Marco Venturi, "Le centre de direction de Bologne: ou comment le PCI gère le problème urbain," in *Espaces et sociétés* 2 (March 1971), pp. 45–52.

17. Bernard Huet, "Les centres historiques face au développement," *Architecture d'Aujourd'hui* 180 (July-August 1975), p. 3.

18. Ibid., p. 44.

19. Jean Castex, Jean-Charles Depaule, and Philippe Panerai, *Formes urbaines: de l'îlot à la barre* (Paris: Dunod, 1977).

20. Ahmet Gülgönen and François Laisney (research advisors), *Morphologie urbaine et typologie architecturale* (Paris: IERAU/Corda, 1977).

21. Christian Devillers, "Typologie de l'habitat et morphologie urbaine," in "Recherche habitat," *Architecture d'Aujourd'hui* 174 (July-August 1974), pp. 18–22. Also see a site study based on the same positions: Christian Devillers, Bernard Huet, *Le Creusot, naissance et développement d'une ville industrielle 1782–1914* (Champ Vallon: Seyssel, 1981).

22. Bernard Huet, editorial, *Architecture d'Aujourd'hui* 174 (July–August 1974), p. vii.

23. Henri Raymond, "Commuter et transmuter: la sémiologie de l'architecture," in "Sémiotique de l'espace," *Communications* 27 (1977), pp. 103–111. This and other articles by Raymond have been reprinted in an anthology which bears the mark of Italian influence: Henri Raymond, *L'architecture: Les aventures spatiales de la raison* (Paris: Centre de Création Industrielle, Centre Georges Pompidou, 1984).

24. Gülgönen and Laisney, *Morphologie urbaine et typologie architecturale*. The three concrete studies deal with Saint-Denis (Jean-Claude Delorme and Jean-Paul Scalabre), the HBM and the *ceinture de Paris* (Jean-François Chiffard and Jean-Claude Delorme), and Nancy (François Laisney and Martine Piétu).

25. Issue titled "Politique industrielle et architecture: le cas Olivetti," *Architecture d'Aujourd'hui* 188 (December 1976).

26. Vittorio Gregotti, "La passion d'Alvaro Siza," in "Portugal," *Architecture d'Aujourd'hui* 185 (May–June 1976), p. 42.

27. "Vie et mort du gratte-ciel," *Architecture d'Aujourd'hui* 178 (March–April 1975).

28. Manfredo Tafuri, "Les cendres de Jefferson," in "New York in White & Gray," *Architecture d'Aujourd'hui* 186 (August-September 1976), pp. 53–58; trans. as "The Ashes of Jefferson," in *The Sphere and the Labyrinth*.

29. Bernard Huet, "Formalisme-réalisme," *Architecture d'Aujourd'hui* 190 (April 1977), pp. 35–36; translated in this volume.

30. Cf. the responses to the above-quoted editorial by Paul Chemetov, Anatole Koop, and Claude Schnaidt (under the title "Bernard Huet entre le rationalisme et le kitsch stalinien") and by Bruno Queysanne, as well as the single letter of support from Giorgio Grassi and the clarification by Bernard Huet, "Le temps des malentendus," *Architecture d'Aujourd'hui* 192, pp. vii–x. Also see the lateral response by Roland Castro, "Se hâter lentement," *Architecture* 403 (June 1977), pp. 68–69.

31. Karel Teige, "Realismus und Formalismus," in "Réalisme," *Archithese* 19 (1976), pp. 49–50. This text is a short excerpt of a long manuscript on the question of socialist realism, written by Teige shortly before his suicide.

32. Aldo Rossi, interview in "Formalisme-réalisme."

33. "L'autre," special issue of *Architecture Mouvement Continuité* 2–3 (February 1975); "Nuove architetture in Francia," special issue of *Controspazio* 1 (January-February 1976).

34. Olivier Gérard, in *Architecture Mouvement Continuité* 2–3 (February 1975), p. 2.

35. Yve-Alain Bois, "On Manfredo Tafuri's *Théories et histoire de l'architecture*," *Oppositions* 11 (Winter 1977), pp. 118–123.

36. Manfredo Tafuri, interview with Françoise Véry, *Architecture Mouvement Continuité* 39 (June 1976), p. 64; English translation in *Casabella* 619–620 (January–February 1995), pp. 37–47.

37. Manfredo Tafuri, *Projet et utopie* (Paris: Dunod, 1979); original Italian edition, *Progetto e utopia* (Bari: Laterza, 1973); English edition *Architecture and Utopia*, trans. Barbara Luigia La Penta (Cambridge: MIT Press, 1976).

38. Walter Benjamin, *Mythe et violence, poésie et révolution* (Paris: Denoël, 1971). For the French bibliography on Walter Benjamin, see "Walter Benjamin," *Revue d'Esthétique*, n.s. 1 (1981), pp. 177–178.

39. Giorgio Ciucci, Francesco Dal Co, Mario Manieri-Elia, and Manfredo Tafuri, "L'architecture et l'avant-garde artistique en URSS de 1917 à 1934," *VH 101*, no. 7–8 (1972).

40. See, for example, the events organized in 1983 on the theme of museum architecture, and specifically on Carlo Scarpa's work in Verona: Luciana Miotto, ed., *Carlo Scarpa et le musée de Vérone* (Paris: Institut Italien de Culture, 1983). Also see, as testimony of the official service reports concerning urban policy, the issue of *Paris-projet* devoted to the two capitals: "Paris-Rome—Protection et mise en valeur du patrimoine architectural," *Paris-projet* 23–24 (1983).

41. *Babylone* 1 (Winter 1982–1983).

42. Vittorio Gregotti, "I vecchietti delle colonne," *La Repubblica*, August 1, 1980.

Peter Eisenman   "The End of the Classical: The End of the Beginning, the End of the End"

Perspecta 21 (1984)

In architectural projects as well as writings, Peter Eisenman has tirelessly sought a space for architecture outside the traditional parameters of the sensuous and the built, concerning himself instead with what may properly be called a conceptual architecture—one that seeks through an aesthetic withdrawal to replace the built object with a diagram of its formative procedures, isolating and elaborating the architectural elements and operations that would resist all encircling determinants of architectural form.[1] "The End of the Classical: The End of the Beginning, the End of the End" cannot be separated from the endgames of Eisenman's House X (1975), House El Even Odd (1980), and the project for the Cannaregio district in Venice (1978).

see Eisenman (236–239)

In Eisenman's view, modern architecture was never fully modern. Though it did produce a certain opacity of the architectural sign (most often referred to as its abstractness), modern architecture was never really free of the burden *to mean*; the referent still survives, albeit problematically, in cherished modernist emblems like the industrial shed, grain silo, and steamship, their workmanlike materials, and their social utility. Though it sought to reprogram our perceptual habits, modern architecture did not produce a cognitive reflection about the nature of architecture on a fundamental level (which Eisenman seems to see as a kind of universal grammar of form, available for elaboration and transgression). For Eisenman to stigmatize this crisis of and commitment to representation as classical or humanist is to characterize modernism as ideological and underscore the way in which its vision of architectural form and its potentials, as well as the possibilities of form's fictional status, remained an anthropological one.

An anti-anthropological, anti-humanist architecture must manage the conflict between the need for a systematic, verifiable geometry and the desire for a random organization of form (which Eisenman calls decomposition). And the only available figure of thought that can hold these oppositions of "timeless," "non-

compare 566–567

representational," "artificial" architecture together is the *text*—a tissue, textile, or texture of referral and delay in which there is neither beginning nor end. Now, whether Eisenman's conceptual architecture, with its textualization of every domain of the practice—the site as text, the program as text, the body as text—is a redemptive detour out of reification (the identification of a possible critical vocation for the tissue of fragmented, floating, reified signs) or a postmodern flattening of architecture's material and historical dimensions is, perhaps, not so much a dilemma of alternatives as a paradox that cannot be escaped: the historical paradox of an era of postsignification, in which Eisenman's work is fully immersed.

In a 1979 essay on Aldo Rossi, Eisenman had already characterized the exigent program for present-day architecture as one of reckoning with postsignification:

The problem [we face now is] choosing between an anachronistic continuance of hope and an acceptance of the bare conditions of survival. . . . Incapable of believing in reason, uncertain of the significance of his objects, *man [has lost] his capacity for signifying.* . . . The context which gave ideas and objects their previous significance is gone. . . . The [modernist proposal of the] "death of art" no longer offers a polemical possibility, because the former meaning of art no longer obtains. There is now merely a landscape of objects; new and old are the same; they appear to have meaning but they speak into a void of history. The realization of this void, at once cataclysmic and claustrophobic, demands that past, present, and future be reconfigured. *To have meaning, both objects and life must acknowledge and symbolize this new reality.*[2]

We must signify the fact that we can no longer signify; Eisenman generalizes the present historical condition of loss and anticipates an architecture exasperated by the desire to mean and forced into an apocalyptic becoming aware of loss — a state charged by a residual tension of minimal difference between signifying *something* and signifying that signification is henceforth impossible.

Notes

1. In an early essay that seeks a definition of conceptual architecture, Eisenman writes: "A conceptual structure is that aspect of the visible form, whether it is an idea, in a drawing, or in a building, which is intentionally put in the form to provide access to the inner form or universal formal relationships. . . . In order to approximate a conceptual intention, the shapes which are perceived would have to contain a structure within their physical presence which would have the capacity to take the viewer from the sense (immediate) perception to a conceptual attitude, and at the same time requiring of this structure a capacity to suppress the possible primacy of a sensual response." "Notes on Conceptual Architecture: Towards a Definition," *Design Quarterly* 78/79 (1970), pp. 1–5.
2. Peter Eisenman, introduction to *Aldo Rossi in America, 1976 to 1979*, ed. Kenneth Frampton (New York: Institute for Architecture and Urban Studies, 1979), p. 3; my emphasis.

Peter Eisenman   The End of the Classical: The End of the Beginning, the End of the End

Architecture from the fifteenth century to the present has been under the influence of three "fictions." Notwithstanding the apparent succession of architectural styles, each with its own label—·classicism, neoclassicism, romanticism, modernism, postmodernism, and so on into the future—these three fictions have persisted in one form or another for five hundred years. They are *representation, reason,* and *history.*[1] Each of the fictions had an underlying purpose: representation was to embody the idea of meaning; reason was to codify the idea of truth; history was to recover the idea of the timeless from the idea of change. Because of the persistence of these categories, it will be necessary to consider this period as manifesting a continuity in architectural thought. This continuous mode of thought can be referred to as *the classical.*[2]

It was not until the late twentieth century that the classical could be appreciated as an abstract system of relations. Such recognition occurred because the architecture of the early part of the twentieth century itself came to be considered part of history. Thus it is now possible to see that, although stylistically different from previous architectures, "modern" architecture exhibits a system of relations similar to the classical.[3] Prior to this time, the "classical" was taken to be either synonymous with "architecture" conceived of as a continuous tradition from antiquity or, by the mid-nineteenth century, an historicized style. Today the period of time dominated by the classical can be seen as an "episteme," to employ Foucault's term—a continuous period of knowledge that includes the early twentieth century.[4] Despite the proclaimed rupture in both ideology and style associated with the modern movement, the three fictions have never been questioned and so remain intact. This is to say that architecture since the mid-fifteenth century aspired to be a paradigm of the *classic,* of that which is *timeless, meaningful,* and *true.* In the sense that architecture attempts to recover that which is classic, it can be called "classical."[5]

The "Fiction" of Representation: The Simulation of Meaning

The first "fiction" is representation. Before the Renaissance there was a congruence of language and representation. The meaning of language was in a "face value" conveyed within representation; in other words, the way language produced meaning could be *represented within* language. Things *were;* truth and meaning were self-evident. The meaning of a Romanesque or gothic cathedral was in itself; it was *de facto.* Renaissance buildings, on the other hand—and all buildings after them that pretended to be "architecture"—received their value by representing an already valued architecture, by being simulacra (representations of representations) of antique buildings; they were *de jure.*[6] The *message* of the past was used to verify the *meaning* of the present. Precisely because of this need to verify, Renaissance architecture was the first simulation, an unwitting fiction of the object.

By the late eighteenth century historical relativity came to supersede the face value of language as representation, and this view of history prompted a search for certainty, for origins both historical and logical, for truth and proof, and for goals. Truth was no longer thought to reside in representation but was believed to exist outside it, in the processes of history. This shift can be seen in the changing status of the orders: until the seventeenth century they were thought to be paradigmatic and timeless; afterwards the possibility of their time-lessness depended on a necessary historicity. This shift, as has just been suggested, occurred because language had ceased to intersect with representation—that is, because it was not *meaning* but a *message* that was displayed in the object.

Modern architecture claimed to rectify and liberate itself from the Renaissance fiction of representation by asserting that it was not necessary for architecture to represent another architecture; architecture was solely to embody its own *function*. With the deductive conclusion that form follows function, modern architecture introduced the idea that a building should express—that is, look like—its function, or like an *idea* of function (that it should manifest the rationality of its processes of production and composition).[7] Thus, in its effort to distance itself from the earlier representational tradition, modern architecture attempted to strip itself of the outward trappings of "classical" style. This process of reduction was called *abstraction*. A column without a base and capital was thought to be an abstraction. Thus reduced, form was believed to embody function more honestly. Such a column looked more like a *real* column, the simplest possible load-carrying element, than one provided with a base and capital bearing arboreal or anthropomorphic motifs.

This reduction to pure functionality was, in fact, not abstraction; it was an attempt to represent reality itself. In this sense functional goals merely replaced the orders of classical composition as the starting point for architectural design. The moderns' attempt to represent "realism" with an undecorated, functional object was a fiction equivalent to the simulacrum of the classical in Renaissance representation. For what made function any more "real" a source of imagery than elements chosen from antiquity? The idea of function, in this case the message of utility as opposed to the message of antiquity, was raised to an originary proposition—a self-evident starting point for design analogous to typology or historical quotation. The moderns' attempt to represent realism is, then, a manifestation of the same fiction wherein meaning and value reside outside the world of an architecture "as is," in which representation is about its own *meaning* rather than being a *message* of another previous meaning.

Functionalism turned out to be yet another stylistic conclusion, this one based on a scientific and technical positivism, a simulation of efficiency. From this perspective the modern movement can be seen to be continuous with the architecture that preceded it. Modern architecture therefore failed to embody a new value in itself. For in trying to *reduce* architectural form to its essence, to a pure reality, the moderns assumed they were transforming the field of referential figuration to that of non-referential "objectivity." In reality, however, their "objective" forms never left the classical tradition. They were simply stripped down classical forms, or forms referring to a new set of givens (function, technology). Thus, Le Corbusier's houses that look like modern steamships or biplanes exhibit the same referential attitude toward representation as a Renaissance or "classical" building. The points of reference are different, but the implications for the object are the same.

The commitment to return modernist abstraction to history seems to sum up, for our time, the problem of representation. It was given its "Post-Modern" inversion in Robert Venturi's distinction between the "duck" and the "decorated shed."[8] A duck is a building that looks like its function or that allows its internal order to be displayed on its exterior; a decorated shed is a building that functions as a billboard, where any kind of imagery (except its internal function)— letters, patterns, even architectural elements—conveys a *message* accessible to all. In this sense the stripped-down "abstractions" of modernism are still referential objects: technological rather than typological ducks.

But the Post-Modernists fail to make another distinction which is exemplified in Venturi's comparison of the Doges' Palace in Venice, which he calls a decorated shed, and Sansovino's library across the Piazza San Marco, which he says is a duck.[9] This obscures the more significant distinction between architecture "as is" and architecture as message. The Doges' Palace is not a decorated shed because it was not representational of another architecture: its significance came directly from the meaning embodied in the figures themselves; it was an architecture "as is." Sansovino's library may seem to be a duck, but only because it falls into the history of library types. The use of the orders on Sansovino's library speaks not to the function or type of the library, but rather to the representation of a previous architecture. The facades of Sansovino's library contain a message, not an inherent meaning; they are sign boards. Venturi's misreading of these buildings seems motivated by a preference for the decorated shed. While the replication of the orders had significance in Sansovino's time (in that they defined the classical), the replication of the same orders today has no significance because the value system represented is no longer valued. A sign begins to replicate or, in Jean Baudrillard's term, "simulate," once the reality it represents is dead.[10] When there is no longer a distinction between representation and reality, when reality is only simulation, then representation loses its a priori source of significance, and it, too, becomes a simulation.

The "Fiction" of Reason: The Simulation of Truth

The second "fiction" of postmedieval architecture is *reason*. If representation was a simulation of the meaning of the present through the message of antiquity, then reason was a simulation of the meaning of the truth through the message of science. This fiction is strongly manifest in twentieth-century architecture, as it is in that of the four preceding centuries; its apogee was in the Enlightenment. The quest for origin in architecture is the initial manifestation of the aspiration toward a rational source for design. Before the Renaissance the idea of origin was seen as self-evident; its meaning and importance "went without saying"; it belonged to an a priori universe of values. In the Renaissance, with the loss of a self-evident universe of values, origins were sought in natural or divine sources or in a cosmological or anthropomorphic geometry. The reproduction of the image of the Vitruvian man is the most renowned example. Not surprisingly, since the origin was thought to contain the seeds of the object's purpose and thus its destination, this belief in the existence of an ideal origin led directly to a belief in the existence of an ideal end. Such a genetic idea of beginning/end depended on a belief in a universal plan in nature and the cosmos which, through the application of classical rules of composition concerning hierarchy, order, and closure, would confer a harmony of the whole upon the parts.

The perspective of the end thus directed the strategy for beginning. Therefore, as Alberti first defined it in *Della pittura*, composition was not an open-ended or neutral process of transformation, but rather a strategy for arriving at a predetermined goal; it was the mechanism by which the idea of order, represented in the orders, was translated into a specific form.[11] Reacting against the cosmological goals of Renaissance composition, Enlightenment architecture aspired to a rational process of design whose ends were a product of pure, secular reason rather than of divine order. The Renaissance vision of harmony (faith in the divine) led naturally to the scheme of order that was to replace it (faith in reason), which was the logical determination of form from a priori types.

Durand embodies this moment of the supreme authority of reason. In his treatises formal orders become type forms, and natural and divine origins are replaced by rational solutions to the problems of accommodation and construction. The goal is socially "relevant" architecture; it is attained through the rational transformation of type forms. Later, in the late nineteenth and early twentieth centuries, function and technique replaced the catalogue of type forms as origins. But the point is that from Durand on, it was believed that deductive reason—the same process used in science, mathematics, and technology—was capable of producing a truthful (that is, meaningful) architectural object. And with the success of rationalism as a scientific method (one could almost call it a "style" of thought) in the eighteenth and early nineteenth centuries, architecture adopted the self-evident values conferred by rational origins. If an architecture *looked* rational—that is, *represented* rationality—it was believed to *represent* truth. As in logic, at the point where all deductions developed from an initial premise corroborate that premise, there is logical closure and, it was believed, certain truth. Moreover, in this procedure the primacy of the origin remains intact. The rational became the moral and aesthetic basis of modern architecture. And the representational task of architecture in an age of reason was to portray its own modes of knowing.

At this point in the evolution of consciousness something occurred: reason turned its focus onto itself and thus began the process of its own undoing. Questioning its own status and mode of knowing, reason exposed itself to be a fiction.[12] The processes for knowing—measurement, logical proof, causality—turned out to be a network of value-laden arguments, no more than effective modes of persuasion. Values were dependent on another teleology, another end fiction, that of rationality. Essentially, then, nothing had really changed from the Renaissance idea of origin. Whether the appeal was to a divine or natural order, as in the fifteenth century, or to a rational technique and typological function, as in the post-Enlightenment period, it ultimately amounted to the same thing—to the idea that architecture's value derived from a source outside itself. Function and type were only value-laden origins equivalent to divine or natural ones.

In this second "fiction" the crisis of belief in reason eventually undermined the power of self-evidence. As reason began to turn on itself, to question its own status, its authority to convey truths, its power to prove, began to evaporate. The analysis of analysis revealed that logic could not do what reason had claimed for it—reveal the self-evident truth of its origins. What both the Renaissance and the modern relied on as the basis of truth was found to require, in essence, faith. Analysis was a form of simulation; knowledge was a new religion. Similarly, it can be seen that architecture never embodied reason; it could only state the desire to do so; there is no architectural image of reason. Architecture presented an aesthetic of the experience of (the persuasiveness of and desire for) reason. Analysis, and the illusion of proof, in a continuous process that recalls Nietzsche's characterization of "truth," is a never-ending series of figures, metaphors, and metonymies.

In a cognitive environment in which reason has been revealed to depend on a belief in knowledge, therefore to be irreducibly metaphoric, a classical architecture—that is, an architecture whose processes of transformation are value-laden strategies grounded on self-evident or a priori origins—will always be an architecture of restatement and not of representation no matter how ingeniously the origins are selected for this transformation, nor how ingeniously the transformation is.

Architectural restatement, replication, is a nostalgia for the security of knowing, a belief in the continuing of Western thought. Once analysis and reason replaced self-evidence as the means by which truth was revealed, the classic or timeless quality of truth ended and the need for verification began.

The "Fiction" of History: The Simulation of the Timeless

The third "fiction" of classical Western architecture is that of history. Prior to the mid-fifteenth century, time was conceived nondialectically; from antiquity to the Middle Ages there was no concept of the "forward movement" of time. Art did not seek its justification in terms of the past or future; it was ineffable and timeless. In ancient Greece the temple and the god were one and the same; architecture was divine and natural. For this reason it appeared "classic" to the Classical epoch that followed. The classic could not be represented or simulated, it could only be. In its straightforward assertion of itself it was nondialectical and timeless.

In the mid-fifteenth century the idea of a temporal origin emerged, and with it the idea of the past. This interrupted the eternal cycle of time by positing a fixed point of beginning. Hence the loss of the timeless, for the existence of origin required a temporal reality. The attempt of the classical to recover the timeless turned, paradoxically, to a time-bound concept of history as a source of timelessness. Moreover, the consciousness of time's forward movement came to "explain" a process of historical change. By the nineteenth century this process was seen as "dialectical." With dialectical time came the idea of the zeitgeist, with cause and effect rooted in presentness—that is, with an aspired-to timelessness of the present. In addition to its aspiration to timelessness, the "spirit of the age" held that an a priori relationship existed between history and all its manifestations at any given moment. It was necessary only to identify the governing spirit to know what style of architecture was properly expressive of, and relevant to, the time. Implicit was the notion that man should always be "in harmony"—or at least in a non-disjunctive relation—with his time.

In its polemical rejection of the history that preceded it, the modern movement attempted to appeal to values for this (harmonic) relationship other than those that embodied the eternal or universal. In seeing itself as superseding the values of the preceding architecture, the modern movement substituted a universal idea of relevance for a universal idea of history, analysis of program for analysis of history. It presumed itself to be a value-free and collective form of intervention, as opposed to the virtuoso individualism and informed connoisseurship personified by the post-Renaissance architect. Relevance in modern architecture came to lie in embodying a value other than the natural or divine; the zeitgeist was seen to be contingent and of the present, rather than as absolute and eternal. But the difference in value between presentness and the universal—between the contingent value of the zeitgeist and the eternal value of the classical—only resulted in yet another set (in fact, simply the opposite set) of aesthetic preferences. The presumably neutral spirit of the "epochal will" supported asymmetry over symmetry, dynamism over stability, absence of hierarchy over hierarchy.

The imperatives of the "historical moment" are always evident in the connection between the representation of the function of architecture and its form. Ironically, modern architecture, by invoking the zeitgeist rather than doing away with history, only continued to act as the "midwife to historically significant form." In this sense modern architecture was not a rupture with history, but simply a moment in the same continuum, a new episode in the evolution of the zeitgeist. And architecture's representation of its particular zeitgeist turned out to be less "modern" than originally thought.

One of the questions that may be asked is why the moderns did not see themselves in this continuity. One answer is that the ideology of the zeitgeist bound them to their present history with the promise to release them from their past history; *they were ideologically trapped in the illusion of the eternity of their own time.*

The late twentieth century, with its retrospective knowledge that modernism has become history, has inherited nothing less than the recognition of the end of the ability of a classical or referential architecture to express its own time as timeless. The illusory timelessness of the present brings with it an awareness of the *timeful* nature of past time. It is for this reason that the representation of a zeitgeist always implies a simulation; it is seen in the classical use of the *replication* of a *past time* to invoke the timeless as the *expression* of a *present time.* Thus, in the zeitgeist argument, there will always be this unacknowledged paradox, a simulation of the timeless through a replication of the timeful.

Zeitgeist history, too, is subject to a questioning of its own authority. How can it be possible, from within history, to determine a timeless truth of its "spirit?" Thus history ceases to be an objective source of truth; origins and ends once again lose their universality (that is, their self-evident value) and, like history, become fictions. If it is no longer possible to pose the problem of architecture in terms of a zeitgeist—that is if architecture can no longer assert its relevance through a consonance with its zeitgeist—then it must turn to some other structure. To escape such a dependence on the zeitgeist—that is, the idea that the *purpose* of an architectural style is to embody the spirit of its age—it is necessary to propose an alternative idea of architecture, one whereby it is no longer the purpose of architecture, but its inevitability, to express its own time.

Once the traditional values of classical architecture are understood as not meaningful, true, and timeless, it must be concluded that these classical values were *always* simulations (and are not merely seen to be so in light of a present rupture of history or the present disillusionment with the zeitgeist). It becomes clear that the classical itself was a simulation that architecture sustained for five hundred years. Because the classical did not recognize itself as a simulation, it sought to represent extrinsic values (which it could not do) in the guise of its own reality.

The result, then, of seeing classicism and modernism as part of a single historical continuity is the understanding that there are no longer any self-evident values in representation, reason, or history to confer legitimacy on the object. This loss of self-evident value allows the timeless to be cut free from the meaningful and the truthful. It permits the view that there is no one truth (a timeless truth), or one meaning (a timeless meaning), but merely the timeless. *When the possibility is raised that the timeless can be cut adrift from the timeful (history), so too can the timeless be cut away from universality to produce a timelessness which is not universal.* This separation makes it unimportant whether origins are natural or divine or functional; thus, it is no longer necessary to produce a classic—that is, a timeless—architecture by recourse to the classical values inherent in *representation, reason,* and *history.*

The Not-classical: Architecture as Fiction

The necessity of the quotation marks around the term "fiction" is now obvious. The three fictions just discussed can be seen not as fictions but rather as simulations. As has been said, fiction becomes simulation when it does not recognize its condition as fiction, when it tries to simulate a condition of reality, truth, or non-fiction. The simulation of representation in architecture has led, first of all, to an excessive concentration of inventive energies in the representational object. When columns are seen as surrogates of trees and windows resemble the portholes of ships, architectural elements become representational figures carrying an inordinate burden of meaning. In other disciplines representation is not the only purpose of figuration. In literature, for example, metaphors and similes have a wider range of application—poetic, ironic, and the like—and are not limited to allegorical or referential functions. Conversely, in architecture only one aspect of the figure is traditionally at work: object representation. The architectural figure always alludes to—aims at the representation of—some *other* object, whether architectural, anthropomorphic, natural, or technological.

Second, the simulation of reason in architecture has been based on a classical value given to the idea of truth. But Heidegger has noted that error has a trajectory parallel to truth, that error can be the unfolding of truth.[13] Thus to proceed from "error" or fiction is to counter consciously the tradition of "mis-reading" on which the classical unwittingly depended—not a presumably logical transformation of something a priori, but a deliberate "error" stated as such, one which presupposes only its own internal truth. Error in this case does not assume the same value as truth; it is *not* simply its dialectical opposite. It is more like a *dissimulation*, a "not-containing" of the value of truth.

Finally, the simulated fiction of modern movement history, unwittingly inherited from the classical, was that any present-day architecture must be a reflection of its zeitgeist: that is, architecture can simultaneously be about presentness and universality. But if architecture is inevitably about the invention of fictions, it should also be possible to propose an architecture that embodies an *other* fiction, one that is not sustained by the values of presentness or universality and, more importantly, that does not consider its purpose to reflect these values. This *other* fiction/object, then, clearly should eschew the fictions of the classical (representation, reason, and history), which are attempts to "solve" the problem of architecture rationally; for strategies and solutions are vestiges of a goal-oriented view of the world. If this is the case, the question becomes: What can be the model for architecture when the essence of what was effective in the classical model—the presumed rational value of structures, representations, methodologies of origins and ends, and deductive processes—has been shown to be a simulation?

It is not possible to answer such a question with an alternative model. But a series of characteristics can be proposed that typify this aporia, this loss in our capacity to conceptualize a new model for architecture. These characteristics, outlined below, arise from that which can *not* be; they form a structure of *absences*.[14] The purpose in proposing them is not to reconstitute what has just been dismissed, a model for a theory of architecture—for all such models are ultimately futile. Rather what is being proposed is an expansion beyond the limitations presented by the classical model to the realization of *architecture as an independent discourse*, free of external values—classical or any other; that is, the intersection of the *meaning-free*, the *arbitrary* and the *timeless* in the artificial.

The meaning-free, arbitrary, and timeless creation of artificiality in this sense must be distinguished from what Baudrillard has called "simulation:"[15] it is not an attempt to erase the classical distinction between reality and representation—thus again making architecture a set of conventions simulating the real; it is, rather, more like a *dissimulation*.[16] Whereas simulation attempts to obliterate the difference between real and imaginary, dissimulation leaves untouched the difference between reality and illusion. The relationship between dissimulation and reality is similar to the signification embodied in the mask: the sign of pretending to be *not* what one is—that is, a sign which seems not to signify anything besides itself (the sign of a sign, or the negation of what is behind it). Such a dissimulation in architecture can be given the provisional title of the *not-classical*. As dissimulation is not the inverse, negative, or opposite of simulation, a "not-classical" architecture is not the inverse, negative, or opposite of classical architecture; it is merely different from or other than. A "not-classical" architecture is no longer a certification of experience or a simulation of history, reason, or reality in the present. Instead, it may more appropriately be described as an *other* manifestation, an architecture *as is*, now as a fiction. It is a representation of itself, of its own values and internal experience.

The claim that a "not-classical" architecture is necessary, that it is proposed by the new epoch or the rupture in the continuity of history, would be another zeitgeist argument. The "not-classical" merely proposes an end to the dominance of classical values in order to reveal other values. It proposes, not a new value or a new zeitgeist, but merely another condition—one of reading architecture as a text. There is nevertheless no question that this idea of the reading of architecture is initiated by a zeitgeist argument: that today the classical signs are no longer significant and have become no more than replications. A not-classical architecture is, therefore, not unresponsive to the realization of the closure inherent in the world: rather, it is unresponsive to representing it.

The End of the Beginning

An origin of value implies a state or a condition of origin before value has been given to it. A beginning is such a condition prior to a valued origin. In order to reconstruct the timeless, the state of *as is*, of face value, one must begin: begin by eliminating the time-bound concepts of the classical, which are primarily origin and end. The end of the beginning is also the end of the beginning of value. But it is not possible to go back to the earlier, prehistoric state of grace, the Eden of timelessness before origins and ends were valued. We must begin in the present without necessarily giving a value to presentness. The attempt to reconstruct the timeless today must be a fiction which recognizes the fictionality of its own task—that is, it should not attempt to simulate a timeless reality.

As has been suggested above, latent in the classical appeal to origins is the more general problem of cause and effect. This formula, part of the fictions of reason and history, reduces architecture to an "added to" or "inessential" object by making it simply an effect of certain causes understood as origins. This problem is inherent in all of classical architectures including its modernist aspect. The idea of architecture as something "added to" rather than something with its own being—as adjectival rather than nominal or ontological—leads to the perception of architecture as a practical device. As long as architecture is primarily a device designated for use and for shelter—that is, as long as it has origins in programmatic functions—it will always constitute an effect.

But once this "self-evident" characteristic of architecture is dismissed and architecture is seen as having no a priori origins—whether functional, divine, or natural—alternative fictions for the origin can be proposed: for example, one that is *arbitrary*, one that has no external value derived from meaning, truths or timelessness. It is possible to imagine a beginning internally consistent but not conditioned by or contingent on historic origins with supposedly self-evident values.[17] Thus, while classical origins were thought to have their source in a divine or natural order and modern origins were held to derive their value from deductive reason, "not-classical" origins can be strictly arbitrary, simply starting points, without value. They can be artificial and relative, as opposed to natural, divine, or universal.[18] Such artificially determined beginnings can be free of universal values because they are merely arbitrary points in time, when the architectural process commences. One example of an artificial origin is a *graft*, as in the generic insertion of an alien body into a host to provide a new result.[19] As opposed to a collage or a montage, which lives within a context and alludes to an origin, a graft is an invented site, which does not so much have object characteristics as those of process. A graft is not in itself genetically arbitrary. Its arbitrariness is in its freedom from a value system of non-arbitrariness (that is, the classical). It is arbitrary in its provision of a choice of reading which brings no external value to the process. But further, in its artificial and relative nature a graft is not in itself necessarily an achievable result, but merely a site that contains *motivation* for action—that is the beginning of a process.[20]

Motivation takes something arbitrary—that is, something in its artificial state which is not obedient to an external structure of values—and implies an action and a movement concerning an internal structure which has an inherent order and an internal logic. This raises the question of the motivation or purpose from an arbitrary origin. How can something be arbitrary and non-goal oriented but still be internally motivated? Every state, it can be argued, has a motivation toward its own being—a motion rather than a direction. Just because architecture cannot portray or enact *reason* as a value does not mean that it cannot argue systematically or reasonably. In all processes there must necessarily be some beginning point; but the value in an arbitrary or intentionally fictive architecture is found in the *intrinsic* nature of its action rather than in the direction of its course. Since any process must necessarily have a beginning and a movement, however, the original origin must be considered as having at least a methodological value—a value concerned with generating the internal relations of the process itself. But if the beginning is in fact arbitrary, there can be no direction toward closure or end, because the motivation for change of state (that is, the inherent instability of the beginning) can never lead to a state of no change (that is, an end). Thus, in their freedom from the universal values of both historic origin and directional process, motivations can lead to *ends* different from those of the previous value-laden *end*.

The End of the End

Along with the end of the origin, the second basic characteristic of a "not-classical" architecture, therefore, is its freedom from a priori goals or ends—the end of the end. The end of the classical also means the end of the myth of the end as a value-laden effect of the progress or direction of history. By logically leading to a potential closure of thought, the fictions of the classical awakened a desire to confront, display, and even transcend the end of history. This desire was manifest in the modern idea of utopia, a time beyond history. It was thought that objects imbued with value because of their relationship to a self-evidently meaningful origin could somehow transcend the present in moving toward a timeless future, a utopia. This idea of progress gave false value to the present; utopia, a form of fantasizing about an "open" and limitless end, forestalled the notion of closure. Thus the modern crisis of closure marked the end of the process of moving toward the end. Such crises (or ruptures) in our perception of the continuity of history arise not so much out of a change in our idea of origins or ends than out of the failure of the present (and its objects) to sustain our expectations of the future. And once the continuity of history is broken in our perception, any representation of the classical, any "classicism," can be seen only as a belief. At this point, where our received values are "in crisis," the end of the end raises the possibility of the invention and realization of a blatantly fictional future (which is therefore non-threatening in its "truth" value) as opposed to a simulated or idealized one.

With the end of the end, what was formerly the process of composition or transformation ceases to be a causal strategy, a process of addition or subtraction from an origin. Instead, the process becomes one of *modification*—the invention of a non-dialectical, non-directional, non-goal oriented process.[21] The "invented" origins from which this process receives its motivation differ from the accepted, mythic origins of the classicists by being *arbitrary*, reinvented for each circumstance, adopted for the moment and not forever. The process of modification can be seen as an open-ended tactic rather than a goal-oriented strategy. A strategy is a process that is determined and value-laden before it begins: it is *directed*. Since the arbitrary origin cannot be known in advance (in a cognitive sense), it does not depend on knowledge derived from the classical tradition and thus cannot engender a strategy.

In this context architectural form is revealed as a "place of invention" rather than as a subservient representation of another architecture or as a strictly practical device. To invent an architecture is to allow architecture to be a cause; in order to be a cause, it must arise from something outside a directed strategy of composition.

The end of the end also concerns the end of object representation as the only metaphoric subject in architecture. In the past the metaphor in architecture was used to convey such forces as tension, compression, extension, and elongation; these were qualities that could be seen, if not literally in the objects themselves, then in the relationship between objects. The idea of the metaphor here has nothing to do with the qualities generated between buildings or between buildings and spaces; rather, it has to do with the idea that the internal process itself can generate a kind of non-representational figuration in the object. This is an appeal, not to the classical aesthetic of the object, but to the potential *poetic* of an architectural text. The problem, then, is to distinguish texts from representations, to convey the idea that what one is seeing, the material object, is a text rather than a series of image references to other objects or values.

This suggests the idea of architecture as "writing" as opposed to architecture as image. What is being "written" is not the object itself—its mass and volume—but the *act* of massing. This idea gives a metaphoric body to the act of architecture. It then signals its reading through an other system of signs, called *traces*.[22] Traces are not to be read literally, since they have no other value than to signal the idea that there is a reading event and that reading should take place; trace signals the idea to read.[23] Thus a trace is a partial or fragmentary sign; it has no objecthood. It signifies an action that is in process. In this sense a trace is not a simulation of reality; it is a dissimulation because it reveals itself as distinct from its former reality. It does not simulate the real, but represents and records the action inherent in a former or future reality, which has a value no more or less real than the trace itself. That is, trace is unconcerned with forming an image which is the representation of a previous architecture or of social customs and usages; rather, it is concerned with the marking—literally the figuration—of its own internal processes. Thus the trace is the record of motivation, the record of an action, not an image of another object-origin.

In this case a "not-classical" architecture begins actively to involve an idea of a reader conscious of his own identity as a reader rather than as a user or observer. It proposes a new reader distanced from any external value system (particularly an architectural-historical system). Such a reader brings no a priori competence to the act of reading other than an identity as a reader. That is, such a reader has no preconceived knowledge of what architecture should be (in terms of its proportions, textures, scale, and the like); nor does a "not-classical" architecture aspire to make itself understandable through these preconceptions.[24]

The competence of the reader (of architecture) may be defined as the capacity to distinguish a *sense of knowing* from *a sense of believing*. At any given time the conditions for "knowledge" are "deeper" than philosophic conditions; in fact, they provide the possibility of distinguishing philosophy from literature, science from magic, and religion from myth. The new competence comes from the capacity to read per se, to know how to read, and more importantly, to know how to read (but not necessarily decode) architecture as a text. Thus the new "object" must have the capacity to reveal itself first of all as a text, as a reading event. The architectural fiction proposed here differs from the classical fiction in its primary condition as a text and in the way it is read: the new reader is no longer presumed to know the nature of truth in the object, either as a representation of a rational origin or as a manifestation of a universal set of rules governing proportion, harmony, and ordering. But further, knowing how to decode is no longer important; simply, language in this context is no longer a code to assign meanings (that *this* means *that*). The activity of reading is first and foremost in the recognition of something as a language (that it *is*). Reading, in this sense, makes available a level of *indication* rather than a level of meaning or expression.

Therefore, to propose the end of the beginning and the end of the end[25] is to propose the end of beginnings and ends of value—to propose an *other* "timeless" space of invention. It is a "timeless" space in the present without a determining relation to an ideal future or to an idealized past. Architecture in the present is seen as a process of inventing an artificial past and a futureless present. It remembers a no-longer future.

This paper is based on three non-verifiable assumptions or values: timeless (originless, endless) architecture; non-representational (objectless) architecture; and artificial (arbitrary, reasonless) architecture.

Notes

1. Jean Baudrillard, "The Order of Simulacra," in *Simulations* (New York: Semiotext(e), 1983), p. 83. Baudrillard portrays the period beginning in the fifteenth century by three different simulacra: counterfeit, production, and simulation. He says that the first is based on the natural law of value, the second on the commercial law of value, and the third on the structural law of value.

2. The term "classical" is often confused with the idea of the "classic" and with the stylistic method of "classicism." That which is classic, according to Joseph Rykwert, invokes the idea of "ancient and exemplary" and suggests "authority and distinction": it is a model of what is excellent or of the first rank. More importantly, it implies its own timelessness, the idea that it is first rank at any time. Classicism, as opposed to the classical, will be defined here as a method of attempting to produce a "classic" result by appealing to a "classical" past. This accords with the definition given by Sir John Summerson, for whom classicism is not so much a set of ideas and values as it is a style. He maintains that while much of Gothic architecture was based on the same proportional relationships as the "classical" architecture of the Renaissance, no one could confuse a Gothic cathedral with a Renaissance palazzo: it simply did not have the look of classicism. In contrast, Demetri Porphyrios argues that classicism is not a style, but instead has to do with rationalism: "as much as architecture is a tectonic discourse, it is by definition transparent to rationality. . . . The lessons to be learned today from classicism, therefore, are not to be found in classicism's stylish wrinkles but in classicism's rationality." Porphyrios here confuses classicism with the classical and the classic, that is, with a set of values privileging the "truth" (that is, rationality) of tectonics over "expression" and error. The fallacy of this approach is that classicism relies on an idea of historical continuity inherent in the classical: therefore it does not produce the timelessness characteristic of the classic. The classical, by implication, has a more relative status than the classic: it evokes a timeless *past*, a "golden age" superior to the modern time or the present.

3. Michel Foucault, *The Order of Things* (New York: Random House, 1973). It is precisely Foucault's distinction between the classical and modern that has never been adequately articulated in relationship to architecture. In contrast to Foucault's epistemological differentiation, architecture has remained an uninterrupted mode of representation from the fifteenth century to the present. In fact, it will be seen that what is assumed in architecture to be classical is, in Foucault's terms, modern, and what is assumed in architecture to be modern is in reality Foucault's classical. Foucault's distinction is not what is at issue

here, but rather the continuity that has persisted in architecture from the classical to the present day.

4. Foucault, *The Order of Things*, p. xxii. While the term "episteme" as used here is similar to Foucault's use of the term in defining a continuous period of knowledge, it is necessary to point out that the time period here defined as the classical episteme differs from Foucault's definition. Foucault locates two discontinuities in the development of Western culture: the classical and the modern. He identifies the classical, beginning in the mid-seventeenth century, with the primacy of the intersection of language and representation: the value of language, its "*meaning*," was seen to be self-evident and to receive its justification within language: the way language provided meaning could be represented within language. On the other hand, Foucault identifies the modern, originating in the early nineteenth century, with the ascendance of historical continuity and self-generated analytic processes over language and representation.

5. "The End of the Classical" is not about the end of the classic. It merely questions a contingent value structure which, when attached to the idea of the classic, yields an erroneous sense of the *classical*. It is not that the desire for a classic is at an end, but that the dominant conditions of the classical (origin, end, and the process of composition) are under reconsideration. Thus it might be more accurate to title this essay "The End of the Classical as Classic."

6. Franco Borsi, *Leon Battista Alberti* (New York: Harper and Row, 1977). The facade of the church of Sant'Andrea in Mantua by Alberti is one of the first uses of the transposition of ancient building types to achieve both verification and authority. It marks, as Borsi says "a decisive turning away from the vernacular to the Latin" (p. 272). It is acceptable in the "vernacular" to revive the classical temple front because the function of the temple in antiquity and the church in the fifteenth century were similar. However, it is quite another matter to overlay the temple front with the triumphal arch. (See Rudolf Wittkower, *Architectural Principles in the Age of Humanism* [New York: Norton, 1971], and also D. S. Chambers, *Patrons and Artists in the Renaissance* [London: Macmillan, 1970].) It is as if Alberti were saying that with the authority of God in question, man must resort to the symbols of his own power to verify the church. Thus the use of the triumphal arch becomes a message on the facade of Sant'Andrea rather than an embodiment of its inherent meaning.

7. Jeff Kipnis, from a seminar at the Graduate School of Design, Harvard University, 28 February 1984. "Form cannot follow function until function (including but not limited to use) has first emerged as a possibility of form."

8. Robert Venturi, Denise Scott Brown, and Steven Izenour, *Learning from Las Vegas: The Forgotten Symbolism of Architectural Form*, rev. ed. (Cambridge: MIT Press, 1977), p. 87.

9. See the film *Beyond Utopia: Changing Attitudes in American Architecture*, Michael Blackwood Productions, New York City, 1983.

10. Baudrillard, *Simulations*, pp. 8–9. In referring to the death of the reality of God, Baudrillard says "metaphysical despair came from the idea that images concealed nothing at all, and that in fact they were not images . . . but actually perfect simulacra."

11. Leon Battista Alberti, *On Painting* (New Haven: Yale University Press, 1966), pp. 68–74.

12. Morris Kline, *Mathematics: The Loss of Certainty* (New York: Oxford University Press, 1980), p. 5.

13. Martin Heidegger, "On the Essence of Truth," from *Basic Writings* (New York: Harper and Row, 1977). "Aberrancy is the essential counteressence to the primordial essence of the truth. Errancy opens itself up as the open region for every opposite essential truth. . . . Errancy and the concealing of what is concealed belong to the primordial essence of truth."

14. Gilles Deleuze, "Plato and the Simulacrum," *October* 27 (1983), pp. 52–52. Deleuze uses a slightly different terminology to address a very similar set of issues: he discusses the Platonic distinction between model, copy and "simulacrum" as a means of assigning value and hierarchical position to objects and ideas. He explains the overthrow of Platonism as the suspension of the a priori value-laden status of the Platonic *copy* in order to: "raise up simulacra, to assert their rights over icons or copies. The problem no longer concerns the distinction Essence/Appearance or Model/Copy. This whole distinction operates in the world of representation. . . . The simulacrum is not degraded copy, rather it

contains a positive power which negates *both original and copy, both model and reproduction*. Of the at least two divergent series interiorized in the simulacrum neither can be assigned as original or copy. It doesn't even work to invoke the model of the Other, because no model resists the vertigo of the simulacrum" (pp. 52–53). Simulation is used here in a sense which closely approximates Deleuze's use of copy or icon, while dissimulation is conceptually very close to his description of the pre-Socratic simulacra.

15. Baudrillard, *Simulations*, p. 2. In the essay "The Precession of Simulacra" Baudrillard discusses the nature of simulation and the implication of present-day simulacra on our perception of the nature of reality and representation: "Something has disappeared: the sovereign difference between them (the real and . . . simulation models) that was the abstraction's charm."

16. Baudrillard, *Simulations*, p. 5. Distinguishing between simulation and what he calls "dissimulation," Baudrillard says that "to dissimulate is to feign to have what one hasn't. . . . 'Someone who feigns an illness can simply go to bed and make believe that he is ill. Someone who simulates an illness produces in himself some of the symptoms.' (Littré) Thus feigning . . . is only masked: whereas simulation threatens the difference between 'true' and 'false,' between 'real' and 'imaginary.' Since the simulator produces 'true' symptoms, is he ill or not?" According to Baudrillard, simulation is the generation by models of a reality without origin: it no longer has to be rational, since it is no longer measured against some ideal or negative instance. While this sounds very much like my proposal of the not-classical, the not-classical is fundamentally different in that it is a dissimulation and not a simulation. Baudrillard discusses the danger in the realization of the simulacra—for when it enters the real world it is its nature to take on the "real" attributes of that which it is simulating. Dissimulation here is defined differently: it makes apparent the simulation with all of its implications on the values of "reality," without distorting the simulacra or allowing it to lose its precarious position, poised between the real and the unreal, the model and the other.

17. What is at issue in an artificial origin is not motivation (as opposed to an essential or originary cause, as in an origin of the classical) but rather the idea of self-evidence. In deductive logic reading backward inevitably produces self-evidence. Hence the analytic process of the classical would always produce a self-evident origin. Yet there are no a priori self-evident procedures which could give one origin any value over any other. It can be proposed in a *not-classical* architecture that any initial condition can produce self-evident procedures that have an internal motivation.

18. The idea of arbitrary or artificial in this sense must be distinguished from the classical idea of architecture as artificial nature, and from the idea of the arbitrariness of the sign in language. Arbitrary in this context means having no natural connection. The insight that origins are a contingency of language is based on an appeal to reading: the origin can be arbitrary because it is contingent on a reading that brings its own strategy with it.

19. Jonathan Culler, *On Deconstruction: Theory and Criticism after Structuralism* (Ithaca: Cornell University Press, 1982). This is basically similar to Jacques Derrida's use of graft in literary deconstruction. He discusses graft as an element which can be discovered in a text through a deconstructive reading: "Deconstruction is, among other things, an attempt to identify grafts in the text it analyses: what are the points of juncture and stress where one scion or line of argument has been spliced with another? . . . Focusing on these moments, deconstruction elucidates the heterogeneity of the text" (p. 135). The three defining qualities of graft as it is used in this paper are: (1) graft begins with the arbitrary and artificial conjunction of (2) two distinct characteristics which are in their initial form unstable. It is this instability which provides the motivation (the attempt to return to stability) and also allows modification to take place. (3) In the incision there must be something which allows for an energy to be cut off by the coming together of the two characteristics. Culler's discussion of deconstructive strategy contains all of the elements of graft: it begins by analysis of text to reveal opposition. These are juxtaposed in such a way as to create movement, and the deconstruction (graft) is identifiable in terms of that motivation. This paper, which concentrates on transposing these ideas from a pure analytic framework to a program for work, is more concerned with what happens in the process of consciously making grafts than finding those that may have been placed unconsciously in a text. Since a graft by definition is a process of modification, it is unlikely that

one could find a static or undeveloped moment of graft in an architectural text: one would be more likely to read only its results. Graft is used here in a way that closely resembles Culler's analysis of Derrida's method for deconstruction of opposition: "To deconstruct an opposition . . . is not to destroy it. . . . To deconstruct an opposition is to undo and displace it, to situate it differently" (p. 150). "This concentration on the apparently marginal puts the logic of supplementarity to work as an interpretive strategy: what has been relegated to the margins or set aside by previous interpreters may be important precisely for those reasons that led it to be set aside" (p. 140). Derrida emphasizes graft as a non-dialectic condition of opposition: this paper stresses the processual aspects which emerge from the moment of graft. The major differences are of terminology and emphasis.

20. Culler, *On Deconstruction*, p. 99. "The arbitrary nature of the sign and the system with no positive terms gives us the paradoxical notion of an 'instituted trace,' a structure of infinite referral in which there are only traces—traces prior to any entity of which they might be the trace."

    This description of "instituted trace" relates closely to the idea of *motivation* as put forth in this paper. Like Derrida's "instituted trace," motivation describes a system which is internally consistent, but arbitrary in that it has no beginning or end and no necessary or valued direction. It remains a system of differences, comprehensible only in terms of the spaces between elements or moments of the process. Thus, motivation here is similar to Derrida's description of *différance*—it is the force within the object that causes it to be the dynamic at every point of a continuous transformation.

21. Jeff Kipnis, "Architecture Unbound," unpublished paper, 1984. Modification is one aspect of extension which is defined by Kipnis as a component of decomposition. While extension is any movement from an origin (or an initial condition), modification is a specific form of extension concerned with preserving the evidence of initial conditions (for example, through no addition or subtraction of materiality). On the other hand, synthesis is an example of extension which does not attempt to maintain evidence of initial conditions but rather attempts to create a new whole.

22. The concept of trace in architecture as put forward here is similar to Derrida's idea in that it suggests that there can be neither a representational object nor representable "reality." Architecture becomes text rather than object when it is conceived and presented as a system of differences rather than as an image or an isolated presence. Trace is the visual manifestation of this system of differences, a record of movement (without direction) causing us to read the *present* object as a system of relationships to other prior and subsequent movements. Trace is to be distinguished from Jacques Derrida's use of the term, for Derrida directly relates the idea of "difference" to the fact that it is impossible to isolate "presence" as an entity. "The presence of motion is conceivable only insofar as every instant is already marked with the traces of the past and future. . . . The present instant is not the past and future. . . . The present instant is not something given but a product of the relations between past and future. If motion is to be present, presence must already be marked by difference and deferral" (Culler, *On Deconstruction*, pp. 94–95). The idea that presence is never a simple absolute runs counter to all of our intuitive convictions. If there can be no inherently meaningful presence which is not itself a system of differences, then there can be no value-laden or a priori origin.

23. We have always read architecture. Traditionally, it did not induce reading but responded to it. The use of arbitrariness here is an idea to stimulate or induce the reading of traces without references to meaning but rather to other conditions of process—that is, to stimulate pure reading without value or prejudice, as opposed to interpretation.

24. Previously, there was assumed to be an a priori language of value, a poetry, existing within architecture. Now we are saying that architecture is merely language. We read whether we know what language we are reading or not. We can read French without understanding French. We can know someone is speaking nonsense or noise. Before we are competent to read and understand poetry we can know something to be language.

25. Compare Franco Rella, "Tempo della fine e tempo dell'inizio" (The Age of the End and the Age of the Beginning), *Casabella* 489/499 (January–February 1984), pp. 106–108. The similarity to the title of Rella's article is coincidental, for we use the terms "beginning" and "end" for entirely different purposes. Rella identifies the present as the

age of the end, stating that the paradoxical result of progress has been to create a culture that simultaneously desires progress and is burdened with a sense of passing and the chronic sense of irredeemable loss. The result is a culture which "does not love what has been but the end of what has been. It hates the present, the existing, and the changing. It therefore loves nothing." Rella's article poses the question of whether it is possible to build today, to design in a way that is with rather than against time. He desires the return to a sense of time-boundedness and the possibility of living in one's own age without attempting to return to the past. The mechanism by which he proposes to re-create this possibility is myth. He differentiates myth from fiction, and it is this difference which illuminates the opposition between his proposal and the propositions of this paper. Myth is defined as a traditional story of ostensibly historical events that serves to unfold part of the worldview of a people in the traditional value-laden sense, giving history and thus value to timeless or inexplicable events. Rella dismisses fiction as verisimilitude, merely creating the appearance of truth. Instead of attempting to return to the past, myth attempts to create a new beginning, merely situating us at an earlier, and less acute, state of anxiety. But a myth cannot alleviate the paradox of progress. Against both of these, "The End of the Beginning and the End of the End" proposes dissimulation, which is neither the simulation of reality as we know it, nor the proposal of an alternate truth, which appeals to the identical terrifying structures of belief—that is, origins, transformation, and ends. "The End of the Classical" insists on maintaining a state of anxiety, proposing fiction in a self-reflexive sense, a process without origins or ends which maintains its own fictionality rather than proposing a simulation of truth.

Paul Virilio   **"The Overexposed City"** "La ville surexposée," from *L' espace critique* (Paris:

Christian Bourgeois, 1984); translated in *Zone* 1–2 (New York: Urzone, 1986), trans.

Astrid Hustvedt

While the train, automobile, and airplane interrupted and distorted the rationalized space of the nineteenth-century city of industrialism, these technologies did not fundamentally challenge the representational paradigm that understands forces of communication and speed to produce visible effects. Architectural surfaces still formed boundaries, cities still comprised clusters of locales, and space was still managed perspectivally. Paul Virilio, guided by his own "law of proximity," argues that, with the passage from mechanical transport of an earlier epoch to the absolute speed of present-day telecommunication, the relevant interval of analysis shifts from space to time and, ultimately, to light—to the electromagnetic waves that permit the interactivity and relativization of space and time. "The city of the future is the pleasure of the interval."[1] And when the interval is light, mechanically proximate space yields to electromagnectic proximity (simultaneous and instantaneous) and the city grid to the informational network; immediate practice is displaced by "teleaction," and geopolitics by chronopolitics. This is the overexposed city, whose images range from the comparatively benign ubiquity of televisions, computer screens, and fax machines to the horrifying penetration of the nuclear flash into Hiroshima's darkest recesses.

For in the overexposed city, the architectural organism is no longer opaque, occlusive, and inscribed with visible information, but, like the human body on which it was formerly based, porous and vulnerable to the intrusion of forces that are no more visible than an electron—and no less real. Here and there, interior and exterior, private and public—these distinctions on which architecture has depended—no longer hold, and the resultant insecurity of territory ranges from the city to one's own body. Virilio's later work, especially *War and Cinema* (1984) and *The Art of the Motor* (1993), would pursue the fusion of teletechnology, biology, and the arrangement of the environment, and remind us that perception and destruction can be disturbingly coterminous.[2] The present essay is a preliminary exploration of the emergent representational paradigm—an "aesthetics of disappearance"—and of new ways of analyzing a city whose structure can no longer be seen in the materials and locations that realize it. Since the world system is now not so much global as *virtual*—like a cinematic shot of Virilio's "night tables" receding into one-dimensional pixels as the skycam is propelled into orbit—information technology becomes the representational solution to the new representational problem.

"The Overexposed City" was republished in 1986 as the first entry in the inaugural issue of *Zone*, an anthology that attempted to further the analysis of the city of timespaces.

compare Koolhaas (**322 ff**), Segrest (**554 ff**), and Kwinter (**588 ff**)

see 586

Notes

1. Kazuo Shinohara, interview with Virginie Luc, *D'Architecture* 17 (August 1991), cited in Paul Virilio, "The Law of Proximity," *D: Columbia Documents of Architecture and Theory* 2 (1993), p. 132. In the same essay, Virilio summarizes his "law of proximity" or "law of the least action": "Where given, side by side, an elevator or escalator and a simple staircase to reach upper stories, no one would take the staircase. Similarly, where, in an excessively long subway corridor, a conveyor belt walkway is provided, no one would walk in the corridor.

So it is with telecommunications: to transmit an electronic impulse is better than to transport a piece of paper; but to transport a letter is better than to send a messenger. And so to the notions, central to architecture, of *within* and *without*, which are gradually losing their importance. In fact, with the immateriality of electromagnetic radiation, even *above* and *below* begin to lose their characteristic distinction in the erection of buildings" (p. 132).

2. Paul Virilio, *War and Cinema: The Logistics of Perception* (1984), trans. Patrick Camiller (London: Verso, 1989); *The Art of the Motor* (1993), trans. Julie Rose (Minneapolis: University of Minnesota Press, 1995).

At the beginning of the 1960s, with the black ghetto revolts in full swing, the mayor of Philadelphia declared: "From now on, state lines cross inside the city." While this sentence expressed a political reality for the victims of American discrimination, it more importantly opened onto a much wider dimension because the Berlin Wall had just been erected, on August 13, 1961, in the Reich's ancient capital. Since then, the mayor's assertion has continued to prove true. Only a few years ago in Belfast and Londonderry, certain streets were marked with a yellow band, dividing Protestants and Catholics, before both moved further apart, leaving behind a fenced in no-man's-land that made for an even stronger separation between their neighborhoods. Beirut came next, with its east and west quarters, its domestic frontiers, its tunnels, its mined boulevards. In fact, this declaration, made by the leader of a large American metropolis, underscored a general phenomenon affecting capitals as well as provincial cities. The phenomenon of obligatory introversion, in which cities, just like industrial companies, suffered the first effects of a multinational economy, led to a significant urban redeployment. On the one hand, it contributed to the disruption of certain working-class cities such as Liverpool or Sheffield in England, Detroit or St. Louis in the United States, and Dortmund in Germany. On the other hand, new urban centers developed around gigantic international airports—the Metroplex—metropolitan complexes such as Dallas–Fort Worth.

With the beginning of the worldwide economic crisis in the 1970s, these airports were constructed in order to conform to defense imperatives against hijacking. Buildings were no longer built according to traditional technical constraints, but were designed to minimize the risk of "terrorist contamination." Sites were planned to discriminate between a sterile zone (departures) and a nonsterile zone (arrivals). All circuits and circuit breaks (i.e., passengers, baggage and freight), as well as the general flow of traffic, were submitted to a discriminatory (interior/exterior) transit system. Consequently, the building's architectural form became less the result of an individual architect's personality than of the necessary precautions taken for public safety. As the state's last gateway, the airport became, like the fort, the harbor or the train station of the past, the place of the necessary regulation of exchange and communication. For this very reason, it also became the perfect field for intense control and high surveillance experimentation. An "air and border patrol" was developed, and their antiterrorist exploits made headlines, as, for example, in the case of the GS.G9 German guards' intervention in the Mogadishu hijacking several thousand kilometers from their jurisdiction.

From that moment on, it was no longer simply a matter of isolating the contagious or suspected person by confinement as in the past, but rather of intercepting him in the course of his journey, in order to examine his baggage and clothing electronically. Thus the sudden proliferation of cameras, radar and detectors at mandatory passageways. French prisons with high-security quarters were also equipped with these same magnetic doors which had been installed in airports several years earlier. Paradoxically, the very equipment designed for the utmost freedom in travel served as a model for penitentiary incarceration. Previously, in several American residential areas, security was carried out only by closed-circuit televisions hooked up to police headquarters. In banks and supermarkets, as well as on highways, where tollbooths simulate the old city gates, the *rites of passage* are no longer intermittent—they have become immanent.

Given such a perspective without horizons, the way one gains access to the city is no longer through a gate, an arch of triumph, but rather through an electronic audiencing system whose users are not so much inhabitants or privileged residents as they are interlocutors in permanent transit. From this moment on, breaks in continuity occur less within the boundary of a physical urban space or its cadastral register than within a span of time, a span that advanced technology and industrial redeployment have incessantly restructured through a series of interruptions (closing of companies, unemployment, variable work schedules, etc.) and through successive or simultaneous transformations which have managed to organize and reorganize the urban milieu to the point of bringing about a decline, an irreversible deterioration of urban sites, as in, for example, the large townhouses near Lyons where the occupant turnover rate became so high (no one stayed more than a year) that it caused the ruin of a residential complex otherwise considered satisfactory.

In fact, since men first began using enclosures, the notion of what a boundary is has undergone transformations which concern both the facade and what it faces, its vis-à-vis. From the fence to the screen, by way of the rampart's stone walls, the *boundary-surface* has been continually transformed, perceptibly or imperceptibly. Its most recent transformation is perhaps that of the *interface*. The question of access to the city, then, should be asked in a new way: Does a greater metropolis still have a facade? At what moment can the city be said to face us? The popular expression "to go into the city," which has replaced last century's "to go to the city," embodies an uncertainty regarding relations of opposites (the vis-à-vis and the face-à-face), as though we were no longer ever in front of the city but always inside it. If the metropolis still occupies a piece of ground, a geographical position, it no longer corresponds to the old division between city and country, nor to the opposition between center and periphery. The localization and the axiality of the urban layout faded long ago. Suburbia was not single-handedly responsible for this dissolution. The very opposition "intramural"/"extramural" was itself weakened by the revolution in transportation and the development of communications and telecommunications, which resulted in the nebulous conurbation of an urban fringe. In effect, we are witnessing a paradoxical phenomenon in which the opacity of construction materials is virtually being eliminated. With the emergence of portative structures, curtain walls made of light and transparent materials (glass, plastics) are replacing the stone facade at the same time that the tracing paper, acetate and plexiglass used in project studies are replacing the opacity of paper.

On the other hand, with the screen interface (computers, television, teleconferencing) the surface of inscription—until now devoid of depth—comes into existence as "distance," as a depth of field of a new representation, a visibility without direct confrontation, without a face-à-face, in which the old vis-à-vis of streets and avenues is effaced and disappears. Thus, differences between positions blur, resulting in unavoidable fusion and confusion. Deprived of objective limits, the architectonic element begins to drift, to float in an electronic ether devoid of spatial dimensions yet inscribed in the single temporality of an instantaneous diffusion. From this moment on, no one can be considered as separated by physical obstacles or by significant "time distances." With the interfacade of monitors and control screens, "elsewhere" begins here and vice versa. This sudden reversion of limits and oppositions introduces into the space of common experience what had previously belonged only to the realm of microscopy. Solid substance no longer exists; instead, a limitless expanse is revealed in the false perspective of the apparatuses' luminous emission. Constructed space now occurs within an electronic topology, where the framing of the point of view and the scanlines of numerical images give new form to the practice of urban mapping. Replacing the old distinctions between public and private and "habitation" and "circulation" is an overexposure in which the gap between "near" and "far" ceases to exist, in the same way that the gap between "micro" and "macro" disappears through electronic microscope scanning.

The representation of the contemporary city is thus no longer determined by a ceremonial opening of gates, by a ritual of processions and parades, nor by a succession of streets and avenues. From now on, urban architecture must deal with the advent of a "technological space-time." The access protocol of telematics replaces that of the doorway. The revolving door is succeeded by "data banks," by new rites of passage of a technical culture masked by the immateriality of its components: its networks, highway systems and diverse reticulations whose threads are no longer woven into the space of a constructed fabric, but into the sequences of an imperceptible planning of time in which the interface man/machine replaces the facades of buildings and the surfaces of ground on which they stand.

Only a short time ago, the opening of the city's gates was determined by the alternating of day and night. Today, however, since we not only open the shutters but also the television,[1] daylight itself has been changed. A false electronic day, whose only calendar is based on "commutations" of information bearing no relationship whatsoever to real time, is now added to the solar day of astronomy, electric light and the dubious "daylight" of candles. Chronological and historical time, which passes, is thus succeeded by a time that instantaneously *exposes itself*. On the terminal's screen, a span of time becomes both the surface and the support of inscription; time literally or, rather, cinematically surfaces. Due to the cathode-ray tube's imperceptible substance, the dimensions of space become inseparable from their speed of transmission. Unity of place without unity of time makes the city disappear into the heterogeneity of advanced technology's temporal regime. Urban form is no longer designated by a line of demarcation between here and there, but has become synonymous with the programming of a "time schedule." Its gateway is less a door which must be opened than an audio-visual protocol—a protocol which reorganizes the modes of public perception.

In this realm of deceptive appearances, where the populating of transportation and transmission time supplants the populating of space and habitation, inertia revives an old sedentariness (the persistence of urban sites). With the advent of instantaneous communications (satellite, TV, fiber optics, telematics) arrival supplants departure: everything arrives without necessarily having to depart. Only yesterday, metropolitan areas maintained an opposition between an "intramural" population and a population outside the city walls; today, the distinctive oppositions between the city's residents occur only in time: first, long historical time spans which are identified less with the notion of a "downtown" as a whole than with a few specific monuments; and second, technological time spans which have no relation to a calendar of activities, nor to a collective memory, except to that of the computer. Contributing to the creation of a permanent present whose intense pace knows no tomorrow, the latter type of time span is destroying the rhythms of a society which has become more and more debased. And the "monument," no longer the elaborately constructed portico, the monumental passageway punctuated by sumptuous edifices, but idleness, the monumental wait for service in front of machinery: everyone bustling about while waiting for communication or telecommunication machines, the lines at highway tollbooths, the pilot's checklist, night tables as computer consoles. Ultimately, the door is what monitors vehicles and various vectors whose breaks of continuity compose less a space than a kind of countdown in which the urgency of work time plays the part of a *time center*, while unemployment and vacation time play the part of the periphery—*the suburb of time*: a clearing away of activities whereby everyone is exiled to a life of both privacy and deprivation.

If, in spite of the wishes of postmodern architects, the city from now on is to be deprived of doors, it is due to the fact that the urban wall has given way to an infinity of openings and ruptured enclosures. While they are less apparent than those of antiquity, they are just as real, constraining and segregating. The illusions surrounding the industrial revolution of transportation have deluded us about the unlimited nature of progress. The industrial structuring of time has imperceptibly compensated for the disruption of rural territory. If in the nineteenth century the lure of the city emptied agrarian space of its substance (cultural, social), at the end of the twentieth century it is urban space which loses in its turn its geographical reality. This reality is lost to the sole benefit of instantaneous deportation systems whose technological intensity continuously upsets social structures: the deportation of people through the redeployment of production modes; the elimination of attention, of human confrontation, of the direct face-à-face, of the urban vis-à-vis, which all takes place at the level of the man/machine interface. In fact, all of this is part of another type of concentration, a nascent transnational and posturban concentration which has been revealed by many recent events.

In spite of continual rises in the cost of energy, middle-class Americans are evacuating eastern metropolitan areas. After the decay of inner cities, which subsequently became ghettoes, comes the current deterioration of the cities themselves as regional centers.

From Washington to Chicago, from Boston to Saint Louis, the great urban centers are depopulating. New York has lost, over the course of the last decade, 10 percent of its population. As for Detroit, it saw more than 20 percent of its inhabitants disappear; Cleveland, 23 percent; Saint Louis, 27 percent. Certain neighborhoods in these cities already resemble the ghost towns immortalized by American cinema.

These are premonitory signs of an imminent postindustrial deurbanization, and this exodus will most likely affect all developed countries. Foreseeable for about 40 years now, this deregulation of urban planning originates from an economic and political illusion about the permanence of sites constructed in the era of time management (automobile) and in the era of audio-visual development of retinal persistence—the afterimage.

"Every surface is an interface between two milieus in which a constant activity prevails, taking the form of an exchange between two substances placed in contact with one another." This new scientific definition illustrates how contamination is at work in the concept of *surface*: the surface-boundary becomes an osmotic membrane, a blotter. Even if this last etymology is more rigorous than preceding ones, it nonetheless points to a change affecting the notion of limitation. The limitation of space becomes commutation, a radical separation, mandatory passageways, a transit of constant activity, nonstop exchanges, a transference between two milieus, two substances. What used to be a substance's boundary line, its "terminal," now becomes an access route concealed in the most imperceptible entity. From this moment on, the appearance of surfaces hides a secret transparency, a thickness without thickness, a volume without volume, an imperceptible quantity.

If this situation corresponds to the outward appearance of the infinitely small, it also reaches that of the infinitely large: if what was visibly nothing becomes "something," then it follows that the longest distance no longer cuts off perception; that is, even the most vast geophysical expanse contracts and becomes concentrated. In the interface of the screen, everything is already there to be seen in the immediacy of instantaneous transmission. When Ted Turner decided, for example, to launch Cable News Network in Atlanta in 1980, a channel providing live news around the clock, he metamorphosed his subscribers' apartments into a type of station of world events.

Because of satellites, the cathode-ray window is capable of presenting antipodes along with the light of a different day to each one of its viewers. If space is that which prevents everything from being in the same place, this abrupt confinement brings everything—absolutely everything—back to that place which has no place. The exhaustion of natural relief and of temporal distances creates a telescoping of any localization, of any position. As in the case of events televised live, places also become interchangeable at will.

The instantaneousness of ubiquity results in the atopia of a single interface. Speed, which replaces the distances of space and time, abolishes the notion of physical dimension. Suddenly, speed returns to a primary scale which resists any kind of measurement, whether it be temporal or spatial. This phenomenon is equivalent to an instant of inertia of the environment. With the intense acceleration of telecommunications, the old city disappears, only to give birth to a new form of concentration: the concentration of residentialization without residence, in which property lines, enclosures and partitions are no longer the result of permanent physical obstacles but of interruptions of an emission or of an *electronic shadow zone* which mimics sunshine and the shadows of buildings. A strange topology is concealed within the conspicuousness of televised images. The sequences of an invisible montage replace the architect's blueprints. It used to be geographical space which was structured according to a geometrical setting of boundaries (urban or rural). Today it is time which is structured according to an imperceptible fragmentation of a technological time span in which cutting—a momentary interruption—replaces lasting disappearances, and in which the "program grid" replaces the grid of wire fences, just as in the past the railway replaced the ephemeris.

"The camera has become our best inspector," John F. Kennedy declared a short while before he was killed on a street in Dallas. Actually, the camera allows us to participate in—live or on tape—certain political events and certain optical phenomena, such as phenomena of breaking into *effraction*, in which the city lets itself be seen through and through, and phenomena of breaking apart *diffraction*, in which its image is reflected beyond the atmosphere to the ends of space. And meanwhile, the endoscope and the scanner are permitting us to see life in its most remote aspects. This *overexposure* attracts our attention inasmuch as it portrays the image of a world without antipodes, without hidden sides, a world in which opacity is no longer anything but a momentary "interlude." It must be noted, however, that the illusion of proximity does not last very long. Where the polis once inaugurated a political theater, with the agora and the forum, today there remains nothing but a cathode-ray screen, with its shadows and specters of a community in the process of disappearing. This "cinematism" conveys the last appearance of urbanism, the last image of an urbanism without urbanity, where tact and contact yield to televisual impact: not only "teleconferencing" which allows for conferring at great distances without having to move, but also "telenegotiating" which, to the contrary, lets one maintain a distance during discussion, even when one's partners are within a close physical range, a little like those telephone maniacs for whom the receiver facilitates belligerency—the anonymity of remote control aggressivity.

Where does the *city without gates* begin? Probably inside the minds of returning vacationers, taking the form of that fleeting anxiety which grabs them when they think about all the unwanted mail and the possibility that their home has been broken into, their property stolen; and perhaps, also, in the desire to flee, to escape temporarily, from an oppressive technological environment in order to find oneself again, to pull oneself together. Then again, while spatial escape is still possible, temporal escape is not. Unless one considers the practice of laying-off as an "exit door," the ultimate form of paid vacation, running away in time is dependent upon a postindustrial illusion, the effects of which are beginning to make themselves felt. The theory of "shared jobs," already introduced into a segment of the community, offers each member an alternative plan in which shared timetables could open onto a whole new sharing of space: the reign of an endless periphery where the homeland and the colony would replace the industrial city and its suburbs. (Concerning this subject, see the Community Development Project, a project which promotes local development using the forces of the community itself and aims at assimilating English inner cities.)

Where does the edge of the outer city begin? Where is the *door without a city* located? Most likely within the new American technology used for the instantaneous destruction (by explosion) of large buildings, and also within the policy of systematic demolition of social housing judged "unfit for the new French way of life," as has been seen in Venissieux, La Courneuve and Gagny. A recent economic study, conducted by the Association for Communications Development, arrived at the following conclusions: "The destruction of 300,000 lodgings over a period of five years would cost 10 billion francs per year, but would provide 100,000 jobs. Better yet, at the end of the operation demolition-reconstruction, the fiscal receipts would be six to ten billion francs more than the sum which the public originally invested."

One last question must now be asked: during a crisis period, will the demolition of cities replace the major public works of traditional politics? If so, it would no longer be possible to distinguish between the nature of recessions (economic, industrial) and the nature of war.

Architecture or postarchitecture? In the end, the debate surrounding the notion of modernity seems to belong to a phenomenon of "derealization" which at once affects means of expression, modes of representation and information. The dispute currently taking place in the media with respect to certain political acts and their social communication, is also being extended to architectural expression, which can never be said to be properly cut off from communication systems inasmuch as it continually experiences the direct or indirect side effects of different "means of communication" (automobile, audio-visual, etc.). Along with the technique of construction, there is, one must not forget, the construction of technique, the ensemble of spatial and temporal mutations which continually reorganize on an everyday basis the aesthetic representations of contemporary territory. Constructed space is thus not simply the result of the concrete and material effect of its structures, its permanence and its architectonic or urbanistic references, but also the result of a sudden proliferation, an incessant multiplying of special effects, which, with consciousness of time and distance, affects perception of the environment.

This technological deregulation of different areas is also "topological" inasmuch as it no longer constructs a perceptible and visible chaos, as was the case with certain processes of degradation and destruction (accident, aging, war); to the contrary and paradoxically, it constructs an imperceptible order that, even though invisible, is just as practical as masonry or road and highway systems. Today, it is more than likely that the basis of so called urbanism is composed/decomposed by these very systems of transfer, transit and transmission, the transportation and transmigration networks whose immaterial configurations renew urban organization and the building of monuments. If "monuments" in fact exist today, they are no longer visible, in spite of the revolutions and convolutions of architectural grandioseness. This "disproportion" is no longer inscribed in the order of perceptible appearances, in the aesthetic of volumes assembled under the sun, but in the terminal's obscure luminosity—the home computer and other electronic "night tables." It is too easily forgotten that more than being an ensemble of techniques designed to shelter us from inclemency, architecture is an instrument of measure, a sum of knowledge capable of organizing society's space and time by pitting us against the natural environment. This "geodesic" capacity of defining a unity of time and place for activities now enters into open conflict with the structural capacities of mass communication.

Two procedures confront each other here: one is material, made up of physical elements, precisely situated walls, thresholds and levels; the other is immaterial, its representations, images and messages possessing neither locale nor stability, since they exist only as vectors of a momentary and instantaneous expression, with all the misinterpretations and manipulation of meanings that this implies.

The first procedure, which is architectonic and urbanistic, organizes and constructs geographic and political space in a durable fashion. The second procedure heedlessly structures and destructures space-time, the continuum of society. Obviously, it is not a question here of a Manichaean dualism opposing physics to metaphysics but rather of trying to discern the status of contemporary architecture, in particular the status of urban architecture, placed within the disconcerting concert of advanced technology. Architectonics, which developed along with the city and the discovery and colonialization of new lands, is now, since this quest has been accomplished, continually regressing, accompanied by the decline of large urban areas. While continually investing in internal technical equipment, architecture has become progressively introverted, turning into a sort of machine gallery, an exhibition hall of science and technology, technology born of industrial "machinism," of revolutions in transportation and finally of the all-too-famous "conquest of space." However, it is symptomatic that when space technology is discussed, it is not in terms of architecture but in terms of engineering, an engineering which propels us beyond the atmosphere.

And all of this exists as though architectonics were merely a subsidiary technology surpassed by other technologies which permit sidereal projections and accelerated displacement. Thus, questions are raised concerning the nature of architectural performance, the telluric function of constructed dwellings and the relationship between a particular conception of technology and the earth. The way in which the city has developed as a conservator for ancient technologies has already contributed to the increase in architecture by projecting it into all different directions. With its demographic concentration and extreme vertical densification, the urban center is structured in a way that is precisely the opposite of agrarian organization. Advanced technology continues to further this trend with the dramatic expansion of architectonics and in particular with the development of means of transportation. At the moment, state-of-the-art technologies, derived from the military conquest of space, are projecting dwellings—and perhaps someday will project even cities—into orbit. With inhabited satellites, space shuttles and orbital stations, high technological research and aeronautical industries, architecture is "flying high," but not without repercussions for the fate of postindustrial society, whose cultural points of reference are disappearing one after the other, bringing about a decline of the arts and a slow regression of basic technology. Is urban architecture in the process of becoming a technology just as outdated as extensive farming? Will architectonics become nothing more than a decadent form of dominating the earth, with consequences analogous to the unbridled exploitation of raw materials? Hasn't the decline in the number of cities also become the symbol of industrial decline and forced unemployment, the symbol of scientific materialism's failure? The recourse to history, proposed by experts of postmodernity is merely a subterfuge to avoid the question of time, the regime of "transhistoric" temporality generated by technological ecosystems. If a crisis exists today, it is first and foremost a crisis of references (ethical, aesthetic), an incapacity to take stock of events in an environment where appearances are against us. The mounting disequilibrium between indirect and direct information, resulting from the development of various means of communication, tends to heedlessly privilege information mediated in such a way as to jeopardize meaning: the effect of reality seems to supplant immediate reality. The crisis of modernity's grand narratives, about which Lyotard speaks, betrays the presence of new technology, with the emphasis being placed, from now on, on the "means" and not on the "ends."

The *grand narratives* of theoretical causality were replaced by the *little narratives* of practical opportunity and finally by the *micro-narratives* of autonomy. The issue therefore is no longer the "crisis of modernity," the progressive degradation of common ideals, the proto-foundation of History's meaning benefiting narratives which are more or less linked to the autonomous development of an individual, but rather a crisis of narrative itself. That is, the crisis of an official discourse or mode of representation bound until now to the universally recognized capacity—inherited from the Renaissance—to assert, describe and inscribe reality. Thus the crisis of "narrative" appears as the flip side of the crisis of "dimension," understood as a geometrical narrative, a discourse—accessible to all—of the measuring of a visible reality.

The crisis of the grand narrative and the rise of micro-narratives are ultimately the crisis of the "grand" as well as the "little," the advent of disinformation in which disproportion and incommensurability are to postmodernity what the philosophic resolution of problems and the resolution of the image (pictorial, architectural) were to the birth of the Enlightenment.

The crisis of dimension thus appears as the crisis of the whole or, in other words, as the crisis of a substantial, homogeneous space, inherited from archaic Greek geometry, to the benefit of an accidental, heterogeneous space where parts and fractions become essential once again. Urban topology has, however, paid the price for this atomization and disintegration of figures, of visible points of reference which promote transmigrations and transfigurations, much in the same way as landscapes suffered in the face of agricultural mechanization. The sudden breaking up of whole forms and the destruction of the entity caused by industrialization is, however, less perceptible within the space of the city—despite the destructuring of suburbia—than it is in time, in the sequential perception of urban appearances. In fact, for a long time now transparency has replaced appearances. Since the beginning of the twentieth century, the depth of field of classical perspective has been renewed by the depth of time of advanced technology. The development of cinematography and aeronautics followed on the heels of the opening of the "grand boulevards": the Haussmann boulevard procession was followed by the Lumière brothers' invention of accelerated motion; the esplanade of the Invalides was followed by the invalidation of urban planning; the screen abruptly became place—the crossroads of mass media.

From the aesthetics of the appearance of stable images, present precisely because of their static nature, to the aesthetics of the disappearance of unstable images, present because of their motion (cinematic, cinemagraphic), a transmutation of representations has taken place. The emergence of form and volume intended to exist as long as their physical material would allow has been replaced by images whose only duration is one of retinal persistence. Ultimately, it seems that Hollywood, much more than Venturi's Las Vegas, merits a study of urbanism, since, after the theaters of antiquity and the Italian Renaissance, it was the first Cinecittà: the city of living cinema where sets and reality, cadastral urban planning and cinematic footage planning, the living and the living dead merge to the point of delirium. Here, more than anywhere, advanced technologies have converged to create a synthetic space-time. The Babylon of film "derealization," the industrial zone of pretense, Hollywood built itself up neighborhood by neighborhood, avenue by avenue, upon the twilight of appearances, the success of illusions and the rise of spectacular productions (such as those of D. W. Griffith) while waiting for the megalomaniacal urbanization of Disneyland, Disneyworld and Epcot Center.

When Francis Ford Coppola directed *One from the Heart* by inlaying his actors, by an electronic process, in the filmic framework of a life-sized Las Vegas reconstructed in Zoetrope Company Studios simply because he did not want his shooting to adapt itself to the city, but for the city to adapt itself to his shooting, he surpassed Venturi by far, not so much by demonstrating contemporary architectural ambiguity but by showing the "spectral" character of the city and its inhabitants.

Ray Harryhausen's and Douglas Turnbull's video-electronic special effects were added to the utopian "architecture on paper" of the 1960s at the same time that computer screens were making their way into architectural firms. "Video does not mean I see, but I fly," explained Nam June Paik. In effect, given this technology, "over-view" is no longer a question of theoretical altitude, of scale designs, but has become an opto-electronic interface operating in real time, with all that this implies about the redefinition of image. If aviation, which began the same year as cinematography, instigated a revision of point of view, a radical change in the perception of the world, infographic techniques will instigate, in their turn, a revision of reality and its presentations. This process can also be seen in the "Tactical Mapping System," a videodisc created by the United States Defense Agency for Advanced Research Projects. This system provides a viewing of Aspen in continuity by accelerating or slowing down the procession pace of 54,000 images, changing direction or season as one changes television channels, transforming the little city into a sort of ballistic tunnel in which the function of eyesight and the function of weapons merge.

In fact, if architectonics used to measure itself against the scale of geology, against the tectonics of natural reliefs with pyramids, towers and other neogothic structures, today it no longer measures itself against anything except state-of-art technologies, whose dizzying prowess exiles all of us from the terrestrial horizon.

A neo-geology, the "Monument Valley" from a pseudolithic era, the metropolis is no longer anything but a ghostly landscape, the fossil of past societies for which technology was still closely associated with the visible transformations of substance, a visibility from which science has gradually turned us away.

Note

1.   [Translator's note: In French, the verb *ouvrir*, "to open," may also be used to mean "to turn on" a television.]

Robert Segrest   **"The Perimeter Projects: Notes for Design"** *Art Papers* 8, no. 4 (July-August 1984),

special issue "Without Architecture," edited by Robert Segrest and Jennifer

Bloomer; revised in *Assemblage* 1 (October 1986)

If taking stock of the trivia and trash of everyday life is epistemological, as Walter Benjamin argued, then one obvious next step is the intentional mapping for cognitive purposes of heretofore unintentional and irrational activities. The construction and use of the American suburb surely qualify as activities of this sort, with the advantage to the would-be cartographer that their analysis entails a concrete, historical content — a particularly American experience of space and its iteration from Herman Melville and Edgar Allan Poe to Laurie Anderson — as well as a form of a new kind not legible with reading habits forged on European capitals.

  Robert Segrest's project to produce a map of the American perimeter began as a prospectus for an architectural design studio at the Georgia Institute of Technology. Yet, in his effort to provide exemplary instances of practicing space adequate to the new system "out there," Segrest also produces a concept of architecture as no longer bound to an object, but rather as a web of transactions among various codes — architecture as a kind of commutation device, moving and sorting among different images given by contemporary culture, trucking and exchanging inventories between the various storehouses of knowledge and ideology; architecture as the *writing* of events rather than as any lived experience. "A suburban architecture . . . is a geography of filaments, of structures in space, of the silent mirage of the drive-in movie (flickers, flicks, Barthes's semic code), the symbiosis not of city and building but of book and building — the playing of the game."

  Though Segrest takes recourse in the old destructive characters of modernism — Poe's man of the crowd, Musil's man without qualities, the generic impersonality of Robbe-Grillet's *nouveau roman* — it is the postcontemporary world of J. G. Ballard's *Crash* and Wim Wenders's *Paris, Texas,* that he intends to map. Architecture's entry into this sensibility — into its geography of incidents and necessarily decentered subjects — requires that architecture's categories be developed in spatial terms rather than in objective ones, cartographic rather than geometrical, chronotopic rather than typological. And it leads not into a joyous discovery of a redemptive postmodernism so much as into a phantasmagoria of fragments no less somber than the anomie typically reserved for the damaged modernists from Piranesi to James Joyce.

| see 642 | It is here that Segrest registers an ambiguity characteristic of architecture theory in the mid-1980s, a skeptical, transgressive kind of writing whose convulsions somehow resemble laughter.

In the wide space of architecture, that which is not the building is of no consequence. Ideas, descriptions, critiques, theories, even ideology—all abstractions—are, in the end, passive and inert, the ether of the architectural space. The object—separate and privileged—is the sole subject of an enclosed and centripetal order. Architecture is a collection of ruins that closes at six o'clock.

Or so the story has gone. These notes seem first as a transgressor in that orderly and well-lit space. These are other, viral spaces, formed after closing, in darkness and silence, behind hidden doors. The ether, etched and marked as a stone, is the space of literature: a separate army enforced with words; the enemy, Hugo said, of architecture. Vandals in the museum, they rearrange the day works, confuse the titles, paint slogans on the bathroom walls. An indelible stain bleeds across the white skin.

The binary clock that organizes the museum (metaphor) is, of course, faulty. Words did not and do not oppose and destroy. There is, rather, in the abyss between, a state of indifference—a demilitarized zone of foray and brief encounter, of tunnels and watchtowers, and of seeing and of the imagination of seeing in a perpetual dawn (or is it dusk?). The records of the zone catalogue the itinerary—actual, possible, desired—like filaments across the abyss. A map that is both *Campo Marzio* and *Finnegans Wake*. From Oedipus to Hopalong, the action occurs at the pass.

1. Space

"Hey Pal!

How do I get to town from here?"

And he said:

"Well, just take a right where they're going to build that new
   shopping mall;

go straight past where they're going to put in the freeway;

take a left at what's going to be the new sports center;

and keep going until you hit the place where they're thinking
   of building that drive-in bank.

You can't miss it."

LAURIE ANDERSON, "Big Science"

On the fringe in America, the postcard is the evoking, organizing trope.

The physical design of the Opryland Hotel is a consummation of classic Southern and Williamsburg architecture highlighted by a warm interior style.

They are signals from displaced presence, imprinting the marginal landscape with emblems and codifying (geographically) its narratives in a mobile history that is successive to nothingness. SPACE, not history, not time, is (still) the totalizing force in the American experience.

It has always been the case. The most American of novels—*Moby Dick* and *Huckleberry Finn*—are about SPACE. It is the landscape of the American imagination; not the time-filled, humanist space of Europe, defined and limited by objects, but the opposite: space unlimited, empty, space as QUANTITY. Charles Olson, the Gloucester poet, found that America in Melville. In the preamble to his study to *Moby Dick*, he wrote:

I take SPACE to be the central fact to man born in America, from Folsom Cave to now. I spell it large because it comes large here. Large and without mercy.[1]

And for Olson and Melville the emptiness was primordial, the locus of another (last) beginning. Histories could be written, geographies traced; Ahab's voyage into the Pacific sea and Huck's journey were itineraries of transgression, forays into the DMZ. ". . . what's going to be."

But Poe was opposite to Melville and Twain. Olson also said:

Some men ride on such space, others have to fasten themselves like a tent stake to survive. As I see it, Poe dug in and Melville mounted. They are the alternatives.[2]

Poe, the man of the street, of the archetypes of fear, imagined man caught in diminishing, malevolent space—the maelstrom, the closing room, the crowded street, the grave. Man lost in *constructions*. Poe's ocean novel—*The Narrative of the Voyage of Arthur Gordon Pym*—is an unfolding map of terror and redemption, a transgression not of space, but of time. Pym is controlled, and his itinerary is set, by what already exists. The shape of his journey is the shape of a history horribly deformed by the architecture of Poe's imagination. So, too, the *flâneur* of "The Man of the Crowd" is trapped, propelled forward through the labyrinth of an urban night by dread and curiosity. Poe's landscape is mapped with these archetypal constructions; Melville's is mapless.

The American suburb is a display of this dialectic—the place forming in primordial space, but haunted by the archetypes of tradition. It is a geography of edges and perimeters, a becoming landscape that is marked by a cartography at once scientific and mythic—trajectory and labyrinth.

The architecture of this order—trajectories and labyrinths—is the subject of the notes that follow, and the *itinerary* of Pym, Ahab, Huckleberry Finn, the *flâneur* is a schema for them. (Are not architecture and writing, after all, a kind of mapping, a spatial and literal cartography?) The elements of the schema—geography and geometry—are constructions—bridges or programs for bridges—across the traditional limits, again spatial and discursive, of these disciplines, architecture and literature: and the resulting structures and the zone they cross become concepts for our architecture of transgression. On the fringe.

And I said:

"This must be the place."

LAURIE ANDERSON, "Big Science"

2. Limits
The Architect/Geometer

Geometers, all measures measure themselves,

none measures the world. Premise and axiom

are terms of the limited case, to limit it.

There is no limited truth: there is no truth.

WILLIAMS BRONK, "On Divers Geometries"

Architecture—Euclidean architecture—is then a system of self-defining limits: the surfaces of orders imposed in SPACE, a measuring (geometry) and a marking (geography) of the world. Skyscraper. Pyramid. Horizon. Labyrinth. Well. The intellectual shape of architecture is the tropological extension of these limits. But limit is privilege. The system measures itself and is its truth. The status of architectural theory is the flux between motives: in one direction consolidation and in the other, transgression. In the first case separateness, the privilege of architecture, is sustained; the coherence of the formation is preserved. It is the course of the mainstream. In a Kuhnian landscape, it is the working of a kind of preparadigmatic discipline in which the building as canon is exemplar. Theory resists anomaly, consolidates, gives shape to the field.

Theories of transgression invite anomaly, fragment, violate the shape of the field. The authority of architecture—the symbiosis of building and city—is undermined by operations that reveal and subvert its limits. The bus to Edge City stops finally, momentarily at a phone booth next to a chain link fence next to nothing. An exchange must take place, a change of phase in this "space of transformation." The metaphor is in flux. The building can no longer be *canon* and exemplar. *Out of Order.*

The intricate works of the philosopher/physicist Michel Serres are, fractionally, a cartography of spaces of transformation that is both method and theme. On the traces of a stonehouse of narrative figures (Homeric Voyages, the Myths of La Fontaine, the Discovery of Thermodynamics, the Northwest Passage), Serres constructs an itinerary that is

a kind of encyclopedia—a series of crossings of varying length, a mosaic of knowledge made up of borrowings, detours, codes and messages that cross each other, creating unforeseeable connections and nodes.[3]

In *The Parasite* Serres leads us outward onto the plain of limits in a compelling architectonic:

At the crossroads, the morals turn around the decision, sometimes murders are committed; bifurcation, that of space and of logic, suddenly rises to a fantastic level and takes charge of old tales where language is as close as possible to its birthplace; one's reason for living—one's reason, quite simply—is changed. The discourse speaks of the path taken and follows its meanderings. The well, the bridge, the labyrinth: these are vignettes of figurings, games, strategies, chances or random occurrences, circumstances, built or constructed monuments, . . .[4]

The suburban fringe is the narrative space of our itinerary. Like Serres's Northwest Passage, it too is a metaphor for the space of intellectual passage, the space of transgression; but it is also different. The fringe is antispace—empty, not filled but to be filled, the space of potential intersection, interference, and disorder. To operate there, Serres's critical theory must be transformed into a theory of design in which, as in Wittgenstein's house, the discursive is embedded in the architectural. There, order is not natural, as in the city, but is created out of the potential structure of experience.

Our movement, really, walking around, there and here, walking around, is not the plane of the skin of the earth, but every way, the way a spider webs a room: the seeming falls, the climbs, the back and forth, the feeling out, to sensitize a space; and hanging there, we rest on tension. What should we make of this, which is the structure of experience—walking around, walking around, nowhere, being like that explosion in silence, those nets of white inside the rot of trees, radiating everywhere?[5]

Benjamin and the Shape of History

It is not for me to ponder what is happening to the "shape of the city."

ANDRÉ BRETON, *Nadja*

To encompass Breton and Le Corbusier—that would mean drawing the spirit of the present-day France like a bow and shooting knowledge to the heart of the moment.

WALTER BENJAMIN, *Arcades Project*

The programs of avant-garde transgression that characterized the early phase of twentieth-century art (futurism, dadaism, surrealism, etc.) were not manifest in the more conservative realm of rationalist and productivist urbanism. The Cartesian utopias of Le Corbusier and others were less prescriptions for radical action and more confirmations of an economic and technological evolution already taking place in Western Europe. The projects for decentralization in postwar Russia were similarly programs of implementation rather than resistance. On the other hand, the "theater" of the avant-garde—the settings of radical action—was a form of virtual architecture: the momentary or temporary transformation of place into event. (Nikolai Eureinov's concept of "theatricalization of everyday life" and Natan Altman's "decorations" for St. Petersburg for the anniversary of the October Revolution are examples.)

In the *Arcades Projects* Walter Benjamin intended to fuse the counterimaginings of the surrealists, particularly Aragon, and the rationalists into a historical present—a chronicle of nineteenth-century Paris, of places, objects, fragments, and textures that would trace and retrace the city like an organizing web and that, allegorically, would represent its present as well. Benjamin, the surrealist philosopher, and Benjamin, the materialist historian, seem to merge. But the elements of the fusion (of the history) would be held in suspension, held apart by the geometry of Benjamin's historiography. In the prologue, "N," he said:

The work must raise to the very highest level the art of quoting without quotation marks. Its theory is intimately linked to that of montage.[6]

The unit of Benjamin's itinerary is the image, the monad, the quotation positioned in the architecture of montage. History, for Benjamin, is a game—element (image) and operation (idea).

History as a structuring, crystallizing web—a secular field—extends from Vico's "gentile" world to Foucault's "genealogies." Edward Said says of Vico:

the fundamental thing is that history and human society are made up of numerous efforts crisscrossing each other, frequently at odds with each other, always untidy in the way they involve each other.[7]

In the face of "traditional" historiography, these histories may be transgressive in the narrative (ideological, political) sense, but, more important, they embody the continuity of a *structural* idea that, purged of narrative, is the order of postmodern thought.

Method of this work: literary montage. I need say nothing. Only show. I won't steal anything valuable or appropriate any witty turns of phrase. But the trivia, the trash: this, I don't want to take stock of, but let it come into its own in the only way possible: use it.
WALTER BENJAMIN, *Arcades Project*

Like all big cities, it consisted of irregularity, change, sliding forward, not keeping in step, collisions of things and affairs and fathomless points of silence in between, of paved ways, and wilderness, of one great rhythmic throb and the perpetual discord and dislocation of all opposing rhythms and as a whole resembled a seething, bubbling fluid in a vessel consisting of the solid material of buildings, laws, regulations, and historical traditions.
ROBERT MUSIL, *The Man without Qualities*

Musil's epic begins with a car wreck. The event, minor in itself, is nonetheless an *image* in the flux of the city, a temporary arrest of history. It is also somehow foreign, a superimposition:

"According to American statistics," the gentlemen observed, "there are over a hundred and ninety thousand people killed on the roads annually over there and four hundred and fifty thousand injured."[8]

Point equals event. The house of the Man without Qualities is similarly an event, caught in the web of history, a "glance":

It was an eighteenth- or even perhaps a seventeenth-century garden, still in parts unspoilt; and passing along its wrought-iron railings one caught a glimpse through the trees of a well-kept lawn and beyond it something like a miniature chateau, hunting lodge, or *pavillon d'amour* from times past and gone. More precisely, its original structure was seventeenth century, the garden and upper story had a eighteenth-century look, and the facade had been restored and somewhat spoilt in the nineteenth century so that the whole thing had a faintly bizarre character like that of a superimposed photograph.[9]

But these images—of "progress" and "tradition"—are now on opposing paths. The city is centrifugal, moving out but without a center (like "the well-known incoherency of ideas, with their way of spreading out without a central point"). History—the chateau and its garden—is enveloped by this "soup." What was once outside and independent is now contained and without meaning ("nothing more than a neglected piece of real estate waiting for a rise in the price of land"). Musil's introduction is an allegory of the modernist's dilemma: the expanding city is increasingly composed of events and traces of events and less of objects, the debris of history.

What holds the city [the Dublin of *Ulysses*] together is not a common conceptual basis but the web of connections which may be formed with the texture of its surfaces.
CLIVE HART, "Wandering Rocks," in *James Joyce's Ulysses: Critical Essays*

Venturi

Beyond the town the only transition between the Strip and the

Mojave Desert is a zone of rusting beer cans.

ROBERT VENTURI, *Learning from Las Vegas*

The canonical theories of modern urbanism withdrew from a tradition-laden present and thereby erased the tension. Le Corbusier's old town was a museum piece in the matrix of the City of Tomorrow. Wright diagnosed the present city as diseased and cancerous and fled to the primeval (deserts and spirals). To design was to separate the chaotic, disordered now from a utopian future or a primal past. The Athens Charter was an agenda for the divided, demystified city—no car wrecks in a unified landscape. Broadacre City was a field of primitive individualism—and secondhand Fords. Both concepts (not transgressions, but displacements) were, paradoxically, captured in the productive mechanisms of the modern city and became its commodity.
    The question of both the discursive and formal limits of architecture was renewed by Robert Venturi in *Complexity and Contradiction in Architecture* and, with Denise Scott Brown and Steven Izenour, in *Learning from Las Vegas*. In the first, the discipline of architecture was represented in a pattern of exchange—primarily metaphoric—with another discipline, literary studies, and the course of architectural history—primarily European—was revived as a reservoir for the present. In the second, a more objective analysis of the popular "nouveau-riche" cityscape was carried out, again aided and abetted by literature (the cultural histories of Tom Wolfe and J. B. Jackson) and historic example. In the first a system of criticism, in the second a prologue for design, energized the expressiveness of architecture in the commingled landscapes of European history and contemporary roadside America. So influenced, architects began to find creative guidance not in the canons of architecture but in a Wallace Stevens poem, an Eliot essay, the theories of I. A. Richards or William Empson, or in a Las Vegas casino. It was a soft revolution couched more in the prevailing pop irony of the time than in the transgressive spirit of the avant-garde.
    The allies of Venturi's architectural polemic were the aging heroes of a literary movement—the New Criticism—which had already been seriously challenged within its own discipline by the emerging philosophy-laden critical theories of structuralism and phenomenology. Ten years later in his *The Shingle Style Revisited*, Vincent Scully, who had championed Venturi in the foreword to *Complexity and Contra-*

diction, shifted (vaguely) the nature of the interdisciplinary alliance to the more current American deconstructionism of Harold Bloom.

So, if it was a revolution at all, Venturi's was a revolution of the *derrière-garde*; nonetheless, the problematic, the substance and the shape of his arguments for an American architecture had a dramatic effect on theory and practice in the 1970s. The shape was derived from a set of extended parallels, the present of architecture reconnected to its history and tradition and positioned relative to the dominant critical sensibility of the immediate Anglo-Saxon past. The norms—the aesthetic principles—of the latter were transferred to architecture and confirmed in its history (and in the literary behavioralism of Richards). Yet the integrity—the object-centered (poem/building) structure—of each discipline was maintained; the exchange occurred across a territory of seemingly mutual and traditional respect. Venturi's centripetal model still stopped at the border, reconfirmed the limits, a geography of noninterference that helped form the essential conservatism of countermodernism. The discursive motive of architecture was consolidation.

Except in the problematic, Venturi's perceived radicalism was, and is, in the shift in the locus of architecture—from city to suburb, from high culture to nouveau riche, from Fifth Avenue to Main Street. This was transgression. "How do you design *out there?*"

The main justification for honky-tonk elements in architectural order is their very existence. They are what we have . . . the short-term plan, which expediently combines the old and the new, must accompany the long-term plan. Architecture is evolutionary as well as revolutionary. As an art it will acknowledge what is and what ought to be, the immediate and the speculative.
ROBERT VENTURI, *Complexity and Contradiction in Architecture*

Out There

An empty amusement park makes a great hideout.

MICHAEL O'HARA (ORSON WELLES), *The Lady from Shanghai*

Venturi's so-called populism is a redirection outward from time into space—desert, suburb, seacoast—and onto the fringes of American culture. It is a geography of lines carved in rock, of signifiers torn from concept, vague monuments in the wilderness and a neon sunrise—a landscape of events. But Venturi, like Poe, ties himself down. With metaphor and irony, Main Street becomes not just "almost all right" but quite all right in the recomposed art of the pop architect. Signs emptied of signification in rational analysis are rejoined to history and to science. Program and event are monumentalized and the traditional "centeredness" of architecture is reconfirmed. Venturi's world is marked by Eliotic monuments, not by Benjamin's debris.

But Las Vegas, Levittown, and Atlantic City are themselves transgressions—anomaly, fragment, violations of the shape of the field. Their "permanence" is not of form but of structure, and their motive is not function but program and event. Their effect is more cinematic than architectural. The geography of the zone of transgression, the game, is not unlike the idea of film as a reconstructive medium.

The idea of transgression is based on notions of interference and transaction—of structure and narrative, of architecture and literature—to produce event. It is a physical and a discursive phenomenon in which signifier and signified are suspended in patterns of separation. In commenting on the work of Swift, Edward Said remarks:

We are then forced to take seriously Swift's discovery that words and objects in the world are not simply interchangeable, since words extend from objects into an entirely verbal world on their own. If words and objects ever coincide, it is because at certain propitious times both converge into what the prevailing polity can readily identify as an event, which does not necessarily involve exchange or communication.[10]

It is a system not of criticism but of performance. A cinematic analogy: following an opening encounter in a deserted Central Park, Welles's film journeys around the underworld of Mexico only to end abruptly in the Magic Maze in San Francisco. The mythical architecture of the film—Eden, the journey, and the labyrinth—is empty, a geography of unexpected encounters, temptations, multiples, disorder through which the wanderer must pass and on which narrative overlay—the sequence of events (scenes) imposed on the structure of the architecture—evolves. The film is a graph of these events; the setting is a program. "Structure organizes the game space" (Serres).

Criss-cross!
BRUNO (ROBERT WALKER), in Hitchcock's *Stranger on a Train*

(In the phrase, Bruno suddenly joins the structure of his crime with the intersecting tracks of the opening scene.)

3. Construction

> In the gathering dusk I draw closer, groping my way and place
> a hand on the hard cold wall where, cutting into the schist with
> the point of the broad-bladed knife I write the word *construction*,
> an illusionist painting, a make-believe construction by which I
> name the ruins of a future deity.
>
> **ALAIN ROBBE-GRILLET,** *Topology of a Phantom City*

The genesis of transgression is a game. Writing as a game. Architecture as a game. The game space is the space of transgression, transaction, and construction. Building. The witches' brew.

Brouillage	1.)	jamming, interference
	2.)	inteference area
	3.)	scramble, scrambling
Brouillon	1.)	disorganized, unmethodical, muddle-headed
	2.)	muddler
	3.)	rough draft, rough copy

Harrap's New Shorter Dictionnaire

A brouillon for *Ulysses* (Frank Budgen suggests) might have been the taxonomy drawn by Joyce from playing a game called "Labyrinth" with his daughter Lucia. "As a result of winning or losing at the game he was enabled to catalog six main errors of judgement into which one might fall in choosing a right, left, or centre way out of the maze."[11] The result is the transformation of a game that is both geographical and geometrical into one that is narrative and linguistic as well. "Reading this chapter ['Wandering Rocks'] is like walking into the maze of a city's streets. One finds oneself continually taking wrong turns, being caught in deadends, having to retrace one's steps."[12] Through a land of Vichian superimpositions, Joyce's narrative consciousness and the particular geography of Dublin are enjoined with the structure of the board game. The book is a paradigm for architecture. (Clive Hart reminds us that "Joyce had said, with allowable hyperbole, that he wanted *Ulysses* to be a documentary source from which Dublin, if destroyed, might be recreated.")[13]

The city (the narrative?) is (was, will be?) destroyed in Robbe-Grillet's *Topology of a Phantom City* but, again, by a game—the defiantly complex system of "intertextual assembly" that Bruce Morrissette, the author's Dr. Watson has carefully interpreted and documented. *Topology* is a *created order* (the term is Robbe-Grillet's), a transgression of the established, the conventional, and the authoritarian generated by "organizing structures that seem to me beautiful, demonstrably provable, even almost pedagogic." These "generative structures"—Robbe-Grillet's *brouillons*—are a map, a schema for the "book." An example:

There are single words, phrases, and small drawings of geometric forms, in a concentrated collection of generative elements to be incorporated into the diegesis. Among the briefly annotated geometric figures are: a vertical triangle, with the annotations "table, trappe, regle du jeu"; an equilateral triangle identified as pubis, temple pediment, and easel; a slender, needle-like triangle, identified as paintbrush, stylus. or engraver's tool, catheter, as well as bar cane, and pointer; a mandala, yantra, or circle with the notes pebble, breast, spectator's circle, sunset, belly, iron ring; a sinuous letter five, as fingers, digits, "1 + 3 + 1"; five divergent slanting lines with the notes sun's rays, "raies du plancher," iron bars; and a curving vertical line identified as road, whip, and serpent.[14]

The taxonomy of the *brouillons* is activated by tactics of transgression—motives of ordering/disordering (they are intertwined like the *caduceus*) that establish the itinerary of the work. In Robbe-Grillet's film *Glissements progressifs du plaisir*, two characters, the criminal/prostitute/transgressor and the magistrate/authority/orderer, recount these devices:[15]

She:	Jeu	*He:*	Récidive
	Viol		Relapse
	Plaisir		Libertaire
	Structure		Désirdre
	Infraction		Paresse
	Sperme		Parricide
	Déboublement		Inversion
	Permutation		

The two are playing the game—the author's game, director's game—of disruption (*clinamen*) and diversion, and, finally, assault.

Of course, game structures and game playing abound in both modern (from Flaubert forward) and postmodern literature, film, music, and painting; but it is the emphasis on structure torn from a narrative (or representative or ideological) dimension that increasingly separates recent work from its precursors (Robbe-Grillet from Joyce, for instance). Interestingly this phenomenon has little characterized contemporary architecture, which, in working itself out of the formal constraints of the various schools of modernism, has, as Venturi and others exemplify, worked backwards into history and ideology rather than forward. Postmodernism in architecture (to generalize) is a reactionary movement, a *countermodernism*.

What is the shape of postmodern architecture in America?

An image (mis)remembered from a Sam Shepard play: things on the prairie at night. The young boy weaves through the labyrinthian rows of high corn toward a white glow at the center. The chimera slowly takes silent form and it is (of course) the earnest face of Spencer Tracy and another of a woman in red, both engaged in frantic pantomime.

The drive-in movie. Coming attractions. "You can't miss it."

For the beginning is assuredly the end—since we know nothing, pure and simple, beyond our own complexities.

WILLIAM CARLOS WILLIAMS

Architecture—Euclidean architecture—is then a system of self-defining limits: the surfaces of order *constructed* in SPACE, a measuring (geometry) and a marking (geography) of the world. Carnivals. K-Mart. The Magic Maze. U.S. 1. The Strip(e), the trajectory and the itinerary is also the hallowed edge, *La Maison Dedalus.*

Arthur Gordon Pym, Poe's penultimate *flâneur,* encountered such an architecture—fragments of a language, glyphs on a stone—near the end of his voyage (or of his narrative, or of Poe's narrative). It is a filament, between two poles, occupying space (difference), visible in the event, a violator and a transgressor of the dark. But, too, connection and transaction.

A suburban architecture (not the binary *disorder* of an urban *order;* not the residual of archetypes, Olmsted's and Howard's) is a geography of filaments, of structures in space, of the silent mirage of the drive-in movie (flickers, flicks, Barthes's semic code), the symbiosis not of city and building but of book and building—the playing of the game. An archaeology of the present: sifting through the refuse pile (like Benjamin) like children

who are particularly fond of haunting any site where things are being visibly worked on. They are irresistibly drawn by the detritus generated by building, gardening, housework, tailoring, or carpentry. In waste products, they recognize the fact that the world of things turns directly and solely to them. In using these things they do not so much imitate *the works of adults as bring together, in the artifact produced in play* [emphasis mine] materials of widely differing kinds in a new intuitive relationship. Children thus produce their own small world of things within the greater one.[16]

The futurists (in ideological as well as formal transgression) had done the same: arranging and imitating the art of children in defiance of the limits of the conventional.

An object: an agit-train, a painted toy, gliding onto the steppe, like a Milanese theater or a Rabelaisian carnival or a ship of fools before, in an ideological trajectory, crisscrossing the landscape. At each stop the object unfolds, poles are connected, and flickers of a distant imagination appear. The *flâneur* (the itinerant) and the commodity (itinerant too), torn from the city, are flung across space to be reprised, reconciled, reconstructed in a created order.

In *Paterson,* William Carlos William's epic collage, a fragment of the genesis:

So far, everything had gone smoothly. The pulley and ropes were securely fastened on each side of the chasm and everything made in readiness to pull the clumsy bridge into position. It was a wooden structure boarded up on both sides, and a roof.

Tim Crane built the bridge because his rival, Fyfield, who kept the tavern on the other side of the falls, was getting the benefit of the "Jacob's Ladder," as it was sometimes called—the "hundred steps," a long rustic, winding stairs in the gorge leading to the opposite side of the river—it making his place more easy to get to. . . .[17]

The scene is enlarged into a bizarre, pun-filled, topological field. The two resorts are popular with the "circus men." The chasm is the site of the Falls and marks the beginning of the career of the famous jumper, Sam Patch, who dives into the river to upstage Tim Crane. A network of chasms and connections emerges and out of it Sam Patch's itinerary (with fox and bear) only to end when he is somehow failed by the emptiness of his pre-jump speech—of language—and falls, tangled Icarus, to his death.

The game structure emerges. ("Structure organizes the game space"; "Structure is a set of elements provided with operations"—Serres.) The mythical space of the American suburb, potential space, is to be organized—as Serres exposes Zola's *Rougon-Macquart* novels—with a game, the "graph of an itinerary," in which the squares, stages, points of chance are necessarily architectural—connectors. For Serres (for Zola): bridge, well, hotel, labyrinth, prison, and death. For us as well as for Poe, Williams, Robbe-Grillet, etc., "connection and non-connection are at stake, space is at stake, an itinerary is at stake."[18]

The fact is that in general a culture constructs in and by its history an original intersection between spatial varieties, a node of very precise and particular connections. This construction, I believe, is that culture's very history.[19]

"How beautiful the world is, and how ugly labyrinths are," I said, relieved. "How beautiful the world would be if there were a procedure for moving through labyrinths," my master replied.
UMBERTO ECO, *The Name of the Rose*

Notes
These notes were written as a prologue to a design studio taught at Georgia Tech in the Fall of 1984.
1. Charles Olson, *Call Me Ishmael* (San Francisco: City Lights Books, 1947), p. 11.
2. Ibid., p. 12.
3. Michel Serres, *Hermes*, ed. Josue V. Harari and David F. Bell (Baltimore: Johns Hopkins University Press, 1982), p. xxxv.
4. Michel Serres, *The Parasite*, trans. Lawrence R. Schehr (Baltimore: Johns Hopkins University Press, 1982), p. 71.
5. Ibid.
6. Walter Benjamin, "N [Theoretics of Knowledge; Theory of Progress]," trans. Leigh Itafrey and Richard Sieburth, *Philosophical Forum* 15, nos. 1–2 (Fall-Winter 1983–1984), p. 3. For the extracts from the *Arcades Project*, above and following, see ibid., pp. 4, 5.
7. Edward Said, "Opponents, Audiences, Constituencies," in *The Anti-Aesthetic: Essays on Postmodern Culture*, ed. Hal Foster (Port Townsend, Washington: Bay Press, 1983), p. 145.
8. Robert Musil, *The Man without Qualities*, vol. 1 (London: Pan Books, 1983), p. 6.
9. Ibid.
10. Edward Said, *The Word, the Text, and the Critic* (Cambridge: Harvard University Press, 1983), p. 58.
11. Frank Budgen, *James Joyce and the Making of "Ulysses" and Other Writings*, rev. ed. (London, 1972), quoted in Clive Hart, "Wandering Rocks," in *James Joyce's Ulysses: Critical Essays*, ed. Clive Hart and David Hayman (Berkeley: University of California Press, 1974), p. 189.
12. Hart, "Wandering Rocks," p. 189.
13. Ibid.
14. Bruce Morrissette, *Intertextual Assemblage in Robbe-Grillet from Topology to the Golden Triangle* (Fredericton, New Brunswick: York Press, 1979), p. 18.
15. Alain Robbe-Grillet, *Glissements progressifs du plaisir* (Paris: Editions de Minuit, 1974), pp. 140–141.
16. Walter Benjamin, *One-Way Street and Other Writings*, trans. Edmund Jephcott and Kingsley

Shorter (London: New Left Books, 1979), pp. 52–53, quoted in Terry Eagleton, *Walter Benjamin, or Towards a Revolutionary Criticism* (London: Verso, 1981), pp. 57–58.

17. William Carlos Williams, *Paterson* (Middlesex: Penguin Books, 1983), p. 16.
18. Serres, *Hermes*, p. 43.
19. Ibid., p. 45.

Jacques Derrida   **"Point de folie — Maintenant l'architecture"** Essay accompanying the portfolio

Bernard Tschumi, *La Case Vide: La Villette 1985* (London: Architectural Association,

1986), essay trans. Kate Linker

What Jacques Derrida calls his double writing (*écriture double*) provokes, on the one hand, an inversion of the general cultural domination he everywhere identifies with Western metaphysics and enacts, on the other hand, a new text that, necessarily, participates in the very principles it deconstructs, but participates as an invasion, releasing the dissonance of the inherited order. In his essay on Bernard Tschumi's *La Case Vide* — the "folio-folie" that presents the conceptual structure of Tschumi's Parc de La Villette — Derrida projects onto architecture the same formulation: *l'architecture double* disrupts the entire given architectural system and, just for a moment, takes over the field.

Architecture theory had already constructed for itself an account of meaning based on a generalized system — an architectural *langue* — understood as necessary for the production and intelligibility of architectural events — *parole*, the messages, usages, and effects of the generalized code. But the relationship between *langue* and *parole* produces an aporia. The norms and regularities of the language, its structure, are a product of all the prior architectural events; yet each event is itself made possible by the prior structure. There can be no originary event that might have produced the structure — an event comprising, say, a point, a line, and a surface — for such an event is already structurally distributed and arranged. Neither is the structure ever present; there are no full, positive elements of meaning but only differentiation and referral to other elements. A point, for example, can function as a signifier only insofar as it differs from a line and a surface and, moreover, traces those forms, refers to those forms, which it is not. Thus meaning is not a presence but rather is the effect of a generalized economy of absences.

Derrida's term for this generalized absence is *différance* (difference-differing-deferring), which alludes to the undecidability of this alternation of structure and event and to the nonoriginary origin of meaning's infinite play. Meaning is not inexhaustible in the sense that there are infinite possible interpretations; rather meanings are maintained in the arrest of unmeaning. An analogous term is spacing, which he uses throughout the following essay. "*Différance*, then, is a structure and a movement no longer conceivable on the basis of the opposition presence/absence. *Différance* is the systematic play of differences, of the traces of differences, of the *spacing* by means of which elements are related to each other. This spacing is the simultaneously active and passive . . . production of the intervals without which the 'full' terms would not signify, would not function."[1]

Deconstruction ordinarily does its work by locating the moment in a text where meaning is supposed to be antecedent to *différance*, exposing the untenable metaphysics of that supposition, and reversing the hierarchy. In the instance of *La Case Vide*, however, the architecture's complex signifying practice is already divided against itself; the undecidability of its meanings (though meaning is the wrong word) is built into the architecture and its workings. Such a text cannot be deconstructed, since its repetitions, substitutions, and gaps have already been "marked" by its author and by the architecture. What Derrida shows, then, is the text's exorbitance — not only its effacements, tracings and retracings, but its excesses, its bursting through conceptual repressions.

Derrida graphs the function of architecture as four points, four traits-traces, four corners of a frame: what he elsewhere terms a *parergon*.[2] Together, "they translate one and the same postulation: *architecture must have a meaning*, it must *present* it and, through it, *signify*. The signifying or symbolical value of this meaning must direct the structure and syntax, the form and function of architecture. It must direct it *from outside*, according to a principle (*archè*), a fundamental or foundation, a transcendence or finality (*telos*) whose locations are not themselves architectural." A *parergon* of architecture is against, above, and beyond the work of architecture, but it is not incidental; rather it cooperates in the inside operations of architecture from the outside. The logic of the *parergon* is the logic of the supplement. It must be convoked because of a lack in the work — its internal indeterminacy — that it comes to frame. The lack that produces the frame is also produced by the frame, and in the moment, precisely, when the work is considered *from the point of view of architecture*. Thus, like *différance*, architecture is never present as an event (not present, not even for a moment) but nevertheless can be recovered by a kind of *Nachträglichkeit*, a deferred action in which architecture is constructed and maintained for a moment in the work of architecture by what can be called only a textual mechanism — a transcription and a translation.[3]

One example of this textual mechanism is the graft, inserting other discourses into one as its iteration and exploring the disruptive repetitions that ensue. "The invention, in this case, consists in crossing the architectural motif with what is most singular and most parallel in other writings which are themselves drawn into the said madness, in its plural, meaning photographic, cinematographic, choreographic, and even mythographic writings. . . . An architectural writing interprets . . . events which are *marked* by photography or cinematography." Even the points, lines, and surfaces are here understood as grafts insofar as each system conflicts with and is superimposed on the others.

see Eisenman
531–532

The graft is included in what Derrida calls "a typology of forms of iteration."[4] In *La Case Vide* it operates along with other forms of iteration like the signature ("the *maintenant* that I speak of will be this, most irreducible, signature") — whose "authenticity" paradoxically depends on its reiterability — and the performative ("the event that I *make* happen or *let* happen by marking it"), whose very productive success depends on its repetition of an already iterable code.[5] Architecture *maintenant* is a signing of the architectural contract ("it does not contravene the charter, but rather draws it into another text"), an iteration of an iterable code.

But Derrida attributes a more generalized disruption to Tschumi's text, for its thematic figure, the point, comes to both describe and arrest the general series to which it belongs and is, therefore, not a theme at all but the arche-theme behind all the thematic effects. This is the point at which the strains to sustain architecture's contract, its promise, its "charter or metaphysical frame" can be felt in an uncanny opacity. It is a point of condensation that maintains the perpetual disruptions and disjunctions, maintains the undecidability of its architecture not in polysemousness but in the affirmative power of its infinite generality and unorganizable energy. This is Tschumi's madness (or better, the madness of *La Case Vide*, for such a system cannot have an intending author): "it maintains the *dis-jointed per se*." It is a text capable of reiteration without exhaustion and, importantly, without keeping anything like meaning in reserve.

A final point. Derrida hints at the nontextual nature of institutions that must always be involved in architecture or deconstruction: "Deconstructions would be feeble . . . if they did not first measure themselves against institutions in their solidity, *at the place of their greatest resistance*: political structures, levers of economic decision, the material and phantasmatic apparatuses which connect state, civil society, capital, bureaucracy, cultural power and architectural education." But he does not resolve how deconstruction can actively reckon with the forces of an extratextual institutional reality.

Notes

"Point de folie—Maintenant l'architecture" was reprinted in *AA Files* 12 (Summer 1986).

1. Jacques Derrida, *Positions*, trans. Alan Bass (Chicago: University of Chicago Press, 1981), p. 27.

2. See Jacques Derrida, *The Truth in Painting*, trans. Geoff Bennington and Ian McLeod (Chicago: University of Chicago Press, 1987).

3. According to the Freudian theory of deferred action, precocious sexual stimulation normally has no psychopathological repercussions at the time of its occurrence, due to the child's psychical incapacity to comprehend the act of seduction. With the physiological change of puberty, however, the mnemic-psychical trace—inscribed in the unconscious as if in an unknown language—would be transformed (rewritten, reiterated) as trauma and displaced as symptom in neurosis.

4. Jacques Derrida, *Speech and Phenomena, and Other Essays on Husserl's Theory of Signs*, trans. David B. Allison (Evanston: Northwestern University Press, 1973), p. 192.

5. The promise is the standard case of a performative utterance, which constitutes the very act to which it refers. Derrida points out that for a promise to constitute itself, however, it must be recognizably a repetition of an iterable model of promising. Ibid., pp. 191–192.

1

Maintenant:[1] this French word will not be translated. Why? For reasons, a whole series of reasons, which may appear along the way, or even at the end of the road.
For here I am undertaking one road or, rather, one course among other possible
and concurrent ones: a series of cursive notations through the *Folies* of Bernard
Tschumi, from point to point, and hazardous, discontinuous, aleatory.

Why *maintenant*? I put away or place in reserve, I set aside the
reason to maintain the seal or stamp of this idiom: it would recall the Parc de la
Villette in France, and that a pretext gave rise to these *Folies*. Only a pretext, no
doubt, along the way—a station, phase, or pause in a trajectory. Nevertheless, the
pretext was offered in France. In French we say that a chance is offered, but also,
do not forget, to offer a resistance.

2

Maintenant: the word will not flutter like the banner of the moment, it will not introduce burning questions: What about architecture today? What are we to think
about the current state of architecture? What is new in this domain? For architecture
no longer defines a domain. *Maintenant:* neither a modernist signal nor even a salute
to post-modernity. The *post*-s and *posters* which proliferate today (post-structuralism,
post-modernism, etc.) still surrender to the historicist urge. Everything marks an
era, even the decentering of the subject: post-humanism. It is as if one again wished
to put a linear succession in order, to periodize, to distinguish between before and
after, to limit the risks of reversibility or repetition, transformation or permutation:
an ideology of progress.

3

Maintenant: if the word still designates what happens, has just happened, promises
to happen *to* architecture as well as *through* architecture, this imminence of the *just*
(*just* happens, *just* happened, is *just* about to happen) no longer lets itself be inscribed
in the ordered sequence of a history: it is not a fashion, a period or an era. The *just
maintenant* [just now] does not remain a stranger to history, of course, but the relation would be different. And if this happens *to us,* we must be prepared to receive
these two words. On the one hand, it does not happen to a constituted *us,* to a
human subjectivity whose essence would be arrested and would then find itself
affected by the history of this thing called architecture. We appear to ourselves only
through an experience of spacing which is already marked by architecture. What
happens through architecture both constructs and instructs this *us.* The latter finds
itself engaged by architecture before it becomes the subject of it: master and pos-
sessor. On the other hand, the imminence of what happens to us *maintenant* announces not only an architectural event but, more particularly, a writing of space,
a mode of spacing which makes a place for the event. If Tschumi's work indeed
describes an architecture of the events it is not only in that it constructs places in

which something should happen or to make the construction itself be, as we say, an event. This is not what is essential. The dimension of the event is subsumed in the very structure of the architectural apparatus: sequence, open series, narrative, the cinematic, dramaturgy, choreography.

4

Is an architecture of events possible? If what happens to us thus does not come from outside, or rather if this outside engages us in the very thing we are, is there a *maintenant* of architecture, and in what sense [*sens*]? Everything indeed [*justement*] comes down to the question of meaning [*sens*]. We shall not reply by indicating a means of access, for example, through a given form of architecture: preamble, *pronaos*, threshold, methodical route, circle or circulation, labyrinth, flight of stairs, ascent, archaeological regression towards a foundation, etc. Even less through the form of a system, that is, through architectonics: the art of systems, as Kant says. We will not reply by giving access to some final meaning, whose assumption would be finally promised us. No, it is justly [*justement*] a question of what happens to meaning: not in the sense of what would finally allow us to arrive at meaning, but of what happens to it, to meaning, to the meaning of meaning. And so—and this is the event—what happens to it through an event which, no longer precisely or simply falling into the domain of meaning, would be intimately linked to something like madness [*la folie*].

5

Not madness [*la folie*], the allegorical hypostasis of Unreason, non-sense, but the *madnesses* [*les folies*]. We will have to account with this plural. The *folies*, then, Bernard Tschumi's *folies*. Henceforth we will speak of them through metonymy and in a metonymically metonymic manner, since, as we will see, this figure carries itself away, it has no means within itself to stop itself, any more than the number of *Folies* in the Parc de la Villette. *Folies*: it is first of all the name, a proper name in a way, and a signature. Tschumi names in this manner the point-grid which distributes a non-finite number of elements in a space which it in fact spaces but does not fill. Metonymy, then, since *folies*, at first, designates only a part, a series of parts, precisely the pinpoint weave of an ensemble which also includes lines and surfaces, a "sound-track" and an "image-track." We will return to the function assigned to this multiplicity of red points. Here, let us note only that it maintains a metonymic relation to the whole of the Parc. Through this proper name, in fact, the *folies* are a common denominator, the "largest common denominator" of this "programmatic deconstruction." But, in addition, the red point of each *folie* remains divisible in turn, a point without a point, offered up in its articulated structure to substitutions or combinatory permutations which relate it to other *folies* as much as to its own parts. Open point and closed point. This double metonymy becomes abyssal when it determines or overdetermines what opens this proper name (the "Folies" of Bernard

Tschumi) to the vast semantics of the concept of madness, the great name or common denominator of all that happens to meaning when it leaves itself, alienates and dissociates itself without ever having been subject, exposes itself to the outside and spaces itself out in what is not itself: not the semantics but first of all, the asemantics of *Folies*.

6

The *folies*, then, these *folies* in every sense—*for once* we can say that they are not on the road to ruin, the ruin of defeat or nostalgia. They do not amount to the "absence of the work"—that fate of *madness in the classical period* of which Foucault speaks. Instead, they make up a work, they put into operation. How? How can we think that the work can possibly *maintain itself* in this madness? How can we think the *maintenant* of the architectural work? Through a certain adventure of the point, we are coming to it, *maintenant* the work—*maintenant* is the point—this very instant, the point of its implosion. The *folies* put into operation a general dislocation; they draw into it everything that, until *maintenant*, seems to have given architecture meaning. More precisely, everything that seems to have given architecture over to meaning. They deconstruct first of all, but not only, the semantics of architecture.

7

Let us never forget that there is an architecture of architecture. Down even to its archaic foundation the most fundamental concept of architecture has been *constructed*. This naturalized architecture is bequeathed to us: we inhabit it, it inhabits us, we think it is destined for habitation, and it is no longer an object for us at all. But we must recognize in it an *artifact*, a *construction*, a monument. It did not fall from the sky; it is not natural, even if it informs a specific scheme of relations to *physis*, the sky, the earth, the human and the divine. This architecture of architecture has a history, it is historical through and through. Its heritage inaugurates the intimacy of our economy, the law of our hearth (*oikos*), our familial, religious and political "oikonomy," all the places of birth and death, temple, school, stadium, agora, square, sepulchre. It goes right through us [*nous transit*] to the point that we forget its very historicity: we take it for nature. It is common sense itself.

8

The concept of architecture is itself an inhabited *constructum*, a heritage which comprehends us even before we could submit it to thought. Certain invariables remain, constant, through all the mutations of architecture. Impassable, imperturbable, an axiomatic traverses the whole history of architecture. An axiomatic, that is to say, an organized ensemble of fundamental and always presupposed evaluations. This hierarchy has fixed itself in stone; henceforth, it informs the entirety of social space. What are these invariables? I will distinguish four, the slightly artificial charter of four traits, let us say, rather, of four points. They translate one and the same postulation: *architecture must have a meaning*, it must *present* it and, through it, *signify*. The signifying or symbolical value of this meaning must direct the structure and syntax, the form and function of architecture. It must direct it *from outside*, according to a principle (*archè*), a fundamental or foundation, a transcendence or finality (*telos*) whose locations are not themselves architectural. The anarchitectural topic of this semanticism from which, inevitably, *four points* of invariance derive:

- The experience of meaning must be *dwelling*, the law of *oikos*, the economy of men or gods. In its non-representational presence which (as distinct from the other arts) seems to refer only to itself, the architectural work seems to have been destined for the presence of men and gods. The arrangement, occupation and investment of locations must be measured against this economy. Heidegger still alludes to it when he interprets homelessness (*Heimatlosigkeit*) as the symptom of onto-theology and, more precisely, of modern technology. Behind the housing crisis he encourages us to reflect properly on the real distress poverty and destitution of dwelling itself (*die eigentliche Not des Wohnens*). Mortals must first learn to dwell (*sie das Wohnen erst lernen müssen*), listen to what *calls* them to dwell. This is not a deconstruction, but rather a call to repeat the very fundamentals of the architecture that we inhabit that we should learn again how to inhabit, the origin of its meaning. Of course, if the *folies* think through and dislocate this origin, they should not give in either to the jubilation of modern technology, or to the maniacal mastery of its powers. That would be a new turn in the same metaphysics. Hence the difficulty of what justly—*maintenant*—arises.

- Centered and hierarchized, the architectural organization had to fall in line with the anamnesis of the origin and the seating of the foundation. Not only from the time of its foundation on the ground of the earth, but also since its juridico-political foundation, the institution which commemorates the myths of the city, heroes or founding gods. Despite appearances, this religious or political memory, this historicism, has not deserted architecture. Modern architecture retains nostalgia for it: it is its destiny to be a guardian. An always hierarchizing nostalgia: architecture will materialize the hierarchy in stone or wood (*hylè*), it is a hyletics of the sacred (*hieros*) and the principle (*archè*), an *archi-hieratics*.

- This economy remains, of necessity, a *teleology* of dwelling. It subscribes to all the rules of finality. Ethico-political finality, religious duty, utilitarian or functional ends: it is always a question of putting architecture *in service*, and *at service*. This end is the principle of the archi-hieratical order.

- Regardless of mode, period or dominant style, this order ultimately depends on the fine arts. The value of beauty, harmony, and totality still reigns. These four points of invariability do not adjoin. They delineate the chart of a system from the angles of a frame. We will not say only that they come together and remain inseparable, which is true. They give rise to a specific experience of *assembling*, that of the coherent totality and continuity of the system. Thus, they determine a network of evaluations; they induce and inform, even if indirectly, all the theory and criticism of architecture, from the most specialized to the most trivial. Such evaluation inscribes the hierarchy in a hyletics, as well as in the space of a formal distribution of values. But this architectonics of invariable points also regulates all of what is called Western culture, far beyond its architecture. Hence the contradiction, the *double bind* or antinomy which at once animates and disturbs this history. On the one hand, this general architectonics *effaces* or *exceeds* the sharp specificity of architecture; it is valid for other arts and regions of experience as well. On the other hand, architecture forms its most powerful metonymy; it gives it its most solid *consistency* objective substance. By consistency, I do not mean only logical coherence, which implicates all dimensions of human experience in the same network: there is no work of architecture without interpretation, or even economic, religious, political, aesthetic, or philosophical decree. But by consistency I also mean duration, hardness, the monumental mineral or ligneous subsistence, the hyletics of tradition. Hence the *resistance*: the resistance of materials as much as of consciousnesses and unconsciouses which instate this architecture as the last fortress of metaphysics. Resistance and transference. Any consequent deconstruction would be negligible if it did not take account of this resistance and this transference, it would do little if it did not go after architecture as much as architectonics. To go after it: not in order to attack,

destroy or de-route it, to criticize or disqualify it. Rather, in order to *think* it in
fact, to detach itself sufficiently to apprehend it in a thought which goes beyond
the theorem—and becomes a work in its turn.

9

Maintenant we will take the measure of the *folies* of what others would call the immeasurable *hybris* of Bernard Tschumi and of what it offers to our thought. These *folies*
destabilize meaning, the meaning of meaning, the signifying ensemble of this powerful architectonics. They put in question, dislocate, destabilize or deconstruct the
edifice of this configuration. It will be said that they are "madness" in this. For in a
polemos which is without aggression, without the destructive drive that would still
betray a reactive affect within the hierarchy, they do battle with the very meaning of
architectural meaning, as it has been bequeathed to us and as we still inhabit it. We
should not avoid the issue: if this configuration presides over what in the West is
called architecture, do these *folies* not raze it? Do they not lead back to the desert of
"anarchitecture," a zero degree of architectural writing where this writing would
lose itself, henceforth without finality, aesthetic aura, fundamentals, hierarchical
principles or symbolic signification, in short, in a prose made of abstract, neutral,
inhuman, useless, uninhabitable and meaningless volumes?

       Precisely not. The *folies* affirm, and engage their affirmation be-
yond this ultimately annihilating, secretly nihilistic repetition of metaphysical architecture. They enter into the *maintenant* of which I speak; they maintain, renew and
reinscribe architecture. They revive, perhaps, an energy which was infinitely anaes-
thetized, walled-in, buried in a common grave or sepulchral nostalgia. For we must
begin by emphasizing this: the charter or metaphysical frame whose configuration
has just been sketched was already, one could say, the end of architecture, its "reign
of ends" in the figure of death.

       This charter had come to arraign the work, it imposes on norms
or meanings which were extrinsic, if not accidental. It made its attributes into an
essence: formal beauty, finality, utility, functionalism, inhabitable value, its religious
or political economy—all the *services*, so many nonarchitectural or meta-architectural
predicates. By withdrawing architecture *maintenant*—what I keep referring to in this
way, using a paleonym, so as to maintain a muffled appeal—by ceasing to impose
these alien norms on the work, the *folies* return architecture, faithfully, to what architecture, since the very eve of its origin, should have signed. The *maintenant* that I speak
of will be this, most irreducible, signature. It does not contravene the charter, but
rather draws it into another text, it even subscribes to, and directs others to subscribe
to, what we will again call, later, a *contract*, another play of the trait, of attraction
and contraction.

       A proposition that I do not make without caution and warnings.
Still, the signal of two red points:

- These *folies* do not destroy. Tschumi always talks about "deconstruction/recon-
  struction," particularly concerning the *folie* and the generation of its cube (formal combinations and transformational relations). What is in question in *The
  Manhattan Transcripts* is the invention of "new relations, in which the traditional
  components of architecture are broken down and reconstructed along other
  axes." Without nostalgia, the most living act of memory. Nothing, here, of that
  nihilistic gesture which would fulfill a certain theme of metaphysics; no reversal
  of values aimed at an unaesthetic, uninhabitable, unusable, asymbolical and
  meaningless architecture, an architecture simply left vacant after the retreat of
  gods and men. And the *folies*—like *la folie* in general—are anything but anarchic

chaos. Yet, without proposing a "new order," they locate the architectural work in another place where, at least in its principle, its essential impetus, it will no longer obey these external imperatives. Tschumi's "first" concern will no longer be to organize space as a function or in view of economic, aesthetic, epiphanic or techno-utilitarian norms. These norms will be taken into consideration, but they will find themselves subordinated and reinscribed in one place in the text and in a space which they no longer command in the final instance. By pushing "architecture towards its limits," a place will be made for "pleasure"; each *folie* will be destined for a given "use," with its own cultural, ludic, pedagogical, scientific and philosophical finalities. We will say more later about its powers of "attraction." All of this answers to a program of transfers, transformations or permutations over which these external norms no longer hold the final word. They will not have presided over the work, since Tschumi has folded them into the general operation.

• Yes, folded. What is the fold? The aim of reestablishing architecture in what should have been specifically its own is not to reconstitute a *simple* of architecture, a simply architectural architecture, through a purist or integratist obsession. It is no longer a question of saving its own in the virginal immanence of its economy and of returning it to its inalienable presence, a presence which, ultimately, is non-representational, non-mimetic and refers only to itself. This autonomy of architecture, which would thus pretend to reconcile a formalism and a semanticism in their extremes, would only fulfill the metaphysics it pretended to deconstruct. The invention, in this case, consists in crossing the architectural motif with what is most singular and most parallel in other writings which are themselves drawn into the said madness, in its plural, meaning photographic, cinematographic, choreographic, and even mythographic writings. As *The Manhattan Transcripts* demonstrated (the same is true, though in a different way, of La Villette), a narrative montage of great complexity explodes, outside, the narrative which mythologies contracted or effaced in the hieratic presence of the "memorable" monument. An architectural writing interprets (in the Nietzschean sense of active productive, violent, transforming interpretation) events which are *marked* by photography or cinematography. Marked: provoked, determined or transcribed, captured, in any case always mobilized in a scenography of passage (transference, translation, transgression from one place to another, from a place of writing to another, graft, hybridization). Neither architecture nor anarchitecture: transarchitecture. It has it out with the event; it no longer offers its work to users, believers or dwellers, to contemplators, aesthetes or consumers. Instead, it appeals to the other to invent, in turn, the event, sign, consign or *countersign*: advanced by an advance made at the other—and *maintenant* architecture.

(I am aware of a murmur: but doesn't this event you speak of, which reinvents architecture in a series of "only onces" which are always unique in their repetition, isn't it what takes place each time not in a church or a temple, or even in a political place—not in them, but rather *as* them, reviving them, for example, during each Mass when the body of Christ, etc., when the body of the King or of the nation presents or announces itself? Why not, if at least it could happen again, happen through (across) architecture, or even up to it? Without venturing further in this direction, although still acknowledging its necessity, I will say only that Tschumi's architectural *folies make us think* about what *takes place* when, *for example*, the eucharistic event goes through [*transir*] a church, *ici, maintenant* [here, now], or when a date, seal, the trace of the other are finally laid on the body of stone, this time in the movement of its dis-appearance.)

10

Therefore, we can no longer speak of a *properly* architectural moment, the hieratic impassability of the monument, this hyle-morphic complex that is given once and for all, permitting no trace to appear on its body because it afforded no chance of transformation, permutation or substitutions. In the *folies* of which we speak, on the contrary, the event undoubtedly undergoes this trial of the monumental moment; however, it inscribes it, as well, in a series of *experiences*. As its name indicates, an experience traverses: voyage, trajectory, translation, transference. Not with the object of a final presentation, a face-to-face with the thing itself, nor in order to complete an odyssey of consciousness, the phenomenology of mind as an architectural step. The route through the *folies* is undoubtedly prescribed, from point to point, to the extent that the point-grid counts on a *program* of possible experiences and new experiments (cinema, botanical garden, video workshop, library, skating rink, gymnasium). But the structure of the grid[2] and of each cube—for these points are cubes—leaves opportunity for chance, formal invention, combinatory transformation, wandering. Such opportunity is not given to the inhabitant or the believer, the user or the architectural theorist, but to whoever engages, in turn, in architectural

Bernard Tschumi, Parc de La Villette, Paris, 1982–1983

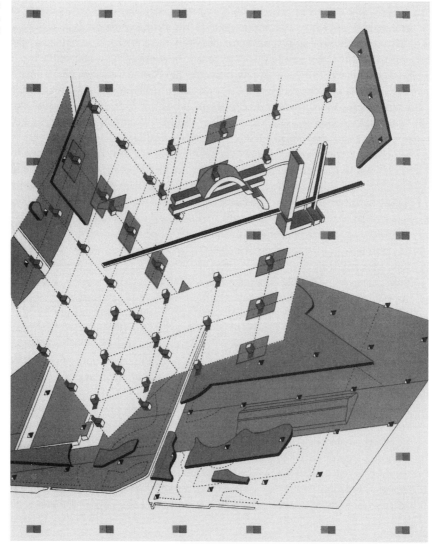

writing: without reservation, which implies an inventive reading, the restlessness of a whole culture and the body's signature. This body would no longer simply be content to *walk*, circulate, stroll around *in* a place or *on* paths, but would transform its elementary motions by giving rise to them; it would receive from this other spacing the invention of its gestures.

11

The *folie* does not stop: either in the hieratic monument, or in the circular path. Neither impassibility nor pace. Seriality inscribes itself in stone, iron or wood, but this seriality does not stop there. And it had begun earlier. The series of *trials* (experiments or artist's proofs) that are naively called sketches, essays, photographs, models, films or writings (for example, what is gathered together for a while in this volume) fully belongs to the *experience* of the *folies: folies at work.* We can no longer give them the value of documents, supplementary illustrations, preparatory or pedagogical notes—*hors d'oeuvre*, in short, or the equivalent of theatrical rehearsals. No—and this is what appears as the greatest danger to the architectural desire which still inhabits us. The immovable mass of stone, the vertical glass or metal plane that we had taken to be the very object of architecture (*die Sache selbst*, or "the real thing"), its indisplaceable effectivity, is apprehended *maintenant* in the voluminous text of multiple writings: superimposition of a *Wunderblock* (to signal a text by Freud—and Tschumi exposes architecture to psychoanalysis, introducing the theme of the transference, for example, as well as the schiz), palimpsest grid, supersedimented textuality, bottomless stratigraphy that is mobile, light and abyssal, foliated, foliiform. Foliated folly, foliage and *folle* [mad] not to seek reassurance in any solidity: not in ground or tree, horizontality or verticality, nature or culture, form or foundation or finality. The architect who once wrote with stones now places lithographs in a volume, and Tschumi speaks of them as *folios*. Something weaves through this foliation whose stratagem, as well as coincidence, reminds me of Littré's suspicion. Regarding the second meaning of the word *folie*, that of the houses bearing their signers' name, the name of "the one who has had them built or of the place in which they are located," Littré hazards the following, in the name of etymology: "Usually one sees in this the word *madness* [*folie*]. But this becomes uncertain when one finds in the texts from the Middle Ages: *foleia quae erat ante domum*, and *domum foleyae*, and *folia Johannis Morelli*; one suspects that this involves an alteration of the word *feuillie* or *feuillée* [foliage]." The word *folie* has no common sense any more: it has lost even the reassuring unity of its meaning. Tschumi's *folies* no doubt play on this "alteration" and superimpose, against common sense, common meaning, this other meaning, the meaning of the other, of the other language, the madness of this asemantics.

12

When I discovered Bernard Tschumi's work, I had to dismiss one easy hypothesis: recourse to the language of deconstruction, to what in it has become coded, to its most insistent words and motifs, to some of its strategies, would only be an analogical transposition or even an architectural application. In any case, impossibility itself. For, according to the logic of this hypothesis (which quickly became untenable), we could have inquired: What could a deconstructive architecture be? That which deconstructive strategies begin or end by destabilizing it, is it not exactly the structural principle of architecture (system, architectonics, structure, foundation, construction, etc.)? Instead, the last question led me towards another turn of interpretation: what *The Manhattan Transcripts* and the *Folies* of La Villette urge us towards is the obligatory route of deconstruction in one of its most intense, affirmative and necessary implementations. Not deconstruction *itself*, since there never was such a thing; rather, what carries its jolt beyond semantic analysis, critique of discourses and ideologies, concepts or texts, in the traditional sense of the term. Deconstructions would be feeble if they were negative, if they did not construct, and above all if they did not first measure themselves against institutions in their solidity, *at the place of their greatest resistance*: political structures, levers of economic decision, the material and phantasmatic apparatuses which connect state, civil society, capital, bureaucracy, cultural power and architectural education—a remarkably sensitive relay; but in addition, those which join the arts, from the fine arts to martial arts, science and technology, the old and the new. All these are so many forces which quickly harden or cement into a large-scale architectural operation, particularly when it approaches the body of a metropolis and involves transactions with the State. This is the case here.

13

One does not declare war. Another strategy weaves itself between hostilities and negotiations. Taken in its strictest, if not most literal, sense, the grid of *folies* introduces a specific device into the space of the transaction. The meaning of "grid" does not achieve assembled totality. It crosses through. To establish a grid is to cross through, to go through a channel. It is the experience of a permeability. Furthermore, such crossing does not move through an already existing texture; it weaves this texture, it invents the histological structure of a text, of what one would call in English a "fabric." Fabric in English recalls *fabrique*, a French noun with an entirely different meaning, which some decisionmakers proposed substituting for the disquieting title of *folies*.

Architect-weaver. He plots grids, twining the threads of a chain, his writing holds out a net. A weave always weaves in several directions, several meanings, and beyond meaning. A network-stratagem, and thus a singular device. Which? A dissociated series of "points," red points, constitutes the grid spacing a multiplicity of matrices or generative cells whose transformations will never let themselves be calmed, stabilized, installed, identified in a continuum. Divisible themselves, these cells also point towards instants of rupture, discontinuity, disjunction. But simultaneously, or rather through a series of mishaps, rhythmed anachromies or aphoristical gaps, the point of *folie* [Fr. *point de folie* = no *folie*] gathers together what it has just dispersed; it reassembles it *as* dispersion. It gathers into a multiplicity of *red* points. Resemblance and reassembly are not confined to color but the *chromographic* reminder plays a necessary part in it.

What then, is a point, *this* point of *folie*? How does it stop *folie*? For it suspends it and, in this movement, brings it to a halt, but *as folie*. Arrest of *folie*: *point de folie*, no or node-*folie*, more *folie*, no more *folie*, no *folie* at all. At the same time it settles the question, but by which decree, which arrest—and which aphoristic justness? What does the law accomplish? Who accomplishes the law? The law divides *and* arrests division; it *maintains* this point of *folie*, this chromosomal cell, as the generative principle. How can we analyze the architectural *chromosome*, its color, this labor of division and individuation which no longer pertains to the domain of biogenetics?

We are getting there, but only after a detour. We must pass through one more point.

14

There are strong words in Tschumi's lexicon. They locate the points of greatest intensity. These are the words beginning with *trans-* (transcript, transference, etc.) and, above all, *de-* or *dis-*. These words speak of destabilization, deconstruction, dehiscence and, first of all, dissociation, disjunction, disruption, difference. An architecture of heterogeneity, interruption, non-coincidence. But who would ever have built in this manner? Who would have counted on only the energies in *dis-* or *de-*? No work results from a simple displacement or dislocation. Therefore, invention is needed. A path must be traced for another writing. Without renouncing the deconstructive affirmation whose necessity we have tested—indeed, on the contrary so as to give it new impetus—this writing *maintains* the dis-jointed *per se*; it joins up the *dis-* by maintaining (*maintenant*) the distance; it gathers together the difference. This assembling will be singular. What holds together does not necessarily take the form of a system; it does not always depend on architectonics and can disobey the logic of synthesis or the order of syntax. The *maintenant* of architecture would be this maneuver to inscribe the *dis-* and make it into a work in itself. Abiding and maintaining [*maintenant*], this work does not pour the difference into concrete; it does not erase the differential trait, nor does it reduce or embed this track, the dis-tract or abs-tract, in a homogeneous mass (*concrete*). Architectonics (or the art of the system) represents only one epoch, says Heidegger, in the history of the *Mitsein*. It is only a specific possibility of the assembling.

This, then, would be both the task and the wager, a preoccupation with the impossible: to give dissociation its due, but to implement it *per se* in the space of reassembly. A transaction aimed at a spacing and at a *socius* of dissociation which, furthermore, would allow the negotiation of *even this*, difference, with received norms, the politico-economic powers of architectonic, the mastery of the *maîtres d'oeuvre*. This "difficulty" is Tschumi's experience. He does not hide it, "this is not without difficulty": "At La Villette, it is a matter of forming, of acting out dissociation. . . . This is not without difficulty. Putting dissociation into form necessitates that the support structure (the Parc, the institution)· be structured as a reassembling system. The red point of *folies* is the focus of this dissociated space." ("Madness and the Combinative," *Précis V*, Columbia University, New York, 1984.)

15

A force joins up and holds together the dis-jointed *per se*. Its effect upon the *dis-* is not external. The *dis-joint* itself, *maintenant* architecture, architecture that arrests the *madness* in its dislocation. It is not only a point: an open multiplicity of red points resists its totalization, even by metonymy. These points might fragment, but I would not define them as fragments. A fragment still signals to a lost or promised totality.

Multiplicity does not open each point *from outside*. In order to understand how it also develops from inside we must analyze the double bind whose knot the point of *folie* tightens, without forgetting what can bind a double bind to schiz and madness.

On the one hand, the point concentrates, folds back towards itself the greatest force of attraction, *contracting* lines towards the center. Wholly self-referential, within a grid which is also autonomous, it fascinates and magnetizes, seduces through what could be called its self-sufficiency and "narcissism." At the same time, through its force of magnetic attraction (Tschumi speaks here of a magnet which would "reassemble" the "fragments of an exploded system"), the point seems to bind, as Freud would say, the energy freely available within a given field. It exerts its attraction through its very punctuality, the *stigmè* of instantaneous *maintenant* towards which everything converges and where it seems to individuate itself; but also from the fact that, in stopping madness, it constitutes the point of transaction with the architecture which it in turn deconstructs or divides. A discontinuous series of instants and *attractions*: in each point of *folie* the attractions of the Parc, useful or playful activities, finalities, meanings, economic or ecological investments, services will again find their place on the program. Bound energy and semantic recharge. Hence, also, the distinction and the transaction between what Tschumi terms the normality and deviation of the *folies*. Each point is a breaking-point: it interrupts, absolutely, the continuity of the text or of the grid. But the interruptor maintains together both the rupture *and* the relation to the other, which is itself structured as both attraction *and* interruption, interference and difference: a relation without relation. What is contracted here passes a "mad" contract between the *socius* and dissociation. And this without dialectic, without the *Aufhebung* whose process Hegel explains to us and which can always reappropriate such a *maintenant*: the point negates space and, in this spatial negation of itself, generates the line in which it maintains itself by cancelling itself (*als sich aufhebend*). Thus, the line would be the truth of the point, the surface the truth of the line, time the truth of space and, finally, the *maintenant* the truth of the point (*Encyclopédie*, §256–257). Here I permit myself to refer to my text, "Ousia et grammè" ("La paraphrase: point, ligne, surface," in *Marges* [Minuit, 1972], *Margins* [University of Chicago Press]). Under the same name, the *maintenant* I speak of would mark the interruption of this dialectic.

But on the other hand, if dissociation does not happen to the point from outside, it is because the point is *both* divisible and indivisible. It appears atomic, and thus has the function and individualizing form of the point according only to a *point of view*, according to the perspective of the serial ensemble which it punctuates, organizes and subtends without ever being its simple support. As it is seen, and seen from outside, it simultaneously scans and interrupts, maintains and divides, puts color and rhythm into the spacing of the grid. But this point of view does not see, it is blind to what happens in the *folie*. For if we consider it *absolutely*, abstracted from the ensemble and in itself (it is also destined to abstract, distract or subtract itself), the point is not a point any more; it no longer has the atomic indivisibility that is bestowed on the geometrical point. Opened inside to a void that gives play to the pieces, it constructs/deconstructs itself like a cube given over to formal combination. The articulated pieces separate, compose and recompose.

By articulating pieces that are more than pieces—pieces of a game, theatre pieces, pieces of an "a-partment" [Fr. *pièce*, room] at once places and spaces of *movement*—the *dis*-joint forms that are *destined* for events: in order for them to take place.

16

For it was necessary to speak of promise and pledge, of promise as affirmation, the promise that provides the privileged example of a performative writing. More than an example: the very condition of such writing. Without accepting what would be retained as presuppositions by theories of performative language and *speech acts*—relayed here by an architectural pragmatics (for example, the value of presence, of the *maintenant* as present)—and without being able to discuss it here, let us focus on this single trait: the provocation of the event I speak of ("I promise," for example), that I describe or trace; the event that I *make* happen or *let* happen by marking it. The mark or trait must be emphasized so as to remove this performativity from the hegemony of speech and of what is called human speech. The performative mark *spaces* is the event of spacing. The red points space, maintaining architecture in the dissociation of spacing. But this *maintenant* does not only maintain a past and a tradition; it does not ensure a synthesis. It maintains the interruption, in other words, the relation to the other *per se*. To the other in the magnetic field of attraction, of the "common denominator" or "hearth," to other points of rupture as well, but first of all to the Other: the one through whom the promised event will happen or will not. For he is called, only called to countersign the pledge [*gage*], the engagement or the wager. This Other never presents itself; he is not present, *maintenant*. He can be represented by what is too quickly referred to as Power, the politico-economic decisionmakers, users, representatives of domains of cultural domination, and here, in particular, of a philosophy of architecture. This Other will be anyone, not yet [*point encore*] a subject, ego or conscience and not a man [*point l'homme*]; anyone who comes and answers to the promise, who first answers for the promise, the to-come of an event which would maintain spacing, the *maintenant* in dissociation, the relation to the other *per se*. Not the hand being held [*main tenue*] but the hand outstretched [*main tendue*] above the abyss.

17

Overlaid by the entire history of architecture and laid open to the hazards of a future that cannot be anticipated, this other architecture, this architecture of the other, is nothing that exists. It is not a present, the memory of a past present, the purchase or pre-comprehension of a future present. It presents neither a constative theory nor a politics nor an ethics of architecture. Not even a narrative, although it opens this space to all narrative matrices to sound-tracks and image-tracks (as I write this, I think of *La folie du jour* by Blanchot, and of the demand for, and impossibility of, narration that is made evident there. Everything I have been able to write about it, most notably in *Parages*, is directly and sometimes literally concerned—I am aware of this after the fact, thanks to Tschumi—with the madness of architecture: step, threshold, staircase labyrinth, hotel, hospital, wall, enclosure, edges, room, the inhabitation of the uninhabitable. And since all of this, dealing with the madness of the trait, the spacing of "dis-traction," will be published in English, I also think of that idiomatic manner of referring to the fool, the absent-minded, the wanderer: *the one who is spacy, or spaced out*).

But if it presents neither theory, nor ethics, nor politics, nor narration ("No, no narrative never again," *La folie du jour*) it gives a place to them all. It writes and signs in advance—*maintenant* a divided line on the edge of meaning, before any presentation, beyond it—the very other, who engages architecture, its discourse, political scenography, economy and ethics. Pledge but also wager, symbolic order and gamble: these red cubes are thrown like the dice of architecture. The throw not only programs a strategy of events, as I suggested earlier; it anticipates the architecture to come. It runs the risk and gives us the chance.

Notes

1. *Maintenant*, Fr., adv., now; from *maintenir*, v., maintaining, keeping in position, supporting, upholding; from *se maintenir*, v., remaining, lasting; from *main tenant*, the hand that holds.
    Folie, Fr., n., madness, delusion, mania; folly; country pleasure-house.
    In general, the French spelling of the word *folie* has been kept in this translation, according to Bernard Tschumi's own usage, so as to retain the connotation of madness. [Translator's note.]
2. *Trame*, Fr., n., woof, weft, web, thread; also plot, conspiracy; (phot. engr.) screen. [Translator's note.]

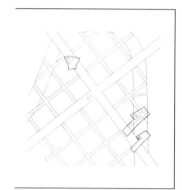
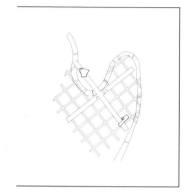

For five centuries the human body's proportions have been a datum for architecture. But due to developments and changes in modern technology, philosophy, and psychoanalysis, the grand abstraction of man as the measure of all things, as an originary presence, can no longer be sustained, even as it persists in the architecture of today. In order to effect a response in architecture to these cultural changes, this project employs an *other* discourse, founded in the process called *scaling*.

The process of scaling entails the use of three destabilizing concepts: *discontinuity*, which confronts the metaphysics of presence; *recursivity*, which confronts origin; and *self-similarity*, which confronts representation and the aesthetic object. Strictly speaking, discontinuity, recursivity, and self-similarity are mutually dependent aspects of scaling. They confront presence, origin, and the aes-

  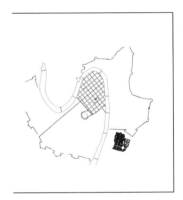

thetic object in three aspects of the architectural discourse: site, program, and representation.

The first aspect which is confronted is that of "the site" as a privileged presence, as a context that is knowable and whole. By treating the site not simply as presence but as both a *palimpsest* and a *quarry,* containing traces of both memory and immanence, the site can be thought of as non-static.

The second aspect which is confronted is the idea of program. The program for this project was to present the dominant themes of the stories of Romeo and Juliet in architecture form at the site of the two castles. There are three important versions of the story of Romeo and Juliet which were taken as the basis of the architectural "program." Each narrative is characterized by three structural relationships: *division* (the separation of the lovers—the bal-

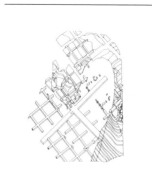
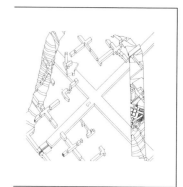

cony); *union* (the marriage of the lovers—the church); and their *dialectical relationship* (the togetherness and apartness of the lovers—Juliet's tomb).

The three structural relationships which pervade the narratives can also be found to exist at a physical level in the plan of the city of Verona: the *cardo* and *decumanus* divide the city; the old Roman grid unites it; and the Adige river creates a dialectical condition of union and division between the two halves. Similarly, places in Verona can be located as key foci in the narrative: supposedly existing in Verona today are Juliet's house (division); the church where the couple was married (union); and Juliet's tomb (the dialectical relationship of togetherness and

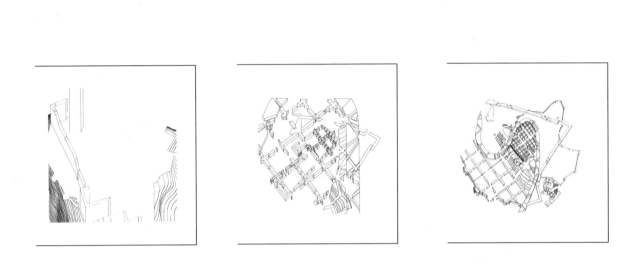

apartness). The project's superpositions of scale and place address the dominant themes. In the overlaps and coincidences of registration arise interrelated elements of present conditions, memory, and immanence, revealing aspects of the structure of the textual narrative.

In reflecting on the two conditions—the "fictional" and the "real"—this architecture denies origin and closure in both fiction (which is seen to have no origin or end in reality) and reality (which has no origin or end in fiction).

Peter Eisenman, *Moving Arrows, Eros and Other Errors: An Architecture of Absence* (London: Architectural Association, 1986)

Sanford Kwinter   **"La Città Nuova: Modernity and Continuity"** *Zone* 1–2 (New York: Urzone, 1986);

slightly revised for this anthology

Though modernist historiographic efforts to link architecture to its technological milieu — Sigfried Giedion's *Space, Time and Architecture* (1941) and Reyner Banham's
Theory and Design in the First Machine Age (1960) are the canonic texts — were regarded by most critics after 1968 as overly deterministic, architecture theory did not
produce its own account of technology until the inaugural issue of *Zone*, wherein
Sanford Kwinter along with Michel Feher assembled some twenty-three essays and

compare Virilio
(542 ff)

projects intended to characterize a new "regime." In contrast to the morphological or
physiological constructs of classical accounts of modern architecture and urbanism,
the new "soft urbanism," as Kwinter would later call it, understands the city as

at once the medium of circulation for populations, information, commodities and rumors; a complex formation of sovereignties and a shifting perceptual field. . . . When considered as a field,
the contemporary city rejoins those irreconcilable questions that overturned classical physics
and the plastic arts at the beginning of the twentieth century. The idea of a space-time continuum, its diffusion throughout scientific and artistic experimentation and the bleak deficiencies
of all maps relying on Euclidean principles betray the emergence of a new perceptual field.[1]

Bound no longer by the limits of three dimensions or the distinc-
tion between interior and exterior, the architecture of the contemporary city comprises
elements — social, economic, biological, and spatial — that are mutually constituted,
an enfolding of insides and outsides, components in an immense global material and
immaterial fluid. Along with the rhizomatic thinking of Gilles Deleuze and Félix Guattari, what enabled this account of architecture and the city was a convergence of
newly recognized chaos theory, global economics, non-Euclidean geometry, and the
nonlinearity of complex thinking.[2] While Kwinter's reading of the projects of Antonio
Sant'Elia, in the essay reprinted here, enunciated the new regime, it also initiated a
theoretical paradigm that, a decade later, is still being played out in architectural
practice and theory alike.[3]

But we should not misunderstand Kwinter's enthusiasm for the
various incorporations of modernity's milieus as an uncritical endorsement of its unstoppable advance. For he has also argued (in a mode that seems parallel to "weak

compare de Solà-
Morales (616 ff)

thought") that, along with soft urbanism, there are "encroaching soft tyrannies and
surreptitious deprivals that are an intimate and necessary complement to the so-
called advances being prepared for us."[4] Because modern thought is unable to separate discourses of emancipation from discourses of technological mastery, the very
possibility of thinking ways to resist modernity or radically reroute its technologies
may not be available in a language intelligible to our society.

Few people would disagree that our civilization, our ethics, and our politics are through and
through technological ones. And yet the horror lies not here, but in the fact that we, as beings,
as animals, as examples of a once human nature, are so fully and irretrievably technological
ourselves that we are today deprived of a language with which to articulate, even to summon a
memory of, the historical passage towards this fate which has claimed us. The Western techno-

logical imperative—the will to mastery of an uncaring nature and of the cruelties of chance—simply cannot be thought separate from the more general (and however apparently noble) dream of the material and spiritual emancipation of humankind. . . . It is for this reason that it may be necessary to think of our technological being, our condition, as *fate*—for we are simply no longer the type of human being we once were, and are today scarcely able to imagine what other type we might become, if not in relation to this all too modern type of embodied freedom.[5]

Notes

1. Michel Feher and Sanford Kwinter, "Forward," *Zone* 1–2 (New York: Urzone, 1986), p. 12.
2. Whereas linearity suggests that small changes result in small effects, that the relationship between a cause and an effect is proportional, nonlinearity argues that perturbations at seemingly insignificant levels can transform the dynamic of an entire system. Manuel Castells, *The Informational City* (Cambridge: Blackwell, 1989), argues that place and geography are being superseded by "the space of flows," an urban and posturban condition that corresponds to the emergence of a new informational mode of development driven by the restructuring of capitalism on a global scale.
3. Among the efforts should be mentioned Rem Koolhaas and Bruce Mau, *Small, Medium, Large, Extra-large* (New York: Monacelli Press, 1995); and Lars Lerup, *After the City* (Cambridge: MIT Press, forthcoming).
4. Sanford Kwinter, "Virtual City, or The Wiring and Waning of the World," *Assemblage* 29 (April 1996), p. 91.
5. Sanford Kwinter, "Architecture and the Technologies of Life," *AA Files* 27 (Summer 1994), p. 3.

The New Plasticity

> We are passing through a stage in a long progress towards in-
> terpenetration, simultaneity, and fusion, on which humanity
> has been engaged for thousands of years.
>
> **UMBERTO BOCCIONI,** December 12, 1913

Technology and Mechanolatria

The two decades beginning in 1876 saw the appearance of the incandescent lamp,
the telephone, hydraulic generators, skyscrapers, electric trolleys, subways and elevators, as well as cinema, X-rays and the first automobiles. By 1903 the spectacle of
the first mechanically powered airships and airplanes had shattered the still inviolate
horizontality of the phenomenological and geopolitical space of the pre–World War
I era. The life-world in Europe and America was being transformed in depth—the
unparalleled technical saturation of the human perceptual apparatus (innovations
in transport and communications) was redefining the body and its relations to the
world beyond it. A new order was emerging whose configuration could be expressed either in terms of a dynamics of force and a relativism or in the privative
terms of nihilism and dissolution. Whatever their ultimate convictions, the philosophies of Bergson and Husserl may be seen to form one axis of this configuration:
Bergson's for its insistence on the nondiscrete nature of the contents of consciousness and on the systematic dissolution of spatial form in the fluid and intensely
subjective multiplicity of *durée*; Husserl's for its attempt to work out the dynamic of
(ap)perception by extending the intentional *horizon* to the vector of internal time
consciousness so that a perceived object (noema)—already defined as partial and
contingent in space—was further relativized in a temporal complex of retained and
anticipated images.

       The first systematic attempt to express these new principles,
however, arose in the realm of aesthetics, first and most fully in the theoretical
program of Italian Futurism, yet realized unequivocally only in the work of one of
its members, Antonio Sant'Elia. The movement's founder, Filippo Tommaso Marinetti, published the Foundation Manifesto in the Paris daily *Le Figaro* in February
1909. Certainly the most literary of any of the several dozen manifestos which
would follow in the next seven years, Marinetti's text recapitulates in its organization and form the same disjunctive pattern it was meant to effect in the real historical world around it. The prologue opens with a description of the Marinetti family
apartment with its precious, saturating *turquerie* and claustrophobic, fin-de-siècle ex-
oticism,[1] then, with scarcely a change in tone turns to a heroic reverie on the new
industrial culture formed by machines and "those who sweat before them." The
text pauses long enough to affirm Futurists' and workers' common affinity to in-

habit the night, before proceeding to the more immediate apprehension of a passing tram, its panoply of artificial lights and finally to an unfavorable comparison of "the arthritic, ivy-bearded old palaces" of the city with the healthy "roar of famished motorcars" that speed among them. The section continues as Marinetti and his companions start out on their famous motorcar race through the streets of Milan. Both the race and the section end abruptly as Marinetti's car capsizes in a ditch, pitching him headlong into the swamp of a factory drain from which he draws at least one "nourishing" draught before emerging to declare himself baptismally delivered into the Futurist world of mechanical splendor.

The main body of the manifesto follows, praising danger, movement, crowds and, above all, speed as a new form of beauty, an *éloge* to mechanism and abstract energy of all kinds including war and automobilism, while denouncing museums, libraries, contemplation, history, old age and stasis in any form, and pronouncing once and for all the abolition of space and time.[2]

In many ways this text marks a turning point in the history of avant-garde culture. Not only was it the first time a call had been made for a complete break with the past and an insistence that the techniques and subject matter of art be drawn solely from the concrete contemporary world around one, but it was the first to have conceived of this concrete world as inseparable from the industrial and scientific technologies which arrange, and are arranged (however abstractly), within it. Correspondingly, the activities and attitudes promulgated by the manifesto were singularly devoid of reference to aesthetic or literary practice. Artistic revolution was conceived only within a more general program of transformation of the totality of human existence. "Dynamism" was the catchword for the entire movement:[3] through it was expressed the will to intervene politically, scientifically and aesthetically in an emerging order of space-time that was already revolutionizing the social environment.

The most significant technical innovations of the era, from the skyscraper to moving pictures and the automobile, were made possible by inventions—electric motor (lifts), incandescent lamp, internal combustion engine, etc.—which themselves depended on more fundamental breakthroughs in the harnessing and exploitation of energy, most notably of the electromagnetic spectrum. Wireless telegraphy and later the wireless home radio set, the electrification of private homes, streets and public spaces, the proliferation of telephones and automobiles together gave a new fluidity, and a new consistency, to everyday space. What once passed unqualified or as insubstantial began to take on a new palpability, dense with wires and waves, kinetic and communicative flows. It was out of this apprehension of space as a kinetic and substantial plenum that the new plasticity emerged, simultaneously in aesthetics and in the Relativity Theory that was revolutionizing physics in the years between 1905 and 1916.

The Field

In his 1905 paper "On the Electrodynamics of Moving Bodies," Einstein first presented his Special Theory of Relativity. The theory's main features were, first, to preserve the Galilean principle of relativity. According to this principle the uniform motion of any inertial system (a time-space reference frame) can be discerned only by referring to a point which lies outside the system. By the same token motion of any kind *within* an inertial system derives its value only in relation to points in that system. And finally it states that the laws which determine the values of any state of motion are invariant for all inertial systems. To this theory—the very cornerstone of classical mechanics—was added Relativity's second important feature, the principles of Lorentz's transformation equations which provided a simple theorem for relating and transforming time and space coordinates from one inertial system to another. Its radicality lay in quantifying the elastic deformation of bodies and the dilation of time at high speeds. By adding a third principle whose derivation goes back to James Clerk Maxwell—the constancy of the velocity of light in empty space—Einstein was able to formulate the Special Theory of Relativity. Its radicality lay in freeing time itself of its metaphysical and absolute character and reducing it to just one more dependent (i.e. variable) coordinate in the kinematical transformation equations.[4] The new four-dimensional continuum developed in this theory differed from that of classical mechanics in the following way: time and space were no longer, at least algebraically, heterogeneous; the continuous 4-dimensional manifold could no longer be separated into a three-dimensional section evolving in one-dimensional time, where "simultaneous" events are contained only in the former; rather, each inertial system would now express its own particular time determined as a mutual relation of events to the frame in which they are registered. Events occurring simultaneously can thus be said to do so only with respect to a single inertial system into which they are arbitrarily grouped and outside of which any notion of "now" becomes meaningless. By making time in this way relative and contingent,[5] space-time and the field were conceived as a new entity, irreducible to their component dimensions, objectively unresolvable with respect to their infinitely varied regions (different speeds = different times), and thickened to consistency by the world-lines[6] that career through them.

This consistency, too, was of an entirely new kind. The concept of space as it developed from antiquity was founded on Euclidean mathematics for which space, as a continuum with its own independent reality, was never fully posited. The elements of which this system was constructed—the point, the line and the plane—were nothing more than idealizations of solid bodies. Space itself emerged only secondarily, that is, only insofar as it could be derived from these idealized forms and the relations produced by their contact—intersections, points lying on lines or planes, etc. Only with Descartes does space finally emerge as autonomous and pre-existing: an infinite and generalized three-dimensional continuum, where points and figures are describable by their coordinates.

If geometrical descriptions in the Euclidean system were reducible to actual objects (point, line and plane) or aggregates and derivations thereof, the Cartesian system permitted "all surfaces [to] appear, in principle on equal footing, without any arbitrary preference for linear structures."[7] In other words, space now existed independently of solid bodies, preceding them and containing them.

Until the introduction of dynamics the Greek system had been adequate for all geometric needs (e.g., Brunelleschi, Desargues, Mercator, etc.), but the new Cartesian system would be absolutely indispensable for Newtonian physics, in which equations of motion and acceleration play a dominant role. This is because acceleration cannot be expressed or defined as a relation between points alone but only in relation to an abstract ground of space as a whole. Events could now be

conceived of as taking place against a fixed backdrop which also served as their unaffected carrier.

Not until the nineteenth century did this concept of space and
the relations between movements and bodies begin to change. First thermodynamics
(problems of heat conduction in solid bodies), then the discovery of the electromagnetic interaction and the wave-theory of light provided both the first treatment of
matter as a continuum (or at least as a vehicle of continuous "intensive" movements
or changes) and the first evidence of states in free or empty space which are propagated in waves. In the first case matter is treated as a *system* of states, characterized by
independent quantitative variables—thermal differences, volume, pressure—expressible as a *function* of space coordinates and, most importantly, of time. In the second it was a simple transposition of these same mathematics—partial differential
equations—to the propagation of magnetic and light phenomena. Passing from a
field theory of masses (thermodynamics) to a field theory of empty space (electrodynamics) meant that classical mechanics had to be superseded.[8] Maxwell's breakthrough in the theory of electromagnetic processes went far in this direction, but
unable to make the final conceptual break he was obliged to posit a material vehicle
or medium for this electromagnetic field: the luminiferous ether. The ether played a
purely mechanical role as the material seat and carrier of all forces acting across
space—though it was imperceptible and only logically derivable, based as it was on
the presupposition that every state is capable of mechanical interpretation and therefore implies the presence of matter. The Michelson-Morley experiment of 1888 failed
to yield any evidence of the material existence of such an ether. Between this event
and the Special Theory of Relativity of 1905 came Lorentz's important work which,
while accounting for the Michelson-Morley results, established, according to Einstein, that ether and physical space "were only different terms for the same thing."[9]
It was a momentous conceptual leap if only a short mathematical step that Einstein
took to emancipate the field concept entirely from any association with a substratum.
For the Special Theory of Relativity Einstein employed the Riemannian conception
of space,[10] whose plastic structure is susceptible both to partaking in physical events
and to being influenced by them. The Einsteinian field, and its corresponding notion
of space-time, dispensed entirely with the need to posit a material substratum as a
carrier for forces and events by identifying the electromagnetic field—and ultimately
gravitational fields as well—with the new metrical one. This notion of "the field"
expresses the complete immanence of forces and events while supplanting the old
concept of space identified with the Cartesian substratum and ether theory. The field
emerges as "an irreducible element of physical description, irreducible in the same
sense as the concept of matter in the theory of Newton."[11]

The field describes a space of propagation, of effects. It contains
no matter or material points, rather functions, vectors and speeds. It describes local
relations of difference within fields of celerity, transmission or of careering points,
in a word, what Minkowski called the *world.* Einstein himself offered as an example
of a field phenomenon nothing other than the description of the motion of a liquid:

At every point there exists at any time a velocity, which is quantitatively described by its three
"components" with respect to the axes of a coordinate system (vector). The components of a
velocity at a point (field components) [fulfill the conditions of the field for they, like the temperature in a system of thermal propagation] are functions of the coordinates (x,y,z) and time (t).

This hydrodynamic model, of course, deserves no particular priority in Einstein's
system for it was still only a rudimentary mechanical model describing a state
of matter, whereas Einstein's physics was an attempt to think the pure event, independent of a material medium or substratum. Yet the field theory it typified was

emerging in other areas of endeavor, often finding expression through similar or related models of dynamics in fluids. Its mysterious charm was none other than the partial differential function through which alone it was possible to express the principles of immanence, dynamism and continuity.

Plastic Dynamism

In aesthetics, no less than in physics, the last years of the nineteenth century and the first of the twentieth brought about a decisive transformation in the concept of space. Beginning with Hildebrand's *Problem of Form* (1893) in which space appears for the first time both as an autonomous aesthetic concept and, more importantly, as a continuum unbroken and indistinct from solid objects,[12] to its development in Riegl and its ultimate identification with the *Kunstwollen*, and finally to the later syntheses of Panofsky's "Die Perspektive als 'symbolische Form'," space emerged with a new positivity as an object of both knowledge and direct experience. One historian situates the emergence of a modern continuum theory of space with Geoffrey Scott's influential *Architecture of Humanism* (1914), tracing it to the psychological theories of Theodor Lipps and the Beaux-Arts compositional theories of Charles Blanc and Julien Guadet.[13] This latter development, however, would not become fully integrated into architectural practice until the mid-1920s, long after Cubism (through which it was transmitted)[14] had elaborated and, to a large extent, exhausted it. A more essential evolution of these problems, and one closer to the scientific movement that emancipated physical theory from the old notion of matter and its correlative space, is the basis of the new plastic theories developed by the Futurist Umberto Boccioni in his writings on Plastic Dynamism.[15]

Following in the wake of Marinetti's Foundation Manifesto there is much, undeniably, in these writings of the rehearsed denunciations that were an integral part of the Futurist public relations enterprise. But more than any other of the movement's exponents, even Marinetti—whose flair for public promotion and the right turn of phrase was less amply sustained by consistency of thought—Boccioni's were cogent and forceful ideas that came to be formed into a complex system of concepts bearing on the nature of the physical world.

In the *Technical Manifesto of Futurist Sculpture*, the first manifesto published solely under his own name, Boccioni develops in a radically unprecedented way the relationship of an object to its environment:

Sculpture must make objects live by rendering apprehensible, plastic and systematic their prolongations into space, since no one can any longer believe that an object finishes where another begins and that there is not an object around us: bottle, automobile, tree, house or street, that does not cut and section us with an arabesque of curved and straight lines. (*Ar.* I, p. 69)

These same relations are expressed in a subsequent text, recast now in the language of (ancient) atomist physics:

Areas between one object and another are not empty spaces but rather *continuing materials of differing intensities*, which we reveal with visible lines which do not correspond to any photographic truth. This is why we do not have in our paintings objects and empty spaces but only *a greater or lesser intensity and solidity of space*. (*Ar.* I, p. 143, italics added)

Leaving the body/nonbody opposition aside altogether, space is also characterized in terms of two interrelated and interpenetrating fields:

Absolute motion is a dynamic law grounded in an object. The plastic construction of the object will here concern itself with the motion an object has within it, be it at rest or in movement.

I am making this distinction between rest and movement, however, only to make myself clear, for in fact, there is no such thing as rest; there is only motion, rest being merely relative, a matter of appearance. This plastic construction obeys a law of motion which characterizes the body in question. It is the plastic potential which the object contains within itself, closely bound up with its own organic substance, and according to its general characteristics: porosity, impermeability, rigidity, elasticity, etc. or its particular characteristics: color, temperature, consistency, form (flat, concave, angular, convex, cubic, conic, spiral, elliptical, spherical, etc.). (SPF, p. 80)

Relative motion is a dynamic law based on the object's movement. . . . Here it is a matter of conceiving the objects in movement quite apart from the motion which they contain within themselves. That is to say we must try to find a form which will express the new absolute—*speed*, which any true modern spirit cannot ignore. (SPF, pp. 82–83)

Boccioni's system reveals a certain dual nature of space: on the one hand, a fixed and extended *milieu* with metrical or dimensional properties and, on the other, a fluid and consistent field of intensities (e.g. forces, speeds, temperatures, color). The resemblance to Bergson's two types of multiplicity, the numerical (discrete) and the qualitative (continuous) or, more generally, that of space and that of *durée*, deserves to be underscored here once again.[16] The basic difference, of course, between Bergson's second, dynamic multiplicity as formulated in the *Essai*, and Boccioni's is that for the latter there is no separate or privileged *internal* domain.[17] Specifically, it is the very problematization of this separation that is the point of departure for Boccioni's work.[18] What remains to both regardless of this difference is the task of giving systematic expression to the world in the modern terms of a *continuous multiplicity*.[19]

For Boccioni such a conception of the world was implicitly sustained by means of what I shall schematize below as three interdependent hypotheses:

1. *The hypothesis of the undividedness of the object field.* According to this hypothesis, the world is at once an aggregate of separate fragments *and* a materially indivisible whole. The main underlying current here is an attack on perspectival space[20] and the correlative "scientific" geometry based on the optical model.[21] "Traditionally a statue cuts into, and stands out from, the atmosphere of the place where it is on view," Boccioni writes; though henceforth sculpture will use "the facts of landscape and the environment which act simultaneously on the human figure and on objects" and "extend its plastic capacities to [these objects] which till now a kind of barbaric crudeness has persuaded us to believe were divided up or intangible" (*Ar.* I, p. 68). This conception yields to positive formulations such as "the interpenetration of planes" (*Ar.* I, pp. 68, 72), the notion, borrowed from Marinetti, of the (*immaginazione*) *senza fili* (both "wireless" as in radio, and "without strings"), and the "absolute and complete abolition of finite lines" (*Ar.* I, p. 70).

Closely connected with the idea of interpenetration is Boccioni's belief that the environment not only conditions and acts on objects but is contained by them, forming labile plastic zones of influence (SPF, pp. 81–82; *Ar.* I, p. 71). Resuscitating Marinetti's *immaginazione senza fili*, he means to insist on an *analogical*[22] (intuitive, immanent) method of reconstructing space, as well as to underscore its technological implications; the wireless radio actualizes and, by this measure, belongs to the invisible electromagnetic plenum which surrounds it.

The third formulation deals with finite lines and closed forms, elements whose plastic possibilities have been eclipsed by a new fluid order of *becoming* ("the law of the unity of universal motion" [FM, p. 94]). This order is one which conceives formed matter as in flux, a momentary and metastable constellation of forces (or force-lines) which originate outside it and continue beyond it.

For all these reasons Futurist art cannot be based on visual principles. Against the fragmenting spectacle[23] of all, even modern, art, Boccioni affirms the fullness of conception (FM, p. 94), dynamic transformation and becoming (Ar. I, p. 144), and the synthesis of all body sensation (Ar. I, pp. 105–106). "In Futurist art," he declares, "the viewpoint has completely changed"; from now on the spectator will live in the center of the picture, embedded in the "simultaneousness of the ambient [amid] the dislocation and dismemberment of objects, the scattering and fusion of details, freed from accepted logic and independent from one another"(Ar. I, p. 105). Vision alone fragments the field because it gives unity and discreteness to bodies: once the integrity of the field is restored, it is "objects" themselves which appear fragmented:

The entire visible world will tumble down on top of us, merging . . . a leg, an arm or an object has no importance except as an element in the overall plastic rhythm, and can be eliminated, not because we are trying to imitate a Greek or Roman fragment, but in order to conform with the general harmony the artist is trying to create. (Ar. I, p. 71)

The substance of the world is not resolvable into pure or integral materials or forms. Rather, these latter shift and fluctuate in and out of the formal arrangements that Boccioni calls "plastic zones"; they have become arrangements of *materials in the generic sense*, formless, random multiplicities. There is now only world-substance—an indeterminate and a-centered aggregate of different materials—no longer "ideal" form, transcendent yet made incarnate in "sublime" or noble material:

Destroy the literary and traditional "dignity" of marble and bronze statuary. Insist that even twenty different materials can be used in a single work of art in order to achieve plastic movement. To mention only a few: iron, cement, hair, leather, cloth, mirrors, electric light, etc. (Ar. I, p. 72)

2. *The hypothesis of universal motion* extends the theory of the continuity of the object field, already more of a fluid than a rigid three-dimensional continuum, onto the axis of time. As we have seen, substance is indissociably linked to motion (absolute), just as motion (relative) is linked to "speed." The world-substance (multiplicity), now animated, describes a field of vectors of differing qualities and intensities. If the formula "interpenetration of planes" adequately expressed the principle of continuity within the object-field, it is no longer adequate to express vectorial quantities in a field of speed or celerity. Only line can express variation or difference in a field of force; line conceived *qua* line, as vector not delimitor of form.[24] Thus the hypothesis of universal motion does not bear on the object-field and its relations.[25] It describes an entirely different cosmos whose substance, conceived within time, is speed itself, ontologically pure and without substrate (the pure "d" in dx/dt). Yet these speeds constellate, decelerate and change quality to create object-effects wholly outside the realm of form: "the object has no form in itself; the only definable thing is the line which reveals the relationship between the object's weight (quantity) and its expansion (quality)." The object is resolved plastically into its component quantae of force which in turn are determined by the qualities of the field—here gravity and centrifugality. Lines, or rather "force-lines" (*linee-forze*) describe the object's *nature* (character and quality of field) not its movement as such (displacement of form against a fixed ground). Force-lines are of an entirely other order; they depict a condition of inter-

face or pure transmission without medium: the becoming-line of matter[26] and the becoming-immanent of both.

This is the essential meaning of *dynamism*, and it is also the reason that cinematographic and chronophotographic division and delay have nothing to do with Futurism or its underlying physics. The ill-guided experiments of Giacomo Balla of 1912–13 are no exception to this rule.[27] Dynamism does not characterize an activity of objects in space but describes the quality of a field of immanence or becoming, where the world, in Boccioni's own words, "is conceived as an infinite prolonging of an evolutionary species" (FM, p. 95).

3. *Time and space are full and have a plastic consistency.* This third hypothesis depends logically on the previous two. As we have seen, Einstein's Special Theory of Relativity introduced the concept of inertial systems into physical theory, and in so doing replaced the absolute time and space of classical mechanics by the concept of the field. Though the laws of classical mechanics are valid within an inertial system they do not apply to events occurring outside it. Thus local events seem to obey Newtonian principles, but they themselves are always embedded in a larger fluid framework of space-time where events can be related only through the Lorentz transformation and not through a fixable or universal coordinate. The fundamental novelty in this theory was twofold: first, space, events and matter ceased to function as substrata for one another and were resolved non-hierarchically as interdependent characteristics of the field; and second, the four-dimensional continuum ceased to be reducible to three space coordinates evolving in one-dimensional time, but became a truly unresolvable four-dimensional whole in which the four coordinates assume their positions, without privilege or qualitative distinction.

What time lost in universality when it ceased to be absolute it gained in concreteness through its new association with space. And this is all the more paradoxical since it was the very insertion of time into the spatial continuum that first permitted physical theory (notably thermodynamics) to proceed to the theory of the field and to abandon the limiting notion of material points. It could be said then that time replaced the physical particle, and in so doing introduced *consistency* as a characteristic of the field, where before there was only space and the mechanical need to posit material carriers.

In this sense the thermo- and electrodynamic field is always a field of consistency, a strange new entity because equally abstract and concrete; it does not exist materially yet it exists everywhere and all at once wherever there is force or matter. The field of consistency, to quote Boccioni's phrase, is "the unique form that gives continuity in space."

Force-lines can now be seen as the abstract units which articulate the object's relation to its consistent field. And as we have already shown this relation is one of immanence, or at least a becoming-immanent. Force-lines (vectors) are to the field (space-time) what the old line was to classical mechanics. They are time-imbued and animate world-substance into plastic zones. Plasticity is a property of these world-lines.

With the field characterized in this way there is no conceivable real occurrence which would not mobilize the abstract consistency to form concrete plastic events. The field however does not pre-exist, but is always present as a virtuality, determined within and by the plastic *events* which articulate it and render it actual. "We reject any a priori reality; this is what divides us from the Cubists" (Ar. I, p. 145).

By incorporating space so deeply into the body of time as to change its very nature thereby, Futurist theory, like that of Einstein, Bergson and others, undertook to resolve the problem of Being through the concept of a continuous multiplicity. From this fact arises what may be the single most important contribution of Futurist theory to our modern conception of the world. The physics of space-time, one could say, gave rise to a fundamental new entity—the event—as well as the new geometry through which it could be expressed. In its own way Futurist theory made of Plastic Dynamism a scientific hypothesis and an artistic technique, allowing this selfsame event to emerge in its full materiality as the sole substance and medium of man's intervention in the world.

The modern world, then, will no longer be resolvable into separate and autonomous realms of value or meaning, i.e., the economic, the social, the phenomenal. Futurist Plasticity is above all a pragmatics which reflects all phenomena—events—through the single screen of a real material consistency. Thus the "swing of a pendulum or the moving hands of a clock, the in-and-out motion of a piston inside a cylinder, the engaging and disengaging of two cogwheels, the fury of a flywheel or the whirling of a propeller, are all plastic and pictorial elements" whose shape and effects can now be diagrammed in their continuity, in their multiple connections to the ever-differentiating outside with which they invariably form a single substance.

La Città Nuova

The last-conscripted member of the pre-war Futurist brigade (the group's composition, ideological predilections and credibility would be altered radically after the war) was the Lombard architect Antonio Sant'Elia. Born in Como in 1888, Sant'Elia was trained in Milan and Bologna, where he received his diploma in 1912, before returning to Milan to set up a practice and, soon after, to establish an association with a group of architects known as the Nuove Tendenze. Sant'Elia's earliest work (prior to Milan, 1912) was heavily inflected by the highly ornamented *stile Liberty* whose popularity was then only beginning to wane.[28] In the two years following his move to Milan he executed a large number of drawings and urban concept studies, largely speculative in nature, which were first grouped together under the heading Milano 2000, and later when exhibited publicly with the Nuove Tendenze group in 1914 were collected under the title La Città Nuova. The exhibition catalogue contained statements from each of the group's members, including the important preface by Sant'Elia on the tasks of modern architecture. Though Sant'Elia was not yet an official member of the Futurist movement, this text, called simply *Messaggio*, was undeniably Futurist in inspiration and was adapted a few months later, with the most minor alterations, as the *Manifesto of Futurist Architecture*.[29]

The *Messaggio* opens dramatically, effecting the first of several fundamental transpositions of the traditionally conceived architectural object into evermore complex, abstract, yet more deeply and historically authentic configurations. Consider the opening passage with its two opposing notions of history:

The problem of modern architecture is not a problem of rearranging its lines; not a question of finding new mouldings, new architraves, for doors and windows; nor of replacing columns, pilasters and corbels with caryatids, hornets and frogs; not a question of leaving a façade bare brick or facing it with stone or plaster; in a word, it has nothing to do with defining formalistic differences between the new buildings and old ones. But to raise the new-built structure on a sound plan, gleaning every benefit of science and technology, settling nobly every demand of our habits and our spirits, rejecting all that is heavy, grotesque and unsympathetic to us (tradition, style, aesthetics, proportion), establishing new forms, new lines, new reasons for existence, solely out of the special conditions of Modern living, and its projection as aesthetic value in our sensibilities.

Such an architecture cannot be subject to any law of historical continuity. It must be as new as our state of mind is new, and the contingencies of our moment in history.

The art of building has been able to evolve through time and pass from style to style while maintaining the general character of architecture unchanged, because in history there have been numerous changes of taste brought on by shifts of religious conviction or the successions of political regimes, but few occasioned by profound changes in our conditions of life, changes that discard or overhaul the old conditions, as have the discovery of natural laws, the perfection of technical methods, the rational and scientific use of materials.

Denounced from the outset is the kind of history which is sedimented and transmitted in the evolution of taste and styles, the narrative of succession, memory and encrusted representations. This history of "differenze formali . . . soggetta a una legge di continuità storica" is renounced in the name of a more authentic and more comprehensive historicity rooted in the "condizioni dell'ambiente" and the "contingenze del nostro momento storico." This disqualification of the past, and the filiative relations whose tenuous claim is to link it with the present, resonates, however superficially, with Nietzsche's repudiation of the disadvantages of history for life made 40 years earlier[30] though in a more profound sense, with the Nietzschean repudiation in general of history as repository and transmitter of anything like absolute truth or meanings. Yet the sudden and quite radical assault on historical epistemology as it was waged systematically by Nietzsche and adopted by the Futurists does not in itself exhaust either of these enterprises' claims to modernity. Of greater importance on this count is the particular kinds of terrain they opened up: for Nietzsche the affirmation of active affects (of which "forgetting" was an integral one) resolved historical time into both a pragmatics and an aesthetics of force (Will to Power); for the Futurists history became inseparable from that transverse line which links concrete social phenomena—technique, science, art, politics—and embeds them indifferently in material life. In one case as in the other the valorization of life itself endowed it with the character of an aesthetic phenomenon; the metaphysical *telos* of history gave way to a reality that was, and indeed had to be, constructed anew at every moment, and from within.[31] For the Futurists, "Man's" new privilege was to have no privilege at all vis-à-vis reality or Being: his history and time were no longer separate from the history of material nor the vicissitudes of force. Tradition was seen as not only disadvantageous for life, to use Nietzsche's phrase, but as simply fraudulent; it offered a metaphysics of perpetuity where really there exist only natural laws, a bourgeois academicism of representations where in fact there is only the chaotic and senseless circumstance of force, and finally the mysticism of lineal continuity—influence, transmission, origin, causality—in place of the palpable immanence of the conjunctural, the aleatory and the simultaneous. Historical consciousness was losing its metaphysical infrastructure—a development entirely at one with the superseding of classical time in physics—only to reaffirm itself through an insistence on a profound historical consciousness of the *present*, an historical consciousness of the world and life *as such*, rather than through representations derived from its self-constituting Grand narratives.[32]

It is no surprise that the rest of the *Messaggio* concerns itself with the specific denunciation of these forms of discredited historical representation:

We have lost the sense of the monumental, the massive, the static, and we have enriched our sensibilities with a taste for the light and the practical. We no longer feel ourselves to be the men of the cathedrals and the ancient moot halls, but men of the Grand Hotels, railway stations, giant roads, colossal harbours, covered markets, glittering arcades, reconstruction areas and salutory slum clearances.

. . . We must abolish the monumental and the decorative, we must resolve the problem of modern architecture without cribbing photographs of China, Persia and Japan nor imbecilizing ourselves with Vitruvian rules. . . . We must depreciate the importance of façades, transfer questions of taste out of the field of petty mouldings, fiddling capitals and insignificant porticos. . . . It is time to have done with funereal commemorative architecture; architecture must be something more vital than that, and we can best begin to attain that something by blowing sky-high all those monuments.

Architectural time for Sant'Elia can no longer be that of historical styles—effete, academic and truncated from the natural forces that were once the source of its life—nor is it the apocryphal time of monuments. Architecture is no longer a vehicle expressing the spurious contents of a singular ("grand") history-in-the-making, no longer a constellation of signs operating externally to culture through the intermediary of a code, but an entirely internal and inhering *mechanism* inseparable from the body of the world and operating on it from within.[33] Thus the classic Futurist theme of elements and materials becomes crucial once again. Wood, stone, marble and brick will be replaced by reinforced concrete, iron, glass, textile fibers and anything else which helps obtain "the maximum of elasticity and lightness." The nobility of the conventional architectural mediums is undermined; instead, architecture follows sculpture toward a more promiscuous (immanent) relation toward material reconceived now according to the framework elaborated by Boccioni, as a deployment of world-substance, or as an operator of whatever (relations, materials, forces, laws) is contemporary and close at hand. At the same time the tendency toward lightness and kinematic plasticity brings the traditional architectural mass to a greater and greater approximation with force, allowing the research of forms to give way to an emphasis on configurations.[34] Architecture undergoes a revaluation in terms of a new state of knowledge and technique, and a new constellation of needs and desires (material, political, and spiritual) while simultaneously assuming its purest artistic role:

True architecture is not an arid combination of practicality and utility, but remains art, that is, synthesis and expression.

Though Sant'Elia did not realize a single building during his mature (post-Liberty) period, he did produce a sufficient number of eloquent studies and drawings[35] which, together with the *Messaggio* and the Manifesto, constitute a rigorous and programmatic reconception of architectural and urbanist practice whose influence would be felt for decades and whose implications are still today being realized. The drawings of this period (1913–1914) will be examined in two main groups: the morphological studies in which single architectonic structures are explored—lighthouses, turbine stations, hangars, bridges and other nonspecific structures named simply *Edifici* and *Dinamismi architettonici*—and those which develop more explicitly relations within whole regions of the city-manifold. In the first group one sees the elaboration of a formal vocabulary whose themes and implications are realized only at a second-order or molar level—the city—whose concrete substance they indeed comprise yet whose units and ultimate organization they in no way reflect. The form studies will be examined first and the more complex city drawings afterward.

One is inevitably struck, when examining Sant'Elia's sketches, by the extraordinary momentum of the draftsmanship, the obsessively precise freehand style with its swift, simplified yet deliberate lines, at once restrained and expressive, volatile and refined. Few historians have failed to remark his predilection for the extreme oblique setting of masses and the close viewpoint which together artificially intensify perspective effects.[36] The orthogonal lines of the depicted buildings pass almost invariably beyond the drawing's frame. This unusual technique makes the depicted forms appear as molecular fragments belonging to greater but indeterminate wholes; the impression is that of masses framed hastily and close up, further suggesting the brute immediacy of photography. Also, one notes the borrowing of a device common to nineteenth-century painting, but just beginning to discover new modes of application in the nascent art of cinema: that of allowing the contents of a frame, no matter how spare or "innocent," to become fraught with whatever occurs or exists beyond it. There is considerable method to this technique: the refusal to make available all the information about a building structure through its visual apprehension shifts the problem of its "meaning" from the expression of interior contents to an exterior syntax of combination and connection. The buildings are often remarkably dissymmetrical—despite the constant use of symmetrically apposed elements at the molecular level; they seem to have positive and negative ends, male and female interlocking parts, open and closed elements distributed almost randomly over their surface, and most importantly, a single building complex deploys its several façades in such a way that they have no apparent relation to one another, but remain completely autonomous with respect to the "building" conceived as an integral organism. These latter are determined rather by specific functions—passage, connection, transmission, reception—defined in terms of specifically located or immediately adjacent external elements—roads, gangways, elevator stacks, landing strips. This general tendency of *atomization* of the building's traditionally irreducible unity is supported further by an array of secondary devices.

The simplest of the morphological studies describe elongated, ascending, elliptical masses either embedded in, or partially penetrated by, rectangular slabs, which together align in paradoxical configurations as if the result of silent, frictionless collisions. Paradoxical here is the combination of the extraordinarily "sovereign" and ballistic power of the collided forms, and their unexpected suppleness and permeability, their seeming lack of material resistance to one another.[37] Paradoxical semiotically as well, for the blatant interference of forms, violently splitting and passing through one another, could logically be translated internally it seems only by introducing the most vertiginous disjunctions and intermittence to their lived space. These studies always contain combinations of both tapering and rectilinear forms whose pronounced differences of inertia create effects of virtual separation and vertical momentum. This kinetic tension is further underscored by the smooth unadorned concrete surfaces on which the accelerated play of light confronts the eye less with a coherent object than with a field or *glacis* unencumbered by the friction of detail, texture or articulated features. The careful combining and wedging together of forms produces a controlled interplay of right angles with oblique surfaces, battered walls with promontory-like abutments. What remains is a simple system of glyptic faces and sharply pronounced arrises whose courses, for all their breakneck precipitousness, provide the eye's only formal guides. Add to this the explicitly narrative "contraforte" theme of the canted surfaces pressing back, and often through other perpendicular ones, shoring up as if to resist great external masses or forces, and one can already intuit the presence of a more comprehensive city vision, based not on aggregation and juxtaposition of separate parts but a differentiating field of *pressures* with its corresponding mechanical language of resistance and transmission.

At the simple morphological level this language expresses a theory of individuated architecture as servomechanism, where individual units are mere operators or commutation devices within a much larger assembly whose greater intensity they modulate and control. The elements of this language include conduits, circuitry, rhythmized cadences and progressions including rotation, nesting, stepbacks, tapers, telescoping and ranked columnar forms, as well as the more literal machine vocabulary of jigs, stops and templates. "Study for a building" (fig. 3) and "Study for a building or a station" (fig. 6) (both 1913) demonstrate the rhetorical use of the conduit theme (over and above literal applications, e.g., bridges, gangways, electrical wires) acting less to buttress than to marshal and translate forces from one section to another. The latter attains a particularly high level of abstraction by forming its own independent (short-) circuit in which the flying beams (A) support—or house—a perforated upright structure (B) themselves supported by arch (C) which in turn both transects and forms the absent base of the main structure (B). In this *mise-en-abyme* system where every element seems in part, only fortuitously there, in part *already* there relaying forces received from other similar elements, the earth as first principle or ground seems no longer to exist at all; rather, a homeostatic system of circulating currents which, thanks to the visionary use of reinforced concrete, seems virtually untouched by gravity or any other *essential* (grounded or original) cause.[38] These same drawings, as well as "Study for a building or a hangar" (1913; fig. 7), employ repeated columnar forms though not in the service of the traditional imperatives of proportion and spatial patterning. Here their positive/negative inter-

Antonio Sant'Elia, sketches for La Città Nuova, 1913–1914

vals are not static but belong to a more procedural sequence of intermittent coupling like the rabbeted digits on a mortise hinge that either espouse one another to form an unbroken surface or rotate fully beyond, opening onto other configurations or conjunctions. The themes of rotation and interpenetration belong to a more general tendency to articulate all conjunctions dynamically. "Study for an electric power station" (1913; fig. 8) provides what is perhaps the most acute example of this tendency, unashamedly miming the conventions of machine assembly with its protruding jig plate acting as guide for an ostensibly movable cylinder and the clear implications of flexion—the jig's acute angle; torsion—the cylinder's counterpoint to its inert squared-off base; and friction—the interaction of shaft and template. Yet it may be said that Sant'Elia's was uniquely *an architecture of conjunction*, one that does not posit forms primordially, but rather *systems* whose very expansivity and acenteredness precludes classical individuated expression. Here the very notion of conjunction takes on its maximal significance: these are conjunctions, not of buildings or isolated structures but of imbricating systems, both at the molecular level of interpenetrating guided, rotating or sliding masses and at the molar level of urban megasystems of transport, hydro-electric and informational lattices.

The combination of the system theory of the urban realm with its dynamic interpretation as a pressurized field gives rise to an assembly language based on impregnation, with system elements existing simultaneously, and at least virtually, everywhere, emerging to actualization only within nodes (conjunctions) of mutually interfering systems. A second "Study for a building" (1913; fig. 9) literalizes this technique formally within a single structure, where three separate plans superimpose like three individual *dispositifs* or running systems on the same site—a point-grid corresponding to the chimney stacks, the square plan base of the teepee structure, and the elliptical collector that seals them all into a solid agglomerate. No one system ever predominates over the others, and though together they undoubtedly form a unit, they singly maintain a certain autonomy and separateness due to their extension and resonance within broader, more comprehensive networks. Interference, like the sporadic invasion of electronic images by foreign frequencies, becomes here a positive expression of spatial complexity allowing several disparate architectures (say telecommunications towers, elevator stacks, tram systems) to articulate themselves in a single and same block of matter.

Thus the dominant technique for ordering the various chains within this multilayered systemic space is a special use of transparency different from the literal and phenomenal versions endemic to visual Modernism. Here the transparency is functional and explicitly concrete: masses are placed seemingly only to be pierced, stratified or disaggregated, in other words, as passive and inarticulate carriers of the movement-bearing systems which traverse and penetrate them, or else huge framelike chassis baring their lading like skeletons yielding to the newly invented X-ray gaze that the Futurists so emulated. Though articulated in often grandiose and imperious sweeps these masses, as we have noted, are in fact remarkably plastic and porous; they are easily incised and punctured, as in the window system of a second "Study for an electric power station" (1913; fig. 10), which is literally punched out of a single inert horizontal slab—note the strong, literal implication of perpendicular momentum in the impact-absorbing triangular niches—which, once transformed by this operation, can be read as a lattice-frame.

At every level the morphological studies assume, rather than represent, an extended field of movement and circulating forces. Each element relates primarily to the "horizontal" chain of which it is a link and secondarily to the transverse or vertical system that concretizes it and weds it, however incompletely, to a discrete and grounded form. It is here, more than in any other body of Futurist work, that the laws of Boccioni's physical theory found their full and unqualified application. It is as if the very nature of an art work, as understood by even the most radical avant-gardes of the time, were yet too primitive or ontologically conventional to express the conditions of a revolutionized cosmos. What clearly was needed was not new objects, but a new orientation toward a phenomenal field of events and interactions, not objects but the abstract regimes of force which organize and deploy them. For Sant'Elia this field was the emerging modern metropolis.

Just as the morphological studies drew their principle inspiration from engineering structures—electrical turbine stations, hangars, factories, lighthouses—the large-scale studies for La Città Nuova developed out of a series of projects to redesign the Milan Central Station. An early study, "Station for trains and airplanes" (1913–14; fig. 11), still bears stylistic resonances from the Liberty period, with its denser, less precise expressionistic rendering, an organic use of materials which gives the almost palpable sensation of weight settling toward the lower regions, a noticeable lack of horizontal or homeostatic tension or pressure, lending the project an almost old-fashioned, earth-based aura. The accuracy of such an impression however comes to an abrupt end, for in many ways this scheme breaks with previous conceptions of urban planning. The most spectacular innovation is unquestionably the airplane landing strip built into the upper level of the station. Here the central thoroughfare which traditionally ascends to and grandly frames the station's main entry is decked over to allow for vertical air access. The ease with which this scandalous idea is accommodated, though it is certainly naive from today's standpoint, is evident from the nonchalance of the parked air vehicles on the runway, not to mention the way the buildings that flank the Viale Vittore Pisani are allowed to frame the runway at such a close distance. This feature sets up another element crucial to Sant'Elia's scheme, its multilayered acentricity. In this exterior perspective alone, one counts seven levels of thoroughfare not including the radio masts, elevators or funiculars, each superimposed like porous grids seeping and flowing into one another. The project exaggerates and develops the nature of its object—a literal commutation point—at once disaggregating its spurious but conventional unity, and multiplying the surfaces of connection within it. It does this by willfully embracing the city block into which it has been literally submerged, continuing its (the city's) present lines of flow (streets, tram routes, passages) through its own, pausing only to effect additional convergences by means of ramps, catwalks and steps. It is difficult to say whether the station system is embedded in the city's fabric or it is the city which runs freely through the station. The novelty of this arrangement has nothing to do with the ambiguity of place produced by such dispersion nor any mere decentering of once integral architectural forms, but with a more fundamental overhaul that permits one to conceive of the architectural object not as a form but as an agglomeration and interaction of *functions*, each with its proper series of system elements whose architectonic value and role is defined only secondarily, and wholly in relation to these functions. Thus the Milan station becomes less a "building" than a field of convergence and linkup for many systems of flow, including air transport, trains, cars, radio signals, trams, funiculars, pedestrians, and necessarily all the secondary flows which they host, i.e., money, goods, information. In this sense, the "station" comes to be seen as an allegorical representation of the city itself, and necessarily, in terms of the transformation of "place" into a swirling manifold of circuitry, switching points and deterritorialized, non-grounded flows.

In "Station for airplanes and railway trains with funiculars on three street levels" (1914; fig. 12), we see a later, clarified version of the station project (whose title incidentally now gives priority to its airport function) where the conventional straining arches have given way to a taut linearity made possible by "new materials." The flanking towers of the main mass have been split into two slabs and mortised into a more finely divided and variegated base system, and finally the heavy monumental quality of the original is throughout refined to more slender platforms and laminae allowing the expression of ductwork to emerge as the dominant. visual theme. This reworking also incorporates many of the assembly motifs from the morphological studies, principally the oscillating beats of serial elements with their implied rotation, folding and sliding. Finally, one should not fail to remark the unusual treatment of the plan in both these drawings for it is identical to much of what we have seen in the morphology studies with respect to the treatment of façades. They are treated indifferently as pierceable slabs of matter, instantly transformable through perforation into space-frames revealing yet other systems (or only potential ones) beyond and beneath. In other words, the plan elements have a construction logic and appearance identical to the elevations, giving the "node theory" of construction here a truly literal, three-dimensional validity. This total indifference to absolute (external) determinations of place and direction has the effect of further denying the earth and its "essential" forces and values both as the metaphysical ground of architecture and the social processes it modulates.

The house . . . must rise from the brink of a tumultuous abyss; the street itself will no longer lie like a doormat at the level of the thresholds, but will plunge storeys deep into the earth, gathering up the traffic of the metropolis connected for necessary transfers to metal catwalks and high-speed conveyor belts.

We must exploit our roofs and put our basements to work . . . dig out our streets and piazzas, raise the level of the city, reorder the earth's crust and reduce it to a servant of our every need and fancy (*Messaggio*).

The most powerful and fully developed of the Città Nuova studies is the drawing entitled "La Città Nuova: Apartment complex with external elevators, galleria, covered passage, three street levels (tramlines, autoway, metallic pedestrian gangway), light beacons and wireless telegraph" (fig. 13). The elaborate subheading very well emphasizes the exterior orientation and almost incidental nature of the building itself with respect to the "public works" structures. Of all the elements in the drawing in fact, only the residential block (due to its sheer inertia) seems to lack autonomy of purpose, becoming a passive receiver of vectors filiating in every direction and at best their infrastructural support. What, after all, could remain, now that its entire organic semiotic system has been laid asunder: the once grand or at least centralizing and frontalizing entrance has given way to a promiscuous panoply of multiple perforations, the "palatial" stairwells torn from its bowels and reconstituted outside as mechanical lifts which "swarm up the façades like serpents of glass and iron," the entire enclosing structure now subordinated to a minor role as collector or distributor of primary currents. The façade itself never assumes an integral form, due in part to the lack of organizational ornament that the manifesto so vehemently eschewed, in part to the atomizing effect of the step-back assembly which defines each floor as a separate and apparently slidable, autonomous module, and in part due to the "frame and mesh" construction that highlights the bold chassis trusses and elevator stacks, leaving the façades simply to recede as mere fenestrated infill. A Città Nuova sketch (fig. 15) depicting a secondary pedestrian thoroughfare (the avenue between two backing buildings) shows the affected preeminence of the newly externalized, and constituted, elevator stack presented as an architectural integer in its own right, here totally disjunct from the building (to which building does it belong?) and embedded in and linked up with the exterior manifold of street levels and its pedestrian and vehicular flows. Thus streets, roads, utility stacks and conveyor ramps are now seen as so many concrete lines, no longer simply connectors of architectural objects and urban blocks, but the very elemental units of which the city is comprised.

       The devaluation of the contained unit with its expressive façade can be seen as part of a more general devaluation of all enclosing planes in favor of superinvested surfaces. Roofs, for example, are now recoded with gardens, landing strips, beacons and electronic transmission equipment; vertical surfaces now support bridges, balconies, gangways, often baying open to permit passage for traffic, or re-consolidating to bear the weight (and form) of a traveling arc or spanning I-beam. But what might be the most important revaluation of all can be seen in "Apartment house with graduated setback and external elevators" (1914; fig. 16), in which a neon publicity panel, explicitly built into the façade of an apartment tower, gives expression, perhaps for the very first time, to the idea that information dissemination processes (ads, signs, graffiti) constitute nothing less than a *material* intervention in the urban continuum. By adding another totally heterogeneous material to those enumerated in the Manifesto (glass, iron, textile), the introduction of language—and presumably later, of images—into the urban/architectural domain would, be-sides having far-reaching consequences for the Russian and Dutch avant-garde of the 1920s and the later Italian work of architects such as Depero, Dazi, and others, create the conditions for the truly polymorphous, procedural—action- or information-based—architectures that began to emerge in the late 1950s and 1960s.[39]

       This same study shows the typical *gradinata* or graduated setback characterizing nearly all the highrise apartment blocs, and the externalized lift tower motif that gives salient expression to the city's third-dimensional axis, a feature that had certainly never found such full development in any previous town-planning scheme.[40] For this reason we feel it would be wrong to attribute the egregious lack of plan studies in Sant'Elia's oeuvre—and the Città Nuova project in particular—to haste, superficial reflection or lack of technical rigor.[41] The lack of plans is at least in part a positive expression of a new form of organization of space, one that resists reduction to two-dimensions, and the conventional planar construction method that derives 3-D representations by combining vertical elevations with their horizontal plans.[42] We have already called attention to the undifferentiated treatment of hori-zontal ("plan") and vertical plane elements in Sant'Elia's work, where they are de-ployed indifferently as surfaces capable of infinite investment, penetrable to a limitless depth, and revealing ever more laminae beneath and behind. Add to this the notions of the pressurized field, the preeminence of linear, vectorial units, the atomization of molar forms, the themes of circulation, sliding, frictionless impacts and wave phe-nomena like interference and flow, and it soon becomes clear that one is dealing with a space characterized more by hydrodynamics and laminar flows than by statics, metrics or the physics of solids.[43] Because such a space is characterized by a non-hierarchical organization—think of a cloud which has no center, ground or exterior cause[44]—any of its sections, whether horizontal or vertical, could express at best only its own very localized configurations or events. In other words, the very idea of a plan(e) would be rendered obsolete; any information it might contain would still have no necessary repercussions on any other part of the building, and besides, which level could be given priority as matrix or master?

       Paolo Portoghesi has characterized the relations of forms in Sant'Elia's work to "jets of water in a fountain," and Reyner Banham has written that Sant'Elia was "the first to give modern architecture "the habit . . . of thinking in terms of circulation, not vistas."[45] The prevalent use of parabolas, ellipses and com-pressed helical forms, while undoubtedly owing something to their Liberty origin, have undergone a profound formal reorientation,[46] now suggesting an arrangement of forces in disequilibrium, crisis and flux. Conventional town plans, organized on axes or in regular (or irregular) metrical bays have here given way to an almost stochastic distribution of elements, where material seemingly gravitates and sediments in random centers of turbulence. If the complex embedded structures are understood in this way it becomes easy to account for the centrifugal and centripetal effects suggested by the refrains of orbiting and constellated masses, the constant nesting motif, and the gradual tapering and lightening of forms as they develop toward their extremities. In what could easily have been a maquette for La Città Nuova, Boccioni's prodigious "Sviluppo di una bottiglia nello spazio" can be read as a tour de force on the hydraulic/turbulence theme.

The most significant innovation brought about by this "new" hydrodynamic model[47] of circulation was the superseding of the most classical though enduring notion of *site* as an essential, causal or pre-existing substratum.[48] Even Le Corbusier's pylons later did no more than affirm the classical site, either by hygienically clearing it in an ultimate gesture of homage or by positing it, in relation to the architecture, as an opposing term.[49] The site, and the hierarchical figure/ground relation it supports, has in La Città Nuova begun to give way to an all-encompassing univocity, where the flows that compose its space are continuous with those actually forming the bodies within it.

What physical theory in science and aesthetics had managed to express in a conceptual framework (neither Hildebrand, Rodin nor Boccioni ever found the definitive sculptural solutions to match their ambitions in this area) Sant'Elia was the first to furnish with a concrete and sensible body. The thermo- and electrodynamic theory at the turn of the century, as we have seen, already contained a preliminary notion of the field made possible then by the introduction of time into the spatial continuum. The hydrodynamic themes of La Città Nuova—the vectors, the concatenating sequences, in a word, its flow—also embody time in a way fundamentally different from previous schemas, including the essentially self-contained spectacle of Baroque architecture or the excessively narrative and romantic Picturesque. Rather, time is put in the service of a certain pantheism. This is first apparent in the inclusivity of the city's networks—one can never be outside them, but always already part of a system experienceable only over time and in pieces,[50] a system in which the observer is either a mobile entity himself, or else the stationary receiver of mobile parts. Second, because the city-system, based on the circulation of force (-lines) wholly disencumbered from reference or relation to an exterior ground or site, must derive its first principle, or principle of *differentiation*, from something inherent to it (turbulence, interference, etc.). This inherent "first principle" is an immanent cause: an infinitely recurring, always virtual cause, based not on the absolute time of a fixed, exterior origin but a mobile and relativistic time that belongs indissociably to the concrete events that give it form. Nor is the city's structure discernable from any hypothetical outside; it has no divisions or sectors that could be combined into a second order unity or whole. Its unity is always present in its local, molecular relations. For this architecture expresses at its elementary level those global and collective urban functions that it modulates and participates in. It does not allegorize "Man's" temporality—day/night, work/rest, public/private, childhood/school/work/family, etc.—by organizing it into overcoded molar units. Here, "the city" in its virtuality and complexity, is the expressed content of each of its single elements—not those received ideas of what actions, and what order of actions, constitutes a human life. The distinction between global and local is elided, pre-empting—for better or for worse—the molar, hierarchical, or centralizing formations endemic to any social and political urban system.[51] Like a three-dimensional crabgrass the city proliferates as if through some internal mechanism—it does not expand along a boundary or front but simply produces more of itself randomly (*nunc hinc, nunc illinc*), differentiating, ramifying and recombining basic elements. The field it develops, like the one described by Einsteinian physics, is radically heterogeneous if viewed globally (though it is precisely this global view that is no longer interesting or even possible), yet the same laws unfailingly hold for every local instance. La Città Nuova is a system then, with no inside or outside, no center and no periphery, merely one virtual circulating substance—force—and its variety of actualized modes—linear, rotating, ascending, combining, transecting.

The implications of such a new temporality were vast. The nineteenth century had already forged an obsessive oeuvre of these and similar changes through the works of Flaubert, Engels, Baudelaire, Dickens and H. G. Wells, to mention only a few. The industrial city was then rapidly multiplying and fragmenting not only as a spatial image but as a temporal one as well; its slow or permanent rhythms, which once seemed to furnish a stable reference or support for man's chaotic and fluid experience, were now themselves, due to industrialization and accelerated technical innovation, beginning to mutate and incorporate change over shorter and shorter periods of time, slowly atomizing and becoming ever more fluid. What once served as a global, stable ground to man's temporal figure was threatening now to become as labile as he, and in this process of drawing forth the ground to embrace the figure—a tactical innovation so well known to Modernist painting—menaced to dissolve him completely.

Generations of critics to this day have interpreted Modernist culture as a specific resistance to this threat of dissolution. And this despite the fact that the unmasterable and chaotic were developed as much as possible on the side of the object, leaving man and his consciousness to the greatest possible extent unmolested. The works of Joyce, Proust, Kafka and Woolf are seen as part apologia, part lament for the modern facts of fragmentation and flux, but only as part of a more resounding and reassuring affirmation of a transcendentality of the subject and internal privatized time. Today we still need to be reminded that these works, more than just mirrors reflecting a prodigiously mutable world, were important spatio-temporal entities themselves, *places* for the dedicated explorer to navigate and apprentice him/ herself, no longer in the techniques of reading, but more properly in the mapping of this very world, and just as it was lapsing forever into illegibility. What we might hope to discover today when returning to the works of this period, alongside all that was valid in the existentialist-humanist view, are principles and remains of rudimentary maps once formed, consciously or not, from some beyond point of representation. To do this, analysis would need bypass, not only traditional notions of "meaning," but also most currently accepted notions of "structure." For even this latter "progressive" term remains victim of a perennial transparency myth: the belief that beneath the shifting profusion of appearances there lies, accessible through proper operations, the finite, essential pattern of the real. At its most sophisticated, structure was understood as the abstract but always immobile framework—perhaps even a true component—of a living signification. Yet even as interest shifted from the analysis of systems of signification to topographical configurations and mapping, what seemed a critical innovation too often fell back on the structuralist bias for spatial systems to the proper exclusion of what I have been calling the "event."

The event belongs to a complex and abstract realm of spacetime; so must the cartographic techniques that sketch out its lines. Difference, a value whose so-called disappearance is today lamented only by those insensible to its subtler yet increasingly insistent effects, becomes the new transcendental principle of the field: the differential equation (dx/dt) with which physics replaced the material point, the perpetual becoming of Boccioni's force-lines, and Sant'Elia's everdifferentiating field of pressures and flows. None of these configurations however would resemble maps in the traditional sense. They are rather what I will call *procedural maps*, made up not of "global" representations, which tend to reduce entire multiplicities to static and finite schemas, but of protocols or formulas for negotiating local situations and their fluctuating conditions. To construct such a procedural map it is necessary, first, to abandon the following two principles: (1) the epistemological prejudice that gives priority to the visual, spatial logic of simultaneity—the "image" of traditional cartography; and (2) the illusory exteriority of the subject vis-à-vis the map and the mapped. Here again it is the insertion of the dimension of time into the field that establishes a relation of continuity between subject and object, figure and ground, observer and event. Time is no longer exclusively subjective and private nor objective and absolute, but forms the seamless plane that gathers and gives consistency to both the subject- and object-effects that are in actuality corollaries or by-products of the event. To call these by-products is not to diminish them in any way, but rather to underscore the fact that they are *derived*, locally and in immanent relation to the event that constitutes them; they are not pre-given entities arriving readymade from without.

What is at stake in the question of modernity is, of course, an ontological problem regarding the nature of Being, but equally important and equally at stake is an epistemological one dealing with the nature of knowing. Today's crisis, as discussed at the beginning of this study, may be seen as an effect of the discrepancy between the steady emergence of a new mode of Being and the failure to evolve adequate modes of knowing that would be proper to it. This situation today is often an extremely confused one. Typical, and symptomatic, is the work of one author who, while acutely eliciting a number of the most trenchant, problematic and richly challenging artifacts of our time (the work of Nam June Paik, Michel Foucault, the analytic of schizophrenia, high technology, the contemporary urban environment . . .) is led to disqualify them routinely in the name of a more overriding need for representational schemas—depth-model hermeneutics, a theory of the social field based on cultural dominants, subject-centered consciousness and cognitive mapping—in short, the resuscitation in every possible way of the subject-object relation that by his own admission had already lapsed into oblivion.[52]

It is, of course, no accident that the city has occupied a privileged position in the emergence of our modernity. It was here where the compounding of technical innovations would have its first and most profound effects on mental and social life. But the culture of cities also belongs to much more fundamental moments in our history—the rise of the first "artificial" (technique-based) civilizations as they break more and more fully from the "organic" earth-based world with its single lived-time and legible naturalistic space; and, of course, the rise of capitalism whose radical reordering of the relations of production made these other revolutions both necessary and possible.

The myth of the machine was more than a metonym of this new culture, it expressed the autonomous, detached, infernal, abstract, self-regulating, euphoric *functioning* that characterized the new order; it was in itself the very recognition that this new order was about the mobilizing and productive possibilities of abstract *functions* rather than the invention and deployment of yet another register of objects and elements. The cultural space occupied by this machine obsession was always an ambiguous one. At one extreme were the excesses of mechanolatria of figures like Marinetti whose understanding of the machine failed to develop the question of productive relations that it on so many levels implied. At the other was the Taylorism of both the Soviet revolutionary and the American capitalist variety, which conspired to draw the social field and the worker's body into the well-oiled delirium of an efficiently producing machine.

La Città Nuova belongs properly to neither of these groups, but rather to a third, open-ended category that left its own powerful though tacit mark on Modernist culture. To this category belong those machines whose task it was to produce other machines, or more precisely the "machinic" itself, and to set this latter loose as some kind of autofunctioning demon that appropriated, combined and connected to itself a limitless array of materials and forces, assembling perverse hybrids and mixtures of social, political and erotic flows. Duchamp's *Large Glass*, but also the procedural *Green Box* that contains its assembly instructions, the infernal bureaucracies and apparatuses of Kafka, the exotic conjugations of Roussel's performing machines, and in both these last two cases, the strange writing machines that subtended them, are among those identified in the 1950s as bachelor machines.[53] La Città Nuova may be understood in this light less as a literal, realizable program than as a set of instructions, governing not only the assembly of isolated modules of (bachelor) machinery, but the composition, in its most pragmatic and concrete form of a universal machinic consistency. It is this consistency alone which is capable of endowing with a substantial body all those events, processes and flows, and all those invisible or "surreptitious" alliances, communications, and even subjugations that once may have seemed, as today they still do to certain modes of thought, so unfathomable and abstract.

Notes

1. "We had stayed up all night, my friends and I, under the mosque-lamps whose filigree copper domes were constellated like our very souls." *Founding and Manifesto of Futurism*, in *Archivi del futurismo*, ed. Maria Drudi Gambillo and Teresa Fiori, 2 vols. (Rome: DeLuca, 1958–1962), 1:15.

2. The text not only dramatizes the passage from an outdated environment to a new and invigorated one, but furnishes in a great number of details sources for dozens of works which would follow in its wake. To mention just a few among them, Giacomo Balla's *Velocità astratta* (1913), Luigi Russolo's *Automobile in corsa* (1913), Carlo Carrà's *Quello que mi disse il tram* (1911), and Umberto Boccioni's *La strada entra nella casa* (1911).

3. Marinetti originally wavered between Dynamism and Futurism as names for his movement; cf. Marianne W. Martin, *Futurist Art and Theory, 1909–1915* (Oxford: Clarendon Press, 1968), p. 40.

4. That is, all of the mathematics in sections 3 and 4 of Part 1 of "On the Electrodynamics" dealing with transformations of (space) coordinates and times between stationary and moving systems. H. A. Lorentz, A. Einstein, H. Minkowski, and H. Weyl, *The Principle of Relativity*, trans. W. Perrett and G. B. Jeffery (New York: Dover, 1952, orig. 1923), pp. 43–50.

5. On three space coordinates, one of which will undergo a change in the dimension parallel to the motion due to the Lorentz contraction, one variable (relative velocity between two reference frames), and one constant (the speed of light).

6. This term was coined by H. Minkowski in his famous article "Space and Time" (1908), which gave the first mathematical formulation to space-time. Minkowski defined a world-point as a point in space at a point in time (a system of values x,y,z,t). Attributing the variations dx, dy, dz to conform to the value dt, this point would describe "an everlasting career" that he named a world-line. "The whole universe is seen to resolve itself into similar world-lines, and I would fain anticipate myself by saying that in my opinion physical laws might find their most perfect expression as reciprocal relations between these world-lines. Lorentz et al., *The Principle of Relativity*, p. 76.

7. "The Problem of Space, Ether and the Field in Physics," in Albert Einstein, *Ideas and Opinions* (New York: Bonanza Books, n.d.), p. 279.

8. "Before Maxwell people conceived of physical reality—in so far as it is supposed to represent events in nature—as material points, whose changes consist exclusively of motions, which are subject to total differential equations. After Maxwell they conceived physical reality as represented by continuous fields, not mechanically explicable, which are subject to partial differential equations. This change in the conception of reality is the most profound and fruitful one that has come to physics since Newton." "Maxwell's Influence on the Evolution of the Idea of Physical Reality," in Einstein, *Ideas and Opinions*, p. 269. Ernst Mach, whose theories exerted a great influence on Einstein, argued the need to abandon the metaphysics of Newtonian mechanics in his 1883 *Die Mechanik in ihrer Entwicklung* (The

Science of Mechanics; Chicago: Open Court, 1902). Cf. Max Jammer's discussion in his *Concepts of Space* (Cambridge: Harvard University Press, 1957), pp. 138–143.

9.   Einstein, "The Problem of Space, Ether and the Field in Physics," p. 281.

10. Einstein asserts this, however, only retrospectively. Cf. Ibid., p. 281.

11. Albert Einstein, *Relativity: The Special and General Theory* (New York: Bonanza Books, 1961), p. 150.

12. Adolf von Hildebrand, *Das Problem der Form in der bildenden Kunst* (Strassburg: J. H. E. Heitz, 1893), pp. 32–33. "Let us imagine total space (*das Raumganze*) as a body of water, into which we may sink certain vessels, and thus be able to define individual volumes of water without however destroying the idea of a continuous mass of water enveloping all."

13. Reyner Banham, *Theory and Design in the First Machine Age* (Cambridge: MIT Press, 1981, orig. 1960), pp. 66–67.

14. Colin Rowe and Robert Slutzky, "Transparency: Literal and Phenomenal," in Colin Rowe, *The Mathematics of the Ideal Villa and Other Essays* (Cambridge: MIT Press, 1976).

15. Umberto Boccioni, *Pittura, scultura futuriste: Dinamismo plastico* (Florence: Vallechi, 1977, orig. 1914) (abbr. PSF in text) ; *Archivi del futurismo* (abbr. Ar. in text). English translations of some of Boccioni's writings were published in *Futurist Manifestos*, ed. Umbro Appolonio (London: Thames and Hudson, 1973) (abbr. FM in text). Because these translations are extremely unreliable, all citations and page numbers given in the body of the text will refer when possible to the Italian originals. All quotes are either my own translations or are altered versions of those given in the latter work.

16. Henri Bergson, *Essai sur les données immédiates de la conscience* (Paris: Presses Universitaires de France, 1927), chap. 2.

17. The rhetoric of Bergsonian intuitionism is, however, to a certain degree maintained. Cf. *Archivi del futurismo*, 1:71, 104, 108, 144.

18. "Les problèmes clefs de l'art moderne [sont] les problèmes de la représentation de l'espace, notamment le problème de la continuité dans l'espace, et ceux de la transition entre l'espace intérieur et l'espace extérieur. Grâce à la spirale, l'espace n'est plus défini par un volume à trois dimensions, mais composé avec une quatrième dimension—celle du temps: la spirale permet . . . une durée réele." Noémi Blumenkranz-Onimus, "La spirale, thème lyrique dans l'art moderne," in *Cahiers d'Esthétique* (1971), p. 296.

19. This notion of multiplicity was first developed by the mathematician Bernhard Riemann. Cf. Gilles Deleuze and Félix Guattari, *Mille plateaux* (Paris: Minuit, 1980), p. 604, n. 15.

20. It is important here to differentiate between those systematic attacks on perspective which were commonplace in the Modernist period (Cubism) and those, such as Boccioni's and Duchamp's, which, more than a simple modification of existing pictorial theory, constitute a critique of the conception of the world as an optical phenomenon. This latter movement goes beyond questions of aesthetic dogma, casting its challenge not just to the Renaissance's rationalizing *costruzione legittima* but to the quasi-entirety of western notions of space back to the time of Euclid and Vitruvius. Erwin Panofsky has demonstrated the constant link between optics and geometry. For his discussion of Euclid, cf. *The Codex Huygens and Leonardo da Vinci's Art Theory: The Pierpont Morgan Library, Codex M.A. 1139* (London: Warburg Institute, 1940); on Vitruvius cf. "Die Perspektive als 'symbolische Form,'" in *Aufsätze zu Grundfragen der Kunstwissenschaft* (Berlin: Verlag Volker Speiss, 1980); and for an interesting reference to Riemann and binocular vision, cf. *Early Netherlandish Painting* (Cambridge: Harvard University Press, 1964), p. 12.

21. *Archivi del futurismo*, 1:105–106, 144; *Futurist Manifestos*, p. 94. Cf. also Carlo Carrà's *Plastic Planes as Spherical Expansions in Space*, in *Archivi del futurismo*, 1:145–147; *Futurist Manifestos*, pp. 91–92.

22. "Analogy is nothing more than the deep love that assembles distant, seemingly diverse and hostile things. . . . Together we will invent what I call the imagination without strings. Someday we will achieve a yet more essential art, when we dare to suppress all the first terms of our analogies and render no more than an uninterrupted sequence of second terms. . . . Syntax was a kind of abstract cipher that poets used to inform the crowd about the color, musicality, plasticity and architecture of the universe. Syntax was a kind of interpreter or monotonous cicerone. This intermediary must be suppressed, in order that literature may enter *directly into the universe and become one body with it*" (italics added).

Technical Manifesto of Futurist Literature (1912), in *Marinetti: Selected Writings*, ed. R. W. Flint (New York: Farrar, Strauss and Giroux, 1971), pp. 85, 89. Cf. also *Destruction of Syntax—Imagination without Strings—Words-in-Freedom*, in *Futurist Manifestos*, pp. 95–106; and the discussion below on point of view.

23. "It is the static qualities of the old masters which are abstractions, and unnatural abstractions at that—they are an outrage, a violation and a separation, a conception far removed from the law of the unity of universal motion." *Futurist Manifestos*, p. 94.

24. Sanford Kwinter, "The Pragmatics of Turbulence," *Arts* (December 1985).

25. "A body in movement is not simply an immobile body subsequently set in motion, but a truly mobile object, which is a reality quite new and original." *Futurist Manifestos*, p. 93.

26. "Every object reveals by its lines how it would resolve itself by following the tendencies of its forces." *Archivi del futurismo*, 1:106.

27. This period included an array of movement studies in which images are multiplied to conform to the optical theory of retinal persistence. The famous *Guinzalio in moto* (1912) is one example. This idea of halting and spatializing movement, rather than temporalizing and mobilizing static form, further underscores Futurism's fundamental difference from Cubism.

28. Note the first projects for the Milano *stazione* (there would be five in all); see note 35 below.

29. The texts of the *Messaggio* and the statements by other members of the Nuove Tendenze as well as the final text of the *Manifesto of Futurist Architecture* are in the *Archivi del futurismo*, 1:122–127 (members' statements), and 81–85 (manifesto). Separate texts of the *Messaggio* and the manifesto can also be found in *Controspazio* 4–5 (April-May 1971), pp. 17–19. Whether Sant'Elia was or was not a true Futurist, and whether he was or was not the sole author of these texts, has given rise to long and tedious debates. That the ideas in question were those of Sant'Elia has never been put in doubt (cf. Banham, *Theory and Design*, pp. 127–128; Martin, *Futurist Art and Theory*, pp. 188–189), which is all that is relevant for the present context. For a bibliography on these debates cf. *La Martinella di Milano* 12, no. 10 (October 1958), pp. 526–539.

30. Friedrich Nietzsche, *The Use and Abuse of History for Life* (Indianapolis: Bobbs-Merrill, 1949).

31. "Our houses will last less time than we do, and every generation will have to make its own." *Manifesto of Futurist Architecture*.

32. On narrative vs. pragmatic history, cf. Jean-François Lyotard, *The Postmodern Condition: A Report on Knowledge*, trans. G. Bennington and B. Massumi (Minneapolis: University of Minnesota Press, 1984). Futurist theory may be read as the first important instance of a pure pragmatics in modernist culture.

33. "I affirm that just as the ancients drew their inspiration from the elements of the natural world we too—materially and spiritually artificial—must draw our inspiration from the elements of the radically new mechanical world we have created, of which architecture must be the most perfect expression, the most complete synthesis and the most effective artistic integration." *Messaggio*.

34. This theme, among many others first adumbrated by Sant'Elia, was most powerfully echoed in László Moholy-Nagy's *Von Materiel zu Architektur* (1929). "The fact that kinetic sculpture exists leads to the recognition of a space condition which is not the result of the position of static volumes, but consists of visible and invisible forces e.g., of the phenomena of motion, and the forms that such motion creates. . . . The phrase 'material is energy' will have significance for architecture by *emphasizing relation, instead of mass*." Cf. Moholy-Nagy, *The New Vision* (New York: Wittenborn, Schultz, 1947), especially pp. 41–63. Of great importance here as well are El Lissitzky, *A. and Pangeometry* (1925), in *Russia: An Architecture for World Revolution* (Cambridge: MIT Press, 1984), and Iakov Chernikhov's pedagogical notebooks (1927–1933) in *Chernikhov: Fantasy and Construction* (London: A.D. Editions, 1984).

35. *Antonio Sant'Elia. Catalogo della mostra permanente a cura di Luciano Caramel e Alberto Longati* (Como: Villa Comunale dell'Olmo, 1962). The catalogue lists nearly 300 drawings. Many of the drawings listed in this work and a host of others from other sources are available in an English edition; cf. *Antonio Sant'Elia*, ed. Dore Ashton and Guido Ballo, trans. and ed. Kate Singleton (New York: Cooper Union, 1986).

36. Fewer than 10 percent of all the drawings employ frontal or attenuated oblique settings. The best descriptive study of Sant'Elia's form language is Paolo Portoghesi, "Il linguaggio di Sant'Elia," in *Controspazio* 4–5 (April-May 1971), pp. 27–30.

37. This device is already embodied in Sant'Elia's drafting style. Lines consistently overshoot the edges of the forms they describe (this had yet to become a standard affectation of architectural rendering), further suggesting the nodal character of "form" as if this latter were constituted only by perpetually remigrating force-lines.

38. Cf. the discussion of immanent cause below.

39. In this category one would certainly place the major exponents of "paper architecture," such as Archigram, Superstudio, Coop Himmelblau, but also the work of Ant Farm, the Situationists and artists like Robert Smithson and Dan Graham, whose use of mirrors, video, photography and print helped effect architecture's definitive migration into abstract space.

40. This is perhaps the time to mention some of the visionary schemes of planners and architects like Antoine Moilin, Henri-Jules Borie, Charles Lamb and Hugh Ferriss. All of these proposed important schemes based on a superimposed transportation net of roads and aerial tracks and catwalks. But these schemes remained always that—superimpositions necessarily exterior to the objects they were meant to link. Sant'Elia was the first to establish movement or circulation as a first principle which does not so much act upon a substratum as meld with and mobilize the city's actual substance (including its architectural elements).

41. All of these charges have been made, either in criticism or in apology. Not untypical of the outlandishness and the triviality of these claims was the publishing of three rather desultory sketches relating to Milan's town plan accompanied by the claim "We now show that Sant'Elia was also a practical town planner." Cf. "Antonio Sant'Elia," presented by Leonardo Mariani in *L'Architettura* 4, no. 9 (January 1959).

42. This technique is the basis of quattrocento perspective theory and originates with Alberti's *De pictura*.

43. An interesting scientific and philosophical history of hydrodynamics in which many of the above themes are developed is Michel Serres, *La naissance de la physique dans le texte de Lucrèce* (Paris: Minuit, 1977).

44. Pierre Rosenstiehl and Jean Petitot, "Automate asocial et systèmes acentrés," *Communications* 22 (1974). The authors propose mathematical models to account for communication and propagation effects in non-hierarchically organized systems.

45. Paolo Portoghesi, "Il linguaggio di Sant'Elia"; Reyner Banham, "Futurism and Modern Architecture," *Royal Institute of British Architects* (February 1957); and "Sant'Elia," *Architectural Review* (May 1955).

46. C. G. Argan, "Il pensiero critico di Sant'Elia," in *Dopo Sant'Elia* (Milan: Editoriale Domus, 1935).

47. The hydrodynamic model of course is not new, but goes back at least to Archimedes. As I have already stressed modernity is not so much about the "new" as the "untimely" in the sense of Nietzsche's *unzeitgemasse* meditations. "Untimely" (and modern) is the emergence of a world-system based on relations of force rather than the qualities of form.

48. We have already seen to what extent space for the Greeks depended on a substratum of real material bodies. For Aristotle space was never dissociated from the notion of place (*topos*), which he defined as an envelope or boundary between an enclosed and an enclosing body. "The continuity of space is transformed [in Aristotelian physics] from a geometrical and ideal determination to a kind of objective determination. The continuity of space is not, as in the idealistic theories of space, founded in 'form' and in its 'principle'; rather it follows from what space is as a substantial and objective entity, as a sub-stratum." Ernst Cassirer, *The Individual and the Cosmos in Renaissance Philosophy* (Philadelphia: University of Pennsylvania Press, 1963), pp. 181–182. Compare the Aristotelian *topos* to Lucretius's *nunc hinc, nunc illinc* (now here, now there) which describes the random appearance of the clinamen (swerve, differentiation) in the universal cascade of atoms. Here place lacks all determination save as a relation of pure difference within an indistinct field. The event is there where space is suddenly differentiated from itself. Cf. Lucretius, *On Nature* (Indianapolis: Bobbs-Merrill, 1965), Book II; and Serres, *Naissance de la physique*.

49. Perhaps the closest he would ever come was in the "artificial sites" of the OBUS linear plan, nearly two decades after La Città Nuova. On the OBUS plan see Mary McLeod, "Le Corbusier and Algiers," *Oppositions* 19–20 (Winter-Spring 1980). Far more radical in this direction were certain experiments in the 1920s by the Russian Constructivists—Tatlin, Lissitzky, Leonidov, Vesnin, the Stenberg brothers—as well as the Dymaxion project of Buckminster Fuller.

50. Though one will object that this is true of all cities it is not true of their individual architectural elements. It is precisely the way these latter are embedded within a temporality of generalized flow that interests us here. The objection moreover is unfounded in another way, for most cities are still today capable of traditional cartographic representation while La Città Nuova is not. One need only consider the difficulty New York City has had in producing an overview map of its relatively simple (maximum two levels) subway system to appreciate this problem. What would be needed for n-dimensional systems are procedural maps or protocols, which again re-introduces the question of time. Cf. the closing discussion of this essay.

51. This is a considerably more optimistic interpretation of La Città Nuova than the one to be found in Sergio Los, "Città macchina gigante," in *La città macchina* (Vicenza: Assessorato Cultura, 1974). Los opposes transmissive (global) to communicational (local) systems, seeing in the former an inevitable reproduction of the "relationship of domination."

52. I am referring to a series of articles and lectures of Fredric Jameson, including the final essay in which these studies culminated called "Postmodernism, or, The Cultural Logic of Late Capitalism," *New Left Review* 146 (July-August 1984). The monotheistic themes propounded throughout are notable and avowed.

53. Michel Carrouges, *Les machines célibataires* (Paris: Arcanes, 1954). Cf. also *Junggesellenmaschinen/ Les machines célibataires* (Venice: Alfieri, 1975).

Ignasi de Solà-   **"Weak Architecture"** "Arquitectura dédil," *Quaderns d'Arquitectura i Urbanisme* 175

Morales   (October-December 1987); translated in de Solà-Morales, *Differences: Topographies*

of Contemporary Architecture, ed. Sarah Whiting, trans. Graham Thompson

(Cambridge: MIT Press, 1996)

Perhaps even before 1980, there existed an architecture that was capable of producing a concept of *il pensiero debole*, or weak thought, though we could not have called it that then. One thinks of the small bank buildings of Alvaro Siza, Frank Gehry's house in Santa Monica, Rafael Moneo's town hall in Logroño, or, just later, Roger Diener's apartment houses in Basel, among others. The extraordinary quality of this work arises from a modernist understanding of production, tectonic density, and compositional rigor but now coupled with what Heidegger called an *Andenken* or recollection — a keeping-in-mind of the modernist tradition, a willingness to traverse it once again, but not to return uncritically to its heroism. There is an acceptance in this work of architecture's aleatory relation to the physical and social city (whose disjunctions and contradictions are inscribed materially in all of these examples) that tends to distort and dissolve modernism's confidence and seek some sort of convalescence in the small, the fragmented, the momentary. Roger Diener speaks of "the registration of the environment and its condition for life [as] the expression of a certain disillusionment."[1] And Siza (in a passage that seems to echo de Solà-Morales's approving citation of Goethe's fluttering to and fro of truth) instructs that "an architectonic proposition whose aim is to go deep . . . can't find support in a fixed image, can't follow a linear evolution. . . . Each design must catch, with the utmost rigor, a precise moment of flittering image in all its shades, and the better you can recognize that flittering quality of reality, the clearer your design will be. It is the more vulnerable as it is true."[2]

Ignasi de Solà-Morales does not specify the architecture that qualifies as "weak," but he is explicit about his desire to construct an apparatus for reading architecture that is legitimate in a world that no longer produces stable, monumental works of the classical or modernist type but, in its ceaseless separation and reshuffling of images, can nevertheless produce a new kind of intensity. For this apparatus, he appeals to the notion of event. "In a world that incessantly consumes images, in a constantly expanding metropolitan culture, in a universe whose buildings are no more than a few of the infinite number of figurative and informative dwellings that surround us, there nonetheless exists the architectonic event. This event is like an extended chord, like an intensity at an energetic crux of streams of communication, a subjective apprehension offered by the architect in the joy of producing a polyphonic instant in the heart of the chaotic metropolis."[3]

The "polyphonic instant" is experienced as multiple interpretations, which is the necessary link in de Solà-Morales's conjunction of hermeneutics and Gilles Deleuze's multiplanar thought, and the source of contemporary architecture's weakness relative to the modernist tradition (with its singularity of vision) that it still prolongs. The "radical desolation" of weak architecture, "a groundlessness emerging out of the singularity of an event," has "nothing to do with a lack of ability to manifest the conditions of the contemporary culture. Quite the contrary. This weakness is precisely the architectonic manifestation of the condition of contemporary culture."[4]

If modernity is essentially characterized by the correlated notions of progress and overcoming, then the idea of simply rejecting modernity — rejecting it, say, for some new stage of history — leads to a double bind: for to reject modernity is also to reject the possibility of overcoming modernity, since the very concept of overcoming belongs to the same system that is being rejected. This is the central insight of Gianni Vattimo's reading of Nietzsche and Heidegger and one of the premises of weak thought. For de Solà-Morales, this insight entails that the perceptions of time and place themselves are now profoundly changed, rendering irrelevant not only the Vitruvian concerns with duration and stability and the phenomenological cultivation of genius loci, but also a purely nihilistic architecture of negation. What is enabled by this changed perception is a sense of architecture's "untimeliness" — the apprehension of "an opening, a window on a more intense reality," and a recollection (*Andenken*, "that which is constituted as pure residuum") that takes as its point of departure the sensuous materiality of the event and the specific circumstances of the interpretive encounter.

compare Cacciari (**394 ff**)

Notes

1. Roger Diener, "On the Uncertainty of the Individual," *Quaderns d'Arquitectura i Urbanisme* 183 (1989), p. 58.
2. Alvaro Siza, "To Catch a Precise Moment of the Flittering Image in All Its Shades," *A + U* 123 (December 1980), p. 9.
3. Ignasi de Solà-Morales, "Place: Permanence or Production," in *Anywhere*, ed. Cynthia C. Davidson (New York: Rizzoli, 1992); reprinted in *Differences: Topographies of Contemporary Architecture* (Cambridge: MIT Press, 1996), pp. 101–102.
4. Ignasi de Solà-Morales, "From Autonomy to Untimeliness," in *Anyone*, ed. Cynthia C. Davidson (New York: Rizzoli, 1991); reprinted in *Differences*, p. 88.

Weak architecture evokes, from the outset, an allusion (not difficult to apprehend) to the terms *weak thought* and *weak ontology* that Gianni Vattimo and subsequently other Italian, as well as French and German, thinkers have put into circulation in recent years. It seems to me that what really lies behind the propositions of weak philosophy is an interpretation of our contemporary culture's international, aesthetic situation. It is this subtext that leads to the question: What role is accorded to architecture in the aesthetic system of contemporary weak thought?

In a recent essay on the question of realism in modern architecture, Manfredo Tafuri posed the problem of interpreting what we commonly refer to as modern architecture, concluding that the contemporary experience, embracing all of twentieth-century architecture, can no longer be read in any linear form. On the contrary, it presents itself to us as a plural, multiform, complex experience in which it is legitimate to cut sectional trajectories that run not only from top to bottom, from beginning to end, but also transversely, obliquely, and diagonally. In some sense, it is only by way of approximations of this kind that the diverse, plural experience of twentieth-century architecture allows us to unstitch and unravel the intrinsic complexity of the modern experience itself.

And it is in this same sense that I propose the utility of the term *weak architecture*. I propose it as a diagonal cut, slanting, not exactly as a generational section but as an attempt to detect in apparently quite diverse situations a constant that seems to me to uniquely illuminate the present juncture. The interpretation of the crisis of the modern project can only be effected from what Nietzsche called "the death of God"; that is to say, from the disappearance of any kind of absolute reference that might in some way coordinate, or "close," the system of our knowledge and our values at the point at which we articulate these in a global vision of reality.

The crisis of the thought of the classical age, as Michel Foucault called it, is a crisis produced by this loss of a ground, together with the loss, in the field of art, of an artistic project, produced on the basis of a desire to represent. In *Les mots et les choses*, Foucault sets out to explain in painstaking detail how the system of representation belongs to the episteme of the classical age: mimesis presents a certain manner of articulating the world of the visual—and thus the world of architecture; in short, it effectively represents a vision of a closed and complete universe as a finished totality.

But the end of the classical age, which Friedrich Nietzsche announced as an end without return, was in reality the exhaustion of something that still inspires—at least to some degree—what we have come to refer to as the modern project. This end is an "illusion," but I wish to bring into play here the ambiguity of that term in Castilian, for it can also express a sense of wishful belief, *ilusión* as simultaneously hope and delusion. Illusion implies a process, and that this process is oriented toward a certain end. In this sense, the project of the Enlightenment, the basis of modernity, still participates in a secular theism, in the idea that it is possible to discover an absolute reality, within which art, science, and social and political praxis can be constructed on the basis of universal rationality. When this system enters into crisis (and it does enter into crisis, precisely as a result of the impossibility of establishing a universal system), we find ourselves faced with the *real* crisis of the modern project and the perplexing—we might say critical—situation of our contemporaneity.

Nietzsche again, in *Human, All Too Human*, speaks of the need for a grounding without ground. In the field of aesthetics, literary, pictorial, and architectonic experience can no longer be founded on the basis of a system: not on a closed, economical system such as that of the classical age; not even on the *ilusión* of a new system such as that which the pioneers of modern design sought to establish. On the contrary, contemporary architecture, in conjunction with the other arts, is confronted with the need to build on air, to build in the void. The proposals of contemporary art are to be constructed not on the basis of any immovable reference, but under the obligation to posit for every step both its goal and its grounding.

I want to emphasize the role assumed by the aesthetic in this situation of the crisis of contemporary culture. Indeed, as is acknowledged in Nietzsche, for example, and also in Martin Heidegger's appropriation of Nietzschean thought, the aesthetic constitutes a particularly significant reference for contemporary experience. In the system of the classical age, the aesthetic was very much a specific area, linked precisely to the practice of the concrete, far removed from any pretensions to the totality of an ontological system. In contemporary experience, the aesthetic has, above all, the value of a paradigm. It is precisely through the aesthetic that we recognize the model of our richest, most vivid, most "authentic" experiences in relation to a reality whose outlines are vague and blurred. If, as Heidegger warned in his meditation on technology, science ultimately becomes routine, it is not difficult to see why culture should have shifted the center of its interests toward those regions formerly regarded as manifestly peripheral. The most "full," the most "alive," that which is felt as being experience itself, that in which the perceiving subject and perceived reality are powerfully fused, is the work of art.

This is not to suggest that in the contemporary world, aesthetic experiences are at the center of the referential system. On the contrary, they continue to occupy a peripheral position; but this peripheral position possesses not a marginal but a paradigmatic value. Aesthetic experiences constitute, in some sense, the most solid, the strongest model of—paradoxically, indeed—a weak construction of the true or the real, and thus assume a privileged position within the system of references and values of contemporary culture.

(We might recall here, parenthetically, the fortunes of the artistic in contemporary mass society. The proliferation of museums, the magnification of the figure of the artist, the existence of a massive consumption of printed and televised artistic images, the widespread appetite for information about the arts, all reflect, of course, an increasingly leisured society, but also relate precisely to the fact that, faced with the tedium of everyday, real, lived experience, of the scientific illusion, of work and production, the world of art appears as a kind of last preserve of reality, where human beings can still find sustenance. Art is understood as being a space in which the fatigue of the contemporary subject can be salved away.)

But we must not forget that this contemporary aesthetic experience is not normative: it is not constituted as a system from which the organization of all of reality might be derived. On the contrary, the present-day artistic universe is perceived from experiences that are produced at discrete points, diverse, heterogeneous to the highest degree, and consequently our approximation to the aesthetic is produced in a weak, fragmentary, peripheral fashion, denying at every turn the possibility that it might ultimately be transformed definitively into a central experience.

The aestheticism of the late nineteenth century consisted precisely in the wishful hope of proposing the experience of art as the backbone of the experience of reality. But it was in this Promethean effort to appropriate to itself something that was fleeting, fugitive, always a little beyond our reach, that the articulating capacity of the aesthetic experience was diluted, and that this experience now presents itself as fragmentary and marginal. It is only from this peripheral position that the aesthetic continues to exercise its seductive influence, its power to unveil, its capacity to imply rather than to constitute the intense apprehension of reality.

This referential framework, which has particularly close links with the thinking of the mature Heidegger, also helps to illuminate certain efforts at interpreting our contemporary architectural milieu. With the hope of clarifying this position, I would like to compare the above exposition with other approaches to and interpretations of the present situation that seem to me to offer much less satisfactory responses to that situation. In the context of architectonic culture, and starting with the experience of crisis, the first responses—the responses we perceive throughout the course of the sixties—are above all fundamentalist in nature. For the phenomenon of fundamentalism is not to be found only in religion, reactionary politics, and certain specific sectors of society; there has also been a fundamentalism in the field of architectural theory and practice.

These fundamentalisms operate in two directions. On the one hand, there are those who, when confronted with the crisis, have called for order in the form of a return to the essentials of the modern experience. Certain theoretical discourses, sustained by leading academics at the influential Istituto Universitario di Architettura in Venice, as well as certain positions adopted by the New York Five group in the late 1960s, put forth the claim that only by going back to what was essential, germinal, and initial in the modern experience—Le Corbusier's *purisme*, in effect—was it possible to find the true path, picking up once again the thread of authentic experience. These voices called for an established line of orthodoxy and correctness to counter the diversion and diversification of the time. This was, in my opinion, a fundamentalist expression of the modern tradition. While it was understood by some as the recovery of the most pristine language of the avant-garde movements of the twenties, for others this experience served to take them further: they sought the lost tradition of the modern in still more primal origins, tracing the founding moments of modernity back to the primary forms of the Enlightenment.

The architecture of the Tendenza in Italy amounted to nothing other than a call to fundamentalism: an attempt at rereading the hardest, most programmatic, most radical architecture of the strictest exponents of rationalism of the interwar years, as well as of the architects of the Enlightenment. It was no accident that the most intensely enlightened architects disseminated some of the most apologetic images in an effort to proclaim origins and a return to original purity. Certainly, figures such as Aldo Rossi have taken it on themselves to deny the possibility of this undertaking. Rossi's work increasingly asks to be seen as a process that is above all self-critical. More and more, he demonstrates a progressive loss of confidence in that fundamentalism that was so decisive in his book *The Architecture of the City*, and that has nevertheless metamorphosed in his recent work into an intimate, private game.

Whether it be through such an enlightened fundamentalism or the fundamentalism of a Richard Meier, repeating over and over the linguistic tropes of twenties purism, these responses, for all their good intentions, amount to nothing more than pure historicism. With their fine words and noble aims, they constitute merely nostalgic attempts to return to supposedly authentic roots, whether in Le Corbusier's Villa Savoye, in Ludwig Hilberseimer's desolate apartment blocks, in Claude-Nicolas Ledoux's drawings, or in any other source of iconography taken for the wellsprings of the true tradition.

In opposition to this fundamentalist illusion, Kenneth Frampton has proposed in recent years a more dialectical and thus less monist, less self-enclosed approach. With his idea of critical regionalism, Frampton has put into circulation a term that I personally consider somewhat unfortunate, but one that has at least introduced a dualist vision into the interpretation of the contemporary situation. Frampton's proposal possesses two clearly differentiated faces. On the one hand there is the idea (in my view, the more attractive) of *resistance*. In this, Frampton has kept faith with the teachings of the Frankfurt School and with his conviction that only by means of a critical attitude toward reality is it possible for contemporary architecture to maintain a rigorous and nonconformist position. It is an attitude capable of distinguishing itself from trivial culture, from the perverse operations of market forces, toward which the only valid response is resistance. But alongside this notion of resistance, the idea of *regionalism* seems a good deal more ingenuous. Frampton's concept, of course, refers to a reading of Heidegger, most directly to the philosopher's text "Bauen, Wohnen, Denken." But one must be cautious when one refers to Heidegger, and that caution is not fully visible in Frampton's articulation of regionalism. On the one hand, Heidegger's writing represents a profound diagnosis of the diseases of the modern world: isolation, provisionality, displacement, and failure. But on the other hand, we now know to what extent the former rector of Freiburg's university was associated with the burgeoning Nazism of the thirties, how much he sustained positions that directly opposed the development of technology, and how much he resisted the loss of traditional values, such as the vernacular, the anti-urban, and the archaic, that had historically formed the basis of a reactionary streak in modernism. When Frampton claims for the new vernacularism the resonances of a reappropriation of the sense of place, of light, of the tectonic, and of the tactile over the purely visual—the categories in terms of which he has characterized the new regionalism— he is undoubtedly engaged in a useful operation: that of understanding that a "system" as such is no longer possible, and that it is therefore necessary to understand architectonic reality from a polycentric strategy. Nevertheless, I believe it is naive to accept at the same time the viability of certain tectonic categories that can only be intelligible within the order of the old political urban culture of the classical age, a culture in which building, dwelling, and thinking constituted a unity. What in Heidegger is a tremulous verification of the disappearance of an already endangered world becomes, in Frampton and in other theoreticians of contemporary architecture, a phenomenologically ingenuous restoration that reveals little or no sense of the contemporary crisis.

Massimo Cacciari, in one of those brilliant and ferocious texts he so often produces, is withering in his dismissal of such excessively immediate interpretations of Heidegger's writings. For Heidegger, Cacciari claims, the metropolitan experience is constructed not through *dwelling* but through *desertion*: a desolation that in some sense constitutes the ground or root of the metropolitan condition. Turning to a late text by Heidegger, Cacciari suggests that, in point of fact, the contemporary metropolitan experience is not one that allows us to speak of dwelling in the same terms as a citizen of Periclean Athens or the Rome of Sixtus V; unlike theirs, our metropolitan dwelling is split, diversified, subject to absence more than to presence. Poetry, that is to say what is vitalizing and grounding, does not construct the entirety of our daily surroundings but is simply the experience of absence. It is the experience of absence, in other words, that draws the contours of the metropolitan subject. If Frampton's proposals are of interest only to the extent that they have expanded the vision of reality and introduced the need to accept as incontrovertible the diversity of modern experiences, Cacciari's critique, underlining as it does the sense of absence, brings us to a concept of central importance in contemporary criticism—a concept that directly stems from this experience of the fragmentary: the archaeological.

The specific use of the term *archaeology* derives from French poststructuralism, primarily from the writings of Foucault, and has been taken up by thinkers such as Jacques Derrida and applied to the analysis of literary communication as a process of deconstruction. But this notion of archaeology comes into its own as a tool for describing, in almost physical fashion, the superimposed reading(s) of tectonic reality: of a reality that can no longer be regarded as a unitary whole but appears instead as the overlapping of different layers. Faced with this reality, the work of art can do no more than reread or redistribute this system of superimpositions. The notion of archaeology evidently introduces the idea that what confronts us is not a reality that forms a closed sphere but a system of interweaving languages. Nobody could be so naive as to imagine that, for archaeology, the system of knowledge of the past can be constituted by a simple accumulation of the objects uncovered by excavation. Rather, these objects present themselves as the outcome of a process of decomposition of superimposed systems, systems that nowhere touch, systems that move independently according to their own logic. Language, too, is a diversity that can no longer be read in a linear fashion. We can no longer believe that the reality of a

Rafael Moneo, Museum for Roman Artifacts, Mérida, Spain, 1980–1984, sketch of the site plan showing theater, amphitheater, and museum site

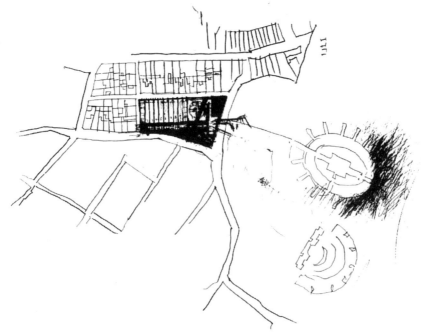

signified responds to the precision of a signifier, as Derrida would say. Instead, it forms a magma that is at once producer and produced. Only a task of deconstruction, a work of analysis and comprehension of the processes of juxtaposition, is capable of elucidating certain relationships.

There is no doubt that this way of thinking has a very direct translation in the experience of the production of form, and thus, by inclusion, of architectonic form. In effect, the experience of certain recent architectures is the experience of superimposition. The signified is not constructed by means of an order but by means of pieces that may ultimately touch; that approach one another, at times without touching; that draw nearer to one another yet never make contact; that overlap, that offer themselves in a discontinuity in time whose reading as juxtaposition is the closest approximation to reality at our disposal.

At the same time, the relationship between archaeology and language has introduced a fundamental innovation into the discourse of contemporaneity: the centrality of the notion of time. This is, expressly, a time different from the time of the classical age. Contemporary time—today's fragmented reality of overlapping virtual and "real" times that was artistically anticipated in the writings of James Joyce, Robert Musil, and Mario Vargas Llosa—is presented precisely as juxtaposition: a discontinuity; something that is in complete contrast to a single, unique, closed and complete system. Time in the architecture of the classical age could be reduced simply to zero (as in the experience of Renaissance centrality) or at most constitute a controlled time—a time with a beginning and an orderly and ordered expansion (which was entirely the experience of baroque temporality). In fact, it is not by chance that Giedion's presentation of modern time in *Space, Time and Architecture* begins by analyzing baroque architecture. In some sense, that means that for the first generation of modern architects, time/space was defined as a continuity more than as a fragment or juxtaposition, as it had already been anticipated and explored in literature, theater, music, and other disciplines.

Contemporary time, however, cannot sustain these classical or baroque illusions. It presents itself as a diffracted explosion in which there is no unique and single time from which we can construct experience. There are, instead, *times*, various times, the times with which our experience of reality produces itself. The confrontation with and the attempt to understand this problem of the diversity of times embraces the whole struggle of art in the twentieth century. Time in the cubist experience, futurist time, time in Dadaism, time in the formalist experiences of the optical and the gestalt experiences of formalism, are versions of a diversified, juxtaposed time that constitutes one of the basic conditions of modernity. It is nevertheless clear that this condition was not always fully understood by the masters of modern architecture, who in many cases thought that what was needed was a time divorced from the centralism of perspectival vision, but which might perfectly well be a time organized from the linear viewpoint, after the fashion of the cinematographic sequence. In Le Corbusier, the *promenade architecturale* is not a diversity but an itinerary that admits the possibility of control. This is the illusory hope that we find not only in Le Corbusier but equally in Giedion and in other foundational architectures and histories of the modern experience. What is abundantly clear is that, increasingly, metropolitan culture offers us times as diversity, and the recognition of this is something that an archaeological approach to the languages of architecture has manifested in a number of ways.

This diversity of times becomes absolutely central in what I have chosen to call weak architecture. In sympathy with the visions of Joyce and others, and in contrast to the idealist narrative sustained by Giedion, these architectures transform the aesthetic experience of the artwork, and specifically of architecture, into *event*. Temporality does not present itself as a system but as an aleatory instant that, responding above all to chance, is produced in an unforeseeable place and moment. In certain works of contemporary art, in dance, in music, in installation, the experience of the temporal as event, occurring once and then gone forever, ably explicates a notion of temporality that finds in the event its fullest form of expression.

If the notion of event allows us to approximate more closely one of the characteristics of weak architecture, the Deleuzean notion of the *pli*, or fold, is no less definitive. Gilles Deleuze published a book that, under the apparently innocuous guise of a summary of Foucault's thought, set out to develop a whole project constitutive of a contemporary vision of reality. The seductive appeal of this text lies, among other things, in its grasp of the fact that in contemporary thought the objective and the subjective are not different and opposing fields but constitute what he calls "folds of a single reality." For architecture, this notion of the fold proves exceptionally illuminating. Reality emerges as a continuum in which the time of the subject and the time of external objects go round together on the same looped tape, with the encounter of objective and subjective only occurring when this continuous reality folds over in a disruption of its own continuity.

Eugenio Trias, in his book *Los límites del mundo*, speaks of the untimely nature of the contemporary situation and contemporary art; untimely in the sense of sudden, unanticipated coagulations of reality, events that are produced not through linear and foreseeable organization but through folds and fissures, as Foucault himself sometimes says, that in some way afford the refuge, the tremulous fluttering of a brief moment of poetic and creative intensity.

Together with the precarious nature of the event and this untimely fold of reality, what I have called weak architecture is always decorative. Let no one be shocked: decoration is a *parole maudite*, a dirty word in the modern tradition, yet there is nonetheless a clear need to go back and reflect on the significance of the term and on the fundamental meaning of the notion of decorum that underlies that of decoration. I am aware of the decisive signification that this term exercises in, for example, the thinking of Leon Battista Alberti and in humanist aesthetics generally. Here, however, I mean to propose a different use of the word. As it is most commonly employed, in the sense it has in the decoration magazines, in its everyday use, the decorative is the inessential; it is that which presents itself not as substance but as accident: something complementary that will even lend itself, in Walter Benjamin's terms, to a reading that is not attentive but distracted, and which thus offers itself to us as something that enhances and embellishes reality, making it more tolerable, without presuming to impose itself, to be central, to claim for itself that deference demanded by totality. Decoration, then, or the decorative condition of contemporary art and architecture, not in the sense of vulgarity, of triviality, of the repetition of established stereotypes, but as a discreet folding back to a perhaps secondary function, a pulling back to a function that projects beyond the hypothetical ground of things. The text in which Heidegger deals with the question of sculpture in space, *Die Kunst und der Raum*—a text based on a conversation with Eduardo Chillida, and in fact published with a series of beautiful etchings by the Basque sculptor—addresses precisely this question: that the decorative is not of necessity a condition of trivialization of the vulgar, but simply constitutes a recognition of the fact that for the work of art—sculptural or architectonic—an acceptance of a certain weakness, and thus of relegation to a secondary position, may possibly be the condition of its greatest elegance and, ultimately, its greatest significance and import.

In conclusion, I would like to gloss one last characteristic of weak architecture: monumentality. We must resort once again here to wordplay. This is not a question of monumentality as representation of the absolute. The monument in the classical age is the center, it is the *imago Dei*, the figuration of a transcendent divinity that guarantees the consistency of time. The figure of the king in the middle of the Royal Square thus constitutes the emblem of the power that hierarchically orders a given public space. The obelisk at the central point of the perspective is the monument that guarantees the coherence and immovability of the representational visual structure. It is not about this monument that I wish to speak, because quite clearly this is the monument that has provoked the crisis in the contemporary situation. The monumentality of weak architecture is not continuous with the monuments of the classical age in either geometric or ideological value, but only in what remains within the present context of that condition of the root term *monitu*; that is to say, of recollection.

Heidegger, once again, in *Die Kunst und der Raum*, quotes some words of Goethe that I would like to repeat here: "It is not necessary for the true always to take on material form, it is enough that it should flutter to and fro, like a spirit, promoting a kind of accord; as when the companionable pealing of a bell rings out, bringing us some little measure of peace." The idea of monument that I want to bring in here is that which we might find in an architectonic object: for all its being an opening, a window on a more intense reality, at the same time its representation is produced as a vestige, as the tremulous clangor of the bell that reverberates after it has ceased to ring; as that which is constituted as pure residuum, as recollection. In his *Architecture of the City*, Aldo Rossi employed the term *monument* to signify permanence, because he was then still operating within a monistic conception of reality and a fixed and static definition of the city. In contrast, the notion of monument I have sought to put forward here is bound up with the lingering resonance of poetry after it has been heard, with the recollection of architecture after it has been seen.

This is the strength of weakness; that strength which art and architecture are capable of producing precisely when they adopt a posture that is not aggressive and dominating, but tangential and weak.

Beatriz Colomina   *"L'Esprit Nouveau*: **Architecture and *Publicité*"** From *Architectureproduction*, ed.

Beatriz Colomina and Joan Ockman (New York: Princeton Architectural Press, 1988)

In his 1936 essay "The Work of Art in the Age of Mechanical Reproduction," Walter Benjamin characterizes the "aura" of traditional art and analyzes its decay under the impact of new cultural technologies such as photographic reproduction and cinematic presentation. Benjamin's central thesis — that the historical and social meanings of art change with the character of its technical production — entails that the ritual, cultic function of traditional art (which produces concentration, absorption, and identification on the part of its audience), the secular humanist cult of beauty (which begins the long struggle for artistic autonomy), and the contemplative perceptual habits and autonomy of nineteenth-century aestheticism (which leads to aesthetic and political passivity) are all negated by the "sense of the universal equality of things" deriving from the trajectory of modern mass culture and technical reproducibility. Rather than maintain the authenticity, originality, and psychological distance of past art, reproducibility demands the *Aufhebung* or sublation of art into life and creates the conditions for a political vocation for artistic practice.[1]

       Peter Bürger draws on Benjamin and develops *Aufhebung* into the defining concept of the historical avant-garde, distinguishing dadaism, surrealism, and the post-1917 Russian avant-garde as practices that closed the gap between art and reality that had been opened by aestheticism's development within bourgeois society.[2] The convergence of these two texts, Benjamin's and Bürger's (the English translation of whose *Theory of the Avant-Garde* appeared in 1984), was the partial inspiration behind the collection of essays gathered by Beatriz Colomina in *Architectureproduction*, the second issue of *Revisions: Papers on Architectural Theory and Criticism*, an occasional publication of essays and discussions by a small study group in New York.[3] Colomina swerves from standard treatments of Benjamin's work, however, in her emphasis on both the material production of the architectural work and the work's dissemination and reception through printed media. The latter emphasis, first broached in her introduction to the volume as well as in the essay reprinted here, has characterized most of her subsequent work.[4]

       What is at stake in the larger context of Colomina's discussion is the negotiation of what Andreas Huyssen has called "the Great Divide," the attempt to hold bourgeois high culture distinct from modern commercial culture and salvage the purity of modernism from the encroachments of mass production, technological modernization, urbanization, and everyday life.[5] Huyssen argues that this interpretive discourse has distorted the understanding of current cultural phenomena (insofar as any theorization of our postmodernism will depend on its characterization of modernism), and that certain postmodern artistic practices — which are continuations of the historical avant-garde and which make their affinities with popular culture thematic — provide the terms for a challenge to that divide. Colomina similarly projects contemporary theoretical insights back onto "classics" of the modern like Le Corbusier and Adolf Loos and documents modern architecture's involvement with mass media, not in order to identify modernism and postmodernism but to make the epistemological break that separates them less than clean. Benjamin's thinking on reproduction, forged out of his knowledge of the progressive art of Germany and the Soviet Union in the 1920s yet presciently available for theorizing the contemporary culture of the simulacrum, is a primary aid, of course, in such mediations.[6]

Such "revisions" were not uncontroversial, however, even within the *Revisions* group. In a response to Colomina's essay *"L' Esprit Nouveau*: Architecture and *Publicité*," in which she emphasizes Le Corbusier's interest in advertising, use of mass media, and cinematic dispersal of vision, Mary McLeod and Joan Ockman argue against what they see as the postmodernization of modernism, which amounts to little more than the commodification of theory. "While such an operation of revisionism, the reading of any historical text through a contemporary conceptual lens, can offer new insights, it also points clearly to problems endemic to such an approach. Among these are the potential for distortion, for deemphasizing original intentionality under the rubric of 'unmasking,' and for decontextualization."[7] Such debates spurred ongoing historical and theoretical research of what Ernst Bloch called the "synchronicity of the nonsynchronous" (*Gleichzeitigkeit des Ungleichzeitigen*)[8] — of the modern as an uneven condition in which production techniques and perceptual conventions from radically different moments of history coexist. They also indicate that one of the deepest subjects of postmodernism is very precisely reproductive technology itself.

Notes

1. "Sublation" is the English approximation of Hegel's notoriously untranslatable term *Aufhebung*, which means simultaneously "negation" and "preservation" in a different, usually "redeemed" form.

2. Peter Bürger, *Theory of the Avant-Garde* (Minneapolis: University of Minnesota Press, 1984).

3. The first (and only other) volume was *Architecture Criticism Ideology*, ed. Joan Ockman (Princeton: Princeton Architectural Press, 1985).

4. See Beatriz Colomina, *Privacy and Publicity: Modern Architecture and Mass Media* (Cambridge: MIT Press, 1994). A revised version of the present essay is the fourth chapter of that book.

5. Andreas Huyssen, *After the Great Divide: Modernism, Mass Culture, and Postmodernism* (Bloomington: Indiana University Press, 1986).

6. In fact, Benjamin saw his own Arcades project in similar terms. Following the Marxian dictum that the key to understanding the anatomy of the ape is through human anatomy (that all precapitalist economic formations could finally be understood only in light of the capitalist economy), Benjamin asserted that an early practice of de-aestheticization like Baudelaire's and the impending demise of auratic art in the nineteenth century could be fully comprehended only if the mature form of anti-auratic art in the age of mechanical reproducibility were projected back onto them.

7. Mary McLeod and Joan Ockman, "Some Comments on Reproduction with Reference to Colomina and Hays," *Architectureproduction*, ed. Beatriz Colomina and Joan Ockman (New York: Princeton Architectural Press, 1988), p. 224.

8. Ernst Bloch, *"Nonsynchronism and Dialectics," New German Critique* 11 (Spring 1977), pp. 22–38.

Le Corbusier and the Everyday Image of the Industrial Age

> At every moment either directly, or through the medium of newspapers and reviews, we are presented with objects of an arresting novelty. All these objects of modern life create, in the long run, a modern state of mind.
>
> LE CORBUSIER, *Vers une architecture*

The archives of *L'Esprit Nouveau* in the Fondation Le Corbusier in Paris indicate that throughout the years of the magazine's publication, 1920 to 1925,[1] Le Corbusier collected a great number of industrial catalogues and manufacturer's publicity brochures lavishly illustrated with photographs of their products. These include not only the automobiles Voisin, Peugeot, Citroën, and Delage; Farman airplanes and Caproni hydroplanes; suitcases and trunks from Innovation; office furniture by Or'mo and file cabinets by Ronéo; hand bags, sport bags, and cigarette cases by Hermès; and Omega watches, but also, among the most extravagant, turbines by Brown-Boweri, high-pressure centrifugal ventilators by Rateau, and industrial equipment by Clermont-Ferrand and Slingsby. Le Corbusier went, in fact, very much out of his way to obtain this material, constantly writing to companies to ask for it. Not only were the catalogues useful in securing advertising contracts for *L'Esprit Nouveau* (the products of most of the companies ended up being advertised in the magazine), but they also had an influence on his work.

Along with the catalogues, he collected department store mail-order brochures (Printemps, Au Bon Marché, La Samaritaine) and clippings from newspapers and magazines of the time, such as *The Autocar, Science et la Vie, Revue du Béton Armé,* and *L'Illustré.* In fact, he seems to have collected everything that struck him visually, from postcards to the cover of a child's school notebook illustrated with the basic geometric volumes.[2] This material, these "everyday images," are the source of many illustrations in *L'Esprit Nouveau* and the five books that came out of this experience: *Vers une architecture, Urbanisme, L'art décoratif d'aujourd'hui, La peinture moderne,* and *Almanach de l'architecture moderne.*[3] The illustrations in *L'art décoratif d'aujourd'hui* especially come from this "disposable" material; here images from department stores catalogues, industrial publicity, and newspapers like *L'Illustré* alternate with ones taken from art history and natural science books. One entire page is devoted to a photograph that was apparently promised but never obtained; in its place one reads the story of the abortive attempt: *on ne se comprend pas.*

Le Corbusier's arguments in L'Esprit Nouveau rely to a great extent on the juxtapositions of image and text. Unlike the representational use of imagery in traditional books, Le Corbusier's arguments are to be understood in terms of never resolved collisions of these two elements. In this unconventional manner of conceiving a book, one can see the influence of advertising techniques. As in advertising, the strongest effect is achieved through the impact of the visual material.

When a low-pressure centrifugal ventilator from the Rateau company is placed on the page opposite the opening of the chapter "Architecture ou Révolution" in *Vers une architecture,* and a turbine from the Centrale Electrique de Gennevilliers placed at the head of the chapter, the message of this chapter derives from the interaction between title and images: it is not social conditions that most preoccupy Le Corbusier, it would seem, but the condition of the architect in an industrial society. The Rateau ventilator puns on the meanings of mechanical revolution in a literal sense and industrial revolution. In the article one reads, "modern society does not recompense its intellectuals judiciously, but it still tolerates the old arrangements as to property, which are a serious barrier to transforming the town or the house." Le Corbusier here is defending public property and the need to address the housing problem through mass production—directing his critique, that is, precisely where a "revolution" in the position of the architect in an industrial society is at stake.[4]

The imagery derived from advertising is proportionately considerably more pervasive in the pages of *L'Esprit Nouveau* than that from strictly architectural sources—for example, Le Corbusier's famous borrowing of photographs of American silos from the Gropius article in the *Werkbund Jahrbuch* of 1913. Whereas the Gropius borrowing (and the subsequent traveling of this image through avant-garde journals) might also be read as a "media phenomenon"—as Banham has noted, none of the architects had seen the silos in question[5]—the presence of this heterodox publicity material in *L'Esprit Nouveau*'s pages suggests a shift in the conventional interpretation of that journal: from an internal exchange among avant-garde movements (as if enclosed in their own "magic circle," uncontaminated by the materials of low culture) to a dialogue with an emerging new reality, namely the culture of advertising and mass media.

Historically speaking, there is nothing very surprising about this impact on Le Corbusier of the visual imagery and techniques of advertising. He witnessed firsthand the passage from an industrial to a consumer society, with the corresponding development of mass media and publicity and the formation of a "culture of consumption." Le Corbusier was very sensitive to this new cultural condition. The production of consumer goods—as Theodor Adorno noted—developed according to a logic completely internal to its own cycle, to its own reproduction; its main mechanism was the "culture industry," the vehicles of which are the mass media—cinema, radio, advertising, and periodical publications.[6]

The media evolved from the technical revolution of the post–World War I years in much the same way as the vehicles of speed, automobiles and airplanes, had emerged from the prewar revolution. Radios and telecommunications had become household items by the beginning of the twenties.[7] The media were developed as part of the technology and instrumentation of war. What made possible the involvement of so many distant countries in World War I was communications, which bridged the distance between the battlefield and the places the news was being transmitted, between the fighting and the decision-making. The battle of the Marne is said to have been won by *coups de téléphone*.[8] The classic accounts of World War I explain the significant role of propaganda built up among nations, especially through the medium of the newspaper.

In contrast to the amount of attention that has been focused on Le Corbusier's architecture in relation to the culture of the machine age, very little has been paid to that of his architecture and the new means of communication, architecture and the culture of the consumer age. The very idea of the "machine age," we can see now, served the period as a symbolic concept, doubtless to say largely induced by the advertising industry.[9] Retrospectively speaking, from the point of view of criticism, the concept of the "machine age" has served the purpose of sustaining the myth of the "modern movement" as an autonomous artistic practice and of the architect as "interpreter" of the new industrial reality.[10]

Le Corbusier not only had an "intuitive understanding of media and a definite feel for news," as Marie-Odile Briot writes in one of the few existing comments on Le Corbusier and the media. Actually, the idea can be advanced (and this is a working hypothesis) that *Purist culture*, by which I understand Le Corbusier and Ozenfant's project of arriving at a theory of culture in industrialized everyday life through *L'Esprit Nouveau*'s pages, is a "reflection," in both the specular and intellectual sense of the word, on the culture of the new means of communication, the world of advertising and mass media.

How Le Corbusier's use of mass-media culture, of the everyday images of the press, industrial publicity, department store mail-order catalogues, and advertisements as "ready-mades" to be incorporated into his editorial work, informed his visual search is a question that belongs to the first meaning of the word "reflection." The architect's tracings and sketches on the catalogues suggest that he was not taking these images in a passive manner; these drawings testify to a formal search ultimately directed to actual practice. But there is more, and this is where the second meaning of the word "reflection" comes in. Le Corbusier identified in the very existence of the printed media an important conceptual shift regarding the function of culture and the perception of the exterior world by the modern individual. In *L'art décoratif d'aujourd'hui* he writes, "The fabulous development of the book, of print, and the classification of the whole of the most recent archaeological era, has flooded our minds and overwhelmed us. We are in a completely new situation. *Everything is known to us.*"[11]

This new condition in which one knows "everything about everything" represents a transformation of traditional culture. Paradoxically, the classical, humanist accumulation of knowledge, a process that was strongly Cartesian and deductive, becomes problematic.[12] Further on I shall discuss Le Corbusier's position vis-à-vis the epistemological break represented by the media. Meanwhile, I shall address one aspect of it, his view of the status of the artwork in an industrial society.

The role of art in society was, in Le Corbusier's view, radically altered by the existence of mass media. In *L'art décoratif d'aujourd'hui* he writes, "Here, in widespread use in books, schools, newspapers, and at the cinema, is the language of our emotions that was in use in the arts for thousands of years before the twentieth century." And in the introduction to *La peinture moderne*, he writes with Ozenfant, "Imitative art has been left behind by photography and cinema. The press and the book operate much more efficiently than art relative to religious, moral, or political aims. What is the destiny of the art of today?"

L'Esprit Nouveau between Avant-Garde and Modernity: The Status of the Artwork and the Everyday Object

One question that presents itself in relation to Le Corbusier's use of publicity images as "ready-mades" is to what extent this is paralleled by Dadaist practices. This question contains a conceptual problem that has become important in recent critical discourse—the difference between modernism and the avant-garde in the context of the first half of this century.[13] A comparison between Le Corbusier's image of a bidet by the manufacturer Maison Pirsoul, published in *L'Esprit Nouveau*, and Marcel Duchamp's *Fountain by R. Mutt* of 1917 will serve as a starting point for this discussion.

These are, if we take representation as a transparent medium, two plumbing fixtures. The origin of the first is its publication in the pages of *L'Esprit Nouveau*; there is no other "original." The second was supposed to have been exhibited in the Salon of the Independents in New York, but never was, as it was rejected and subsequently lost; what remains is only the photograph of it. Nevertheless, it is this document together with a piece of contemporary criticism by Beatrice Woods in *The Blind Man*, a New York Dada journal, that has assured this piece a place in history. Thus both of these objects conceived by Duchamp and Le Corbusier exist only as "reproductions." Another aspect of the lack of an original has to do with the objects each reproduction represents. Duchamp's artwork is a mass-produced object turned upside-down, signed, and sent to an art exhibition. Le Corbusier's prime matter is an advertising image, obviously taken from an industrial catalogue, and placed in the pages of an art journal.

These are the superficial similarities between the two documents. Their difference, however, resides in the meaning of each gesture and the context in which it is placed. The context of the *Fountain by R. Mutt* is the exhibition space. It does not matter that it was never exhibited there. It has to be thought of in that setting; its interpretation is inseparable from it. As Peter Bürger says in his book *Theory of the Avant-Garde*, the meaning of Duchamp's gesture derives from the contrast between mass-produced objects on the one hand and signature and art exhibits on the other. In signing a mass-produced object, Duchamp is negating the category of individual creation and unmasking the art market, where a signature means more than the quality of the work. The avant-garde gesture, in Bürger's definition, is an attack on art as an institution.[14]

To what extent can we consider Le Corbusier's bidet an avant-garde gesture? The context of the Le Corbusier bidet is *L'Esprit Nouveau*. The image heads an article titled "Other Icons: The Museums," which belongs to a series published between 1923 and 1924, later reprinted in *L'art décoratif d'aujourd'hui* in 1925. The series was issued in preparation for the 1925 Exposition des Arts Décoratifs in Paris. In the article Le Corbusier writes, "Museums have just been born. There were none in other times. In the tendentious incoherence of museums the model does not exist, only the elements of a point of view. The true museum is the one that contains everything."

These observations on museums again seem close to Duchamp. The museum viewer can only perform an intellectual operation; contemplation is no longer possible. When the *Fountain by R. Mutt* was rejected by the Independents as "plagiarism, a plain piece of plumbing," Beatrice Woods (presumably in agreement with Duchamp) wrote in *The Blind Man*, "Whether Mr. Mutt with his own hands made the fountain or not has no importance. He CHOSE it. He took an ordinary article of life, placed it so that its useful significance disappeared under the new title and point of view—created a new thought for that object." If the museum transforms the work of art—in fact, creates it as such—and allows the viewer only an intellectual experience of it, Marcel Duchamp's act consists in putting this condition in evidence: creating a new thought for an ordinary product.

The Maison Pirsoul bidet is an everyday object, an industrial product, and Le Corbusier never intended it to abandon this status. His statement that it should be in a museum does not mean he intended to present it as an art object. That the bidet should be in a museum—to be precise, in the museum of decorative arts—means to Le Corbusier that the bidet speaks of our culture, as the folklore of a certain place spoke of that place's culture in other times. But in the places where the railway had already arrived, as Le Corbusier realized, after Loos, folklore could no longer be preserved. The industrial product had become the folklore of the age of communications.[15] Both folklore and industrial production are collective phenomena. *L'art décoratif moderne* did not have the individual character of artistic creation but the anonymous one of industrial production, of folklore.

While Duchamp was questioning the institution of art and artistic individual production, Le Corbusier, more in line with Adolf Loos (who was also fascinated with sanitary material), was distinguishing between the object of use and the art object. Indeed, Le Corbusier's arguments in *L'art décoratif d'aujourd'hui* are strongly indebted to Loos, who not only wrote the famous essay "The Plumbers" (1898), but in 1908 wrote another essay called "The Superfluous." This text is devoted to the architects of the Werkbund. Loos writes:

Now they have all gathered together in a congress in Munich. They want to demonstrate their importance to our craftsmen and industrialists. . . . Only the products of industries that have managed to keep away from the superfluous have attained the style of our times: our automobile industry, our production of glass, our optical instruments, our canes and umbrellas, our suitcases and trunks, our saddles and our silver cigarette cases, our jewelry and our dresses are modern. Certainly, the cultivated products of our time do not have any relation to art. The nineteenth century will pass into history as having effected a radical break between art and industry.

Contrary to the received view of Loos, it is not only the unselfconscious craftsman, the master saddler, who is "modern." Modern, for Loos, includes everything we do not know as such: anonymous collective production. Le Corbusier, like Loos, distinguishes between art and life, between the art object and the everyday object. He does not deny the individuality of artistic creation. In *L'art décoratif d'aujourd'hui* he writes:

Permanence of the decorative arts? or more precisely, of the objects that surround us? It is there that we have to pass judgment: the Sistine Chapel first, then chairs and file cabinets—to tell the truth, problems of a second order, as the cut of a man's suit is a second-order problem in his life. Hierarchy. First the Sistine Chapel, that is, works where passion is inscribed. Then, machines for sitting, for classifying, for illuminating, *machines-types*, problems of purification, of cleanliness, of clarification, before problems of poetry.[16]

There are three key words in this passage: *permanence*, *passion*, and *purification*. The first two are associated with art, the third one with the everyday object. For Le Corbusier the essential thing about art is its permanence, lastingness. As Banham has noted, Le Corbusier rejected the Futurist theory of the *caducità* or ephemerality of the work of art. He distinguishes works of art from works of technology and insists that only the latter are perishable.[17]

Against the products of reason Le Corbusier sets the products of passion, the passion of a creative man, a genius. The capacity of a work of art to provoke an emotion, qualitatively different from the pleasures of a beautiful object, for Le Corbusier lies in recognizing the passionate gesture of the artist who created it, in any time or place. He thus sets apart the artwork from the everyday object, the artist from all the other "producers" in society.

Finally, *L'art décoratif moderne* promotes cleanliness, purification. This notion reminds us once again of Loos, when in "The Plumbers," after commenting on America in a manner reminiscent of Duchamp[18] ("the most remarkable difference between Austria and America is the plumbing"), he goes on to say:

We don't really need art. We don't even have a culture of our own yet. This is where the state could come to the rescue. Instead of putting the cart before the horse, instead of spending money on art, let's try producing a culture. Let's put up baths next to the academies and employ bath attendants along with professors.

However, Loos's caustic and irreverent writings should be distinguished from the shock tactics of Dada. A comment made by Walter Benjamin in reference to Karl Kraus is applicable here to Loos, who predicted that in the twentieth century a single civilization would dominate the earth: "Satire is the only legitimate form of regional art." "The greatest type of satirist," continues Benjamin, "never had firmer grounds under his feet than amid a generation about to board tanks and put on gas masks, a mankind that has run out of tears but not of laughter."[19] Le Corbusier is a post–World War I figure, Loos a prewar one. While it is possible to establish relations between their work, a crucial question remains unanswered: how much does this demarcation line of the war cause them to be such different historical witnesses?

Faut-il brûler le Louvre?

The key to Le Corbusier's position on universal culture is to be found in his idea of the museum: "The true museum is the one that contains everything." Le Corbusier makes this comment in the context of his publication of the bidet. With this definition, however, the museum and the world become conflated with each other. Perhaps, then, Le Corbusier is not talking about museums after all, at least not in the literal sense, especially since, as we have seen, he is not suggesting that the bidet is an art object. In this respect, it is interesting to notice the way in which he twists his argument later, in *L'art décoratif d'aujourd'hui*, to talk about popular literature (*Je sais tout*, *Sciences et vie*, *Sciences et voyages*), cinema, newspapers, photography, and everything from the new culture industry that brings, as it were, the world into our living rooms.[20]

What makes the museum obsolete as a nineteenth-century accumulative institution is the mass media. Thus when Le Corbusier says the true museum should contain everything he is talking about an imaginary museum, a museum that comes into being with the new means of communication, something close to what Malraux will later call a "museum without walls."[21] "For a long time," says Le Corbusier in a document called "Lettre de Paris" conserved in the Fondation Le Corbusier, "painting had as its main objective the creation of documents. Those documents were the first books. . . . But a hundred years ago photography arrived, and thirty years ago, cinema. Documents are obtained today by an objective click, or by a film that rotates."[22]

Since everything is known to us through the media the problem is no longer that of mere documentation, but of the classification of information. The question of museums gives way, in Le Corbusier's argument, to that of classification. As he says of Ronéo file cabinets, "In the twentieth century we have learned to classify."

Malraux begins his "Museum without Walls" by reflecting on the transformation of the "work of art" in the context of the museum:

A Romanesque crucifix was not regarded by its contemporaries as a work of sculpture, nor Cimabue's *Madonna* as a picture. . . . Museums have imposed on the spectator a wholly new attitude toward the work of art. For they have tended to estrange the works they bring together from their original functions and to transform even portraits into pictures.[23]

The museum, Malraux argues, is the place where the work of art is constituted as such. Walter Benjamin takes somehow the reverse route when he writes:

By the absolute emphasis on its cult value, it [the work of art in prehistoric times] was, first and foremost, an instrument of magic. Only later did it come to be recognized as a work of art. In the same way today, by the absolute emphasis on its exhibition value, the work of art becomes a creation with entirely new functions, among which the one we are conscious of, the artistic function, later may be recognized as incidental.[24]

Mechanical reproduction, suggests Benjamin, qualitatively modifies the nature of art in modifying the relation of the public with it. Something of this order was understood by Le Corbusier when he wrote (in response to Marcel Temporal, who was heading a group of painters attempting to recuperate the fresco as an artistic medium):

The fresco wrote history upon the walls of churches and palaces, told stories of virtue or of vanity. There were no books—one read the frescoes. (In passing, a quick homage to Victor Hugo: "This will kill that."). . . . The poster is the modern fresco, and its place is in the street. It lasts not five centuries but two weeks, and then it is replaced.[25]

"L'art est partout dans la rue qui est le musée du présent et du passé," writes Le Corbusier in *L'art décoratif d'aujourd'hui*. The works in this imaginary "museum" are the poster, fashion, the industrial design object, advertising; they are the equivalent in our time of the madonnas, crucifixes, and frescoes of medieval society. That is to say, we do not perform in front of them an intellectual operation. We perceive them in a mood of relaxation that, among other things, allows advertising to become effective. They constitute the objects of a cult, the cult of consumption, as necessary to the reproduction of the social system as religion was in medieval times. They embody the values and myths of our society. As Adorno and Horkheimer have noted, they are not only the vehicles of an ideology, they are ideology itself.

Any critical reassessment of Le Corbusier's position in the light of a "critique of ideology" must take into account this structural condition of capitalist society, and the role of media and advertising. Particularly in the case of Le Corbusier, perhaps the first architect fully to understand the nature of the media (to put it bluntly, he published some fifty books), critical theories exclusively founded on the notion of traditional building production are insufficient. I shall return to this subject shortly: the architect as (re)producer. In the meantime, a pending question: if "the press and the book operate much more efficiently than Art relative to religious, moral, or political aims, what destiny is left to art in an industrial society?"

As we have seen, for Le Corbusier the everyday object, the industrial product, the engineer's construction were not works of art:

I discard, I discard. . . . My life isn't meant to preserve dead things. I discard Stevenson's locomotive. . . . I will discard everything, for my twenty-four hours must be productive, brilliantly productive. I will discard everything of the past, everything except that which still serves. Certain things serve forever: they are Art.[26]

With such a statement, Le Corbusier distinguishes himself from the avant-garde, understood as an attack on High Art. For him, permanence still differentiates the artwork from the everyday object, architecture from engineering, painting from posters. The artist as maker is set apart from the rest of producers in industrial society. The institution of art, its autonomy from everyday life, remains intact. Nor is Le Corbusier the quintessentially modernist figure we are accustomed to see portrayed in conventional histories. Perhaps the best evaluation is still Manfredo Tafuri's when, in his *Theories and History of Architecture*, he notes in passing that Le Corbusier did not accept the new industrial conditions as an external reality, did not relate to them as an "interpreter," but rather aspired to enter into them as a "producer."

Interpreters are those who perpetuate the figure of the *artist-magician*, in the Benjaminian definition, those who, faced by the "new nature of artificial things" to be used as raw material in their artistic work, remain anchored to the principle of mimesis. On the opposite side is the *artist-surgeon*, again in the Benjaminian sense, one who has understood that reproduction techniques create new conditions for the artist, the public, and the media of production. Instead of passively admiring the "equipment," they go behind it and use it.[27]

The Architect as (Re)producer

In his books and articles Le Corbusier borrows the rhetoric and techniques of persuasion of modern advertising for his own theoretical arguments and manipulates actual advertisements to incorporate his own vision, thus blurring the limits between text and publicity. He does this consciously, arguing that in this way persuasion is most effective: "*L'Esprit Nouveau*," he announces in the publicity brochure sent to industrialists, "is read calmly. You surprise your client into calmness, distance from business, and he listens to you because he doesn't know you are going to solicit him."

In obtaining advertising contracts Le Corbusier often reversed the usual procedure. Once he had incorporated images from industrial catalogues in his articles, or even published actual advertisements in the review, he would send the company a letter with a copy of *L'Esprit Nouveau* and request payment for the publicity the company was receiving. Of course, the request was not made so crudely, but rather wrapped up in Le Corbusier's flattering rhetoric: the product had been singled out as representative of the spirit of the times, and so forth.

The strategy was not always effective: "Les bagages Moynat thank *L'Esprit Nouveau*'s administration very much for the free publicity given to them in issues 11 and 13 . . . but we cannot commit ourselves for the moment to an advertising contract." In some cases, however, as with the company Innovation, Le Corbusier not only obtained an advertising contract for *L'Esprit Nouveau* but a commission to redesign and publish its catalogue. This type of commission, also pursued with other companies such as Ingersoll-Rand and Ronéo, was part of a wider project conceived by Le Corbusier as *Catalogues spéciaux de L'Esprit Nouveau*: "We have thus conceived a kind of publicity that is almost editorial, but it can only be applied—this is evident—to products whose fabrication and use are consistent with a certain *esprit nouveau*." (Note that it is not the product itself, its formal qualities, that count, but its fabrication and use.) "*L'Esprit Nouveau* itself comments on the product of the advertising firm, and, with respect to the clientele, this will certainly have an effectiveness that is far different from ordinary publicity."[28]

The company was to have a full page with a different text and illustration published in each issue of *L'Esprit Nouveau* for a year. At the end of the year, the twelve pages thus constituted would be printed "in an edition of 3,000 (or more) on fine paper, put together to form a brochure or catalogue called 'L'Esprit Nouveau'" that the advertising firm "will be able to distribute usefully to a certain segment of its clientele."

Innovation's first page of "editorial publicity" appeared in *L'Esprit Nouveau* 18. Instead of the conventional text of an Innovation catalogue—"An

Innovation armoire holds three times as much as an ordinary armoire. Makes order. Avoids unnecessary folds"—one reads, "Construction in series is necessary to setting up house. . . ." This is followed in *L'Esprit Nouveau* 19 by "To construct in series is to dedicate oneself to the pursuit of the element. . . . By analyzing the element one arrives at a standard. We must establish the standards of construction—windows, doors, plans, distribution, and all the interior mechanics that modern man requires for its comfort and hygiene." This tone seems to intensify progressively. A double page in *L'Esprit Nouveau* 20, laid out in the shape of an hour glass, starts with, "The war has shaken us out of our torpor. Taylorism has been spoken of and achieved." Throughout those pages specific references to Innovation products are practically nonexistent.

While this is not the place to attempt a complete analysis of these pages of publicity produced by Le Corbusier—an analysis, I should note in passing, that would prove very fruitful not only for an understanding of Le Corbusier's ideology, but also for tracing the source of certain of his architectural concepts such as the horizontal window—I shall try to relate this strategy of Le Corbusier's to contemporary advertising strategies.

In his book *The Making of Modern Advertising* Daniel Pope divides the history of advertising into three periods. The third one, the modern era, extends from 1920 to the present, and is defined as the "era of market segmentation." At this point the marketplace begins to be transformed from production for mass consumption—that is, for an undifferentiated group of consumers—to one of production for consumption in a stratified marketplace characterized by consumers organized into relatively well-defined subgroups. *L'Esprit Nouveau's* special catalogues fall clearly into this category. The audience becomes in this context the "product" to be sold to advertisers. Thus the contract with Innovation states, "Mr. Jeanneret will himself take responsibility for the writing of the text and the choice of images to accompany it, thereby furnishing you with a catalogue that can favorably influence your clientele and especially architects."[29]

Another publicity strategy employed by Le Corbusier includes the portrayal of his own work in actual advertisements, as often occurs in the *Almanach de l'architecture moderne* (the content of the *Almanach* was originally intended to be issue 29 of *L'Esprit Nouveau*, which never appeared). The image used in the text and in the advertisement is the same. Sometimes an image of a built work by the architect is placed in the advertisement of a company that has been involved in its construction (Summer, Euboolith, etc.), a strategy that clearly illustrates the previous point—publicity addressed to a targeted group, in this case architects.

Another dimension is added when the process is reversed, as happens with the Immeubles-Villas. The image in the *Almanach* text and in the advertisement is again the same. But since the Immeubles-Villas do not actually exist, their appearance in an advertisement confers on them a degree of legitimacy (beyond that which publishing already confers). The advertising context elides the realm of ideas with the world of facts. Something of the same order also happens when Le Corbusier associates himself with industrialists for his visionary projects. Le Corbusier, as Stanislaus von Moos has pointed out, tried to involve the Michelin tire company in the Plan Voisin for Paris. The plan was to have been called *Plan Michelin et Voisin du Centre de Paris* (the Michelin and Voisin Plan for the Center of Paris). In a letter to Michelin Le Corbusier wrote, "Through association of the name Michelin with our plan, the project will acquire considerable mass appeal. It will become possible to motivate public opinion in a much more fundamental way than would be possible through books, for example."[30] As this statement reveals, Le Corbusier's interest in industrial publicity was twofold: on the one hand, the industrialists were to provide economic support for his projects, editorial or otherwise; on the other, the association with such concerns would have a multiplying effect owing precisely to the reputation of their names and products within mass culture. Of course, the blurring of the limits between publicity and content in *L'Esprit Nouveau* was more effective not only for the advertised product but also for the dissemination of the review's theories. Every time its readers were confronted in another context with, for instance, a Ronéo advertisement, they would inevitably associate it with Le Corbusier's ideas.

      L'Esprit Nouveau was effectively used by Le Corbusier to publicize his own work. In the archives of the review in the Fondation, there is a box containing numerous letters from potential clients. These were readers of the magazine or visitors to the L'Esprit Nouveau pavilion in the Exposition des Arts Décoratifs. As Roberto Gabetti and Carlo del Olmo have noted, the pavilion was used by Le Corbusier not to launch the magazine but to attract a professional clientele.[31] Le Corbusier answered the letters he received, sending sketches and preliminary budgets and, in some cases, proposing an actual site. While this is a subject for detailed study, it is sufficient for our purposes to note that some readers of *L'Esprit Nouveau* became actual clients.

      When *L'Esprit Nouveau* ceased publication in 1925 ("Five years is a lot for a magazine," Le Corbusier declared, "one ought not to repeat oneself continuously. Others, younger people, will have younger ideas"), he emerged from the experience as an established architect. This maturation process was abetted by his production of the review and the nature of the audience it was reaching. Statistics included in a letter to the Ateliers Primavera, a subsidiary of the Printemps department store, in an effort to obtain an advertising contract, state that only 24.3% of *L'Esprit Nouveau's* subscribers were artists (painters and sculptors). The rest comprised "people occupying active positions in society." Architects, of course, were included in the latter category, together with doctors, lawyers, teachers, engineers, industrialists, and bankers. While these statistics are not entirely reliable—Le Corbusier also asserted that *L'Esprit Nouveau* had a circulation of 5,000 copies when the maximum ever reached was 3,500—his statement in the same letter that "*L'Esprit Nouveau* finds its most sympathetic response precisely in the active milieu of society" not only was a stratagem to sell *L'Esprit Nouveau* readership as a "product" to the Ateliers Primavera, but it also reveals Le Corbusier's relentless desire to integrate his work into the contemporary conditions of production. The largest group of subscribers was, as he claims, constituted by industrialists and bankers—31%; architects made up 8%.[32] Financing for the magazine, which it was Le Corbusier's responsibility to produce, also came largely from industrialists and bankers, many of Swiss origin.[33]

      Le Corbusier's understanding of the media also secured his review a place in the international architectural circuits. A map published in *L'Esprit Nouveau* 17 shows the distribution of subscribers by country of origin. Le Corbusier and Ozenfant even attempted at one point to come out with an English-language version of the review, but "L'affaire Américaine," as they themselves called the project, was never realized.[34] *L'Esprit Nouveau* was part of an exchange network with avant-garde magazines such as *MA, Stavba, De Stijl, Veshch/Gegenstand/Objet, Disk,* and others. Correspondence in the Fondation illuminates Le Corbusier's relations with El Lissitzky, Ilya Ehrenburg, Walter Gropius, László Moholy-Nagy, Theo van Doesburg, Karel Teige. Perhaps the most telling document in this respect, not only on a symbolic level, is a card Sigfried Giedion wrote to Le Corbusier in 1925 mentioning that he was preparing a book on modern architecture and that Moholy-Nagy had recommended that he visit Le Corbusier.

      We can already see in this the network of the avant-garde engaged in its own historical legitimation, something Giedion would carry out on full scale as the first "operative critic" of the modern movement.[35]

Le Corbusier between Modernity and Tradition

A drawing by Le Corbusier with the heading "Ronéo," found in the archives of *L'Esprit Nouveau*, provides the occasion for the last section of this essay. Le Corbusier appears to have been in the process of making a "Special Catalogue *L'Esprit Nouveau*" for the Ronéo company. What the drawing illustrates, however, is the famous Perret–Le Corbusier debate over the horizontal window, concerning which Bruno Reichlin has made an insightful analysis.[36] Perret maintained that the vertical window, the *porte-fenêtre*, "reproduces an impression of complete space" because it permits a view of the street, the garden, and the sky, giving a sense of perspectival depth. The horizontal window, on the other hand, diminishes one's perception and correct appreciation of the landscape. In fact, Perret argues, it cuts out precisely that which is most interesting.[37]

Perret expresses here with an exceptional clarity the authority of the traditional notion of representation within a realistic epistemology, representation defined as the subjective reproduction of an objective reality. In these terms, Le Corbusier's concept of the horizontal window, as well as other aspects of his work, undermines this concept of representation. Classical painting attempted to identify images with their models. Purist paintings, built up with shapes and images of recognizable objects—bottles, glasses, books, pipes, and so forth—eschew this identification, as Ozenfant and Jeanneret claim. In *La peinture moderne* they define the standard objects that they chose to represent in their paintings as "objects of the most perfect banality," which have "the advantage of a perfect readability." That is, they avoid being dispersed by their own allusiveness, by deviation of attention.

The terms of Le Corbusier's "pictorial frontality" have been read by Rosalind Krauss as threefold:

First, the object is registered as pure extension, as flat shape which never breaks rank with the picture's frontality to suggest a turning of one of its facets into depth. Second, the constellation of objects wedge together in that insistent continuity of edges which the Purists called *mariage de contours*. Third, color and texture are handled in a manner that calls attention to the inherent superficiality of these "secondary qualities"—so that distance or depth in the painting becomes no longer a matter of representing the space separating one object from another in the real world. Instead distance is transformed into a representation of the caesura between the appearance of the object and the object itself.[38]

Viewing a landscape through a window implies a separation. A window, any window, breaks the connection between being in a landscape and seeing it. Landscape becomes visual, and we depend on memory to know it as a tangible experience.[39] Le Corbusier's horizontal window works to put this condition, this caesura, in evidence.

Perret's window corresponds, as Reichlin has shown, to the traditional space of perspectival representation in Western art. Le Corbusier's window corresponds, I would argue, to the space of the camera. It is not by chance that Le Corbusier continues the polemic with Perret in an argument in *Précisions*, demonstrating "scientifically" that the horizontal window illuminates better, by relying on a photographer's chart that gives times of exposure.[40] Photography and film, based on single-point perspective, are "transparent" mediums; their derivation from the classical system of representation is obvious. But between perspective and photography there is an epistemological break. The point of view of photography is that of the camera, a mechanical eye. The painterly convention of perspective centers everything on the eye of the beholder and calls this appearance "reality." The camera—and more particularly the movie camera—implies that there is no center.

Using Walter Benjamin's metaphor one could conclude that Le Corbusier's architecture is the result of his positioning himself behind the camera.

But we are not referring now to these larger metaphorical implications: Le Corbusier as "producer" and not as "interpreter" of the industrial reality. Rather we intend a more literal reading, emphasizing the deliberate dispersal of the eye in Le Corbusier's villas of the twenties, effected through the promenade, together with the shrinkage of depth of the landscape outside the horizontal window—the architectural correlative of the space of the movie camera.

On this basis, may we therefore say that Perret's architecture falls within the humanist tradition and Le Corbusier's within the modernist? The following reflection stems from an observation by Kerry Shear on the paradoxical nature of the Ronéo drawing. While Le Corbusier intends by his drawing to illustrate the superiority of the horizontal window, in fact the intensity and detail with which he draws Perret's *porte-fenêtre*, in contrast to the sketchiness of the horizontal window, show it to be much more emotionally charged. Above all this may be seen in the way Le Corbusier draws the human figure in each. In the *porte-fenêtre*, a carefully drawn man holds open his window, recalling Perret's assertion that "a window is man himself, it accords with his outlines. . . . The vertical is the line of the upright human being, it is the line of life itself." In contrast, the diminutive man drawn in the horizontal window occupies a peripheral position; the window opens by sliding. Le Corbusier wrote in the *Almanach*, "fenêtre, élément type—élément mécanique type: nous avons serré de près le module anthropocentrique."

Whether Le Corbusier's work falls within the humanist or the modernist tradition cannot be answered conclusively here. Certainly he understood the crisis of values resulting from the introduction of reproduction into the processes of architecture. His work is precisely about the tension between a classical conception of the world and the shattering of this hierarchical order by the new processes of mass (re)production and the culture industry.

Notes

I have chosen to keep the word *publicité* in French in my title to avoid the loss that occurs in its translation into the English "publicity." The word in French, as in all Romance languages, means (1) advertising (methods and techniques), (2) advertisement, (3) publicity. The notion of publicity as used in this article embraces all these meanings. It is also consistent with its root in the word "public." In relation to Le Corbusier and *publicité*, see Stanislaus von Moos, *Le Corbusier: Elements of a Synthesis* (Cambridge: MIT Press, 1979), and his later article, "Standard und Elite. Le Corbusier, die Industrie und der Esprit Nouveau," in Tilmann Buddensieg and Henning Rogge, eds., *Die nützlichen Künste* (Berlin: Quadriga, 1981), pp. 306–323.

1. *L'Esprit Nouveau* was published in Paris between 1920 and 1925 by Le Corbusier and the French painter Amédée Ozenfant. Initially the editor of this magazine was the Dadaist poet Paul Dermée, but he was dismissed by number 4 amid a polemic among the editorial group that ended up in a court trial. Ozenfant would later write in his memoirs, "Dermée had gotten it into his head to make a Dada journal: we eliminated him." The subtitle of the magazine changed significantly with Dermée's dismissal, from *Revue internationale d'esthétique* to *Revue internationale de l'activité contemporaine*. This change implies a shift from "aesthetics," as a specialized field separate from everyday life, to "contemporary activity," which included not only painting, music, literature, and architecture, but also "lower" forms of art: theater, music hall entertainment, sports, cinema, and book design.

2. At the back of this "found object," the child's school notebook, Le Corbusier wrote: "Ceci est imprimé sur les cahiers des écoles de France/C'est la géométrie/La géométrie est notre langage/C'est notre moyen de mesure et d'expression/La géométrie est la base." A fragment of this image was to find its way into "Nature and Creation" (*L'Esprit Nouveau* 19), an article by Ozenfant and Le Corbusier, later reprinted in *La peinture moderne* (1925). The complete image appears again in *Urbanisme* (1925), reproducing the above comment. The illustrations of an article in *The Autocar*, called "The Harmony of Outline," were trans-

planted into *L'Esprit Nouveau* in the form of a photo essay called "Evolution des formes de l'automobile" (*L'Esprit Nouveau* 13).

3. The content of these books was first published as a series of articles in *L'Esprit Nouveau*, with the exception of the chapter "Architecture ou révolution," which was added to *Vers une architecture*. The *Almanach de l'architecture moderne* was supposed to have been number 29 of *L'Esprit Nouveau*, an issue entirely devoted to architecture, but it never appeared.

4. There is never only one reading in Le Corbusier's work. The Rateau ventilator can also be interpreted as a spiral, one of the images that obsesses Le Corbusier throughout his life, and that in modern psychology is bound to the process of individuation. The spiral may be seen as the expression of a path that goes from life to death to reenter life The renaissance of man (of the architect) is possible through the death of a part of his previous being. "Architecture or Revolution" could from this point of view also be read as initiating a spiritual-cultural rebirth. Without exhausting the complex significance of the spiral, one might also mention the myth of Daedalus, builder of the labyrinth: "d'après une tradition antique il aurait été capable de tendre un fil à travers un coquille de limaçon." Karl Kerenyi, *Labyrinth-Studien* (Zurich: Rhein-Verlag, 1950), p. 13.

5. Reyner Banham, *A Concrete Atlantis: U.S. Industrial Building and European Modern Architecture* (Cambridge: MIT Press, 1986), p. 11. In addition to the sources mentioned by Banham, it should be noted that Theo van Doesburg borrowed some images of silos from *L'Esprit Nouveau* for publication in *De Stijl* 4 and 6 (1921). Le Corbusier and Ozenfant wrote to van Doesburg reprimanding him for not crediting *L'Esprit Nouveau* as the source of the material. The same photographs of the silos reappeared in Kassak and Moholy-Nagy's *Uj Müveszek Könyve* (Vienna; republished in Berlin as *Buch neuer Künstler*, 1922) and afterward in *MA* (nos. 3–6, 1923). See Gladys C. Fabre, "The Modern Spirit in Figurative Painting: From Modernist Iconography to a Modernist Conception of the Work of Art," in *Léger et l'esprit moderne* (Paris: Musée d'Art Moderne de la Ville de Paris, 1982), pp. 99–100.

6. Max Horkheimer and Theodor Adorno, *Dialectic of Enlightenment* (New York: Seabury Press, 1972). See esp. the chapter "The Culture Industry." Also see Sergio Moravia, *Adorno e la teoria critica della società* (Florence, 1974), pp. 33–37.

7. Cf. Marie-Odile Briot, "L'Esprit Nouveau and Its View of the Sciences," in *Léger et l'esprit moderne*, p. 62.

8. Stephen Kern, *The Culture of Time and Space: 1880–1918* (Cambridge: Harvard University Press, 1983), p. 309.

9. "At about the same time that serious artists were discovering in the industrial landscape new religious symbols, businessmen were learning about the power of advertising. To stave off the perils of overproduction, their advertising agencies turned to machine age imagery to stimulate consumption." Alan Trachtenberg, "The Art and Design of the Machine Age," *New York Times Magazine*, September 21, 1986.

10. The term "machine age" was coined in 1927 with the exhibition organized by the *Little Review* in New York and is hardly adequate to characterize the artistic practices of the earlier part of the twentieth century in Europe. Critics interested in sustaining the myth of the "modern movement" as an autonomous artistic practice are those who under labels such as "machine age" put together such different attitudes toward the industrial reality as, for instance, the Futurist, the Dadaist, and Le Corbusier's. The differences, however, are more striking than the similarities. While Le Corbusier is showing airplanes, for instance, he is talking about mass-production houses. It is important to note how much airplanes were part of the popular imagination, occupying vast pages in the illustrated newspapers. Le Corbusier is deploying a well-known publicity technique: grabbing the attention of readers through their eyes in order to direct them, then, to the important matter. The Futurists, on the other hand, were indifferent to the processes of industrialization.

11. Le Corbusier, *L'art décoratif d'aujourd'hui* (Paris: Editions Crès, 1925), p. 23.

12. Abraham Moles, in his *Sociodynamique de la culture* (Paris and The Hague: Mouton, 1967), notes: "The role of culture is to provide the individual with a screen of concepts in which he projects his perceptions of the exterior world. This conceptual screen had in traditional culture a rational reticular structure, organized in an almost geometrical fashion . . . we knew how to place new concepts with reference to old ones. Modern culture, mosaic culture, offers us a screen which is like a series of fibers glued together at random. This

screen is established by the submersion of the individual in a flux of disparate messages, with no hierarchies of principles: he knows everything about everything; the structure of his thought is extremely reduced." Le Corbusier's constant attempts to classify his knowledge do not exempt his work from this cultural condition described by Moles, but rather make it one of its possible manifestations. The conventionality with which Le Corbusier constructs the table of contents in his books, in an almost nineteenth-century fashion, stands dramatically in opposition to their actual content, which is drawn from all kinds of sources of information and manifested according to the new "visual thinking" strongly indebted to the new condition of printed mass-information.

13. "The problem I address . . . is not what modernism 'really was,' but rather how it was perceived retrospectively, what dominant values and knowledge it carried, and how it functioned ideologically and culturally after World War II. It is a specific image of modernism that has become the bone of contention for the postmoderns, and that image has to be reconstructed if we want to understand postmodernism's problematic relationship to the modernist tradition and its claims to difference." Andreas Huyssen, "Mapping the Postmodern," *New German Critique* 33 (1984), p. 13. The usual equation of the avant-garde with "modernism" is part of this received view. The "ism" in this sense is particularly telling—it reduces everything to a style. Against this heritage we should indeed try to understand the specificity of the different projects that fall within the modern period—or perform, in Manfredo Tafuri's words, "a thorough investigation of whether it is still legitimate to speak of a Modern Movement as a monolithic corpus of ideas, poetics and linguistic traditions." Manfredo Tafuri, *Theories and History of Architecture* (1969; New York: Harper and Row, 1980), p. 2.

14. Peter Bürger, *Theory of The Avant-Garde* (Minneapolis: University of Minnesota Press, 1984), p. 52. Burger also remarks how easily Duchamp's gesture is consumed: "It is obvious that this kind of provocation cannot be repeated indefinitely: here, it is the idea that the individual is the subject of artistic creation. Once the signed bottle drier has been accepted as an object that deserves a place in a museum, the provocation no longer provokes, it turns into its opposite . . . it does not denounce the art market but adapts to it." Manfredo Tafuri also gives priority to the question of architecture as an institution. He writes: "One cannot 'anticipate' a class architecture; what is possible is the introduction of class criticism into architecture. . . . Any attempt to overthrow the institution, the discipline, with the most exasperated rejections or the most paradoxical ironies—let us learn from Dada and Surrealism—is bound to see itself turned into a positive contribution, into a 'constructive' avant-garde, into an ideology all the more positive as it is dramatically critical and self-critical." *Theories and History of Architecture*, note to the second (Italian) edition. See also, in this regard, Lionello Venturi, *History of Art Criticism* (New York: Dutton, 1964).

15. Le Corbusier, *L'art décoratif d'aujourd'hui*, p. 57.

16. Ibid., p. 77.

17. Reyner Banham, *Theory and Design in the First Machine Age* (New York: Praeger, 1978), p. 250.

18. I am referring to the comment, "The only works of art America has created are its installations and its bridges," in *The Blind Man*, 2 (1917).

19. Walter Benjamin, "Karl Kraus," in *Reflections* (New York: Harcourt Brace Jovanovich, 1979), p. 260.

20. Le Corbusier, *L'art décoratif d'aujourd'hui*, p. 128.

21. André Malraux, "The Museum without Walls," in *The Voices of Silence* (Garden City, N.Y.: Doubleday, 1953).

22. "Lettre de Paris," undated manuscript, Fondation Le Corbusier, A1(16). The document is part of the *L'Esprit Nouveau* archives. The argument is so close to that of *L'art décoratif d'aujourd'hui* as to suggest a 1924–1925 date.

23. Malraux, "The Museum without Walls," pp. 13–14.

24. Walter Benjamin, "The Work of Art in the Age of Its Mechanical Reproduction," in *Illuminations* (New York: Schocken Books, 1969), p. 225.

25. "Fresque," *L'Esprit Nouveau* 19. The posters that Le Corbusier was admiring were those of Cassandre. However, he did not know at the time, or did not acknowledge, their authorship. Instead, he wrote to the company the posters were advertising, Le Boucheron, in an effort to obtain a publicity contract for *L'Esprit Nouveau*. See letters of June 6 and 14, 1924, in Fondation Le Corbusier, Al (17). Of course, Cassandre's posters were not "Art" for Le

Corbusier, but one more instance of the beautiful objects that industrialized everyday life was producing.

26. Le Corbusier, *L'art décoratif d'aujourd'hui*, p. 182.

27. Benjamin studies film as an example of an art in which the reproduction techniques confer a new condition on the artist, the public, and the media of production. He writes: "The magician and the surgeon behave respectively like the painter and the operator. The painter keeps, in his work, a natural distance from what he is given, while the operator penetrates deeply into the texture of the data. . . . [The image] of the painter is total, that of the operator is multifragmented, and its parts are rearranged according to a new law. Therefore the cinematic representation of reality is vastly more meaningful for the modern man because, precisely on the basis of its intense penetration through the equipment, it offers him that aspect free from the equipment, that he can legitimately ask from the work of art." "The Work of Art in the Age of Its Mechanical Reproduction," p. 233. Tafuri finds in this passage a principle by which to identify the distinctive features of the twentieth-century avant-gardes. It is interesting to note that he includes Marcel Duchamp among those who perpetuate the figure of the artist-magician. *Theories and History of Architecture*, p. 32.

28. Fondation Le Corbusier, A1 (7), 194.

29. Fondation Le Corbusier, A1 (17), 1.

30. Stanislaus von Moos, "Urbanism and Transcultural Exchanges, 1910–1935: A Survey," in H. Allen Brooks, ed., *The Le Corbusier Archive*, vol. 10 (New York: Garland, 1983), p. xiii.

31. Fondation Le Corbusier, A1 (5). See also Roberto Gabetti and Carlo del Olmo, *Le Corbusier e L'Esprit Nouveau* (Turin: Einaudi, 1975), pp. 215–225.

32. Fondation Le Corbusier, A1 (10).

33. Fondation Le Corbusier, A1 (18). See also Gabetti and del Olmo, *Le Corbusier e L'Esprit Nouveau*, pp. 215–225.

34. Fondation Le Corbusier, A1 (17), 105.

35. "What is normally meant by 'operative criticism' is an analysis of architecture (or of the arts in general) that, instead of an abstract survey, has as its objective the planning of a precise poetical tendency, anticipated in its structure and derived from historical analyses programmatically distorted and finalized." Manfredo Tafuri, *Theories and History of Architecture*, p. 141. The relations between "operative criticism" and a "consumerist" cultural situation are clear: differences are canceled by the process of labeling, and the product in turn becomes marketable.

36. Bruno Reichlin, "The Pros and Cons of the Horizontal Window," *Daidalos* 13 (1984). For the debate between Le Corbusier and Perret, see *Paris Journal*, December 1, December 14, and December 28, 1923, in Fondation Le Corbusier.

37. Marcel Zahar, *Auguste Perret* (Paris: Vincent Fréal, 1959).

38. Rosalind Krauss, "Léger, Le Corbusier and Purism," in *Artforum*, April 1972, pp. 52–53.

39. For insightful comments on the nature of the "window" and "landscape," see Raoul Bunschoten, "Wor(l)ds of Daniel Libeskind," *AA Files* 10 (Autumn 1985), pp. 79–84.

40. Le Corbusier, *Précisions sur un état présent de l'architecture et de l'urbanisme* (Paris: Editions Crès, 1930), p. 74.

Catherine Ingraham **"The Burdens of Linearity: Donkey Urbanism"** Paper presented 1988; published in

Strategies in Architectural Thinking, ed. John Whiteman, Jeffrey Kipnis, and Richard

Burdett (Cambridge: MIT Press, 1992); revised for this anthology

In September 1988 a group conferred at the Chicago Institute for Architecture and Urbanism to discuss the current state of architectural theory through presentations of theoretical works in process. The group comprised academics, all of a generation born around 1950, many loosely associated with the journal *Assemblage,* and all self-declared "theorists" as distinct from critics or historians or practicing architects who occasionally write. The event put a point to a repositioning of architectural theory relative to architectural practice and of architecture relative to poststructuralist thought, emergent for several years, whose importance was threefold.[1]

First was the shift from the linguistics- and semiotics-based problematic dominant in the 1970s to new affinities with cultural criticism, including concerns with textual strategies, constructions of subjectivity and gender, power and property, geopolitics, and other themes that were already part of the general post-structuralist repertoire but whose spatial dimension was now foregrounded. This entailed, second, that the emphasis of the earlier theory—much of it written by practicing architects—on the production of architectural objects should give way to an emphasis on the production of architecture as a *subject* of knowledge. While the former aimed to visibly lay bare architecture's productive procedures, the latter revealed the unintended presumptions that architectural techniques alternately enabled or tried to remove from the possibility of thinking. The theorization of the internal, autonomous workings of architecture—whose concerns are mainly synchronic, synthetic, and projective—was not abandoned so much as folded into various discourses of context and exteriority, recalibrated according to what was sayable or thinkable in the idiolects of deconstruction, psychoanalysis, critical theory, and
❚ *see* x–xii ❚ other imported systems. These systems were not merely yoked together with architecture. Rather, something of a shift of level (as much as perspective) took place in which, third, architecture's specific forms, operations, and practices could now more clearly be seen as producing concepts whose ultimate horizon of effect lay outside of architecture "proper," in a more general sociocultural field. This is not to deny that earlier theoretical activities had contextualized their material. But by 1988 different devices for situating architecture were available, and architecture theory deployed them with renewed energy.

This dialectical reversal of interiority and exteriority was a fruitful and necessary modulation of previous trends in architecture theory and its relation to practice, which had tended to understand theory as providing methods and motives for architectural design (and whose more directly instrumental intentions seemed to have converged with Reagonomics to produce a "Po-Mo" building boom). What the reversal meant was that, since the assimilation and transcoding of terms and concepts from other fields, and the management of those fields' disciplinary histories along with architecture's own, require quite different operations than the formulation of a design theory, henceforth architecture theory need not necessarily achieve or even intend the sort of synthesis required by the realization of a building (as it had, for the most part, in the 1970s), even if such a synthesis was crucial to preserving or reconstructing the history of the discipline or might be developed as a resource for some future practice. This new activity of theory demanded not new buildings, but the invention of altogether new techniques for thinking architectural concepts and discursive relations.

Such is the case with Catherine Ingraham's "The Burdens of Linearity"—a meditation on the marks made by humans but also by animals, and a criticism of received forms of reason—which branches out from her ongoing interest in the issue of the proper and power. For, if the theme of the proper and its inflections, property and propriety, had already been part of the general poststructuralist repertoire, that of linearity and its corollaries had not.[2] And if the transcoding of the first into architecture required an activity of comparing and exchanging the conceptual possibilities from one preexisting code to another, the development of the theme of linearity produced a new concept not controlled or even recognized by any of the "imported" discourses alone. Linearity is a figure that permits one discourse to interpret the other, opening up Le Corbusier's commitment to rectitude and rationality to Claude Lévi-Strauss's perceptions of the relations between writing, architecture, and exploitation and both to Jacques Derrida's argument that culture in itself is an act of suppression, all of which Ingraham construes as an inescapable condition of architecture—its inscription-construction of culture through labor and reproduction.

Such impracticalities of line as errant paths and wavy navigations can then be thought as traverses *within* architecture that infiltrate the clean, articulate, mensurable space of orthogonal thought with something unwieldy, speechless, animal. It is not a matter of simply switching the improper for the proper, anarchy for rightness. The animal escapes the eminently proper and civilized orthogonal space by wandering through it, leaving outlines of its subaltern dumbness. Ingraham would later link this to the way architecture generally manages the threat of undifferentiated space (and thought) to absorb all morphological and subjective specificity, to obliterate our sense of place in the world. "Architecture 'animalizes' space by maintaining its distinctness. It acts as animal, as repository of the classifiable. Architecture thus makes culture much as the animal makes it—by filling in, with classifiable differences, the place of the inert, the speechless. It gives meaningful materiality to the speechless, which might also be a kind of repression of the 'life' of a material in order to give it certain form."[3]

Notes

A later version of this essay was published as chapter 3 in Catherine Ingraham, *Architecture and the Burdens of Linearity* (New Haven: Yale University Press, 1998).

1. The incipient institutionalization of architecture theory was signaled shortly afterward by the Symposium on Architectural Theory and Practice, Museum of Modern Art, New York, April 1990, with Jennifer Bloomer, Beatriz Colomina, Michael Hays, Catherine Ingraham, Jeffrey Kipnis, Robert Somol, John Whiteman, and Mark Wigley.

2. Ingraham addressed the theme of the proper and its inflections in an essay of the same year, "The Faults of Architecture: Troping the Proper," *Assemblage* 7 (October 1988).

3. Catherine Ingraham, "Animals 2: The Problem of Distinction," *Assemblage* 14 (April 1991), p. 28.

I refer in this essay to three overworked (by critics) and, for me, strangely inter-twined pieces of writing: the first piece is Claude Lévi-Strauss's "A Writing Lesson,"[1] which I read through the second, Jacques Derrida's commentary on that essay in "The Violence of the Letter";[2] and the third, the first chapter of *The City of Tomorrow*[3] by Le Corbusier.

Derrida's critique of Lévi-Strauss's writing lesson is an exemplary[4] critical commentary on the problem of writing and the limitations of structuralist analysis. And Le Corbusier's writings are, in their own way, exemplary modernist polemics. However, none of these texts are exemplary in any sense that would allow me to connect them to each other in the way I have in mind. In other words, even though I am playing, in a less than exemplary way, Derrida's own (exemplary) game by linking these texts through their oddness, the result is somewhat ancillary to the range of Derrida's concerns. The result only concerns certain internal debates in architecture. I am referring to Le Corbusier's and Derrida's (and implicitly, Lévi-Strauss's) interest in lines and linearity; and to Le Corbusier's and Lévi-Strauss's (and implicitly Derrida's) curious encounters with "beasts of burden"—specifically mules and donkeys.

Lines and beasts occupy fundamentally different orders—the inanimate versus the animate is only the most obvious. And yet both Lévi-Strauss and Le Corbusier, and in a different way Derrida, use the inscription (or failed inscription) of lines on the one hand, and the antics of beasts on the other, to speak of nature, culture, rationality, ethnology, and metaphysics. Just as the donkey in *The City of Tomorrow* is a recurrent figure of classical resistance to modernity, of ornamental fruh-fruhness and dilatory historicism, so the mule in "A Writing Lesson" induces a certain confusion and humiliation—a waywardness—that opens into a meditation on the origins of writing, empires and architecture. Derrida's critique of Lévi-Strauss's essay remarks, in turn, on the curious paraphernalia of Lévi-Strauss's ethnographic journey into the Brazilian jungle, the (im)possibility of a "path" (made by oxen, mules and men), ruined lines of communication (fallen telegraph lines), and inscriptionality and violence.

I am reminded here of at least two other taxonomies where things radically different become things alike (a contamination through proximity): Emerson's obsession in his famous essay "Nature" with the phenomena of "language, sleep, madness, dreams, beasts [and] sex"[5] and Borges's "Chinese Encyclopedia" cited by Foucault at the beginning of *The Order of Things* in which animals "drawn with a very fine camelhair brush" are listed next to animals "innumerable," and animals "belonging to the Emperor," "stray dogs," "et cetera."[6] These lists (series) are provocative because they suggest, indeed remark exquisitely upon, the possibility/inevitability of everything being brought into relation with everything else—although this is, of course, both a wonderful and terrible dream. Taxonomies are neither endless or unfixed: an infinite number of relations are hypothetically possible but only a few, very specific, connections are ever actually made. Taxonomies are only as persuasive as the institutional, cultural, linguistic, conventions that frame them—although here, especially in Borges, there is some kind of fragile interplay going on between taxonomic conventions themselves (alphabetic, numeric).

So what is the framework here? What permits a connection between lines and beasts in Derrida's, Lévi-Strauss's and Le Corbusier's texts? Neither a strictly historical nor scientific tradition would put lines and beasts on the same list. A certain critical license granted by poststructural critical theory might permit one, in general, to construct homologous worlds where the lines made by certain beasts (in this case, mules and donkeys) on the landscape—the paths they make/follow, the direction they take, the marks/spoor they leave behind as they navigate the terrain, their willingness or stubbornness in all this—are intimately and significantly related to the lines (the marks) that one might draw or write or otherwise inscribe on paper and/or the lines and paths inscribed on a landscape by a building, more precisely, by architecture.[7] But it takes neither a special "critical license" nor a revisionist history to trace bestial paths back to the layout of cities. It is easy to forget that the track of the car, another kind of beast, is only about one hundred years old (1885), whereas the track of the beast is, well, extremely old. The connection between this bestial urbanism and "modern urbanism"—and the implications for lines and linearity in architecture— is, of course, what directly concerns, and is therefore authorized by, Le Corbusier himself.

Le Corbusier argues that orthogonality, the "orthogonal state of mind," best expresses the spirit of the modern age. And he opposes the "regulating line" of humankind—orthogonal, geometric, measured (architectural, urbanistic)—to the path of the pack-donkey. Le Corbusier's remarks are easily recalled:

Man walks in a straight line because he has a goal and knows where he is going; he has made up his mind to reach some particular place and he goes straight to it. The pack-donkey meanders along, meditates a little in his scatter-brained and distracted fashion, he zigzags in order to avoid the larger stones, or to ease the climb, or to gain a little shade; he takes the line of least resistance.[8]

Man thinks only of his goal. The pack-donkey thinks only of what will save him trouble. "The Pack-Donkey's Way," Corbusier goes on, "is responsible for the plan of every continental city."[9]

According to Corbusier's mytho-poetical account of the history of the city, covered wagons of an invading population "lumbered along at the mercy of bumps and hollows, of rocks or mire [and] in this way were born roads and tracks." These early tracks are made according to a "donkey's idea" of how to move from one point to another. Along these tracks houses are "planted" and eventually these houses are enclosed by city walls and gates. "Five centuries later another larger enclosure is built, and five centuries later still a third yet greater." The great cities, built according to this first track heedlessly traced out on an inhospitable land-scape, have a multitude of small connective capillaries and, in order to cure the prob-lems of a city suffocated by these intersecting capillaries, Le Corbusier recommends "surgery"—cutting out central corridors (arteries) so the "bodily fluids" of the cities can flow. The straight line that cuts through the congestion of the "Pack-Donkey's Way" is, according to Le Corbusier, "a positive deed, the result of self-mastery. It is sane and noble."[10]

    The pack-donkey recurs as a motif throughout *The City of Tomor-row*; in a later account of "nature" whose material body is chaotic (the beast) but whose spirit is orderly (human rationality); again in an account of the human body as a "fragmentary and arbitrary shape" but a pure and orderly idea; in an account of nations "overcoming their animal existence"; in an account of the supremacy of orthogonality[11] and so on. And the pack-donkey also frequents *Towards a New Architec-ture*, although it remains unnamed, subsumed under the order of the "bestial." The pack-donkey is the figure, in these (and other) fables, of a disorderly nature, of the chaotic and diseased body, of a barbaric architectural and urban past. The don-key makes the "ruinous, difficult and dangerous curve of animality," and typifies the "looseness and lack of concentration" of human beings in distraction, that is, the primitive/non-modern human being. The donkey in all of these guises threatens the triumph of geometry, an urbanism and an architecture of geometry, of positive action, of overcoming and ascending to power (nationhood), of sanity, nobility and self-mastery.

    The "orthogonality" that Le Corbusier polemicizes in these parts of *The City of Tomorrow* and *Towards A New Architecture*[12] does not refer simply to the rectilinearity that one finds, almost, in Corbusier's Unité d'Habitation, although Cor-busier remarks extensively on the "rightness" of the right angle. According to Le Corbusier, the "orthogonal state of mind," which defines modern urbanism/archi-tecture for Le Corbusier,[13] governs all urbanistic/architectural thought and action that is devoted to self-mastery and the "rational" line (which is not necessarily straight in a literal or graphic sense, although always straight in an ideological sense). Orthogonality is a theory about how to win architecture and the city away from the irrational forces arrayed against them.[14] It extends beyond the (merely) rectilinear to any form that is erected against the monstrous, speechless, wandering, pathless incoherence of the genealogical "line" itself, the history of the city and architecture itself.[15] Orthogonality keeps culture hegemonically superior to nature and attempts to obliterate the trace of nature in culture. The orthogonal/non-orthogonal opposi-tion is at work everywhere in Le Corbusier's urbanistic and architectural projects—indeed, one might say that it is operative in all urbanism and architecture. The Modu-lor, in particular, in spite of its oddly contortionist posture, is the Corbusian figure of resistance to the collapse of this opposition and it stands opposed to the misbehav-ing donkey.[16]

    The beast of burden, of course, must oppose orthogonality in order to give orthogonality its force—at least in this cartoon version of the pack-donkey and the founding of urban culture. But the cartoon only makes sense if one can first imagine a proper path from which the donkey has deviated, and not just a proper path but an economy and organization of labor, an human economy within which the beast is structured as a cultural, rather than a natural (or wild) entity. The covert manner in which the beast of burden (the donkey) also stands as an oblique measure of human work,[17] transgression and laziness, while retaining all the faults of an animal of "nature"—"instinctive" rather than "rational" motivations, indirec-tion, enigmatic behavior, apparent mindlessness and so on—complicates the orthog-onal/non-orthogonal opposition immeasurably. The allegorical collapse of the donkey into the transgressive (human) body and, simultaneously, Le Corbusier's repeated surgeries, by which the animal body is separated from the mind and spirit in the modern city, reiterate an ancient nature/culture drama. Whether this drama is between two urbanisms, the orthogonal (proper) and the non-orthogonal (improper), or between a "natural" production (beast/donkey) and a "cultural" production (line/architecture), its power is to forestall the collapse of the division between the proper and the improper, the cultural and the natural.[18]

In the early version of this essay, the distinction between the ideology of orthogonality in urbanism and this ideology in architecture—a distinction animated by Le Corbusier in, on the one hand, The City of Tomorrow and, on the other, in Towards a New Architecture—did not seem particularly significant. The same words—particularly the words "mastery" and "uprightness"—underwrite both texts. Le Corbusier also repeatedly unites the "house" and the "town." But now the issue seems more difficult. The "dangerous curve" of the animal does not seem to be a problem in the numerous architectural examples offered by Le Corbusier (and in his own work)—indeed, the curve is often evidence of the "mathematical" and the "rhythmic." And, of course, geometry itself is not only made up of right angles. At the same time, modern architecture, along with modern urbanism, privileges the geometry of the right angle and, also, the *ethos* of geometry is the *ethos* of the right angle. And, in another way, modern urbanism and architecture meet each other—as geometric, right-angled, linear practices—inside the projective drawing system that connects the plan and the elevation.[19] This encounter is less the historical "invention" of the projective drawing system itself than the coalescence of geometry and philosophy in what Derrida calls "Cartesian Intellectualism." Donkey urbanism, or donkey architecture, is not merely curved, it is swerved. That is, it deviates (and suffers the consequences of deviance) from a system of production that allows houses (architecture) and towns (urbanism) to be jointly conceived and represented. "It" is neither wholly urbanistic nor wholly architectural in the traditional sense. One of the (felt) powers of this donkey*ism* is the power to introduce the confusing force of distraction into the generation, the inscription, of either an urbanistic or architectural scheme/body of thought. Certainly "distraction," considered urbanistically, would be different from architectural distraction,[20] but for the moment I want to bring the donkey to a kind of pause at this idea of the "distracted."

Because donkey urbanism/architecture depends on the (prior) possibility of representing the city graphically (as gridded, for example)—and the possibility of bringing the urban and the architectural together by means of the graphic system of projection—what Le Corbusier notices, when he notices the pack-donkey "state" of the ancient city, is not a pure history of the city (as something that evolved through an "animal state"). He sees, in a sense, through a mass of lines already criss-crossing and crossing his vision (because he is, after all, an architect). But to help me explain this kind of "seeing" I need to branch off from the linear *graphics* of projection to another *graphics*, mainly, writing. Bluntly, Le Corbusier's writing about urbanism/architecture is a paragon of heedlessness, lack of self-mastery, lack of direction. This is true generally—all writing twists out of the straight line that is its graphic expression into the non-straight line of interpretation and signification.[21] And it is true specifically—The City of Tomorrow and Towards a New Architecture thematize the opposition between the straight and the crooked so their failure, as writing, to (pretend to) "act rationally" is particularly significant. This is a tricky point because it relies on a "reading" of Le Corbusier that emanates from the donkey side of the equation—a donkey reading. In the chapter "Eyes Which Do Not See," with the subheading "I: Liners," Le Corbusier proposes the ocean liner as a machine of functional purity, free from specious decoration and ornament. But we could easily, following certain rules of the game—it would be a child's game—hear the confusion of the "eye" and the "I" in order to swerve "I: Liners" into "eye-liner"—"eyes which do not see" because they have too much ornament, eye-liner, on them—or "I Liners," a parody of the linings of the self and authorial identity. But we wouldn't even have to play this, perhaps too linguistically torqued, game in order to see that Le Corbusier's "seeing" is already laden with massive preconceptions, summarized by all the attendant problematic oppositions: ornament/structure, straight/crooked, proper/improper, donkey/line, etc. We could ask, for example, what it means for Le Corbusier to talk about straight lines since no lines, except the "ideal" ones, which I will discuss shortly, are absolutely straight. Does Le Corbusier really mean "relatively straight lines"? And exactly how far off the true is a straight line before it becomes a donkey line? Two degrees? Ten degrees? Not to mention the usual stuff, of course, about mastery, master planning, self-mastery—all of which are defunct, but still amazingly operative, terms of totalization.

But the line and the donkey of Le Corbusier's text are only half the story. The other half is the anthropologist and the mule. Genetically speaking, mules are the cross (point of intersection) of a horse mating with a donkey. The horse, through the discipline of dressage as well as lesser disciplines, is, at least mythologically, capable of being accurately directed by reins held in human hands. Mules, although often ridden, are bred for the strength and indirect guidance of the pack animal (who is frequently driven rather than ridden). Further, mules cannot reproduce their own kind and must be produced over and over again by the pairing between the two other species. The move from the donkey of Le Corbusier's text to the mule of Lévi-Strauss's text may seem slight (in genetic terms); indeed, it is very slight on one level. Both Le Corbusier and Lévi-Strauss use the movements of these animals as a counterpoint to another discourse about lines. As we have seen in Le Corbusier's text, this discourse on lines had to do with the "straightness" of modernity versus the "crookedness" of the past; a straight urbanism versus a bent urbanism. And yet, on another level, the move from the donkey to the mule is as drastic and as absolute as the move from the animal as a piece of nature to the animal as a piece of culture. Donkeys and mules, in this sense, are as different from each other as horses and cars. One reproduces. The other is produced. As allegorical figures that oppose the line, it matters that a mule opposes the line in the same way a circle opposes a line—as one construction opposing another—whereas a donkey opposes a line, say, in the way a plant opposes a line—as something "natural" opposes something "artificial." But we must double back again because these words, these symmetries, are misleading. What would it mean, in the context of this discussion, to talk about the difference between things that reproduce—donkeys and humans—and things that are produced—mules and lines?[22]

Claude Lévi-Strauss, like Le Corbusier, is concerned with reflecting on (and upsetting) a genealogy, specifically, the origin of writing, empires and architecture. The line of descent that Lévi-Strauss claims for writing in "A Writing Lesson" ignores, according to Jacques Derrida's subsequent critique, the "writing" (colloquial writing, empires, and architecture) that begins at the same moment as the beginning of culture. Derrida does not correct Lévi-Strauss in favor of another point of origin, another history, for writing. Instead, as we know, Derrida characterizes "writing," and, in related but different ways, "history," as *originless*—as *multioriginaled*. Derrida's argument focuses on Lévi-Strauss's belief that there are cultures with writing and cultures without writing and that cultures without writing are somehow "innocent," uncorrupted by the exploitation and violence that he (Lévi-Strauss) thinks writing inaugurates. Writing, cities, architecture are re-situated in Derrida's critique as multiple genealogies and grammatologies that bend around and nest within each other, producing horizon lines here and there that provisionally shape the adventuresome path of knowledge.[23]

I want to consider Lévi-Strauss's essay only briefly. At the beginning of his short piece, "The Writing Lesson," it appears that Lévi-Strauss and his fellow anthropologists cannot take the usual *picada*, the path in the forest, because the oxen carrying gifts for the natives cannot get through the heavy underbrush. The expedition is thus forced to take a route over the plateau, a route unfamiliar even to Lévi-Strauss's native guides, with the result that the whole expedition gets lost in the bush somewhere around the fifth paragraph of the account. After a crisis of authority having to do with the chief's inability to provide his people with direction and food, the Indians reorient themselves and the expedition pushes on to their rendezvous. Lévi-Strauss and his men effect their exchanges, count about seventy-five Indians gathered (since the purpose of his expedition in the first place was to take a census of the Indian population) and leave as quickly as possible. The situation directly after the exchange of goods is, as Lévi-Strauss remarks, always fraught with danger. However, it turns out that the danger for Lévi-Strauss does not lie in the latent violence of the "natives" but in the recalcitrance of his mule. Shortly after leaving the gathering Lévi-Strauss somehow finds himself alone and lost in the jungle with only his mule for a companion. He stops and gets off the mule in order to fire a shot for help, which in turn causes the mule to bolt. Lévi-Strauss spends the next several hours trying to catch the mule, but by the time he does, he has become more thoroughly lost. "Demoralized by this episode," Lévi-Strauss writes, he decides to rely on his mule to get him out of this predicament. "Neither my mule nor I knew where they [the band] had gone," he goes on, "sometimes I would head him in a direction that he refused to take; sometimes I would let him lead, only to find that he was simply turning in a circle. . . . I was not, admittedly, the first white man to penetrate that hostile zone. But none of my predecessors had come back alive and, quite apart from myself, my mule was a tempting prey for people who rarely have anything very much to get their teeth into."

Fortunately, however, it seems that several of the Lévi-Strauss's Indian guides had turned back as soon as they noticed his absence and had been following him all day (presumably because they found his wanderings amusing, or instructive). They now rescue him, lead him back to where he left his belongings at the foot of a tree, and together they rejoin the main party.

This episode is the central trauma of "A Writing Lesson." And it conditions Lévi-Strauss's reflections on something that happened earlier in the expedition. As the result of a sleepless night (caused by the "torment" of the mule episode), Lévi-Strauss thinks back on an episode with the chief of the tribe. During the transfer of gifts from whites to Indians, this chief pulled forth a piece of paper upon which he began to draw wavy lines. (Both paper and pencil were routinely given as gifts by the anthropologists.) The chief pretends in front of his people to be the one who is authorizing the exchanges. He confers with Lévi-Strauss about each gift according to his "false" list. Lévi-Strauss in a sense gets lost in this "false discourse" which does not correspond with anything that, for him, counts as writing, and has to be rescued by the chief's commentary, "which was prompt in coming." The wavy lines count as neither writing nor drawing for Lévi-Strauss.[24] Reflecting on this episode the evening after his fiasco with the mule in the jungle, Lévi-Strauss concludes that the chief understood how writing "works" as a controlling mechanism without actually understanding *how* to write. He goes on to utter these amazing observations:

If we want to correlate the appearance of *writing* with certain other characteristics of civilization, we must look elsewhere. The one phenomenon which has invariably accompanied it is the *formation of cities and empires*: the integration into political systems, that is to say, of those individuals into a hierarchy of castes and classes. Such is, at any rate, the type of development which we find, from Egypt right across to China, at the moment when writing makes its debut; it seems to favor rather the exploitation than the enlightenment of mankind. This exploitation made it possible to assemble workpeople by the thousand and set them tasks that taxed them to the limits of their strength: to this, surely, we must attribute the *beginnings of architecture* as we know it [my emphasis].[25]

Now it is precisely the link between writing and urbanism and architecture that interests me—embedded, as it is, in this reflection about the origins of writing, which itself occurs as a kind of nightmare, or perturbance, as a result of Lévi-Strauss's episode with his mule. For one thing, when Derrida critiques Lévi-Strauss's perceptions of the relation between writing, exploitation, violence, and cultural origins, he seems to leave the triadic "arrival" of writing, cities, architecture untouched. For another thing, in some obvious way writing, urbanism and architecture rely on the making of lines, and Lévi-Strauss's text is a continuous lament about how lines (paths, marks, inscriptions, writing, communication) are in the process of disintegration or loss. I want to suggest that the surreptitious figure of connection between writing, cities, architecture in Lévi-Strauss's, and subsequently Derrida's, and retroactively Le Corbusier's, text, is the recalcitrant mule. The mule—a cross between two poorly urbanized creatures (the donkey and the horse, which will become "horse-power")—is the cross-roads, the *chiasmas*, for urbanism, architecture, and, now, writing.

Now perhaps I am speaking (merely) allegorically. Perhaps I am telling an animal story in order to smuggle in a story about architecture, urbanism and writing. What I would like to suggest is that it is not coincidental that Le Corbusier chooses to level his accusations against classical and nineteenth-century architecture by refusing an urbanism and architecture built according to the "Pack-Donkey's Way." Nor is it coincidental that Lévi-Strauss is forced to his musings about writing, cities and architecture while riding a mule. It is not surprising that in the presence of animals, in general, (metaphorical, mythical or otherwise) we are forced to a consideration of the mechanisms of control and, simultaneously, waywardness—and thus to considerations of morality, rationality, order, civilization, cities and architecture. At the same time, the banality of these particular animals, donkeys and mules, constrains these large commentaries (by Le Corbusier and Lévi-Strauss) and reduces them to the local problems of how to find your way through the jungle, or how to lay out a city street. These more local issues become, in both accounts, issues of how to follow, draw, interpret, account for, lines. But whereas the donkey still falls (genetically) on the side of "nature," the mule is entirely cultural. So the mule, in the hands of the anthropologist, is an "improvement" on the donkey—that is, the mule produces a subtler confusion than the donkey in the midst of linear practices because it itself already belongs to the order of the line[26]—it has been bred to the line. But what is "the order of the line?" One might say, loosely, that the line is simultaneously of and against these beasts since, on the one hand, like the mythical beast, lines just start in the middle of things—they have aimless beginnings—and, on the other, lines are hyper-directed according to the forces of the ideal.

The "ideal model" for lines in both urbanism and architecture is Euclidean geometry. Euclid defines the line as "breadthless length."[27] A "straight line" is "a line which lies evenly with the points on itself." And a "point" is "that which has no part." It is interesting to look at these definitions—and to note that they are definitions rather than proofs—because the problem of the ideal, in architecture and elsewhere, is partially constructed by means of these definitions. For example, the ideal points (vanishing point and viewer position) in projective drawing systems are, of course, Euclidean in their ideality. The two oxymorons: "*breadthless length*" and "*that which has no part*" must take the form of a priori propositions—from which the rest of the geometric system develops—because Euclidean definitions and postulates (and what Euclid calls "Common Notions") are the occasion for controlling, in advance, contradictions in the system. This is an over-simplification, of course, because the economy of the definitions is crucial to the economy of the whole system. It matters that there are almost one hundred definitions, all of them a priori reductions and, therefore, repositories of conflict, rather than, say, one thousand definitions or only two definitions. From these definitions and postulates, and a few others, the thirteen books of Euclid's *Elements*, which comprise the basics of solid geometry, are derived. Here I want to look not at the specifics of a geometric system but at the idea of the "geometric ideal."

It is pertinent, in this regard, to look at Derrida's seminal text on Husserl's *Origin of Geometry*. Derrida draws out, in Husserl's text, a necessary failure in the search for an "origin" in geometry. These are remarkable texts, both the *Origin of Geometry* and Derrida's *Introduction*. Husserl claims that geometry was a "quantum leap" in understanding, a "genesis" that does not belong to the "adventure of humanity" but to a "higher reason." As Derrida characterizes it:

> *The Origin of Geometry* . . . concerns the status of the ideal objects of science (of which geometry is one example), their production, by identifying acts, as "the same," and the constitution of exactitude through idealization and passage to the limit—a process which starts with the life-world's sensible, finite, and prescientific materials.[28]

For Husserl, the question of pure geometry—the pure geometric tradition—lies outside the "sense" of the world, the "life-world" of multiple variations of forms and culture. Geometry cannot be treated historically, according to Husserl:

> The question of origin will not be a "philological-historical . . . search" in the investigation of "particular propositions" [*Origin*, p. 158] that the first geometers discovered or formulated. There, it would only be a matter for the history of science in the classical sense . . . to take stock of the already constituted contents of geometrical cognitions, in particular of the first postulates, axioms, theorems, and so forth, contents that must be explored and determined as precisely and as completely as possible from archeological documents. Despite its incontestable interest, such an investigation can teach us nothing about the geometrical sense of the first geometrical acts.[29]

The study of the history of the origin of geometry, Derrida writes, is "the history of an operation, and not of a founding."[30] In Derridean terms, ideal geometry is always already in place by the time the geometers first wield their instruments. The "origin" of geometry predates the moment when Euclid and other geometers (Thales, for example) consolidate their propositions. The geometer per se always arrives too late at the scene of the birth. The "always already" construction, of course, is a "classical" Derridean technique of passing through the boundary layer that classical origins, and classical theories of origin, put in place as absolute barriers.[31]

Before the exactitude of forms appeared in history, before the origin of geometry, Husserl argues, "an essential form becomes recognizable through a method of variation." As Derrida summarizes the sense of this remark:

> By imaginary variation we can obtain inexact but pure morphological types: "roundness," for example, *under* which is *constructed* the geometrical ideality of the "circle." In a pregeometrical world, the ideal shapes we attain are not the geometrically "pure" shapes which can be inscribed in ideal space—"pure" bodies, "pure" straight lines, "pure" planes, other "pure" figures, and the movements and deformations which occur in "pure" figures.[32]

But the power to imagine "essential shapes" is "not to be con-fused" with "pure geometrical ideality, which in itself is released from all sensible or imaginative intuitiveness. The imagination is what gives me the pure morphological type, and it 'can transform sensible shapes only into other sensible shapes.'"[33] Derrida goes on: The "institution of geometry could only be a *philosophical* act."

[The] physical thing, the body, the vague morphological and phoronomic types, the art of measure,[34] the possibility of imaginary variation, and preexact spatiotemporality already had to be located in the cultural field that was offered "to the philosopher who did not yet know geometry but who should be conceivable as its inventor." The philosopher is a man who inau-gurates the theoretical attitude [which] . . . makes idealization's decisive "passage to the limit" possible.[35]

Thus does Derrida arrive at "infinitization," the "going beyond every sensible and factual limit" that must take place for the constitution, or institution, of the geomet-ric ideal. And, simultaneous with this "radical freedom" of the philosophical spirit is the need to limit, in advance, the system of "infinite production."[36]

Here we are, then, as a last recourse, before an idealizing operation whose activity has never been studied for itself and whose conditions are never to be so studied, since we are dealing with a radically institutive operation. This idealization is that which, on the basis of sensible ideality (the morphological type of "roundness," for example), makes a higher, absolutely objective, exact, and nonsensible ideality occur—the "circle," a "similarly named [but] new" formation [the pure geometric circle].[37]

Pure geometry becomes possible through what Derrida calls "Cartesian intellectu-alism," which necessarily suppresses certain questions and structures, questions of "imagination" and "sensibility," for example, and the "origin of the ability to idealize."[38]

Derrida's point, his drive here, is toward a theory of "multiple births" of geometry rather than one "origin":

Does not geometry have an infinite number of births (or birth certificates) in which, each time, another birth is announced, while still being concealed? Must we not say that geometry is on the way towards its origin, instead of proceeding from it?[39]

The disruption of a secure sense of origin for geometry has to do with what has been left out of the game. In this case, what has been left out of the game is the act of "reduction itself . . . the origin of philosophy and history themselves,"[40] that is the origin of the "theoretical attitude" itself.

To ask the question of the line within the question of the geo-metric ideal, then, is to instantly invoke and become entangled in these problems.[41] The "origin" that Lévi-Strauss claims for writing will receive the same scrutiny, the same treatment, as Husserl's "origin of geometry." But it is important that it is writ-ing—the "origin of language" and Derrida's paradigmatic discussions of the "origin of language"—that ultimately dismantles the possibility of a "pure" geometry, or a pure science of any kind, and for this reason the word "writing" in Lévi-Strauss's passage receives privileged attention from Derrida. But the "large tasks" of cities and empires, and the "beginnings of architecture," have already criss-crossed the path of (the origin of) writing, and vice versa, by the time we get to Derrida's account. Otherwise, why would this "reflection" occur as a reaction to, on the one hand, the curiosity of the Chief's "wavy" drawings and, on the other, to the "wayward" path of Lévi-Strauss's mule?

One of the working assumptions of an earlier section in this essay was that at least one of the consequences of mixing up geometric lines (straight lines) with urbanistic/architectural lines (paths, plans/elevations) with mules and donkey lines (paths and lines of descent) and, finally, with the lines of writing, was that this "mix-up" (the chiasmas represented by the genetic "mix-up" of the mule) offered a certain resistance to the various tactics of "ideality." The mule (which can have no single origin—cannot be classified as a species) and the donkey, insofar as they both advance perturbed "technologies" for representing the line in space (as city or architecture), participate in the anexact measure of the everyday. In this scheme, "linearity"—an ideal system based on the same "passage to the limit" as pure geometry—must be perpetually won away, through philosophical means (Cartesian intellectualism, for example), from animality, irrationality, impropriety and disease and death.

But this "winning away" cannot be understood in any simple or heroic sense. The geometric or philosophical attitude of urbanism or architecture cannot be heroic in the sense that, perhaps, the protogeometer is/was. Urbanism and architecture, as we have already seen through the strange narratives of Le Corbusier and Lévi-Strauss, come (in a state of considerable hegemony) to the geometric (straight) line in the immediate presence of the animal (swerving, making a path), which irrevocably perturbs the hegemonic and the straight. And, lest we forget, the animal is not "The Animal," but the principle of animality that belongs entirely to human culture.

Returning, at last, to Derrida's discussion of Lévi-Strauss's "A Writing Lesson," Derrida remarks:

One should mediate on all of the following together: writing as the possibility of the road and of difference, the history of writing and the history of the road, of the rupture, of the *via rupta*, of the path that is broken, beaten, *fracta*, of the space of reversibility and of repetition traced by the opening, the divergence from, and the violent spacing, of nature, of the natural, savage forest. The *silva* is savage, the *via rupta* is written, discerned, and inscribed violently as difference, as form imposed on the *hyle*, in the forest, in wood as matter.[42]

The "path," thus made, produces a crisis of origin; a crisis of spontaneous "arrival" (of certain forms of consciousness, such as "pure geometry" or "history"); a crisis of the "line" that is outline (Alberti), wall (Alberti), path (Le Corbusier), crossroads (Lévi-Strauss). It substitutes for the singularity of these moments the plural complication of difference, divergence, repetition, cross-roads, and violent spacing.

The line, as Derrida writes in another place, is the very thing that philosophy could not see "when it had its eyes open on the interior of its own history." "The end of linear writing is indeed the end of the book, even if . . . it is within the form of the book that new writings . . . allow themselves to be . . . encased."[43] What is not so clear—what is in the state of suspension and suggestion here—is how architecture and cities are built at the bestial crossroads of their own lines (urban and architectural) and the lines of writing. This is intimately related to the question of how the violence of spacing (urbanism/architecture) is thought before, or at the same time as, the violence of writing.

Notes

1. Claude Lévi-Strauss, *Tristes Tropiques* (New York: Atheneum, 1972).
2. Jacques Derrida, *Of Grammatology*, trans. Gayatri C. Spivak (Baltimore: Johns Hopkins University Press, 1976).
3. Le Corbusier, *The City of Tomorrow*, trans. Frederick Etchells (Cambridge: MIT Press, 1971).

4. The word "exemplary" is meant to reflect on the invitation issued to the people attending the "working session," from which the publication *Strategies in Architectural Thinking* emerged. We were invited to do "exemplary" architectural criticism. But since the word "exemplary" expresses and represses a will-to-the-transcendental, the word is also an opening gambit in a long game that only Derrida could win. But I am also speaking in a more local sense here. I mostly mean that within the horizon of Derrida's work—beginning with the other Derridean text that I deal with in this chapter, the *Introduction* to Edmund Husserl's *The Origin of Geometry*, which is quite explicitly about the problem of the exemplary (see Jacques Derrida, *Edmund Husserl's Origin of Geometry, an Introduction*, trans. John P. Leavey, Jr. [Lincoln: University of Nebraska Press, 1989], p. 30)—certain techniques of inquiry become recognizable as Derridean and, among these, the techniques used in Derrida's critical commentary on Lévi-Strauss are exemplary.

5. See Eric Cheyfitz, *The Transparent: Sexual Politics in the Language of Emerson* (Baltimore: Johns Hopkins University Press, 1981).

6. Michel Foucault, *The Order of Things: An Archaeology of the Human Sciences* (New York: Vintage, 1973), p. xv.

7. This is, without question, a glib way to invoke the "critical license" granted by "poststructural theory." Nothing has been granted to anyone. But the homologous affiliation—like structures related to like structures—is quite specifically offered as a structuralist technique of investigation in Lévi-Strauss's *Totemism* (New York: Beacon Press, 1963) when Lévi-Strauss considers the relationship between "nature" and "culture." The stunning instance of this in that text is the following: "The relation thus postulated between twins and birds is explained neither by a principle of participation after the manner of Lévy-Bruhl, nor by utilitarian considerations such as those adduced by Malinowski, nor by the intuition of perceptible resemblances proposed by Firth and by Fortes. What we are presented with is a series of logical connections uniting mental relations. Twins 'are birds,' not because they are confused with them or because they look like them, but because twins, in relation to other men, are as 'persons of the above' to 'persons of below,' and, in relation to birds, as 'birds of below' are to 'birds of the above.' They thus occupy, as do birds, an intermediary position between the supreme spirit and human beings" (pp. 80–81).

8. Le Corbusier, *The City of Tomorrow*, p. 11.

9. Ibid., p. 12.

10. Ibid. The passages in this paragraph are taken from pp. 12–18.

11. Ibid. Passages in this paragraph are taken from pp. 41–43.

12. Le Corbusier, *Towards a New Architecture*, trans. Frederick Etchells (New York: Dover, 1986), p. 3. "The regulating line is a guarantee against wilfulness. It brings satisfaction to the understanding."

13. Le Corbusier, *The City of Tomorrow*, p. 43. Le Corbusier's statements are even more dramatic than this. "When man begins to draw straight lines he bears witness that he has gained control of himself and that he has reached a condition of order. Culture is an orthogonal state of mind. Straight lines are not deliberately created. They are arrived at when man is strong enough, determined enough, sufficiently equipped and sufficiently enlightened to desire and to be able to trace straight lines. In the history of forms, the moment which sees the straight line is a climax; behind it and within it lie all the arduous effort which has made possible this manifestation of liberty." Like the Yoruba culture—which Le Corbusier would no doubt call "primitive"—Le Corbusier believes that lines, particularly straight lines, express the moment when art reaches its apotheosis in culture. In Le Corbusier's case, of course, it is architecture that reaches its climax.

14. "Orthogonality," which means "lying at right angles" or in a "linear transformation," conjures up the related word "orthographic," which means the proper spelling of a word. This "ortho-", or proper, state of the architectural and urban "mind" is what interests Le Corbusier.

15. "Line" is picking up its (more than) double sense here as both a line of descent from Greece and Rome, i.e. the architectural legacy that Le Corbusier is most interested in launching an attack against, and a "line" that Le Corbusier feels has been fed to the modern world by antiquated and irrational forces. This sense is not automatic but, to some degree, it has been prepared for by Chapter 1 and "Lear's Architectural Theory."

16. The Modulor, as Hashim Sarkis pointed out to me, is a hybrid figure comprised of the module plus the "or," i.e., the golden rule or the golden section. The golden state of measurement is won away from the bestiality of the donkey. This brings to mind another donkey, the gold-excreting donkey of Perrault's "Peau d'âne," who is sacrificed for the sake of the princess. Here the donkey skin cloaks the princess, making her ugly, until her "prince" comes along and sees the "gold" beneath the skin. Louis Marin talks about this story as a fable of kingly power in *Portrait of the King* (Minneapolis: University of Minnesota Press, 1988). Also see "Comic Lines" by Robin Evans in *The Projective Cast* (Cambridge: MIT Press, 1995) for a discussion of the "invention" of the Modulor as a figure of measurement and ideology (on the eve of the design of Ronchamp).

17. The importance of "measure" cannot be underestimated. In Derrida's commentary on Husserl, systems of measurement are necessary to the formation of a "pregeometric" geometry: "This sensible and, to a certain degree, empirical anticipation (although in comparison with facts submitted to variation, imaginative ideality of the morphological type can no longer be merely empirical) is true not only for geometrical forms but also for geometrical measurement. The latter comes to the fore in and through praxis: for example 'where just distribution is intended. . . . An empirical technique of measurement (in surveying, in architecture, and so forth) must necessarily belong to every prescientific culture. Husserl does not elaborate on that in the *Origin*. In *The Crisis [of European Sciences and Transcendental Phenomenology]*, he seems to consider empirical measure as a stage further than sensible morphology on the path toward pure geometrical ideality. Measure initiates an advance in the sense of the univocal, intersubjective, therefore ideal-objective determination of the geometrical thing" (Derrida, *Edmund Husserl's Origin of Geometry*, p. 126).

18. See Jeffrey Kipnis's essay "/Twisting the Separatrix/," *Assemblage* 14 (1991). This remarkable essay, which discusses Peter Eisenman's and Jacques Derrida's collaboration on Bernard Tschumi's La Villette park project in Paris, articulates the power of the "separatrix," "that divider whose ability to separate the inside from the outside establishes the solid ground upon which all the foundations of discourse rest."

19. There is certainly a history of drawing techniques and certainly the plan—and later the section—have been theorized in interesting directions. But the problem of origin is the same problem that Damisch cites in *The Origin of Perspective* and that Derrida cites in his introduction to Husserl, mainly, the problem of speaking of a single "origin" of complex practices (such as drawing or geometry). Speaking loosely one might situate the beginning of the projective drawing system at the same time perspectival drawing is "invented" by Brunelleschi in the fifteenth century.

20. Urban "distraction" is the theme of another piece I wrote several years ago on John Hejduk's work. Cf. Catherine Ingraham, "Errand, Detour and the Wilderness Urbanism of John Hejduk," delivered at a conference on John Hejduk at the Canadian Centre for Architecture, April 1992.

21. The "linearity" of writing itself is, of course, implicit in all this. The seminal discussions around the point of writing, hermeneutics, language, and the linguistic model are, of course, in Jacques Derrida's *Of Grammatology*.

22. As an example of how this relationship ties in with the other issues confronting us here, Le Corbusier uses the pack donkey as an allegorical figure (a figure of "reproduction"), whereas Lévi-Strauss buys and sells pack animals (mules) for his expeditions (figures of "production"). At the same time, there is no "animal of nature" in the sense that all animals, and particularly pack animals, are produced by mechanisms and technologies of work that draft them into a human production system. And while I do not want to adopt a strictly Marxist position with respect to the ideological character of this drafting—a position that ignores the relation of the animal to its own technologies—I think the Marxist position is the only one that addresses the axis of labor that connects these animals to human production.

23. Michel Foucault also contributes substantially to the contemporary sense of the word "genealogy." Derrida and Foucault were contemporaries, of course, both commanding large audiences adhering to their "philosophies." Foucault's "archaeologies" are not Derrida's "grammatologies." Foucault, while, of course, operating under the "aura" of "linguistic model" is far more interested in certain institutional histories, the formation of "disciplines," the history of sexuality and so forth. "In France," Foucault wrote in *The*

Order of Things, "certain half-witted 'commentators' persist in labelling me a 'structuralist.' I have been unable to get it into their tiny minds that I have used none of the methods, concepts, or key terms that characterize structural analysis" (xiv).

24. At another point in the narrative, Lévi-Strauss remarks that many of the Indians would draw wavy horizontal lines on the paper when given pencils and paper. This he claims is neither writing nor drawing (*Tristes Tropiques*, p. 288). Lévi-Strauss goes on to say, "The Nambikwara . . . do not know anything about design, if one excepts some geometric sketches on their calabashes. . . . They imitated the only use that they had seen us make of our notebooks, namely writing, but without understanding its meaning or its end. They called the act of writing iekariukedjutu, namely: 'drawing lines.'" Derrida notes this passage with surprise. "It is," he remarks, "as if one said that such a language has no word designating writing—and that therefore those who practice it do not know how to write—just because they use a word meaning 'to scratch,' 'to engrave,' 'to scribble,' 'to scrape,' 'to incise,' 'to trace,' 'to imprint,' etc. As if 'to write' in its metaphoric kernel, meant something else. Is not ethnocentrism always betrayed by the haste with which it is satisfied by certain translations" (*Of Grammatology*, p. 123).

25. Lévi-Strauss, *Tristes Tropiques*, p. 292.

26. As before, the "line" carries within it the notion of the genealogical. It is common to speak of lines of descent, and, with the mule, these lines are a "cross" between two other lines. Because the mule must be reproduced each generation—i.e., the mule is sterile, not a self-perpetuating species—it is completely a production of this X, this cross.

27. Euclid, *The Thirteen Books of Euclid's Elements*, trans. Sir Thomas L. Heath (Chicago: Encyclopedia Britannica, 1952), p. 1.

28. Derrida, *Edmund Husserl's Origin of Geometry*, p. 25.

29. Ibid., p. 37.

30. Ibid., p. 41.

31. This "introduction" was Derrida's first "major published essay," and, as such, it is (using Derrida's own words about the birth of geometry) the "birth certificate" for those formulations that we now associate routinely with Derrida's work. See ibid., p. 8.

32. See ibid., pp. 123–124 (italics are Derrida's). It is important to remember that Derrida is here investigating the "pregeometrical" account of ideal forms in Husserl. This "pure ideality" is of a sensible order, he remarks, and must be distinguished from a "pure geometrical ideality, which in itself is released from all sensible or imaginative intuitiveness. . . . According to Husserl, then, pure sensible ideality is situated on a premathematical level. *Once constituted*, pure mathematics will thus be accessible only to 'understanding'. . . an activity conceivable in the sense of Cartesian intellectualism."

33. Ibid., p. 124.

34. "An empirical technique of measurement (in surveying, in architecture, and so forth) must necessarily belong to every prescientific culture. . . . Measure initiates an advance in the sense of the univocal, intersubjective, therefore ideal-objective determination of the geometrical thing" (ibid., p. 126).

35. Ibid., p. 127.

36. Ibid. It is necessary to quote at length on the matter of infinitization because its implications are so great: "If the primordial infinitization opens the mathematical field to infinite fecundities for the Greeks, it no less first limits the a priori system of that productivity. The very content of an infinite production will be confined within an a priori system which, for the Greeks, will always be *closed*. The guide here is Euclidean geometry, or rather the "ideal Euclid," according to Husserl's expression. . . . Later, at the dawn of modern times, the a priori system will itself be overthrown by a new infinitization" (ibid., p. 128).

37. Ibid., p. 133.

38. Ibid., p. 134. Also see Jacques Derrida, "Structure, Sign and Play" in *The Structuralist Controversy* (Baltimore: Johns Hopkins University Press, 1972), for Derrida's early remarks on the problem of "the structurality of structure."

39. Derrida, *Edmund Husserl's Origin of Geometry*, pp. 130–131.

40. Ibid., p. 132.

41. See ibid., pp. 53–54. As Derrida remarks here, "all the questions about the possibility or impossibility of maintaining Husserl's demands—either as an essentially inaccessible

regulative ideal or as a methodological rule and actual technique . . . are they not asked precisely within this unity of the geometrico-mathematical horizon in general, within the open unity of a science? And it is within the horizon that Husserl here questions that the preoccupation with decidability belongs. . . . This whole debate is only understandable within something like the geometrical or mathematical science, whose unit is still to come on the basis of what is announced in its origins. . . . The objective thematic field of mathematics must already be constituted in its mathematical sense, in order for the values of consequence and inconsistency to be rendered problematic" (italics are Derrida's).

42. Derrida, *Of Grammatology*, p. 108.

43. Ibid., p. 7.

Mark Wigley **"The Translation of Architecture, the Production of Babel"** Paper presented at the Chicago Institute for Architecture and Urbanism, September 1988; published in *Assemblage* 8 (February 1989)

The hype and hysteria surrounding the 1988 "Deconstructivist Architecture" exhibition at the Museum of Modern Art blurred an important distinction of terms in the relation of architecture and deconstruction. On the one hand was the ongoing problematic of architectural representation or meaning, the legacy of the architectural theory of the 1970s. In many ways so-called deconstructivist architecture continued the research of meaning but shifted from attempts to develop stable and controllable architectural meanings, adequate to a broad cultural consensus, to attempts to disrupt and disperse meaning, to seize on the fragmentation of present culture and the impossibility of consensus. On the other hand were the facts that an architectural metaphor had dominated the history of philosophy from Plato to Kant to Heidegger to Derrida, and that Derrida had declared: "Deconstruction itself resembles an architectural metaphor. . . . It is not simply the technique of an architect who knows how to de-construct what has been constucted, but a probing that touches upon the technique itself, upon the authority of the architectural metaphor and thereby constitutes its own architectural rhetoric. . . . One could say that there is nothing more architectural than deconstruction, but also nothing less architectural."[1] If his curatorial and editorial roles in the "Deconstructivist Architecture" exhibition associated Mark Wigley with the former understanding of the architecture/deconstruction relation, his most important theoretical work places him squarely within the latter, in questions of philosophy's use of architecture as a figure of its own practices of building and interrogating structures.

compare Hollier (192 ff)

Wigley turns the probing of the authority of the architectural metaphor back on the writings of Derrida, in an attempt to show that central (Heideggerian) notions of deconstruction like ground, structure, ornament, domestication, tomb, and institution cannot but produce an "architecture," and that architectural thinking — so implicated is it in the economy of translation of such notions — at once preserves and threatens philosophy. The translation of deconstruction in architecture, in fact, constitutes what it claims to simply reproduce. "The architectural translation of deconstruction, which appears to be the last-minute, last-gasp application, turns out to be part of the very production of deconstructive discourse from the beginning, an ongoing event organized by the terms of an ancient contract between architecture and philosophy that is inscribed within the structure of both discourses."[2]

see 642

"The Translation of Architecture" is one mark of an important moment in architectural theory, a moment when architecture was understood as, inter alia, a way of doing philosophy — not representing or illustrating philosophical concepts but rather thinking philosophical problems *through architecture*. That the philosophical problems are now architectural (ornament/structure) rather than linguistic (form/content) entails that questions of meaning give way to questions of grounding (fixing, stabilizing, authorizing) and the ways in which architecture and philosophy constantly appeal to one another for the ground they cannot generate out of their own internal economies.

Notes

1. Jacques Derrida, "Architecture Where the Desire May Live," *Domus* 671 (1986), p. 18.
2. Mark Wigley, *The Architecture of Deconstruction: Derrida's Haunt* (Cambridge: MIT Press, 1993), p. 6. A revised version of the present essay formed the core of that book.

How then to translate deconstruction in architectural discourse? Perhaps it is too late to ask this preliminary question. What is left to translate? Or, more important, what is always left by translation? Not just left behind but left specifically for architecture. What remains of deconstruction for architecture? What are the remains that can be located only in architecture, the last resting place of deconstruction? The question of translation is, after all, a question of survival. Can deconstruction survive architecture?

1.

It is now over twenty years since Derrida's first books were published. Suddenly his work has started to surface in architectural discourse. This appears to be the last discourse to invoke the name of Derrida. Its reading seems the most distant from the original texts, the final addition to a colossal stack of readings, an addition that marks in some way the beginning of the end of deconstruction, its limit if not its closure.

After such a long delay—a hesitation whose strategic necessity must be examined—there is now such haste to read Derrida in architecture. But it is a reading that seems at once obvious and suspect. Suspect in its very obviousness. Deconstruction is understood to be unproblematically architectural. There seems to be no translation, but just a metaphoric transfer, a straightforward application of theory from outside architecture to the practical domain of the architectural object. The hesitation does not seem to have been produced by some kind of internal resistance on the part of that object. On the contrary, there is no evidence of work, no task for the translator, no translation. Just a literal application, a transliteration. Architecture is understood as a representation of deconstruction, the material representation of an abstract idea. The recent reception of Derrida's work follows the classical teleology from idea to material form, from initial theory to final practice, from presence to representation. Architecture, the most material of the discourses, seems the most detached from the original work, the most suspect of the applications, the last application, the representational ornament that cannot influence the tradition it is added to, a veneer masking as much as it reveals of the structure beneath. The last layer, just an addition, no translation. Yet.

But how to translate? Deconstruction is no more than a subversion of the architectural logic of addition which sets into play a certain thought of translation. But one cannot simply consider translation outside and above either deconstruction or architecture. The question immediately becomes complicated. There is no hygienic starting point, no superior logic to apply. There are no principles to be found in some domain that governs both deconstructive discourse and architectural discourse. Nevertheless, certain exchanges are already occurring between them. Architecture, translation and deconstruction are already bound together, already defining an economy whose pathological symptoms can be studied. It is a matter of identifying the logic of translation that is already in operation. Since there is no safe place to begin, one can only enter the economy and trace its convoluted geometry in order to describe this scene of translation.

This can be done by locating that moment in each discourse where the other is made thematic, where the other comes to the surface. The line of argument that surfaces there can then be folded back on the rest of the discourse to locate other layers of relations. These hidden layers are not simply below the surface. They are within the surface itself, knotted together to form the surface. To locate them involves slippage along faultlines rather than excavation. As there are no principles above or below the convoluted folds of this surface, it is a matter of following some circular line of inquiry, of circulating within the economy, within the surface itself.

2.

Translation surfaces in deconstructive discourse when Derrida, following Walter Benjamin's *The Task of the Translator*, argues that translation is not the transference, reproduction, or image of an original. The original only survives in translation. The translation constitutes the original it is added to. The original calls for a translation which establishes a nostalgia for the innocence and the life it never had. To answer this call, the translation abuses the original, transforming it.

And for the notion of translation, we would have to substitute a notion of *transformation*: a regulated transformation of one language by another, of one text by another. We never will have, and in fact never have had, a "transport" of pure signifieds from one language to another, or within one and the same language, that the signifying instrument would leave virgin and untouched.[1]

There is some kind of gap in the original which the translation is called in to cover over. The original is not some organic whole, a unity. It is already corrupted, already fissured. The translation is not simply a departure from the original, as the original is already exiled from itself. Language is necessarily impure. Always divided, it remains foreign to itself. It is the translation that produces the myth of purity and, in so doing, subordinates itself as impure. In constructing the original as original, the translation constructs itself as secondary, exiled. The supplementary translation which appears as a violation of the purity of the work is actually the possibility of that very purity. Its violence to the original is a violent fidelity, a violence called for by the original precisely to construct itself as pure. The abuse of the text is called for by an abuse already within the text. Translation exploits the conflict within the original to present the original as unified.

Consequently, in translation, the text neither lives nor dies, it neither has its original life-giving intention revived (presentation) nor is it displaced by a dead sign (representation). Rather, it just lives on, it survives. This survival is organized by a contract that ensures that translation is neither completed nor completely frustrated.[2] The contract is the necessarily unfulfilled promise of translation. It defines a scene of incomplete translation, an incompletion that binds the languages of the original and the translation together in a strange knot, a double bind. This constitutional bond is neither a social contract nor a transcendental contract above both languages. Neither cultural nor acultural, it is other than cultural without being outside culture. The negotiable social contracts within which language operates presuppose this nonnegotiable contract which makes language possible, establishing the difference between languages while making certain exchanges between them possible.

This translation contract is not independent of the languages whose economy it organizes. It is inscribed within both languages. Not only is the original already corrupt, already divided, but translation is already occurring across those divisions. The gap between languages passes through each language. Because language is always already divided, inhabited by the other, and constantly negotiated with it, translation is possible.[3] The translation within a language makes possible translation outside it. Which is to say that one language is not simply outside the other. Translation occurs across a gap folded within rather than between each language. It is these folds that constitute language. The contract is no more than the geometry of these folds, the organization of the gaps.

Consequently, any translation between architecture and deconstruction does not occur between the texts of architectural discourse and those of philosophical discourse.[4] Rather, it occupies and organizes both discourses. Within each there is an architectural translation of philosophy and a philosophical translation of architecture. To translate deconstruction in architectural discourse is not, therefore, to faithfully recover some original, undivided sense of deconstruction.[5] Rather, it is one of the abuses of the texts signed by Derrida that constitutes them as originals. To translate deconstruction in architectural discourse is to examine the gaps in deconstructive writing that demand an architectural translation in order that those texts be constituted as deconstructive. The architectural translation of deconstruction is literally the production of deconstruction.

This production must be organized by the terms of a contract between architecture and philosophy which is inscribed within the structure of both in a way that defines a unique scene of translation.

3.

A preliminary sketch of this scene can be drawn by developing Heidegger's account of the relationship between architecture and philosophy. Heidegger examines the way in which philosophy describes itself as architecture. Kant's *Critique of Pure Reason*, for example, describes metaphysics as an "edifice" erected on secure foundations laid on the most stable ground. Kant criticizes previous philosophers for their tendency to "complete its speculative structures as speedily as may be, and only afterwards to enquire whether these foundations are reliable."[6] The edifice of metaphysics has fallen apart and is "in ruins" because it has been erected on "groundless assertions" unquestioningly inherited from the philosophical tradition. To restore a secure foundation, the critique starts the "thorough preparation of the ground"[7] with the "clearing, as it were, and levelling of what has hitherto been wasteground."[8] The edifice of metaphysics is understood as a grounded structure.

Heidegger argues that Kant's attempt to lay the foundations is the necessary task of all metaphysics. The question of metaphysics has always been that of the ground (*Grund*) on which things stand even though it has been explicitly formulated in these terms only in the modern period inaugurated by Descartes. Metaphysics is no more than the attempt to locate the ground. Its history is that of a succession of different names (*logos*, *ratio*, *arche*, etc.) for the ground. Each of them designates "Being," which is understood as presence. Metaphysics is the identification of the ground as "supporting presence" for an edifice. It searches for "that upon which everything rests, what is always there for every being as its support."[9] For Heidegger, metaphysics is no more than the determination of ground-as-support.

Metaphysics is the question of what the ground will withstand, of what can stand on the ground. The motif of the edifice, the grounded structure, is that of standing up. Philosophy is the construction of propositions that stand up. The ability of its constructs to stand is determined by the condition of the ground, its supporting presence. Heidegger repeatedly identifies presence with standing. The "fundamental" question of metaphysics (why there are beings rather than nothing) asks of a being "on what does it stand?"[10] Standing up through construction makes visible the condition of the ground.

But in Heidegger's reading, construction does not simply make visible a ground that precedes it. The kind of ground clearing Kant attempts does not simply precede that construction of the edifice. The ground is not simply independent of the edifice. The edifice is not simply added to the ground; it is not simply an addition. For Heidegger, a building does not stand on a ground that preceded it and on which it depends. Rather, it is the erection of the building that establishes the fundamental condition of the ground. Its structure makes the ground possible.[11] The ground is constituted rather than revealed by that which appears to be added to it. To locate the ground is necessarily to construct an edifice. Consequently, philosophy's successive relayings of the foundation do not preserve a single, defined edifice.[12] Rather, it is a matter of abandoning the traditional structure by removing its foundations.[13] The form of the edifice changes as the ground changes.

Having cleared the ground, Kant must reassess its loadbearing capacity and "lay down the complete architectonic plan" of a new philosophy in order to "build upon this foundation."[14] The edifice must be redesigned. Relaying the foundations establishes the possibility of a different edifice. For Heidegger, the laying of the foundation is the "projection of the intrinsic possibility of metaphysics"[15] through an interrogation of the condition of the ground. This interrogation is the projection of a plan, the tracing of an outline, the drawing, the designing of an edifice, the drawing of the design out of the ground. Interrogating the condition of the ground defines certain architectonic limits, certain structural constraints within which the philosopher must work as a designer. The philosopher is an architect, endlessly attempting to produce a grounded structure.

In these terms, the history of philosophy is that of a series of substitutions for structure. Every reference to structure is a reference to an edifice erected on a ground, an edifice from which the ground cannot simply be removed. The motif of the edifice is that of a structure whose free play is constrained by the ground. The play of representations is limited, controlled, by presence: "The concept of centered structure is in fact the concept of a play based on a fundamental ground, a play constituted on the basis of a fundamental immobility and a reassuring certitude, which itself is beyond the reach of play.[16] Philosophy is the attempt to restrain the free play of representation by establishing the architectonic limits provided by the ground. It searches for the most stable ground in order to exercise the greatest control over representation.

The metaphor of grounded structure designates the fundamental project of metaphysics to produce a universal language that controls representation, a logos. Heidegger identifies the original sense of the word logos as "gathering" in a way that lets things stand, the standing of construction. The link between structure and presence organizes traditional accounts of language. The means by which language is grounded is always identified with structure.

Metaphysics maintains its protocol of presence/presentation/representation with an account of language that privileges speech over writing. While speech is promoted as presentation of pure thought, writing is subordinated as representation of speech. Speech is identified with structure which makes visible the condition of the ground it is bonded to. Phonetic writing, as the representation of speech, is identified with ornament that represents the structure it is added to. If writing ceases to be phonetic, if it loses its bond with speech, it becomes representation detached from pure presence, attached to the structure like an ornament referring away from the structure. The protocol of metaphysics sustained by the traditional account of language as thought/speech/phonetic writing/nonphonetic writing is established by the architectural motif of ground/structure/ornament.

Metaphysics is dependent on an architectural logic of support. Architecture is the figure of the addition, the structural layer, one element supported by another. Metaphysics's determination of the ground-as-support presupposes a vertical hierarchy from ground through structure to ornament. The idea of support, of structure, is dependent on a certain view of architecture which defines a range of relationships from fundamental (foundational) to supplementary (ornamental). With each additional layer, the bond is weaker. The structure is bonded to the ground more securely than the ornament is bonded to the structure. But as the distance from the ground becomes greater, the threat to the overall structure diminishes. The vertical hierarchy is a mechanism of control that makes available the thought of the ground-as-support which is metaphysics.

Structure makes present the ground. Structure is grounding, submission to the authority of presence. Ornament either represents the grounding of structure or deviates from the line of support, detaching itself from the ground in order to represent that which is other than the structure. Philosophy attempts to tame ornament in the name of the ground, to control representation in the name of presence. The philosophical economy turns on the status of ornament. It is the structure/ornament relationship that enables us to think of support, and thereby, to think of the ground.

4.

The strategic importance of the architectural metaphor discussed above emerges when Heidegger examines the status of art. Metaphysics's determination of ground-as-support also determines art as a merely representative "addition" to a utilitarian object, a "superstructure" added to the "substructure" which, in turn, is added to the ground. The architectural metaphor organizes this relationship: "It seems almost as though the thingly element in the art work is like the substructure into and upon which the other, authentic element is built."[17] It is the "support" to which the artwork is added, the presentation of the ground to which the artwork is added as a representation.

But it is not just the internal structure of the art object that is understood in these architectural terms, it is also the status of art as a discourse. Heidegger notes that metaphysics treats art itself as a superstructure added to the substructure of philosophy. Metaphysics understands itself as a grounded structure to which is attached the representational ornament of art. It subordinates the arts, and therefore architecture, by employing the vertical hierarchy dependent on a certain understanding of architecture. Art is subordinated by being located furthest from the ground. Architecture, then, plays a curious strategic role. It is able to pass between philosophy and art in a unique way. It is involved in a kind of translation. The metaphor circulates between and within the two systems, complicating them as it folds back on itself. A convoluted economy is sustained by the description of architecture as ornamented structure, which enables art to be subordinated to philosophy, even while philosophy describes itself as architecture. Philosophy describes itself in terms of that thing which it subordinates.

Heidegger argues that art is actually "foundational" to the philosophical tradition that subordinates it to the level of ornament. This convolution is doubled in the case of architecture itself. Metaphysics organizes itself around an account of the object as grounded structure. It projects an account of architecture outside itself which it then appeals to as an outside authority. It literally produces an architecture. As Derrida argues, in reading Kant's use of the architectural metaphor, philosophy "*represents* itself as part of its part, as an art of Architecture. It re-presents itself, detaches itself, dispatches an emissary, one part of itself outside itself to bind the whole, to fill up or to heal the whole which has suffered detachment."[18] It does so to cover up some kind of gap, some internal division. Metaphysics produces the architectural object as the paradigm of ground-as-support in order to veil its own lack of support, its ungrounded condition. Philosophy represents itself as architecture, it translates itself as architecture, producing itself in the translation. The limits of philosophy are established by the metaphorical status of architecture.

Philosophy draws an edifice, rather than draws on an edifice. It produces an architecture of grounded structure which it then uses for support, leaning on it, resting within it. The edifice is constructed to make theory possible, then subordinated as a metaphor in order to defer to some higher, non-material truth. Architecture is constructed as a material reality in order to liberate some higher domain. As material, it is but a metaphor. The most material condition is used to establish the most ideal order, which is then bound to reject it as merely material. The status of material oscillates. The metaphor of the ground, the bedrock, the base, the fundamental, inverts to become base in the sense of degraded, material, less than ideal. The vertical hierarchy inverts itself. In this inversion, architecture flips from privileged origin to gratuitous supplement, from foundation to ornament.

Philosophy treats its architectural motif as but a metaphor that can and should be discarded as superfluous. The figure of the grounded structure is but an illustration, a useful metaphor that illustrates the nature of metaphysics but outlives its usefulness and must be abandoned in the final form of metaphysics, a representation to be separated from the fundamental presentation, a kind of scaffolding to be discarded when the project is complete, a frame that traces the outline of the building, a trace that lacks substance but is structurally necessary, an open frame that is the very possibility of a closed structure to which it then becomes an unnecessary appendage. Scaffolding is that piece of structure which becomes ornamental. When philosophy reflects upon its own completion, it defines architecture as metaphorical. Metaphysics is the determination of architecture as metaphor.

But can architecture be so simply discarded? The use of the figure of structure "is only metaphorical, it will be said. Certainly. But metaphor is never innocent. It orients research and fixes results. When the spatial model is hit upon, when it functions, critical reflection rests within it."[19] The very attempt to abandon metaphor involves metaphors. Even the concept that the metaphorical can be detached from the fundamental is itself metaphorical. Metaphysics grounds itself in the metaphors it claims to have abandoned. Metaphor "is the essential weight which anchors discourse in metaphysics"[20] rather than a superfluous ornament. Metaphor is fundamental. The metaphor of the grounded structure in particular cannot be discarded in order to reveal the ground itself. The "fundamental" is an architectural metaphor, so architecture cannot be abandoned in favor of the fundamental.

Thus, the criteria for a classification of philosophical metaphors are borrowed from a derivative philosophical discourse. . . . They are metaphorical, resisting every meta-metaphorics, the values of a concept, foundation, and theory. . . . What is fundamental corresponds to the desire for a firm and ultimate ground, a terrain to build on, the earth as the support for an artificial structure.[21]

Philosophy can define only a part of itself as nonmetaphorical by employing the architectural metaphor. This metaphor organizes the status of metaphor. In so doing, it organizes the tradition of philosophy that claims to be able to discard it. Architectural figures cannot be detached from philosophical discourse. The architectural metaphor is not simply one metaphor among others. More than the metaphor of foundation, it is the foundational metaphor. It is therefore not simply a metaphor.

The architectural motif is bound to philosophy. The bond is contractual, not in the sense of an agreement signed by two parties, but a logical knot of which the two parties are but a side effect. More than the terms of exchange within and between these discourses, it produces each discourse as a discourse. The translation contract between architecture and philosophy works both ways. Each constructs the other as an origin from which they are detached. Each identifies the other as other. The other is constructed as a privileged origin which must then be discarded. In each there is this moment of inversion.

This primal contract, which is neither a contingent, cultural artifact nor an atemporal, acultural principle, establishes the possibility of a social contract that separates architecture and philosophy and constitutes them as discourses. The eventual status of architecture as a discipline began to be negotiated by the first texts of architectural theory, which drew on the canons of the philosophical tradition to identify the proper concern of the newly constituted figure of the architect with drawing (*disegno*) that mediates between the idea and the building, the formal and the material, the soul and the body, the theoretical and the practical. Architecture—architectural drawing—is neither simply a mechanical art bound to the bodily realm of utility, nor a liberal art operating in the realm of ideas, but is their reconciliation, the bridge between the two. Architectural theory thus constructs architecture as a bridge between the dominant oppositions of metaphysics and constitutes itself by exploiting the contractual possibility already written into the philosophical tradition wherein it describes itself as architecture.

It is not simply that architecture has some familiar unambiguous material reality that is drawn upon by philosophy. Rather, philosophy draws an architecture, presents a certain understanding, a certain theory, of architecture. The terms of the contract are the prohibition of a different description of the architectural object, or rather, the dissimulation of the object.

To describe the privileged role of architecture in philosophy is not to identify architecture as the origin from which philosophy derives, but rather to show that the condition effected when philosophy infects itself from outside by drawing on architecture is internal to architecture itself. Architecture is cut from within, and philosophy unwittingly appeals to architecture precisely for this internal torment.

The concern here is to locate certain discursive practices repressed within the pathological mechanisms of this economy, to trace the impact of another account of architecture hidden within the tradition. Deconstruction is not outside the tradition. It achieves its force precisely by inhabiting the tradition, and thereby operating in terms of the contract. The question is, what relationship does deconstruction assume with the account of architecture repressed by that tradition?

The translation of deconstruction in architecture does not simply occur across the philosophy/architecture divide. It is occurring within each discourse. It is not a matter of simply generating a new description of the architectural

object in architectural discourse but rather of locating the account of architecture
already operative within deconstructive writing. It is the difference between this account and that of traditional philosophy that marks the precise nature of deconstruction's inhabitation of philosophy. The limits of deconstruction are established by the
account of architecture it unwittingly produces.

5.

As architecture is bound up into language,[22] this account can be located precisely
in the discussion of translation itself. Inasmuch as deconstruction tampers with the
philosophical ideal of translation, it tampers with the ideal of architecture.

Derrida's account of translation is organized around an architec-
tural figure: the tower of Babel. The failure of the tower marks the necessity for translation, the multiplicity of languages, the free play of representation, which is to say
the necessity for controlling representation. The collapse of the tower marks the necessity for a certain construction. The figure of the tower acts as the strategic intersection of philosophy, architecture, deconstruction, and translation.

The tower is the figure of philosophy because the dream of phi-
losophy is that of translatability.[23] Philosophy is the ideal of translation. But the univocal language of the builders of the tower is not the language of philosophy; it is an
imposed order, a violent imposition of a single language.[24] The necessity of philosophy is defined in the collapse rather than in the project itself. As the desire for translation produced by the incompletion of the tower is never completely frustrated, the
edifice is never simply demolished. The building project of philosophy continues but
its completion is forever deferred.

The tower is also the figure of deconstruction. Since deconstruc-
tion inhabits philosophy, subverting it from within, it also inhabits the figure of the
tower. It is lodged in the tower, transforming the representation of its construction.
Inasmuch as philosophy is the ideal of translation, deconstruction is the subversion
of translation.[25] That subversion is found within the conditions for philosophy, the
incompletion of the tower: "The deconstruction of the Tower of Babel, moreover,
gives a good idea of what deconstruction is: an unfinished edifice whose half-
completed structures are visible, letting one guess at the scaffolding behind them."[26]
Deconstruction identifies the inability of philosophy to establish the stable ground,
the deferral of the origin which prevents the completion of the edifice by locating
the untranslatable, that which lies between the original and the translation.

But the tower is also the figure of architecture. The necessity of
translation is the failure of building that demands a supplementation by architecture.
Just as it is the precondition for philosophy, understood as building (presentation),
translation also marks the necessity for architecture (representation), but as a representation that speaks of the essence of building, an architecture that represents the
ground in its absence: "If the tower had been completed there would be no architecture. Only the incompletion of the tower makes it possible for architecture as well as
the multitude of languages to have a history."[27] The possibility of architecture is
bound up with the forever incomplete project of philosophy. Philosophy requires the
account of building as grounded and architecture as detached precisely because of
this incompletion. Structural failure produces the need for a supplement, the need
for a building/architecture distinction, the need for architecture. Architecture is
the translation of building that represents building to itself as complete, secure,
undivided.

Since the tower is the figure of deconstruction, architecture, and
translation, the question shifts from identifying the common ground between them,
the identity, to locating the difference. The once discrete domains become entangled

to the extent that the task becomes to identify the convoluted mechanism of translation that produces the sense of separate identities. This mechanism must be embedded in the scene of translation which bears on the status of structure.

Translation between the discourses is made possible by a breakdown in the sense of structure that is the currency within them. Derrida argues that the incompletion of the tower is the very structure of the tower. The tower is deconstructed by establishing that "the structure of the original is marked by the requirement to be translated"[28] and that it "in no way suffers from not being satisfied, at least it does not suffer insofar as it is the very structure of the work."[29] There is a gap in the structure that cannot be filled, a gap that can only be covered over. The tower is always already marked by a flaw inasmuch as it is a tower. This is a displacement of the traditional idea of structure. Structure is no longer simply grounding. It is no longer a vertical hierarchy, but a convoluted line. The structure is no longer simply standing on the ground. The building stands on an abyss.

This argument follows Heidegger's attempt to dismantle the edifice of metaphysics in order to reveal the condition of the ground on which it stood. In doing so, he raises the possibility that the ground (*Grund*) might actually be a concealed "abyss" (*Abgrund*) so that metaphysics is constructed in ignorance of the instability of the terrain on which it is erected: "we move over this ground as over a flimsily covered abyss."[30] Metaphysics becomes the veiling of the ground rather than the interrogation of it.

Heidegger's later work developed this possibility into a principle. He argues that philosophy has been in a state of "groundlessness" ever since the translation of the ancient Greek terms into the language of metaphysics. This translation substituted the original sense of ground with that of the sense of ground as support, ground as supporting presence to which the world is added.[31] For Heidegger, metaphysics is groundless precisely because it determines the ground as support. The original sense of *logos* has been lost. With metaphysics, the origin is seen as a stable ground rather than an abyss. The "modern" crisis, the groundlessness of the age of technology, is produced by philosophy's ancient determination of the ground as support for a structure to which representations are added.[32] The crisis of representation is produced by the very attempt to remove representations in order to reveal the supporting presence of the ground. Man is alienated from the ground precisely by thinking of it as secure.

Because of the very familiarity of the principle of ground-as-support, "we misjudge most readily and persistently the deceitful form of its violence."[33] Metaphysics conceals this violence. The architectural motif of the grounded structure is articulated in a way that effects this concealment. The vertical hierarchy is a mechanism of control that veils its own violence.

Heidegger attempts to subvert this mechanism by rereading the status of the architectural motif. He argues that the thought of architecture as a simple addition to building actually makes possible the thought of the naked ground as support. Undermining the division between building and architecture displaces the traditional sense of the ground: "But the nature of the erecting of buildings cannot be understood adequately in terms either of architecture or of engineering construction, nor in terms of a mere combination of the two."[34] The thought of that which is neither building nor architecture makes possible the original ground that precedes the ground as support. The linear logic of addition is confused. The building is not simply added to the ground, the ornament is not simply added to the structure, art is not simply added to philosophy. The vertical hierarchy of ground/structure/ornament is convoluted. The architectural motif undermines itself.

But while certain Heideggerian moves subvert the logic of addition by displacing the traditional account of architecture, Heidegger ultimately contradicts that possibility, confirming the traditional logic by looking for a stable structure. Derrida argues that Heidegger is unable to abandon the tradition of ground-as-support. Indeed, he retains it in the very account of translation he uses to identify its emergence.

> At the very moment when Heidegger is denouncing translation into Latin Words, at the moment when, at any rate, he declares Greek speech to be lost, he also makes use of a "metaphor." Of at least one metaphor, that of the foundation and the ground. The ground of the Greek experience is, he says, lacking in this "translation." What I have just too hastily called "metaphor" concentrates all the difficulties to come: does one speak "metaphorically" of the ground for just anything?[35]

The thought of ground-as-support is not just produced by a mistranslation. It is itself no more than a certain account of translation. Translation is understood as presentation of the ground, and mistranslation is understood as loss of support, detachment from ground. The collapse of the tower establishes the necessity of translation as one of reconstruction, edification.[36] Heidegger's account of translation undermines itself when dealing with the translation of the original ground into the idea of the edifice. Heidegger appears to employ an account of translation similar to Derrida's inasmuch as he argues that the violation of the original ground is already there in the Greek original. But then he attempts to go beneath this sense in order to erase the violation, and, in so doing, restores a traditional account of translation.[37] He rebuilds the edifice he appears to have undermined.

6.

Derrida departs from Heidegger precisely by following him. He takes the Heideggerian line further until it folds back on itself, transforming itself. "Deconstruction" is a "translation" of two of Heidegger's terms: *Destruktion*, meaning "not a destruction but precisely a destructuring that dismantles the structural layers in the system," and *Abbau*, meaning "to take apart an edifice in order to see how it is constituted or deconstituted."[38] Derrida follows Heidegger's argument that this "destructuring" or "unbuilding" disturbs a tradition by inhabiting its structure in a way that exploits its metaphoric resources against itself.

> The movements of deconstruction do not destroy structures from the outside. They are not possible and effective, nor can they take accurate aim, except by inhabiting those structures. Inhabiting them *in a certain way*, because one always inhabits, and all the more when one does not suspect it. Operating necessarily from the inside, borrowing all the strategic and economic resources of subversion from the old structure, borrowing them structurally.[39]

The concern here is with the way deconstruction inhabits the structure of the edifice, that is, the structure of structure. Deconstruction is neither unbuilding nor demolition. Rather, it is the "soliciting" of the edifice of metaphysics, the soliciting of structure "in the sense that *sollicitare*, in old Latin means to shake as a whole, to make tremble in entirety."[40] Solicitation is a form of interrogation which shakes structure in order to identify structural weaknesses, weaknesses that are structural.

Derrida destabilizes the edifice by arguing that its fundamental condition, its structural possibility, is the concealment of an abyss. The edifice of metaphysics claims to be stable because it is founded on the bedrock exposed when all the sedimentary layers have been removed. Deconstruction destabilizes metaphysics by locating in the bedrock the fractures that undermine its structure. The threat to metaphysics is underground. The subversion of presence is an underground operation. Deconstruction subverts the edifice it inhabits by demonstrating that the ground on which it is erected is insecure: "the terrain is slippery and shifting, mined and undermined. And this ground is, by essence, an underground."[41] But the fissures in the ground that crack the structure are not flaws that can be repaired. There is no more stable ground to be found. There is no unflawed bedrock.

Consequently, deconstruction appears to locate in metaphysics the fatal flaw that causes its collapse. It appears to be a form of analysis that dismantles or demolishes structures. It appears to be an undoing of construction. It is in this sense that it is most obviously architectural. But this obvious sense misses the force of deconstruction. Deconstruction is not simply architectural. Rather, it is a displacement of traditional thought about architecture.

Now the concept of de-construction itself resembles an architectural metaphor. It is often said to have a negative attitude. Something has been constructed, a philosophical system, a tradition, a culture, and along comes a de-constructor and destroys it stone by stone, analyses the structure and dissolves it. Often enough this is the case. One looks at a system—Platonic/Hegelian—and examines how it was built, which keystone, which angle of vision supports the authority of the system. It seems to me, however, that this is not the essence of deconstruction. It is not simply the technique of an architect who knows how to de-construct what has been constructed, but a probing which touches upon the technique itself, upon the authority of the architectural metaphor and thereby constitutes its own architectural rhetoric. Deconstruction is not simply—as its name seems to indicate—the technique of a reversed construction when it is able to conceive for itself the idea of construction. One could say that there is nothing more architectural than de-construction, but also nothing less architectural.[42]

Deconstruction leads to a complete rethinking of the supplemental relationship organized by the architectural motif of ground/structure/ornament. To disrupt metaphysics in this way is to disrupt the status of architecture. But it is not to simply abandon the traditional architectonic. Rather, it demonstrates that each of its divisions are radically convoluted. Each distinction is made possible by that which is neither one nor the other. The architectural logic of addition is subverted by demonstrating that it is made possible by precisely that which frustrates it.

This subversion of structure does not lead to a new structure. Flaws are identified in the structure but do not lead to its collapse. On the contrary, they are the very source of its strength. Derrida identifies the constitutional force of the weakness of a structure, that is, the strength of a certain weakness. Rather than abandoning a structure because its weakness has been found (which would be to remain in complicity with the ideal of a grounded structure), Derrida displaces the architectural motif. Structure becomes "erected by its very ruin, held up by what never stops eating away at its foundations."[43] Deconstruction is a form of interrogation that shakes structure in order to identify structural flaws, flaws that are structural. It is not the demolition of particular structures. It displaces the concept of structure itself by locating that which is neither support nor collapse.

Structure is perceived through the incidence of menace, at the moment when imminent danger concentrates our vision on the keystone of an institution, the stone which encapsulates both the possibility and the fragility of its existence. Structure then can be *methodically* threatened in order to be comprehended more clearly and to reveal not only its supports but also that secret place in which it is neither construction nor ruin but lability. This operation is called (from the Latin) *soliciting*.[44]

The edifice is erected by concealing the abyss on which it stands. This repression produces the appearance of solid ground. The structure does not simply collapse because it is erected on, and fractured by, an abyss. Far from causing its collapse, the fracturing of the ground is the very possibility of the edifice. Derrida identifies the "structural necessity" of the abyss:

And we shall see that this abyss is not a happy or unhappy accident. An entire theory of the structural necessity of the abyss will be gradually constituted in our reading; the indefinite process of supplementarity has always already *infiltrated* presence. . . . Representation *in the abyss* of presence is not an accident of presence; the desire of presence is, on the contrary, born from the abyss (the indefinite multiplication) of representation, from the representation of the representation, etc.[45]

The abyss is not simply the fracturing of the ground under the edifice. It is the internal fracturing of the edifice, the convolution of the distinction between building and architecture, structure and ornament, presentation and representation. Architecture always already inhabits and underpins the building it is supposedly attached to. It is this convolution that makes possible the thought of a ground that precedes the edifice, a thought that subordinates architecture as merely an addition. Architecture makes possible its own subordination to building.

Deconstruction is concerned with the untranslatable, the remainder that belongs neither to the original nor to the translation, but nevertheless resides within both. Deconstruction marks the structural necessity of a certain failure of translation. That is to say, the structural necessity of architecture. Architecture becomes the possibility of building rather than a simple addition to it. Inasmuch as translation is neither completed nor completely frustrated, the edifice of metaphysics is neither building nor architecture, neither presentation of the ground nor detachment from it, but the uncanny effacement of the distinction between them, the distinction that is at once the contractual possibility of architectural discourse and the means by which to repress the threat posed by that discourse. Deconstruction traces architecture's subversion of building, a subversion that cannot be resisted because architecture is the structural possibility of building. Building always harbors the secret of its constitutional violation by architecture. Deconstruction is the location of that violation. It locates ornament within the structure itself, not by integrating it in some classical synthetic gesture, but, on the contrary, by locating ornament's violation of structure, a violation that cannot be exorcised, a constitutional violation that can only be repressed.

7.

Such a gesture does not constitute a method, a critique, an analysis, or a source of legitimation.[46] It is not strategic. It has no prescribed aim. Which is not to say that it is aimless. It moves very precisely, but not to some end. It is not a project. It is neither an application of something nor an addition to something. It is, at best, a strange structural condition, an event. It is a displacement of structure that cannot be evaluated in traditional terms because it frustrates the logic of grounding or testing. It is precisely that which is necessary to structure but evades structural analysis (and all analysis is structural); it is the breakdown in structure that is the possibility of structure.

The repression of certain constitutional enigmas is the basis of the social contract that organizes the discourse. Rather than offering a new account of the architectural object, deconstruction unearths the repressive mechanisms by which that figure of architecture operates. Hidden within the traditional architectural figure is another: the architectural motif is required by philosophy not simply because it is a paradigm of stable structure; it is also required precisely for its instability.

For this reason, to translate deconstruction in architecture is not simply to transform the condition of the architectural object. As metaphysics is the definition of architecture as metaphor, the disruption of architecture's metaphoric condition is a disruption of metaphysics. But this is not to say that this disruption occurs outside the realm of objects. The teleologies of theory/practice, ideal/material, etc. do not disappear. Rather, there is a series of nonlinear exchanges within and between these domains, exchanges which problematize, but do not abandon, the difference. It is thereby possible to operate within the traditional description of architecture as the representation of structure in order to produce objects that make these enigmas thematic.

Such gestures are neither simply theoretical, nor simply practical. They are neither a new way of reading familiar architecture, nor the means of producing a new architecture. Objects are already bisected into theory and practice. To translate deconstruction in architecture does not lead simply to a formal reconfiguration of the object. Rather, it calls into question the condition of the object, its objecthood; it problematizes the condition of the object without simply abandoning it. Deconstruction is a concern with theoretical objects, objects whose theoretical status and objecthood are problematic, slippery objects that make thematic the theoretical condition of objects and the objecthood of theory.

Such gestures do not simply inhabit the prescribed domains of philosophy and architecture. While philosophical discourse and architectural discourse depend on an explicit account of architecture, they have no unique claim on that account. The translation contract on which those discourses are based underpin a multiplicity of cultural exchanges. The concern becomes the strategic play of the architectural motif in these exchanges. This cultural production of architecture does not take the form specified in the architectural discourse; architecture does not occupy the domain allotted to it. Rather than the object of a specific discourse, architecture is a series of discursive mechanisms whose operations can be traced in ways that are unfamiliar to architectural discourse.

Consequently, the status of the translation of deconstruction in architecture needs to be rethought. A more aggressive reading is required, an architectural transformation of deconstruction that draws on the gaps in deconstruction that demand such an abuse, sites that already operate with a kind of architectural violence. There is a need for a strong reading which locates that which deconstruction cannot handle of architecture.

Possibilities emerge within architectural discourse that go beyond the displacement of architecture implicit in deconstructive writing. To locate these possibilities is to (re)produce deconstruction by transforming it. Such a transformation must operate on the hesitation deconstruction has about architecture, a hesitation that surfaces precisely within its most confident claims about architecture. Derrida writes:

The "Tower of Babel" does not merely figure the irreducible multiplicity of tongues; it exhibits an incompletion, the impossibility of finishing, of totalizing, of saturating, of completing something on the order of edification, architectural construction, system and architectonics What the multiplicity of idioms actually limits is not only a "true" translation, a transparent and adequate interexpression, it is also a structural order, a coherence of construct. There is then (let us translate) something like an internal limit to formalization, an incompleteness of the constructure. It would be easy and up to a certain point justified to see there the translation of a system in deconstruction.[47]

This passage culminates symptomatically in a sentence that performs the classical philosophical gesture. Architecture is at once given constitutive power and has that power frustrated by returning its status to mere metaphor. Here the tower, the figure of translation, is itself understood as a translation, the architectural translation of deconstruction. Which, in Derridean terms, is to say a figure that does not simply represent deconstruction, but is its possibility. But an inquiry needs to focus on why an architectural reading of deconstruction is "easy" and what is the "certain point" beyond which it becomes unjustified, improper. A patient reading needs to force the convoluted surface of deconstructive writing and expose the architectural motif within it. But perhaps even such an abusive reading of Derrida is insufficient. Inasmuch as deconstruction is abused in architectural discourse, its theory of translation, which is to say its theory of abuse, needs to be rethought. Because of architecture's unique relationship to translation, it cannot simply translate deconstruction. It is so implicated in the economy of translation that it threatens deconstruction. There is an implicit identity between the untranslatable remainder located by deconstruction and that part of architecture that causes deconstruction to hesitate—the architecture it resists. Consequently, deconstruction does not simply survive architecture.

Notes

1. Jacques Derrida, *Positions*, trans. Alan Bass (Chicago: University of Chicago Press, 1981), p. 20.
2. "A text lives only if it lives on [sur-vit], and it lives on only if it is *at once* translatable *and* untranslatable. . . . ͲTotally translatable, it disappears as a text, as writing, as a body of language [*langue*]. Totally untranslatable, even within what is believed to be one language, it dies immediately. Thus triumphant translation is neither the life nor the death of the text, only or already its living on, its life after life, its life after death." Jacques Derrida, "Living On: Border Lines," trans. James Hulbert, in *Deconstruction and Criticism* (New York: Seabury Press, 1979), p. 102.
3. Cf. Jacques Derrida, "Me—Psychoanalysis: An Introduction to 'The Shell and the Kernel' by Nicolas Abraham," trans. Richard Klein, *Diacritics* (Spring 1979).
4. Deconstruction is considered here in the context of philosophy. While Derrida repeatedly argues that deconstruction is not philosophy, he also notes that it is not nonphilosophy either. To simply claim that deconstruction is not philosophy is to maintain philosophy by appealing to its own definition of its other. It is to participate in the dominant reading of Derrida that resists the force of deconstruction. That force is produced by identifying the complicity of the apparently nonphilosophical within the philosophical tradition. Deconstruction occupies the texts of philosophy in order to identify a nonphilosophical site within them. Deconstruction cannot be considered outside the texts of philosophy it inhabits, even as a foreigner.
5. "For if the difficulties of translation can be anticipated . . . one should not begin by naively believing that the word 'deconstruction' corresponds in French to some clear and univocal signification. There is already in 'my' language a serious ('somber') problem of translation between what here or there can be envisaged for the word, and the usage itself, the reserves of the word." Jacques Derrida, "Letter to a Japanese Friend," in *Derrida and Différance*, ed. David Wood and Robert Bernasconi (Coventry: Parousia Press, 1985), p. 1.
6. Immanuel Kant, *Critique of Pure Reason*, trans. Norman Kemp Smith (London: Macmillan, 1929), p. 47.
7. Ibid., p. 608.
8. Ibid., p. 14.
9. Ibid., p. 219.
10. Martin Heidegger, *An Introduction to Metaphysics*, trans. John Macquarrie and Edward Robinson (New York: Harper and Row, 1962), p. 2.
11. Cf. the Greek temple in "The Origin of the Work of Art": "Truth happens in the temple's standing where it is. This does not mean that something is correctly represented and rendered there, but that what is as a whole is brought into unconcealedness and held therein." Martin Heidegger, "The Origin of the Work of Art," in *Poetry, Language, Thought*, trans. Albert Hofstadter (New York: Harper and Row, 1971). The edifice is neither a representation of the ground, nor even a presentation, but is the production of the world.

12. "It is precisely the idea that it is a matter of providing a foundation for an edifice already constructed that must be avoided." Martin Heidegger, *Kant and the Problem of Metaphysics*, trans. James S. Churchill (Bloomington: Indiana University Press, 1962), p. 4.

13. "The foundation of traditional metaphysics is shaken and the edifice . . . begins to totter." Heidegger, *Kant and the Problem of Metaphysics*, p. 129.

14. Kant, *Critique of Pure Reason*, p. 60.

15. Heidegger, *Kant and the Problem of Metaphysics*, p. 5.

16. Jacques Derrida, "Structure, Sign and Play in the Discourse of the Human Sciences," in *Writing and Difference*, trans. Alan Bass (Chicago: University of Chicago Press, 1978), p. 279.

17. Heidegger, "The Origin of the Work of Art," p. 19.

18. Jacques Derrida, "The Parergon," trans. Craig Owens, *October* 9 (1979), p. 7.

19. Jacques Derrida, "Force and Signification," in *Writing and Difference*, p. 17.

20. Ibid., p. 27.

21. Jacques Derrida, "White Mythology: Metaphor in the Text of Philosophy," in *Margins of Philosophy*, trans. Alan Bass (Chicago: University of Chicago Press, 1982), p. 224.

22. Not in the sense of the structuralist concern for architecture as a kind of language, a system of objects to which language theory can be applied, but as the possibility of thought about language.

23. "With this problem of translation we will thus be dealing with nothing less than the problem of the very passage into philosophy." Jacques Derrida, *Dissemination*, trans. Barbara Johnson (Chicago: University of Chicago Press, 1981), p. 72.

24. "Had their enterprise succeeded, the universal tongue would have been a particular language imposed by violence, by force. It would not have been a universal language—for example in the Leibnizian sense—a transparent language to which everyone would have access." Jacques Derrida, *The Ear of the Other*, ed. Christie V. McDonald (New York: Schocken Books, 1985), p. 101. Cf. Jacques Derrida, "Languages and the Institutions of Philosophy," *Recherche et Sémiotique/Semiotic Inquiry* 4, no. 2 (1984), pp. 91–154.

25. "And the question of deconstruction is also through and through the question of translation. . . ." Derrida, "Letter to a Japanese Friend," p. 6.

26. Derrida, *The Ear of the Other*, p. 102.

27. Jacques Derrida, "Architecture Where the Desire May Live," *Domus* 671 (1986), p. 25.

28. Jacques Derrida, "Des Tours de Babel," trans. Joseph F. Graham, in *Difference in Translation*, ed. Joseph F. Graham (Ithaca: Cornell University Press, 1985), p. 184.

29. Ibid., p. 182.

30. Heidegger, *An Introduction to Metaphysics*, p. 93.

31. This degenerate translation is based on a degeneration that already occurred within the original Greek, requiring a return to a more primordial origin: "But with this Latin translation the original meaning of the Greek word is destroyed, this is true not only of the Latin translation of this word but of all other Roman translations of the Greek philosophical language. What happened in this translation from the Greek into the Latin is not accidental and harmless; it marks the first stage in the process by which we cut ourselves off and alienated ourselves from the original essence of Greek philosophy. . . . But it should be said in passing that even within Greek philosophy a narrowing of the word set in forthwith, although the original meaning did not vanish from the experience, knowledge, and orientation of Greek philosophy." Heidegger, *An Introduction to Metaphysics*, p. 13.

32. "The perfection of technology is only the echo of the claim to the . . . completeness of the foundation. . . . Thus, the characteristic domination of the principle of ground then determines the essence of our modern technology age." Martin Heidegger, "The Principle of Ground," trans. Keith Hoeller, *Man and World* 7 (1974), p. 213.

33. Ibid., p. 204.

34. Martin Heidegger, "Building, Dwelling, Thinking," in *Poetry, Language, Thought*, p. 159.

35. Jacques Derrida, "Restitutions of the Truth in Pointing," in *The Truth in Painting*, trans. Geoff Bennington and Ian McLeod (Chicago: University of Chicago Press, 1987), p. 290.

36. Note how Derrida argues that the university is "built" on the ideal of translation (Derrida, "Living On: Border Lines," pp. 93–94) in the same way that he argues that it is "built" on the ideal of ground as support (Jacques Derrida, "Principle of Reason: The University in the Eyes of Its Pupils," *Diacritics*, Fall 1983, pp. 11–20).

37. "*Beneath* the seemingly literal and thus faithful translation there is concealed . . . a trans-

lation without a corresponding, equally authentic experience of what they say. The root-lessness of Western thought begins with this trans-lation." Heidegger, "The Origin of the Work of Art," p. 23 (emphasis added). "We are not merely taking refuge in a more literal translation of a Greek word. We are reminding ourselves of what, unexperienced and unthought, *underlies* our familiar and therefore outworn essence of truth." Ibid., p. 52 (emphasis added).

38. Jacques Derrida, "Roundtable on Autobiography," trans. Peggy Damuf, in *The Ear of the Other*, p. 86. Of the word "deconstruction": "Among other things I wished to translate and adapt to my own ends the Heideggerian word *Destruktion* or *Abbau*. Each signified in this context an operation bearing on the structure or traditional architecture of the fundamental concepts of ontology or of Western metaphysics." Derrida, "Letter to a Japanese Friend," p. 1.

39. Jacques Derrida, *Of Grammatology*, trans. Gayatri Chakravorty Spivak (Baltimore: Johns Hopkins University Press, 1976), p. 24.

40. Jacques Derrida, "Difference," in *Margins of Philosophy*, p. 21.

41. Jacques Derrida, *Limited Inc.* (Baltimore: Johns Hopkins University Press, 1977), p. 168.

42. Derrida, "Architecture Where the Desire May Live," p. 18.

43. Jacques Derrida, "Fors," trans. Barbara Johnson, *Georgia Review* 31, no. 1 (1977), p. 40.

44. Derrida, "Force and Signification," p. 6.

45. Derrida, *Of Grammatology*, p. 163.

46. "In spite of appearance, deconstruction is neither an analysis nor a critique and its translation would have to take that into consideration, it is not an analysis in particular because the dismantling of a structure is not a regression toward a *simple* element, toward an *indissoluble* origin. These values, like that of analysis, are themselves philosophemes subject to deconstruction." Derrida, "Letter to a Japanese Friend," p. 4.

47. Derrida, "Des Tours de Babel," p. 165.

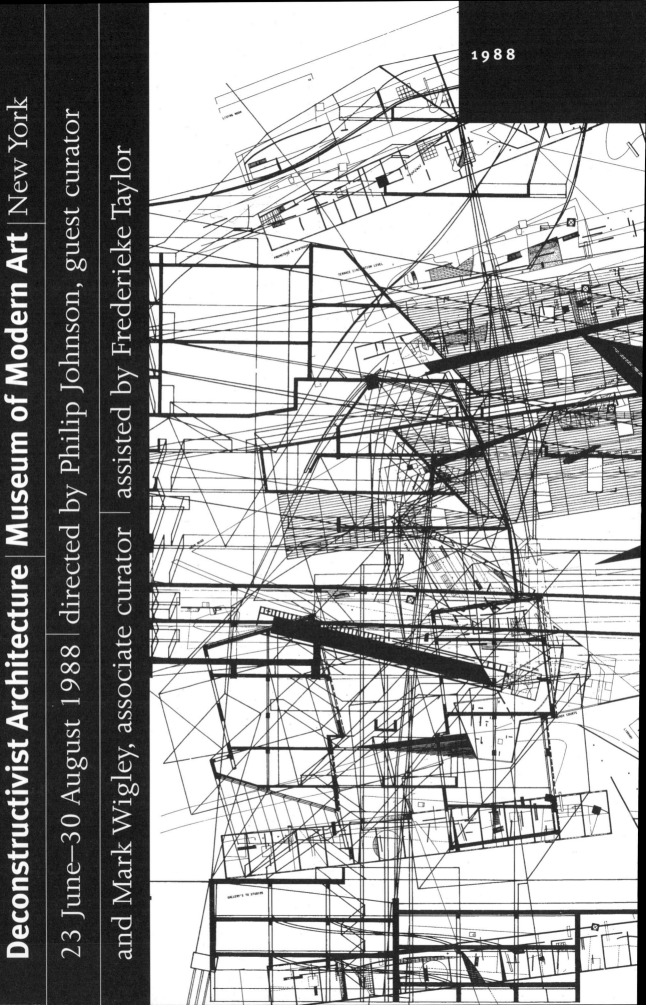

Deconstructivist Architecture | Museum of Modern Art | New York

23 June–30 August 1988 | directed by Philip Johnson, guest curator | assisted by Frederieke Taylor

and Mark Wigley, associate curator

1988

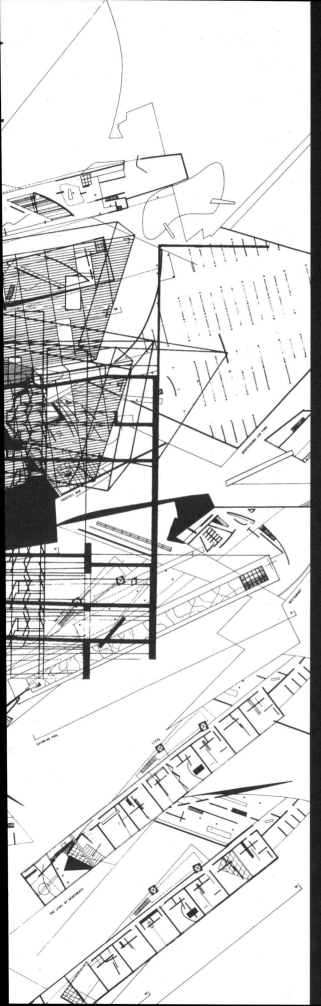

It is now about sixty years since Henry-Russell Hitchcock, Alfred Barr, and I started our quest for a new style of architecture which would, like Gothic or Romanesque in their day, take over the discipline of our art. The resulting exhibition of 1932, "Modern Architecture," summed up the architecture of the twenties—Mies van der Rohe, Le Corbusier, Gropius, and Oud were the heroes—and prophesied an International Style in architecture to take the place of the romantic "styles" of the previous century.

With this exhibition, there are no such aims. As interesting to me as it would be to draw parallels to 1932, however delicious it would be to declare again a new style, that is not the case today. Deconstructivist architecture is not a new style. We arrogate to its development none of the messianic fervor of the modern movement, none of the exclusivity of that catholic and Calvinist cause. Deconstructivist architecture represents no movement; it is not a creed. It has no "three rules" of compliance. It is not even "seven architects."

It is a confluence of a few important architects' work of the years since 1980 that shows a similar approach with very similar forms as an outcome. It is a concatenation of similar strains from various parts of the world.

Philip Johnson

Critical work today can be done only in the realm of building: to engage with the discourse, architects have to engage with building; the object becomes the site of all theoretical inquiry. Theorists are forced out of the sanctuary of theory, practitioners are roused from sleepwalking practice. Both meet in the realm of building, and engage with objects.

This should not be understood as a rejection of theory. Rather, it indicates that the traditional status of theory has changed. No longer is it some abstract realm of defense that surrounds objects, protecting them from examination by mystifying them. Architectural theory generally preempts an encounter with the object. It is concerned with veiling rather than exposing objects. With these projects, all the theory is loaded into the object: propositions now take the form of objects rather than verbal abstractions. What counts is the condition of the object, not the abstract theory. Indeed the force of the object makes the theory that produced it irrelevant. . . .

The nightmare of deconstructivist architecture inhabits the unconscious of pure form rather than the unconscious of the architect. The architect merely countermands traditional formal inhibitions in order to release the suppressed alien. Each architect releases different inhibitions in order to subvert form in radically different ways. Each makes thematic a different dilemma of pure form.

In so doing they produce a devious architecture, a slippery architecture that slides uncontrollably from the familiar into the unfamiliar, toward an uncanny realization of its own alien nature: an architecture, finally, in which form distorts itself in order to reveal itself anew. The projects suggest that architecture has always been riddled with these kinds of enigmas, that they are the source of its force and its delight— that they are the very possibility of its formidable presence.

Mark Wigley

Mary McLeod **"Architecture and Politics in the Reagan Era: From Postmodernism to Deconstructivism"** *Assemblage* 8 (February 1989)

One account of postmodernism associates efforts to retrieve cultural memory through formal, historical allusions with neoconservative politics, while holding out the possibility, as Mary McLeod puts it in her essay here, that forms of "fragmentation, dispersion, decentering, schizophrenia, [and] disturbance" can imbue architecture with a "critical" power associated with poststructuralist theoretical practices. But another view understands both the pastiche of historical representations and the poststructuralist critique of the same as secondary to the accelerated culture of consumption that characterized the 1980s. For something like the binary logic of an earlier, structural linguistics-based formalism still bleeds through the fabric of later theories that otherwise claim a more radically proliferated and destabilizing force. In most versions of so-called poststructuralist or deconstructivist architecture, the negativity of modernism is reconstituted as a specific sign system in its own right, which is then "critically," even "violently" opposed (such words were prevalent in the 1980s) to the context into which it is inserted. The strident freshness of the new architecture still seeks to perform an essentially modernist function of renewal of perception but substitutes for modernism's totalized socio-aesthetic-productive package a practice of signs that shares the same techniques of building production and delivery with *another* practice of signs that it opposes. And as the 1980s came to an end, doubts arose about whether an architecture that is nothing more than a practice of signs could ever escape the destiny of becoming one more degraded form of the commodification of information.

The discourse of architectural postmodernism pushed into full view a deeply felt struggle in progressive architecture theory. The wholesale deprecation of postmodernism as a symptom of capitalism is as reductive as earlier leftist dismissals of modernism (Lukács's attack on expressionism in the 1930s, for example, or even Adorno's writing off of jazz); yet one cannot deny that postmodern architecture, in all its forms, is solidly anchored in consumer culture. When even those experiments (whether cynical or sincere) allegedly aimed at undermining the system seem inevitably to draw their life from the same kind of insatiable desire that keeps the consumer system going in the first place, theory is confronted with the impossibility of even imagining *something else*, of projecting a space outside the structures of commodification.

As what was for some the most radical architecture of the 1980s was being disseminated through the publicity machine of Philip Johnson and the Museum of Modern Art, architecture theory had to wrestle with such problems. McLeod's close attention to the specific, historical dynamics of architecture in the age of universal surrender to market ideology gives shape to an earnest call for architecture theory to shake itself out of its fixation on the critical or liberative power of form and to include considerations of commodity production and institutional constraints along with its formal analyses. Though her essay does not produce solutions (perhaps it could not have in 1989), it has the advantage of reminding us that, lest they turn into mere moralism or desperate handwringing, critical reflections on commodification and consumption must hold out the possibility of projecting alternative interpretive systems to capitalism—must offer, that is, some utopian proposition—something that architecture theory in the 1980s was not generally accustomed to doing.

"Postmodern architecture is the architecture of Reaganism." Among many leftist architects and critics, this kind of statement has become a cliché. The pseudohistorical nostalgia, the fabricated traditions, the pandering to a nouveau-riche clientele, the populist rhetoric that often sounds more paternalistic than democratic, the abandonment of any social vision—all seem related in some way to the conservative turn in American politics. On the other hand, neoconservative critics Daniel Bell and Hilton Kramer have vehemently attacked postmodernism from their perspective, claiming that it undermines social stability and fundamental spiritual values.[1] This attack on disparate fronts immediately reveals the difficulties of any simple equation between postmodernism and a political position. The relation between style and ideology has always been a complex one, but in the instance of postmodernism the problem is compounded: first, by the confusion surrounding what postmodernism is and, second, by the ever-quickening cycle of consumption that seems to cause political meanings to change with increasing rapidity, raising more fundamental questions about the nature of architecture's political power.

Postmodern Architecture: Some Definitions

Almost inevitably, any essay about postmodernism must confront the problems of defining this diverse and pluralistic movement. Attempts at definition have varied from broad-scale historical periodization (Fredric Jameson), to philosophical equations (postmodernism as the cultural equivalent of poststructuralism), to specific stylistic trends or intentions, open at odds from one field to another (autonomy and formalism, for example, are seen as modern in one field, postmodern in another). In American architecture, where the word was first popularized, the critic has the potential advantage of its widespread usage. The first, and still the most common, understanding of the term refers to the tendency that rejects the formal and social constituents of the modern movement and embraces a broader formal language, which is frequently figurative and historically eclectic. While advocates of postmodern architecture have often agreed more about what they reject than about what they endorse, certain themes have consistently been explored: historical styles, regionalism, decoration, urban contextualism and morphologies, among others. If there is any single objective that unites these various concerns, it is the search for architectural communication, the desire to make architecture a vehicle of cultural expression. Postmodern practitioners and critics have tended to seek ideological justification, not in program, function, or structure, but in *meaning*. A manifesto by the editors of the *Harvard Architectural Review* declared that postmodernism is "an attempt, and an important one, to respond to the problem of meaning which was posed but never solved by the modern movement."[2]

As architects themselves have been influenced by critical discourse and events in other fields, another understanding of postmodernism has arisen in the past few years: one that attempts to link architecture to a general epistemological situation, frequently associated with poststructuralism. Here, the objective seems almost the inverse of that of the earlier postmodernists. Whereas the first group criticized modern architecture for being abstract, arcane, and inaccessible—for having forsaken architecture's traditional communicative role—this second group accepts, even celebrates, this same disintegration of communication and consensus—the impossibility, in fact, of postulating any meaning at all. Although these two positions are dialectically opposed, the territory of debate remains the same: meaning and its dissolution. At first, this later interpretation of postmodernism seemed, in architecture, to be a one-man movement, advanced by Peter Eisenman; but in recent years a number of other architects, most notably several young "neoconstructivists," have been grouped with him in this alternative reaction to the failings of modernism. How "postmodern" this phenomenon actually is remains suspect as new labels ("schismatic postmodernism," "decomposition," "deconstructivism") are continually being introduced, juxtaposing this group to the other "postmodernists."[3]

What is immediately apparent in either of these conceptions of postmodernism, however, is that some of the distinctions that can be drawn between modernism and postmodernism in other fields cannot be sustained in architecture. Although modern architects were frequently engaged in highly sophisticated, abstract formal explorations, modernism in architecture was never commonly conceived, as it was in painting after World War II, as being "art about art" or as implying autonomy of the discipline. The modern movement was seen by both its early practitioners and its historians as intrinsically involving new techniques, mass culture, and a broader social role.[4] And if postmodern advocates have produced their own more reductive, monolithic version of modern architecture, it is one that asserts, even exaggerates, the modern movement's social concerns. Thus the commonly assumed polarity of modernism/artistic autonomy and postmodernism/mass culture (cultural "contamination") simply does not hold. Indeed, postmodern currents, whether historicist or poststructuralist, can be viewed as a return to architecture as a primarily formal and artistic pursuit, one that rejects the social engagement of the modern movement;[5] with few exceptions, the eclecticism and pluralism of postmodern architecture have operated almost entirely in the formal sphere. And yet, in delineating this retreat to traditional boundaries, it is also important to acknowledge architecture's more visible cultural role. Postmodernism has coincided with the public's increased attention to architecture. More buildings in the United States are now designed by architects; more students are enrolled in architecture schools;[6] more design criticism appears routinely in magazines and newspapers; and at least a few architects have achieved the celebrity status that earns them advertising endorsements and *Time* magazine covers.

Architecture and Politics

Linking architecture and politics presents certain difficulties. Neither field can be reduced to the other: nor is it self-evident that architecture's relation to politics has any major impact on power relations. It might appear that architecture is always political in the sense that anything is political, the meaning of politics being diluted to some generalized cultural association; or else that architecture is rarely political, in which case the definition is narrowly confined to those activities directly influencing power relations.[7] Notwithstanding these qualifications, it would be impossible to deny that some real, if ambiguous connection exists between the two realms. The intersections between architecture and politics can be seen as twofold: the first involves architecture's role in the economy; the second, its role as a cultural object.

What, in fact, immediately distinguishes architecture from other arts—notably painting, music, and writing—is the enormous expense it entails.[8] Although an art form can be seen as reflecting market pressures, architecture's dependence on the sources of finance and power extends to nearly every facet of the design process: choice of site, program, budget, materials, and production schedules. These economic and utilitarian parameters ordinarily limit architecture's transgressive and transformative power, but they also inscribe areas for potential social action. In other words, architecture's production processes imply possibilities of institutional change itself. Here, architecture's connection to politics appears more direct than that of other arts.

But just as architecture is intrinsically joined to political and economic structures by virtue of its production, so, too, its form—its meaning as a cultural object—carries political resonances. In this sense, owing to its utilitarian value, its political impact may be more diffuse, if more sustained, than that of other arts. Buildings are rarely perceived at once for their aesthetic qualities and "content"; rather their impact occurs gradually through use and repeated contact.[9] From this perspective, spatial configurations, tackle qualities, and functional relations are as important as figurative dimensions in architecture's reception. And as with art, this reception is always closely tied to a particular social context and historical moment.[10] These two political dimensions of architecture, production processes and formal reception, are, of course, not unrelated—building techniques can convey meanings—but their political roles can operate independently, each exerting influence at different moments and on different groups.[11]

The modern movement in architecture was deeply concerned with the first of these political dimensions. The advocacy of standardization and serial production, the emphasis on housing as a social program, the concern for a mass clientele—all were examples of the modern architect's attempt to redefine architecture's economic and social role. When Le Corbusier made his passionate plea "Architecture or Revolution. Revolution can be avoided," he was arguing not for formal isolation, but rather for an expansion of architecture's role to address social problems.[12] If in the case of Le Corbusier this position remained an issue of polemics more than practice, in the instance of many German practitioners the production of architecture radically changed. Ernst May's program for mass-produced housing in Frankfurt and Walter Gropius's experiments with standardization in Dessau are two obvious examples.

In retrospect, the forms of the modern movement can also be seen as embodying ideological positions. The rejection of monumental imagery in public buildings, the radical reorganization of the home, the elimination of explicit gender references in interior design, all challenged existing social patterns. Occasionally, such ideological intentions were specifically stated (for example, Hannes Meyer's claim that the open glazed rooms of his League of Nations project would eliminate "backstairs diplomacy," or the frequent associations of the free plan with democracy);[13] but for the most part, the architects of the modern movement did not conceive of form as an *independent* critical or utopian tool. It was seen as either the result of structural and functional concerns or an expression of the zeitgeist of the machine age. In other words, the new forms reflected either materially or symbolically the changes in production. Architecture's political role was conceived first as a question of process, and only secondarily as a question of form, although to separate the two would have been virtually impossible in the minds of the early pioneers.[14] Both necessitated radical change, if architecture *and* society were to be transformed.

Postmodernism (in its first sense) emerged in part from a disillusionment with this social vision. The unprecedented brutality of Nazi Germany, the purges of Stalinist Russia, the advent of the atom bomb, and the increasing dominance of multinational capitalism all undermined hopes of architecture's redemptive power. But just as significant to this loss of faith were the manifestations of modernism itself. By the 1960s architects and social critics no longer saw the revolutionary zeal of the modern movement as productive, but as destructive; they cited the desolate mass-housing projects, the wasteland of urban renewal, the alienation resulting from an architectural language that now seemed arcane, mute, and of little appeal outside a narrow cultural elite. Advocacy planning and the self-help projects of the 1960s were one response to modernism's apparent failure, but the collapse of those efforts only contributed further to the architect's sense of political impotence. What both the activists of the 1960s and the first postmodern critics of the early 1970s were reacting to was, in fact, the evolution of modernism in the postwar decades into a routinized corporate modernism that seemed headed in two equally unpromising directions: the expressionistic excesses of a Stone or a Saarinen, on the one hand, and the "scientific" determinism epitomized by the researches of Christopher Alexander or the technological fantasies of Archigram, on the other.[15] But if this modernism already stripped of most of its revolutionary content spawned the first criticisms of modern architecture, the focus of the attack soon reverted to the modern movement, which was seen as instigating the demise of architectural meaning and artistic expression.[16] And just as form and content were inseparably intertwined in the minds of the early modern pioneers, so too were they inextricably linked in the postmodern reaction. What was considered wrong with the modern movement was equally its forms *and* its political content. Together they had produced the failures of public housing complexes and the destruction of the center city.

In the United States, this critique of modernism appears to be related to the economic cycle of construction itself. Numerous International Style skyscrapers were built in the 1950s and 1960s, when the economy was booming and, not coincidentally, when modernism had its first real opportunity to manifest itself in the United States (the Depression and World War II had severely limited private construction). The theoretical reassessment of modern architecture only emerged in full force during the early 1970s when young architects were almost without work. Designers such as Peter Eisenman and Michael Graves were making professional careers of an annual house addition or interior renovation (leading to epithets such as "the cubist kitchen king"); frequently, they were busier writing than building. The dismal economy not only permitted theoretical speculation, but also further fueled perceptions of the architect's diminished social role.

The result, all too familiar today, was a return to the concept of architecture as art. Architecture's value no longer lay in its redemptive social power, its transformation of productive processes, but rather in its communicative power as a cultural object. If this new perspective harked back to traditional aesthetic parameters, it also reflected a new interest in cultural signs, spurred by semiology and communication theories. Meaning, not institutional reform, was now the objective.

Postmodernism and Politics

What is immediately apparent in any survey of architectural developments of the 1960s and 1970s is that the political impulses linked to this change in perspective had mixed connotations. To critics of the traditional Left, most notably Tomás Maldonado, Kenneth Frampton, and Martin Pawley, the rejection of social engagement represented an abdication of the architect's responsibility. They criticized the split between form and social institutions as invalid and argued that a rigorous structural rationalism and functionalism were still essential to answering the mass's needs in an age of late capital. But to the early critics of modernism, not yet dubbed "postmodernists," it was exactly this position that had led to the public's alienation and to the disintegration of any sense of urban community. In the early 1970s, influenced by the social theories of Karl Popper, Colin Rowe condemned the utopianism of modernism as a form of totalitarianism akin to the apocalyptic visions of Marxism. He claimed that the universal rationalism of modernism suppressed diversity and complexity; the objective instead should be a city of fragments, a "collage city."[17] Robert Venturi and Denise Scott Brown also attacked the "environmental megalomania" of modern architects "as a curse on the city." In a response to Pawley in 1970 they stated, "We suggest that the architect who starts with what *is* . . . will be less harmful and more effective than the petulant rhetorician grandly and dryly continuing to evoke 'the impact of technology on Western civilization' and 'the relationship of the nascent science of design to human goals and aspirations.' We are in favor of science in architecture but not of science-voodooism, twenties or sixties style."[18]

This debate echoed the running argument among leftists in the late 1960s and early 1970s between those believing in the instrumentality of technology yet condemning commodity culture and those rejecting the determinacy of technology but finding in popular culture the impulses of a new order. Following Herbert Marcuse, many Marxists believed that technology was essential to alleviating oppressive work conditions and improving social life, but that the masses were so manipulated by advertising and the media that it was impossible to determine from contemporary culture any genuine needs or values. Many of the New Left, however, found in mass culture the stirrings of a grass-roots populism that embodied legitimate needs and aspirations, regardless of the economic and political institutions that generated them. At the heart of this conflict was the critics' relation to mass opinion: the issue of elitism vs. populism. Did the masses know what they wanted or were social aspirations to be determined only by a critical, educated elite shrewd to the forces of capital? Or were the so-called populists denying the masses' needs by restricting their vision to the image presented by a media culture? It was exactly over this issue that architectural debate took its most acerbic form. Frampton charged that Venturi and Scott Brown's interest in Las Vegas was "elitist" and "conservative," a "de facto rationalization of the polluted environment," and Maldonado condemned their position as "cultural nihilism."[19] In the pages of *Casabella*, Scott Brown caustically returned the charges, stating that European-based "armchair-revolutionary pot shots" reflected a disdain for American culture and legitimized a "repressed upper-middle-class prejudice" against a "hard-hat majority."[20]

Even among the early critics of modernism, however, the position concerning audience was hardly cohesive. Although *Learning from Las Vegas* (1972) embodied clear populist sympathies, Venturi's earlier and more influential work *Complexity and Contradiction in Architecture* (1966) vividly illustrated the tensions between an elitist appreciation of high art and a populist embrace of Main Street that would be so characteristic of the later postmodern movement. Indeed, the balance of the argument and the number of plates (346 of 350) in the book clearly favors the former. Throughout the 1970s, Charles Moore consistently and enthusiastically embraced popular culture; but Rowe was steeped in a kind of nostalgia for nineteenth-century bourgeois culture, while Michael Graves longed for a public who could appreciate the world of Poussin and Roman villas. Whether elitist or populist, what these factions shared, however, was a sense that modernism was failing to communicate to any group besides design professionals; in this respect, the architects' critique of the modern movement allied itself with earlier criticism in the social sphere, most notably Jane Jacobs's *The Death and Life of the Great American Cities* of 1961 and Herbert Gans's *The Levittowners* of 1966.[21] The populism of the 1960s led to advocacy efforts; conversely, in the early 1970s, these same impulses were channeled to the formal sphere.

A passivity vis-à-vis economic and political power has continued to be one of the major reasons for leftists' unease with postmodern architecture. However critical postmodern architects were of corporate skyscrapers and government housing projects, it was soon apparent that their focus was on form and style. With amazing rapidity, postmodernism became the new corporate style, after Philip Johnson's notorious Chippendale top for AT&T instantly convinced patrons of its marketability and prestige value. The office building boom, which followed on the heels of New York City's financial recovery, further fueled the acceptance of the new style. If the reassessment of modernism occurred in a tight economy, which encouraged reflection and criticism, postmodernism began to flourish in the boom economy of the early 1980s. Architects seemed to stop writing and theorizing; most reacted hungrily to the opportunities to build.

The domination of American political life by conservative forces since the advent of postmodernism has only reinforced the Left's assessment. In the private sector, the proliferation of luxury apartment towers, amenity-packed condominium developments, planned resort communities, larger suburban homes, and ubiquitous shopping centers,[22] all spurred by the emergence of the new "yuppie" class, have given postmodernism a fertile field in which to grow. In the public sector the Reagan administration's ninety-percent reduction of funds for public housing and its drastic curtailment of social programs have virtually eliminated commissions oriented toward the poor and minority groups.[23] The only public commissions have been for traditional institutions such as museums. Although nothing in the polemics of postmodernism has precluded architects from addressing social programs, neither has there been anything to encourage architects to challenge their elimination. Collectively, postmodern architects have exhibited a marked indifference to economic and social policy.

Thus, if any dialectical tension with the dominant power structures exists in postmodern architecture, it resides not in institutions but in the content of architectural forms. As already noted, most postmodern architects hold as a basic assumption some concept of architecture's communicative power; and, indeed, it is here that a few critics and architects have made political claims for their discipline.[24] After acknowledging the difficulties of finding "uplifting social content" to include in contemporary architecture, Charles Jencks states that the architect can "design dissenting buildings that express the complex situation. He can communicate the values which are missing and ironically criticize the ones he dislikes."[25] And in *Complexity and Contradiction in Architecture*, Venturi more modestly asserts, "The architect who would accept his role as combiner of significant old cliches—valid banalities— in new contexts as his condition within a society that directs its best efforts, its big money, and its elegant technologies elsewhere, can ironically express in this indirect way a true concern for society's inverted scale of values."[26] This raises immediate questions, however, about the legibility of architectural forms: Do buildings convey clear messages? Is it appropriate to discuss buildings as critical or constructive in political terms at all? For our purposes here, it is probably sufficient to mention the difficulties of equating architectural forms with words, the problems of consensus concerning architectural meaning, the distracted mode of architecture's reception, and the shifting nature of any meanings that might be conveyed.[27] All of this challenges Jencks's claims that architecture can communicate clear political positions. But if it is difficult to grasp what architectural meaning might entail, it also refutes everyday experience to deny the connotative and suggestive power of forms. Architectural meaning is shifting and ambiguous, which inevitably results in ambiguous, and double-edged, political readings. Thus any analysis of architectural ideology must go beyond simplistic labels of good and bad, and must search to discover in this complex matrix instances of both social entrenchment and genuine critique.

Historical Styles

These ambiguities become immediately apparent in one of the fundamental themes of postmodernism: the rediscovery of history. Postmodern architects universally rejected the modern movement's messianic faith in the *new* and condemned the notion of a zeitgeist that obliterated the past and wiped out differences in tradition and experience. Their motives for embracing historical styles, however, varied considerably. Some postmodernists, notably Robert Stern, Allen Greenberg, and Thomas Beeby, sought to establish cultural continuities and a renewed sense of community. Quoting Daniel Bell, Stern stated that the central issue facing postmodernists was "whether culture can regain coherence, a coherence of substance and experience, not only form."[28] History provided a more communicative language; it was a means for architecture to regain the public role that the hermeticism of modernist abstraction had denied it. This historical revivalism emerged from the egalitarian and populist impulses of the 1960s critique, but its assumptions were largely social integration and preservation, not social change. In contrast, other postmodernists, such as Venturi, Johnson, and Stanley Tigerman, saw history as promising freedom and change, if only on an aesthetic plane. Technological progress did not mandate one style but made possible many styles, and the past offered an infinite field of possibilities. This was hardly the eclecticism of nineteenth-century architects who sought a moral fit between style and social function. Instead, for Venturi, the model was the eighteenth-century garden.[29] Historical styles offered a means to represent a variety of experiences, moods, and allusions; in other words, history provided the material for a complex and diverse vision of the present. For Johnson, stylistic eclecticism meant simply aesthetic liberation: an invitation to a new art for art's sake. As early as 1961, he declared to Jürgen Joedicke, "There are no rules, absolutely no given truths in any of the arts. There is only the sensation of a marvelous freedom, of an unlimited possibility to explore, of an unlimited past of great examples of architecture from history to enjoy. . . . Structural honesty for me is one of those infantile nightmares from which we will have to free ourselves as soon as possible."[30]

There was something at once exhilarating and resigned in this rediscovery of history. On the one hand, it meant freedom and a chance to recoup lost values; on the other, it suggested that the present was no better than the past, that aesthetic and political choices might be arbitrary. In the most successful postmodern works, such as Venturi's Vanna Venturi house (1961) and James Stirling and Michael Wilford's Stuttgart Museum (1977–1984), historical references are used to express just this tension.[31] Reinstating a dialogue with the past, the architecture installs and then subverts conventions in parodic ways that make explicit the inherent paradoxes and provisionality of a historical moment. The dualities of tradition and innovation, order and fragmentation, figuration and abstraction help articulate the contradictions of modernism and its ideological context. In Venturi's work especially, the very emphasis on surface and image elucidates the discursive and contingent dimensions of our present historicity. But in most postmodern architecture, such insight appears too painful to acknowledge. Historical allusion rapidly becomes nostalgia, escape, or enjoyable simulacrum—a denial of history itself. In the case of literal revivalists, such as Greenberg and John Blatteau, tension and parody are eliminated in academic recreations of the past. And all too often, the references to Lutyens, colonial plantations, and imperial monuments evoke a one-sided past, a "history of victors." For other practitioners, such as Stern and Johnson, irony looses its critical edge, as historical caricatures are openly acknowledged as diversions from the routine of daily existence. Cartooned exaggeration alternates with esoteric, mannered quotation; history is randomly scavenged to create an aura of historical depth.

But whether in literal copybook recreations or in exuberant displays of random quotation, the rediscovery of history has reflected with uncanny ease the interests of the marketplace. More than the stripped-down forms of modernism, revived historical styles signaled the desire for the instant acquisition of the values of family, tradition, and social status that surfaced with a vengeance in the 1980s. The marketing tactics of Ralph Lauren, the period revivals in furnishings and fashion, the long-standing eclecticism of suburban development—all found aesthetic allies within the architectural establishment. Paradoxically, as the market increasingly co-opted postmodernism, the value of variety itself became suspect. Many styles and many pasts began to appear as one style and one past. By the mid-1980s, the real-estate ads had designated postmodernism a historical style in itself.

Regionalism

Postmodernism's interest in regionalism, closely linked to its historicist focus, is yet another response to the modern movement's universalizing tendencies: the latter's postulation of a method (mass production) and an aesthetic (the International Style) that would obliterate cultural differences. It is on these grounds that such ideologically opposed critics as Jencks and Frampton have placed hopes of political dissent and resistance. Jencks claims that in order to design "dissenting buildings," the architect "must make use of the language of the local culture; otherwise his message falls on deaf ears, or is distorted to fit this local language."[32] Although Frampton rejects Jencks's emphasis on sign and image, he too turns to regionalism in the early 1980s as a locus for creating an "architecture of resistance," one that will answer Paul Ricoeur's quest of "how to become modern and to return to the sources."[33]

Leaving aside difficulties of what might constitute a "dissenting" architectural message, two problems immediately present themselves: first, the paucity in the United States of vital "local" languages—especially in the major areas of new construction—and second, the difficulties of convincingly recreating or transforming these languages, given financial constraints, changes in construction processes, and new building types—often of a radically different scale. Although buildings such as Venturi's Nantucket houses or Graves's library at San Juan Capistrano are less obtrusive in traditional surroundings than the brutal structures of the two preceding decades, the postmodern use of regionalism rarely extends beyond surface image; such designs are mere fabrications, without any real cultural roots.[34] And given the conciliatory aspirations of most designers, only occasionally do these designs gain a self-consciously critical dimension; more often they seem to be the architectural equivalents to conservative yearnings for a simpler American past.

Nor have Frampton's more abstract criteria of light, topography, and technique been widely adopted; his essay "Towards a Critical Regionalism" omits American examples. And those buildings that he does cite as models—works by Mario Botta, Tadao Ando, Jørn Utzon—often share more with each other than with their respective locales.[35] This raises the question of whether "region" or some more universal criteria of artistic quality—craftsmanship, detail, quality of materials—are the source of their "resistant" qualities.[36] The homogenizing forces of mass media and the increasingly multinational scale of finance and the construction industry certainly leave little regional heritage to recover. In the United States, the large size, low budget, and rapid timetable of most (nonluxury) contemporary developments further mitigate against the kind of attentive design that Frampton prescribes.

The one regional attribute of pressing political concern in this energy-consuming society is climate. But postmodernism's rejection of "biological" determinism and its emphasis on style have generally precluded the investigations of sun orientation and ventilation that were of such concern to modern architects. (As one critic at a conference on regionalism caustically noted, "The air conditioner is Florida's regional identity.")[37]

Decoration

The emphasis on ornament, color, texture, and pattern in postmodern architecture is still another response to what many architects have considered the excessive limitations of modernism: its formal monotony, repetitiveness, and narrow expressive range. By the 1960s the austerity of modern architecture no longer represented a critique of bourgeois values and oppressive stereotypes; it reflected instead the relentless rationalization and routinization of the business world. Again advocates of postmodernism claimed that advanced technology need not be so restrictive or determinate. Rather than preclude ornament or traditional styles, it made them potentially available to a broad range of people. And where costs remained prohibitive, signage and simulacra might successfully substitute for traditional forms. The initial embrace of decoration, like the rediscovery of history, thus appeared as a liberating gesture; it opened up new possibilities and broke down traditional hierarchies, whether between architecture and interior design, structure and ornament, abstraction and figuration, or "educated" taste and popular taste (as well as the "purported" modernist bias toward the former in each of these pairings). Postmodernism sanctioned a new appreciation of sensuality, comfort, and the body—almost a hedonism, which challenged the mundane, the prosaic, the matter-of-fact rationality of modernism. Even dimensions stereotypically condemned as feminine, weak, or frivolous—pink, chintz, boudoir chairs—received validation. Just as the abstract forms of the modern movement could be seen in the 1920s as dissolving traditional images of gender identity, the more sensuous, decorative forms of postmodernism could be seen in the 1970s as challenging this same abstract language, which was now associated with a masculine, corporate world—severe, removed, and mechanistic. In a tone foreign to a previous generation, Charles Moore notes, "If our century's predominant urge to erect high-rise macho objects was nearly spent, I thought we might now be eligible for a fifty-year-long respite of yin, of absorbing and healing and trying to bring our freestanding erections into an inhabitable community."[38]

Thus the first phase of postmodernism played a role somewhat akin to modernism itself after World War I: it reinvigorated architecture's vocabulary by discovering new "pasts," new vernaculars, and new aspects of mass culture. If in the 1920s the sources were the Acropolis, the automobile, and Mediterranean villages, in the 1970s they were Ledoux, Levittown, and Las Vegas. Some architects, such as Graves, Greenberg, and Blatteau, drew on classicism and a high-art heritage; but others, such as Venturi and Moore mined suburbia and the "strip" for new aesthetic images. And probably, it is in the realm of ornament that postmodern architecture has come the closest to the spirit of pop culture and contamination that one equates with the postmodernism of other fields.[39] But if all of this raised certain hopes, the flip side revealed another picture: pretensions, blatant materialism, pseudoculture, a level of ostentatious display that would make Veblen shiver. And what first emerged as endless freedom, by the mid-1960s seemed rigidified and codified. Mauve and gray, falling keystones, giant pilasters, and temple fronts had all become ubiquitous clichés, now mass-produced by the culture industry.

Urban Contextualism and Typology

The postmodern urban critique recapitulates the themes expressed earlier—the universalizing, homogenizing, dehumanizing qualities of modern architecture—only now on a much larger scale. Although the American post-modern movement was initially more concerned with image than with urban form, by the mid-1970s both Rowe's theories of contextualism and the Italian investigations of type had had a major impact. And if Rowe's politics conjure up images of Disraeli and Queen Victoria, the Italian Rationalist movement identified itself firmly with the Left; in fact, Paolo Portoghesi cites Solidarity's document on architecture as a defense of postmodern urban aspirations.[40] In the United States the postmodern critique joined widespread public disenchantment with urban renewal, itself partially a product of leftist protests and grass-roots action in the 1960s.

It is in its rejection of the modern movement's urban vision that postmodernism has probably had its most positive social impact. It has all but eliminated the isolated block, the vast terrains of concrete, the ne'er-traveled pedestrian bridge as urban solutions; and it has contributed to the meteoric rise in preservation. Although contextualism has produced boring buildings—notably, the numerous brick boxes of Boston and the Upper West Side—it has frequently produced better urbanism, reversing the earlier priorities of building over city, private over public. This is not to deny that it may have also inhibited more exciting and challenging urban solutions: how often has Battery Park City generated the remarks "It could have been better" or "It could have been worse?" Postmodernism's urban interventions are not so much regenerative as simply resistant, an attempt to preserve, not transform, areas of community life.

But even this claim to resistance can be challenged if one looks further at that area excluded from postmodern theories: architecture's relation to the powers at large. The revitalization of the urban metropolis has coincided with the return to the city of a young professional class. This so-called good contextualism is almost exclusively the province of the prosperous and upwardly mobile. Whatever its merits, it has contributed to the gloss of gentrification, itself slowly eroding neighborhoods and producing another more insidious kind of uniformity. In the past decade, few opportunities have been taken to explore what contextualism might mean in poorer neighborhoods or in the endless sprawl of suburbia. Certainly here, change, not continuity, of context is sometimes in order.

Affirmation and Commodification

From the 1960s to the present, postmodernism seems to have changed from being essentially a movement that criticized aesthetic and social parameters to one that affirms the status quo. However contradictory its generating impulses, postmodernism's interests in tradition and regional cultures emerged from more than a desire for novelty and spectacle; they embodied a genuine dissatisfaction with the course of modernization, one that pointed to the failures of technology and artistic novelty as social panaceas.[41] By the early 1980s, however, postmodern architecture largely abandoned its critical and transgressive dimensions to create an eclectic and largely affirmative culture, one strikingly in accord with the tone of contemporary political life. It was a trajectory traced by the careers of many architects: for Robert Stern, from a critique of public housing in the Roosevelt Island Competition to luxury suburban developments; for Charles Moore, from a sensitive search for place and a regionally responsive vocabulary at Sea Ranch to outlandish walls and amusement parks at the New Orleans World's Fair; for Michael Graves, from the startling forms of Fargo-Moorhead to the cartooned imagery of Disney Dolphin hotels; and for Andres Duany, Elizabeth Plater-Zyberk, and developer Robert Davis, from the 1960s idealism that inspired Seaside to its present Victorian condominiums for Atlanta lawyers. If there were bumps and jags in this course, and moments of genuine quality and insight, the potential for opposition was soon exhausted. By the time the AT&T building was completed—the initial shock of its historicist forms dissipated—the battle with modernism was largely won; but by that time, too, postmodernism itself became subject to the forces of consumption and commodification.

This is probably nowhere clearer than in the architecture culture itself. It is almost as if the populist bias of the movement invited new levels of publicity and promotion. The proliferation of books and labels—five different editions of Jencks's *The Language of Post-Modern Architecture*, architecture drawings in the art market, editions of the complete works of architects under fifty, architect-designed teapots and doghouses, glossy magazine articles, advertising endorsements for Dexter shoes—signaled architecture's new popularity and marketability. The image of the architect shifted from social crusader and aesthetic puritan to trendsetter and media star. This change in professional definition had ramifications throughout architectural institutions. In the 1980s most schools stopped offering regular housing studios; gentlemen's clubs, resort hotels, art museums, and vacation homes became the standard programs. Design awards and professional magazine coverage have embodied similar priorities. Advocacy architecture and pro bono work are almost dead.

If this bleak picture of commodification threatens to overshadow postmodernism's contributions—its critique of modernization and its renewed sense of the city and public space—it poses much broader problems about the power of architecture to counter the forces of capital, indeed, its capacity to sustain any critical role at all. Certainly, as the first critics of the modern movement revealed, architecture's role has been increasingly diminished by larger economic and social processes.[42] But it is also important to consider what role the theoretical and formal assumptions of postmodernism may have played in these processes. Commodification suggests the importance of cultural signs: that the consumption of objects is as integral to questions of power as their production. But it also suggests a process that automatically vitiates any sustained critique, a recycling of images that leaves material forces untouched. Could it be that postmodernism, by focusing exclusively on image, by detaching meaning from other institutional issues, might have lent itself readily to commodification, even potentially spurring its development in architecture?

Poststructuralism, Deconstructivism
A new architectural tendency, associated both with poststructuralist theory and constructivist forms (in school jargon, the slash-crash projects and the Russian train wrecks), is in part a vehement reaction against postmodernism and what are perceived as its conservative dimensions: its historicist imagery, its complacent contextualism, its conciliatory and affirmative properties, its humanism, its rejection of technological imagery, and its repression of the new.[43] This recent wave of critics and designers claims that postmodern architecture does not confront the present and the current impossibility of cultural consensus (here, despite their rejection of any concept of history, many poststructuralist advocates fall into zeitgeist and periodizing rhetoric). Instead of seeking cultural communication, architecture, in their view, should make explicit its purported obliteration. Fragmentation, dispersion, decentering, schizophrenia, disturbance are the new objectives; it is from these qualities that architecture is to gain its "critical" edge.

But the question arises of whether the political role of this new architectural avant-garde—this second strain of "postmodernism"—differs significantly from that of the first movement. Is deconstructivism, with its iconoclastic rhetoric, its blatant defiance of structural and material conventions, any more potent than postmodernism in countering the dominant conservatism of the Reagan era? Or is it yet another, perhaps even more extreme, manifestation of the social retreat of recent years?

Before examining some of the political claims of this new tendency and their possible ramifications, however, several qualifications must be made. Like the earlier postmodern architects, these practitioners comprise a disparate group with different styles and intentions; but unlike their predecessors, who shared a critical assessment of the modern movement and recognized their own similarities over a decade of debate and criticism, these individuals have worked independently for years—and in some instances before the full emergence of historicist tendencies. They have been connected to each other not by themselves but by a handful of critics, and through the institutional sanction of New York's Museum of Modern Art. The categorization "deconstructivists" itself presents numerous problems, not the least of which is that many of the participants in the recent MoMA exhibition "Deconstructivist Architecture" themselves reject the label. Among those included (Coop Himmelblau, Peter Eisenman, Frank Gehry, Zaha Hadid, Rem Koolhaas, Daniel Libeskind, and Bernard Tschumi), only Eisenman and Tschumi publicly espouse an interest in the philosophy of Jacques Derrida; yet his theory of deconstruction—which argues that meaning is infinitely deferred and that there exists no extralinguistic beginning or end—has been widely used by critics to explain the philosophical underpinnings of this new formal trend.[44] At the same time, the implication of a single formal source—early Russian constructivism—is similarly misleading: other important formal influences on these designers include Russian constructivism of the mid and late 1920s (Koolhaas, Tschumi), German expressionism (Coop Himmelblau), the architecture of the 1950s (Hadid, Koolhaas), and contemporary sculpture (Gehry). Of the MoMA participants, only Coop Himmelblau, Hadid, and Libeskind are involved with the extreme fragmentation of diagonal forms—the dismantling of constructivist imagery—that curator Mark Wigley claims as a basic attribute of deconstructivism.[45] Nor do these practitioners share a common cultural heritage or architectural background. In contrast to the first postmodern critique, which started as a particularly American movement and only later became associated with contemporary developments in Europe, this second tendency has been explicitly international from the beginning, with the Architectural Association in London and the former Institute for Architecture and Urban Studies in New York, both international exchange centers, being the largest common bonds. At this moment, as only a few of these designs have been realized, "deconstructivism" exists primarily as a theoretical debate, and it remains questionable whether it will gain the widespread currency of the earlier postmodern movement—whether, in fact, it warrants the designation "movement" at all. The cost of constructing these "antigravity" fantasies will undoubtedly either inhibit deconstructivism's extension or temper its present aesthetic.

As a reaction to postmodernism, deconstructivism shares certain aspects with modernism. Its preference for abstract forms, its rejection of continuity and tradition, its fascination with technological imagery, its disdain for academicism, its polemical and apocalyptical rhetoric—are all reminiscent of an earlier modern epoch. But deconstructivism, as already suggested, also emerged from many of the same impetuses as postmodernism.[46] Like postmodernism this new tendency rejects the fundamental ideological premises of the modern movement: functionalism, structural rationalism, and a faith in social regeneration. For all its rhetoric against historical quotation, deconstructivism also looks to the past for formal sources, only now the search centers on modernism and machine-age forms. Finally, deconstructivism, too, emphasizes the formal properties of architecture. (In this regard, it is ironic that Russian constructivism, with its political and social programs, is considered the primary source.)

Formal Hermeticism

The focus on form in deconstructivist architecture, as in postmodern architecture, suggests that here, too, any political role that would challenge existing structures must reside in architecture's nature as an object. And indeed, this would seem to be the thrust of explorations by such diverse practitioners as Coop Himmelblau, Hadid, and Libeskind as well as by poststructuralist apologists such as Wigley and Jeff Kipnis. Site, client, production process, and program are rarely the subject of investigation or radical transformation.[47] In built work, existing institutional boundaries are generally accepted; in theoretical projects, they are simply ignored.

It should also be noted, however, that two of the architects in the MoMA show, Eisenman and Tschumi, have claimed to stress process over form and have used the poststructuralist notion of intertextuality to assert a new contamination that challenges the autonomy of the designed object. Initially a reaction in library circles to the formalism of the New Critics, this idea holds that meaning begins before and extends beyond the text; in other words, not only is literature indebted to previous texts, but a text's very existence depends on all texts. Eisenman translates this concept in architecture through a metaphor of the palimpsest; Tschumi works literally with superimpositions of systems. These excavations and layerings, however, almost always operate on a compositional rather than on an institutional plane, and all involve the architect's (as opposed to the client's or user's) role in the design process. The combining of conventional functional programs in the Follies at Tschumi's La Villette perhaps comes closest to challenging institutional boundaries; but even here it must be acknowledged that in the initial competition brief the government had largely conceded the definition of program to the architect and, further, that parks themselves lie outside of traditional strictures of utility (hence follies—and their long history in landscape design).

One could, in fact, readily argue that the poststructuralist influence has led to an even greater focus on form as an end in itself than was the case in the earlier postmodern experiments. The notion of communication embraced by many of the historicist postmodernists, however naïve, countered a completely hermetic conception of architecture. In contrast, architects influenced by poststructuralist theory have intentionally stressed abstract compositional procedures that tend to preclude references beyond form. In the essay "The End of the Classical: The End of the Beginning, the End of the End," Eisenman describes his objective as "*architecture as independent discourse*, free of external values—classical or any other; that is, the intersection of the *meaning-free*, the *arbitrary*, and the *timeless* in the artificial."[48] Similarly, Tschumi states that "La Villette . . . aims at an architecture that *means* nothing, an architecture of the signifier rather than the signified, one that is pure trace or play of language."[49] In its continual deferral of meaning, in its celebration of the endless signifier, poststructuralist theory appears to have produced another kind of aestheticization, which privileges form (language) and "textuality" and which refuses any reality outside the object (text). Andreas Huyssen has written that "American poststructuralist writers and critics . . . call for self-reflexiveness, not, to be sure, of the author-subject, but of the text; . . . they purge life, reality, history, society from the work of art and its reception, and construct a new autonomy, based on a pristine notion of textuality, a new art for art's sake which is presumably the only kind possible after the failure of all and any commitment."[50] This formal hermeticism seems to be doubly problematic in architecture, which, as already suggested, does not lend itself readily to the linguistic analogy. The poststructuralist literary critic can assert that the very process of meaning's displacement involves content, even if its presence is ultimately—and solipsistically—denied; but for the architecture critic involved with the abstract formal explorations of deconstructivist design, even this modest claim is difficult. Although architecture never completely escapes referentiality, highly abstract architecture, like instrumental music, refers essentially to itself. In other words, signification may not be so much displaced as nonexistent from a conventional linguistic perspective; instead of an endless signifier, the result may be a self-reflexive or static signifier. Intertextuality, then, is constricted to the realm of architectural form.

The aestheticization of deconstructivist architecture is certainly a further retreat from social processes, but it would be a mistake to dismiss its formal explorations as politically neutral or irrelevant. Even artistic abstraction has social implications, and, given the increasingly conservative connotations of postmodern figuration, deconstructivism may well be an instance where abstraction takes on progressive resonances, as modernism did initially. Nor are the forms always as mute as their practitioners sometimes claim them to be.[51] Compared to the tired classical images of postmodernism, these neoconstructivist forms possess for the moment a freshness and energy that embrace the present and the future. Even when the imagery harks back to Russian constructivism, it invokes (however self-consciously) the Revolution's dream of a heroic future. Technology is here a source of pleasure and play— something to be exploited and stretched in order to realize new spatial possibilities. Similarly, steel, glass, corrugated sheet metal, chain link—the signs of industrial economy—offer new options and imagery. Some of the designs in the MoMA exhibition, such as Hadid's and Libeskind's, are arcane, almost precious, space-age displays of refinement; others, particularly those of Frank Gehry, gain power from their matter-of-factness—their rough joints and inexpensive materials. Whatever despair these projects may ultimately convey on the social front, they project a vigorous optimism on the artistic front.

But the implications of other aspects of deconstructivism's formal hermeticism are more problematic. One consequence is a potential narrowing of audience. Although the general public might respond to the images' aesthetic exuberance and technological bravura, most likely only a small cultural elite will appreciate the iconoclasm of forms, the inversions of common sense and everyday expectations. This is not to suggest that this hermeticism will allow deconstructivism to escape commodification, but rather that its marketing appeal may well be to a narrower group than that of postmodern designs. Indeed, deconstructivist architecture risks the elitist charges that modern architecture faced with the postmodern critique.

Another consequence of deconstructivism's formal hermeticism has been a denial of urban context and a renewed focus on the building as object. The fragmentation and formal explosion of these works means that not only do they contrast radically with a traditional urban fabric, but they cannot join readily with other buildings to form defined public space.[52] The single building once again becomes more important than the city, individual creation more important than collective accretion. In cities such as Los Angeles this may be a realistic position, perhaps just a conformist one; in older urban fabrics it becomes an act of rebellion and opposition. And here the power of the vision is paramount. Just as in a few of the earlier postmodern works historical references could illuminate the tensions between continuity and fissure, past and present, in certain deconstructivist projects the fragmentation stands as a telling comment on banality, loss, and poverty of context. It is an urban vision of negation, rejecting past solutions and denying possibilities of reconstituted community. As marginal avant-garde gestures, these projects promise a certain critical power, but as larger endeavors—as a general strategy for the numerous and repetitive problems confronting urban space—they represent a closure, one at odds with the exuberance of many of the forms themselves.

Politics and Formal Subversion

It is in this moment of negation, the disruption of both the traditional city and the conventions of architecture, that several poststructuralist advocates have made their political claims. Using such words as "unease," "disintegration," "decentering," "dislocation," Eisenman, Tschumi, and Wigley have stated that this work challenges the status quo, not from the outside, but through formal disruptions and inversions within the object. In other words, formal strategies themselves have the power, in their view, to undermine codes and preconceptions—in fact, the entire apparatus of Western humanism itself. If architecture forsakes a political role in the sense espoused by the modern movement—one seeking the transformation of production processes and institutional boundaries—it now gains political power simply through the cultural sign, or more precisely, through revealing the disintegration of that sign. This objective is indeed an inversion of the optimistic claims of the earlier postmodern movement. Practitioners such as Moore, Graves, and Stern thought that they could reconstitute community and regional identity through the formal properties of architecture; some deconstructivist practitioners believe that they can reveal the impossibility of such reconstitutions through the cultural object. Like Jean-François Lyotard, they proclaim the death of master narratives: equality, reason, truth, notions of collective consensus, and so forth.[53] With this collapse of values, art gains a new redemptive role, one that negates utopian aspirations but finds hope within contemporary disintegration. Quite clearly this is no longer the negation of Theodor Adorno and certain members of the Frankfurt School, who called for artistic retreat in order to preserve a utopian vision of the social and political sphere.

The introduction of deconstruction to architecture has contributed to an attitude of critical skepticism and scrutiny, a questioning of existing conventions of composition and form. Already, deconstructivism has played a major role in undermining the pseudohistoricism, mindless contextualism, and conciliatory values of postmodernism. Here its impact can be compared to that of traditional avant-garde practices of negation and subversion. But outside of the formal sphere, the critical role of deconstructivism remains elusive; indeed, many of the more progressive political contributions of poststructuralist theory have disappeared in its application to architecture. While in literary criticism poststructuralist analyses have pointed out internal inconsistencies and irrationalities in oppressive discourse and have thus brought to light strategies of racism, sexism, colonialism, and the like, in architecture these critical possibilities are largely precluded once again by the difficulties of the linguistic analogy. To the extent that architectural meaning is ambiguous, the connections between architectural form and political oppression are rarely as self-evident as those between language and political oppression. And in those situations where the connections are more obvious (for instance, in the monumental architecture of Nazi Germany), the political and economic circumstances often mitigate against change in a purely representational sphere. Certainly in the present American context, any claims linking the formal fragmentation of deconstructivist architecture to political subversion remain suspect; any critical properties center on architecture itself.[54]

Beyond these particular problems of translation from literary theory to architecture, deconstruction raises deeper political and ethical questions that are at the heart of some of the difficulties of allying this philosophical position with political praxis. In a world of endless textuality, how can the institutional and material causes of representation—and oppression—ever be determined or examined sufficiently to be countered? In a world without truth, history, or consensus, what is the basis or criterion for action? In other words, how does one choose the objects, strategies, and goals of subversions? Is there any way to avoid total relativism—a sense that anything goes?

It does not, of course, take much imagination to envision sub-versions of the status quo resulting in greater inequities and injustices. Regardless of epistemological questions, some values, however provisional, and some notion of collective identity are probably essential to political action and social betterment.[55] But if these issues seem to place an unjust burden on form, it may be because post-structuralist advocates are caught in delusions of architecture's transformative power, a situation strangely reminiscent of an earlier modern period. Even more than the problem of total relativism, the political problems posed by a poststructuralist archi-tecture reside in the paradox whereby the architect is absolved of obligations of au-thorship but the object is granted considerable subversive power.

Such absolution underestimates the architect's power and pre-cludes a political actor. Following Michel Foucault's and Roland Barthes's famous dec-larations of the death of the author, poststructuralists have denounced authorial subjectivity and its concomitant claims of intentionality, originality, truth, and trans-parent communication.[56] In part this position is an elaboration of modernism's own denunciation of idealist and romantic notions of creation. But as the critic Huyssen has asked, how radical or even useful is such a stand when few today would deny the role of external forces in creation and reception? Is it a refusal of responsibility? An inadvertent acceptance of the status quo—allied with, rather than opposed to, the processes of modernization?[57] And, finally, does the denial of authorship prohibit the emergence of alternative voices that would challenge the ideology of the architect (almost always male, white, and middle class)?[58]

At the same time, the overestimation of form's role does not take into account the power of capital to numb acts of subversion. Uneasiness, fright, a sense of disruption are hardly alien to contemporary society; they are in fact so much a part of our everyday life that they can be easily ignored or consumed—common fates of avant-garde culture. Any sensations, pleasurable or painful, instantly become fodder for both high culture and mass consumption. The brief history of deconstructivism leaves little grounds for political optimism. Just as the progressive impulses of the postmodern critique became largely swallowed by the movement's own success, so too the critique posed by these frenzied forms threatens to be under-mined by its sudden fashionability. If anything, the cycle seems ever more rapid; proclamation and consumption are almost simultaneous. How subversive can a movement be when it gains simultaneous sanction from two major museums in New York City? How sustained can any challenge be when the forces that have promoted it (Philip Johnson, Century Club lunches, Princeton University, Max Protetch, and MoMA) have uncanny similarities to those that helped institutionalize what it pur-ports to criticize—postmodern architecture? Ironically, the rhetoric of the death of the author seems not to dampen the spirit of self-promotion, hype, and commodifi-cation that became so integral to the dissemination of postmodernism.

Should deconstructivism, however, manage to sustain any sub-versive qualities in the face of these forces, other questions arise: Are radical formal statements necessarily the most appropriate means to shelter people whose lives are already filled with the disruption and frustration that deconstructivist architecture celebrates? Would scarce resources for public housing be more appropriately spent on day-care centers, sports facilities, and larger housing units than on structural acro-batics? The avant-garde desire "épater la bourgeoisie" may fulfill the architect's need for a radical self-image, but it does little in this era of social retrenchment to improve the everyday life of the poor and dispossessed.

Perhaps not surprising, women, blacks, and other minorities have been notably silent voices in these recent theoretical debates. While the reasons are complex and diverse, a few immediately come to the fore: the elitist atmosphere induced by both the hermetic forms and an obscure discourse, the aggressive rhetoric of subversion that rings of a new machismo, the exclusionary forums of promotion, and probably most fundamental, the denial of real institutional transformation.[59] Deconstructivist forms reject nostalgia, historicist fabrication, and the postmodern denial of the present, but they embody another kind of forgetting—a forgetting of the *social* itself. A tendency that began as a reaction against the conservative ethos of postmodernism and contemporary political life threatens to become an even more extreme embodiment of that same ethos.

A Fin de Siècle?

In 1980, summarizing architecture's new political cast, Robert Stern wrote, "Postmodernism is not revolutionary in either the political or artistic sense; in fact, it reinforces the effect of the technocratic and bureaucratic society in which we live— traditional post-modernism by accepting conditions and trying to modify them, schismatic postmodernism [i.e., Eisenman] by proposing a condition *outside* Western Humanism, thereby permitting Western Humanist culture to proceed uninterrupted though not necessarily unaffected."[60] However disturbing, Stern's assessment, made on the eve of the Reagan era, seems on the mark. But what Stern and most of his contemporaries overlooked is that the initial critique of modern architecture stemmed from a dissatisfaction with the forces that in fact constitute "technocratic and bureaucratic society." In other words, the reification and reductivism of modernism were partly a product of those forces that both strains of postmodernism have "reinforced." From the same perspective, historicist and poststructuralist advocates could not have anticipated the power of an increasingly commercialized society to control the evolution of an artistic movement, how rapidly efforts to preserve and modify a cultural situation would themselves become sterile and commodified.

What seems to be operating in recent architectural developments is a process by which a movement, whose initial critique and experimentation is vigorous and challenging, becomes increasingly lifeless and routinized as it becomes part of the dominant culture. Thomas Crow has described the avant-garde as "a kind of research and development arm of the culture industry."[61] Both postmodernism and deconstructivism can be seen as having staked out areas of cultural practice that retain some vitality in an increasingly administered and rationalized society: the postmodernists by looking to forms that predate the hegemony of bureaucratic modernization; the poststructuralists by challenging the precepts of rationality and of order itself. But just as both these tendencies discover areas not yet part of commodity culture, they make their existence discrete and visible, and thus subject to the market's manipulation.[62]

This cycle of appropriation can easily be used to justify the cynicism and social passivity that are such strong components of postmodernism in all of its colors. Indeed, it is precisely this cycle that has bred the split between politics and aesthetics: "There's nothing to be done"; hence "Anything goes." But these conclusions assume the total impotence of the cultural sphere, an impotence that is belied by the fears of both Right and Left and by the initial vitality of postmodernism itself. In some ways, the political resignation of contemporary architecture is simply a reversal of the utopian aspirations of the modern movement. Both fall into an either/or mentality that obscures the complexity of relations between form and politics. It would appear that part of the problem lies in postmodernism's criticism of modernism itself. Both the historicist and poststructuralist tendencies correctly pointed to the failures of the modern movement's instrumental rationality, its narrow teleology, and its overblown faith in technology, but these two positions have erred in another direction in their abjuration of all realms of the social and in their assumption that form remains either a critical or affirmative tool independent of social and

economic processes. That contemporary architecture has become so much about surface, image, and play, and that its content has become so ephemeral, so readily transformable and consumable, is partially a product of the neglect of the material
dimensions of architecture—program, production, financing, and so forth—that
more directly invoke questions of power. And by precluding issues of gender, race,
ecology, and poverty, postmodernism and deconstructivism have also forsaken the
development of a more vital and sustained heterogeneity. The formal *and* the social
costs are too high when the focus is so exclusively on form.

Notes

I would like to thank Alan Colquhoun, Stephen Frankel, Robert Heintges, Marc Treib,
Bernard Tschumi, and, especially, Joan Ockman, who all generously reviewed and commented on an earlier draft of this article. I am also extremely grateful for the insightful
criticism and encouragement of Richard Pommer, Michael Hays, and Alicia Kennedy.

1. Daniel Bell's criticisms of postmodernism predate most architectural developments and
    consequently focus on literary and philosophical trends, which are often at odds in their
    rejection of representation, history, and humanism with those in architecture. Robert
    Stern has, in fact, cited Bell's cultural criticism as justification for his own postmodern
    position. But Bell's attack on the populism of Herbert Gans and his general disapproval
    of hedonism and experimentation suggest that he would not be in sympathy with the
    subsequent development of postmodern architecture. See Daniel Bell, *The Cultural Contradic-
    tions of Capitalism* (New York: Basic Books, 1976), pp. 51–55, 264; idem, "Beyond Modern-
    ism, Beyond Self," in *The Winding Passage: Essays and Sociological Journeys 1960–1980* (Cambridge,
    Mass.: ABT Books, 1980), pp. 288–289; and Robert Stern, "The Doubles of Post-
    Modern," *Harvard Architecture Review* 1 (1980), p. 87. Hilton Kramer's attacks on postmodern
    architecture can be found throughout the pages of the *New Criterion*.
2. "Beyond the Modern Movement," *Harvard Architecture Review* 1 (1980), p. 4. For a more
    extended discussion of the role of "meaning" in postmodern architecture, see Mary
    McLeod, "Architecture," in *The Postmodern Moment: A Handbook of Contemporary Innovation in the Arts*
    (Westport, Conn.: Greenwood Press, 1985), pp. 19–46.
3. Stern uses the term "schismatic postmodernism" in his essay "The Doubles of Post-
    Modern," pp. 75–87, citing as examples the work of John Cage, William Gass, and Peter
    Eisenman. Eisenman himself employs the term "decomposition" to describe his own
    work, beginning with his book *House X*. The term "deconstructivism" recently received
    official sanction with the Museum of Modern Art's exhibition "Deconstructivist Architec-
    ture." Joseph Giovannini claims to have first coined the term. See Joseph Giovannini,
    "Breaking All the Rules," *New York Times Magazine*, 12 June 1988.
4. In many instances, of course, these themes were more visible on a formal than a material
    plane. There is no equivalent in architecture criticism to Clement Greenberg's or Theodor
    Adorno's theories of modernism as artistic autonomy. In the first generation of historians
    of modernism, Nikolaus Pevsner and Sigfried Giedion created genealogies that incorpo-
    rated the social vision of the Arts and Crafts movement, the structural rationalism of engi-
    neering, and the aesthetic innovations of cubism (the first two for Pevsner, the latter two
    for Giedion). In the second generation, historians such as Reyner Banham and William
    Jordy place greater stress on the symbolic dimensions and academic heritage of the mod-
    ern movement, which undoubtedly more strongly emphasizes its artistic interpretation.
    Neither group, however, presents a teleology of form that stresses architecture's isolation
    as a discipline. Colin Rowe perhaps comes closest to the formalism of some art critics of
    the postwar period, but the social and symbolic aspirations of the modern movement are
    fully acknowledged in many of his essays (see especially his introduction to *Five Architects*
    [New York: Wittenborn, 1972] and his essay "The Architecture of Utopia," in *The Mathe-
    matics of the Ideal Villa and Other Essays* [Cambridge: MIT Press, 1976]) and in fact become a
    subject of criticism in the setting forth of his own polemical agenda. The involvement of
    the modern movement with technology and mass culture has been a topic of considerable
    interest among contemporary scholars, including Manfredo Tafuri, Stanislaus von Moos,
    Nikolaus Bullock, and Jean-Louis Cohen.

5. The word "historicist" refers in this instance, as it commonly does in discussions of post-modern architecture, to the use of historical forms and styles in designs. Until the emergence of postmodernism, the term was most frequently associated with revivalist and eclectic tendencies in nineteenth-century architecture, which rejected the static ideal embraced by the previous classical concept. Nineteenth-century stylistic eclecticism was linked to the emergence of the philosophical concept of historicism in late-eighteenth-century and early-nineteenth-century Germany, but it did not result necessarily in an acceptance of relativism. For a discussion of historicism in architecture, see Alan Colquhoun, "Three Kinds of Historicism," *Oppositions* 26 (Spring 1984), pp. 29–39.

6. See Robert Gutman, *Architectural Practice: A Critical View* (Princeton: Princeton Architectural Press, 1988), esp. pp. 3–12, 21–22.

7. The growing public presence of architecture is itself an indication of a broader dissolution of the boundaries between culture, economics, and politics brought on by commodity capitalism. This dissolution (underscored in very concrete terms by the transformation of a movie star into a president) can be seen as having made power more diffuse, but also as having made issues of control in everyday life more critical from a political perspective.

8. See Alan Colquhoun, "Postmodernism and Structuralism: A Retrospective Glance," *Assemblage* 5 (1988), p. 7.

9. See Walter Benjamin, "The Work of Art in the Age of Mechanical Reproduction," in *Illuminations*, ed. Hannah Arendt, trans. Harry Zohn (New York: Schocken Books, 1969), pp. 239–240.

10. What may appear oppressive and totalitarian in one situation—for instance, the stripped classicism of Nazi Germany—may appear progressive and democratic in another—for instance, the similar forms of Roosevelt's New Deal America. Within different contexts, the same forms might serve as propaganda, criticism, or tacit affirmation of values.

11. Here I intentionally do not invoke Walter Benjamin's aspiration to a complete integration of technique and content, expressed in his essay "The Author as Producer," in *Reflections*, ed. Peter Demetz (New York: Harcourt Brace Jovanovich, 1979), pp. 220–238. Benjamin's objective is not unrelated to that of some modern architects, especially Hannes Meyer, Ernst May, and Mart Stam, but the interface between art and politics has rarely been so clean. Often what is a progressive tendency in terms of technique may not be such in terms of content, and vice versa; and depending on the context, one dimension may take on more political importance than another. The total separation of the two, however, raises other political issues, to be discussed later in the essay.

12. Le Corbusier, *Vers une architecture* (Paris: Editions Crès, 1923); translated as *Towards a New Architecture*, trans. Frederick Etchells (New York: Praeger, 1960), p. 211.

13. Claude Schnaidt, *Hannes Meyer: Bauten, Projekte und Schriften: Buildings, Projects and Writings* (Teufen: Verlag Arthur Niggli, 1965), p. 25.

14. There are, of course, exceptions to this, notably the De Stijl group and some of the Russian constructivists of the early 1920s. Paradoxically, we might see modern architecture's challenge to existing social patterns (particularly outside Germany) as more successful on a formal rather than an economic level. The new forms and compositional strategies raised questions about traditional hierarchies that elevated the monumental over the everyday, the public over the private, the formal over the informal, the male over the female.

15. For a discussion of this division, see George Baird, "'La Dimension Amoureuse' in Architecture," in *Meaning in Architecture*, ed. Charles Jencks and George Baird (New York: Braziller, 1969), pp. 79–99 [reprinted in this volume]; and McLeod, "Architecture," pp. 27–28.

16. Several historical reasons exist for the failure of the first postmodern critics to distinguish between the modernism of the 1950s and that of the 1920s and 1930s. First, the continuing presence of Gropius and Mies gave to most Americans an impression of modernism's continuity. Second, many American practitioners of the 1950s (in contrast to those in Italy, for instance) did not themselves distinguish their work from that of the prewar period, even if the forms were radically different. Third, there was little modern architecture in the United States of the 1920s and 1930s against which to compare the later works.

17. See Rowe, "Addendum, 1973," to "The Architecture of Utopia," pp. 213–217, and Colin Rowe and Fred Koetter, *Collage City* (Cambridge: MIT Press, 1978). Rowe's language of

"fragment" and "collage" in many respects presages contemporary poststructuralist discourse.

18. Robert Venturi and Denise Scott Brown, "'Leading from the Rear': Reply to Martin Pawley," *Architectural Design* 40 (July 1970), pp. 320, 370; reprinted in *A View from the Campidoglio: Selected Essays 1953–84*, ed. Peter Arnell, Ted Bickford, and Catherine Bergart (New York: Harper and Row, 1984), p. 24.

19. Kenneth Frampton, "America 1960–1970: Notes on Urban Images and Theory," *Casabella* 35, nos. 359–360 (December 1971), pp. 25–37. In this essay Frampton's solution is a far cry from the "critical regionalism" that he professes a decade later. Here he questions how much legitimate populism remains in American culture and proposes the "semi-indeterminate" infrastructures of Shadrach Woods as urban design models that simultaneously accommodate technology and the specificities of place.

Tomás Maldonado's critique of Scott Brown and Venturi's position is similar to Frampton's. In a chapter entitled "Las Vegas and the Semiological Abuse," he writes: "There is also a kind of cultural nihilism which, consciously or unconsciously, exalts the status quo. We find an example of it among those who are singing paeans to die 'landscape' of certain American cities, which are among the most brutal, degrading, and corrupt that consumer society has ever created. . . . Las Vegas is not a creation by the people, but for the people. It is the final product . . . of more than half a century of masked manipulatory violence." Tomás Maldonado, *Design, Nature and Revolution: Toward a Critical Ecology*, trans. Mario Domandi (New York: Harper and Row, 1972), pp. 60, 65.

20. Denise Scott Brown, "Pop Off: Reply to Kenneth Frampton," in *A View from the Campidoglio*, pp. 34–37. Scott Brown argues that Frampton is caught between two contradictory positions, an endorsement of Marcuse's social critique and a rejection of Gropius's social architecture, and that he does not acknowledge their shared rejection of populist culture.

21. Also of importance were Herbert Gans's two other books *The Urban Villagers: Group and Class in the Life of Italo-Americans* (New York: Free Press, 1962), and *Popular Culture and High Culture: An Analysis and Evaluation of Taste* (New York: Basic Books, 1974). Another sociologist frequently mentioned during this period was Melvin Webber. See, especially, Melvin M. Webber, "The Urban Place and the Nonplace Urban Realm," in *Explorations into Urban Structure* (Philadelphia: University of Pennsylvania Press, 1964). Scott Brown and Venturi often cited Gans and Webber in their early writings.

22. Shopping centers have provided one of the most important sites for the dissemination of postmodern architecture outside of major metropolitan areas.

23. See Richard L. Berke, "Dukakis Says He Would Commit $3 Billion to Build New Housing," *New York Times*, 29 June 1988.

24. Many (including Michael Graves, Thomas Gordon Smith, and Steven Peterson), of course, have not. One of the strongest defenses of postmodern architecture coming from the Left is Linda Hutcheon's article "The Politics of Postmodernism: Parody and History," *Cultural Critique* 5 (Winter 1986–1987), pp. 179–207. Hutcheon claims here that postmodern works are "resolutely historical and inescapably political precisely because they are parodistic" and that they expose "the contradictions of modernism in an explicitly political light." The ease with which parody loses its critical edge will be addressed later.

25. Charles Jencks, *The Language of Post-Modern Architecture*, 3d ed. (New York: Rizzoli, 1981), p. 37.

26. Robert Venturi, *Complexity and Contradiction in Architecture* (New York: Museum of Modern Art, 1966), p. 44.

27. For a more extended discussion of some of these issues, see McLeod, "Architecture," pp. 31–42. Paradoxically, for Walter Benjamin the distracted mode of architecture's reception is paradigmatic of the new media—film, photography, journalism—on which he places so much political hope. But in contrast to the postmodernists who stress architecture's reception as art, Benjamin seeks transformation through a gradual, almost unconscious, change of habit and expectation; in other words, a reception of distraction rather than of attention is now to architecture's political advantage. See Benjamin, "The Work of Art in the Age of Mechanical Reproduction," pp. 239–240.

28. Stern, "The Doubles of Post-Modern," p. 87.

29. Robert Venturi, "The RIBA Annual Discourse," *Transactions* 1 (1981–1982); reprinted in *A View from the Campidoglio*, p. 109.

30. Quoted in Paolo Portoghesi, *Postmodern: The Architecture of the Postindustrial Society* (New York: Rizzoli, 1983), p. 33. Johnson wrote this letter after having read Jürgen Joedicke's *History of Modern Architecture*.

31. The word "postmodern" should be qualified in reference to Venturi's work. Certainly, his mother's house predates any public acknowledgment of the movement, although it probably influenced the subsequent development of postmodernism in the United States more than any other design. Venturi himself has been extremely critical of most postmodern architecture for its "simplistic, esoteric" use of historicist forms and for its dependence on a high-art heritage. See, especially, Venturi, "The RIBA Annual Discourse," and idem, "Diversity, Relevance and Representation in Historicism, or *Plus ça Change* . . . Plus a Plea for Pattern All over Architecture with a Postscript on My Mother's House," *Architectural Record* (June 1982), pp. 114–119; reprinted in *A View from the Campidoglio*, pp. 104–118.

32. Jencks, *The Language of Post-Modern Architecture*, p. 37.

33. Paul Ricoeur, "Universal Civilization and National Cultures" (1961), in *History and Truth*, trans. C. A. Kelbey (Evanston: Northwestern University Press, 1965), p. 277; quoted in Kenneth Frampton, "Towards a Critical Regionalism: Six Points for an Architecture of Resistance," in *The Anti-Aesthetic: Essays on Postmodern Culture*, ed. Hal Foster (Port Townsend, Wash.: Bay Press, 1983), pp. 16–17.

34. For instance, the last decade has brought a proliferation of "Charleston Place," whether the context is a Westchester suburb or a Florida resort community.

35. Ando does not appear in the original essay, but is often cited in Frampton's lectures.

36. These qualities could, of course, be regional, if techniques and materials were particular to a region. But that hardly seems to be the case with the materials, such as concrete block and metal paneling, used by Ando and Botta.

37. Marc Treib, "Regionalism and South Florida Architecture," conference paper, The Architectural Club of Miami, 1986. In Florida, for example, compare the regionally responsive designs of Paul Rudolph, Rufus Nim, and Robert Brown of the 1950s and the early 1960s to the conventional wall surfaces and roof details of most contemporary postmodern architecture. Of course, some modern architects did experiment with air conditioning as one response to climatic conditions, and in the case of Le Corbusier's Salvation Army Pavilion the results were disastrous.

38. The quote continues: "I like that, but am growing impatient with fifty-year swings, and wonder whether a more suitable model for us might be Goldilocks, of Three Bears fame, who found some things (Papa Bear's) too hot or too hard or too big, and other things (Mama Bear's) too cold, too soft, or too small, but still other things (Baby Bear's) just right, inhabitable, as we architects would say." *Charles Moore: Buildings and Projects 1949–1986*, ed. Eugene J. Johnson (New York: Rizzoli, 1986).

39. Critics coming from other disciplines, such as Fredric Jameson and Andreas Huyssen, seem, however, to exaggerate the importance to architects of *Learning from Las Vegas*, perhaps in a desire to make connections to their own disciplines. *Complexity and Contradiction in Architecture* had a much greater impact on architects, and the vast majority of its examples are from high culture. It was really only at the Yale University School of Architecture that Scott Brown and Venturi's interest in pop culture stimulated a major response. It is probably fair to say that most figurative imagery in postmodernism derives from historical architectural styles rather than popular culture.

40. The document states: "The architect is neither the omnipotent master nor the slave of spaciocultural models, universal or local. His proposed role is to interpret them within the framework of the continuity of civilization. Reducing architecture to its utilitarian function is to remove its role as a means of social communication. From the moment the language of models was replaced with the newspeak of towers, bars and *grands ensembles*, the town has become monotonous, illegible and dead for its inhabitants. A town must be built on the basis of elemental housing models, roads and squares." Quoted in Portoghesi, *Postmodern*, p. 46.

41. See Andreas Huyssen's more general, and extremely insightful, comments about the trajectory of postmodernism, "Mapping the Postmodern," in *After the Great Divide: Modernism, Mass Culture, Postmodernism* (Bloomington and Indianapolis: Indiana University Press, 1986), esp. p. 188.

42. Venturi, for instance, writes: "Industry promotes expensive industrial and electronic research but not architectural experiments, and the Federal government diverts subsidies toward air transportation, communication, and the vast enterprises of war or, as they call it, national security, rather than toward the forces for the direct enhancement of life. The practicing architect must admit this." *Complexity and Contradiction*, p. 44.

43. In choosing to discuss postmodernism and deconstructivism, which have both been placed by critics under a broader rubric of postmodernism, I do not mean to suggest that I am addressing the entire contemporary field. In the United States numerous architectural firms, in fact, still practice a form of "late modernism," whose vocabulary of stripped-down forms is highly indebted to the International Style. As well, among other currents, numerous practitioners are exploring an abstract architectural vocabulary, which cannot readily be classified as either deconstructivist or modernist.

44. Libeskind's philosophical stance derives from phenomenology, and Koolhaas's eclectic position seems more indebted to surrealism and the hedonism of the 1960s than to post-structuralist theories. Both Hadid and Gehry are loath to give philosophical labels to their work. The differences between Eisenman and Libeskind's position are articulated clearly in Libeskind's essay "Peter Eisenman and the Myth of Futility," *Harvard Architecture Review* 3 (1984), pp. 61–63.

45. Certainly, Koolhaas's and Eisenman's architecture has been largely orthogonal, and any diagonals that appear (one suspects MoMA must have been hard pressed to find the "right" Koolhaas project) are within standard modern formal practice. But Eisenman's combination of orthogonal forms and diagonal "events" is more reminiscent of Le Corbusier and early Stirling than of some of his deconstructivist peers. Perhaps most problematic is the inclusion of Gehry in this group, as his use of the diagonal stems more from perceptual concerns in contemporary sculpture than from a revivalism of constructivist imagery. Influenced by the work of this group, however, a trend toward formal fragmentation can be observed among younger architects and students: the postmodern historicist forms of the late 1970s and early 1980s have virtually disappeared from student drafting boards.

46. In fact, at various moments both Tschumi and Eisenman have called for a broader conception of the term "postmodernism," one that would embrace all contemporary movements that reject the rational instrumentality of modernism and its concomitant claims of universality. See especially Peter Eisenman, "The Futility of Objects: Decomposition and the Processes of Difference," *Harvard Architecture Review* 3 (1984), pp. 66, 81; and Bernard Tschumi, *Cinegramme Folie: Le Parc de la Villette* (Princeton: Princeton Architectural Press, 1987), p. 7. Among the critics who have attempted to link these two tendencies is Hal Foster. See especially his essay "(Post)Modern Polemics," *Perspecta* 21 (1984); reprinted in *Recodings: Art, Spectacle, Cultural Politics* (Port Townsend, Wash.: Bay Press, 1987), pp. 121–136. Like Stern's essay "The Doubles of Post-Modern," Foster's "(Post)Modern Polemics" outlines two kinds of postmodernism: neoconservative (eclectic historicism) and poststructuralist (decentering of the object), with Eisenman's work, again, serving as the only example of architecture in the latter category.

47. Both Tschumi and Koolhaas have focused on program in their urban projects; in this respect their work differs from that of the other designers in the MoMA exhibition and from most student work that embraces a neoconstructivist aesthetic.

48. Peter Eisenman, "The End of the Classical: The End of the Beginning, the End of the End," *Perspecta* 21 (1984), p. 166.

49. Tschumi, *Cinegramme Folie*.

50. See especially the critiques of Huyssen, "Mapping the Postmodern," pp. 206–211, and Edward W. Said, "The Problem of Textuality: Two Exemplary Positions," in *Aesthetics Today*, ed. Morris Philipson and Paul J. Gudel, rev. ed. (New York: New American Library, 1980), pp. 113–129. One of the most cogent political critiques of deconstruction is Barbara Foley, "The Politics of Deconstruction," in *Rhetoric and Form: Deconstruction at Yale*, ed. Robert Con Davis and Ronald Schleifer (Norman: University of Oklahoma Press, 1985), pp. 113–134.

51. Here, the deconstructivist model of "no meaning/endless meaning" risks being as deceptive as the postmodern assumption of "transparent communication."

52. Eisenman specifically precludes the creation of place as an objective. In an unpublished manuscript of 1987, he states that "if architecture traditionally has been about 'topos,' that is, an idea of place, then to be 'between,' is to search for 'atopos,' the atopia within topos" (Eisenman, "The Blueline Text," p. 5). I am grateful to Sharon Haar for alerting me to this text.

53. Jean-François Lyotard, *The Postmodern Condition: A Report on Knowledge*, trans. Geoff Bennington and Brian Massumi (Minneapolis: University of Minnesota Press, 1984).

54. That efforts to construct an architectural model of "logocentrism" exclude more of architectural history than they include raises doubts about whether anything other than the latest architectural style is being "deconstructed" or disturbed at all. For instance, in the exhibition catalogue for the MoMA show Mark Wigley writes, "Buildings are constructed by taking simple geometric forms—cubes, cylinders, spheres, cones, pyramids, and so on—and combining them into stable ensembles, following compositional rules which prevent any one form from conflicting with another. No form is permitted to distort another; all potential conflict is resolved." Mannerist, baroque, picturesque, and German expressionist architecture—not to mention many areas of non-Western architecture—are ignored in this reductive and ahistorical account. See Mark Wigley, "Deconstructivist Architecture," in *Deconstructivist Architecture*, ed. Philip Johnson and Mark Wigley (New York: Museum of Modern Art, 1988).

55. Gayatri Chakravorty Spivak's term "strategic essentialism" seems especially appropriate in this context. See *In Other Worlds: Essays in Cultural Politics* (New York: Methuen, 1987).

56. See Michel Foucault, "What Is an Author?" in *Language, CounterMemory, Practice: Selected Essays and Interviews*, ed. Donald F. Bouchard, trans. Donald F. Bouchard and Sherry Simon (Ithaca: Cornell University Press, 1977), pp. 113–138; and Roland Barthes, "The Death of the Author," in *Image, Music, Text*, ed. and trans. Stephen Heath (New York: Hill and Wang, 1977), pp. 142–148.

57. Huyssen argues that the rejection of authorship in poststructuralist theory "merely duplicates on the level of aesthetics and theory what capitalism as a system of exchange relations produces tendentially in everyday life: the denial of subjectivity in the very process of its construction. Poststructuralism thus attacks the appearance of capitalist culture—individualism writ large—but misses its essence." Huyssen, "Mapping the Postmodern," p. 213.

58. Ibid. The feminist Sandra Gilbert has labeled such "subjectless" theory "father speech," because it once more refuses women a public basis for speech and solidarity. See Gerald Gruff, "Feminist Criticism in the University: An Interview with Sandra M. Gilbert," in *Criticism in the University*, ed. Gerald Graff and Reginald Gibbons (Evanston: Northwestern University Press, 1985), p. 119; see also Bruce Robbins, "The Politics of Theory," *Social Text* 18 (Winter 1987–1988), p. 11. Although many feminist and minority critics have found aspects of poststructuralist theory liberating as far as it dismantles unspoken assumptions of patriarchal discourse—older, oppressive categories such as "race," "women," "the people"—many of these same individuals also fear that poststructuralist theory subverts the categories of resistance itself.

59. For an insightful analysis of recent deconstructionist rhetoric in architectural discourse, see Joan Ockman's paper "Some Rhetorical Questions/In Response to Mark Rakatansky," Conference on Architectural Theory, SOM Foundation, Chicago, 9–11 September 1988.

60. Stern, "The Doubles of Post-Modern," pp. 82–83.

61. Thomas Crow, "Modernism and Mass Culture," in *Modernism and Modernity, The Vancouver Conference Papers*, ed. Benjamin H. D. Buchloh, Serge Guilbaut, and David Solkin (Halifax: Press of the Nova Scotia College of Art and Design, 1983), p. 253. The following argument draws on Crow's analysis.

62. The same, of course, can be said of the critic, and in writing this article, I have often wondered whether I am only fueling the fashionability of deconstructivism by giving it so much attention. But for the critic, as for the architect, the only means to counter this cycle is continual scrutiny and questioning. This may not prevent cooptation, but it may slow its processes and raise new possibilities for cultural and political exploration.

1989

 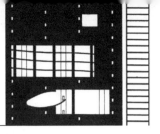 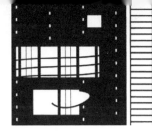 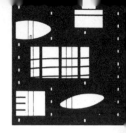

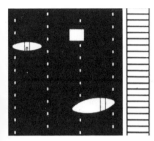 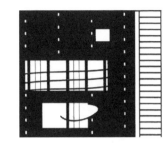 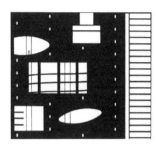 

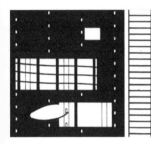 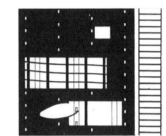 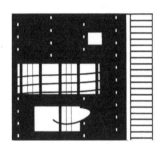 

 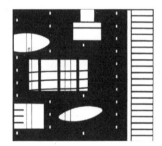 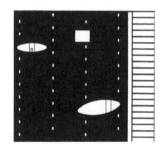 

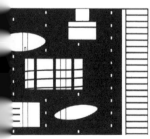 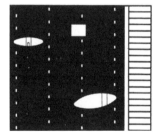 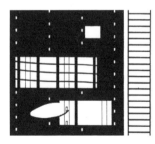 

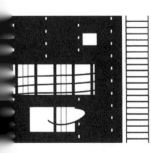 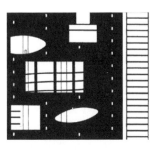 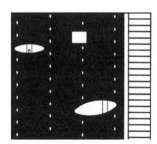 

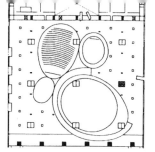 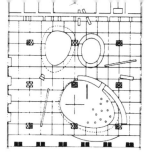 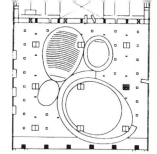 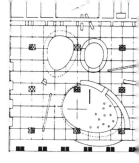

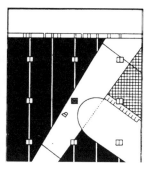 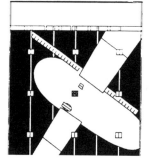 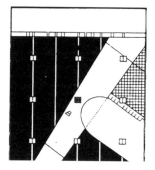 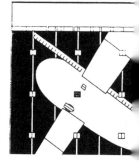

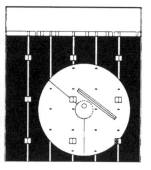 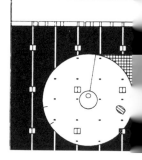

The library is interpreted as a solid block of information, a storehouse for all forms of memory: books, laserdiscs, microfiches, computers. In this block, public spaces are defined as *absences of the built,* voids dug out of the mass of information. These absences are presented as multiple embryos floating in the stacks—each one endowed with a technological placenta of its own. Defined as holes, the spatialities of the individual libraries can be explored according to their inherent logic, independently from one another, the exterior envelope, and the usual constraints of architecture, including the laws of gravity. Together, they imply a spectrum of spatial experiences that runs from the conventional to the experimental.

The revolutionary potential of the elevator has always been to introduce—by its capacity to establish mechanical rather than architectural relationships—a new era of liberated and problematic relationships between diverse components of a building. This is why the connection between the principal interior spaces of the library is a group of nine elevators which cross the block at regular intervals.

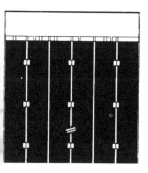 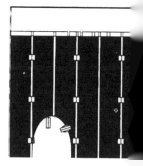

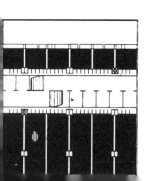 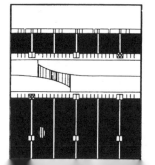 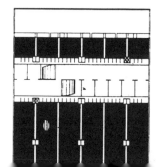 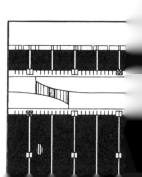

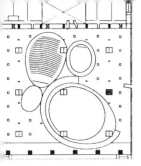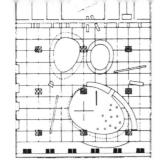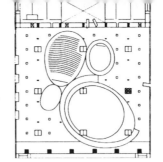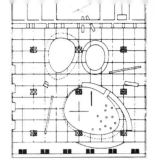

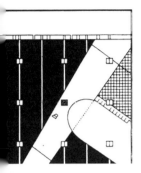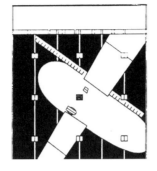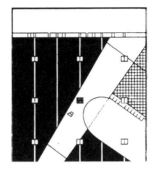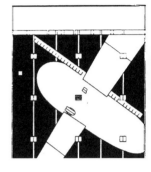

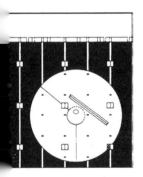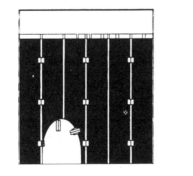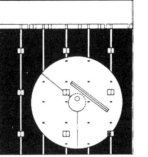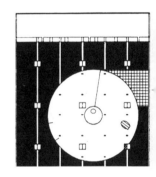

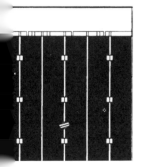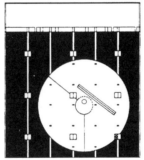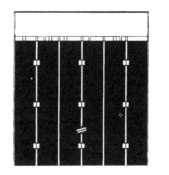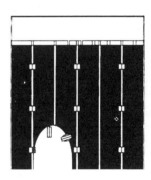

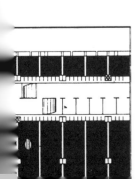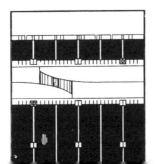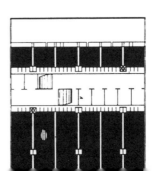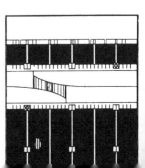

Jeffrey Kipnis   **"/Twisting the Separatrix/"** *Assemblage* 14 (April 1991)

"Deconstruction in three easy lessons: a) The meaning of any work is undecidable. b) In as much as they aspire to the meaningful, conventional ways of working, whether radical or conservative, always seek to repress undecidability. c) It is both possible and desirable to work in such a way as to respect undecidability, that is, to produce a work which is neither meaningful nor meaningless."[1] This, the third aphorism in Jeffrey Kipnis's *In the Manor of Nietzsche*, summarizes a theme to which he returns again and again in both his occasional essays — most notably on the work of Peter Eisenman, Daniel Libeskind, John Hejduk — and his general considerations of the workings of architecture theory and design. The attempt to determine an architectural object comprehensively — whether through the practice of history, criticism, theory, or design — does not "respect" the object (appreciate it, look at it again) but rather the opposite, since internal to what an object "is" is its indeterminacy.

In order for any meaning to be possible, Kipnis instructs, a signifier must be able to refer and a signified must be able to be referred to. Yet any unit of meaning, including architectural meaning, can both refer to and be referred to by other units. Meaning is an interminable web of referral and deferral, which the term *text* and its inflections, *texture*, *textile*, and *context*, are used to invoke. Thus decidability is not the result of exigencies of circumstance (incorrect information, prejudice, and so forth), but rather an intrinsic property of the work itself. Deconstruction, nevertheless, does not attempt to render a work meaningless but rather to keep in motion its contingent and provisional status, respecting the work by unwinding meaning's repressed threads.[2]

Another important aspect of Kipnis's theoretical position is his insistence that any history or theory, intentionally or not, draws in the wake of its retrospective project an agenda for present design. He outlines two possibilities for playing out the design effect of histories and theories, which are related to his concerns with undecidability. First and foremost is a Hegelian one, in which architecture is understood as metaphysically complete, its general principles known; all themes that can be taken up by architecture have been taken up already, and all that is left to do, no matter how creatively, is to elaborate those themes. A second possibility, infrequently if ever explored, is a challenge, in the manner of Nietzsche, to the hegemony in architectural history and theory of such foundational constraints as representation and rationality, beauty and truth, which must now be understood not as historical or theoretical ideals at all but as moral prohibitions.[3] To exercise the Nietzschean challenge is not to substitute the opposite constraints of irrationality and ugliness, but to shake the structure (the structure of the separatrix) that makes such oppositions thinkable.

That Jacques Derrida had taken up the Nietzschean alternative in philosophy, that Peter Eisenman had already experimented with procedures that defer the traditional constraints of representational and rational architecture, and that the two proposed to collaborate made doubly interesting the case that came to be called *Choral Work*, a design process in which Kipnis participated and which he analyzes here.[4] That, despite their efforts, Derrida and Eisenman ultimately leave the

compare Derrida (570 ff)

see Eisenman (524 ff)

institution of architecture undisturbed only reconfirms that the control of meaning is not a local and limited urge but fundamental to what Kipnis calls architectural design's metaphysic.

Notes

"/Twisting the Separatrix/" was reprinted in *Chora L Works: Jacques Derrida and Peter Eisenman*, ed. Jeffrey Kipnis and Thomas Leeser (New York: Monacelli Press, 1997).

1. Jeffrey Kipnis, *In the Manor of Nietzsche: Aphorisms around and about Architecture* (New York: Calluna Farms Press, 1990), §3.

2. Jeffrey Kipnis, "Nolo Contendere," *Assemblage* 11 (April 1990).

3. "All architectural theories and histories always also operate, beneath their veil of objectivity and aside from their announced intent, in the service of a design agenda despite their frequent protestations to the contrary." Jeffrey Kipnis, "Forms of Irrationality," in *Strategies in Architectural Thinking*, ed. John Whiteman, Jeffrey Kipnis, and Richard Burdett (Cambridge: MIT Press, 1992), p. 149.

4. Another noteworthy account of that collaboration is Ann Bergren, "Architecture Gender Philosophy," in *Strategies in Architectural Thinking*.

From the moment Bernard Tschumi invited Peter Eisenman and Jacques Derrida to collaborate on a design for one of the gardens along the *promenade cinématique* of the Parc de la Villette in Paris, all were agreed. In fact, their collaboration was so obvious that its latecoming felt oddly conspicuous, like an augury that though prepared at a beginning could only mean its meanings at an end. A collaboration between Peter Eisenman and Jacques Derrida would be a golden opportunity if the chemistry proved right. Allow me to add immediately that the chemistry between the two was exactly right, better than one could have imagined. It was the right chemistry for the opportunity—the chemistry of gold.

      Derrida, of course, is the architect of deconstruction, that contemplation of writing and reading which has shaken and forever destabilized the "solid foundations" of all the humanities, particularly the "serious" disciplines such as philosophy, law, psychoanalysis, literary criticism, and now, at last, architecture. At the risk of repeating a no longer necessary summary of deconstruction, let us accent certain of its themes to better situate the discussion to follow. First, despite the invectives of nihilism hurled at it from the right and the more recent charges of a complicity with conservativism emerging from the traditional left, deconstruction is neither radical nor conservative, at least in the familiar sense of a radical/conservative opposition. A general positioning of its motifs for architectural design: Do not destroy; maintain, renew, and reinscribe. Do battle with the very meaning of architectural meaning without proposing a new order. Avoid a reversal of values aimed at an unaesthetic, uninhabitable, unusable, asymbolic, and meaningless architecture. Instead, destabilize meaning. To destabilize meaning does not imply progression toward any new and stable end, and thus can neither mean to end meaning nor to change meaning. Nor, obviously, does it mean to conserve a "true" meaning. To destabilize meaning is to maintain (a respect for) all of the meanings possible, as a consequence of the congenital instability of writing.[1] "One does not declare war: another strategy weaves itself between hostilities and negotiation."[2]

      One of the most powerful techniques of deconstruction is to search out and destabilize the *separatrix*, that divider whose ability to separate the inside from the outside establishes the solid ground upon which all of the foundations of discourse rest. The separatrix is the /, aka *solidus, virgule, slash, slant, diagonal,* and, in French, *ligne, barre oblique, trait.* It marks among its many punctuations: ratios and fractions (2/3), simultaneity (president/commander-in-chief), choice (and/or), opposition (nonserious/serious, inside/outside), and all other manner of structured relationships (signifier/signified, ornament/structure). The separatrix is the incision of decision, the cut that is the possibility of management, of rendering complexity manageable (from the French, *traitable*) of keeping things in line, keeping things straight. Throughout his work, Derrida relentlessly tracks the separatrix in all its operations, overt or covert, so as to twist it, turn it back on itself, and poke holes in it in order to expose the inseparability of those terms that it separates.

Like Holmes on the trail of Moriarity, Derrida pursues his quarry, *le trait*, with a compulsive, icy calculation that often causes his readers to shiver—with excitement of course, but always also with dread and revulsion. Lest we think his chase a matter of mere academic exercise, let us eavesdrop on one of the author's private postcards, sent to a lover but destined for Eisenman: "The *trait* in itself is indiscreet; whatever it traces or represents, it is indecent (my love, free me from the *trait*). And to these obscene *traits* I immediately want to erect a monument or a *house of cards*" (emphasis added).[3] What drives Derrida against the separatrix, against *le trait*, is a violent, puritanical passion. And can it fail to interest us that in this private, expressive moment, Derrida's abhorrence of the separatrix moves him to contemplate committing architecture, Eisenman's architecture?[4] Thanatos and architecture are familiar bedfellows, of course, and, as voyeurs of this postcard well know, eros is always close behind.

Having dogged and disrupted the separatrix, deconstruction can then inquire into the hidden agendas that underlie its efficacy of simple difference. It thereby recovers, and gains respect for, the undecidability that this mark represses so as to make decision possible.[5] Thus, for example, deconstruction deconstructs the project of radicality as well as that of conservativism by destabilizing the network of separatrices that construct the simple directionalities, inclusions, and exclusions of either project, of any project as such. Other than in this sense, deconstruction has no project.[6]

Above all, deconstruction is nothing new. According to its principles, deconstruction is possible only because it is always already occurring. What is new about it, what gets named with the new name "deconstruction," is a new respect for the instability that is always already at work, that is irrepressible and yet that every totality, radical or conservative, and every scene of stability must attempt to repress, to disrespect. Architecture is a major test for deconstruction precisely because it is a scene of the proper, a scene of stability unlike any other—physical, aesthetic, historic, economic, social, and political.

If it is unnecessary to introduce Derrida and deconstruction, then in this context it is even less necessary to identify Peter Eisenman, who throughout his career has been the foremost advocate of a "depth" architecture. In recent years, largely through the stimulus of Derrida's work, this has come to mean, for Eisenman, an architecture that admits of the clay feet of its own "stable" (historical) foundations of familiarity, orderliness, beauty—all of which he assembles under the term "anthropocentric." What he desires is an architecture that no longer writes the one anthropocentric text that sponsors all traditional theories and processes of architectural design. In Eisenman's view, the architect does not write differently that writes by mere contradiction or idiosyncrasy. Instead, the architect must find methods that at once embody complex organizations of multiple and contradictory meanings and meet the responsibility to shelter, function, and stand.

Thus, rather than merely symbolizing a lack of confidence in the traditional terms of architectural stability with a traditional design process given to a contradictory aesthetic (fragments, nonorthogonal angles, sculptural collage, etc.), Eisenman seeks nontraditional design processes that might yield another architecture.

While there are clear allegiances between Eisenman's and Derrida's work, there are also conspicuous tensions and disagreements.[7] The field of these differences may be circumscribed by noting that Derrida has tenaciously worked to render fathomless the "depth," which always means the deeper truths, sought by depth practices. Thus that deconstruction should become the intellectual stimulus of a depth practice—and Eisenman's is always that, above all else—is one of the many contradictions that we will leave to others to ravel. Of course, to stimulate is not the same as to instruct.

Let us pause for a moment, then, to consider the promise of this collaboration before we take up the question of its results. For though the relationship produced exactly what it was prepared for, it is not clear that it produced what was anticipated. In this sense, we might say that the event was fecund but infertile, from it came offspring, but not progeny. Thus if we hoped for a clear and definitive discourse in both text and design on the relationship between architecture and deconstruction, one that would end the anxious ambiguity and difficulty of this issue, then we would be disappointed. If we desired some demonstration of how simply rigid disciplinary boundaries could be dissolved, as if such boundaries were arbitrary conventions and carried no stakes, then we would be thwarted. If we dreamed of two authorities cutting through all resistances, habits, and vested interests to focus on a common task then we would be rudely awakened by the defensiveness, duplicity, and conflict in this relationship—most of which has operated through the conduit of an intimate friendship. These were the loftier aspirations for the collaboration, but there were other stakes, more vulgar perhaps, yet stakes nonetheless. So the litany continues: if we hoped that Derrida could be convinced, coerced, tricked, or seduced into anointing one architectural effort from those put forward under his name—and in 1985 that meant Tschumi or Eisenman—then we would be deflected. And if some anticipated that Derrida would, if not vindicate, then at least grant dispensation to Eisenman's misreading of deconstruction and his argument by casual analogy and non sequitur. While others looked forward to this forbidding intellect excommunicating Eisenman and his theories, then both parties would receive their just desert.

Aside from its naïveté, an irony resides in asking, from whatever position, what the presence "in person" of Derrida "himself" in collaboration would do to, or for, Eisenman. One of the concerns of Derrida's work is to disrupt from within what he terms the "metaphysics of presence," the insatiable desire for an unambiguous standard for truth that shapes the conceptual structure of all that stands and has the status of serious discourse. Derrida argues that such a standard, a "transcendental signified," does not exist. The principal vector for this desire, belief in the possibility of the unambiguous truth of the word, he names "logocentrism," and within logocentrism the particularly important status of the authority of the spoken word he names "phonocentrism."[8] The most disturbing aspects of Derrida's work evolve from these ideas, including the deconstruction of the separatrix that produces the ordered relationships that constitute all discourse as discourse, the analytic of the undecidables such as *différance* and trace,[9] and, ultimately, his call to "write in another way."

Can we, then, avoid a certain discomfort with the very premise of an event whose main attraction is the copresence of these two figures in particular? Moreover, if we overcome this discomfort we immediately face another. Since Derrida ostensibly operates as the authority on discourse in this joint effort, should we not, according to him, have the deepest suspicion of that which is taken for granted in this event as a unit—that is, "Derrida himself"—but which, in fact, is one of those insidious systems most vulnerable to deconstruction: (Derrida's) writing (Derrida's) speech. In this event, it seems that logocentrism, phonocentrism, and the metaphysics of presence could not be more dominant—unless we somehow find a way to refuse them. At the very least, let us bear this issue in mind as we ask the question, What are these things (themselves) called Eisenman and Derrida?

To be sure, however, the issues are by no means connected to what Derrida would do to, or for, Eisenman; for some, the reverse is perhaps more interesting. Could Eisenman dislodge what seemed to be an absent-minded architectural conservatism expressed by Derrida? This conservatism, were it that, took several forms, the most conspicuous being a certain suspect voice he gave to public responsibility and the inviolability of domesticity. Consider Eisenman's remarks, made at a conference on deconstruction and architecture in Chicago in 1987:

He wants architecture to stand still and be what he assumes it appropriately should be in order that philosophy can be free to move and speculate. In other words, he wants architecture to be real, to be grounded, to be solid, not to move around—that is what Jacques wants. And so when I made the first crack at the project we were doing together—a public garden in Paris—he said things to me that filled me with horror: "How can it be a garden without plants?" "Where are the trees?" Where are the benches for people to sit on?" This is what philosophers want, they want to know where the benches are.

The minute architecture begins to move away from its traditional role as the symbolization of customary use, that is when philosophy starts to shake. [Such movement] starts to question its philosophical underpinnings and starts to move it around and suggests that what is under philosophy may be architecture and something that isn't so nice. In other words, perhaps it's not so solid, not so firm, not so well constructed.[10]

To give a deserved benefit of doubt, perhaps all that is evident in this more pedestrian conservativeness that Derrida displays is a struggle between this thinker's intellectual commitment to the consequences of his work and an initial reluctance to face these consequences in architecture, where, as he now often repeats, the stakes are among the highest. In this case, Derrida's conflict would merely be representative of the vested interest in architectural inertia that confirms these stakes as highest, even for those most committed to overcoming this inertia. Let us recall how often Eisenman has asserted his own lack of interest in living in residences designed in the spirit of his work. Is this, too, "wanting architecture to stand still and be what he assumes it appropriately should be in order that he can be free to move and speculate?" If the stakes are truly so high, then none, including Derrida and Eisenman, is immune.

Hence, Eisenman's claim to the contrary, any conservatism of particular interest on Derrida's part will not be found at the level of the humane concerns he expresses during the project. Nor can much be made of the mild xenophobia the philosopher demonstrates when he first encounters Eisenman's efforts to work at the limits of architecture. He was, after all, not at home in architecture, though a certain irony or two sounds here, considering how much abuse his "too foreign" writings have received. To his credit, in fact, Derrida quickly set aside these early resistances—perhaps even too quickly.[11]

But Derrida exhibits another form of conservativeness that is worth closer attention. In the beginning, he assumes as self-evident that architecture, in its essence, is limited to very narrow modes of meaning, namely, depiction or symbolization. Thus, for example, when the discussion turns to the representation of *chora* by the design, Derrida's suggestions always stay close to sculptural depiction.[12] Because *chora* is something of a radical void (though not a void), he recommends that the project be simple, even empty. The role of the four elements—earth, air, fire, water—in Plato's text on *chora*, leads him to propose that they be symbolized in the project (sand for earth, light for fire, and so on). When called upon to contribute form to the design, he draws a picture derived from one of the descriptions of *chora* in the *Timaeus*. Likewise, as the collaboration proceeds, Derrida becomes distressed by the complex, narrative-loaded, and labyrinthine architecture that Eisenman pursues in the name of *chora*. This is all the more curious when we consider what he has to say about the history of the interpretations of *chora* in his own essay on the subject:

Everything happens as if the yet-to-come history of the interpretations of *chora* were written or even prescribed in advance, in advance reproduced and reflected in a few pages of the *Timaeus* "on the subject" of *chora* "herself" ("itself"). *With its ceaseless relaunchings, this history wipes itself out in advance since it programs itself, reproduces itself, and reflects itself by anticipation. Is a prescribed, programmed, reproductive, reflexive history still a history?* (second emphasis added)[13]

Here it is almost as though he were trying to describe Eisenman's design process. While we must point out that at this moment in the essay Derrida is raising questions about the efficacy and agenda of this history, he by no means intends to call for an interpretation that would be somehow more representational.

In putting forward this axiomatic of architecture's limited talents, Derrida repeats a familiar theme found in philosophy's contemplation of the nonlinguistic fine arts. Let us remember that Hegel uses precisely the "self-evidence" of architecture's limited and insufficient possibilities of meaning to relegate it forevermore to the irrelevant. It is particularly conspicuous that Derrida should casually repeat Hegel, since, as the most powerful philosopher of totalization, Derrida endlessly grapples with his thought. Beyond this contradiction, two others are worth attending. First, Derrida knows that such representational strategies are wrong for *chora*. *Chora* is that which cannot be shown, described, or positively represented. He not only says as much in his meetings with Eisenman, but in his essay "Chora" brilliantly conveys both the error of trying to represent *chora* "properly" and the underlying agenda in a history of those efforts in philosophy to do so. Moreover, his essay paradoxically seems to get closer to *chora* by moving away from it in a complex, labyrinthine writing that, like all of this writer's work, is neither philosophy nor literature but something else again. A third kind of writing, a bastard writing, we might say, as long as we avoid meaning a new kind of writing, a bad seed come to flower in the letters. To the issues of this essay we will return. But here we must point out that it is exactly his writing technique wherein lies the last contradiction. Derrida feels no conflict in the labyrinthine complexity of his writing on *chora*, no need to present blank pages or to use simple representational descriptions, in other words, to depict *chora* in his essay. Quite to the contrary.

Consider these three contradictions: first, the comfortable repetition of themes from a philosophical tradition that he, above all, discomforts; second, the proposition of ideas that he knows are wrong but other than which he cannot conceive; and third, the employment of techniques in his own medium, writing, that he resists in the medium of architecture. If a more complex writing can say something about *chora* that could not otherwise be said, why not a more complex architecture? Certainly, it seems in the end that Derrida agrees or at least stipulates the possibility. At least he says in retrospect that he is comfortable with cosigning the work. We will check to make sure.

Before we do so, though, let us note that to challenge the self-evidence of the limitations of architectural meaning to the "aesthetic" and the "representational" is the most persistent theme in Eisenman's work. In his view, these limitations are not due to any essential aspect of architecture; rather, they constitute a resistance, a received value-structure by which architecture is repressed. His concepts of "presence of absence" and "absence of presence," his development of "scaling" processes, and so forth evidence his effort to articulate the terms of and produce another mode of meaning in architecture. Eisenman was attracted to deconstruction, correctly or not, for this reason. Most alluring to him have been its theme of the return of the repressed and such Derridean notions as "arché-writing" and "text," which, in Eisenman's eyes, confirmed that architecture was a writing in its own right, not merely and inferiorly a "writing" by analogy to linguistic models. Deconstruction said to Eisenman that architecture could do something more, something of what writing does, even if that is not what deconstruction says. It promised him the possibility of another architectural meaning and—it must always be repeated—a new relevance for architecture. Thus we might say that the scene of Derrida's resistance coincided with that of Eisenman's greatest interest.

We should return, then, to examine Derrida's signature. But again not yet. Let us look first at Eisenman's resistance. Without doubt, the design process and final project of this collaboration are, in every way, situated firmly within Eisenman's work of the period: it belongs among his so-called scalings. From this angle, the design process and the "choral work" scheme are interesting enough. The multiple relationships among Tschumi's La Villette scheme, Eisenman's Cannaregio scheme, Paris, and Venice within which the design process operates are rich, highly charged, and provide a fascinating scenario for an architectural text. As a polemic design process, however, the work here is not particularly distinguishable from the others in its species, such as *Romeo and Juliet* or the Long Beach Museum. Hence it cannot be said that the garden evidences any significant directional change for Eisenman that can be expressly attributed to Derrida's participation. Eisenman prevented that from happening, as we shall see, though he and Derrida agreed that it must happen.

Throughout their meetings, Derrida reluctantly deferred to Eisenman on each step of the design process ("OK, so we have to do so"). From the transcript of their conversations, we can follow as Eisenman ignores his collaborator, usually by seeming to go along with him ("I hear you"), while Derrida abandons every one of the specific ideas and desires for the design that he had proffered: that it be a place where "something should be printed by reflection and erased as soon as it is printed"; that it be simple ("it will be a simple scheme," "the operation must be simple"); that it be naked—not too labyrinthine, too emotional, or too historical; that it not be a masterwork, an ultimate place, but a place among others; that it provide some mechanism for the user to "affect the forms without leaving a stable trace"; that it make use of material analogies for earth, air, fire, and water, particularly water; that it employ light and sound through photographic and phonographic devices; that, above all, it not be circular, self-contained, totalizing ("now, it is my wish to avoid any kind of totalization, and the metonymic structure of which you are speaking approaches such a totalization"). Though scaling is circular, is self-contained, we will leave open for a moment the question of its totalization. Regardless, all of these suggestions, whatever their merits in retrospect, are absent from the garden.

Most conspicuously, Eisenman kept Derrida from affecting the work even when, near the end of their collaboration, Derrida seemed finally to insist on somehow disrupting the circular closure of the process ("what is needed here is some heterogeneity, something impossible to integrate into the scheme"). They arrived at a tactic. Some will say it was too little too late; it hardly matters, for it, too, was deflected. Derrida was to send a drawing for a contribution that would have nothing to do with Eisenman's design process, making all decisions as to materiality, scale, shape, and location in the scheme, thereby breaching the project's circularity. As agreed, he sent by letter a contribution that was quite specific, if somewhat short of the requested specificity of scale, location, and so on. Upon receiving it, Eisenman and Thomas Leeser, principal design associate on the project, quickly formed a way to ignore the contract, to violate both the spirit and the form of the contribution. In brief, they rationalized a loose analogy between Derrida's drawing and the shape of the site, and integrated the site, not the drawing, into the circularity of the scaling scheme, reiterating the closure Derrida desired to break.

It almost seems as if an obsessed Eisenman wanted nothing from Derrida but an endorsement of scaling, wanted, that is, Derrida's signature. In turn, it almost seems as if Derrida would sign anything in this project but scaling. A closer look at the movements of this signature is thus called for. Derrida, after he and Eisenman concur on the tactic of his contribution, says of it:

And this will be the place of the real signature. Some little something, I don't mean names, but some signature would be there. So *your work* would be, *on the one hand*, read as a combination of those three elements continually expanding, as an exercise in, reconstructing in a sophisticated way, and then, *in the margin, something totally alien* from which and toward which everything had been or would be written [emphasis added].

"On the one hand," "your work." On the other hand, his signature as "something totally alien," "in the margin." At this point, at least, Derrida is less than willing to sign the design. Can we imagine where Derrida wants to be, where the margin of this project is? Perhaps it is the grid become gridiron, the no-man's-land between Tschumi proper(ty) and Eisenman proper(ty). Indeed, that would be a fascinating place for a separatrix, an Eisenman/Tschumi come to be written:

Eisenman Tschumi

One way or the other, the reader will discover the skirmishes over this border to be well rehearsed.

Derrida has elsewhere placed his signature on this project, most conspicuously in his essay "Why Peter Eisenman Writes Such Good Books." Once we delve into this text and others associated with it, however, any aspiration of finding a simple solution to the problem of the role and place of Derrida's signature in this collaboration quickly evaporates. Instead, we confront a complex, dizzying structure—a double labyrinth at least—of signatures and autographs, inclusions and omissions, insides and outsides. Keeping in mind all that Derrida has written on the operations of quotation marks, signatures, autographs, and letters, we might have expected as much.

If, to clarify his position, we attempt to compare the idea that Derrida's contribution hosts the signatures as that idea occurs in the meetings with its appearance in "Why Peter Eisenman Writes Such Good Books," we immediately discover the difficulty at hand.

I believe that nothing else should be inscribed on this sculpture (for this is a sculpture) save perhaps the title, and a signature might figure somewhere (*Choral Work*, by . . . 1986), as well as one or two Greek words (*plokanon, seiomena*, etc.) To be discussed, among other things. . . .[14]

The cited passage appears within the essay as the end of an extended extract from the letter Derrida sent to Eisenman discussing his contribution. To be precise, however, what Derrida sent to Eisenman was two versions of the same letter differing slightly in the pertinent passage: one, handwritten and unsigned (no doubt a draft, though it, too, was dispatched); another, the one "quoted" in the essay, typed and signed. So, at the very least, a thorough reading must trace the ins and outs of the question of Derrida's signature as it circulates through four variously signed representations of this question: one "in his own words" (the conversation transcript), one unsigned but in his autograph (the draft of the letter), one typed but autographed with his personal signature (the letter), and one retyped with autograph eliminated and placed within an essay that bears his name as author. We begin to wonder whether or not there is any meaning to the questions, what, and where, is Derrida's signature?

Let us outline a portion of one of the several labyrinthine structures at work here. Among the three letters, the typed version is ostensibly the "original." It is the one authorized to appear in the essay; as well, though actually a copy of the original draft, it bears the author's handwritten signature. On the other hand, the handwritten draft sans signature is in the author's autograph; though merely a draft, it is a letter in autograph. And, after all, both were dispatched to Eisenman at the same time. Furthermore, Derrida introduces the letter within the essay thus: "I write therefore to Eisenman, in the airplane, this letter from which one will permit me to cite a fragment."[15] What is the antecedent of "this"? The fragment "quoted" is not from the draft written on the airplane, but from the version typed later—almost. Additional material (in both autograph and type!) appears in the margins of the typed rewrite, that is, as marginal to the body of the letter. In the letter as it appears in the essay this material has been brought into the body of the letter as parenthetical; thus, strictly speaking, the essay letter is "original." This original letter is inside the essay, but is inside as outside, as a quotation. It is an inside-outside as outside-inside, since it appears as the representation of Derrida's private communication to Eisenman. Clearly, this trail winds a vertiginous, indissoluble labyrinth that no Ariadne's thread can lead out of. Each line that appears as such a thread is but the lure of Arachne's web. Were we to consider all of the translations, changes, omissions, strikeovers, and other inside-outside mechanisms at work here, which become even more augmented in their complexity as they bear upon to whom these various letters were dispatched (the draft to himself, the draft plus typed letter to Eisenman, the quoted letter to an audience), we could fill a large volume.

Yet for our purpose, let us attend to a few details alone. First, under one of Derrida's signatures, that of the letter, one event is represented as having occurred inside a conversation between Eisenman and Derrida, while another, also part of this conversation, has been removed from this event to appear in the letter as if for the first time. We refer, of course, to the question of Derrida's contribution as the site of the signature. In all versions of the letter, what is to be remembered from the meeting that generated the letter is the agreement for a contribution. "You will recall what we envisaged together at Yale: that in order to finish, I 'write,' if one can say, without a word, a heterogeneous piece."[16] What is forgotten, or to be forgotten, is that the question of this piece as the site for a signature was also an issue within the meeting. The issue resides in the tense of the letter: "I believe that nothing else should be inscribed on this sculpture." The signature is never a topic for collaboration, it is always in Derrida's hands.

Compare now the two versions of Derrida's contribution as a site for the signature and other things. In the meeting: the real signature, though perhaps not names. In the letter: the title (*Choral Work*), names ("by . . ."), and some Greek words. But perhaps not names. Derrida skirts the issue yet again; though his parenthetical inscription suggests names, he refers to "*une signature*," seemingly leaving room for it with three dots. Or is he suggesting three dots as the signature? So far, neither his signature nor his thoughts on this signature will be pinned down. At the very least, however, he seems willing to have the title, *Choral Work*, signed.

Before engaging this willingness, let us raise another point or two. Turning back to Derrida's introduction of the letter in the essay, we read: "I write therefore to Eisenman, in the airplane, this letter." Now consider the first sentence of the letter, which immediately follows: "'You will recall what we envisaged together at Yale: that in order to finish, I 'write,' if one can say, without a word, a heterogeneous piece.'" Note the quotation marks that distinguish the *I write* of the essay from the *I "write"* of the letter. For Derrida, to write a contribution to architecture requires a not quite writing, an outside of writing proper, a "writing." Not so for letters.

Derrida is comfortable with "real" writing, having rehabilitated writing from its exclusion, its metaphysical exteriorization and repression vis-à-vis speech. This he was able to do by putting forward a concept of arché-writing—that is, a generalized writing anterior to speech—in large part based on such notions as trace and *différance*. Trace is a materialless, indeed, strictly speaking, nonexistent, condition that, as Derrida has demonstrated, is nevertheless necessary for and always anterior to any production of meanings—including architectural meanings.[17] The original trace frustrates the desire for a transcendental origin, a first and final "actual meaning," and thus guarantees the infinite openness of writing and reading. Yet, though architecture is a zone of the trace and thus within arché-writing, it seems nonetheless to require a hierarchical mark, a trace of its difference (in value) from "real" writing, hence the quotation marks.

In fact, as he himself emphasizes, Derrida never makes an architectural contribution. In the handwritten draft of his letter, he writes of his contribution: "I believe that nothing should be inscribed on this *sculpture*." In the typed version, the emphatic underline is insufficient and is replaced by a parenthetical mark: "nothing should be inscribed on this sculpture (for this is a sculpture)." What is Derrida trying to write so emphatically? Permit another digression to situate this question.

Among other places, Derrida confronts and undoes the metaphysical distinction between speech and writing as it is made in the works of Hegel.[18] Operating in and between Hegel's *Encyclopedia* and his *Aesthetics*, Derrida focuses on two issues—the difference between sign and symbol and the differing materiality of speech and writing—both of which are central to Hegel's privileging of speech. Hegel privileges hearing and speech over sight and writing because the materiality of the former, the breath, internalizes the temporality of the concept, something that the latter cannot do. Hence, like the plastic arts, writing holds back the progress of the spirit. Derrida is able to disrupt this argument by rendering the question of materiality immaterial, that is, by finding again the immaterial originary trace, the spacing that makes possible both writing and speech, as a necessary but repressed aspect of Hegel's argument. Of greater interest here, however, is Derrida's identification of the agenda behind this repression: "This *relevant*, spiritual, and ideal excellence of the phonic makes every spatial language—and in general all spacing—remain *inferior* and *exterior*."[19] Including architecture.

We have already touched on this issue. As an aspect of the question of materiality, Hegel, in his *Aesthetics*, invokes as an essential limitation of the plastic arts a production of meaning restricted to the aesthetic and the representational. From this, he can argue their inferiority and irrelevance within the arts as compared to poetry. Architecture, for example, confined to the massive and immobile material of stone and wood, is thus connected to the symbol. Poetry, to the contrary, living in the mobile and fluid materiality of language, of writing and, even better, of speech, operates with the *sign*. According to Hegel (and many others), the distinction between sign and symbol is that, unlike the symbol, which is motivated and thus limited by its referent, the sign is an unmotivated vector of meaning, arbitrarily related to its referent. Therefore the sign alone can express the infinite elaboration that is the spirit. Along the way of this linear Hegelian path from the irrelevant to the relevant, from architecture to poetry and eventually out of the arts to philosophy, architecture—not quite the first art but, in any case, the first expression of the spirit to itself—is superseded by sculpture. Sculpture, the *Aufhebung* of architecture, kills architecture as a relevant activity.[20]

Is Derrida's contribution a monument to the death of architecture, one upon which he would be willing to write, as one does upon a headstone, here lies "*Choral Work*, by . . . 1986," after which he would say a few Greek words"? If so, he would have created a marvelous symbol, ironically representing not only the death of architecture and its supercession by sculpture, but the death of sculpture and its supercession by music—for what is more musical than a choral work?—the death of music and its supercession by poetry—the play on words—and, finally, the death of the arts in general and their supercession by philosophy: for the "few Greek words," drawn from the *chora* passage in Plato's *Timaeus*, are to be inscribed, are they not, to symbolize Plato's texts, where poetry and myth move toward philosophy. In other words, he would have created a monument to Hegel's *Aesthetics*.

Let us be neither so rash nor so harsh. Derrida subverts Hegel's simple sign/symbol distinction precisely by tracking the operations in his writings of the *pyramid*, for Hegel, the quintessence of architecture and proof of its power and its limitation. Though the particulars of the argument are beyond the scope of this essay, suffice it to say that Derrida follows the pyramid as both concept and object in Hegel's work to show that Hegel himself cannot sustain the simple difference sign/symbol. Yet another separatrix crumbles.

As we have said, Hegel's philosophy is totalization itself and therefore the constant target of Derrida and deconstruction in every one of its arguments and manifestations. Yet in this collaboration, again and again, we run across a latent Hegelian tendency in Derrida that surfaces in his confrontation with architecture. Whether in stipulating architecture's restriction to the symbolic or in preferring to situate his signature closer to writing than to design, he casts a Hegelian shadow.

Derrida's critique of Eisenman's scaling process as totalizing is, on its surface, accurate and consistent with his attack on totalization in any form. A glance at the scaling diagram for the project reveals that the circular relationships it proposes among Tschumi's design scheme for La Villette and Eisenman's for Cannaregio are not only closed but determined by fact and presence: a fourth permutation of the cycle returns the system to its origin, a statement of the current condition of the presence of Tschumi's scheme and the absence of Eisenman's.

Eisenman counterargues that the scaling scheme proposes a design process motivated by other criteria than those that have dominated architecture throughout its history, or, more accurately, as its history. From Eisenman's point of view the history of architecture's limitation to the aesthetic and the representational is the history of architecture as totalization. In this view, the history of architecture is a univocal text of *uomo universale*, the universal man, man the measure of all things. While the metric of measurement changes and produces what we call architectural history, the origin of that metric—"man"—remains the same. Thus all of the considerations that dominate traditional design processes—attention to the whole, symmetry, order, ornamentation (whether prescribed or proscribed), function, and so on—are always grounded in the self-evidency that the purpose and meaning of architecture is to express (what is considered to be) the timeless and universal condition of man (at any time). To be sure, throughout Eisenman's writings, particularly those on scaling, we encounter an inconsistent and self-contradictory strain of argument. Eisenman typically grounds his call for a "textual architecture," one that writes of other than the universal man, on the post-Freudian condition. In other words, he argues that, since Freud, man has discovered himself to be more complex and multivalent than he is represented to be in traditional architecture. Therefore architecture should do something new and different—represent this complexity and multivalency. Hence, at the very moment Eisenman demands an end to the domination of the *uomo universale* he reinvokes it.[21]

The "should do something new and different" tone of Eisenman's writings is antithetical to the position of deconstruction and supports Derrida's criticism, directed not only at the closure of scaling but at scaling as the flagship of this revolutionary aspect of the entire Eisenman enterprise. To summarize, scaling is totalizing first because it is structured as a closed narrative entirely determined by origin and end; thus, though it can be made to read differently—a central dogma of deconstruction being that every text is essentially undecidable and so open to different readings—it does not respect textual openness. Secondly, scaling is the vehicle by which Eisenman seeks to replace one totality, traditional design, with a new and different totality. If we grant this last point, and we must, we have nevertheless said nothing of scaling as a design process, merely commented on Eisenman's pronouncements about it. The key question is whether or not Derrida's first criticism is valid.

Certainly, were Eisenman to write the fictional story contained in the recursive diagram of this project in literary language, it would be suspect as totalizing in all of the terms discussed. Yet, Eisenman argues, this is not true of the design process, nor necessarily of its final result. Scaling is not the discussion of scaling or the literary motif within the scaling diagram, but rather, these taken together with the manipulation of drawings and forms as one text. The process uses the linear fictional scheme to direct a play with the materials of architecture. In using a linear motive to direct design, scaling is akin to traditional design methods; however, it seeks to avoid the trap of architectural (not literary) totalization by replacing the universalizing discourse that drives traditional design with a local fiction. Scaling also engages aesthetics and representation, scale, solid and void, simultaneity and materiality, in such a way as to stay within the tradition of architectural design while displacing the underlying "anthropocentrism" of this tradition. It searches architecture for something that remains architecture yet is other than a discreet, unified, and universalizing whole. In this regard, Eisenman argues, scaling meets the criteria for design as writing in deconstruction's sense of the term.

Derrida's uneasiness with the linearity and closure of scaling is only legitimate if architectural design results in nothing more, and nothing other than an exemplification of the ideas that motivate it—a signifier/signified thesis strongly at odds with the themes of deconstruction. Derrida aims his criticism at neither the process nor the final design, but at what is said of them: "Now, it is my wish to avoid any kind of totalization, and the *metonymic structure* of which you are *speaking* approaches such a totalization" (emphasis added). In these terms, his criticism is completely accurate: however, in targeting the word rather than the entire text, is it off target?

Discourse, literary writing, and architectural design are different; they each do things the other cannot. If, before, we took Derrida to task for distinguishing between literary writing and architectural writing (writing vs. "writing"), it was not to suggest that they are identical. Rather, it was to ask why their difference required the hierarchy of quotation marks, which suggest the Hegelian theme of literary writing, "real" writing, as more important and more able than architectural design. Scaling is not a hierarchical chain, a discourse that produces a narrative that then produces drawings and models. It is a text in which discourse, narrative, and design all operate simultaneously to motivate and disrupt each other in their separate realms.

As we indicated, one of the traditions of hierarchical difference between architectural design and writing turns on the question of sign versus symbol. This is not to say that the structure sign/symbol correctly articulates the difference between language and architecture, but that the differences between the two have been incorrectly and hierarchically subsumed under that distinction. Derrida has disturbed the sign/symbol distinction by demonstrating that the unmotivated trace, the required condition for the arbitrariness of the sign, does not exist: "In fact, there is no unmotivated trace: the trace is indefinitely its own becoming-unmotivated . . . there is neither symbol nor sign, but the becoming-sign of symbol."[22] Thus deconstruction respects, and depends on, the irreducible nonarbitrariness—the formality and materiality—of language. It makes its necessary essay and serious point by playing with spelling, anagrams, puns, homophones, homonyms, formal analogies, in other words, by emphasizing the residual symbolic always within the signification of language.

Architecture poses, in a sense, the opposite problem. If, in language, the "arbitrary signifier" would like to disappear completely into its signified but cannot quite do so, always leaving open the door for deconstruction, then, in architecture, the symbol would like to appear exactly as its referent, be its (own) referent, though neither can it quite do so. Hence, though architecture is another field of the becoming-unmotivated trace, unlike writing, it is the one that has been constituted historically as entirely motivated, that is, symbolic. Architecture is the scene in which, so to speak, the always-becoming-symbolic of the ("arbitrary") sign is repressed. Scaling attempts to respect and play with the becoming-symbolic of the arbitrary. Not, of course, the truly arbitrary, which does not exist: scaling does not aspire to invent new forms out of nowhere. Rather it produces a more playful disposition of the sources of the symbolic (reference, scale, and so forth). Hence it results in neither an entirely arbitrary sign nor an architectural symbol. It seeks to subvert:

the autocratic and authoritative relationship of the word over the object, figure/ ground relations, the hierarchy of scale, the hierarchy of solid versus void, the privilege of the "now" of perception, and the traditional presence of the architectural whole. In short, it seeks to subvert ail of the bastions of architectural totalization without simply negating these issues.

It must be admitted that, by the end of the collaboration, Derrida, if still somewhat wary, addresses these issues as they apply to scaling. In "Why Eisenman . . . ," he says of the final design, "In this *abyssal* palimpsest, no truth can establish itself on any primitive or final presence of meaning, and later notes "the discontinuous structure of scaling."[23] However, even as he takes up the question of whether or not to sign scaling, he always leans toward, if not on, the word. On the way to a final look at Derrida's contribution in these terms, at his reading of the ongoing text implied by the emphatic sculpturality of this contribution, we should pass by another excerpt from his writings.

One must then, in a single gesture, but doubled, read and write. And that person would have understood nothing of the game who, at this, would feel himself authorized merely to add on: that is, to add any old thing. He would add nothing: the seam would not hold. Reciprocally, he who through "methodological prudence," "norms of objectivity," or "safeguards of knowledge" would refrain from committing anything of himself, would not read at all. The same foolishness, the same sterility, obtains in the "not serious" as in the "serious." The reading or writing supplement must be rigorously prescribed, but by the necessities of a *game*, by the logic of *play*, signs to which the system of all textual powers must be accorded and attuned.[24]

If all that we have written is wrong, if, contrary to these arguments, the scaling process failed to meet the criteria of rigorously prescribed play and, indeed, was too closed, too circular, too totalizing, was it correct to add "something totally alien," a "sculpture" to introduce "some heterogeneity"? Was not this proposition an example of any old thing merely added on? In restoring the figure ground relationship by reducing the scaling held to a pedestal for a "totally alien" "sculpture," Derrida's contribution would have homogenized more than heterogenized—just as the Choragic Monument of Lysicrates in Athens does to its famous pedestal. At the very least, the absence of any mention of the Derridean treatment of "supplement" during the discussion of Derrida's contribution is a conspicuous silence.[25]

In a certain sense, Derrida's tactic was, as always, precise and to the point. The idea of contributing an image extracted from the *chora* passage of Plato's *Timaeus* would have introduced, through rigorous play, a heterogeneity into the discussion of a process designed around *chora* that at the same time had nothing of *chora* in it. It would not, in fact, have been adding any old thing. But the drawings and models were of the text, not exemplifications of it. To avoid adding any old thing, to put aside his anaclitic relationship to the word, would it not have been necessary to read in such a way as to respect the drawings and models as text rather than as examples? Then the contribution could have played its game with the entire text, formally, materially, discursively, and so on.

Without having decided anything, then, let us return to the scene that we were reading, return, that is, to the question of Derrida's signature. In his essay "Why Eisenman . . . ," though he praises much of Eisenman's work, again particularly as it concerns writing, Derrida extends his criticism of the architect's totalizing tendencies with stinging irony, thus distinguishing his work from deconstruction proper. The very title of the essay indicates what is to come. Consider what Derrida writes in a chapter, entitled "The End of the Book and the Beginning of

Writing," from Of Grammatology, held by many to be the premier textbook of deconstruction:

The idea of the book is the idea of a totality, finite or infinite, of the signifier: this totality of the signifier cannot be a totality, unless a totality constituted by the signified preexists it, supervises its inscriptions and its signs, and is independent of it in its ideality. The idea of the book, which always refers to a natural totality, is profoundly alien to the sense of writing. It is the encyclopedic protection of theology and logocentrism against the disruption of writing, against its aphoristic energy, and against difference in general [emphasis added].[26]

Does such a writer entitle an essay "Why Peter Eisenman Writes Such Good Books" without irony? Lest we think that, in the case of Eisenman, Derrida could be referring to "books," not books, and thus perhaps that the text/book distinction does not play here, consider how quickly it arises in the essay. In the second paragraph the distinction is revived in terms that suggest a choice be made between Derrida and Eisenman. Referring to his own writing strategy, Derrida remarks, "Is this not the best condition for writing good texts?" (emphasis added).[27]

The title also opens the door to several other participants in the discussion; some enter forthrightly, some obliquely. Derrida reveals some, conceals others: as he says, this is the best condition for writing good texts; certainly, it is the best condition for writing ironic texts. Besides Jacques Derrida and Peter Eisenman, who for a time we require in name only, we will want some of these participants on hand in this reading. Let us call them by name. The most obvious is Nietzsche, for the title to this essay is a play on a chapter title, "Why I Write Such Good Books," from Nietzsche's Ecce Homo.[28] Then there is, of course, Wagner, for beyond the Case of Wagner, what and who is Nietzsche, in any case, without Wagner? Almost as obvious is John, the Gospel According to St. John: after all, Pontius Pilate in John 19:5 delivers Jesus to his accusers and to his eventual crucifixion with the ironic words "Ecce Homo." In that text and this one, we also find, among other things, the denial of Peter. Jesus himself has a small role, at least insofar as he knew how to stop a spear, if not an arrow. We need a cameo from Plato, a safecracker, a wrinkle or two to be ironed out, some ice, some diamonds, and, above all, laughter for this irony of ironies.

In "Why Eisenman . . . ," Derrida employs a technique found in much of his writing, though with a twist. Many of this writer's essays play on the name of their underlying subject: Signéponge on the poet Ponge and "Parergon" on Kant (Kante in German means "border" or "edge") come to mind as obvious examples. Such is the case for this essay as well, with the twist that the play extends into the work's very tone. It is an ironic essay first because of what it has to say, but it is also an iron-y essay about Peter Eisenman (Eisen is German for "iron").[29] The irony to be worked out, perhaps even heard as a plaint within the title (Why Eisenman?), is at once how very similar and how very different the two are to and from each other, and not only in their work. The lever of intervention, the pivot between the two that is also a gap, is ostensibly Nietzsche. The Eisenman/Nietzsche is the old Nietzsche, the simple, radical Nietzsche, the one traditionally read as critic of the human-all-too-human, as nihilist, as revaluer of all values, as the philosopher of the end of the "truth" of everything, which is to say, the end of everything. La fin de tout, particularly the end of God, la fin de Dieu. Versus the Derrida/Nietzsche, the Nietzsche who would read a text as a text, the complex Nietzsche who not only abolishes the "true" world, but also in the same gesture abolishes the apparent world, the "apparency" of the apparent world.

But I ask, Do we not hear a hint of another voice in the opening strains of the essay, when, as Derrida summons Nietzsche's Ecce Homo to bear witness, he takes it upon himself to clear Eisenman of all suspicion? Suspicion of what? At the very least, do we not hear a whisper of Pontius Pilate, who did everything he could to evade the entanglement in which he found himself, who tried to put his responsibility on someone else, who summoned a bearing-witness with the ironic words "Ecce Homo," who took it upon himself to clear someone of all suspicion, but, above all, himself? And Pilate who removed his signature from the act, washed his hands of it, so to speak? Do we not hear him? No? Perhaps not.

Derrida draws the lines among Eisenman, Nietzsche, and himself quickly, and equally quickly seems to take sides. Though Eisenman's antianthropocentric words sound like Nietzsche's, "we should not, however, simply conclude that such an architecture will be Nietzschean." Rather, Derrida suggests that Eisenman is "the most anti-Wagnerian creator of our time."[30] He, Derrida, is more like the real Nietzsche; he writes on a computer as Nietzsche wrote on his typewriter. With Nietzsche, Wagner and I-rony are never far away. It is in the chapter of *Ecce Homo* concerning his "Case of Wagner" that Nietzsche writes of his "love of irony, particularly world-historical irony." What is it to be the most anti-Wagnerian creator of our time? Wagner was the foremost creator of artistic totalities, the composer par excellence of whole worlds. To be the most anti-Wagnerian creator of the time: is this to be, like Derrida an arch-deconstructionist totally against all totalization, or is it to be the foremost creator of new totalities, the creator of whole antiworlds? In the end, we must consider the possibility that these are the same.

Great care is called for here, for we are sending letters to "the wrong address" if we think we have a simple twosome in this essay, a Derrida versus an Eisenman. When Derrida writes that "it is not he who speaks, it is I. I who write; I who, using displacements, borrowings, fragmentations, play with identities, with persons and their titles, with the integrity of their proper names," be warned.[31] The initial play from first person to third person, from "I" to "Eisenman" is played back and forth again and again, intentionally and/or not. Throughout, wherever Derrida says "I" listen for "Eisenman." Whenever he writes "Eisenman" listen for "I," as in "I's a man" or "I's de man."

Beyond the tone of the work, the play on the proper name becomes a specifically ironic theme in the essay. Derrida writes, "Peter Eisenman, whose own name embodies both stone and metal," and, a moment later, "it is the truth that this man of iron, determined to break with the anthropocentric scale, with its 'man the measure of all things,' writes such good books! I swear it to you!"[32] As might be expected both in principle and in these particular circumstances, nothing in this essay permits of a conclusion that Derrida is simply opposed to Eisenman's work; to the contrary, much in it explores Eisenman's machinations with both respect and admiration. Yet the reader will be hardpressed to find such ironic heat elsewhere in Derrida's writing, which is usually as cool as ice. As a writer, Derrida is an iceman. If we look deeply enough at the play of proper names, beyond those that Derrida engages, we can discover within them barely imaginable ironies that confirm and overdetermine many themes in this collaboration, including the fluidity of identities. If, for example, Peter comes from the Greek word meaning stone and Eisenman means iron-man, what does Jacques Derrida mean?

Consider the French verb *dérider*, is it close enough to Derrida? An English-speaking reader might guess from the looks of it that *dérider* means "to deride," perhaps ironically. Happily, it does not; it means "to brighten up," "to make less serious." Certainly, in French, Derrida *déride*. Further, since *rider* is the French verb meaning "to wrinkle," *dérider* (de-rider) can also mean "to remove wrinkles," "to unfurrow the brow." To remove wrinkles: could that be "to iron"? And Jacques? Like the English Jack, nickname of John. Does John 19:5 anticipate Derrida's signature, especially since the collaboration began in 1985? No doubt that is too farfetched.[33] Let us treat Jacques a bit more properly. Jacques, French equivalent to Jacob, comes from the Hebrew word meaning "supplanter," one who takes the place of through force or scheming. Jacques Derrida: one who schemes to supplant iron, "I" take the place of "Eisenman"!? One wonders whether "supplant" is ever used to translate Hegel's *Aufhebung*.

Almost at the very beginning of this paper, we introduced the theme of gold, which we will mine further, in particular, as we engage the question of *chora*. In anticipation, however, let us read a passage about gold from the *Timaeus* in order to extend our thought on the proper names of this event.

Of all these fusible varieties of water, as we have called them, one that is very dense, being formed of very fine and uniform particles, unique in its kind, tinged with shining and yellow hue is gold, the treasure most highly prized, which has been filtered through rock and compacted.

The "scion of gold," which is very hard because of its density and is darkly coloured, is called *adament*.[34]

In his commentary on the *Timaeus*, Francis Cornford outlines a debate on the meaning here of *"adament"*: some say iron, some say diamond. In the end, what difference does it make? In German *Eis* means "ice," American criminal slang for diamonds. At least, as we have seen, Eisenman is adamant about the scaling process, to Derrida's chagrin. And if ice is criminal slang for diamond, a peterman is criminal slang for a safecracker. Is not Peter (Eisen)man one who seeks to crack the illusion of safety in anthropocentrism, to crack the safe of architecture, break into its pyramid, so to speak? None of this improper play, which nevertheless confirms and elaborates themes within the text proper, would be possible without the originary trace, that is, without writing. Moreover, we are guaranteed by the trace that the proliferation of meaning cannot peter out.[35]

This is why in his essay Derrida stays close to writing and close to Eisenman's play with writing. In the very last sentence of the essay, the climax of his ironic criticism of Eisenman as architectural totalist, as the anti-Wagner—"Ecce homo: end, the end of all, *la fin de tout*"—Derrida is at play. He not only plays with the termination of his essay, but as well, extends the many plays on another of Eisenman's wordplay titles, *Fin d'Ou T Hou S*. Therein also are the conflated identities. Derrida: the end of all (I have to write). Eisenman: the end of everything (the anti-Wagner). And Nietzsche: *la fin de Dieu*.

While we play, however, we should not lose sight of our elusive quarry, Derrida's signature. Very early in the essay Derrida introduces the collaboration as "one of Eisenman's works in progress." Not until after he elaborates Eisenman's skill with titles and wordplay and turns his attention to the title *Choral Work* does the collaboration become a joint effort, "our common work." And the title alone is entitled to the honor of being of a joint effort: "This title is more than a title. It also designates a signature, a plural signature, written by both of us in concert." The ever-present qualifier is there, however. In a parenthetical, in the essay as not in the essay, we find that this "(. . . was also a way not to sign while signing)."[36] Until this moment, there was no collaboration. Even though Derrida made an earlier contribution, a fragment of his *chora* text, until the title emerged no duet existed. Eisenman "appropriated by himself and for himself" from this fragment. In fact, after this point, after "our" title, Derrida is reluctant to refer again to the collaboration as a joint effort. Without doubt correctly, despite his efforts: we already know what happened to his final contribution. Moreover, Derrida's analysis of the title *Choral Work* is very much to the point of the collaboration at the level of discourse, as his unfolding of it more than amply demonstrates. The title did open the work to readings and extensions that were resisted by the discourse of the collaboration before its inception. And it is truly a collaborative moment: though it is spoken by Eisenman, its possibility and desirability come from Derrida.

Throughout "Why Eisenman . . . ," Derrida lends his signature to Eisenman's *play with words* while furrowing his brow at the architect's inclinations toward a totalizing architecture, at his *work with words*. He is virtually silent on the drawings and models; if he describes them or uses them as examples of discourse, he never reads them as text. What interests Derrida most is how Eisenman's wordplay "participates with full legitimacy in the invention of architecture without being submitted to the order of discourse."[37] What interests him least, besides the themes of totalization already discussed, is Eisenman's reliance on traditional rhetorical modes. He stops short of crucifying the architect on this issue, though he comes very close: "And we could say something *analogous* on the subject of this active/passive opposition in the texts of Eisenman, something analogous as well on what he says about analogies. But one must also know how to stop an arrow. He, too, knows how to do that."[38]

If our conjecture on the interplay of "I's" is to the point, Derrida also stops short of allowing his arrow to strike home because he must stop short of suicide. This is not a Freudian question of unconscious projection or identification; that moment was reserved for Eisenman. During the first meeting, following upon a period spent apologizing for their respective lack of expertise in each other's discipline, was this exchange:

Derrida: I will stop apologizing for not being an architect.
Eisenman: And I will stop apologizing for not being an architect.

It is telling that no one in the meeting heard the slip. Derrida stopped short rather because, as he well knows and despite his effort to the contrary, *he writes such good books*.

So what are our conclusions; where is Derrida's signature, does he sign the project?

In this collaboration, Derrida, master of the word as an open door, is somewhat of a victim of words. Eisenman's words. He believes them and is upset by them. He hears closure, dialectic, circularity, allegory, etc., and closes his eyes.[39] He signs most easily some of Eisenman's words, but other of Eisenman's words stop him short of simply signing the project. He chooses his words carefully, so carefully, in fact, that he comes close to choosing nothing but words. Thus, despite what he has done for writing, Derrida never moves very far either from his name or from the book of John. Though he has done much to unfetter writing from its false bondage to a desire for the truth of the word, Derrida remains devoted to the power and priority of the word. "In the beginning was the word" is the haunting opening of John, as we all know. It is also worth recalling that the Gospel According to St. John is a text concerned with logocentrism versus anthropocentrism.[40] Let us also remember that in the Old Testament, at least, logocentrism as phonocentrism in mortal man was first a question of power, not truth. In Genesis 27 the metaphysical power of the word extends from God's breath to man's, even though what is spoken is false. Though he was tricked into giving his blessing to the wrong son, Isaac could do nothing to take back his word. It was through the power of the word, not the truth, that *Jacob* supplanted Esau.

Clearly, to the question, Where is Derrida's signature? the answer must be that it is always with the word. Equally clearly, that this is the case does not indicate merely some trivial failing on Derrida's part. Rather, it speaks to the stakes of a deeply problematic issue in architecture: the role and privilege of the word with/in design. Does he sign the project? The answer to that must be both yes and no, neither yes nor no. That is the final irony, for this familiar double bind is his most genuine, most authentic signature. It is the one signature of Derrida that is absolutely resistant to deconstruction. Irreducible in every reduction, it is Derrida's transcendental signature itself.

Thus far we have outlined the expectations for this collaboration and pointed out the deflections and deferrals that they inevitably encountered. Are we gaining much? Or have we taken the path of least resistance by following the paths of most resistance through this event? Everyone that studies the transcripts of their meetings and the designs will no doubt quickly and correctly identify many more fascinating defenses and resistances than we have discussed. And it must be said, in this regard, that Eisenman and Derrida each exceed the typical in their capability of and givenness to the inert, above and beyond the machinations of this joint effort. If elsewhere Derrida has proclaimed this potential inertness of his work, has written that he risks not meaning anything, not a few in architecture would say that Eisenman has for some time now repeatedly accomplished the fact.

Though we recognize now a collaboration on the word, however convoluted, do we claim that there was never an effort at collaboration on design? No. Let us run a risk and try to identify one point in this event when a mutual commitment to work together, to become a duet, came briefly to fruition only to dissolve again into an "aggregate of solos." For such a moment, certain preliminary criteria would have to be met out of respect for the players. It could not be a singular origin, the singularity of a beginning, the point of the big bang; rather, it would have to be a moment of originary coincidence. A coincidence, a co-incident, the doubling of a co-inside, of an originary two, the condition made possible by the originary trace, which is to say, all conditions. It would thus leave traces, footprints that rippled both ways in the event, forward and backward.

Our nomination for such a moment would be the conversation between Eisenman and Derrida that took place in Trento, Italy, on 16 December 1985, during the third of their six meetings. As in the early stages of all such opera, in the first two meetings the universe had begun to take shape. Which Eisenman and which Derrida would perform: the program, Plato's *chora* in a new scoring by Derrida; the choreography, Eisenman's scaling; the cast; the scenery—all these had undergone a first negotiation and had been preliminarily endorsed. The first act, then, of this opera occurs in scene three. Staged as a pas de deux with chorus, it is the sparest scene in the entire opera, the one and only time the two are alone together and at one together, almost. If it is correct that this is the scene of two become one become two again, it could not have been better staged in any other form, keeping in mind that in French *pas de deux*, a ballet duet—literally, a "step of two"—means at the same time, coincidentally, "not of two" or "no two." Here we find the classical form of the pas de deux, consisting of an entrée, an adagio, a set of variations for each of the two, and a coda. For the question at hand, we turn our attention to the variations that begin with Derrida, "Repeat it once more, I'm not sure I got it," to which Eisenman responds, "Look, you are pushing me to invent this as I go along." Thus the curtain rises on a set of variations on metaphorical and literal language played out through misunderstandings of the meaning of words. It is a scene with both the hilarity of Abbott and Costello's "Who's on First" and the sadness engendered by all of the hitches, contretemps, and misunderstandings of *Romeo and Juliet*.

Eisenman is attempting to convey metaphorically how the scaling he has in mind might be related to *chora*, in particular, to the theme of imprinting: "Our writing leaves a trace on a palimpsest, *whatever the material*, and we freeze that. Now, the imprint could be the plan of La Villette" (emphasis added). Derrida, perhaps confused by the mention of a specific, is no longer sure whether Eisenman speaks metaphorically or literally. To confirm his thought that the conversation may have moved to specifics, he interjects: "In concrete." To a French-speaking philosopher, his remark is unambiguous; it means "I take it we are speaking literally now, no longer figuratively." To an English-speaking architect, it is equally unambiguous and means "in the material concrete." Thus Eisenman answers, "Let's say concrete," confirming to Derrida that they are now speaking of reality while confirming to himself that they continue to speak metaphorically. Though Derrida hears the variation on concrete, he now talks of reality: "The problem is, what substance will you use for this? If the floor layer is concrete, then you need something which is not hard." Eisenman, still completely within metaphor, says, "That is correct . . . let's say paste," elaborating the false confirmations and the slippages among materiality, the real, and the metaphorical. And so ensues an extraordinary conversation that climaxes in the moment of unstable unity in which Derrida makes an effort at concrete design, or should we say paste design? As funny and sad as this exchange may be, what is important is that, however short-lived, in this attempt, Derrida abandons the traditional design assumptions he came with and tries to design in Eisenman's terms.

The variations are brief, and the pas de deux soon moves to the beginning of the end, the coda, the tail that tells the tale of the rest of the opera. Derrida: "It is as if you were the dreamer and I were the architect, the technician. So, you are the theoretician and I am thinking all the time of the practical consequences of everything in the place," and indeed will be for the rest of the story. There will be fluidities of identity, as we have seen, but never again an effort at unity. Later in the same scene, Eisenman will strongly protest when Derrida asserts that the work has moved from a duet to an "aggregate of solos."

Derrida: I am less sure that the rest of our, your . . .
Eisenman: No! No! Of OUR.
Derrida: . . . is physically possible for the moment.

Derrida never recants his "your." *La fin de deux*.

So, now that we have acquitted our responsibility to take the presence of these two figures seriously, to consider their personalities, inclinations, and disinclinations, let us simply grant the obvious. Defenses and resistances abound: above all, the mark of an implied contract of noninteraction is inscribed in this event. In fact, come to think of it, how could this have been otherwise, considering the chemistry of gold? Therefore, can we be satisfied merely to continue this litigation? To do so would be to stipulate the question of presence: psychological presence, artistic and intellectual presence, and, especially, the "metaphysics of presence" that, as we noted early on, could render this potent event mundane, if not mute, unless we find a way to refuse it. We need a place of refusal, a way to sift through this collaboration and shake more out of it. Shake out of it what it was prepared for rather than what we anticipated for it. Shake out of it something for architecture.

Chora

is a common word in ancient Greek for place. It differs though from *topos*, "the place where something is located." Neither does it mean "finite void," *kenon*, or "infinite space," *apeiron*. *Chora* designates the container of something and has associations with words that convey "to hold" or "to have room for." It is used for the post, station, office, the place that a person holds, or a room that is filled. For Derrida and this event, however, the word takes on special significance for the unthinkable place it holds in the *Timaeus*, Plato's account of the cosmogeny, the making of the known universe. According to Plato, the universe that we know was born as the Demiurge, architect of the cosmos, forged the sensible, material universe while contemplating the Forms (the Ideas, the *eidos*, the members of the true, perfect, immutable, and intelligible realm of being) as models (*paradigmata*) for the creation.⁴¹ Though the Demiurge did the best possible job in making the universe, the necessities of his work—that is, materiality—insured that the sensible universe would be inferior to, and other than, the realm of true and ideal being; the sensible universe, then, is the realm of becoming. During the course of this discussion, a problematic question arises: Into what place does the Demiurge inscribe the copies?⁴² As Plato takes up this question, a wonderfully obscure and conflicted discourse emerges, unlike any other in the philosopher's writings. Generations of philosophers have struggled to make more precise Plato's problematic treatment of this dizzying question.

Before we examine Derrida's meditation on *chora* and take a second look at the collaboration through this lens, let us review some of the characteristics of this place unlike any other. When Plato turns his attention to *chora*, he does so as a retelling of the cosmogeny, having discussed it once already in terms of the paradigms and the copies, being and becoming. As a prelude to this first telling, Plato says that any account of the physical world is, at best, a "likely story" because the world itself is a likeness: he reiterates this contingency before turning to this second "strange and unfamiliar exposition." In his first account, Plato distinguishes only two types, the intelligible and the sensible, the paradigm and the copy. In his second, his thought of *chora* requires that it be a "third kind," neither sensible nor intelligible, a form "difficult and obscure." What is its nature? "This more than anything else: that it is the Receptacle—as it were, the nurse—of all Becoming." After arguing that a figure molded in gold should always be referred to as "gold," for gold remains the same though the figure may be remolded, Plato notes that the same principle applies to that which receives all:

It must be called always the same: for it never departs at all from its own character; since it is always receiving all things, and never in any way whatsoever takes on any character that is like any of the things that enter it. By nature it is there as a matrix for everything, changed and diversified by the things that enter it, and on their account it *appears* to have different qualities at different times; it takes impressions from [the copies] in a strange manner that is hard to express.

Plato goes on to compare the receptacle to a mother, the paradigm to a father, and the copy to a child. Yet the receptacle/mother/nurse is neuter; it has no qualities of its own. It is "free from all those characters which it is to receive from elsewhere"; "that which is to receive in itself all kinds must be free from all characters." Thus it is not earth, air, fire, or water; rather, "it is invisible and characterless, all-receiving, partaking in some very puzzling way of the intelligible and very hard to apprehend."

This third genus, *chora*, is everlasting, indestructible. "It provides a situation for all things that come into being, but (is) hardly an object of belief"; *chora* can only be thought "as in a dream." Not (exactly) one of the Forms yet nevertheless everlasting, *chora* was of the chaos before the Demiurge brought forth the ordered universe. Before the ordering by the Demiurge, *chora*, receptacle of the chaos, "had every sort of diverse appearance to the sight" and "was everywhere swayed and unevenly shaken by these things and by its motion shook them in turn." "And they, being thus moved, were perpetually being separated and carried in different directions, just as things are shaken and winnowed by means of winnowing-baskets. . . . The dense and heavy go one way, while the rare and light are carried to another place and settle there." Thus *chora* moved and ordered the chaos before the origin of true motion and ordering: "whereby the different kinds came to have different regions, even before the ordered whole consisting of them came to be."

The problem of *chora* is an anomaly in Plato's oeuvre: *chora* is therefore an outside that is inside—an irresistible temptation for Derrida. Let us skim quickly his reading of this enigma to situate some of the issues that arise in the discussions and to extract some guidelines for another look at the Eisenman/Derrida event. Derrida first attends to the history of the interpretations of *chora*, all of which aspire to speak the terms of *chora*'s existence, or at least its condition, better than Plato, that is, more seriously, more philosophically.

Rich, numerous, inexhaustible, the interpretations come, in short, to give form to the meaning of *chora*. They always consist by giving it form by determining it—it which, however, can offer itself only by removing itself from any determination, from all the marks or impressions to which we said it was exposed.[43]

All "serious" interpretations, then, try to recover the philosophic essence of *chora* from the apparent metaphoricity of Plato's descriptions and the mythological form of his argument, assuming, first, that the structures metaphor/referent and mythos/logos exist, second, that from these structures metaphor and myth can be identified as such and isolated, and (therefore), third, that the logos and referent as such can be recovered, disencumbered from myth or metaphor. Thus, and we might finally begin to say as always, this history, the history of the interpretations of *chora*, is a metonymy for history as the production of logocentrism.

Operating strictly with and within Plato's text, Derrida determines that the difficulty is not a failure of interpretation that might someday be overcome with more powerful exegetical or hermeneutic technique, but that the assumptions underlying what is called serious philosophic interpretation are precisely those resisted essentially by *chora*. Chora, as what, above all, is not, but what also is not nothing, emerges as that which cannot not be thought, but cannot be thought as such. To think toward a recovery of *chora-itself* is to re-cover *chora*. Thus, on the one hand, though we can write about *chora*, we cannot get to, achieve, expose, define, determine, or reveal *chora*, we cannot "give form to the meaning of *chora*." Beyond the negative rule, however, Derrida writes to us that, on the other hand, we cannot but write *chora*, something that all writing as inscription will always do.

The history of interpretations seeking to correct the "problems" of Plato's treatment of *chora* begin by criticizing Plato's reliance on metaphor and myth: metaphor and myth are philosophically inadequate forms of argument. Derrida demonstrates that the concepts of metaphor and myth, strictly speaking, cannot apply to a meditation on *chora*. There is no metaphor, at least in the structure metaphor/referent, nor is there myth, at least in the structure mythos/logos, if there is no referent, no logos. Chora is always anterior to inscription, though it is always anterior after the fact; it is after the fact as before the fact, after the fact as such. Chora has no existence, no pure being anterior to and free from inscription, outside of rhetoric and trope: it *is*, though it *is* only and always in the text as before it.

In a lengthy digression to and against Hegel, Derrida reminds us that the mythos/logos structure embodies one of the underlying oppositions within Western philosophy, nonserious/serious. His reading of *chora* here twists this opposition into a form that can no longer be taken seriously. Moving from and with his thought on *chora* and the problematic of its history of interpretations, Derrida then develops a new strategy for reading (Plato), one that finds the evidence of *chora* already at work in (Plato's) text. In brief, he combs out formal analogies between the textual structures of the *Timaeus* and what is said of *chora* within the text. Thus, for example, he locates compelling analogies to what is said there of *chora* in an extended consideration of the place of Socrates in the early passages of the *Timaeus*. As Derrida writes, "Socrates is not *chora* but he would look a lot like it/her if it/she were someone or something." So, too, of the architecture of the text, which occurs as a "theater of irony where the scenes interlock in a series of receptacles without end and without bottom."[44]

Derrida stops short of it, but his reading seems to insist that *chora* be inscribed into his list of undecidables. We can at least draw the vector of such a conclusion by connecting those points in his essay where *chora* takes on the traits of the other, more familiar undecidables—the contradiction in terms notwithstanding. Like the others, *chora* is neither word nor concept, neither proper noun nor common noun, and it is a condition of absolute anteriority. Moreover, though Derrida treats of it only in passing, *chora* shakes, shakes the whole, separating before the separation; it is a movement before movement begins, since in the *Timaeus* all true movement begins with the world-soul and comes after the Demiurge does his work. Yet *chora* shakes and orders even the chaos. Thus *chora* solicits, in the Derridean sense of the term.[45]

For the sake of expediency, let us limit ourselves to extracting from Derrida's reading only a few directions. The first comes by way of a caution: "these formal analogies are not considered . . . as artifices, boldnesses, or secrets of formal composition: the art of Plato the writer!" His reading is not of a Plato who, with totalizing skill deploys his discourse on *chora* in both the content and the structural form of the *Timaeus*, but of a Plato who, as he engages the question of the space of inscription, is inextricably bound by the very fact of his inscription to repeat by resemblance and before the fact his discourse on *chora*, as do all those who follow him. Including Derrida and Eisenman. *By resemblance and before the fact.* Recalling that his reading depends on formal analogy and authorizes this dependence in the name of *chora*, we find in Derrida's essay that *chora* is also the inevitability, the structural law, of anachronism in all inscriptions, including events. 'We would like to show that [*chora*] is the structure that makes them inevitable, makes of them something other than accidents, weaknesses, or provisional moments," Derrida writes, "*Chora* 'is' the anachrony within being, or better, the anachrony of being, it anachronizes being." We might add, it analogizes being.

Our guide, our Greek chorus, then, shall be the law of the *ana-* that *chora* reflects into every inscription. Though we concentrate on but two paragraphs of that law, *analogy* and *anachronism*, we should not lose sight of its dimension, which would embrace the evidence of *chora* in an entire field of *ana-*: anabiosis, anabolism, anaclisis, anagnoresis, anaglyph, anagram, analysis, anamnesis, anastrophe, anastylosis, anatomy, and so forth, even extending by formal analogy to Ananke, Anaximander, and Anaxgoras, each of which operates in this event and could lead to yet another reading. Even more care is necessary here, however. Though not incorrect, it would underestimate the breadth of this law if all we read in it was that *chora* guarantees that no chronology be free of anachrony, that no logic be free of analogy. The law of *ana-* is not merely a law of impropriety; it is not a law of the contamination of the proper (*logos*, *chronos*) by the improper (*ana-logos*, *ana-chronos*), but a law anterior to the separation of the proper from the improper, a law anterior to the possibility of law, a law of laws. The law of *ana-* is the law of originary *ana-*, of originary anachrony, originary analogy.

Today we think of anachronism as error or, at best, as a form of literary play or joke. We treat analogy as an illegitimate, bastard form of reasoning.[46] Similarly, we consider coincidence to be merely a striking analogy arising by accident. Yet, since *chora* is the meeting place in which things that are not together in time or space nevertheless participate in one another in time and space, the place in which others co-inside, it reflects a law of analogy, anachrony, and coincidence that is not only their possibility but their necessity.[47] *Chora* makes inevitability of what we call mere accident and error.

On the way to an end, then, let us test our law with respect to analogies, anachronies, and coincidences in this event, test it with a second look, remembering that *chora* is in evidence only in a second look, a re-spect of the text. To inscribe *chora*, the Demiurge took a second look at the Forms,[48] Plato a second look at the Demiurge, the history of interpretations a second look at Plato, Derrida a second look at the history of interpretations, Tschumi a second look at Derrida,[49] and Eisenman a second look at Tschumi. As Eisenman says, "In retrospect, we were already working toward *chora*" and, later, "I feel I was actually making *chora* before I ever knew about it."

We begin again with the separatrix.

Though cautioned by Derrida not to dare too much with plays on feminine suffices, note that, like *chora*, the separatrix is an it/she.[50] The ending *-trix*, as in *aviatrix*, is the feminine form of the suffix of action, *-or*, as in *aviator*. That is, except in geometry where *-trix* is neutered and used to name various straight lines, not without irony, as in *directrix*. Like Derrida's Socrates, the separatrix is not *chora* but it/she would look a lot like it/her if *chora* were something. The separatrix is the third kind in those tripartite systems called "binary," such as word/meaning, becoming/being, or copy/paradigm. It forms all manner of relationships, yet it is "always called the same" and "never departs from its own character"; it "never in any way whatsoever takes on any character that is like any of the things that enter it." The separatrix is there as "a matrix for everything," though in its ability to forge different relationships it "appears to have different qualities at different times." Moreover, though it never belongs to one side or the other—for example, it is neither signifier nor signified—nevertheless, the separatrix "partakes in some very puzzling and hard to apprehend way of the intelligible: though it does not mean anything, it is the place and possibility of meaning, of something meaning something else." As Derrida says of *chora*, so may we say of the separatrix: "Giving place to oppositions, it would itself not submit to any reversal. And this, another consequence would not be because it would inalterably be *itself* but because in carrying beyond the polarity of sense (metaphorical or proper), it would no longer belong to the horizon of sense, nor to that of meaning as the meaning of being." No logic can put the separatrix into opposition; although without it there is no meaning, no meaningful /// is possible.

If earlier we characterized deconstruction as preying upon the separatrix to destabilize it and here we draw an analogy between the separatrix and *chora* that seems to valorize the former, there is, nonetheless, no contradiction or paradox. Deconstruction is not destruction, it does not pursue the separatrix to destroy it and the laws it enables; it does not seek the chaos that would result from destruction of either the separatrix or *chora*. It seeks, instead, to expose the hidden agenda behind an untenable reification of the order that the separatrix imposes. Deconstruction questions the repressions of the instability that the separatrix, like *chora*, reflects into order, making order possible. Deconstruction, returning to Nietzsche's question, What if truth were a woman? respects the mark for what it/she is.

And so it seems, in a bit of bastard reasoning, does Eisenman. Is it not the separatrix as *chora* that Eisenman struggles to articulate during the fourth meeting, right in the middle of the dialogues, in his strange and unfamiliar exposition of the "wedge," the cut between metonymy and metaphor? We may be uncomfortable when he uses "allegory" as a metaphor for this between, this wedge, but have we not read a similar exposition on such a "between" already, one also strange, also in the middle of a dialogue, also confined to, yet discomfited by, inadequate metaphor? To be sure, the proliferating analogies among the themes and structures of the dialogue of the *Timaeus* and those that occurred during this event are uncanny. The curtain rising, the introductory conversations among Socrates, *Timaeus*, Critias, and Hermocrates, and those among Eisenman, Derrida, Rizzi, and myself, each shaped around the identification of expertise and incompetence, render these dialogues as virtual mirror images.

As mirrors reverse left and right, so does the analogic/anachronistic mirror between these dialogues, *chora*, reverse before and after. Just *after* Socrates discusses what Derrida demonstrates to be a key structural analogy for *chora* in the early part of the *Timaeus*, he states his own incompetence to conduct this dialogue: "My judgment upon myself is that to celebrate our city and its citizens as they deserve would be beyond my powers. My incapacity is not surprising." Socrates goes on to relate his unsurprising incompetence to his resemblance to the poets, the artists, the imitators. Though he is not an imitator, he is incompetent because he feels like one; thus Socrates silences himself, preparing to receive all. Derrida uses this very moment in the dialogue to begin constructing his analogy between Socrates and *chora*. Now, in his first meeting with Eisenman, just *before* he introduces *chora*, Derrida mirrors Socrates with startling precision. First, he states his incompetence for the dialogue: "I have no competence in architecture at all." Then he adds that he is like an imitator, an architect: "Yet, I have always had the feeling of being an architect." Finally, as in the case of Socrates, Derrida constructs himself in terms belonging to *chora*. He says, "When Tschumi first asked me to participate in this project, I was excited, but, at the same time, I was totally, totally empty. I mean, I had no ideas at all."

Let us simply list a few more of these analogies.

Early in the *Timaeus*, Socrates states the desirability of contriving so that no parent "should recognize his own offspring." This theme recurs in the first meeting: it is noted that one of the most interesting and important features of the scaling process is that, when finished, no one knows the results, no one person understands all of the features in the final design, not even Eisenman.

The question in the *Timaeus* that leads to the discussion of *chora* concerns the relationship between idea and necessity—the very issue that governs the collaboration. Countless times during the event necessity encroaches upon the idea: 'in the end, it must be sensible, it must have physicality.'"

The *Timaeus* itself was to be the first of a trilogy; it stands now with the partially finished *Critias* and the never-begun *Hermocrates*. The final design was also to be the first of a trilogy, a three-site scheme; need we point out that the second site was started but left unfinished and the third site never begun?

Consider Eisenman's initial speech on the anthropocentrism of architecture. He takes as his principle motif that function, considered by many to be the primary cause of architecture, is only accessory to its deeper cause, the manifestation of meaning, of the idea. Compare this to the discussion of accessory cause in the *Timaeus*: "Now all these things are among the accessory causes which the god uses as subservient in achieving the best result that is possible. But the great mass of mankind regards them, not as accessories, but as the sole cause of things." Plato, too, goes on to privilege the idea as first cause.

And just as the Demiurge, after beginning the process of making the sensible universe, delegates it to those lesser gods he has created, so Eisenman turns the design process over to his protégés, Thomas Leeser and Renato Rizzi: "These people work full-time on it, I have only been overseeing."

Where analogy reigns, anachronism cannot be far behind. One of the most striking anachronistic analogies concerns the much-discussed title of this collaboration, *Choral Work*. The law of *ana-* should guarantee that this title was already at work as architecture in the *Timaeus*. And, in fact, is not the name of the architect in the *Timaeus* already like *Choral Work*, a likeness that emerges after the fact as before the fact? Demiurge (*demi-urgos*) is a word constructed from the Greek roots *demos* meaning "a group of people," such as a chorus, and *ergon* meaning "work."

If we made much of Derrida adding a sculpture to the scheme to introduce some heterogeneity, we cannot now be surprised that before this issue arose in the meetings, Renato Rizzi simply added a diagonal ground line to the scaling diagram for the very same reason, to add some heterogeneity. This is the source of the skew to the ground in the scheme. Like Derrida, he derived this addition by rereading a source text, Eisenman's Cannaregio project.

Also worth attending is the anachronism of authorship in the dialogue of the final meeting. When he first sees the second model, Derrida remarks, "It's really a creative space; so many things about it call for going in and under." Afterwards, a discussion ensues concerning whether or not people will be allowed onto the scheme. Derrida wants access so that the design will not become a precious object. Several suggestions are made and rejected, when Rizzi finally says, "Or we could create an access level beneath." Derrida: "I do not understand. Under?" Eisenman: "Like a tunnel." Derrida: "Yes, it's a wonderful idea." On this occasion, it is Derrida who has Rizzi's "original" idea first.

There can be little doubt, then, that in reflecting the wonders of the law of *ana*- the event of the collaboration is inscribed in *chora*. Yet does the law operate within the design produced by this event? Scaling, of course, is a design process entirely constructed around anachronism, analogy, and coincidence. In this case, a fictional narrative anachronizes the relationship between Eisenman's housing project for Cannaregio and Tschumi's design for the Parc de la Villette. This narrative gains its foothold by taking opportunistic advantage of the formal analogy that exists between the point grids in these two designs. Elements from (the history of) Venice and Paris and Eisenman's and Tschumi's projects coincide at three different scales and in various notations for presence, absence, and "time." For instance, the Paris of Louis-Philippe is represented in a fragment of the last Parisian wall raised by Thiers, while a subsequent Paris is represented by the forms of the abattoirs that took the place of the wall on this site after it was razed by Haussmann.

As well, we see at differing scales a positive representation of the Cannaregio Canal, positive and negative representations of Eisenman's housing blocks, imprints of Tschumi's plan, the analogous point grids characteristic of these two schemes, and the lyre/site form that displaced Derrida's contribution. These are made to participate in one another by registering one ensemble of forms to another along the seam of an analogic feature. Thus, for example, the dominant axes of the two point grids serve to register Tschumi's scheme to Eisenman's. Decisions as to scale, solid (positive) or void (negative), and so forth derive from the scaling diagram as modified by Rizzi's rotation of the ground datum.

These aspects of the scaling process are straightforward, and with a little study the reader could easily understand the process and confirm its results in the second model. Yet merely to affirm that anachronism and analogy have been built into the design process is not to test the process in terms of the law of *ana*-. Indeed, if the final design closes off an extended held of reading, if it interrupts the proliferation of analogy, anachronism, and coincidence as it seeks to take control of them, then we must acknowledge that, though scaling as a process symbolizes *chora*, it does not respect it/her. As we now know, symbolization is particularly antithetical to the undecidability of the place that this event seeks.

So, for our purposes, a test of the final design cannot stand either on its beauty or on the legibility of the fictional history that was its nominal genealogy.[51] These are insufficient to determine whether or not this work finds its place. For this measurement, we must turn our attention to a feature within the design that nevertheless eludes the clarifying grasp of the design's history and logic, an inside that is outside. We can then track this feature to read what, if any, internal analogies, anachronies, and coincidences unfold from it.

In examining the second model, we soon notice the color, which participates as a design notation. Most of the elements remain the natural color of basswood. The reds of the Eisenman housing forms, the silver of the lyre/ site forms, and the gold of the Paris wall and abattoirs are the exceptions. The reds recall the original color of the housing for Cannaregio; the silver indicates aspects of the discussion of the lyre form in the meetings and in Derrida's letter. In all these discussions, it was thought that Derrida's sculpture should be in metal. In fact, in his letter, the philosopher specifically suggests it be gold, noting that gold appears both in relevant passages of the *Timaeus* and in one of the models of the Cannaregio project. Instead, the golden sections of the second *Choral Work* model belong to the Paris forms. Nothing in the discussions or the scaling logic accounts for this notation, yet it is one of the most prominent features of the model. Let us choose this feature, then, for our test.

As we have said, gold is not arbitrary, not simply outside of the motifs of this event. Beyond the several appearances of gold in the *Timaeus* already noted, in certain ways, in fact in its very heart, *chora* already heralds gold. Gold opens a place for a key analogy in Derrida's essays "Chora" and "Why Eisenman . . ." Derrida also attends gold in other of his writings on Plato, most notably in his essay group "Plato's Pharmacy." And if we trust our ear, surely we can hear that what we began by calling a golden opportunity became exactly that, an aural opportunity an oral exchange become choral. Yet, in the model, gold fails to mold any of these possible figures; considering this, it seems rather oddly unmotivated.

In Eisenman's Cannaregio project, gold and Venetian red appear for symbolic reasons, gold symbolizing the alchemical pursuits of Giordano Bruno and red the blood of his execution. After Cannaregio, however, something else takes place in Eisenman's designs. Some projects, such as the Wexner Center for the Visual Arts and the Berlin housing, are dominated by multiple grids. In the rest, including *Romeo and Juliet*, the Long Beach museum, and the Progressive Corporation project, an anomalous golden area appears in one or more of their representations. If the grid is Eisenman's most famous signature, we must begin to wonder whether gold is becoming another, alternative, signature. Remembering that Hebrew law forbids the name of God to be spoken or written, a prohibition that requires English-speaking Jews to write "G-d" in the word's place, then perhaps the g-d structure that persists as Eisenman's signature moves from grid to gold suggests that the "arbitrary" gold in this project is Eisenman's signature as Architect/Demiurge.[52]

Yet this reading of the golden section of the model as Eisenman's signature is, at first glance, somewhat disappointing in that, unlike *chora* and its law of *ana-*, it seems to have a precise beginning at the Cannaregio project. It thus lacks the anachrony that should be inscribed in the movement of the signature. An endpoint enters the reading, blocking off the proliferation of analogies and coincidences that we seek. Or does it? Are there golden sections at work in this model and in Eisenman's signature before the fact? A paradoxical lapse in Eisenman's early houses might help us to break through this block.

From his earliest endeavor, Eisenman was interested in using intellectualized processes to move away from the anthropocentrism of architecture. In keeping with this interest, he venerated the rational design process of Le Corbusier while criticizing the unabashed anthropocentrism that motivated the Paris-based Swiss architect. Le Corbusier's "Modulor," avatar of the rationalized anthropocentrism underlying his processes, should therefore have been an anathema to Eisenman; yet his early houses each deployed proportional systems drawn from the Modulor. Of interest to us here, however, is that Corb based his proportional analysis of man on the Fibonacci series, the mathematical extension of the geometric proportion known as the *golden ratio* or *golden section*. A well-known signature device in several of Le Corbusier's drawings is the boldly proclaimed algebraic ratio of the golden section, $A/B = B/A+B$. Thus, from his beginning and before he first signs with an anomalous golden section, Eisenman was already signing his works with anomalous golden sections.

The golden section does not occur in the *Timaeus* as such, but Plato opens a place for it in his discussion of the most perfect triangle out of which the Demiurge is to build perfect bodies. Before stating his nominations for the best of the isosceles and scalene triangles, he writes that "if anyone can tell us of a better kind . . . his will be the victory, not of an enemy, but of a friend" (54a–b). Now, the geometry and mathematics of the *Timaeus* are thoroughly Pythagorean. The symbol of the Pythagorean Society, which the Pythagoreans named *health*—they, too, posited the relationships among triangles, ratios, and the perfect body—is today called the *triple triangle*. It consists of three identical one-hundred-eight-degree isosceles triangles superimposed to create a two-pointed star with a regular pentagram as its center. Other than its cosmological symbolism, the most outstanding feature of this figure, and a source of its mystical power for the Pythagoreans, is the extraordinary number of golden sections that it contains, well over two hundred. At the very least, armed with the golden section, we could ably take up Plato's challenge to name a better triangle.

Through the lens of the golden section, a second look at the project unfolds yet another series of startling anachronisms and coincidences. Eisenman has already spoken of the analogy between Le Corbusier and Tschumi, another Swiss-born architect based in Paris. And it was Corb's unrealized project for a hospital in Cannaregio that provided the source of the point grid in Eisenman's housing design. Recalling Plato's problematic metaphors for *chora*, mother/nurse, can we resist the coincidental presence of absence in this project of the house/hospital, those architectural places par excellence for the mother/nurse that already occupied Eisenman's Cannaregio scheme before being reinscribed and multiplied here, even before Eisenman feels as though he is already "making *chora*"? Lest the reader think this track of the golden section a contrivance imposed upon the event by a mere play on words, note Eisenman's remarks in the second meeting as he describes the details of the scaling he has in mind:

In this case we also have three texts: Bernard Tschumi's, Jacques Derrida's, and Peter Eisenman's, which is not yet given. Interestingly, each of these is a text on a text: Bernard's can be seen as a text on mine for Venice, mine will be a text on Jacques Derrida's; his is a text on Plato's *Timaeus*. We therefore have both a closed and an open circle. Derrida opens the circle, changing it into a *spiral*. But the process will be as much conditioned by Tschumi's text as by Derrida's. Let's see. Tschumi is to Eisenman as Eisenman is to Tschumi plus Eisenman. Then, Plato is to Derrida as Derrida is to Plato plus Derrida. Then a third which connects the two. Something like that.

"Tschumi is to Eisenman as Eisenman is to Tschumi plus Eisenman. Then, Plato is to Derrida as Derrida is to Plato plus Derrida." This is, of course, $A/B = B/A+B$, the classical algebraic statement of the golden section. Eisenman here extends this ratio from its geometric beginnings through its mathematization into the realm of textual analogy.

If the reader remains unconvinced, if he or she still finds this only a coincidence of words, then consider the design process itself. Though the details of scaling as a process varied in each of the projects in which it was employed, nevertheless, one characteristic remained constant: the notion of recursivity. In every case, the texts—the ensembles of forms—in question were recapitulated at three spiraling scales to destabilize any dominant, original scale. Yet such spiraling is one of the characteristic features of the golden section as embodied in the golden rectangle. This analogic spiraling can easily he seen in the second model if we follow the lyre/site form at its three scales. Eisenman disrupts the self-same repetition of the golden rectangle diagram by employing, instead, a temporal notion of self-similarity; but does this not actually improve the architectural translation of the regress of the golden section by embodying in it one of the most important factors distinguishing architecture from geometry—time?

If this brief excursion along a golden pathway is to be trusted, then perhaps we have found what we were looking for. Clearly, in the context of the event, the design does operate as a signpost for many readings, does, that is, obey the law of *ana-* with respect to anachronisms, analogies, and coincidences Considering that no event has a true beginning or a true end, we can expect more readings to unfold, readings unanticipated by the project but for which it will have always been prepared. On the other hand, *chora* and the law of *ana-* guaranteed this result from the beginning, guaranteed it absolutely, not only in this project but in any and all projects, any and all inscriptions. What was at stake in the collaboration was therefore less a work in which undecidability could be found than a work that began to explore, to celebrate, *to respect* undecidability as an essential aspect of architectural design. Did Eisenman's scaling accomplish this respect, or was it yet another, more sophisticated version of architecture's traditional desire to exercise complete control? Let us, for the time being, leave these questions without answers. They must be discussed and elaborated at length, perhaps in terms not yet conceived and not restricted to the circles of Eisenman and Derrida.[53]

As we bring our second telling to a close, then, let us remind ourselves that the motive for our reimbarkation was not to determine the success or failure of this collaboration. Rather, we wanted to shake something out of it for architecture. And it does seem that we have winnowed a positive possibility. We have at least begun to articulate the terms, not of a new architecture or anarchi-tecture, new first principles or anarchy, but of a new respect for the imprint that *chora* reflects into all writing, including architecture. The respect is nothing other, but nothing less, than the recognition that what marks and makes possible the opposition arché/anarchy is the entire held of *ana-*, ana-architecture. To close without ending, let us call up one last separatrix for a twist, let us shake a bit the massive structure of lie/truth. Perhaps then we will understand that this respect is not a new possibility, but only the movement that always already lies within what we call the truth of architecture.

Notes

1. This congenital instability is the necessary consequence of the "originary trace," the condition that Derrida finds preceding all writing, making it possible. Derrida's meditation on writing, extended to the notion of "arché-writing," includes not only what we call writing, but as well, speech, reading, and, in general, all acts and ensembles from which meanings flow. Contrary to the tradition in which thought on architectural meaning derives from thought on linguistic meaning, the notion of arché-writing is, or should be, a thought of architectural design necessarily and from the beginning. Moreover, in that the thought of arché-writing is from its outset a questioning of status and repression vis-à-vis meaning, it interrogates the agendas that underlie the privilege of the linguistic model over other disciplines. See text below.

2. This paragraph has been reconstructed from phrases extracted from Derrida's essay on the work of Bernard Tschumi "Point de folie: Maintenant l'architecture," trans. Kate Linker, in *La Case Vide* (London: Architectural Association, 1985). I have refrained from using quotation marks on these phrases, with the exception of the last sentence, because

my extraction and reconstruction has been violent. For example, the context of each phrase has been ignored. In deciding how to notate this reconstruction, I have considered it the lesser of evils to elect not to put these words forward under quotation marks, that is, under Derrida's signature.

3. "Le trait en lui-même est indiscret; quoi qu'il trace ou représente, il est indécent (mon amour, libère-moi du trait). Et à ces traits obscènes j'ai tout de suite envie d'élever un monument, ou un château de cartes." Jacques Derrida, *La carte postale: De Socrate à Freud et au-delà* (Paris: Flammarion, 1980), p. 22; trans. Alan Bass as *The Post Card: From Socrates to Freud and Beyond* (Chicago: University of Chicago Press, 1987), p. 17.

4. Beyond, and because of, its idiomatic use, "house of cards" is strongly associated with Eisenman. The architect first employed it as a sobriquet for his work in the essays on Houses I and II, and it subsequently appeared as the title of his book concerning the early houses: *House of Cards* (New York: Oxford University Press, 1987).

5. Throughout this essay, I always employ *respect* toward two meanings. First, I use it in its most familiar sense as indicating appreciation and consideration. In addition, I intend it to echo its etymology: "to re-spect," "to look again," "to take a second look." In this sense, the term reflects not only an important particular theme of the essay but the necessary condition for any deconstruction, which always consists in taking a second look at a text to see what other meanings unfold in it. In this combined sense, deconstruction is always a form of respect.

6. See Jacques Derrida, "Fifty-five Aphorisms on the Aphorism," in the forthcoming publication on the collaborative work of Derrida and Eisenman entitled *Choral Works*.

7. For an excellent discussion of these differences, see Geoff Bennington, "Complexity without Contradiction in Architecture," *AA Files* 15 (Summer 1987), pp. 15–18.

8. For example, consider these themes as they unfold in the first two chapters of Derrida's *Of Grammatology*, trans. Gayatri Spivak (Baltimore: Johns Hopkins University Press, 1976), pp. 3–73:

    ". . . that logocentrism which is also a phonocentrism: absolute proximity of voice and being, of voice and the meaning of being, of voice and the ideality of meaning."

    "We have already a foreboding that phonocentrism merges in general with the historical determination of the meaning of being in general as *presence*, with all the subdeterminations which depend on this general form and which organize within it their system and their historical sequence (*presence of the thing to the sight as eidos, presence as substance/ essence/existence, temporal presence as point of the now or the moment, the self-presence of the cogito, consciousness, subjectivity, the co-presence of the other and of the self, intersubjectivity as the intentional phenomenon of the ego, and so forth*). Logocentrism would thus support the determination of the being of the entity as presence" (emphasis added).

    "I have identified logocentrism and the metaphysics of presence as the exigent, powerful systematic and irrepressible desire for such a [transcendental] signified."

    "There is thus no phenomenality reducing the sign or representer so that the thing signified may be allowed to glow finally in the luminosity of its presence. The so-called 'thing-itself' is always already a *representamen*."

9. In one sense, an *undecidable* is a thing that appears to be a word and/or a concept but, because within it is its own destabilization, it is best thought of as a mark within a text. As a simple example, *ravel* means both to entangle and to disentangle, to confuse and to make clear. Thus when an argument uses the mark *ravel* with the intention of invoking one of these meanings, the other is repressed, though a careful reading can find hints of its continuing to operate within the text, a condition Derrida refers to as the return of the repressed, borrowing from Freud. One tactic of deconstruction is to seek out the multiple and covert operations of such marks within a text, respecting all the meanings of undecidable marks on which every text relies (notice, for example, that *relies* can mean both "depends on" and "tells a lie again"). In doing so, a reading produces irresolvable gaps within a text and exposes its apparent meaning as dependent on the operation of an untenable metaphysics, an assumption that the context reveals the correct or intended meaning. Beyond this, however, the "list of undecidables" refers to some three dozen or so marks, including *différance, trace, remark,* and *supplement*, that Derrida has produced in his analysis of that which resides between the members of apparently self-evident oppositional pairs. Such pairs—same/other, in/out, etc.—seem to consist of unambiguous

poles of a switch, free from the undecidability that plagues (or enriches) marks such as *ravel*. All philosophical argument can be shown to rely on the unambiguous hierarchy and decidability of these pairs. In his analysis of these oppositions, Derrida demonstrates that their seeming clarity depends on the repression of an undecidable condition that must be thought anterior to the opposition, producing it and residing within it. His list of undecidables consists of marks for those conditions that he has shown to be always operating in all apparently decidable texts. He thus extends the tactic of deconstruction discussed above with a more powerful technique able to render undecidable even the most resistant texts. For further discussion, see nn. 11, 20, and 39 below.

10. Eisenman's comments are quoted with modification from Ann Bergren's essay "Architecture Gender Philosophy," in *Papers in Architectural Theory*, ed. Richard Burdett and John Whiteman (Chicago: Chicago Institute for Architecture and Urbanism, forthcoming). This essay, delivered in 1988 at a CIAU conference on architectural theory, weaves its three themes through a reading of classical texts that blends philological considerations with contemporary gender-structure analysis. It adds an invaluable dimension to the reading of this event and thus, though it does not appear herein, forms part of this present work.

     As the reader will confirm in the transcripts of their discussions to be published in *Choral Works*, though Derrida exhibits some of the conservatism indicated by Eisenman's statement, nevertheless, Eisenman takes a good deal of liberty in dramatizing this point. All future citations from the meetings of Derrida and Eisenman refer to these unpublished transcripts.

11. In light of this discussion, it is interesting to note how easily some of Derrida's writings and comments on architecture lend themselves to arguments for an architectural conservatism. At the CIAU conference on architectural theory, Giovanna Borradori, proponent of Italian "weak thought," delivered a response to an essay by Catherine Ingraham, with a decidedly deconstructive flavor, that concerned the role of the proper in architecture (see *Assemblage* 7 [October 1988]). Weak thought is one of the philosophical countermovements to deconstruction; it claims to locate and criticize a modernist residue of global idealism and ideologism in the poststructuralist discourse and to offer alternatives. Weak thought would direct architecture, if Borradori's remarks are representative, toward a somewhat conservative, mildly historical, domesticated design with a dash of the safely liberal. Borradori's propositions were grounded on a nonglobal notion of the "architecturally good" that isolates architectural judgment from the interrogation of the foundations of judgments as such, thereby immunizing the architectural tradition from scrutiny and doubt. Thus it was fascinating to hear Borradori construct her response to Ingraham—a response that was conservative, if not reactionary, in its views on dwelling, domesticity, and history—around an argument authorized entirely by quotations from Derrida's writings and interviews about architecture. Though these quotations suffered all of the abuses one might expect (removal from context, systematic misconstrual, etc.), nevertheless, one could ignore neither the availability of the material for such an argument nor its persuasiveness.

12. A well-known and problematic segment of Plato's *Timaeus* (48e–53a) concerns the place (*chora*) into which the universe was inscribed at the time of its creation. Derrida's treatment of this issue provided the program for the collaboration. See his essay "Chora," to be published in *Choral Works*; *chora* is also discussed extensively throughout the transcripts in *Choral Works* as well as in the latter part of this essay.

13. All quotations from Derrida's essay "Chora" are from the as yet unpublished manuscript.

14. Jacques Derrida, "Why Peter Eisenman Writes Such Good Books," *Threshold* 4 (Spring 1988), pp. 102–103 (translation modified).

15. Ibid., p. 102 (translation modified). In French, "J'écris donc à Eisenman, dans l'avion, cette lettre dont on me permettra de citer un fragment."

16. Ibid. (translation modified). In French, "Vous vous rappelez ce que nous avons envisagé ensemble à Yale: que pour finir j'"écrive,' si on peut dire, sans un mot, un pièce hétérogène. . . ."

17. "*The (pure) trace is différance*. It does not depend on any sensible plenitude, audible or visible, phonic or graphic. It is, on the contrary, the condition of such a plenitude. Although it *does not exist*, although it is never a *being-present* outside of all plenitude, its possibility is by

rights anterior to all that one calls sign (signifier/signified, content/expression, etc.), concept or operation, motor or sensory." Derrida, *Of Grammatology*, p. 62.

18. Cf. Jacques Derrida, "The Pit and the Pyramid: Introduction to Hegel's Semiology," in *Margins of Philosophy*, trans. Alan Bass (Chicago: Chicago University Press, 1982).

19. Ibid., 94.

20. *Aufhebung*, a key term in Hegel's work, is the process by which the spirit fulfills its telos, coming to know itself in itself as itself. In *Aufhebung* an insufficient representation of the spirit for itself to itself is at once suppressed as insufficient but retained in an elevated second term. By virtue of its abstraction, architecture is an insufficient representation of the spirit to itself. Sculpture retains the residue of architecture's limited capacity, but in the *Aufhebung* resolves the insufficiency by raising the representation to a new and higher level. Because of the retention, the verb is often, but not quite adequately, translated into English as *sublimation* or *sublation*.

21. Cf. Eisenman's essay in *Moving Arrows, Eros and Other Errors* (London: Architectural Association, 1986).

22. Derrida, *Of Grammatology*, p. 47.

23. Derrida, "Why Eisenman . . . ," pp. 103, 104 (translation modified).

24. Jacques Derrida, "Plato's Pharmacy," in *Dissemination*, trans. Barbara Johnson (Chicago: University of Chicago Press, 1981), p. 64.

25. Mark Wigley has observed that the very notion of "to add" presupposes a totality to which the addition is made. For example, it is under the logic of addition that an "ornament" is "added to" an independent, self-contained, and whole receiver, such as "the building itself." The metaphysics of presence operating in the logic of such "additions" is exposed under Derrida's scrutiny of the supplement, one of the aforementioned undecidables. In his analysis, Derrida shows that the classical addition logic of the supplement presupposes the presence of existences that cannot exist. Thus, in the most famous example, "culture" can only supplement "nature" if the latter always already lacks, that is, if nature is always already naturally supplemented. "The supplement comes naturally to put itself in Nature's place." The logic of addition is but a desire for a whole nature, without need of supplementation, to which culture comes as an external exigent, and is thus another manifestation of the dream of a transcendental signified. An entire family of separatrices traceable to the culture/nature structure (disease/health, evil/good, etc.) is shaken by this reading of the supplement.

      Wigley has observed as well that the "translation" of Derrida's contribution letter as a writing within which a drawing, nominally "the contribution," stands incorporated as nonwriting also evidences familiar mechanisms of the metaphysics of presence. Another translation, perhaps a better deconstructive reading in that it would not violate the letter, but at the same time would not obey its properties, would have been to treat the entire letter as the contribution; *"cette sculpture"* would then have referred not to a drawing of an object within a letter, but to the letter itself. Ample and well-known precedent for this treatment was available, considering the proliferation of "correspondence art." Too, this tactic would have emphasized that Derrida, ostensible origin and author of the letter, was also always "translating," even at the moment of first writing. The theme of translation can be found throughout Derrida's work, for example, in the essays "Les Tours de Babel," trans. Joseph F. Graham, in *Difference in Translation*, ed. Joseph F. Graham (Ithaca: Cornell University Press, 1985), and "Fors: The Anglish Words of Nicolas Abraham and Maria Torok," introduction to Abraham and Torok's *The Wolf Man's Magic Word: A Cryptonymy*, trans. Barbara Johnson (Minneapolis: University of Minnesota Press, 1986). The latter essay is especially interesting here for its discussion of "incorporation."

26. Derrida, *Of Grammatology*, p. 18.

27. Derrida, "Why Eisenman . . . ," p. 99.

28. In Derrida's "Otobiographies: The Teaching of Nietzsche and the Politics of the Proper Name," trans. Avital Ronell, in *The Ear of the Other: Otobiography, Transference, Translation* (New York: Schocken Books, 1985), particularly in the first section "The Logic of the Living Feminine," the reader will find further elaboration of Nietzsche's *Ecce Homo*. The signature, *le trait*, even life and death are therein considered.

29. Derrida's interest in the proper name derives, in part, from his discussion of writing as the always-becoming-sign of symbol. The history of writing as the phoneticization of

speech is intimately connected to the name, the proper noun. Thus, for example, foreign names in the cartouches of Egypt were "spelled out" by a series of hieroglyphs in which the initial sounds of the nominal symbol combined to produce the name. Recall that a key issue in his meditation on writing is the destabilization of the privilege of speech over writing, a manifestation of the metaphysics of presence. This privilege seems confirmed as long as writing is nothing other than and nothing but the picture of speech. Derrida first demonstrates that, strictly speaking, a purely phonetic writing does not exist and then turns his attention to reading texts by emphasizing the nonphonetic content that always resides within any writing, including speech. His reading and writing of texts in terms of the proper name is therefore a tactic in this strategy and works to destabilize the repression of the symbol within the sign. Cf. Gregory Ulmer, *Applied Grammatology: Post(e)-Pedagogy from Jacques Derrida to Joseph Beuys* (Baltimore: Johns Hopkins University Press, 1985), pp. 3–153.

30. Derrida, "Why Eisenman . . . ," p. 99.

31. Ibid.

32. Ibid., 104.

33. But why does the play between the colon and the 8 in 19:5 seem too farfetched, seem out of bounds even for textual play? This reading uses the forms within text other than letters, and perhaps the properties of punctuational form, like architecture, must remain inviolate. Clearly, the "ornamental" scale and other aspects of the architectonics of punctuation are necessary for it to be outside of the "text itself" yet irreplaceably within the text, the condition that always calls for a deconstruction.

34. See Francis M. Cornford, *Plato's Cosmology* (New York: Harcourt, Brace, 1937). All excerpts from the *Timaeus* herein are from the Cornford translation.

35. The play of proper names also suggests interventions into the design that might have avoided the problem of "adding a sculpture," discussed above, by unfolding the proper name into the design. Thus, as proposed in the meetings, coral or a corral might have been used. But might not consideration have been given as well to iron, peat, and/or jade?—JA cques DE rrida; the French word *déjà* is already a well-known Derridean signature. For Plato's sake, perhaps something could have been made of the Khorat Plateau in Thailand, and not only in respect of the play on names that it affords, but also because this plateau has an uncanny similarity to the project: its shape is roughly the same and it, too, is skewed with respect to the ground plane. Finally, though it may be inexcusably frivolous, the important dialogue of the "homogenous paste," discussed later in the text, almost demands naming a material that not only meets all the characteristics sought in this conversation, but moreover, inscribes a proper name, namely *Playdough.*

36. Derrida, "Why Eisenman . . . ," p. 101.

37. Ibid., p. 100.

38. Ibid., p. 104 (translation modified).

39. There should be little doubt that Derrida can not only "see" but read drawings as text brilliantly. For example, consider his extended reading of the engraved frontispiece from Mathew Paris's thirteenth-century fortune-telling book. This image, which Derrida discovered reprinted on a postcard, provides the armature for the "Envois" in his *Carte postale.* To say the least, his translations of this image are astonishing.

40. Cf. William Barclay, *The Gospel of John* (Philadelphia: Westminster Press, 1975), pp. 29–37.

41. In the *Timaeus,* the Demiurge is the creator of the sensible universe. In most English translations, the word is rendered as god or God, but to preserve interesting connections—for example, at certain times and locations in ancient Greece the architect was termed *demiurge*—I have maintained the term in transliterated Greek.

42. We might liken the difficulty of this problem to the question that young students often ponder after learning that the universe is expanding. It is a familiar conundrum: If the universe is everything—all matter, energy, and space—then *into what* does it expand? Another version of the same problem is, If the all-inclusive universe was infinitesimally small at the time of the Big Bang, in what space was it located? Of course, the problem of the space of inscription that Plato contemplates is not identical to the problem of the bound universe. Indeed, it is even more difficult and subtle, yet the two problems share conceptual similarities.

43. Derrida, "Chora," unpublished manuscript.

44. The architecture of the text, particularly its center, seems to intrigue Derrida as he reads Plato. In "Chora," he appeals to the appearance of *chora* in the *Timaeus* as a theme "right in the middle of the book." In "Plato's Pharmacy," written some twelve years earlier, this architectural argument is even more emphatic as Derrida reads Plato's *Phaedrus*: "Let us read this more closely. At the precisely calculated center of the text—the reader can count the lines—the question of logography is raised." Other similar architectures might interest us. Consider, for example, that, though Derridean thought is devoted to destabilizing the metaphysics and status of the Idea, there is, nonetheless, an idea imbedded inextricably within Derridean thought.

45. Derrida writes of deconstruction as a *soliciting* of the text, a shaking of the wholeness of the text to see what falls out. This play derives from the Latin etymology of *solicit*, from *sollus*, "the whole," and *citus*, from *ciere*, "to arouse."

46. Yet in the *Timaeus* (31c) *analogia* was calculation par excellence and opposed to bastard reasoning, *logismoi nothoi*, which was calculation leading to impossible results. In reading this passage, an analogy between analogy and *chora* is evident: "But two things alone cannot be satisfactorily united without a third, for there must be some bond between them drawing them together." *Chora*, of course, does not unite the Forms (Ideas, *eidos*) to the copies (*eidolon*); rather it is the place in which one participates in the other.

47. Derrida alluded to this in "Why Eisenman . . .": "I would rather speak of meetings, and of what takes *place* at the intersection of chance and program, of risk and necessity" (p. 100; translation modified).

48. In this regard, consider an interesting anachrony implied in the *Timaeus*. As we have said, the Forms constitute the permanent, timeless realm of being. The Demiurge, looking upon them and using them as models (*paradigmata*), forges the material universe, the realm of becoming. Yet, strictly speaking, there must be becoming in the realm of being before the realm of becoming is created in order for the Forms to *become* Paradigms in the eyes of the Demiurge. Clearly, this has profound implications for all of metaphysics: it implies that translation is of the essence and, moreover, that the essence is not fulfilled until translation occurs. The "thing itself" is always already translated.

49. Tschumi's first look at Derrida and deconstruction was in his highly regarded *Manhattan Transcripts* of 1981. His second look was the publication of his La Villette project in the *AA Files* folio, *La Case Vide*, which included the essay by Derrida cited earlier. *Case vide*, French for "empty box," can be taken as an obvious if somewhat coarse metaphor for *chora*. Thus, in a sense, before Eisenman and Derrida became the first architect/philosopher pair to collaborate on *chora*, Tschumi and Derrida had already done so.

50. "In the final l, choral, *chora* becomes more liquid, more aerial, I do not dare to say more feminine," playing on the French *elle* (Derrida, "Why Eisenman . . . ," p. 101 (translation modified).

51. As is well known, beauty is one of the three canonic conjugates of Platonic perfection, the True, the Good, and the Beautiful. For many reasons touched upon herein, not least of which is the collaboration's interest in shaking (soliciting) the Platonic foundation of architecture that continues to operate even today, beauty, though not excluded as such, cannot be a measure of the results. In this regard, it is noteworthy to find Eisenman and Derrida in the sixth meeting beginning their assessment of the final design with a discussion of its beauty. I examine this moment and the question of beauty in further detail in an unpublished essay entitled "The Irrelevance of Beauty."

52. It is interesting to note the relationship between this movement of gold in Eisenman's work from motivated symbol to the (almost) arbitrary sign of a signature, a proper name, and Derrida's interest in this same movement. See note 24.

53. Eisenman and Derrida have continued their discussions on these matters in an open correspondence published in *Assemblage* 12 (August 1990). While taking issue with some of Derrida's inferences about the possible implications of the philosopher's work for architecture, Eisenman tacitly acknowledges Derrida's critique of the architect's scaling work and begins to outline a new design response, a belated "collaboration," which he terms "weak form." For a discussion of weak form, see my "A Matter of Respect," *A+U* 232 (January 1990), pp. 134–137. Further writings on the Derrida/Eisenman collaboration include Gregory Ulmer's treatment in a forthcoming collection of his essays as well as my reading of the recent correspondence in "Aweful Architecture," also forthcoming.

Anthony Vidler   From *The Architectural Uncanny: Essays in the Modern Unhomely* (Cambridge:

MIT Press, 1992)

see **174–175** and
Foucault (**430**
ff)

"Space may be the projection or the extension of the psychical apparatus," Freud noted.[1] Had it been intended as a prolegomenon to future theorizations of space, his note could not have been more astute. For treatments of space, as Anthony Vidler reminds us, have moved from Sigfried Giedion's modernist notion of space-time to Henri Lefebvre's Marxian "production of space" to a Foucauldian linking of space, knowledge, and power to, most recently, a concern shared by those interested in constructions of gender, sexuality, and difference with space and its psychical internalization.

In 1985–1987, during architecture theory's most intense affiliation with deconstruction, Vidler, working on the architecture of romanticism, was inevitably led to Freud and the principle of the uncanny, *das Unheimliche*, itself a veritable deconstructionist concept that initiates an osmotic and fearful mixing of opposites — analysis/paralysis, composition/decomposition, site/parasite, even life/ death. Vidler:

At once a psychological and an aesthetic phenomenon, it simultaneously established and de-stablized. Its effects were guaranteed by an original authenticity, a first burial, and made all the more potent by virtue of a return that, in civilization, was in a real sense out of place. Something was not, then, merely haunted, but rather revisited by a power that was thought long dead. To such a force the romantic psyche and the romantic aesthetic sensibility were profoundly open; at any moment what seemed on the surface homely and comforting, secure and clear of superstition, might be reappropriated by something that should have remained secret but that neverthe-less, through some chink in the shutters of progress, had crept back into the house, of all topoi in literature and art, the *locus suspectus* of the uncanny."[2]

From its origins in romantic thought, Vidler's later work traces the theme of the architectural uncanny to contemporary questions of the psychopathologies of modern space, such as agoraphobia and claustrophobia, and the haunting of modernism by the myth of a transparency that is at once social, epistemological, and spatial.[3] Such themes may be — if one might join Freud in a prediction — among the primary ones for the problematic of architecture theory in the next decades.

Notes

"Dark Space" was originally published in *The Interrupted Life,* ed. France Morin (New York: New Museum of Contemporary Art, 1991); "Transparency" was originally published in *Any-one,* ed. Cynthia C. Davidson (New York: Rizzoli, 1992). The articles appear as chapters in *The Architectural Uncanny* and are reprinted here as a single essay.

1. *The Standard Edition of the Complete Psychological Works of Sigmund Freud* (London: Hogarth Press, 1955), vol. 23, p. 30.
2. Anthony Vidler, "The Architecture of the Uncanny: The Unhomely Houses of the Romantic Sublime," *Assemblage* 3 (July 1987), p. 12.
3. See, for example, Anthony Vidler, "Bodies in Space/Subjects in the City: Psychopathologies of Modern Urbanism," *Differences: A Journal of Feminist Cultural Studies* 5, no. 3 (1993).

Dark Space

> A whole history remains to he written of *spaces*—which would at the same time be the history of *powers* (both these terms in the plural)—from the great strategies of geo-politics to the little tactics of the habitat, institutional architecture from the classroom to the design of hospitals, passing via economic and political installations.
>
> **Michel Foucault,** "The Eye of Power"

Space, in contemporary discourse, as in lived experience, has taken on an almost palpable existence. Its contours, boundaries, and geographies are called upon to stand in for all the contested realms of identity, from the national to the ethnic; its hollows and voids are occupied by bodies that replicate internally the external conditions of political and social struggle, and are likewise assumed to stand for, and identify, the sites of such struggle. Techniques of spatial occupation, of territorial snapping, of invasion and surveillance are seen as the instruments of social and individual control.

Equally, space is assumed to hide, in its darkest recesses and forgotten margins, all the objects of fear and phobia that have returned with such insistency to haunt the imaginations of those who have tried to stake out spaces to protect their health and happiness. Indeed, space as threat, as harbinger of the unseen, operates as medical and psychical metaphor for all the possible erosions of bourgeois bodily and social well being. The body, indeed, has become its own exterior, as its cell structure has become the object of spatial modeling that maps its own sites of immunological battle and describes the forms of its antibodies. "Outside," even as the spaces of exile, asylum, confinement, and quarantine of the early modern period were continuously spilling over into the "normal" space of the city, so the "pathological" spaces of today menace the clearly marked out limits of the social order. In every case "light space" is invaded by the figure of "dark space," on the level of the body in the form of epidemic and uncontrollable disease, and on the level of the city in the person of the homeless. In other words, the realms of the organic space of the body and the social space in which that body lives and works, domains clearly enough distinguished in the nineteenth century, as François Delaporte has shown, no longer can be identified as separate.[1]

In what follows I want to examine only one aspect of this new condition, one that touches on its implications for monumental architecture and more generally on the theorization of spatial conditions after Foucault. I will, that is, analyze the visual construction of images and objects that refer to this dark side of space in the modern period, as a way of approaching a more complex and (I hope) more politically subtle interpretation of subject-space relations than that offered by the conventional wisdom of modern urbanism (flood dark space with light) or architecture (open up all space to vision and occupation).

      In the elaboration of the complex history of modern space following the initiatives of Foucault, historians and theorists have largely concentrated their attention on the overtly political role of *transparent* space—that paradigm of total control championed by Jeremy Bentham and recuperated under the guise of "hygienic space" by modernists led by Le Corbusier in the twentieth century. Transparency, it was thought, would eradicate the domain of myth, suspicion, tyranny, and above all the irrational. The rational grids and hermetic enclosures of institutions from hospitals to prisons; the surgical opening up of cities to circulation, light, and air; the therapeutic design of dwellings and settlements; these have all been subjected to analysis for their hidden contents, their capacity to instrumentalize the politics of surveillance through what Bentham termed "universal transparency." Historians have preferred to study this myth of "power through transparency," especially in its evident complicity with the technologies of the modern movement and their "utopian" applications to architecture and urbanism.

      Yet such a spatial paradigm was, as Foucault pointed out, constructed out of an initial fear, the fear of Enlightenment in the face of "darkened spaces, of the pall of gloom which prevents the full visibility of things, men and truths." It was this very fear of the dark that led, in the late eighteenth century, to the fascination with those same shadowy areas—the "fantasy-world of stone walls, darkness, hideouts and dungeons"—the precise "negative of the transparency and visibility which it is aimed to establish."[2] The moment that saw the creation of the first "considered politics of spaces" based on scientific concepts of light and infinity also saw, and within the same epistemology, the invention of a spatial phenomenology of darkness.

      Late eighteenth-century architects were entirely aware of this double vision. Etienne-Louis Boullée, who was among the first to apply the newly outlined precepts of the Burkean sublime to the design of public institutions, exploited all the visual and sensational powers of what Burke had called "absolute light" to characterize his projects for metropolitan cathedrals and halls of justice. He was equally obsessed with absolute darkness as the most powerful instrument to induce that state of fundamental terror claimed by Burke as the instigator of the sublime. His design for a Palace of Justice confronted the two worlds, light and dark, in a telling allegory of enlightenment; the cubiform justice halls, lit from above, are set on top of a half buried podium containing the prisons. "It seemed to me," Boullée wrote, "that in presenting this august palace raised on the shadowy lair of crime, I would not only be able to ennoble architecture by means of the oppositions that resulted, but further present in a metaphorical way the imposing picture of vice crushed beneath the feet of justice."[3]

      It was perhaps not by chance that Boullée's reflections on the dark were elaborated during the period of his enforced withdrawal from public life under the real Terror—one that Robespierre himself had described as predicated on the necessities of the "political sublime." During this internal exile, sometime in the mid 1790s, Boullée recounted his "experiments" in light and shade as he walked by night in the woods surrounding his home:

Finding myself in the countryside, I skirted a wood by the light of the moon. My effigy produced by its light excited my attention (assuredly this was not a novelty for me). By a particular disposition of the mind, the effect of this simulacrum seemed to me to be of an extreme sadness. The trees drawn on the ground by their shadows made the most profound impression on me. This picture grew in my imagination. I then saw everything that was the most somber in nature. What did I see? The mass of objects detached in black against a light of extreme pallor. Nature seemed to offer itself, in mourning, to my sight. Struck by the sentiments I felt, I occupied myself, from this moment on, in making its particular application to architecture.

Out of his experiences, Boullée formed a notion of an architecture that would speak of death. It should be low and compressed in proportions—a "buried architecture" that literally embodied the burial it symbolized. It should express the extreme melancholy of mourning by means of its stripped and naked walls, "deprived of all ornament." It should, finally, following the model of the architect's shadow, be articulated to the sight by means of shadows:

One must, as I have tried to do in funerary monuments, present the skeleton of architecture by means of an absolutely naked wall, presenting the image of buried architecture by employing only low and compressed proportions, sinking into the earth, forming, finally, by means of materials absorbent to the light, the black picture of an architecture of shadows depicted by the effect of even blacker shadows.

Boullée gave the example of a Temple of Death, a temple front etched, so to speak, in shadow form on a flat plane of light absorbent material—a virtual architecture of negativity. Boullée was proud of his "invention": "This genre of architecture formed by shadows is a discovery of the art that belongs to me. It is a new career that I have opened up. Either I fool myself, or artists will not disdain to follow it."[4] Certainly his younger contemporaries were quick to seize on the sublime potentials of this abyssal vision of mortuary form. Claude-Nicolas Ledoux, in particular, made the architecture of death a point of departure for a reverie on the infinite scale of the universe and the absolute "nothingness" of the void after life.

And yet, in retrospect, what is fascinating about Boullée's account is not so much its commonplace references to darkness, nor its fashionable appeal to Egyptian motifs on the eve of Napoleon's expedition, but rather its projection of a "skeleton" of architecture from the basis of the human shadow. This shadow, or "effigy" as Boullée called it, prefiguring the disappearance of the body into darkness, was both a haunting "double" for Boullée himself and a model for imitation in architecture. On one level, Boullée was following the traditional idea of architecture "imitating" the perfection of the human body in massing and proportions, inverting the theory in order to make an architecture based on the "death form" of the body, shadowed on the ground. But beyond this Boullée created a veritable "simulacrum" of the buried body in architecture: the building, already half sunken, compressed in its proportions as if by a great weight from above, imitated not a standing figure (as classical Vitruvian theory would have demanded) but a form that was already recumbent, itself depicted on the ground as a negative space. This prone figure was then raised up, so to speak, in order to mark the facade of Boullée's temple, now become an image of a specter: a monument to death that represented an ambiguous moment, somewhere between life and death, or, rather, a shadow of the living dead. In this way, Boullée prefigured the nineteenth-century preoccupation with the double as the harbinger of death, or as the shadow of the unburied dead.

In this doubling of the double, Boullée was thus setting up a play between architecture (art of imitation, of doubling) and death (imaged in the double) in a way that gave tangible force to Enlightenment fears. As Sarah Kofman has argued in her analysis of Freud's essay on "The Uncanny," "erected to conquer death, art, as a 'double', like any double, itself turns into an image of death. The game of art is a game of death, which already implies death in life, as a force of saving and inhibition." Boullée's death image, with its shadow inscription mirroring the shape of its dark facade or "ground," plays insistently on this theme that, as Freud pointed out, has to do with "the constant recurrence of the same thing," or repetition. Kofman comments,

[Freud's] "The Uncanny" indicates this transformation of the algebraic sign of the double, its link with narcissism and death as the punishment for having sought immortality, for having wanted to "kill" the father. It is perhaps no accident that the model of the "double," erected for the first time by the Egyptians, is found in the figuration of castration in dreams, the doubling of the genital organ.[5]

Boullée, in these terms, might well have invented, if not the first architectural figuration of death, certainly the first self-conscious architecture of the uncanny, a prescient experiment in the projection of "dark space." For by flattening his shadow, so to speak, on the surface of a building that was itself nothing but (negative) surface, Boullée had created an image of an architecture not only without real depth, but one that deliberately played on the ambiguities between absolute flatness and infertile depth, between his own shadow and the void. The building, as the double of the death of the subject, translated this disappearance into experienced spatial uncertainty.

Here the limits of Foucault's interpretation of Enlightenment space become evident. Still tied to the Enlightenment's own phenomenology of light and dark, clear and obscure, his insistence on the operation of power through *transparency*, the panoptic principle, resists exploration of the extent to which the pairing of transparency and obscurity is essential for power to operate. For it is in the intimate associations of the two, their uncanny ability to slip from one to the other, that the sublime as instrument of fear retains its hold—in that ambiguity that stages the presence of death in life, dark space in bright space. In this sense, all the radiant spaces of modernism, from the first Panopticon to the Ville Radieuse, should be seen as calculated not on the final triumph of light over dark but precisely on the insistent presence of the one in the other.

Indeed, on another level, Boullée's design puts into question the generally assumed identity of the spatial and the monumental in Foucault's system. Foucault posited a virtual homology between title institutional politics of panopticism and their monumental crystallizations in the form of building types from the hospital to the prison and beyond, thus setting in motion the critique of modernist typologies that began in the late 1960s; the *spatial* dimension here seems to act as a universal flux bonding political and architectural or monumental. But our analysis of Boullée might suggest that the spatial is rather a dimension that incipiently opposes the monumental: not only does it work to contextualize the individual monument into a general map of spatial forces that stretch from the building to the city and thence to entire territories—something recognized by the situationists, and, in another context, by Henri Lefebvre—but it also operates, by way of the negative bodily projection we have described, to absorb the monument altogether.

Boullée's relentless desire to mimic the "engulfing" of the subject into the void of death, a desire itself mimicked by Ledoux when he speaks of composing "an image of nothingness" in his Cemetery project of 1785, thus ends in the engulfing of monumentality itself. For the rational grids and spatial orders that mark the laying out of the panoptical system in the late eighteenth century are, in the Temple of Death, nowhere present; there is literally no *plan* for this monument to nothingness. Its sole mark is a facade as infinitely thin and insubstantial as the idea of redoubled darkness—a facade moreover that is precariously balanced between above and below, vertical and horizontal. Here the bodily substantiality of the traditional monument and the palpable spatial identity of the controlling institution dissolve into a mirror of the projection of a disappearing subject. Space, that is, has operated as an instrument of monumental dissolution.

The homology thus established between subject and space seems, on the subjective as well as on the monumental level, to emulate what Roger Caillois referred to as "legendary psychasthenia," that "temptation by space" that seemed to operate in the realm of insect mimicry and that offered so many analogies to human experience. Caillois was fascinated by the loss of any distinction between the insect and its surroundings during the process of camouflaging identity, its tendency to assimilate to its milieu; he pointed out that this did not always correspond to the best possible defense against death. The insect that looked like the leaf on which it was seated could equally be destroyed or eaten along with the leaf. Such loss of identity, he argued, would be a kind of pathological luxury, even "a dangerous luxury." As in imitation in the arts, such mimicry depended on the distortion of spatial vision, on the breaking down of the normal process by which spatial perception situates the subject clearly in space and in opposition to it:

There can be no doubt that the perception of space is a complex phenomenon: space is indissolubly perceived and represented. From this standpoint it is a double dihedral changing at every moment in size and position: a *dihedral of action* whose horizontal plane is formed by the ground and the vertical plane by the man himself who walks and who, by this fact, carries the dihedral along with him; and a *dihedral of representation* determined by the same horizontal plane as the previous one (but represented and not perceived) intersected vertically at the distance where the object appears. It is with represented space that the drama becomes specific, since the living creature, the organism, is no longer the origin of the coordinates, but one point among others; it is dispossessed of its privilege and literally *no longer knows where to place itself.* One can already recognize the characteristic scientific attitude and, indeed, it is remarkable that represented spaces are just what is multiplied by contemporary science: Finsler's spaces, Fermat's spaces, Riemann-Christoffel's hyper-space, abstract, generalized, open, and closed spaces, spaces dense in themselves, thinned out, and so on. The feeling of personality, considered as the organism's feeling of distinction from its surroundings, of the connection between consciousness and a particular point in space, cannot fail under these conditions to be seriously undermined; one then enters into the psychology of psychasthenia, and more specifically of *legendary psychasthenia*, if we agree to use this name for the disturbance in the above relations between personality and space.[6]

Following the psychological studies of Pierre Janet, Caillois compared such a disturbance to that experienced by certain schizophrenics when, in response to the question "where are you?," they invariably responded "I know where I am, but I do not feel as though I'm at the spot where I find myself." Caillois seemed to be relating such spatial disorientation to the pathology of derealization discussed by Freud, and beyond this to the host of spatial phobias, from agoraphobia to acrophobia and claustrophobia, identified in the late nineteenth century. Like sufferers from agoraphobia, described by Carl Otto Westphal in 1871, Caillois saw the schizo-phrenic literally eaten up by space:

To these dispossessed souls, space seems to be a devouring force. Space pursues them, encircles them, digests them in a gigantic phagocytosis. It ends by replacing them. Then the body separates itself from thought, the individual breaks the boundary of his skin and occupies the other side of his senses. He tries to look at *himself from any point whatever* in space. He feels himself becoming space, *dark space where things cannot be put*. He is similar, not similar to something, but just *similar*. And he invents spaces of which he is "the convulsive possession."[7]

This spatial condition of the devoured subject Caillois assimilated to the experience, described by Eugène Minkowski, of "dark space," a space that is lived under the conditions of depersonalization and assumed absorption. Minkowski, distinguishing between "light space" and "dark space," saw dark space as a living entity, experienced, despite its lack of visual depth and visible extension, as deep: "an opaque and unlimited sphere wherein all the radii are the same, black and mysterious."[8] For Caillois, Minkowski's formulation approximated his own self-induced experience of psychasthenia, explaining among other symptoms his (much intensified) "fear of the dark," rooted once more in "the peril in which it puts the opposition between the organism and the milieu." In Minkowski and Caillois, darkness is not the simple absence of light:

There is something positive about it. While light space is eliminated by the materiality of objects, darkness is "filled," it touches the individual directly, envelops him, penetrates him, and even passes through him: hence "the ego is *permeable* for darkness while it is not so for light"; the feeling of mystery that one experiences at night would not come from anything else. Minkowski likewise comes to speak of *dark space* and almost of a lack of distinction between the milieu and the organism: "Dark space envelops me on all sides and penetrates me much deeper than light space; the distinction between inside and outside and consequently the sense organs as well, insofar as they are designed for external perception, here play only a totally modest role."[9]

The notion of an impulsion toward a loss of the subject into dark space, linked directly by Caillois both to the death drive and to certain forms of aesthetic mimicry, thus returns us to Boullée's experience of impending death in the forest outside Paris, and more directly to its monumental mimicry. We might now say that the Temple of Death, as monument, mimics the subject's own impulsion to be tempted by space, a monument that suffers, so to speak, from legendary psychasthenia.

Transparency
Modernity has been haunted, as we know very well, by a myth of transparency: transparency of the self to nature, of the self to the other, of all selves to society, and all this represented, if not constructed, from Jeremy Bentham to Le Corbusier, by a universal transparency of building materials, spatial penetration, and the ubiquitous flow of air, light, and physical movement. As Sigfried Giedion observed in his *Bauen in Frankreich* of 1928,

The houses of Le Corbusier define themselves neither by space nor by forms: the air passes right through them! The air becomes a constitutive factor! For this, one should count neither on space nor forms, but uniquely on relation and compenetration! There is only a single, indivisible space. The separations between interior and exterior fall.[10]

Walter Benjamin, who copied this citation in his monumental compilation of quotes, the *Passagen-Werk*, heard in this urge for transparency a death knell for the ancient art of dwelling:

In the imprint of this turning point of the epoch, it is written that the knell has sounded for the dwelling in its old sense, dwelling in which security prevailed. Giedion, Mendelssohn, Le Corbusier have made the place of abode of men above all the transitory space of all the imaginable forces and waves of air and light. What is being prepared is found under the sign of transparency.[11]

On another level, transparency opened up machine architecture to inspection—its functions displayed like anatomical models, its walls hiding no secrets; the very epitome of social morality. In this vein, André Breton criticized the hermeticism of Huysmans and the interiority of symbolism:

As for me, I continue to inhabit my glass house [*ma maison de verre*], where one can see at every hour who is coming to visit me, where everything that is suspended from the ceilings and the walls holds on as if by enchantment, where I rest at night on a bed of glass with glass sheets, where *who I am* will appear to me, sooner or later, engraved on a diamond.[12]

Reading this passage, which does not entirely, as we might imagine, join Breton to his modernist contemporaries, Walter Benjamin was drawn to remark, "To live in a glass house is a revolutionary virtue par excellence. It is also an intoxication, a moral exhibitionism, that we badly need. Discretion concerning one's own existence, once an aristocratic virtue, has become more and more an affair of petit-bourgeois parvenus."[13] Such an ideology of the glass house of the soul, a psychogeographic glass house one might say, parallels the ideology of the glass house of the body—the aerobic glass house—and together the two themes inform the twenties with dialectical vigor. No wonder that Marcel Duchamp, Man Ray, and of course Georges Bataille were all in favor of a little dust. In Bataille's ironic encomium of dust:

The storytellers have not imagined that the Sleeping Beauty would be awakened covered by a thick layer of dust; no more have they dreamed of the sinister spiders' webs that at the first movement of her brown hair would have torn. Nevertheless the sad *nappes de poussière* endlessly invade earthly dwellings and make them uniformly dirty; as if attics and old rooms were planned for the next entry of obsessions, of phantoms, of larvae living and inebriated by the worm-eaten smell of the old dust. When the big girls "good for anything" arm themselves, each morning, with a big feather duster, or even with a vacuum cleaner, they are perhaps not entirely ignorant that they contribute as much as the most positive savants to keeping off the evil phantoms that sicken cleanliness and logic. One day or another, it is true, dust, if it persists, will probably begin to gain ground over the servants, invading the immense rubbish of abandoned buildings, of deserted docks: and in this distant epoch there will be nothing more to save us from nocturnal terrors.[14]

Glass, once perfectly transparent, is now revealed in all its opacity.

Indeed, it was under the sign of opacity that the universalism of modernism, constructed on the myth of a universal subject, came under attack in the past twenty-five years. Beginning with Colin Rowe's and Robert Slutzky's sly undermining of modernist simplicities in their "Transparency: Literal and Phenomenal," transparency was gradually discredited by the critique of the universal subject in politics and psychoanalysis.[15] In its place, opacity, both literal and phenomenal, became the watchword of the postmodern appeal to roots, to tradition, to local and regional specificity, to a renewed search for domestic security. A few years ago one might have concluded that, if the old art of dwelling had not been entirely revived, save in kitsch imitation, certainly transparency was dead.

Yet in the last few years, as if confirming the penchant of the century for uncanny repetition, we have been once again presented with a revived call for transparency, this time on behalf of the apparently "good modernism," patronized by the French state in its Parisian *grands projets. La transparence* is now the rage in France, represented by the winning schemes for the new national library and the Palais des Expositions near the Eiffel Tower, reopening questions originally posed in the context of the first of François Mitterand's monuments—the pyramid of the Louvre. But what seemed, in the case of the pyramid, to be an ostensibly practical problem of making a new monument disappear in relation to its context has been raised to the status of principle. Transparency, in the form of the four towers proposed for the book stacks of Dominique Perrault's library and the three box-shaped pavilions for the expo building, is now, at least in the minds of Mitterand, his administration, the juries and apologists for the schemes, and, of course, the architects themselves, firmly identified with progressive modernity. And is thus posed against what is regarded as a regressive postmodern tendency of historical atavism. The association is made confidently, with the apparent faith of the first avant-gardes of the twenties.

On one level, the connection transparency/modernity is easy enough to understand. Following a decade of historical and typological exploration of "false walls" and fake stones, postmodernism, the argument goes, has been seen for what it was—the Potemkin City of the present—to be purified only by a renewed adhesion to the spirit of the age. In France at least, the spirit of the age is still haunted by the ghosts of technocratic "rational" architecture from Durand and Viollet-le-Duc to Pierre Chareau, continued in the sixties with the technological expressionism of the Centre Pompidou, and, more recently, Norman Foster's Town Hall for Nîmes, next door to the Maison Carrée.

Literal transparency is of course notoriously difficult (as Pei himself admitted) to attain; it quickly turns into obscurity (its apparent opposite) and reflectivity (its reversal). Despite all the researches of the Saint-Gobain glass company, the pyramid remains a glass pyramid, no more or less transparent than Bruno Taut's glass block pavilion of 1914. As for the library, the claim of transparency— books exposed to the world as symbols of themselves—was quickly suppressed in the face of professional librarians asking simple questions. The solution has been twofold: either to "fake" transparency—a falsely lit wall beyond the walls protecting the stacks from daylight—or to embrace its mirror image, so to speak, reflectively.

Why then transparency in the first place? To make huge cubic masses, monumental forms, urban constructions of vast scale—disappear? A crisis of confidence in monumentality? Certainly it seems significant that the projects were selected from models, without structure or scale—and conceptual models at that, where the expo "boxes" seem (and are) like giant perspex boxes. The conclusion would be that to work effectively, the ideology of the modern, either as *bête noire* of the postmodern or its recent replacement, would have to be a fiction in practice. Public monumentality would then be in the same position as in the 1940s when Giedion posed the question of whether a "new monumentality" was indeed possible in modern materials.

We are presented with the apparently strange notion of a public monumentality that is more than reticent—indeed wants literally to disappear, be invisible—even as it represents the full weight of the French state. And perhaps the underpinnings of the present revival should indeed be sought in the difficult area of representation, one that is no doubt joined to the problematic outlined by Gianni Vattimo, that of a "weak" or background monumentality, but also, and perhaps more fundamentally, to the self-perceived role of architecture in the construction of identity. For if it was in the task of constructing a new and modern subject that transparency in architecture was first adduced, the present passion for see-through buildings is indubitably linked to the attempt to construct a state identity of technological modernity against a city identity (Paris, Chirac) enmeshed in the tricky historicism of preservation.

Yet, coupled with this tendency, we may begin to discern the emergence of a more complex stance, one that, without rejecting the technological and ideological heritage of modernism, nevertheless seeks to problematize its premises, recognizing that the "subject" of modernity has indeed been destabilized by its worst effects. In this vein, the cube of glass envisaged by Rem Koolhaas in his competition entry for the French national library, with its internal organs displayed, so to speak, like some anatomical model, is at once a confirmation of transparency and its complex critique. For here the transparency is conceived of as solid, not as void, with the interior volumes carved out of a crystalline block, so as to float within it, in amoebic suspension. These are then represented on the surface of the cube as shadowy presences, their three-dimensionality displayed ambiguously and flattened, superimposed on one another, in a play of amorphous densities. Transparency is thus converted into translucency, and this into darkness and obscurity. The inherent quality of absolute transparency to turn into its opposite, reflectivity, is thrown into doubt; the subject can no longer lose itself in l'espace indicible of infinite reason or find itself in the narcissism of its own reflection. Rather, it is suspended in a difficult moment between knowledge and blockage, thrust into an experience of density and amorphism, even as it is left before an external surface that is, to all intents and purposes, nothing more than a two-dimensional simulacrum of interior space.

The qualities of estrangement that result are, on one level, similar to the uncanny effects of all mirroring, apparent to writers from Hoffmann to Maupassant. In the latter's story "Le Horla" (1887), which served as an exemplary model for Otto Rank in his book The Double, the narrator is tormented by the thought that he is ever accompanied by an invisible other, a spirit that he cannot see but that nevertheless resides in his house, drinks his wine, controls his actions and thoughts; he is obsessed with the idea of catching it out, often running into his room in order to seize his mysterious double and kill it. Once, on an impulse, he turned around quickly, to face a tall wardrobe with a mirror; but, as he recalled, "I did not see myself in my mirror. The glass was empty, clear, deep, brightly lit, but my reflection was missing, though I was standing where it would be cast." Then, after gazing at this large clear mirrored surface from top to bottom for some time, he was terrified, for "suddenly I saw myself in a mist in the center of the mirror, through a sort of watery veil; and it seemed to me as if the water were slipping very slowly from left to right." Convinced he had seen his double, he develops a case of what, in the context of our analysis, might be called advanced agoraphobia: barricading the windows and doors of his room with iron; leaving and setting fire to the room in order to kill the apparently trapped other. But beset with doubts as to whether he had actually killed this invisible specter, he was finally forced to kill himself.[16]

Such themes of mirror reflection and its uncanny effects were noted by Freud, who tells the amusing but disturbing story of sitting alone in his compartment in a wagon-lit, when a jolt of the train caused the door of his washing cabinet to swing open; "an elderly gentleman in a dressing gown and traveling cap came in." Jumping up angrily to protest this unwonted intrusion, Freud at once realized to his dismay "that the intruder was nothing but my own reflection in the looking glass of the open door. I can still recollect that I thoroughly disliked his appearance" (U 244). Interpreting this scene, Sarah Kofman has concluded:

Repetition, like repression, is originary, and serves to fill an originary lack as well as to veil it: the double does not double a presence but rather supplements it, allowing one to read, as in a mirror, originary "difference," castration, death, and at the same time the necessity of erasing them.[17]

The psychoanalyst Mahmoud Sami-Ali has gone further in explaining this association of the uncanny with reflection, taking Lacan's notion of the mirror stage and arguing that the proximity, noted by Freud, of the familiar and the strange causes "a profound modification of the object, which from the familiar is transformed into the strange, and as strange something that provokes disquiet because of its absolute proximity." Sami-Ali proposes that space itself is deformed by this experience. If, as Freud had implied, "the feeling of the uncanny implies the return to that particular organization of space where everything is reduced to inside and outside and where the inside is also the outside," then the space of the mirror would precisely meet this condition: a space of normal binocular, three-dimensional vision, modified by being deprived of depth. This would lead to the conflation, on the same visual plane, of the familiar (seen) and the strange (projected). In the case of the mirror stage, this would involve a complex superimposition of the reflected image of the subject and, conflated with this, the projected image of the subject's desire—the other: "Being simultaneously itself and the other, familiar and nevertheless strange, the subject is that which has no face and whose face exists from the point of view of the other."[18]

But, while the presence of such an uncanny in Koolhaas's library project is undeniable, we have yet to account for its equally evident refusal of mirroring, its absorbency to both interior representation and external reflection. Here the unexpected manifestation of this as yet undefinable condition, erupting suddenly out of an apparently simple play of transparencies, should be distinguished from the qualities of reflectivity found in modernism as well as from any "postmodern" surface play of simultaneity and seduction. The architect allows us neither to stop at the surface nor to penetrate it, arresting us in a state of anxiety.

This condition seems to approximate not the mirror stage itself but that moment, described by Lacan, of the *accomplishment* of the stage. "This moment in which the mirror stage comes to an end inaugurates, through identification with the *imago* of the counterpart and the drama of primordial jealousy . . . the dialectic that will henceforth link the I to socially elaborated situations." Such socially elaborated situations were, he concluded, characterized by "paranoiac alienation, which dates from the deflection of the specular I into the social I.[19]

With this swerve from the self to the social, the subject is no longer content to interrogate its face in the mirror in the search for transparency of the soul but, following Lacan's deliberately chosen metaphor, desires to stage its self in its social relations. Here two-dimensional physiognomy, the representation of the "face," is transformed into the three-dimensional space of subjectivity, place for the staging of social activity. That is, the plane of the mirror becomes the space of a theater: "The *mirror stage* is a drama" asserts Lacan.[20]

In Lacan's wordplay, the mirror stage is staged, or, following the connotations of the French, the *stade* (or biological stage) acts in the space of a *stade* (or stadium):

The formation of the I is symbolized oneirically by a fortified camp, a stadium indeed—establishing, from the interior arena to its outer enclosure, its periphery of rubbish and marshes, two opposed fields of struggle where the subject is caught up in the quest for the lofty and distant chateau, whose form (sometimes juxtaposed in the same scenario) symbolizes the id in a striking fashion. And in the same way we find realized, here on the mental level, those structures of the fortified work the metaphor of which rises up spontaneously, and as a result of the very symptoms of the subject, to designate the mechanisms of inversion, of isolation, of reduplication, of annulation, of displacement, of obsessional neurosis.[21]

In this image of the self, fortified and surrounded by garbage dumps, staged in an arena, is established the parameters of what Victor Burgin in a recent article also following Lacan, has termed "paranoiac space."[22]

In the light of Rem Koolhaas's preoccupation, outlined in *Delirious New York*, with the "paranoid critical method" of Salvador Dalí, a method that anticipates Lacan's first publications on paranoia, we might be tempted to apply such a designation to the facade of the Koolhaas library project. The paranoiac space of the library would then be that which is staged through the anxiety instigated at its surface.

In his seminar on *angoisse* conducted between 1962 and 1963, Lacan himself tied anxiety directly to the experience of the uncanny, claiming, indeed, that it was through the very structure of the *unheimlich* that anxiety might be theorized. The "field of anxiety" is framed by the uncanny, so to speak, even as the uncanny itself is framed as a sudden apparition seen, as it were, through a window: "The horrible, the suspicious, the uncanny, everything by which we translate as we can into French this magisterial word 'unheimlich,' presenting itself through the skylights [lucarnes] by which it is framed, situates for us the field of anxiety." The notion of "suddenness," of the "all at once," is fundamental for Lacan in setting this scene of uncanny anxiety: "you will always find this term at the moment of entry of the phenomenon of the *unheimlich*!" In this space of the sudden, as in "that brief, quickly extinguished moment of anxiety" before the curtain goes up in the theater—the moment of the three taps of the conductor's baton—anxiety is framed; it is for a moment collapsed into waiting, preparation, "a state of alert." But, beyond the frame, anxiety is, in a real sense, in the frame; it is something already known, and therefore anticipated: "Anxiety is when, in this frame, something appears that was already there, much closer to the house, the *Heim*: the host." The host, suddenly appearing at the door of the home or on the scene of the stage, is both expected and hostile, foreign to and yet embedded in the house: "It is this rising up of the *heimlich* in the frame that is the phenomenon of anxiety."[23]

The anxiety of the subject confronted with the "soft" space of Koolhaas's surfaces is then the manifestation of an uncanny based on the newly formulated conditions of interiority and exteriority, where the "ghosting" of the functionalist "interior" on the exterior mirrors not the outward appearance of the subject but its own, now transparent biological interior. Paranoiac space is transformed then into panic space, where all limits become blurred in a thick, almost palpable substance that has substituted itself, almost imperceptibly, for traditional architecture.

Notes

1. François Delaporte, in *Disease and Civilization: The Cholera Epidemic in Paris, 1832*, trans. Arthur Goldhammer (Cambridge: MIT Press, 1986), characterized these realms as follows (p. 80): "Living conditions affect two distinct areas, one within the body, the other outside it: organic space and social space. Social space is the space within which the organism lives and labors, and the conditions of existence within that space—living conditions—determine the probability of life and death."
2. Michel Foucault, "The Eye of Power," in *Power/Knowledge: Selected Interviews and Other Writings 1972–1977*, ed. Colin Gordon (New York: Pantheon Books, 1980), pp. 153, 154.
3. Etienne-Louis Boullée, *Architecture. Essai sur l'art*, texts selected and presented by Jean-Marie Pérouse de Montclos (Paris: Hermann, 1968), p. 113.
4. Boullée, *Architecture*, pp. 136, 78.
5. Sarah Kofman, *The Childhood of Art: An Interpretation of Freud's Aesthetics*, trans. Winifred Woodhull (New York: Columbia University Press, 1988), p. 128.
6. Roger Caillois, "Mimicry and Legendary Psychasthenia," trans. John Shepley, in *October: The First Decade, 1976–1986*, ed. Annette Michelson, Rosalind Krauss, Douglas Crimp, and Joan Copjec (Cambridge: MIT Press, 1987), p. 70. Caillois's essay was first published

in *Le mythe et l'homme* (Paris: Gallimard, 1938), and in a shortened version in *Minotaure* a year before.

7. Caillois, "Mimicry and Legendary Psychasthenia," p. 72.

8. Eugène Minkowski, *Lived Time: Phenomenological and Psychopathological Studies*, trans. and with an introduction by Nancy Metzel (Evanston: Northwestern University Press, 1970), p. 427.

9. Caillois, "Mimicry and Legendary Psychasthenia," p. 72. Caillois is quoting from Eugene Minkowski, "Le temps vécu," *Etudes phénoménologiques et psychopathologiques* (Paris, 1933), pp. 382–398.

10. Sigfried Giedion, *Bauen in Frankreich* (Berlin, 1928), p. 85, quoted in Benjamin, *Passagen-Werk*, in *Gesammelte Schriften*, 7 vols., ed. Rolf Tiedemann and Hermann Schweppenhauser (Frankfurt: Suhrkamp, 1972ff.), 5:533.

11. Walter Benjamin, "Die Wiederkehr des Flaneurs," in *Gesammelte Schriften*, 3:168.

12. André Breton, *Nadja* (Paris: Gallimard, 1964), pp. 18–19.

13. Benjamin, "Surrealism," in *Reflections: Essays, Aphorisms, Autobiographical Writings*, ed. Peter Demetz, trans. Edmund Jephcott (New York: Harcourt Brace Jovanovich, 1978), p. 180.

14. Bataille, *Oeuvres complètes*, 9 vols. (Paris: Gallimard, 1970), 1:197.

15. Colin Rowe, "Transparency: Literal and Phenomenal" (with Robert Slutzky), in *The Mathematics of the Ideal Villa and Other Essays* (Cambridge: MIT Press, 1976), pp. 160–176.

16. Guy de Maupassant, "Le Horla," in *Le Horla et autres contes d'angoisse* (Paris: Garnier-Flammarion, 1984), pp. 77–80.

17. Kofman, *The Childhood of Art*, p. 128.

18. Mahmoud Sami-Ali, "L'espace de l'inquiétante étrangeté," *Nouvelle Revue de Psychanalyse* 9 (Spring 1974), pp. 33, 43.

19. Jacques Lacan, *Ecrits, a Selection*, trans. Alan Sheridan (New York: Norton, 1977), p. 5.

20. Lacan, *Ecrits*, p. 4.

21. Jacques Lacan, "Le stade du miroir," in *Ecrits*, 2 vols. (Paris: Seuil, 1966), 1:94, my translation.

22. Victor Burgin, "Paranoiac Space," *New Formations* 12 (Winter 1990), pp. 61–75.

23. Jacques Lacan, unpublished seminar, "L'angoisse," 19 December 1962.

Jennifer Bloomer   **"Abodes of Theory and Flesh: Tabbles of Bower"** *Assemblage* 17 (April 1992)

❙ *see* 642❙

Feminism in architecture theory began, like American "women's studies" generally, with the perception of the glaring absence of women's experiences, histories, and design projects from the history of architecture, and with attempts to fill in or set the record straight by resurrecting the work of women designers—their methods, materials, and sources—who had been ignored by the masculine canon. But the close involvement of architecture theory in the second half of the 1980s with the discourses of French deconstruction, literary theory, and psychoanalysis led another kind of feminist architecture theory to posit the feminine as that condition which is always already repressed, misrepresented, and violated in the very structure of architectural thought. Not only has "women's work" been marginalized and denigrated by architectural history, but even work by and about women has been reduced and distorted through phallocentric codes of analysis and production such as rationality, objectivity, hierarchies, dualisms, and conclusions. For male sexual identity (and by extension, the masculine canon) is based on the dualistic perception of the self and the "other"—she who lacks, she who is only absent—whom the masculine economy then seeks to reduce to sameness or complement.

What is called for, then, is a new architecture "written" out of the radical alterity of woman's difference, a "minor architecture" that reverses the traditional desire for identity and mastery,[1] an architecture that enunciates, against phallocentric thought, the sexual embodiment of woman as a general model of signification: *l'architecture féminine*, we might call it, following the model of *l'écriture féminine*—the architectural inscription of the "marked" sexual-textual body. For the structures of architectural signifying practices—based as they are on masculinity as an "unmarked" (presumed to be neutral) condition—are as reductive and oppressive as material and social structures, and the body is as much a text, a theory, as it is a piece of flesh.

Thus the appropriation and valorization of woman's bodily experiences in pregnancy and childbirth in Jennifer Bloomer's "Tabbles of Bower." Pregnancy is itself *prior* to the separation of the self and the other, a continuity of differentiated otherness within the self, a libidinal fusion that, importantly, cannot be presided over by the male gaze. Thus, too, her interest in allegory and metonymy over symbol and metaphor. For "the opposition of symbol and allegory involves the centered, bright unity of the one and the eccentric, dark assemblage of the other. . . . Allegory is the other."[2] Following from this interest is a concern for collaboration over individual authority, for detail, ornament, *supplément*, abjection, and in general the metonymy of "the not male, the not Caucasian, the not heterosexual, the not homeowner/head of house, the not Christian." Bloomer's characteristic excessive punning, etymological play, and oversupply of intertexts, and her deconstruction of boundaries between those texts and her architectural object ("theory and flesh"), refuse traditional modes of presentation and exegesis even at a stylistic level. In fact, Bloomer's texts achieve another level of emotional and epistemological significance when she performs them in public, using different accents, even different voices, to further articulate the material and make it more immediate.

It should be noted that, despite the inscription of a specifically feminine discourse, the terms masculine/feminine do not correspond to men/women as strictly biologically conceived. For Bloomer, intimations of an *architecture féminine* can be found in male authors like James Joyce, Walter Benjamin, and Jacques Derrida, who also seek to undermine phallocentric discourse. Nevertheless, the fearful threat of feminism to architecture and its theory as traditionally practiced is perhaps best put by Bloomer herself: "A feminist architecture is not architecture at all."[3]

Notes

1. See Jennifer Bloomer, *Architecture and the Text: The (S)crypts of Joyce and Piranesi* (New Haven: Yale University Press, 1993).
2. Ibid., p. 39.
3. Ibid., p. 142.

The bulk of this essay was written when I was pregnant with my second daughter. At the time, the fact of the pregnancy was so all-encompassing that I scarcely could see beyond my belly, and I used it as a structuring metaphor. A year later, I realize that the metaphor is, in an important sense, inappropriate. While the bearing of a child is an essentially hermetic and private enterprise, the production of this project has been thoroughly collaborative and has been possible only because of many individuals who have put untold hours, ideas, and material into it. It is that kind of production that necessitates a foregrounding of acknowledgments to the major collaborators—Nina Hofer, Mikesch Muecke, Bob Heilman, and Jimmie Harrison— and others to whom I am most grateful.

Style is an indispensable adjunct to architectural knowledge, and . . . the cultivation of a sense of appropriate detail is immensely more significant than any pursuit of pure 'proportion' or 'form.' . . . Only certain approaches to form and detail answer to the demands of the aesthetic sense, and these approaches all lead away from prevailing fashions to some more settled 'classical' style.
ROGER SCRUTON, *The Aesthetics of Architecture*

A true understanding of the self led us to uphold, not only the primacy of aesthetic values, but also the objectivity which they implicitly claim. It became possible to arrive at a conception of critical reasoning, reasoning which is at once aesthetic and moral but which remains, for all that, free from the taint of moralism. We were drawn tentatively to conclude that some ways of building are right, and others (including many that are currently practised) wrong.
SCRUTON, final paragraph of *The Aesthetics of Architecture*

To not be probative is to be trivial.
JEFFREY KIPNIS, from a conversation recorded in Chicago

Preface: To bring forth allegory as a construct for theory is to point to a deconstruction of theory itself and, particularly, to a disacknowledgment of the separability of theory and practice. Theory and practice are suspended in the construction; theory is embedded, or disseminated, in it. Uncircumscribed by such concepts as foundation, regulation, or validation, theory becomes a potentiality, a possible pattern; it is dynamic, tracing a fragmentary process of object making. This essay and the project it attends are about such a tracing; they are, as well, objects resulting from the process.

One of the moments when it becomes abundantly clear what a peculiar construct time is occurs during the so-called nine months in which one holds a tiny, developing project within one's own body. Toward the end, time, which yesterday flew like a hurricane, full of the debris of everyday life, flows like the proverbial molasses in January. And this restructuring of time does not go without its concomitant reconfiguration of space. By this I mean something beyond the very present fact that one can no longer reach the triangle on the far side of the drafting table or the normal–permanent-press–delicate button on the now distant horizon of the clothes drier. It is more metaphysical than that; it is how the space takes on an anticipatory otherness. I tell you (many of you I do not need to tell, for you know well already), the furniture waits. Stark, empty, ticking. Waiting, waiting, waiting for "something that is about to happen."[1]

In the room where my husband and I slept and waited, there is a particularly compelling piece of furniture on either side of our bed. On his side (the right, nearest the door), there is a small bench, which, when it is not festooned with cast-off underwear and socks, is recognizable as the handicraft of Gustav Stickley: a simple, unornamented dark-stained oak frame with recessed pad, cased in a rather overly sat-upon, tanned and oiled hide of a cow. On my side (the left, nearest the gapingly empty, nagging space of the bassinet), there is an ancient wicker rocker. Festooned with the elaborate twisting and interlacing lines and swollen rolled edges of its own structure, and not recognizable as the work of any proper name, it is known simply as "Miss Eleanor's Rocker." The fact of the matter is that both of these pieces belonged to Miss Eleanor in another place in time. Miss Eleanor, you see, was our child's great-grandmother's closest and dearest friend. In the Athens, Georgia, before REM and the B-52s were born, before their parents and even their grandparents were born.

A photograph of Miss Eleanor presents the very image of turn-of-the-century Southern femininity: young, demurely posed, eyes downcast, dressed in white, layers of fabric so fine it could float, edged with gossamer lace, lace that also encrusts her prettily held fan. Beneath the airiness and lightness of the fabric and facial expression, her body is deformed in the fashion of the time. Confined in a posttensioned construction of bone, metal, and fabric, her chest is thrust upward and outward from a waist so tiny it is no wonder Mr. Bishop's son fell in love with and married her. An entirely artificial construction, she, so beautiful and horrible it is hard to take your eyes away.

Miss Eleanor was given by her father (in marriage) to Mr. Bishop's son. Mr. Bishop had once owned the house on Milledge Avenue in Athens in which my child's great-grandfather and grandmother and father lived and grew up, the house that now hosts the Phi Mu sorority at the University of Georgia. Family legend has it that Mr. Bishop, having moved to Athens from Chicago on the advice of his physician, detested the un-Chicago-like summer browning of the grass on his lawn and ordered a railroad car of evergreen nutgrass shipped from Africa. The windborne seeds of the nutgrass carried it all over the South, where it is currently viewed as a great regional pest.

Before becoming an importer of deleterious plants, Mr. Bishop had been a Chicago merchant, the proprietor of A. Bishop and Company, purveyors of fine furs. Mr. Bishop sold habitable and ornamental constructions made from the hides of animals. And this is where the nine-months-plus "project," which I, my feet propped for leverage on the Stickley bench, now on many evenings soothe to sleep in Miss Eleanor's rocker, meets another project that has been inhabiting the same space in time.[2]

This other enterprise, the subject of this essay, is a project for and about Chicago and is an effect of the Great Fire of October 1871. Mr. Bishop provides a joint between the two. For Mr. Bishop and his hides survived the Great Fire. The story goes that Mr. Bishop, minding his store when the fire came whipping down the way, realized that he hadn't enough time to procure a conveyance to rescue his merchandise. In desperation, he offered one of the fleeing throng in the street outside a very large sum of money to dump the contents of his wagon, his own domestic treasures, and take on the furs. Keepsakes, heirlooms, and necessities went out; sable, mink, and chinchilla skins went in. Mr. Bishop and his furs set up shop in another part of Chicago before the smoke had cleared.[3]

I shall return to the fire and address a certain unconscionable domestic animal, the responsibility of a certain blameworthy housewife, that started it all. But first let us recall those two pieces of restive furniture, which, after all, were never presented as benign objects merely decorating this manuscript. You will remember that the one is solid, rectilinear, and sturdy, while the other is airy, curvaceous, and lacy. And so you will begin to perceive, had you not already, a certain dichotomy in the works, a duo that might be construed as some sort of metaphor, were one so disposed to do.

The ornament/structure pair has intrigued architects for many centuries and has certainly been a great architectural bugaboo of this one; and so I am by no means the first, nor will I be the last, to consider these, for some reason, uneasy bedfellows. I am not concerned with making yet another argument for the privileging of one over the other. What interests me is the why and how of the urge to privilege and the possibilities for architecture when this urge is absent. I am interested in how the work of Louis Sullivan that had more to do with structure (for example, the articulation of the basic structures of classical orders in the stacking of tall buildings or the development of the Chicago window and its freeing up of the structural frame to expose itself) has given greater weight to his reputation as the "dean of American architects" than has his prodigious body of work on ornament— for which the former has served more or less as an excuse to forgive. I am interested in how the pair ornament/structure has throughout the history of Western culture had an acritical relationship with the pair feminine/masculine and in the ramifications of this for architecture as cultural production. As Naomi Schor points out, neoclassical aesthetics and its successors are bound up in the conventions of classical rhetoric, in which the ornamental and the idea of feminine duplicity are practically synonymous:

This imaginary femininity weighs heavily on the fate of the detail as well as of the ornament in aesthetics, burdening them with the negative connotations of the feminine: the decorative, the natural, the impure, and the monstrous.[4]

A brief excursion into the work on ornament of two canonical architectural writers will suggest the particular territory. But I would like to suggest from the beginning that what is construed as "feminine" can also be read as a much broader category. For the duplicity and degeneracy of the feminine is a metaphor for many forms of alterity to the dominant. Throughout our project, this convention is mined and exploited. And so, in the Joycean (*Wakean*) mode, the not male, the not Caucasian, the not heterosexual, the not homeowner/head of house, the not Christian slide into identity under this metaphor.

In reading Alberti's *De re aedificatoria*, four of whose ten books are devoted to the subject of ornament, it is easy to construe ornament as a *supplément* to beauty. (I am using the French word *supplément* in the sense in which it is exploited by

Jacques Derrida: an entity that is added to another entity, which is both in excess of that to which it is added, that is, is excessive, and which by nature of being added points to, by supplying, a lack in the original entity.) In the Sixth Book, Alberti defines beauty as "that reasoned harmony of all the parts within a body, so that nothing may be added, taken away, or altered, but for the worse."[5] But he then goes on to state that

ornament may be defined as a form of auxiliary light and complement to beauty. From this it follows, I believe, that beauty is some inherent property, to be found suffused all through the body of that which may be called beautiful; whereas ornament, rather than being inherent, has the character of something attached or additional.[6]

Thus if the "inherent property" is a sufficient condition for beauty, ornament, as an addition that is for Alberti a positive one ("Who would not claim to dwell more comfortably between walls that are ornate . . . ?"),[7] at once is in excess of the conditions for beauty and points to a lack in the essentially beautiful (unornamented) object. A temporal condition is also suggested here: the beautiful object is beautiful prior to ornament. When ornament is added after the establishment of the beautiful object, there must logically be a slipping away of beauty, since, for the object to possess beauty in the first place, "nothing may be added . . . but for the worse." So when something (ornament) is added, the beautiful object becomes both worse (no longer its pure self) and better ("more delightful").

Our second canonical writer demonstrates great faith in the intimate connections of architecture with all aspects of cultural production, from ladies' fashion to plumbing. Adolf Loos, who as a young man visited Chicago for the World's Columbian Exposition of 1893, who remained in Chicago for some time thereafter, and who left an invisible mark on the history of the city with his entry to the Chicago Tribune Competition of 1923, is peculiarly incisive on the topic of ornament, femininity, nature, and degeneracy:

The lower the cultural level of a people, the more extravagant it is with its ornament, its decoration. The Indian covers every object, every boat, every oar, every arrow with layer upon layer of ornament. To see decoration as a sign of superiority means to stand at the level of the Indians. But we must overcome the Indian in us. The Indian says, "This woman is beautiful because she wears gold rings in her nose and ears." The man of high culture says, "This woman is beautiful because she does not wear rings in her nose and ears." To seek beauty only in form and not in ornament is the goal toward which all humanity is striving.[8]

Although Loos here indulges in the classical identification of the feminine and ornament, he elsewhere "excuses" woman for her barbaric degeneracy, claiming that, in turn-of-the-century European society, because of her forced economic dependency, woman must fetishistically adorn herself as a sexual object in order to "hold on to her place by the side of the big, strong man."[9] In the famous "Ornament and Crime" essay, Loos writes, "The urge to decorate one's face . . . is the babbling of painting. All art is erotic."[10] He goes on to explain how the first ornament ever invented, the cross, was pornographic in its intentions: "A horizontal line: the woman. A vertical line: the man penetrating her. The man who created this felt the same creative urge as Beethoven."[11] Regardless of what this wonderful passage tells us about Loos's own peculiar psychological makeup, it is of enormous import to the topic at hand because it marks a connection of the sacred/profane, writing, and ornament (alterity) in the tidy conjunction of a drawing, a hieroglyph that is also a symbol, that offers itself up, in oversignification, to florid undecidability. And this leads us directly into the territory of allegory.

Schor notes that

> the detail with an allegorical vocation is distinguished by its "oversignification" (Baudrillard); this is not a matter of realism, but of surrealism, if not hyperrealism. Finally, the allegorical detail is a disproportionately enlarged ornamental detail; bearing the seal of transcendence, it testifies to the loss of all transcendental signifieds in the modern period. In short, the modern allegorical detail is a parody of the traditional theological detail. It is the detail deserted by God [an un-Miesian detail, certainly]. . . . The allegorical detail is a disembodied and destabilized detail.[12]

Roger Scruton underscores this observation, from another viewpoint: "Certainly, there is nothing more meaningless or repulsive in architecture than detail used . . . outside the control of any governing conception or design."[13]

What happens when we assemble such Nietzschean details into construction?[14] The mode of such assembly must, to preserve the destabilized aspect of the detail, be something akin to collage. In writing of collage and allegory, the realm of both Walter Benjamin and Jacques Derrida, Gregory Ulmer cites Derrida on the resulting undecidability of reading the assembly that is a collage. Each heterogeneous element, or detail, of the collage, because of its position both as a fragment that can be connected to its original context and as a part of a new whole, shuttles between "presence and absence" and thus disallows a linear or univocal reading of the whole.[15]

The phenomenon cited by Schor and labeled "oversignification" by Baudrillard is one of the mechanisms of the *gram*, that which is to grammatology as the *sign* is to semiology. One of the corollaries of the *gram* as Derrida approaches it is the notion of the *supplément*. Ulmer notes that Craig Owens, in a definitive article linking the allegorical mode to postmodern art, identified allegory with the *supplément* and thus with writing, in its supplementarity to speech.[16] Of course, Benjamin had already made this correspondence when he identified baroque allegory with hieroglyphs and other forms of script.

In addressing objections to the possibility of sustaining the distinction that Owens drew—and that Derrida's work suggests—between the self-referential (through metaphor) image of modernism and the problematized reference of postmodernism, Ulmer rescues grammatology and, more important for present purposes, allegory as articulated and used by Benjamin and Derrida from the realm of formalism:

> Grammatology has emerged on the far side of the formalist crisis and developed a discourse which is fully referential, but referential in the manner of "narrative allegory" rather than of "allegoresis." "Allegoresis," the mode of commentary long practiced by traditional critics, "suspends" the surface of the text, applying a terminology of "verticalness, levels, hidden meaning, the hieratic difficulty of interpretation," whereas "narrative allegory" (practiced by post-critics) explores the literal—letteral—level of the language itself, in a horizontal investigation of the polysemous meanings simultaneously available in the words themselves—in etymologies and puns—and in the things the words name. . . . In short, narrative allegory favors the material of the signifier over the meanings of the signifieds.[17]

In tracking these possibilities in architecture, with its grand and enduring, however limited, canon of symbolic materiality, we are once again shuttling between: maintaining the veiled/layered possibilities of allegoresis while playing over them at the level of the detail with the tools of narrative allegory. This movement maintains the fetish: something, an absence, is being hidden here, but revealed at the same time that it is being covered up. The fetish apparatus is excessive to its object, and yet, in its addition, points to a lack in the object. This mechanism of simultaneous concealment and revelation is the mechanism of both fetishism and allegory, and it will be the connection through which to pursue a positive fetishism in architecture.[18]

Benjamin likens baroque allegory to texts written in intertwined Egyptian, Greek, and Christian pictorial languages. This kind of writing could provide, in addition to "a refuge for many ideas which people were reluctant to voice openly before princes," a place for theology to preserve the power of sacred things by embedding them in the profane.[19] Benjamin quotes Martin Opitz:

Because the earliest rude world was too crude and uncivilised and people could not therefore correctly grasp and understand the teachings of wisdom and heavenly things, wise men had to conceal and bury what they had discovered for the cultivation of the fear of God, morality, and good conduct, in rhymes and fables, to which the common people are disposed to listen.[20]

What lies hidden in the allegorical is theological, the sacred buried in the profane. But this aspect of the sacred, the spiritual, has been carved away properly from religion—now a cagey structure of domination. Mark Taylor observes,

Bataille maintains that art now provides a more effective access to the uncanny time-space of the sacred. . . . In Lascaux, or the Birth of Art, he argues that art "begins" in the bowels of mother earth. . . . From the beginning (if indeed there is a beginning), there is something grotto-esque and dirty about art. Bataille is convinced that the dirt of art's grotesque, subterranean "origin" can never be wiped away. Art [we might add architecture, "mother of the arts"], like religion, emerges from the filth of the sacred.[21]

Allegory for Benjamin, like the Dionysian orgy for Bataille, is a "harsh disturbance of the peace and a disruption of law and order" that occurs where the sacred and the profane are indistinguishable.[22] And this place can be allegorized (or emblematized) as allegory itself. Because in allegory "any person, any object, any relationship can mean absolutely anything else," the profane world—the material world—is rendered a world in which each person, object, or relationship is of no particular significance.[23] At the same time, these "things" that are used to signify acquire a power that locates them on a "higher plane," in the realm of the sacred. As Benjamin puts it, "Considered in allegorical terms, the profane world is both elevated and devalued."[24] This apparent paradox (which is, of course, not unrelated to supplementarity) is one of the processes at work in our project. The things of the conventionally constituted profane world of the other, in being foregrounded into signification, are brought out of convention into expression; that is, they are simultaneously elevated and devalued, shuttled between the sacred and the profane.

This phenomenon of foregrounding the profane world into signification in the domain of the sacred is also at work in George Hersey's The Lost Meaning of Classical Architecture. Hersey's thesis is that the elements of classical temples derive from the residual constructions of pagan sacrificial rites; more precisely, that the remains of the sacrificial victims and the accoutrements of the ritual as they were arranged about the sacred place constitute the origins of the structure and arrangement of ornamental parts of the Greek temple. Hersey carries out this work by way of rhetorical operations on the words for the various elements and their accepted as well as some creative (Viconian) etymologies. As in Vico's philosophy of history, words become the historical documents that provide evidence of the thesis. One example will remain germane to the larger topic at hand: In writing of the caryatid as woman punished for sexual misconduct, Hersey notes what he calls the trope between *caryatid* and *Corinthian*, which contains the phoneme *cor*, meaning both "heart" and "horn," body parts of a sacrificed animal.[25] Here language is a switching mechanism, a time machine. Regardless of how such creative scholarship and the ends to which it is applied might be judged, the fact remains that these kinds of moves, which treat words almost as material constructions themselves, suggest a methodology for assembling architectural material.

For an inhabitant of the Hellenistic world, the words "Doric," "echinus," or "Ionic fascia," in Greek, did not have the purely workaday associations they have for us. They suggested *bound and decorated victims, ribboned exuviae* set on high, gods, cults, *ancestors, colonies.* Temples were read as concretions of sacrificial matter, of the things that were put into graves and laid on walls and stelai [written]. This sense of architectural ornament is very different from the urge to beauty. But indeed the word ornament, in origin, has little to do with beauty. It means something or someone that has been equipped or prepared, like a hunter, soldier, or priest [or a woman, through fashion, makeup, jewelry, manners].[26]

Classical ornaments, for Hersey, are thus trophies/tropes of sacrifice. The assemblage of details in the project mimes this operation, but indulges in tropes of the tropes, letting them slide from their origins in classicism to become allegorical and richly undecidable (for instance, elements here both do and do not adhere to the ideas of the classical temple in Hersey's terms).

This exploration of and play in the territory between the sacred and the profane, sanctity and sensuality, links the project to baroque art and architecture.[27] A historical assemblage of the use of the word *baroque* serves as an approximate description of the aesthetic milieu in which it is situated:

The word *baroque* appeared in current speech in France at the end of the sixteenth century, to designate something unusual, bizarre, even badly made. Montaigne uses it in this sense in his *Essais.* It is still used by jewellers to describe those irregular pearls known . . . in Portuguese as *barroco*; in the mannerist and baroque periods these odd shapes were used . . . in precious settings to form figures of sirens, centaurs and other fabulous creatures.[28]

The Swiss historian Jacob Burckhardt characterized the baroque as "wild" and "barbarous" (think of Loos) when compared to the ideal beauty of the Renaissance. Quatremère de Quincy called it "bizarre to a degree," a definition that Francesco Milizia repeated. In the *Dictionnaire de la Musique*, Jean-Jacques Rousseau used it to suggest a "confused harmony." In the twentieth century, Benedetto Croce called it "the art of bad taste."[29] But it is the project's generative tie to baroque tragic drama, the *Trauerspiel*, the subject of Walter Benjamin's *Habilitationsschrift*, that is most profound:

The *Trauerspiel* . . . is not rooted in myth but in history. Historicity, with every implication of political-social texture and reference, generates both content and style. . . . The baroque dramatist clings fervently to the world. The *Trauerspiel* is countertranscendental; it celebrates the immanence of existence even where this existence is passed in torment. It is emphatically "mundane," earth-bound, corporeal.[30]

The Project
The project encompasses a constellation of barnaclelike corner structures that would explore the structure/ornament pair. This investigation enters into two significant territories. First, these structures are constituted as parasitical and habitable and are therefore, by conventional definition, both ornamental and structural; they exist in a realm of blurred boundaries. Second, they are constituted as structures of signifi-

cance; that is, they convey messages. They serve dual functions: as places for people who might otherwise be out on the street to rest or take shelter from bad weather and as signs of the condition of rampant homelessness in the city—at the most general level, they signify the presence of alterity to the status quo.

This project is figured as Louis Sullivan's revenge, a Louis Sullivan who serves as trope of the *alter*. Sullivan and "Dora," both of whose "unconscious" homosexual tendencies were treated—Dora's by Freud, Sullivan's by a herd of architectural historians—become tropes for each other.[31] They are connected as well through their given names, both of which allude to gold. The project of joyous revenge is also a twisted delivery of Adolf Loos's promise to the world, given when his entry to the Chicago Tribune Competition, an enormous black Doric column, failed to win: "The great, Greek Doric column will one day be built. If not in Chicago, then in another city. If not for the Chicago Tribune, then for someone else. If not by me, then by another architect."[32] This Greek gift, this (now) disseminated rage of Louis/Dora, this other Doric *colon*, by *other* architects, appears, mapped onto Chicago as a great mantle of Tabbles of Bower. The center of this maelstrom is the site of the Chicago Tribune Building.

The Structure of the Project

The generating structure of this collection of proposed constructions is a web with five major interconnecting nodes: colon, fire, cow, temple, and Dora. In this temporally perceived text it is impossible to denote sufficiently the flows among the nodes of the nonlinear structure. These flows are suggested below by lists of generative facts and ideas that adhere to each node and begin to build conduits among them—a process by which the (disordered) metaphoric is projected onto the metonymic structure of the project.

Colon

Colon, French for "column" or "order," is the surname of Cristóbal Colón, or Cristoforo Colombo, or Christopher Columbus, who "discovered" "America" in 1492. The colonization of the North American continent by Europeans, with its corollary displacement and murder of the human communities that occupied it, was the result of this "discovery," which was commemorated in 1893 by the World's Columbian Exposition in Chicago.

The root of the word *columba* is suggestive of color: *kel*, "blackness" or "grayness," and *umbra*, "shade"; thus the *columba*, the dove, is named by its color. Color is an omnipresent coding device of difference in this culture. Blondes. Blacks. Mulattoes. Pink is for girls; blue is for boys.

The first thing a person who is not an architect notices about a building is what color it is.
CRAIG SAPER, Assistant Professor of English, University of Pennsylvania

Chicago was first settled (in 1779) by Jean-Baptiste Pointe DuSable, a black man from Jamaica, who married a Native American woman after his arrival. At the World's Columbian Exposition, no reference was made to the contributions of African-Americans to the history of this country. Black women were not represented at the Women's Congresses. In reaction to this slight, Ida B. Wells founded the first Black Women's Club in Chicago in 1894.

The root *kel* also branches into words suggestive of "hill" or "prominence" (to stick out or project), producing "column," and "excel." George Hersey notes that the Greek *coria* connotes "hill, mound, blood clot, or altar."[33]

In Hersey's terms, we might also note that the caryatid both is and represents the colonization, or ordering, of the female.

Colony and *bucolic* share the same Indo-European root, *-kwel*, which suggests circling (of humans, on the one hand, of cows, on the other). Thus the Greek *-kolos*, "herd," and the Latin *colere*, "to cultivate" or "to inhabit." The Latin *colonus* is a farmer, for which the German word is *Bauer*. *Bau*, in the same language, is a building or construction.

In 1900, a full two decades before Loos conceived his Doric column, a monument commemorating the bicentenary of the founding of Detroit was in the works: a "proper" expression of Detroit, an erection, "the largest in the world," of a gigantic Doric column, from the top of which would spew a "great flame of natural gas, so characteristic of the West, and impossible elsewhere." "As though," Sullivan adds with derisive scatological humor, "there were not 'natural gas' enough in this Doric column itself."[34]

Dora died from cancer of the colon.

Fire

The balloon frame is one of two construction techniques to bracket the Great Chicago Fire of October 1871. To whom the credit for the invention of the balloon frame belongs seems open to question, but there is no doubt that it originated in Chicago. Called "Chicago construction" before the fire, it was praised as a significant technological event, allowing for the mass production of parts that unskilled labor could assemble into inexpensive housing. In this context, Sigfried Giedion deduces its invention in 1832 by one George W. Snow, a building contractor educated in civil engineering who owned the local lumber yard as well as a real estate business.[35] But the balloon frame, being light timber construction surrounded by lots of oxygen, is highly ignitable, as the Great Fire proved. In this context, its invention has been credited to a Mrs. Albertine Taylor in 1837, the year of Chicago's official founding.[36]

A second, more infamous woman is faulted with the fire's destruction: Mrs. Patrick O'Leary left a burning lantern in the shed that housed Mr. O'Leary's other dull-witted, and clumsy, domestic animal.

In the multitude of etchings that document the horror of the fire, it is virtually impossible to find a black face among the fleeing crowds, although this was the decade following the mass exodus of former slaves from the South to Chicago.

After the fire, a hundred thousand people were living on the streets. Wooden shanties were quickly thrown up in the corners of what had been cellars (providing two ready-made walls). In 1871 in Chicago, homelessness was an impetus to build.

Grotesquely shaped pieces of glass and iron, relics of the fire, were sold by children as a means of livelihood.

"Whether or not a cow did indeed kick over a lantern in the barn is impossible to say, but there were a cow and a lantern in the shed where the blaze started."[37]

Cow

All history looks pretty much the same to cows.
JOHN IRVING[38]

The cow represents a crucial joint, a turning of the corner, between the two American construction methods that originated in Chicago: balloon-frame construction and skeleton construction.

The Indo-European root of *corner* is *ker*, "horn," with derivatives that refer to horned animals, horn-shaped objects, and projecting parts. From *ker* come "cervix," "carrot," "rhinoceros," and "cerebrum." The corner, then, has intimate associations with grotesque body parts.

Cow O'Leary is but one among the many bovines important to Chicago's history: the millions that have populated the stockyards and made the transmogrifying journey through the slaughterhouses.

The Greek *bous* is an ox or cow. A trinity of bovinity underlies the *Chicago Tribune* and its site, smack in the middle of the black zone of the Great Fire.

The cow is a domesticated animal, used as a form of currency, an object of exchange. The cow is a gift, source, of milk or meat.

The verb *cow* comes from an Old Norse word meaning "to oppress." The verb is active, the noun the passive recipient. Through punning, the metonymic figure of the cow, her "udderness," oscillates to metaphor.

Everyone knows that cows are stupid, placid, contented, but sometimes stubborn.

The *American Heritage Dictionary* tells us that a cow is "a fat and slovenly woman." Charlotte Perkins Gilman writes,

The wild cow is a female. She has healthy calves, and milk enough for them. And that is all the femininity she needs. Otherwise than that she is bovine rather than feminine. She is a light, strong, swift, sinewy creature, able to run, jump, and fight, if necessary. We, for economic uses, have artificially developed the cow's capacity for producing milk. She has become a walking milk-machine, bred and tended to that express end, her value measured in quarts.[39]

Louis Sullivan himself offers a final insult to cows, when he uses them as metaphors for architects:

The Roman temple can no more exist in fact on Monroe Street, Chicago, U.S.A., than can Roman civilization exist there. Such a structure must of necessity be a simulacrum, a ghost. Of course you and I know well enough that the reason why the bank building is an imitation Roman temple is because it is easy and cheap to make that sort of thing—but the people at large do not know it. They do not know how easy it is for the architect to turn to a book of plates, pick out what he wants, and pass it on to a draughtsman who will *chew this particular architectural cud* for a stipend.[40]

In a declaration that underlines his personal penchant for simplicity without self-denial, Adolf Loos juxtaposed himself to those who would opt for decorated gourmet concoctions: "I eat roast beef."[41]

Temple

Temple comes from the Latin *templum*, which comes from a root meaning "to cut." *Templum* suggests both a place cut out (a special, sacred place) and a small piece of wood cut out from a larger one. Thus the manifestations of the English word *temple* as a container of the sacred and as the mundane device in a loom that keeps the cloth stretched to a consistent width are related.

My body is the temple of the Lord.
SHIRLEY COTHRAN, former Miss America

The metaphor of the body has persisted as a ruling paradigm throughout the history of Western architecture, but generally this has involved the image or figure of the (male) body, not an analogue of the body as a messy assemblage of flows, both material and immaterial.[42]

Consider the balloon frame of Mrs. Albertine Taylor. How easy it might be to see the economical beauty of the balloon frame as a construction while cleaning and gutting a chicken for Sunday dinner. Balloon-frame construction is a metonymy of the body: not the image of the body, but the stuff of the body. The economy, the *oikos*, of the body. This is neither the Renaissance body nor the Corbusian body.

In *Moby Dick*, Melville described a temple, "a Bower in the Arsacides," presided over by "my royal friend Tranquo, being gifted with a devout love for all matters of barbaric virtue." This temple was formed of the skeleton of a great sperm whale

all woven over with the vines, . . . with his head against a cocoa-nut tree, whose plumage-like, tufted droopings seemed his verdant jet. . . . The ribs were hung with trophies; the vertebrae were carved with Arsacidean annals in strange hieroglyphics; in the skull, the priests kept up an unextinguished aromatic flame, so that the mystic head again sent forth its vapory spout; while, suspended from a bough, the terrific lower jaw vibrated over all the devotees, like the hair-hung sword that so affrighted Damocles. . . . Life folded Death; Death trellised Life.[43]

Sullivan wrote of the Roman temple, "And so the temple was created by its own people; blood of their blood, flesh of their flesh, bone of their bone, and gold of their gold."[44]

The chrysalis, a body enclosure formed from the body's own secretions, receives its name from the Greek *khrusos*, "gold."

Interlude: Helen of Troy

One day, when this project was beginning, we chanced to find a very fat caterpillar in our herb garden. My husband thought it would be a fine lesson for nine-year-old Sarah to watch the caterpillar do what comes naturally and put it in a large glass jar in our kitchen window. The skin of the caterpillar was so beautifully variegated with subtle spots of color that we named her Helen of Troy. Over the next few weeks, Helen of Troy consumed all of our garden's dill (her herb of choice), generously placed bit by bit in the jar by her human servants, and she grew even more enormous. One afternoon, I returned home from an out-of-town trip to discover Helen missing from the jar; in a distressed state, I called my husband to report this wretched fact. "Look more closely," he advised. I returned to the kitchen window and, after puzzling over the clearly caterpillarless jar for a moment, discovered, eight inches above, just on the corner of the window frame, adhering to the intricacies of the wooden molding, a magnificent construction: a symmetrical, grotesque golden-grey figure, the head piece bowing out vertiginously from the frame, but held in place by a gossamer cable suspended from above. The chrysalis of Helen of Troy. A barnaclelike corner construction with a body inside. And two weeks later, the wet, messy emergence of the imago.

Dora/Doric/D'or

Dora, like the original Helen of Troy, was treated by her father as an object of exchange, as a gift, as gold.[45] In 1900 Freud was treating her hysterical symptoms, including respiratory problems and "unconscious lesbian tendencies":

The hysterical symptom arises as a compromise between two opposing affects or instinctual trends, of which one is attempting to express a partial impulse or component of the sexual constitution, while the other tries to suppress it.[46]

"Dora" was the pseudonym for a young woman whose real name was Ida Bauer. The Middle English *bour* means a "dwelling" or "inner apartment." A bower is an inner chamber, locked up, where family secrets are encrypted. When the chamber gets too full, it moves around; this is the classical cause of hysteria, or "wandering womb." A bower is also "a shaded, leafy recess, an arbor," and "a private chamber, a boudoir."[47]

771 BLOOMER | 1992 | 771

Dora's mother suffered from what Freud termed "housewife's psychosis," an obsession with keeping things clean so absolute that she ignored the "needs" and behavior of her husband and the plight of her daughter. (It was her fault.)

Doric is the adjectival form of Dora. Loos's great Doric column, now readable as Dora's missing phallus, becomes Sullivan's return of the repressed. This project takes up Louis's beef with classicism and, through Hersey, meets it on its own terms in a doubling, reversing move.

As Dora's death returns us to *colon*: Hersey notes the positions of women's arms in the *caryatis* dance: "The women raised their arms during the dance, just as women at sacrifices raised theirs when the god came into their presence."[48] He goes on to show the connection between the raised arms of the dancers and the body motion of supporting weight. (In another story, the origin of the caryatid lies in the depiction of the punishment inflicted by the Caryan men on the Caryan women, who took rape over death when given the choice by invading troops: they were pilloried and forced to hold heavy weights over their heads for extended periods of time in the public gathering place). In this context, it is intriguing to note Freud's interpretation of one of the symptoms of the "hysterical attack":

For instance, in an hysterical attack an embrace may be represented by the arms being drawn back convulsively until the hands meet above the spinal column. Possibly the well-known *arc de cercle* of major hysterical attacks is nothing but an energetic disavowal of this kind, by antagonistic innervation of the position suitable for sexual intercourse.[49]

Parts of the Project

Amulets

The stone is the conventional emblem of the allegorist; its ponderous inertia is associated with melancholy, the allegorist's temperamental attribute.[50] With its grand tradition of stone piling, architecture is thus always already an allegorical enterprise. In the generation of this project, stones (bits of material from which architecture is made) take the form of amulets called *fascini*. The *fascinus* is defined as an amulet made in the shape of a phallus, whose power is directed toward holding motionless (like a stone) under a spell. (This is the root of the word *fascinate*. Fascination is traditionally held as the province of a woman—or other beautiful object—and often associated with evil: bewitchment. A *fascinator* is a woman's head covering made of net or lace.)

The *fascini* serve as tiny generative models for the project, bits of three-dimensional research that explore the possibilities of barnacle construction that emerge from Sullivan's work. These amulets are shaped with thought not to form, but *technique*. The techniques derive from Sullivan: symmetrical placement of parts, interweaving, swirling, overlay, repetitious alternation, use of organic material. The materials come from the everyday domestic sphere, much having to do with ornamenting the body: copper and brass wire, buttons, beads, baubles, hooks, eyes, straps, false fingernails, makeup, hair, ribbons, lace, thread, shells, feathers, and bones.[51] The amulets are fetishes, beautiful ornamental objects, and they are connected to the fetishism of architectural representation.

Drawings

Three kinds of drawings are at work in the project. Two are tools: sketchbook drawings, which examine and document construction techniques, signification of material, and form; and "shop" drawings, from which a full-scale construction was built. The third, "dirty" drawings, document the project ex post facto. The dirty drawing aims both to exploit the power of the pornographic image and to mark the connection between it and the conventions of architectural representation. It occupies the territory between a working drawing and a pornographic photograph (I have in mind that famous, lush image of the flesh of Marilyn Monroe dished up on red satin). Thus it is both technically correct and "improperly" ornamental. In its oscillation between poles that might be considered those of sanctity and sensuality, and in its bizarre and emphatic mundaneness, the dirty drawing is baroque. The dirty drawing addresses architectural representation by colliding the rendering with the working drawing (the sacred with the profane), while at the same time pointing to the fetishistic role of the image in architecture. It comments as well on the contemporary phenomenon of the architectural drawing as art commodity.

Full-Scale Construction

The full-scale demonstrative construction is an assemblage of thirteen allegorical details that together form a laboratory condition of the project as a whole. The thirteen parts are the residual of an exploration of techniques of blurring the ornament/structure boundary that would be used in building the corner barnacles. In their assemblage, they serve as an exhibitional armature for models and drawings, as well as an allegorical emblem of the Tabbles of Bower.

Thirteen Parts of the Construction
Cowslab

The cowslab constitutes the floor of the construction. It is a two-and-a-half-inch-thick concrete slab in the shape of two cows placed nose-to-nose, miming the symmetrical form of Louis Sullivan's seedpod motif and recalling his use of paired animals at the corners of buildings. The figure of the cows comes from a photograph that appeared on the front page of the *Gainesville* (Florida) *Sun*, depicting the plight of two cows that had fallen into a sinkhole, a ubiquitous local geological condition.[52] Each cow has been divided into four sections, suggestive of the drawings that demonstrate how cows become cuts of beef. Their bellies have been incised with slits to receive the door posts. The cows are gilded, for they are golden calves. The undulatory orifice between them is filled with red seed.

Hersey writes, "Let us note that many of these myths about reconstructed victims are foundation myths for religious rituals; in other words, they are a precondition for the erection of temples."[53]

"Dirty" drawing

Cowhide

A map of the project has been "drawn" on a cowhide suspended belly out and down from a lacy steel frame before and above the opening into the construction. The frame, welded together from short lengths of # 2 rebar,[54] then wrapped in treated muslin and coated in shellac, is modeled on a hybrid of bustle and steel-bridge construction (back-to-back camelback trusses triangulated so as to accommodate the bending moment of swinging bridges). It bears traces of Sullivan's tympana, mammalian skeletons, and the imago, the ultimate state of the chrysalis. It is bound in the position of a vertiginous canopy by a steel centerline, which is stabilized laterally by tension cables emerging from the bases of two concrete (tabby) columns, and from which suspends a great, ornamental plumb bob that maintains the steel frame in tension.

The cowhide map connects simultaneously to the traditional drawing medium of parchment (the skin of a sheep or goat) and to the "ribboned" exuviae to which Hersey refers. It merges as well with one of the famous constructions of Daedalus, "the first architect," the hollow cow that he made for Pasiphae to facilitate her copulation with the father of the Minotaur.[55]

The cowhide was a weapon of braided leather, related to the cat-o'-nine-tails, used to beat disobedient slaves during the considerable portion of the history of this continent given over to slavery's exploitation.

Upon the cowhide are superimposed three maps of different scales:

First, a map of the earth, cut as a globe's surface must be in order to render it flat (as well as the skin of the cow, which, after all, is not a two-dimensional animal).[56] This map, however, is "cut" so that all the oceans remain intact as one body of water, reconfiguring the continents so as to fling them, unfamiliar, to the edges of the map. The oceans are depicted as flows painted into the twisted cow hair in gold. On the now marginal scraps of land are mapped, in their correct locations, the origins of all the stony fragments embedded in the base of the Chicago Tribune Building. Each origin is denoted by a gold map tack punched through the hide and secured on the back by an earring post.

Second, a map of the Chicago Loop, North Michigan Avenue, and the surrounds as far north as Lincoln Park. This map consists of the points of the street intersections marked by brass fishhooks. Particular historical sites germane to the project (the locations of Sullivan's buildings both extant and demolished, for example) are noted by amulets suspended from the hooks. The remainder of the hooks are embedded in "Cretan skirts," small corks coated in sea-green wax and wrapped and knotted with delicate brass wire: lures. The whorl from which the hair pattern originates locates the Tribune Building. The longer white hair that occurs on the hide at what was the back of the cow indicates the flow of the Chicago River. Its length is exaggerated by being twisted and braided into a large *fascinus* full of signifying accretions, at once bringing the Chicago River into identity with the feminine figure of *Finnegans Wake*, Anna Livia Plurabelle, the River Liffey, and all others,[57] and underlining Freud's explanation for women's one contribution to the industry of civilization, weaving.[58]

Third, a map of a Sullivanian tympanum woven in brass wire as an exoskeleton over the entire belly of the hide.

When we first went to Mr. L's, they had a cowhide which she used to inflict on a little slave girl she previously owned, nearly every night. . . . As they stinted us for food my mother roasted the cowhide. It was rather poor picking, but it was the last cowhide my mother ever had an opportunity to cook while we remained in his family.
MATTIE JACKSON[59]

Cornerstone

The stone which the builders refused is become the headstone of the corner.
PSALMS 118:22

The steel cornerstone,[60] which forms the common nose of the two cows of the cow-slab (or the germ of Sullivan's seedpod), takes the shape of an extruded plan of a *vesica piscis*, the fish's bladder, a Euclidean device for the generation of an equilateral triangle. One side of the *vesica* extrudes more than the other. The cornerstone was lined inside with small copper tubes to receive the warp of the interior mantle;[61] it was then filled with Portland cement and topped off with plaster carved in significant relief and encrusted with gilded seeds.

No house worth living in has for its cornerstone the hunger of those who built it.
URSULA LEGUIN[62]

Maple Frame

The framing condition that occurs at the corner is suggestive of a balloon frame, but clearly is not. Maple members of graduated sizes that have been planed, beveled, sanded, and given nine coats of tung oil form the L-shaped frame, which is assembled with cross-lapped joints and with perforated end-lap joints at the corner, where it is suspended above the center point of the cornerstone. The vertical members, on the interior, are ten feet eight and a half inches tall; the horizontal members, on the exterior, are five feet two inches long. The geometry of the structure derives from the layers of a local geological catastrophe called the Devil's Millhopper, a sinkhole that has fallen thirteen times and has as many distinct layers.[63] The cross-lapped joints are bound by nylon and cotton cord dyed scarlet, evocative of flayed flesh, tied with surgeon's knots, and wrapped with brass wire. These bindings provide points of attachment for the armature of the interior mantle.

Tabby Columns

This first of two pairs of *colons* is described by a word, *tabby*, that refers at the primary level to the material from which the columns are built. Tabby is a type of concrete that has long been used in domestic construction in the southeastern coastal regions of the United States, a concrete the aggregate of which comprises oyster shells. The surfaces of tabby walls have a sensuous texture and a faintly pearlescent glow in dim light. *Tabby* also means "a rich watered silk," "a plain weave fabric," "a striped or brindled domestic cat," "a female domestic cat," "an old maid," and "a prying woman," "a gossip" (who chatters or babbles).[64] In a word, then: material, pattern, weave, domestic animal, derogatory female stereotype referring to domestic animal. The domestic animal is Louis Sullivan's cat. Tabby houses are cat houses.

Each column is in plan an irregular segment of a circle and consists of seven segments of reinforced concrete of varying sinkhole-derived heights. It was poured into a horizontal Sonotube with six particle board dividers and styrofoam ribs laid in to create the slots and ledges into/onto which the maple frame members and bony ribs rest. The tabby column is a receiver of ribs. Before the pour, the tube was prepared by smearing on a three-eighths-inch layer of clay into which the ornamental aggregate was laid (crisscrossing lines of buttons with intersections marked by alligator vertebrae and thirteen layers of aggregate representative of the constituents of the Millhopper's geological layers—coal, bone, terra-cotta, phosphorescent marbles, glass, shell). Over this a coating of ground graphite was distributed in a tabby pattern. The segments were then reinforced with chicken wire and the concrete poured. As it began to set up, a quarter-inch layer of cement and plaster pigmented grey was poured onto the concrete, to create a smooth drawing surface on one side of each column.

The heavy concrete column is the least stable part of the construction; because of its slender proportions, it relies on structural bracing by other parts (the cowhide map frame, the maple frame, and the door) for its stability. Its seven segments are strung, like beads, on a threaded posttensioning rod, which fits into a steel base through whose slots it is tightened. The base is filled with grotesquerie ("base" objects). The cap of the rod emerges from a flat perforated steel top plate, from which also spring seven bound # 2 rebars. Some provide lateral bracing for the cowhide map frame, the others simply quiver and tremble in space, like insect antennae.

Tower of Babel, or Lallypop, Columns

The base of each of these columns is a steel disc to which has been welded, on the one side, a short steel post that may be inserted into any one of the belly slits of the cowslab and, on the other, a threaded steel tube that receives a large eye screw. Onto the eye screw are bound eighteen lengths of twisted copper wire that have been threaded up through the shaft of a seven-foot Lally column. From six trios of wire are suspended, at intervals corresponding to the ribs of the door, six steel rings with protruding double ribs. Like all the steel elements, the column shafts and rings have been ground and polished, rubbed with asphaltum in a tabby pattern, and given three coats of polyurethane. The result is a staged pole festooned with decreasing densities of wire, formally suggestive in many directions.

The Tower of Babel emblematizes the relationship among architecture, language, the sacred, and the profane.

Remember Loos's dictum: "The urge to decorate one's face and everything in reach . . . is the babbling of painting. All art is erotic."[65]

Column Capitals

The column capitals function as pads over which the tension wires traverse the verges of the shafts. Their undecidability is clear: udders, Medusas, fingers, sea anemones, the feeders of the barnacle, Vitruvius's tale of the origin of the Corinthian column, hysterical catalepsies. Fashioned from pink lycra spandex using a newspaper pattern cut from the stock market page, stitched, and stuffed with quilt batting, the capitals were then reinforced with steel wire and beeswax and bound to the lallypops with lead fillets. The "fingers" are covered with gold reinforcing rings.

Dory Door

Although he claimed to call "un chat un chat," Freud made much of the metaphor of door and key as displacements of certain gendered body parts. In this project, the door, which opens onto Dora, Doric, and D'or,[66] is figured as an unsullied object of exchange: a figure in white on the outside that, once entered, shifts to living color. This door is assembled from the sides of a dory, a boat with deep sides and a V-shaped transom; only, not having access to a dory, we have salvaged a cast-off flat-bottomed boat and rendered it a dory otherwise.[67]

Fiberglass resin reinforces the sides of the boat. All barnacles have been lovingly retained. Ribs and straps attach to the structural ribs of the boat; the steel footing of each side, fitted with a rolling caster to allow the door to move, is bolted in place. The exterior of each side has been coated with two layers of fine white papier-mâché, sanded down to reveal the barest top layer of the bare boat, then covered with an elegant lace pattern of a ghostly grey. An astute observer will recognize this pattern as that of the "bad ornament" of Louis Sullivan, the pattern on the soffits of the arches at the National Farmers' Bank at Owatonna, Minnesota.[68]

This door swings both ways.

V-Shaped Transom

The addition of the transom makes the boat a proper dory and the door a proper door. The transom is a pink triangle of lace stretched and bound within a V-shaped portion of the steel frame from which the cowhide map is suspended.

Ribs and Straps

Two series of bonelike ribs, one long and one short, secure the sides of the dory to the babel columns on one side and to the tabby columns on the other. The ribs are constructed from flat steel plates to which wood strips have been epoxied, smoothed over with joint compound, wrapped in gauze soaked in wood glue, then slathered with alternating layers of a fine but strong papier-mâché and amber shellac. They have been sanded, incised, and wrapped in "Hot Mama Pink" cord triangles. The steel plates protrude slightly from each end and are here perforated for receiving bolts and hinges. The ribs are kept in place by "Hot Mama Pink" resin-reinforced canvas sleeves held in suspension by "Hot Mama Pink" nylon straps bolted to the boat structure and secured with rows of aluminum angles—a brassiere-inspired detail.

Mantle

The mantle forms the interior lining of the construction. It suggests the mantle of the barnacle, the middle of its three layers, which generates the outer shell. Related etymologically to *mantilla*, it is a lacelike textile: "Lace: . . . [Middle English *lace, laas, las,* ornamental braid, cord, from Old French *laz, las,* from Vulgar Latin *lacium* (unattested), from Latin *laqueus,* noose, trap, probably related to *lacere,* to allure. See delight]."[69]

  An interior frame of bustlelike construction supports this diaphanous cocoon of white organza; wrapped aluminum ribs tie into three vertical wrapped wooden busks from which the swaths, "laced with gilt," radiate.[70]

  "Freud's project was to dismantle Dora's anger."[71]

  "The master's tools will never dismantle the master's house."[72]

Plumb Bob

This large and heavy amulet serves as the counterweight to the cowhide in its bony steel frame. It is formed of sea detritus—an ancient buoy filled with concrete and sea glass—and petrified mammoth bones, held together by a crocheted mantle of brass wire and glass beads from which hang other small accretions. Referring both to the *cathetos,* the invention of Daedalus, and to the "dead man" of conventional construction, it is also a bower, the heaviest anchor on a sea-going vessel. Cantilevered and suspended away from the corner of the construction, it is a lure and a lodestone.

Guided by the wondrous North Star, that blessed lodestone of a slave people, my mother finally reached Chicago.
LUCY A. DELANEY[73]

Centerline

Swerving out of the center of the steel frame, a twenty-foot-long bundle of gilded steel pipe and # 2 rebar marks the centerline of the construction. It rests on a wooden cradle-shaped acroterion atop the corner of the maple frame and projects, tail-like, behind to support the plumb bob. This counterweighting assemblage keeps the cowhide's steel frame, through which it is threaded, in place. The repetitive bindings of brass wire that hold it together consist formally of short and long segments (dots and dashes) that both identify it as the centerline and encode half of the key to the project.[74]

Postface. The building, or any other artifact of the creative impulse seen as offspring, as childbearing surrogate, is clean, whole, and ordered. It appears, complete and full-blown, at the end of an uncertain period of gestation. The "real thing" is not only a triumphant production of a complete, but still-developing project at the end of nine months, but a messy, bloody, erotic event. An other architecture is an architecture of abjection (the thrown away). At the moment of birth, the body gives forth excrement, vomit, blood, mucous, as well as a human being. Abject offerings, gifts, they are the products of flows. The abject products of the body might be metaphorized in the abject products of the body politic—detritus of street and home—toward a project of positive fetishizing, supplementing excrement, vomit, and blood to the phallus.

P. S. On 8 April 1991 Laura Barrett Bloomer-Segrest emerged, wet and messy, fearless and hungry.[75] Both projects continue in ever-unfolding collaborations.

Notes
1. The words of Aldo Rossi, now well-worn by a generation of architecture students.
2. I have been criticized for using the word *project* on the basis of its "phallocentrism." Although I prefer the words *construction* and *assemblage* to refer to complex inventions of various media, I have chosen here to remain within the convention of architecture that maintains a distinction between a project (unbuilt) and a construction (built).
3. I am grateful to Laura Ann Segrest, my mother-in-law, for the story of Mr. Bishop and his furs.
4. Naomi Schor, *Reading in Detail: Aesthetics and the Feminine* (New York: Methuen, 1987), p. 45.
5. Leon Battista Alberti, *On the Art of Building in Ten Books* (c. 1450), trans. Joseph Rykwert, Neil Leach, and Robert Tavernor (Cambridge: MIT Press, 1988), p. 156.
6. Ibid.
7. Ibid.
8. Adolf Loos, "The Luxury Vehicle" (1898) in *Spoken into the Void: Collected Essays 1897–1900*, trans. Jane O. Newman and John H. Smith (Cambridge: MIT Press, 1982), p. 40.
9. Adolf Loos, "Ladies' Fashion" (1898) in *Spoken into the Void*, p. 103. Note that this passage reiterates the gendering of the ornament/structure pair.
10. Adolf Loos, "Ornament and Crime" (1908), in Yehuda Safran and Wilfried Wang, eds., *The Architecture of Adolf Loos*, exhibition catalogue (London: London Arts Council, 1987), p. 100.
11. Ibid.
12. Schor, *Reading in Detail*, p. 61.
13. Roger Scruton, *The Aesthetics of Architecture* (Princeton: Princeton University Press, 1979), p. 207.
14. In the present context, it is interesting to note the closing of Nietzsche's preface to the 1887 edition of *On the Genealogy of Morals*, where he writes of the need to decipher, not simply to read, his work: "To be sure, one thing is necessary above all if one is to practice reading as an art in this way, something that has been unlearned most thoroughly nowadays—and therefore it will be some time before my writings are 'readable'—something for which one has almost to be a cow and in any case not a 'modern man': *rumination.*" Friedrich Nietzsche, *On the Genealogy of Morals*, trans. Walter Kaufmann and R. J. Hollingdale (New York: Vintage Books, 1969), 23.
15. Gregory Ulmer, "The Object of Post-Criticism," in Hal Foster, *The Anti-Aesthetic: Essays on Postmodern Culture* (Port Townsend, Washington: Bay Press, 1983), p. 88.
16. Craig Owens, "The Allegorical Impulse: Toward a Theory of Postmodernism," *October* 12 (Spring 1980), pp. 67–86, and 13 (Summer 1980), pp. 59–80.
17. Ulmer, "The Object of Post-Criticism," p. 95.
18. This is a concept I have explored at greater length in "Big Jugs," in *The Hysterical Male: New Feminist Theory*, ed. Arthur and Marilouise Kroker (New York: St. Martin's Press, 1991), to be reprinted in *Fetish: The Princeton Journal* 4 (forthcoming). Also see Ann Bergren's article "Mouseion," in the same journal, for a stunning map for positive fetishism.
19. Walter Benjamin, *The Origin of German Tragic Drama*, trans. John Osborne (London: New Left Books, 1977), p. 172.
20. Ibid.
21. Mark C. Taylor, *Altarity* (Chicago: University of Chicago Press, 1987), pp. 141–142.

22. Benjamin, *German Tragic Drama*, p. 177. Benjamin is here quoting Carl Horst.

23. Ibid., p. 175.

24. Ibid.

25. George Hersey, *The Lost Meaning of Classical Architecture: Speculations on Ornament from Vitruvius to Venturi* (Cambridge: MIT Press, 1989), pp. 72–73.

26. Ibid., p. 149 (emphasis mine).

27. Although Walter Benjamin's text on baroque drama articulates the notions of allegory that have informed my work over the last seven years, it took Laura Ann Segrest's sharp eye to bring to my attention the "baroqueness" of this project, and, once again, I am grateful to her.

28. Germain Bazin, *The Baroque: Principles, Styles, Modes, Themes* (London: Thames and Hudson, 1968), p. 15.

29. Ibid., pp. 15–17. It seems significant to the context of the work that Eugenio d'Ors was (along with Heinrich Wölfflin) one of the twentieth-century redeemers of the aesthetics of the baroque.

30. George Steiner, introduction to Benjamin, *German Tragic Drama*, p. 16.

31. Dora is the pseudonym of the subject of Freud's *Fragment of an Analysis of a Case of Hysteria* of 1905.

32. Safran and Wang, *The Architecture of Adolf Loos*, p. 60.

33. Hersey, *The Lost Meaning of Classical Architecture*, p. 71.

34. Louis H. Sullivan, "A Doric Column," in *Kindergarten Chats and Other Writings* (1918; reprint, New York: Dover Publications, 1979), p. 58. All citations but the last are Sullivan quoting the report of the architect of the Detroit monument.

35. Sigfried Giedion, *Space, Time and Architecture* (Cambridge: Harvard University Press, 1949), pp. 281–288.

36. This remarkable fact was unearthed by Nina Hofer.

37. David Lowe, *The Great Chicago Fire* (New York: Dover Publications, 1979), p. 1.

38. John Irving, *The One-Hundred-Fifty-Eight-Pound Marriage* (New York: Ballantine, 1990), p. 179.

39. Charlotte Perkins Gilman, *Women and Economics*, ed. Carl Degler (reprint, New York: Harper and Row, 1966), pp. 43–44.

40. Sullivan, "A Roman Temple (2)," in *Kindergarten Chats*, p. 39 (emphasis mine).

41. Loos, "Ornament and Crime," p. 101.

42. See Diana Agrest, "Architecture from Without: Body, Logic, and Sex," *Assemblage* 7 (October 1988), pp. 29–41.

43. Herman Melville, *Moby Dick* (1851; New York: Norton, 1976), pp. 441–443.

44. Sullivan, "A Roman Temple (1)," in *Kindergarten Chats*, p. 36.

45. At its simplest level, the story of Dora is one of an adolescent daughter being given to a man by her father in exchange for the man's wife. See Sigmund Freud, *Dora: An Analysis of a Case of Hysteria* (1905; New York: Macmillan, 1963).

46. Freud, *Dora*, p. 150.

47. *The American Heritage Dictionary.*

48. Hersey, *The Lost Meaning of Classical Architecture*, p. 72.

49. Freud, *Dora*, p. 154.

50. See Benjamin, *German Tragic Drama*.

51. Following some exploratory "exemplars" constructed by Nina Hofer and myself, the amulets, which number many dozen, were made one weekend by the graduate students whose names appear in my acknowledgments. Significantly, this endeavor changed its name from a "charrette" to a "bee" (as in a quilting bee or a barn-raising bee), which has a more domestic, mundane, and collective character associated with it. The bee also privileges *constructing* over *designing.*

52. I have explored the sinkhole, and its suggestions about vessels and voids, in "Big Jugs."

53. Hersey, *The Lost Meaning of Classical Architecture*, p. 16.

54. One of the more satisfying discoveries of this project was the liberating potential of "drawing in the air," that is, producing with these quarter-inch strands of steel and an arc welder large three-dimensional line drawings that inscribe a spatiality unapproachable with ink or even computer drawings.

55. A canny move on the part of Daedalus, as it necessitated an even larger commission: to design the labyrinth to contain the horrible offspring of this coupling.

56. I would like to thank Jimmie Harrison for pointing this out to me as we pondered the relationship between the flat hide and the rounded form that it was to take.

57. A major methodological source of this project is the last work of James Joyce; it is also the generator and subject of *Desiring Architecture* (forthcoming from Yale University Press) in which I lay out the territory from which this material project emerges.

58. Freud's explanation was that woman invented weaving to mask what she lacks—plaiting her pubic hair into a masking phallus.

59. *Six Women's Slave Narratives, 1831–1909* (London: Oxford University Press, 1988), p. 10.

60. It is important to note that the major component of steel is iron, and this is all I shall have to say on that subject. Decoders will find here a secret as proper as the name of the father. *J'appelle un chatterer un chatterer.*

61. Note that the placing of a foundation stone is called "fixing the warp."

62. Ursula K. Le Guin, "Hunger," in *Dancing at the Edge of the World: Thoughts on Words, Women, Places* (New York: HarperCollins, 1990), p. 50.

63. The Devil's Millhopper also plays a large structuring role in "Greg Ulmer Reads Reading on TV," 1988, a videotape from Paper Tiger. The Millhopper is present in the project as a structurally suggestive "other" to the Great Doric Column.

64. *The American Heritage Dictionary.*

65. Loos, "Ornament and Crime," p. 100.

66. I explore the further ramifications of D'or in a companion piece to this, "D'Or," in *Sexuality and Space*, ed. Beatriz Colomina (New York: Princeton Architectural Press, 1992).

67. In editing this text, Alicia Kennedy has added another layer of brocade. She notes that the progenitrix of *dory* is a Moskito word for "dugout," a tree or log from which a section has been removed. Dory thus connects to colon and to temple; and, as significantly, to my collaborator Mikesch Muecke, whose surname is German for "mosquito."

68. This is the appraisal of George Elmslie, Sullivan's assistant and chief draftsman, who designed all the ornament for the National Farmers' Bank except this particular motif. The motif, significantly, involves a repetition of an OXOXOXOX pattern. The bank is also notable in this context for its large mural, which Sullivan commissioned from a Viennese painter named Oskar Gross; the mural depicts a herd of cows grazing. I am grateful to Amy Landesberg for bringing this cowfact to my attention. See Larry Millett, *The Curve of the Arch: The Story of Louis Sullivan's Owatonna Bank* (St. Paul: Minnesota Historical Society Press, 1985), pp. 80, 98.

69. *The American Heritage Dictionary.*

70. A busk is a thin strip of bone, wood, or metal that stiffens a woman's undergarments so that her body is held in its proper place.

71. From Philip Rieff's introduction to Freud, *Dora*, p. 13.

72. Audre Lord, "The Master's Tools Will Never Dismantle the Master's House," in *This Bridge Called My Back: Writings by Radical Women of Color*, ed. Cherrie Moraga and Gloria Anzaldua (New York: Kitchen Table: Women of Color Press, 1983), p. 99.

73. *Six Women's Slave Narratives*, p. 22.

74. The Morse Code centerline appears in one other location (on the door, in red, where it bisects the OXOXOXOX ornament) and there provides the other half of the key.

75. I thank Herb Gottfried for this perfect phrase.

R. E. Somol **"One or Several Masters?"** Paper presented at a colloquium at the Canadian

Centre for Architecture, Montreal, 1993; published in *Hejduk's Chronotope*,

ed. K. Michael Hays (New York: Princeton Architectural Press, 1996)

The architectural practices that constitute the American neo-avant-garde developed hand in hand with the reformation of architecture theory itself in what might properly be called the linguistic research of the 1960s and 1970s: the attempt not only to codify architecture as a language but, further, to collapse the distinction between the architectural object and the theoretical text. First, the identification of what counted as the architectural object was shifted away from a single, purely phenomenological mode of perception toward multiple and differentiated "textual" structures, resonances, and plays of signification (this had actually begun as early as John Hejduk's Texas houses in the mid-1950s and their textualization of the work of Mies and Le Corbusier). Simultaneously, as the newly constructed object-text's internal powers of constructing meaning and its intertextual plays were stressed, architects' written texts (expositions, interviews, poems, fictions) — formerly an appurtenance to the autonomous architectural object — took on the status of an equally important, interwoven object-text, a combination of a wide range of signs and codes. Nowhere is this more true than in the work of John Hejduk. Consequently, Robert Somol observes, "it is difficult to tell what does not count in the work of John Hejduk, to distinguish the central focus from the peripheral, the totality from the vignette."

    Architecture's urban vocation was theorized in this structuralist-formalist discourse as a liberal reconciliation of heterogeneity and autonomy or of fragmented, individual forms and events against a coordinating, grammatical ground, which in its canonical form, that of Colin Rowe's "collage city," manifested itself both physically and conceptually in a planimetric grid. Somol argues that Hejduk, in prosecuting his own architectural and urban tasks, turns this logic ninety degrees, as it were — from the figure-ground, plan gestalt of architectural collage to "the elevational pair subject-object" and from *langue* to *parole*, grammar to performance, grid to holey surface. What is thus initiated is not only a return to the positive narrative potentials of architecture after the structuralist-formalist prohibition but also the proposition of a radical figurality — a figurality without a ground — and an "urbanism" (if it is right to call it that) in which inhabitants are deterritorialized into their vocations, buildings likewise are exchangeable pieces of movable mechanical equipment, and the city itself becomes a smooth space of directional traces (both registering past events and projecting possible future ones) rather than a mensurable, regulating grid.

    This "elevational pair subject-object" must constantly produce itself, continually exchanging contexts, programs, subjects, and objects. It is a smooth screen of continuous narrative projection, which means that Hejduk's refusal to posit "solutions," on the order of architecture as social service, is integral to the new conception of time-space produced by his work. And it is important to add that this smooth space includes not only new forms of presentation of architectural concepts (through painting, scriptwriting, cryptography, cataloging, etc.), but also new forms of distribution in commercially mass-produced books (*Mask of Medusa, Vladivostok, Victims, Lancaster/Hanover Masque,* et al., which invariably are assigned the status of "works"), thus polemically, promiscuously affiliating the conventional

see Rowe and Koetter (**92 ff**)

spaces of architectural production, architectural publication, and commodity.[1] The very theatricality or boundary-displacing effects of these elements must be emphasized, for as Somol reminds us, it is the theatrical and aleatory nature of this architecture that bleeds off the autonomy and heroic monumentality of form — precisely those attributes that traditionally have been most valued.

It is in the same dissociation from Rowe and the politico-architectural model of one ground/many figures that Somol finds the possibility of a "minor urbanism," adapted from Gilles Deleuze and Félix Guattari's minor literature.[2] For if Hejduk's can be construed as an architecture where the reconciliation of the many within the one is dissolved into a state of the-many-becoming-one, then cannot the promise of his excessive, positively promiscuous affiliations be extended to the city itself?

Somol's essay stands as representative of what may well turn out to be a fundamental shift of interest in architecture theory, a quarter of a century after its inauguration: "While the first generation of the neo-avant-garde in the early 1960s began to investigate the *semiotics of form*, its progeny (specifically, in the generation that came of age after the events of May 1968) have indulged a *diagrammatics of function and structure*."[3] This shift does not entail an abandonment of the linguistic model, still less a retreat from the discourse of form, so much as an expansion of the model beyond the binary unit of the sign, a double articulation of expression and content, so that each term is understood to have both form and substance (the form *and* content of expression, the substance *and* form of content). A diagrammatics of function and structure would attend to the ways in which architecture organizes and distributes activities, events, and affects that are coextensive with the larger social field too often bracketed off by earlier formal models — this in an effort to "recuperate from tradition such formerly taboo topics as program, structure, materials, the body, context, and, most recently, the earth, the ground, and gravity itself."[4]

The notion of diagram is derived from Deleuze and Guattari's "abstract machine." For the influence that this concept continues to have on a generation of architecture theorists, it is worth an extended quotation.

We must say that the abstract machine is necessarily "much more" than language. When linguists (following Chomsky) rise to the idea of a purely language-based abstract machine, our immediate objection is that their machine, far from being too abstract, is not abstract enough because it is limited to the form of expression and to alleged universals that presuppose language. Abstracting content is an operation that appears all the more relative and inadequate when seen from the viewpoint of abstraction itself. A true abstract machine has no way of making a distinction within itself between a plane of expression and a plane of content because it draws a single plane of consistency, which in turn formalizes contents and expressions according to strata and reterritorializations. The abstract machine in itself is destratified, deterritorialized; it has no form of its own (much less substance) and makes no distinction within itself between content and expression, even though outside itself it presides over that distinction and distributes it in strata, domains, and territories. An abstract machine in itself is not physical or corporeal, any more than it is semiotic; it is *diagrammatic*. . . . It operates by *matter* [a substance that is unformed either physically or semiotically], not by substance [which is formed matter]; by *function* [which has only "traits"], not by form. Substances and forms are of expression "or" of content. But functions are not yet "semiotically" formed, and matters are not yet "physically" formed. The abstract machine is pure Matter-Function—a diagram independent of the forms and substances, expressions and contents it will distribute.[5]

Deleuze finds diagrams, for example, in Michel Foucault's analysis of disciplinary and punitive systems like Panopticism which "*impose a particular conduct on a particular human multiplicity*. We need only insist that the multiplicity is reduced and confined to a tight space and that the imposition of a form of conduct is done by distributing in space, laying out and serializing in time, composing in space-time, and so on. . . . [A diagram] is a machine that is almost blind and mute, even though it makes others see and speak."[6] Deleuze also finds diagrams in the paintings of Francis Bacon. Here the diagram is "the operative set of lines and areas, of asignifying and nonrepresentative brushstrokes and daubs of color. And the operation of the diagram, its function, as Bacon says, is to 'suggest.' Or, more rigorously, it is the introduction of 'possibilities of fact.'"[7] Neither abstract in the sense of Mondrian nor expressionist in the sense of action painting, Bacon's painting breaks from traditional figuration in order, exactly, to produce a new figure. "It is like the emergence of another world."

In one sense, perhaps any architecture is an abstract machine, insofar as any architecture enables certain functions and constrains others, produces certain effects and forecloses others. But the intensity with which certain recent architectures (including that of younger architect-theorists like Stan Allen and Greg Lynn) pursue this particular dimension of architecture must be underscored as a re-emergent desire stretching toward genuine *praxis*—the unity of theory and practice—which is also properly utopian. Once again Deleuze and Guattari: "The diagrammatic or abstract machine does not function to represent, even something real, but rather constructs a real that is yet to come, a new type of reality. Thus when it constitutes points of creation or potentiality it does not stand outside history but is instead always 'prior to' history."[8]

Notes

1. Part of what is meant by "promiscuous affiliation," a locution that arises often in discussions of the work of Hejduk, is simply that Hejduk's forms *create* categories that can then be filled by other items. For example, when you see a concrete column with reinforcing rods coming out of its top and think of an angel, or when you find that you notice water towers more than you used to, it's probably because of Hejduk's category-constitutive architecture.
2. Gilles Deleuze and Félix Guattari, *Kafka: Toward a Minor Literature*, trans. Dana Polan (Minneapolis: University of Minnesota Press, 1986).
3. Robert Somol, "Oublier Rowe," *ANY* 7/8 (1994), p. 8.
4. Somol, "Oublier Rowe," p. 9.
5. Gilles Deleuze and Félix Guattari, *A Thousand Plateaus*, trans. Brian Massumi (Minneapolis: University of Minnesota Press, 1987), p. 141.
6. Gilles Deleuze, *Foucault*, trans. Seán Hand (Minneapolis: University of Minnesota Press, 1988), p. 34.
7. Gilles Deleuze, "The Diagram," in *The Deleuze Reader*, ed. Constantin V. Boundas (New York: Columbia University Press, 1993), p. 194.
8. Deleuze and Guattari, *A Thousand Plateaus*, p. 142.

This personality rapidly takes shape, an unknown but not an indefinite figure, a master builder, a Master of Lockhart, whom one equips with the attributes one feels he should possess—an unsubverted integrity, an innate capacity, tastes which are uncomplicated and definite, an understanding of necessity. . . . But stubbornly, this ideally anonymous, quasi-medieval character whom one has educed refuses to take shape. The Master of Lockhart resists formulation as a myth. Indeed, was there one or were there several Masters?[1]

haiduk or **heyduck** [G heiduck, haiduck, fr. Hung hajduk, pl. of hajdu robber] 1. A Balkan outlaw opposed to Turkish rule 2. A Hungarian mercenary foot soldier of a class eventually given the rank of nobility and a territory in 1605 3. a liveried personal follower; a male attendant or servant
zanni [It, fr. It dial. Zanni, nickname fr. the It name Giovanni JOHN] 1. a madcap clown in masked comedy traditionally from Bergamo, Italy, usu. playing the part of a comic servant 2. stock servant characters in the Italian improvisational theatre known as the commedia dell'arte who initiated the action of the play and produced comic impact based on repeated comic actions, topical jokes, and practical jokes, often directed against the smug, the proud, and the pretentious 3. one of two zanni who often played contrasting roles, the first clever and adept at confounding, the second a dull-witted foil

"The fox knows many things but the hedgehog knows one big thing." . . . If one might sometimes feel that fox propensities are less than moral and, therefore, not to be disclosed, of course there still remains the job of assigning to Le Corbusier his own particular slot, "whether he is a monist or a pluralist, whether his vision is of one or of many, whether he is of a single substance or compounded of heterogeneous elements."[2]

hodge 1. an English rustic or farm laborer
hodgepodge 1. a heterogeneous mixture often of incongruous and ill-suited elements
Hodges, Tom S. 1. local Lockhart architect and builder responsible for many of the public buildings in Lockhart including the Dr. Eugene Clark Library (1889), the First Christian Church (1898), and the Caldwell County Jail (1908).

The Master of Lockhart is ninety-six today . . .[3]

It is difficult to tell what does not count in the work of John Hejduk, to distinguish the central focus from the peripheral, the totality from the vignette. While there are any number of subjects that draw immediate speculation in Hejduk's work, it is perhaps the subject *as* number that prevents these quick fixes from registering this impasse of accounting, for criticism is always anxious to frame its object and settle its debts, to believe that it has its subject's number.[4] As Hejduk remarks in conjunction with the Accountant of *Victims*, "for each number there is a name." But the connection between subject and number can be imagined classically or otherwise, the difference between the subject thought as interiority, as an identity or unity (the number One), and the "subject" (if it can be called that anymore) as a function of exteriority, as multiplicity, as both more and less than one. A question difficult to answer in the case of Corbusier—"whether he is of a single substance or compounded of heterogeneous elements"—is even more tricky and pointed in the case of Hejduk who has precisely and self-consciously figured Rowe's alternatives of the fox and the hedgehog.[5]

From his Texas House series to the more recent urban masques, Hejduk's work continues to investigate the relation of part to whole, the status or character of connection, the significance of number and numbering. His thirty-five year "Theory of Accumulation," moving methodically from the individual house to collective arrangement, begins with the early pedagogy of Texas and Cooper Union that establishes the high modern series 1, 4, 9, 16: the single square of four points, the four-square with nine points, and the nine-square with sixteen. As exercises in opposed spatial organization—the homogenous seriality of the four-square (aa) and the hierarchically centered symmetry of the nine-square (aba)—this oscillating modernist and classical series has now been collapsed through the associative laws of Hejduk's *Vladivostok*, appropriately ending in its 36-square cemetery (which operates as both 4 nine-squares and 9 four-squares, and is thus exhausted by neither serial nor symmetrical assignments). It should be noted that this Theory of Accumulation is not merely additive, as Hejduk's reflections on unity, connection, and number have also found expression through the functions of subtraction (e.g., the fractional 1/4, 1/2, and 3/4 houses) and abandonment (e.g., New Town for the New Orthodox). In his architectural/aesthetic and political/social enunciations, everything counts without the necessity of adding up or making a difference; everything matters without being essential.

It is this theme of dumb enumeration that marks Hejduk's deviation from the discourse of American high modernism as articulated by his early colleague and collaborator, Colin Rowe. If *colin-rowe* denotes the proper name of the grid, of classical-modernist definition and clarity, then Hejduk reads this mechanic of orthogonality obliquely, as in the "diagonal sciences" Roger Caillois advances in his own *The Mask of Medusa* from 1960.[6] Even before his Diamond House series, Hejduk's "diagonal" reading operates in the first Texas houses where the grid of points, the structural members, are hollow containers for the mechanical systems, an elemental "hollowness" that progressively expands or swells to become the entire figure in the more recent work, exposing potential anthro- or zoomorphic viscera. While Rowe abstracts the column so that it emerges as the generic structural grid,[7] Hejduk proceeds in an alternate direction, by specifying the column's sacrificial and militaristic character, revealing the animal and captive figures "trapped" within its classical ordination.[8] From the hollow grid of columns to its becoming-animal or figure, Hejduk identifies multiple forms of domestication and occupation (in the *colonizing* sense of the imposition of order) as the center, the innards, of the most familiar architectural elements. In Hejduk's accounting, the detail emerges as the understudy to the city, and the suspicion arises that urbanism amounts to warfare conducted by other means.[9]

The alternate treatments to which the column has been subjected (as either the mathematical grid that establishes the neutral field for plan geometries, or as the source for repressed narrative and vertical figuration) begin to chart Hejduk's complex relationship to Rowe and his version of high modernism. More generally, this instance of the column serves as an emblem for diverse attempts to correlate or align "architecture and language" in the postwar period, to establish the possibility (however contradictory that goal would become) for an architecture of both *autonomy* and *heterogeneity* against the modern rhetoric and experience of anonymous and homogenous "building." This academic and critical quest in postwar American architecture for autonomy and heterogeneity—or, again, identity and multiplicity—was seen to require the construction of the discipline as a self-conscious language.[10] Thus, beginning in the late 1950s, diverse critics and practitioners (such as Rowe and Robert Venturi) came to invoke the historical metalanguage of Mannerism while at the same time pushing architecture in the direction of painting and poetry, the two privileged media in the discourse of high modernism and the New Criticism. Not surprisingly, these same models (poetry and painting) have remained in the work of Hejduk, though significantly no longer as *discrete and external analogies* from other disciplines but as *cohesive and intensive anomalies.* They serve as neither examples nor footnotes, but are inseparable (despite attempts by various critics) from the entire ensemble of production.

Just as Hejduk's practices might be seen as continuous differentiations from the work of Rowe and Venturi, so, along another trajectory, they can be distinguished from the related reflections of Peter Eisenman. In fact, Hejduk's position seems to emerge as the complementary response to the extension and critique of Rowe's formalism found in Eisenman. In contrast to Eisenman's early search for the deep structure of the architectural *langue*, Hejduk enumerates specific utterances, performing architecture's *parole*, suggesting that there can be no abstracted ideal, no generalized theory of architectural meaning, divorced from its particular embodiment.[11] Rather than pursue a codified *language of architecture*, Hejduk more accurately engages the *writing of architecture*, soliciting writing's potential for disaster, its aspects of materiality and contingency, its undecidable confection as both toxin and cure. His speculative and specified productions constitute a *spec writing* of which it remains uncertain as to whether it multiplies and counts on risk, or contains, contracts and insures against it. This uncertainty reflects the more fundamental aporia in Hejduk's work, for—while the systemic and fixed institution of *la langue* constructs itself precisely through its ability to separate the essential from the accidental, the typical (or typological) from the idiosyncratic—with the advent of *parole*, relevance and irrelevance become difficult to distinguish. This larger shift from *syntax* to *usage* (or grammar to performance) in Hejduk's mutation of postwar American formalism accompanies other movements: from plan to elevation, geometry to narrative, type to token, the proportional model to the anomalous, categorizing and distinguishing species to processes of speciation. Hejduk wittily plays on the mathematics and linguistics of formalism where numbers come to double as "figures," and letters as "characters."

The traits of accumulation and speciation (or figuration and characterization) in Hejduk's thought can perhaps best be observed in the masques he has performed in (for) various cities. As suggested above, in place of the transcendental figure-ground *gestalt* of Rowe's planar collage urbanism, Hejduk substitutes the elevational pair subject-object, suggesting an experiential relation on the ground datum rather than a conceptual view from the air. Thus, rather than identifying with the mathematical and measuring concerns of geography, he situates his work within the artistic and descriptive tradition of chorography. This distinction dates back to Ptolemy who analogizes geographical plan-making of the world as the rendering of an entire head, while chorographic views of particular places are seen as the depiction of individual features, such as ear or eye. Moreover, chorography implies place, abandonment and musicality,[12] a triad of concerns repeatedly mixed in Hejduk's work, particularly as they emanate from his reflections on the "widow's walk," an architectural element that immediately provides both subject (character) and program (narrative). Again, it is only from a particular conflation of form, material, function, context and subject that expression is possible, that words and forms can be seen to relate. In Hejduk's work, objects with the same name may have different forms in different cities, while those with the same form often have different names, thus revealing new traits.[13] As demonstrated in his continuing reflections on the otherness of the widow's walk, the "Sea Captain's House" in *Vladivostok* "looks like" *Lancaster/Hanover*'s "Music House" more than its "Widow's House," whereas *Vladivostok*'s "Musician" appears more like the house of the Widow than that of Music. As elsewhere in Hejduk's work, the formal and structural logics of analogy and homology are at once solicited and frustrated. More importantly—and in contrast to the dominant reception of his work by his disciples or its consumption as an institutionalized ethic—Hejduk's obsession with renaming, staging encounters, and establishing instructions suggests that he is engaged in a practice of architectural nominalism, one where "the *idea of an inscription* replaces the *idea of fabrication*."[14] More significant than the official institutional rhetoric of crafting the detail, then, is the act of signing the detail as readymade, revealing its potential to vibrate through larger institutional and disciplinary mechanisms.

If the detail is the understudy to urbanism in Hejduk's work, it is as it approaches the condition of the borderline. In distinction to both Aldo Rossi's analogous city and Rowe's collage city, Hejduk ventures a city of the anomalous.[15] One result of this investigation of the borderline is an urbanism that oscillates between the conditions of synecdoche and spectacle.[16] By focusing on discrete elements and details (e.g., awnings, balconies, water towers, smokestacks, stairs and landings, exhaust ducts, satellite dishes, etc.) Hejduk exposes the fragmented unit of architectural activity (the anonymous, machine-made, or "off the shelf"), where the part stands in for the whole. Equally, however, Hejduk revisits an auratic vision of production, one which emphasizes gesture, passion, and the expressive symbolism of the hand, resulting in an organic totality, an ultimately bounded and composed whole. The question arises, then, whether Hejduk's concern with accumulation and number comprehends multiplicity and contagion, or merely sustains familial and contracted relations, whether or not it is contained by a humanist aesthetic and liberal-legal vision of individual to collective (and part to whole) articulations. These, of course, are political matters as well as aesthetic, and it is precisely in pursuing an explicitly political line of inquiry that Hejduk's speculations display a lineage similar to that of Rowe.[17] In distinguishing his early work from his "first city plan"—the Cemetery for the Ashes of Thought (1975)—Hejduk comments that the "first real shift in the work was political." As will be seen later, however, this political dimension was already present in his early study with Colin Rowe on the town of Lockhart, Texas from 1957.

At about the same time as the collaborative work on Lockhart, Rowe was examining the development of architectural vocabulary in the nineteenth century through aspects of "character" and "composition," terms which did not exist before the late eighteenth century and which had disappeared from architectural discussions by the time modernism was canonized in the 1930s.[18] For designers like J. B. Papworth, Sir John Soane, and Andrew Jackson Downing, character consisted of the subjective expression of the building's purpose and was located specifically in the elements or details of architecture—roof, chimney, porch, veranda. During the nineteenth century, character and composition were associated with the Picturesque tradition as a resistance to academic architecture and ideal types, a dispute which also exhibited a shift away from the work itself to its effect on the spectator. In part, then, one can begin to understand Hejduk's focus on aspects of both detail and "character" (i.e., the heterogeneous subject that is neither abstracted nor idealized) as an equivalent resistance to high modernism. In viewing Hejduk through the lens of the Picturesque, it becomes possible to relate his work to the contemporary practices of the minimalists, as Yve-Alain Bois has connected the work of Richard Serra, for example, to that same tradition, particularly in its concern with one-to-one scale, the avoidance of plan in favor of elevation, an emphasis on the temporal dimension, and the effect on the viewing subject as a species of performer.[19] Like the minimal ("literalist") sculpture Michael Fried criticized for its unconscious biomorphism and its theatrical (and borderline or "between") status, Hejduk's "hollow" objects refigure the late 1960s debate between the roles of contemplation and participation.[20] In addition to celebrating the figurative possibilities within elemental geometries and background tectonics, Hejduk's work operates between Fried's opposed terms of art and objecthood, an uneasy terrain that restates the dilemma of unity (or the contained unique) and multiplicity (the dispersed iteration of the seemingly banal).

While it is true that Rowe has been critical of the picturesque—especially in its postwar guise as townscape, which he has characterized as "sensation without plan"—there remains a major aesthetic and political point of contact between the picturesque and Rowe's collage urbanism. Just as the picturesque attempted to mediate tyranny and license (order and chaos) and produce the "third term" of liberty, so too Rowe's urbanism is a balance between structure and event (or scaffold and exhibit, which makes explicit his metaphor of the "city as museum") for which he appropriates at a crucial juncture, once again, a significantly political, and eminently "reasonable," model—that of the law: "it is the notion of the law, the neutral background which illustrates and stimulates the particular . . . which equips itself with both empirical and ideal . . . it is this very public institution which must now be gainfully employed in commentary upon the scaffold-exhibit relationship."[21] For Rowe, the "elementary and enlivening duplicities of law" along with "the idea of free trade" serve as emblems for the "balancing act" of structure and event as well as the technique of collage. As forces opposed to his promotion of this legal-capitalist (i.e., contractual) economy, Rowe dismisses "accident" and "gifts of chance" which he associates with debtorship and theft, attributes of the unfortunate servant or the outlaw. Like the picturesque, Rowe's collage would contain chance and the accident, pulling back far enough to cover its risk and spread its losses. An insurance company for liberalism, postmodern collage (with its vision of heterogeneity as contained pluralism) ultimately maintains the arrangements of self and society. This political and legal theme—divergently extended in the later reflections on the city by Rowe and Hejduk—finds its first explicit site for articulation in the solitary, unrelenting landscape of central Texas and, not surprisingly, it is here aligned with the question of unified or multiple subjectivity.

It is in Lockhart that Rowe and Hejduk find a specific "representative" of the American courthouse town, an urban type which itself was earlier adduced in their article as "a more representative illustration" of settlement patterns in the West than, for example, the mining town. Through layers of representation and exemplification, a typical situation is described that by necessity avoids the bizarre or the random:

This is a town dedicated to an idea, and its scheme is neither fortuitous nor whimsical. The theme of centralized courthouse in central square is—or should be—a banal one. And it is in fact one of great power. . . . Here it is the law which assumes public significance; and it is around the secular image of the law, like architectural illustrations of a political principle, that these towns revolve. In each case the courthouse is both visual focus and social guarantee; and in each square the reality of government made formally explicit provides the continuing assurance of order. . . . Urbanistic phenomena they palpably are, but they are also the emblems of a political theory. A purely architectural experience of their squares is therefore never possible. Within these enclosures the observer can never disentangle his aesthetic response from his reaction as a social animal.[22]

It is with regard to this theme of the political theories and implications of the city, the polis, that Rowe and Hejduk have continually returned over the succeeding thirty years in their urban thought, twin practices that form a real debate over the liberal-legal vision of the city and modernism. While Rowe would emphasize the reasonable, judicious, orderly, and decisive aspects as the preconditions for an exemplary urbanism, Hejduk has recovered other traits with very different political, social, and formal implications. Only now is it possible, perhaps, to foreground the awnings, power lines, "angelic" streetlights, and cruciform telephone poles in Hejduk's Lockhart photographs, to appreciate the potential for a peripheral and residual vision; only now is it possible to account for the central courthouse squares, jails, and water towers that have come to populate several European cities, to understand the generative potential in the dossier of Lockhart and reconfigure it as a description of Hejduk's later characters *avant la lettre*:

The first view of the town affords the characteristic visual competition. In approaching from the south the dominant intricacies of courthouse silhouette struggle for attention with the aluminum painted spheroid of the water tower; and a concentration of interest upon either is further disturbed by the appearance to the right of a small castellated building of curiously Vanbrughian profile. A toy fort, brick and machicolated, partly Romanesque and partly Italianate, evidently the jail, its disarming self-assurance sets the mood for the entire town.[23]

At the time, Rowe and Hejduk associated Lockhart and other Texas courthouse towns with French *bastides* (medieval towns built for defensive purposes) and credited them with presenting "minor triumphs of urbanity." With slight inflections, these cues can be seen to exhaust Hejduk's preoccupation with number, subject, and the city: namely, the medieval, practices of warfare and siege, and the chance for a minor urbanism. In each case there is a dissociation from Rowe's legalistic model.

In their work on Kafka, Deleuze and Guattari list three characteristics of a minor literature: (1) "language is affected with a high coefficient of deterritorialization"; (2) "everything in them is political"; (3) "everything takes on a collective value."[24] First, language is "deterritorialized" through an intensive usage, a kind of *arte povera*, where one acts as a foreigner in "one's own" tongue, a situation that Deleuze and Guattari associate primarily with the recognition of "impossibility."[25] It is the experience of just such an impossibility that repeatedly blocks and prompts Hejduk's work at both the architectural and urban scales, condemning it (or enabling it) to proceed through fits and starts. Confronted with a New England site surrounded by old shingle-style houses, for example, Hejduk finds he can neither produce something new nor copy in an historicist or modern manner.[26] More to the point with respect to a minor urbanism, Hejduk remarks: "I don't believe that there has been any really creative or essentially new town planning or city planning since the 19th century. This is the first time I've become interested in town planning, with the knowledge, let's say, that I have the real sense that it's an impossibility."[27] In dating the last viable urban project at the end of the nineteenth century, Hejduk provides a clue as to how he will confront the impossibility of urban visions. Rather than promoting the ideal permanence (and real obsolescence) of the White City, Hejduk's traveling circus—the rides, Ferris wheels, sideshows, and games of chance—will take their cue from the temporary events and distractions of the midway.

Here, the carnival aspects of Hejduk's nomadic troupes (troops) reverberate with the second criterion of a minor practice. In advancing an argument for the political space of a minor literature, Deleuze and Guattari explain, "its cramped space forces each individual intrigue to connect immediately to politics. The individual concern thus becomes all the more necessary, indispensable, magnified, because a whole other story is vibrating within it."[28] As in various masquerade traditions—e.g., the mumming plays of England or the *commedia dell'arte* of Italy— Hejduk employs stock characters to elicit a cross-section of society, at once highly particularized and de-individuated through stylized object-forms (*masks*), which eliminate the organized *faciality* of liberal, individualist politics, as well as through the specific improvisation of the company at a given performance through which traditional scenarios are enacted (*masque*). As this traditional opposition between form (object) and function (performance) is mutated through the homonymic collapse of mask/masque, the liberal contradictions that came to identify postwar modernism (and which were highly articulated by Rowe) are elided and rearranged by Hejduk. In a sense, before any cultural practice or form (e.g., architecture or the city) could be rendered political, it first had to be purged of its liberal psychology and economy. In order to counter the way in which modernism had been made safe for liberal-capitalism since the 1930s, Hejduk revisits pre-liberal "mixed" forms to advance another possibility for modernism,[29] it being no coincidence that cultural expressions such as the *commedia dell'arte* could not withstand the rise of bourgeois legalism any more than could the monarchy or the city as an independent political entity. As the development of a political chorography in Hejduk becomes incompatible with the plans of liberalism, a new form of (extra-legal) subjectivity must be imagined as well.

In addition to manifesting an engagement with "impossibility" and the political, Hejduk's work also stresses collective expression, a trait that Deleuze and Guattari explicitly associate with the "passing" of the master: "in a minor literature, there are no possibilities for an individuated enunciation that would belong to this or that 'master' and that could be separated from a collective enunciation."[30] As suggested earlier, Hejduk's practices constitute a continuous reflection on the impossibility of originality for a generation "twice removed" from the "masters of twentieth century architecture."[31] For Hejduk, these masters (Corbusier, Wright, Mies) completed their work in a panoramic sense, leaving for Hejduk (and presumably his generation) the minor task of becoming a winged insect:

I am like a fly that comes in and says, "Ok, here is one aspect that has been left out, yet which has great potentiality, it should be wrapped up." . . . All my work has been completing pieces. Corb should have done a Diamond House. So and so should have done a Wall House, but didn't. In other words, the panoramic views of the great architects, which are panoramic, they didn't conclude. And I come like a fly and fill in the pieces, the logical pieces, then they are cleaned up.[32]

In developing this minor territory, this fly space between the categories of fox and hedgehog (as two proper forms of master), Hejduk's practice approximates that of Henry Adams, whose own form of antimodernism (or dispute with the Protestant liberalism of his well-established paternity) likewise led him to the medieval, the primitive, the childlike, the celebration of feminine qualities, and the cult of the Virgin. Moreover, the model of Adams's *Education* seems to be repeated in private and public forms by Hejduk, with the autobiographical *Mask of Medusa* and the more institutional *Education of an Architect*. In both instances, a medieval, guild-like knowledge, politics, and subjectivity emerge that come to dispute the terms of the so-called formalist (or liberal proceduralist) modernism of Hejduk's one-time collaborator, Colin Rowe.

In many ways, the city exists as *the* battleground in this dispute between medieval and liberal visions of society and politics.[33] Liberalism constructs its vision of the world on the basis of complex (but articulate) contradictions, mediated by the neutral instrumentality of "the law." As a corollary to this principle, the liberal vision is opposed to intermediate entities or associations that would exist *between* the individual and the State. In contrast, medieval practice relied on associations (e.g., corporations like cities, towns, churches, and guilds) that operated precisely between and in excess of individual and State, event and structure, the exclusive duality on which liberalism would stake its claim for freedom, rights, and security. In the medieval community, the ideas of the autonomy of the town and its citizens were merged so that there was no imagined fundamental contradiction "between personal property rights and town sovereignty rights," between freedom and security, "the town as a collection of individuals and the town as a collective whole."[34] Thus, the medieval city exists as a different species (or species of difference) that is reducible neither to a prior collection of individuals nor to the post-facto creation of the State. While liberal visions emphasize an abstract equality (with its objective "reasonable man" standard present in Rowe and his source, Karl Popper), pre-liberal visions of community count on differences of caste or status among its members which are nonetheless dissolved in the singular functioning or performance of the "pack," an entity often conditioned by martial or violent means. While the medieval city has been characterized as existing under "a permanent state of siege," it also tended to mix what liberalism has posited as distinct spheres: the political (with its now diminished public life) and the economic (an increasingly far from equal realm of privatization). As Gerald Frug argues, it is this artificial distinction within liberalism that has contributed to the powerlessness of contemporary cities.

Based on the radical subjectivity of value, the goal of liberalism (as its name would suggest) is individual liberty, an ideal middle term existing between tyranny and license, or totalitarian structure and anarchic event. In contrast, a minor practice wagers only on a line of flight, a becoming, a way out (like the Ape in Kafka's "A Report to an Academy"). As in the medieval city, one set of jurisdictions are escaped (deterritorialized or decoded), only to be replaced by a different set (reterritorialization), a politics of continuous movement, perpetual performance, which will never dream of ultimate liberation via the structure of the law. In this way, Hejduk's figures of speech have escaped the judgment and execution of formalism; urban parolees, they are no longer confined, but not quite free, either. They have simply found a way out. In the Masques, there is an involution, a becoming or exchange of figure and ground, as a collection of interventions establish a new territory, a heaving plane of consistency, that will expand, contract, and move on. Unlike the diverse urban analyses of others (e.g., Rowe and Manfredo Tafuri, as well as Rem Koolhaas's reflections on New York) where the structured grid establishes the precondition for the freedom of form, in Hejduk the figure precedes its disposition; it has no structured or static position but only a loose set of scenarios. Still, the precise valence between traits of occupation and deterritorialization remains unmeasured. What is more certain, however, is that given the fusion of liberalism and the modern in postwar discourse, Hejduk's "way out" consists of grafting the medieval with surrealism to salvage historical avant-garde procedures and paradigms that had been devalued if not obliterated within the canons of high modernism.

In their discussion of the state apparatus and the war machine, Deleuze and Guattari identify two figures with the former bureaucratic organization: the jurist-priest and the magician-king. While the liberal-legal reading of Rowe outlined above places him within the "jurist-priest" type (the commentator or critic), conventional accounts of Hejduk, by his critics and followers alike, tend to characterize him as a "magician-king" (the heroic poet). While any such attribution is never simply right or wrong, the near universal acceptance of this view has obstructed other potentialities within the work. Regardless of whether the pair Rowe-Hejduk is elaborated as complicit (in terms of sharing a mannered humanism) or oppositional (as a debate between the formalist and the phenomenological), it is precisely the identity of *the pair* that frustrates further development. If one is to advance an other project from Hejduk's chats, one must extrapolate from what he simply shows and tells. Hejduk's spec writing—e.g., the emphasis on materiality, refiguring and iterating background tectonics and details, the *parole* aspects of the event, the politicization of program, the dissolution of subject-object relations, etc.—at least sustains *the possibility* for an escape from the legality or conjugality of the pair toward the promiscuity of the double.

What begins as a nascent mode of promiscuous affiliation in Hejduk's work (an implicit trajectory aimed at the borderline), however, often supports subjectivity, interiority, and the propriety of form in many of his would-be successors. At every turn, the chance for a minor practice appears to have been defeated: through a fetishization of materiality that supplants a real interest in the specificity of materials; the triumphant celebration of a renewed phenomenological subject in place of the continued dismantling of any discrete notion of subjectivity; the construction of an heroic category of the genius-master rather than the weakening of the status of author through the "vita minor"; the symbolic and mythic interpretation of form that displaces its potential to recharge context through its own disappearance; the embodiment of ultimate meaning in narrative instead of its usage as an index of contingency and event; a dependence on the logic of the body, proportion, and analogy that avoids an engagement with the borderline and the anomalous; an architecture and urbanism of the colon where the relation of one to many is never one *too* many. In place of the all-too-loyalist reception of Hejduk, then, an improper alternative might be warranted, one which would impair the conjunction of Rowe

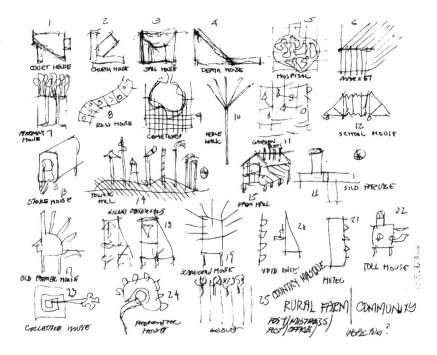

John Hejduk,
Characters, from
*Lancaster/Hanover
Masque*, 1992

and Hejduk (or the state dialectics of jurist-priest and magician-king), one that could speciate or germinate Hejduk's production, bastardizing it if necessary, in order to avoid its being rendered still-born.

The political and aesthetic distinctions drawn earlier between Hejduk and Rowe—along the lines of the medieval and the liberal, the avant-garde and the high modern—were never quite of the same order, were somehow always disproportionate. They never truly formed a pair, their functions never ideally split between the speaking-critic and producing-architect, at least in the case of Hejduk who (like other practitioners of his generation, if in a somewhat different idiom) collapsed these distinct categories which were themselves constructs of the liberal reception of modernism. It is in this way that the dialectical relations of state space—the striated roles of jurist-priest and magician-king—are inadequate with regard to Hejduk, the effects of whose work may now be more productively aligned with the nomadic space of the war machine. As a third figure of inequivalence, it is the "warrior-outlaw" who is associated with this smooth space within the schema of Deleuze and Guattari.[35]

It is Hejduk's war machine, then, that descends upon several European cities in its eastern sweep from Venice to Vladivostok, at once a force of occupation and deterritorialization that would momentarily subvert the juridical and royalist poles of the state and political sovereignty. Of course, since Vitruvius, the "education of the architect" has always included a knowledge of the construction of military machines for siege and assault (machinery being one of the three departments of architecture for the classical theorist, along with the "art of building" and "the making of time-pieces," an area covered by Hejduk with his clock/collapse of time built in London). Beyond this tradition, however, Hejduk's masques, his movable and hollow "gifts," bear a more than passing resemblance to the figural construction of Epeius, wheeled into the city by day as an offering and evacuated by night as an apparatus of war. Finally, the affects of the war machine connect with two principles developed earlier in Hejduk's work: the establishment of a minor science or practice, and the project of reimagining the relationship of number and subject. While the number of the State is linked to metric magnitudes in order to gain mastery over matter (to divide and possess), there exists an other kind of number, the autonomous "numbering number" that operates in the war machine:

These numbers appear as soon as one distributes something in space, instead of dividing up or distributing space itself. *The number becomes a subject.* The independence of the number in relation to space is a result not of abstraction but of the concrete nature of smooth space, which is occupied without being counted. The number is no longer a means of counting or measuring but of moving: it is the number itself that moves through smooth space. There is undoubtedly a geometry of smooth space: but as we have seen, it is a minor, operative geometry, a geometry of the trait. . . . Geometry as a royal science has little importance for the war machine. . . . The number becomes a principle whenever it occupies a smooth space, and is deployed within it as subject, instead of measuring a striated space. *The number is the mobile occupant, the moveable in smooth space, as opposed to the geometry of the immovable in striated space.*[36]

Hejduk's masques, the distribution of entities which occupy without counting, produce a directional rather than a dimensional space. In a related military metaphor, Hejduk has fashioned a kind of "stone soup" urbanism. Like the soldiers in that fable (where roles of guest and host are exchanged), Hejduk has provided the recipe and the stone, word and form, but these vague attractors or connectors will serve only as a mute index of their inadequacy if abandoned in the abstract. Existing conditions in the city (contexts, programs, events, subjects, objects, etc.) are the "real" ingredients, and the success of the fable depends on whether the insertion of what largely amounts to an urban placebo (or is it a *pharmakon?*) can transform behaviors, institutions, and ways of seeing, and whether new means of deciding what counts can be developed.

As the war machine infiltrates the city limits—between the dominant (major) axes of the political, proliferating series of becomings—so too Hejduk's masques compromise the borders of the architectural. Traditionally, the category architecture has constituted itself on the basis of satisfying a double negation, namely that it is not-urbanism (which is without site or structure) and not-sculpture (which is without function). Additionally, architecture is seen to be "bigger" than sculpture and "smaller" (or less numerous) than urbanism. Hejduk's constructions, however, emerge as a positive exhaustion of this dichotomy since they can be provisionally framed under all three discourses and scales, *sculpture-architecture-urbanism*. His arrangements actually exceed the collapse of object, setting, and subject provided by minimalism, and refuse the dream of an existentially integrated beholder maintained by many of its more phenomenologically-minded advocates. In Hejduk, the exchange among forms, functions, and subjects is continuous and monstrous. His work soberly maps a condensed genealogy where professions become proper names which in turn designate structures (e.g., as in the line carpenter, Carpenter, Carpenter Center, or, for that matter, cooper, Cooper, Cooper Union) while at the same time proposing a condition where one would assume the (pre)occupations or the characteristics of one's inhabitation, and vice versa. In the near-dark milieu of several European cities, Hejduk's masques serve as switching mechanisms, providing the opportunity for an exchange, a flutter. Outside the jurisdiction of identification where form, subject, context, and function are distinct, the masque event-forms enable the reading of a new aggregate, one without organized parts that construct determinate wholes, the kind of singularity Deleuze and Guattari refer to as a *haeccity*.

Climate, wind, season, hour are not of another nature than the things, animals, or people that populate them, follow them, sleep and awaken within them. This should be read without a pause: the animal-stalks-at-five-o'clock. The becoming-evening, becoming-night of an animal, blood nuptials. Five o'clock is this animal! This animal is this place![37]

As a political and social model of connection, of course, the recognition of *haeccity* has existed only as the nightmare of liberalism given that the assemblage it envisions escapes the categories of the one (the individual/event) and the many (the State/structure). Previously permitted only in the fascinated warnings of horror and science fiction films, this "invasion of the subject snatchers" constitutes Hejduk's urban proposals and "cross-over" spaces, an architectural becoming of subject and object in the manner that pets and their owners are said to come to resemble one another. Hejduk's urban tales begin in 1975—with his "first urban plan," The New Town for the New Orthodox, and his assumption of the Deanship at Cooper Union—and are reminiscent of a film from the same year, Roman Polanski's *The Tenant*, where the actor-director, a Kafkaesque clerk, evolves with his new apartment, "becoming" its previous female occupant and disappearing into its walls, ultimately reenacting, twice over, her jump from the window. Here, a becoming-other ends in suicide, or a potential suicide brings about a becoming-other. Perhaps more than any other figure, then, it is the House of the Suicide that occupies the borderline of the liberal polis and subjectivity, the limit condition of a becoming, a line of flight merely rehearsed by the angels and other hybrid species of Hejduk's spec-writing machine.

Avoiding the logic of contradiction or dialectics (of subject and object, function and form), the experience of *haeccity* in Hejduk's work marks the end of pluralism and an identity-based politics. Consequently, it potentially ventures a form of collage or model of alliance quite opposed to the high modern form canonized by the legalism of Rowe, with its organizational balance between structure and event. And it is these two forms of collage that allow the postwar desire for autonomy and heterogeneity (or identity and difference) to be reassessed, for it is ultimately around opposed conceptions of this desire that the diverse politics and aesthetics of Rowe and Hejduk have revolved. For Rowe, heterogeneity or difference can only flow from a prior autonomy or previous identity. This begins to explain the proliferation of parity within Rowe's work, for here a "difference" (like right and left) is only conceivable as the fallout of a previous identity, the pair. In this model, difference often operates through the tone of nostalgia (for a lost or broken totality, a tone familiar to those advancing the "city as museum"). In one reading of Hejduk's work, however, the possibility is maintained that difference can precede autonomy or identity horizontally, that differences are in a state of becoming identical (e.g., the surrealist encounter of the sewing machine and umbrella or the exchange of the wasp and the orchid) through the construction of a singularity (or a *haeccity*) that lacks the liberal-humanist articulations of part-to-whole. Here, difference (and the heterogeneity of the city) may exist as the house of the amnesiac, always in the process of becoming something else in conjunction with something else. Hejduk obviates the need for choosing between Rowe's pair "singular substance" (the space of the king, the hedgehog) and "heterogeneous elements" (the space of the jurist, the fox), by developing a third species, the fly (or flea) that infects both figures and dissolves their categorical difference (itself founded on a previous "being," *the raven*, Corbu) in a singular plane of consistency and affect. In any case, "filling in" to abandon is quite different than preserving in order to memorialize. But, despite all clues to the contrary, it is the latter reading to which Hejduk's work has been largely subjected and contained.

Earlier it had been suggested that a series of institutional discourses had neglected the minor initiatives in Hejduk's production and captured his reception for various established interests (briefly, a craft fetishism, the subject of phenomenology, the authorial master, mytho-symbolic form, narrative embodiment, and a proportional humanism). While the varied uses to which Hejduk's thought and production have been put by the still "major sciences" of architecture and urbanism are instructive to catalogue—a case study in how a subtle and almost arid critique of such institutional forms can nevertheless emerge as their ideal model—there remains an oversight that unites all these major forms of reception, and for which Hejduk himself may share some complicity. Each of these reconstructions has taken him *all-too-seriously*. Like the *commedia dell'arte* the effects of which were dependent upon the laughter provoked by the juxtaposition of the sublime with the banal, the Hejduk-effect requires its own outburst. As a *parole* practice it cannot be satisfied with diagramming the joke (as with the geometry of the fold), but must produce the sound. It is significant that in Kafka, too, the element of humor has been overlooked, and the discussion of this by Deleuze and Guattari is illuminating in the case of Hejduk as well:

There is a Kafka laughter, a very joyous laughter, that people usually understand poorly. It is for stupid reasons that people have tried to see a refuge far from life in Kafka's literature, and also an agony, the mark of an impotence and a culpability, the sign of a sad interior tragedy. Only two principles are necessary to accord with Kafka. He is an author who laughs with a profound joy, a *joie de vivre*, in spite of, or because of, his clownish declarations that he offers like a trap or a circus. And from one end to the other, he is a political author, prophet of the future world because he has two poles that he will know how to unify in a completely new assemblage: far from being a writer withdrawn into his room, Kafka finds that his room offers him a double flux, that of bureaucrat with a great future ahead of him . . . and that of a nomad who is involved in fleeing things in the most contemporary way . . . . Never has there been a more comic and joyous author from the point of view of desire; never has there been a more political and social author from the point of view of enunciation.[38]

In Hejduk as in Kafka, laughter and the political are intimately related. Moreover, both laughter and politics were precisely the terms repressed in the liberal-modernist reconstruction of architecture and urbanism after the war. To advance a post-legal practice of the city and modernism, to reinvigorate the polis, the politics of laughter must be reconsidered. It is as one of the few sustained reflections on this problem in postliberal imagination that Hejduk's masques have contributed, realigning the post-war concerns for autonomy and heterogeneity. To the contemporary repertoire of design concerns and procedures Hejduk has offered an early vision of an architectural animation, both as the pursuit of non-static effects and the use of cartoon techniques. While his attempt to specify the abstraction of program through performance may ultimately be more committed to ritual than event—a project that would remain to be taken up by his successors with their investigations of the postnarrative possibilities provided by cinema, video, and hypertext—his singular crossing of the medieval-alchemical and avant-garde-surrealist agendas has redirected the imperatives and humors of architecture: namely (if not literally), to inform objecthood and to animate matter. Among his generation, then, Hejduk emerges most fully as a hinge figure—precisely through his nominalism—in establishing the preconditions that would enable a later neo-avant-garde to move from the semiotic critique of the first generation (his own) to a more direct practice of institutional projection. In the near-dark of the twentieth century, the nomadic space of the "warrior-outlaw" figure might now more accurately be characterized as belonging solely to the madcap-brigand, *zanni-haiduk*.

Notes

1. Colin Rowe and John Hejduk, "Lockhart, Texas," *Architectural Record*, March 1957, p. 205.
2. Colin Rowe, *Collage City* (Cambridge: MIT Press, 1978), p. 92. Earlier in this text, in his dispute with Disney World's "packaging" of Main Street, Rowe returns to Lockhart as an example of the authentic, the real thing: "The Greek temple, the false Victorian facade, the Palladian portico, the unused Opera-House, the courthouse sanctioned by the glamour of Napoleon III's Paris, the conspicuous monument to the Civil War or to the Fearless Fireman, these are the evidence of almost frenzied effort, via the movingly ingenious reconstitution of stable cultural images, to provide stability in an unstable scene, to convert frontier flux into established community." Ibid., p. 46 and p. 182 n. 13. In contrast to Rowe's celebration of the "desperate" structuring-event as a guarantee to a community of liberalism (i.e., a balance between the desire of the people and the reason of science), the event-figures of Hejduk's recent urban proposals seem to wager on the frontier flux of a temporary occupation.
3. John Hejduk, in "Texas," *The Silent Witnesses and Other Poems* (1980), reprinted in *Mask of Medusa* (New York: Rizzoli, 1985), p. 111.
4. Paradoxically, this is especially true in the case of Hejduk, where the determination of what counts by critics and commentators is made categorically: i.e., it is all essential; it is all frivolous; he is important, but not the work; the institution is significant, but not him; the drawings are central, but not the building; the early work is serious, and the more recent a sham, etc. From the tendency of most criticism, it would appear that making distinctions and evaluations—particularly along the simplest categorical lines (subject, genre, technique, period)—is least problematic with respect to Hejduk's production.
5. Besides its early appearance in his illustrations for Aesop's *Fables*, the fox-figure in Hejduk's work can be seen in the Conservation Office, Cemetery of the Mothers, Building for Juries, Town Hall, and Angel Watcher. Hedgehog attributes are displayed in the Chinese Consulate, Chief of Police, House of the Suicide, and Scare-Crow House.
6. Caillois argues that, given the dominant system of classification, attempts "to relate phenomena belonging to different 'kingdoms' and consequently to different sciences" are

condemned to being marginalized, and suggests as an example of such a transverse approach the potential desire to study "winged creatures," a topic of some interest to Hejduk. See Caillois, *The Mask of Medusa*, trans. George Ordish (New York: Clarkson N. Potter, 1964), p. 10, originally published as *Meduse et Cie* (Paris: Gallimard, 1960). Caillois continues: "Man, by a thousand triumphs, by eluding a thousand cunning traps, has unquestionably classified the attributes of the natural world into a system at once the most fruitful, the most rational and the most exact. But this arrangement by no means exhausts all the different possible combinations. It ignores the 'diagonal' relationships in nature which occur in those domains apparently least related. . . . Science has been the less able to countenance them since, by definition, they cross boundaries between disciplines." Ibid., p. 12. Caillois's postulate of a "diagonal science" appears to share characteristics with the "minor sciences" of Deleuze and Guattari. Like Hejduk, too, Caillois seems to be interested in exploring non-essential properties, but traits that matter nonetheless.

7. In "The Chicago Frame," Rowe argues that "without stretching the analogy too far, it might be fair to say that the frame has come to possess a value for contemporary architecture equivalent to that of the column for classical antiquity and the Renaissance. Like the column, the frame establishes throughout the building a common ratio to which all the parts are related." In *The Mathematics of the Ideal Villa and Other Essays* (Cambridge: MIT Press, 1976), p. 90. These linguistic and arithmetic themes of *analogy, ratio,* and *proportion* rely on the functions of the colon: and the series column, colon, Colin. This exchange of column and grid is further discussed and diagrammed by Rowe in his analysis of Michelangelo's facade for San Lorenzo where he suggests that a "skeletal organization" of columns, pilasters, string courses and architraves "might be seen as contributing to the existence of a grid." Colin Rowe and Robert Slutzky, "Transparency: Literal and Phenomenal . . . Part II," *Perspecta* 14 (1971), p. 293. In a final "reading" of Michelangelo's now gridded facade (numbered 10m), Rowe succeeds in transforming San Lorenzo into Corbusier's Villa Savoye.

8. See, e.g., George Hersey's *The Lost Meaning of Classical Architecture* (Cambridge: MIT Press, 1988), where he traces the history of columns as prisoners, columns that "may be thought of as containing, and even sealing in (as if they were sarcophagi), human figures" (p. 80). Earlier, he discusses the "echinus" (a part of the column capital) which is shown to connote several objects composed of "compound curves broken into spines or projections," such as the sea urchin. "Echinus" also names the hedgehog.

9. This relates to Paul Virilio's "minor" school of thought on urban planning that understands the city as the result of war and its preparation rather than the effect of commerce. Virilio and Lotringer, *Pure War* (New York: Semiotext(e), 1983), p. 3. At a later point in the discussion, the comment is made that "cinema is war pursued by other means," thus establishing a connection between the city and cinema, both existing as the bastards or simulacra of war.

10. In general, the two primary contemporary devices or techniques for the exploration of the linguistic capacities of architecture have been the grid and collage, both of which have ties to Rowe and his progeny, beginning with essays on the "Ideal Villa" and "Collage City." While the grid has been largely associated with the condition of autonomy, collage has emerged as the analogous model or emblem for heterogeneity. Nevertheless, there is no natural, necessary, or privileged connection between these relations: e.g., collage may be deployed for effects of autonomy (and this begins to account for the diverse ways in which collage has been recovered in the postwar situation, by both historicist postmodern and neo-avant-garde practices), while geometry increasingly serves as the site for the heterogeneous. Similarly, whereas traditionally the grid (and geometry) has been seen as "descriptive" and collage as "narrative," there are also attempts today to involve a "descriptive collage." The two procedures of grid and collage are also ambiguously associated with Rowe's distinction between "structure" and "event," as will be suggested later.

11. Although I only became aware of the comment after reading Peggy Deamer's paper in *Hejduk's Chronotope*, a form of this parole/langue distinction has been more poetically rendered by Daniel Libeskind: "*Masque space* stands to *architectural space* as does a meal to a menu." *Mask of Medusa*, p. 12 n. 3. Having overlooked this text initially, I have returned to Libeskind's introduction to find a prescient observation, a question of both the anomaly

and the servant, which has come to inform (after the fact of its being written) what will follow: "What then is one to think of an anomaly: of an architect who refuses to enter into anyone's service and who remains aloof from the duties of a vassal?" Ibid., p. 9.

12. Etymologically, *Chor-* and *choro-* derive from the Greek *choras*, meaning "place" or "clear space," but interestingly are also akin to *cheros*, indicating abandoned or bereaved. While *choro* in some contemporary Romance languages (such as Portuguese) has connections to weeping, crying out, or wailing, it also denotes a dance band, or musical piece in the style of Brazilian folk music.

13. E.g., The Painter of Vladivostok, the Old Farmer's House of Lancaster/Hanover, and the House of the Eldest Citizen in Berlin.

14. Thierry de Duve, "Echoes of the Readymade: Critique of Pure Modernism," *October* 70 (Fall 1994), p. 73. For more on de Duve's explication of Duchamp's nominalist practice, see *Pictorial Nominalism: On Marcel Duchamp's Passage from Painting to Readymade* (Minneapolis: University of Minnesota Press, 1991). Not surprisingly, many of Hejduk's advocates and recruits mistake the project of nominalism for a new essentialism, just as they in turn supplant inscription with an overemphasis on fabrication, thus inevitably leading to the call for a new ontology of architecture as well as to the series of small compromises which end in the destitute call for "design-build," a capitulation to economic convenience that masquerades as political resistance. To put the matter somewhat differently, it may be more productive, at least for the argument advanced here, to think the detail in *diagrammatic* rather than *tectonic* terms. This may account for the discomfort or disappointment, expressed by supporters as well as critics, toward the built manifestations of Hejduk's projects as "realized" by his followers.

15. Hejduk's investigation of the detail is couched exactly in terms of this issue of the borderline, a calculation that permits awnings to be used but not shutters. In some cases a material (or alchemical) transformation allows an element to be deployed, as in the steel verandas of the Texas houses that "become something else." As Hejduk states, "I'm not certain of the borderline. And that's my question." *Mask of Medusa*, p. 130 n. 3. Here, the themes of uncertainty, the borderline, and becoming converge. As borderline instances are approached and multiplied, an irregular landscape of the anomalous is produced, that which deviates from the general rule, outbids analogy, and resides on the other side of the law. This exorbitant alliance of the borderline with the anomalous is explicitly taken up by Deleuze and Guattari: "Sorcerers . . . use the old adjective 'anomalous' to situate the positions of the exceptional individual in the pack. It is always with the Anomalous, Moby-Dick or Josephine, that one enters into alliance to become-animal. . . . The anomalous is neither an individual nor a species; it has only affects. . . . It is a phenomenon, but a phenomenon of bordering. This is our hypothesis: a multiplicity is defined not by the elements that compose it in extension, not by the characteristics that compose it in comprehension, but by the lines and dimensions it encompasses in 'intension.' If you change dimensions, if you add or subtract one, you change multiplicity. . . . That the anomalous is the borderline makes it easier for us to understand the various positions it occupies in relation to the pack or the multiplicity it borders, and the various positions occupied by a fascinated Self." Gilles Deleuze and Félix Guattari, *A Thousand Plateaus* (Minneapolis: University of Minnesota Press, 1987), pp. 244–245. It is thus the anomalous that provides a clue to out-maneuvering the liberal antinomies of individual and collective, identity and multiplicity. It is this extra-legal functioning of the anomalous that exists as "the cutting edge of deterritorialization." Ibid., p. 244.

16. These terms are borrowed from Benjamin Buchloh who uses them to characterize the oppositional tendencies within the history of modernist painting. See "Gerhard Richter's Facture: Between the Synecdoche and the Spectacle," *Art and Design* (1989), pp. 41–45. Buchloh's distinction is very close to the "centrifugal" (scientific and fragmented) and "centripetal" (spiritual and organic) attitudes Rosalind Krauss identifies as the dual possibilities contained within the use of the grid in modern art. See "Grids," in *The Originality of the Avant-Garde and Other Modernist Myths* (Cambridge: MIT Press, 1985). For Krauss, "The work of Mondrian, taken with its various and conflicting readings, is a perfect example of this dispute. Is what we see in a particular painting merely a section of an implied continuity, or is the painting structured as an autonomous, organic whole?" Ibid., p. 19. In extending the "cubist analogy" of Rowe and Slutzky, Hejduk significantly moves to the

rotation of Mondrian's "diamond" canvases as a source for his early work. For Hejduk, "modernism ends with Mondrian." *Mask of Medusa*, p. 36 n. 3.

17. This despite Rowe's more widely discussed and understood connection to Eisenman's investigations (their likely disagreement over formal conclusions notwithstanding). In other words, while Eisenman elaborates and transforms Rowe's techniques of formal abstraction, Hejduk develops his practice as a political enunciation, which always constituted the other aspect of Rowe's reflections, and the one largely neglected by Eisenman. Perhaps it would be more accurate to say, however, that Eisenman's *anti*-liberal critique of Rowe's modernism—in contrast to Hejduk's *pre*-liberal critique—has too often been dismissed or misunderstood as being simply *apolitical*, not least by the architect himself.

18. See Rowe, "Character and Composition; or Some Vicissitudes of Architectural Vocabulary in the Nineteenth Century," in *Mathematics of the Ideal Villa*, note 7. While the following discussion will suggest the implicit theme of "character" in Hejduk's work, it would perhaps be possible to make a similar connection to the work of Frank Gehry as a parallel reflection on "composition" as evidence of their related dispute with postwar modernism. Like Hejduk, Gehry, too, seems preoccupied with "the isolation of parts" as an American phenomenon. Whereas Hejduk's early domestic schemes geometricize, parody, and attenuate the functionalist bubble diagram (pulling the elemental event-pieces along an infrastructural corridor), Gehry's residences seem to result from a figural sculpting of the bubbles, where for each shape there is a function (as in Hejduk), which are then pushed together to compose a community.

19. Yve-Alain Bois, "A Picturesque Stroll around *Clara-Clara*," *October* 29 (Summer 1984), pp. 32–62.

20. In this way, Hejduk's work can be seen as complicit with diverse attempts by other members of the neo-avant-garde (e.g., Venturi, Eisenman, Libeskind, etc.) to register their new professional role as "architect-critic." Hejduk's particular manner of figuring this collapse of interiority and exteriority entails establishing a series of dual characters and functional relations such as observer and participant, watcher and inhabitant, witness and victim. For an initial discussion of this theme see "My Mother the House," *Fetish* (New York: Princeton Architectural Press, 1992), esp. p. 61, and, "RE: The Subject of Disappearance," *Anyone* (New York: Rizzoli, 1991), pp. 128–129.

21. Rowe and Koetter, *Collage City*, p. 146 n. 2.

22. Rowe and Hejduk, "Lockhart, Texas," pp. 202–203 n. 1.

23. Ibid., pp. 203–204.

24. Gilles Deleuze and Félix Guattari, *Kafka: Toward a Minor Literature* (Minneapolis: University of Minnesota Press, 1986), pp. 16–17. Technically, a minor literature can only operate within and through a dominant language, and is therefore more accurately a minor usage of a major code, and thus has a *parole* aspect. They reprise the three traits briefly as "the deterritorialization of language, the connection of the individual to a political immediacy, and the collective assemblage of enunciation." Ibid., p. 18.

25. For example, Kafka's writing serves as the index of a specific impasse for the Jews of Prague: "the impossibility of not writing, the impossibility of writing in German, and the impossibility of writing otherwise." Ibid., p. 16.

26. "And how are you going to put a new house in there? So I cannot copy and put an old house style in there, it's not my nature. So then I can't put a modern house there." Hejduk, *Mask of Medusa*, p. 131 n. 3.

27. Ibid., p. 85. Since "The New Town for the New Orthodox," his first explicit commentary on town planning (a future perfect cemetery, a will-have-been-abandoned city), Hejduk has continued to pursue this impossibility. For a quite similar prognosis (which illustrates a second form of minor practice) see Rem Koolhaas's introduction of his La Défense project: "I won't talk as an architect, but as a planner, in other words, as someone representing a discipline that no longer exists." "Gridding the New," *Anywhere* (New York: Rizzoli, 1992), p. 154.

28. Deleuze and Guattari, *Kafka*, p. 17 n. 23.

29. As pre-operatic and popular mixed media, the masques combined theater, dance, mime, acrobatics, and magic. Moreover, as "minor" practice, each character-type spoke his or her own dialect (the ambiguity of words providing one cause for the misunderstanding that might direct the narrative) while regional events of the day would often instigate

satirical and critical commentary. The important thing to note here is that it was precisely the argument against mixed or multi-media that was used to defend a limited conception of modernism ("art as such") by postwar critics like Michael Fried: "what lies between the arts is theatre." See "Art and Objecthood," reprinted in Gregory Babcock, ed., *Minimal Art* (New York: Dutton, 1968), p. 142. For Fried "theatre" (i.e., the art form produced by the minimalists which required a "beholder") was at war with modernism, as quality and value within the postwar canon of high modernism could only obtain within a discrete and autonomous medium. Significantly, Fried indicts surrealism along with minimalism due to its "theatrical" (i.e., boundary displacing) aspirations and effects, conditions that were antithetical to the postwar (or, for the purposes here, liberal) reconstruction of modernism. Not surprisingly, then, Hejduk's particular repetition of historical avant-garde propositions repressed within modernism entails a related pre-liberal political model: thus, his now readily explicable hybrid of "medieval surrealism," which he relates to a peculiarly futurist sounding slogan, "a metalizing of the universe." Hejduk, *Mask of Medusa*, p. 122 n. 3. Beyond its futurist overtones, however, Hejduk's metallurgic project connects his work to aspirations and forms of knowledge pursued by alchemists.

30. Deleuze and Guattari, *Kafka*, note 23, p. 17. It is this "scarcity of talent" that necessitates an intensive usage of given forms, and that Deleuze and Guattari claim "allows the conception of something other than a literature of masters."

31. See, e.g., the Hejduk's opening text in *Mask of Medusa* , p. 26 n. 3, which follows the brief parable "The Fox and the Goat."

32. Ibid., pp. 129–131.

33. For more on this debate and an extended consideration of the following discussion, see Gerald Frug's comprehensive and suggestive study in "The City as Legal Concept," *Harvard Law Review* 93 (1980), p. 1057.

34. Ibid., p. 1087.

35. In describing the "warrior" figure, they write, "he is like a pure and immeasurable multiplicity, the pack, an irruption of the ephemeral and the power of metamorphosis. . . . He bears witness, above all, to other relations with women, with animals, because he sees all things in relations of becoming, rather than implementing binary distributions between 'states': a veritable becoming-animal of the warrior, a becoming-woman, which lies outside dualities or terms as well as correspondences between relations. In every respect, the war machine is of another origin than the State apparatus." Deleuze and Guattari, *A Thousand Plateaus*, p. 352 n. 14.

36. Ibid., p. 389. Emphasis added.

37. Ibid., p. 263.

38. Deleuze and Guattari, *Kafka*, pp. 41–42 n. 23.

Index